Eighth Edition

SERVICES MARKETING

People   Technology   Strategy

Jochen Wirtz
Christopher Lovelock

World Scientific

NEW JERSEY · LONDON · SINGAPORE · BEIJING · SHANGHAI · HONG KONG · TAIPEI · CHENNAI · TOKYO

Published by

World Scientific Publishing Co. Inc.

27 Warren Street, Suite 401-402, Hackensack, NJ 07601, USA

Head office: 5 Toh Tuck Link, Singapore 596224

UK office: 57 Shelton Street, Covent Garden, London WC2H 9HE

For orders of individual copies, course adoptions, bulk purchases: sales@wspc.com
For orders for individual chapters, customized course packs: sales@wspc.com
For adaptions or translation rights, permissions to reprint: rights@wspc.com

Library of Congress Cataloging-in-Publication Data

Names: Lovelock, Christopher H., author. | Wirtz, Jochen, author.
Title: Services marketing : people, technology, strategy / Jochen Wirtz, Christopher Lovelock.
Description: Eighth edition. | New Jersey : World Scientific, [2016] | Includes index.
Identifiers: LCCN 2016003724| ISBN 9781944659004 (hardcover) | ISBN 9781944659011 (pbk.)
Subjects: LCSH: Marketing--Management. | Professions--Marketing. | Service industries--Marketing. |
   Customer services--Marketing.
Classification: LCC HF5415.13 .L5883 2016 | DDC 658.8--dc23
LC record available at http://lccn.loc.gov/2016003724

British Library Cataloguing-in-Publication Data
A catalogue record for this book is available from the British Library.

Desk Editor: Karimah Samsudin

Printed in Singapore

To Jeannette, the light of my life, for your love
and support, and all the fun and laughter.

– JW

Services Marketing: People, Technology, Strategy

Brief Contents

Contents

About the Authors

As a team, Christopher Lovelock and Jochen Wirtz provide a blend of skills and experience ideally suited to writing an authoritative and engaging services marketing text. Since first meeting in 1992, they've worked together on a variety of projects, including cases, articles, conference papers, and two books — *Services Marketing: People, Technology, Strategy* and *Essentials of Services Marketing.*

Jochen Wirtz is Professor of Marketing at the National University of Singapore (NUS), an international fellow of the Service Research Center at Karlstad University, Sweden, and academic scholar at the Cornell Institute for Healthy Futures (CIHF) at Cornell University, USA.

Professor Wirtz was the founding director of the dual degree UCLA–NUS Executive MBA Program (ranked fourth globally in the *Financial Times* 2015 EMBA rankings, and third in the EIU 2015 rankings) from 2002 to 2014, an Associate Fellow at the Saïd Business School, University of Oxford from 2008 to 2013, and a founding member of the NUS Teaching Academy (the NUS think-tank on education matters) from 2009 to 2015.

Professor Wirtz's research focuses on service marketing and has been published in over 200 academic articles, book chapters, and industry reports. He is author or co-author of more than 10 books, including *Services Marketing — People, Technology, Strategy* (World Scientific, 8th edition, 2016), co-authored with Professor Lovelock, which has become one of the world's leading services marketing textbook, translated and adapted for more than 26 countries and regions, and with sales of some 800,000 copies. His other books include *Flying High in a Competitive Industry: Secrets of the World's Leading Airline* (McGraw Hill, 2009), *Essentials of Services Marketing* (Prentice Hall, 3rd edition, 2016), and *Winning in Service Markets: Success Through People, Technology and Strategy* (World Scientific, 2016).

In recognition of his excellence in teaching and research, Professor Wirtz has received more than 40 awards, including the prestigious Academy of Marketing Science (AMS) 2012 Outstanding Marketing Teacher Award (the highest recognition of teaching excellence of AMS globally), and the top university-level Outstanding Educator Award at NUS. He was also the winner of the inaugural Outstanding Service Researcher Award 2010, and the Best Practical Implications Award 2009, both by Emerald Group Publications. He serves on the editorial review boards of more than 10 academic journals, including the *Journal of Service Management, Journal of Service Research, Journal of Service Science,* and *Cornell Hospitality Quarterly* and is also an ad hoc reviewer for the *Journal of Consumer Research* and *Journal of Marketing.* Professor Wirtz chaired the American Marketing Association's biennial Service Research Conference in 2005 when it was held for the first time in Asia.

Professor Wirtz was a banker and took the banking exam at Chamber of Commerce and Industry in Munich. He has since been an active management consultant, working with international consulting firms, including Accenture, Arthur D. Little and KPMG, and major service firms in the areas of strategy, business development, and customer feedback systems.

Originally from Germany, Professor Wirtz spent seven years in London before moving to Asia. Today, he shuttles between Asia, the United States, and Europe. For further information, see www.JochenWirtz.com.

The late **Christopher Lovelock** was one of the pioneers of services marketing. He consulted and conducted seminars and workshops for managers all around the world, with a particular focus on strategic planning in services and managing the customer experience. From 2001 to 2008, he had been an adjunct professor at the Yale School of Management, where he taught services marketing in the MBA program.

After obtaining a B Com and an MA in economics from the University of Edinburgh, he worked in advertising with the London office of J. Walter Thompson Co., and then in corporate planning with Canadian Industries Ltd. in Montreal. Later, he earned an MBA from Harvard and a PhD from Stanford, where he was also a postdoctoral fellow.

Professor Lovelock's distinguished academic career included 11 years on the faculty of the Harvard Business School and two years as a visiting professor at IMD in

Switzerland. He has also held faculty appointments at Berkeley, Stanford, and the Sloan School at MIT, as well as visiting professorships at INSEAD in France and the University of Queensland in Australia.

Author or co-author of more than 60 articles, 100 teaching cases, and 27 books, Professor Lovelock saw his work translated into 16 languages. He served on the editorial review boards of the *Journal of Service Management, Journal of Service Research, Service Industries Journal, Cornell Hospitality Quarterly*, and *Marketing Management,* and was also an ad hoc reviewer for the *Journal of Marketing.*

Widely acknowledged as a thought leader in services, Professor Lovelock has been honored by the American Marketing Association's prestigious Award for Career Contributions in the Services Discipline. This award has been renamed the *SERVSIG Christopher Lovelock Career Contribution Award* in his honor. His article with Evert Gummesson "Whither Services Marketing? In Search of a New Paradigm and Fresh Perspectives" won the AMA's Best Services Article Award in 2005. Earlier, he received a best article award from the *Journal of Marketing*. Recognized many times for excellence in case writing, he has twice won top honors in the *Business Week*'s "European Case of the Year" Award.

About the Contributors of the Case Studies

Karla Cabrera is a senior researcher at the Service Management Research & Education Group at EGADE Business School, Tecnologico de Monterrey, Mexico.

Mark Colgate is a professor at University of Victoria, Canada.

Lorelle Frazer is a professor at Griffith University, Australia.

Roger Hallowell is affiliated professor of strategy at HEC Paris and former professor at Harvard Business School, US.

Christopher W. Hart is a former professor at Harvard Business School, US.

Loizos Heracleous is a professor at Warwick Business School, UK.

James L. Heskett is an Emeritus Professor at Harvard Business School, US.

Ron Kaufman is founder and chairman of UP! Your Service Pte. Ltd.

Sheryl E. Kimes is a professor at the School of Hotel Management, Cornell University, US.

Suzanne Lowe is President, Expertise Marketing LLC, US.

Michael Mahoney is a former writer at Harvard Business School, US.

Youngme Moon is Donald K. David Professor of Business Administration at Harvard Business School, US.

Paul E. Morrison is a professor at Boston University, US.

John A. Quelch is Senior Associate Dean and Lincoln Filene Professor of Business Administration at Harvard Business School, US.

Javier Renoso is the Chair of the Service Management Research & Education Group at EGADE Business School, Tecnologico de Monterrey, Mexico.

Roy D. Shapiro is a professor at Harvard Business School, US.

Robert Simons is a professor at Harvard Business School, US.

Christopher Tang is a UCLA Distinguished Professor and the Edward W. Carter Chair in Business Administration at the Anderson School of Management, UCLA, US.

Rohit Verma is a professor at School of Hotel Management, Cornell University, US.

Lauren K. Wright is a professor of marketing, California State College, Chico, US.

Preface

Services dominate the expanding world economy like never before, and technology continues to evolve in dramatic ways. Established industries and their often famous and old companies decline, and may even disappear, as new business models and industries emerge. Competitive activity is fierce, with firms often using new strategies and technologies to respond to changing customer needs, expectations, and behaviors. This book has been written in response to the global transformation of our economies to services. Clearly, the skills in marketing and managing services have never been more important!

Creating and marketing value in today's increasingly service and knowledge-intensive economy requires an understanding of the powerful design and packaging of "intangible" benefits and products, high-quality service operations, and customer information management processes, a pool of motivated and competent frontline employees, building and maintaining a loyal and profitable customer base, and the development and implementation of a coherent service strategy to transform these assets into improved business performance. This textbook provides this knowledge. Specifically, its main objectives are to:

1. Provide an appreciation and understanding of the unique challenges inherent in the marketing, management, and delivery of service excellence at a profit. Readers are introduced to and have the opportunity to work with tools and strategies that address these challenges.

2. Develop an understanding of the "state of the art" of services marketing and management thinking.

3. Promote a customer service-oriented mind-set.

As the field of services marketing has evolved, so too has this book, with each successive edition representing a significant revision over its predecessor. The new eighth edition is no exception. You can be confident that it captures the reality of today's world, incorporates recent academic and managerial thinking, and illustrates cutting-edge service concepts.

Preparing this new edition has been an exciting challenge. Services marketing, once a tiny academic niche championed by just a handful of pioneering professors, has become a thriving area of activity for both research and teaching. There's growing student interest in taking courses in this field, which makes good sense from a career standpoint, as most business school graduates will be going to work in service industries.

WHAT'S NEW IN THIS EDITION?

The eighth edition represents a significant revision. Its contents reflect ongoing developments in the service economy, dramatic developments in technology, new research findings, and enhancements to the structure and presentation of the book in response to feedback from reviewers and adopters.

New Structure, New Topics

- Almost all chapters are now structured around an **organizing framework** that provides a pictorial overview of the chapter's contents and line of argument.

- New **applications of technology** are integrated throughout the text, ranging from apps, M-commerce, and social networks, to robots, artificial intelligence, and biometrics.

- Each of the 15 chapters has been revised. All chapters incorporate **new examples** and references to **recent research**. Significant changes in chapter content are highlighted below.

- Chapter 1 "Creating Value in the Service Economy" now explores the nature of the modern service economy more deeply and covers B2B services, outsourcing and offshoring. The Service–Profit Chain, featured in Chapter 15 in the previous editions, was moved here to serve as a guiding framework for the book.

- Chapter 2 "Understanding Service Consumers" covers the post-consumption behaviors, including service quality, its dimensions and measurement (SERVQUAL), and how quality relates to customer loyalty. This was in Chapter 14 in the previous edition.

- Chapter 7 "Service Marketing Communications" is now tightly organized around the **5 W**s model, a new section on the services marketing communications funnel was added, and the coverage of new media (including social media, mobile, apps, and QR codes) is significantly expanded.

- Chapter 8 "Designing Service Processes" has a new section on emotionprints, and covers service blueprinting in more detail.

- Chapter 11 "Managing People for Service Advantage" has new sections on a service-oriented culture and how to build a climate for service, a section on effective leadership in service organization and leadership styles. Part of this content was previously covered in Chapter 15 in the previous editions.

- Chapter 14 "Improving Service Quality and Productivity" now integrates key concepts in the main body of the chapter instead of including them in the Appendix as seen in the previous editions. They are TQM, ISO 9000, Six Sigma and the Malcolm-Baldrige and EFQM.

- Chapter 15 "Building a World-Class Service Organization" was completely restructured to provide a recap and integration of key themes of this book. It now features an auditing tool to assess the service level of an organization. It emphasizes on the impact of customer satisfaction on long-term profitability and closes with a call to action.

FOR WHAT TYPES OF COURSES CAN THIS BOOK BE USED?

This text is designed for advanced undergraduates, MBA and EMBA students. *Services Marketing* places marketing issues within a broader general management context. The book will appeal to both full-time students headed for a career in management and to EMBAs and executive program participants who are combining their studies with ongoing work in managerial positions.

Whatever a manager's specific job may be, we argue that he or she has to understand and acknowledge the close ties that link the functions of marketing, human resource, and operations. With that in mind, we've designed this book so that instructors can make selective use of chapters and cases to teach courses of different lengths and formats in either services marketing or service management.

WHAT ARE THE BOOK'S DISTINGUISHING FEATURES?

Key features of this highly readable book include:

- A **strongly managerial perspective**, yet is **rooted in solid academic research**, complemented by memorable frameworks. Our goal is to bridge the all-too-frequent gap between theory and the real world.

- Text that is **organized around an integrated framework** that the reader immediately can relate to. The framework cascades across the entire book. Each chapter also provides a succinct **chapter overview in pictorial form**.

- Text that is **clear, readable, and focused**.

- A **global perspective**, with examples carefully selected from America, Europe, and Asia.

- A **systematic learning approach**, with each chapter having clear **learning objectives**, an **organizing framework providing a quick overview** of the chapter's contents and lines of argument, and **chapter summaries in bullet form** that condense the core concepts and messages of each chapter.

- **Opening vignettes** and **boxed inserts** within the chapters are designed to capture student interest and provide opportunities for in-class discussions. They describe significant research findings, illustrate practical applications of important service marketing concepts, and describe best practices by innovative service organizations.

We've designed this textbook to complement the materials found in traditional marketing management texts. Recognizing that the service sector of the economy can best be characterized by its diversity, we believe that no single conceptual model suffices to cover marketing-relevant issues among organizations ranging from huge international corporations (in fields such as airlines, banking, insurance, telecommunications, freight transportation, and professional services) to locally owned and operated small businesses such as restaurants, laundries, taxis, optometrists, and many business-to-business services. In response, the book offers a carefully designed "toolbox" for service managers, teaching students how different concepts, frameworks, and analytical procedures can best be used to examine and resolve the varied challenges faced by managers in different situations.

Acknowledgments

Over the years, many colleagues in both the academic and business worlds have provided us with valuable insights into the marketing and management of services through their publications, conference or seminar discussions, and stimulating individual conversations. In addition, both of us have benefited enormously from in-class and after-class discussions with our students and executive program participants.

We're much indebted to those researchers and teachers who helped to pioneer the study of services marketing and management, and from whose work we continue to draw inspiration. Among them are John Bateson of Cass Business School; Leonard Berry of Texas A&M University; Mary Jo Bitner and Stephen Brown of Arizona State University; David Bowen of Thunderbird Graduate School of Management; Richard Chase of the University of Southern California; Bo Edvardsson of University of Karlstad; Pierre Eiglier of Université d'Aix-Marseille III; Raymond Fisk of the Texas State University; Christian Grönroos of the Swedish School of Economics in Finland; Stephen Grove of Clemson University, Evert Gummesson of Stockholm University; James Heskett and Earl Sasser of Harvard University; A. "Parsu" Parasuraman of University of Miami; Roland Rust of the University of Maryland; and Benjamin Schneider formerly of the University of Maryland. We salute, too, the contributions of the late Eric Langeard, Robert Johnston, and Daryl Wyckoff.

Although it's impossible to mention everyone who has influenced our thinking, we particularly want to express our appreciation to the following: Tor Andreassen, Norwegian School of Management; Steve Baron of University of Liverpool; Ruth Bolton of Arizona State University; John Deighton, Theodore Levitt, and Leonard Schlesinger, all currently or formerly of Harvard Business School; Michael Ehret of Nottingham Trent University; Dominik Georgi of Lucerne School of Business; Loizos Heracleous of University of Warwick; Douglas Hoffmann of Colorado State University; Irene Ng of University of Warwick; Jay Kandampully of Ohio State University; Ron Kaufman of UP! Your Service College; Sheryl Kimes of Cornell University; Tim Keiningham of Rockbridge Associate; Jean-Claude Larréché of INSEAD; Jos Lemmink of Maastricht University; Kay Lemon of Boston College; David Maister of Maister Associates; Anna Mattila of Pennsylvania State University; Ulrich Orth of Kiel University; Chiara Orsingher of University

of Bologna; Anat Rafaeli of Technion-Israeli Institute of Technology; Ram Ramaseshan of Curtin University; Frederick Reichheld of Bain & Co; Jim Spohrer of IBM; Bernd Stauss formerly of Katholische Universität Eichstätt; Christopher Tang of UCLA; Rodoula Tsiotsou of University of Macedonia; Charles Weinberg of the University of British Columbia; Lauren Wright of California State University, Chico; George Yip of London Business School; Ping Xiao of the National University of Singapore; and Valarie Zeithaml of the University of North Carolina.

We've also gained important insights from our co-authors on international adaptations of *Services Marketing*, and are grateful for the friendship and collaboration of Guillermo D'Andrea of Universidad Austral, Argentina; Harvir S. Bansal of University of Waterloo, Canada; Jayanta Chatterjee of Indian Institute of Technology at Kanpur, India; Xiucheng Fan of Fudan University, China; Miguel Angelo Hemzo, Universidade de São Paulo, Brazil; Hean Tat Keh of the University of Queensland, Australia; Luis Huete of IESE, Spain; Laura Iacovone of University of Milan and Bocconi University, Italy; Denis Lapert of Telecom École de Management, France; Barbara Lewis of Manchester School of Management, UK; Xiongwen Lu of Fudan University, China; Paul Maglio of University of California, Merced, USA; Annie Munos, Euromed Marseille École de Management, France; Jacky Mussry of MarkPlus, Inc., Indonesia; Javier Reynoso of Tec de Monterrey, Mexico; Paul Patterson of the University of New South Wales, Australia; Sandra Vandermerwe of Imperial College, London, UK; and Yoshio Shirai of Takasaki City University of Economics, Japan.

It's a pleasure to acknowledge the insightful and helpful comments of reviewers of this and previous editions: David M. Andrus of Kansas State University; Charlene Bebko of Indiana University of Pennsylvania; Michael L. Capella of Villanova University; Susan Carder of Northern Arizona University; Frederick Crane of the University of New Hampshire; Harry Domicone of California Lutheran University; Lukas P. Forbes of Western Kentucky University; Bill Hess of Golden Gate University; Ben Judd of the University of New Haven; P. Sergius Koku of Florida Atlantic University; Robert P. Lambert of Belmont University; Martin J. Lattman of Johns Hopkins University; Daryl McKee of Louisiana State University; Terri Rittenburg of the University of Wyoming; Cynthia Rodriguez Cano of Augusta State

University; and Lisa Simon of California Polytechnic State University. They challenged our thinking and encouraged us to include many substantial changes. In addition, we benefited from the valued advice of Sharon Beatty of the University of Alabama and Karen Fox of Santa Clara University, who provided thoughtful suggestions for improvement.

It takes more than authors to create a book and its supplements. Warm thanks are due to the editing and production team who worked hard to transform our manuscript into a handsome published text. They include Chua Hong Koon, Publishing Director; Karimah Samsudin, Desk Editor, Munira Alhad and Shirley Ng, Graphic Designers. Thanks also to Shanti Venkatesh,

Associate Professor of Marketing at Loyola Institute of Business Administration, author of the eighth edition test bank.

Finally, we'd like to thank you, our reader, for your interest in this exciting and fast-evolving field of services marketing. If you have any feedback, interesting research, examples, stories, cases, videos, or any other materials that would look good in the next edition of this book, please contact us via www.JochenWirtz.com. We'd love to hear from you!

Jochen Wirtz
Christopher Lovelock

PART 1

The Services Marketing Framework

Part I

Understanding Service Products, Consumers, and Markets

1. Creating Value in the Service Economy
2. Understanding Service Consumers
3. Positioning Services in Competitive Markets

Part II

Applying the 4 Ps of Marketing to Services

4. Developing Service Products and Brands
5. Distributing Services Through Physical and Electronic Channels
6. Service Pricing and Revenue Management
7. Service Marketing Communications

Part III

Managing the Customer Interface

8. Designing Service Processes
9. Balancing Demand and Capacity
10. Crafting the Service Environment
11. Managing People for Service Advantage

Part IV

Developing Customer Relationships

12. Managing Relationships and Building Loyalty
13. Complaint Handling and Service Recovery

Part V

Striving for Service Excellence

14. Improving Service Quality and Productivity
15. Building a World-Class Service Organization

Figure I Organizing framework for services marketing

UNDERSTANDING SERVICE PRODUCTS, CONSUMERS, AND MARKETS

Part I lays the building blocks for studying services and learning how one can become an effective service marketer. It consists of the following three chapters:

CHAPTER 1

Creating Value in the Service Economy

Chapter 1 highlights the importance of services in our economies. We also define the nature of services and how they create value for customers without transfer of ownership. The chapter highlights some distinctive challenges involved in marketing services and introduces the 7 Ps of services marketing.

The framework shown in Figure I on the facing page will accompany us throughout as it forms the basis for each of the four parts in this book. It describes systematically what is involved in developing marketing strategies for different types of services. The framework is introduced and explained in Chapter 1.

CHAPTER 2

Understanding Service Consumers

Chapter 2 provides a foundation for understanding consumer needs and behaviors related to services. The chapter is organized around the three-stage model of service consumption that explores how customers search for and evaluate alternative services, make purchase decisions, experience and respond to service encounters, evaluate service performance, and finally, develop loyalty.

CHAPTER 3

Positioning Services in Competitive Markets

Discusses how to develop a customer-driven services marketing strategy and how a value proposition should be positioned in a way that creates competitive advantage for the firm. This chapter first links the customer, competitor, and company (commonly referred to as "3 C"s) analysis links to a firm's positioning strategy. The core of the chapter is then organized around the three key elements of positioning — *s*egmentation, *t*argeting, and *p*ositioning (commonly referred to as 'STP') — and shows how firms can segment a service market, position their value proposition, and finally focus on attracting their target segment.

Creating Value in the Service Economy

Ours is a service economy and has been for some time.

Karl Albrecht and Ron Zemke,
Thought leaders in business and service

In today's marketplace, consumers have the power to pick and choose as never before.

From the article "Crowned At Last",
published in **The Economist**, 31 March 2005

It's never enough to just tell people about some new insight… Instead of pouring knowledge into people's heads, you need to help them grind a new set of eyeglasses so that they can see the world in a new way. That involves challenging the implicit assumptions that have shaped the way people have historically looked at things.

John Seely Brown,
Thought leader on innovation

LEARNING OBJECTIVES (LOs)

By the end of this chapter, the reader should be able to:

LO 1 Understand how services contribute to a country's economy.

LO 2 Know the principal industries of the service sector.

LO 3 Identify the powerful forces that are transforming service markets.

LO 4 Understand how B2B services improve the productivity of individual firms and drive economic development.

LO 5 Be familiar with the difference between outsourcing and offshoring of services.

LO 6 Define services using the non-ownership service framework.

LO 7 Identify the four broad "processing" categories of services.

LO 8 Be familiar with the characteristics of services and the distinctive marketing challenges they pose.

LO 9 Understand the components of the traditional marketing mix applied to services.

LO 10 Describe the components of the extended marketing mix for managing the customer interface.

LO 11 Appreciate that the marketing, operations, and human resource management functions need to be closely integrated in service businesses.

LO 12 Understand the implications of the Service–Profit Chain for service management.

LO 13 Know the framework for developing effective service marketing strategies.

Figure 1.1 Tertiary education may be one of the biggest service purchases in life

OPENING VIGNETTE

Introduction to the World of Services Marketing

Like every reader of this book, you're an experienced service consumer. You use an array of services every day, although some — such as talking on the phone, using a credit card, riding a bus, downloading music, using the Internet, or withdrawing money from an ATM — may be so routine that you hardly ever notice them unless something goes wrong. Other service purchases may involve more thought and be more memorable — for instance, booking a cruise vacation, getting financial advice, or having a medical examination. Enrolling in college or graduate school may be one of the biggest service purchases you will ever make. A typical university is a complex service organization that offers not only educational services, but also libraries, student accommodation, healthcare, athletic facilities, museums, security, counseling, and career services.

On campus you may find a bookstore, a bank, a post office, a photocopying shop, Internet cafes, a grocery store, entertainment, and more. Your use of these services is an example of service consumption at the individual or business-to-consumer (B2C) level.

Organizations use a wide array of business-to-business (B2B) services, which usually involve purchases on a much larger scale than those made by individuals or households.

Nowadays, organizations outsource more and more tasks to external service providers in order to focus on their core business. Without being able to buy these services at a good value, these organizations can't hope to succeed. Unfortunately, consumers aren't always happy with the quality and value of the services they receive. You too may not always be delighted with your service experiences; in fact, at times, you may be very disappointed.

Both individual and corporate consumers complain about broken promises, poor value for money, rude or incompetent personnel, inconvenient service hours, bureaucratic procedures, wasted time, malfunctioning self-service technologies (SSTs), complicated websites, a lack of understanding of their needs, and various other problems.

Suppliers of services, who often face stiff competition, appear to have a very different set of concerns. Many owners and managers complain about how difficult it is to find skilled and motivated employees, to keep costs down and make a profit, or to satisfy customers, who, they sometimes grumble, have become unreasonably demanding.

Fortunately, there are service companies that know how to please their customers while also running a productive and profitable operation, staffed by pleasant and competent employees, and accessible through user-friendly SSTs, websites, and apps.

You probably have a few favorite service firms you like to patronize. Have you ever stopped to think about the way they succeed in delivering services that meet and sometimes even exceed your expectations? This book will show you how service businesses can be managed to achieve customer satisfaction and profitability.

In addition to studying key concepts, organizing frameworks, and tools of services marketing, you will also be introduced to many examples from firms across the United States and around the world. From the experiences of other firms, you can draw important lessons on how to succeed in increasingly competitive service markets.

Figure 1.2 Happy people on a cruise vacation

Why Study Services

- Services dominate the global economy
- Most new jobs are generated by services
- Understanding services offers personal competitive advantage

Definition of Services

- Services provide benefits without ownership
- Services are economic activities performed by one party to another. Often time-based, these performances bring about desired results to recipients, objects, or other assets. In exchange for money, time, and effort, service customers expect value from access to labor, skills, expertise, goods, facilities, networks, and systems.

Service Sector Industries

In order of contribution to US GDP:

- Government services
- Real estate
- Business and professional services
- Wholesale & retail trade
- Transport, utilities, & communications
- Finance & insurance
- Healthcare services
- Accommodation & food services
- Arts, entertainment, & recreation service
- Other private sector services

Categories of Services by Type of Processing

- People processing (e.g., passenger transport, hairstyling)
- Possession processing (e.g., freight transport, repair services)
- Mental stimulus processing (e.g., education)
- Information processing (e.g., accounting)

Key Trends

General Trends

- Government policies
- Social changes
- Business trends
- Advances in IT
- Globalization

B2B Services Growth

- Outsourcing
- Offshoring
- Firms increasing focus on core competencies
- Increasing specialization of economies
- Increasing productivity through R&D

Services Pose Distinct Marketing Challenges

Services tend to have four frequently cited characteristics: *i*ntangibility, *h*eterogeneity (variability of quality), *i*nseparability of *p*roduction and consumption, and perishability of output, or *IHIP* for short. Key implications of these features include the following:

- Most services cannot be inventoried (i.e., output is perishable).
- Intangible elements typically dominate value creation (i.e., services are physically intangible).
- Services are often difficult to understand (i.e., services are mentally intangible).
- Customers are often involved in co-production (i.e., if people processing is involved, the service in inseparable).
- People (service employees) may be part of the service product and experience.
- Operational inputs and outputs tend to vary more widely (i.e., services are heterogeneous).
- The time factor often assumes great importance (e.g., capacity management).
- Distribution may take place through nonphysical channels (e.g., information processing services).

Functions

Need to be tightly integrated as together they shape the customer experience, especially:

- Marketing
- Operations
- Human resources
- Information technology

Service–Profit Chain

Shows the tight links between

- Leadership
- Internal quality and IT
- Employee engagement
- Customer value, satisfaction, & loyalty
- Profitability & growth

Putting Service Strategy Into Action

This books is structured around an integrated model of services marketing and management that covers:

- Understanding Service Products, Consumers, & Markets
- Applying the 4 Ps of Marketing to Services
- Designing & Managing the Customer Interface using the additional 3 Ps of Services Marketing (Process, People, & Physical Environment)
- Developing Customer Relationships
- Striving for Service Excellence

Figure 1.3 Introduction to services marketing.

Figure 1.3 provides an overview of Chapter 1. In this chapter, we describe today's ever-changing service economy, define the nature of services, and highlight some challenges involved in marketing services. We conclude the chapter with a framework for developing and implementing service marketing strategies. This framework also establishes the structure for this book

WHY STUDY SERVICES?

➲ **LO 1**
Understand how services contribute to a country's economy.

Consider this paradox: While we live in a service-driven economy, most business schools continue to teach marketing from a manufacturing perspective. If you have already taken a course in marketing, you would have most likely learned more about marketing manufactured products, especially consumer goods, rather than marketing services. Fortunately, a growing and enthusiastic group of scholars, consultants, and educators, including the authors of this book, has chosen to focus on services marketing and build on the extensive research conducted in this field over the past four decades. This book aims to provide you with the knowledge and skills that are necessary and relevant in tomorrow's business environment.

Services Dominate the Global Economy

The size of the service sector is increasing in almost all countries around the world. As an economy develops, the relative share of employment between agriculture, industry (including manufacturing and mining), and services changes dramatically[1]. Even in emerging economies, the service output is growing rapidly and often represents at least half of the Gross Domestic Product (GDP). *Figure 1.4* shows how the evolution to a service-dominated economy is likely to take place over time as the per capita income rises. In developed economies, knowledge-based services — defined as having intensive users of high technology or relatively skilled workforces — have been the most dynamic component[2]. *Figure 1.5* shows that the service sector already accounts for almost two-thirds of the value of the global GDP.

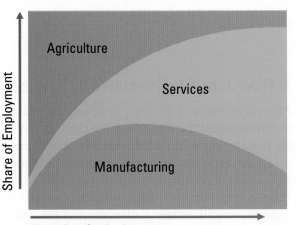

Figure 1.4 Changing structure of employment as an economy develops

Source
International Monetary Fund, 1997

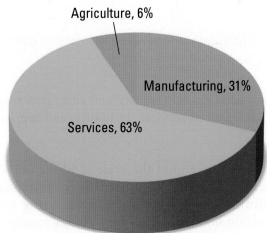

Figure 1.5 Contribution of services industries to GDP globally

Source
The World Factbook 2015, Central Intelligence Agency, www.cia.gov, accessed January 22, 2015.

Figure 1.6 shows the relative size of the service sector in various large and small economies. For most of the highly developed nations, services account for 65–80% of the GDP. One exception is South Korea, a manufacturing-oriented country with its service sector contributing only 58% to the GDP. Which are the world's most service-dominated economies? The answer would be Jersey, the Bahamas, and Bermuda — all small islands with a similar economic mix — which are equally service-dominated. Luxembourg (86%) has the most service-dominated economy in the European Union. Panama's strong showing (78%) reflects not only the operation of the Panama Canal, which is widely used by cruise ships as well as freight vessels, but also related services such as

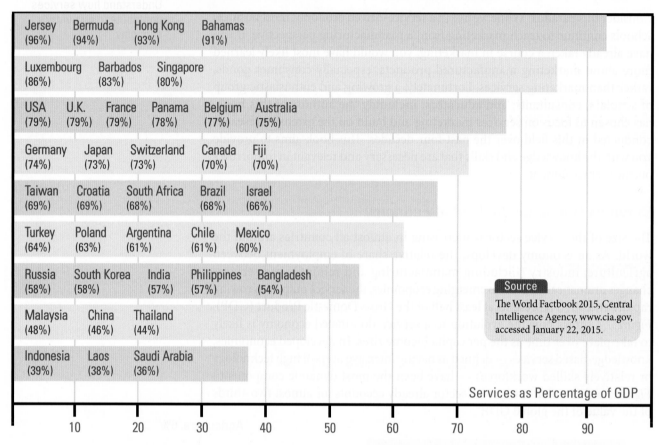

Figure 1.6 Estimated size of service sector in selected countries as a percentage of GDP

container ports, flagship registry, and a free port zone, as well as financial services, insurance, and tourism (*Figure 1.7*).

On the opposite end of the scale is China (46%), an emerging economy dominated by a substantial agricultural sector, booming manufacturing and construction industries. However, China's economic growth is now leading to an increase in demand for business and consumer services. China's government is investing heavily in service infrastructure, including shipping facilities and new airport terminals. Among the relatively affluent countries is Saudi Arabia with its oil-dominated economy, where services account for only 36% of the GDP.

Most New Jobs Are Generated by Services

Since the service sector is growing so rapidly in virtually all countries around the world, new job creation comes mainly from services. In fact, this shift in employment to the service sector has been seen as one of the longest and most stable of economic trends[3]. Service jobs do not just refer to relatively lowly paid frontline jobs such as in restaurants or call centers. Rather, some of the fastest economic growth is in knowledge-based industries — such as professional and business services, education, and healthcare[4]. These jobs tend to be well-paid, require good educational qualifications, and offer attractive careers.

Many manufacturing firms too have moved from just bundling supplementary services with their physical products to marketing certain elements as standalone services. See *Service Insights 1.1* to find out how Rolls-Royce achieved that transformation.

Just like Rolls-Royce, IBM was also previously known mainly as a manufacturer. The company made the transformation to a service provider and has become the world's largest business and technology services provider offering management consulting, systems integration, and application management services as part of IBM Global Services[5]. Not only has IBM moved into delivering services, it is also at the forefront of the movement to ensure that it trains workers for the service economy. Reflecting the ever tighter integration of value creation in the service economy, IBM coined the term Service Science, Management and Engineering (SSME), often called **service science** for short, which integrates key disciplines required to design, improve, and scale service systems. To be effective in today's service-driven economies, IBM believes future graduates should be 'T'-shaped. That is, they need a deep understanding of their own discipline such as business, engineering, or computer science (the vertical part of the T) as well as a basic understanding of service-related topics in other disciplines (the horizontal part of the T)[6].

Figure 1.7 The Panama Canal forms the backbone of Panama's service economy

SERVICE INSIGHTS 1.1
Rolls-Royce Sells Power by the Hour

Many manufacturing firms increase their competitive edge by providing superior value to their customers in the form of service. Rolls-Royce is one such example. Rolls-Royce, which makes world-class aircraft engines, is a successful company because it focuses on technical innovation. Rolls-Royce engines power about half of the latest wide-bodied passenger jets and a quarter of all single-aisle aircrafts in the world. A very important factor for its success has been the move from manufacturing to selling "power by the hour"— a bundle of goods and services that keeps the customers' engines running smoothly.

Imagine this — high above the Pacific, passengers doze on a long-haul flight from Tokyo to Los Angeles. Suddenly, there is a bolt of lightning. Passengers may not think much of it, but on the other side of the world in Derby, England, engineers at Rolls-Royce get busy. Lightning strikes on jets are common and usually harmless, but this one has caused some problems in one of the engines. The aircraft will still be able to land safely and could do so even with the affected engine shut down. The question is whether it will need a full engine inspection in Los Angeles, which would be normal practice but would also inconvenience hundreds of passengers waiting in the departure lounge.

A stream of data is beamed from the plane to Derby. Numbers dance across screens, graphs are drawn, and engineers scratch their heads. Before the aircraft lands, word comes that the engine is running smoothly, will not need a physical inspection, and the plane will be able to take off on time.

Industry experts estimate that manufacturers of jet engines can make about seven times the revenue from servicing and selling spare parts than they do from just selling the engines. Since it is so profitable, many independent servicing firms compete with companies like Rolls-Royce and offer spare parts for as low as one-third of the price charged by the original equipment manufacturers (OEMs). This is where Rolls-Royce has used a combination of technology and service to make it more difficult for competitors to steal its clients. Instead of selling engines first and parts and service later, Rolls-Royce has created an attractive bundle, which it branded TotalCare®. Customers are charged for every hour that an engine runs. Its website advertizes it as a solution ensuring "peace of mind" for the lifetime of an engine. Rolls-Royce promises to maintain the engine and replace it if it breaks down. The operations room in Derby continuously monitors the performance of some 3,500 engines, enabling it to predict when engines are likely to fail and let airlines schedule engine changes efficiently, reduce repairs and unhappy passengers. Today, about 80% of the engines shipped to its customers are covered by such contracts! Although Rolls-Royce had engines troubles on its A380, they fixed the problem quickly and bounced back from the incident with many more orders for their engines.

© Rolls-Royce plc

Leading research centers have followed IBM's call and have increasingly focused on the integration of key disciplines to better equip future service professionals. Some of the leading centers that have embraced service science include (in alphabetical order): the Center for Excellence in Service of Robert H. Smith School of Business at University of Maryland (www.rhsmith.umd.edu/ces), the Center for Services Leadership at the W. P. Carey School of Business at Arizona State University (http://wpcarey.asu.edu/csl), and The Service Research Center at Karlstad University in Sweden (www.ctf.kau.se). Recently, even an academic journal called *Service Science* has been launched to provide a publication outlet for service science research[7].

Understanding Services Offers Personal Competitive Advantage

This book is in response to the global transformation of our economies towards services. Learning about the distinctive characteristics of services and how they affect both customer behavior and marketing strategy will give you important insights and perhaps create a competitive advantage for your own career. Unless you are predestined to work in a family manufacturing or agricultural business, the probability is high that you will spend most of your working life in service organizations. You may also find yourself serving as a volunteer or board member for a nonprofit organization. The knowledge gained from studying this book may even encourage you to think about starting your own service business!

WHAT ARE THE PRINCIPAL INDUSTRIES OF THE SERVICE SECTOR?

⊃ LO 2
Know the principal industries of the service sector.

What industries make up the service sector and which are the biggest? The latter may not be the ones you would imagine at first, because this diverse sector includes many services targeted at business customers, some of which are not very visible unless you happen to work in that industry. National economic statistics are a useful starting point. To provide a better understanding of today's service-dominated economy, government statistical agencies have developed new ways to classify industries. In the United States, the manufacturing-oriented Standard Industrial Classification (SIC) system, developed in the 1930s, has been replaced by the new North American Industry Classification System (NAICS)[8], with Canada and Mexico adopting it too (*Service Insights 1.2*).

SERVICE INSIGHTS 1.2

NAICS: A New Way to Classify the Economies of North America

The North American Industry Classification System — developed jointly by the statistical agencies of Canada, Mexico, and the United States — offers a new approach to classifying industries in the economic statistics of the three North American Free Trade Agreement (NAFTA) countries. It replaces previous national systems, such as the SIC codes formerly used in the United States.

NAICS (pronounced "nakes") includes many new service industries that have emerged in recent decades and also reclassifies services as "auxiliary" establishments that provide services to manufacturing industries — examples include accounting, catering, and transportation. Every sector of the economy has been restructured and redefined. NAICS includes 358 new industries that the SIC did not identify, 390 that are revised from their SIC counterparts, and 422 that continue substantially unchanged. These industries are grouped into sectors and further subdivided into subsectors, industry groups, and establishments.

Among the new sectors and subsectors devoted to services are: *Information,* which recognizes the emergence and uniqueness of businesses in the "information economy"; *Health Care and Social Assistance; Professional, Scientific and Business Services; Educational Services;* and *Accommodation and Food Services; and Arts, Entertainment and Recreation* (which includes most businesses engaged in meeting consumers' cultural, leisure, or entertainment interests).

NAICS uses a consistent principle for classification, grouping businesses that use similar production processes. Its goal is to make economic statistics more useful and to capture developments that encompass applications of high technology (e.g., cellular telecommunications), new businesses that previously did not exist (e.g., environmental consulting), and changes in the way business is done (e.g., warehouse clubs).

NAICS codes are set up in such a way that researchers can drill down within broad industry sectors to obtain information on tightly defined types of service establishments. For instance, the NAICS code 71 designates arts, entertainment and recreation. Code 7112 designates spectator sports, and code 711211 designates sports teams and clubs. By looking at changes over time in "real" dollars (adjusted for inflation), it's possible to determine which industries have been growing and which have not. The NAICS codes are also being used to categorize employment statistics and numbers of establishments within a particular industry. And a new North American Product Classification System (NAPCS) thus defines thousands of service products. If you want to research service industries and service products, NAICS data is a great place to start.

Source

Economic Classification Policy Committee, "NAICS—North American Industry Classification System: New Data for a New Economy". Washington, DC: Bureau of the Census, October 1998; North American Industry Classification System, United States 2002 [Official NAICS manual], Washington, D.C.: National Technical Information Service, PB2002101430*SS, 2002. http://www.census.gov/eos/www/naics/, accessed January 22, 2015.

Contribution to Gross Domestic Product

To see how much value each of the major service industry groups contributes to the U.S. GDP, take a look at *Figure 1.8*. Would you have guessed that real estate and rental and leasing would be the largest for-profit service industry sector in the United States, accounting for 13% in 2013, almost one-eighth of GDP? Over 90% of this figure comes from activities such as renting residential or commercial property; managing properties on behalf of their owners; providing realty services to facilitate purchases, sales, and rentals; and appraising property to determine its condition and value. The balance is accounted for by renting or leasing a wide variety of other manufactured products, ranging from heavy construction equipment (with or without operators) to office furniture, tents, and party supplies. Another large cluster of services provides for distribution of physical products. Wholesale and retail trade accounts for about 11.8% of GDP.

Other substantial industry sectors or subsectors are professional and business services (11.8%), finance and insurance (7.2%), and healthcare (7.1%). Accommodation and food services constitute 2.7%, while the arts, entertainment, and recreation services — which includes high-profile consumer services such as spectator sports, fitness centers, skiing facilities, museums and zoos, performing arts, casinos, golf courses, marinas, and theme parks — collectively represent a mere 1.0% of GDP. Nevertheless, in an economy with an output of over $17.1 trillion, this last group of services was still valued at an impressive $164 billion in 2013.

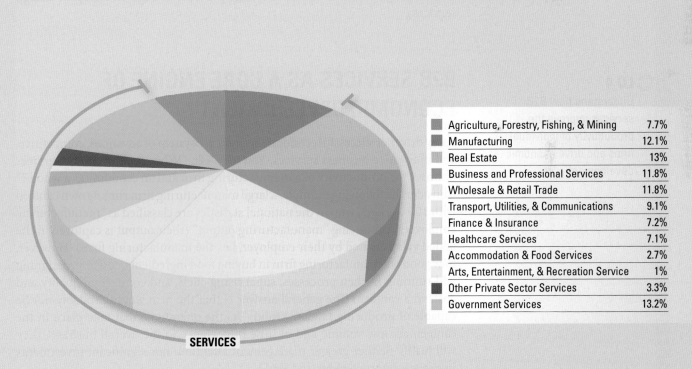

Agriculture, Forestry, Fishing, & Mining	7.7%
Manufacturing	12.1%
Real Estate	13%
Business and Professional Services	11.8%
Wholesale & Retail Trade	11.8%
Transport, Utilities, & Communications	9.1%
Finance & Insurance	7.2%
Healthcare Services	7.1%
Accommodation & Food Services	2.7%
Arts, Entertainment, & Recreation Service	1%
Other Private Sector Services	3.3%
Government Services	13.2%

SERVICES

Figure 1.8 Value added by service industry categories to US GDP.

Source

Adapted from: U.S. Department of Commerce, Bureau of Economic Analysis, GDP by Industry Accounts for 2013, 2007, www.bea.gov; accessed January 22, 2015.

POWERFUL FORCES ARE TRANSFORMING SERVICE MARKETS

What are the factors causing this rapid growth of the service sector? Government policies, social changes, business trends, globalization, and advances in information technology (IT) and communications in particular, are among the powerful forces transforming today's service markets (*Figure 1.9*). Collectively, these forces reshape demand, supply, competitive landscape, and even the way customers buy and use services.

Of these forces, the dramatic development of IT and communications is perhaps the most important at the moment. Innovations in big data, cloud computing, user-generated content, mobile communications, networking technologies, artificial intelligence, and increasingly app-based SSTs bring their own service revolution. These technologies enable firms to deepen the relationships with their customers, offer multi-way information flow and more personalized services, improved analytics, and increase productivity and profitability[9]. More importantly, these new technologies also lead to a vast array of highly innovative business models, ranging from peer-to-peer services (e.g., Airbnb for short-term accommodation and Lending Club for personal loans), integrators (e.g., Uber connects passengers with independent drivers through apps), to crowd-based services (e.g., crowdSPRING, a leading provider of logo and graphic design services).

LO 4

Understand how B2B services improve the productivity of individual firms and drive economic development.

B2B SERVICES AS A CORE ENGINE OF ECONOMIC DEVELOPMENT[10]

A key driver of successful economies is their ecosystem of advanced, competitive, and innovative business services. You may ask, "Why would business services improve the productivity of a manufacturing firm and an economy as a whole?" Consider the following example: a large manufacturing firm runs its own canteen with 100 workers, who in the national statistics are classified as "manufacturing employees" producing "manufacturing output" (their output is captured in the added value created by their employer, i.e., the manufacturing firm). However, how good is a manufacturing firm in buying food ingredients, cooking, designing and running kitchen processes, supervising chefs, and controlling quality and costs in a canteen? The general answer is that the firm would probably not be capable of producing fantastic food. As the operations that take place in the canteen are low volume and of little importance to the overall business, they will justify neither greater management attention, nor significant investments in process improvements and R&D.

Many manufacturing firms have recognized this problem and outsourced their canteen operations, most likely via a tendering process with a renewal period of every few years. The winning bidder is likely to be a firm that specializes in running canteens and kitchens across many sites or branches. That company makes "operating canteens" its core competency. As such, the operation is managed with an emphasis on the quality of the services and food provided, and the efficiency of its cost structure. Branches can be benchmarked internally, and the overall operation has economies of scale, and is way down the learning curve.

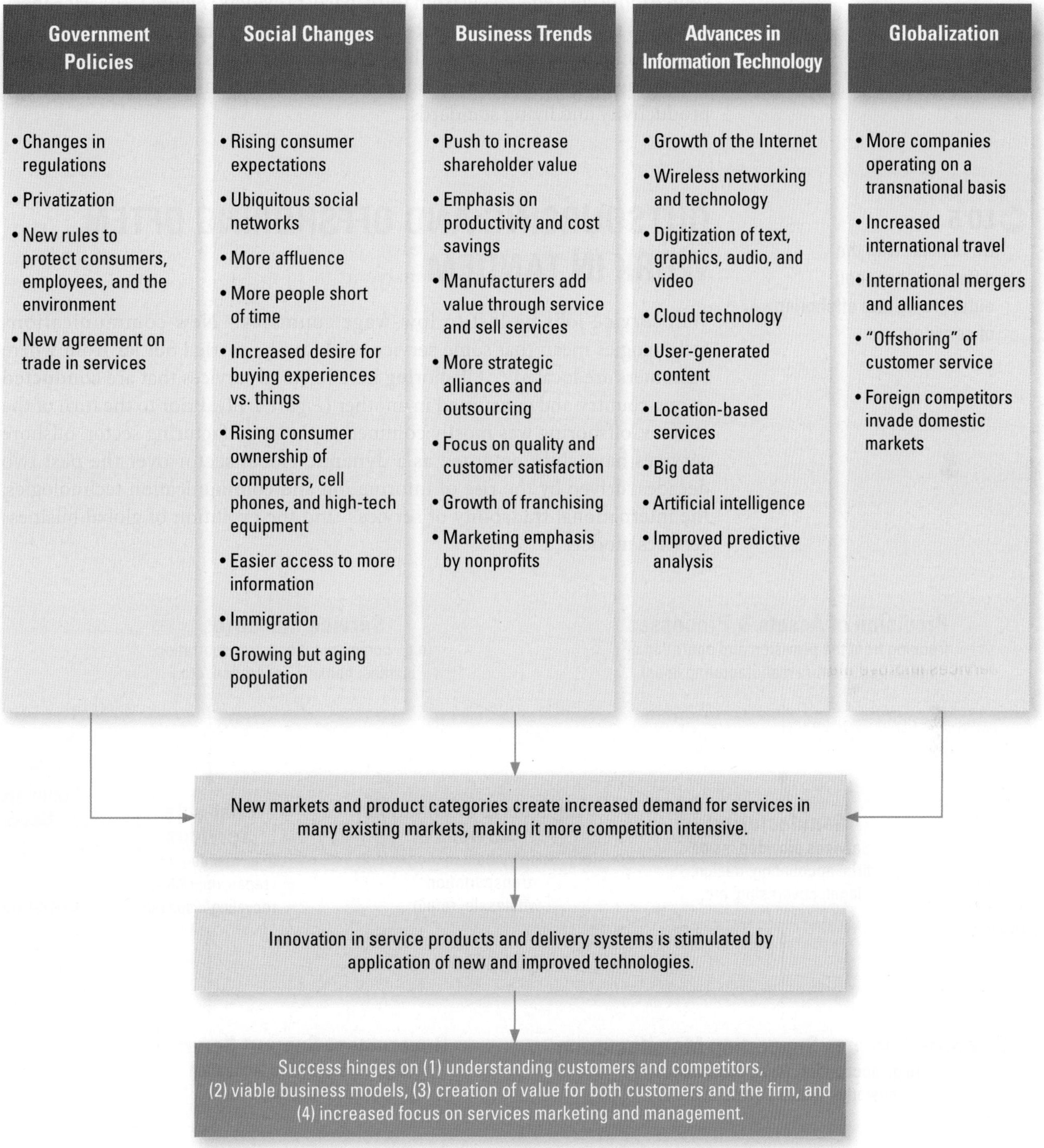

Government Policies	Social Changes	Business Trends	Advances in Information Technology	Globalization
• Changes in regulations • Privatization • New rules to protect consumers, employees, and the environment • New agreement on trade in services	• Rising consumer expectations • Ubiquitous social networks • More affluence • More people short of time • Increased desire for buying experiences vs. things • Rising consumer ownership of computers, cell phones, and high-tech equipment • Easier access to more information • Immigration • Growing but aging population	• Push to increase shareholder value • Emphasis on productivity and cost savings • Manufacturers add value through service and sell services • More strategic alliances and outsourcing • Focus on quality and customer satisfaction • Growth of franchising • Marketing emphasis by nonprofits	• Growth of the Internet • Wireless networking and technology • Digitization of text, graphics, audio, and video • Cloud technology • User-generated content • Location-based services • Big data • Artificial intelligence • Improved predictive analysis	• More companies operating on a transnational basis • Increased international travel • International mergers and alliances • "Offshoring" of customer service • Foreign competitors invade domestic markets

New markets and product categories create increased demand for services in many existing markets, making it more competition intensive.

Innovation in service products and delivery systems is stimulated by application of new and improved technologies.

Success hinges on (1) understanding customers and competitors, (2) viable business models, (3) creation of value for both customers and the firm, and (4) increased focus on services marketing and management.

Figure 1.9 Factors stimulating the transformation of the service economy

It also makes sense for the firm to invest in process improvements and R&D as the benefits can be reaped across multiple sites. What used to be a neglected support activity within a manufacturing firm has become a management focus and core competency of an independent service provider. The same logic applies to almost all non-core activities, assets, goods, and services a company can source more cost-effectively from third-party providers (*Figure 1.10*). McKinsey estimates that such service inputs to manufacturing output are about 20–25%, offering much potential for further outsourcing[11]. This development leads to an increasing specialization of our economies with significant gains in overall productivity and living standards.

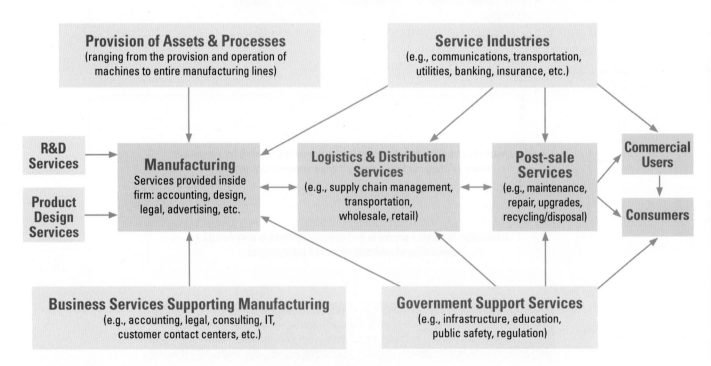

⊃ LO 5
Be familiar with the difference between outsourcing and offshoring of services.

OUTSOURCING AND OFFSHORING OFTEN WORK IN TANDEM

Will service jobs be lost to low-wage countries? New communications technologies mean that some service work can be carried out far from where customers are located[12]. Offshoring here refers to services that are **conducted** in one country and **consumed** in another (*Figure 1.11*). Prior to the turn of the century, offshoring was mostly confined to the manufacturing sector, offshore services have since emerged as a dynamic global sector over the past two decades, driven by the rise of information and communication technologies, the international tradability of services, and the evolution of global business services models.

Figure 1.10 Outsourcing is an important driver for the growth of the service sector.

Source

Jochen Wirtz and Michael Ehret, "Service-Based Business Models: Transforming Businesses, Industries and Economies," in Raymond P. Fisk, Rebekah Russell-Bennett, and Lloyd C. Harris, eds. *Serving Customers: Global Services Marketing Perspectives* (Tilde University Press, Melbourne, Australia), 28–46.

Figure 1.12 shows different business models that can develop in the outsourcing and offshoring of services[13]. The first scenario (**Arrow 1**) describes a firm's decision to outsource services domestically. **Arrow 2** describes a situation where a firm switches from a domestic supplier to a foreign supplier. In some cases, firms make the decision to outsource and to offshore to a foreign supplier simultaneously (**Arrow 3**). The fourth scenario is when firms source from foreign locations by establishing a subsidiary abroad (**Arrow 4**). This is often referred to as "captive offshoring." Finally, combining outsourcing and offshoring implies shifting the service provision from a foreign affiliate to a foreign-owned supplier (**Arrow 5**).

A study by the international consulting firm McKinsey & Company estimated that 11% of service jobs around the world could be carried out remotely. In practice, however, McKinsey predicted that the percentage of service jobs that could actually be "offshored" will prove to be much more limited — only 1% of the total service employment in developed countries[14]. Of course, loss of even that small percentage can affect a large number of workers, including some well-paid professionals whose work can be performed much more cost-effectively by, say, highly qualified engineers working in India, the Philippines, or Belarus[15].

Figure 1.11 Many services today can be outsourced to lower cost destinations

"We found someone overseas who can drink coffee and talk about sports all day for a fraction of what we're paying you."

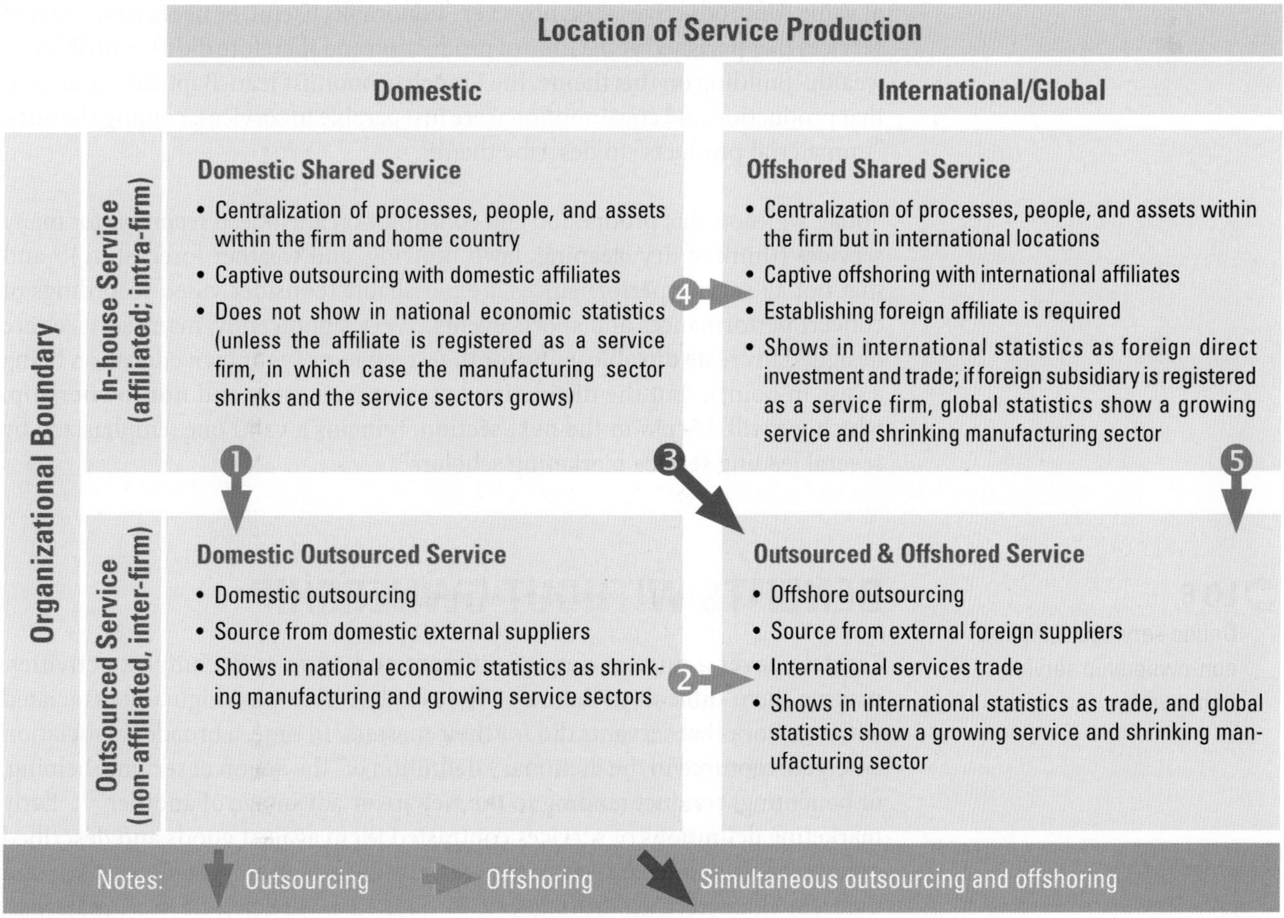

Location of Service Production

		Domestic	International/Global
Organizational Boundary	**In-house Service (affiliated; intra-firm)**	**Domestic Shared Service** • Centralization of processes, people, and assets within the firm and home country • Captive outsourcing with domestic affiliates • Does not show in national economic statistics (unless the affiliate is registered as a service firm, in which case the manufacturing sector shrinks and the service sectors grows)	**Offshored Shared Service** • Centralization of processes, people, and assets within the firm but in international locations • Captive offshoring with international affiliates • Establishing foreign affiliate is required • Shows in international statistics as foreign direct investment and trade; if foreign subsidiary is registered as a service firm, global statistics show a growing service and shrinking manufacturing sector
	Outsourced Service (non-affiliated, inter-firm)	**Domestic Outsourced Service** • Domestic outsourcing • Source from domestic external suppliers • Shows in national economic statistics as shrinking manufacturing and growing service sectors	**Outsourced & Offshored Service** • Offshore outsourcing • Source from external foreign suppliers • International services trade • Shows in international statistics as trade, and global statistics show a growing service and shrinking manufacturing sector

Notes: ⬇ Outsourcing ➡ Offshoring ⬊ Simultaneous outsourcing and offshoring

Figure 1.12 Outsourcing and offshoring are independent, but often work in tandem.

Source

Jochen Wirtz, Sven Tuzovic, and Michael Ehret (2015), "Global Business Services: Increasing Specialization and Integration of the World Economy as Drivers of Economic Growth," *Journal of Service Management*, Vol. 26, No.4, pp. 565--587.

WHAT ARE SERVICES?

Thus far, our discussion of services has focused on different types of service industries and their development. But now it's time to ask the question: What exactly is a service?

The Historical View

Attempts to describe and define services go back more than two centuries. In the late eighteenth and early nineteenth centuries, classical economists focused on the creation and possession of wealth. They contended that goods (initially referred to as "commodities") were objects of value over which ownership rights could be established and exchanged. Ownership implied tangible possession of an object that had been acquired through purchase, barter, or gift from the producer or a previous owner, and was legally identifiable as the property of the current owner.

Adam Smith's famous book *The Wealth of Nations,* published in Great Britain in 1776, distinguished between the outputs of what he termed "productive" and "unproductive" labor[16]. The former, he stated, produced goods that could be stored after production and subsequently exchanged for money or other items of value. Unproductive labor, however "honorable, useful, or necessary," created services that **perished** at the time of production and therefore didn't contribute to wealth. Building on this theme, the French economist Jean-Baptiste Say argued that production and consumption were inseparable in services, coining the term "immaterial products" to describe them[17].

Today, we know that production and consumption are indeed *separable* for many services (think of dry cleaning, lawn mowing, and weather forecasting)[18] and that not all service performances are perishable (consider video recordings of concert performances and sports events). Very significantly, many services are designed to create **durable value** for their recipients (your own education being a case in point). But the distinction between ownership and **non-ownership**, which we will discuss in the next section, remains a valid one, emphasized by several leading service marketing scholars[19].

BENEFITS WITHOUT OWNERSHIP

⊃ **LO 6**
Define services using the non-ownership service framework.

Services cover a huge variety of different and often very complex activities, making them difficult to define[20]. The word **service** was originally associated with the work that servants did for their masters. In time, a broader association emerged, captured in the dictionary definition of "the action of serving, helping, or benefiting; conduct tending to the welfare or advantage of another"[21]. Early marketing definitions of services contrasted them against goods and described services as "acts, deeds, performances, or efforts" and argued that they had different characteristics from goods — defined as "articles, devices, materials, objects, or things"[22]. But we believe that services need to be defined in their own right, not in relation to goods. A short and snappy definition, like the oft-repeated "something which can be bought and sold but which cannot be dropped on your foot"[23] is amusing and memorable, but may not be particularly helpful as a guide to marketing strategy. Today, our thinking has advanced and focuses on the lack of transfer of ownership when buying a service.

Consider this: you didn't acquire ownership of the hotel room where you stayed last weekend, you didn't have ownership over the physical therapist who worked on your injured knee, and you didn't receive ownership of the concert you just attended. None of these purchases resulted in actual ownership. If you didn't receive a transfer of ownership the last time you purchased a service, then what did you buy?

Christopher Lovelock and Evert Gummesson argue that services involve a form of **rental** through which customers can obtain benefits[24]. What customers value and are willing to pay for are desired experiences and solutions. We use the term **rent** as a general term to describe payment made for use of something or access to skills and expertise, facilities or networks (usually for a defined period of time), instead of buying it outright (which may not even be possible in many instances).

We can identify five broad categories within the non-ownership framework that focus on (1) use of labor, skills, and expertise, (2–4) various degrees of use of goods and facilities (exclusive, defined, or shared), and (5) access and use of networks and systems:

1. **Labor, skills, and expertise rentals.** Here, other people are hired to perform work that customers either cannot or choose not to do themselves. Some of these include:
   - Car repair
   - Medical check-up
   - Management consulting

2. **Rented goods services.** These services allow customers to obtain the exclusive temporary right to use a physical object that they prefer not to own. Examples include:
   - Boats
   - Fancy dress costumes
   - Construction and excavation equipment

3. **Defined space and facility rentals.** This is when customers obtain the use of a certain portion of a larger facility such as a building, vehicle, or area. They usually share this facility with other customers. Examples of this kind of rental include:
   - A seat in an aircraft
   - A suite in an office building
   - A storage container in a warehouse

4. **Access to shared facilities**. Customers rent the right to share the use of the facility. The facilities may be a combination of indoors, outdoors, and virtual. Examples include:
   - Theme parks
   - Golf clubs
   - Toll roads *(Figure 1.13)*

5. **Access and use of networks and systems**. Customers rent the right to participate in a specified network. Service providers offer a variety of terms for access and use, depending on customer needs. Examples include:
   - Telecommunications
   - Utilities and banking
   - Social online networks and games (e.g., League of Legends)

The difference between ownership and non-ownership affects the nature of marketing tasks and strategy. For example, the criteria for a customer's choice of service differ when something is being rented instead of owned. For a rental car to be used on vacation in Hawaii, for example, customers may focus on the ease of making reservations, the rental location and hours, the attitudes and performance of service personnel, the cleanliness and maintenance of vehicles, etc. If the customers are looking to own a car, then they are more likely to consider price, brand image, ease of maintenance, running costs, design, color, upholstery, etc.

Figure 1.13 Customers rent the right to use toll roads

Defining Services

Based on the non-ownership perspective of services, we offer the following comprehensive definition of services:

> ## DEFINITION OF SERVICES
>
> Services are economic activities performed by one party to another. Often time-based, these performances bring about desired results to recipients, objects, or other assets.
>
> In exchange for money, time, and effort, service customers expect value from access to labor, skills, expertise, goods, facilities, networks, and systems. However, they do not normally take ownership of the physical elements involved[25].

Note that we define services as **economic activities** between two parties, implying an exchange of value between the seller and buyer in the marketplace. We describe services as **performances** that are most commonly **time-based**. We emphasize that purchasers buy services because they are looking for **desired results**. In fact, many firms explicitly market their services as "solutions" to prospective customers' needs. And finally, our definition emphasizes that while customers *expect to obtain value* from their service purchases *in exchange for their money, time, and effort,* this value comes from *access to a variety of value-creating elements rather than transfer of ownership.* (Spare parts installed during repairs and restaurant-prepared food and beverages are among the few exceptions, but the value added by these items is usually less than that of the accompanying service elements).

Service Products versus Customer Service and After-Sales Service

With the growth of the service economy, and the emphasis on adding value-enhancing services to manufactured goods, the line between services and manufacturing increasingly becomes blurred. Many manufacturing firms — from carmakers Toyota, aerospace engine producers GE and Rolls-Royce to high-tech equipment manufacturers Samsung and Siemens — are moving aggressively into service businesses[26]. Quite a few firms have transitioned from simply bundling supplementary services with their physical products to reformulating and enhancing certain elements so that they can be marketed as standalone services (see the example of Gulfstream in *Figure 1.14*)[27]. Another success story is Rolls-Royce featured in *Service Insights 1.1*.

The principles and tools discussed in services marketing (e.g., how to price a service, manage capacity in a call center, improve service quality or manage service employees) are equally applicable to manufacturing firms that increase the service component of their offering. As Theodore Levitt long ago observed, "There are no such things as service industries. There are only industries whose service components are greater or less than those

Figure 1.14 Gulfstream advertises its award-winning maintenance and support services

of other industries. Everybody is in service[28]." More recently, Roland Rust and Ming-Hui Huang suggested that "the 'product versus services' conceptualization is out-of-date and that service is everywhere, not just in the service sector[29]." An even more radical view has been advanced by Stephen Vargo and Robert Lusch in their award-winning article on a new mindset, the **service-dominant (S-D) logic**. S-D logic suggests that all products are valued for the service they provide, and that the value derived from a physical good, for example, is not the good itself, but the service it provides during consumption (which they termed "**value-in-use**"[30]).

FOUR BROAD CATEGORIES OF SERVICES — A PROCESS PERSPECTIVE

 LO 7
Identify the four broad "processing" categories of services.

Did you notice that the definition of services emphasizes not only value creation through rental and access, but also the desired results that can be brought about to recipients of the service, objects, and other assets? There are major differences among services depending on what is being processed. Services can "process" people, physical objects, and data, and the nature of the processing can be tangible or intangible. Tangible actions are performed on people's bodies or to their physical possessions. Intangible actions are performed on people's minds or to their intangible assets. This gives rise to the classification of services into four broad categories. They are **people-processing, possession-processing, mental stimulus processing,** and **information processing** (*Figure 1.15*)[31]. Although the industries within each category may appear at first sight to be very different, analysis will show that they do, in fact, share important process-related characteristics. As a result, managers from different industries within the same category may obtain useful insights by studying another to generate useful innovations for their own organization. Let's examine why these four different types of processes often have distinctive implications for marketing, operations, and human resource management.

Name of the Service Act	Name of the Service Act	
	People	**Possessions**
Tangible Actions	**People processing** (services directed at people's bodies): • Hairstylist • Passenger Transportation • Healthcare	**Possession processing** (services directed at physical possessions): • Freight Transportation • Laundry and Dry Cleaning • Repair and Maintenance
Intangible Actions	**Mental stimulus processing** (services directed at people's mind): • Education • Advertising/PR • Psychotherapy	**Information processing** (services directed at intangible assets): • Accounting • Banking • Legal Services

Figure 1.15 Four broad categories of services

People Processing

From ancient times, people have sought out services directed at themselves, including transportation, food, lodging, health restoration, or beautification (*Figure 1.16*). To receive these types of services, customers must physically enter the service system. Why? Because they are an integral part of the process and cannot obtain the desired benefits by dealing at arm's length with service suppliers. In short, they must enter the **service factory**, a physical location where people or machines (or both) create and deliver service benefits to customers. Of course, service providers are sometimes willing to come to customers, bringing the necessary tools of their trade to create the desired benefits at the customers' preferred location. Implications of people processing services include:

Figure 1.16 A customer getting treated to a luxurious manicure

- Service production and consumption are simultaneous, which means that the customers typically must be present in the physical location (service factory). This requires planning about the location of the service operation, careful design of service processes and the service environment, and demand and capacity management.

- Active cooperation of the customer is needed in the service delivery process. For example, for a manicure service, you would have to cooperate with the manicurist by specifying what you want, sitting still, and presenting each finger for treatment when requested.

- There is a need for managers to think carefully about the location of the service operation, the design of service processes and the service environment, demand and capacity management, and output from the customer's point of view. Apart from financial costs, non-financial costs such as time, mental and physical effort need to be taken into account.

Possession Processing

Often, customers ask a service organization to provide tangible treatment for some physical possession — a house that has been invaded by insects, a hedge that has grown too high, a malfunctioning elevator (*Figure 1.17*), a broken screen of a smartphone, a parcel that needs to be sent to another city, or a sick pet. The implications of such services are:

- Unlike for people-processing services, production and consumption are not necessarily simultaneous, giving more flexibility to the service firm in designing such services for cost-efficiency.

- Customers tend to be less involved in these services, compared to people-processing services. The involvement may be limited to just dropping off or collecting the item. In such instances, production and consumption can be described as **separable**. However, in some instances, the customer may prefer to be present during service delivery, perhaps wishing to supervise cutting of the hedge or comfort the family dog while it receives an injection at the veterinary clinic.

Figure 1.17 Elevator repair is a possession processing service

Mental Stimulus Processing

These services touch people's minds and have the power to shape attitudes and influence behavior. Mental stimulus processing services include education, news and information, professional advice, and some religious activities. Obtaining the full benefit of such services requires an investment of time and a degree of mental effort on the customer's part. However, recipients don't necessarily have to be physically present in a service factory — just mentally in communication with the information being presented. There's an interesting contrast here with people-processing services. Passengers can sleep through a flight and still arrive at their desired destination. But if you fall asleep during an online lecture, you won't be any wiser at the end than at the beginning!

Because the core content of services in this category is information-based (whether text, speech, music, visual images, or video), it can be digitized and made available via downloads, YouTube, and the like. For instance, the Boston Symphony Orchestra's concerts can be attended live, viewed or heard live, pre-recorded on TV, or sold as digital recordings (*Figure 1.18*). Services in this category can thus be "inventoried," for consumption at a later date than their production. In fact, the same performance can be consumed repeatedly. For some students, accessing a lecture online and perhaps viewing key parts repeatedly may be a better solution than taking a physical class. Key implications that arise from these kinds of services are as follows:

- Customers do not have to be physically present in the service factory. They only access the information remotely when they need it.

- Services in this category can be "inventoried" for consumption at a later date, or consumed repeatedly.

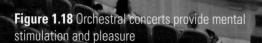

Figure 1.18 Orchestral concerts provide mental stimulation and pleasure

Information Processing

Information can be processed by information and communications technology (often referred to as ICT), and/or by professionals who use their brains to perform information processing and packaging. Information is the most intangible form of service output. However, it can be transformed into more permanent and tangible forms like letters, reports, books, or files in any type of format. Some services that are highly dependent on the effective collection and processing of information are financial and professional services such as accounting (*Figure 1.19*), law, marketing research, management consulting, and medical diagnosis.

It is sometimes difficult to tell the difference between information processing and mental stimulus processing services. For example, if a stockbroker performs an analysis of a client's brokerage transactions, it seems like information processing. However, when the results of the analysis are used to make a recommendation about the most suitable type of investment strategy for the future, it would seem like mental stimulus processing. Therefore, for simplicity, we will periodically combine our coverage of mental stimulus and information processing services under the umbrella term of **information-based services**.

Figure 1.19 A young couple getting financial advice on buying a new home looking at insurance.

LO 8

Be familiar with the characteristics of services and the distinctive marketing challenges they pose.

SERVICES POSE DISTINCT MARKETING CHALLENGES

Can the marketing concepts and practices developed in manufacturing companies be directly transferred to service organizations where no transfer of ownership takes place? The answer is often "no." Services tend to have different features from goods, including the frequently cited four characteristics of *i*ntangibility, *h*eterogeneity (variability of quality), *i*nseparability of production and consumption, and *p*erishability of output[32], or **IHIP** for short[33]. *Table 1.1* explains these characteristics, and other common differences between services and goods. Together, these differences cause the marketing of services to differ from that of manufactured goods in several important respects.

Table 1.1 Managerial implications of eight common features of service

Differences	Implications	Marketing-related Topics
Most service products cannot be inventoried (i.e., output is perishable)	• Customers may be turned away or have to wait	• Smooth demand through promotions, dynamic pricing, and reservations • Work with operations to adjust capacity
Intangible elements usually dominate value creation (i.e., service is physically intangible)	• Customers cannot taste, smell, or touch these elements and may not be able to see or hear them • Harder to evaluate service and distinguish from competitors	• Make services tangible through emphasis on physical clues • Employ concrete metaphors and vivid images in advertising and branding
Services are often difficult to visualize and understand (i.e., service is mentally intangible)	• Customers perceive greater risk and uncertainty	• Educate customers to make good choices, explain what to look for, document performance, offer guarantees
Customers may be involved in co-production (i.e., if people processing is involved, the service is inseparable)	• Customers interact with providers' equipment, facilities, and systems • Poor task execution by customers may hurt productivity, spoil the service experience, and curtail benefits	• Educate customers to make good choices, explain what to look for, document performance, offer guarantees
People may be part of the service experience	• Appearance, attitude, and behavior of service personnel and other customers can shape the experience and affect satisfaction	• Recruit, train, and reward employees to reinforce the planned service concept • Target the right customers at right times; shape their behavior
Operational inputs and outputs tend to vary more widely (i.e., services are heterogeneous)	• Harder to maintain consistency, reliability, and service quality or to lower costs through higher productivity • Difficult to shield customers from results of service failures	• Set quality standards based on customer expectations; redesign product elements for simplicity and failure-proofing • Institute good service recovery procedures • Automate customer–provider interactions; perform work while customers are absent
The time factor often assumes great importance	• Customers see time as a scarce resource to be spent wisely, dislike wasting time waiting, want service at times that are convenient	• Find ways to compete on speed of delivery, minimize burden of waiting, offer extended service hours
Distribution may take place through non-physical channels	• Information-based services can be delivered through electronic channels such as the Internet or voice telecommunications, but core products involving physical activities or products cannot • Channel integration is a challenge; that is to ensure consistent delivery of service through diverse channels, including branches, call centers and websites.	• Seek to create user-friendly, secure websites and free access by telephone • Ensure that all information-based service elements are delivered effectively and reliably through all key channels

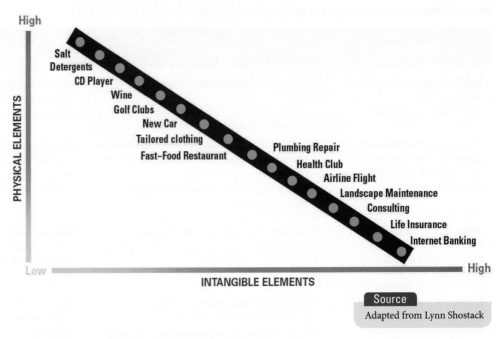

Figure 1.20 Relative value added by physical versus intangible elements in goods and services

It is important to recognize that these differences, while useful generalizations, **do not apply equally to all services**. Intangibility for example, ranges from tangible-dominant to intangible-dominant (see *Figure 1.20* for a scale that presents a variety of examples)[34]. Large differences also exist between the four categories of services we discussed in the previous section. For example, people tend to be part of the service experience only if the customer has direct contact with service employees. This is usually the case for people-processing services but not for many information-processing service transactions such as online banking. You will recognize these differences as we discuss the marketing mix for services throughout this book.

THE 7 PS OF SERVICES MARKETING

When developing strategies to market manufactured goods, marketers usually address four basic strategic elements: *p*roduct, *p*rice, *p*lace (or distribution), and *p*romotion (or communication). As a group, these are usually referred to as the "4 Ps" of the marketing mix[35]. As is evident from *Table 1.1*, the nature of services poses distinct marketing challenges. Hence, the **4 Ps** of goods marketing are not adequate to deal with the issues arising from marketing services and have to be adapted and extended. We will therefore revisit the traditional **4 Ps** of the marketing mix in this book to focus on service-specific issues.

Furthermore, the traditional marketing mix does not cover the customer interface. We therefore need to extend the marketing mix by adding three Ps associated with service delivery — **process, physical environment,** and **people**[36]. Collectively, these seven elements are referred to as the "7 Ps" of services marketing. You can think of these elements as the seven strategic levers of services marketing used to develop strategies for meeting customer needs profitably in competitive marketplaces. Now, let's look briefly at each of the **7 Ps**.

THE TRADITIONAL MARKETING MIX APPLIED TO SERVICES

⊃ **LO 9**
Understand the components of the traditional marketing mix applied to services.

Product Elements

Service products lie at the heart of a firm's marketing strategy. If a product is poorly designed, it won't create meaningful value for customers, even if the rest of the **7 Ps** are well executed. Planning the marketing mix begins with creating a service product that will offer value to target customers and satisfy their needs better than competing alternatives. Service products consist of a core product that meets the customers' primary need and a variety of supplementary service elements that are mutually reinforcing, and add value to help customers to use the core product more effectively. Supplementary service elements include providing information, consultation, order taking, hospitality, handling exceptions, etc.

Place and Time

Service distribution may take place through physical or electronic channels (or both), depending on the nature of the service (*Table 1.1*). For example, today's banks offer customers a wide range of distribution channels, including visiting a bank branch, using a network of ATMs, doing business by telephone, online banking on a desktop, and using apps on a smartphone. In particular, many information-based services can be delivered almost instantaneously to any location in the world that has Internet access. Furthermore, firms may also deliver their services directly to end-users or through intermediary organizations such as retail outlets that receive a fee or commission to perform certain tasks associated with sales, service, and customer-contact. To deliver service elements to customers, companies need to decide where and when these services are delivered, as well as the methods and channels used[37].

Distribution of Core versus Supplementary Services. The Internet is reshaping distribution strategy for numerous industries. However, we need to distinguish between its potential for delivering information-based **core products** (those that respond to customers' primary requirements) and simply providing **supplementary services** that facilitate purchase and use of physical goods. Examples of information-based core products include online educational programs offered by the Khan Academy and Coursera, and automobile insurance coverage from Progressive Casualty Co.

In contrast, if you buy an outdoor gear or book a flight online, the delivery of the core product itself must still take place through physical channels. The tent and sleeping bag that you bought from REI (Recreational Equipment Inc.) will be delivered to your home. And you'll have to go to the airport in person to board your United Airlines flight. Much e-commerce activity concerns supplementary services that are based on **transfer of information, making reservations and payments,** as opposed to downloading the core product itself.

Importance of the Time Factor. Speed and convenience of place and time have become important determinants of effective distribution and delivery of services (*Table 1.1*). Many services are delivered in real time while customers are physically present. Today's customers are highly time-sensitive, mostly in a hurry, and see wasted time as a cost to avoid[38]. You probably do, too. They may be willing to pay extra to save time, such as taking a taxi when a city bus serves the same route (*Figure 1.21*), or to get a needed task performed faster. Increasingly, busy customers expect service to be available when it suits them, rather than when it suits the supplier. If one firm responds by offering extended hours, its competitors often feel obliged to follow suit. Nowadays, a growing number of services are available 24/7, and via more delivery channels.

Figure 1.21 Taking a taxi can save time for busy commuters

Price and Other User Outlays

Like product value, payment is very important in allowing a value exchange to take place. For firms, the pricing strategy affects how much income is generated. Pricing strategy is often highly dynamic, with price levels adjusted over time according to factors like customer segment, time and place of delivery, level of demand, and available capacity.

For customers, price is a key part of the costs they must incur to obtain desired benefits. To calculate whether a particular service is "worth it," they may go beyond just money and assess how much time and effort are involved

(*Figure 1.22*). Service marketers, therefore, must not set only prices that target customers are willing and able to pay, but also understand — and seek to minimize, where possible — other burdensome outlays that customers incur in using the service. These outlays may include additional monetary costs (such as travel expenses to a service location), time spent, unwanted mental and physical effort, and exposure to negative sensory experiences.

Figure 1.22 Money is not the only consideration when measuring the cost of a service

Most Service Products Cannot be Inventoried. Since services involve actions or performances, they are temporary and perishable. Therefore, they usually cannot be stocked as inventory for future use (*Table 1.1*). Although facilities, equipment, and labor can be held in readiness to create the service, each represents productive capacity, not the product itself. If there is no demand, unused capacity is wasted and the firm loses the chance to create value from these assets. During periods when demand exceeds capacity, customers may be turned away or asked to wait until later. A key task for service marketers, therefore, is to find ways of smoothing demand levels to match available capacity using dynamic pricing strategies.

Promotion and Education

What should we tell customers and prospects about our services? Few marketing programs can succeed without effective communications. This component plays three vital roles: providing needed information and advice, persuading target customers to buy the service product, and encouraging them to take action at specific times. In services marketing, much communication is educational in nature, especially for new customers. Suppliers need to teach their customers about the benefits of the service, where and when to obtain it, and how to participate in service processes to get the best results.

Services are Often Difficult to Visualize and Understand as Intangible Elements Tend to Dominate Value Creation. Intangibility can consist of both mental and physical dimensions. Mental intangibility means that it is difficult for customers to visualize the experience in advance of purchase and to understand the value and benefits they will be getting, while physical intangibility is that which cannot be touched or experienced by the other senses[39]. It is often the intangible elements — such as processes, Internet-based transactions, and the expertise and attitudes of service personnel — that create the most value in service performances. When customers can't taste, smell, or touch these elements and may not be able to see or hear these elements (i.e., they are physically intangible), it may be more difficult for them to assess important service features in advance of purchase and evaluate the quality of the service performance itself (Table 1.1).

Therefore, an important role of a service firm's communications is to create confidence in the firm's experience, credentials, and expertise of its employees. For example, firms can use physical images and metaphors to promote service benefits and demonstrate the firm's competencies (*Figure 1.23*). In personal interactions, the role of well-trained service employees in communications is crucial in reducing the perceived risk of purchase by helping prospective customers to make good choices, by educating them on what to expect both during and after service delivery, and by helping them to move smoothly through the service process. Documenting performance, explaining what was done and why, and offering guarantees are additional ways to reassure customers and reduce anxiety. Service firms have much to gain from helping customers to appreciate the service offering, become more competent and productive[40]. After all, if you know how to use a service well, you'll not only have a better service experience and outcome, but your greater efficiency may boost the firm's productivity, lower its costs, and even enable it to reduce the price you pay.

Customer–Customer Interactions Affect the Service Experience. When you encounter other customers at a service facility, they too can affect your satisfaction. How they're dressed, who they are, and how they behave can reinforce or negate the image a firm is trying to project and the experience it is trying to create. The implications are clear: we need to use marketing communications to attract the right customer segments to the service facility, and once there, also to educate them on the proper behavior.

Figure 1.23 A customer is co-producing the service when working out at the gym under the direction of a personal trainer

LO 10

Describe the components of the extended marketing mix for managing the customer interface.

THE EXTENDED SERVICES MARKETING MIX FOR MANAGING THE CUSTOMER INTERFACE

Process

Smart managers know that where services are concerned, **how** a firm does things is as important as **what** it does. Therefore, creating and delivering product elements requires design and implementation of effective processes. Badly designed service processes lead to slow, bureaucratic, and ineffective service delivery, wasted time, and a disappointing experience for customers. Poor service process design also makes it difficult for frontline employees to do their jobs well, resulting in low productivity and employee dissatisfaction.

Operational Inputs and Outputs Can Vary Widely. Operational inputs and outputs tend to vary more widely for services, and can make customer service process management a challenge (*Table 1.1*). When a service is delivered face to face and consumed as it is produced, final "assembly" must take place in real time. However, operations are often distributed across thousands of sites or branches. When operations are distributed (rather than centralized in a factory), it is difficult for service organizations to ensure reliable delivery, control quality, and improve productivity. As a former packaged goods marketer once observed after moving to a new position at Holiday Inn:

> We can't control the quality of our product as well as a Procter and Gamble control engineer on a production line can...When you buy a box of Tide, you can reasonably be 99 and 44/100 percent sure that it will work to get your clothes clean. When you reserve a Holiday Inn room, you're sure at some lesser percentage that it will work to give you a good night's sleep without any hassle, or people banging on the walls and all the bad things that can happen in a hotel[41].

Nevertheless, the best service firms have made significant progress in reducing variability by carefully designing customer service processes, adopting standardized procedures and equipment, implementing rigorous management of service quality, training employees more carefully, and automating tasks previously performed by humans.

Customers Are Often Involved in Co-production. Some services require customers to participate actively in co-producing the service product (*Table 1.1*). For example, you're expected to help the investment banker understand what your needs are, how much you want to invest financially, the kind of risks you are willing to take, and the expected returns. This will enable the banker to advise you on what to invest in. In fact, service scholars argue that customers often function as **partial employees**[42]. Increasingly, your involvement takes the form of self-service, often using SSTs facilitated by smart machines, telecommunications, and the Internet[43]. Whether customers co-produce or use SSTs, well-designed customer service processes are needed to facilitate service delivery.

Demand and Capacity Need to be Balanced. Manufacturing can ensure a smooth process flow by having an inventory of materials and parts ready for use. For services, such buffering means having customers wait in the service process! Therefore, areas closely related to service process management involve the balancing of demand and capacity, design of waiting and queuing systems, and management of the impact of waiting on the customer's psychology.

Physical Environment

If your job is in a service business that requires customers to enter the service factory, you'll also have to spend time thinking about the design of the physical environment or servicescape[44]. The appearance of buildings, landscaping, vehicles, interior furnishings, equipment, staff members' uniforms, signs, printed materials, and other visible cues provide tangible evidence of a firm's service quality. The servicescape also facilitates service delivery, and guides customers through the service process. Service firms need to manage servicescapes carefully, since they can have a profound impact on customer satisfaction[45] and service productivity.

People

Despite advances in technology, many services will always need direct interaction between customers and service employees (*Table 1.1*). You must have noticed many times how the difference between one service supplier and another lies in the attitude and skills of their employees. Service firms need to work closely with their human resources (HR) departments and devote special care in selecting, training, and motivating their service employees (*Figure 1.24*). In addition to possessing the technical skills required by the job, these individuals also need good interpersonal skills and a positive attitude. HR managers who think strategically recognize that having loyal, skilled, motivated employees who can work well independently or together in teams represent a key competitive advantage.

Figure 1.24 Hospitality is shown through employees wearing a ready smile and being ready to serve customers

LO 11

Appreciate that the marketing, operations, and human resource management functions need to be closely integrated in service businesses.

MARKETING MUST BE INTEGRATED WITH OTHER MANAGEMENT FUNCTIONS

In the previous section, we described the **7 Ps** as the strategic levers of services marketing. As you think about these different elements, it should quickly become clear that marketers working in a service business cannot expect to operate successfully in isolation from managers in other functions. In fact, four management functions play central and interrelated roles in meeting the needs of service customers: marketing, operations, HR, and IT. *Figure 1.25* illustrates this interdependency. One of the top management's responsibilities is to ensure that managers and other employees in each of these functions don't operate in departmental silos.

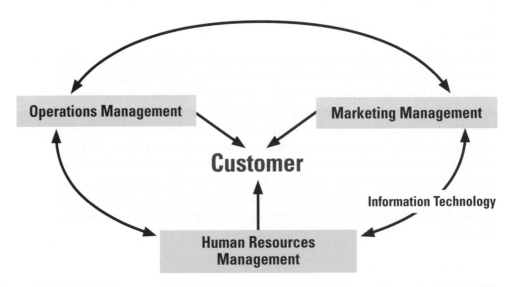

Figure 1.25 Marketing, Operations, Human Resources, and IT departments must collaborate to serve the customer

Operations is the primary line function in a service business, responsible for managing service delivery through equipment, facilities, systems, and many tasks performed by customer-contact employees. In most service organizations, you can also expect to see operations managers actively involved in product and process design, many aspects of the physical environment, and implementation of productivity and quality improvement programs.

HR is often seen as a staff function, responsible for job definition, recruitment, training, reward systems, and quality of work life — all of which are, of course, central to the people element. But in a well-managed service business, HR managers view these activities from a strategic perspective. They understand that the quality and commitment of the front line have become a major source of competitive advantage. Service organizations cannot afford to have HR specialists who do not understand customers. When employees understand and support the goals of their organization, have the skills and training needed to succeed in their jobs, and recognize the importance of creating and maintaining customer satisfaction, both marketing and operations activities are easier to manage and are more likely to be successful.

IT is a key function as service processes are information-heavy — at almost every customer touch point, real-time information is needed (from customer data to prices and available capacity). Operations, HR, and marketing are critically dependent on IT to manage their functions and create value for the organization's customers.

For these reasons, we don't limit our coverage exclusively to marketing in this book. In many of the chapters you'll also find us referring to service operations, human resource management, and IT. Some firms deliberately rotate their managers among different job functions, especially between marketing and operations positions, precisely so that they will be able to appreciate different perspectives. Your own career in services might follow a similar path.

Imagine yourself as the manager of a small hotel. Or, if you like, think big and picture yourself as the chief executive officer (CEO) of a major bank. In both instances, you need to be concerned about satisfying your customers on a daily basis, about operational systems running smoothly and efficiently, and about making sure that your employees are not only working productively, but are also delivering good service. In short, integration of activities between these functions is the name of the game in services. Problems in any one of these areas can negatively affect the execution of tasks in other functions and might result in dissatisfied customers. Only a minority of people who work in a service firm are employed in formal marketing positions. However, Evert Gummesson argues that all those whose work affects the customer in some way — either through direct contact or the design of processes, IT systems, and policies that shape customers' experiences — need to think of themselves as **part-time marketers**[46].

THE SERVICE–PROFIT CHAIN

LO 12
Understand the implications of the Service–Profit Chain for service management.

A conceptual framework that shows how marketing, operations, HR, and IT are integrated in high-performance service organizations is the Service–Profit Chain. James Heskett and his colleagues at Harvard argue that when service companies put employees and customers first, there is a big change in the way they manage and measure success. They relate profitability, customer loyalty, and customer satisfaction to the value created by satisfied, loyal, and productive employees, and supported by customer- and employee-centric operations and technology:

> *Top-level executives of outstanding service organizations spend little time setting profit goals or focusing on market share... Instead they understand that in the new economics of service, frontline workers and customers need to be the center of management concern. Successful service managers pay attention to the factors that drive profitability... investment in people, technology that supports frontline workers, revamped recruiting and training practices, and compensation linked to performance for employees at every level.*

The service–profit chain, developed from analyses of successful service organizations, puts "hard" values on "soft" measures. It helps managers target new investments to develop service and satisfaction levels for maximum competitive impact, widening the gap between service leaders and their merely good competitors[47].

The Service–Profit Chain (*Figure 1.26*), shows the links in a managerial process that are proposed to lead to success in service businesses.

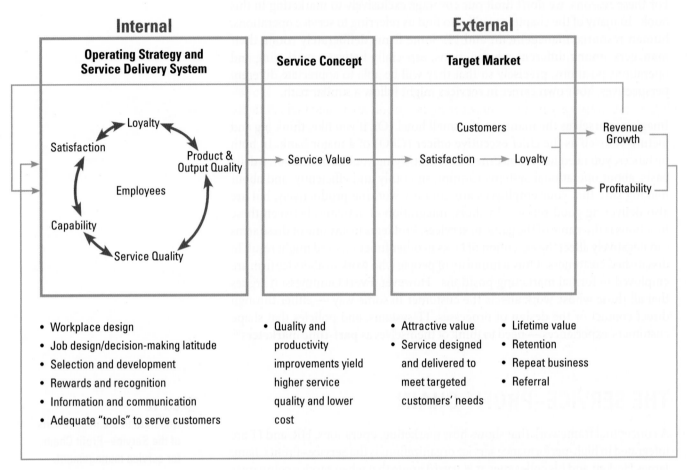

Figure 1.26 The Service–Profit Chain

Source

Reprinted by permission of Harvard Business Review: Heskett, JL., Jones, T.O., Loveman, G.W., Sasser Jr., W.E., and Schlesinger, L.A. (March–April 1994), "Putting the Service–Profit Chain to Work," *Harvard Business Review*, p.166. Copyright © 1994 by the Harvard Business School Publishing Corporation; all rights reserved.

Table 1.2 provides a useful summary, highlighting the behaviors required of service leaders in order to manage their organizations effectively. Working backwards, from the desired end results of revenue growth and profitability, links 1 and 2 focus on customers. The links include an emphasis on identifying and understanding customer needs, making investments to ensure customer retention, and having a commitment to adopt new performance measures that track such variables as satisfaction and loyalty among both customers and employees. Link 3 focuses on the value for customers created by the service concept and highlights the need for investments to continually improve both service quality and productivity.

Another set of service leadership behaviors (links 4–7) relate to employees and include organizational focus on the front line. The design of jobs should offer greater freedom for employees. Managers with potential should be developed. This category also stressed the idea that paying higher wages can actually decrease labor costs because of reduced turnover, higher productivity, and higher quality. Underlying the chain's success (link 8) is top management leadership. The Service–Profit Chain is an important guiding philosophy for this book, with core chapters explaining how to successfully implement the Service–Profit Chain.

Table 1.2 Links in the Service–Profit Chain

1. Customer loyalty drives profitability and growth
2. Customer satisfaction drives customer loyalty
3. Value drives customer satisfaction
4. Quality and productivity drive value
5. Employee loyalty drives service quality and productivity
6. Employee satisfaction drives employee loyalty
7. Internal quality as delivered by operations and IT drives employee satisfaction
8. Top management leadership underlies the chain's success.

Source

Heskett, JL., Jones, T.O., Loveman, G.W., Sasser Jr., W.E., and Schlesinger, L.A., (March-April 1994), "Putting the Service–Profit Chain to Work," *Harvard Business Review*; James L. Heskett, W. Earl Sasser, and Leonard L. Schlesinger, *The Service Profit Chain* (Boston: Harvard Business School Press, 1997).

A FRAMEWORK FOR DEVELOPING EFFECTIVE SERVICE MARKETING STRATEGIES

The **7 Ps** and the Service–Profit Chain are integrated into the wider organizing framework of this book. It shows how each of the chapters fits together with the others as they address related topics and issues. *Figure 1.27* presents the organizing framework for this book, which is divided into five parts: (1) understanding service products, consumers, and markets; (2) applying the **4 Ps** of marketing to services; (3) designing and managing the customer interface (i.e., the additional **3 Ps** of services marketing); (4) developing customer relationships; and (5) striving for service excellence. Note that the arrows link the different boxes in the model: They stress the interdependences between the different parts. Decisions made in one area must be consistent with those taken in another, so that each strategic element will mutually reinforce the rest.

Part I

Understanding Service Products, Consumers, and Markets

1. Creating Value in the Service Economy
2. Understanding Service Consumers
3. Positioning Services in Competitive Markets

Part II

Applying the 4 Ps of Marketing to Services

4. Developing Service Products and Brands
5. Distributing Services Through Physical and Electronic Channels
6. Service Pricing and Revenue Management
7. Service Marketing Communications

Part III

Managing the Customer Interface

8. Designing Service Processes
9. Balancing Demand and Capacity
10. Crafting the Service Environment
11. Managing People for Service Advantage

Part IV

Developing Customer Relationships

12. Managing Relationships and Building Loyalty
13. Complaint Handling and Service Recovery

Part V

Striving for Service Excellence

14. Improving Service Quality and Productivity
15. Building a World-Class Service Organization

Figure 1.27 Integrated model of Services Marketing

The key contents of the five parts of this book are:

Part I

Understanding Service Products, Consumers, and Markets

Part I of the book lays the building blocks for studying services and learning how to become an effective services marketer.

- **Chapter 1:** defines **services** and shows how we can create value without transfer of ownership.
- **Chapter 2:** discusses **consumer behavior** in both high- and low-contact services. The three-stage model of service consumption is used to explore how customers search for and evaluate alternative services, make purchase decisions, experience and respond to service encounters, and evaluate service performance.
- **Chapter 3:** discusses how a service **value proposition should be positioned** in a way that creates competitive advantage for the firm. The chapter shows how firms can segment a service market, position their value proposition, and focus on attracting their target segment.

Part II

Applying the 4Ps of Marketing to Services

Part II revisits the 4 Ps of the traditional marketing mix taught in your basic marketing course. However, the 4 Ps are expanded to take into account the characteristics of services that are different from goods.

- **Chapter 4:** **product** includes both the core and supplementary service elements. The supplementary elements facilitate and enhance the core service offering.
- **Chapter 5:** **place** and **time** elements refer to the delivery of the product elements to the customers.
- **Chapter 6:** **prices** of services need to be set with reference to costs, competition and value, and revenue management considerations.
- **Chapter 7:** **promotion** and **education** explains how firms should inform customers about their services. In services marketing, much communication is educational in nature to teach customers how to effectively move through service processes.

Part III

Managing the Customer Interface

Part III of the book focuses on managing the interface between customers and the service firm. It covers the additional 3 Ps that are unique to services marketing.

- **Chapter 8:** **processes** create and deliver the product elements. The chapter begins with the design of effective delivery processes, specifying how the operating and delivery systems link together to deliver the value proposition. Very often, customers are involved in these processes as co-producers, and well-designed processes need to account for that.

- Chapter 9: this chapter also relates to **process management** and focuses on balancing demand and capacity for each step of a customer service process. Marketing strategies for managing demand involve smoothing demand fluctuations, inventorying demand through reservation systems, and formalized queuing. Managing customer waiting is also explored in this chapter.

- Chapter 10: **physical environment**, also known as the *servicescape*, needs to be engineered to create the right impression and facilitate effective service process delivery. The *servicescape* provides tangible evidence of a firm's image and service quality.

- Chapter 11: **people** play a key role in services marketing when direct interaction between customers and service personnel is part of the service. The nature of these interactions strongly influences how customers perceive service quality. Hence, service firms devote a significant amount of effort to recruit, train, and motivate employees. How to get all this right is explained using the Service Talent Cycle as an integrative framework.

Part IV

Developing Customer Relationships

Part IV focuses on how to develop customer relationships and build loyalty.

- Chapter 12: achieving profitability requires creating **relationships with customers** from the right segments and then finding ways to build and reinforce their loyalty. This chapter introduces the Wheel of Loyalty, which shows three systematic steps in building customer loyalty. The chapter closes with a discussion of customer relationship management (CRM) systems.

- Chapter 13: a loyal customer base is often built from effective **complaint handling** and **service recovery**, which are discussed in this chapter. Service guarantees are explored as a powerful way of institutionalizing service recovery and as an effective marketing tool to signal high-quality service.

Part V

Striving for Service Excellence

Part V focuses on how to develop and transform a firm to achieve service excellence.

- Chapter 14: **productivity** and **quality** are both necessary and are strongly related to financial success in services. This chapter focuses on service quality, diagnosing quality shortfalls using the Gaps model, and strategies to close quality gaps. Customer feedback systems are discussed as an effective tool for systematically listening to and learning from customers. Productivity is introduced as closely related to quality, and it is emphasized that in today's competitive markets, firms need to simultaneously improve both quality and productivity — not one at the expense of the other.

- Chapter 15: this final chapter discusses how we can move a service organization to **higher levels of performance** in each functional area.

CONCLUSION

Why study services? Because modern economies are driven by individual service businesses operating within a remarkable array of industries. Collectively, services are responsible for the creation of a substantial majority of all new jobs, both skilled and unskilled, around the world. Many of these industries are undergoing dramatic transformations, driven by advances in technology, globalization, changes in government policies, evolving consumer needs, and lifestyles (*Figure 1.28*). In such an environment, effective marketing plays a vital role in determining whether an individual organization survives and thrives — or declines and fails.

In this chapter, we've demonstrated that services require a distinctive approach to marketing, because the context and the tasks often differ in important aspects from those in the manufacturing sector. Succeeding as a marketing manager in a service business requires you not only to understand key marketing concepts and tools, but also know how to use them effectively. Each of the **7 Ps** — the strategic levers of services marketing — has a role to play, but it's how well you tie them together that will make the difference. As you study this book, attend classes, and undertake projects, remember that the winners in today's highly competitive service markets succeed by continually rethinking the way they do business, by looking for innovative ways to serve their customers better, by taking advantage of new developments in technology, and by embracing a disciplined and well-organized approach to developing and implementing services marketing strategy.

Figure 1.28 Advances in technology are changing the ways in which the service industry works

CHAPTER SUMMARY

➲ **LO 1** Services represent an important and growing contribution to most economies in the world. As economies develop, services form the largest part of the GDP of those economies. Globally, most new jobs are generated in the service sector.

➲ **LO 2** The principal industries of the service sector include (in order of contribution to GDP):
- Government services
- Real estate services
- Business and professional services
- Wholesale and retail trade
- Transport, utilities, and communications services
- Finance and insurance
- Healthcare services
- Accommodation and food services
- Arts, entertainment, and recreation services

➲ **LO 3** Many forces are transforming our economies, making them more *services-oriented*. They include government policies, social changes, business trends, advances in IT, and globalization.

➲ **LO 4** Business services allow manufacturing firms and other service organizations to outsource non-core activities, processes, and assets. What used to be a neglected support activity in a client organization has become the management focus and core competency of an independent service provider. The benefits include:
- Economies of scale and scope, an operation that is way down the learning curve that therefore operates at high quality and productivity levels.
- Tight cost and quality control (performance can be benchmarked across many sites).
- Process improvements and R&D are applied to these services as the benefits can be reaped across multiple sites.
- The rapid growth of business services leads to an increasing specialization of advanced economies with significant gains in overall productivity and standards of living.
- Intangible elements usually dominate value creation (i.e., physically intangible).
- Distribution may take place through nonphysical channels (especially for information processing-type services).
- Services often are difficult to visualize and understand (i.e., mentally intangible).

- Operational inputs and outputs tend to vary widely (i.e., heterogeneous).
- People may be part of the service experience.
- Customers may be involved in co-production (i.e., if people processing is involved, the service is inseparable).
- Most service products cannot be inventoried (i.e., perishable).
- Time factor often assumes great importance.

➲ **LO 5** Outsourcing refers to the contracting of services that were previously conducted internally in an organization to an external service provider. Offshoring refers to services that are conducted in one country and consumed in another. Outsourcing and offshoring are independent (e.g., firms can outsource without offshoring to a domestic service provider; or offshore without outsourcing to a foreign subsidiary), but often work in tandem (e.g., a U.S.-based firm outsources a customer contact center to a service provider in the Philippines).

➲ **LO 6** What exactly is a service? The key distinguishing feature of a service is that it is a form of rental rather than ownership. Service customers obtain the rights to hire the labor, skills and expertise of personnel, use a physical object or space, or access shared facilities, networks, and systems. Services are performances that bring about the desired results or experience for the customer.

➲ **LO 7** Services vary widely and can be categorized according to the nature of the underlying process: Is the service directed at customers or their possessions? Are service actions tangible or intangible in nature? These distinctions have important marketing implications and lead to four broad categories of services:
- People processing
- Possession processing
- Mental stimulus processing
- Information processing

Mental stimulus and information processing can be combined into what is called information-based services.

➲ **LO 8** Services have unique characteristics that make them different from goods, including the frequently cited four characteristics of *i*ntangibility, *h*eterogeneity (variability of quality), *i*nseparability of production and consumption, and *p*erishability of output, or *IHIP* for short. These characteristics lead to the following marketing and management challenges:

- Intangible elements usually dominate value creation (i.e., physically intangible).
- Distribution may take place through nonphysical channels (especially for information processing-type services).
- Services often are difficult to visualize and understand (i.e., mentally intangible).
- Operational inputs and outputs tend to vary widely (i.e., heterogeneous).
- People may be part of the service experience
- Customers may be involved in co-production (i.e., if people processing is involved, the service is inseparable).
- Most service products cannot be inventoried (i.e., are perishable).
- Time factor often assumes great importance.

LO 9 Due to the unique characteristics of services, the traditional marketing mix of the **4 Ps** needs to be amended. Some important amendments include:

- Product elements include more than just the core elements.
- They also include supplementary service elements such as the provision of consultation, hospitality, or handling of exceptions.
- Place and time elements refer to the delivery of the product elements to the customer; many information-processing elements are delivered electronically.
- Pricing includes non-monetary costs to the consumer and revenue management considerations.
- Promotion is also viewed as a form of communication and education that guide customers through service processes, rather than focusing mainly on advertising and promotion.

LO 10 Services marketing requires three additional Ps that cover management of the customer interface:

- Process refers to the design and management of customer service processes, including managing demand and capacity and related customer waits.
- Physical environment, also known as the servicescape, facilitates process delivery, and provides tangible evidence of a firm's image and service quality.
- People covers the recruiting, training, and motivating of service employees to deliver service quality and productivity.

LO 11 To be successful, the marketing, operations, human resource, and IT management functions need to be tightly integrated and work closely together in well-coordinated ways.

- Integration means that the key deliverables and objectives of the various functions are not only compatible but also mutually reinforcing.

LO 12 The Service–Profit Chain shows how successful service firms integrate key management functions and deliver high performance in several related areas:

- Customer relationships must be managed effectively and there must be strategies to build and sustain loyalty.
- Value must be created and delivered to the target customers in ways that lead them to see the firm's offering as superior to competing offerings.
- Service quality and productivity must be continuously improved through better processes, systems and tools, and IT.
- Service employees must be enabled and motivated.
- Top management's leadership needs to drive and support all the components of the Service–Profit Chain.

LO 13 A framework for services marketing strategy forms the underlying structure of this book. The framework consists of the following five interlinked parts:

- Part I begins with the need for service firms to understand their markets, customers, and competition.
- Part II shows us how to apply the traditional **4 Ps** to services marketing.
- Part III covers the 3 Ps of the extended services marketing mix and shows how to manage the customer interface.
- Part IV illustrates how to develop lasting customer relationships through a variety of tools ranging from the Wheel of Loyalty and CRM to effective complaint management and service guarantees.
- Part V discusses how to improve service quality and productivity. This part closes with a discussion on how change management and leadership can propel a firm to become a service leader.

Review Questions

1. What are the main reasons for the growing share of the service sector in all major economies of the world?

2. What are the five powerful forces transforming the service landscape, and what impact do they have on the service economy?

3. Is it possible for an economy to be almost entirely based on services? Is it a sign of weakness when a national economy manufactures few of the goods that it consumes?

4. Why would growth in business services help individual firms and entire economies become more productive?

5. "A service is rented rather than owned." Explain what this statement means, and use examples to support your explanation.

6. Describe the four broad "processing" categories of services, and provide examples for each.

7. What is so special about services marketing that it needs a special approach?

8. "The **4 Ps** are all a marketing manager needs to create a marketing strategy for a service business." Prepare a response that argues against this, and support it with examples.

9. What types of services do you think are (a) most affected and (b) least affected by the problem of variable inputs and outputs? Why?

10. Why do the marketing, operations, HR management, and IT functions need to be closely coordinated in service organizations?

11. What are the implications of the Service–Profit Chain for service management?

12. What are the key elements in the framework for developing effective service marketing strategies?

Application Exercises

1. Visit the websites of the following national statistical bureaus: U.S. Bureau of Economic Analysis (www. bea.gov); Eurostat (http://ec.europa.eu/eurostat/ web/national-accounts/data/database); and the respective websites for your country if they are not covered here. In each instance, obtain data on the latest trends in services as (a) a percentage of the GDP; (b) the percentage of employment accounted for by services; (c) breakdowns of these two statistics by type of industry; and (d) service exports and imports. Looking at these trends, what are your conclusions for the main sectors of these economies, and within services, for specific service sectors?

2. Legal and accounting firms now advertise their services in many countries. Search for a few advertisements and review the following: What do these firms do to cope with the intangibility of their services? What could they do better? How do they deal with consumer quality and risk perceptions, and how could they improve this aspect of their marketing?

3. Review IBM's annual report, *www.ibm.com/ annualreport*, recent quarterly reports, *www.ibm. com/investor*, and other information on its website describing its different businesses. What conclusions do you draw about future opportunities in different markets? What do you see as competitive threats?

4. Give examples of how Internet and telecommunications technologies (e.g., mobile commerce (M-Commerce) and apps) have changed some of the services you use.

5. Choose a service company you are familiar with, and show how each of the **7 Ps** of services marketing applies to one of its service products.

6. Explain how concepts in Chapter 1 are relevant to the marketing of a religious institution, or a nonprofit organization such as World Wildlife Fund.

Endnotes

1   Organization for Economic Co-operation and Development, *The Service Economy.* Paris (OECD, 2000).

2   Michael Peneder, Serguei Kaniovsky, and Bernhard Dachs (2003), "What Follows Tertiarisation? Structural Change and the Rise of Knowledge-Based Industries," *The Service Industries Journal*, Vol. 23, March, pp. 47–66; Jochen Wirtz, Sven Tuzovic, and Michael Ehret (2015), "Global Business Services: Increasing Specialization and Integration of the World Economy as Drivers of Economic Growth," *Journal of Service Management.* Vol.26, No.4, pp. 565–587.

3   Roland Rust and Ming-Hui Huang (2014), "The Service Revolution and the Transformation of Marketing Science," *Marketing Science*, Vol. 33, No. 2, pp. 206–221.

4   Marion Weissenberger-Eibl and Daniel Jeffrey Koch (2007), "Importance of Industrial Services and Service Innovations," *Journal of Management and Organization*, No. 13, pp. 88–101; Jochen Wirtz and Michael Ehret (2009), "Creative Restruction — How Business Services Drive Economic Evolution," *European Business Review*, Vol. 21, No. 4, pp. 380–394.

5   http://www.ibm.com/us/en/ and http://en.wikipedia.org/wiki/IBM_Global_Services, accessed January 22, 2015.

6   For more information on SSME, see IFM and IBM, *Succeeding through Service Innovation: A Discussion Paper.* (Cambridge, UK: University of Cambridge Institute for Manufacturing, 2007); Paul P. Maglio and Jim Spohrer (2008). "Fundamentals of Service Science," *Journal of the Academy of Marketing Science*, Vol. 36, No. 1, pp. 18–20; R. C. Larson, "Service Science: At the Intersection of Management, Social, and Engineering Sciences," *IBM Systems Journal*, Vol. 47, No. 1, pp. 41–52; R. J. Glushko (2008), "Designing a Service Science Discipline with Discipline," *IBM Systems Journal*, Vol. 47, No. 1, pp. 15–27; Roberta S. Russell (2009). "Collaborative Research in Service Science: Quality and Innovation," *Journal of Service Science*, Vol. 2, No. 2, pp. 1–7. See also http://researcher.watson.ibm.com/researcher/view_group.php?id=1230, accessed January 22, 2015.

7   See the website of Service Science for the latest research in this field: http://pubsonline.informs.org/journal/serv, accessed January 22, 2015.

8   U.S. Department of Commerce, *North American Industry Classification System — United States.*

(Washington, DC: National Technical Information Service, # PB 2002-101430, 2002).

9   Roland Rust and Ming-Hui Huang (2014), "The Service Revolution and the Transformation of Marketing Science," *Marketing Science*, Vol. 33, No. 2, pp. 206–221.

10 This section is based on: Michael Ehret and Jochen Wirtz (2010), "Division of Labor between Firms: Business Services, Non-ownership-value and the Rise of the Service Economy," *Service Science*, Vol. 2, No. 3, pp. 136–145; and Jochen Wirtz and Michael Ehret, "Service-based Business Models: Transforming Businesses, Industries and Economies," in Raymond P. Fisk, Rebekah Russell-Bennett, and Lloyd C. Harris, eds. *Serving Customers: Global Services Marketing Perspectives*, (Melbourne, Australia: Tilde University Press, 2013), pp. 28–46. For firms' motivation to use non-ownership services see also: Kristina Wittkowski, Sabine Möller, and Jochen Wirtz (2013), "Firms' Intentions to Use Non-Ownership Services," *Journal of Service Research*, Vol. 16, No. 2, pp. 171–185.

11 McKinsey & Company, *Manufacturing the Future: The Next Era of Global Growth and Innovation* (McKinsey Global Institute, November 2012).

12 This section was adapted from Jochen Wirtz, Sven Tuzovic and Michael Ehret (2015), "Global Business Services: Increasing Specialization and Integration of the World Economy as Drivers of Economic Growth," *Journal of Service Management.* Vol. 26, No. 2, pp. 565–587.

13 This section is based on: Gereffi, G. and Fernandez-Stark, K. (2010), *The Offshore Services Global Value Chain* (Center on Globalization, Governance & Competitiveness, Duke University, March); Massini, S. and Miozzo, M. (2010), Outsourcing and Offshoring of Business Services: Challenges to Theory, Management and Geography of Innovation, Manchester Business School Working Paper, No. 604, Manchester; Sako, M. (2005), "Outsourcing and Offshoring: Key Trends and Issues," Emerging Markets Forum, November, Oxford, UK, http://brie.berkeley.edu/conf/Sako.pdf, accessed on January 22, 2015.

14 Diana Farrell, Martha A. Laboissière, and Jaeson Rosenfeld (2005), "Sizing the Emerging Global Labor Market," *The McKinsey Quarterly*, No. 3, pp. 93–103.

15 Thomas H. Davenport and Bala Iyer (2009), "Should You Outsource Your Brain?" *Harvard Business Review,* February, p. 38; Paul Sergius Koku (2013), "A View from the Street: An Exploratory Study of Consumer

Attitudes Toward Offshoring of Professional Services in the United States", *Journal of Services Marketing*, Vol. 29, No. 2, pp. 150–159.

See also the following study on the consumer perception of outsourced and offshored services: Piyush Sharma (2012), "Offshore Outsourcing of Customer Services — Boon or Bane?" *Journal of Services Marketing*, Vol. 26, No. 5, pp. 352–364.

16   Smith, Adam (1776), *The Wealth of Nations, Books I-III*, with an Introduction by Alan B. Krueger. (London: Bantam Classics, 2003).

17   Say, Jean Baptiste (1803), *A Treatise on Political Economy: or. The Production Distribution and Consumption of Wealth. Translated by and with notes from C.R. Prinsep. M.A* (Ann Arbor, MI: Scholarly Publishing Office, University of Michigan Library, 2005).

18   Hean Tat Keh and Jun Pang (2010), "Customer Reactions to Service Separation," *Journal of Marketing*, Vol. 74, pp. 55–70.

19   Robert C. Judd (1964), "The Case for Redefining Services," *Journal of Marketing*, Vol. 28, January, p. 59; John M. Rathmell, *Marketing in the Service Sector* (Cambridge, MA: Winthrop, 1974); Christopher H. Lovelock and Evert Gummesson (2004), "Whither Services Marketing? In Search of a New Paradigm and Fresh Perspectives," *Journal of Service Research*, Vol. 7, August, pp. 20–41.

20   Robin G. Qiu, "Service Science: Scientific Study of Service Systems," *Service Science*. Retrieved at http://www.sersci.com/ServiceScience/paper_details.php?id=1, published on November 22, 2008.

21   Lesley Brown (ed.), *Shorter Oxford English Dictionary*, 5th ed., 2002.

22   Rathmell, John M. (1966), "What Is Meant by Services?" *Journal of Marketing*, Vol. 30, October, pp. 32–36.

23   Evert Gummesson (1987), (citing an unknown source) "Lip Service: A Neglected Area in Services Marketing," *Journal of Consumer Services*, No. 1, Summer, pp. 19–22.

24   Christopher H. Lovelock and Evert Gummesson (2004), "Whither Services Marketing? In Search of a New Paradigm and Fresh Perspectives," *Journal of Service Research*, Vol. 7, August, pp. 20–41.

25   Adapted from a definition by Christopher Lovelock (identified anonymously as Expert 6, Table II, p. 112)

in Bo Edvardsson, Anders Gustafsson, and Inger Roos (2005), "Service Portraits in Service Research: A Critical Review," *International Journal of Service Industry Management*, Vol. 16, No. 1, pp. 107–121.

26   Rogelio Oliva and Robert L. Kallenberg (2003), "Managing the Transition from Products to Services," *International Journal of Service Industry Management,* Vol. 14, No. 2, pp. 160–172; Mohanbir Sawhney, Sridhar Balasubramanian, and Vish V. Krishnan (2004), "Creating Growth with Services," *MIT Sloan Management Review*, Vol. 45, Winter, pp. 34–43; Wayne A. Neu and Stephen A. Brown (2005), "Forming Successful Business-to-Business Services in Goods-Dominant Firms," *Journal of Service Research*, 8, August; Bernhard Dachs, Sabiene Biege, Martin Borowiecki, Gunter Lay, Angela Jäger, and Doris Schartinger (2014), "Servitisation of European Manufacturing: Evidence from a Large Scale Database," *The Service Industries Journal*, Vol. 34, No. 1, pp. 5–23.

27   For recommendations for manufacturing firms to successfully offer services see: Werner Reinartz and Wolfgang Ulaga (2008), "How to Sell Services Profitably," *Harvard Business Review,* May, pp. 90–96; Wolfgang Ulaga and Werner Reinartz (2011), "Hybrid Offerings: How Manufacturing Firms Combine Goods and Services Successfully," *Journal of Marketing*, Vol. 75, November, pp. 5–23; Andreas Eggert, Jens Hogreve, Wolfgang Ulaga, and Eva Muenkhoff (2014), "Revenue and Profit Implications of Industrial Service Strategies," *Journal of Service Research*, Vol. 17, No. 1, pp. 23–39.

28   Theodore Levitt, *Marketing for Business Growth* (New York: McGraw-Hill, 1974), p. 5.

29   Roland Rust and Ming-Hui Huang (2014), "The Service Revolution and the Transformation of Marketing Science," *Marketing Science,* Vol. 33, No. 2, pp. 206–221.

30   Stephen L. Vargo and Robert R. Lusch, "Evolving to a New Dominant Logic for Marketing (2004)," *Journal of Marketing*, Vol. 9, No. 2, pp. 1–21; Stephen L. Vargo and Robert R. Lusch (2008), "Service-dominant Logic: Continuing the Evolution," *Journal of the Academy of Marketing Science*, Vol. 36, No. 1, pp. 1–10. For a recent review of the S–D logic, see Stephen L. Vargo, Robert R. Lusch and Cristina Mele (2012), "Service-for Service Exchange and Value Co-Creation," in: *Serving Customers: Global Services Marketing Perspectives* (Melbourne, Australia: Tilde University Press), pp. 208–228; Ingo O. Karpen, Liliana L. Bove, and Bryan A. Lukas (2012), "Linking Service-Dominant Logic and Strategy Business Practice: A Conceptual Model of a Service-Dominant Orientation," *Journal of Service Research*, Vol. 15, No. 1, pp. 21–38.

31 These classifications are derived from Christopher H. Lovelock (1983), "Classifying Services to Gain Strategic Marketing Insights," *Journal of Marketing*, Vol. 47, Summer, pp. 9–20.

32 Valarie A. ZeithamI, A. Parasuraman, and Leonard L. Berry (1985), "Problems and Strategies in Services Marketing." *Journal of Marketing*, Vol. 49, Spring, pp. 33–46.

33 Christopher H. Lovelock and Evert Gummesson (2004), "Whither Services Marketing? In Search of a New Paradigm and Fresh Perspectives," *Journal of Service Research*, Vol. 7, August, pp. 20–41.

34 G. Lynn Shostack (1977), "Breaking Free from Product Marketing," *Journal of Marketing*, Vol. 41, April, pp. 73–80.

35 The 4 Ps classification of marketing decision variables was created by E. Jerome McCarthy, *Basic Marketing: A Managerial Approach,* (Homewood, IL: Richard D. Irwin, Inc., 1960). It was a refinement of the long list of ingredients included in the marketing mix concept, created by Professor Neil Borden at Harvard in the 1950s. Borden got the idea from a colleague who described the marketing manager's job as being a "mixer of ingredients."

36 An expanded 7 Ps marketing mix was first proposed by Bernard H. Booms and Mary Jo Bitner, "Marketing Strategies and Organization Structures for Service Firms," in J. H. Donnelly and W.R. George, eds. *Marketing of Services* (Chicago, IL: American Marketing Association, 1981), pp. 47–51.

37 Philip J. Coelho and Chris Easingwood (2004), "Multiple Channel Systems in Services: Pros, Cons, and Issues," *The Service Industries Journal*, Vol. 24, September, pp. 1–30.

38 Gary Stix (2002), "Real Time," *Scientific American,* Vol. 287, September, No. 3, pp. 36–3.

39 John E. G. Bateson, "Why We Need Service Marketing" in O. C. Ferrell, S. W. Brown and C. W. Lamb Jr., eds. *Conceptual and Theoretical Developments in Marketing* (Chicago, IL: American Marketing Association, 1979), pp. 131–146.

40 Bonnie Farber Canziani (1997), "Leveraging Customer Competency in Service Firms," *International Journal of Service Industry Management,* Vol. 8, No. 1, pp. 5–25; Paul Flanagan, Robert Johnston, and Derek Talbot

(2005) "Customer Confidence: The Development of 'Pre-Experience' Concept", *International Journal of Service Industry Management,* Vol. 16, No.4, pp. 373–384.

41 Gary Knisely, "Greater Marketing Emphasis by Holiday Inns Breaks Mold," *Advertising Age*, January 15, 1979.

42 The term "partial employee" was coined by P. K. Mills and D. J. Moberg (1982), "Perspectives on the Technology of Service Operations," *Academy of Management Review*, Vol. 7, No. 3, pp. 467–478. For further research on this topic, see: Karthik Namasivayam (2004), "The Consumer as Transient Employee: Consumer Satisfaction through the Lens of Job-performance Models", *International Journal of Service Industry Management*, Vol. 14, No. 4, pp. 420–435. An-Tien Hsieh, Chang-Hua Yen, and Ko-Chien Chin (2004), "Participative Customers as Partial Employees and Service Provider Workload", *International Journal of Service Industry Management*, Vol. 15, No. 2, pp. 187–200.

43 For research on SST, see Matthew L. Meuter, Mary Jo Bitner, Amy L. Ostrom, and Stephen W. Brown (2005), "Choosing Among Alternative Delivery Modes: An Investigation of Customer Trial of Self Service Technologies," *Journal of Marketing*, Vol. 69, April, pp. 61–84.

44 The term "servicescape" was coined by Mary Jo Bitner (1992), "Servicescapes: The Impact of Physical Surroundings on Customers and Employees," *Journal of Marketing*, Vol. 56, April, pp. 57–71.

45 Hei-Lim Michael Lio and Raymond Rody (2009), "The Emotional Impact of Casino Servicescape," *UNLV Gaming Research and Review Journal,* Vol. 13, No. 2, October, pp. 17–25.

46 The term "part-time marketer" was coined by Evert Gummesson (1987), "The New Marketing: Developing Long-Term Interactive Relationships," *Long Range Planning*, Vol. 4. See also, Christian Grönroos, *Service Management and Marketing, 3rd ed.* (Hoboken, NY: John Wiley & Sons, Ltd., 2007) and Evert Gummesson, *Total Relationship Marketing, 3rd ed.* (Routledge, 2008).

47 James L. Heskett, Thomas O. Jones, Gary W. Loveman, W. Earl Sasser Jr., and Leonard A. Schlesinger (1994), "Putting the Service Profit Chain to Work," *Harvard Business Review*, Vol. 72, March/April; James L. Heskett, W. Earl Sasser, Jr., and Leonard A. Schlesinger, *The Service Profit Chain* (New York: The Free Press, 1997).

CHAPTER
02 **Understanding Service Consumers**

I can't get no satisfaction.

> From the song "(I Can't Get No) Satisfaction"
> **Mick Jagger**, lead singer of The Rolling Stones

An individual who seeks out the necessary information and chooses wisely has a better chance of getting satisfaction than Mick Jagger.

> **Claes Fornell**
> Distinguished Donald C. Cook Emeritus Professor of Business at the University of Michigan and Founder of the American Customer Satisfaction Index

All the world's a stage and all the men and women merely players; they have their exits and their entrances and one man in his time plays many parts.

> From "As You Like It" by **William Shakespeare**
> English poet, playwright, and actor.

LEARNING OBJECTIVES (LOs)

By the end of this chapter, the reader should be able to:

➲ **LO 1** Understand the three-stage model of service consumption.

➲ **LO 2** Use the multi-attribute model to understand how consumers evaluate and choose between alternative service offerings.

➲ **LO 3** Learn why consumers often have difficulties evaluating services, especially those with many experience and credence attributes.

➲ **LO 4** Know the perceived risks customers face in purchasing services and the strategies firms can use to reduce consumer risk perceptions.

➲ **LO 5** Understand how customers form service expectations and the components of these expectations.

➲ **LO 6** Know the *moment-of-truth* metaphor.

➲ **LO 7** Contrast how customers experience and evaluate high- versus low-contact services.

➲ **LO 8** Be familiar with the servuction model and understand the interactions that together create the service experience.

➲ **LO 9** Obtain insights from viewing the service encounter as a form of theater.

➲ **LO 10** Know how role, script, and perceived control theories contribute to a better understanding of service encounters.

➲ **LO 11** Describe how customers evaluate services and what determines their satisfaction.

➲ **LO 12** Understand service quality, its dimensions and measurement, and how quality relates to customer loyalty.

Figure 2.1 New York University is the gateway for a brighter future for students like Susan Munro

OPENING VIGNETTE
Susan Munro, Service Customer[1]

Susan Munro, a final-year business student, had breakfast and then checked the weather app on her iPhone. It predicted rain, so she grabbed an umbrella before leaving the apartment. On the way to the bus stop, she dropped a letter in a mailbox. The bus arrived on schedule. It was the usual driver, who recognized her and gave a cheerful greeting as she showed her commuter pass.

Arriving at her destination, Susan left the bus and walked to the College of Business. Joining a crowd of other students, she found a seat in the lecture theater where her marketing class was held. The professor was a dynamic individual who believed in having an active dialog with the students. Susan made several contributions to the discussion and felt that she learned a lot from listening to others' analyses and opinions.

Susan and her friends ate lunch at the recently renovated Student Union. It was a well-lit and colorfully decorated new food court, featuring a variety of small stores. These included both local suppliers and brand-name fast-food chains, which offered different types of cuisine. There were stores selling sandwiches, crepes, health foods, a variety of Asian cuisine and desserts. Although she had wanted a sandwich, there was a long queue of customers at the Subway outlet. Thus, Susan joined her friends at Burger King and then splurged on a café latte from the Have-a-Java coffee stand. The food court was unusually crowded that day, perhaps because of the rain pouring outside. When they finally found a table, they had to clear away the dirty trays. "Lazy slobs!" commented her friend Mark, referring to the previous customers.

After lunch, Susan stopped at the cash machine, inserted her bank card, and withdrew some money. When she remembered that she had a job interview at the end of the week, she telephoned her hairdresser and counted herself lucky to be able to make an appointment for later. This was because of a cancellation by another client. When she left the Student Union, the rain had stopped and the sun was shining.

Susan looked forward to her visit to the hairdresser. The store, which had a bright, trendy décor, was staffed by friendly hairdressers. Unfortunately, the hairstylist was running late and Susan had to wait for 20 minutes. She used that time to review a human resources course. Some

Figure 2.2 Susan is just another customer facing a large selection of services out there

of the other waiting customers were reading magazines provided by the store. Eventually, it was time for a shampoo, after which the hairstylist proposed a slightly different cut. Susan agreed, although she drew the line at the suggestion to lighten her hair color as she had never done it before and was unsure how it would look. She did not want to take the risk, especially not just before her job interview. She sat still, watching the process in the mirror and turning her head when asked. She was very pleased with the result and complimented the hairstylist on her work. She tipped the hairstylist and paid at the reception desk.

On the way home, she stopped by the cleaners to pick up some clothes. The store was rather gloomy, smelled of cleaning solution, and the walls badly needed repainting. She was annoyed to find that although her silk blouse was ready as promised, the suit that she needed for the interview was not. The assistant, who had dirty fingernails, mumbled an apology in an insincere tone. Although the store was convenient and the quality of work was quite good, Susan considered the employees unfriendly and not very helpful, and was unhappy with their service. However, she had no choice but to use them as there were no other dry cleaners close by.

Back at her apartment building, she opened the mailbox in the lobby. Her mail included a bill from her insurance company. However, it required no action since payment was deducted automatically from her MasterCard. She was about to throw away the junk mail when she noticed a flyer promoting a new dry-cleaning store nearby, which included a discount coupon. She decided to try the new firm and kept the coupon.

Since it was her turn to cook dinner, she looked in the kitchen to see what food was available. Susan sighed when she realized that there was nothing much. Maybe she could make a salad and call for the delivery of a large pizza.

This story of Susan's day as a service consumer will follow us throughout this chapter to illustrate service-related consumer behavior concepts and theories.

LO 1

Understand the three-stage model of service consumption.

THE THREE-STAGE MODEL OF SERVICE CONSUMPTION

The story of Susan Munro shows consumer behavior in a variety of situations and stages. In marketing, it is very important to understand why customers behave the way they do. How do they make decisions about buying and using a service? What determines their satisfaction with it after consumption? Without this understanding, no firm can hope to create and deliver services that will result in satisfied customers who will buy again.

Service consumption can be divided into three main stages. They are the prepurchase, service encounter, and post-encounter stages. *Figure 2.3* shows that each stage consists of several steps. The prepurchase stage includes need-awareness, information search, evaluation of alternatives, and making a purchase decision. During the service encounter stage, the customer initiates, experiences, and consumes the service. The post-encounter stage includes evaluation of the service performance, which determines future intentions such as wanting to buy again from the same firm, and recommending it to friends. The rest of this chapter is organized around the three stages and the related key concepts of service consumption.

PREPURCHASE STAGE

The prepurchase stage begins with **need-awareness** and continues through to information search and evaluation of alternatives to deciding whether or not to buy a particular service.

Pre-purchase Stage

Stages of Service Consumption

- ▶ Awareness of need
  - Information search
  - Clarify needs
  - Explore solutions
  - Identify alternative service products and suppliers

- ▶ Evaluation of alternatives (solutions and suppliers)
  - Review supplier information (e.g., advertising, brochures, websites)
  - Review information from third parties (e.g., published reviews, ratings, comments on the Web, blogs, complaints to public agencies, satisfaction ratings, awards)
  - Discuss options with service personnel
  - Get advice and feedback from third-party advisors and other customers

- ▶ Make decisions on service purchase and often make reservations

Key Concepts

- ▶ Need arousal
- ▶ Evoked set
- ▶ Consideration set

- ▶ Multi-attribute model
- ▶ Search, experience, and credence attributes
- ▶ Perceived risk

- ▶ Formation of expectations: desired service level, predicted service level, adequate service level, zone of tolerance

Service Encounter Stage

Stages of Service Consumption

- ▶ Request service from a chosen supplier or initiate self-service (payment may be upfront or billed later)

- ▶ Service delivery by personnel or self-service

Key Concepts

- ▶ Moments of truth
- ▶ Service encounters
- ▶ Servuction system
- ▶ Theater as a metaphor
- ▶ Role and script theories
- ▶ Perceived control theory

Post-encounter Stage

Stages of Service Consumption

- ▶ Evaluation of service performance

- ▶ Future intentions

Key Concepts

- ▶ Confirmation/ Disconfirmation of expectations
- ▶ Dissatisfaction, satisfaction, and delight
- ▶ Service Quality
- ▶ Word-of-mouth
- ▶ Repurchase
- ▶ Loyalty

Figure 2.3 The Three Stage Model of Service Consumption

Need Awareness

When a person or organization decides to buy or use a service, it is triggered by an underlying need or **need arousal**. The awareness of a need will lead to information search and evaluation of alternatives before a decision is reached. Needs may be triggered by:

- People's unconscious minds (e.g., personal identity and aspirations).

- Physical conditions (e.g., Susan Munro's hunger drove her to Burger King).

- External sources (e.g., social media or a service firm's marketing activities)

When a need is recognized, people are likely to be motivated to take action to resolve it. In Susan Munro's case, her need for hairstyling was triggered when she remembered she had a job interview at the end of the week and wanted to look her best. Needs and wants are continuously developing, for example, the need for increasingly novel and innovative service experiences in extreme sports, such as guided mountain climbing,

paragliding, white-water rafting , mountain biking, and bungee jumping (*Figure 2.4*).

Information Search

Once a need has been recognized, customers are motivated to search for solutions to satisfy that need. Several alternatives may come to mind, and these form the **evoked set**. The evoked set can be derived from past experiences or external sources such as social media, online reviews, online searches, advertising, retail displays, news stories, and recommendations from service personnel, friends, and family. However, a consumer is unlikely to use all the alternatives in the evoked set for decision-making. The consumer is likely to narrow it down to a few alternatives to seriously consider, and these alternatives form the **consideration set**. For Susan, her consideration set for a quick lunch included the sandwich store and Burger King. During the search process, consumers also learn about service attributes they should consider and form expectations of how firms in the consideration set perform on those attributes.[2]

Figure 2.4 Activities like paragliding are becoming more popular so there is an increase in the number of service providers offering that sport

Evaluation of Alternative Services

Once the consideration set and key attributes are understood, the consumer typically makes a purchase decision. In marketing, we often use multi-attribute models to simulate consumer decision-making.

Multi-attribute Model

This model holds that consumers use service attributes important to them to evaluate and compare alternative offerings in their consideration set. Each attribute has an importance weight. A higher weight means the attribute is more important. For example, let's assume Susan has three alternative dry cleaners in her consideration set. *Table 2.1* shows the alternatives as well as the attributes she would use to compare them. The table shows that the quality of the dry cleaning is most important to her, followed by convenience of location, and then price (*Table 2.1*). Susan can use these two common decision rules to decide. They are the very simple linear compensatory rule and the more complex, but also more realistic, conjunctive rule. Using the same information, Susan can end up choosing different alternatives if she uses different decision rules. It is therefore important for firms to understand which rule their target customers are using through careful market research!

Using the linear compensatory rule, Susan mentally computes a global score for each dry cleaner, with scores ranging from 1 to 10. This is done by multiplying the score for the dry cleaner on each attribute by the importance weight. The scores are then added up. For example, the current dry cleaner would score 9 x 30% for quality of dry cleaning, plus 10 x 25% for convenience of location, plus 8 x 20% for price, etc. If you do this computation for all three alternatives, you will get a total score for the current dry cleaner of 7.7, the campus dry cleaner of 9.2, and 9.0 for the new dry cleaner. Therefore, the choice would be the on-campus dry cleaner.

⊃ LO 2

Use the multi-attribute model to understand how consumers evaluate and choose between alternative service offerings.

Table 2.1 Modeling Consumer Choice — Susan Munro's Multi-attribute Model for Choosing a Dry Cleaner

	Current Dry Cleaner	Campus Dry Cleaner	New Dry Cleaner	Importance Weight (%)
Quality of Dry Cleaning	9	10	10	30
Convenience of Location	10	8	9	25
Price	8	10	8	20
Opening Hours	6	10	9	10
Reliability of On-time Delivery	2	9	9	5
Friendliness of Staff	2	8	8	5
Design of Shop	2	7	8	5
Total Score	7.7	9.2	9.0	100

In the conjunctive rule, the consumer will make the decision based on the total overall score in conjunction with minimum performance levels on one or several attributes. For example, Susan may only consider a dry cleaner that scores a minimum of 9 on convenience of location as she does not want to carry her dry cleaning over longer distances. In that case, the choice is between the current and new dry cleaner in her neighborhood. She will pick the new dry cleaner of the two as it has the higher overall score. If none of the brands meet all the cutoffs in a conjunctive model, then Susan may delay making a choice, change the decision rule, or modify the cutoffs.

Service providers who understand the decision-making process of their target customers can then try to influence that decision-making process in a number of ways to enhance their chance of being the chosen provider:

- First, firms need to ensure that their service is in the consideration set, as without being considered, a firm cannot be chosen! This can be done through advertising or viral marketing (Chapter 7).

- Next, firms can change and correct consumer perceptions (e.g., if a clinic has superior performance on personalized and special care offered by their doctors but customers do not see this, it can focus its communications on correcting customer perceptions).

- They can also shift importance weights (e.g., communicate messages that increase weights of attributes the firm excels in, and de-emphasize those the firm is not so strong at).

- Firms can even introduce new attributes such as what Hertz did when advertising its environmental-friendly car. Consumers who are eco-conscious would consider the environment aspect when deciding which car rental company to use.

The objective is to shape the target customers' decision-making so that they make the "right" choice, that is, choose the firm's service offering.[3]

⊃ **LO 3**

Learn why consumers often have difficulties evaluating services, especially those with many experience and credence attributes.

Service Attributes

The multi-attribute model assumes that consumers can evaluate all important attributes before purchase. However, this is often not the case as some attributes are harder to evaluate than others. There are three types of attributes[4]. They are:

- **Search attributes** – they are tangible characteristics that customers can evaluate before purchase. For example, search attributes for a restaurant include type of food, location, type of restaurant (e.g., fine dining, casual or family-friendly), and price. You can also check out a golf course before actually playing a round, or take a tour of a health club and try working out with one or two pieces of the gym equipment. These tangible search attributes help customers better understand and evaluate a service, therefore reducing the sense of uncertainty or risk associated with the purchase.

- **Experience attributes** – they cannot be evaluated before purchase. Customers must "experience" the service before they can assess attributes such as reliability, ease-of-use, and customer support. In our restaurant example, you won't know how much you actually like the food, the service provided by your waiter, and the atmosphere in the restaurant until you are actually using the service.

Vacations (*Figure 2.5*), live entertainment performances, and many medical procedures all have high experience attributes. Although people can scroll through websites describing a specific holiday destination, view travel films, read reviews by travel experts and past guests, or hear about the experiences from family and friends, they cannot really evaluate or feel the dramatic beauty associated with, say, hiking in the Canadian Rockies or snorkeling in the Caribbean until they experience these activities themselves.

Figure 2.5 Holiday-makers hiking up the mountains

Finally, reviews and recommendations cannot possibly account for all situation-specific circumstances. For example, the excellent chef may be on a vacation or a boisterous birthday party at the neighboring table may spoil the romantic candlelight dinner you came for to celebrate an anniversary.

- **Credence attributes** are characteristics that customers find hard to evaluate even after consumption. Here, the customer is forced to believe or trust that certain tasks have been performed at the promised level of quality. In our restaurant example, credence attributes include the hygiene conditions in the kitchen, the nutritional quality and the freshness of ingredients used (e.g., "Do they really use the higher grade olive oil for cooking?").

It's not easy for a customer to determine the quality of repair and maintenance work performed on a car, and patients can't usually evaluate how well their dentists have performed complex dental procedures. Also, consider the purchase of professional services. People seek such assistance precisely because they lack the necessary training and expertise themselves — think about counseling, surgery, legal advice, and consulting services. How can you really be sure that the best possible job was done? Often it comes down to a matter of having confidence in the provider's skills and professionalism.

All products can be placed on a continuum ranging from "easy to evaluate" to "difficult to evaluate," depending on whether they are high in search, experience, or credence attributes. As shown in *Figure 2.6*, most physical goods are located somewhere toward the left of the continuum because they rank high in search attributes. Most services tend to be located from the center to the right of the continuum as they tend to be high in experience and credence attributes.

The harder it is to evaluate a service, the higher is the perceived risk associated with that decision. We will discuss perceived risk next.

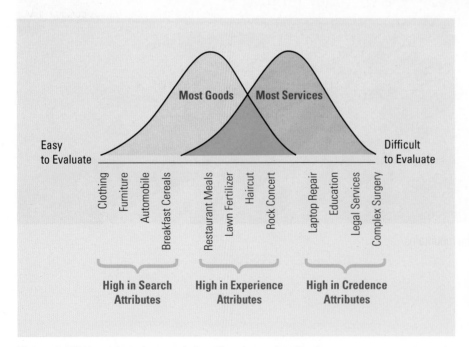

Source

Adapted from Valarie A. Zeithaml, "How Consumer Evaluation Processes Differ Between Goods and Services," in J. H. Donnelly and W. R. George, *Marketing of Services* (Chicago: American Marketing Association, 1981).

Figure 2.6 How product characteristics affect ease of evaluation

Perceived Risk

If you buy a physical good that is unsatisfactory, you can usually return or replace it. With services, this option may not be possible. Susan Munro had not tried coloring her hair before and was uncertain how it would turn out. Hence, when the hairstylist suggested she lighten her hair color, she declined. Her uncertainty increased her **perceived risk**. Perceived risk is usually greater for services that are high in experience and credence attributes, and first-time users are likely to face greater uncertainty. Think about how you felt the first time you had to make a decision about an unfamiliar service, especially one with important consequences such as choosing a college or a health insurance plan. It is likely that you were worried about the possibility of not making the best choice, or not even a good choice. The worse the possible consequences and the higher likelihood of these negative consequences happening, the higher the perception of risk. *Table 2.2* shows seven categories of perceived risks.

 LO 4
Know the perceived risks customers face in purchasing services and the strategies firms can use to reduce consumer risk perceptions.

Table 2.2 Perceived Risks in Purchasing and Using Services

Type of Risk	Examples of Customer Concerns
Functional (unsatisfactory performance outcomes)	• Will this training course give me the skills I need to get a better job? • Will this credit card be accepted wherever and whenever I want to make a purchase? • Will the dry cleaner be able to remove the stains from this jacket?
Financial (monetary loss, unexpected costs)	• Will I lose money if I make the investment recommended by my stockbroker? • Could my credit card details be stolen if I register with this website? • Will repairing my car cost more than the original estimate?
Temporal (wasting time, consequences of delays)	• Will I have to wait in line for a long time before I can enter the exhibition? • Will service at this restaurant be so slow that I will be late for my afternoon meeting? • Will the renovations to our bathroom be completed before our friends come to stay with us?
Physical (personal injury or damage to possessions)	• Will there be complications or scars if I go for this cosmetic surgery? • Will the contents of this package get damaged in the mail? • Will I get an upset stomach if I eat at this roadside stall?
Psychological (personal fears and emotions)	• How can I be sure that this aircraft will not crash? • Will the consultant make me feel embarrassed or stupid? • Will the doctor's diagnosis upset me?
Social (how others think and react)	• What will my friends think of me if they learned that I registered for the dating service? • Will my relatives approve of the restaurant I have chosen for the family reunion dinner? • Will my business colleagues disapprove of my selection of an unknown law firm?
Sensory (unwanted effects on any of the five senses)	• Will I get a view of the parking lot rather than the beach from my restaurant table? • Will I be kept awake by noise from the guests in the room next door? • Will my room smell of stale cigarette smoke?

How might consumers handle perceived risk? People usually feel uncomfortable with perceived risks and use a variety of methods to reduce them, including:

- Seeking information from trusted and respected personal sources such as family, friends, and peers.[5]

- Using the Internet to compare service offerings, to search for independent reviews and ratings, and to explore discussions on social media.

- Relying on a firm that has a good reputation.

- Looking for guarantees and warranties.

- Visiting service facilities or trying aspects of the service before purchasing, and examining tangible cues or other physical evidence such as the feel and look of the service setting or looking out for awards won by the firm (*Figure 2.7*).

- Asking knowledgeable employees about competing services to learn about what to look out for when making this decision.

Customers are risk-averse and — all else being equal — will choose the service with the lower perceived risk. Therefore, firms need to proactively work on reducing customer risk perceptions. Suitable strategies vary according to the nature of the service and may include all or some of the following:

- Encourage prospective customers to preview the service through their company websites and videos.

Figure 2.7 Winning awards is a cue for service excellence

- Encourage prospective customers to visit the service facilities before purchase.

- Offer free trials suitable for services with high experience attributes. Many caterers and restaurants allow potential wedding customers to have free food tasting sessions before making a booking for their wedding banquet.

- For services with high credence qualities and high customer involvement, advertising helps to communicate the benefits, usage, and how consumers can enjoy the best results.

Figure 2.8 Doctor displays his credentials

- Display credentials. Professionals such as doctors, architects, and lawyers often display their degrees and other certifications because they want customers to "see" they are qualified to provide expert service (*Figure 2.8*). Many professional firms' websites inform prospective clients about their services, highlight their expertise, and even showcase successful past engagements.

- Use **evidence management**, an organized approach where customers are presented with coherent evidence of the company's targeted image and its value proposition. This includes the appearance of furnishings, equipment and facilities; and employees' dress and behavior[6]. For example, the bright and trendy decor at the hairdressing salon may have helped Susan Munro choose the salon on her first visit. Now, it probably contributes to her feeling satisfied in the end, even though her stylist kept her waiting for 20 minutes.

- Have visible safety procedures that build confidence and trust.

- Give customers access to online information about the status of an order or procedure. Many courier service providers use this (e.g., FedEx, DHL, and UPS).

- Offer service guarantees such as money-back guarantees and performance warranties.

When a company does a good job in managing potential customers' risk perceptions, uncertainty is reduced, thereby increasing the chances of them being the chosen service provider. Also important to consumer choice (and subsequently satisfaction) are customer expectations, which we shall discuss next.

Service Expectations

Expectations are formed during the search and decision-making process, through a customer's search and evaluation of information and alternatives. If you do not have any previous experience with the service, you may base your prepurchase expectations on online searches and reviews, word-of-mouth comments, news stories, or a firm's own marketing efforts. Expectations can even be situation-specific. For example, if it is peak period, expectations of service delivery timing will be lower than during non-peak periods.

Expectations change and can be managed, as discussed in the section on multi-attribute models. Firms try to shape expectations through their communications and the introduction of new services and technologies. Increased access to information through the media and the Internet can also change expectations. For instance, today's healthcare consumer is well-informed and often seeks a participative role in decisions relating to medical treatment. *Service Insights 2.1* describes a new assertiveness among parents of children with serious illnesses.

 LO 5

Understand how customers form service expectations and the components of these expectations.

SERVICE INSIGHTS 2.1

Parents Seek Involvement in Medical Decisions Affecting Their Children

Many parents want to participate actively in decisions relating to their children's medical treatment. Thanks partly to in-depth media and online coverage of medical advances and health-related issues, as well as the educational efforts of consumer groups, parents are better informed and more assertive than those of previous generations. They are no longer willing to simply accept the recommendations of medical specialists. In particular, parents whose child was born with congenital defects or has developed a life-threatening illness are often willing to invest immense amounts of time and energy to learn everything they can about their child's condition. Some have even founded nonprofit organizations centered on a specific disease to bring together other families facing the same problems and to help raise money for research and treatment.

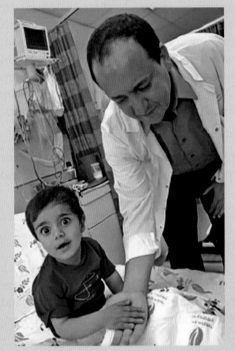

The Internet has made it much easier to access healthcare information and research findings. A study by the Texas-based Heart Center of 160 parents who had Internet access and children with cardiac problems found that 58% obtained information related to their child's diagnosis. Four out of five users searching for cardiology-related information stated that locating the information was easy. Of those, half could name a favorite cardiology website. Almost all felt the information was helpful in better understanding their child's condition. The study reported that six parents even created interactive personal websites about their child's congenital heart defect.

Commenting on the phenomenon of highly-informed parents, Norman J. Siegel, MD, former chair of pediatrics at Yale New Haven Children's Hospital, observed:

It's a different practice today. The old days of "Trust me, I'm going to take care of this" are completely gone. I see many patients who come in carrying a folder with printouts from the Internet and they want to know why Dr. So-and-So wrote this. They go to chat rooms, too. They want to know about the disease process, if it's chronic. Some parents are almost as well informed as a young medical student or house officer.

Dr. Siegel said he welcomed the trend and enjoyed the discussions but admitted that some physicians found it hard to adapt.

Source

Christopher Lovelock and Jeff Gregory, "Yale New Haven Children's Hospital," New Haven, CT: Yale School of Management, 2003 (case).

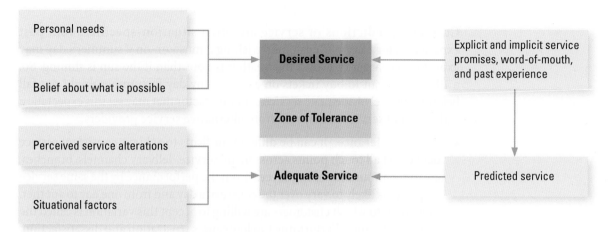

```
Personal needs ──────┐
                     ├──→  Desired Service  ←──  Explicit and implicit service
Belief about what is possible ──┘                promises, word-of-mouth,
                                                 and past experience
                          Zone of Tolerance              │
                                                         ↓
Perceived service alterations ──┐
                     ├──→  Adequate Service  ←──  Predicted service
Situational factors ──┘
```

Figure 2.9 Factors influencing customer expectations of service

Source

Adapted from Valarie A. Zeithaml, Leonard A. Berry, and A. Parasuraman (1993), "The Nature and Determinants of Customer Expectations of Service," *Journal of the Academy of Marketing Science*, Vol. 21, No. 1, pp. 1–12.

What are the components of customer expectations? Expectations embrace several elements, including desired, adequate and predicted service, and a zone of tolerance that falls between the desired and adequate service levels[7]. The model in *Figure 2.9* shows the factors influencing the different levels of customer expectations. These factors are:

- **Desired service.** The type of service customers hope to receive is termed desired service. It's a "wished for" level — a combination of what customers believe can and should be delivered in the context of their personal needs. Desired service could also be influenced by explicit and implicit promises made by service providers, word-of-mouth, and past experiences[8]. However, most customers are realistic.

Recognizing that a firm can't always deliver the "wished for" level of service, they also have a threshold level of expectations, termed adequate service, and a predicted service level.

- **Adequate service.** The minimum level of service customers will accept without being dissatisfied.

- **Predicted service.** This is the level of service that customers actually anticipate to receive. Predicted service can also be affected by service provider promises (*Figure 2.10*), word-of-mouth, and past experiences. The predicted service level directly affects how customers define "adequate service" on that occasion. If good service is predicted, the adequate level will be higher than when poorer service is predicted.

Courtesy of Singapore Airlines

Figure 2.10 This advertisement creates high expectations for Singapore Airline Suites on its A380 Airbus aircraft

Customer predictions of service are often situation-specific. From past experience, for example, customers visiting a museum on a summer's day may expect to see larger crowds if the weather is poor than if the sun is shining. So, a 10-minute wait to buy tickets on a cool, rainy day in summer might not fall below their level of adequate service. Another factor that may set this expectation is the level of service anticipated from alternative service providers.

- **Zone of tolerance.** It can be difficult for firms to achieve consistent service delivery at all touch points across many service delivery channels, branches, and often thousands of employees. Even the performance by the same service employee is likely to vary over the course of a day and from one day to another. The extent to which customers are willing to accept this variation is called the zone of tolerance. Performing too low causes frustration and dissatisfaction, whereas exceeding the zone of tolerance can surprise and delight customers. Another way of looking at the zone of tolerance is to think of it as the range of service within which customers don't pay explicit attention to service performance. When service falls outside this range, customers will react, either positively or negatively[9].

The size of the zone of tolerance can be larger or smaller for individual customers, depending on factors such as competition, price, or importance of specific service attributes — each of which can influence the expectation of adequate service levels. In contrast, desired service levels tend to move up very slowly in response to accumulated customer experiences. Consider a small business owner who needs some advice from her accountant. Her ideal level of professional service may be receiving a thoughtful response by the following day. However, if she makes her request at the time of year when all accountants are busy preparing corporate and individual tax returns, she will know from experience not to expect a fast reply. Although her ideal service level probably won't change, her zone of tolerance for response time may be broader because she has a lower adequate service threshold at busy periods of the year.

The predicted service level is the most important level for the consumer choice process, which we shall discuss in the next section. Desired and adequate levels, and the zone of tolerance become important determinants to customer satisfaction, which we will discuss in the postencounter purchase stage section.

Purchase Decision

After consumers have evaluated possible alternatives by, for example, comparing the performance of the important attributes of competing service offerings; assessed the perceived risk associated with each offering; and developed their desired, adequate, and predicted service level expectations, they are ready to select the option they like best.

Many purchase decisions for frequently purchased services are quite simple and can be made quickly without too much thought — the perceived risks are low, the alternatives are clear, and, because they have been used before, their characteristics are easily understood. If the consumer already has a favorite supplier, he or she will probably choose it again in the absence of a compelling reason to do otherwise. In many instances, however, purchase decisions involve tradeoffs. Price is often a key factor. For example, is it worth paying more for faster service, a larger room with a better view, or a better seat in a theater performance (*Figure 2.11*)?

For more complex decisions, tradeoffs can involve multiple attributes, as we have seen in the section on consumer choice based on the multi-attribute model. In choosing an airline, convenience of schedules, reliability, seating comfort, attentiveness of cabin crew, and availability and quality of meals may well vary among different carriers, even at the same rates.

Once a decision is made, the consumer is ready to move to the service encounter stage. This next step may take place immediately, as it is in deciding to enter a fast-food restaurant, or it may first involve an advance reservation, as what usually happens with taking a flight or attending a live theater performance.

Figure 2.11 Consumers have to see whether it is worthwhile to pay a higher price for better seats

SERVICE ENCOUNTER STAGE

After making a purchase decision, customers move on to the core of the service experience. The service encounter stage is when the customer interacts directly with the service firm. We use a number of models and frameworks to better understand the consumers' behavior and experience during the service encounter. First, the "moments of truth" metaphor shows the importance of effectively managing service touch points. A second framework, the high- or low-contact service model, helps us to better understand the extent and nature of points of contact. A third concept, the servuction model, focuses on the various types of interactions that together create the customer's service experience. Finally, the theater metaphor together with the script, role, and perceived control theories communicate effectively how one can look at "staging" service performances to create the experience customers desire.

➲ **LO 6**

Know the *moment-of-truth* metaphor.

Service Encounters Are "Moments of Truth"

Richard Normann borrowed the *moment of truth* metaphor from bullfighting to show the importance of contact points with customers (*Figure 2.12*):

> [W]e could say that the perceived quality is realized at the moment of truth, when the service provider and the service customer confront one another in the arena. At that moment they are very much on their own... It is the skill, the motivation, and the tools employed by the firm's representative, and the expectations and behavior of the client which together will create the service delivery process[10].

In bullfighting, the life of either the bull or the matador (or possibly both) is at stake. The message in a service context is that at the *moment of truth*, the relationship between the customer and the firm is at stake.

Figure 2.12 The service provider is the matador who skillfully manages the service encounter

Jan Carlzon, former chief executive of Scandinavian Airlines System (SAS), used the *moment of truth* metaphor as a reference point for transforming SAS from an operations-driven business into a customer-driven airline. Carlzon made the following comments about his airline:

> *Last year, each of our 10 million customers came into contact with approximately five SAS employees, and this contact lasted an average of 15 seconds each time. Thus, SAS is "created" 50 million times a year, 15 seconds at a time. These 50 million "moments of truth" are the moments that ultimately determine whether SAS will succeed or fail as a company. They are the moments when we must prove to our customers that SAS is their best alternative[11].*

Each service business faces similar challenges in defining and managing the "moments of truth" its customers will encounter.

Service Encounters Range From High Contact to Low Contact

Services involve different levels of contact with the service operation. Some of these encounters can be very brief and may consist of a few steps, such as when a customer calls a customer contact center or uses a service app. Others may extend over a longer time frame and involve multiple interactions of varying degrees of complexity. For example, a visit to a theme park might last all day. In *Figure 2.13*, we group services into three levels of customer contact. These represent how much customers interact with service personnel, physical service elements, or both. Although we recognize that the level of customer contact covers a spectrum, it's useful to examine the differences between services at the high and low ends, respectively. For example, you'll notice that traditional retail banking, person-to-person phone banking, and Internet banking are located in very different parts of the chart but may deliver the same basic banking transaction such as a funds transfer.

⊃ **LO 7**
Contrast how customers experience and evaluate high- versus low-contact services.

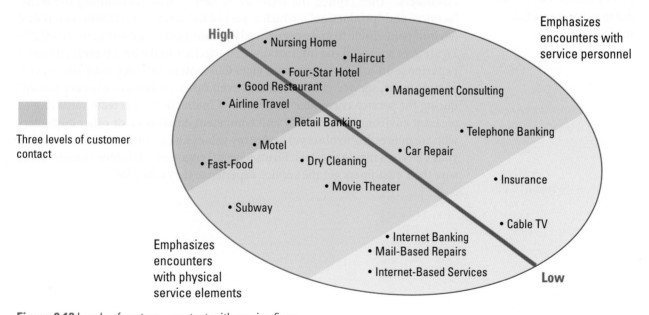

Three levels of customer contact

Figure 2.13 Levels of customer contact with service firms

- **High-Contact Services.** Using a high-contact service means there is direct contact between customers and the firm throughout the entire service delivery. When customers visit the facility where service is delivered, they enter a service "factory" — something that rarely happens in a manufacturing environment. From this perspective, a hospital is a health treatment factory, and a restaurant is a food service factory. Because each of these industries focuses on "processing" people rather than inanimate objects, the marketing challenge is to make the experience appealing for customers in terms of both the physical environment and their interactions with service personnel. During the course of service delivery, customers are usually exposed to many physical clues about the organization — the exterior and interior of its buildings, the equipment and furnishings, the appearance and behavior of service personnel, and even other customers. For Susan Munro, the clues at the dry cleaners, such as the gloomy interior and the walls that need repainting contributed to her experience of a bad service. Even the pace of service encounters can affect customer satisfaction[12].

- **Low-Contact Services.** At the opposite end of the spectrum, low-contact services involve little, physical contact if any, between customers and service providers. Instead, contact takes place at arm's length through electronic or physical distribution channels. For example, customers conduct their insurance and banking transactions by mail, telephone, and Internet; or buy a variety of information-based services online (e.g., buy songs from iTunes or download books to their Kindle) rather than from brick-and-mortar stores. In fact, many high-contact and medium-contact services are being transformed into low-contact services as part of a fast-growing trend whereby convenience plays an increasing importance in consumer choice.

The Servuction System

⊃ LO 8

Be familiar with the servuction model and understand the interactions that together create the service experience.

French researchers Pierre Eiglier and Eric Langeard were the first to conceptualize the service business as a system that integrates marketing, operations, and customers. They coined the term *servuction system* (combining the terms "service" and "production"), which is part of the service organization's physical environment visible to and experienced by customers[13]. The servuction model in *Figure 2.14* shows all the interactions that together make up a typical customer experience in a high-contact service. Customers interact with the service environment, service employees, and even other customers who are present during the service encounter. Each type of interaction can create value (e.g., a pleasant environment, friendly and competent employees, or other customers who are interesting to observe) or destroy value (e.g., another customer blocking your view in a movie theater). Firms have to "engineer" all interactions to make sure their customers get the service experience they came for.

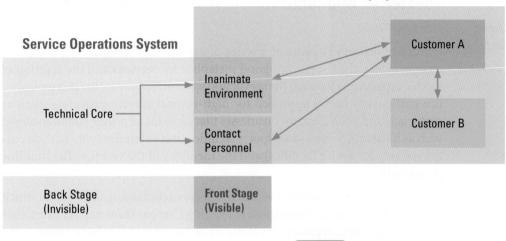

Service Delivery System

Service Operations System

- Technical Core
- Inanimate Environment
- Contact Personnel
- Customer A
- Customer B

Back Stage (Invisible) | Front Stage (Visible)

Source

Adapted and expanded from an original concept by Eric Langeard and Pierre Eiglier

Figure 2.14 The servuction system

The servuction system consists of a technical core and the service delivery system:

- **Technical core** — where inputs are processed and the elements of the service product are created. This technical core is typically back-stage and invisible to the customer (e.g., think of the kitchen in a restaurant). Like in the theater, the *invisible* components can be termed "back-stage" or "back office," while the *visible* components can be termed "front-stage" or "front office."[14] What goes on back-stage usually is not of interest to customers (*Figure 2.15*). However, if what goes on back-stage affects the quality of front-stage activities, customers will notice. For example, if a kitchen reads orders wrongly, diners will be upset.

- **Service delivery system** — where the final "assembly" takes place and the product is delivered to the customer. This subsystem includes the visible part of the service operations system — buildings, equipment, and personnel — and possibly other customers. Using the theater analogy, the visible front office is like a live theater where we stage the service experience for our customers.

The proportion of the overall service operation that is visible to customers varies according to the level of customer contact. Because high-contact services directly involve the physical person of the customer, the visible component of the entire service operation tends to be substantial, and many interactions — or "moments of truth" — have to be managed. In contrast, low-contact services usually have most of the service operations system back-stage with front-stage elements limited to online, telephone, or mail contacts. Here, customers normally do not see the "factory" where the work is performed, making the design and management of such facilities much easier. For example, credit card customers may never have to visit a physical bank — they only transact online and may once in a while talk to a service employee on the phone if there is a problem, and there is very little left of the "theater" performance.

Figure 2.15 Back-office operations are typically not seen by the customer

Theater as Metaphor for Service Delivery: An Integrative Perspective

As service delivery consists of a series of events that customers experience as a *performance,* the theater is a good metaphor for services and the creation of service experiences through the servuction system[15] (*Figure 2.16*). This metaphor is a particularly useful approach for high-contact service providers, such as physicians and hotels, and for businesses that serve many people simultaneously, such as hospitals, professional sports facilities, and entertainment. Let's discuss the stages (i.e., service facilities) and the members of the cast (i.e., the frontline personnel):

- **Service facilities.** Imagine service facilities as containing the *stage* on which the drama unfolds. Sometimes, the setting changes from one act to another (e.g., when airline passengers move from the entrance to the terminal to the check-in stations and then on to the boarding gate and finally step inside the aircraft). Some stages have minimal "props," such as a taxi for instance. In contrast, other stages have more elaborate "props," such as resort hotels with elaborate architecture, luxurious interior design, and lush landscaping.

- **Personnel.** The front-stage personnel are like the members of a cast playing roles as *actors* in a drama supported by a back-stage production team. In some instances, service personnel are expected to wear special costumes when on stage (such as the fanciful uniforms often worn by hotel doormen (*Figure 2.17*), or the more basic brown uniforms worn by UPS drivers).

The theater metaphor also includes the roles of the players on stage and the scripts they have to follow, which we will discuss next.

Figure 2.16 When service facilities and personnel are all in place, the stage is set for a memorable service performance for the customer

Role and Script Theories

The actors in a theater need to know what roles they play and familiarize themselves with the script. Similarly, in service encounters, knowledge of role and script theories can help organizations better understand, design, and manage both employee and customer behaviors during service encounters.

Role Theory. If we view service delivery from a theatrical perspective, then both employees and customers act out their parts in the performance according to predetermined roles. Stephen Grove and Ray Fisk define a role as "a set of behavior patterns learned through experience and communication, to be performed by an individual in a certain social interaction in order to attain maximum effectiveness in goal accomplishment"[16]. Roles have also been defined as combinations of social cues or expectations of society that guide behavior in a specific setting or context[17]. The satisfaction and productivity of both parties depend on role congruence, or the extent to which each person acts out his or her prescribed role during a service encounter. Employees must perform their roles in accordance to customer expectations or risk dissatisfying customers. As a customer, you too must "play by the rules" or risk causing problems for the firm, its employees, and even other customers. If either party is uncomfortable in their role or if they do not act accordingly, it will affect the satisfaction and productivity of both parties.

Script Theory. Much like a movie script, a service script specifies the sequences of behavior employees and customers are expected to learn and follow during service delivery. Employees receive formal training. Customers learn scripts through experience, through communication with others, and through designed communications and education[18]. The more experience a customer has with a service company, the more familiar that particular script becomes. Unwillingness to learn a new script may be a reason not to switch to a competing organization. Any deviations from this known script may frustrate both customers and employees, and can lead to dissatisfaction. If a company decides to change a service script (for example, by using technology to transform a high-contact service into a low-contact one), service personnel and customers need to be educated about the new approach and the benefits it provides.

Many service dramas are tightly scripted (like the flight attendants' scripts for economy class), which reduces variability and ensures uniform quality. However, not all services involve tightly scripted performances. Scripts tend to be more flexible for providers of highly customized services — designers, educators, consultants — and may vary by situation and by customer.

Figure 2.18 shows a script for teeth cleaning and a simple dental examination, involving three players — the patient, the receptionist, and the dental hygienist. Each has a specific role to play, reflecting what he or she brings to the encounter. The role of the customer (who is probably not looking forward to this encounter) is different from that of the two service providers, and the receptionist's role differs from the hygienist's, reflecting their distinctive jobs. This script is driven partly by the need to run an efficient dental office, but even more importantly, by the need to perform a technical task proficiently and safely (note the mask and gloves). The core service of examining and cleaning teeth can only be accomplished satisfactorily if the patient cooperates during the delivery of the service.

LO 10
Know how role, script, and perceived control theories contribute to a better understanding of service encounters.

Figure 2.17 Hotel doorman in a fanciful uniform contributes to the performance staged for the guests.

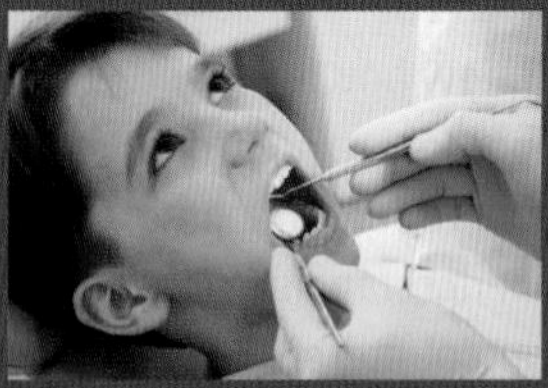

Patient	Receptionist	Dental Hygienist
1. Phone for appointment		
	2. Confirms needs and sets date	
3. Arrive at dental office		
	4. Greets patient; verify purpose; direct to waiting room; notify hygienist of arrival	
		5. Review notes on patient
6. Sits in waiting room		
		7. Greets patient and leads way to treatment room
8. Enters room, sits in dental chair		
		9. Verify medical and dental history; ask about any issues since previous visit
10. Respond to hygienist's questions		
		11. Place protective cover over patient's clothes
		12. Lower dental chair, put on own protective face mask, gloves and glasses
		13. Inspect patient's teeth (option to ask questions)
		14. Place suction device in patient's mouth
		15. Use high-speed equipment and hand tools to clean teeth in sequence
		16. Remove suction device; complete cleaning process
		17. Raise chair to sitting position; ask patient to rinse
18. Rinse mouth		
		19. Remove and dispose of mask and gloves; remove glasses
		20. Complete notes on treatment; return patient file to receptionist
		21. Remove cover for patient
		22. Give patient free toothbrush; offer advice on personal dental care for future
23. Rise from chair		
		24. Thank patient and say good-bye
25. Leave treatment room		
	26. Greet patient; confirm treatment received; present bill	
27. Pay bill		
	28. Give receipt; agree on date for next appointment; document agreed-upon date	
29. Take appointment card		
	30. Thank patient and say good-bye	
31. Leave dental office		

Figure 2.18 Script for teeth cleaning and simple dental examination

Role and Script Theory Complement Each Other.
Think, for example, of professor and student *roles* in the classes that you've attended. What is the role of the professor? Typically, it's to deliver a well-structured lecture, focusing on the key topics assigned for that day, making them interesting, and engaging students in discussion. What is the role of a student? Basically, it's to come to class prepared and on time, listen attentively, participate in discussions, and not disrupt the class. By contrast, the opening portion of the *script* for a lecture describes specific actions to be taken by each party. For instance, students should arrive at the lecture hall before class starts, select a seat, sit down, and open their laptops; the professor enters, puts notes on the table, turns on the notebook and LCD projector, greets the class, makes any preliminary announcements needed, and starts the class on time. As you can see, the frameworks offered by the two theories are complementary and describe the behavior during the encounter from two different perspectives. Excellent service marketers understand both perspectives and proactively define, communicate and train their employees and customers in their roles and service scripts to achieve a performance that yields high customer satisfaction and service productivity.

We will explore the core components of the service delivery system and the design of scripts and roles in detail in the later chapters of this book. Specifically, Chapter 7, "Services Marketing Communications" focuses on educating customers to move through the service delivery process to play their part in the service performance; Chapter 8, "Designing Service Processes," covers how to design scripts and roles; Chapter 10, "Crafting the Service Environment," discusses the process of designing the service environment, and Chapter 11, "Managing People for Service Advantage," explores how to manage service employees.

Perceived Control Theory

Another underlying dimension of every service encounter is perceived control[19], which holds that customers have a need for control during the service encounter, and that control is a major driving force of their behavior and satisfaction[20]. The higher the level of perceived control during a service situation, the higher their level of satisfaction will be. The perception of control can be managed via different types, including behavioral, decisional, and cognitive control.

Behavioral control means that the customer can change the situation and ask for customization beyond what the firm typically offers (e.g., by asking frontline employees to accommodate a special arrangement for a romantic candle light dinner). Decisional control means that the customer can choose between two or more standardized options, but without changing either option (e.g., choose between two tables in a restaurant). Cognitive control refers to the customer understanding why something happens (e.g., a flight delay due to a technical problem with the aircraft), and knowing what will happen next (also called predictive control, e.g., know how long the flight will be delayed). We are often mollified when someone keeps us informed about the situation[21].

If you imagine yourself in these situations, you can quickly understand how having these types of control immediately makes one feel better. In contrast, imagine you do not have control and how it would make you feel — for instance, you do not know why the flight is delayed or how long it will be. The same applies also to online services — users want to know where they are on a website, whether their transaction is being processed or whether the site "died" on them (that is why websites usually have a moving icon or processing bar to show that it is still processing). Even self-service machines like ATMs are designed to make you feel in control. Did you notice they make noises to indicate that they are processing and haven't simply swallowed your card? These sounds are often generated by a chip, as the machine alone would be silent for much of the process.

In short, it is important to design perceived control into service encounters. However, if processes, scripts and roles are tightly defined (as is the case for self-service technologies and highly scripted services such as fast-food and consumer banking), the scope for customization is limited. This means, firms cannot give much behavioral control as carefully designed processes would simply collapse, and productivity and quality would suffer. In those cases, firms can focus on giving customers decisional control (e.g., offer two or more fixed options), cognitive control (e.g., hospitals often go through great lengths to explain what is being done and why), and predictive control (e.g., never let the customer wait without giving an indication how long the wait will be). The good news is that perceived control is largely a compensatory additive, which means that a reduction in behavioral control can be compensated through higher decisional and cognitive control.

POST-ENCOUNTER STAGE

The last stage of service consumption is the post-encounter stage[22] which involves consumers' attitudinal and behavioral responses to the service experience. Important consumer responses are customer satisfaction, service quality perceptions, repeat purchase, and customer loyalty. We will discuss each concept next.

⊃ **LO 11**

Describe how customers evaluate services and what determines their satisfaction.

Customer Satisfaction

In the post-encounter stage, customers evaluate the service performance they have experienced and compare it with their prior expectations. Let us explore in more detail how service expectations relate to customer satisfaction and delight.

The Expectancy-Disconfirmation Model of Satisfaction. Satisfaction is a judgment following a series of consumer product interactions. Most customer satisfaction studies are based on the expectancy-disconfirmation model of satisfaction (*Figure 2.19*)[23]. In the model, confirmation or disconfirmation of pre-consumption expectations is the essential determinant of satisfaction.

Where do service expectations in our satisfaction model come from? During the decision-making process, customers assess the attributes and risks related to a service offering. In the process, they develop expectations about how the service they choose will perform (i.e., our predicted, desired, and adequate service levels discussed in the consumer decision-making section). The zone of tolerance can be narrow and firm if they are related to attributes important in the choice process. For example, if a customer paid a premium of $350 for a direct flight rather than one that has a four-hour stopover, the customer will not take it lightly if there is a six-hour flight delay. A customer will also have high expectations if he paid a premium for high-quality service, and will be deeply disappointed when the service fails to deliver. Smart firms manage customers' expectations at each step in the service encounter so that customers expect what the firm can deliver[24].

During and after consumption, consumers experience the service performance and compare it to their expectations. Satisfaction judgments are then formed based on this comparison. If performance perceptions are worse than expected, it is called **negative disconfirmation**. Susan Munro's expectations were negatively disconfirmed when her suit was not ready for pick up at the dry cleaner, leading to her dissatisfaction and her intention to give another dry cleaner a try in the future. If performance is better than expected, it is called **positive disconfirmation**, and if it is as expected, then it is simply called **confirmation of expectations**[25].

Source

Adapted from Richard L. Oliver (1997), *Satisfaction: A Behavioral Perspective on the Consumer*, (New York: McGraw-Hill) 110.

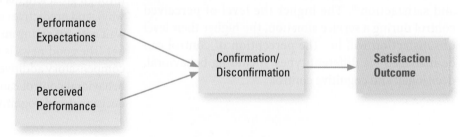

Figure 2.19 The expectancy-disconfirmation model of satisfaction

Customers will be reasonably satisfied as long as perceived performance falls within the zone of tolerance, that is, above the adequate service level. As performance perceptions approach or exceed desired levels, customers will be very pleased. Satisfied customers are more likely to make repeat purchases, remain loyal, and spread positive word-of-mouth[26]. However, if the service experience does not meet their expectations, customers may suffer in silence, complain about poor service quality, or switch providers in the future[27].

You can see that the attributes used in the choice process are again used in the satisfaction evaluation, whereby satisfaction judgments of the individual attributes are aggregated by the consumer to an overall customer satisfaction evaluation. Satisfaction with service attributes thus results from the experience of attribute-specific performance and strongly influences consumers' overall satisfaction.

Multi-attribute models help to better understand the formation process of customer satisfaction. Specifically, they help managers identify specific attributes with strong impacts on overall satisfaction, which is especially important if customers are satisfied with some attributes but dissatisfied with others[28]. Understanding this helps managers to cement the strengths of the firm's services and to focus improvement efforts on where it matters most.

Are Expectations Always the Right Comparison Standard? Comparing performance to expectations works well in reasonably competitive markets where customers have sufficient knowledge to choose a service that meets their needs and wants. Then, when expectations are met, customers are satisfied. However, in uncompetitive markets or in situations in which customers do not have free choice (e.g., because of time or location constraints, or because switching costs are prohibitive as it would be for many students once they have enrolled in a degree program), there are risks to defining customer satisfaction relative to their prior expectations. For example, if customer expectations are low and actual service delivery meets the dismal level that was expected, customers will hardly feel they are receiving good service quality. In such situations, it is better to use needs or wants as the standard for comparison, and to define satisfaction as meeting or exceeding customer wants and needs rather than expectations[29].

Furthermore, the disconfirmation-of-expectations model works very well for search and experience attributes (e.g.,

"I know whether you kept your promise and delivered by 1 p.m."), but less so for credence attributes. For example, when customers are asked to evaluate the quality of services with many credence attributes, such as complex legal cases or medical treatments, they find it difficult to evaluate the performance of that service even after the delivery is completed. Here, customers may be unsure of what to expect in advance and may not know for years — if ever — how good the job done by the professional actually was. A natural tendency in such situations is for clients or patients to use tangible cues and their experience as proxies to evaluate quality. Experience factors include customers' feelings about the personal style of individual providers (e.g., their friendliness, making eye contact, showing compassion and interest in the patient, and explaining medical treatments in simple terms) and satisfaction levels with those service elements they feel competent to evaluate (e.g., the service environment, waiting times in clinics, and the tastiness of hospital meals). As a result, customers' perceptions of service quality may be strongly influenced by their evaluation of process attributes and tangible elements of the service — also called halo effect[30].

Finally, customers rely on their expectations (e.g., "I expected to receive the best surgery money can buy") to form their satisfaction evaluations. If no tangible evidence contradicts their expectations, customers tend to evaluate credence attributes as meeting expectations and will be satisfied. Firms therefore have to understand how customers evaluate their service to proactively manage those aspects of their operations that have a strong effect on customer satisfaction, even if these attributes may be unrelated to the core attributes (e.g., the quality of a surgery).

How Is Customer Delight Different From Satisfaction? Customer delight is a function of three components: (1) unexpectedly high levels of performance, (2) arousal (e.g., surprise, excitement), and (3) positive affect (e.g., pleasure, joy, or happiness)[31]. In contrast, high satisfaction alone is a function of positively disconfirmed expectations (better than expected) and positive affect. So, achieving a customer's delight requires focusing on what is currently unexpected. Once a customer is delighted, it has a strong impact on a customer's loyalty[32]. One thing to note is that once customers have been delighted, their expectations are raised. They may be dissatisfied if service levels return to the previous levels, and it probably will take more effort to "delight" them again in future[33].

Based on the analysis of 10 years of data from the American Customer Satisfaction Index (ACSI), Claes Fornell and his colleagues caution against trying to exceed customer expectations on a continual basis, arguing that reaching for unobtainable objectives may backfire. They note that such efforts often come close to the point of diminishing returns[34]. More importantly, most firms have to first consistently meet their customers' needs and expectations before they even try to delight them — as was highlighted in a recent article published in Harvard Business Review on the context of call center services: "...what customers really want (but rarely get) is just a satisfactory solution to their service issue"[35]. Nevertheless, a few innovative and customer-centric firms seem to be able to delight customers even in seemingly mundane fields like insurance (*Service Insights 2.2*).

SERVICE INSIGHTS 2.2
Progressive Insurance Delights Its Customers

Progressive Insurance Corp. prides itself on providing extraordinary customer service — and its accomplishments in the area of claims processing are particularly impressive. To improve customer satisfaction and retention, and simultaneously lower its costs, the company introduced its Immediate Response service, offering customers 24/7 access to claims handling. Adjusters work out of mobile claims vans instead of offices, and Progressive has a target of nine hours for an adjuster to inspect a damaged vehicle. In many instances, claims representatives actually arrive at the scene of an accident while the evidence is still fresh.

Consider the following scenario. The crash site in Tampa, Florida, is chaotic and tense. Two cars are damaged and although the passengers aren't bleeding, they are shaken up and scared. Lance Edgy, a senior claim representative for Progressive Corp., arrives on the scene just minutes after the collision. He calms the victims and advises them on medical care, repair shops, police reports, and legal procedures. Edgy invites William McAllister, Progressive's policyholder, into an air-conditioned van equipped with comfortable chairs, a desk, and two cell phones. Even before the tow trucks have cleared away the wreckage, Edgy is able to offer his client a settlement for the market value of his totaled Audi. McAllister, who did not appear to have been at fault in this accident, later stated in amazement: "This is great — someone coming right out here and taking charge. I didn't expect it at all."

The shortened time cycle has advantages for Progressive too. Costs are reduced, there's less likelihood of lawyers being involved when settlement offers are made promptly, and it's easier to prevent fraud. Progressive continues to find new ways to delight its customers. Its website, www.progressive.com, has consistently been rated as the top overall among Internet-based insurance carriers by Gómez.com (an Internet quality measurement firm), which places a priority on a site's educational, purchasing, and servicing capabilities. Progressive has also been cited repeatedly for pleasantly surprising its customers with consumer-friendly innovations and extraordinary customer service.

Figure 2.20 Drivers involved in accidents do not have to worry with Progressive's Immediate Response Service

Source

R Henkoff (27 June 1994), "Service is Everybody's Business," *Fortune*, p. 50; M Hammer (April 2004), "Deep Change: How Operational Innovation Can Transform Your Company," *Harvard Business Review*, Vol. 82, pp. 84–95; www.progressive.com, accessed January 2015.

Service Quality

What do we mean when we speak of service quality? Since services are intangible, it is hard to evaluate the quality of a service compared to a good. In addition, customers often experience the servuction process, so a distinction needs to be drawn between the process of service delivery and the actual output (or outcome) of the service[36]. We define excellent service quality as a high standard of performance that **consistently** meets or exceeds customer expectations. As suggested humorously by the restaurant illustration in *Figure 2.21*, service quality can be difficult to manage, even when failures are tangible in nature. Nevertheless, it is critical to improve service quality and keep it at high levels, as it is a key driver of important customer behaviors, including word-of-mouth recommendations, repurchasing, and loyalty.

LO 12
Understand service quality, its dimensions and measurement, and how quality relates to customer loyalty.

Figure 2.21 service quality is difficult to manage

Customer Satisfaction versus Service Quality[37]. Both customer satisfaction and service quality are defined as contrasting customers' expectations with their performance perceptions. Yet, satisfaction and service quality are very different constructs. Specifically, satisfaction is an evaluation of a single consumption experience, a fleeting judgment, and a direct and immediate response to that experience. In contrast, service quality refers to relatively stable attitudes and beliefs about a firm, which can differ significantly from satisfaction. To illustrate, you may have been dissatisfied with a particular visit to your favorite Starbucks outlet, but you still think this café is fantastic with great service. Of course, satisfaction and quality are linked. While the perceptions of a firm's overall service quality is relatively stable, it will change over time in the same direction as transaction-specific satisfaction ratings[38]. And it is service quality that in turn influences behavioral intentions (e.g., positive word-of-mouth, and repurchase intentions).

Sometimes people also refer to the transaction quality (e.g., the quality of food, the friendliness of the server, and the ambiance of a restaurant), which then relates to attribute satisfaction (e.g., satisfaction with food and service in a restaurant). Both are transaction-specific and determine overall customer satisfaction, which in turn drives service quality beliefs (whether at the attribute or overall level). It is the interchangeable use of these terms that confuses people. When you distinguish between transaction-specific judgments and the more stable beliefs and attitudes, you can clearly see the difference in meaning. That is, attribute-specific transaction quality and satisfaction precedes overall consumer satisfaction, which in turn influences the formation of beliefs regarding a firm's service quality for specific attributes and overall.

Note that consumers' repurchase intentions are influenced by their general beliefs about the service quality of the firm at the time of their next purchase decision, and less so by individual, transaction-specific satisfaction judgments formed during and after consumption. That is, consumers try to predict how good the next service transaction will be, as was discussed in context of the multi-attribute choice model. For example, consumers might return to a hairstylist if they think the stylist is generally fantastic, even if they were unhappy at their last visit. They may view the poor experience as an exception. However, a second or even third dissatisfaction evaluation will reduce the overall perception of the firm's service quality more dramatically and jeopardize repeat visits (*Figure 2.22*).

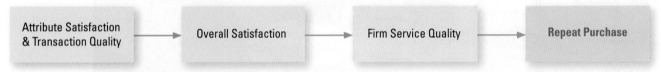

Figure 2.22 From attribute satisfaction to repeat purchase

Dimensions of Service Quality. Valarie Zeithaml, Leonard Berry, and A. Parasuraman have conducted intensive research on service quality and identified 10 dimensions used by consumers in evaluating service quality (*Table 2.3*). In subsequent research, they found a high degree of correlation between several of these variables and consolidated them into five broad dimensions:

1. *Tangibles* (appearance of physical elements)

2. *Reliability* (dependable and accurate performance)

3. *Responsiveness* (promptness and helpfulness)

4. *Assurance* (credibility, security, competence, and courtesy)

5. *Empathy* (easy access, good communications, and customer understanding)[39]

Measuring Service Quality. To measure service quality, Valarie Zeithaml and her colleagues developed a survey instrument called SERVQUAL[40]. It is based on the premise that customers evaluate a firm's service quality by comparing their perceptions of its service with their own expectations. SERVQUAL is seen as a generic measurement tool that can be applied across a broad spectrum of service industries. In its basic form, respondents answer 21 questions measuring their

Table 2.3 Generic Dimensions Used by Customers to Evaluate Service Quality

Dimensions of Service Quality	Definition	Sample Illustrations
Tangibles	Appearance of physical facilities, equipment, personnel, and communication materials	Are the hotel's facilities attractive? Is my accountant dressed appropriately? Is my bank statement easy to understand?
Reliability	Ability to perform the promised service dependably and accurately	Does my lawyer call me back when promised? Is my telephone bill free of errors? Is my TV repaired right the first time?
Responsiveness	Willingness to help customers and provide prompt service	When there is a problem, does the firm resolve it quickly? Is my stockbroker willing to answer my questions? Is the cable TV company willing to give me a specific time when the installer will show up?
Assurance • Credibility	Trustworthiness, believability, honesty of the service provider	Does the hospital have a good reputation? Does my stockbroker refrain from pressuring me to trade? Does the repair firm guarantee its work?
• Security	Freedom from danger, risk, or doubt	Is it safe for me to use the bank's ATMs at night? Is my credit card protected against unauthorized use? Can I be sure that my insurance policy provides complete coverage?
• Competence	Possession of the skills and knowledge required to perform the service	Can the bank teller process my transaction without fumbling around? Is my health insurance able to obtain the information I need when I call? Does the dentist appear to be competent?
• Courtesy	Politeness, respect, consideration, and friendliness of contact personnel	Does the flight attendant have a pleasant demeanor? Are the telephone operators consistently polite when answering my calls? Does the gardener take off his muddy shoes before stepping on my carpet?
Empathy • Access	Approachability and ease of contact	How easy is it for me to talk to a supervisor when I have a problem? Does the airline have a 24-hour, toll-free phone number? Is the hotel conveniently located?
• Communication	Listening to customers and keeping them informed in the language they can understand	When I have a complaint, is the manager willing to listen to me? Does my doctor avoid using technical jargon? Does the electrician call when he or she is unable to keep a scheduled appointment?
• Understanding the customer	Making the effort to know customers and their needs	Does someone in the hotel recognize me as a regular guest? Does my stockbroker try to determine my specific financial objectives? Is the moving company willing to accommodate my schedule?

expectations of companies in a particular industry on a wide array of specific service characteristics (*Table 2.4*). Subsequently, they are asked a matching set of questions on their perceptions of a specific company whose services quality they assess. When perceived performance ratings are lower than expectations, service quality is poor, while the reverse indicates good quality.

Customizing SERVQUAL. SERVQUAL has been widely used in its generic form as shown in *Table 2.4*. However, many managers found that the measure provides more insights if it is adapted to their specific industry and context. Therefore, the majority of researchers omits from, adds to, or changes the list of statements used to measure service quality[41]. Other research suggests that SERVQUAL mainly measures two factors: intrinsic service quality (resembling what Grönroos termed functional quality) and extrinsic service quality (which refers to the tangible aspects of service delivery and resembles what Grönroos referred to as technical quality")[42].

Table 2.4 The SERVQUAL Scale

The SERVQUAL scale includes five dimensions: tangibles, reliability, responsiveness, assurance and empathy. Within each dimension, several items are measured. There are many different formats in use, and we show the most basic 21 items for ideal perceptions below. The statements are accompanied by a seven-point scale, ranging from "strongly disagree = 1" to "strongly agree = 7".

The firm's performance is measured by rewording the same items (e.g., for item 1 in the table below: "XYZ firm has modern-looking equipment"). The difference between the scores for each item, dimension and for overall service quality is the computed and used as an indicator of a firm's level of service quality.

If measuring both ideal (or expected) and actual performance perceptions is not possible due to time constraints during the interview, both measures can also be combined by using the same 21 items (e.g., "modern looking equipment") and scale anchors "Lower than my desired service level", "The same as my desired service level", and "Higher than my desired service level".

Tangibles
- Excellent banks (refer to cable TV companies, hospitals, or the appropriate service business throughout the questionnaire) will have modern-looking equipment.
- The physical facilities at excellent banks will be visually appealing.
- Employees at excellent banks will be neat in appearance.
- Materials (e.g., brochures or statements) associated with the service will be visually appealing in an excellent bank.

Reliability
- When excellent banks promise to do something by a certain time, they will do so.
- Excellent banks will perform the service right the first time.
- Excellent banks will provide their services at the time they promise to do so.
- Excellent banks will insist on error-free records.

Responsiveness
- Employees of excellent banks will tell customers exactly when service will be performed.
- Employees of excellent banks will give prompt service to customers.
- Employees of excellent banks will always be willing to help customers.
- Employees of excellent banks will never be too busy to respond to customer requests.

Assurance
- The behavior of employees of excellent banks will instill confidence in customers.
- Customers of excellent banks will feel safe in their transactions.
- Employees of excellent banks will be consistently courteous with customers.
- Employees of excellent banks will have the knowledge to answer customer questions.

Empathy
- Excellent banks will give customers individual attention.
- Excellent banks will have operating hours convenient to all their customers.
- Excellent banks will have employees who give customers personal attention.
- The employees of excellent banks will understand the specific needs of their customers.
- Excellent banks have your best interest at heart.

Source

Adapted from Parasuraman, A., Zeithaml, V. A., and Berry, L (1988). "SERVQUAL: A Multiple Item Scale for Measuring Consumer Perceptions of Service Quality," *Journal of Retailing*, Vol. 64, pp. 12–40.

SERVICE INSIGHTS 2.3
New Thinking on Defining and Measuring E-Service Quality

SERVQUAL was developed to measure service quality mostly in a face-to-face service encounter context. To measure service quality of online retailers, Parasuraman, Zeithaml, and Malhotra created a 22-item scale called E-S-QUAL, reflecting the four key dimensions of *efficiency* (i.e., is navigation easy, can transactions be completed quickly, and does the website load fast?), *system availability* (i.e., is the site always available, does it launch right away, and is it stable and does not crash?), *fulfillment* (i.e., are orders delivered as promised, are offerings described truthfully?), and *privacy* (i.e., is information privacy protected and personal information not shared with other sites?).

Further research integrated service quality measurement across both virtual and physical channels. "To managers of companies with a Web presence," say Joel Collier and Carol Bienstock, "an awareness of how customers perceive service quality is essential to understanding what [they] value in an online-service transaction." E-service quality involves more than just interactions with a website — described as process quality — it extends to outcome quality and recovery quality, and each must be measured. The separation of customers from providers during online transactions highlights the importance of evaluating how well a firm handles customers' questions, concerns, and frustrations when problems arise.

- **Process Quality.** Customers initially evaluate their experiences with an e-retailing website against five process quality dimensions: *privacy, design, information, ease of use,* and *functionality*. This last construct refers to quick page loads, links that aren't dead-end, payment options, accurate execution of customer commands, and the ability to appeal to a universal audience (including the disabled and those who speak other languages).

- **Outcome Quality.** Customers' evaluations of process quality have a significant effect on their evaluation of outcome quality, made up of *order timeliness, order accuracy,* and *order condition*.

- **Recovery Quality.** In the event of a problem, customers evaluate the recovery process against *interactive fairness* (ability to locate and interact with technology support for a website, including telephone-based assistance), *procedural fairness* (policies, procedures, and responsiveness in the complaint process), and *outcome fairness*. How the company responds has a significant effect on the customer's satisfaction level and future intentions.

Both measurement scales emphasize the importance of tailoring service quality measures to their specific contexts.

Source

A. Parasuraman, Valarie A. Zeithaml, and Arvind Malhotra (2005), "E-S-QUAL: A Multiple-Item Scale for Assessing Electronic Service Quality." *Journal of Service Research*, Vol. 7, No. 3, pp. 213–233; Joel E. Collier and Carol C. Bienstock (February 2006), "Measuring Service Quality in E-Retailing." *Journal of Service Research*, Vol. 8, pp. 260–275

These findings highlight the difficulty of measuring customer perceptions of service quality and the need to adapt dimensions and measures to specific research contexts. In any case, it is important for firms to understand how the dimensions of service quality apply to their business context (see *Service Insights 2.3* relating to E-services) so that they can measure service quality, diagnose shortfalls, and then take actions to improve (this will be discussed in Chapter 14, "Improving Service Quality and Productivity").

Customer Loyalty

Loyalty is a customer's willingness to continue patronizing a firm over the long-term, preferably on an exclusive basis, and recommending the firm's products to friends and associates. Customer loyalty extends beyond behavior and includes preference, liking, and future intentions.

The opposite of loyalty is defection, which is used to describe customers who drop off a company's radar screen and transfer their loyalty to another supplier. Not only does a rising defection rate indicate that something is wrong with quality (or that competitors offer better value), it may also be a leading indicator signaling a fall in profits. Big customers don't necessarily disappear overnight; they often may signal their mounting dissatisfaction by steadily reducing their purchases and shifting part of their business elsewhere.

Loyalty is an important outcome of satisfied customers who believe that the firm delivers great service. Customers are not inherently loyal to any one firm! Rather, we need to give our customers a reason to consolidate their buying with us and then stay with us. Delivering great service experiences that satisfy your customers and build positive service quality perceptions is the first and probably the most important step toward building a loyal customer base. Later in this book, we discuss in-depth a number of strategies and tools that are key for driving loyalty, such as the Wheel of Loyalty in Chapter 12, and complaint management and service recovery in Chapter 13.

CONCLUSION

The three-stage model of service consumption — prepurchase, service encounter, and post-encounter — helps us to understand how individuals recognize their needs; search for alternative solutions; address perceived risks; choose, use, and experience a particular service; and finally, evaluate their service experience resulting in a customer satisfaction outcome. The various models we explored for each of the stages are complementary and together provide a rich and deep understanding of consumer behavior in a services context. In all types of services, managing customer behavior in the three stages of service consumption effectively is central to creating satisfied customers who will be willing to enter into long-term relationships with the service provider. As such, gaining a better understanding of customer behavior should lie at the heart of all services marketing strategies, which we discuss in the remainder of this book.

CHAPTER SUMMARY

LO 1
- Service consumption can be divided into the following three stages: (1) prepurchase stage, (2) service encounter stage, and (3) post-encounter stage.
- The **prepurchase stage** consists of the following four steps: (1) need awareness, (2) information search, (3) evaluation of alternative solutions and suppliers, and (4) making a purchase decision.

LO 2 The following theories help us to better understand consumer behavior in this stage:
- Recognizing a need motivates customers to search for solutions to satisfy that need. Several alternatives may come to mind, and these form the evoked set, which is further narrowed down to a few alternatives to seriously consider, that is, the consideration set.
- During the search process, consumers also learn about service attributes they should consider and form expectations about how firms in the consideration set will perform on those attributes.
- **Multi-attribute model.** Many decisions involve complex trade-offs along several attributes. The multi-attribute model simulates this decision-making by combining customers' attribute performance expectations for each firm in the consideration set and the importance weights of each attribute.
- Two common consumer decision rules in the multi-attribute model are the linear compensatory rule and the conjunctive rule. Given the same attribute ratings, consumers can arrive at different decisions when different decision rules are applied.
- Firms should actively manage key variables in the multi-attribute model to increase the chances of their service being the one chosen. This includes ensuring that the firm's services are in the consideration set and shaping their target customers' attribute performance perceptions, attribute weights and even decision rules towards the firm's strengths.

LO 3 Service attributes. People often have difficulty in evaluating services as they tend to have a low proportion of search attributes and a high proportion of experience and credence attributes. This makes it difficult for consumers to evaluate services before purchase. Tangible cues then become important, and firms need to manage them carefully to shape their customer's expectations and perceptions of experience and credence attributes.

LO 4 Perceived risk. As many services are hard to evaluate, consumers perceive higher risk when buying services. Successful firms employ risk reduction strategies such as offering free trials and service guarantees to assuage the customers' perceived risks.

LO 5
- **Service expectations.** These are shaped by the information search and evaluation of service attributes. The components of expectations include desired, adequate, and predicted service levels. Between the desired and adequate service levels is the zone of tolerance, within which customers are willing to accept variations in service levels.
- **Purchase decision.** The outcome of the prepurchase stage is a purchase decision, based largely on expectations of the likely performance of a service based on important attributes and associated risk perceptions. Many decisions involve complex tradeoffs along several attributes, typically including price.

LO 6 In the **service encounter stage**, the customer initiates, experiences, and consumes the service. A number of concepts and models help us better understand customer behavior in this stage:
- The **moments-of-truth** metaphor refers to customer touch points that can make or break a customer relationship.

LO 7 We distinguish between **high-** and **low-contact services.** High-contact services are challenging as they have many points of contact and "moments of truth" that have to be managed. In contrast, low-contact services are mostly delivered via websites, equipment (e.g., ATMs), or call centers with relatively few customer interfaces.

LO 8
- The **servuction model** encompasses a technical core and a service delivery system.
- The **technical core** is back-stage and **invisible** to the customers, but what happens back-stage can affect the quality of front-stage activities. Therefore, back-stage activities have to be coordinated with front-stage activities.

- The **service delivery system** is front-stage and visible to the customer. It encompasses all the interactions that together create the service experience. In a high-contact service, it includes customer interactions with the service environment, service employees, and with other customers. Each type of interaction can create or destroy value. Firms have to orchestrate all these interactions to create a satisfying service experience.

↪ **LO 9 Theater can be used as a metaphor** for service delivery, and firms can view their service as "staging" a performance with props and actors, and manage them accordingly. The props are the service facilities and equipment. The actors are the service employees and customers.

↪ **LO 10**
- Each of the actors needs to understand their roles and scripts in order to perform their part of the service well. Firms can make use of the **role** and **script theories** to better design, train, communicate, and manage both employee and customer behaviors.
- Consumers have a need to feel in **control**. There are three types of control that can be designed into a service encounter: **behavioral control** (customers can change the service encounter to their individual preferences), **decisional control** (they can choose between fixed options), and **cognitive control** (they understand what and why something happens, and they know what will happen next; also known as **predictive control**).
- However, if processes, scripts and roles are tightly defined (e.g., as in fast-food restaurants or in consumer banking settings), the scope for behavioral control is limited. Here, firms can focus on giving customers more decisional, cognitive, and predictive control.

↪ **LO 11** In the post-encounter stage, customers evaluate the service performance and compare it to their prior expectations.
- The **expectancy-disconfirmation model of satisfaction** holds that satisfaction judgments formed are based on a comparison of expectations with performance perceptions.

- Satisfaction is a continuum ranging from very high satisfaction to deep dissatisfaction. As long as perceived performance falls within the zone of tolerance, that is, above the adequate service level, customer will be reasonably satisfied. As performance perceptions approach or exceed desired levels, customer will be very satisfied. Customers will be delighted at unexpectedly high levels of performance. Performance below the adequate service level will result in dissatisfaction.
- Customer delight occurs when positive disconfirmation is coupled with pleasure and surprise.

↪ **LO 12**
- Excellent **service quality** means that a firm **consistently** meets or exceeds customer expectations.
- In contrast to customer satisfaction (which is transaction-specific and refers to a single service experience), service quality is a consumer's belief and attitude about the general performance of a firm.
- Consumers use five broad dimensions to evaluate service quality: (1) tangibles, (2) reliability, (3) responsiveness, (4) assurance, and (5) empathy.
- In situations where customer satisfaction and service quality deviate (e.g., "I think the firm in general is great, but the last transaction was poor"), it is service quality as the more stable belief that is being used by customers to form their performance expectations for the next purchase. However, a second or third dissatisfaction evaluation will reduce the overall service quality perception of the firm more dramatically and jeopardize repeat visits.
- **SERVQUAL** is a 22-item scale designed to measure the five dimensions of service quality. The scale is frequently adapted to the specific context of a particular service, including Internet shopping and online services.

Review Questions

1. Explain the three-stage model of service consumption.

2. How can customer choice between services in their consideration set be modeled?

3. What is the difference between the linear compensatory rule and the conjunctive rule?

4. Describe search, experience, and credence attributes, and give examples of each.

5. Explain why services tend to be harder for customers to evaluate than goods.

6. Why do consumer's perceptions of risk play an important role in choosing between alternative service offers? How can firms reduce consumer risk perceptions?

7. How are customers' expectations formed? Explain the difference between desired service and adequate service with reference to a service experience you've had recently.

8. What are "moments of truth"?

9. Describe the difference between high-contact and low-contact services, and explain how the nature of a customer's experience may differ between the two.

10. Choose a service you are familiar with, and create a diagram that represents the servuction system. Define the "front-stage" and "back-stage" activities.

11. How do the concepts of theater, role theory, and script theory help to provide insights into consumer behavior during the service encounter?

12. Describe the relationship between customer expectations and customer satisfaction.

13. What is service quality? How is it different from customer satisfaction?

14. What are the five dimensions of service quality?

15. How can you measure service quality?

Application Exercises

1. Construct a multi-attribute model to compare three different restaurants for an important celebration in your family. Apply the two different decision rules and determine the choices that arise from that.

2. Select three services: one high in search attributes, one high in experience attributes, and one high in credence attributes. Specify what product characteristics make them easy or difficult for consumers to evaluate, and suggest specific strategies that marketers can adopt in each case to facilitate evaluation and reduce perceived risk.

3. Develop a simple questionnaire designed to measure the key components of customer expectations (i.e., desired, adequate and predicted service, and the zone of tolerance). Conduct 10 interviews with key target customers of a service of your choice to understand the structure of their expectations. Based on your findings, develop recommendations for firms offering this service.

4. What are the back-stage elements of (a) a car repair facility, (b) an airline, (c) a university, and (d) a consulting firm? Under what circumstances would it be appropriate or even desirable to allow customers to see some of these back-stage elements, and how would you do it?

5. What roles are played by front-stage service employees in low-contact organizations? Are these roles more or less important to customer satisfaction than in high-contact services?

6. Visit the facilities of two competing service firms in the same industry (e.g., banks, restaurants, or gas stations) that you believe have different approaches to service. Compare their approaches using suitable frameworks from this chapter.

7. Apply the script and role theories to a service of your choice. What insights can you gain that would be useful for management?

8. How can a firm design perceived control into a service encounter? Apply it to one face-to-face encounter and one online encounter.

9. Describe a low-contact service encounter respectively via email and via phone, and a high-contact, face-to-face encounter that you had recently. How satisfied were you with each of the encounters? What were the key drivers of your overall satisfaction with these encounters? In each instance, what could the service provider have done to improve the service?

10. Describe an unsatisfactory encounter you experienced recently with (a) a low-contact service provider via email, mail, or phone and (b) a high–contact, face-to-face service provider. What were the key drivers of your dissatisfaction with these encounters? In each instance, what could the service provider have done to improve the service?

11. Review the five dimensions of service quality. What do they mean in the context of (a) an industrial repair shop, (b) a retail bank, (c) a "Big 4" accounting firm?

12. How would you define "excellent service quality" for an enquiry/information service provided by your cell phone or electricity service provider? Call a service organization and go through a service encounter and evaluate it against your definition of "excellence."

Endnotes

1   Adapted and updated from *Principles of Services Marketing and Management*, 2nd ed., (Upper Saddle River, NJ: Prentice Hall, 2001).

2   Recent research focuses on customer learning so that customers can acquire the necessary knowledge and skills to be effective in choosing and in integrating resources to facilitate value-creation. See: Sally Hibbert, Heid Winklhofer, and Mohamed Sobhy Temerak (2012), "Customers as Resource Integrators: Toward a Model of Customer Learning," *Journal of Service Research*, Vol. 15, No. 3, pp. 247–261

3   An excellent example of using customer choice modeling to drive firm strategy is: Peter J. Danaher, John H. Roberts, Ken Roberts, and Alan Simpson (2011), "Applying a Dynamic Model of Consumer Choice to Guide Brand Development at Jetstar Airways," *Marketing Science,* Vol. 30, No. 4, pp. 586–594. See also the electronic companion to this paper at http://mktsci.pubs.informs.org/.

4   Valarie A. Zeithaml, "How Consumer Evaluation Processes Differ Between Goods and Services," in J. A. Donnelly and W. R. George, eds. *Marketing of Services,* (Chicago, IL: American Marketing Association, 1981), 186–190.

5   Interestingly, when buying credence services, consumers do not necessarily undertake a more comprehensive information search. Rather, they rely more on word-of-mouth from friends and family, credible publications such as consumer reports, and the recommendations by sales people; see: Kathleen Mortimer and Andrew Pressey (2013), "Consumer Information Search and Credence Services: Implications for Service Providers", *Journal of Services Marketing*, Vol. 27, No. 1, pp. 49–58.

6   Leonard L. Berry and Neeli Bendapudi (2003), "Clueing in Customers," *Harvard Business Review*, Vol. 81, February, pp. 100–107.

7   Valarie A. Zeithaml, Leonard L. Berry, and A. Parasuraman (1996), "The Behavioral Consequences of Service Quality," *Journal of Marketing,* Vol. 60, April 1996, pp. 31–46; R. Kenneth Teas and Thomas E. DeCarlo (2004), "An Examination and Extension of the Zone-of-Tolerance Model: A Comparison to Performance-Based Models on Perceived Quality," *Journal of Service Research*, Vol. 6, No. 3, pp. 272–286.

8   Cathy Johnson and Brian P. Mathews (1997), "The Influence of Experience on Service Expectations," *International Journal of Service Industry Management*, Vol. 8, No. 4, pp. 46–61.

9   Robert Johnston (1995), "The Zone of Tolerance: Exploring the Relationship between Service Transactions and Satisfaction with the Overall Service," *International Journal of Service Industry Management*, Vol. 6, No. 5, pp. 46–61; Michael Stodnick and Kathryn A. Marley (2013), "A Longitudinal Study of the Zone of Tolerance," *Managing Service Quality*, Vol. 23, No. 1, pp. 25–42.

10 Normann first used the term "moments of truth" in a Swedish study in 1978; subsequently it appeared in English in Richard Normann, *Service Management: Strategy and Leadership in Service Businesses*, 2nd ed. (Chichester, UK: John Wiley & Sons, 1991), 16–17.

11 Jan Carlzon, *Moments of Truth* (Cambridge, MA: Ballinger Publishing Co., 1987), p. 3.

12 Breffni M. Noone, Sheryl E. Kimes, Anna S. Mattila, and Jochen Wirtz (2009), "Perceived Service Encounter Pace and Customer Satisfaction," *Journal of Service Management*, Vol. 20, No. 4, pp. 380–403.

13 Pierre Eiglier and Eric Langeard, "Services as Systems: Marketing Implications," in Pierre Eiglier, Eric Langeard, Christopher H. Lovelock, John E. G. Bateson, and Robert F. Young, eds. *Marketing Consumer Services: New Insights.* (Cambridge, MA: Marketing Science Institute, Report #77–115, November 1977), pp. 83–103; Eric Langeard, John E. Bateson, Christopher H. Lovelock, and Pierre Eiglier, *Services Marketing: New Insights from Consumers and Managers* (Cambridge, MA: Marketing Science Institute, Report #81–104, August 1981).

14 Richard B. Chase (1978), "Where Does the Customer Fit in a Service Organization?" *Harvard Business Review,* Vol. 56, November–December, pp. 137–142; Stephen J. Grove, Raymond P. Fisk, and Joby John, "Services as Theater: Guidelines and Implications," in Teresa A. Schwartz and Dawn Iacobucci, eds. *Handbook of Services Marketing and Management* (Thousand Oaks, CA: Sage, 2000), pp. 21–36.

15 Stephen J. Grove, Raymond P. Fisk, and Joby John, "Services as Theater: Guidelines and Implications," in Teresa A. Schwartz and Dawn Iacobucci, eds. *Handbook of Services Marketing and Management* (Thousand Oaks, CA: Sage, 2000), pp. 21–36; Steve Baron, Kim Harris, and Richard Harris (2003), "Retail Theater: The 'Intended Effect' of the Performance," *Journal of Service Research*, Vol. 4, May, pp. 316–332; Richard Harris, Kim Harris, and Steve Baron (2003), "Theatrical Service Experiences: Dramatic Script Development with Employees," *International Journal of Service Industry Management*, Vol. 14, No. 2, pp. 184–199.

See also F. Ian Stuart (2006), "Designing and Executing Memorable Service Experiences: Lights, Camera, Experiment, Integration, Action", *Business Horizons*, Vol. 49, pp. 149–159.

16 Stephen J. Grove and Raymond P. Fisk, "The Dramaturgy of Services Exchange: An Analytical Framework for Services Marketing," in L. L. Berry, G. L. Shostack, and G. D. Upah, eds. *Emerging Perspectives on Services Marketing* (Chicago, IL: The American Marketing Association, 1983), pp. 45–49.

17 Michael R. Solomon, Carol Suprenant, John A. Czepiel and Evelyn G. Gutman (1985), "A Role Theory Perspective on Dyadic Interactions: The Service Encounter," *Journal of Marketing*, Vol. 49, Winter, pp. 99–111.

18 See R. P. Abelson, "Script Processing in Attitude Formation and Decision-Making," in J. S. Carrol and J. W. Payne, eds. *Cognitive and Social Behavior* (Hillsdale, NJ: Erlbaum, 1976), pp. 33–45; Richard Harris, Kim Harris, and Steve Baron (2003), "Theatrical Service Experiences: Dramatic Script Development with Employees," *International Journal of Service Industry Management*, 14, No. 2, pp. 184–199.

19 Parts of this section were adapted from K. Douglas Hoffman and John E.G. Bateson, *Services Marketing: Concepts, Strategies, & Cases.* 4th ed. (Mason, OH: South Western Cengage Learning, 2011), pp. 100–101.

20 The research in consumer behavior was based on earlier work in psychology, see Averill, J.R. (1973), "Personal Control Over Aversive Stimuli and Its Relationship to Stress," *Psychological Bulletin,* Vol. 80, No. 4, pp. 286–303; Langer, E.J., *The Psychology of Control.* (Beverly Hills, CA: Sage). The following studies applied perceived control to service encounters: John E.G. Bateson, "Perceived Control and the Service Encounter," in John A. Czepil, Michael R. Solomon, and Carol F. Surprenant, eds., *The Service Encounter* (Lexington, MA: Lexington Books, 1982), 67–82; Michael K. Hui and John E.G. Bateson (1991), "Perceived Control and the Effects of Crowding and Consumer Choice on the Service Experience," *Journal of Consumer Research*, Vol. 18, No. 2, pp. 174–184. Michael K. Hui, and Roy Toffoli (2006), "Perceived Control and Consumer Attribution for the Service Encounter", *Journal of Applied Psychology*, Vol 32. No. 9, pp. 1,825–1,844.

21 Richard B. Chase and Sriram Dasu (2014), "Experience Psychology — A Proposed New Subfield of Service Management," *Journal of Service Management*, Vol. 25, No. 5, pp. 574–577.

22 For an excellent and comprehensive review of the extant literature on customer satisfaction and its outcomes, see: Richard L. Oliver, *Satisfaction: A Behavioral Perspective on the Consumer.* 2nd ed. (Armonk, NY: Armonk, M.E. Sharpe, 2010).

23 Richard L. Oliver (1980), "A Cognitive Model of the Antecedents and Consequences of Satisfaction Decisions," *Journal of Marketing Research*, Vol. 17, November, pp. 460–469; Richard L. Oliver and John E. Swan (1989), "Consumer Perceptions of Interpersonal Equity and Satisfaction in Transactions: A Field Survey Approach," *Journal of Marketing,* Vol. 53 April, pp. 21–35; Eugene W. Anderson and Mary W. Sullivan (1993), "The Antecedents and Consequences of Customer Satisfaction for Firms," *Marketing Science*, Vol. 12, Spring, pp. 125–143.

24 Ray W. Coye, "Managing Customer Expectations in the Service Encounter (2004)," *International Journal of Service Industry Management*, Vol. 15, No. 4, pp. 54–71; see also: Chiara Orsingher, Gian Luca Marzocchi, and Sara Valentini (2011), "Consumer (Goal) Satisfaction: A

Means-End Chain Approach," *Psychology & Marketing*, Vol. 28, No. 7, pp. 730–748.

25 Richard L. Oliver, *Satisfaction: A Behavioral Perspective on the Consumer*. 2nd ed. (Armonk, NY: Armonk, M.E. Sharpe), 2010.

26 Gour C. Saha and Theingi (2009), "Service Quality, Satisfaction and Behavioral Intentions," *Managing Service Quality*, Vol. 19, No. 3, pp. 350–372; Jochen Wirtz and Patricia Chew (2002), "The Effects of Incentives, Deal Proneness, Satisfaction and Tie Strength on Word-of-Mouth Behavior," *International Journal of Service Industry Management*, Vol. 13, No. 2, pp. 141–162; V. Kumar, Ilaria Dalla Pozza, and Jaishankar Ganesh (2013), "Revisiting the Satisfaction-Loyalty Relationship: Empirical Generalizations and Directions for Further Research," *Journal of Retailing*, Vol. 89, No. 3, pp. 246–262; Timothy L. Keiningham, Larzan Aksoy, Edward C. Malthouse, Bart Lariviere, and Alexander Buoye (2014), "The Cumulative Effect of Satisfaction with Discrete Transactions on Share of Wallet," *Journal of Service Management*, Vol. 25, No. 3, pp. 310–333.

27 Jaishankar Ganesh, Mark J. Arnold, and Kristy E. Reynolds (2000), "Understanding the Customer Base of Service Providers: An Examination of the Differences Between Switchers and Stayers," *Journal of Marketing*, Vol. 64, No. 3, pp. 65–87.

28 Mittal, V., W.T. Ross, and P.M. Baldasare (1998),"The Asymmetric Impact of Negative and Positive Attribute-Level Performance on Overall Satisfaction and Repurchase Intentions," *Journal of Marketing*, Vol. 62, No.1, pp. 33–47; Mittal, V., P. Kumar and M. Tsiros (1999), "Attribute-Level Performance, Satisfaction, and Behavioral Intentions Over Time: A Consumption-system Approach," *Journal of Marketing*, Vol. 63, No. 2, pp. 88–101; Thomas Falk, Maik Hammerschmidt, and Joeron J.L. Schepers (2010), "The Service Quality-Satisfaction Link Revisited: Exploring Asymmetries and Dynamics," *Journal of the Academy of Marketing Science*, Vol. 38, No. 3, pp. 288–301.

29 Jochen Wirtz and Anna S. Mattila (2001), "Exploring the Role of Alternative Perceived Performance Measures and Needs-Congruency in the Consumer Satisfaction Process," *Journal of Consumer Psychology*, Vol. 11, No. 3, pp. 181–192.

30 Jochen Wirtz (2003), "Halo in Customer Satisfaction Measures — The Role of Purpose of Rating, Number of Attributes, and Customer Involvement," *International Journal of Service Industry Management*, Vol. 14, No. 1, pp. 96–119)

31 Richard L. Oliver, Roland T. Rust, and Sajeev Varki (1997), "Customer Delight: Foundations, Findings, and Managerial Insight," *Journal of Retailing*, Vol. 73, Fall, pp. 311–336; For delight in an online context, see Christopher Bartl, Matthias H.J. Gouthier, and Markus Lenker (2013), "Delighting Customers Click by Click: Antecedents and Effects of Online Delight", *Journal of Service Research*, Vol. 16, No. 3, pp. 386–399.

32 Adam Finn (2012), "Customer Delight: Distinct Construct or Zone of Nonlinear Response to Customer Satisfaction?", *Journal of Service Research*, Vol. 15, No. 1, pp. 99–110. Christopher Bartl, Matthias H.J. Gouthier, and Markus Lenker (2013), "Delighting Customers Click by Click: Antecedents and Effects of Online Delight", *Journal of Service Research*, Vol. 16, No. 3, pp. 386–399.

33 Roland T. Rust and Richard L. Oliver (2000), "Should We Delight the Customer?," *Journal of the Academy of Marketing Science*, Vol. 28, No. 1, pp. 86–94. A recent study has explored how rising expectations as part of a firm's delight strategy could be avoided. The authors found that providing an explanation that the surprise is an exception is effective in avoiding higher expectations and at the same time, increasing delight. The authors recommend that delight strategies should be offered infrequently and randomly; see: Min Gyung Kim and Anna S. Mattila (2013), "Does a Surprise Strategy Need Words? The Effect of Explanations for a Surprise Strategy on Customer Delight and Expectations", *Journal of Services Marketing*, Vol. 27, No. 5, pp. 361–370.

34 Claes Fornell, David VanAmburg, Forrest Morgeson, Eugene W. Anderson, Barbara Everitt Bryant, and Michael D. Johnson, *The American Customer Satisfaction Index at Ten Years — A Summary of Findings: Implications for the Economy, Stock Returns and Management*. (Ann Arbor, MI: National Quality Research Center, University of Michigan, 2005), 54.

35 Matthew Dixon, Kareen Freeman, and Nicholas Toman (2010), "Stop Trying to Delight Your Customers: To Really Win Their Loyalty, Forget the Bells and Whistles and Just Solve Their Problems," *Harvard Business Review*, (July-August), Vol. 88, No.7/8, pp. 116–122.

36 Christian Grönroos, *Service Management and Marketing*. 3rd ed. (Chichester, NY: Wiley, 2007).

37 For a detailed discussion on the difference between customer satisfaction and service quality at the encounter (or individual transaction level) and the global overall constructs, see: Richard L. Oliver, *Satisfaction: A Behavioral Perspective on the Consumer*. 2nd ed. (Armonk, NY: M.E. Sharpe, 2010), 173–185.

38 Boulding, W., A. Kalia, R. Staelin, and V.A. Zeithaml (1993), "A Dynamic Process Model of Service Quality: From Expectations to Behavioral Intentions," *Journal of Marketing Research*, Vol. 30, No. 1, pp. 7-27; Palmer, A. and M. O'Neill (2003), "The Effects of Perceptual Processes on the Measurement of Service Quality," *Journal of Services Marketing*, Vol. 17, No. 3, pp. 254–274.

39 Valarie A. Zeithaml, A. Parasuraman, and Leonard L. Berry, *Delivering Quality Service* (New York: The Free Press, 1990). See alsoValarie A. Zeithaml, Mary Jo Bitner, and Dwayne D. Gremler, *Services Marketing: Integrating Customer Focus Across the Firm*. (New York: McGraw-Hill, 2013), pp. 49–105.

40 A. Parasuraman, Valarie A. Zeithaml, and Leonard Berry (1988), "SERVQUAL: A Multiple Item Scale for Measuring Consumer Perceptions of Service Quality," *Journal of Retailing*, Vol. 64, pp. 12–40.

41 See, for instance, Anne M. Smith (1995), "Measuring Service Quality: Is SERVQUAL Now Redundant?" *Journal of Marketing Management*, Vol. 11, Jan/Feb/April, pp. 257–276; Francis Buttle (1996), "SERVQUAL: Review, Critique, Research Agenda," *European Journal of Marketing*, Vol. 30, No. 1, pp. 8–32; Simon S.K. Lam and Ka Shing Woo (1997), "Measuring Service Quality: A Test-Retest Reliability Investigation of SERVQUAL," *Journal of the Market Research Society*, Vol. 39, April, pp. 381–393; Terrence H. Witkowski, and Mary F. Wolfinbarger (2002), "Comparative Service Quality: German and American Ratings Across Service Settings," *Journal of Business Research*, Vol. 55, pp. 875–881; Lisa J. Morrison Coulthard (2004), "Measuring Service Quality: A Review and Critique of Research Using SERVQUAL," *International Journal of Market Research*, Vol. 46, Quarter 4, pp. 479–497.

There is also significant research that adapted SERVQUAL to specific contexts, including self-service technology, see: Jiun-Sheng Chris Lin and Pei-Ling Hsieh (2011), "Assessing the Self-Service Technology Encounters: Development and Validation of SSTQUAL Scale", *Journal of Retailing*, Vol. 87, No. 2, pp. 194–206.

42 Gerhard Mels, Christo Boshoff, and Denon Nel (1997), "The Dimensions of Service Quality: The Original European Perspective Revisited," *The Service Industries Journal*, Vol. 17, January, pp. 173–189; see also: Christian Grönroos, *Service Management and Marketing. 3rd.* (Chichester, NY: Wiley, 2007), pp. 84–86.

CHAPTER 03 Positioning Services in Competitive Markets

To succeed in our overcommunicated society, a company must create a position in the prospect's mind, a position that takes into consideration not only a company's own strengths and weaknesses, but those of its competitors as well.

Al Reis and Jack Trout,
Thought leaders who coined the term "positioning" as related to marketing

The essence of strategy is choosing to perform activities differently than rivals do.

Michael Porter,
Professor at Harvard Business School and leading authority on competitive strategy

LEARNING OBJECTIVES (LOs)

By the end of this chapter, the reader should be able to:

➲ **LO 1** Understand how the **c**ustomer, **c**ompetitor, and **c**ompany analysis (i.e., the **3 Cs**) helps to develop a customer-driven services marketing strategy.

➲ **LO 2** Know the key elements of a positioning strategy (i.e., **STP**), and explain why these elements are so crucial for service firms to apply.

➲ **LO 3** **S**egment customers on needs first before using other common bases to further identify and profile the segments.

➲ **LO 4** Distinguish between important and determinant attributes for segmentation.

➲ **LO 5** Use different service levels for segmentation.

➲ **LO 6** **T**arget service customers using the four focus strategies for competitive advantage.

➲ **LO 7** **P**osition a service to distinguish it from its competitors.

➲ **LO 8** Understand how to use positioning maps to analyze and develop competitive strategy.

➲ **LO 9** Develop an effective positioning strategy.

OPENING VIGNETTE

Positioning a Chain of Child Care Centers Away From the Competition

Roger Brown and Linda Mason met at business school, following previous experience as management consultants. After graduation, they operated programs for refugee children in Cambodia and then ran a "Save the Children" relief program in East Africa. When they returned to the US, they saw a need for childcare centers that would provide caring, educational environments and give parents confidence in their children's well-being.

Through research, they discovered an industry that had many weaknesses. There were no barriers to entry, profit margins were low, the industry was labor intensive, there were low economies of scale, there was no clear brand differentiation, and there was a lack of regulation in the industry. Brown and Mason developed a service concept that would allow them to turn these industry weaknesses into strengths for their own company, Bright Horizons. Instead of marketing their services directly to parents — a one-customer-at-a-time sale — Bright Horizons formed partnerships with companies seeking to offer an on-site day-care center for employees with small children. The advantages included:

- A powerful, low-cost marketing channel.

- A partner/customer who supplied the funds to build and equip the center and would therefore want to help Bright Horizons to achieve its goal of delivering high-quality care.

- Benefits for parents who would be attracted to a Bright Horizons center (rather than competing alternatives) as a result of its nearness to their own workplace, thus decreasing traveling time and offering a greater peace of mind.

Bright Horizons offered a high pay and benefits package to attract the best staff so that they could provide quality service, one aspect that was lacking in many of the other providers. Since traditional approaches to childcare either did not have a proper teaching plan, or had strict, cookie-cutter lesson plans, Bright Horizons developed a flexible teaching plan. It was called "World at Their Fingertips" and had a course outline, but it also gave teachers control over daily lesson plans.

The company sought accreditation for its centers from the National Association for the Education of Young Children (NAEYC) and actively promoted this. Bright Horizons' emphasis on quality meant that it could meet or exceed the highest local and state government licensing standards. As a result, the lack of regulation became an opportunity, not a threat, for Bright Horizons and gave it a competitive edge.

With the support and help from its clients, which included many high-tech firms, Bright Horizons developed innovative technologies such as streaming video of its classrooms to the parents' desktop computers; digitally scanned or photographed artwork; electronic posting of menus, calendars, and student assessments; as well as online student assessment capabilities. All of these served to differentiate Bright Horizons and helped it to stay ahead of the competition.

Bright Horizons sees labor as a competitive advantage. It seeks to recruit and retain the best people. In 2014, it had been listed for the fourteenth time as one of the "100 Best Companies to Work for in America" by *Fortune* magazine. By then, Bright Horizons had some 20,000 employees globally and was operating for more than 700 clients organizations in the US, Canada, and Europe. These clients are the world's leading employers, which include corporations, hospitals, universities, and government offices. Clients want to hire Bright Horizons as a partner because they know they can trust the staff.

Figure 3.1 Happy children at a childcare center

Source

Roger Brown (2001), "How We Built a Strong Company in a Weak Industry," *Harvard Business Review*, pp. 51–57; www.brighthorizons.com, accessed February 3, 2015.

CUSTOMER-DRIVEN SERVICES MARKETING STRATEGY

In an industry with low barriers of entry and a lot of competition, Bright Horizons managed to find a niche position and differentiate itself from the competition. They linked up with employers instead of individual parents, emphasized service quality, and used accreditation as a selling point. As competition intensifies in the service sector, it is becoming ever more important for service organizations to differentiate their products in ways that are meaningful to customers. This is especially so for many mature service industries (e.g., banking, insurance, hospitality, and education), where for a firm to grow, it has to take market share from its competitors or expand into new markets. However, ask a group of managers from different service businesses on how they compete, and chances are many will say simply, "on service". Press them a little further, and they may add words and phrases such as "value for money", "service quality", "our people", or "convenience." None of this is very helpful to a marketing specialist who is trying to develop a meaningful value proposition and a viable business model for a service product that will enable it to compete profitably in the marketplace.

What makes consumers or institutional buyers select — and remain loyal to — one supplier over another? Terms such as "service" typically subsume a variety of specific characteristics, ranging from the speed with which a service is delivered to the quality of interactions between customers and service personnel; and from avoiding errors to providing desirable "extras" to supplement the core service. Likewise, "convenience" could refer to a service that is delivered at a convenient location, available at convenient times, or easy to use. Without knowing which product features are of specific interest to customers, it is hard for managers to develop an appropriate strategy. In a highly competitive environment, there is a risk that customers will perceive little real difference between competing alternatives and therefore make their choices based on who offers the lowest price.

Managers thus need to think systematically about all aspects of the service offering and to emphasize competitive advantage on attributes that will be valued by customers in their target segment(s). A systematic way to do this typically starts with an analysis of customers, competitors, and the company, collectively often referred to as the **3 Cs**. This analysis then helps a firm to determine the key elements of its services positioning strategy, which are segmentation, targeting, and positioning, frequently called *STP* by marketing experts. The basic steps involved in identifying a suitable market position are shown in *Figure 3.2*. The desired positioning has wide-reaching implications on the firm's services marketing strategy, including the development of its **7 Ps** of Services Marketing (as discussed in Parts II and III of this book), its customer relationship strategy (as discussed in Part IV), and its service quality and productivity strategies (as discussed in Part V).

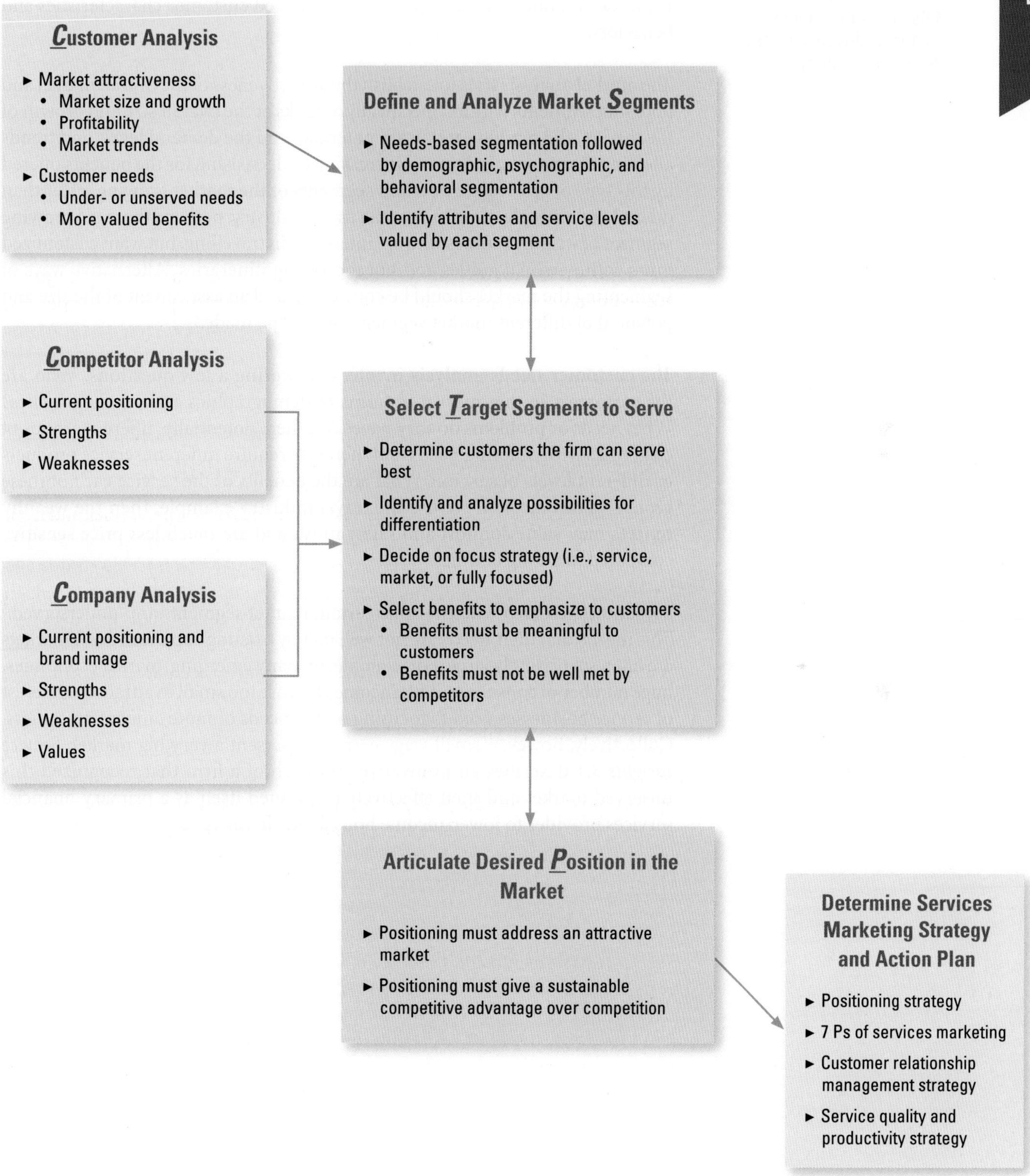

Customer Analysis

▶ Market attractiveness
  • Market size and growth
  • Profitability
  • Market trends
▶ Customer needs
  • Under- or unserved needs
  • More valued benefits

Define and Analyze Market Segments

▶ Needs-based segmentation followed by demographic, psychographic, and behavioral segmentation
▶ Identify attributes and service levels valued by each segment

Competitor Analysis

▶ Current positioning
▶ Strengths
▶ Weaknesses

Select Target Segments to Serve

▶ Determine customers the firm can serve best
▶ Identify and analyze possibilities for differentiation
▶ Decide on focus strategy (i.e., service, market, or fully focused)
▶ Select benefits to emphasize to customers
  • Benefits must be meaningful to customers
  • Benefits must not be well met by competitors

Company Analysis

▶ Current positioning and brand image
▶ Strengths
▶ Weaknesses
▶ Values

Articulate Desired Position in the Market

▶ Positioning must address an attractive market
▶ Positioning must give a sustainable competitive advantage over competition

Determine Services Marketing Strategy and Action Plan

▶ Positioning strategy
▶ 7 Ps of services marketing
▶ Customer relationship management strategy
▶ Service quality and productivity strategy

Figure 3.2 Developing a services marketing positioning strategy

LO 1

Understand how the **c**ustomer, **c**ompetitor, and **c**ompany analysis (i.e., the **3 Cs**) helps to develop a customer-driven services marketing strategy.

Customer, Competitor, and Company Analysis (3Cs)

Customer Analysis. The customer analysis is typically done first and this includes an examination of overall market characteristics, followed by an in-depth exploration of customer needs and related customer characteristics and behaviors.

The **market analysis** tries to establish the attractiveness of the overall market and potential segments within. Specifically, it looks at the overall size and growth of the market, the margins and profit potential, and the demand levels and trends affecting the market. Is demand increasing or decreasing for the benefits offered by this type of service? Are certain segments of the market growing faster than others? For example, if we look at the travel industry, perhaps there is a growing segment of wealthy retirees who are interested in travelling, but want customized tours with personal guides and not too taxing itineraries. Alternative ways of segmenting the market should be considered and an assessment of the size and potential of different market segments should be made.

The **customer needs analysis** involves answering a few questions. Who are the customers in that market in terms of demographics and psychographics? What needs or problems do they have? Are there potentially different groups of customers with differing needs and therefore require different service products or different levels of service? What are the benefits of the service each of these groups values most? If we use the travel industry example, then the wealthy retirees may value comfort and safety most, and are much less price sensitive compared to young families.

Sometimes research will show that certain market segments are "underserved." This means that their needs are not well met by existing suppliers. Such markets are often surprisingly large. For example, in many emerging-market economies, huge number of consumers have incomes that are too small to attract the interest of service businesses used to focusing on the needs of more affluent customers. Collectively, however, small wage earners represent a very big market. *Service Insights 3.1* describes an innovative approach of a firm that recognized this unserved market and then effectively positioned itself as a primary financial services provider to lower-income households in Mexico.

SERVICE INSIGHTS 3.1

Banco Azteca Caters to the Little Guy

Banco Azteca, which opened in 2002, was Mexico's first new bank in nearly a decade. It initially targeted the 16 million households in the nation who earned the equivalent of $250–$1,300 a month, working as taxi drivers, factory workers, and teachers among others. Despite their combined annual income of $120 billion, these individuals were of little interest to most banks, which considered small accounts a nuisance. Not surprisingly, only one in 12 of these households had a savings account.

Banco Azteca was the brainchild of Mexican billionaire Ricardo Salinas Pliego, head of a retail-media-telecommunications empire that includes Grupo Elektra, Mexico's largest appliance retailer. Its branches, located within the more than 900 Elektra stores, were decorated in the green, white, and red colors of the Mexican flag. They aimed to create a welcoming atmosphere and featured posters with the Azteca slogan, which translated as "A bank that's friendly and treats you well."

Azteca's relationship with Elektra aimed to take advantage of the retailer's 50-year track record in consumer finance and the fact that some 70% of its merchandise is sold on credit. Elektra had an excellent record in credit sales, with a 97% repayment rate, and a rich database of customers' credit histories. So top management felt it made sense to convert Elektra credit departments in each store into Azteca branches with an expanded line of services.

The new bank invested heavily in information technology, including high-tech fingerprint readers that eliminated the need for customers to present printed identification or passbooks. It also took its services to the people through a 3,000-strong force of loan agents on motorcycles. The bank offered personal loans and time deposits, and rolled out used-car loans, low-income mortgages, and debit cards. Loans often used customers' previously purchased possessions as collateral.

In 2003, Grupo Elektra purchased a private insurance company, which it renamed Seguros Azteca. This firm offered basic insurance products at very low prices to a population segment that has historically been ignored by the Mexican insurance industry. Policies were distributed through Banco Azteca's branch network. The following year, the bank expanded its activities to finance individuals who wished to start or expand a small business.

More recently, however, Banco Azteca has been criticized for profiteering from the poor through charging high effective annual percentage rates of 50%–120% interest and of using high-pressure employee quotas and incentives to persuade customers to take loans, ideally with the longest possible period of 104 weeks. Has the bank been gorging its customers, or is it just common business practice in Mexico to charge high interest for micro loans? Do a search online to find out the latest updates on this issue.

By 2015, Banco Azteca became one of the largest banks in Mexico in terms of coverage with over 6.8 million savings and 9 million credit accounts, and it was expanding in Latin America with operations in Brazil, Panama, Guatemala, Honduras, and Peru.

Source

Geri Smith (January 13, 2003), "Buy a Toaster, Open a Banking Account," *Business Week*, p. 54; Keith Epstein and Geri Smith (December 12, 2007), "The Ugly Side of Microlending: How Big Mexican Banks Profit as Many Poor Borrowers Get Trapped in a Maze of Debt," *Business Week*; http://en.wikipedia.org/wiki/Banco_Azteca and , accessed February 3, 2015.

Competitor Analysis. Identification and analysis of competitors can provide a marketing strategist with a sense of competitors' strengths and weaknesses. Relating these to the company analysis in the next section should suggest what the opportunities for differentiation and competitive advantage might be, and thereby enabling managers to decide which benefits could be emphasized to which target segments.

Company Analysis. In an internal corporate analysis, the objective is to identify the organization's strengths in terms of its current brand positioning and image, and the resources the organization has (financial, human labor and know-how, and physical assets). It also examines the organization's limitations or constraints, and how its values shape the way it does business. Using insights from this analysis, management should be able to select a limited number of target market segments that can be served with either existing or new services. The core question is: How well can our company and our services address the needs and problems faced by each customer segment?

Segmentation, Targeting, and Positioning (STP)

⊃ LO 2
Know the key elements of a positioning strategy (i.e., **STP**), and explain why these elements are so crucial for service firms to apply.

Linking customer and competitor analysis to company analysis allows the service organization to develop an effective positioning strategy. Here, the basic steps involved in identifying a suitable market position and developing a strategy to reach it are:

- **Segmentation** — dividing the population of possible customers into groups. A market segment is composed of a group of buyers who share common characteristics, needs, purchasing behavior, and/or consumption patterns. Effective segmentation groups buyers into segments in ways that result in as much similarity as possible on the relevant characteristics within each segment. Once customers with similar needs are grouped together, demographic, geographic, psychographic, and behavioral variables can be used to describe them. Customers in the same segment should have as similar needs as possible, but between segments, their needs should be as different as possible.

- **Targeting** — Once a firm's customers have been segmented, the firm has to assess the attractiveness of each segment, and decide which segment(s) would most likely be interested in its service, and focus on how to serve them well.

- **Positioning** — the unique place that the firm and/or its service offerings occupy in the minds of its consumers. Before a firm can create a unique position for its service, it must first differentiate the service from that of its competitors. Hence, differentiation is the first step towards creating a unique positioning for a service.

Table 3.1 shows the key elements of a services positioning strategy on the left-hand side and related concepts on the right-hand side. We will discuss each concept in the remainder of this chapter.

Table 3.1 Elements and Key Concepts of a Services Positioning Strategy

Elements of a Positioning Strategy	Key Concepts

Segmentation	• Segmenting service markets
	• Service attributes and service levels relevant for segmentation
	  – Important versus determinant attributes
	  – Establishing service levels

Targeting	• Targeting service markets through four focus strategies:
	  – Fully focused
	  – Market focused
	  – Service focused
	  – Unfocused

Positioning	• Positioning services in competitive markets • Using positioning maps to plot competitive strategy • Developing an effective positioning strategy

SEGMENTING SERVICE MARKETS

 LO 3

Segment customers on needs first before using other common bases to further identify and profile the segments.

Segmentation is one of the most important concepts in marketing. Service firms vary widely in their abilities to serve different types of customers. Hence, rather than trying to compete in an entire market, perhaps against superior competitors, each firm should adopt a strategy of market segmentation, identifying those parts, or segments, of the market that it can serve best.

There are many ways to segment a market, and marketing experts typically combine and integrate several approaches. Traditionally, **demographic segmentation** (e.g., based on age, gender, and income) has frequently been used. However, this often does not result in meaningful segmentation as two people in the exact same demographics can exhibit very different buying behaviors (e.g., not all 20-year-old middle-class males feel and behave the same way). As a result, **psychographic segmentation** has become more popular as it reflects people's lifestyles, attitudes, and aspirations. Psychographic segmentation can be very useful in strengthening brand identity and creating an emotional connection with the brand, but may not necessarily map to behaviors and sales. **Behavioral segmentation** addresses this shortcoming as it focuses on observable behaviors, such as people being non-users, light users, or heavy users. **Needs-based segmentation** focuses on what customers truly want in a service and maps closely to the multi-attribute decision models we discussed in Chapter 2 (e.g., a time and quality sensitive segment versus a price sensitive segment). In addition, you need to recognize that often people have different needs and their decision-making criteria vary according to:

- The purpose of using the service.

- Who makes the decision.

- The timing of use (time of day/week/season).

- Whether the individual is using the service alone or with a group, and if the latter, the composition of that group.

Consider the criteria that you might use when choosing a restaurant for lunch when you are (1) on vacation with friends or family, (2) meeting with a prospective business client, or (3) going for a quick meal with a coworker. Given a reasonable selection of alternatives, it is unlikely that you would choose the same type of restaurant in each instance, let alone the same one. It is possible too, that if you left the decision to another person in the party, he or she would make a different choice. It is therefore important to be quite specific about the occasion and context a service is purchased for and explicitly include that in the segmentation analysis.

For companies to effectively segment a market, it is often best to start with a deep understanding of customers' needs. The availability of big data and marketing analytics on the cloud enables marketers to collect accurate and detailed information at the individual consumer level, allowing for very narrow and specific segmentation analyses[1]. Marketers can then overlay this understanding with demographic, psychographic, behavioral, and consumption context variables to further define and describe key segments in a market[2].

Contiki Holiday is an example of a company that uses needs-based segmentation as a foundation, and then fine-tunes it with other types of segmentation. It found that some singles do not want to join tours where there are families. They prefer holidays where they can meet others with similar preferences (needs-based segmentation). Contiki serves this special group of people. In fact, it is a worldwide leader in holidays for the 18–35 age group (demographic segmentation) (*Figure 3.3*). Some of its holiday packages are aimed at fun-loving youths. Contiki further segments its packages by catering to different lifestyles and budgets (psychographic segmentation). For example, those going to Europe can choose "High Energy" (for people who are outgoing and want event-packed day and night itineraries), "Camping" (for the budget-conscious exploring the same Europe for less), or "Discovery Plus" (with lots of sightseeing, extra excursions and more choices of accommodation and destinations).

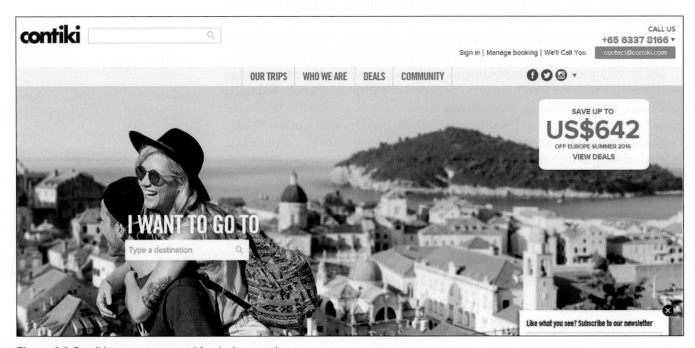

Figure 3.3 Contiki targets young and fun-loving travelers

Important versus Determinant Service Attributes

➲ **LO 4**
Distinguish between important and determinant attributes for segmentation.

It is important to select the right needs and their corresponding service attributes for segmentation. Consumers usually make their choices among alternative service offerings on the basis of perceived differences between them. However, the attributes that distinguish competing services from one another may not always be the most important ones. For instance, many travelers rank "safety" as a very important attribute in their choice of an airline and avoid traveling on airlines with a poor safety reputation. However, after eliminating such alternatives from consideration, a traveler flying on major routes is still likely to have several choices of carriers available that are perceived as equally safe. Hence, safety is not usually an attribute that influences the customer's choice at this point.

Determinant attributes (i.e., those that actually determine buyers' choices between competing alternatives) are often lower on the list of service characteristics important to purchasers. However, they are the attributes where customers see significant differences among competing alternatives. For example, convenience of departure and arrival times (*Figure 3.4*), availability of frequent flyer miles and related loyalty privileges, quality of in-flight service, or the ease of making reservations might be determinant characteristics for business travelers when selecting an airline. For budget-conscious vacation travelers, on the other hand, price might assume primary importance.

Figure 3.4 Convenient departure times are determinant attributes for business travelers

In Chapter 2, we saw that consumers may use different decision rules and therefore arrive at different decisions even though the important attributes are all the same. For example, in *Table 2.1*, the most important attribute is the quality of dry cleaning. However, if the consumer uses the conjunctive rule, depending on what the cut-offs are, the determinant attribute may actually be price, which is the third most important variable. Identifying determinant attributes is therefore crucial for effective positioning to make a firm's service stand out in the minds of its target customers.

Segmentation Based on Service Levels

Aside from identifying attributes to be used for segmentation, decisions must also be made on the service levels to offer on each attribute[3]. Some service attributes are easily quantified, while others are qualitative. Price, for instance, is a quantitative attribute. Punctuality of transport services can be expressed in terms of the percentage of trains, buses, or flights arriving within a specified number of minutes from the scheduled time. Both of these attributes are easy to understand and are therefore quantifiable. However, characteristics such as the quality of personal service or a hotel's degree of luxury are subject to individual interpretation. To facilitate both service design and performance measurement, each attribute needs to be operationalized and standards established. For instance, if customers say they value physical comfort, what does that mean for a hotel or an airline, beyond the size of the room or the seat? In a hotel context, does it refer to ambient conditions, such as absence of noise? Or to more visible, tangible elements such as the bed (e.g., Westin Hotels & Resorts use their "Heavenly Bed" to tangibalize their superior beds). In practice, hotel managers need to address both the ambient conditions and tangible elements.

Customers often can be segmented according to their willingness to give up some level of service for a lower price. Price-insensitive customers are willing to pay a relatively high price to obtain higher levels of service on each of the attributes important to them. In contrast, price-sensitive customers will look for an inexpensive service that offers a relatively low level of performance on many key attributes (see *Service Insights 3.2*).

Segmentation helps to identify potential attributes and service levels that have different degrees of relevance for key market segments. Once the segment structure of a market is understood, the firm can then move on to determining which of those segments should be targeted.

SERVICE INSIGHTS 3.2
Capsule Hotels

Capsule hotels consist of small rooms almost the size of large cupboards. Some of these capsule-like rooms cost as little as $20 a night. The main benefits of these hotels are convenience and price. They started in space-constrained Japan in the 1980s but did not take off in other parts of the world until recently. Now, capsule hotel chains have been launched in many countries and include The Pod Hotel in New York, Yotel in London, and Citizen M in Amsterdam.

These new chains have also modified their service offerings, differentiating themselves from the early capsule hotels in Japan. For example, the Yotel group offers different classes of rooms which they call cabins. This concept came from the capsule hotels of Japan and the first-class cabins in British Airways airplanes. Yotel's premium cabin includes a double bed that can be changed into a couch at the touch of a button. It has tables that accommodate hand luggage, a luxury bathroom, and a study desk that unfolds. Yotel also offers free Internet access, flat-screen TV, premium coffee, and 24-hour in-cabin service. The cost of a premium room at Yotel's location at the London Heathrow Airport starts from £55 for four hours, and £8 per hour after that. The cost for a standard room per day is only £89, a fraction of the typical price for a hotel room in London.

Yotel and Qbic have aggressive growth plans, and we can expect capsule hotels to become a mainstream choice for budget-conscious travelers in the future.

Source

www.yotel.com; http://www.thepodhotel.com/; http://en.wikipedia.org/wiki/Capsule_hotel, accessed February 3, 2015; *The Economist*, "Capsule Hotel: Thinking Small," November 17, 2007.

LO 6

*T*arget service customers using the four focus strategies for competitive advantage.

TARGETING SERVICE MARKETS

Service firms vary widely in their abilities to serve different types of customers well. Hence, achieving competitive advantage usually requires a firm to be more focused, which is what we will discuss next. Rather than trying to compete in an entire market, each company ideally focuses its efforts on those customers it can serve best — its **target segment**. Nearly all successful service firms apply this concept.

Achieving Competitive Advantage Through Focus

It is usually not realistic for a firm to try to appeal to all potential buyers in a market, because customers are varied in their needs, purchasing behavior, and consumption patterns, and often too numerous and geographically widely spread. Service firms also vary widely in their abilities to serve different types of customers well. Hence, rather than trying to compete in an entire market, each company needs to focus its efforts on those customers it can serve best.

In marketing terms, **focus** means providing a relatively narrow product mix for a particular target segment. Nearly all successful service firms apply this concept. They identify the strategically important elements in their service operations and concentrate their resources on them. The extent of a company's focus can be described along two dimensions: market focus and service focus[4]. **Market focus** is the extent to which a firm serves few or many markets, while **service focus** describes the extent to which a firm offers few or many services. These two dimensions define the four basic focus strategies (*Figure 3.5*):

Breadth of Service Offerings

	Wide	**Narrow**
Few	Market focused	Fully focused (Service and market focused)
Many	Unfocused (Everything for everyone)	Service focused

Numbers of Markets Served

Source

Achieving Focus in Service Organizations, Johnson, R. *The Service Industries Journal* (January): 10–12. January 1, 1995.

Figure 3.5 Basic focus strategies for services

Figure 3.6 Private air charter services for VIPs

- **Fully-focused**. A fully-focused organization provides a limited range of services (perhaps just a single core product) to a narrow and specific market segment. For example, private jet charter services may focus on the high-net-worth individuals or corporations (*Figure 3.6*). Developing recognized expertise in a well-defined niche may provide protection against would-be competitors and allows a firm to charge premium prices. An example of a fully focused firm is Shouldice Hospital, featured in *Service Insights 3.3*. The hospital performs only a single surgery (hernia) on otherwise healthy patients (mostly men in their 40s to 60s). Because of their focus, their surgery and service quality are superb.

There are key risks associated with pursuing the fully-focused strategy. The market may be too small to get the volume of business needed for financial success, and the firm is vulnerable should new alternative products or technologies substitute their own.

- **Market-focused**. In a market-focused strategy, a company offers a wide range of services to a narrowly defined target segment. *Service Insights 3.3* features the example of Rentokil Initial, a provider of business-to-business services. Rentokil has profited from the growing trend in outsourcing of services related to facilities maintenance, which has enabled it to develop a large range of services for its clients.

Following a market-focused strategy often looks attractive because the firm can sell multiple services to a single buyer. However, before choosing a market-focused strategy, managers need to be sure their firms are capable of doing an excellent job of delivering each of the different services selected.

- **Service-focused**. Service-focused firms offer a narrow range of services to a fairly broad market. Lasik eye surgery clinics and Starbucks coffee shops follow this strategy, serving a broad customer base with a largely standardized product. However, as new segments are added, the firm needs to develop expertise in serving each segment. Furthermore, this strategy is likely to require a broader sales effort and greater investment in marketing communication — particularly in B2B markets.

- **Unfocused**. Finally, many service providers fall into the unfocused category, because they try to serve broad markets and provide a wide range of services. The danger with this strategy is that unfocused firms often are "jacks of all trades and masters of none". In general, that's not a good idea, although public utilities and government agencies may be obliged to do so. A few departmental stores followed this strategy, and as a result, have been struggling against more focused competitors (e.g., hypermarkets and specialty stores).

It is recommended that firms have some sort of focus, whether on market segments or on services. How then should a firm select which of the three "focused" strategies to pursue? This decision relates back to the 3 Cs, segmentation and targeting analyses. For example, a market-focused strategy may be appropriate if (a) customers value the convenience of one-stop shopping, (b) the firm has the capabilities of delivering these multiple services better than competition, and/or (c) there are significant synergies in selling multiple services to the same customer (as is often the case in B2B services, see Rentokil Initial in *Service Insights 3.3*), which then enables the firm to either lower its price or provide better service.

A service-focused strategy can work best if the firm has a unique set of capabilities and resources to deliver a particular service exceptionally well or cost-effectively. The firm may then want to ride on its advantage to deliver the service to a broad market (i.e., many customer segments at the same time).

Finally, a fully-focused strategy may work well if a particular segment has very specific needs and requires unique design of the service environment, service processes and interaction with the firm's frontline employees. Here, a fully-focused strategy can deliver superb quality and at low costs because of its focus and experience. The Shouldice Hospital is a good example. The entire hospital is designed around the needs of hernia patients who are otherwise well and do not have to stay in bed. Patients get their perfect hospital experience and outstanding surgery quality all at a low price. This makes Shouldice Hospital the perfect hospital for people who have hernia but are otherwise healthy. However, this hospital cannot deal with any other types of patients.

The decision on focus is very important for service firms as they have distributed operations (i.e., each Starbuck's café is like a mini-factory), and any additional service offered increases the complexity of processes and the costs of the operation significantly. Likewise, even if a firm wants to sell the same basic service to different segments, it will find often that each additional segment may require some changes to the facility and processes to cater to their different needs and requirements. They also need to understand customer purchasing practices and preferences. In a B2B context, when trying to cross-sell additional services to the same client, many firms have been disappointed to find that decisions on purchasing the new service are made by an entirely different group within the client company[5].

Inherent in focus and excellence are tradeoffs. According to Frances Frei and Anne Morriss, there are a lot of heroic people in service organizations who feel compelled to be the best at everything. However, trying to do that will almost inevitably lead to mediocrity. The authors argue that excellence requires sacrifice (another way of looking at focus), and service firms should excel where it matters. For example, the Mayo Clinic decided to focus on reducing the time it takes for patients from scheduling an examination, to being examined by a doctor, and receiving a diagnosis in 24 hours or less. That is important for anxious patients who want to know fast what is wrong with them. However, focusing on speed does not allow patients anymore to select a specific physician. It is important to decide on areas where the firm does not have to perform as well (i.e., where their customers care less about) with the knowledge that it gives it the resources to excel where it matters most to their target customers[6].

SERVICE INSIGHTS 3.3
Market-Focused Brand Across Multiple Services at Rentokil Initial

With revenue for 2015 at over £2.3 billion, Rentokil Initial is one of the world's largest business support service companies. The company has about 27,000 employees in over 50 countries where the "Rentokil" and "Initial" brands have come to represent innovation, deep expertise, and consistent quality of service. The UK-based firm has grown and developed from its origins as a manufacturer of rat poison and a

pesticide for killing wood-destroying beetles. When the firm realized it could make more money by providing a service to kill rodents than by selling products customers would use themselves, it shifted to pest control and extermination services.

Through organic growth and acquisitions, Rentokil Initial has developed an extensive product range that includes testing and safety services, security, package delivery, interior plants landscaping (including sale or rental of tropical plants), specialized cleaning services, pest control, uniform rental and cleaning, clinical waste collection and disposal, personnel services, and a washroom solutions service that supplies and maintains a full array of equipment, dispensers, and consumables. The firm sees its core competence as "the ability to carry out high-quality services on other people's premises through well-recruited, well-trained, and motivated staff."

Promoting use of additional services to existing customers is an important aspect of the firm's strategy. Initial Integrated Services offer clients the opportunity to move beyond the established concept of "bundling" services — bringing together several free-standing support services contracts from one provider — to full integration of services. Clients purchase sector-specific solutions that deliver multiple services, but feature just "one invoice, one account manager, one help desk, one contract, and one motivated service team."

According to former chief executive, Sir Clive Thomson: *Our objective has been to create a virtuous circle. We provide a quality service in industrial and commercial activities under the same brand-name, so that a customer satisfied with one Rentokil Initial Service is potentially a satisfied customer for another... Although it was considered somewhat odd at the time, one of the reasons we moved into [providing and maintaining] tropical plants [for building interiors] was in fact to put the brand in front of decision makers. Our service people maintaining the plants go in through the front door and are visible to the customer. This contrasts with pest control where no one really notices unless we fail... The brand stands for honesty, reliability, consistency, integrity and technical leadership.*

Investment in research and development (R&D) ensures constant improvement in its many service lines. For example, the company has built the RADAR intelligent rodent trap. RADAR attracts rats and mice into a sealable chamber and kills them humanely by injecting carbon dioxide. Using Rentokil's unique "PestConnect" technology, the trap causes emails to be sent to the customer and the local branch when a rodent is caught, and a Rentokil technician receives a text message identifying which unit has been activated at which customer's premises, and its precise location. PestConnect checks each individual RADAR unit every 10 minutes, 24/7. Getting information in real time enables technicians to remove dead rodents promptly and to control future infestation better.

Rentokil Initial's success lies in its ability to position each of its many business services in terms of the company's core brand values, which include providing superior standards of customer care and using the most technologically advanced services and products. The brand image is strengthened through physical evidence in terms of distinctive uniforms, vehicle color schemes, and use of the corporate logo.

Source

Clive Thompson, "Rentokil Initial: Building a Strong Corporate Brand for Growth and Diversity," in F. Gilmore (ed.) *Brand Warriors* (London: HarperCollinsBusiness, 1997), 123–124; http://www.rentokil-initial.com/, accessed February 3, 2015.

LO 7

*P*osition a service to distinguish it from its competitors.

PRINCIPLES OF POSITIONING SERVICES

Positioning strategy is concerned with creating, communicating, and maintaining distinctive differences that will be noticed and valued by those customers the firm would most like to develop a long-term relationship with. Successful positioning requires managers to understand their target customers' preferences, their conception of value, and the characteristics of their competitors' offerings. Price and product attributes are the two of the 4 Ps of marketing most commonly associated with positioning strategy. For services, however, positioning often relates also to other Ps of the services marketing mix, including service processes (e.g., their convenience, ease of use), distribution systems, service schedules, locations, the services environment, and service personnel. Competitive strategy can take many different routes. George Day observes:

> *The diversity of ways a business can achieve a competitive advantage quickly defeats any generalizations or facile prescriptions... First and foremost, a business must set itself apart from its competition. To be successful, it must identify and promote itself as the best provider of attributes that are important to target customers*[7].

Jack Trout distilled the essence of positioning into the following four principles[8]:

1. A company must establish a position in the minds of its targeted customers.

2. The position should be singular, providing one simple and consistent message (*Figure 3.7*).

3. The position must set a company apart from its competitors (*Figure 3.8*).

4. A company cannot be all things to all people — it must focus its efforts.

These principles apply to any type of organization that competes for customers. Firms must understand the principles of positioning in order to develop an effective competitive position. The concept of positioning offers valuable insights by forcing service managers to analyze their firm's existing offerings and to provide specific answers to the following six questions:

1. What does our firm currently stand for in the minds of current and potential customers?

2. What customers do we serve now, and which ones would we like to target in the future?

3. What is the value proposition for each of our current service offerings, and what market segments is each one targeted at?

4. How does each of our service products differ from those of our competitors?

5. How well do customers in the chosen target segments perceive our service offerings as meeting their needs?

6. What changes do we need to make to our service offerings in order to strengthen our competitive position within our target segment(s)?

Figure 3.8 For powerful positioning, a firm needs to set itself apart from its competitors

"In hindsight, I'd say my first mistake was letting my competitors advertise on my website."

Figure 3.7 Visa has one simple message globally

One of the challenges in developing a viable positioning strategy is to avoid the trap of investing too much in points of difference that can easily be copied. As researchers Kevin Keller, Brian Sternthal, and Alice Tybout note: "Positioning needs to keep competitors out, not draw them in"[9]. When Roger Brown and Linda Mason, founders of the Bright Horizons chain of childcare centers featured in the opening vignette of this chapter, were developing their service concept and business model, they took a long, hard look at the industry[10]. Discovering that for-profit childcare companies had adopted low-cost strategies, Brown and Mason selected a different approach that competitors would find very difficult to copy.

Similarly, it used to be that when large companies were looking for auditing services, they typically turned to one of the Big Four accounting firms (*Figure 3.9*). Now, a growing number of clients are switching to the so-called "Tier Two" accounting firms in a search for better service, a lower bill, or both[11]. Grant Thornton, the fifth largest firm in the industry, has successfully positioned itself

as offering easy access to their partners and having "a passion for the business of accounting". Its advertising promotes an award from J. D. Powers, a global market research company, ranking it as achieving the "Highest Performance Among Audit Firms Serving Companies with up to $12 billion in Annual Revenue".

Figure 3.9 The Big Four accounting firms refers to PricewaterhouseCoopers, Deloitte Touche Tohmatsu, Ernest & Young, and KPMG

Figure 3.10 Dubai's Burj Al Arab is favorably positioned along many determinant attributes like personal service, level of physical extravagance and location

USING POSITIONING MAPS TO PLOT COMPETITIVE STRATEGY

⊃ **LO 8**
Understand how to use positioning maps to analyze and develop competitive strategy.

Positioning maps are great tools to visualize competitive positioning along key aspects of its services marketing strategy, to map developments over time, and to develop scenarios of potential competitor responses. Developing a positioning map — a task sometimes referred to as perceptual mapping — is a useful way of representing consumers' perceptions of alternative products graphically. A map usually has two attributes, although three-dimensional models can be used to show three of these attributes. When more than three dimensions are needed to describe product performance in a given market, then a series of separate charts needs to be drawn.

Information about a product (or company's position relative to any one attribute) can be inferred from market data, derived from ratings by representative consumers, or both. If consumer perceptions of service characteristics differ sharply from "reality" as defined by management, then communications efforts may be needed to change these perceptions, which we will discuss in Chapter 7.

An Example of Applying Positioning Maps to the Hotel Industry

The hotel business is highly competitive, especially during seasons when the supply of rooms exceeds demand. Within each class of hotels, customers visiting a large city find that they have many alternatives to choose from. The degree of luxury and comfort in physical amenities will be one choice criterion; others may include attributes like location, safety, availability of meeting rooms and a business center, restaurants, a swimming pool and gym, and loyalty programs for frequent guests (*Figure 3.10*).

Let's look at an example, based on a real-world situation of how to apply positioning maps. Managers of The Palace, a successful four-star hotel, developed a positioning map showing their own and competing hotels, to get a better understanding of future threats to their established market position in a large city that we will call Belleville.

Located on the edge of the booming financial district, the Palace was an elegant old hotel that had been renovated to a great extent and modernized a few years earlier. Its competitors included eight four-star establishments, and The Grand, one of the city's oldest hotels, which had a five-star rating. The Palace had been very profitable in recent years and has had an above average occupancy rate. For many months of the year, it was sold out on weekdays, reflecting its strong appeal to business travelers, who were very attracted to the hotel because of their willingness to pay a higher room rate than tourists or conference delegates. However, the general manager and his staff saw problems on the horizon. Planning permissions had recently been granted for four large new hotels in the city, and The Grand had just started a major renovation and expansion project, which included the construction of a new wing. There was a risk that customers might see The Palace as falling behind.

To better understand the nature of the competitive threat, the hotel's management team worked with a consultant to prepare charts that displayed The Palace's position in the business traveler market both before and after the entrance of new competition. Four key attributes were selected for study: room price, level of personal service, level of physical luxury, and location.

Data Sources. In this instance, management did not conduct new consumer research. Instead, they got their customer perceptions data from various sources:
- Published information.
- Data from past surveys done by the hotel.
- Reports from travel agents and knowledgeable hotel staff members who frequently interacted with guests.

Information on competing hotels was not difficult to obtain, because the locations were known. Information was obtained through:

- Visiting and evaluating the physical structures.
- Having sales staff who kept themselves informed on pricing policies and discounts.
- To evaluate service level, they used the ratio of rooms per employee. It is easily calculated from the published number of rooms and employment data provided to the city authorities.
- Data from surveys of travel agents conducted by The Palace provided additional insights the quality of personal service at each competitor.

Scales and Hotel Ratings. Scales were then created for each attribute and each hotel was rated on each of the attributes so the positioning maps could be drawn:

- Price was simple because the average price charged to business travelers for a standard single room at each hotel was already quantified.
- The rooms-per-employee ratio formed the basis for a service level scale, with low ratios equated to high service. This rating was then fine-tuned because of what was known about the quality of service actually delivered by each major competitor.
- Level of physical luxury was more subjective. The management team identified the hotel that members agreed was the most luxurious (The Grand) and then the four-star hotel they viewed as having the least luxurious physical facilities (the Airport Plaza). All other four-star hotels were then rated on this attribute relative to these two benchmarks.
- Location was defined using the stock exchange building in the heart of the financial district as a reference point. Past research had shown that a majority of The Palace's business guests were visiting destinations in this area. The location scale plotted each hotel in terms of its distance from the stock exchange. The competitive set of 10 hotels lay within a four-mile, fan-shaped radius, extending from the exchange through the city's principal retail area (where the convention center was also located) to the inner suburbs and the nearby airport.

Two positioning maps were created to portray the existing competitive situation. The first (*Figure 3.11*) showed the 10 hotels on the dimensions of price and service level; the second (*Figure 3.12*) displayed them on location and degree of physical luxury.

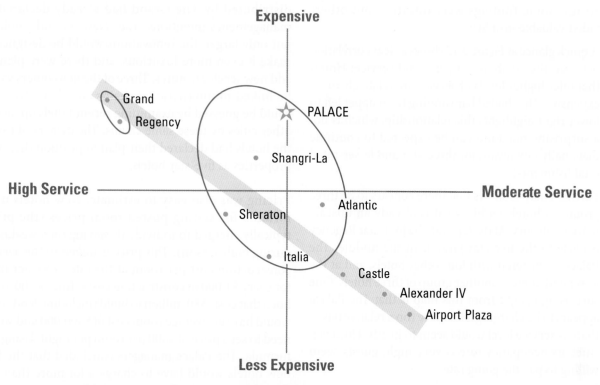

Figure 3.11 Positioning map of Belleville's principal business hotels: service level versus price level

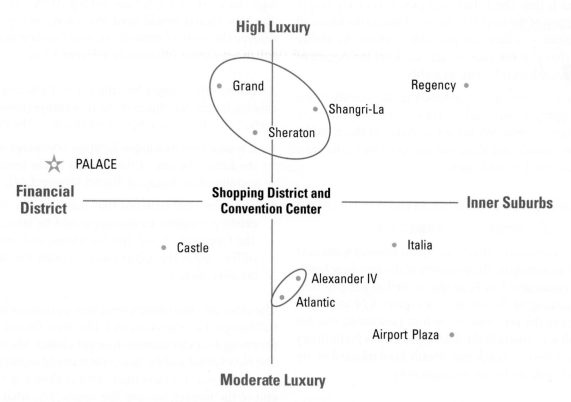

Figure 3.12 Positioning map of Belleville's principal business hotels: location versus physical luxury

Findings. Some findings were intuitive, but others provided valuable insights:

- A quick glance at *Figure 3.12* shows a clear correlation between the attributes of price and service: Hotels that offer higher levels of service are relatively more expensive. The shaded bar running from upper left to lower right highlights this relationship, which is not a surprising one (and can be expected to continue diagonally downward for three-star and lesser-rated establishments).

- Further analysis shows that there appears to be three groups of hotels within what is already an upscale market category. At the top end, the four-star Regency is close to the five-star Grand. In the middle, The Palace is clustered with four other hotels, and at the lower end, there is another group of three hotels. One surprising insight from this map is that The Palace appears to be charging a lot more (on a relative basis) than its service level would seem to justify. However, since its occupancy rate is very high, guests seem willing to pay the going rate.

- *Figure 3.13* shows how The Palace is positioned relative to the competition on location and degree of luxury. We don't expect these two variables to be related, and they don't appear to be so. A key insight here is that The Palace occupies a relatively empty portion of the map. It is the only hotel in the financial district — a fact that probably explains its ability to charge more than its service level (or degree of physical luxury) seems to justify.

- There are two groups of hotels in the vicinity of the shopping district and convention center (*Figure 3.13*). There is a relatively luxurious group of three, led by The Grand, and a second group of two offering a moderate level of luxury.

Mapping Future Scenarios to Identify Potential Competitive Responses

What of the future? The Palace's management team next sought to anticipate the positions of the four new hotels being constructed in Belleville as well as the probable repositioning of The Grand (see *Figures 3.14* and *3.15*). Predicting the positions of the four new hotels was not difficult for experts in the field, especially as preliminary details of the new hotels had already been released to city planners and the business community.

The construction sites were already known; two would be in the financial district and two in the vicinity of the convention center, under expansion. Press releases distributed by The Grand had already declared its management's intentions: The "New" Grand would be not only larger, the renovations would be designed to make it even more luxurious, and there were plans to add new service features. Three of the newcomers would be linked to international chains and their strategies could be guessed by examining recent hotels opened in other cities by these same chains. The owners of two of the hotels had declared their plan to position their new properties as five-star hotels.

Pricing was also easy to estimate. New hotels use a formula for setting posted room prices (the prices typically charged to individuals staying on a weeknight during high season). This price is linked to the average construction cost per room at the rate of $1 per night for every $1,000 of construction costs. Thus, a 200-room hotel that costs $80 million to build (including land costs) would have an average room cost of $400,000 and would need to set a price of $400 per room per night. Using this formula, The Palace managers concluded that the four new hotels would have to charge a lot more than The Grand or Regency. This would establish a *price umbrella* above existing price levels, thereby giving competitors the option of raising their own prices. To justify their high prices, the new hotels would have to offer customers very high standards of service and luxury. At the same time, The New Grand would need to raise its own prices to recover the costs of renovation, new construction, and enhanced service offerings (see *Figure 3.13*).

Assuming no changes by either The Palace or other existing hotels, the effects of the new competition in the market clearly posed a significant threat to The Palace:

- It would lose its unique location advantage and, in the future, be one of three hotels in the immediate vicinity of the financial district (*Figure 3.14*).

- The sales staff believed that many of The Palace's existing business customers would be attracted to The Continental and The Mandarin, and would be willing to pay the higher rates to obtain the superior benefits offered.

The other two newcomers were seen as more of a threat to Shangri-La, Sheraton, and The New Grand in the shopping district/convention center cluster. Meanwhile, The New Grand and the newcomers would create a high-price/high-service (and high-luxury) cluster at the top end of the market, leaving The Regency in what might prove to be a distinctive — and therefore defensible — space of its own.

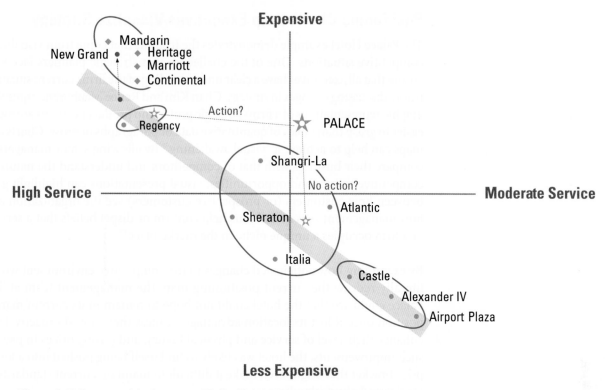

Figure 3.13 Future positioning map of Belleville's business hotels: service level versus price level

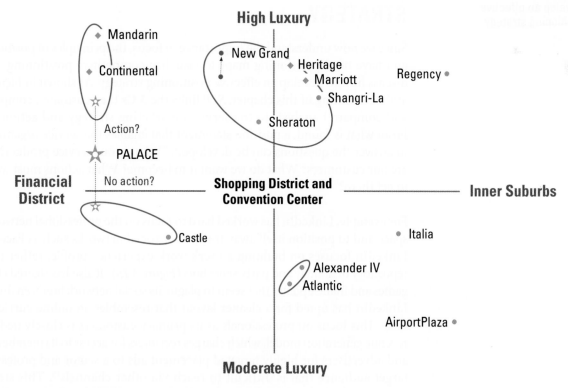

Figure 3.14 Future positioning map of Belleville's business hotels: location versus physical luxury

Positioning Charts Help Executives Visualize Strategy

The Palace Hotel example demonstrates the insights that come from visualizing competitive situations. One of the challenges that strategic planners face is to ensure that all executives have a clear understanding of the firm's current situation before discussing changes in strategy. Chan Kim and Renée Mauborgne argue that graphic representations of a firm's strategic profile and product positions are much easier to grasp than tables of quantitative data or paragraphs of prose. Charts and maps can help to achieve a "visual awakening." By allowing senior managers to compare their business with that of competitors and understand the nature of competitive threats and opportunities, visual presentations can highlight gaps between how customers (or prospective customers) see the organization and how management sees it, and thus help confirm or dispel beliefs that a service or a firm occupies a unique niche in the marketplace[12].

By examining how anticipated changes in the competitive environment would literally redraw the current positioning map, the management team at The Palace could see that the hotel could not hope to remain in its current market position once it lost its location advantage. Unless they moved proactively to enhance their level of service and physical luxury, and raising prices to pay for such improvements, the hotel was likely to find itself being pushed into a lower price bracket that might even make it difficult to maintain current standards of service and physical upkeep.

DEVELOPING AN EFFECTIVE POSITIONING STRATEGY

LO 9
Develop an effective positioning strategy.

Since we now understand the importance of focus, the principles of positioning, and have used positioning maps to visualize competitive positioning, let us discuss how to develop an effective positioning strategy. As shown in *Figure 3.2* at the beginning of this chapter, *STP* links the **3 Cs** (i.e., customer, competitor, and company) analysis to the services marketing strategy and action plan. From what is found, a position statement that enables the service organization to answer the questions can be developed: "What is our service product? Who are our customers? What do we want it to become? What actions must we take to get there?"

For example, LinkedIn has worked hard to focus on the professional networking space and to position itself away from other social networks such as Facebook. LinkedIn focuses on building a user's work experience profile, rather than a repository of holiday and party snapshots (*Figure 3.15*). It also has steered clear of games and inane updates that seem to plague its social network brethren. Instead, LinkedIn has opted for a cleaner layout that resembles an online curriculum vitae. This focus on professionals as its primary customers is closely tied to its revenue generation model, which charges recruiters for access to its member base, and advertisers for highly targeted placement ads to a senior and professional target audience that is difficult to reach via other channels[13]. This strategy clearly worked. As of 2015, LinkedIn had more than 300 million members in over 200 countries and territories, significantly ahead of its competitors Viadeo from France and XING from Germany, which had 70 million and 10 million members, respectively.

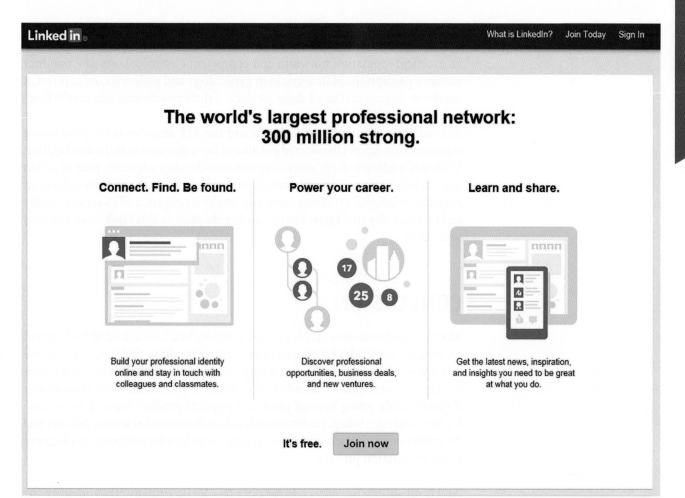

Figure 3.15 LinkedIn positioned itself away from social networks by focusing exclusively on professional networking and career development

There are four basic elements to writing a good positioning statement[14], and we use the LinkedIn example to illustrate them:

- Target audience — the specific group(s) of people that the brand wants to sell to and serve (e.g., professionals as primary target customers, and employers and advertisers as secondary target audiences).

- Frame of reference — the category in which the brand is competing (e.g., in the social networking space).

- Point of difference — the most compelling benefit offered by the brand that stands out from its competition (e.g., largest network of professionals and recruiters to help advance your career, develop your business acumen, industry knowledge, and personal development).
- Reason to believe — proof that the brand can deliver the benefits that are promised. (e.g., our network is many times bigger than that of our nearest competitor).

Developing a positioning strategy can take place at several different levels, depending on the nature of the business in question. Among other multi-site, multi-product service businesses, a position might be established for the entire organization, for a given service outlet or for a specific service offered at that outlet. There must be consistency between the positioning of different services

Understanding Service Products, Consumers, and Markets **115** offered at the same location, because the image of one may spill over onto the others, especially if it is perceived to be related. For instance, if a hospital has an excellent reputation for warm and competent obstetrical services, that may enhance perceptions of its services in gynecology and pediatrics. By contrast, it would be detrimental to all three services, if their positioning was conflicting.

The outcome of integrating the **3 Cs** and the *STP* analyses is the positioning statement that defines the desired position of the organization in the marketplace. With this understanding, marketers can now develop a specific plan of action that includes its positioning strategy along the **7 Ps** of services marketing, its customer relationship management and loyalty strategies, and its service quality and productivity strategies. The remaining chapters in this book show you how to do this!

CONCLUSION

Most service businesses face active competition. Marketers need to find ways of creating meaningful value propositions for their products that stake a distinctive and defensible **position** in the market against competing alternatives. The nature of services introduces a number of distinctive possibilities for competitive differentiation, going beyond price and physical product features to include: location and scheduling, performance levels such as speed of service delivery and the caliber of service personnel, and a range of options for customer involvement in the production process.

Nearly all successful service firms pursue a focus strategy. They identify the strategically important elements in their service operations and concentrate their resources on them. They target segments which they can serve better than other providers, offering and promoting a higher level of performance on those attributes particularly valued by their target customers.

CHAPTER SUMMARY

LO 1 Developing an effective positioning strategy links **customer**, **competitor**, and **company analysis**, often called the **3 Cs**.

- **Market analysis** looks at the market attractiveness (e.g., market size and growth, and trends) and customer needs (e.g., desired service levels, level of contact, delivery channel, time of consumption, and price sensitivity).
- **Competitor analysis** examines the competitors' current positioning, strengths and weaknesses to spot opportunities for the firm.
- **Company analysis** focuses on a firm's brand positioning and image, the firm's strengths and weaknesses (e.g., its resources and constraints), and how its values shape the way it does business.

LO 2 The key elements of developing a customer-driven services marketing strategy are **segmentation**, **targeting**, and **positioning**, commonly referred to as *STP*.

LO 3 **Segmentation** is the division of a market into groups. Those customers within the same segment share common service-related needs. Segmentation is often based on customer needs first to focus the firm on what customers truly want and what drives their purchase decision. Subsequently, demographic, psychographic and behavioral variables can be used to further define and describe key segments.

LO 4 It is crucial for segmenting customers to understand the difference between important and determinant attributes for consumer choice.

- **Important attributes** are important to the consumer, but may not be important for the buying decisions (e.g., safety is important, but all airlines a traveler considers are seen as safe). If that is the case, such an attribute should not be used as a basis for segmentation.
- **Determinant attributes** often are further down on the list of service characteristics important to customers. However, they are attributes where customers see significant differences between competing alternatives (e.g., convenience of departure times, or quality of in-flight service), and will determine the final purchase. Differences between customers regarding determinant attributes are therefore crucial for segmentation.

LO 5 Once the important and determinant attributes are understood, management needs to decide which **service level** different customers prefer on each of the attributes. Service levels often are used to differentiate customer segments according to their willingness to trade off price and service level.

LO 6 Next, each company needs to focus its efforts on those customers it can serve best – its **target segment**. Firms must have a competitive advantage on attributes valued by their target segment. To achieve competitive advantage, firms need to be focused. There are three focused strategies firms can follow to achieve competitive advantage. They are:

1. **Fully-focused:** A firm provides a limited range of services (perhaps only one) to a narrow target segment (e.g., Shouldice Hospital).
2. **Market-focused:** A firm concentrates on a narrow market segment, but offers a wide range of services to address the many diverse needs of that segment (e.g., Rentokil).
3. **Service-focused:** A firm offers a narrow range of services to a fairly broad market (e.g., Lasik eye surgery clinics, Starbucks cafés, or LinkedIn).
4. There is a fourth, the unfocused strategy. However, it is generally not advisable for firms to choose an unfocused strategy as they might spread themselves too thin to remain competitive (e.g., some departmental stores).

LO 7 Once we have understood determinant attributes and related service levels of our target segment(s), we can decide how to best position our service in the market. **Positioning** is based on establishing and maintaining a distinctive place in the market for a firm's offerings. The essence of positioning is:

- A company must establish a position in the minds of its targeted customers.
- The position should be singular, providing one simple and consistent message.
- The position must set a company apart from its competitors.
- A company cannot be all things to all people — it must focus its efforts.

⊃ **LO 8 Positioning maps** are an important tool to help firms develop their positioning strategy. They provide a visual way of summarizing customer perceptions of how different services are performing on determinant attributes compared to competition. They can help firms to see where they might reposition themselves and also to anticipate competitors' actions.

⊃ **LO 9** The outcome of these analyses is the position statement that articulates the desired position of the firm's offering in the marketplace. With this understanding, marketers can then develop a specific plan of action that includes its positioning strategy along the **7 Ps** of services marketing, its customer relationship management and loyalty strategies, and its service quality and productivity strategies.

Review Questions

1. What are the elements of a customer-driven services marketing strategy?

2. In segmentation, what are the most common bases to use? Provide examples for each of these bases.

3. What is the distinction between important and determinant attributes in consumer purchase decisions?

4. How are service levels of determinant attributes related to positioning services?

5. Why should service firms focus their efforts? Describe the basic focus strategies, and give examples of how these work.

6. What are the six questions for developing an effective positioning strategy?

7. How can positioning maps help managers better understand and respond to competitive dynamics?

8. Describe what is meant by positioning strategy and how do the market, customer, internal, and competitive analyses relate to positioning strategy?

Application Exercises

1. Select a company of your choice. Identify the variables that the company has used to segment their customers. Support your answers with examples from the company.

2. Provide two examples of service firms that use service levels (other than airlines, hotels, and car rentals) to differentiate their products. Explain the determinant attributes and service levels used to differentiate the positioning of one service from another?

3. Find examples of companies that illustrate the four focus strategies discussed in this chapter.

4. Travel agencies are losing business to passengers booking their flights directly on airline websites. Identify possible focus options open to travel agencies wishing to develop new lines of business that would make up for the loss of airline ticket sales.

5. Imagine you have been hired as a consultant to give advice to The Palace Hotel. Consider the options for the hotel based on the four attributes in the positioning charts (*Figures 3.14* and *3.15*). What actions do you recommend The Palace take? Explain your recommendations.

6. Choose an industry you are familiar with (such as cell phone service, credit cards, or online music stores), and create a perceptual map showing the competitive positions of different service providers in that industry. Use attributes you believe are determinant attributes. Identify gaps in the market, and generate ideas for a potential "blue ocean" strategy.

Endnotes

1   Roland Rust and Ming-Hui Huang (2014), "The Service Revolution and the Transformation of Marketing Science," *Marketing Science,* Vol. 33, No. 2, pp. 206–221.

2   Daniel Yankelovich and David Meer (2006), "Rediscovering Marketing Segmentation," *Harvard Business Review*, Vol. 84, No. 2, pp. 122–131. A best-practice example in a B2B context is discussed in: Ernest Waaser, Marshall Dahneke, Michael Pekkarinen, and Michael Weissel (2004), "How You Slice It: Smarter Segmentation for Your Sales Force," *Harvard Business Review*, Vol. 82, No. 3, pp. 105–111.

3   Frances X. Frei (May 2008), "The Four Things a Service Business Must Get Right," *Harvard Business Review*, Vol. 86, No. 4, pp. 70–80, 136.

4   Robert Johnston (January 1996), "Achieving Focus in Service Organizations," *The Service Industries Journal*, Vol. 16, pp. 10–20.

5   For a detailed approach to exploring synergies in marketing or production, see Michael E. Porter, "A Framework for Competitor Analysis," in (New York: The Free Press, 1980), Chapter 3, pp. 47–74.

6   Frances Frei and Anne Morriss, *Uncommon Service: How to Win by Putting Customers at the Core of Your Business* (Boston, MA: Harvard Business Review Press, 2012).

7   George S. Day, *Market Driven Strategy (*New York: The Free Press, 1990), p. 164.

8   Jack Trout, *The New Positioning: The Latest on the World's #1 Business Strategy* (New York: McGraw-Hill, 1997).

9   Kevin Lane Keller, Brian Sternthal, and Alice Tybout (September 2002), "Three Questions You Need to Ask about Your Brand," *Harvard Business Review*, Vol. 80, p. 84.

10 Roger Brown (February 2001), "How We Built a Strong Company in a Weak Industry," *Harvard Business Review*, Vol. 79, pp. 51–57.

11 Nanette Byrnes (August 22/29, 2005), "The Little Guys Doing Large Audits," *BusinessWeek*, p. 39.

12 W. Chan Kim and Renée Mauborgne (June 2002), "Charting Your Company's Future," *Harvard Business Review*, Vol. 80, pp. 77-83.

13 Robert Simons (2014), "Choosing the Right Customer: The First Step in a Winning Strategy," *Harvard Business Review*, Vol. 92, No. 3, pp. 49–55. https://www.linkedin.com/company/linkedin, accessed February 2, 2015.

14 http://www.brandeo.com/positioning%20statement, accessed February 2, 2015

PART 2

The Services Marketing Framework

Part I

Understanding Service Products, Consumers, and Markets

1. Creating Value in the Service Economy
2. Understanding Service Consumers
3. Positioning Services in Competitive Markets

Part II

Applying the 4 Ps of Marketing to Services

4. Developing Service Products and Brands
5. Distributing Services Through Physical and Electronic Channels
6. Service Pricing and Revenue Management
7. Service Marketing Communications

Part III

Managing the Customer Interface

8. Designing Service Processes
9. Balancing Demand and Capacity
10. Crafting the Service Environment
11. Managing People for Service Advantage

Part IV

Developing Customer Relationships

12. Managing Relationships and Building Loyalty
13. Complaint Handling and Service Recovery

Part V

Striving for Service Excellence

14. Improving Service Quality and Productivity
15. Building a World-Class Service Organization

Figure II Organizing framework for services marketing

APPLYING THE 4 Ps OF MARKETING TO SERVICES

Part II revisits the **4 Ps** of the traditional marketing mix (*P*roduct, *P*lace, *P*rice, and *P*romotions). However, they are expanded to take into account the specific characteristics of services that make them different from goods marketing. It consists of the following four chapters:

CHAPTER 4
Developing Service Products and Brands

Chapter 4 discusses the meaningful service concept that includes both the core and supplementary elements. The supplementary elements both facilitate and enhance the core service offering. This chapter also covers branding, tiered servicer products, and explains how service firms can build brand equity.

CHAPTER 5
Distributing Services Through Physical and Electronic Channels

Chapter 5 examines the time and place elements. Manufacturers usually require physical distribution channels to move their products. However, some service businesses are able to use electronic channels to deliver all (or at least some) of their service elements. For the services delivered in real time with customers physically present, speed, and convenience of place and time have become important determinants of effective service delivery. This chapter also discusses the role of intermediaries, franchising, and international distribution and market entry.

CHAPTER 6
Service Pricing and Revenue Management

Chapter 6 provides an understanding of pricing from both the firm and customer's point of view. For firms, the pricing strategy determines income generation. Service firms need to implement revenue management to maximize the revenue generated from available capacity at any given time. From the customer's perspective, price is a key part of the costs they must incur to obtain the desired benefits. However, the cost to the customer often includes significant nonmonetary costs too. This chapter also discusses ethics and fairness in service pricing and how to develop an effective pricing strategy.

CHAPTER 7
Service Marketing Communications

Chapter 7 deals with how firms should communicate with their customers about their services through the use of promotion and education. As customers are co-producers and they contribute to how others experience a service performance, much communication in services marketing is educational in nature so as to teach customers how to effectively move through a service process. This chapter covers the service marketing communications funnel, the services marketing communications mix, and communications through online, mobile, and social networks.

CHAPTER 04 Developing Service Products and Brands

"Each and every one of you will make or break the promise that our brand makes to customers."

An American Express manager speaking to his employees

LEARNING OBJECTIVES (LOs)

By the end of this chapter, the reader should be able to:

⊃ **LO 1** Understand what constitutes a service product.

⊃ **LO 2** Be familiar with the Flower of Service model.

⊃ **LO 3** Know how facilitating supplementary services relate to the core product.

⊃ **LO 4** Know how enhancing supplementary services relate to the core product.

⊃ **LO 5** Understand branding at the corporate and individual service product level.

⊃ **LO 6** Examine how service firms use different branding strategies.

⊃ **LO 7** Understand how branding can be used to tier service products.

⊃ **LO 8** Discuss how firms can build brand equity.

⊃ **LO 9** Understand what is required to deliver a branded service experience.

⊃ **LO 10** List the categories of new service development, ranging from simple style changes to major innovations.

⊃ **LO 11** Describe how firms can achieve success in new service development.

OPENING VIGNETTE[1]

Unequivocally the globally dominant specialty-coffee brand, Starbucks — before anything else — is a place you would associate with coffee, hand-crafted for you by one of its baristas. Starbucks attributes its Cinderella success story to three core components — (1) what it believes is the highest-quality coffee in the word, (2) its customer service, which aims to create an uplifting experience every time you walk through the door; and (3) the ambiance of its stores; upscale, yet inviting for those who want to linger.

However, did you know that Starbucks has been making many retail and service innovations completely unrelated to coffee? It was one of the first coffee chains to offer free wireless broadband in many of its outlets around the world. Later, Starbucks tied-up with Apple's iTunes Wi-Fi Music Store to allow for the songs played at selected cafes to be browsed, purchased, and downloaded wirelessly onto customers' iPhones or iPads. Since then, Starbucks has continued experimenting with innovative services that its customers may want to use while enjoying their

coffee. It launched its Starbucks Digital Network, which offers exclusive movie trailers and a bounty of premium media content, as well as Android and Apple apps that allow customers to pay, check card balances and reload cards, track stars and redeem rewards, leave digital tips for the barista, find and redeem personalized offers, view menu choices and nutritional content, and much more. Recently, Starbucks partnered with Spotify to allow its baristas and customers to pick the songs played at the shops by incorporating Spotify into Starbucks' mobile app. According to Howard Schultz, Starbucks CEO, "By connecting Spotify's world-class streaming platform into our world-class store and digital ecosystem, we are reinventing the way our millions of customers discover music."

Starbucks is a company that has developed service innovations with great success. However, competition continues to be intense and Starbucks has to continue reinventing itself to maintain its edge.

LO 1
Understand what constitutes
a service product.

CREATING SERVICE PRODUCTS

In recent years, more and more service firms have started talking about their **products** — a term previously largely associated with manufactured goods. What is the distinction between these two terms in today's business environment? What is a product? A **product** implies a defined and consistent "bundle of output" as well as the ability to differentiate one bundle of output from another. In a manufacturing context, the concept is easy to understand and visualize. Service firms can also differentiate their products in a similar fashion using the various "models" offered by manufacturers. For example, fast-food restaurants display a menu of their products, which are, of course, highly tangible. If you are a burger connoisseur, you can easily distinguish Burger King's Whopper from its Whopper with Cheese, or from McDonald's Big Mac.

Providers of more intangible services, also offer various "models" of products, representing an assembly of carefully prescribed value-added supplementary services built around a core product. For instance, credit card companies develop different cards that each comes with a distinct bundle of benefits and fees; insurance companies offer different types of policies; and universities offer different degree programs, each composed of a mix of required and elective courses. The objective of product development is to design bundles of output that are distinct and can be easily differentiated from another.

All service organizations face choices concerning the types of products to offer and how to deliver them to customers. To better understand the nature of services, it's useful to distinguish between the core product and the supplementary elements that facilitate its use and enhance its value for customers. Designing a service product is a complex task that requires an understanding of how the core and supplementary services should be combined, sequenced, and delivered to create a value proposition that meets the needs of target segments.

What Are the Components of a Service Product?

What do we mean by a service "product"? Service performances are experienced rather than owned. Even when there are physical elements to which the customer takes a title of ownership — such as a meal (which is promptly consumed), a surgically implanted pacemaker, or a replacement part for a car — a significant portion of the price paid by customers is for the value added by the service elements, including expert labor and the use of specialized equipment. A service product comprises of all the elements of the service performance, both physical and intangible, that create value for customers.

How should you go about designing a service product? Experienced service marketers recognize the need to take a holistic view of the entire performance that they want customers to experience. The value proposition must address and integrate three components: (1) **core product**, (2) **supplementary services**, and (3) **delivery processes**.

Core Product. The core product is "what" the customer is fundamentally buying. When buying a one-night stay in a hotel, the core service is accommodation and security. When paying to have a package delivered, the core service is for the package to arrive at the correct address, on time and undamaged. In short, a core product is the central component supplying the principal benefits and solutions that customers seek. The core product is the main component that supplies the desired experience (e.g., a rejuvenating spa treatment or an exhilarating roller coaster ride) or the problem-solving benefit (e.g., a management consultant provides advice on how to develop a growth strategy, or a repair service restores a piece of equipment to proper working condition) that customers are looking for.

Some core products are highly intangible. Think of credit card and travel insurance products and their innovative design of features, benefits, and pricing (note that many fees are hidden transaction costs, especially if used abroad). Equally, if not more intangible, are exchange traded funds (ETFs) which revolutionized the mutual fund industry. An ETF is essentially a low-cost mutual fund that usually tracks an index (e.g., the Dow Jones or Nikkei 225) and is listed on a stock exchange so that investors can trade in and out as they like. These funds are cheap, tax-efficient and allow retail investors to buy a diversified portfolio. The development of ETF products has been an exciting journey with major product innovation involved[2].

Supplementary Services. Delivery of the core product is usually accompanied by a variety of other service-related activities we refer to collectively as supplementary services, which augment the core product, both facilitating its use and enhancing its value[3]. Core products tend to become commoditized as an industry matures and competition increases. So the search for competitive advantage often emphasizes supplementary services, which can play an important role in differentiating and positioning the core product against competing services.

Delivery Processes. The third component in designing a service concept concerns the processes used to deliver both the core product and each of the supplementary services. The design of the service offering must address the following issues:

- How the different service components are delivered to the customer.
- The nature of the customers' role in those processes.
- How long delivery lasts.
- The prescribed level and style of service to be offered.

The integration of the core product, supplementary services, and delivery processes is captured in *Figure 4.1*, which illustrates the components of the service offering for an overnight stay at a luxury hotel. The core product — overnight rental of a bedroom — dimensioned by service level, scheduling (how long the room may be used before another payment becomes due), the nature of the process (in this instance, people processing), and the role of customers (in terms of what they are expected to do themselves and what the hotel will do for them, such as making the bed, supplying bathroom towels, and cleaning the room).

Surrounding the core product is a variety of supplementary services. These range from reservations to meals to in-room service elements. Delivery processes must be specified for each of these elements. The more expensive the hotel is, the higher the level of service is required of each element. For example, very important guests might be received at the airport and transported to the hotel in a limousine. Check-in arrangements can be done on the way to the hotel. By the time the guests arrive at the hotel, they are ready to be escorted to their rooms, where a butler is on hand to serve them. We will discuss the service process aspect in detail in Chapter 8, and focus on core and supplementary services, branding and new product development in this chapter. An overview of the structure of this chapter is provided in *Figure 4.2*.

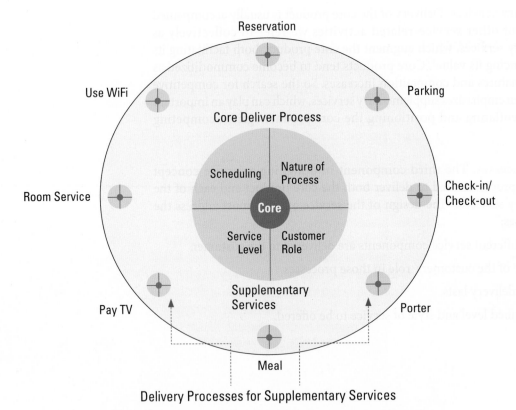

Figure 4.1 Depicting the Service Offering for an Overnight Hotel Stay

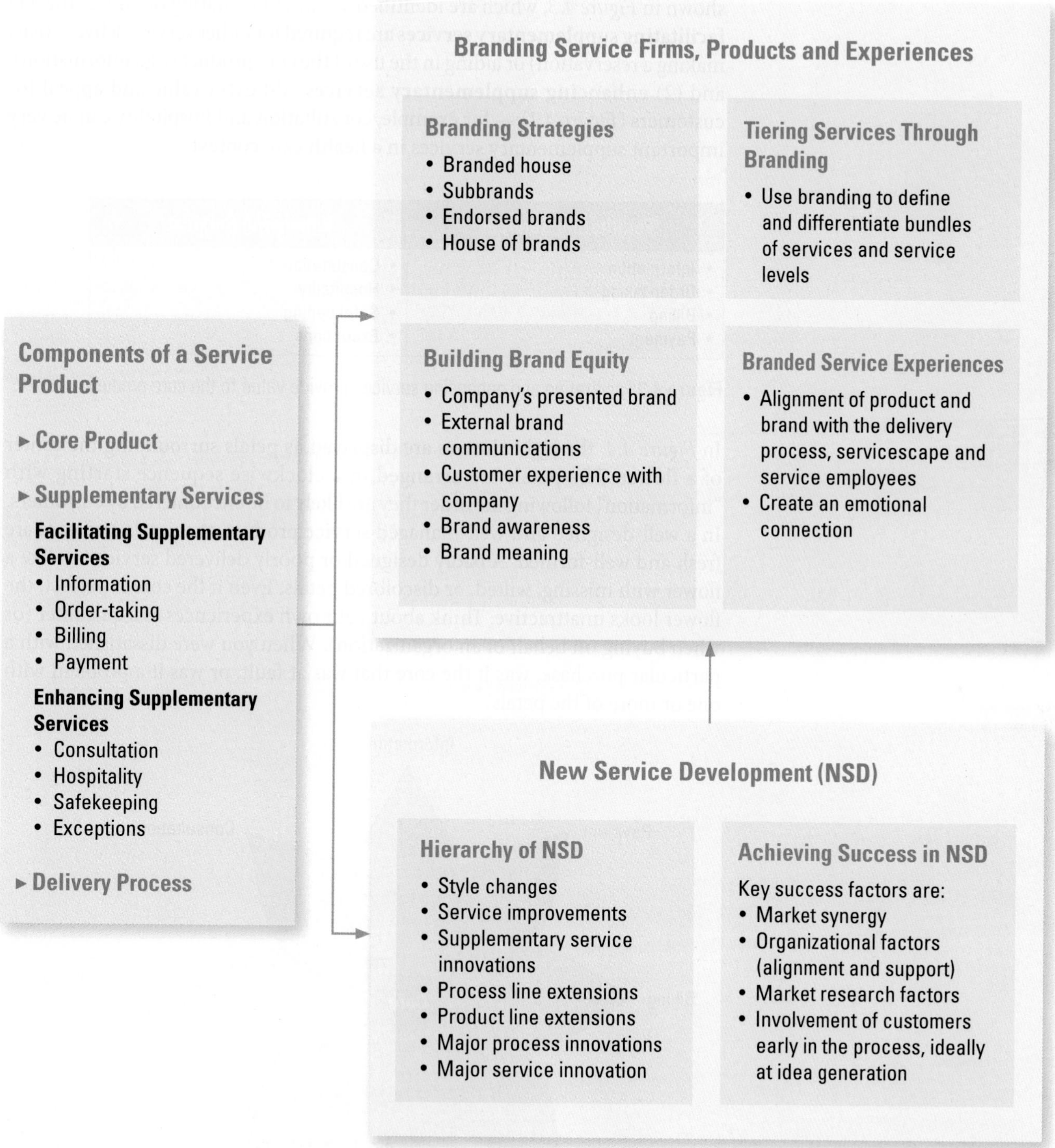

Components of a Service Product

▶ Core Product

▶ Supplementary Services

Facilitating Supplementary Services
- Information
- Order-taking
- Billing
- Payment

Enhancing Supplementary Services
- Consultation
- Hospitality
- Safekeeping
- Exceptions

▶ Delivery Process

Branding Service Firms, Products and Experiences

Branding Strategies
- Branded house
- Subbrands
- Endorsed brands
- House of brands

Tiering Services Through Branding
- Use branding to define and differentiate bundles of services and service levels

Building Brand Equity
- Company's presented brand
- External brand communications
- Customer experience with company
- Brand awareness
- Brand meaning

Branded Service Experiences
- Alignment of product and brand with the delivery process, servicescape and service employees
- Create an emotional connection

New Service Development (NSD)

Hierarchy of NSD
- Style changes
- Service improvements
- Supplementary service innovations
- Process line extensions
- Product line extensions
- Major process innovations
- Major service innovation

Achieving Success in NSD
Key success factors are:
- Market synergy
- Organizational factors (alignment and support)
- Market research factors
- Involvement of customers early in the process, ideally at idea generation

Figure 4.2 Overview of Chapter 4

LO 2
Be familiar with the Flower
of Service model.

THE FLOWER OF SERVICE[4]

The Flower of Service consists of the core service and a range of supplementary services. There are potentially dozens of different supplementary services, but almost all of them can be classified into one of the following eight clusters shown in *Figure 4.3*, which are identified as either facilitating or enhancing: (1) **facilitating supplementary services** are required for either service delivery (e.g., making a reservation) or aiding in the use of the core product (e.g., information), and (2) **enhancing supplementary services** add extra value and appeal for customers (*Figure 4.1*) — for example, consultation and hospitality can be very important supplementary services in a health care context.

Facilitating Services	Enhancing Services
• Information • Order-taking • Billing • Payment	• Consultation • Hospitality • Safekeeping • Exceptions

Figure 4.3 Facilitating and enhancing services provide value to the core product

In *Figure 4.4*, the eight clusters are displayed as petals surrounding the center of a flower. The petals are arranged in a clockwise sequence starting with "information", following the order they are likely to be encountered by customers. In a well-designed and well-managed service product, the petals and core are fresh and well-formed. A badly designed or poorly delivered service is a like a flower with missing, wilted, or discolored petals. Even if the core is perfect, the flower looks unattractive. Think about your own experiences as a customer (or when buying on behalf of an organization). When you were dissatisfied with a particular purchase, was it the core that was at fault, or was it a problem with one or more of the petals?

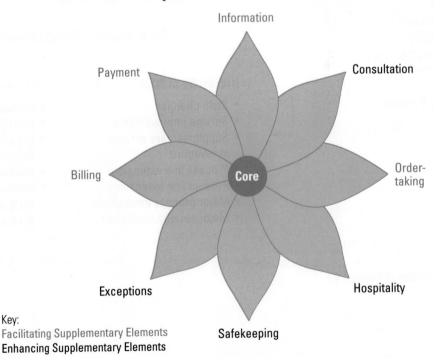

Key:
Facilitating Supplementary Elements
Enhancing Supplementary Elements

Figure 4.4 The Flower of Service: Core product surrounded by cluster of supplementary services

Facilitating Supplementary Services

Information. To obtain full value from any good or service, customers need relevant information. Information includes the following:

- Direction to service site
- Schedules/service hours
- Price information
- Terms and conditions of sale/service (*Figure 4.5*)
- Advice on how to get the most value from a service
- Warnings and advice on how to avoid problems
- Confirmation of reservations
- Receipts and tickets
- Notification of changes
- Summaries of account activities

⊃ **LO 3**
Know how facilitating supplementary services relate to the core product.

Twitter Terms of Service

These Terms of Service ("**Terms**") govern your access to and use of our Services, including our various websites, SMS, APIs, email notifications, applications, buttons, widgets, ads, commerce services (the "**Twitter Services**"), and our other covered services that link to these Terms (collectively, the "**Services**"), and any information, text, graphics, photos or other materials uploaded, downloaded or appearing on the Services (collectively referred to as "**Content**"). Your access to and use of the Services are conditioned on your acceptance of and compliance with these Terms. By accessing or using the Services you agree to be bound by these Terms.

1. Basic Terms

You are responsible for your use of the Services, for any Content you post to the Services, and for any consequences thereof. Most Content you submit, post, or display through the Twitter Services is public by default and will be able to be viewed by other users and through third party services and websites. Learn more here, and go to the account settings page to control who sees your Content. You should only provide Content that you are comfortable sharing with others under these Terms.

Tip: What you say on the Twitter Services may be viewed all around the world instantly. You are what you Tweet!

Language: English ▾ Sign in

Twitter, Tweet and Twitter Bird Logo are trademarks of Twitter, Inc. or its affiliates.

Figure 4.5 Twitter.com provides conditions of service to users

Figure 4.6 Parcels can be tracked around the world with their identity code

New customers are especially information-hungry. Companies should make sure the information they provide is both timely and accurate. If not, it is likely to cause customers inconvenience, make them feel irritated and perceive a lack of control.

Traditional ways of providing information include using company websites, mobile apps, front-line employees, signs, printed notices, and brochures. Information can also be provided through videos or software-driven tutorials, touch-screen video displays on tablets and self-service machines. Many business logistics companies offer shippers the opportunity to track the movements of their packages — each of which has been assigned a unique identification number (*Figure 4.6*). For example, Amazon.com provides its customers with a reference number that allows tracking of the goods so that customers know when to expect them.

Order-Taking. Once customers are ready to buy, a key supplementary element comes into play — order-taking. Order-taking includes:

- Order entry
  - On-site order entry
  - Mail/telephone/email/online/mobile app order
- Reservations or check-ins
  - Seats/tables/rooms
  - Vehicles or equipment rental
  - Professional appointment (*Figure 4.7*)
- Applications
  - Memberships in club/programs
  - Subscription services (e.g., utilities)
  - Enrolment-based services (e.g., financial credit, college enrolment)

Order entry can be received through a variety of sources such as through sales personnel, phone and email, or online (*Figure 4.8*). The process of order-taking should be polite, fast, and accurate so that customers do not waste time and endure unnecessary mental or physical effort.

Reservations (including appointments and check-in) represent a special type of order-taking that entitles customers to a specified unit of service. These can be an airline seat, a restaurant table, a hotel room, time with a qualified professional, or admission to a facility such as a theater or sports arena with designated seating.

Technology can be used to make order-taking and reservations easier and faster for both customers and

Figure 4.7 The services of a professional emcee have to be reserved

suppliers. For example, airlines now make use of ticketless systems, based on email and mobile apps. Customers receive a confirmation number when they make the reservation and need only show identification (or the ticket as shown on a mobile app) at the airport to claim their seats and receive a boarding pass.

Banks, insurance companies, and utilities require prospective customers to go through an application process so that they can gather relevant information and screen out those who do not meet basic enrollment criteria (such as a bad credit record or serious health problems). Universities also require prospective students to apply for admission.

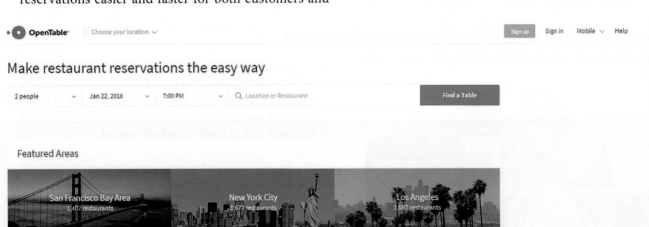

Figure 4.8 Websites like OpenTable take dining reservations to a whole new level by allowing diners to bypass the traditional call-and-book experience, with a mere click

Billing. Billing is common to almost all services (unless the service is provided free-of-charge). Inaccurate, illegible, or incomplete bills risk disappointing customers who may, up to that point, have been quite satisfied with their experience. If customers are already dissatisfied, the billing mistake may make them even angrier. Billing should also be timely, because it encourages people to make faster payment. Billing can be:

- Periodic statements of account activity.
- Invoices for individual transactions.
- Verbal statements of amount due.
- Online or machine display of amount due for self-payment transactions.

Perhaps the simplest approach is self-billing, by which the customer tallies up the amount of an order and authorizes a card payment. In such instances, billing and payment are combined into a single act, although the seller may still need to check for accuracy.

Customers usually expect bills to be clear and informative, and itemized in ways that make it clear how the total was computed. Unexplained, arcane symbols that have all the meaning of hieroglyphics on an Egyptian monument (and are decipherable only by the high priests of accounting and data processing) do not create a favorable impression of the service firm, but unfortunately, are all too common (think of your cell phone service or a hospital bill). The same goes for fuzzy printing or illegible handwriting. Online or emailed statements, and laser printers with their ability to switch fonts and typefaces, to box and to highlight, can produce statements that are not only more legible but also organize information in useful ways. Marketing research can help here, by asking customers what information they want and how they would like it to be organized and presented.

Figure 4.10 Tokens allow self-service payment

Busy customers hate to be kept waiting for a bill to be prepared in a hotel, restaurant, or rental car lot. Many hotels and car rental firms have created express check-out options, taking customers' credit card details in advance and documenting charges later by email. However, accuracy is essential. Even though customers use the express check-outs to save time, they certainly don't want to waste time later with corrections and refunds. An alternative express check-out procedure is used by some car rental companies. An agent meets customers as they return their cars, checks the mileage on the odometer and the fuel gauge readings, and then prints a bill on the spot using a portable wireless terminal (*Figure 4.9*). Many hotels push bills under guestroom doors on the morning of departure showing the charges to date. Others offer customers the option of previewing their bills on the TV monitor in their room before checking out.

Payment. In most cases, a bill requires the customer to take action on payment (and such action may be very slow in coming!). Exceptions include bank statements and other direct debit payment services, which shows the charges to be deducted from a customer's account.

A variety of payment options exist, but customers expect them to be easy to use and convenient. They include:

- Self-service
  - Inserting card, cash, or token into machine (*Figure 4.10*)
  - Electronic funds transfer
  - Mailing a check

Figure 4.9 A wireless handheld terminal allows car rental bills to be printed on the spot

- Entering credit card information online
- Online payment systems such as PayPal, Google Wallet, or Bitcoins

- Direct to payee or intermediary
  - Cash handling or change giving
  - Check handling
  - Credit/charge/debit card handling
  - Coupon redemption

- Automatic deduction from financial deposits
  - Automated systems (e.g., machine-readable tickets that operate entry gate)
  - Pre-arranged automatic deduction for bill payment through direct debit (e.g., for bank loans and post-paid cell phone subscription plans)

Self-service payment systems, for instance, require insertion of coins, banknotes, tokens, or cards in machines. Equipment breakdowns will destroy the whole purpose of such a system, so good maintenance and rapid-response troubleshooting are essential. Most payment still takes the form of cash or credit cards. Other alternatives include vouchers, coupons, or prepaid tickets, and other electronic means such as PayPal, which offers a fuss-free and secure way to make payments especially since more shopping is done online.

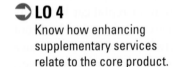

LO 4

Know how enhancing supplementary services relate to the core product.

Enhancing Supplementary Services

Consultation. Now we move on to enhancing supplementary services, led by consultation. In contrast to information, which suggests a simple response to customers' questions (or printed information that anticipates their needs), consultation involves a dialog to probe for customer requirements and then develop a tailored solution. At its simplest, consultation consists of advice from a knowledgeable service person in response to the request: "What do you suggest?" For example, you might ask your hairstylist for advice on different hairstyles and products. Effective consultation requires an understanding of each customer's current situation, before suggesting a suitable course of action. Examples of consultation include:

- Customized advice
- Personal counseling
- Tutoring/training in service use
- Management or technical consulting (*Figure 4.11*)

Figure 4.11 An auditor provides a human touch during the process of consultation

Counseling represents a more subtle approach to consultation because it involves helping customers to better understand their situations so they can come up with their "own" solutions and action programs. This approach can be a particularly valuable supplement to services such as health treatments, in which part of the challenge is to get customers to make significant lifestyle changes and live healthily. For example, diet centers like Weight Watchers use counseling to help customers change behaviors so that weight loss can be sustained after the initial diet is completed (*Figure 4.12*).

Figure 4.12 Counseling for weight reduction is a form of consultation

More formalized efforts to provide management and technical consulting for corporate customers include "solution selling" for expensive industrial equipment and services. The sales engineer researches a customer's situation and then offers advice about what particular package of equipment and systems will yield the best results. Some consulting services are offered free of charge in the hopes of making a sale. In other instances, however, the service is "unbundled" and customers are expected to pay for it (e.g., for diagnostic tests before a surgery, or a feasibility study before a solution is being proposed). Advice can also be offered through tutorials, group training programs, and public demonstrations.

Hospitality. Hospitality-related services should ideally reflect pleasure at meeting new customers and greeting old ones when they return. Well-managed businesses try, at least in small ways, to ensure that their employees treat customers as guests. Courtesy and consideration for customers' needs apply to both face-to-face encounters and telephone interactions. Hospitality elements include:

- Greeting
- Food and beverages
- Toilets and washrooms
- Waiting facilities and amenities
  - Lounges, waiting areas, seating
  - Weather protection
  - Magazines, entertainment, newspapers
- Transport

Hospitality finds its fullest expression in face-to-face encounters. In some cases, it starts (and ends) with an offer of transport to and from the service site on courtesy shuttle buses. If customers must wait outdoors before the service can be delivered, then a thoughtful service provider will offer weather protection. If customers have to wait indoors, a waiting area with seating and even entertainment (TV, newspapers, or magazines) may be provided to pass the time. Recruiting customer-contact employees who are naturally warm, welcoming, and considerate helps to create a hospitable atmosphere. Shoppers at retailers such as Abercrombie & Fitch, a global clothing retailer, are given a welcoming "hello" and "thank you" when they enter and leave the store, even if they did not buy anything (*Figure 4.13*).

Figure 4.13 Abercrombie & Fitch provides hospitality with a smile

The quality of the hospitality services offered by a firm plays an important role in determining customer satisfaction. This is especially true for people-processing services, because one cannot easily leave the service facility until the delivery of the core service is completed. Private hospitals often seek to enhance their appeal by providing a level of room service that might be expected in a good hotel (*Figure 4.14*). This includes the provision of quality meals. Some airlines seek to differentiate themselves from their competitors with better meals and a more attentive cabin crew; Singapore Airlines is well-recognized on both counts[5].

Although pre-flight and in-flight hospitality is important, an airline journey doesn't really end until passengers reach their final destination. Air travelers have come to expect departure lounges, but British Airways (BA) came up with the novel idea of an arrivals lounge for its terminals at London's Heathrow and Gatwick airports to serve passengers arriving early in the morning after a long, overnight flight from the Americas, Asia, Africa, and Australia. The airline offers holders of first and business class tickets or a BA Executive Club gold card

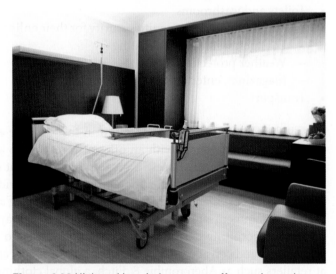

Figure 4.14 High-end hospitals can now offer service and rooms like a 5-star hotel

(which is awarded to the airline's most frequent flyers) the opportunity to use a special lounge where they can take a shower, change their clothes, use a spa, have breakfast, make phone calls, and check their emails before continuing to their final destination feeling a lot fresher. It's a nice competitive advantage, which BA actively promotes. Other airlines have since felt obliged to copy this innovation, although few can match the array of services offered by BA.

Safekeeping. When customers are visiting a service site, they often want assistance with their personal possessions. In fact, some customers may not visit at all unless certain safekeeping services are provided (such as safe and convenient parking for their cars). Safekeeping includes caring for:

- Child care, pet care (*Figure 4.15*)
- Parking for vehicles, valet parking
- Coat rooms
- Baggage handling
- Storage space
- Safe deposit boxes
- Security personnel

Responsible businesses pay close attention to safety and security issues for customers who are visiting the firm's premises. Wells Fargo Bank mails a brochure with its bank statements containing information about using its ATM machines safely, educating its customers about how to protect both their ATM cards and themselves from theft and personal injury. The bank also makes sure that its machines are in brightly lit, highly visible locations, and are equipped with CCTV. It takes a similarly careful

Figure 4.15 Pet care services is a form of safekeeping

approach to customer privacy and security for their online services. Have a look at https://www.wellsfargo.com and search for "online security".

Additional safekeeping services may involve physical products that customers buy or rent. They may include packaging, pick-up and delivery, assembly, installation, cleaning, and inspection. These services may be offered free or for an additional fee.

Exceptions. Exceptions involve supplementary services that fall outside the routine of normal service delivery. Astute businesses anticipate such exceptions and develop contingency plans and guidelines in advance. That way, employees will not appear helpless and unprepared when customers ask for special assistance. Well-defined procedures make it easier for employees to respond promptly and effectively (*Figure 4.16*). There are several types of exceptions:

- **Special requests.** A customer may request service that requires a departure from normal operating procedures. Common requests relate to personal needs, including the care of children, dietary requirements, medical needs, religious observance, and personal disabilities. Such requests particularly are common in the travel and hospitality industries.

Figure 4.16 Well-established procedures allow customers' requests for online hotel reservations to be registered and handled properly by employees

- **Problem-solving.** Sometimes normal service delivery (or product performance) fails to run smoothly as a result of accident, delay, equipment failure, or a customer having difficulty in using a product.

- **Handling of complaints/suggestions/compliments.** This activity requires well-defined procedures. It should be easy for customers to express dissatisfaction, offer suggestions for improvement, or pass on compliments, and service providers should be able to make an appropriate response quickly (see Chapter 13 on complaint handling and service recovery).

- **Restitution.** Many customers expect to be compensated for serious performance failures. Compensation may take the form of repairs under warranty, legal settlements, refunds, an offer of free service, or other form of payment-in-kind.

Managers need to keep an eye on the level of exception requests. Too many requests may indicate that standard procedures need revamping. For instance, if a restaurant frequently receives requests for special vegetarian meals as there are none on the menu, it may be time to revise the menu to include at least one or two such dishes. A flexible approach to exceptions is generally a good idea, because it reflects responsiveness to customer needs. On the other hand, too many exceptions may compromise safety, negatively impact other customers, and overburden employees.

Managerial Implications

The eight categories of supplementary services that form the "Flower of Service" collectively provide many options for enhancing core products. Most supplementary services do (or should) represent responses to customer needs. As noted earlier, some are facilitating services — such as information and reservations — that enable customers to use the core product more effectively. Others are "extras" that enhance the core or even reduce its non-financial costs (e.g., meals, magazines, and entertainment are hospitality elements that help pass the waiting time). Some elements — notably billing and payment — are, in effect, imposed by the service provider. Even if they are not actively desired by the customer, they still form part of the overall service experience. Any badly handled element may negatively affect customers' perceptions of service quality. The "information" and "consultation" petals illustrate the emphasis in this book on the need for education as well as promotion in communicating with service customers (see Chapter 7 on "Services Marketing Communications").

Not every core product is surrounded by supplementary elements from all eight petals of the Flower of Service. Each of the four categories of processes introduced in Chapter 2 — people, possession, mental stimulus and information processing — has different implications for operational procedures, the degree of customer contact with service personnel and facilities, and requirements for supplementary services. As you might anticipate, people-processing services tend to be the most demanding in terms of supplementary elements, as they involve close and often extended interactions with customers, especially in the hospitality industry. Similarly, high-contact services usually have more supplementary elements than low-contact services. When customers don't visit the service factory, the need for hospitality may be limited to simple courtesies in communications. Possession-processing services sometimes place heavy demands on safekeeping elements, but there may be less need for this particular "petal" when providing information-processing services in which customers and suppliers deal entirely at arm's length. However, many services deal with sensitive information (e.g., healthcare providers and financial services) — these companies must ensure that their customers' intangible financial assets and privacy are carefully safeguarded in transactions that occur via phone or the Internet[6] (*Figure 4.17*).

Figure 4.17 Security features ensure that online transactions are safe

A company's market positioning strategy helps to determine which supplementary services should be included. A strategy of adding benefits to increase customers' perceptions of quality will require more supplementary services, as well as a higher level of performance on all such elements, than what a strategy of price-competitiveness requires. Furthermore, offering progressively higher levels of supplementary services around a common core may offer the basis for a product line of differentiated offerings, similar to the various classes of travel offered by airlines.

B2B service firms were found to simply add layer upon layer of services to their core offerings without knowing what customers really valued[7]. Managers surveyed in the study indicated that they did not understand which services should be offered to customers as a standard package accompanying the core, and which could be offered as options for an extra charge. Without this knowledge, developing effective pricing policies can be tricky. There are no simple rules governing pricing decisions for core products and supplementary services, but managers should continually review their own policies and those of their competitors to make sure they are in line with both market practice and customer needs. We'll discuss these and other pricing issues in more detail in Chapter 6.

In summary, the Flower of Service and its petals discussed here can serve as a checklist in the continuing search for new ways to augment existing core products and to design new offerings. Regardless of which supplementary services a firm decides to offer, all of the elements in each petal should receive the care and attention needed to consistently meet defined service standards. That way, the resulting "flower" will always have a fresh and appealing appearance.

LO 5

Understand branding at the corporate and individual service product level.

BRANDING SERVICE FIRMS, PRODUCTS, AND EXPERIENCES

Branding plays an important role in services, as explained by Leonard Berry:

Strong brands enable customers to better visualize and understand intangible products. They reduce customers' perceived monetary, social, or safety risk in busying services, which are difficult to evaluate prior to purchase. Strong brands are surrogates when the company offers no fabric to touch, no trousers to try on, no watermelons or apples to scrutinize, no automobile to test drive[8].

Branding can be employed at both the corporate and product levels by almost any service business. In a well-managed firm, the corporate brand is not only easily recognized but also has meaning for customers, representing a particular way of doing business. Applying distinctive brand names to individual products enables the firm to communicate the distinctive experiences and benefits associated with a specific service concept to the target market. In short, it helps marketers to establish a mental picture of the service in customers' minds and to clarify the nature of the value proposition.

Branding individual service products helps to differentiate one bundle of output from another. One example is Banyan Tree Hotels & Resorts (featured in *Case x*), which carefully crafted specified products for its various target segments branded as "Heavenly Honeymoon", "Spa Indulgence", or "Intimate Moments"[9]. The latter is a product specially created for couples who may celebrate their wedding anniversary. It is presented as a surprise to the partner or spouse when guests return to find their villas decorated with lid candles, incense burning, flower petals spread throughout the room, satin sheets on the decorated bed, chilled champagne or wine, and a private outdoor pool decorated with a variety of aromatic massage oils to further inspire those intimate moments. Having "packaged" and "branded" this product allows Banyan Tree to sell it via its website, distributors, and reservations centers, and train it at the individual hotels. Without specifying exactly what this product means and giving it a name, marketing, selling, and delivery would not be effective. Let's next look at alternative branding strategies for services.

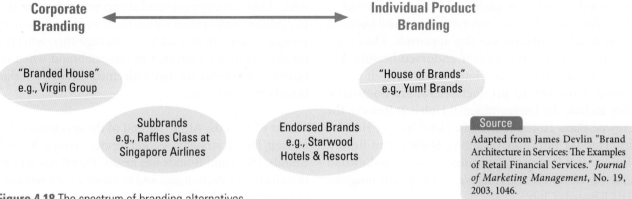

Figure 4.18 The spectrum of branding alternatives

Source

Adapted from James Devlin "Brand Architecture in Services: The Examples of Retail Financial Services." *Journal of Marketing Management*, No. 19, 2003, 1046.

Branding Strategies for Services

Most service organizations offer a line of products rather than just a single product. As a result, they must choose from among four broad branding alternatives: Branded house (i.e., using a single brand to cover all products and services), house of brands (i.e., using a separate stand-alone brand for each offering), or sub-brands and endorsed brands which are both some combination of these two extremes[10]. These alternatives are represented as a spectrum in *Figure 4.18*, and are discussed in the following sections.

Branded House. The term **branded house** is used to describe a company, such as the Virgin Group, that applies its brand name to multiple offerings in often unrelated fields[11]. Virgin's core business areas are travel, entertainment, and lifestyle, but it also offers financial services, healthcare, media, and telecommunications services. The danger of such a branding strategy is that the brand gets overstretched and weakened.

Sub-brands. Next on the spectrum are **sub-brands**, for which the corporate or the master brand is the main reference point, but the product itself has a distinctive name too. Examples are the Singapore Airlines Raffles Class, denoting the company's business class, and the Singapore Airlines Suits, its "beyond first class" service on the A380.

FedEx has been successfully using a sub-branding strategy. When the company decided to rebrand a ground delivery service it had purchased, it chose the name FedEx Ground and developed an alternative color for the standard logo (purple and green rather than purple and orange). Its goal was to transfer the positive image of reliable, on-time service associated with its air services to its less expensive, small-package ground service. The well-known air service was then rebranded as FedEx Express. Its other sub-brands, in what the firm refers to as "the FedEx family of companies", include FedEx Home Delivery (which delivers to US residential addresses), FedEx Freight (regional, less-than-truckload transportation for heavyweight freight), FedEx Custom Critical (nonstop, door-to-door delivery of time-critical shipments), FedEx Trade Networks (customs brokerage, international freight forwarding, and trade facilitation), Fedex Supply Chain (comprehensive suite of solutions that synchronize the movement of goods), and Fedex Office (office and printing services, technology services, shipping supplies, and packing services located at both city and suburban retail stores)[12].

LO 6
Examine how service firms use different branding strategies.

Endorsed Brands. For **endorsed brands**, the product brand dominates but the corporate name is still featured. Many hotel companies use this approach. They offer a family of subbrands and/or endorsed brands. For instance, Intercontinental Hotel Group in itself is well known. However, its product brands are dominant. They include the Intercontinental Hotels & Resorts, the Crowne Plaza Hotels & Resorts, Hotel Indigo, Holiday Inn, Holiday Inn Club Vacations, Holiday Inn Resort, Holiday Inn Express, Staybridge Suites, Candlewood Suites, Even Hotels, and Hualuxe, and its loyalty program IHG Rewards Club[13].

For a multi-brand strategy to succeed, each brand must promise a distinctive value proposition, targeted at a different customer segment. It is important to note that in some instances, segmentation is situation-based: The same individual may have different needs (and willingness to pay) under differing circumstances, such as when traveling with family or traveling on business. A multi-brand strategy is aimed at encouraging customers to continue buying from within the brand family. Loyalty programs are often used to encourage this, whereby loyalty points are collected in one subbrand when on business travel, but are then redeemed through another brand on leisure trips.

House of Brands. At the far end of the spectrum is the *house of brands* strategy. A good service example is Yum! Brands, Inc. Yum! Brands has nearly 43,000 restaurants in more than 130 countries and territories, with revenues of more than $13 billion in 2015. While many may not have heard of Yum! Brands, people certainly are familiar with their restaurant brands — KFC, Pizza Hut and Taco Bell — the global leaders of the chicken, pizza and Mexican-style food categories. Worldwide, the Yum! Brands system opens over six new restaurants per day on average, making it a leader in global retail development (*Figure 4.19*).

Photo Courtesy of Yum! Brands, Inc.

Figure 4.19 KFC, Pizza Hut and Taco Bell are just some of the few popular fast-food brands under Yum! Brands.

TIERING SERVICE PRODUCTS WITH BRANDING

⟲ **LO 7**
Understand how branding can be used to tier service products.

In a number of service industries, branding is not only used to differentiate core services, but also to clearly differentiate service levels. This is known as **service tiering**. It is common in industries such as hotels, airlines, car rentals, and computer hardware and software support. *Table 4.1* shows examples of the key tiers within each of these industries. Other examples of tiering include healthcare insurance, cable television, and credit cards.

In the airline industry, individual carriers decide what levels of performance should be included with each class of service. Innovative carriers, such as British Airways and Virgin Atlantic, are continually trying to add new service features like business class seats that unfold flat into beds for overnight travel. In other industries, tiering often reflects an individual firm's strategy of bundling service elements into a limited number of packages, each priced separately. In other industries, tiering often reflects an individual firm's strategy of bundling service elements into a limited number of packages, rather than offering a broad *a la carte* menu of options, each priced separately. Let's examine a few examples next.

- **Avis Car Rental.** Avis focuses on two kinds of customers — consumer customers and business customers. For consumer customers, they tier their service based on different car classes (e.g., subcompact, compact, intermediate, standard, full size, specialty, signature, premium, luxury, standard elite SUV, intermediate SUV, full size SUV, premium SUV, convertible, minivan, and passenger van) and also service. For example, if a customer does not want to drive, they can opt for Avis Chauffeur Drive. The chauffeur not only drives, but also acts as a mobile concierge. Business customers have four programs that cater to different types of business customers (small- and mid-sized business, entertainment and productions, meeting and group services, and government and military) to choose from[14].

Table 4.1 Examples of Service Tiering

Industry	Tiers	Key Service Attributes and Physical Elements Used in Tiering
Lodging	Star or diamond rating (5 to 1)	Architecture; landscaping; room size; furnishings, and décor; restaurant facilities and menus, room service hours; array of services and physical amenities; staffing levels' calibre and attitudes of employees
Airline	Classes (intercontinental); first, business, premium economy, economy[a]	Seat pitch (distance between rows), seat width, and reclining capability; meal and beverage service, staffing ratios; check-in speed; departure and arrival lounges; baggage retrieval speed
Car rental	Class of vehicle[b]	Based on vehicle size (from subcompact to full size), degree of luxury, plus special vehicle types (minivan, SUV, convertible)
Hardware and software support	Support levels	Hours and days of service; speed of response; speed of delivering replacement parts; technician-delivered service versus advice on self-service; availability of additional services

[a] Only a few airlines offer as many as four classes of intercontinental service; domestic services usually feature one or two classes.
[b] Avis and Hertz offer seven classes based on size and luxury, plus several special vehicle types

- **British Airways.** A comprehensive example of strong sub-branding of service tiers in the airline industry comes from British Airways (BA), which offers a number of distinct air travel products: First (deluxe service), Club Europe (business class for flights within Europe), Club World (business class for longer international flights), Club World London City (business class for flights between London City and New York JFK), World Traveller Plus (premium economy class), World Traveller (economy class on longer international flights); Euro Traveller (economy class on flights within Europe), and UK Domestic (economy class on flights within the UK). Each BA sub-brand represents a specific service concept and a set of clearly stated product specifications for preflight, in-flight, and on-arrival service elements. To provide additional focus on product, pricing, and marketing communications, the responsibility for managing and developing each service is assigned to separate management teams. Through internal training and external communications, staff and passengers alike are kept informed of the characteristics of each service. Except for the UK Domestic, most aircrafts in BA's fleet are configured in several classes. For instance, the airline's intercontinental fleet of Boeing 777-300s is equipped to serve First, Club World, World Traveller Plus, and World Traveller passengers.

  On any given route, all passengers traveling on a particular flight receive the same core product — say, a 10-hour journey from Los Angeles to London — but the nature and extent of most of the supplementary elements both on the ground and in the air can differ widely. Passengers in Club World, for instance, not only benefit from better tangible elements, they also receive more personalized service from airline employees and benefit from faster service on the ground at check-in, passport control in London (special lines), and baggage retrieval (priority handling). First class passengers are even more pampered[15].

- **Sun's Hardware and Software Support.** Sun, a brand of Oracle, is an example of branding different tiers in a high-tech, B2B product line. The company offers a full range of hardware and software support in a program branded as "SunSpectrum Support"[16]. Four different levels of support are available, sub-branded from platinum to bronze. The objective is to give buyers the flexibility to choose a level of support consistent with their own organization's needs (and willingness to pay), ranging from expensive, mission-critical support at the enterprise level (Platinum Service Plan) to relatively inexpensive assistance with self-service maintenance support (Bronze Service Plan):
  - Platinum: Mission-critical support with onsite service 24/7 and a two-hour response time.
  - Gold: Business critical support with onsite service from Monday to Friday, 8 a.m. to 8 p.m., telephone service 24/7 and a four-hour response time.
  - Silver: Basic support with on-site service from Monday to Friday, 8 a.m. to 5 p.m., telephone service from Monday to Friday, 8 a.m. to 8 p.m., and a four-hour response time.
  - Bronze: Self-support with phone service 8 a.m. to 5 p.m.

BUILDING BRAND EQUITY

→ **LO 8**
Discuss how firms can build brand equity.

To build a strong brand, we need to understand what contributes to brand equity. Brand equity is the value premium that comes with a brand. It is what customers are willing to pay for the service, beyond what they are willing to pay for a similar service that has no brand. *Figure 4.21* shows the following six key components:

1. **Company's presented brand** — mainly through advertising, service facilities and personnel.

2. **External brand communications** — from word of mouth and publicity. These are outside of the firm's control.

3. **Customer experience with the company** — what the customer has gone through when they patronized the company.

4. **Brand awareness** — the ability to recognize and recall a brand when provided with a cue.

5. **Brand meaning** — what comes to the customer's mind when a brand is mentioned.

6. **Brand equity** — the degree of marketing advantage that a brand has over its competitors.

From *Figure 4.20*, we can see that a company's marketing and external communications help to build brand awareness. However, it is the customer's actual experience with the brand, or the "moments of truth", which are more powerful in building brand equity. Firms need to focus on customers, deliver great experiences, and create an emotional connection with their customers. We discuss how they can do that next.

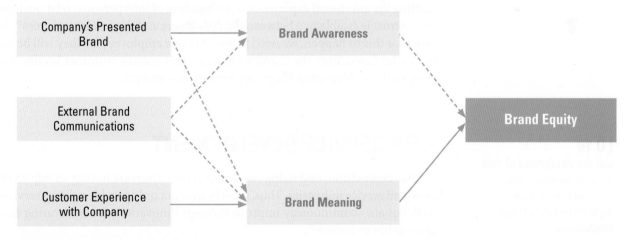

Figure 4.20 A service-branding model

Source
Adapted from Leonard L. Berry, "Cultivating Service Brand Equity," *Journal of the Academy of Marketing Science*, Vol. 28, No. 1, pp. 128–137.

Legend:
——————▸ strong relationships
- - - - - -▸ weaker relationships

LO 9

Understand what is required to deliver a branded service experience.

DELIVERING BRANDED SERVICE EXPERIENCES

Around the world, many financial service firms continue to create and register brand names to distinguish the different accounts and service packages that they offer. Their objective is to transform a series of service elements and processes into a consistent and recognizable service experience, offering a definable and predictable output at a specified price. Unfortunately, there is often little discernible difference — other than the name — between one bank's branded offering and another's, and their value proposition may be unclear. Don Shultz emphasizes: "The brand promise or value proposition is not a tagline, an icon, or a color or a graphic element, although all of these may contribute. It is, instead, the heart and soul of the brand…"[17].

An important role for service marketers is to become brand champions, familiar with and responsible for shaping every aspect of the customer's experience. We can relate the notion of a branded service experience to the "Flower of Service" metaphor by emphasizing the need for consistency in the color and the texture of each petal. Unfortunately, many service experiences remain very haphazard and create the impression of a flower stitched together with petals drawn from many different plants! We will return to a discussion of branding in the context of marketing communications strategy in Chapter 7.

Besides designing great service products and giving them a brand name, how else can we deliver branded service experiences[18]? It starts with aligning the service product and brand with its delivery process, servicescape, and people with the brand proposition. To start off, we need to have great processes in place (see Chapter 8 — Developing Service Processes). Next, creating the emotional experience can be done effectively through the servicescape, (which we will learn in Chapter 10 — Crafting the Service Environment). The hardest part of crafting the emotional experience is the building of interpersonal relationships, where trust is established between the consumers and the firm's employees[19]. In order for this to happen, we need to invest in our employees for they will be the ones who can deliver the brand experience that creates customer loyalty (see Chapter 11 — Managing People for Service Advantage).

LO 10

List the categories of new service development, ranging from simple style changes to major innovations.

NEW SERVICE DEVELOPMENT

Intense competition and rising consumer expectations are having an impact on nearly all service industries. Thus, great brands not only provide existing services well, but also continuously improve through innovation and by creating new approaches to service[20].

A Hierarchy of New Service Categories

There are many ways for a service provider to innovate. Below, we identify seven categories of new services, ranging from simple style changes to major innovations.

1. **Style changes** represent the simplest type of innovation, typically involving no changes in either processes or performance. However they often are highly visible, create excitement, and may serve to motivate employees. Examples include redesigning retail branches, websites or new uniforms for service employees.

2. **Service improvements** are the most common type of innovation. They involve small changes in the performance of current products, including improvements to either the core product or to existing supplementary services. Often, it is the little things that matter and customers appreciate it. For example, the Lydmar hotel in Stockholm has a series of buttons where passengers can choose their music from a choice of garage, funk, and rhythm and blues. This is just a simple improvement that can add to a customer's experience as it is unique and surprising[21].

3. **Supplementary service innovations** take the form of adding new facilitating or enhancing service elements to an existing core service or significantly improving an existing supplementary service. Low-tech innovations for an existing service can be as simple as adding parking at a retail site or agreeing to accept payment via smartphone for payment.

4. **Process line extensions** often represent distinctive new ways of delivering existing products. The intention is to offer more convenience and a different experience for existing customers, or attract new customers who find the traditional approach unappealing. Often, they involve adding a lower-contact distribution channel to an existing high-contact one, such as having self-service to complement delivery by service employees, or creating online or app-based service delivery.

5. **Product line extensions** are additions to a company's current product lines. The first company in a market to offer such a product may be seen as an innovator. The others are merely followers, often to defend themselves. These new services may be targeted at existing customers to serve a broader variety of needs or are designed to attract new customers with different needs, or both. For example, a restaurant may extend the product line to offer dog lovers a menu as well, so both the owners and their dogs are able to dine in the same restaurant.

6. **Major process innovations** consist of using new processes to deliver existing core products in new ways with additional benefits. For example, online courses are transforming higher education by using cutting edge technology, the Internet and smart devices. Sebastian Thrun, while still a tenured professor at Stanford University, launched for-profit educational organization Udacity in 2012, while Andrew Ng and Daphne Koller, also from Stanford, launched Coursera, a non-profit competitor using massive open online courses (MOOCS) to completely redesign education (*Figure 4.21*).

Major redesign was required to make online courses effective and successful, and today, these courses take full advantage of the interactivity of online, video, short assessment tasks, simulations, and discussion forums. Students can watch and do any part of a course as often as they want until they internalize the content. According to Salman Khan, founder of Khan Academy and former hedge fund analyst, "If people are meeting, they don't need a lecture; if you don't need them to interact, information should just be in a video or a memo"[22]. Sebastian Thrun also predicts that in 50 years, there will be only 10 universities left in the world. If not quite on that scale, online education will clearly mean upheaval for universities around the world, and for students, education will be transformed[23].

Figure 4.21 Online courses and MOOCS are transforming education.

7. **Major service innovations** are new core products for markets that have not been previously defined. They usually include both new service characteristics and radical new processes. For example, Amazon diversified into providing on-demand computing power and became a leader in cloud computing services. Other examples are Virgin Galactic and XCOR Aerospace, hoping to create demand for suborbital space tourism. Space Adventures, a leading company in the spaceflight industry, flew the first space tourist on the Russian Soyuz spacecraft to the International Space Station in 2001. Today, they provide different space experiences, including lunar missions, orbital space flights, suborbital space flights, and a spacewalk program (*Figure 4.22*). These experiences do not come cheap. Suborbital space flights for example, start from over $100,000 and the lunar mission costs $100 million per seat [24].

Major service innovations are relatively rare. More common is the use of new technologies to deliver existing services in new ways, enhancing or creating new supplementary services, and greatly improving performance on existing ones through process redesign. However, technology is improving so fast that we will see major service innovations as is discussed in *Service Insights 4.1*.

⟳ **LO 11**
Describe how firms can achieve success in new service development.

ACHIEVING SUCCESS IN NEW SERVICE DEVELOPMENT

Consumer goods have high failure rates, with more than 90% of the 30,000 new products introduced each year ending in failure [25]. Services are not immune to the high failure rates either. For example, Delta Airlines was one of several major carriers attempting to launch a separate low-cost carrier designed to compete with discount airlines such as Jet Blue and Southwest Airlines. However, none of these operations were successful. In banking, many banks have tried to sell insurance products in the hopes of increasing the number of profitable relationships with existing customers, but many of these product extensions also failed.

There are various reasons for failure, including not meeting a consumer need, inability to cover costs from revenues, and poor execution. For example, a study in the restaurant business found a failure rate of about 26% during the first year rising to close to 60% within three years [26]. How then can we successfully develop new services? A number of studies have found that the following three factors contribute most to success [27]:

1. **Market synergy** — The new product fits well with the existing image of the firm, its expertise, and resources; it is better than competing products in terms of meeting customers' needs, as the firm has a good understanding of its customers' purchase behavior and receives strong support during and after the launch from the firm and its branches.

2. **Organizational factors** — There are strong inter-functional cooperation and coordination. Development personnel need to be fully aware of why they are involved and of the importance of new products to the company. Before the launch, staff must understand the new product and its underlying processes, as well as details about direct competitors.

3. **Market research factors** — Detailed and scientifically designed market research studies are conducted early in the development process with a clear idea of the type of information to be obtained. A good definition of the product concept is developed before undertaking field surveys.

This research supports the notion that a highly structured development process increases the chances of success for a complex service innovation. However, it is worth noting that there are limits to the degree of structure that can and should be imposed. Swedish researchers Bo Edwardsson, Lars Haglund, and Jan Mattson reviewed new service development in telecommunications, transport, and financial services and concluded that:

> [C]omplex processes like the development of new services cannot be formally planned altogether. Creativity and innovation cannot only rely on planning and control. There must be some elements of improvisation, anarchy, and internal competition in the development of new services... We believe that a contingency approach is needed and that creativity on the one hand and formal planning and control on the other can be balanced, with successful new services as the outcome.[28]

An important conclusion from subsequent research in Sweden concerns the role of customers in service innovation. Researchers found that in the idea-generation stage, the nature of submitted ideas differed significantly depending on whether they were created by professional service developers or by the users themselves. Users' ideas were judged to be more original and to have a higher perceived value for customers. However, on average, these ideas were harder to convert into commercial services[29]. The emergence of crowds as innovation partners provides additional exciting opportunities for cost-effective innovation that can lead to breakthroughs in new service development[30]. We will discuss the role of customer feedback in improving and developing (new) services in more detail in Chapter 8 on process design, and Chapter 14 on improving service quality and productivity.

Figure 4.22
Spacewalk program offered by Space Adventures

SERVICE INSIGHTS 4.1

Major Service Innovation Enables by Technology

Digital startups are bubbling up in an astonishing variety of services, penetrating every nook and cranny of our economies. They are reshaping entire industries and according to Marc Andreessen, a Silicon Valley venture capitalist, "Software is eating the world". Just think of recent successes such as Uber's taxi, private car and rideshare service (www.uber.com), or Airbnb's platform that lets people rent out their homes for holidays and short-term stays (www.airbnb.com). This digital frenzy has given rise to a global movement, with most big cities, from London to Berlin and Singapore to Shanghai, having sizeable startup ecosystems. Between them they have hundreds of startup schools (i.e., "accelerators") and thousands of co-working spaces where caffeinated folk in their 20s and 30s toil hunched over their laptops. All these ecosystems are highly interconnected, making them a global crowd. They travel from city to city, and a few of them spend a semester with "Unreasonable at Sea," an accelerator on a ship which cruises the world while its passengers work on their business models and write code. "Anyone who writes code can become an entrepreneur — anywhere in the world," says Simon Levene, a venture capitalist in London.

Today's entrepreneurial boom is based on solid foundations which makes it likely to continue for the foreseeable future. The basic building blocks for digital services or, in the words of Josh Lerner of Harvard Business School, "the technologies for startup production" have become so evolved, cheap and ubiquitous that they can be easily combined, build upon and reconfigured. These building blocks include snippets of code that can be copied free from the Internet, easy-to-learn programming frameworks (e.g., Ruby on Rails), services for finding developers (eLance, oDesk), sharing code (GitHub) and testing usability (UserTesting.com), and application programming interfaces (APIs). Others include services that can be used as inputs such as voice calls (Twilio), maps (Google), and payments (PayPal). Probably the most important are platform services that can host startup's services (e.g., Amazon's cloud computing), distribute them (app

© HUIS TEN BOSCH/J-17116

Figure 4.23 Robots serve guests at Henn-na Hotel, Japan

stores by Apple, Samsung or Google), and market them (Facebook, Twitter, and LinkedIn).

Thanks to the Internet, even information on how to do a startup has become easily accessible. Global standards are emerging for all things related to startups, from term sheets for investments to business plans.

Innovation does not stop at the virtual world. Hardware, from processors to cameras to sensors, is getting better, smaller, and cheaper! Technologies such as robots, drones, wearable computers and sensors, self-driving cars, virtual reality, speech recognition, biometrics, artificial intelligence, and the Internet of things will bring opportunities for a wide range of service innovations that will dramatically improve the customer experience, service quality, and productivity.

For example, the Henn-na Hotel in Nagasaki, Japan is run by robots. It aims to have 90% of hotel services provided by robots (*Figure 4.23*), including porter service, room cleaning, front desk, and other services to reduce costs and ensure comfort. Many other processes were also redesigned such as using facial recognition to give access to the hotel, rooms, and other facilities, effectively replacing cumbersome room card systems.

Source

The Economist, "A Cambrian Moment," January 18, 2014, p. 4; *The Economist*, "The Third Great Wave," October 4, 2014, p. 3. *Mail Online*, "Japan Opens Hotel Run by Robots that Will Welcome Guests, Carry Bags and Even Clean Your Room," http://www.dailymail.co.uk/sciencetech/article-2946103/FAULTY-towers-Japan-opens-hotel-multi-lingual-ROBOTS-welcome-guests-carry-bags-clean-room.html, accessed February 17, 2015.

CONCLUSION

A service product comprises all the elements of the service performance that create value for the customer, and it consists of a core product bundled with a variety of supplementary service elements and their delivery processes. In mature industries where the core service tends to become commoditized, the search for competitive advantage often centers on creating new supplementary services or significantly improving the performance on existing ones. Another important differentiator can be the way the product is delivered, that is, the service delivery processes. It is not the outcome of a service delivery, but the way this outcome is achieved that often differentiates one service provider from another.

Designing a service product is a complex task that requires an understanding of how the core and supplementary services should be combined, sequenced, delivered, and branded to create a value proposition that meets the needs of target market segments. To do this, we discussed the "Flower of Service", branding strategies, and new service development as key tools for product development.

CHAPTER SUMMARY

LO 1 A service product consists of three components:
- Core product delivers the principle benefits and solutions customers seek.
- Supplementary services facilitate and enhance the core product.
- Delivery processes determine how the core and supplementary service elements are being delivered to the customer.

LO 2 The Flower of Service consists of two components:
- Core product delivers the main benefits and solutions customers look for.
- Supplementary services facilitate and enhance the value of the core product.

The core product often becomes commoditized, and supplementary services can then play an important role in differentiating and positioning the core product.

LO 3 The Flower of Service concept categorizes supplementary services into facilitating and enhancing supplementary services:
- Facilitating supplementary services such as information, order-taking, billing, and payment are needed for service delivery or they help in the use of the core product.

LO 4 Enhancing supplementary services add value for the customer. They include consultation, hospitality, safekeeping, and dealing with exceptions.

LO 5 Branding can be used at both the corporate and individual service level:
- The corporate brand is not only easily recognized but also has meaning for the customer by representing a particular way of doing business.
- Branding of individual service products helps firms to differentiate one bundle of output from another. Most service firms offer a line of products, with each one having a different combination of service attributes and their respective performance levels. Branding of individual service products is used to increase the tangibility of the service offering and value proposition.

LO 6 Firms can use a variety of branding strategies, including:
- **Branded house:** applying a brand to multiple, often unrelated services (e.g., Virgin Group).
- **Sub-brands:** using a master brand (often the firm name) together with a specific service brand (e.g., FedEx Ground service).
- **Endorsed brands:** the product brand dominates but the corporate brand is still featured (e.g., Starwood Hotels & Resorts).
- **House of brands:** individual services are promoted under their own brand name without the corporate brand (e.g., KFC of Yum! Brands).

LO 7 In many industries, branding is not only used to differentiate core services, it also differentiates service levels, called service tiering. There are some industries where service tiering is common and they include hotels, airlines, car rentals, and credit cards.

LO 8 Branding is not just about applying distinctive brand names and market communications:
- Rather, a service firm's presented brand (e.g., through advertising, facilities, and service employees) is more effective in building brand awareness rather than brand equity.
- Ultimately, it is the customer's service experience with the brand (i.e., the "moments of truth") that is more powerful in building brand equity. To build great brands, firms need to align processes, servicescapes, and people with its brand positioning.

LO 9 A branded service experience transforms a series of service elements and processes into a consistent and recognizable service experience. It aligns the service product and brand with its delivery process, servicescape and people with the brand proposition.

LO 10 Firms need to improve and develop new services to maintain a competitive edge. The seven levels in the hierarchy of new service development are:
- **Style changes**: highly visible, create excitement (e.g., repainting retail branches and vehicles in a new color scheme), but typically do not involve changes in service performance or processes.
- **Service improvements**: involve modest changes in the performance of current products.
- **Supplementary service innovations**: significantly improving or adding new facilitating or enhancing service elements.
- **Process line extensions**: new ways of delivering existing services products, such as creating self-service options.

- **Product line extensions**: adding new services that typically deliver the same core service but are specified to satisfy different needs.
- **Major process innovations**: using new processes to deliver current products, such as adding online courses to traditional class-room delivered lectures.
- **Major service innovations**: development of new core products for markets that have not been previously defined. Major service innovations are relatively rare. More common is the use of new technologies to deliver existing services in new ways, enhancing or creating new supplementary services, and greatly improving performance on existing ones through process redesign.

However, digital startups, quickly improving hardware (from processors to cameras to sensors), and new technologies such as robots, self-driving cars, virtual reality, speech recognition, artificial intelligence, and the Internet of things, bring opportunities for service innovations that will dramatically improve the customer experience, service quality, and productivity.

LO 11 Key factors that enhance the chances of success in new service development can be described as:
- **Market synergy**: the new product fits well with the firm's existing image, expertise, and resources, is better at meeting customers' needs over competing services, and receives strong support during and after the launch from the firm and its branches.
- **Organizational factors**: strong cooperation between the different functional areas in a firm, staff are aware of the importance of the new products in the company, and understand the new product and its underlying processes.
- **Market research**: customer ideas and research are already incorporated early in the new service design process. There is a clear idea of the type of information to be obtained. A good definition of the product concept is developed before undertaking field surveys.

Review Questions

1. Explain what is meant by core product and supplementary services.

2. Explain the Flower of Service concept and identify each of its petals. What insights does this concept provide for service marketers?

3. What is the difference between enhancing and facilitating supplementary services? Give several examples of each, relative to services you have used recently.

4. How is branding used in services marketing? What is the distinction between a corporate brand such as Marriott and the names of its various inn and hotel chains?

5. How can service firms build brand equity?

6. What is meant by using brands to tier service products?

7. What are the approaches firms can take to create new services?

8. Why do new services often fail? What factors are associated with successful development of new services?

Application Exercises

1. Select a specific service product you are familiar with and identify its core product and supplementary services. Then, select a competing service and analyze the differences in terms of core product and supplementary services between the two services.

2. Identify two examples of branding in financial services (e.g., specific types of retail bank accounts or insurance policies), and define their characteristics. How meaningful are these brands likely to be to customers?

3. Select a service firm you believe is highly successful and has strong brand equity. Conduct a few interviews to find out how consumers experience its service. From the findings, identify the factors that helped that service firm to build strong brand equity.

4. Using a firm you are familiar with, analyze what opportunities it might have to create product line extensions for its current and/or new markets. What impact might these extensions have on its present services?

5. Identify two failed new service developments. Analyze the causes for their failure.

6. Select a service brand you consider to be outstanding. Explain why you think it is outstanding. Also explore any weaknesses of this brand. You should select an organization you are very familiar with.

Endnotes

1 Bruce Horovitz "Starbucks Aims Beyond Lattes to Extend Brand," *USA Today*, May 18, 2006; Youngme Moon and John Quelch, *Starbucks: Delivering Customer Service*, Harvard Business School, Case Series, 2003; Joseph A. Michelli, *The Starbucks Experience: 5 Principles for Turning Ordinary into Extraordinary* (New York: McGraw Hill, 2007). www.starbucks.com, accessed February 17, 2015.

2 If you want to build a nest egg, do have a look at ETFs as they tend to be an excellent financial product for this purpose for retail investors. According to Salim Ramji, a consultant at McKinsey: "If you were inventing the mutual fund industry today, it would look like this [ETFs]." "Exchange-traded Funds: From Vanilla to Rocky Road", *The Economist*, February 25, 2012; https://investor.vanguard.com and http://en.wikipedia.org/wiki/Exchange-traded_fund; accessed February 16, 2015.

   For an excellent overview for retail investors, see: Burton G. Malkiel, *A Random Walk Down Wall Street: The Time-Tested Strategy for Successful Investing,* 11th ed. (W. W. Norton & Company).

3 The notion of a core service enhanced by supplementary services was advanced by: Pierre Eiglier and Eric Langeard, "Services as Systems: Marketing Implications," in P. Eiglier, E. Langeard,

C.H. Lovelock, J.E.G. Bateson, and R.F. Young, eds. *Marketing Consumer Services: New Insights,* ed. P. Eiglier, E. Langeard, C.H. Lovelock, J.E.G. Bateson, and R.F. Young (Cambridge, MA: Marketing Science Institute, 1977), pp. 83–103. Note: An earlier version of this article was published in French in *Révue Française de Gestion*, March–April, 1977, pp. 72–84; G. Lynn Shostack (1977), "Breaking Free from Product Marketing," *Journal of Marketing,* Vol. 44, April, pp. 73–80; Christian Grönroos, *Service Management and Marketing* (Lexington, MA: Lexington Books, 1990), p. 74.

4 The "Flower of Service" concept was first introduced in Christopher H. Lovelock, "Cultivating the Flower of Service: New Ways of Looking at Core and Supplementary Services," in P. Eiglier and E. Langeard, eds. *Marketing, Operations, and Human Resources: Insights into Services* (Aix-en-Provence, France: IAE, Université d'Aix-Marseille III, 1992), pp. 296–316.

5 Loizos Heracleous and Jochen Wirtz (2010), "Singapore Airlines' Balancing Act — Asia's Premier Carrier Successfully Executes a Dual Strategy: It Offers World-class Service and Is a Cost Leader," *Harvard Business Review*, Vol. 88, No. 7/8, pp. 145–149; Loizos Heracleous and Jochen Wirtz (2014), "Singapore Airlines: Achieving Sustainable Advantage Through Paradox," *The Journal of Applied Behavioral Science*, Vol. 50, No. 2, pp. 150–170.

6   Jochen Wirtz and May O. Lwin (2009), "Regulatory Focus Theory, Trust and Privacy Concern," *Journal of Service Research*, Vol. 12, No. 2, 190–207; May O. Lwin, Jochen Wirtz, and Jerome D. Williams (2007), "Consumer Online Privacy Concerns and Responses: A Power-Responsibility Equilibrium Perspective," *Journal of the Academy of Marketing Science*, Vol. 35, No. 4, pp. 572–585.

7   James C. Anderson and James A. Narus (1995), "Capturing the Value of Supplementary Services," *Harvard Business Review*, Vol. 73, January–February, pp. 75–83.

8   Leonard L. Berry (2000), "Cultivating Service Brand Equity," *Journal of the Academy of Marketing Science*, Vol. 28, No. 1, pp. 128–137.

9   See www.banyantree.com, accessed February 17, 2015.

10 James Devlin (2003), "Brand Architecture in Services: The Example of Retail Financial Services," *Journal of Marketing Management,* Vol. 19, pp. 1043–1065.

11 David Aaker and Erich Joachimsthaler (2000), "The Brand Relationship Spectrum: The Key to the Brand Challenge," *California Management Review*, Vol. 42, No. 4, pp. 8–23.

12 www.fedex.com, http://en.wikipedia.org/wiki/FedEx_Office, accessed February 17, 2015.

13 www.ihgplc.com, accessed February 17, 2015.

14 www.avis.com, accessed February 17, 2015.

15 www.britishairways.com, accessed February 17, 2015

16 http://www.sun.com/service/serviceplans/sunspectrum/index.jsp accessed May 7, 2009.

17 Don E. Shultz (2001), "Getting to the Heart of the Brand," *Marketing Management*, September–October, pp. 8–9.

18 For an excellent and detailed introduction to the development of customer experience strategies, see: Phillip Klaus (2014), *Measuring Customer Experience: How to Develop and Execute the Most Profitable Customer Experience Strategies.* Palgrave Macmillian.

For a review of experience marketing in general, see Bernd Schmitt (2010), "Experience Marketing: Concepts, Frameworks and Consumer Insights," *Foundations and Trends in Marketing*, Vol. 5, No. 2, pp. 55–112.

19 Sharon Morrison and Frederick G. Crane (2007), "Building the Service Brand by Creating and Managing an Emotional Brand Experience," *Brand Management*, Vol. 14, No. 5, pp. 410–421.

20 For an overview of service innovation research, see: Per Carlborg, Daniel Kindström, and Christian Kowalkowski (2014), "The Evolution of Service Innovation Research: A Critical Review and Synthesis," *The Service Industries Journal*, Vol. 34, No. 5, pp. 373–398.

For recent research on the impact of Internet- and people-enabled innovation on customer satisfaction and firm value, see: Thomas Dotzel, Venkatesh Shankar, and Leonard L. Berry (2013), "Service Innovativeness and Firm Value", *Journal of Marketing Research*, Vol. 50, April, pp. 259–276.

For research that integrated service innovation networks, organization- and customer co-creation, see: Luis Rubalcaba, Stefan Michel, Jon Sundbo, Stephen W. Brown, and Javier Reynoso (2012), "Shaping, Organizing, and Rethinking Service Innovation: A Multidimensional Framework," *Journal of Service Management*, Vol. 23, No. 5, pp. 696–715.

For research examining the integration of planning and innovation see: Jaakko Siltaloppi and Marja Toivonen (2015), "Integration of Planning and Execution in Service Innovation," *The Service Industries Journal*, Vol. 35, No. 2, pp. 197–216.

For research on the elements of service innovation that are classified along the three core innovation types of new service concepts, new service processes, and new service business models, see: Jung-Kuei Hsieh, Hung-Chang Chiu, Chih-Ping Wei, HsiuJu Rebecca Yen, and Yu-Chun Cheng (2013), "A Practical Perspective on the Classification of Service Innovations", *Journal of Services Marketing*, Vol. 27, No. 5, pp. 371–384.

21 Talk by Rory Sutherland: Sweat the Small Stuff, http://www.ted.com/talks/lang/eng/rory_sutherland_sweat_the_small_stuff.html, accessed February 17, 2015.

22 *Harvard Business Review*, "Life's Work, Salman Khan," 2014, Vol. 92, No. 1/2, p. 124.

23 *The Economist*, "Learning New Lessons: Online Courses are Transforming Higher Education, Creating New Opportunities for the Best and Huge Problems for the Rest," December 22, 2012, pp. 95–96.

24 http://en.wikipedia.org/wiki/Space_tourism and http://www.spaceadventures.com/, accessed February 17, 2015.

25 Clayton M. Christenson, Scott Cook, and Taddy Hall (2012), "Marketing Malpractice: The Cause and the Cure," *Harvard Business Review*, Vol. 83. No. 12, pp. 4–12.

26 H.G. Parsa, John T. Self, David Njite, and Tiffany King (2005), "Why Restaurants Fail," *Cornell Hotel and Restaurant Administration Quarterly*, Vol. 46, August, pp. 304–322.

27 Scott Edgett and Steven Parkinson (1994), "The Development of New Financial Services: Identifying Determinants of Success and Failure," *International Journal of Service Industry Management*, Vol. 5, No. 4, pp. 24–38; Christopher D. Storey and Christopher J. Easingwood (1993), "The Impact of the New Product Development Project on the Success of Financial Services," *Service Industries Journal*, Vol. 13, No. 3, July, pp. 40–54; Michael Ottenbacher, Juergen Gnoth, and Peter Jones (2006), "Identifying Determinants of Success in Development of New High-Contact Services," *International Journal of Service Industry Management*, Vol. 17, No. 4, pp. 344–363.

28 Bo Edvardsson, Lars Haglund, and Jan Mattsson (1995), "Analysis, Planning, Improvisation and Control in the Development of New Services," *International Journal of Service Industry Management,* Vol. 6, No. 2, pp. 24–35 (at page 34).

See also Bo Edvardsson and Jan Olsson (1996), "Key Concepts for New Service Development," *The Service Industries Journal,* Vol. 16, April, pp. 14–164.

29 Peter R. Magnusson, Jonas Matthing, and Per Kristensson (2003), "Managing User Involvement in Servive Innovation: Experiments with Innovating End Users," *Journal of Service Research*, Vol. 6, November, pp. 111–124; Jonas Matthing, Bodil Sandén, and Bo Edvardsson (2004), "New Service Development: Learning from and with Customers," *International Journal of Service Industry Management,* Vol. 15, No. 5, pp. 479–498.

30 Kevin J. Boudreau and Karim R. Lakhani (2013), "Using the Crowd as an Innovation Partner," *Harvard Business Review,* Vol. 91, No. 4, pp. 61–69.

Distributing Services Through Physical and Electronic Channels

Think globally, act locally.

John Naisbitt
American author of best-seller "Megatrends"

One thing we're not trying to drive is the proliferation of more and more apps... customers don't want that. We want to create that single platform that's device agnostic.

Simon Pomeroy
Chief Digital Officer, Westpac New Zealand Limited

LEARNING OBJECTIVES (LOs)

By the end of this chapter, the reader should be able to:

➲ **LO 1** Know the four key questions that form the foundation of any service distribution strategy: What, How, Where, and When.

➲ **LO 2** Describe the three interrelated flows that show **what** is being distributed.

➲ **LO 3** Be familiar with **how** services can be distributed using three main options, and understand the importance of distinguishing between distributing core and supplementary services.

➲ **LO 4** Recognize the issues of delivering services through electronic channels and discuss the factors that have fueled the growth of service delivery via cyberspace.

➲ **LO 5** Understand the determinants of customers' channel preferences.

➲ **LO 6** Know the importance of channel integration.

➲ **LO 7** Describe the **where** (place) decisions of physical channels and be familiar with the strategic and tactical location considerations.

➲ **LO 8** Describe the **when** (time) decisions of physical channels and the factors that determine extended operating hours..

➲ **LO 9** Understand the role, benefits, and costs of using intermediaries in distributing services.

➲ **LO 10** Know why franchising is a common way of delivering services to end users.

➲ **LO 11** Understand the challenges of distributing services in large domestic markets.

➲ **LO 12** Be familiar with the forces that drive service firms to go international.

➲ **LO 13** Appreciate the special challenges of distributing services internationally.

➲ **LO 14** Understand the key barriers to international trade in services.

➲ **LO 15** Explain the determinants of international market entry strategies.

OPENING VIGNETTE

Being Global in an Instant? …Or Does It Take Forever?

Some services spread like wildfire and at incredible speed. For example, Michelle Phan's YouTube channel became one of the world's most popular channels in less than 24 months when it went viral (*Figure 5.1*). Today, with over 1 billion views, Michelle Phan is widely known all around the world.[1] Likewise, diverse business models such as Airbnb, Uber, TripAdvisor, and Coursera went global within a few years.

Other services, however, may take decades to achieve global distribution. Think of how long it took Starbucks or supply chain solution providers such as FedEx or DHL to achieve a global presence! These contrasting examples show both the diversity of the service sector and the importance of differentiating information processing and people- or possession-processing services. Information-processing services can be distributed rapidly. People- or possession-processing services require development of facilities in every market where they want presence. There is also the need for the growing firm to deal with local labor, building, food hygiene regulations, and more. That requires a lot of finances and management time! Just think about all the decision that had to be made by Starbucks to make its service accessible around the world.

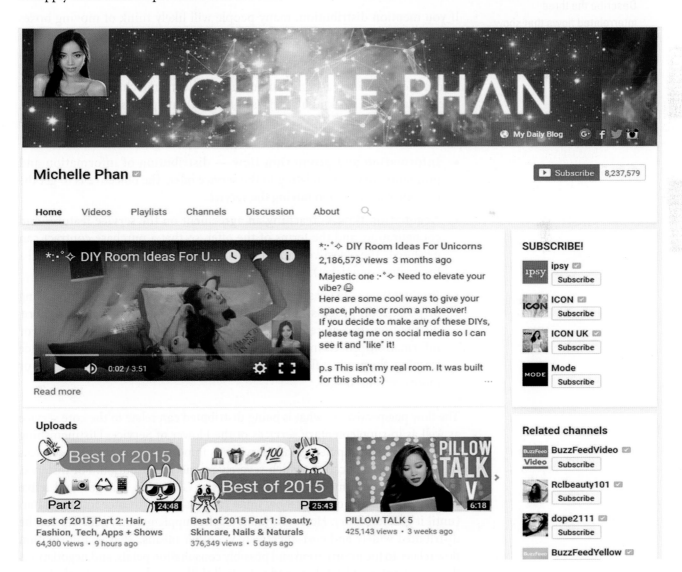

Figure 5.1 Michelle Phan's makeup videos on YouTube are viewed by millions of audiences globally

LO 1

Know the four key questions that form the foundation of any service distribution strategy: What, How, Where, and When.

DISTRIBUTION IN A SERVICES CONTEXT

What? How? Where? When? Responses to these four questions form the foundation of any service distribution strategy. They determine the customer's service experience, which is a function of how the different elements of the Flower of Service (Chapter 4) are distributed and delivered through physical and electronic channels. We summarize these questions in the Flow Model of Service Distribution in *Figure 5.2*. The "what" determines what exactly will flow through the distribution channel (i.e., information, negotiation, and the core and other supplementary services), and a distribution strategy needs to cover for each of these flows the remaining three questions of how, where and when. This model is the organizing framework for this chapter, and the following sections describe each of the components of this model.

LO 2

Describe the three interrelated flows that show **what** is being distributed.

WHAT IS BEING DISTRIBUTED?

If you mention distribution, many people will likely think of moving boxes through physical channels to distributors and retailers for sale to end-users. In services though, often there is nothing to move. Experiences, performances, and solutions are not physically shipped and stored. Meanwhile, informational transactions are increasingly conducted via electronic channels. How then does distribution work in a services context? In a typical service sales cycle, distribution embraces three interrelated flows, which partially address the question of *what* is being distributed:

- **Information and promotion flow** — distribution of information and promotion materials relating to the service offer. The objective is to get the customer interested in buying the service.

- **Negotiation flow** — reaching an agreement on the service features and configuration, and the terms of the offer, so that a purchase contract can be closed. The objective is often to sell the **right** to use a service (e.g., sell a reservation or a ticket).

- **Product flow** — many services, especially those involving people processing or possession processing, require physical facilities for delivery. Here, distribution strategy requires development of a network of local sites. For information-processing services, such as Internet banking and distance learning, the product flow can be via electronic channels, employing one or more centralized sites.

The flow perspective on what is being distributed can relate to the core service as well as to supplementary services of the Flower of Service. Distinguishing between core and supplementary services is important, as many core services require a physical location, which severely restricts distribution. For instance, you can only consume Club Med holidays at Club Med Villages, and a live performance of a Broadway show must take place at a theater in Manhattan (until it goes on tour). However, many of the supplementary services can be distributed widely and cost-effectively via other means. That is, information flow relates to the information and possibly consultation petals, and negotiations flow is present in order-taking and potentially billing and payment petals. In our example, prospective Club Med customers can get information and consultation from a travel agent, either face-to-face, online, by phone, or by email, and then

Key questions for designing an effective service distribution strategy:

What	**How**	**Where**	**When**
"What flows through the channel?"	"How should service reach the customer?"	"Where should service be delivered?"	"When should service be delivered?"

What
"What flows through the channel?"

- Information & promotion flow (e.g., promotional materials)
- Negotiation flow (e.g., make a reservation or sell a ticket)
- Product flow (e.g., core & remaining supplementary services)*

How
"How should service reach the customer?"

- Customers visit the service site
- Service providers go to their customers
- Transaction is conducted remotely (e.g., via the Internet, telephone, mail, and email)
- Channel integration is key

Where
"Where should service be delivered?"

- Strategic location considerations (e.g., customer needs and type of service)
- Tactical considerations (i.e., specific location characteristics)
- Location constraints (e.g., due to required economies of scale)

When
"When should service be delivered?"

- Customer needs
- Economics of incremental opening hours (fixed vs. variable costs)
- Availability of labor
- Use of self-service facilities

Intermediaries
"What tasks should be delegated to intermediaries?"

- Roles
- Benefits
- Costs (e.g., of franchisees, agents, and distributors)

Distributing Service Internationally
"How should the service be distributed?"

- Export the service concept
- Import customers /possessions
- Deliver remotely

Entering International Markets
"How can the value-add be protected?"

- Export the service
- Licensing, franchising, joint venture
- Foreign direct investment

Note that information and negotiations are types of supplementary services, but were listed separately here to emphasize their importance in any service distribution strategy.

Figure 5.2 The Flow Model of Service Distribution

make a booking through one of these same channels. Similarly, you can purchase theater tickets through an agency without the need for an advance trip to the physical facility itself.

⊃ **LO 3**

Be familiar with **how** services can be distributed using three main options, and understand the importance of distinguishing between distributing core and supplementary services.

HOW SHOULD A SERVICE BE DISTRIBUTED?

How should services be distributed? Here, a key question is: Does the service or the firm's positioning strategy require customers to be in direct physical contact with its personnel, equipment, and facilities? (As we saw in Chapter 1, this is unavoidable for people-processing services, but may not be necessary for other categories.) If so, do customers have to visit the facilities of the service organization, or will the service organization send personnel and equipment to customers' own sites? Alternatively, can transactions between provider and customer be completed at arm's length through the use of either telecommunications or physical channels of distribution? (The three possible options are shown in the first column of *Table 5.1*.) For each of these three options, should the firm maintain just a single outlet or offer to serve customers through multiple outlets at different locations?

Table 5.1 Six Options for Service Delivery

Nature of Interaction Between Customer and Service Organization	Availability of Service Outlets	
	Single Site	Multiple Sites
Customer goes to service organization	Theater Car service workshop	Café house chain Car rental chain
Service organization comes to customer	House painting Mobile car wash	Mail delivery Auto club road service
Customer and service organization transact remotely (mail or electronic communication)	Credit card company Local TV station	Broadcast network Telephone company

Customers Visit the Service Site

When customers have to visit the service site, key factors that need to be considered include costs (e.g., rental), customer catchment areas, and the convenience of service outlet locations for customer. Elaborate statistical analysis including retail gravity models are used to help firms make decisions on where to locate supermarkets or similar large stores, relative to the homes and workplaces of future customers.

Service Providers Go to Their Customers

For some types of services, the service provider visits the customer. Compass Group, the largest food service organization in the United Kingdom and Ireland, provides catering and support services to over 8,500 locations in 50 countries with over 500,000 employees. They must visit the customer's site, because the need is location-specific. When should service providers go to their customers?

- Going to the customer's site is unavoidable whenever the object of the service is some immovable physical item, such as a tree to be pruned (*Figure 5.3*), installed machinery to be repaired, or a house that requires pest control treatment.

- There may be a profitable niche in serving individuals who are willing to pay a premium for the convenience of receiving personal visits or home delivery. Think of Domino's Pizza's delivery service, or Starbucks which only started in 2015 to offer delivery to office buildings. The service was launched in Manhattan and Seattle, with workers in the Empire State Building being the first who were able to enjoy the convenience of having their favorite Espresso Frappuccino blended coffee and other energy boosters delivered directly to their desks.

Figure 5.3 Tree pruning is a service that has to be provided onsite

Another example is a young veterinary doctor who has built her business around house calls to care for sick pets. She found that customers are glad to pay extra for service that not only saves them time, but is less stressful for their pets, compared to waiting in a crowded veterinary clinic, full of other animals and their worried owners. Other consumer services of this kind include mobile car-washing, office and in-home catering, and made-to-measure tailoring services for business people.

- In remote areas like Alaska or Canada's Northwest Territory, service providers often fly to visit their customers, because the latter find it so difficult to travel. Australia is famous for its Royal Flying Doctor Service, in which physicians fly to make house calls at farms and sheep stations in the outback.

  - In general, service providers are more likely to visit corporate customers at their premises than individuals in their homes, reflecting the larger volume associated with business-to-business transactions.

A growing service activity involves the rental of both equipment and labor at the customer's site for special occasions or in response to customers who need to expand their capacity during busy periods. *Service Insights 5.1* describes the B2B services of Aggreko, an international company that rents generating and cooling equipment around the world.

SERVICE INSIGHTS 5.1
Power and Temperature Control for Rent

You probably think of electricity as coming from a distant power station, and air conditioning and heating as fixed installations. So how would you deal with the following challenges?

- At the 2014 FIFA World Cup in Brazil, they needed temporary power to support the broadcasting of the 64 matches in 12 host cities to over three billion people worldwide.
- A tropical cyclone has devastated the small mining town of Pannawonica in Western Australia, destroying everything in its path, including power lines, and electrical power must be restored as soon as possible so that the town and its infrastructure can be rebuilt.

- In Amsterdam, organizers of the World Championship Indoor Windsurfing competition need to power 27 wind turbines that will be installed along the length of a huge indoor pool to create winds of 20–30 miles per hour (32–48 kilometers per hour).
- A US Navy submarine needs a shore-based source of power when it is docked at a remote Norwegian port.
- Sri Lanka faces a great shortage of electricity-generating capability after water levels fall dangerously low at major hydroelectric dams due to insufficient monsoon rains for two years in a row.

- Hotels in Florida need to be dried out following water damage from a hurricane.
- A large, power-generating plant in Oklahoma urgently seeks temporary capacity to replace one of its cooling towers, destroyed in a tornado the previous day.
- The Caribbean island of Bonaire requires a temporary power station to stabilize its grid after a fire damages the main power plant and results in widespread blackouts.

These are all challenges that were faced by a company called Aggreko, which describes itself as "The World Leader in Temporary Utility Rental Solutions". Aggreko serves customers around the world and generated $2.4 billion in revenue. It rents a "fleet" of mobile electricity generators, oil-free air compressors, and temperature control devices ranging from water chillers and industrial air conditioners, to giant heaters and dehumidifiers.

Aggreko's customer base is dominated by large companies and government agencies. Although much of its business comes from predicted needs, such as backup operations during planned factory maintenance or the filming of a James Bond movie, the firm is ready to resolve problems that arise unexpectedly from emergencies or natural disasters.

Much of the firm's rental equipment is contained in soundproofed, box-like structures that can be shipped anywhere in the world to create the specific type and level of electrical power output or climate-control capability required by the client. Consultation, installation, and ongoing technical support add value to the core service. Emphasis is placed on solving customer problems rather than just renting equipment. Some customers have a clear idea of their needs in advance, others require advice on how to develop innovative and cost-effective solutions to what may be unique problems, and still others are desperate to restore power that was lost because of an unexpected disaster. In the last-mentioned instance, speed is essential because downtime can be extremely expensive and lives may depend on the promptness of Aggreko's response.

Delivering service requires Aggreko to ship its equipment to the customer's site. Following the Pannawonica cyclone, Aggreko's West Australian team swung into action, rapidly setting up some 30 generators ranging from 60 to 750 kVA, as well as cabling, refueling tankers, and other equipment. The generators were transported by four "road trains," each comprising a giant tractor unit pulling three 40-foot (13-meter) trailers. Technicians and additional equipment were flown in on two Hercules aircraft. The Aggreko technicians remained on-site for six weeks, providing 24/7 service while the town was being rebuilt.

Courtesy of Aggreko plc. Unauthorized use not permitted.

Source

Aggreko's "International Magazine," 1997, www.aggreko.com and http://en.wikipedia.org/wiki/Aggreko, accessed February 21, 2015.

The Service Transaction Is Conducted Remotely

Developments in telecommunications, online technology, and sophisticated logistics solutions have spurred many new approaches to service delivery. A customer may never see the service facilities or meet service personnel face-to-face when dealing with a service firm through remote transactions. Service encounters with service personnel are more likely via a customer contact center, mail, email, chat, or Twitter, and should physical products, documents or other tangibles (e.g., credit cards or membership cards) need to reach a customer, logistics providers offer service firms integrated, reliable, and cost-effective solutions. Examples of service transactions at arm's length are as follows:

- Repair services for small pieces of equipment sometimes require customers to ship the product to a maintenance facility, where it is serviced and then returned by mail (with the option of paying extra for express shipment). Many service providers offer solutions with the help of integrated logistics firms such as FedEx, TNT, or UPS. These solutions range from the storage and express delivery of spare parts for aircraft (B2B delivery) to the pickup of defective cell phones from customers' homes and the return of the repaired phones to the customers (B2C pickup and delivery, also called "reverse logistics").

- Any information-based product can be delivered almost instantly through the Internet from almost any point on the globe to any smart device, phone, tablet, and their apps connected via high-speed Internet technology.

When you look at the eight petals of the Flower of Service, you can see that no fewer than five supplementary services are information based (*Figure 5.4*).

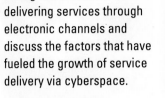

→ LO 4
Recognize the issues of delivering services through electronic channels and discuss the factors that have fueled the growth of service delivery via cyberspace.

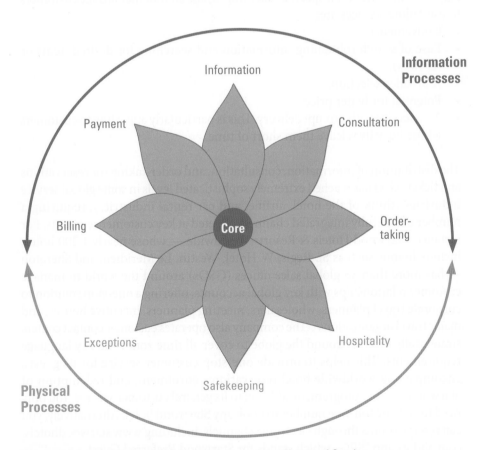

Figure 5.4 Information and physical processes of the Flower of Service

Figure 5.5 Many companies have moved their customers to online channels

Information, consultation, order-taking, billing, and payment (e.g., via credit card) can all be transmitted using online channels. Even service businesses that involve physical core products, such as retailing and repair, are shifting delivery of many supplementary services to the Internet, closing physical branches, and relying on speedy business logistics to enable a strategy of arm's-length transactions with their customers (*Figure 5.5*).

Web and app-delivered services are becoming increasingly sophisticated, but also more user-friendly. They often simulate the services of a well-informed sales assistant in steering customers toward items that are likely to be of interest. Some even provide the opportunity for "live" email or chat dialog with helpful customer service personnel. Facilitating searches is another useful service on many sites, ranging from browsing available books by a particular author, to finding flight schedules between two cities on a specific date. Important factors that attract customers to use online services are:

- Convenience.
- Ease of search (obtaining information and searching for desired items or services).
- A broader selection.
- Potential for better prices.
- 24/7 service with prompt delivery. This is particularly appealing to customers whose busy lives leave them short of time.

The distribution of information, consultation, and order-taking (or reservations and ticket sales) has reached extremely sophisticated levels in some global service industries (think of the hotel, airline, and car rental industries), requiring a number of carefully integrated channels targeted at key customer segments. For instance, Starwood Hotels & Resorts Worldwide — whose nearly 1,200 hotels include brands such as St. Regis, W Hotel, Westin, Le Méridien, and Sheraton — has more than 33 global sales offices (GSOs) around the world to manage customer relationships with key global accounts, offering a one-stop solution to corporate travel planners, wholesalers, meeting planners, incentive houses, and major travel organizations[2]. The company also operates customer contact centers strategically located around the globe to cover all time zones and key language requirements. This helps to provide one-stop customer service for its guests, encompassing worldwide hotel reservations, enrolment, and redemption of Starwood's loyalty program, in addition to its general customer service. You only need to call one toll-free number to book any Starwood hotel. Alternatively, you can reserve rooms through electronic channels, including www.starwoodhotels.com and its app "SPG", which stands for Starwood Preferred Guest.

Channel Preferences Vary Among Customers

The use of different channels to deliver the same service not only has vastly different cost implications for a service organization; it also drastically affects the nature of the service experience for the customer. Although electronic self-service channels tend to be the most cost-effective, not all customers like to use them. This means that if we want to migrate customers to new electronic channels, we may require different strategies for different segments[3]. We also need to recognize that some proportion of customers will never voluntarily change from their preferred high-contact delivery environments. Recent research has explored how customers choose among personal, impersonal, and self-service channels and has identified the following key drivers[4]:

- For complex and perceived high-risk services, people tend to rely on personal channels. For example, customers are happy to apply for credit cards using remote channels, but prefer a face-to-face transaction when obtaining a mortgage.

- Individuals with higher confidence and knowledge about a service and/or the channel are more likely to use impersonal and self-service channels (*Figure 5.6*).

- Customers who look for the functional aspects of a transaction prefer more convenience. This often means the use of impersonal and self-service channels. Customers with social motives tend to use personal channels.

- Convenience is a key driver of channel choice for the majority of consumers. Service convenience means saving time and effort rather than saving money. A customer's search for convenience is not just confined to the purchase of core products but also extends to convenient times and places. People want easy access to supplementary services too — especially information, reservations, and problem solving.

Figure 5.6 Frequent travelers are often willing to use self-check-ins so as to avoid queues

Channel Integration is Key

Singly or in combination, electronic channels offer a complement or alternative to traditional physical channels for delivering information-based services. However, channel integration is key for successfully delivering through multiple channels[5]. As consumers are using more devices while still using traditional channels (e.g., automated teller machines (ATMs), branches, and call centers), it is important for service organizations to deliver a seamless and consistent user experience across channels. New delivery channels have created an inconsistent and frequently disjointed experience for many customers.

Finally, service providers have to be careful when channels are priced differently. Increasingly, customers take advantage of price variation among channels and markets, a strategy known as channel arbitrage[6]. For example, customers can ask the expensive full-service broker for advice (and perhaps place a small order) and then conduct the bulk of their trades via the much lower-priced discount broker. Service providers need to develop effective pricing strategies that will enable them to deliver value and capture it through the appropriate channel.

LO 7

Describe the **where** (place) decisions of physical channels and be familiar with the strategic and tactical location considerations.

WHERE SHOULD A SERVICE FACILITY BE LOCATED?

Unless a service is delivered remotely, location decisions for physical sites have to be made.[7] A physical site location requires a sizable investment and a long-term commitment. Due to its fixed nature as a result of long leases and high investments into a site, a firm cannot easily move to another site or convert to another format. Even if sunk costs are written off, moving to another location causes the problem of a proportion of loyal customers and employees being lost; the farther the distance between the new and old locations, the bigger the loss.

How then should service managers make decisions on the places **where** service is delivered? Frequently, a two-step approach is used; first, strategic location considerations are developed to help identify the general types of location a service firm should aim for. Second, tactical considerations are used to choose between specific sites of a similar type that fit the overall location strategy.

Strategic Location Considerations

The site location is an integral part of the overall service strategy; it must be at a location that is consistent with its marketing strategy and target segments for an extended period of time. To develop a location strategy, start by understanding customer needs and expectations, competitive activity, and the nature of the service operation. As we noted earlier, the distribution strategies used for some of the supplementary service elements may differ from those used to deliver the core product itself. For instance, as a customer, you're probably willing to go to a particular location at a specific time to attend a sporting or entertainment event. But you probably want greater flexibility and convenience when reserving a seat in advance, so you may expect the reservations service to be open for extended hours, to offer booking and credit card payment by phone or the Internet (*Figure 5.7*), and to deliver tickets through postal or electronic channels.

Figure 5.7 Customers can opt to pay by phone or the Internet

Likewise, firms should make it easy for people to access frequently purchased services, especially those that face active competition[8]. Examples include retail banks and fast-food restaurants. However, customers may be willing to travel further from their homes or workplaces to reach specialty services (*Figure 5.8*).

In general, firms have to trade-off between ease of access and convenience for their customers versus the cost of providing that access and convenience! Markets can often be segmented by accessibility preferences and price sensitivity. There will always be segments that are willing to pay premium for ease of access and convenience (even if that applies only to certain consumption situations such as the occasional pizza TV dinner at home for home delivery services), and segments that are willing to travel and spend time for a lower price.

Tactical Location Considerations

In the second step for selecting a specific site, key factors that need to be considered include:

- Population size and characteristics (i.e., to assess the density and number of target customers that could be served with this site).

- Pedestrian and vehicular traffic and its characteristics (i.e., to assess the number of target customers passing a site that could be served with this outlet).

- Convenience of access for customers (e.g., public transportation, availability of parking).

- Competitors in this area.

- Nature of nearby businesses and stores.

- Availability of labor.

- Availability of site locations, rental costs, and contractual conditions (e.g., length of lease, legal restrictions) and regulations (e.g., on zoning and opening hours).

Elaborate statistical analyses and models are used to help firms make decisions on where to locate supermarkets or similar large stores, relative to the homes and workplaces of future customers. Geographic information system (GIS) tools combine maps with key location data, including population demographics, purchase data, and listing of current and proposed competitor locations. Mapping software can be accessed or leased for as little as $100 to several thousands of dollars. Have a look at the websites of a few of these vendors such as Autodesk (http://usa.autodesk.com) or Nielsen Site Reports (www. claritas.com/sitereports/default.jsp). These tools help firms to find locations with the most desirable attributes and derive the sales potential of these sites. For example, Starbucks uses GIS software as part of its site selection. Patrick O'Hagan, Starbucks' manager of global market planning, said:

Figure 5.8 Millions of people from around the world are willing to travel to Munich to experience the Oktoberfest

My team provides analytics, decision support, business intelligence, and geospatial intelligence to our real-estate partners... We need tools that provide decision support to answer critical questions — what's going on in this trade area; what are general retail trends in this area; where are competitors; who are those competitors; where is business generated; where's the highest traffic volume; where are people living; where are they working; and how are they travelling to work[9]?

Locational Constraints

Although customer convenience is important, the need for economies of scale and operational requirements may restrict choice of locations.

- Major hospitals offer many different healthcare services at a single location, requiring a very large facility. Customers requiring complex, in-patient treatment must go to the service factory rather than be treated at home. However, an ambulance — or even a helicopter — can be sent to pick them up. Medical specialists, as opposed to general practitioners, often find it convenient to locate their offices close to a hospital because it saves them time when they need to treat their patients.

- Airports, for instance, are often inconveniently located relative to travelers' homes, offices, or destinations. Because of noise and environmental factors, finding suitable sites for construction of new airports or expansion of existing ones is a very difficult task. A governor of Massachusetts was once asked what would be an acceptable location for a second airport to serve Boston; he thought for a moment and then responded, "Nebraska!" One way to make airport access more convenient is to install fast rail links, such as San Francisco's BART service (*Figure 5.9*), or London's Heathrow Express.

Innovative Location Strategies

Innovative distribution strategies can be at the core of powerful new service models. We highlight mini-stores and related location strategies, and locating in multi-purpose facilities in the following sections. What these strategies have in common is that accessibility is a key component of these services' value propositions.

Mini-stores. An interesting innovation among multi-site service businesses involves creating numerous small service factories to maximize geographic coverage. Examples include:

Figure 5.9 San Francisco's BART service helps passengers get to the city from the airport more conveniently

SFO BART station photo courtesy of Bay Area Rapid Transit District.

- Automated kiosks are one example. ATMs offer many of the functions of a bank branch within a self-service machine that can be located within stores, hospitals, colleges, airports, and office buildings. Automated vending machines for stamps purchase and payment of bills is another example (*Figure 5.10*).

- Another approach results from separating the front and back stages of the operation. Taco Bell's innovative K-Minus strategy involves restaurants without kitchens. Food preparation takes place in a central location. The meals are then shipped to restaurants (which can now devote more of their expensive floor area to customer use) and to other "points of access" (such as mobile food carts), where the food can be reheated before serving.

- Increasingly, firms offering one type of service business are purchasing space from another provider in a complementary field. Perhaps you've noticed small bank branches inside supermarkets, and food outlets such as Dunkin Donuts and Subway sharing space with a fast-food restaurant such as Burger King.

Figure 5.10 Automated kiosks selling stamps are a form of mini-store

Locating in Multi-Purpose Facilities. The most obvious locations for consumer services are close to where customers live or work. Modern buildings are often designed to be multi-purpose, featuring not only office or production space but also services such as a bank (or at least an ATM), a restaurant, a hair salon, several stores, and maybe a health club (*Figure 5.11*). Some companies even include a children's day-care facility to make life easier for busy working parents.

Entire new business models are based on co-location strategies. For example Walgreens, a US-pharmacy chain, is locating clinics increasingly in shopping malls vying to offer convenient and low(er) cost health services. Its clinics look like a doctor's office, but do not operate like one. Patients can check waiting times online before coming to the store, see a nurse for a diagnosis in a private room, and at kiosks, they use touch screens to pull up prescriptions and pay for them. The pharmacists devote their time to patients' questions, whereas pharmacy clerical work is done centrally elsewhere. Some doctors and their lobbyists huff that such clinics are doomed to provide substandard healthcare. However, there is little evidence of this — a study by the RAND Corporation found that retail clinics were less expensive for treating common health conditions, without any apparent loss in quality[10].

Figure 5.11 Many office buildings now include shops

Interest is growing in locating retail and other services on transportation routes and in bus, rail, and air terminals. Most major oil companies have developed chains of small retail stores to complement the fuel pumps at their service stations, thus offering customers the convenience of one-stop shopping for fuel, vehicle supplies, food, and a selection of basic household products. Truck stops on major highways often include laundry centers, restrooms, ATMs, Internet access, restaurants, and inexpensive accommodation in addition to a variety of vehicle maintenance and repair services. Airport terminals — designed as part of the infrastructure for air transportation services — have been transformed into vibrant shopping malls.

⊃ **LO 8**

Describe the **when** (time) decisions of physical channels and the factors that determine extended operating hours.

WHEN SHOULD SERVICE BE DELIVERED?

In the past, most retail and professional services in industrialized countries followed a traditional schedule of being available about 40 or 50 hours a week. In large measure, this routine reflected social norms (and even legal requirements or union agreements) as to what were appropriate hours for people to work and for enterprises to sell things. Historically, Sunday opening was strongly discouraged in most Christian cultures and was often prohibited by law, reflecting a long tradition based on religious practice. The situation inconvenienced working people who had to shop either during their lunch break or on Saturdays. Today, the situation has changed. For some highly responsive service operations, the standard has become 24/7 service — 24 hours a day, 7 days a week, around the world.

Key factors determining the opening hours of a service facility include customer needs and wants, and the economics of opening hours whereby the fixed costs of the facility and the variable costs of extending opening hours (including labor and energy costs) are weighted against the expected contribution generated from incremental sales and potential operational benefits (e.g., shifting demand from peak periods to extended opening hours). For a more detailed overview of the factors behind the move to more extended hours, see *Service Insights 5.2*.

Some firms, however, have resisted the trend to seven-day operations. Atlanta-based Chick-fil-A, a highly successful restaurant chain, declares that "being closed on Sunday is part of our value proposition" and claims that giving managers and crew a day off is a factor in the firm's extremely low turnover rate.

SERVICE INSIGHTS 5.2
Factors That Encourage Extended Operating Hours

There are at least five factors driving the move towards extended operating hours and seven-day operations. The trend that originated in the US and Canada has since spread to many other countries around the world.

- **Pressure from consumers.** The growing number of two-income families and single wage-earners who live alone need time outside normal working hours to shop and use other services. Other customers like to enjoy the convenience to go shopping and do their service transactions at any time of the day and the week. Once one store or firm in any given area extends its hours to meet the needs of these market segments, competitors often feel the need to follow. Chain stores have frequently led the way.

- **Changes in legislation.** Support has declined for the traditional religious view that a specific day (Sunday in predominantly Christian cultures) should be legalized as a day of rest for one and all, regardless of religious affiliation. In a multicultural society, of course, it's a moot point which day should be designated as special for observant Jews and Seventh Day Adventists, Saturday is the Sabbath; for Muslims, Friday is the holy day; and agnostics or atheists are presumably indifferent. There has been a gradual erosion of such legislation in Western nations in recent years.

- **Economic incentives to improve asset utilization.** A great deal of capital is often tied up in service facilities. The incremental cost of extending hours tends to be relatively modest, and if it reduces crowding and increases revenues, then it is economically attractive. There are costs involved in shutting down and reopening a facility such as a supermarket, yet climate control and some lighting must be left running all night, and security personnel must be paid 24/7. So, even if the number of extra customers served is minimal, there are both operational and marketing advantages to remaining open 24 hours.

- **Availability of employees to work during "unsocial" hours.** Changing lifestyles and a desire for part-time employment have created a growing labor pool of people who are willing to work evenings and nights. They include students looking for part-time work outside classroom hours, people working second jobs, parents juggling childcare responsibilities, and others who simply prefer to work at night and relax or sleep in the day.

- **Automated self-service facilities.** Self-service equipment has become increasingly reliable and user-friendly. Many machines now accept card- and cellphone-based payments, in addition to coins and banknotes. Therefore, installing unattended machines may be economically feasible alternative for locations that cannot support a staffed facility. Unless a machine requires frequent servicing or is particularly vulnerable to vandalism, the incremental cost of going from limited hours to 24-hour operation is minimal. In fact, it may be simpler to leave machines running continuously than to turn them on and off.

LO 9

Understand the role, benefits and costs of using intermediaries in distributing services.

THE ROLE OF INTERMEDIARIES

Having discussed **what** is being distributed and **how**, let's discuss *who* should be involved in delivering which parts of the service (i.e., information, negotiation, and the core and remaining supplementary services) to the customer. Should a service organization deliver all aspects of its service itself, or should it involve intermediaries to take on certain parts of service delivery? In practice, many service organizations find it cost-effective to outsource certain aspects of distribution. Most frequently, this delegation concerns supplementary service elements. For instance, despite their increased use of telephone call centers and the Internet, cruise lines and resort hotels still rely on travel agents to handle a significant portion of their customer interactions such as giving out information, taking reservations, accepting payment, and ticketing.

Benefits and Costs of Alternative Distribution Channels

How should a service provider work in partnership with one or more intermediaries to deliver a complete service package to customers? In *Figure 5.12*, we use the Flower of Service framework to show an example in which the core product and certain supplementary elements such as information, consultation, and exception are delivered by the original supplier. The delivery of other supplementary services is delegated to an intermediary to complete the offering as experienced by the customer. In other instances, several specialist outsourcers might be involved as intermediaries for specific elements. The challenge for the original supplier is to act as the guardian of the overall process, ensuring that each element offered by the intermediaries fits the overall service concept in order to create a consistent and seamless branded service experience.

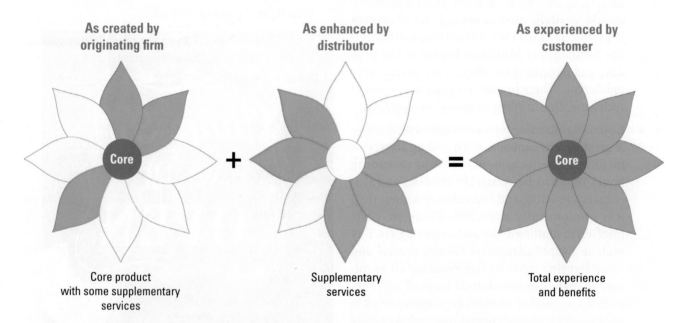

As created by originating firm

Core

Core product with some supplementary services

As enhanced by distributor

+

Supplementary services

As experienced by customer

=

Core

Total experience and benefits

Figure 5.12 Splitting responsibilities for service delivery

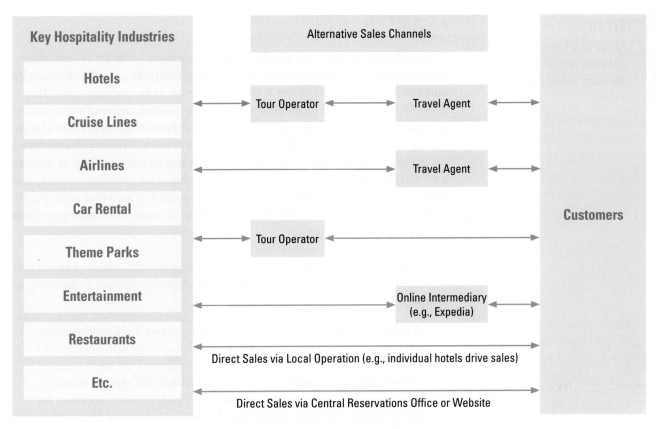

Figure 5.13 Alternative sales channels in the hospitality industry

In addition to "outsourcing" certain tasks to intermediaries, they are frequently used to achieve reach and generate business. Think of the various sales and reservation channels that are used in the travel industry (*Figure 5.13*). Each channel offers different benefits and also has vastly different costs. The lowest cost distribution channel would be the service firm's own website (incremental costs are typically less than $1 per sales transaction), followed by its call center-based central reservations systems (typically between $5 and $25 per sales transaction — note that one sales transaction can involve more than one call). Retail travel agents usually charge 10% commission, and tour operators typically mark-up to 20–30% of the transaction value. The most expensive channels are often online distributors such as Expedia and Priceline, which can charge up to 30% of the transaction value. Therefore, many service firms that have achieved brand equity aim to migrate their customers and sales to lower cost channels to circumvent or remove intermediaries, a process also called disintermediation. Just imagine the profit implications if a firm can save up to 30% by distributing to end customers directly.

An example of an early campaign to switch transactions to direct distribution channels, Swissôtel Hotels & Resorts executed an entire campaign to increase online bookings, especially among the important business traveler segment. Within seven months of launch, its revamped website (www.swissotel.com) more than doubled online revenues. Apart from the enhanced express reservation functions (with fewer clicks), user-friendly navigation, and online promotions and incentives, the hotel company's "Best Rate Guarantee" was a key driver of its success[11].

Leading low-cost carriers relied on direct sales channels to minimize distribution costs often from the onset. For example, easyJet claims to have almost 100% of its customers book through its website and promotes with the tagline "Book cheap flights at the official easyJet.com site for our guaranteed best prices to over 140 destinations", and Southwest Airlines says that its website is the "only place to find Southwest Airlines fares online"[12].

This discussion shows, the role and value-add (i.e., benefits) and costs of every intermediary has to be carefully considered when designing a firm's distribution strategy. Franchising is one of the most commonly used distribution strategies in service, which we will discuss in detail next.

LO 10

Know why franchising is a common way of delivering services to end users.

FRANCHISING

Even delivery of the core product can be outsourced to an intermediary. Franchising has become a popular way to expand delivery of an effective service concept, embracing all of the **7 Ps** (see Chapter 1) to multiple sites. This is done without the level of monetary investment needed for rapid expansion of company-owned and -managed sites. A franchisor recruits entrepreneurs who are willing to invest their time, effort, and equity in managing a previously developed service concept. In return, the franchisor provides training on how to operate and market the business, sells necessary supplies, and provides promotional support at a national or regional level. Local marketing activities are typically paid for by the franchisee, but they must adhere to copy and media guidelines prescribed by the franchisor[13].

The International Franchise Association, the world's oldest and largest organization representing franchising worldwide, has defined franchising as follows:

> *A franchise is the agreement or license between two legally independent parties which gives: (a) a person or group of people (franchisee) the right to market a product or service using the trademark or trade name of another business (franchisor); (b) the franchisee the right to market a product or service using the operating methods of the franchisor; (c) the franchisee the obligation to pay the franchisor fees for these rights, and (d) the franchisor the obligation to provide rights and support to franchisees*[14].

Franchising is a particularly attractive strategy for service firms when:

- The firm has limited resources and fast growth is necessary to preempt competition. Service firms often have little protection beyond their brand as almost everything else they do can be copied by others. The firm that first managed to become top of mind in their target segments for a particular category (e.g., coffee chain) tends to become the market leader in the long run. Franchisees often invest significant funds into their franchise and thereby facilitate fast growth of the overall chain.

- The long-term commitment of the store manager is crucial. Franchisees tend to be highly motivated to ensure high customer satisfaction, build customer loyalty, and run high-quality service operations[15].

- Local knowledge is important. Franchisees tend to be from the local community and therefore can be highly effective in dealing with local authorities (e.g., during the construction and renovation of facilities), labor markets, media, and customers.

The US is the global leader in franchising, a position it has held since the 1930s when it first used the approach for fast-food restaurants, inns, and, slightly later, for motels. Although franchising is still most commonly associated with fast-food restaurants (for an example, see *Figure 5.14*), the concept has been applied to a wide variety of both consumer and B2B services, and now spans some 300 different product categories. New concepts are created and commercialized all the time in most countries around the world. The fastest-growing categories of concepts are related to health and fitness, publications, security, and consumer services. The franchise industry accounts for approximately 50% of all retail sales and services in the US. One out of every 12 businesses is a franchised business. Some 900,000 franchise businesses in the US provide jobs for more than 18 million people and create over $2.1 trillion in economic activity[16]. Among the cases featured in this book is "Aussie Pooch Mobile", which describes a successful Australian-based franchised dog washing service (see *Pages 658)*. In your own role as a consumer, you probably patronize more franchises than you realize (*Table 5.2*).

From a franchisee perspective, a longitudinal study in the restaurant industry has shown that buying a franchise is, on average, more profitable that starting an independent restaurant[17]. Nevertheless, there is a high drop-out rate among franchisors in the early years of a new franchise system, with one-third of all systems failing within the first four years and no less than three-quarters of all franchisors ceasing to exist after 12 years[18]. Success factors for franchisors include:

- The ability to achieve a larger size with a more recognizable brand name.

- Offering franchisees fewer supporting services but longer-term contracts.

- Having lower overhead per outlet.

- Providing accurate and realistic information about expected characteristics of franchise operations, and support given.

- Building a cooperative rather than controlling relationship[19].

Figure 5.14 Subway is a popular American fast-food franchise

Table 5.2 The Top 10 Franchises in the United States in 2015 and Their Start-Up Costs

Rank	Franchise Name	Type	Startup Costs (US$ in thousands)
1	Hampton Hotels	Hotel	$4,000 – $14,000
2	Anytime Fitness	Fitness	$79 – $371
3	Subway	Fast-food	$117 – 263
4	Jack in the Box	Fast-food	$1,000 – $2,000
5	Supercuts	Hair-salon	$114 – $234
6	Jimmy John's Gourmet Sandwiches	Restaurant	$331 – $520
7	Servpro	Fire and water cleanup and restoration	$139 – $187
8	Denny's Inc.	Restaurant	$1,000 – $3,000
9	Pizza Hut Inc.	Restaurant	$297 – $2,000
10	7-Eleven Inc.	Convenience store	$37 – $2,000

Source

Adapted from: http://www.entrepreneur.com/franchise500/index.html, accessed February 18, 2015.

Because growth is very important to achieve an efficient scale, some franchisors adopt a strategy known as "master franchising," which involves delegating the responsibility for recruiting, training, and supporting franchisees within a given geographic area. Master franchisees are often individuals who have already succeeded as operators of one or several individual franchise outlets. They have the responsibility for recruiting, training, and supporting franchisees within a given geographic area.

While franchising has many success stories, it also has some disadvantages.

- It entails some loss of control over the delivery system and, consequently, over how customers experience the actual service.

- Ensuring that an intermediary adopts exactly the same priorities and procedures as prescribed by the franchisor is difficult, yet it's vital for effective quality control. Franchisors usually seek to exercise control over all aspects of the service performance through a contract that specifies adherence to tightly defined service standards, procedures, scripts, and physical presentation. Franchisors frequently control not only output specifications, but also the appearance of the servicescape, employee performance, and elements such as service timetables.

- An ongoing problem is that as franchisees gain experience, they may start to resent the various fees paid to the franchisor and instead, begin to believe they can operate the business better without the constraints imposed by the agreement, often resulting in legal disputes between the two parties.

Figure 5.15 Trucking companies license jobs to local firms in remote areas

Other Intermediaries

Service intermediaries take on many forms in terms of their role, structure, legal status, and relationship with the service firm (often referred to as "principle"). Franchising is one of the most common distribution strategies used, but a range of alternative distribution intermediaries are also available. One is licensing another supplier to act behalf on the original supplier's to deliver the core product. Trucking companies regularly make use of independent agents (*Figure 5.15*), instead of locating company-owned branches in each of the different cities they serve. They may also choose to contract with independent "owner-operators" who drive their own trucks[20].

Other service distribution agreements can be contractual such as those used in financial services. Banks seeking to move into investment services will often act as the distributor for mutual fund products created by an investment firm lacking extensive distribution channels of its own. Many banks also sell insurance products underwritten by an insurance company. They collect a commission on the sale, but are normally not involved in handling claims.

THE CHALLENGE OF DISTRIBUTION IN LARGE DOMESTIC MARKETS

LO 11
Understand the challenges of distributing services in large domestic markets.

There are important differences between marketing services within a compact geographic area and marketing services in a federal nation covering a large geographic area, such as the US, Canada, or Australia. In these cases, physical logistics immediately become more challenging for many types of services, because of the distances involved and the existence of multiple time zones. Multiculturalism is also an issue, because of the growing proportion of immigrants and the presence of indigenous peoples. Firms that market across Canada have to work in two official languages, English and French (the latter is spoken throughout Québec, where it is the only official language; in parts of New Brunswick, which is officially bilingual; and in northeastern Ontario). Finally, there are differences within each country between the laws and tax rates of the various states or provinces and those of the respective federal governments. The challenges in Australia and Canada, however, pale in comparison to those facing service marketers in the mega-economy of the US.

Visitors from overseas who tour the US are often overwhelmed by the immense size of the country, surprised by the diversity of its people, astonished by the climatic and topographic variety of the landscape, and impressed by the scale and scope of some of its business undertakings. Consider some of the statistics. Marketing at a national level in the "lower 48" states of the US involves dealing with a population of some 300 million people and transcontinental distances that exceed 2,500 miles (4,000 kilometers). If Hawaii and Alaska are included, the market embraces even greater distances, covering six time zones, incredible topographic variety, and all climatic zones from arctic to tropical. From a logistical standpoint, serving customers in all 50 states might seem at least as complex as serving customers throughout, say, Europe, North Africa, and the Middle East, were it not for the fact that the US has an exceptionally well-developed communications, transportation, and distribution infrastructure.

Figure 5.16 Service businesses operating nationwide need to conform to the different state and municipal laws, and allow for variations in tax policies

The US is less homogeneous than national stereotypes might suggest. As a federal nation, it has a diverse range of government practices. In addition to observing federal laws and paying federal taxes, service businesses operating nationwide may also need to conform to relevant state and municipal laws, and plan for variations in tax policies from one state to another. However, US law firms operating in multiple states may find this exposure an advantage when expanding overseas (*Figure 5.16*). Because cities, counties and special districts (such as regional transit authorities) have taxing authority in many states, there are also thousands of variations in sales tax across the US!

As the US population becomes increasingly mobile and multicultural, market segmentation issues have become more complex for the service marketers operating on a national scale as they encounter growing populations of immigrants (as well as tourists) who speak many languages. The US economic statistics show a wider range of household incomes and personal wealth (or lack thereof) than almost anywhere else on earth. Corporate customers too present considerable diversity, although the relevant variables may be different.

Faced with an enormous and diverse domestic marketplace, most large US service companies simplify their marketing and management tasks by targeting specific market segments (Chapter 3). Some firms segment on a geographic basis. Others target certain groups based on demographics, lifestyle, needs, or — in a corporate context — on industry type and company size. Smaller firms wishing to operate nationally usually choose to seek out narrow market niches, a task made easier today by the ubiquitous reach of the Internet. However, the largest national service operations face tremendous challenges as they seek to serve multiple segments across a huge geographic area. They must strike a balance between the standardization of strategies across all the elements embraced by the 7 Ps, and adaptation to different segments and local market conditions — decisions are especially challenging when they concern high-contact services in which customers visit the delivery site.

DISTRIBUTING SERVICES INTERNATIONALLY

Many firms distribute their services internationally, including CNN, Reuters, Google, AMEX, Starbucks, Hertz, Citibank, and McKinsey. What are the driving forces pushing these firms to go international or even global? And when service companies plan to go international, how should they enter new markets[21]?

Factors Favoring Adoption of Transnational Strategies

Several forces or **industry drivers** influence the trend toward globalization and the creation of transnationally integrated strategy[22]. As applied to services, these forces are market drivers, competition drivers, technology drivers, cost drivers, and government drivers. Their relative significance may vary by type of service.

Market Drivers. Market factors stimulating the move toward transnational strategies include common customer needs across many countries, global customers who demand consistent service from suppliers around the world, and the availability of international channels in the form of efficient physical supply chains or electronic networks.

As large corporate customers become global, they often seek to standardize and simplify the suppliers used in different countries for a wide array of B2B services. For instance, they may seek to minimize the number of auditors they use around the world, expressing a preference for the "Big Four" accounting firms (i.e., PricewaterhouseCoopers, Deloitte Touche Tohmatsu, Ernst & Young, and KPMG) that can apply a consistent approach (within the context of the national rules prevailing within each country of operation). The use of globalized corporate banking, insurance, and management consulting are further examples. Similarly, the development of global logistics and supply chain management capabilities among firms such as DHL, FedEx, and UPS has encouraged many manufacturers to outsource responsibility for their logistics function to a single firm (*Figure 5.17*). In each instance, there are real advantages in consistency, ease of access, consolidation of information, and accountability. Similarly, international business travelers and tourists often feel more comfortable with predictable international standards of performance for travel-related services such as airline and hotel services.

⊃ **LO 12**
Be familiar with the forces that drive service firms to go international.

Figure 5.17 DHL combines multiple transport modes to create integrated logistics solutions for its global customer base

Competition Drivers. The presence of competitors from different countries, interdependence of countries, and the transnational policies of competitors themselves are among the key competition drivers that exercise a powerful force in many service industries. Firms may be obliged to follow their competitors into new markets in order to protect their positions elsewhere. Similarly, once a major player moves into a new foreign market, a scramble for territory among competing firms may ensue.

Technology Drivers. Technology drivers tend to center around advances in information technology — such as enhanced performance and capabilities in telecommunications, computerization, and software; miniaturization of equipment; and the digitization of voice, video, and text — so that all can be stored, manipulated, and transmitted in the digital language of computers. For information-based services, the growing availability of broadband telecommunication channels with their capability of moving vast amounts of data at great speed is playing a major role in opening up new markets.

Cost Drivers. Big is sometimes beautiful from a cost standpoint. There may be economies of scale to be gained from operating on an international or even global basis, in addition to sourcing efficiencies as a result of favorable logistics and lower costs in certain countries. Lower operating costs for telecommunications and transportation, accompanied by improved performance, facilitate entry into international markets. The effects of these drivers vary according to the level of fixed costs required to enter an industry and the potential for cost savings. Barriers to entry caused by the upfront cost of equipment and facilities may be reduced by strategies such as equipment leasing (as many airlines do), seeking investor-owned facilities such as hotels, and then obtaining management contracts or awarding franchises to local entrepreneurs. However, cost drivers may be less applicable for services that are primarily people-based. When most elements of the service factory are replicated in multiple locations, scale economies tend to be lower and experience curves flatter.

Government Drivers. Government policies can serve to encourage or discourage the development of a transnationally integrated strategy. Among these drivers are favorable trade policies, compatible technical standards, and common marketing regulations. For instance, the actions taken by the European Commission to create a single market throughout the EU is a stimulus to the creation of pan-European service strategies in numerous industries.

Furthermore, the World Trade Organization (WTO) and its focus on the internationalization of services has pushed governments around to world to create more favorable regulatory environments for transnational service strategies. The power of the drivers for internationalization can be seen in the case of the Qantas airliner arriving in Hong Kong described in *Service Insights 5.3*.

Many of the factors driving internationalization and the adoption of transnational strategies also promote the trend to have nationwide operations. The market, cost, technological, and competitive forces that encourage creation of nationwide service businesses or franchise chains are often the same as those that subsequently drive some of the same firms to operate transnationally.

SERVICE INSIGHTS 5.3
Flight to Hong Kong: A Snapshot of Globalization

A white and red Boeing 777-300ER, sporting the flying kangaroo of Qantas, banks low over Hong Kong's dramatic harbor, crowded with merchant vessels, as it nears the end of its 10-hour flight from Australia. Once landed, the aircraft taxis past a kaleidoscope of tail-fins, representing airlines from more than a dozen different countries on several continents — just a sample of all the carriers that offer service to this remarkable city.

The passengers include business travelers and tourists, as well as returning residents. After passing through immigration and customs, most visitors will be heading first for their hotels, many of which belong to global chains (some of them, Hong Kong-based). Some travelers will be picking up cars, reserved earlier from Hertz or one of the other well-known rental car companies with facilities at the airport. Others will take the fast train into the city. Tourists on packaged vacations are actively looking forward to enjoying Hong Kong's renowned Cantonese cuisine. Parents, however, are resigned to having their children demand to eat at the same fast-food chains found back home. Many of the more affluent tourists are planning to go shopping, not only in distinctive Chinese jewelry and antiques stores, but also in the internationally branded luxury stores found in most world-class cities.

What brings the business travelers to this SAR ("special administrative region") of China? Many are negotiating supply contracts for manufactured goods ranging from clothing, toys to computer components, whereas others come to market their own goods and services. Some are in the shipping or construction businesses, others in an array of service industries ranging from telecommunications to entertainment and international law. The owner of a large Australian tourism operation has come to negotiate a deal for package vacations on Queensland's famous Gold Coast. The Brussels-based, Canadian senior partner of a Big Four accounting firm is halfway through a grueling round-the-world trip to persuade the offices of an international conglomerate to consolidate all its auditing business on a global basis with his firm alone. An American executive and her British colleague, both working for a large Euro-American telecom partnership, are hoping to achieve similar goals by selling a multinational corporation on the concept of employing their firm to manage all of

its telecommunications activities worldwide. And more than a few of the passengers either work for international banking and financial service firms or have come to Hong Kong, one of the world's most dynamic financial centers, to seek financing for their own ventures.

In the Boeing's freight hold not only can passengers' bags be found, but also cargo for delivery to Hong Kong and other Chinese destinations. The freight includes mail, Australian wine, some vital spare parts for an Australian-built high-speed ferry operating out of Hong Kong, a container full of brochures and display materials about the Australian tourism industry for an upcoming trade promotion, and a variety of other high-value merchandise. Waiting at the airport for the aircraft's arrival are local Qantas personnel, baggage handlers, cleaners, mechanics and other technical staff, customs and immigration officials, and, of course, people who have come to greet individual passengers. A few are Australians, but the great majority are local Hong Kong Chinese, many of whom have never traveled very far afield. Yet in their daily lives, they patronize banks, fast-food outlets, retail stores, and insurance companies whose brand names — promoted by global advertising campaigns — may be equally familiar to their expatriate relatives living in countries such as Australia, Britain, Canada, Singapore, and the US. Welcome to the world of global services marketing!

How Does the Nature of a Service Affect International Distribution?

Are some types of services easier to internationalize than others? What are the alternative ways a service company can tap on the potential of international markets? Depending in part on the nature of the service, international distribution strategies have vastly different requirements. *Table 5.3* summarizes important variations in the impact of each of the five groups of globalization drivers on three broad categories of services: people-processing services, possession-processing services and information-based services.

Table 5.3 Impact of Globalization Drivers on Various Service Categories

Globalization Drivers	People Processing	Possession Processing	Information-based
Competition	Simultaneity of production and consumption limits leverage of foreign-based competitive advantage in front stage of service factory, but advantage in management systems can be basis for globalization.	Lead role of technology creates driver for globalization of competitors with technical edge (e.g., Singapore Airlines' technical servicing for other carriers' aircraft).	Highly vulnerable to global dominance by competitors with monopoly or competitive advantage in information (e.g., BBC, Hollywood, CNN), unless restricted by governments.
Market	People differ economically and culturally, so needs for service and ability to pay may vary. Culture and education may affect willingness to do self-service.	Less variation for service to corporate possessions, but level of economic development affects demands for services to individually-owned goods.	Demand for many services is derived to a significant degree from economic and educational levels. Cultural issues may affect demand for entertainment.
Technology	Use of IT for delivery of supplementary services may be a function of ownership and familiarity with technology, including telecommunications and intelligent terminals.	Need for technology-based service delivery systems is a function of the types of possessions requiring service and the cost tradeoffs in labor substitution.	Ability to deliver core services through remote terminals may be a function of investments in computerization, quality of telecommunications infrastructure and education levels.
Cost	Variable labor rates may affect pricing in labor-intensive services (consider self-service in high-cost locations).	Variable labor rates may favor low-cost locations if not offset by shipment costs. Consider substituting equipment for labor.	Major cost elements can be centralized and minor cost elements localized.
Government	Social policies (e.g., healthcare) vary widely and may affect labor costs, role of women in front-stage jobs, and hours/days on which work can be performed.	Tax laws, environmental regulations, and technical standards may decrease/increase costs and encourage/discourage certain types of activity.	Policies on education, censorship, public ownership of communications, and infrastructure standards may affect demand and supply and distort pricing.

People-Processing Services. People-processing services require direct contact with the customer. The service provider needs to have a local geographic presence, stationing the necessary personnel, buildings, equipment, vehicles, and supplies within reasonably easy reach of target customers. There are two options for people-processing services:

- **Export the service concept.** Acting alone or in partnership with local suppliers, the firm establishes a service factory in another country. The objective may be to reach out to new customers, or to follow existing corporate or individual customers to new locations (or both). This approach is commonly used by chain restaurants[23], hotels, car rental firms, and weight-reduction clinics, for which a local presence is essential in order to be able to compete.

For corporate customers, the industries are likely to be in fields such as banking, professional services, and business logistics. If the customers themselves are mobile, as in the case of business travelers and tourists, then the same customers may patronize a company's offerings in many different locations, and make comparisons between them.

- **Import customers.** Customers from other countries are invited to come to a service factory with distinctive appeal or competences in the firm's home country. People will travel from abroad to ski at outstanding North American resorts, such as Whistler-Blackcomb in British Columbia or Vail in Colorado. If they can afford it, they may also travel for specialized medical treatment at famous hospitals and clinics, such as Massachusetts General Hospital or the Mayo Clinic in Rochester, Minnesota. Increasingly, a two-way traffic is developing in healthcare, with a growing number of patients from North America, Europe, and Australasia traveling to custom-build modern hospitals in Asian countries for an array of medical interventions by Western-trained specialists, ranging from hip replacements to cosmetic surgery. Even after paying for travel and accommodation, the total cost usually amounts to far less than what patients would pay in their home countries, with the added attraction of recuperating under vacation-like conditions at often exotic locations.

Possession-processing Services. Possession-processing services may also be geographically constrained in many instances. This category involves services to the customer's physical possessions and includes repair and maintenance, freight transport, cleaning and warehousing. Most services in this category require an ongoing local presence, regardless of whether customers drop off items at a service facility or having a personnel visit the customer's site. Sometimes expert personnel may be flown in from a base in another country. However, smaller, transportable items can be shipped to distant service centers for repair, cleaning and maintenance. Certain types of service processes can be applied to physical products through electronic diagnostics and transmission of "remote fixes."

Information-based Services. This group includes two categories, **mental-processing services** (services to the customer's mind, such as news and entertainment) and **information-processing services** (services to the customers' intangible assets, such as banking and insurance). They are perhaps the most interesting category of services from the point of view of global strategy development. This is because data is transmitted or changed to create value. Information-based services can be distributed internationally in one of three ways:

- **Export the service to a local service factory.** The service can be made available in a local facility that customers visit. For instance, a film made in Hollywood can be shown in movie theaters around the world, or a college course can be designed in one country and then offered by approved teachers elsewhere.

- **Import customers.** Customers may travel abroad to visit a specialist facility, in which case the service takes on the characteristics of a people-processing service. For instance, large numbers of foreign students study in the US and Canadian universities.

- **Export the information via telecommunications and transform it locally.** Rather than ship object-based services stored on physical media such as DVDs from the country of origin, the data are increasingly downloaded from the company's website in that country by customers themselves.

In theory, none of these information-based services require face-to-face contact with customers, because all can potentially be delivered at arm's length through telecommunications or mail. Banking and insurance are good examples of services that can be delivered from other countries. Bank customers requiring cash in another country need only visit a local ATM connected to a global network such as VISA. In practice however, a local presence may be necessary to build personal relationships, conduct on-site research (such as in consulting or auditing), or even to fulfill legal requirements.

In addition to industries such as financial services, insurance, news and entertainment, education is becoming a likely candidate for globalized distribution using a combination of channels. Many universities already have international campuses, extension courses delivered by both local and traveling faculty, and long-established correspondence programs. On a national basis, the University of Phoenix in the US and the Open University in the United Kingdom are among the national leaders in electronically distributed programs. A truly globalized service is the next logical step. For example, Netflix aims to be, according to its CEO Reed Hastings, in "every county but North Korea. Under the US law, we're still blocked there"[24].

Barriers to International Trade in Services

The marketing of services internationally has been the fastest-growing segment of international trade[25]. Transnational strategy involves the integration of strategy formulation and its implementation across all the countries in which the company does business in. Barriers to entry, historically a serious problem for foreign firms wishing to do business abroad, are slowly diminishing. The passage of free trade legislation in recent years has been an important facilitator of transnational operations. Notable developments include NAFTA, linking Canada, Mexico, and the US; Latin American economic blocs such as Mercosur and Pacto Andino; and the European Union (EU), now 28 countries strong (see *Service Insights 5.4*).

However, operating successfully in international markets remains difficult for some services. Despite the efforts of the WTO and its predecessor, GATT (General Agreement on Trade and Tariffs), there are many hurdles to overcome. Airline access is a sore point — many countries require bilateral (two-country) agreements on establishing new routes. If one country is willing to allow entry by a new carrier, but the other is not, then access will be blocked. Compounding government restrictions of this nature are capacity limits at certain major airports, which lead to the denial of new or additional landing rights for foreign airlines. Both passenger and freight transport are affected by such restrictions. Financial, healthcare and telecommunications service markets are typically also highly regulated, which makes it difficult for international players to enter those markets.

Companies entering more mundane markets, such as Uber in the taxi market and Airbnb in the accommodation space, try to offer a global reservation service and connect this with local facilities and/or micro-entrepreneurs also often face regulatory roadblocks. The incumbents in those industries were used to regulatory protection and fought back by lobbying regulators in many markets. Ironically, they often use customer protection and service standards as arguments against these new entrants (e.g., passenger safety, security, and insurance in the case of taxi services). In the end, when customers vote with their feet and put pressure on their regulators, incumbent operators are likely to improve their service and probably also cut prices, and local governments will work on a regulatory framework that accommodates innovative business models.

SERVICE INSIGHTS 5.4
The European Union: Moving to Borderless Trade

Many of the challenging strategic decisions facing service marketers in pan-European markets are extensions of decisions already faced by firms operating on a national basis in the US. Although it is geographically more compact than the US, the 28-country EU has an even larger population (500 million versus 320 million), and is culturally and politically more diverse, with distinct variations in tastes and lifestyles, in addition to the added complication of 24 official national languages and a variety of regional tongues, from Catalan to Welsh. As new countries join the EU, the "single market" will become even larger. The admission of several Eastern European countries such as Romania and Bulgaria, and the possibility of a formal link to Turkey (whose land area straddles Europe and Asia), added further cultural diversity and brought the EU market closer to Russia and the countries of Central Asia.

Although the potential for freer trade in services within the EU continues to increase, you should recognize that "Greater Europe" — ranging from Iceland to European Russia, west of the Ural Mountains — includes many countries that are likely to remain outside the Union for some years to come. Some of these countries, such as Switzerland and Norway (which both rejected membership), tend to enjoy much closer trading relations with the EU than others. Whether there will ever be full political union — a "United States of Europe" — remains a hotly debated and contested issue. However, from a services marketing standpoint, the EU is certainly moving toward the US model in terms of both scale and freedom of movement. See *http://europa.eu* and *http://en.wikipedia.org/wiki/European_Union* for more information on the EU.

Within the EU, the European Commission has made huge progress in harmonizing standards and regulations to level the competitive playing field and discourage efforts by individual member countries to protect their own service and manufacturing industries. The results are already evident, with many service firms operating across Europe as well as overseas.

Another important economic step facilitating transnational marketing on a pan-European basis is monetary union. In January 1999, the exchange values of 11 national European currencies were linked to a new currency, the Euro, which completely replaced all European currencies in 2002. Today, services are priced in Euros from Finland to Portugal.

LO 15

Explain the determinants of international market entry strategies.

How to Enter International Markets?

The strategy most suitable for entering a new international market depends on (1) how a firm can protect its intellectual property (IP) and control its key sources of value creation and (2) whether the level of desired interaction with the customer is high or low (*Figure 5.18*).

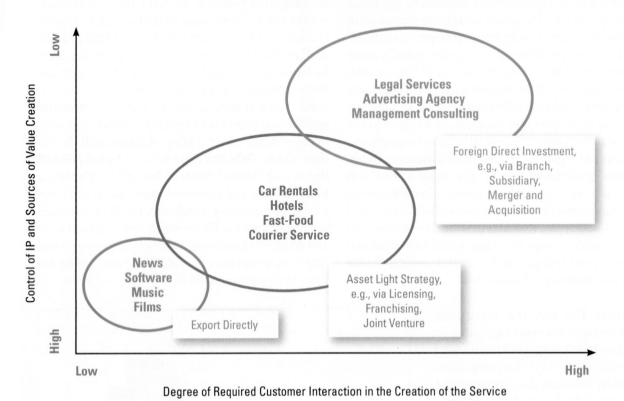

Figure 5.18 How to go international?

In the case where a firm's IP and value creation sources can be protected through copyright or other legal means, and if only low customer contact is required (i.e., the service is distributed at arm's length via the Internet or telephone), then a company can simply export the service. In these cases, there is little risk of losing the business to local competitors, distributors, or other local partners. Examples include database services (e.g., Thomson Reuters' Web of Science and Social Sciences Citation Index-related services), online news (e.g., those offered by CNN or the Financial Times), online advertising (e.g., sold globally by Google or Facebook), and the downloading of music, films, e-books, and software. If these firms do establish a local presence in international markets, it is usually to organize their local corporate sales and marketing (e.g., Google, Facebook, and LinkedIn have sales teams in many countries that sell their advertising services) rather than deliver the service itself[26].

Some services like fast-food restaurants, global hotel chains, and courier services allow a firm to control its IP and sources of value creation. This is done through branding, having a global customer base, and global resources, capabilities, and networks. Without these, it would become impossible, or at least very difficult, to deliver the service at a level customers are expecting. Here, customer contact is often at a moderate level. Firms in this category can expand globally through licensing, franchising, or joint ventures without losing control. For example, brands such as Starbucks and Hard Rock Café add value, and outlets without these brands don't have the same attraction for customers. Large global hotel chains such as Starwood Hotels & Resorts and Hilton "own" the customer relationships with millions of customer through their loyalty programs and global sales offices (GSOs). These offices then feed business to locally owned and operated properties. These properties need the customer traffic from the global chain.

To cite another example, unlike the global courier service firm with global resources, capabilities and an extensive network, a local courier service provider is not able to source for inbound shipments from around the world. They also cannot deliver outbound shipments on a global level. Thus, the global courier service firm can safely appoint a local agent without having to fear that that agent will, at some point, become a competitor.

Finally, there are services where the value-add comes mainly from the skills and knowledge of the service provider, and where a high degree of customer contact is needed to deliver value. These are often knowledge-based, professional services. Examples include creative design of advertising campaigns and management consulting projects. For such services, value is typically created by the firm's employees through their knowledge and the relationship built with their clients. It is difficult to control the sources of value creation for such services. For example, if a firm worked through a licensee or joint-venture partner, it would face the risk that once skill transfer to that partner has happened after a few years of operation, the partner would be able to deliver the service without the support of the firm. When this happens, the partner is likely to show increasing resistance to paying licensing fees or sharing profits. They are then likely to renegotiate the terms of the venture, and could even threaten to

go "independent" and cut out the original service firm. Hence, it is necessary for firms in this category to have tight control over its local resources. This usually includes having the local staff on its own payroll, with carefully written contracts that protect the firm's IP and customer base. Here, the most effective ways to enter a new market are typically through foreign direct investment by setting up a branch office, a subsidiary, or through mergers and acquisitions[27].

CONCLUSION

What? How? Where? When? Responses to these four questions form the foundation of any service distribution strategy. The customer's service experience is a function of how the different elements of the Flower of Service are distributed and delivered through selective physical and electronic channels. In addition to "what" and "how," service marketing strategy must address issues of place and time, paying as much attention to speed, scheduling, and electronic access as to the more traditional notion of physical location. Here, the rapid growth of the Internet and broadband mobile communications is especially exciting for service firms, and many elements of service are informational in nature. Furthermore, in the heat of globalization, important questions are raised concerning the design and implementation of franchising and international service distribution strategies.

CHAPTER SUMMARY

⟳ **LO1 What? How? Where? When?** Responses to these four questions form the foundation of any service distribution strategy.

⟳ **LO2 What** is distributed? The flow model of distribution can be mapped onto the Flower of Service concept and includes the following flows of service distribution:
- Information and promotion flows (includes the information and potentially consultation petals).
- Negotiation flow (includes the order-taking and potentially also billing and payment petals).
- Product flow (includes the core product and the remaining petals of the Flower of Service).

A service distribution strategy encompasses all three flows.

⟳ **LO3 How** can services be distributed? Services can be distributed through three main modes:
- Customers visit the service site (e.g., for people-processing services such as an MRI scan).
- Service providers go to their customers (e.g., as for high net-worth private banking services).
- Service transactions conducted remotely (i.e., at arm's length such as through Skype or buying a travel insurance online).

Some core services require a physical location (e.g., people-processing services), which severely restricts their distribution. However, information-based core services and many supplementary services can be distributed and delivered remotely.

⟳ **LO4** Developments in telecommunications, online technology, service apps, and sophisticated logistics solutions have spurred innovation in remote service delivery.
- All information-based supplementary services (i.e., information, consultation, order-taking, billing, and payment) and information-based core products and many possession-based services can be delivered remotely.
- Key drivers of the growth of service delivery via cyberspace are: (1) convenience, (2) ease of search, (3) a broader selection, (4) potential for lower prices, and (5) 24/7 service with prompt delivery.

⟳ **LO5** Customer preferences drive channel choice:
- Customers often prefer remote channels because of their convenience, when they have high confidence and knowledge about the product, and are technology-savvy.
- However, consumers rely more on personal channels when the perceived risk is high and when there are social motives behind the transaction.

⟳ **LO6** Customers are likely to use different service channels with the same service organization (e.g., bank customers use the gamut of channels ranging from mobile banking apps and websites to ATMs and bank branches). To deliver consistent and seamless service experiences, channel integration is key.

⟳ **LO7 Where** should service be delivered is an important decision for services that require physical locations:
- First, strategic location considerations are involved as the site location is an integral part of the overall service strategy; the location strategy must be consistent with the firm's marketing strategy and the needs and expectations of its target customers.
- Second, tactical location considerations are used to choose between specific sites. They include: population size and characteristics, traffic, convenience of access, competitors in the area, nature of nearby businesses, availability of labor and sites, and rental costs, conditions and regulation. Geographic information systems (GISs) are frequently used to help firms make specific location decisions.
- Locational constraints such as a need for economy of scale (e.g., because of high fixed costs such as in specialized medical facilities) and operational requirements (e.g., airports or distribution centers) limit a firm's location choice.
- Innovative location strategies can be at the core of new service models. Recent trends include mini-stores, sharing retail space with complementary providers, and locating in multi-purpose facilities (e.g., locating clinics in shopping malls).

LO8 When should service be delivered?

- Key factors determining opening hours of a service channel include customer needs and wants, and the economics of opening hours (fixed costs of a facility, variable costs of extending opening hours and incremental sales or contribution expected and potential operational gains by shifting demand from peak periods to extended opening hours).
- There is a move toward extended operating hours, with the ultimate goal of 24/7 service every day of the year, often achieved through the use of self-service technology.
- Information-based core and supplementary services can be offered 24/7. Recent technological developments link customer relationship management (CRM) systems, mobile telephones, apps, websites, and smart cards to provide increasingly convenient and sophisticated electronic services.

LO9 Service firms frequently use intermediaries to distribute some of the supplementary services (e.g., cruise lines still use travel agencies to provide information, take reservations, collect payment, and often bundle complementary services such as air travel).

- Service organizations may find it cost-effective to outsource certain tasks, and intermediates often add reach and generate incremental sales.
- However, there are vast cost differences between channels, with a firm's own website typically costing a fraction of transactions via intermediaries such as Travelocity in the travel industry. A careful cost-benefit analysis is needed, which generally leads strong brands to shift transactions toward their own channels, and brands that lack recognition and reach relying more on intermediaries.
- In either case, the challenge for the service firm is to ensure that overall service is seamless and experienced as desired.

LO10 Franchising is frequently used to distribute even the core service. There are advantages and disadvantages to franchising:

- It allows for fast growth, and franchisees are highly motivated to ensure customer orientation, high-quality service operations, and cost-effective operations.

- Disadvantages of franchising include the loss of control over the delivery system and the customers' service experience. Hence, franchisors often enforce strict quality controls over all aspects of the operation.

LO11 Large domestic markets (e.g., the US, Canada, or Australia) are less homogeneous than national stereotypes suggest. Careful market segmentation, focusing on specific segments, and balancing standardization and adaptation strategies enhance a firm's chances of succeeding in developing large national service penetration.

LO12 Five important forces drive service firms to go international. They are:

- Market drivers (e.g., customers expect a global presence).
- Competitive drivers (e.g., competitors become global and put pressure on domestic firms).
- Technology drivers (e.g., the Internet allows global distribution and cost arbitrage).
- Cost drivers (e.g., economies of scale push toward adding markets).
- Government drivers (e.g., countries joining the WTO have to open many service sectors to international competition).

LO13 How does the nature of service affect international distribution? People-processing, possession-processing, and information-based services have very different requirements.

- People-processing services require direct contact with the customer. There are several options, including (1) export the service concept, and (2) import customers.
- Most possession-processing services require an ongoing local presence. However, in some instances, the crew and equipment can be flown to the customer's site or the customer's possessions can be transported to the provider's location.
- Information-based services are the most flexible as they don't require face-to-face contact or contact with possessions or equipment. They can be distributed in several ways: (1) export the service to a local service factory, (2) import customers, and (3) export the service via telecommunications and, if required, transform it locally.

LO14 Regulation remains a major challenge for many services as their markets are often highly regulated such as in the air travel, healthcare and financial services However, new business models in more mundane markets, such as Uber in the taxi and Airbnb in the accommodation market also face stiff regulatory hurdles around the world.

LO15 The strategy for entering international markets depends on:

- How a firm can control its intellectual property (IP) and its sources of value creation.
- The degree of customer interaction required for the creation of the service.

- If the value lies in the IP, then the service can simply be exported directly, like for e-books, music, and software.
- If IP control and customer contact requirements are moderate, then a firm can use licensing, franchising, or joint ventures.
- If a high degree of interaction is required and control of IP is low, then a firm should have foreign direct investments through setting up a branch, a subsidiary, or going in through mergers and acquisitions.

Review Questions

1. What is meant by "distributing services?" How can an experience or something intangible be distributed?

2. Why is it important to consider the distribution of core and supplementary services both separately and jointly?

3. What are the different options for service delivery? For each of the options, what factors do service firms need to take into account when using it?

4. What are the key factors driving place and time decisions of service distribution?

5. What risks and opportunities are entailed for a retail service firm in adding electronic channels of delivery (a) paralleling a channel involving physical stores, or (b) replacing the physical stores with a combined Internet and call center channel? Give examples.

6. Why should service marketers be concerned with new developments in mobile communications?

7. What marketing and management challenges are raised by the use of intermediaries in a service setting?

8. Why is franchising a popular way to expand distribution of an effective service concept? What are some disadvantages of franchising, and how can they be mitigated?

9. What can service marketers who are planning transnational strategies learn from studying existing practices within the US?

10. What are the key drivers for the increasing globalization of services?

11. How does the nature of the service affect the opportunities for globalization?

12. What factors do service companies need to understand to choose a distribution strategy for going international that still allows it to control its IP and sources of value creation?

Application Exercises

1. An entrepreneur is thinking of setting up a new service business (you can choose any specific business). What advice would you give regarding the distribution strategy for this business? Address the **What? How? Where? When?** of service distribution.

2. Think of three services you buy or use either mostly or exclusively via the Internet. What is the value proposition of this channel over alternative channels (e.g., phone, mail, or branch network)?

3. What advice would you give to a) a weight reduction clinic, b) a pest control company, and c) a university offering undergraduate courses about going international?

4. Select three different service industries, one each for people-processing, possession-processing and information-based services. For each, assess the five globalization drivers and their impact on these three industries.

5. Obtain recent statistics for international trade in services for the US and another country of your choice. What are the dominant categories of service exports and imports? What factors do you think are driving trade in specific service categories? What differences do you see between the countries?

6. Which market entry strategy into a new international market should (1) an architectural design firm, (2) an online discount broker, and (3) a satellite TV channel consider and why?

Endnotes

1   https://en.wikipedia.org/wiki/Michelle_Phan and http://michellephan.com accessed September 8, 2015.

2   Jochen Wirtz and Jeannette P. T. Ho, "Westin in Asia: Distributing Hotel Rooms Globally," in Jochen Wirtz and Christopher H. Lovelock, eds. *Services Marketing in Asia — A Case Book* (Singapore: Prentice Hall, 2005), 253–259. www.starwoodhotels.com, accessed February 21, 2015.

3   Research on the adoption of self-service technologies (SSTs) includes: Matthew L. Meuter, Mary Jo Bitner, Amy L. Ostrom, and Stephen W. Brown (2005), "Choosing Among Alternative Service Delivery Modes: An Investigation of Customer Trial of Self-Service Technologies," *Journal of Marketing*, Vol. 69, April, pp. 61–83; James M. Curran and Matthew L. Meuter (2005), "Self-Service Technology Adoption: Comparing Three Technologies," *Journal of Services Marketing*, Vol. 19, No. 2, pp. 103–113.

4   The section was based on the following research: Nancy Jo Black, Andy Lockett, Christine Ennew, Heidi Winklhofer, and Sally McKechnie (2002), "Modelling Consumer Choice of Distribution Channels: An Illustration from Financial Services," *International Journal of Bank Marketing*, Vol. 20, No. 4, pp. 161–173; J inkook Lee (2002), "A Key to Marketing Financial Services: The Right Mix of Products, Services, Channels and Customers," *Journal of Services Marketing*, Vol. 16,

No. 3, pp. 238–258; Leonard L Berry, Kathleen Seiders, and Dhruv Grewal (2002), "Understanding Service Convenience," *Journal of Marketing*, Vol. 66, No. 3, July, pp. 1–17; Jiun-Sheng C. Lin and Pei-ling Hsieh (2006), "The Role of Technology Readiness in Customers' Perception and Adoption of Self-Service Technologies," *International Journal of Service Industry Management*, Vol. 17, No. 5, pp. 497–517.

5   Madhumita Banerjee (2014), "Misalignment and Its Influence on Integration Quality in Multichannel Services," *Journal of Service Research*, Vol. 17, No. 4, pp. 460–474.

    Regarding optimizing the integration of physical and electronic channels in retailing, see: Stephen Mahar, P. Daniel Wright, Kurt M. Bretthauser, and Ronald Paul Hill (2014), "Optimizing Marketer Costs and Consumer Benefits Across 'Clicks' and 'Bricks,'" *Journal of the Academy of Marketing Science*, Vol. 42, No. 6, pp. 619–641.

6   Paul F. Nunes and Frank V. Cespedes (2003), "The Customer has Escaped," *Harvard Business Review*, Vol. 81, No. 11, pp. 96–105.

7   Locating a service outlet is in many ways akin to locating a retail facility. A detailed discussion on location in a retail context is provided in Barry Berman and Joel R. Evans, *Retail Management: A Strategic Approach.* 12th ed. (Upper Saddle River, NJ:

Prentice Hall, 2013). Of particular interest are Chapter 9 "Trading-Area Analysis" and Chapter 12 "Site Selection." Parts of this section were adapted from these two chapters.

8   Michael A. Jones, David L. Mothersbaugh, and Sharon E. Beatty (2004), "The Effects of Locational Convenience on Customer Repurchase Intentions across Service Types," *Journal of Services Marketing*, Vol. 17, No. 7, pp. 701–712.

9   Erin Harris, "Inside Starbucks' GIS Strategy," www.retailsolutionsonline.com, published April 22, 2011, accessed February 24, 2015.

10 *The Economist*, "Health Care in America: Medicine at the Mall," April 6, 2013, p. 66.

11 www.swissotel.com, and http://www.eyefortravel.com/node/9187, accessed February 25, 2015.

12 http://www.easyjet.com/en/cheap-flights, https://www.southwest.com/flight, accessed February 24, 2015.

13 For special issues on franchising in services that feature the latest academic thinking on this topic, see: *The Service Industries Journal*. Special Double Issue: Franchising in Services, editors: Domingo Ribeiro and Gary Akehurst, 2014, Vol. 34, No. 9–10; and *Journal of Retailing*. Special Issue: Franchising and Retailing, editors Rajiv P. Dant, Marko Grünhagen and Josef Windsperger 2011, Vol. 87, No. 3.

14 www.franchise.org, accessed February 18, 2015. If you are interested in potentially starting your own business as a franchisee, you should carefully research the franchise industry, the franchise model and the pros and cons of owning any particular franchise. The International Franchise Association has developed a resource full of tips and information to help you get started. Have a look at their website and at the posted franchising opportunities at http://www.franchise.org/franchise-opportunities.

15 James Cross and Bruce J. Walker, "Addressing Service Marketing Challenges Through Franchising," in Teresa A. Swartz and Dawn Iacobucci, eds. *Handbook of Services Marketing & Management*. (Thousand Oaks, CA: Sage Publications, 2000), 473–484; Lavent Altinay (2004), "Implementing International Franchising: The Role of Intrapreneurship," *International Journal of Service Industry Management*, Vol. 15, No. 5, pp. 426–443.

16 Quick Franchise Facts, Franchising Industry Statistics, http://www.azfranchises.com/franchisefacts.htm, accessed February 25, 2015.

17 Melih Madanoglu, Kyuho Lee, and Gary J. Castrogiovanni (2011), "Franchising and Firm Financial Performance Among U.S. Restaurants," *Journal of Retailing*, Vol. 87, No. 3, pp. 406–417.

18 Scott Shane and Chester Spell (1998), "Factors for New Franchise Success," *Sloan Management Review*, Vol. 39, Spring, pp. 43–50.

19 Firdaus Abdullah and Mohd Rashidee Alwi (2008), "Measuring and Managing Franchisee Satisfaction: A Study of Academic Franchising," *Journal of Modelling in Management*, Vol. 3, No. 2, pp. 182–199.

For more research on factors that affect the success of franchises, see Scott Weaven and Debra Grace (2009) "Franchisee Personality: An Examination in the Context of Franchise Unit Density and Service Classification," *European Journal of Marketing*, Vol. 43, No. 1/2, pp. 90–109; Markus Blut, Christof Backhaus, Tobias Heussler, David M. Woisetschläger, Heiner Evanschintzky, and Dieter Ahlert (2011), "What to Expect After the Honeymoon: Testing a Lifecycle Theory of Franchise Relationships", *Journal of Retailing*, Vol. 87, No. 3, pp. 306–319; Levent Altinay, Maureen Brookes, Ruth Yeung, and Gurhan Aktas (2014), "Franchisees' Perceptions of Relationship Development in Franchise Partnerships," *Journal of Service Research*, Vol. 28, No. 6, pp. 509–519.

For a conceptual discussion and review on the critical role of knowledge management in franchising, see: Scott Weaven, Debra Grace, Rajiv Dant, and James R. Brown (2014), "Value Creation through Knowledge Management in Franchising: A Multi-level Conceptual Framework," *Journal of Services Marketing*, Vol. 28, No. 2, pp. 97–104.

20 For a discussion on what to look out for when parts of the service are outsourced, see Lauren Keller Johnson (2005), "Outsourcing Postsale Service: Is Your Brand Protected? Before You Spin Off Repairs, or Parts Distribution, or Customer Call Centers, Consider the Cons as well as the Pros," *Supply Chain Strategy*, Vol. 1, No. 5, July, pp. 3–5.

21 A recent study ranked the attractiveness of international markets for US-based franchise firms. The study concluded that key factors that determine a market's attractiveness were size of the market, country risks, and cultural and geographic distance. This made large European countries, Canada, Japan, and Australia the most attractive markets, while the small and unstable African counties were the least attractive. China and the other BRIC countries (i.e., Brazil, Russia, and India) were not so highly ranked in spite of their size because of their significant risks and large cultural and geographic distances.

Source: E. Hachemi Aliouche and Udo A. Schlentich (2011), "Towards a Strategic Model of Global Franchise Expansion," *Journal of Retailing*, Vol. 87, No. 3, pp. 345–365.

22 John K. Johansson and George S. Yip (1994), "Exploiting Globalization Potential: US and Japanese Strategies," *Strategic Management Journal,* Vol. 15, No. 8, October, pp. 579–601; Christopher H. Lovelock and George S. Yip (1996), "Developing Global Strategies for Service Businesses," *California Management Review*, Vol. 38, Winter, pp. 64–86; May Aung and Roger Heeler (2001), "Core Competencies of Service Firms: A Framework for Strategic Decisions in International Markets," *Journal of Marketing Management,* Vol. 17, pp. 619–643; Rajshkhar G. Javalgi, and D. Steven White (2002), "Strategic Challenges for the Marketing of Services Internationally," *International Marketing Review,* Vol.19, No. 6, pp. 563–581.

23 For a discussion of the market penetration in China by McDonald's and KFC, see Qiaowei Shen and Ping Xiao (2014), "McDonld's and KFC in China: Competitors or Companions?" *Marketing Science*, Vol. 33, No. 2, pp. 287–307.

24 *The Business Times*, "Nexflix Shares Up on Talk of Profit Stream after Rollout," January 22, 2015, p. 23.

25 Rajshkhar G. Javalgi, and D. Steven White (2002), "Strategic Challenges for the Marketing of Services Internationally," *International Marketing Review,* Vol. 19, No. 6, pp. 563–581; Jochen Wirtz, Sven Tuzovic, and Michael Ehret (2015), "Global Business Services: Increasing Specialization and Integration of the World Economy as Drivers of Economic Growth," *Journal of Service Management,* Vol. 26, No. 4. pp. 565–587.

26 For more information on foreign market entry modes, read Shawn M. Carraher and Dianne H. B. Welsh, *Global Entrepreneurship* (Des Moines, IA: Kendall Hunt Publishing Inc., 2009).

27 J. J. Boddewyn, Marsha Baldwin Halbrich and A. C. Perry (1986), "Service Multinationals: Conceptualization, Measurement and Theory," *Journal of International Business Studies*, Fall, pp. 41–58; Sandra Vandermerwe and Michael Chadwick (1989), "The Internationalization of Services," *The Services Industries Journal*, Vol. 9, No. 1, January, pp. 79–93.

Service Pricing and Revenue Management

What is a cynic? A man who knows the price of everything and the value of nothing.

Oscar Wilde
Irish author, playwright, and poet (1854–1900)

There are two fools in any market: One does not charge enough. The other charges too much.

Russian Proverb

LEARNING OBJECTIVES (LOs)

By the end of this chapter, the reader should be able to:

➲ **LO 1** Recognize that effective pricing is central to the financial success of service firms.

➲ **LO 2** Outline the foundations of a pricing strategy as represented by the pricing tripod.

"That 'give it away free' strategy certainly worked well."

➲ **LO 3** Define different types of financial costs and explain the limitations of cost-based pricing.

➲ **LO 4** Understand the concept of net value and how gross value can be enhanced through value-based pricing and reduction of related monetary and non-monetary costs.

➲ **LO 5** Describe competition-based pricing and situations where service markets are less price-competitive.

➲ **LO 6** Define revenue management and describe how it works.

➲ **LO 7** Discuss the role of rate fences in effective revenue management.

➲ **LO 8** Be familiar with the issues of ethics and consumer concerns related to service pricing.

➲ **LO 9** Understand how fairness can be designed into revenue management policies.

➲ **LO 10** Discuss the six questions marketers need to answer to design an effective service pricing strategy.

OPENING VIGNETTE
Dynamic Pricing Is Here to Stay

Service firms are often faced with the problem of maximizing revenue and capacity, and one way to solve that is through dynamic pricing.[1] But just what is dynamic pricing? Have you been on a plane chatting with your neighbor and discovered that you both paid very different prices for the same air ticket in the same class of seats? That's dynamic pricing at work.

Dynamic pricing is a pricing strategy that varies the prices for different customers at different times, based on demand conditions. It is commonly used in the airline industry, but has also gained popularity in other industries. For example, the Eagles, the highest selling American band in US' history, started a system in early 2010 to increase prices for the best seats, and to lower prices of cheaper seats for their show in Sacramento, California. Their highest priced tickets cost $250, but the cheapest ticket was priced as low as $32. They cooperated with Live Nation Entertainment Inc. to use dynamic pricing for their tickets. Ten categories of ticket prices were set based on anticipated demand. With that, the band hoped to fill more seats and at the same time, make the tickets more affordable for more fans.

Lion King's success in turning its once-shaky fortunes around and becoming one of Broadway's top grossing shows has been largely attributed to dynamic pricing too. Similarly, in the sporting industry, the San Francisco Giants, a professional baseball team, sold 25,000 extra tickets in the first year they experimented with dynamic pricing, which earned them an extra $500,000 in revenue. Officials from the Major League Basketball and the National Basketball Association are expecting dynamic pricing to become the norm for the industry.

Companies such as ScoreBig Inc. are hoping to tap on this trend. It has been estimated that about 25–35% of seats for sports events and 40–50% of concert tickets remain unsold every year. ScoreBig Inc. aims to become the Priceline.com in this space by using demand-based dynamic pricing to help find buyers for these tickets. Dynamic pricing is certainly here to stay!

LO 1

Recognize that effective pricing is central to the financial success of service firms.

EFFECTIVE PRICING IS CENTRAL TO FINANCIAL SUCCESS

Importantly, marketing is the only function that brings operating revenues into the organization. All other management functions incur costs. A **business model** is the mechanism whereby, through effective pricing, sales are transformed into revenues, costs are covered, and value is created for the owners of the business. As noted by Joan Magretta:

> *A good business model answer [American management consultant] Peter Drucker's age-old questions: Who is the customer? And what does the customer value? It also answers the fundamental questions that every manager must ask: How do we make money in this business? What is the underlying economic logic that explains how we can deliver value to customers at an appropriate cost[2]?*

Creating a viable service requires a business model that allows for the costs of creating and delivering the service, in addition to a margin for profits, to be recovered through realistic pricing and revenue management strategies.

However, the pricing of services is complicated. Consider the bewildering fee schedules of many consumer banks or cell phone service providers, or the fluctuating fare structure of a full-service airline. Service organizations even use different terms to describe the prices they set. Universities talk about tuition, professional firms collect fees, banks impose interest and service charges, brokers charge commissions, some expressways impose tolls, utilities set tariffs, and insurance companies determine premiums — the list goes on. Consumers often find service pricing difficult to understand (e.g., insurance products or hospital bills), risky (when you enquire about an intercontinental flight on three different days, you may be offered three different prices), and sometimes even unethical (e.g., many bank and credit card users complain about a variety of fees and charges they consider to be unfair). Examine your own purchasing behavior; how did you feel the last time when you had to decide on booking a vacation, reserving a rental car, or opening a new bank account? In this chapter, you will learn how to set an effective pricing and revenue management strategy that fulfills the promise of the value proposition so that a value exchange takes place (i.e., the consumer decides to buy your service). An overview of this chapter is provided in *Figure 6.1.*

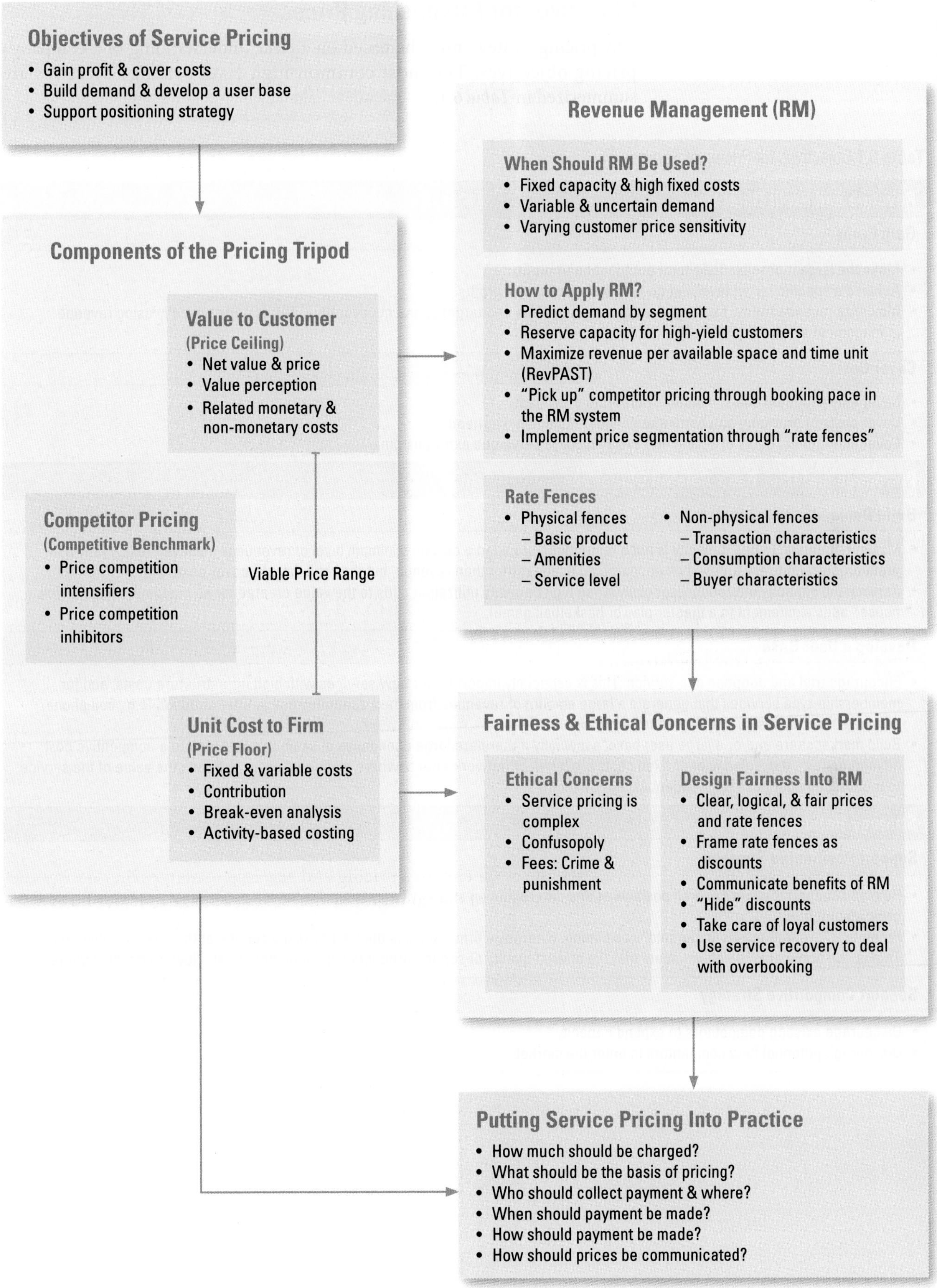

Objectives of Service Pricing

- Gain profit & cover costs
- Build demand & develop a user base
- Support positioning strategy

Components of the Pricing Tripod

Value to Customer
(Price Ceiling)
- Net value & price
- Value perception
- Related monetary & non-monetary costs

Competitor Pricing
(Competitive Benchmark)
- Price competition intensifiers
- Price competition inhibitors

Viable Price Range

Unit Cost to Firm
(Price Floor)
- Fixed & variable costs
- Contribution
- Break-even analysis
- Activity-based costing

Revenue Management (RM)

When Should RM Be Used?
- Fixed capacity & high fixed costs
- Variable & uncertain demand
- Varying customer price sensitivity

How to Apply RM?
- Predict demand by segment
- Reserve capacity for high-yield customers
- Maximize revenue per available space and time unit (RevPAST)
- "Pick up" competitor pricing through booking pace in the RM system
- Implement price segmentation through "rate fences"

Rate Fences
- Physical fences
  - Basic product
  - Amenities
  - Service level
- Non-physical fences
  - Transaction characteristics
  - Consumption characteristics
  - Buyer characteristics

Fairness & Ethical Concerns in Service Pricing

Ethical Concerns
- Service pricing is complex
- Confusopoly
- Fees: Crime & punishment

Design Fairness Into RM
- Clear, logical, & fair prices and rate fences
- Frame rate fences as discounts
- Communicate benefits of RM
- "Hide" discounts
- Take care of loyal customers
- Use service recovery to deal with overbooking

Putting Service Pricing Into Practice

- How much should be charged?
- What should be the basis of pricing?
- Who should collect payment & where?
- When should payment be made?
- How should payment be made?
- How should prices be communicated?

Figure 6.1 Organizing Framework for Pricing of Services

Objectives for Establishing Prices

Any pricing strategy must be based on a clear understanding of a company's pricing objectives. The most common high-level pricing objectives are summarized in *Table 6.1*.

Table 6.1 Objectives for Pricing of Services

Revenue and Profit Objectives
Gain Profit
• Make the largest possible long-term contribution or profit. • Achieve a specific target level, but do not seek to maximize profits. • Maximize revenue from a fixed capacity by varying prices and target segments over time. This is done typically using revenue management systems.
Cover Costs
• Cover fully allocated costs, including corporate overhead. • Cover costs of providing one particular service, excluding overhead. • Cover incremental costs of selling one extra unit or to serve one extra customer.
Patronage and User Base-Related Objectives
Build Demand
• Maximize demand (when capacity is not a restriction), provided a certain minimum level of revenue is achieved (e.g., many non-profit organizations are focused on encouraging usage rather than revenue, but they still have to cover costs). • Achieve full capacity utilization, especially when high capacity utilization adds to the value created for all customers (e.g., a "full house" adds excitement to a theater play or basketball game).
Develop a User Base
• Encourage trial and adoption of a service. This is especially important for new services with high infrastructure costs, and for membership-type services that generate a large amount of revenues from their continued usage after adoption (e.g., cell phone service subscriptions, or life insurance plans). • Build market share and/or a large user base, especially if there are large economies of scale that can lead to a competitive cost advantage (e.g., if development or fixed costs are high), or network effects where additional users enhance the value of the service to the existing user base (e.g., Facebook and LinkedIn).
Strategy-Related Objectives
Support Positioning Strategy
• Help and support the firm's overall positioning and differentiation strategy (e.g., as a price leader, or portrait a premium image with premium pricing). • Promote a "We-will-not-be-undersold" positioning, whereby a firm promises the best possible service at the best possible price. That is, the firm wants to communicate that the offered quality of service products cannot be bought at a lower cost elsewhere.
Support Competitive Strategy
• Discourage existing competitors to expand capacity. • Discourage potential new competitors to enter the market.

PRICING STRATEGY STANDS ON THREE FOUNDATIONS

Once the pricing objectives are understood, we can focus on pricing strategy. The foundations of pricing strategy can be described as a tripod, with costs to the provider, competitors' pricing, and value to the customer as the three legs (*Figure 6.2*). In many service industries, pricing used to be viewed from a financial and accounting standpoint, and therefore cost-plus pricing was used. Today, however, most service firms have a good understanding of value-based and competitive pricing. In the pricing tripod, the costs a firm needs to recover usually sets a minimum price, or price floor, for a specific service offering, and the customer's perceived value of the offering sets a maximum price, or price ceiling.

The price charged by competing services typically determines where the price can be set within the floor-to-ceiling range. The pricing objectives of the organization then determine where actual prices should be set, given the possible range provided by the pricing tripod analysis. Let's look at each leg of the pricing tripod in more detail, starting with costs to the provider.

Cost-Based Pricing

Pricing typically is more complex in services than it is in manufacturing. Because there's no ownership of services, it's usually harder to determine the financial costs of creating a process or intangible real-time performance for a customer than it is to identify the labor, materials, machine time, storage, and shipping costs associated with producing and distributing a physical good. In addition, due to the labor and infrastructure needed to create performances, many service organizations have a much higher ratio of fixed costs to variable costs than is typically found in manufacturing firms. Service businesses with high fixed costs include those with expensive physical facilities (such as hospitals or colleges), or a fleet of vehicles (such as airlines or trucking companies), or a network (such as railroad, telecommunications, and gas pipeline companies; see *Figure 6.3*).

⊃ LO 2
Outline the foundations of a pricing strategy as represented by the pricing tripod.

Figure 6.2 The pricing tripod

⊃ LO 3
Define different types of financial costs and explain the limitations of cost-based pricing.

Figure 6.3 Train services have very high infrastructure costs and variable costs of transporting an additional passenger are insignificant

Establishing the Costs of Providing Service. Even if you have already taken a marketing course, you may find it helpful to review how service costs can be estimated, using fixed, semi-variable, and variable costs, as well as how the notions of contribution and break-even analysis can help in pricing decisions (see *Marketing Review 6.1*). These traditional cost-accounting approaches work well for service firms with a large proportion of variable costs and/or semi-variable costs (e.g., many professional services).

Activity-Based Costing.[3] For service firms with high fixed costs and complex product lines with shared infrastructure such as in retail banking, it may be worthwhile considering the more complex activity-based costing (also called the "ABC") approach. For such firms, the ABC is a more accurate way to allocate indirect costs (i.e., overheads).

ABC links resources needed to perform an activity. A set of activities that comprises the processes needed to create and deliver a particular service is then combined. When determining the indirect cost of a service, a firm looks at the resources needed to perform each activity, and then allocates the indirect cost to a service based on the quantities and types of activities required to perform the service. Thus, resource expenses (or indirect costs) are linked to the variety and complexity of services produced and not just on physical volume.

If implemented well, firms will be in a better position to estimate the costs of its various services, activities, and processes — and about the costs of creating specific types of services, delivering services in different locations (even different countries), or serving specific customers. The net result is a management tool that can help companies to pinpoint the profitability of different services, channels, market segments, and even individual customers.

Pricing Implications of Cost Analysis. To make a profit, a firm must set its price high enough to recover the full costs of producing and marketing the service and add a sufficient margin to yield the desired profit at the predicted sales volume.

Managers in businesses with high fixed and marginal variable costs may feel that they have tremendous pricing flexibility and be tempted to set low prices in order to boost sales. Some firms promote **loss leaders**, which are services sold at less than full cost to attract customers, who (it is hoped) will then be tempted to buy profitable service offerings from the same organization in the future. However, there will be no profit at the end of the year unless all relevant costs have been recovered. Many service businesses have gone bankrupt because they ignored this fact. Hence, firms that compete on low prices need to have a very good understanding of their cost structure and of the sales volumes needed to breakeven.

MARKETING REVIEW 6.1

Understanding Costs, Contribution, and Break-Even Analysis

Fixed costs are economic costs a supplier would continue to incur (at least in the short run) even if no services were sold. These costs are likely to include rent, depreciation, utilities, taxes, insurance, salaries and wages for managers and long-term employees, security, and interest payments.

Variable costs refer to the economic costs associated with serving an additional customer, such as making an additional bank transaction or selling an additional seat on a flight. In many services, such costs are very low. For instance, very little labor or fuel cost is involved in transporting an extra passenger on a flight. In a theater, the cost of seating an extra patron is close to zero. More significant variable costs are associated with activities such as serving food and beverages or installing new parts when undertaking repairs, as they often include providing costly physical products in addition to labor. Just because a firm has sold a service at a price that exceeds its variable cost doesn't mean the firm is now profitable, since there are still fixed and semi-variable costs to be recouped.

Semi-variable costs fall in between fixed and variable costs. They represent expenses that rise or fall in a stepwise fashion as the volume of business increases or decreases. Examples include adding an extra flight to meet increased demand on a specific route or hiring a part-time employee to work in a restaurant on busy weekends.

Contribution is the difference between the variable cost of selling an extra unit of service and the money received from the buyer of that service. It goes to cover fixed and semi-variable costs before creating profits.

Determining and allocating economic costs can be a challenging task in some service operations because of the difficulty of deciding how to assign fixed costs in a

Figure 6.4 Housekeeping services contribute to the cost of hotel rooms

multi-service facility such as a hospital. For instance, certain fixed costs are associated with running the emergency department in a hospital. Beyond that, there are fixed costs of running the hospital. So how much of the hospital's fixed costs should be allocated to the emergency department? A hospital manager might use one of several approaches to calculate the emergency department's share of overhead costs. These could include (1) the percentage of total floor space it occupies, (2) the percentage of employee hours or payroll it accounts for, or (3) the percentage of total patient contact hours involved. Each method is likely to yield a totally different fixed-cost allocation. One method might show the emergency department to be very profitable, while the other might flag it as a loss-making operation.

Breakeven analysis allows managers to know at what sales volume a service will become profitable. This is called the breakeven point. The necessary analysis involves dividing the total fixed and semi-variable costs by the contribution obtained on each unit of service. For example, if a 100-room hotel needs to cover fixed and semi-variable costs of $2 million a year, and the average contribution per room-night is $100, then the hotel will need to sell 20,000 room-nights per year out of a total annual capacity of 36,500. If prices are cut by an average of $20 per room-night (or if variable costs rise by $20), then the contribution will drop to $80, and the hotel's breakeven volume will rise to 25,000 room-nights.

LO 4

Understand the concept of net value and how gross value can be enhanced through value-based pricing and reduction of related monetary and non-monetary costs.

Value-Based Pricing

Another leg of the pricing tripod is value to the customer. No customer will pay more for a service than he or she thinks it is worth. So, marketers need to understand how customers perceive service value in order to set an appropriate price[4].

Understanding Net Value. When customers purchase a service, they are weighing the perceived benefits of the service against the perceived costs they will incur. However, customer definitions of value may be highly personal and idiosyncratic. Valarie Zeithaml proposes four broad expressions of value:

1. Value is a low price.
2. Value is whatever I want in a product.
3. Value is the quality I get for the price I pay.
4. Value is what I get for what I give[5].

In this book, we focus on the fourth category and use the term **net value**, which is the sum of all perceived benefits (gross value) minus the sum of all the perceived costs of the service. The greater the positive difference between the two, the greater the net value. Economists use the term **consumer surplus** to define the difference between the price customers pay and the amount they would actually have been willing to pay to obtain the desired benefits (or "utility") offered by a specific product. If the perceived costs of a service are greater than its perceived benefits, then the service in question will possess negative net value, and the consumer will not buy it. You can think of calculations that customers make in their minds as being similar to weighing with a pair of old-fashioned scales, with product benefits in one tray and the costs associated with obtaining those benefits in the other tray (*Figure 6.5*). When customers evaluate competing services, they are basically comparing the relative net values (see also multi-attribute models in Chapter 2 where we discuss to quantify net value through a scoring system). As we discussed in Chapter 4, a marketer can increase the value of a service by adding benefits to the core product and by improving supplementary services, which typically entails enhancing the benefits while reducing the burdens for customers.

Figure 6.5 Net value equals perceived benefits minus perceived costs

Figure 6.6 Blondie seeks her money's worth from the plumber

Managing the Perception of Value[6]. Since value is subjective, not all customers have the skills or knowledge to judge the quality and value they receive. This is true especially for credence services (discussed in Chapter 2), for which customers cannot assess the quality of a service even after consumption[7]. Marketers of services such as strategy consulting must find ways to communicate the time, research, professional expertise, and attention to detail, that go into, for example, completing a best practice consulting project. The invisibility of back-stage facilities and labor makes it hard for customers to see what they're getting for their money. Therefore, the firm will have to manage the perception of value. Consider a homeowner who calls an electrician to repair a defective circuit. The electrician arrives, carrying a small bag of tools. He disappears into the closet where the circuit board is located, locates the problem, replaces a defective circuit breaker, and presto! Everything works. A mere 20 minutes have elapsed. A few days later, the homeowner is horrified to receive a bill for $150, most of it for labor charges. Not surprisingly, customers are often left feeling they have been taken advantage of — take a look at Blondie's reaction to the plumber in *Figure 6.6*.

To manage the perception of value, effective communications and even personal explanations are needed to help customers understand the value they receive. What customers often fail to recognize are the fixed costs that business owners need to recoup. The electrician in our earlier example has to cover the costs for his office, telephone, insurance, vehicles, tools, fuel, and office support staff. The variable costs of a home visit are also higher than they appear. To the 20 minutes spent at the house, 15 minutes of driving each way might be added, plus five minutes each to unload and reload needed tools and supplies from the van, thus effectively tripling the labor time to a total of 60 minutes devoted to this call. The firm still has to add a margin in order to make a profit.

Reducing Related Monetary and Non-monetary Costs

When we consider customer net value, we need to understand the customers' perceived costs. From a customer's point of view, the price charged by a supplier is only part of the costs involved in buying and using a service. There are other **costs of service**, which are made up of the **related monetary** and **non-monetary costs**.

Related Monetary Costs. Customers often incur significant financial costs in searching for, purchasing, and using the service, above and beyond the purchase price paid to the supplier. For instance, the cost of an evening at the theater for a couple with young children usually far exceeds the price of two tickets, because it can include expenses such as hiring a babysitter, travel, parking, food and beverages.

Non-monetary Costs. Non-monetary costs reflect the time, effort, and discomfort associated with the search, purchase, and use of a service. Like many customers, you may refer to them collectively as "effort" or "hassle." Non-monetary costs tend to be higher when customers are involved in production (which is particularly important in people-processing services and in self-service) and must travel to the service site. Services high on experience and credence attributes may also create psychological costs such as anxiety. There are four distinct categories of non-monetary costs: time, physical, psychological, and sensory costs.

- **Time costs** are part of the service delivery. Today's customers often complain that they do not have enough time and therefore are reluctant to waste time on non-enjoyable and non-value adding activities such as travelling to a government office and waiting in a queue. Customers may even use similar terms to define time usage as they do for money; for instance, consumers talk about budgeting, spending, investing, wasting, losing, and saving time. Time spent on one activity represents an opportunity cost because it could be spent more pleasurably or profitably in other ways. Internet users are often frustrated by the amount of time they spend looking for information on a website. Many people loath visiting government offices to obtain passports, driving licenses, or permits, not because of the fees involved, but because of the time "wasted"[8].

- **Physical costs** (such as effort, fatigue, discomfort) may be part of the costs of obtaining services, especially if customers must go to the service factory, if waiting and long queues are involved, if body treatments are involved such as for medical treatments, piercing or waxing (*Figure 6.7*), and if delivery is through self-service.

Figure 6.7 Anxiety is an important psychological cost in medical treatment

- **Psychological costs** such as mental effort (e.g., filling in account opening forms requesting for detailed information), perceived risk and anxiety ("Is this the best treatment?", "Is he the right surgeon?", or "Is this be best mortgage for me?", *Figure 6.8*), cognitive dissonance ("Was it good to sign up for this life insurance, this annual gym membership?"), feelings of inadequacy and fear ("Will I be smart enough to succeed in this MBA program?") are sometimes attached to buying and using a particular service.

- **Sensory costs** relate to unpleasant sensations affecting any of the five senses. In a service environment, these costs may include putting up with crowding, noise, unpleasant smells, drafts, excessive heat or cold, uncomfortable seating, and visually unappealing environments.

As shown in *Figure 6.9*, service users can incur costs during any of the three stages of the service consumption model as introduced in Chapter 2. Consequently, firms have to consider (1) **search costs**, (2) **purchase and service encounter costs**, and (3) **post-purchase** or **after costs**. When you were looking at colleges and universities, how much money, time, and effort did you spend before deciding where to apply? How much time and effort would you put into selecting a new cell phone service provider or a bank, or planning a vacation?

Figure 6.8 Does adding options always create value or will it confuse the customer?

"As an alternative to the traditional 30-year mortgage, we also offer an interest-only mortgage, balloon mortgage, reverse mortgage, upside down mortgage, inside out mortgage, loop-de-loop mortgage, and the spinning double axel mortgage with a triple lutz."

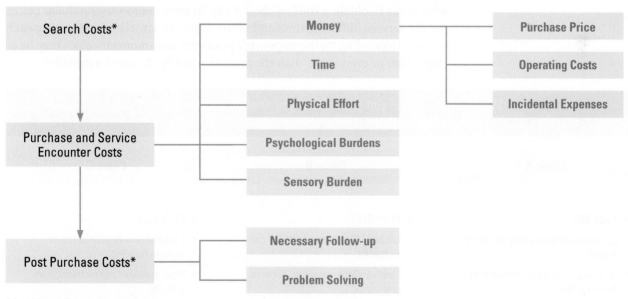

* Includes all five cost categories

Figure 6.9 Defining total user costs

A firm can create competitive advantage by minimizing those non-monetary and related monetary costs, and thereby increase consumer value. Possible approaches include:

- Working with operations experts to reduce the time required to complete service purchase, delivery and consumption; become "easy-to-do-business-with".

- Minimizing unwanted psychological costs of service at each stage by eliminating or redesigning unpleasant or inconvenient procedures, educating customers on what to expect, and retraining staff to be friendlier and more helpful.

- Eliminating or minimizing unwanted physical effort, notably during search and delivery processes. Improve signage and "road mapping" in facilities and on webpages can help customers to find their way and prevent them from getting lost and frustrated.

- Decreasing unpleasant sensory costs of service by creating more attractive visual environments, reducing noise, installing more comfortable furniture and equipment, and curtailing offensive smells.

- Suggesting ways in which customers can reduce associated monetary costs, including discounts with partner suppliers (e.g., parking) or offering mail or online delivery of activities that previously required a personal visit.

Perceptions of net value may vary widely among customers and from one situation to another for the same customer. Most services have at least two segments — one segment that spends time to save money, and another that spends money to save time. Therefore, many service markets can be segmented according to the sensitivity to time savings and convenience versus price sensitivity[9]. Consider *Figure 6.10*, which identifies a choice of three clinics available to an individual who needs to obtain a routine chest x-ray. In addition to varying dollar prices for the service, different time and effort costs are associated with using each service. Depending on the customer's priorities, non-monetary costs may be as important, or even more, than the price charged by the service provider.

Which clinic would you patronize if you needed a chest x-ray (assuming that all three clinics offer good technical quality)?		
Clinic A	**Clinic B**	**Clinic C**
• Price $85	• Price $145	• Price $225
• Located one hour away by car or transit	• Located 15 minutes away by car or transit	• Located next to your office or college building
• Next available appointment is in three weeks	• Next available appointment is in one week	• Next available appointment is in one day
• Hours: Monday to Friday, 9.00 a.m. to 5.00 p.m.	• Hours: Monday to Friday, 8.00 a.m. to 10.00 p.m.	• Hours: Monday to Saturday, 8.00 a.m. to 10.00 p.m.
• Estimated waiting time is about two hours	• Estimated waiting is about 30–45 minutes	• By appointment; estimated waiting time is 0–15 minutes

Figure 6.10 Trading off monetary and non-monetary costs

Competition-based Pricing

LO 5
Describe competition-based pricing and situations where service markets are less price-competitive.

The last leg of the pricing tripod is competition. Firms with relatively undifferentiated services need to monitor what competitors are charging and should to try to price accordingly[10]. When customers see little or no difference between competing offerings, they may just choose what they perceive to be the cheapest. In such a situation, the firm with the lowest cost per unit of service enjoys an enviable market advantage and often assumes **price leadership**. Here, one firm acts as the price leader, with others taking their cue from this company. You can sometimes see this phenomenon at the local level when several gas stations compete within a short distance of one another. As soon as one station raises or lowers its prices, others follow suit.

Price Competition Intensifiers. Price competition intensifies with:
- Increasing number of competitors.
- Increasing number of substituting offers.
- Wider distribution of competitor and/or substitution offers.
- An increasing surplus capacity in the industry.

Price Competition Inhibitors. Although some service industries can be fiercely competitive (e.g., airlines and online banking), not all are, especially when one or more of the following circumstances reduce price competition:

- **Non-price related costs of using competing alternatives are high.** When saving time and effort are of equal or greater importance to customers than price in selecting a supplier, the intensity of price competition is reduced. Competitor services have their own set of related monetary and non-monetary costs. In such cases, the actual prices charged sometimes become secondary for competitive comparisons.

- **Personal relationships matter.** For services that are highly personalized and customized, such as hairstyling (*Figure 6.11*) or family medical care, relationships with individual providers often are very important to customers, thus discouraging them from responding to competitive offers. Many global banks, for example, prefer to focus on wealthy customers in order to form long-term personal relationships with them.

Figure 6.11 Personalized hairstyling may prevent customers from switching to competing providers

- **Switching costs are high.** When it takes effort, time, and money to switch providers, customers are less likely to take advantage of competing offers[11]. Cell phone service providers often require one- or two-year contracts from their subscribers and charge significant financial penalties for early cancellation of service. Likewise, life insurance firms charge administrative fees or cancellation charges when policy holders want to cancel their policy within a certain time period.

- **Services are often time and location specific.** When people want to use a service at a specific location or at a particular time or perhaps both, simultaneously, they usually find they have fewer options, which reduces price competition[12].

Firms that always react to competitors' price changes run the risk of pricing *lower* than what might really be necessary. Managers should be aware of falling into the trap of comparing competitors' prices dollar for dollar and then seeking to match them. A better strategy is to take into account the entire cost to customers of each competitive offering, including all related monetary and non-monetary costs, plus potential switching costs. Managers should also assess the impact of distribution, time and location factors, as well as estimating competitors' available capacity before deciding what response is appropriate.

LO 6
Define revenue management and describe how it works.

REVENUE MANAGEMENT: WHAT IT IS AND HOW IT WORKS

Many service businesses now focus on strategies to maximize the revenue[13] (or contribution) that can be obtained from available capacity at any given point in time. Revenue management is important in value creation as it ensures better capacity utilization and reserves capacity for higher-paying segments. It's a sophisticated approach to managing supply and demand under varying degrees of constraint.

Airlines, hotels, and car rental firms, in particular, have become adept at varying their prices in response to the price sensitivity and needs of different market segments at different times of the day, week, or season. More recently, hospitals, restaurants, golf courses, on-demand IT services, data processing centers, concert organizers (*Figure 6.12*), and even nonprofit organizations increasingly use revenue management[14]. It is most effective when applied to service businesses characterized by:
- High fixed cost structure and relatively fixed capacity resulting in perishable inventory.
- Variable and uncertain demand.
- Varying customer price sensitivity.

Figure 6.12 Golf courses have high fixed cost structure so it benefits them to implement revenue management

Reserving Capacity for High-yield Customers

In practice, revenue management (also known as yield management) involves setting prices according to predicted demand levels among different market segments. The least price sensitive segment is the first to be provided capacity, paying the highest price; other segments follow at increasingly lower prices. Because higher-paying segments often book closer to the time of actual consumption, firms need a disciplined approach to save capacity for them instead of simply selling on a first-come, first-served basis. For example, business travelers often reserve airline seats, hotel rooms, and rental cars at short notice, but vacationers may book leisure travel months in advance, and convention organizers often block hotel space years in advance for big events.

Figure 6.13 illustrates the capacity allocation in a hotel setting, where demand from different types of customers varies not only by day of the week but also by season. These allocation decisions by segment, captured in reservation databases accessible worldwide, tell reservations personnel when to stop accepting reservations at certain prices, even though many rooms may still remain available. Loyalty program members, who are mainly business travelers who pay high corporate rates, are obviously a very desirable segment, followed by transient guests, and weekend packages. Airline contracts typically offer the lowest rates per room, as airlines book large volumes far in advance and can therefore negotiate attractive rates.

Similar charts can be constructed for most capacity-constrained businesses. In some instances, capacity is measured in terms of seats for a given performance, seat-miles, or rooms-nights; in others it may be in terms of machine time, labor time, billable professional hours, vehicle miles, or storage volume, whichever is the scarce resource.

A well-designed revenue management system can predict with reasonable accuracy how many customers will use a given service at a specific time at each of several different price levels and then block the relevant amount of capacity at each level (known as a **price bucket**). Sophisticated firms use complex mathematical models for this purpose and employ revenue managers to make decisions about inventory allocation. This information can also be used to predict periods of excess capacity with the aim to increase usage through promotions and incentives. The objective is to maximize revenues on a day-to-day basis.

In the case of airlines, these models integrate massive historical databases on past passenger travel and can forecast demand of up to one year in advance for each individual departure. At fixed intervals, the revenue manager — who may be assigned specific routes at a large airline — checks the actual pace of bookings (i.e., sales at a given time before departure) and compares it with the forecasted pace. If significant deviations exist between actual and forecasted demand, the manager will adjust the size of the inventory buckets. For example, if the *booking*

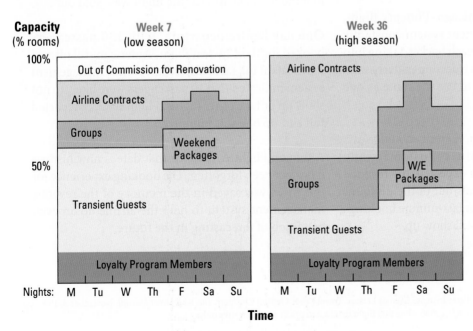

Figure 6.13 Setting capacity allocation targets by segment for a hotel

pace for a higher paying segment is stronger than expected, additional capacity is allocated to this segment and taken away from the lowest paying segment. The objective is to maximize the revenues from the flight. *Service Insights 6.1* shows how revenue management has been implemented at American Airlines, an industry leader in this field.

SERVICE INSIGHTS 6.1
Pricing Seats on Flight AA 333

Revenue management departments use sophisticated revenue management software and powerful computers to forecast, track and manage each flight on a given date separately. Let's look at American Airlines (AA) Flight 333, a popular flight from Chicago to Phoenix, Arizona, which departs daily at 4.50 p.m. on the 1,440–mile (2,317–kilometer) journey.

The 124 seats in coach (economy class) are divided into different fare categories, referred to by revenue management specialists as "buckets". There is enormous variation in ticket prices among these seats: round-trip fares range from $298 for a bargain excursion ticket (with various restrictions and a cancellation penalty attached) all the way up to an unrestricted fare of $1,065. Seats are also available at an even higher price in the small first-class section at $1,530. Scott McCartney tells how ongoing analysis by the computer program changes the allocation of seats between each of the seven buckets in economy class.

In the weeks before each Chicago–Phoenix flight, American's revenue management system constantly adjusts the number of seats in each bucket, taking into account tickets sold, historical ridership patterns, and connecting passengers likely to use the route as one leg of a longer trip.

If advance bookings are slim, American adds seats to low-fare buckets. If business customers buy unrestricted fares earlier than expected, the revenue management system takes seats out of the discount buckets and preserves them for last-minute bookings that the system predicts will still show up.

With 69 of 124 coach seats already sold four weeks before one recent departure of Flight AA333, American's revenue management system begins to limit the number of seats in lower-priced buckets. A week later, it totally shut off sales for the bottom three buckets, priced $300 or less. To a Chicago customer looking for a cheap seat, the flight was "sold out".

One day before departure, with 130 passengers booked for the 124-seat flight, American still offered four seats at full fare because its revenue management system indicated that 10 passengers were likely to not show up or take other flights. Flight AA333 departed full and no one was bumped.

Although Flight AA333 for that date is now history, it has not been forgotten. The booking experience for this flight was saved in the memory of the revenue management system to help the airline do an even better job of forecasting in the future.

Source

Scott McCartney, "Ticket Shock: Business Fares Increase Even as Leisure Travel Keeps Getting Cheaper," *The Wall Street Journal*, November 3, 1997, pp. A1, A10. http://www.aa.com, accessed March 02, 2015. Note that flight details and prices are illustrative only.

How Can We Measure the Effectiveness of a Firm's Revenue Management?

Many capacity-constrained service organizations use percentage of capacity sold as a basic indicator of success. For instance, airlines talk of "load factor" achieved, hotels of "occupancy rate" and hospitals of "census". Similarly, professional firms monitor the proportion of their partners' and associates' time that is "billable hours". However, these percentages by themselves tell us little of the relative profitability of the business attracted, since high usage rates may simply be a reflection of heavy discounting.

Therefore, success in revenue management is generally defined as maximizing the revenue per available capacity for a given space and time unit (RevPAST). For example, airlines seek to maximize revenue per available seat kilometer (RevPASK); hotels try to maximize their revenue per available room-night (RevPAR); and performing arts centers try to maximize their revenue per available seat performance. These indices show the interplay between capacity utilization and average rate or price achieved, and can be tracked over time and benchmarked across operating units within a service firm (e.g., across hotel properties in a larger chain) and across firms. Success in revenue management means increasing RevPAST.

How Does Competitors' Pricing Affect Revenue Management?

Because revenue management systems monitor booking pace, they indirectly pick up the effects of competitors' pricing. For example, if an airline prices a flight too low, it will experience a higher booking pace, and its cheaper seats fill up quickly. That is generally not desirable, as it means a higher share of late-booking as well as high fare-paying customers not being able to get their seats confirmed, and therefore fly on competing airlines. If the initial pricing is too high, the firm will get too low a share of early booking segments (which still tend to offer a reasonable yield) and may later have to offer deeply discounted "last-minute" tickets to sell excess capacity. Some of the sales of distressed inventory, as it is called in industry, may take place through reverse auctions, using intermediaries such as Priceline.com.

Price Elasticity

For revenue management to work effectively, there need to be two or more segments that attach different values to the service and have different price elasticities. The concept of elasticity describes how sensitive demand is to changes in price and is computed as follows:

$$\text{Price elasticity} = \frac{\text{Percentage change in demand}}{\text{Percentage change in price}}$$

When price elasticity is at "unity," sales of a service rise (or fall) by the same percentage that price falls (or rises). If a small change in price has a big impact on sales, demand for that product is said to be **price elastic**. If a change in price has little effect on sales, demand is described as **price inelastic**. The concept is illustrated in the simple chart presented in *Figure 6.14*, which shows the price elasticity for two segments, one with a highly elastic demand (a small change in price results in a big change in the amount demanded) and the other with a highly inelastic demand (even big changes in price have little impact on the amount demanded). To allocate and price capacity effectively, the revenue manager needs to find out how sensitive demand is to price and what net revenues will be generated at different price points for each target segment.

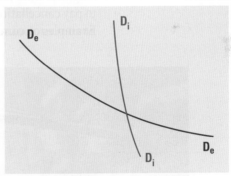

D_e : Demand is *price elastic*. Small changes in price lead to big changes in demand.

D_i : Demand for service is *price inelastic*. Big changes in price have little impact on demand.

$$\text{Price elasticity} = \frac{\text{Percentage change in demand}}{\text{Percentage change in price}}$$

Figure 6.14 Illustration of price elasticity

Designing Rate Fences

Inherent in revenue management is the concept of **price customization** — that is, charging different customers different prices for what is actually the same product. As noted by Hermann Simon and Robert Dolan,

> *The basic idea of price customization is simple: Have people pay prices based on the value they put on the product. Obviously you can't just hang out a sign saying "Pay me what it's worth to you," or "It's $80 if you value it that much but only $40 if you don't." You have to find a way to segment customers by their valuations. In a sense, you have to "build a fence" between high-value customers and low-value customers so the "high" buyers can't take advantage of the low price*[15].

How can a firm make sure that customers who are willing to pay higher prices are unable to take advantage of lower-price buckets? Properly designed rate fences allow customers to self-segment on the basis of service characteristics and willingness to pay. Rate fences help companies to restrict lower prices to customers willing to accept certain restrictions on their purchase and consumption experiences.

Fences can be either physical or non-physical. Physical fences refer to tangible product differences related to the different prices, such as the seat location in a theater (*Figure 6.15*), the size and furnishing of a hotel room, or the product bundle (e.g., first class is better than economy). In contrast, non-physical fences refer to differences in consumption, transaction, or buyer characteristics, but the service is basically the same (e.g., there is no difference in an economy class seat or service whether a person bought a heavily discounted ticket or paid the full fare for it). Examples of non-physical fences include having to book a certain length of time ahead, not being able to cancel or change a booking (or having to pay cancellation or change penalties), or having to stay over a weekend night. Examples of common rate fences are shown in *Table 6.2*.

Figure 6.15 Expect higher prices for seats that have a better view of your favorite musicals on Broadway

Table 6.2 Key Categories of Rate Fences

Rate Fences	Examples
Physical (product-related) Fences	
Basic product	• Class of travel (business/economy class) • Size of rental car • Size and furnishing of a hotel room • Seat location in a theater or stadium
Amenities	• Free breakfast at a hotel, airport pick up, etc. • Free golf cart at a golf course • Valet parking
Service level	• Priority wait-listing, separate check-in counters with no or only short queues • Improved food and beverage selection • Dedicated service hotlines • Personal butler • Dedicated account management team
Other physical characteristics	• Table location pricing (e.g., restaurant table with view in a high-rise building), seat location pricing (e.g., a window or aisle seat in an aircraft cabin) • Extra legroom on an airline
Non-Physical Fences	
Transaction Characteristics	
– Time of booking or reservation	• Discounts for advance purchase
– Location of booking or reservation	• Passengers booking air tickets for an identical route in different countries are charged different prices (e.g., prices tend to be higher at an airline's hub because of higher frequency flights and more direct flights). • Customers making reservations online are charged a lower price than those making reservations by phone
– Flexibility of ticket usage	• Fees/penalties for canceling or changing a reservation (up to loss of entire ticket price) • Non-refundable reservation fees
Consumption Characteristics	
– Time or duration of use	• Happy hour offer in a bar, early-bird special in a restaurant before 6:00 p.m., and minimum required spending during peak periods. • Must stay over a Saturday night for a hotel booking. • Must stay at least for five nights
– Location of consumption	• Price depends on departure location, especially in international travel. • Prices vary by location (between cities, city center versus edges of the city)
Buyer Characteristics	
– Frequency or volume of consumption	• Members of certain loyalty tier with the firm (e.g., platinum member) get priority pricing, discounts or loyalty benefits • Season tickets
– Group membership	• Child, student, senior citizen discounts • Affiliation with certain groups (e.g., alumni) • Membership with the firm's loyalty program • Corporate rates
– Size of customer group	• Group discounts based on size of group
– Geographic location	• Local customers are charged lower rates than tourists • Customers from certain countries are charged higher prices

In summary, based on a detailed understanding of customer needs, preferences, and willingness to pay, product and revenue managers can design effective products comprising the core service, physical product features (physical fences), and non-physical product features (non-physical fences). In addition, a good understanding of the demand curve is needed so that "buckets" of inventory can be assigned to the various products and price categories. An example from the airline industry is shown in *Figure 6.16* and an interview with a senior executive with a career in revenue management is featured in *Service Insights 6.2*.

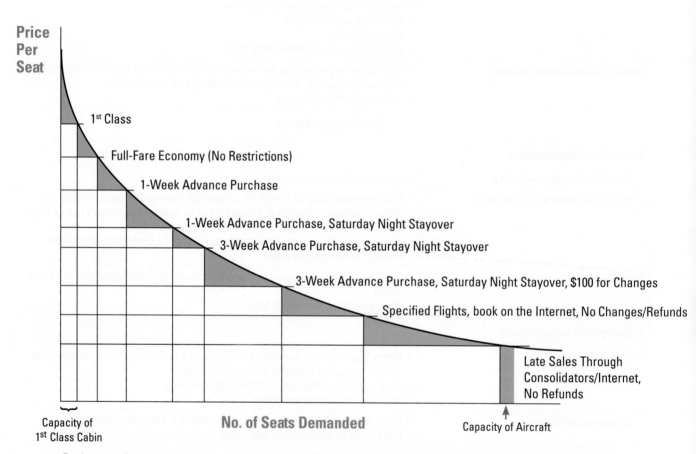

Dark areas denote amount of consumer surplus (goal of segmented pricing is to reduce this).

Figure 6.16 Relating price buckets to the demand curve

SERVICE INSIGHTS 6.2

Interview With a Vice President Revenue Management and Analytics

Q: What is the role of a revenue manager?

A: When I started my career, the primary focus was on forecasting, inventory control, pricing, market segment and geographic mix, and allotment control. The Internet changed the scene significantly and several global giants, such as Expedia and Travelocity, emerged after 9/11 when travel bookings plummeted and the industry realized the power of the Internet to help them sell distressed inventory. But airlines and hotels want to control their own inventory and pricing to cut costs and reduce reliance on intermediaries, so there's increasing focus on driving bookings via direct channels such as their own branded websites, building online brands, and implementing CRM programs to build loyalty and encourage repeat purchase. Responsibilities have also broadened beyond mainstream hotel rooms to include revenue management of secondary income sources such as function space, restaurants, golf courses, and spa.

Q: What differences do you see between revenue management for airlines and hotels?

A: Fundamentally, the techniques of forecasting and optimizing pricing and inventory controls are the same. However, some key differences exist. Airlines have a larger ability to use pricing to expand travel demand from their key markets. By contrast, pricing practices in hotels can shift market share within a location but, as a rule, not overall market size. Consumers are also more likely to view many pricing practices — such as advance purchase restrictions and discounts — as fair practice for the airline industry, but less so when applied by the hotel industry.

Organizational structure also tends to be different. The airlines adopt central revenue management control for all flights, and revenue managers have little interaction with the reservations and sales teams in the field. A precise and statistical application of pricing and inventory control is thus the focus.

Jeannette Ho

In the hotel industry, revenue management is still often decentralized to every hotel, requiring daily interaction with reservations and sales. The human element is key for successful implementation in hotels, requiring a more cohesive culture of revenue management across multiple hotel departments such as reservations, sales, catering and even front office, to gain the biggest impact on hotel performance.

Q: What skills do you need to succeed as a revenue manager?

A: Strong statistical and analytical skills are essential, but to be really successful, revenue managers need to have equally strong interpersonal and influencing skills for their decisions and analyses to be embraced by other departments. Traditional ways of segmenting customers via their transactional characteristics such as booking lead time, channel of reservation, and type of promotion are insufficient. Both behavioral characteristics (such as motive for travel, products sought, spending pattern, and degree of autonomy) and emotional characteristics (such as self-image, conspicuous consumer or reluctant traveler, impulse or planned) need to be incorporated into revenue management considerations.

Q: How are revenue management practices perceived by customers?

A: The art of implementation is not to let the customers feel that your pricing and inventory control practices are unfair and meant primarily to increase the top and bottom line of the company. Intelligent and meaningful rate fences and product packaging have to be used to allow customers to self-segment so that they retain a feeling of choice. Now with the importance of Big Data application, intelligent integration of individual customer needs and wants to create personalized pricing and product offer is key to not only maximizing the revenue for a given period, but maximizing the share of wallet from a loyal customer over their lifecycle.

Q: What is the daily nature of the job?

A: The market presents a lot of demand changes and you need to monitor your competitors' price as it fluctuates daily across the various distribution changes. The customer needs and willingness to pay are also changing over time. It's definitely a prerequisite to be quick in analysis and decisive. One needs to feel comfortable taking calculated risks and choose from a plethora of revenue management and pricing tools to decide on the best fit for the situation.

Source

We thank Jeannette Ho, who was Vice President Revenue Management and Distribution at Fairmont Raffles Hotels International when this interview was conducted on June 25, 2013. Jeannette was responsible for spearheading and implementing the revenue management initiatives for the Group. Her team drove the company's global distribution strategy, oversaw its E-commerce channels and Central Reservations System, and developed its performance intelligence capabilities. Prior to her current role, Jeannette has been working in revenue management, distribution, and CRM with various international companies such as Singapore Airlines, Banyan Tree, and Starwood Hotels & Resorts.

⊃ LO 8

Be familiar with the issues of ethics and consumer concerns related to service pricing.

FAIRNESS AND ETHICAL CONCERNS IN SERVICE PRICING

Do you sometimes have difficulty understanding how much it is going to cost you to use a service? Do you believe that many prices are unfair? If so, you're not alone[16]. The fact is, service users can't always be sure in advance what they will receive in return for their money. There's an implicit assumption among many customers that a higher-priced service should offer more benefits and greater quality than a lower-priced one. For example, a professional, say, a lawyer who charges very high fees is assumed to be more skilled than one who is relatively inexpensive. Although price can serve as an indication of quality, it is sometimes hard to be sure if the extra value is really there.

Service Pricing Is Complex

Pricing for services tend to be complex and hard to understand. Comparison across providers may even require complex spreadsheets or even mathematical formulas. Consumer advocates sometimes charge that this complexity represents a deliberate choice on the part of service suppliers who don't want customers to be able to determine who offers the best value for money and therefore reduce price competition. In fact, complexity makes it easy (and perhaps more tempting) for firms to engage in unethical behavior. The quoted prices typically used by consumers for price comparisons may be only the first of several charges that can be billed.

For example, cell phone companies have a confusing variety of plans to meet the distinct needs and usage patterns of different market segments. Plans can be national, regional, or purely local in scope. Monthly fees vary according to the number of minutes and mobile data capacity selected in advance. There can be separate allowances for peak and off-peak minutes. Overtime minutes and "roaming minutes" on other carriers are charged at higher rates. Some plans allow unlimited off-peak calling, others have free incoming calls. Some providers charge calls per second, per 6-second block, or even per-minute block, resulting in vastly different costs per month. Data plans (including features such as being allowed to roll over unused mobile data to the next month), handset subsidies for new phones, roaming fees, family and bundled plans that can include several cell phones and other mobile devices, landline, and Internet services add to this complexity. On top of complex pricing plans, many people find it difficult to forecast their own usage, which makes it even harder to compute comparative prices when evaluating competing suppliers whose fees are based on a variety of usage-related factors.

In addition, puzzling new fees have started to appear on bills (*Figure 6.17*). Phone bills, of course, include real taxes (e.g., sales tax), but on many bills, the majority of surcharges, which users often misread as taxes, go directly to the phone company. For instance, the "property tax allotment" is nothing more than a factor for the property taxes the carrier pays, the "single bill fee" charges for consolidated billing of the mobile and land line service, and the "carrier cost recovery fee" is a catch-all for all sorts of operating expenses. In an editorial entitled "Cell Hell," Jim Guest, Consumer Union's president, observed:

Figure 6.17 Puzzling new fees have started to appear on the bills of many service providers

> *In the 10 years since Consumer Reports started rating cell phones and calling plans, we've never found an easy way to compare actual costs. From what our readers tell us, they haven't either. Each carrier presents its rates, extra charges, and calling areas differently. Deciphering one company's plan is hard enough, but comparing plans from various carries is nearly impossible[17].*

It seems no coincidence that humorist Scott Adams (the creator of Dilbert) used exclusively service examples when he "branded" the future of pricing as "confusopoly." Noting that firms such as telecommunication companies, banks, insurance firms, and other financial service providers, offer nearly identical services, Adams remarks:

> *You would think this would create a price war and drive prices down to the cost of providing it (that's what I learned between naps in my economics classes), but it isn't happening. The companies are forming efficient confusopolies so customers can't tell who has the lowest prices. Companies have learned to use the complexities of life as an economic tool[18].*

Figure 6.18 Firms would rather confuse customers than compete on price. How far can firms go before such behavior becomes unethical?

"Oh, it's a great healthcare plan ... well worth selling the house to pay for."

One of the roles of effective government regulation, says Adams, should be to discourage this tendency for certain service industries to develop into "confusopolies" (*Figure 6.18*).

Piling on the Fees

Not all business models are based on generating income from sales. There is a growing trend today to impose fees that sometimes have little to do with usage. In the US, the car rental industry has attracted some notoriety for advertising bargain rental prices and then telling customers on arrival that other fees such as collision insurance and personal insurance are compulsory. Also, staff sometimes fail to clarify certain "small print" contract terms such as a high mileage charge that is added once the car exceeds a very low limit of free miles. The "hidden extras" for car rentals in some Florida resort towns got so bad at one point that people were joking: "The car is free, the keys are extra!"[19]

There has also been a trend to adding (or increasing) fines and penalties. Banks have been heavily criticized for using penalties as an important revenue-generating tool

as opposed to using them merely to educate customers and achieve compliance with payment deadlines. Chris Keeley, a New York University student, used his debit card to buy $230 worth of Christmas gifts. His holiday mood soured when he received a notice from his bank that he had overdrawn his checking account. Although his bank authorized each of his seven transactions, it charged him a fee of $31 per payment, totaling $217 for only $230 in purchases. Keeley maintained that he had never requested the so-called overdraft protection on his account and wished his bank had rejected the transactions, because he would then simply have paid by credit card. He fumed, "I can't help but think they wanted me to keep spending money so that they could collect these fees[20]." In fact, for some banks, such fees and penalties now exceed earnings from mortgages, credit cards, and all other lending combined.

The Consumer Financial Protection Bureau (CFPB) has repeatedly raised concerns about overdraft protections and its study found that the majority of debit card overdraft fees are incurred on transactions of $24 or less and the majority of overdrafts are repaid within three days[21]. Put in lending terms, if a consumer borrowed $24 for three days and paid the median overdraft fee of $34, such a loan would carry a 17,000% annual percentage rate (APR). Richard Cordray, CFPB Director, said "Consumers who opt in to overdraft coverage put themselves at serious risk when they use their debit card... Despite recent regulatory and industry changes, overdrafts continue to impose heavy costs on consumers who have low account balances and no cushion for error. Overdraft fees should not be '*gotchas*' when people use their debit cards."

Some banks don't charge for overdraft protection. Said Dennis DiFlorio, President for Retail Banking at Commerce Bancorp Inc. in Cherry Hill, New Jersey: "It's outrageous. It's not about customer convenience. It's just a way for banks to make money off customers." Some banks now offer services that cover overdrafts automatically from savings accounts, other accounts, or even the customer's credit card, and don't charge fees for doing so[22].

It's possible to design fees and even penalties that do not seem unfair to customers. *Service Insights 6.3* describes what drives customers' fairness perceptions with service fees and penalties[23].

SERVICE INSIGHTS 6.3
Crime and Punishment: How Customers Respond to Fines and Penalties

Various types of "penalties" are part and parcel of many pricing schedules to discourage undesirable consumer behaviors, ranging from late fees for DVD rentals to cancellation charges for hotel bookings and charges for late credit card payments. Customer responses to penalties can be highly negative, and can lead to switching providers and poor word-of-mouth. Young Kim and Amy Smith conducted an online survey using the Critical Incident Technique (CIT) in which 201 respondents were asked to recall a recent penalty incident, describe the situation, and then complete a set of structured questions based on how the respondents felt and how they responded to that incident. Their findings showed that negative consumer responses can be reduced significantly by following these three guidelines:

1. **Make Penalties Relative to the Crime Committed.** The survey showed that customers' negative reaction to a penalty increased greatly when they perceived that the penalty was out of proportion to the "crime" committed. Customers' negative feelings were further aggravated if they were "surprised" by the penalty being charged to them suddenly and they had not been aware of the fee or the magnitude of it. These findings suggest that firms can reduce negative customer responses significantly by exploring which amounts are seen as reasonable or fair for a given "customer lapse", and the fines/fees are communicated effectively even before a chargeable incident happens (e.g., in a banking context through a clearly explained fee schedule, and through frontline staff that explain at the point of opening an account or selling additional services the potential fines or fees associated with various "violations", such as overdrawing beyond the authorized limits, bounced checks, or late payments).

2. **Consider Causal Factors and Customize Penalties.** The study showed that customers' perceptions of fairness were lower and negative responses were higher when they perceived the causes that led to the penalty to be out of their control ("I mailed the check on time — there must have been a delay in the postal system"), rather than when they felt it was within their control

and really their fault (e.g., "I forgot to mail the check"). To increase the perception of fairness, firms may want to identify common penalty cases that typically are out of the customer's control and allow the frontline to waive or reduce such fees.

In addition, it was found that customers who generally observe all the rules, and therefore have not paid fines in the past, react particularly negatively if they are fined. One respondent said, "I have always made timely payments and have never been late with a payment — they should have considered this fact and waived the fee." Service firms can improve fairness perceptions by taking into account customers' penalties history in dealing with penalties, and offer different treatments based on past behavior — perhaps waiving the fine for the first incident, at the same time communicating that the fee will be charged for future incidents.

3. **Focus on Fairness and Manage Emotions During Penalty Situations.** Consumers' responses are heavily driven by their fairness perceptions. Customers are likely to perceive penalties as excessive and respond negatively, if they find that a penalty is out of proportion compared to the damage or extra work caused by the penalized incident to the service firm. One consumer complained, "I thought this particular penalty (credit card late payment) was excessive. You are already paying high interest; the penalty should have been more in line with the payment. The penalty was more than the payment!" Considering customers' perceptions of fairness might mean, for example, that the late fee for a keeping a DVD or library book should not exceed the potentially lost rental fees during that period.

Service companies can also make penalties seem fairer by providing adequate explanations and justifications for the penalty. Ideally, penalties should be imposed for the good of other customers (e.g., "We kept the room for you which we could have given to another guest on our wait list") or community (e.g., "others are already waiting for this book to be returned"), but not as a means for generating significant profit. Finally, frontline employees should be trained to handle customers who are angry or distressed and complain about penalties (see Chapter 13 for recommendations on how to deal with such situations).

Source

Young "Sally" K. Kim and Amy K. Smith (2005), "Crime and Punishment: Examining Customers' Responses to Service Organizations' Penalties," *Journal of Service Research*, Vol. 8, No. 2, pp. 162–180.

Understand how fairness
can be designed into
revenue management
policies.

Designing Fairness Into Revenue Management

Like pricing plans and fees, revenue management practices can be perceived as highly unfair, and customer perceptions have to be carefully managed. Therefore, a well-implemented revenue management strategy cannot mean a blind pursuit of short-term yield maximization. Rather, the following approaches can help firms to reconcile revenue management practices with customers' fairness perceptions, satisfaction, trust, and goodwill[24]:

- **Design price schedules and fences that are clear, logical, and fair.** Firms should proactively spell out all fees and expenses (e.g., no-show or cancellation charges) clearly in advance so that there are no surprises (*Figure 6.19*). A related approach is to develop a simple fee structure so customers can more easily understand the financial implications of a specific usage situation. For a rate fence to be perceived as fair, customers must understand them easily (i.e., fences have to be transparent and upfront) and see the logic in them.

- **Use high published prices and frame fences as discounts.** Rate fences framed as customer gains (i.e., discounts) are generally perceived as fairer than those framed as customer losses (i.e., surcharges), even if the situations are economically equivalent. For example, a customer who patronizes her hair salon on Saturdays may perceive the salon as profiteering if she finds herself facing a weekend surcharge. However, she is likely to find the higher weekend price more acceptable if the hair salon advertises its peak weekend price as the published price and offers a $5 discount for weekday haircuts. Furthermore, having a high published price helps to increase the reference price and related quality perceptions in addition to the feeling of being rewarded for the weekday patronage.

Figure 6.19 Limousine service providers usually charge for no shows

- **Communicate consumer benefits of revenue management.** Marketing communications should position revenue management as a win–win practice. Providing different price and value enables a broader spectrum of customers to self-segment and enjoy the service. It allows each customer to find the price and benefits (value) that best satisfies his or her needs. For example, charging a higher price for the best seats in the theater recognizes that some people are willing and able to pay more for a better location and makes it possible to sell other seats at a lower price. Furthermore, perceived fairness is affected by what customers perceive as normal. Hence, when communication makes customers more familiar with a particular revenue management practices, unfairness perceptions are likely to decrease over time[25].

- **"Hide" discounts through bundling, product design, and targeting.** Bundling a service into a package effectively obscures the discounted price. When a cruise line includes the price of air travel or ground transportation in the cruise package (*Figure 6.20*), the customer knows only the total price, not the cost of the individual components. Bundling usually makes price comparisons between the bundles and its components impossible, and thereby side-steps potential unfairness perceptions and reductions in reference prices. This reduces unfairness perceptions[26].

Figure 6.20 Cruise packages bundle land tours into their total package price

Service products can be designed to hide discounts. Instead of varying the prices of food, which makes it difficult to increase once it has been lowered, restaurants can vary the product. For example, restaurants can offer smaller portions for lower-cost set-lunches, and they can impose a minimum spending level during peak periods. Diners having a set-lunch feel they are getting a good deal. When demand is high, a minimum spending per diner can be set at a high level. That is, menu prices will not be changed and price perceptions of diners are unaffected. These two tactics give restaurants flexibility in adjusting effective revenue per seat according to demand levels[27].

Finally, instead of widely advertising low prices and thereby reducing the reference price and potentially quality perceptions, special deals can be offered only to members of a firm's loyalty program and be positioned as a benefit of the program. Members are likely to feel appreciated and the firm can generate incremental demand without reducing its published prices.

- **Take care of loyal customers.** Firms should build in strategies for retaining valued customers, even to the extent of not charging the maximum feasible amount on a given transaction. After all, customer perceptions of price gouging do not build trust. Revenue management systems can be programmed to incorporate "loyalty multipliers" for regular customers, so that reservations systems can give them "special treatment" status at peak times, even when they are not paying premium rates.

- **Use service recovery to compensate for overbooking.** Many service firms overbook to compensate for anticipated cancellations and no-shows. Profits increase but so does the incidence of being unable to honor reservations. Being "bumped" by an airline or "walked" by a hotel can lead to a loss of customer loyalty and adversely affect a firm's reputation[28]. So it's important to back up overbooking programs with well-designed service recovery procedures, such as:

    1. Giving customers a choice between retaining their reservation or receiving compensation (e.g., many airlines practice voluntary offloading at check-in against cash compensation and a later flight).
    2. Providing sufficient advance notice for customers to make alternative arrangements (e.g., preemptive offloading and rescheduling to another flight the day before departure, often in combination with cash compensation).
    3. Offering a substitute service that delights customers if possible (e.g., upgrading a passenger to business or first class on the next available flight, often in combination with options 1 and 2 above).

A Westin beach resort found that it can free up capacity by offering guests who are departing the next day the choice of spending their last night in a luxury hotel near the airport or in the city at no cost. Guest feedback on the free room, upgraded service, and a night in the city after a beach holiday has been very positive. From the hotel's perspective, this practice trades the cost of getting a one-night stay in another hotel against that of turning away a multiple-night guest arriving that same day.

⊃ **LO 10**

Discuss the six questions marketers need to answer to design an effective service pricing strategy.

PUTTING SERVICE PRICING INTO PRACTICE

The first thing a manager has to realize is that service pricing is multi-faceted. It's not just about "How much do I charge?" There are other important decisions to be made that have a major impact on the behavior and value perceptions of customers. *Table 6.3* summarizes the questions service marketers need to ask themselves to develop a well-thought-out pricing strategy. Let's look at each in turn.

Table 6.3 Issues to Consider When Developing a Service Pricing Schedule

1.	**How much should be charged for this service?** • What costs is the organization attempting to recover? Is the organization trying to achieve a specific profit margin or return on investment by selling this service? • How sensitive are customers to various prices? • What prices are charged by competitors? • What discount(s) should be offered from basic prices? • Are psychological pricing points (e.g., $4.95 vs. $5.00) customarily used? • Should auctions and dynamic pricing be used?
2.	**What should be the basis of pricing?** • Execution of a specific task • Admission to a service facility • Units of time (hour, week, month, year) • Percentage commission on the value of the transaction • Physical resources consumed • Geographic distance covered, weight or size of object serviced • Outcome of service or cost-saving generated for the client • Should each service element be billed independently? • Should a single price be charged for a bundled package? • Should discounting be used for selective segments? • Is a freemium pricing strategy beneficial?
3.	**Who should collect payment and where?** • The organization that provides the service collects payment at the location of service delivery or at arm's length (e.g., by mail, phone, or online). • A specialist intermediary (travel or ticket agent, bank, retail, etc.) with a convenient retail outlet location. • How should the intermediary be compensated for this work — flat fee or percentage commission?
4.	**When should payment be made?** • In advance or after-service delivery? • In a lump sum or by installments over time?
5.	**How should payment be made?** • Cash (exact change or not?) • Token (where can these be purchased?) • Stored value card • Check (how to verify?) • Electronic funds transfer • Charge card (credit or debit) • Credit account with service provider • Vouchers • Third-party payment (e.g., insurance company or government agency?)
6.	**How should prices be communicated to the target market?** • Through what communication medium? (advertising, signage, electronic display, salespeople, customer service personnel) • What message content (how much emphasis should be placed on price?) • Can the psychology of pricing presentation and communications be used?

How Much to Charge?

Realistic decisions on pricing are critical for financial solvency. The pricing tripod model discussed earlier (*Figure 6.3*) provides a useful starting point. First, all the relevant economic costs need to be recovered at different sales volumes and these set the relevant floor price. Next, the elasticity of demand of the service from both the providers' and customers' perspectives will help to set a "ceiling" price for any given market segment. Finally, firms need to analyze the intensity of price competition among the providers, before they come to a final price.

A specific figure must be set for the price itself. This task involves several considerations, including the need to consider the pros and cons of setting a rounded price and the ethical issues involved in setting a price exclusive of taxes, service charges, and other extras.

More recently, auctions and dynamic pricing have become increasingly popular as a way to price according to demand and the value perceptions of customers, as seen in the examples of dynamic pricing in the Internet environment in *Service Insights 6.4*.

SERVICE INSIGHTS 6.4
Dynamic Pricing on the Internet

Dynamic pricing — also known as customized or personalized pricing — is a version of the age-old practice of price discrimination. It is popular with service providers because of its potential to increase profits and at the same time provide customers with what they value. E-tailing, or retailing over the Internet, lends itself well to this strategy because changing prices electronically is a simple procedure. Dynamic pricing enables service firms to charge different customers different prices for the same product based on information collected about their purchase history, preferences, price sensitivity, and so on. However, customers may not be happy.

E-tailers are often uncomfortable about admitting to use of dynamic pricing due to the ethical and legal issues associated with price discrimination. Customers of Amazon.com were upset when they learned the online mega-store, in its early days of e-commerce, was not charging everyone the same price for DVDs of the same movie. A study of online consumers by the University of Pennsylvania's Annenberg Public Policy Center found that 87% of respondents did not think dynamic pricing was acceptable.

Reverse Auctions

Travel e-tailers such as Priceline.com and Hotwire.com follow a customer-driven pricing strategy known as a reverse auction. Each firm acts as an intermediary between potential buyers who ask for quotations for a product or service, and multiple suppliers who quote the best price they're willing to offer. Buyers can then compare the offers and choose the supplier that best meets their needs. For example, if a buyer is looking for a flight and accommodation package, search results often show a variety of combinations of packages one can choose from. All the different airlines and hotels are listed by brand, and the price of each package is listed clearly.

Different business models underlie these services. Although some are provided free to end-users, most e-tailers either receive a commission from the supplier or do not pass on the whole savings to their customers. Others charge customers either a fixed fee or a percentage of the savings.

Traditional Auctions

Other e-tailers, such as eBay, uBid, or OnlineAuction, follow the traditional online auction model in which bidders place bids for an item and compete with each other to determine who buys it. Marketers of both consumer and industrial products use such auctions to sell obsolete or overstocked items, collectibles, rare items, and secondhand merchandise. This form of retailing has become very successful since eBay first launched it in 1995.

Shopbots and Metasearch Engines Help Consumers to Benefit From Dynamic Pricing

Consumers now have tools of their own to prevent them from being taken advantage of by practices of dynamic pricing. One approach involves using shopbots and metasearch engines to do a comparison of prices and find the cheapest prices available. Shopbots, or shopping robots, basically are intelligent agents that automatically collect price and product information from multiple vendors. A customer has only to visit a shopbot site, such as Dealtime.com, and run a search for what they are looking for. In the travel industry, Kayak is a leading metasearch engine. These shopbots instantly query all the associated service providers to check availability, features, and price, and then presents the results in a comparison table. Different shopbots have links to different retailers. There is even a shopbot site called MegaShopBot.com, which searches for deals within the best shopbots!

There's little doubt that dynamic pricing is here to stay. With further advances in technology and wider application, its reach will extend to more and more service categories.

Source

Laura Sydell, "New Pricing Plan Soon to Be at Play For Online Music," 27 July 2009, http://www.npr.org/templates/story/story.php?storyId=111046679&ft=1&f=1006, accessed March 2, 2015; Jean-Michel Sahut (2009), "The Impact of Internet on Pricing Strategies in the Tourism Industry" *Journal of Internet Banking and Finance*, Vol. 14, No. 1, pp. 1–8; Promotional Pricing: Dynamic Pricing (2015). From Setting Price: Part 2 Tutorial. KnowThis.com. http://www.knowthis.com/setting-price-part-2/promotional-pricing-dynamic-pricing , accessed March 2, 2015; Thad Rueter (2014), "The Price is Right — Then it's Not," *https://www.internetretailer.com/2014/08/04/price-rightthen-its-not-2?p=1*, accessed March 2, 2015; Max Starkov and Tara Dyer (2013), "Meta Search Marketing: The New Revenue Frontier in Hospitality," http://blog.hebsdigital.com/meta-search-marketing-the-new-revenue-frontier-in-hospitality, accessed March 12, 2015.

What Should Be the Specified Basis for Pricing?

It's not always easy to define a unit of service as the specified basis for pricing. There may be many options. For instance, should price be based on completing a promised service task — such as repairing a piece of equipment or cleaning a jacket? Should it be based on admission to a service performance — such as an educational program, a concert, or a sports event? Should it be time-based — for instance, using an hour of a lawyer's time? Alternatively, should it be related to a monetary value linked to the service delivery, such as when an insurance company scales its premiums to reflect the amount of coverage provided, or a real estate company takes a commission that is a percentage of the selling price of a house?

Some service prices are tied to the consumption of physical resources such as food, drinks, water, or natural gas. Transport firms have traditionally charged by distance, with freight companies using a combination of weight or cubic volume and distance to set their rates (*Figure 6.21*). For some services, prices may include separate charges for access and for usage. Recent research suggests that access or subscription fees are an important driver of adoption and customer retention, whereas usage fees are much more important drivers of actual usage[29]. And consumers of hedonic services such as amusement parks tend to prefer flat rates for access rather than by individual usage as they don't like to be reminded of the pain of paying while they enjoy the service. This is also called the taximeter effect, as customers don't want to "hear" the price ticking upward — it lowers their consumption enjoyment[30]!

In B2B markets in particular, innovative business models charge based on outcomes rather than services provided. For example, Rolls-Royce's "Power-by-the-Hour" service does not charge for services such as maintenance, repairs and materials, but based on the outcome of these activities, that is, the number of flying hours[31]. Some supply chain service providers, such as DHL Supply Chain, charge a base price and then add a variable component that depends on the cost-saving generated for the client. In effect, generated cost savings are shared between the provider and their client.

Figure 6.21 Shipment of goods are typically charged by a combination of distance (miles, kilometers or zones) and weight or size (such as cubic volume)

Price Bundling. An important question for service marketers is whether to charge an inclusive price for all elements (referred to as a "bundle") or to price each element separately. If customers prefer to avoid making many small payments, then bundled pricing may be preferable. However, if they dislike being charged for product elements they do not use, itemized pricing is preferable. Bundled prices offer firms a certain level of guaranteed revenue from each customer, while providing customers a clear idea in advance of how much they can expect to pay. Unbundled pricing provides customers with the freedom to choose what to buy and pay for[32]. For instance, many US airlines now charge economy class passengers for meals, drinks, check-in baggage, seat selection, and surcharges for credit card payment on their domestic flights. However, customers may be angered if they discover that the actual price of what they consume, inflated by all the "extras", is substantially higher than the advertised base price that attracted them in the first place[33].

Discounting. Selective price discounting targeted at specific market segments can offer important opportunities to attract new customers and fill the capacity that would otherwise go unused. However, unless it is used with effective rate fences that allow specific segments to be targeted cleanly, a strategy of discounting should be approached with caution. It reduces the average price and contribution received and may attract customers whose only loyalty is to the firm that can offer the lowest price on the next transaction. Volume discounts are sometimes used to cement the loyalty of large corporate customers who might otherwise spread their purchases among several different suppliers.

Freemium. Over the past decade, "freemium", a combination of "free" and "premium" has become a popular pricing strategy for online and mobile services. Users get the basic service at no cost (typically funded by advertising) and can upgrade to a richer functionality for a subscription fee. If you have shared files on Dropbox, networked on LinkedIn, or streamed music from Spotify, you have experienced this business model firsthand. As marginal costs for technology and bandwidth are dropping, "freemium" models are likely to become more attractive[34].

Who Should Collect Payment and Where Should Payment Be Made?

As discussed in Chapter 4, supplementary services include information, order-taking, billing, and payment. However, service delivery sites are not always conveniently located. Airports, theaters, and stadiums, for instance, often are situated some distance from where potential customers may live or work. When consumers need such services and/or have to purchase a service before using it and there is no convenient online channel available, there are benefits to using intermediaries that are more conveniently located. Therefore, firms sometimes delegate these services to intermediaries such as travel agents who make hotel and transport bookings and collect payment from customers and ticket agents who sell seats for theaters, concert halls, and sports stadiums.

Although the original supplier pays a commission, the intermediary is usually able to offer customers greater convenience in terms of where, when, and how payment can be made. Using intermediaries may also result in savings in administrative costs. However, many service firms nowadays are promoting their websites and apps with best rate guarantees as direct channels for customer self-service, thus bypassing the traditional intermediaries and avoiding the payment of commissions. Tickets are then simply delivered to an email account or a smartphone.

When Should Payment Be Made?

Two basic ways are to ask customers to pay in advance (as with an admission charge, airline ticket, or postage stamps), or to bill them once service delivery has been completed (as with restaurant bills and repair charges). Occasionally, a service provider may ask for an initial payment in advance of service delivery, with the balance due later (*Figure 6.22*). This approach is quite common for expensive repair and maintenance jobs, when the firm — often a small business with limited working capital — must buy and pay for materials.

Asking customers to pay in advance means the buyer is paying before the benefits are received. However, pre-payments may offer advantages to the customer and the provider. Sometimes, it is inconvenient to pay each time a regularly patronized service — such as the Postal Service or public transport — is used. To save time and effort, customers may prefer the convenience of buying a book of stamps or a monthly travel pass. Performing arts organizations with heavy up-front financing requirements can also offer discounted subscription tickets in order to bring in money before the season begins.

Finally, the timing of payment can determine usage patterns. From an analysis of the payment and attendance records of a Colorado-based health club, John Gourville and Dilip Soman found that its members' usage patterns were closely related to their payment schedules. When members made payments, their use of the club was highest during the months immediately following payment and then slowed down steadily until the next payment; members with monthly payment plans used the health club much more consistently and were more likely to renew, perhaps because each month's payment encouraged them to use what they were paying for (*Figure 6.23*)[35].

Figure 6.23 Payment schedules can drive health club usage and renewal of membership

Gourville and Soman concluded that the timing of payment can be used more strategically to manage capacity utilization. For instance, if a golf club wants to reduce the demand during its busiest time, it can bill its fees long before the season begins (e.g., in January rather than in May or June), as the member's pain of payment will have faded by the time the peak summer months come, thereby reducing the need to get his or her "money's worth". A reduction in peak demand during the peak period would then allow the club to increase its overall membership.

Conversely, the timing of payment can also be used to boost consumption. Consider the Boston Red Sox (i.e., the famous American professional baseball team) season ticket holders, who are billed five months before the season starts. To build attendance and strong fan support throughout the season, Red Sox could spread out this large annual payment to four installments that coincide with their games. The team would garner a high game attendance and fan support, and their fans might prefer the lower and financially more manageable installments.

Figure 6.22 Some firms do not leave their customers with much flexibility in dealing with late payment

© 1999 Randy Glasbergen.
www.glasbergen.com

"**Unless we receive the outstanding balance within ten days, we will have no choice but to destroy your credit rating, ruin your reputation, and make you wish you were never born. If you have already sent the seven cents, please disregard this notice.**"

How Should Payment Be Made?

There are many different forms of payment. Cash may appear to be the simplest method, but it raises security problems and is inconvenient when exact change is required to operate machines. Credit and debit cards can be used around the world as their acceptance has become almost universal. Other payment procedures include tokens or vouchers as supplements to, or instead of, cash. Vouchers are sometimes provided by social service agencies to the elderly or individuals in the low-income bracket. Such a policy achieves the same benefits as discounting, but avoids the need to publicize different prices and to require cashiers to check eligibility.

Service marketers should remember that the simplicity and speed with which payment is made may influence the customer's perception of overall service quality. Coming into broader usage are prepayment systems based on cards that store value on a magnetic strip or in a microchip embedded within the card. Contactless payments systems based on credit and debit cards with radio-frequency identification (RFID) technology are increasingly used. Starbucks launched a smartphone app-based payment system integrated with its "My Starbucks Reward Program", which allows its customers to earn special discounts and freebies. Soon, order-taking will be integrated to cut wait time at the counter. Apple users can pay by holding their device to the point of sale system and authenticating the transaction by holding their fingerprint to the phone's Touch ID sensor. Suppliers of these systems claim transactions can be up to twice as fast as conventional cash, credit, or debit card purchases.

Interestingly, a recent study found that the payment mechanism has an effect on the total spending of customers, especially for discretionary consumption items such as spending in cafes[36]. The less tangible or immediate the payment mechanism, the more consumers tend to spend. Cash is the most tangible (i.e., consumers will be more careful and spend less), followed by credit cards, prepayment cards, and finally more sophisticated and even less tangible and immediate mechanisms such as payment via one's cell phone service bill.

How Should Prices Be Communicated to the Target Markets?

The final task, once each of the other issues has been addressed, is to decide how the organization's pricing policies can best be communicated to its target market(s). Consumers need to know the price they are expected to pay before purchase. They may also need to know how, where, and when that price is payable. This information must be presented in intelligible and unambiguous ways so that customers will not be misled and question the ethical standards of the firm. Managers must decide whether or not to include information on pricing in advertising for the service. It may be suitable to relate the price to the costs of competing products. Salespeople and customer service representatives should be able to give immediate, accurate responses to customer queries about pricing, payment, and credit. Good signage at retail points of sale will save staff members from having to answer basic questions on prices.

How to communicate prices is important and shapes buying behavior. For example, in a restaurant context, menu psychology looks at how diners respond to pricing information on a menu (*Service Insights 6.5*).

Finally, when the price is presented in the form of an itemized bill, marketers should make sure that it is both accurate and easy to understand. Hospital bills, which may run up to several pages and contain dozens or even hundreds of items, have been much criticized for inaccuracy. Hotel bills, despite containing fewer entries, are also notoriously inaccurate. One study estimated that business travelers in the US may be overpaying for their hotel rooms by half-a-billion dollars a year, with 11.6% of all bills incorrect, resulting in an average overpayment of $11.36[37].

SERVICE INSIGHTS 6.5
The Psychology of Menu Pricing in Restaurants

Have you ever wondered why you choose certain dishes on the menu and not others? It could be due to the way the dish is displayed. Menu psychology is a growing field of research. Menu engineers and consultants research on the most effective ways to design a menu, including layout and pricing information, in the hope that the diner will spend more money. What can we do to get people to spend more money, and to order items with high profit margins?

- When showing prices on the menu, avoid using a dollar sign. Prices that come with dollar signs will result in customers spending less, compared to when there are no dollar signs on the menu.

- Prices that end with "9", like $9.99, make diners feel that they are getting value for money. This is good for a low price and for good value positioning, but should not be used by high-end restaurants.

- The best position to place prices should be at the end of the description of an item and it should not be highlighted in any way.

- In terms of the order of items, place the most expensive item at the top of the menu so the price of the other items looks lower in comparison.

- For layout, the most profitable item on the menu should be placed at the top right-hand corner of the page because people tend to look there first.

- A longer description of a dish tends to encourage people to order it. Therefore, menus can be designed to have more detailed and more appetizing descriptions of dishes that are more profitable, and have less description for the less profitable dishes.

- What kind of names should be given to dishes? Using names of mothers, grandmothers, and other relatives (e.g., Aunty May's beef stew) has been shown to encourage people to order that item.

The next time you have selected a dish from the menu, you may want to stop and see how it was displayed, and whether that potentially swayed you towards a dish the restaurant wanted you to order.

	€
La Soupe à l'Oignon	11.80
La Soupe de Légumes	11.80
La Soupe de Poissons	11.80
Le Croque Monsieur, salade	9.80
Lasagne Bolognaise	13.50
Les deux oeufs au plat, jambon blanc	9.90
La Blanquette de Veau	15.80
Cuisses de Poulet à la crème	15.80
Le Boeuf Bourguignon	15.80
Le Hamburger Charolais, frites	13.80
L'Entrecôte Charolaise (300 grammes)	19.00
Le Tartare de Boeuf Charolais	15.90
Le Filet de Boeuf Charolais	17.50
La Côte de Porc	13.80

Source
Sarah Kershaw, "In Search of a Formula to Entice Mind, Stomach and Wallet," *The New York Times*, December 23, 2009.

CHAPTER SUMMARY

LO1 Effective pricing is central to the financial success of service firms. The key objectives for establishing prices can be to (1) gain profits and cover costs, (2) build demand and develop a user base, and/or (3) support the firm's positioning strategy. Once a firm sets its pricing objectives, it needs to decide on its pricing strategy.

LO2 The foundations of a pricing strategy are the three legs of the pricing tripod:
- The costs the firm needs to recover set the minimum or floor price.
- The customer's perceived value of the offering sets a maximum or ceiling price.
- The price charged for competing services determines where, within the floor-to-ceiling range, the price can be set.

LO3 The first leg of the pricing tripod is **the cost to the firm**.
- Costing services often is often complex. Services frequently have high fixed costs, varying capacity utilization, and large shared infrastructures that make it difficult to establish unit costs.
- If services have a large proportion of variable and/or semi-variable costs, cost-accounting approaches work well (e.g., using contribution and breakeven analysis).
- However, for complex services with shared infrastructure, activity-based costing (ABC) is often more appropriate.

LO4 The second leg of the pricing tripod is **the value to the customer**.
- Net value is the sum of all perceived benefits (gross value) minus the sum of all the perceived costs of a service. Customers will only buy if the net value is positive. The net value can be enhanced by either increasing value or reducing costs.
- Since value is perceived and subjective, it can be enhanced through communication and education to help customers better understand the value they receive.
- In addition to the price customers pay for the service, costs include related monetary costs (e.g., the taxi fare to the service location) and non-monetary costs (e.g., time, physical, psychological, and sensory costs) during the search, purchase and service encounter, and post-purchase stages. Firms can enhance net value by reducing these related monetary and non-monetary costs.

LO5 The third leg of the pricing tripod is **competition**.
- Price competition can be fierce in markets with relatively similar services. Here, firms need to closely observe what competitors charge and then price accordingly.
- Price competition intensifies with the (1) number of competitors, (2) number of substituting offers, (3) distribution density of competitor and substitution offers, and (4) amount of surplus capacity in the industry.
- Price competition is reduced if one or more of the following applies: (1) Non-price related costs of using competing alternatives are high, (2) personal relationships are important, (3) switching costs are high, and service consumption is time and location specific.

LO6 Revenue management increases revenue for the firm through better use of capacity and reservation of capacity for higher paying segments. Specifically, RM:
- Designs products using physical and non-physical rate fences, and prices them for different segments according to their specific reservation prices.
- Sets prices according to predicted demand levels of different customer segments.
- Works best in service businesses characterized by (1) high fixed costs and perishable inventory, (2) several customer segments with different price elasticities, and (3) variable and uncertain demand.
- Measures success by revenue per available capacity for a given space and time unit (RevPAST). For example, airlines seek to maximize revenue per available seat kilometer (RevPASK) and hotels try to maximize their revenue per available room-night (RevPAR).

LO7 Well-designed rate fences are needed to define "products" for each target segment so that customers with high value for a service offer are unable to take advantage of lower price buckets. Rate fences can be physical and non physical:
- Physical fences refer to tangible product differences related to different prices (e.g., seat location in a theater, size of a hotel room, or service level).

- Non physical fences refer to consumption (e.g., a hotel stay must be over a weekend), transaction (e.g., weeks' advance booking with cancellation and change penalties), or buyer characteristics (e.g., student and group discounts). The service experience is identical across fence conditions although different prices are charged.

○ **LO8** Customers often have difficulties understanding service pricing (e.g., RM practices with their many fences and fee schedules). Service firms need to be careful that their pricing does not become so complex and so riddled with hidden fees that customers perceive them as unethical and unfair.

○ **LO9** The following ways help firms to improve customers' fairness perceptions:
- Design price schedules and fences that are clear, logical, and fair.
- Use published prices and frame fences as discounts.

- Communicate consumer benefits of revenue management.
- "Hide" discounts through bundling, product design, and targeting.
- Take care of loyal customers.
- Use service recovery or deal with overbooking.

○ **LO10** To put service pricing into practice, service marketers need to consider seven questions to have a well-thought-out pricing strategy. The questions are:
1. How much to charge?
2. What should be the specified basis for pricing?
3. Who should collect payment, and where should payment be made?
4. When should payment be made?
5. How should payment be made?
6. How should prices be communicated to the target markets?

Review Questions

1. Why is the pricing of services more difficult as compared to the pricing of goods?

2. How can the pricing tripod approach to service pricing be useful to come to a good pricing point for a particular service?

3. How can a service firm compute its unit costs for pricing purposes? How does predicted and actual capacity utilization affect unit costs and profitability?

4. What is the role of nonmonetary costs in a business model, and how do they relate to the consumer's value perceptions?

5. Why can't we compare competitor prices dollar-for-dollar in a service context?

6. What is revenue management, how does it work, and what type of service operations benefit most from good revenue management systems and why?

7. Explain the difference between physical and non-physical rate fences using suitable examples.

8. Why are ethical concerns important issues when designing service pricing and revenue management strategies? What are potential consumer responses to service pricing or policies that are perceived as unfair?

9. How can we charge different prices to different segments without customers feeling cheated? How can we even charge the same customer different prices at different times, contexts, and/or occasions, and at the same time, be seen as fair?

10. What are the six key decisions managers need to make when designing an effective pricing schedule?

Application Exercises

1. Select a service organization of your choice and find out what its pricing policies and methods are. In what respects are they similar to or different from what has been discussed in this chapter?

2. From the customer perspective, what serves to define value in the following services: (a) a hair salon, (b) a legal firm specializing in business and taxation law, and (c) a nightclub?

3. Review recent bills you have received from service businesses, such as those for telephone, car repair, cable TV, and credit cards. Evaluate each one against the following criteria: (a) general appearance and clarity of presentation, (b) easily understood terms of payment, (c) avoidance of confusing terms and definitions, (d) appropriate level of detail, (e) unanticipated ("hidden") charges, (f) accuracy, and (g) ease of access to customer service in case of problems or disputes.

4. How might revenue management be applied to (a) a professional service firm (e.g., a law firm), (b) a restaurant, and (c) a golf course? What rate fences would you use and why?

5. Collect the pricing schedules of three leading cell phone service providers. Identify all the pricing dimensions (e.g., airtime, subscription fees, free minutes, per second/6 seconds/minute billing, airtime and data rollover plans) and pricing levels for each dimension (i.e., the range offered by the players in the market). Determine the usage profile for a particular target segment (e.g., a young executive who uses the phone mostly for personal calls, or a full-time student). Based on the usage profile, determine the lowest cost provider. Next, measure the pricing schedule preferences of your target segment (e.g., via conjoint analysis). Finally, advise the smallest of the three providers how to redesign its pricing schedule to make it more attractive to your target segment.

6. Explore two highly successful business models that are based on innovative service pricing and/or revenue management strategies, and identify two business models that failed due to major issues in their pricing strategy. What general lessons can you learn from your analysis?

7. Consider a service of your choice, and develop a comprehensive pricing schedule. Apply the six questions marketers need to answer for designing an effective pricing schedule.

Endnotes

1   Joshua Brustein, "Star Pitchers in a Duel? Tickets Will Cost More," *The New York Times*, June 27, 2010; Adam Satariano, "Eagles Pinch Scalpers With Live Nation Price Hikes (Update 1), *Businessweek*, February 24, 2010; Ethan Smith, "Start-Up Scoops Up Unsold Tickets," *The Wall Street Journal*, December 16, 2010; Patrick Healy (2014), "Ticket Pricing Puts 'Lion King' Atop Broadway's Circle of Life," *The New York Times*, March 17, 2014, p. A1.

2   Joan Magretta (2002), "Why Business Models Matter." *Harvard Business Review*, Vol. 80, May, pp. 86–92.

3   This section is based on: Robin Cooper and Robert S. Kaplan (1991), "Profit Priorities from Activity-Based Costing," *Harvard Business Review*, Vol. 69, No. 3, pp. 130–135; Craig A. Latshaw and Teresa M. Cortese-Daniele (2002), "Activity-Based Costing: Usage and Pitfalls," *Review of Business*, Vol. 23, Winter, pp. 30–32; Robert S. Kaplan and Steven R. Anderson (2004), "Time-Driven Activity Based Costing," *Harvard Business Review*, Vol. 82, November, pp. 131-138; Daniel J. Goebel, Greg W. Marshall, and William B. Locander (1998), "Activity Based Costing: Accounting for a Marketing Orientation," *Industrial Marketing Management*, Vol. 27, No. 6, pp. 497–510; Thomas H. Stevenson and David W.E. Cabell (2002), "Integrating Transfer Pricing Policy and Activity-Based Costing," *Journal of International Marketing*, Vol. 10, No. 4, pp. 77–88.

4   Gerald E. Smith and Thomas T. Nagle (2002), "How Much Are Customers Willing to Pay?" *Marketing Research*, Vol. 14, Winter, pp. 20–25.

5   Valarie A. Zeithaml (1998), "Consumer Perceptions of Price, Quality, and Value: A Means-End Model and Synthesis of Evidence," *Journal of Marketing*, Vol. 52, July, pp. 2–21. For alternative conceptualizations of value, see Chien-Hsin Lin, Peter J. Sher, and Hsin-Yu Shih (2005), "Past Progress and Future Directions in Conceptualizing Customer Perceived Value," *International Journal of Service Industry Management*, Vol. 16, No. 4, pp. 318–336.

6   Parts of this section are based on Leonard L. Berry and Manjit S. Yadav (1996), "Capture and Communicate Value in the Pricing of Services," *Sloan Management Review*, Vol. 37, Summer, pp. 41–51.

7   Anna S. Mattila and Jochen Wirtz (2002), "The Impact of Knowledge Types on the Consumer Search Process — An Investigation in the Context of Credence Services," *International Journal of Service Industry Management*, Vol. 13, No. 3, pp. 214–230.

8   It has even been shown that music piracy can be reduced by making the purchase and use of music more convenient. Ironically, the use of digital rights management (DRM), which has the aim to reduce unauthorized copying and piracy, actually increases piracy not because of consumers' unwillingness to pay but because of the inconvenience entailed in using DRM protected files. See Rajiv K. Sinha, Fernando S. Machado, and Collin Sellman (2010), "Don't Think Twice, It's All Right: Music Piracy and Pricing in a DRM-Free Environment," *Journal of Marketing*, Vol. 74, No. 2, pp. 40–54.

9   Leonard L. Berry, Kathleen Seiders, and Dhruv Grewal (2002), "Understanding Service Convenience," *Journal of Marketing*, Vol. 66, July, pp. 1–17. For study examining the tradeoff between price and effort (i.e., self-service), see Lan Xia and Rajneesh Suri (2014), "Trading Effort for Money: Consumers' Cocreation Motivation and the Price of Service Options," *Journal of Service Research*, Vol. 17, No. 2, pp. 229–242.

10 Laurie Garrow (2009), "Online Travel Data: A Goldmine of New Opportunities," *Journal of Revenue and Pricing Management*, Vol. 8, No. 2/3, pp. 247–254.

11 Jochen Wirtz, Ping Xiao, Jeongwen Chiang, and Naresh Malhotra (2014), "Contrasting Switching Intent and Switching Behavior in Contractual Service Settings," *Journal of Retailing*, Vol. 90, No. 4, pp. 463–480.

12 Kristina Heinonen (2005), "Reconceptualizing Customer Perceived Value: The Value of Time and Place," *Managing Service Quality*, Vol. 14, No. 3, pp. 205–215.

13 For a review of the extant revenue management literature, see Sheryl E. Kimes and Jochen Wirtz (2015), "Revenue Management: Advanced Strategies and Tools to Enhance Firm Profitability," *Foundations and Trends in Marketing*, Vol. 8, No. 1, pp. 1–68.

14 For airline and hotel revenue management, see: Yoon Sook Song, Seong Tae Hong, Myung Sun Hwang, and Moon Gil Yoon (2010), "MILP Model for Network Revenue Management in Airlines," *Journal of Business & Economics Research*, Vol. 6, No. 2, pp. 55-62; and demand for different fare classes, see Guillermo Gallego, Lin Li, and Richard Ratliff (2009), "Choice-based EMSR Methods for Single-leg Revenue Management with Demand Dependencies," *Journal of Revenue and Pricing Management*, Vol. 8, No. 2/3, pp. 207-240; Sunmee Choi and Anna S. Mattila (2004), "Hotel Revenue Management and Its Impact on Customers'

Perception of Fairness," *Journal of Revenue and Pricing Management*, Vol. 2, No. 4, pp. 303–314.

For application of yield management to industries beyond the traditional airline, hotel and car rental contexts, see: Frédéric Jallat and Fabio Ancarani (2008), "Yield Management, Dynamic Pricing and CRM in Telecommunications," *Journal of Services Marketing*, Vol. 22, No. 6, pp. 465–478; Sheryl E. Kimes and Jochen Wirtz (2003), "Perceived Fairness of Revenue Management in the US Golf Industry," *Journal of Revenue and Pricing Management*, Vol. 1, No. 4, pp. 332–344; Sheryl E. Kimes and Jochen Wirtz (2003), "Has Revenue Management Become Acceptable? Findings from an International Study and the Perceived Fairness of Rate Fences," *Journal of Service Research*, Vol. 6, November, pp. 125–135; Richard Metters and Vicente Vargas (1999), "Yield Management for the Nonprofit Sector," *Journal of Service Research*, Vol. 1, February, pp. 215–226; Alex M. Susskind, Dennis Reynolds, and Eriko Tsuchiya (2004), "An Evaluation of Guests' Preferred Incentives to Shift Time-Variable Demand in Restaurants," *Cornell Hotel and Restaurant Administration Quarterly*, Vol. 44, No. 1, pp. 68–84; Parijat Dube, Yezekael Hayel, and Laura Wynter (2005), "Yield Management for IT Resources on Demand: Analysis and Validation of a New Paradigm for Managing Computing Centres," *Journal of Revenue and Pricing Management*, Vol. 4, No. 1, pp. 24–38; and Sheryl E. Kimes and Sonee Singh (2009), "Spa Revenue Management," *Cornell Hospitality Quarterly*, Vol. 40, No. 1, pp. 82–95. Ting Li, Eric van Heck, and Peter Vervest (2009), "Information Capability and Value Creation Strategy: Advancing Revenue Management through Mobile Ticketing Technologies," *European Journal of Information Systems*, Vol. 18, No. 1, pp. 38–51.

15 Hermann Simon and Robert J. Dolan (1998), "Price Customization," *Marketing Management*, Vol. 7, Fall, pp. 11–17.

16 Lisa E. Bolton, Luk Warlop, and Joseph W. Alba (2003), "Consumer Perceptions of Price (Un)Fairness," *Journal of Consumer Research*, Vol. 29, No. 4, pp. 474–491; Lan Xia, Kent B. Monroe, and Jennifer L. Cox (2004), "The Price is Unfair! A Conceptual Framework of Price Fairness Perceptions," *Journal of Marketing*, Vol. 68, October, pp. 1–15. Christian Homburg, Wayne D. Hoyer, and Nicole Koschate (2005), "Customer's Reactions to Price Increases: Do Customer Satisfaction and Perceived Motive Fairness Matter?" *Journal of the Academy of Marketing Science*, Vol. 33, No. 1, pp. 36–49.

17 Jim Guest (2003), "Cell Hell" (p. 3) and "Complete Cell-Phone Guide," *Consumer Reports*, February, pp. 11–27; Ken Belson, "A Monthly Mystery," *New York Times*, August 27, 2005.

18 Scott Adams, *The Dilbert™ Future - Thriving on Business Stupidities in the 21st Century* (New York: Harper Business, 1997), p. 160.

19 Ian Ayres and Barry Nalebuff (2003), "In Praise of Honest Pricing," *Sloan Management Review*, Vol. 45, Fall, pp. 24–28.

20 Dean Foust (2005), "Protection Racket? As Overdraft and Other Fees Become Huge Profit Sources for Banks, Critics See Abuses," *Business Week*, Vol. 5, February, pp. 68–89.

21 Consumer Financial Protection Bureau (2014), Data Point: Checking Account Overdraft, http://files.consumerfinance.gov/f/201407_cfpb_report_data-point_overdrafts.pdf, accessed March 2, 2015.

22 The banking examples and data in this section were from Dean Foust (2005), "Protection Racket? As Overdraft and Other Fees Become Huge Profit Sources for Banks, Critics See Abuses," *Business Week*, Vol. 5, February, pp. 68–89.

23 For the effect of charging or waiving penalties on loyalty and word-of-mouth behaviors, see: Lan Xia and Monika Kukar-Kinney (2013), "Examining the Penalty Resolution Process: Building Loyalty Through Gratitude and Fairness," *Journal of Service Research*, Vol. 16, No. 4, pp. 518–532.

24 Parts of this section are based on Jochen Wirtz, Sheryl E. Kimes, Jeannette P. T. Ho, and Paul Patterson (2003), "Revenue Management: Resolving Potential Customer Conflicts," *Journal of Revenue and Pricing Management*, Vol. 2, No. 3, pp. 216–228.

25 Jochen Wirtz and Sheryl E. Kimes (2007), "The Moderating Role of Familiarity in Fairness Perceptions of Revenue Management Pricing," *Journal of Service Research*, Vol. 9, No. 3, pp. 229–240.

26 Judy Harris and Edward A. Blair (2006), "Consumer Preference for Product Bundles: The Role of Reduced Search Costs," *Journal of the Academy of Marketing Science*, Vol. 34, No. 4, pp. 506–513.

27 Rafi Mohammed (2011), "A Better Way to Make Deals on Meals," *Harvard Business Review*, January–February, pp. 25.

28 Florian v. Wangenheim and Tomas Bayon (2007), "Behavioral Consequences of Overbooking Service Capacity," *Journal of Marketing*, Vol. 71, No. 4, pp. 36–47.

29 Peter J. Danaher (2002), "Optimal Pricing of New Subscription Services: An Analysis of a Market Experiment," *Marketing Science*, Vol. 21, Spring, pp. 119–129; Gilia E. Fruchter and Ram C. Rao (2001), "Optimal Membership Fee and Usage Price Over Time for a Network Service," *Journal of Services Research,* Vol. 4, No. 1, pp. 3–14.

30 Fabian Uhrich, Jan H. Schumann, and Florian von Wangenheim (2012), "The Impact of Consumption Goals on Flat-Rate Choice: Can "Hedonizing" a Service Increase Customers' Propensity to Choose a Flat Rate?" *Journal of Service Research*, Vol. 16, No. 2, pp. 216–230.

31 Irene C.L. Ng, David Xing Ding, and Nick Yip (2013), Outcome-based Contracts as New Business Model: The Role of Partnership and Value-driven Relational Assets," *Industrial Marketing Management*, Vol. 42, No. 5, pp. 730–743; Irene C. L. Ng, Roger Maull, and Nick Yip (2009), Outcome-based Contracts as a Driver for Systems Thinking and Service-Dominant Logic in Service Science: Evidence from the Defence Industry," *European Management Journal*, Vol. 27, No. 6, pp. 377–387

32 Avery Johnson, "Northwest to Charge Passengers in Coach for Meals," *Wall Street Journal*, February 16, 2005.

33 Eoghan Macguire (2012), "'Hidden' Airline Charges: Dirty Tricks or Customer Choice?" for CNN, http://edition.cnn.com/2012/07/10/travel/airline-charges/index.html, accessed February 27, 2015.

34 Vineet Kumar (2014), "Making 'Freemium' Work," *Harvard Business Review*, Vol. 92, No. 5, pp. 27–29.

35 John Gourville and Dilip Soman (2002), "Pricing and the Psychology of Consumption," *Harvard Business Review,* Vol. 9, September, pp. 90–96.

36 Dilip Soman (2003), "The Effect of Payment Transparency on Consumption: Quasi-Experiments from the Field," *Marketing Letters*, Vol. 14, No. 3, pp. 173–183.

37 See, for example, Anita Sharpe, "The Operation Was a Success; The Bill Was Quite a Mess," *Wall Street Journal,* September 17, 1997, p. 1; Gary Stoller, "Hotel Bill Mistakes Mean Many Pay Too Much," *USA Today,* July 12, 2005.

Service Marketing Communications

Life is for one generation; a good name is forever.

Japanese proverb

Education costs money, but then so does ignorance.

Sir Claus Moser
British statistician

We don't have a choice on whether we do social media;
the question is how well we do it.

Erik Qualman
Author of Socialnomics

LEARNING OBJECTIVES (LOs)

By the end of this chapter, the reader should be able to:

⊃ **LO 1** Know the 5Ws of the Integrated Service Communications Model, that is, **W**ho, **W**hat, **H**ow, **W**here, and **W**hen.

⊃ **LO 2** Be familiar with the three broad target audiences ("**W**ho") for any service communications program.

⊃ **LO 3** Understand the most common strategic and tactical service communications objectives ("**W**hat").

⊃ **LO 4** Be familiar with the Service Marketing Communications Funnel and key objectives in that funnel.

⊃ **LO 5** Know a few important specific roles service marketing communications can assume.

⊃ **LO 6** Understand the challenges of service communications and how service communications can overcome those ("**H**ow").

⊃ **LO 7** Be familiar with the marketing communications mix in a services context ("**W**here").

⊃ **LO 8** Know the communications mix elements of the traditional marketing communications channels.

⊃ **LO 9** Know the role of the Internet, mobile, apps, QR code, and other electronic media in service marketing communications.

⊃ **LO 10** Know the communications mix elements available via service delivery channels.

⊃ **LO 11** Know the communications mix elements that originate from outside the firm.

⊃ **LO 12** Understand when communications should take place ("**W**hen"), how to set budgets for service communications programs, and how to evaluate these programs.

⊃ **LO 13** Appreciate ethical and consumer privacy-related issues in service marketing communications.

⊃ **LO 14** Understand the role of corporate design in communications.

⊃ **LO 15** Know the importance of integrated marketing communications to deliver a strong brand identity.

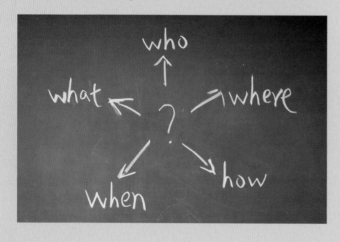

OPENING VIGNETTE

Oscar Is Having the Time of His Life

Employees of the Kilronan Castle Hotel in Ireland found a bright orange and yellow monkey soft toy in a linen bin, which clearly would be missed by its owner. Rather than putting it into the lost property shelf, the employees had the great idea of starting a social media campaign to reunite Oscar, the name the employees gave to the toy, with his rightful owner, and they had a lot of fun in the process as seen in the photos!

They took photos showing Oscar living the high life, and uploaded them to Facebook. The message was that Oscar is looking for his owner, and although he is lost, he has the time of his life at this luxury castle hotel. The photos show him enjoying afternoon tea, having beauty treatments, and having a buffet prepared for him by the executive chef. It almost seemed as if Oscar didn't mind not being found for a little while longer…

Have a look online whether he was eventually reunited with his owner.

While the employees hoped that Oscar's owner would come forward, there is no doubt about the significant social media publicity generated for the Kilronan Castle Hotel. Speed, creativity, and fun are some of the attributes that can make a social media campaign go viral.

Notice put up by staff of Kilronan Castle on its Facebook Page

LOST CUDDLY TOY ALERT
Kilronan Castle are launching an appeal to find the owner of a very cute and cuddly monkey found here at the castle…

Little Oscar (named by the staff at Kilronan) was found in a linen bin and we are now asking any guests who stayed here over the weekend if they have any information on Oscars owner.

Please help us find Oscar's owner… in the meantime he is being well looked after and experiencing the exceptional customer experience here at Kilronan Castle.

Figure 7.1 Oscar is having the time of his life (photo collage)

Source
Kilronan Castle Facebook Page, https://www.facebook.com/media/set/?set=a.913675381980829.1073741840.125951937419848&type=3

LO 1

Know the 5 Ws of the Integrated Service Communications Model, that is, **W**ho, **W**hat, How, **W**here, and **W**hen.

INTEGRATED SERVICE MARKETING COMMUNICATIONS

The "Oscar" campaign in our opening vignette was successful in creating a following on its Facebook pages as a result of the hotels employees who were quick and innovative. Social media has become an integral part of many service organizations.[1] However, such campaigns still have to be integrated and form a part of a larger communications strategy. This chapter focusses on how to plan and design an effective marketing communications strategy for services. Through communications, marketers explain and promote the value proposition their firm is offering.

Communication is the most visible or audible — and some would say intrusive — form of marketing activities, but its value is limited unless it is used intelligently in conjunction with other marketing efforts. An old marketing axiom says that the fastest way to kill a poor product is to advertise it heavily. By the same token, an otherwise well-researched and well-planned marketing strategy is likely to fail if prospects don't learn of a service firm's existence, what it has to offer, the value proposition of each of its products, and how to use them to their best advantage. Customers might be more easily lured away by competitive offerings, and there would be no proactive management and control of the firm's identity. Marketing communications, in one form or another, is essential to a company's success.

There is a lot of confusion over the scope of service marketing communications, with many people still defining it too narrowly. Communications must be viewed more broadly than just as media advertising, public relations (PR), social media, and professional salespeople. There are many other ways for a service business to communicate with current and prospective customers. The location and atmosphere of a service delivery facility, corporate design features such as the consistent use of colors and graphic elements, the appearance and behavior of employees, the design of a website — all these contribute to an impression in the customer's mind that reinforces or contradicts the specific content of formal communication messages.

The past few years have seen the emergence of new and exciting opportunities for reaching prospects through the Internet and mobile apps with degrees of targeting and message specificity that were previously unimaginable. All these media have to be effectively synchronized to attract new customers and to affirm the choice of existing customers while educating them on how to proceed through a service process. It is for good reason that we define the marketing communication element of the **7 Ps** as **Promotion** and **Education**.

How should we develop an effective service marketing communications strategy? It starts with a good understanding of the service product and their prospective buyers. It's essential to understand target market segments and their exposure to different media, consumers' awareness of the service product, their attitudes toward it, and how easily they can evaluate the products characteristics in advance of purchase, and during and after consumption. Decisions include determining the content, structure, and style of the message to be communicated, its manner of presentation, and the media most suited to reaching the intended audience. To integrate all these considerations, we developed the Integrated Service

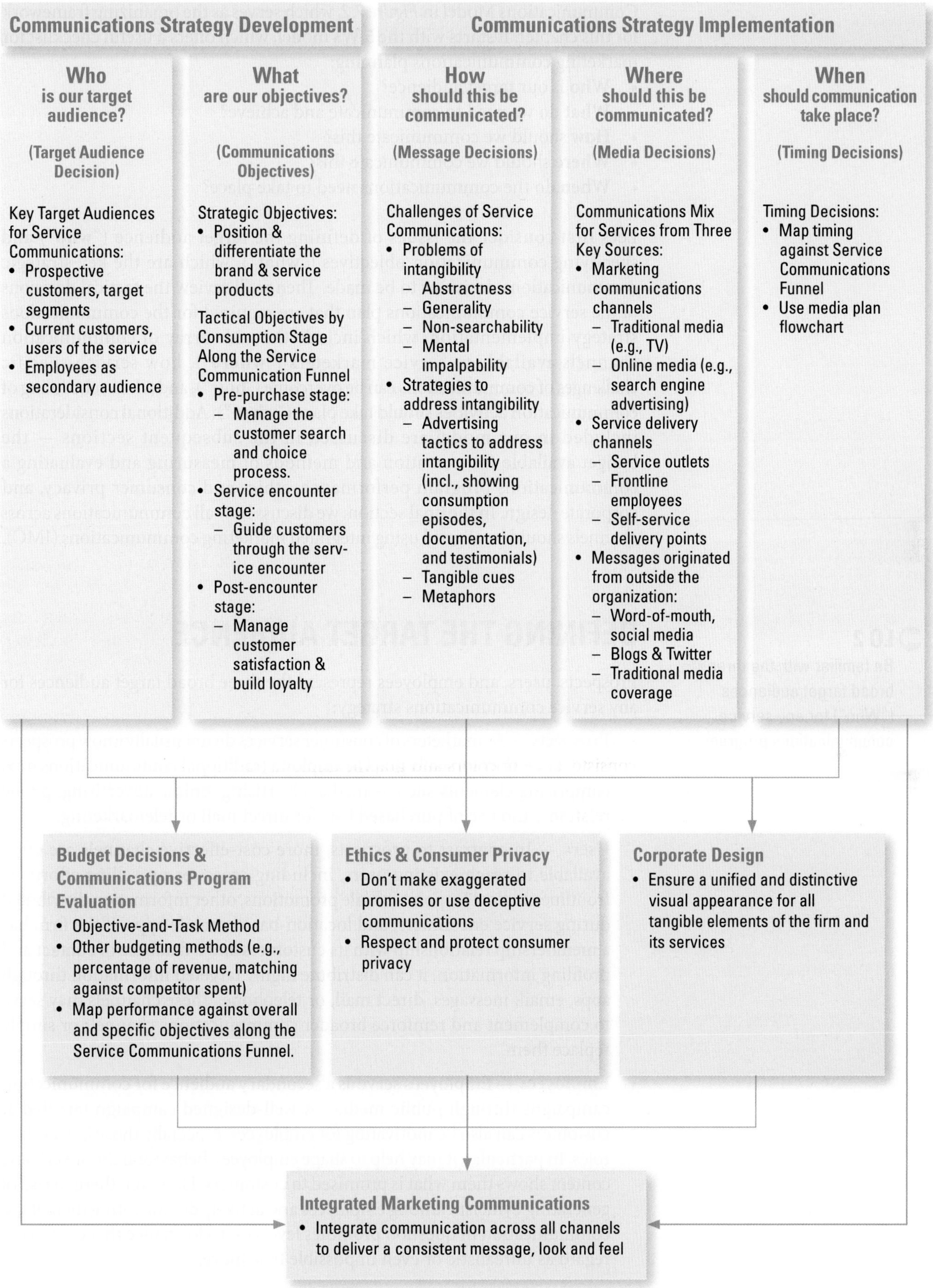

Communications Strategy Development

Who is our target audience? (Target Audience Decision)	What are our objectives? (Communications Objectives)

Key Target Audiences for Service Communications:
• Prospective customers, target segments
• Current customers, users of the service
• Employees as secondary audience
	Strategic Objectives:
	• Position & differentiate the brand & service products
	
	Tactical Objectives by Consumption Stage Along the Service Communication Funnel
	• Pre-purchase stage:
	  – Manage the customer search and choice process.
	• Service encounter stage:
	  – Guide customers through the service encounter
	• Post-encounter stage:
	  – Manage customer satisfaction & build loyalty

Communications Strategy Implementation

How should this be communicated? (Message Decisions)	Where should this be communicated? (Media Decisions)	When should communication take place? (Timing Decisions)

Challenges of Service Communications:
• Problems of intangibility
  – Abstractness
  – Generality
  – Non-searchability
  – Mental impalpability
• Strategies to address intangibility
  – Advertising tactics to address intangibility (incl., showing consumption episodes, documentation, and testimonials)
  – Tangible cues
  – Metaphors
	Communications Mix for Services from Three Key Sources:
	• Marketing communications channels
	  – Traditional media (e.g., TV)
	  – Online media (e.g., search engine advertising)
	• Service delivery channels
	  – Service outlets
	  – Frontline employees
	  – Self-service delivery points
	• Messages originated from outside the organization:
	  – Word-of-mouth, social media
	  – Blogs & Twitter
	  – Traditional media coverage
		Timing Decisions:
		• Map timing against Service Communications Funnel
		• Use media plan flowchart

Budget Decisions & Communications Program Evaluation
- Objective-and-Task Method
- Other budgeting methods (e.g., percentage of revenue, matching against competitor spent)
- Map performance against overall and specific objectives along the Service Communications Funnel.

Ethics & Consumer Privacy
- Don't make exaggerated promises or use deceptive communications
- Respect and protect consumer privacy

Corporate Design
- Ensure a unified and distinctive visual appearance for all tangible elements of the firm and its services

Integrated Marketing Communications
- Integrate communication across all channels to deliver a consistent message, look and feel

Figure 7.2 Integrated Service Communications Model

Communications Model in *Figure 7.2*, which serves as the organizing framework for this chapter. It starts with the **5 Ws** model, which offers a useful checklist for marketing communications planning:

- **Who** is our target audience?
- **What** do we need to communicate and achieve?
- **How** should we communicate this?
- **Where** should we communicate this?
- **When** do the communications need to take place?

Let's first consider the issues of defining the target audience ("**who**") and specifying communication objectives ("**what**"), which are the key strategic communications decisions to be made. Then we'll review the tactical decisions of the service communications plan that are required for the communications strategy implementation, which include the wide array of communication channels available to service marketers ("**where**"), how service-specific challenges of communications can be overcome ("**how**"), and when scheduling of communication activities should take place ("**when**"). Additional considerations included in our model are discussed in the subsequent sections — the budget available for execution and methods of measuring and evaluating a communications program performance, ethics and consumer privacy, and corporate design. In the final section, we discuss how all communications across channels should be aligned using integrated marketing communications (IMC).

⤵ **LO 2**

Be familiar with the three broad target audiences ("**W**ho") for any service communications program.

DEFINING THE TARGET AUDIENCE

Prospects, users, and employees represent the three broad target audiences for any service communications strategy:

- **Prospects** — As marketers of consumer services do not usually know prospects in advance, they typically need to employ a traditional communications mix, comprising elements such as media advertising, online advertising, public relations, and use of purchased lists for direct mail or telemarketing.

- **Users** — In contrast to prospects, more cost-effective channels are often available to reach existing users, including cross- or up-selling efforts by frontline employees, point-of-sale promotions, other information distributed during service encounters, and location-based mobile apps. If the firm has a membership relationship with its customers and a database of contact and profiling information, it can distribute highly targeted information through apps, email, messages, direct mail, or telephone. These channels may serve to complement and reinforce broader communications channels or simply replace them.

- **Employees** — Employees serve as a secondary audience for communication campaigns through public media[2]. A well-designed campaign targeted at customers can also be motivating for employees, especially those in frontline roles. In particular, it may help to shape employees' behavior if the advertising content shows them what is promised to customers. However, there's a risk of generating cynicism among employees and actively demotivating them if the communication in question promotes levels of performance that employees regard as unrealistic or even impossible to achieve.

Communications directed specifically at staff are typically part of an internal marketing campaign, using company-specific channels, and so are not accessible to customers. We will discuss internal communications in Chapter 11, "Managing People for Service Advantage".

SPECIFYING SERVICE COMMUNICATION OBJECTIVES

After we are clear about our target audience, we now need to specify what exactly we want to achieve with this target audience. At the most general level, marketing communications objectives are to inform, educate, persuade, remind, shape behavior, and build relationships. These objectives are, of course, at too high a level to be operationalizable. Communications objectives answer the question of what we need to communicate and achieve. Objectives can be strategic and tactical in nature, and are often an amalgamation of both.

Strategic Service Communications Objectives

Strategic objectives include building a service brand, and positioning it and its service products against competition. That is, companies use marketing communications to persuade target customers that their service product offers the best solution to meet those customers' needs, relative to the offerings of competing firms. Communication efforts serve not only to attract new users but also to maintain contact with an organization's existing customers and build relationships with them. That is, marketing communications is used to convince potential and current customers about the firm's overall superior performance.

To document the superior quality and reliability of its small package delivery services, a FedEx advertisement showcased the awards it received for being rated as highest in customer satisfaction for air, ground, and international delivery from J.D. Power and Associates, widely known and respected for its customer satisfaction research in numerous industries[3]. To reposition a service relative to competitive offerings is also a common strategic objective of communications.

 LO 3
Understand the most common strategic and tactical service communications objectives ("**W**hat").

LO 4

Be familiar with the Service
Marketing Communications
Funnel and key objectives in
that funnel.

TACTICAL SERVICE COMMUNICATIONS OBJECTIVES

Tactical objectives relate to shaping and managing customer's perceptions, beliefs, attitudes, and behavior in any of the three stages of the service consumption process we discussed in Chapter 2 (i.e., the prepurchase, service encounter, and post-encounter stages). We show in the Service Marketing Communications Funnel in *Figure 7.3* how common tactical communications objective map against the three stages of the service consumption (left column in *Figure 7.3*) and related key consumer behavior concepts and theories (right column in *Figure 7.3*).

You may be familiar with models that deal with the prepurchase phase, generally referred to as sales funnel (or purchase funnel from the customer's perspective) and models that depict the stages a consumer typically passes through from not being aware of a product to all the way of actually buying it. Probably the oldest model is "AIDA", standing for **A**wareness, **I**nterest, **D**esire, and **A**ction, which was developed almost a century ago, and holds that persuasion to buy a product occurs over time, and explains how customers move from cognitive (awareness), to affective (interest and desire) to behavioral (action) responses[4]. As with many basic models, it has stood the test of time and is still being used. Today, the **hierarchy of effects model** is probably the most widely used framework to describe this process by extending the steps described in the AIDA model as follows: The hierarchy of effects model starts with a cognitive stage of awareness and knowledge, followed by an affective stage that leads to liking, preference, and conviction, and finally, a behavioral stage of buying[5]. Along each of those stages and the individual steps within, marketing communications assumes different roles to guide consumers towards the purchase decision (*Figure 7.4*).

The Service Marketing Communications Funnel is aligned to the AIDA and hierarchy of effects models in the prepurchase stage, and extends them by incorporating a wider range of service-specific objectives in the prepurchase stage. Furthermore, as neither of the two models covers the service encounter and post-encounter stages, we added service communications objectives relating to the service encounter itself (which can include the full gamut of customer behaviors that needs to be managed, ranging from queuing behaviors to performance perceptions), and to the post-encounter stage (e.g., many services are membership-type or contractual in nature, which therefore includes a host of post-encounter behaviors that can be shaped by communications).

Three–Stage Model of Service Consumption	Common Communication Objectives Along the Services Marketing Communications Funnel	Key Consumer Behavior Concepts and Theories

Pre-purchase Stage

Awareness of need
- Information search
- Clarify needs
- Explore solutions
- Identify alternative service products

Evaluation of alternatives
- Review supplier information (e.g., advertising, website)
- Review information from third parties (e.g., published reviews, ratings, blogs)
- Discuss options with service personnel
- Get advice from third-parties
- Make purchase decision

Customer Acquisition

- Move customers along the key stages of the sales funnel
- Build awareness, knowledge, and interest in the service or brand
  - Encourage to explore the firm's website or social media sites
  - Register for your online newsletter, service updates, or YouTube channel
- Develop liking, preference, and conviction for the service or brand
  - Compare a service favorably with competitors' offerings
  - Convince potential customers about the firm's superior performance on determinant attributes
- Encourage potential customers to purchase
  - Reduce perceived risk by providing information and service guarantees
  - Encourage trial by offering promotional incentives
- Create memorable images of brands and services
- Stimulate and shift demand to match capacity

Pre-purchase Stage

- Need arousal
- Evoked set
- Consideration set

Multi-attribute choice model
- Search, experience, and credence attributes
- Perceived risk
- Formation of expectations
- Purchase decision

Service Encounter Stage

- Request service from the chosen supplier or initiate self-service
- Experience the service encounter

Service Encounter Management

- Familiarize customers with service processes in advance of use (e.g., what to prepare & expect)
- Guide customers through the service process
- Manage customer behavior and perceptions during the service encounter (e.g., teach roles, script for queuing, inject perceived control)
- Manage quality perceptions
- Cross-sell & upsell services

Service Encounter Stage

- Moments of truth
- Service encounters
- Servuction system
- Theatre as metaphor
- Role and script theories
- Perceived control theory

Post-encounter Stage

- Evaluation of service performance
- Future intentions
- Future behaviors

Customer Engagement

- Manage customer satisfaction
- Manage service quality perceptions
- Build loyalty
- Encourage WOM (offline and online)
- Encourage referrals
- Build a brand community

Post-encounter Stage

- Confirmation/disconfirmation of expectations
- Dissatisfaction, satisfaction, and delight
- Service quality
- WOM and referrals
- Online reviews
- Repurchase
- Customer loyalty

Figure 7.3 Common communications objectives along the Service Marketing Communications Funnel

Figure 7.4 This Chicago School advert creates awareness and interest

The Service Marketing Communications Funnel starts with a broad target audience at the top (i.e., all prospects in the firm's target segments), narrows down to customers who actually buy and consume the service, and finally, even for loyalty initiatives, firms typically do not target all their customers with the same intensity — the focus tends to be on their "platinum" or premium customers with high purchase volumes (see also Chapter 12 "Managing Relationships and Building Loyalty"). As you can see, marketing communications plays specific roles during all three stages of the service consumption process and not just the prepurchase stage.

A key takeaway from *Figure 7.3* should be that your communications objectives can be highly specific and can address any aspect of service consumer behavior. Do go back to Chapter 2 "Consumer Behavior in a Service Context", and consider how communications can be used to shape consumer behavior in the firm-desired direction in any of the stages. For example, in the prepurchase stage, how can communications be used to trigger a need, get a service into the evoked and then into the consideration set, reduce perceived risk, and shape multi-attribute model-type processing (e.g., shifting attribute performance perceptions, attribute weightings, and decision rules in the favor of the firm's services). During the service encounter stage, how can communications be employed to shape performance perceptions, help customers move effectively through the service encounter, shape quality perceptions, teach service roles and scripts, and inject perceived control into the service encounter? Finally, how can communications be used in the post-encounter stage to shape customer satisfaction and service quality evaluations, and encourage word-of-mouth (WOM), referrals, repurchase, and loyalty.

To discuss all possible objectives that can be derived from the Services Marketing Communications Funnel is beyond the scope of this chapter. However, we highlight a few important communications objectives in the following sections.

Promote Tangible Cues to Communicate Quality

Even if customers understand what a service is supposed to do, they may find it hard to tell the difference between offerings from different suppliers. Companies can use concrete cues to communicate service performance by highlighting the quality of equipment and facilities and by emphasizing employee characteristics such as qualifications, experience, commitment, and professionalism. Some performance attributes are easier or more appropriate to communicate than others. Airlines and hospitals do not advertise safety because even the suggestion that things might go wrong makes many people nervous. Instead, they approach this ongoing customer concern indirectly by communicating the overall high quality of their people, facilities, equipment, and processes.

LO 5
Know a few important specific roles service marketing communications can assume.

Add Value Through Communication Content. Information and consultation represent important ways to add value to a product. Prospective customers may need information and advice about what service options are available to them (*Figure 7.5*); where and when these services are available; how much they cost; and what specific features, functions, and service benefits there are. (See the Flower of Service framework in Chapter 4 on how this information can add value.)

Facilitate Customer Involvement in Service Production. When customers are actively involved in service production, they need training to help them perform well — just as employees do. Improving productivity often involves making innovations in service delivery. However, the desired benefits won't be achieved if customers resist new, technologically based systems or avoid self-service alternatives.

Marketers often use sales promotions as incentives to encourage customers to make the necessary changes in their behavior. For example, giving price discounts or running lucky draws are some ways to encourage customers to try and switch to self-service. And if necessary, well-trained service personnel can provide one-to-one tutoring to help customers adapt to new procedures.

One way to train customers, as recommended by advertising experts, is to show service delivery in action. Television and videos are effective because of their ability to engage the viewer and display a seamless sequence of events in visual form. Some dentists show their patients videos of surgical procedures before the surgery takes place so that customers know what to expect. Shouldice Hospital in Toronto featured in *Case 9* specializes in hernia repair. It offers potential patients an opportunity to view an online simulation on hernia and explains the hospital experience on its website (see www.shouldice. com). This educational technique helps patients mentally prepare for the experience and shows them what role they need to play in service delivery to ensure a successful surgery and speedy recovery.

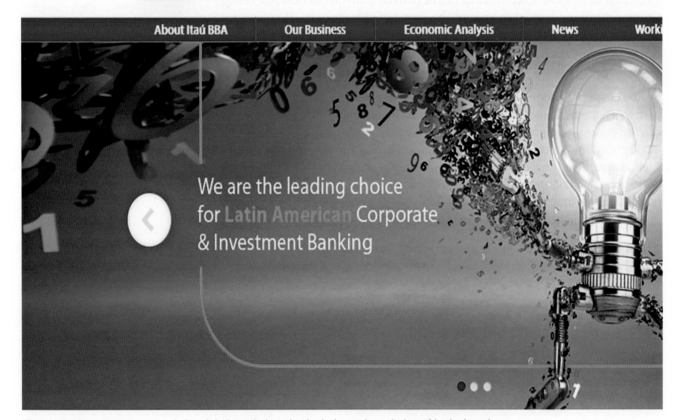

Figure 7.5 Itau stresses not only its global reach, but also its intimate knowledge of Latin America

Figure 7.6 The Starbucks website tells us what goes on behind the scenes in creating a new blend of coffee

Promote the Contribution of Service Personnel and Backstage Operations. High quality, frontline staff, and backstage operations can be important differentiators for services. In high-contact services, frontline personnel are central to service delivery. Their presence makes the service more tangible and, in many cases, more personalized. An ad that shows employees at work helps prospective customers understand the nature of the service encounter and implies a promise of the personalized attention that they can expect to receive.

Advertising, brochures, websites, and videos on YouTube can also show customers the work that goes on "backstage" to ensure good service delivery. Highlighting the expertise and commitment of employees whom customers normally never encounter may enhance trust in the organization's competence and commitment to service quality. For example, Starbucks has publicity materials and videos that show customers what service personnel do behind the scenes. Starbucks shows how coffee beans are cultivated, harvested, and produced — highlighting its use of the finest and freshest (*Figure 7.6*)[6].

Advertising messages set customer expectations, so advertisers must be reasonably realistic in their depictions of service personnel. They should also inform employees about the content of new campaigns that promise specific attitudes and behaviors so that employees know what is expected of them.

Stimulate and Shift Demand to Match Capacity. Low demand outside peak periods is a serious problem for service industries with high fixed costs, such as hotels. One strategy is to run promotions that offer extra value — such as room upgrades or free breakfasts — to encourage demand without decreasing price. When demand increases, the number of promotions can be reduced or eliminated (see also Chapter 6 on revenue management and Chapter 9 on managing demand).

Advertising and sales promotions can also help to shift usage from peak to lower demand periods and thus help to match demand with the available capacity at a given time.

LO 6

Understand the challenges of service communications and how service communications can overcome those ("How").

CRAFTING EFFECTIVE SERVICE COMMUNICATION MESSAGES

Now that we've discussed service communications objectives, let's explore some of the communications challenges service firms face when developing their communications messages. For goods and services alike, messages have to break through the clutter as communications can only succeed if it gains the attention of its target group. Marketers have to make decisions on what they want to say (i.e., the message content) and how to say that (i.e., the message structure and format)[7]. While any good marketing and communications book deals with these questions, traditional marketing communication strategies were shaped largely by the needs and practices associated with marketing manufactured goods. However, several of the differences that distinguish services from goods also have a significant effect on the ways we approach the design of message and creative strategy of service marketing communication programs. This is especially so for intangibility which is discussed next.

Problems of Intangibility

The benefits of services can be difficult to communicate to customers as they are "performances" rather than objects, especially when the service in question does not involve tangible actions to customers or their possessions[8]. Intangibility creates four problems for marketers seeking to promote its attributes or benefits: abstractness, generality, non-searchability, and mental impalpability[9]. Each problem has implications for service communications[10]:

- **Abstractness** refers to concepts such as financial security or investment-related matters (*Figure 7.7*), expert advice, or safe transportation do not have one-to-one correspondence with physical objects. It can therefore be challenging for marketers to connect their services to those intangible concepts.

Figure 7.7 A bank shows how the intangibility of providing balanced banking solutions can be communicated

- **Generality** refers to items that comprise a class of objects, persons, or events — for instance, airline seats, flight attendants, and cabin service. There may be physical objects that can show these services, so abstractness is not a problem. However, it is general and not specific enough, so even though most consumers of the service know what they are, it is difficult for marketers to create a unique value proposition is to communicate what makes a specific offering distinctly different from — and superior to — competing offerings.

- **Non-searchability** refers to the fact that many of the service attributes cannot be searched or inspected before they are purchased. Physical service attributes, such as the appearance of a health club and the type of equipment installed, can be checked in advance, but the experience of working with the trainers can only be determined through extended personal involvement. As noted in Chapter 2, services usually have more experience and credence attributes than search attributes. Experience attributes are those that need consumers to go through the service to understand it. Services high in credence attributes, such as surgeon expertise, must be taken on faith.

- **Mental impalpability** refers to services that are sufficiently complex, multi-dimensional, or novel so much so that it is difficult for consumers — especially new prospects — to understand what the experience of using them will be like and what benefits will result.

Overcoming the Problems of Intangibility

How should service messages be communicated? Here, the intangibility of service presents problems for advertising that need to be overcome. *Table 7.1* suggests specific communications strategies marketers can follow to create messages that help to overcome each of the four problems created by the intangibility of services.

Table 7.1 Advertising Strategies for Overcoming Intangibility

Intangibility Problem	Advertising Strategy	Description
Abstractness	Service consumption episode	Capture and show typical customers benefiting from the service, e.g., by smiling in satisfaction at a staff going out of his way to help
Generality • For objective claim	System documentation	Document facts and statistics about the service delivery system. For example, in the UPS website, they state that they have 227 aircraft in operation
	Performance documentation	Document and cite past service performance statistics, such as the number of packages that have been delivered on time
• For subjective claim	Service performance episode	Present actual service delivery being performed by the service personnel. The video mode is best for showing this
Non-searchability	Consumption documentation	Obtain and present testimonials from customers who have experienced the service
	Reputation documentation	If the service is high in credence attributes, then document the awards received, or the qualifications of the service provider
Mental impalpability	Service process episode	Present a clear step-by-step documentation of what exactly will happen during the service experience
	Case history episode	Present an actual case history of what the firm did for a specific client and how it solved the client's problem
	Service consumption episode	A story or depiction of a customer's experience with a service

In addition to using the strategies presented in *Table 7.1*, using tangible cues and metaphors are two other methods firms can use to overcome the four challenges of intangibility. Both tangible cues and metaphors help to clearly communicate intangible service attributes and benefits to potential customers.

Tangible Cues. Commonly used strategies in advertising include the use of tangible cues whenever possible, especially for services that involve few tangible elements. It's also helpful to include "vivid information" that catches the audience's attention and produces a strong, clear impression on the senses, especially for services that are complex and highly intangible[11]. For example, many business schools feature successful alumni to make the benefits of their education tangible and communicate what their programs could do for prospective students in terms of career advancement, salary increases and lifestyle.

Service Insights 7.1 shows how visualization and comparative advertising affect consumer perceptions of both hedonic services (those that bring pleasure and enjoyment) and utilitarian services (those that are consumed for practical or functional purposes).

Use Metaphors. Some companies have created metaphors that are tangible in nature to help communicate the benefits of their service offerings and to emphasize key points of differentiation. Insurance companies often use this approach to market their highly intangible products. Allstate advertises that "You're in Good Hands" and Prudential uses the Rock of Gibraltar as a symbol of corporate strength. The Merrill Lynch bull has been a symbol for the wealth manager's business philosophy, which suggests both a bullish market and a strong commitment to financial performance of its clients (*Figure 7.8*).

Where possible, advertising metaphors should highlight *how* service benefits are actually provided[12]. Consulting firm AT Kearney emphasizes that it includes all management levels in seeking solutions, not just higher-level management. Its clever advertisement, showing bear traps across the office floor, draws attention to the way in which the company differentiates its service through careful work with all levels in its client organizations, thus avoiding the problems left behind by other consulting firms who work mostly with senior management (*Figure 7.9*).

Figure 7.8 The Merrill Lynch bull shows a strong commitment to the financial performance of its clients

WHAT DID YOUR CONSULTANTS LEAVE BEHIND?

When a consultancy works only with the senior executives, they often leave you with more problems than they solved. A.T. Kearney, however, collaborates with your entire team. So you not only get big ideas, but an organization prepared to implement them—and deliver even more.

Figure 7.9 AT Kearney uses bear traps as a metaphor for problems

SERVICE INSIGHTS 7.1
Visualization and Comparative Advertising for Services

Experts often recommend using visual stimuli to convey a vivid mental picture, and documentation of facts and figures in order to overcome service intangibility and better communicate the value proposition of a service. To test the effectiveness of visualization and documentation strategies for hedonic and utilitarian services, four academics conducted a laboratory experiment.

They showed the 160 participating student subjects one print advertisement each, and then measured their responses. An ad for a spring-break travel service was used as the hedonic service, and one for a bank with specific student offers was used for the utilitarian service. In the visualization condition, one picture of the hotel and one of young adults in an ocean-side pool were added to the text for the hedonic service. For the bank, photos of the exterior of the bank building and an ATM were shown. The text-only documentation condition used an indirect comparative advertising copy stating the high performance of the service provider along the three most important attributes for the respective two services. The study then compared the text-only documentation condition with the ad that contained the pictures (visualization condition).

The findings showed that for both types of services, ads based on a visualization strategy were perceived as more informative than text-only ads. Participants who viewed the visualization ads perceived the services as higher quality and were more likely to say they intended to use these services. Documentation worked well for the hedonic service but not the utilitarian one (further research is needed to explain why). The study has two important managerial implications:

1. **Use pictures to increase tangibility of the value proposition.** Whether you market a hedonic or a utilitarian service, you should use pictures and photos to communicate the potential benefits of your service. For example, Hilton Hotels Corp. started using photos to market its Chef's Signature Catering Collection, replacing its more traditional method of sending text-only menu information to clients who wanted to plan a dinner at the hotel. One Hilton executive noted, "People eat with their eyes, and when they see something they can relate to, something they can recognize, it develops a level of confidence and comfort for the customer."

2. **Comparative data help readers to visualize especially hedonic services.** The study indicated that hedonic services can benefit from adding comparative information into their ads. For example, if Six Flags Great America advertises that its Déjà vu roller coaster is 196-feet tall compared to only 120-feet of other top roller coasters, and that its speed is up to 65 miles per hour (104 kilometers per hour), compared to only 50–60 miles per hour for other roller coasters, then one should expect readers to better visualize the Déjà vu as one of the tallest and fastest roller coasters in the world. Simply listing the height and speed alone wouldn't be as effective — readers need the benchmarking provided by the comparative information.

Source

Donna J. Hill, Jeff Blodgett, Robert Baer, and Kirk Wakefield (2004), "An Investigation of Visualization and Documentation Strategies in Service Advertising," *Journal of Service Research*, Vol. 7, No. 2, pp. 155-166.

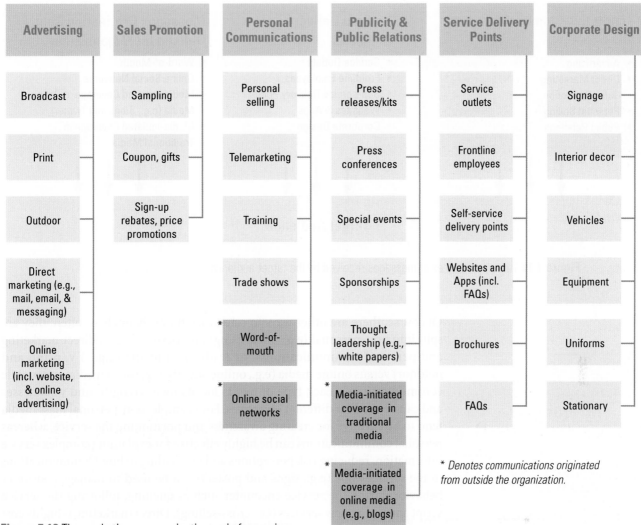

Advertising	Sales Promotion	Personal Communications	Publicity & Public Relations	Service Delivery Points	Corporate Design
Broadcast	Sampling	Personal selling	Press releases/kits	Service outlets	Signage
Print	Coupon, gifts	Telemarketing	Press conferences	Frontline employees	Interior decor
Outdoor	Sign-up rebates, price promotions	Training	Special events	Self-service delivery points	Vehicles
Direct marketing (e.g., mail, email, & messaging)		Trade shows	Sponsorships	Websites and Apps (incl. FAQs)	Equipment
Online marketing (incl. website, & online advertising)		*Word-of-mouth	Thought leadership (e.g., white papers)	Brochures	Uniforms
		*Online social networks	*Media-initiated coverage in traditional media	FAQs	Stationary
			*Media-initiated coverage in online media (e.g., blogs)		

Denotes communications originated from outside the organization.

Figure 7.10 The marketing communications mix for services

THE SERVICES MARKETING COMMUNICATIONS MIX

After understanding our target audience, our specific communications objectives and message strategy, we now need to select a mix of cost-effective communication channels. Most service marketers have access to numerous forms of communication, referred to collectively as the **service marketing communications mix**. Different communication elements have distinctive capabilities relative to the types of messages they can convey and the market segments most likely to be exposed to them, and the mix needs to be optimized to achieve the best possible results for a given budget[13].

Figure 7.10 provides an overview of the wide range of communications channels available to service firms. Note that these media can be categorized in several ways. For example, service employees providing service are, at the same time, part of the service delivery point and a type of personal communications. We categorized each communications mix element according to the most suitable category for the purpose of discussing the overall media strategy of service organizations.

⊃ **LO 7**
Be familiar with the marketing communications mix in a services context ("**W**here").

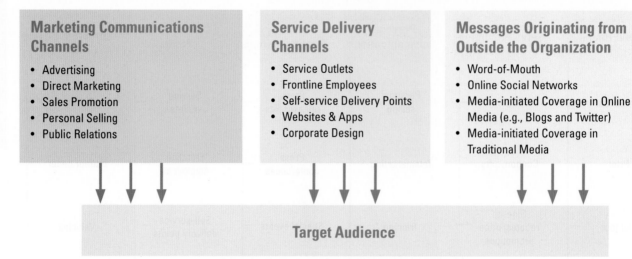

Figure 7.11 Three key sources of messages received by the target audience

Of course, there are other ways to categorize these channels — often, they are split into non-personal (e.g., advertising) and personal (e.g., direct marketing and personal communications), or traditional media (e.g., TV, print, and outdoor) versus online media (e.g., online advertising, social media, and mobile communications). Each type of media has its own strengths and weaknesses and can be used for different objectives. For example, non-personal mass media tend to be effective for creating awareness and positioning the service, whereas personal communications can be highly effective for explaining complex service information, reducing risk perceptions and persuading to buy. Communications in the servicescape (e.g., signs and posters) can be used to manage consumer behavior during the service encounter such as queuing, following the service script and trying new services (i.e., cross-selling). Direct marketing is highly cost effective in the post-encounter stage, such as to encourage customers to come back and to recommend the service to their friends and family.

Communications Originate from Different Sources

As shown in *Figure 7.11*, the services marketing communications mix featured in *Figure 7.10* can also be categorized into three broad categories of sources of communications: (1) marketing communications channels, which include traditional media and online channels, (2) service delivery channels, and (3) messages that originate from outside the organization[14]. Let's look at key options within each of these three originating sources, whereby we discuss traditional media and online media separately as they have vastly different characteristics and applications.

⊃ **LO 8**

Know the communications mix elements of the traditional marketing communications channels.

Messages Transmitted Through Traditional Marketing Channels

As shown in *Figure 7.10*, service marketers have a wide array of communication tools at their disposal. Let's briefly review the principle elements.

Advertising. A wide array of paid advertising media is available, including broadcast (TV and radio), print (magazines and newspapers), movie theaters, and many types of outdoor media (posters, billboards, electronic message boards, and the exteriors of buses or bicycles). Some media are more focused than others, targeting specific geographic areas or audiences with a particular interest. Advertising messages delivered through mass media are often reinforced by direct marketing tools like mailings, telemarketing, or email.

As the most dominant form of communication in consumer marketing, advertising is often the first point of contact between service marketers and their customers, serving to build awareness, inform, persuade, and remind. It plays a vital role in providing factual information about services and educating customers about product features and capabilities. For instance, a review of 11,543 television ads and 30,940 newspaper ads found that ads for services were significantly more likely to contain factual information on price, guarantees/warranties, documentation of performance, and availability (where, when, and how to acquire products) compared to ads for goods[15].

One of the challenges facing advertisers is how to get their messages noticed. In general, people are getting tired of ads in all their forms. A study by Yankelovich Partner, a US marketing services consulting firm, found that consumer resistance to advertising has reached an all-time high. The study found that 65% of people feel "constantly bombarded" by ad messages, and 59% feel that ads have very little relevance to them[16]. Television and radio broadcasts, websites, and online games are cluttered with ads, while newspapers and magazines sometimes seem to contain more ads than news and features. Robert Shaw of Cranfield School of Management runs a forum in which large companies try to monitor the "marketing payback" from advertising. According to Shaw, the results were "never terribly good," with less than half of the ads generating a positive return on their investment[17].

How can a firm hope to stand out from the crowd? Longer, louder commercials and larger format ads are not the answer. Marketers are trying to be more creative with their advertising to allow their messages to be more effective. For example, when customers have low involvement with a service, firms should focus on more emotional appeals and the service experience itself[18]. Some advertisers stand out by using striking designs or a distinctively different format. Others, like Comcast, seek to catch the audience's attention through use of humor as it seeks to show how slow competing services are compared to its own high-speed Internet cable access. Some firms are now placing advertisements in video games and multiplayer online role-playing games, which can be dynamic advertisements if the games are connected to the Internet (*Figure 7.12*)[19]. Furthermore, mobile apps are becoming increasingly important avenues for communication with potential and current customers.

Direct Marketing. This category embraces tools such as mailings, email, and text messaging. These channels offer the potential to send personalized messages to highly targeted microsegments. Direct strategies will most likely succeed when marketers possess a detailed database of information about prospects and customers.

Figure 7.12 Virtual video game worlds like *Second Life* lead the wave of in-game advertising.

Commercial services that combine company-collected data with rich, third-party online and offline data sources are available. Experian, one of the globally leading providers in this market, stated on its website: "We can help you to build a richer picture of your customers' behavior so you can predict and engineer how they behave in the future. Using internal and external data sources, our proven customer management tools allow you to tailor strategies to an individual…powered by up to 6,000 variables…uses lifestyle, demographic, transaction, permissible credit and consumer classification data.[20]"

Advances in on-demand technologies such as email spam filters, TiVo, podcasting, and pop-up blockers allow consumers to decide how and when they like to be reached and by whom. Because a 30-second television spot interrupts a viewer's favorite program and a telemarketing call interrupts a meal, customers increasingly use such technologies to protect their time, thereby reducing the effectiveness of mass media. These developments give rise to **permission marketing**, where customers are encouraged to "raise their hands" and agree to learn more about a company and its products in anticipation of receiving useful marketing information or

something else of value. Instead of annoying prospects by interrupting their personal time, permission marketing allows customers to self-select into the target segments.

In the permission marketing model, the goal is to persuade consumers to volunteer their attention. By reaching out only to individuals who have expressed prior interest in receiving a certain type of message, permission marketing enables service firms to build stronger relationships with their customers. In particular, email and messaging, in combination with websites and mobile apps, can be merged into a one-to-one permission-based medium. For instance, people can be invited to register at the firm's website or download an app and state what type of information they would like to receive[21].

These messages can be designed at the start of a more interactive, multilayered communication process in which customers can request regular information about topics of their interest. In addition, if they are particularly excited about a new service or piece of information, they can click through a link embedded in the message to access more in-depth information and video materials. Finally, they can subscribe for additional services, communicate with other customers, recommend the service to their friends, and like it on Facebook or LinkedIn.

Many service firms increased their focus on permission-based marketing because of its high effectiveness combined with the falling prices and improving quality of customer relationship management (CRM) systems, big data, social media and communications technology, which together power permission-based marketing. To see how some firms have implemented excellent permission-based marketing strategies, just see Amazon.com or Hallmark.com and register at these websites or download their apps.

Sales Promotion. A useful way of looking at sales promotions is as a communication with an incentive. Sales promotions usually are specific to a time period, price, or customer group — sometimes all three as in direct marketing. Typically, it is employed for short-term objectives such as to accelerate the purchasing decision or motivate customers to use a specific service sooner, in greater volume with each purchase, or more frequently[22]. Sales promotions for service firms may take forms such as samples, coupons and other discounts, gifts, and competitions with prizes. Used in these forms, sales promotions increase sales during periods when demand would otherwise be weak, speed up the introduction and acceptance of new services, and generally get customers to act faster than they would in the absence of any promotional incentive[23]. However, sales promotions need to be used with care because research shows that customers acquired through sales promotions may have lower repurchase rates and lower lifetime values[24].

Some years ago, SAS International Hotels devised an interesting sales promotion targeted at older customers. If a hotel had vacant rooms, guests over 65 years of age could get a discount equivalent to their years (e.g., a 75-year-old could save 75% of the normal room price). All went well until a Swedish guest checked into one of the SAS chain's hotels in Vienna, announced his age as 102, and asked to be paid 2% of the room rate in return for staying the night. This request was granted, whereupon the spry centenarian challenged the general manager to a game of tennis — and got that, too. (The results of the game, however, were not disclosed!) Events like these are the stuff of dreams for public relations people. In this case, a clever promotion led to a humorous, widely reported story that placed the hotel chain in a favorable light.

Personal Selling. Interpersonal encounters in which efforts are made to educate customers and promote a particular brand or product are referred to as personal selling. Many firms, especially those marketing business-to-business services, maintain a sales team or employ agents and distributors to undertake personal selling efforts on their behalf. For services that are bought less often like property, insurance, and funeral services, the firm's representative may act as a consultant to help buyers make their selections. For industrial and professional firms that sell relatively complex services, customers may have an account manager they can turn to for advice, education, and consultation.

However, face-to-face selling to new prospects is expensive. A lower-cost alternative is **telemarketing**, involving use of the telephone to reach prospective customers. At the consumer level, there is growing frustration with the intrusive nature of telemarketing, which is often timed to reach people when they are home in the evening or on weekends (*Figure 7.14*). Today, many people in the US subscribe to a "Do Not Call Registry" which has dramatically reduced the number of solicitor calls that reach their prospects[25].

Public Relations. PR involves efforts to stimulate positive interest in an organization and its products by sending out news releases, holding press conferences, staging special events, and sponsoring newsworthy activities put on by third parties. A basic element in PR strategy is the preparation and distribution of press releases (including photos and/or videos) that feature stories about the company, its products, and its employees.

Figure 7.14 Telemarketers call in the evenings

© 1999 Randy Glasbergen.

GLASBERGEN

"Before you hang up, Mrs. Johnson, are you aware that you can lose up to 50 pounds a year by listening to telemarketers instead of eating your dinner?"

Other widely used PR techniques include recognition and reward programs, obtaining testimonials from public figures, community involvement and fund raising, and obtaining favorable publicity for the organization through special events and *pro bono* work. These tools can help a service organization build its reputation and credibility, form strong relationships with its employees, customers, and the community, and secure an image conducive to business success.

Firms can also gain wide exposure through sponsorship of sporting events and other high-profile activities like the Olympics and the World Cup where banners, decals, and other visual displays provide continuing repetition of the corporate name and symbol. Furthermore, unusual activities can present an opportunity to promote a company's expertise. FedEx gained a lot of positive publicity when it safely transported two giant pandas from Chengdu, China, to the National Zoo in Washington, DC. The pandas flew in specially designed containers aboard a FedEx aircraft renamed "FedEx PandaOne." In addition to press releases, the company also featured information about the unusual shipment on a special page on its website (*Figure 7.13*).

⊃ LO 9

Know the role of the Internet, mobile, apps, QR code, and other electronic media in service marketing communications.

Messages Transmitted Online

Online and mobile advertising using the Internet, social media, and apps[26] allow companies to complement and sometimes even substitute traditional communications channels at a reasonable cost. However, like any of the elements of the marketing communications mix, online and mobile advertising should be part of an integrated, well-designed communications strategy[27].

Figure 7.13 The FedEx Panda Express arriving into Edinburgh direct from Chengdu, China with Edinburgh Zoo's new residents, Tian Tian and Yang Guang

Company's Website

Marketers use their own website for a variety of communications tasks:

- Creating consumer awareness and interest.
- Providing information and consultation.
- Allowing two-way communications with customers through email and chat rooms.
- Encouraging product trial.
- Enabling customers to place orders.
- Measuring the effectiveness of specific advertising or promotional campaigns.

Innovative companies continue to constantly look for ways to improve the appeal and usefulness of their websites. Suitable communication content varies widely from one type of service to another. A B2B site may offer visitors access to a library of technical information (e.g., Oracle or SAP both provide substantial information on their CRM solutions at their respective websites). By contrast, a B2C website for an MBA program might include attractive photographs and videos featuring the university, its professors and facilities, student testimonials, information on alumni, the location, and even a graduation ceremony.

Marketers must also address other factors such as downloading speed that affect website "stickiness" (i.e., whether visitors are willing to spend time on the site and will revisit it in the future). A sticky site is:

- **High in quality content.** Relevant and useful content is king. A site needs to contain what visitors are looking for.

- **Easy to use.** Easy to use means it is easy to find their way around the site with good navigation, and a site structure that is well signposted, neither overcomplicated nor too big.. Customers do not get lost in good sites!

- **Quick to download.** Viewers don't want to wait, and will often give up if it takes too long for pages to download from a site. Good sites download quickly, and bad sites are slow; which means that the content has to be "light".

- **Updated frequently.** Good sites look fresh and up-to-date. They include recently posted information that visitors find relevant and timely[28].

A memorable Web address helps to attract visitors to a site. Ideally, they are based on the company's name (e.g., www.citibank.com or www.aol.com). Ensuring that people are aware of the address requires displaying it prominently on business cards, letterhead stationery, email templates, brochures, advertising, promotional materials, and even vehicles.

Online Advertising. There are two main types of online advertising, namely banner advertising and search engine advertising.

- **Banner Advertising:** Many firms pay to place advertising banners and buttons on portals like Yahoo or CNN, social media websites such as Facebook and LinkedIn, and apps, online games, and advertising-funded content websites. The usual goal is to draw online traffic to the advertiser's own site. In many instances, websites include advertising messages from other marketers with services that are related but not competing. For example, Yahoo's stock quotes page has a sequence of advertisements for various financial service providers.

Simply getting a large number of exposures ("eyeballs") to a banner (a thin horizontal ad running across all or part of a web page), or a skyscraper (a long skinny ad running vertically down one side of a website) doesn't necessarily lead to an increase in awareness, preference, or sales for the advertiser. Even when visitors click through to the advertiser's site, this act doesn't necessarily result in sales. Consequently, there is now more emphasis on advertising contracts that link fees to marketing-relevant behavior by these visitors, such as providing the advertiser with some information about themselves or when making a purchase. More Internet advertisers pay only if a visitor to the host site clicks through to the link onto the advertisers' site. This is similar to paying for the delivery of junk mail only to households that read it[29].

- **Search Engine Advertising:** Search engines are a form of a reverse broadcast network. Instead of advertisers broadcasting their messages to consumers, search engines let advertisers know exactly what consumers want through their keyword search, and advertisers can then target relevant marketing communications directly at these consumers. Search engine advertising is currently the most popular online advertising instrument[30], and Google is the leader in this space (*Service Insights 7.2*), with firms like Blink and Yahoo! seeking to increase their market share.

SERVICE INSIGHTS 7.2
Google — the Online Marketing Powerhouse

Larry Page and Sergey Brin, who were both fascinated by mathematics, computers, and programming from an early age, founded Google in 1998 while they were Ph.D. students at Stanford University. Seven years later, following Google's successful public offering, they had become multibillionaires and Google itself had become one of the world's most valuable companies.

Google and the Google logo are registered trademarks of Google Inc., used with permission.

The company has the grand vision "to organize the world's information and make it universally accessible and useful." The utility and ease of its search engine has made it immensely successful, almost entirely through word-of-mouth from satisfied users. Few company names have become verbs, but "to google" has now entered common use in English.

Its popularity has enabled Google to become a highly targeted advertising medium, allowing advertisers two important ways to reach their customers — through sponsored links and through content ads.

Sponsored links appear at the top of search results on Google's website and are identified as "sponsored links". Google prices its sponsored links service as "cost per click", using a sealed-bid auction (i.e., where advertisers submit bids for a search term without knowing the bids of other advertisers for the same term). This means prices depend on the popularity of the search terms with which the advertiser wants to be associated. Heavily used terms such as "MBA" are more expensive than less popular terms such as "MSc in Business". Advertisers can easily keep track of their ad performance using the reports in Google's online account control center.

Google allows **content ads** to be highly targeted through a number of ways via its Google AdWords service. Ads can be placed next to search results on Google.com (e.g., they are displayed as banner ads). These ads allow businesses to connect with potential customers at the precise moment when looking at related topics or even specific product categories. Here, firms buy the opportunity to be associated with particular search categories or terms. To explore this part of Google's advertising business model, just "google" a few words and observe what appears on your screen in addition to the search results.

AdWords also allows advertisers to display their ads at websites that are part of the Google content network rather than only on Google.com. This means these ads are not initiated by a search, but are simply displayed when a user browses a website. Such ads are called "placement-targeted ads". Advertisers can specify either individual websites or website content (e.g., about travel or baseball). Placement targeting allows advertisers to handpick their target audiences, which can be really large (e.g., all baseball fans in the US or even in the world) or small and focused (e.g., people interested in fine dining in the Boston area). Google places the ads alongside relevant content of a Google partner's websites. For example, if you read an article on a partner website, you will see an ad block at the foot of the article. These ads have been dynamically targeted to the content of that article by Google. They can be the same ads that appear on Google.com alongside searches, but they are distributed in a different way here and appear on websites of publishers of all sizes in the Google partner network.

AdWords is complemented by a second service, called AdSense, which represents the other side of Google's advertising model. AdSense is used by website owners who wish to make money by displaying ads on their websites. In return for allowing Google to display relevant ads on their content pages, these website owners receive a share of the advertising revenue generated. An important side effect of AdSense has been that it has created advertising income streams for thousands of small and medium online publishers and blogs, making those businesses sustainable. Although big media companies like *The New York Times* and CNN also use AdSense, it generates a smaller portion of their total online advertising revenue compared to the typical niche website- or blogs.

Google's ability to deliver an advertising medium that is highly targeted, contextual, and results-based has been very attractive to advertisers leading to rapid revenue growth and profits. It's no surprise that Google's success frightens other advertising media.

Source

https://www.google.com.sg/intl/en/about/ and http://en.wikipedia.org/wiki/AdWords, accessed on March 21, 2015.

A key advantage of online advertising is that it provides a very clear and measurable return on investment, especially when compared to other forms of advertising. Particularly in performance-priced online advertising (e.g., pay-per-click), the link between advertising costs and the customers who were attracted to a company's website or offer is trackable[31]. Contrast this to traditional media advertising on TV or in magazines where it is notoriously difficult to assess the success and return of investment of an advertisement. Advertisers have several options; they can:

- Buy top rankings in the display of search results through "pay-for-placement". Since users expect the rankings to reflect the best fit with the keywords used in the search, Google's policy is to shade paid listings that appear at the top of the rankings column and identify them as "sponsored links". Pricing for these ads and placements can be based on either the number of impressions (i.e., eyeballs) or clickthroughs.

- As sponsored links aim to connect to customers just before they make a purchase decision, some firms buy keywords that are closely related to their competitor's offering. This allows them to "poach" customers and freeride on the market created by the other firm[32].

- Pay for the targeted placement of ads to keyword searches related to their offer.

- Sponsor a short text message with a clickthrough link, located next to the search results.

- Pay for performance online advertising. The advertiser is charged on the basis of pre-agreed results of their communication campaign, which could include actions such as a registration on a website, the downloading of a brochure and even sales.

- Regularly conduct search engine optimization (SEO) of the firm's website. SEO improves the ranking of a website in organic (i.e., unsponsored) search lists. Doing this should be a "no-brainer" as firms do not have to spend advertising dollars to get the attention of potential customers. But do note that SEO only works well if the website is well designed, contains relevant information, and is aligned with target customers' interests[33].

Moving from Impersonal to Personal Communications. Communication experts divide impersonal communications — where messages move in only one direction and are generally targeted at a large group of customers and prospects rather than at a single individual — and personal communications such as personal selling, telemarketing, and word-of-mouth (WOM). Technology, however, has created a gray area between personal and impersonal communications. Think about the email messages you've received, containing a personal salutation and perhaps some reference to your specific situation or past use of a particular product. Similarly, interactive software can simulate a two-way conversation. For example, a few firms are beginning to experiment with Web-based agents — on-screen simulations that move, speak, and even change expression.

Through the widespread use of smart mobile devices coupled with social networking platforms, firms have unprecedented opportunities to communicate with their customers and to facilitate firm-relevant communications between customers. Based on the analysis of customer data, highly targeted and personalized services and messages can be generated for each customer. These messages supplement, or in some cases replace, traditional marketing communications[34]. For a brief description of important new media and their implications, see *Service Insights 7.3.*

SERVICE INSIGHTS 7.3
New Media and Their Implications for Marketing Communications

Technology has created exciting new communication channels that offer important opportunities for targeting. Among the key developments are mobile advertising, mobile apps, Web 2.0, social media and social networks, and podcasting.

Mobile Advertising

Mobile advertising[35] through cell phones and other mobile wireless devices is one of the fastest-growing form of advertising, and is expected to exceed US$62.8 billion by 2017. Mobile advertising is quite complex as it can include the Internet, video, text, gaming, music, and much more. For example, advertisements can come in the form of SMSes, advertisements in mobile games, and videos. Through mobile advertising and the use of a global positioning system, customers can walk into shopping malls and receive targeted advertisements with discounts when they visit a particular store within the mall. The most prevalent type is still mobile display advertising (MDA), which takes the form of banners on mobile web pages and in mobile applications. What will such messages mean for the consumer? It might be greater convenience and more relevant advertising — or it might mean the invasion of privacy.

2D codes, better known as QR (for "quick response") codes appear on many ads, allowing those interested to learn more to take a photo of the code with their smart phone and get connected to an in-store promotion, coupons, or a real-world treasure hunt. For firms, QR codes bridge its offline and online communication channels and help to funnel potential customers from other media to the firm's online channels and richer content.

Mobile Apps

Apps have become an increasingly popular tool to help customers navigate extended service encounters, get the most out of the experience, while at the same time pursuing the firm's objectives such as cross-sell, up-sell, manage demand, and queuing. For example, major cruise lines such as Disney, Norwegian, and Royal Caribbean all have their own apps to help passengers navigate their large ships and explore their onboard entertainment options, spa services, and ports of call[36].

Web 2.0, Social Media and Social Networking

Web 2.0 technology[37] helps the rise of user-generated content and combines it with the power of peer-to-peer communications. It is an umbrella term for various media including Facebook (the grandpa of social networks), Google+, LinkedIn, YouTube, Vine, Twitter, Instagram, Snapchat, Pinterest, Wikipedia, Flickr, and other social networks. In Web 2.0, content is generated, updated, and shared by multiple users. Social networking is the fastest growing media behavior online.

Service firms use social media for various purposes, which includes learning from the market, targeting potential customers, creating buzz, and shaping customer behavior. They do this by advertising on social media, listening to what is being discussed, and selectively also participating in conversations. Given the importance of social media, marketers need to understand and carefully integrate them into their communications mix.

Figure 7.15 This social network is constantly connected via various technologies and apps, but also meets face-to-face.

Podcasting

Podcasting comes from the words "iPod" and "broadcasting." It refers to a group of technologies for distributing audio or video programs over the Internet using a publisher/subscriber model. Podcasting gives broadcast radio or television programs a method of distribution. Once someone has subscribed to a certain feed, they will automatically receive new "episodes" that become available.

Podcasting has several forms. These include video podcasting for delivery of video clips, mobilecast for downloads onto a cell phone, and blogcast for attachment of an audio or video file to a blog. It is beneficial to include podcasting as part of a firm's marketing communications program because once a listener has subscribed to a specific show, it means the listener is interested in the topic. Hence, podcasts can reach a wide audience of listeners that have a narrow focus, more like "narrowcasting" than broadcasting. When the advertising message is more targeted, this leads to a higher return on investment for the advertising dollars spent.

YouTube HQ photo: https://commons.wikimedia.org/wiki/File:901cherryave.jpg

Figure 7.16 YouTube's headquarters is in this office building at 901 Cherry Avenue, San Bruno, California

Integrating Online and Traditional Media. To show the complexity for integration of mostly online channels, see the potential integration of various media in a budget carrier context. The largest budget carriers in the US (Southwest Airlines), Europe (Ryanair), and Asia (AirAsia) each has a different strategy, but their common goal is to have travelers book directly at their own websites. Southwest Airlines integrates heavy TV advertising in its communications mix. Ryanair focuses heavily on search engine optimization (SEO) and buys strategic keywords for its online ad campaigns. AirAsia has been highly active on various social media platforms such as Twitter and Facebook to update its followers on a regular basis, push promotions, and collect customer feedback. Although each airline has a different emphasis of its communications campaigns, most use all of the channels shown in *Figure 7.17* to drive online traffic to its website to generate ticket sales.

LO 10

Know the communications mix elements available via service delivery channels.

Messages Transmitted Through Service Delivery Channels

Unlike most goods marketers, service firms typically control the point-of-sale and the service delivery channels, which offer service firms particularly powerful and cost-effective communications opportunities. Specifically, messages can be transmitted through service outlets, frontline employees, and self-service delivery points and location-enabled apps.

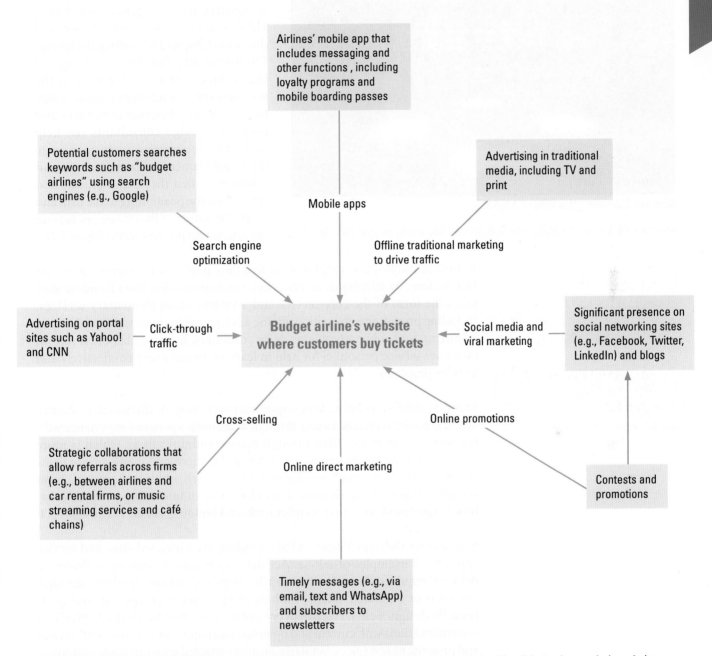

Figure 7.17 Budget carriers are excellent at integrating a vast array of mostly online channels to drive ticket sales on their websites

Bodegas Salentein – Uco Valley – Argentina

Figure 7.18 The Selentein Winery in Argentine has a very unique servicescape

Service Outlets. Both planned and unintended messages reach customers through the medium of the service delivery environment itself. Impersonal messages can be distributed in the form of banners, posters, signage, brochures, video screens, and audio. As we will discuss in Chapter 10 "Crafting the Service Environment", the physical design of the service outlet — what we call the **servicescape** — sends important messages to customers. Interior architects and corporate design consultants can help to design the servicescape to coordinate the visual elements of both interiors and exteriors so that they communicate and strengthen the positioning of the firm and shape the nature of the customers' service experiences in positive ways (*Figure 7.18*).

Frontline Employees. Employees in frontline positions may serve customers face-to-face, by telephone, or via email. Communication from frontline staff takes the form of the core service and a variety of supplementary services, including providing information, giving advice[38], taking reservations, receiving payments, and solving problems. New customers, in particular, often rely on customer service personnel for help in learning to use a service effectively and to solve problems.

Frontline employees have a very important part to play. As discussed in Chapter 4, brand equity is created largely through a customer's personal experience with the service firm rather than through mass communications, which is more suitable for creating awareness and interest. Furthermore, many service firms encourage their customer service staff to cross-sell additional services, or to up-sell to higher value services. Tony Hsieh has an interesting perspective on how to use customer contact centers for brand building, see *Service Insights 7.4*.

Self-Service Delivery Points. ATMs, vending machines, websites, and service apps are all examples of self-service delivery points. Promoting self-service delivery requires clear signage, step-by-step instructions (perhaps through diagrams or animated videos) on how to operate the equipment, and user-friendly design. Self-service delivery points can often be used effectively in communications with current and potential customers, and to cross-sell services and promote new services. Similarly, location-enabled apps can guide customers through complex servicescapes such as cruise ships, airports, hospitals, and shopping malls, while also selling to and informing customers.

Messages Originating From Outside the Organization

⊃ LO 11

Know the communications mix elements that originate from outside the firm.

Some of the most powerful messages about a company and its products come from outside the organization and are not controlled by the marketer. They include word-of-mouth (both in person and in electronic form on social media), online reviews on third-party websites, blogs, twitter, and media coverage.

SERVICE INSIGHTS 7.4

Using the Call Center for Building Brand Equity

Have you ever tried to call Google, or EBay or even Amazon.com, the company that owns Zappos? More likely than not, the phone number is buried many links deep, if it can be found at all! Zappos takes the exact opposite approach and puts its customer service hotline at the top of every single page of its website.

Tony Hsieh, the founding CEO of the highly successful multi-billion dollar revenue e-tailer Zappos, thinks it is funny that when he attends marketing conferences and hears companies talking about customers being bombarded with thousands of advertising messages every day, and that there is a lot of buzz about social media. He feels that "as unsexy and low-tech as it may sound, the telephone is one of the best branding devices out there. You have the customers' undivided attention for five to 10 minutes, and if you get the interaction right, what we've found is that the customer remembers this experience for a very long time." He explains that "a lot of people may think it's strange that an Internet company would be so focused on the telephone, when only 5% of our sales happen by phone. But we've found that on average, our customers telephone us at least once at some point, and if we handle the call well, we have an opportunity to create an emotional impact and a lasting memory. We receive thousands of phone calls and e-mails every day, and we view each one of them as an opportunity to build the Zappos brand… Our philosophy has been that most of the money we might ordinarily have spent of advertising should be invested in customer service, so that our customers will do the marketing for us through word-of-mouth."

In contrast, many service firms view their call centers through an expense-minimizing lens and focus on managing carefully average handling times and how many calls an agent can handle a day, which makes customer service representatives worry about how quickly they can get a customer off the phone, which in the eyes of Zappos is not delivering great service. Zappos' longest phone call from a customer, till this day, took almost six hours to help go through what seemed like thousands of pairs of shoes. Zappos representatives also don't use scripts or upsell, and handling customer calls is viewed as an investment in marketing and branding, and not an expense. Hsieh's view is that call centers are "a huge untapped opportunity for most companies, not only because it can result in word-of-mouth marketing, but because of its potential to increase the lifetime value of the customer."

Zappos CEO Tony Hsieh

Source

Tony Hsieh (2010), "How I Did It: Zappos's CEO on Going to Extremes for Customers," *Harvard Business Review*, Vol. 88, No. 7/8, pp. 41–45; Tony Hsieh, Delivering Happiness: A Path to Profits, Passion, and Purpose. ((New York: Grand Central Publishing, 2010).

Word-of-Mouth (WOM). Recommendations from other customers are generally viewed as more credible than firm-initiated promotional activities and can have a powerful influence on people's decisions to use (or avoid using) a service. In fact, the greater the risk customers perceive in purchasing a service,

Figure 7.19 Word-of-mouth can be an effective promotional tool

the more actively they will seek and rely on WOM to guide their decision-making[39], and customers who are less knowledgeable about a service rely more on WOM than expert consumers do[40] (*Figure 7.19*). WOM even takes place during service encounters. When customers talk with each other about some aspect of service, this information can influence both their behavior and their satisfaction with the service[41], and this has been found to be an important predictor of top-line growth[42]. There are now ways to measure WOM and allow firms to test the effect of WOM on sales and market share for brands, individual promotions campaign and also for the company as a whole[43].

Research shows that the extent and content of WOM is related to satisfaction levels. Customers who hold strong views are likely to tell more people about their experiences than those with milder views, and extremely dissatisfied customers tell more people than those who are highly satisfied[44]. Interestingly, even customers who were initially dissatisfied with a service can end up spreading positive WOM if they are delighted with the way the firm handled service recovery[45] (read more in Chapter 13 "Complaint Handling and Service Recovery").

Positive WOM is particularly important for service firms, as services tend to have a high proportion of experience and credence attributes, and are therefore associated with high perceived risk by potential buyers. In fact, many successful service firms such as Starbucks and Mayo Clinic have built powerful brands largely by relying on WOM of their satisfied customers. As Ron Kaufman, bestselling author, and founder of UP Your Service! College says: "Delighted customers are the only advertisement everyone believes[46]." Because WOM can act as such a powerful and highly credible selling agent, marketers use a variety of strategies to stimulate positive and persuasive comments from existing customers[47]. These include:

• Creating exciting stories, promotions, and competitions that get people talking about the great service the firm provides. Richard Branson of Virgin Atlantic Airways has repeatedly generated global news that got people talking about his airline. For example, Branson abseiled off a 407-feet Las Vegas hotel dressed like James Bond in a tuxedo to promote his, then new, Virgin America airline. More and more firms are running creative promotions on social media that can get global attention in a few days.

- Offering promotions that encourage customers to persuade others to join them in using the service (for instance "bring two friends, and one of you eats for free" or offering a household with several family members to "subscribe to three cell phone service plans or more, and we'll extend a 35% discount off the monthly bill").

- Developing referral reward programs that incentivize existing customers to make referrals with units of free service, a voucher, or even cash for introducing new customers to the firm. Such programs can be highly effective and profitable, so much that they have become ubiquitous — just type "recommend a friend program" into your browser you will get hundreds of millions of hits[48]. Such programs work offline (e.g., clubs, credit card companies, and even diving schools use it) and online (think of Dropbox's highly effective viral incentive scheme, see *Figure 7.20*).

Referral reward programs work well for close friends and family because they trust that you will recommend the service not for the incentive but because you have the best interest of your friends and family at heart. However, firms have to be more careful using referral reward programs when targeting acquaintances and colleagues of current customers as the latter may worry what the people they recommend the service to will think of them and about the impression they create[49]. Think about a finance professor who gets an incentive for recommending a discount broker to his students or colleagues — probably, she would rather not recommend the broker than being seen as receiving an incentive! Creative program design can change these programs so that the person who is being referred receives the reward and not the recommendation giver. In our example, the finance professor's students would get the reward, not her, and the professor would look good by recommending a great service firm and facilitating her students to get this great deal. Sometimes, it is more important for customers to look good and knowledgeable, and receiving an incentive may only achieve the opposite!

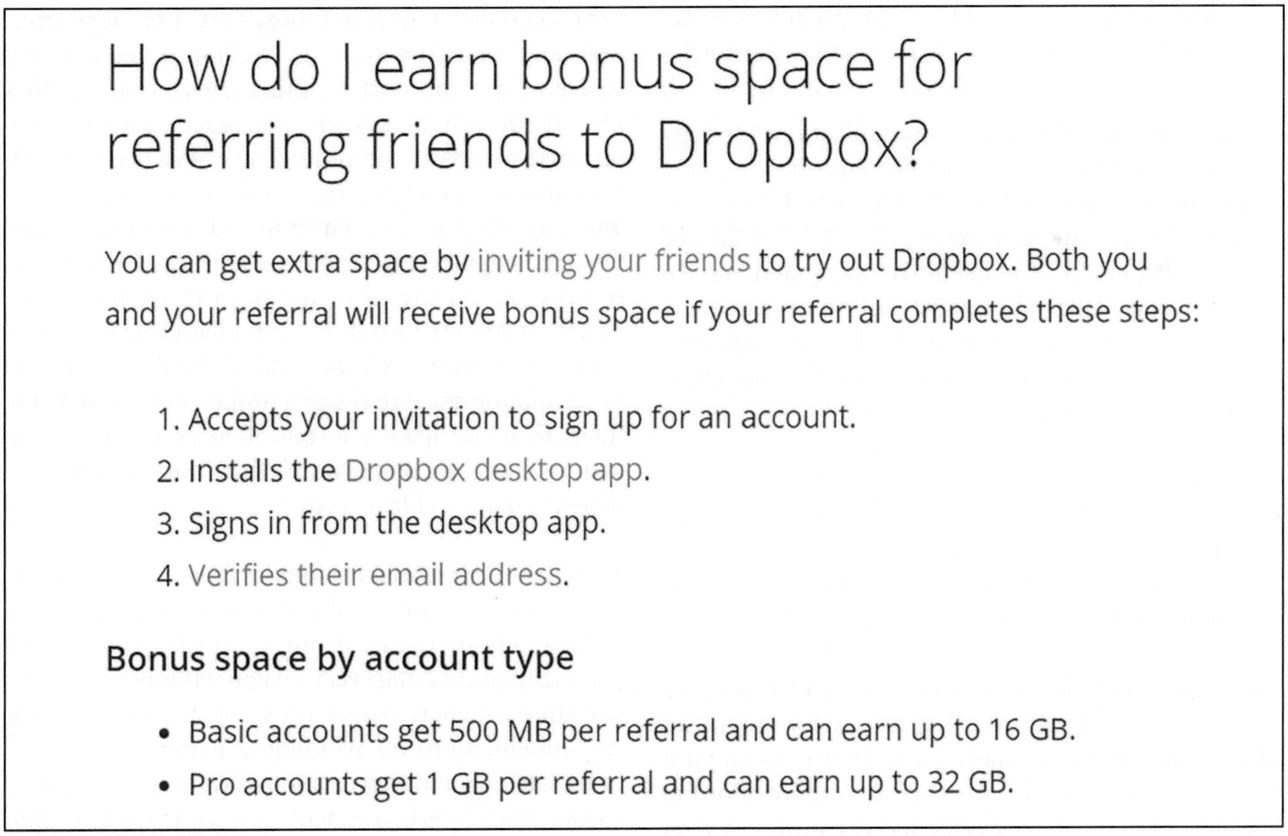

How do I earn bonus space for referring friends to Dropbox?

You can get extra space by inviting your friends to try out Dropbox. Both you and your referral will receive bonus space if your referral completes these steps:

1. Accepts your invitation to sign up for an account.
2. Installs the Dropbox desktop app.
3. Signs in from the desktop app.
4. Verifies their email address.

Bonus space by account type

- Basic accounts get 500 MB per referral and can earn up to 16 GB.
- Pro accounts get 1 GB per referral and can earn up to 32 GB.

Note: Services Marketing: People, Technology, Strategy is not affiliated with or otherwise sponsored by Dropbox, Inc.

Figure 7.20 Dropbox's online referral reward program.

- Referencing other purchasers and knowledgeable individuals, for instance: "We have done a great job for ABC Corp., and if you wish, feel free to talk to Mr. Cabral, their MIS manager, who oversaw the implementation of our project."

- Presenting and publicizing testimonials. Advertising and websites sometimes feature comments from satisfied customers.

- Provide opportunities for online reviews, and support and respond to them frequently. As online reviews become ubiquitous, positive postings help and negative ones damage a firm's brand equity and sales. For example, a study set in the London metropolitan area showed that while all hotels benefit, luxury hotels were particularly strongly influenced by the valence of reviews (and not so much by the volume; that is, a few highly positive or negative reviews had a strong impact and potential discerning guests seem to read those reviews carefully), whereas those of lower-end hotels were more driven by the volume of reviews (a hotel needed a lot of positive or negative reviews before those reviews had impact; potential guests seemed to scan the reviews to see whether the hotel is of acceptable quality and they trust volume for that)[50].

In either case, the firm's communications strategy should be to encourage satisfied customers to post positive reviews, while ideally dissatisfied customers complain to the firm and get a service recovery (see Chapter 13, "Complaint Handling and Service Recovery") instead of going online to vent their frustration[51]. A small hair stylist shop was trying to precisely achieve this by posting the following sign at the exit: "If you like our service, please tell a friend; if you don't like it, please tell us."

- Support brand communities, which can be done with relatively low costs online[52]. See, for example, the successful online brand communities supported by Google and LinkedIn in *Figure 7.21*.

In addition to WOM, we also have "word-of-mouse" or viral marketing. The Internet has accelerated the spread of personal influence, causing it to evolve into a viral marketing phenomena that businesses cannot afford to ignore[53]. One of the very early success stories of viral marketing was the Hotmail free email service, which grew from zero to 12 million users in just 18 months while on a miniscule advertising budget, mostly thanks to the inclusion of a promotional message that included the Hotmail's URL in every email sent by its users[54]. Today, virtually every online startup relies on viral marketing in one way or another. Similarly, eBay and other electronic auction firms rely on users to rate sellers and buyers in order to build trust in the items offered on their websites and thereby facilitate transactions between strangers who, without access to such peer ratings, might be reluctant to transact on these sites.

Besides email, WOM is spread by service reviews on third-party websites, chat, social media, and online communities that have potential for global reach in a matter of days! Companies are taking advantage of this. Swipely is a company that allows users to conveniently upload their purchases whenever they swipe their credit or debit card, and their friends can then immediately see these transactions and discuss the purchase[55]. It is one way users can update their friends on what they are buying. There are constantly new types of social networks emerging which all feed into the online ecosystem where consumers share their experiences.

Blogs, Twitter, and Other Social Media as a Type of Online WOM. Web logs, usually referred to as blogs, have become ubiquitous. Blogs are web pages best described as online journals, diaries, or news listings where people can post anything about whatever they like. Their authors, known as bloggers, usually focus on narrow topics, and quite a few have become self-proclaimed experts in certain fields. Blogs can be about anything, ranging from baseball and sex, to karate and financial engineering. There are a growing number of travel-oriented sites, ranging from Hotelchatter.com (focused on boutique hotels), CruiseDiva.com (reporting on the cruise industry), and pestiside.hu ("the daily dish of cosmopolitan Budapest"). Some sites, such as the travel-focused tripadvisor.com, allow users to post their own reviews or ask questions that more experienced travelers may be able to answer.

Marketers are interested in the way blogs have developed into a new form of social interaction on the Internet; a massively distributed but completely connected conversation covering every imaginable topic, including consumers' experiences with service firms and their recommendations on avoiding or patronizing certain firms. One can find conversations on any topic, including consumers' experiences with service firms and their recommendations on avoiding or patronizing certain firms. A byproduct of this online communication is a set of hyperlinks between weblogs created in the exchange of dialog. These links allows customers to share information with others and influence opinions of a brand or product

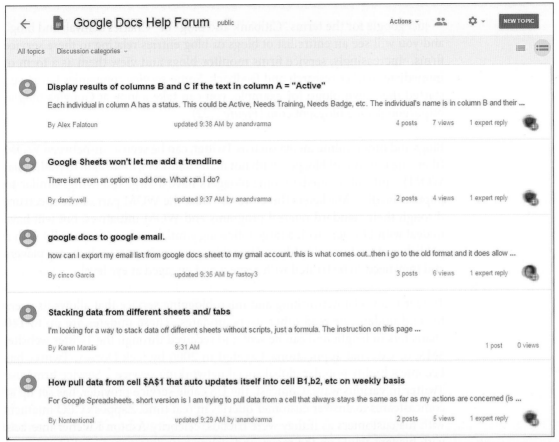

Google and the Google logo are registered trademarks of Google Inc., used with permission.

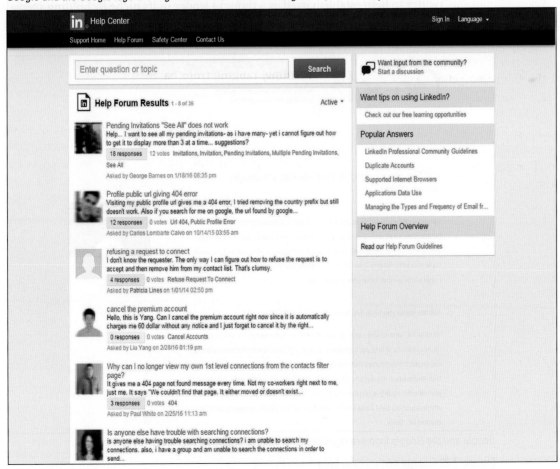

Figure 7.21 Online brand communities as seen on the Google and LinkedIn websites

— just google for the terms "Citibank and blog" or "Charles Schwab and blog", and you will see an entire list of blogs or blog entries relating to these service firms. Increasingly, service firms monitor blogs and view them as a form of immediate market research and feedback. Some service companies have even started their own blogs; for example, you can take a look at Google's blog at http://googleblog.blogspot.com (*Figure 7.22*).

Blogs and other online media such as Twitter, can be seen as in-between WOM (there are millions of bloggers with not many followers, more akin to traditional WOM), and online media (some bloggers have a large following, similar to popular media). Marketers therefore can treat the WOM part of the spectrum through their standard referral programs and WOM initiatives, but will have to deal with bloggers with a large following similar as how they would with a publisher of traditional media[56]. These bloggers are important industry players and they need to be treated with respect and engaged at eye level.

Twitter is a social networking and microblogging service that allows its users to send updates or read other users' updates. These updates are up to 140 characters in length and can be sent and received through the Twitter website, SMS, or external applications. Created in 2006 by Jack Dorsey, Twitter has become a highly popular global social networking service[57]. Service firms use Twitter in various ways. Comcast, the US cable service provider, has set up @ comcastcares to answer customer queries in real time. Zappos's CEO interacts with his customers as if they were friends, celebrity Ashton Kutcher interacts with his fans while on the move, and airline branding firm SimpliFlying used Twitter to help establish itself as a thought leader in its niche by holding special trivia quizzes and competitions for its followers around the world.

Google and the Google logo are registered trademarks of Google Inc., used with permission.

Figure 7.22 Google has its own blog

Media Coverage. Although the online world is rapidly increasing in importance, coverage on traditional media cannot be neglected, especially as newsworthy events are often first discussed in the online world, and are then picked up and reported in the traditional media that then reach the broad masses. Media coverage of firms and their services is often through a firm's PR activity, but broadcasters and publishers also often initiate their own coverage.

In addition to news stories about a company and its services, editorial coverage can take several other forms. For example, journalists responsible for consumer affairs often contrast and compare service offerings from competing organizations, identifying their strong and weak points, and offering advice on "best buys." In a more specialized context, *Consumer Reports,* the monthly publication of Consumers' Union, periodically evaluates services that are offered on a national basis, including financial services and telecommunications, and commenting on the strengths and weaknesses of different service providers and seeking to determine the true cost of their often confusing fee schedules and pricing plans.

Furthermore, investigative reporters may conduct an in-depth study of a company, especially if they believe it is putting customers at risk, cheating them, employing deceptive advertising, damaging the environment, or taking advantage of poor workers in developing countries. Some columnists specialize in helping customers who have been unable to get complaints resolved.

TIMING DECISIONS OF SERVICES MARKETING COMMUNICATIONS

 LO 12
Understand when communications should take place ("**W**hen"), how to set budgets for service communications programs, and how to evaluate these programs.

Goods such as champagne, jewelry, and Christmas pudding are heavily promoted in the three months leading up to Christmas, as often half of their annual sales will happen then. Service firms, in contrast, are capacity constrained and therefore generally do not promote during heavy usage periods. Rather, timing is closely matched to the various perceptions and behaviors the firm wants to manage in the service communications funnel. Often, different communications channels are used to move a customer along from awareness, preference all the way to the post-consumption stage.

Timing of communications is typically managed in a media plan flowchart which looks like a large Excel spreadsheet. It gives a bird's-eye view of the media where and when communications is planned. Software is often used to assist with tedious tasks to crunch numbers to get toward an optimal media mix and media plan, and it computes key numbers such as reach of the target audience and cost per thousand contacts of the target segment. Professional firms such as Telmar (http://www.telmar.com) help companies with their planning.

BUDGET DECISIONS AND PROGRAM EVALUATION

Most service firms will allocate more budget to services marketing communications as long as they believe it will increase sales and profits.[58] However, the optimal point of communications expenditure is difficult to predict, and setting a budget is one of the hardest decisions to make. In practice, service firms use a number of methods to determine their communications budget, including allocating a percentage of sales or profit, matching competitors' spent, and using last year's budget and adding to or subtracting from it, depending on the success of last year's communications and the firm's future plans.

The most logical method, however, is the objective-and-task method, which is also known as the budget buildup method. This method entails three steps: (1) defining the communications objectives along the services marketing communications funnel, (2) determining the tasks needed to achieve these objectives, and (3) estimating the costs of the program. The estimated costs become the basis for the proposed promotions budget. Of course, a firm's financial position and estimated returns on these investments always need to be integrated as well. If costs are too high or expected returns too low, the budget needs to be scaled back. The key challenge though remains that it is difficult to determine in advance the intensity of communications required to achieve a certain goal.

Finally, the empirical research method can be used alone or in combination with the objective-and-task method. The empirical research method runs a series of tests or field experiments with different communications budgets to determine the optimum level of communications spent. Online, of course, such experiments can be done easily and fast, and are regularly used in professional campaign management.

Once the budget is spent, how can firms evaluate the success of the communications program? For specific objectives, it is easy to measure. For example, if specific communications programs were targeted at changing customer behavior (e.g., shifting usage away from peaks, teaching customers how to keep their PINs safe, shifting customers from paper-based statements to e-statements and upselling to a higher-level service) the results are directly measurable. The same applies to direct response marketing such as email campaigns or online marketing where clickthroughs, newsletter signups, followers, registrations, lead generation, and sales can be matched directly to specific marketing communications.

Similarly, advertising and research agencies have become experts at measuring whether wider communications objectives (e.g., awareness, knowledge, and preference) have been achieved. However, the effect of market communications on sales and profit is notoriously hard to measure. A key reason is that marketing communications affects sales, but it is only one of the many drivers of sales which range from service features and service quality to price and competitor activities. You must keep this in mind when preparing your communications plans and budgets.

ETHICAL AND CONSUMER PRIVACY ISSUES IN COMMUNICATIONS

⊃ **LO 13**
Appreciate ethical and consumer privacy related issues in service marketing communications.

We have been focusing on how to reach, persuade, and manage the behavior of prospects and customers. Firms, however, also need to consider the ethical and privacy issues associated with communications, especially as few aspects of marketing are so easily misused (and even abused), such as advertising, selling, and sales promotion. The fact that customers often find it hard to evaluate services makes them more dependent on marketing communication for information and advice. Communication messages frequently include promises about the benefits that customers will receive and the quality of service delivery. When promises are made and then broken, customers will be disappointed.

Some unrealistic service promises result from poor internal communications between operations and marketing personnel concerning the level of service performance that customers can reasonably expect. In other instances, unethical advertisers and salespeople deliberately make exaggerated promises to secure sales. Finally, there are deceptive promotions that lead people to think that they have a much higher chance of winning prizes or awards than is really the case. Fortunately, many consumer watchdog groups are on the lookout for these deceptive marketing practices. They include consumer protection agencies, trade associations within specific industries, and journalists seeking to expose cheating schemes and misrepresentations.

A different type of ethical issue concerns unwanted intrusion by aggressive marketers into people's personal lives. The increase in telemarketing, direct mail, email, and messaging is frustrating for those who receive unwanted sales communications. How do you feel when your dinner at home is interrupted by a telephone call from a stranger trying to get you to buy services in which you have no interest? Even if you are interested, you may feel, as many do, that your privacy has been violated (*Service Insights 7.5*). See also the earlier section on direct marketing where we discussed the concept of permission marketing as one way to address consumer concerns.

To address growing hostility toward these practices, both government agencies and trade associations have acted to protect consumers. In the US, the Federal Trade Commission's National "Do Not Call" Registry enables consumers to remove their home and mobile numbers from telemarketing lists for a five-year period. People who continue to receive unauthorized calls from commercial telemarketers can file a complaint, and the telemarketing firm can be subjected to heavy fines for such violations[59]. Similarly, the Direct Marketing Association helps consumers remove their names from mailing, telemarketing, and e-mail lists[60].

SERVICE INSIGHTS 7.5
Consumer Concerns About Online Privacy

Technological advances have made the Internet a threat to consumer privacy. Information is collected on not only people who register, shop, or use email, but also on those who just surf the Internet, participate in social networks, or contribute to blogs! Individuals are increasingly fearful of databases and concerned about their online privacy. Hence, they use several ways to protect themselves, including:

- Providing false information about themselves (e.g., disguising their identity).

- Using technology like Microsoft's InPrivate Browsing, anti-spam filters, email shredders, and cookie-busters to hide the identity of their computers from websites.

- Refusing to provide information and avoiding websites that require personal information to be disclosed.

Such consumer responses will make information used in CRM systems inaccurate and incomplete, thereby reducing the effectiveness of a firm's customer relationship marketing and its efforts to provide more customized, personalized, and convenient service. Firms can take several steps to reduce consumer privacy concerns, including:

- Customers' fairness perceptions are key — marketers need to be careful about how they use the information they collect and whether consumers see their treatment and outcomes as fair. In particular, marketers should continually provide the customer with enhanced value such as customization, convenience, and improved offers and promotions to increase fairness perceptions of the information exchange.

- The information asked for should be perceived to be related to the transaction, especially if it is highly sensitive. Therefore, firms should clearly communicate why the information is needed, and how information disclosure will benefit the consumer.

- Firms should have a good privacy policy in place, one that can be readily found on its websites, is easily understood and is comprehensive enough to be effective. Ideally, websites should give customers control over how their information can be used.

- Fair information practices need to be embedded in the work practices of all service employees to prevent any situation whereby an employee may allow personal customer information to be misused.

- Firms should have high ethical standards of data protection. They can use third party endorsements like TRUSTe or the Better Business Bureau and have recognizable privacy seals displayed clearly on their website.

Source

M. Lwin, J. Wirtz, and J. D. Williams (2007), "Consumer Online Privacy Concerns and Responses: A Power-Responsibility Equilibrium Perspective," *Journal of the Academy of Marketing Science*, Vol. 35, No. 2, pp. 572–585; Jochen Wirtz and May O. Lwin (2009), "Regulatory Focus Theory, Trust, and Privacy Concern," *Journal of Service Research*, Vol. 12, No. 2, pp. 199–207; Catherine E. Tucker (2014), "Social Networks, Personalized Advertising, and Privacy Controls," *Journal of Marketing Research*, Vol. 51, October, pp. 546–562.

THE ROLE OF CORPORATE DESIGN

➲ LO 14
Understand the role of corporate design in communications.

So far, we have focused on communications media and content but not much on design. Corporate design is key to ensure a consistent style and message is communicated through all of a firm's communications mix channels. Corporate design is particularly important for companies operating in competitive markets where it's necessary to stand out from the crowd to be instantly recognizable in different locations. Have you noticed how some companies stand out in your mind because of the colors they use, the widespread application of their logos, the uniforms worn by their employees, or the design of their physical facilities?

Many service firms employ a unified and distinctive visual appearance for all tangible elements to facilitate recognition and reinforce a desired brand image. Corporate design strategies are usually created by external consulting firms, and include stationery and promotional materials, retail signage, uniforms, and color schemes for painting vehicles, equipment, and building interiors. The objective is to provide a unifying and recognizable theme that links all the firm's operations in a branded service experience through the strategic use of physical evidence. Companies can do that by using the following approaches either individually or in combination:

- Companies in the highly competitive express delivery industry tend to use their name as a central element in their corporate design. When Federal Express changed its trading name to the more modern "FedEx," it featured the new name in a distinctive, new logo.

Figure 7.23 The Golden Arches of a McDonald's restaurant is instantly recognisable

- Many companies use a trademarked symbol, rather than a name, as their primary logo. Shell makes a pun of its name by displaying a yellow scalloped shell on a red background, which has the advantage of making its vehicles and service stations instantly recognizable. McDonald's "Golden Arches" (*Figure 7.23*) is said to be the most widely recognized corporate symbol in the world and is featured at all touchpoints, including its restaurants, on employee uniforms and packaging, and in all the company's communications materials.

- Some companies have succeeded in creating tangible, recognizable symbols to associate with their corporate brand names. Animal motifs are common physical symbols for services. Examples include the eagles of the US Postal Service and AeroMexico, the lions of ING Bank and the Royal Bank of Canada, and the ram of the investment firm T. Rowe Price, and the Chinese dragon of Hong Kong's Dragonair.

- Many companies use colors in their corporate designs (*Table 7.2*). If we look at gasoline retailing, we see BP's immediately recognizable bright green and yellow service stations; Texaco's red, black, and white; and Sunoco's blue, maroon, and yellow.

Table 7.2 Corporate Design Strategies

Examples of Corporate Design Strategies			
Name as central element	Trademarked symbol	Tangible recognizable symbol	Distinctive color used in corporate design
FedEx	McDonald's "Golden Arches"	ING Bank's lion	DHL's yellow (Pantone 116) and red (Pantone 200) colors of its logo.
DHL	Shell's yellow scalloped shell	Hong Kong's Dragon Air's Chinese dragon	BP's bright green and yellow service stations

INTEGRATED MARKETING COMMUNICATIONS

➲ **LO 15**
Know the importance of integrated marketing communications to deliver a strong brand identity.

Have you ever seen a new, exciting service promotion being touted at a firm's website, only to find that the counter staff was not aware of the promotion and couldn't sell it to you when you visited a branch office? What went wrong? In many service firms, different departments look after different aspects of a firm's market communications. For example, the marketing department is in charge of advertising, the PR department of public relations, functional specialists look after a company's website and its direct marketing and promotions activities, operations of customer service, and human resource of training. The service failure described above is a consequence of these various departments not coordinating their efforts effectively.

With so many channels delivering messages to customers and prospects, it becomes more and more important for firms to adopt the concept of integrated marketing communications (IMC). IMC ties together and reinforces all communications to deliver a strong brand identity. It means that a firm's various media deliver the same messages and have the same look and feel, and the communications from the different media and communications approaches all become part of a single, overall message about the service firm and its products. Firms can achieve this by giving the ownership of IMC to a single department (e.g., marketing), or by appointing a marketing communications director who has overall responsibility for all of the firm's market communications.

CONCLUSION

The **promotion** and **education** element of the **7 Ps** requires a somewhat different emphasis from the communication strategy used to market goods. The communication tasks facing service marketers include emphasizing tangible clues for services that are difficult to evaluate, clarifying the nature and sequence of the service performance, highlighting the performance of customer contact personnel, and educating the customer about how to effectively participate in service delivery. A key takeaway point is that effective service marketers are good educators who can use a variety of communication media in cost-efficient ways, not only to promote their firm's value propositions but also to teach both prospects and customers what they need to know about selecting and using the firm's services.

CHAPTER SUMMARY

○ **LO1** Service marketers need to design an effective communications strategy. To do this, they can use the Integrated Service Communications Model as a guiding framework which is organized around the **5 Ws** model. The **5 Ws** are:

- *Who* is our target audience? Are they prospects, users, and/or employees?
- *What* do we need to communicate and achieve? Do the objectives relate to consumer behavior in the prepurchase, service encounter, or postencounter stage?
- *How* should we communicate this? How can we overcome the challenges caused by the intangibility of services?
- *Where* should we communicate this? Which media mix should we use?
- *When* should the communications take place?

○ **LO2** There are three broad target audiences (*Who*) of service communications. They are (1) prospects, which can be reached via traditional communications media just like in goods marketing, (2) current users, which can be reached via more cost-effective communications channels such as the firm's service delivery channels (e.g., service employees, branch network, account statements, and self-service channels), and (3) employees as a secondary audience who can be highly motivated with the right communications messaging.

○ **LO3** At the most generic level, marketing communications objectives (*What*) are to inform, educate, persuade, remind, shape behavior, and build relationships. Communications objectives can be strategic and tactical in nature, and are typically an amalgamation of both.

  - **Strategic objectives** include building brand equity, positioning a brand against competition, and repositioning it.

○ **LO4 Tactical objectives** can be organized according to the Services Marketing Communications Funnel that details a range of potential objectives using the three-stage model of service consumer behavior as a guiding framework. A key takeaway of this funnel is that communications objectives can be highly specific and address any aspect of service consumption behavior in the (1) prepurchase stage (e.g., emphasize the importance of attributes in which the firm outperforms, and reduce perceived

risk), (2) service encounter stage (e.g., guide customers through service process, encourage proper queuing behavior, and manage performance perceptions), and (3) post-encounter stage (e.g., shape customer satisfaction and encourage referral and loyalty behaviors).

○ **LO5** Examples of a few important specific roles service marketing communication can assume are:

- Promote the tangible cues to communicate quality.
- Add value through communication content (e.g., provide information and consultation as discussed in the Flower of Service model).
- Facilitate customer involvement in production.
- Promote the contribution of service personnel.
- Stimulate and shift demand to match capacity.

○ **LO6** How can services best be communicated, especially as the intangibility of services presents challenges for communications. These challenges are:

- Abstractness — no one-to-one correspondence with a physical object.
- Generality — items are part of a class of persons, objects, or events and are not specific to the firm's performance.
- Non-searchability — cannot be inspected, or searched before purchase.
- Mental impalpability — difficult to understand and interpret.

There are a number of ways to overcome the communications problems posed by intangibility.

- Abstractness — use service consumption episode and show typical customers experiencing the service.
- Generality — for objective claims, use system documentation showing facts and statistics about the service delivery system and performance documentation that cites past performance statistics, such as the percentage of packages delivered on time. For subjective claims, service performance episodes can be used, where the actual service delivery being performed by service personnel is shown.
- Non-searchability — Consumption documentation can be used where testimonials are obtained from customers who have experienced the service. For services high in credence attri-

butes, use reputation documentation showing the awards received or the qualifications of the service provider.

- Impalpability — use service process episode by presenting what exactly will happen during the service experience, feature a case history episode of what the firm did for a client and how it solved the client's problem or show a service consumption episode showing the customer's experience with a service.

Two additional ways to help overcome the problems of intangibility are:

- Emphasize tangible cues such as its employees, facilities, certificates, and awards, or its customers.
- Use metaphors to communicate the value proposition. For example, Prudential uses the Rock of Gibraltar as a symbol of corporate strength.

LO7 To reach our target audiences and achieve the communications objectives, we can use a variety of communications channels (*Where*), including:

- Traditional marketing channels (e.g., advertising, direct marketing, online advertising), apps and social media (e.g., Web 2.0, and social media).
- Service delivery channels (e.g., service outlets, frontline employees, service apps, and self-service websites).
- Messages originating from outside the organization (e.g., WOM, social media, and blogs and coverage in traditional media).

LO8 The traditional marketing channels include advertising, public relations, direct marketing (including permission marketing), sales promotions, and personal selling. These communication elements are typically used to help companies create a distinctive position in the market and reach prospective customers.

LO9 Online communications channels include the firm's websites and online advertising (e.g., banner advertising, and search engine advertising and optimization).

- Developments in technology are driving innovations such as permission marketing resulting in exciting possibilities of highly targeted communications using online and mobile advertising, apps, Web 2.0, social media, and podcasting.

LO10 Service firms usually control service delivery channels and point-of-sale environments that offers them cost-effective ways of reaching their current customers (e.g., through its service employees, service outlets, and self-service delivery points).

LO11 Some of the most powerful messages about a company and its services originate from outside the organization and are not controlled by the marketer. They include traditional WOM, blogs, Twitter and other social media, and coverage in traditional media.

- Recommendations from other customers are generally viewed as more credible than firm-initiated communications, and are usually more sought by prospects, especially for high-risk purchases.
- Firms can stimulate WOM from its customers through a number of means including creating exciting promotions, referral reward programs, and referencing customers, all of which are increasingly being shifted to the online environment.

LO12 Unlike in goods marketing where much of the communications happens before periods of heavy buying (e.g., before Christmas), service firms typically cannot cater for additional demand during peak periods. Therefore, communications tends to be more spread out and connected to the specific objectives and their timing in the Service Communications Funnel (*When*). Budget decisions and performance management are mapped against these objectives (if the objective-and-task method is used).

LO13 When designing their communication strategy, firms need to bear in mind ethical and privacy issues in terms of promises made, possible intrusion into people's private lives (e.g., through telemarketing or e-mail campaigns), and protecting the privacy and personal data of customers and prospects.

LO14 Besides communication media and content, corporate design is key to achieving a unified image in customers' minds. Good corporate design uses a unified and distinctive visual appearance for tangible elements including all market communications mix elements, stationery, retail signage, uniforms, vehicles, equipment, and building interiors.

LO15 With so many channels delivering messages to customers and prospects, it becomes crucial for firms to adopt the concept of IMC.

Review Questions

1. What are the **5 Ws** along which the Integrated Service Communications Model is structured?

2. Who are the three broad target audiences of service communications?

3. In what ways do the objectives of services communications differ substantially from those of goods marketing? Describe four common educational and promotional objectives in service settings, and provide a specific example for each of the objectives you list.

4. What can you learn from the Service Marketing Communications Funnel?

5. What are some challenges in service communications and how can they be overcome?

6. Why is the marketing communications mix larger for service firms compared to firms that market goods?

7. What roles do personal selling, advertising, and public relations play in (a) attracting new customers to visit a service outlet and (b) retaining existing customers?

8. What are the different forms of online marketing? Which do you think would be the most effective online marketing strategies for (a) an online broker and (b) a new high-end club in Los Angeles?

9. Why is permission-based marketing gaining so much focus in service firms' communications strategies?

10. Why is WOM important for the marketing of services? How can a service firm that is the quality leader in its industry induce and manage word-of-mouth?

11. How can companies use corporate design to differentiate themselves?

12. What are the potential ways to implement IMC?

Application Exercises

1. Which elements of the marketing communications mix would you use for each of the following scenarios? Explain your answers.
   - A newly established hair salon in a suburban shopping center.
   - An established restaurant facing declining patronage because of new competitors.
   - A large, single-office accounting firm in a major city that serves primarily business clients and wants to grow its client base aggressively.

2. Identify one advertisement (or other means of communications) aimed mainly at managing consumer behavior in the (a) choice, (b) service encounter, and (c) post-consumption stage. Explain how they try to achieve their objectives and discuss how effective they may be.

3. Legal and accounting firms now advertise their services in many countries. Search for a few advertisements and review the following: What do these firms do to cope with the intangibility of their services? What could they do better? How do they deal with consumer quality and risk perceptions, and how could they improve this aspect of their marketing?

4. Discuss the significance of search, experience, and credence attributes for the communications strategy of a service provider. Assume the objective of the communications strategy is to attract new customers.

5. If you were explaining your current university or researching the degree program you are now in, what could you learn from blogs and any other online WOM you can find? How would that information influence the decision of a prospective applicant to your university? Given that you are an expert on the school and degree you are pursuing, how accurate is the information you found online?

6. Identify an advertisement that runs the risk of attracting mixed segments to a service business. Explain why this may happen, and state any negative consequences that could result.

7. Describe and evaluate recent public relations efforts made by service organizations in connection to three or more of the following: (1) launching a new offering, (2) opening a new facility, (3) promoting an expansion of existing services, (4) announcing an upcoming event, or (5) responding to a negative situation that has arisen. Pick a different organization for each category.

8. What tangible cues could a diving school or a dentistry clinic use to position itself as appealing to upscale customers?

9. Explore the websites of a management consulting firm, an Internet retailer, and an insurance company. Assess them for ease of navigation, quality of content, and visual design. What, if anything, would you change about each site?

10. Register at Amazon.com and Hallmark.com and analyze their permission-based communications strategy. What are their marketing objectives? Evaluate their permission-based marketing for a specific customer segment of your choice — what is excellent, what is good, and what could be further improved?

11. Conduct a Google search for (a) MBA programs and (b) vacation (holiday) resorts. Examine two or three contextual ads triggered by your searches. What are they doing right, and what can be improved?

Endnotes

1   Note that this chapter was not written to provide the reader with an in-depth understanding of marketing communications in general. Rather, the focus is on service-specific issues, while covering the basics of marketing communications.

    For a detailed coverage of marketing communications in general, refer to William F. Arens, Michael F. Weigold, and Christian Arens, *Contemporary Advertising & Integrated Marketing Communications.* 14th ed. (New York, NY: McGraw Hill, 2013); and George E. Belch and Michael A. Belch, *Advertising and Promotion: An Integrated Marketing Communications Perspective.* 10th ed. (New York, NY: McGraw Hill, 2015).

2   Daniel Wentzel, Sven Henkel and Torsten Tomczak (2010), "Can I Live Up to That Ad? Impact of Implicit Theories of Ability on Service Employees' Responses to Advertising," *Journal of Service Research*, Vol. 13, No. 2, pp. 137-152; Mary Wolfinbarger Celsi and Mary C. Gilly (2010), "Employees as Internal Audience: How Advertising Affects Employees' Customer Focus," *Journal of the Academy of Marketing Science*, Vol. 38, No. 4, pp. 520–529.

3   JD Power's Consumer Center website includes ratings of service providers in finance and insurance, healthcare, telecommunications, and travel, plus useful information and advice; see http://www.jdpower.com/, accessed March 22, 2015.

4   Edward K. Strong (1925), "Theories of Selling," *Journal of Applied Psychology*, Vol. 9, No. 1, pp. 75–86.

5   Robert .J. Lavidge and Gary A. Steiner (1961), "A Model for Predictive Measurement of Advertising Effectiveness", *Journal of Marketing*, Vol. 25, October, pp. 59–62.

6   For the Starbucks story on how coffee beans are grown and harvested, see videos on YouTube such as: https://news.starbucks.com/multimedia/file/761, and https://news.starbucks.com/news/a-photo-journey-to-coffee-farms-in-costa-rica, accessed March 21, 2015.

7   For a good overview of message strategy, execution and styles, see Philip Kotler and Gary Armstrong, *Chapter 14: Communicating Customer Value: Integrated Marketing Communications Strategy;* and *Chapter 15: Advertising and Public Relations,* in Principles of Marketing, 15th ed. (Upper Saddle River, NJ: Person Education, 2014). See also: William F. Arens, Michael F. Weigold, and Christian Arens, *Contemporary Advertising & Integrated Marketing Communications.* 14th ed. (New York, NY: McGraw Hill, 2013); and George E. Belch and Michael A. Belch, *Advertising and Promotion: An Integrated Marketing Communications Perspective.* 10th ed. (New York, NY: McGraw Hill, 2015).

8   For a review, see Kathleen Mortimer and Brian P. Mathews (1998), "The Advertising of Services: Consumer Views v. Normative Dimensions," *The Service Industries Journal,* Vol. 18, July, pp. 14–19. See also James F. Devlin and Sarwar Azhar (2004), "Life Would be a Lot Easier if We Were a Kit Kat: Practitioners' Views on the Challenges of Branding Financial Services Successfully," *Brand Management*, Vol. 12, No. 1, pp. 12–30.

9   Banwari Mittal (1999), "The Advertising of Services: Meeting the Challenge of Intangibility," *Journal of Service Research*, Vol. 2, August, pp. 98–116.

10 Banwari Mittal and Julie Baker (2002), "Advertising Strategies for Hospitality Services," *Cornell Hotel and Restaurant Administration Quarterly*, Vol. 43, April, pp. 51–63.

11 Donna Legg and Julie Baker (1987), "Advertising Strategies for Service Firms," in C. Surprenant (ed.), *Add Value to Your Service*. Chicago: American Marketing Association, pp. 163–168. See also Donna J. Hill, Jeff Blodgett, Robert Baer, and Kirk Wakefield (2004), "An Investigation of Visualization and Documentation Strategies in Service Advertising," *Journal of Service Research*, Vol. 7, November, pp. 155–166; Debra Grace and Aron O'Cass (2005), "Service Branding: Consumer Verdicts on Service Brands," *Journal of Retailing and Consumer Services*, Vol. 12, pp. 125–139.

12 Banwari Mittal (1999), "The Advertising of Services: Meeting the Challenge of Intangibility," *Journal of Service Research*, Vol. 2, August, pp. 98–116.

13 See how a non-profit organization optimized its marketing mix by shifting budget spent online to TV: "Boosting Demand in the Experience Economy," *Harvard Business Review*, 2015, Vol. 93, No. 1/2, pp. 24–26.

14 Adrian Palmer (2011), *Principles of Services Marketing*, 6th ed., London: McGraw-Hill, 6th edition, p. 450.

15 Stephen J. Grove, Gregory M. Pickett, and David N. Laband (1995), "An Empirical Examination of Factual Information Content among Service Advertisements," *The Service Industries Journal*, Vol. 15, April, pp. 216–233.

16 "The Future of Advertising — The Harder Hard Sell," *The Economist*, June 24, 2004.

17 *Ibid*.

18 Penelope J. Prenshaw, Stacy E. Kovar, and Kimberly Gladden Burke (2006), "The Impact of Involvement on Satisfaction for New, Nontraditional, Credence-based Service Offerings," *Journal of Services Marketing*, Vol. 20, No. 7, pp. 439–452.

19 "Got Game: Inserting Advertisements into Video Games Holds Much Promise," *The Economist*, June 9, 2007, p. 69.

20 Experian, www.experian.co.uk, accessed January 14, 2009.

21 Seth Godin and Don Peppers (1999), *Permission Marketing: Turning Strangers into Friends and Friends into Customers*. New York, NY: Simon & Schuster; Ray Kent and Hege Brandal (2003), "Improving Email Response in a Permission Marketing Context," *International Journal of Market Research*, 45, Quarter 4, pp. 489–503; for recent work exploring customer opt-in and opt-out behaviors see: V. Kumar, Xi (Alan) Zhang, and Anita Luo (2014), "Modeling Customer Opt-In and Opt-Out in a Permission-Based Marketing Context," *Journal of Marketing Research*, Vol. 51, No. 4, pp. 403–419.

22 Gila E. Fruchter and Z. John Zhang (2004), "Dynamic Targeted Promotions: A Customer Retention and Acquisition Perspective," *Journal of Service Research*, Vol. 7, August, pp. 3–19.

23 Ken Peattie and Sue Peattie (1995), "Sales Promotion — A Missed Opportunity for Service Marketers," *International Journal of Service Industry Management*, Vol. 5, No. 1, pp. 6–21.

24 Michael Lewis (2006), "Customer Acquisition Promotions and Customer Asset Value," *Journal of Marketing Research*, Vol. 43, No. 2, pp. 195–203.

For research on how to optimize promotion campaign based on customer lifetime value, see: Yeliz Ekinci, Füsun Ulengin, and Nimet Uray (2014), "Using Customer Lifetime Value to Plan Optimal Promotions," *The Service Industries Journal*, Vol. 34, No. 2, pp. 103–122.

25 For instructions on how to register, refer to https://www.donotcall.gov/register/registerinstructions.aspx, accessed March 21, 2015.

26 For more detailed chapters on marketing on the internet and in social media, see: William F. Arens, Michael F. Weigold, and Christian Arens, Chapter 17: Introducing Social Media, in *Contemporary Advertising & Integrated Marketing Communications*. 14th ed. (New York, NY: McGraw Hill, 2013), 526–541; and George E. Belch and Michael A. Belch, Chapter 15: The Internet: Digital and Social Media, in: *Advertising and Promotion: An Integrated Marketing Communications Perspective*. 10th ed. (New York, NY: McGraw Hill, 2015), pp. 497–524.

27 Stefan Lagrosen (2005), "Effects of the Internet on the Marketing Communication of Service Companies," *Journal of Services Marketing*, Vol. 19, No. 2, pp. 63–69; Thorsten Hennig-Thurau, Edward C. Malthouse, Christian Friege, Sonja Gensler, Lara Lobschat, Arvind Rangaswamy and Bernd Skiera (2010), "The Impact of New Media on Customer Relationships," *Journal of Service Research*, Vol. 13, No. 3, pp. 311–330; Koen Pauwels, Peter S.H. Leeflang, Marije L. Teerling, and K.R. Eelko Huizingh (2011), "Does Online Information Drive Offline Revenues? Only for Specific Products and Consumer Segments", *Journal of Retailing*, Vol. 87, No. 1, pp. 1–17.

For an overview of direct digital marketing, see: Alan Tapp, Ian Whitten, and Matthew Housden, *Principles of Direct, Database and Digital Marketing*. 5th ed. (Harlow, United Kingdom: Pearson Education, 2014).

28　Paul Smith and Dave Chaffey (2005), *eMarketing Excellence*. Oxford, UK: Elsevier Butterworth-Heinemann, p. 173.

29　"The Future of Advertising — The Harder Hard Sell," *The Economist*, June 24, 2004.

30　Nadia Abou Nabout, Markus Lilienthal, and Bernd Skiera (2014), "Empirical Generalizations in Search Engine Advertising," *Journal of Retailing*, Vol. 90, No. 2, pp. 206–216.

31　Initial research also seems to suggest that customers acquired through search advertising have a higher lifetime value than customers acquired through traditional media, see: Tat Y. Chan, Chunhua Wu, and Ying Xie (2011), "Measuring the Lifetime Value of Customers Acquired from Google Search Advertising," *Marketing Science*, Vol. 30, No. 5, pp. 837–850.

32　Amin Sayedi, Kinshuk Jerath, and Kannan Srinivasan (2014), "Competitive Poaching in Sponsored Search Advertising and Its Strategic Impact on Traditional Advertising," *Marketing Science*, Vol. 33, No. 4, pp. 586–608.

33　Ron Berman and Zsolt Katona (2013), "The Role of Search Engine Optimization in Search Marketing," *Marketing Science*, Vol. 32, No. 4, pp. 644–651.

It has even been shown that click through for common search terms is heavily concentrated on the organic list rather than sponsored links. This makes SEO critical, see Kinshuk Jerath, Liye Ma, and Young-Hoon Park (2014), "Consumer Click Behavior at a Search Engine: The Role of Keyword Popularity," *Journal of Marketing Research*, Vol. 51, August, pp. 480–486.

34　Roland Rust and Ming-Hui Huang (2014), "The Service Revolution and the Transformation of Marketing Science," *Marketing Science*, Vol. 33, No. 2, pp. 206–221.

35　Yakov Bart, Andrew T. Stephen, and Miklos Sarvary (2014), "Which Products are Best Suited to Mobile Advertising? A Field Study of Mobile Display Advertising Effects on Consumer Attitudes and Behaviors," *Journal of Marketing Research*, Vol. 51, June, pp. 270–285.

For a detailed discussion on mobile marketing, see: Daniel Rowles (2014), *Mobile Marketing: How Mobile Technology is Revolutionizing Marketing, Communications, and Advertising*. London, United Kingdom: Kogan Page.

36　Stephanie Rosenbloom (2015), "Apps to Help Navigate Cruise Lines," *The New York Times*, p. TR2.

37　V. Kumar and Rohan Mirchandani (2012), "Increasing the ROI of Social Media Marketing," *Sloan Management Review*, Vol. 54. No. 1, pp. 55–61; Roxane Divol, David Edelman, and Hugo Sarrazin (2012), "Demystifying Social Media," *McKinsey Quarterly*, April.

38　Kathleen Seiders, Andrea Godfrey Flynn, Leonard L. Berry, and Kelly L. Haws (2015), "Motivating Customers to Adhere to Expert Advice in Professional Services: A Medical Service Context," *Journal of Service Research*, Vol. 18, No. 1, pp. 39–58.

39　Harvir S. Bansal and Peter A. Voyer (2000), "Word-of-Mouth Processes Within a Services Purchase Decision Context," *Journal of Service Research*, Vol. 3, No. 2, November, pp. 166–177.

40　Anna S. Mattila and Jochen Wirtz (2002), "The Impact of Knowledge Types on the Consumer Search Process — An Investigation in the Context of Credence Services," *International Journal of Research in Service Industry Management*, Vol. 13, No. 3, pp. 214–230.

41　Kim Harris and Steve Baron (2004), "Consumer-to-Consumer Conversations in Service Settings," *Journal of Service Research*, Vol. 6, No. 3, pp. 87–303.

42　Frederick F. Reichheld (2003), "The One Number You Need to Grow," *Harvard Business Review*, Vol. 81, No. 12, pp. 46–55.

43　See Jacques Bughin, Jonathan Doogan and Ole Jorgen Vetvik (2010), "A New Way to Measure Word-of-Mouth Marketing," *McKinsey Quarterly*, April, pp. 1–9.

For online WOM, see: Shyam Gopinath, Jacquelyn S. Thomas, Lakshman Krishnamurthi (2015), "Investigating the Relationship Between the Content of Online Word of Mouth, Advertising and Brand Performance," *Marketing Science*, Vol. 33, No. 2, pp. 241–258.

44　Eugene W. Anderson (1998), "Customer Satisfaction and Word of Mouth," *Journal of Service Research*, Vol. 1, August, pp. 5–17; Magnus Söderlund (1998), "Customer Satisfaction and Its Consequences on Customer Behavior Revisited: The Impact of Different Levels of Satisfaction on Word of Mouth, Feedback to the Supplier, and Loyalty, *International Journal of Service Industry Management*, Vol. 9, No. 2, pp. 169–188. Srini S. Srinivasan, Rolph Anderson and Kishore Ponnavolu (2002), "Customer Loyalty in e-Commerce: An Exploration of its Antecedents and Consequences," *Journal of Retailing*, Vol. 78, No. 1, pp. 41–50; Chatura Ranaweera and Kalyani Menon (2013), "For Better or Worse? Adverse Effects of Relationship Age and Continuance Commitment on Positive and Negative

Word of Mouth", *European Journal of Marketing*, Vol. 47, No. 10, pp. 1598–1621.

For a meta-analysis of research on word of mouth, see: Celso Augusto de Matos and Carlos Alberto Vargas Rossi (2008), "Word-of-Mouth Communications in Marketing: A Meta-Analytic Review of the Antecedents and Moderators," *Journal of the Academy of Marketing Science,* Vol. 36, No. 4, pp. 578–596.

45 Jeffrey G. Blodgett, Kirk L. Wakefield, and James H. Barnes (1995), "The Effects of Customer Service on Consumers Complaining Behavior," *Journal of Services Marketing*, Vol. 9, No. 4, pp. 31–42; Jeffrey G. Blodgett, and Ronald D. Anderson (2000), "A Bayesian Network Model of the Consumer Complaint Process," *Journal of Service Research,* Vol. 2, No. 4, May, pp. 321–338; Stefan Michel (2001), "Analyzing Service Failures and Recoveries: A Process Approach," *International Journal of Service Industry Management*, Vol. 12, No. 1, pp. 20–33. James G Maxham III and Richard G Netemeyer (2002), "A Longitudinal Study of Complaining Customers' Evaluations of Multiple Service Failures and Recovery Efforts," *Journal of Marketing*, Vol. 66, No. 4, pp. 57–72.

46 http://en.wikiquote.org/wiki/Ron_Kaufman, accessed March 21, 2015.

47 Jochen Wirtz and Patricia Chew (2002), "The Effects of Incentives, Deal Proneness, Satisfaction and Tie Strength on Word-of-Mouth Behaviour," *International Journal of Service Industry Management*, Vol. 13, No. 2, pp. 141–162; Tom J. Brown, Thomas E. Barry, Peter A. Dacin, and Richard F. Gunst (2005), "Spreading the Word: Investigating Antecedents of Consumers' Positive Word-of-Mouth Intentions and Behaviors in a Retailing Context," *Journal of the Academy of Marketing Science,* Vol. 33, No. 2, pp. 123–138; John E. Hogan, Katherine N. Lemon, and Barak Libai (2004), "Quantifying the Ripple: Word-of-Mouth and Advertising Effectiveness," *Journal of Advertising Research*, September, pp. 271–280; Jonah Berger and Raghuram Iyengar (2013), "Communication Channels and Word of Mouth: How the Medium Shapes the Message," *Journal of Consumer Research*, Vol. 40, October, pp. 567–579.

To understand how different types of epidemics, including word-of-mouth epidemics, develop, see: Malcom Gladwell, *The Tipping Point* (Little, NY: Brown and Company, 2000), p. 32.

For an award-winning book on how you can get people to share your message, read also: Jonah Berger (2013), *Contagious: Why Things Catch On*. Simon & Schuster; and view an interview with Berger at: http://knowledge. wharton.upenn.edu/article/contagious-jonah-berger-on-why-things-catch-on/.

For a study that identifies brand characteristics that stimulate WOM, see Mitchell J. Lovett, Renana Peres, and Ron Shachar (2013), "On Brands and Word of Mouth," *Journal of Marketing Research*, Vol. 50, August, pp. 427–444.

For an excellent review on the interplay between WOM and advertising, see: Guillermo Armelini and Julian Villanueva (2010), "Marketing Expenditures and Word-of-Mouth Communications: Complements or Substitutes?" *Foundations and Trends in Marketing*, Vol. 5, No. 1, pp. 1–53.

48 Phillipp Schmitt, Bernd Skiera, and Christophe Van den Bulte (2011), "Referral Programs and Customer Value," *Journal of Marketing*, Vol. 75, No. 1, pp. 46–59; V. Kumar, J. Andrew Petersen, and Robert P. Leone (2010), "Driving Profitability by Encouraging Customer Referrals: Who, When, and How," *Journal of Marketing*, Vol. 74, No. 5, pp. 1–17.

It has even been shown that customers who make referrals via reward programs increases their loyalty. That is, recommenders' defection rates fell and average monthly expenditure increases, see: Ina Garnefeld, Andreas Eggert, Sabrina V. Helm, and Stephen S. Tax (2013), "Growing Existing Customers' Revenue Streams through Customer Referral Programs," *Journal of Marketing*, Vol. 77, No. 4, pp. 17–32.

49 Ping Xiao, Christopher S. Tang and Jochen Wirtz (2011), "Optimizing Referral Reward Programs Under Impression Management Considerations," *European Journal of Operational Research*, Vol. 215, No. 3, pp. 730–739; Jochen Wirtz, Chiara Orsingher, Patricia Chew and Siok Tambyah (2013), "The Role of Metaperception on the Effectiveness of Referral Reward Programs," *Journal of Service Research*, Vol. 16, No. 1, pp. 82–98; Peeter W.J. Verlegh, Gangseok Ryu, Mirjam A. Tuk, and Lawrence Feick (2013), "Receiver Responses to Rewarded Referrals: The Motive Inferences Framework," *Journal of the Academy of Marketing Science*, Vol. 41, No. 6, pp. 669–682.

50 Inès Blal and Michael C. Sturman (2014), "The Differential Effects of the Quality and Quantity of Online Reviews on Hotel Room Sales," *Cornell Hospitality Quarterly*, Vol. 55, No. 4, pp. 365–375.

51 For research on online reviews see: Kristopher Floyd, Ryan Freling, Saad Alhoqail, Hyun Young Cho, and Traci Freling (2014), "How Online Product Reviews Affect Retail Sales: A Meta-Analysis," *Journal of Retailing*, Vol. 90, No. 2, pp. 217–232; Nga N. Ho-Dac, Stephen J. Carson, and William L. Moore (2013), "The Effects of Positive and Negative Online Customer Reviews: Do Brand Strength and Category Maturity Matter?" *Journal of Marketing*, Vol. 77, No. 6, pp.

37–53; Eric T. Anderson and Duncan I. Simester (2014), "Reviews Without a Purchase: Low Ratings, Loyal Customers, and Deception," *Journal of Marketing Research*, Vol. 51, June, pp. 249–269; Andreas Munzel and Werner H. Kunz (2014), "Creators, Multipliers, and Lurkers: Who Contributes and who Benefits at Online Review Sites," *Journal of Service Management*, Vol. 25, No. 1, pp. 49–74.

52 Jochen Wirtz, Anouk den Ambtman, Josee Bloemer, Csilla Horváth, B. Ramaseshan, Joris Van De Klundert, Zeynep Gurhan Canli, and Jay Kandampully (2013), "Managing Brands and Customer Engagement in Online Brand Communities," *Journal of Service Management*, Vol. 24, No. 3, pp. 223–244; Richard L. Gruner, Christian Homburg, and Bryan A. Lukas (2014), "Firm-Hosted Online Brand Communities and New Product Success," *Journal of the Academy of Marketing Science*, Vol. 42, No. 1, pp. 29–48.

53 Renee Dye (2000), "The Buzz on Buzz," *Harvard Business Review*, November–December, pp. 139–146. Sandeep Krishnarmurthy (2001), "Viral Marketing: What Is It and Why Should Every Service Marketer Care?" *Journal of Services Marketing*, Vol. 15; Joseph E. Phelps, Regina Lewis, Lynne Mobilio, David Perry, and Niranjan Raman (2004), "Viral Marketing or Electronic Word-of-Mouth Advertising: Examining Consumer Responses and Motivations to Pass Along Emails," *Journal of Advertising Research,* December, pp. 333–348; Robert V. Kozinets, Kristine de Valck, Andrea C. Wojnicki, and Sarah J.S. Wilner (2010), "Networked Narratives: Understanding Word-of-Mouth Marketing in Online Communities," *Journal of Marketing*, Vol. 74, No. 2, pp. 71–89; Jonah Berger and Katherine L. Milkman (2012), "What Makes Online Content Viral?" *Journal of Marketing Research*, Vol. 49, April, pp. 192–205.

For a review of generation Y and their social media use see: Ruth N. Bolton, A. Parasuraman, Ankie Hoefnagels, Nanne Migchels, Sertan Kabadayi, Thorsten Gruber, Yuliya Komarova Loureiro, and David Solnet (2013), "Understanding Generation Y and Their Use of Social Media: A Review and Research Agenda," *Journal of Service Management*, Vol. 24, No.3, pp. 245–267.

54 Steve Jurvetson (2000), "What Exactly Is Viral Marketing?" *Red Herring*, Vol. 78, pp. 110–112.

55 "Selling Becomes Sociable," *The Economist*, September 11, 2010.

56 See also Barak Libai, Eitan Muller, and Renana Peres (2013), "Decomposing the Value of Word-of-Mouth Seeding Programs: Acceleration Versus Expansion," *Journal of Marketing Research*, Vol. 50, April, pp. 161–176.

57 http://en.wikipedia.org/wiki/Twitter, accessed March 21, 2015.

58 This section draws on Philip Kotler and Gary Armstrong, *Chapter 14: Communicating Customer Value: Integrated Marketing Communications Strategy,* in Principles of Marketing, 15th ed. (Upper Saddle River, NJ: Person Education, 2014), 426–453; and William F. Arens, Michael F. Weigold, and Christian Arens, "Marketing and IMC Planning," in *Contemporary Advertising & Integrated Marketing Communications.* 14th ed. (New York, NY: McGraw Hill, 2013), pp. 263–267.

59 https://www.donotcall.gov/default.aspx, accessed March 21, 2015.

60 https://www.dmachoice.org, accessed March 21, 2015.

PART 3

The Services Marketing Framework

Part I

Understanding Service Products, Consumers, and Markets

1. Creating Value in the Service Economy
2. Understanding Service Consumers
3. Positioning Services in Competitive Markets

Part II

Applying the 4 Ps of Marketing to Services

4. Developing Service Products and Brands
5. Distributing Services Through Physical and Electronic Channels
6. Service Pricing and Revenue Management
7. Service Marketing Communications

Part III

Managing the Customer Interface

8. Designing Service Processes
9. Balancing Demand and Capacity
10. Crafting the Service Environment
11. Managing People for Service Advantage

Part IV

Developing Customer Relationships

12. Managing Relationships and Building Loyalty
13. Complaint Handling and Service Recovery

Part V

Striving for Service Excellence

14. Improving Service Quality and Productivity
15. Building a World-Class Service Organization

Figure III Organizing framework for services marketing

MANAGING THE CUSTOMER INTERFACE

Part III focuses on managing the interface between customers and the service organization. It covers the additional **3 Ps** (*P*rocess, *P*hysical environment, and *P*eople) that are unique to services marketing. It consists of the following four chapters:

CHAPTER 8

Designing Service Processes

Chapter 8 begins with design of an effective service delivery process, specifying how operating and delivery systems link together to create the promised value proposition. Very often, customers are actively involved in service creation, especially if acting as co-producers, and the process becomes their experience.

CHAPTER 9

Balancing Demand and Capacity

Chapter 9 relates to process management with a focus on widely fluctuating demands and how to balance the level and timing of customer demand against available productive capacity. Well-managed demand and capacity leads to smooth processes with less waiting time for customers. Marketing strategies for managing demand involve smoothing demand fluctuations and inventorying demand through reservation systems and formalized queuing. Understanding customer motivations in different segments is also important for successful demand management.

CHAPTER 10

Crafting the Service Environment

Chapter 10 focuses on the physical environment also known as the servicescape. It needs to be engineered to create the right impression and to facilitate the effective delivery of service processes. The servicescape needs to be managed carefully as it can have a profound impact on customers' impressions, guide their behavior throughout the service process, and provide tangible clues of a firm's service quality and positioning.

CHAPTER 11

Managing People for Service Advantage

Chapter 11 introduces people as a defining element of many services. Many services require direct interaction between customers and contact personnel. The nature of these interactions strongly influence how customers perceive service quality. Hence, service firms devote a significant amount of effort to recruiting, training, and motivating their employees. Satisfied and engaged employees who perform well are often a source of competitive advantage for a firm.

Designing Service Processes

Well done is better than well said.

Benjamin Franklin,
one of the Founding Fathers of the United States,
1706–1790

Ultimately, only one thing really matters in service encounters — the customer's perceptions of what occurred.

Richard B. Chase and **Sriram Dasu**,
Professors at University of Southern California

The new frontier of competitive advantage is the customer interface. Making yours a winner will require the right people and, increasingly, the right machines — on the front lines.

Jeffrey Rayport and Bernard Jaworski
(Professor at Harvard Business School, founder and chairman of Marketspace LLC and Professor at Claremont Graduate University, respectively)

LEARNING OBJECTIVES (LOs)

By the end of this chapter, the reader should be able to:

- **LO 1** Know the difference between a service experience and a service process.

- **LO 2** Tell the difference between flowcharting and blueprinting.

- **LO 3** Develop a blueprint for a service process with all the typical design elements in place.

- **LO 4** Understand how to use fail-proofing to design fail points out of service processes.

- **LO 5** Know how to set service standards and performance targets for customer service processes.

- **LO 6** Appreciate the importance of consumer perceptions and emotions in service process design.

- **LO 7** Explain the necessity for service process redesign.

- **LO 8** Understand how service process redesign can help improve both service quality and productivity.

- **LO 9** Understand the levels of customer participation in service processes.

- **LO 10** Be familiar with the concept of service customers as "co-creators" and the implications of this perspective.

- **LO 11** Understand the factors that lead customers to accept or reject new self-service technologies (SSTs).

- **LO 12** Know how to manage customers' reluctance to change their behaviors in service processes, including the adoption of SSTs.

OPENING VIGNETTE
Redesigning Customer Service in a Small Hospital Practice

Things were not going smoothly at Family Medicine Faculty Practice (FMFP), a small practice within a hospital system. Its patients were often placed on hold for long times when they called; there was a lack of available and convenient appointment slots; the waiting room was frequently crowded with lengthy delays before patients could see their doctors.

Dr. Schwartz, the medical director, and Dr. Bryan, the assistant medical director, decided to change this situation and engaged Coleman Associates, a consulting firm that specializes in redesigning processes. Over the course of four days, a Coleman Associates team worked closely with the clinic's staff on-site, shoulder-to-shoulder, and radically redesigned work processes. It was an amazing transformation; the redesign started on a Monday afternoon, and by Friday morning the Faculty Practice was operating in a whole new way!

The Redesigned Service Model

FMFP had altogether 12 staff, of which nine were support staff and three were physicians. The clinic was considered lean with only three support staff per physician, which is much lower than the national average of 4.8. As a central part of the redesign, staff were reorganized into three Patient Care Teams. Each Patient Care Team consisted of a clinician, a medical assistant, and a receptionist who acted like a one-stop shop for all the patients in their care. The Patient Care Teams took care of all tasks related to their patients, including walk-ins, collection of co-payments, filing of medical charts, confirming the next day's appointments, checking insurance eligibility, and any other patient transactions.

The three Patient Care Teams shared three "back-office" staff which had the following redesigned roles: a medical records staffer, a phone attendant, and a flowmaster not specifically assigned to any of the three teams. The medical records staff was in charge of getting medical charts 24 hours in advance of clinic sessions and filing lab results in charts on a real-time basis so that no work was left to accumulate. If a patient phoned FMFP for an appointment, the call would be answered by the phone attendant. The flowmaster was in charge of moving patients from the front waiting room into the exam rooms, and out as smoothly and as fast as possible. The flowmaster communicated with each Patient Care Team's medical assistant to get an accurate estimate of the wait time for each patient. Basically, the flowmaster solved any flow problems occurring in the clinic to keep the visit cycle time within 45 minutes for 90% of all visits.

After the redesign, the phone attendant picked up calls and passed it to the relevant Patient Care Team receptionist. In future, they had further plans for direct lines to each Patient Care Team to eliminate the traffic to the phone attendant. The receptionists would be given wireless phones so that patient calls could still be picked up even as they filed medical charts from visits already completed. Patient Care Team receptionists filed charts immediately after visits, thus reducing the incidence of lost charts.

During the booking of appointments, if a patient had a question the receptionist could not answer, she would communicate directly, via walkie-talkie, with the Patient Care Team's medical assistant to get an immediate answer so that work was handled on a real-time basis and not stacked up to be dealt with later.

New tools and equipment helped to stretch FMFP's available resources. For example, digital floor scales were placed in every exam room to weigh adult patients quickly and privately, so there was no need for an extra stop at a vitals station. In fact, all work was done in the exam room reflecting the redesign principle: "Organize our work around the patient, not the patient around our work."

As staff gained more experience working together every day in their Patient Care Teams, they also became stronger and more adept in handling variations in patient flow. Stacks of paper seemingly melted during the week when work was redesigned.

FMFP's staff worked harder than ever, but they were also thrilled with the results and all the compliments they received from delighted patients about the new service processes.

WHAT IS A SERVICE PROCESS?

From the customer's perspective, services are experiences. From the organization's perspective, services are processes that have to be designed and managed to create the desired customer experience. This makes processes the architecture of services. Processes describe the method and sequence in which service operating systems work, specify how they link together to create the value proposition promised to the customers. Badly designed processes are likely to annoy customers because they often result in slow, frustrating, and poor quality service delivery. Similarly, poor processes make it difficult for frontline employees to do their jobs well, thus resulting in low productivity, and increasing the risk of service failures. In this chapter, we discuss how we can design and improve service processes so that they deliver the promised value proposition.

DESIGNING AND DOCUMENTING SERVICE PROCESSES

The first step in designing or analyzing any process is documenting or describing it. Flowcharting and blueprinting are two key tools used for documenting and redesigning existing service processes and for designing new ones. How do we distinguish between flowcharting and blueprinting in a service context? A flowchart describes an existing process, often in a fairly simple form. Specifically, flowcharting is a technique for displaying the nature and sequence of the different steps involved when a customer "flows" through the service process. It is an easy way to quickly understand the total customer service experience. By flowcharting the sequence of encounters customers have with a service organization, we can gain valuable insights into the nature of an existing service. *Figures 8.2* and *8.3* display two simple flowcharts that demonstrate what is involved in each of the featured services.

Blueprinting is a more complex form of flowcharting and specifies in detail how a service process is constructed, including what is visible to the customer and all that goes on in the back-office. It's no easy task to create a service, especially one that must be delivered in real time with customers present in the service factory. To design services that are both satisfying for customers and operationally efficient, marketers and operations specialists need to work together, and a blueprint can provide a common perspective and language for the various departments involved.

Perhaps you're wondering where the term blueprinting comes from and why we use it here. The design for a new building or a ship is usually captured on architectural drawings called blueprints as reproductions have traditionally been printed on special paper on which all the drawings and annotations appear in blue. These blueprints show what the product should look like and they detail the specifications to which it should conform. In contrast to the physical architecture of a building or a piece of equipment, service processes have a largely intangible structure. That makes them all the more difficult to visualize. The same is also true of processes such as logistics, industrial engineering, decision theory, and computer systems analysis, each of which employs blueprint-like techniques to describe processes involving flows, sequences, relationships, and dependencies.

Service Processes

- Are the service experience from the customer's perspective
- Are the architecture of service from the firm's perspective

Mapping & Designing Service Processes

Flowcharting of Service Processes

- Maps a service process
- Shows the nature and sequence of steps involved
- Is an easy way to visualize the customer experience

Blueprinting of Service Processes

- A more complex form of flowcharting
- Shows how a service process is constructed
- Maps the customer, employee, and service system interactions
- Design elements:
  - Front-stage activities
  - Physical evidence
  - Line of visibility
  - Backstage activities
  - Support processes & supplies
  - Potential fail points
  - Common customer waits
  - Service standards & targets
  - Details preprocess, in-process, and postprocess stages of service delivery

Process Design Considerations

- Use poka-yokes to design fail points out of processes
- Set service standards and targets to manage processes
- Design customer emotions into the process:
  - Start strong
  - Build an improving trend
  - Create a peak
  - Get bad experiences over with early
  - Segment pleasure, combine pain
  - Finish strong

Redesigning Service Processes

Indicators for Redesign Need

- Excessive information exchange
- High degree of control activities
- Increased processing of exceptions
- Growing number of customer complaints about inconvenient and unnecessary procedures

Objectives of Redesign

- Reduced number of service failures
- Reduced cycle time
- Enhanced productivity
- Increased customer satisfaction

How to Redesign Service Processes?

- Examine the blueprint with key stakeholders (i.e., customers, frontline and back office employees and IT) and see how to reconstruct, rearrange and substitute tasks
- Eliminate non-value adding steps
- Address bottlenecks, balance process
- Shift to self-service

Manage Customer Participation in Service Processes

Customers as Co-creators

- Educate, train and motivate customers to do their part well
- Use customer poka-yokes to reduce failures caused by customers
- Consider peer-to-peer problem solving as part of online brand communities

Self-Service Technologies (SSTs)

- Customer benefits
  - Convenience & speed
  - Control, information & customization
  - Cost savings
- Disadvantages & barriers
  - Poorly designed SSTs
  - Unreliable SSTs
  - Poor service recovery procedures
  - Inadequate customer education
- Assessing & improving SSTs
  - Does the SST work reliably?
  - Is the SST better than the interpersonal alternative?
  - If it fails, are systems in place to recover the service?

Managing Customers' Reluctance to Change

- Develop customers' trust
- Understand customers' habits & expectations
- Pretest new procedures & equipment
- Publicize the benefits
- Teach customers to use innovations & promote trial
- Monitor performance & improve the SST

Figure 8.1 Chapter overview – designing and managing service processes

People Processing — Stay at Motel

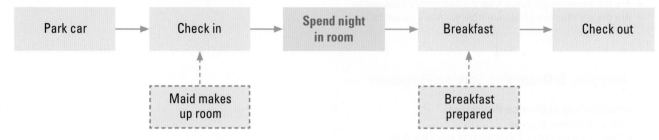

Figure 8.2 Simple flowchart for delivery of motel service

Information Processing — Health Insurance

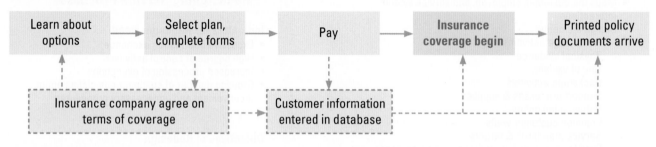

Figure 8.3 Simple flowchart for delivery of health insurance service

Service blueprints map customer, employee, and service system interactions. Importantly, they show the full customer journey from service initiation to final delivery of the desired benefit, which can include many steps and service employees from different departments. For example, in the context of a cable service, it may involve a sales agent, an installation team, a call center employee to do the scheduling, and the back-office officers to set up the billing and payment; all are equally responsible for a trouble-free installation[1]. Blueprints show the key customer actions, how customers and employees from different departments interact (called the line of interaction), the front-stage actions by those service employees, and how these are supported by back-stage activities and systems. By showing interrelationships among employee roles, operational processes, supplies, information technology, and customer interactions, blueprints can help bring together marketing, operations, and human resource management within a firm. Together, they can then develop better service processes, including defining service scripts and roles to guide interactions between staff and customers (as discussed in Chapter 2); designing fail points and excessive customer waits out of processes; and finally, setting the service standards and targets for service delivery teams.

DEVELOPING A SERVICE BLUEPRINT

⟳ **LO 3**
Develop a blueprint for a service process with all the typical design elements in place.

How should you get started on developing a service blueprint? First, you need to identify all the key activities involved in creating and delivering the service in question, and then specify the linkages between these activities. Initially, it's best to keep activities relatively aggregated in order to define the "big picture". This can be done by first developing a simple flowchart documenting the process from the customer's perspective. You can then refine any given activity by drilling down to obtain a higher level of detail. In an airline context for instance, the passenger activity of "boards aircraft" actually represents a series of actions and can be broken down into such steps as "wait for seat rows to be announced, give agent boarding pass for verification, walk down jetway, enter aircraft, let flight attendant verify boarding pass, find a seat, stow carry-on bag, sit down" (*Figure 8.4*).

Next, the more details can be added. Typical service blueprints have the following design characteristics that help to see how a blueprint should be developed[2]:

- **Front-stage activities** map the overall customer experience, the desired inputs and outputs, and the sequence in which delivery of that output should take place.

- **Physical evidence of front-stage activities** is what the customer can see and use to assess service quality.

- **Line of visibility** is a key characteristic of service blueprinting that distinguishes between what customers experience "front-stage" and the activities of employees and support processes "back-stage" where customers can't see them, between the two lines of what is called the line of visibility. When a firm clearly understands the line of visibility, it is able to better manage physical and other evidence for front-stage activities to give customers the desired experience and quality signals. Some firms are too focused on operations and neglect the customer's purely front-stage perspective. Accounting firms, for instance, often have detailed documented procedures and standards for how to conduct an audit, but may lack clear standards for hosting a meeting with clients, or for how staff members should answer the telephone.

- **Back-stage activities** that must be performed to support a particular front-stage step.

Figure 8.4 Baggage collection is one of the last steps in an air travel service process

- **Support processes and supplies** — Many support processes involve a lot of information. The information needed at each step in the blueprint is usually provided by information systems. For example, without the right information at the frontline staff's fingertips, processes such as banking, online broking, or even borrowing a book from your university library could not be completed and the service process could break down. Supplies required to be made available for both front-stage and back-stage steps are also necessary for many services. For example, restaurants need to have the supplies of the right fresh produce and wines; and car rental firms of vehicles, global positioning systems (GPSs) and child seats. Supplies are essential to delivering high quality core services.

- **Potential fail points** — Blueprinting gives managers the chance to identify potential fail points in the process. Fail points are where there is a risk of things going wrong, resulting in diminished service quality. When managers are aware of these fail points, they are better able to design them out of a process (such as using poka-yokes, as discussed later in this chapter) and have backup plans (such as for service recovery, as discussed in Chapter 13) for failures that are not preventable (e.g., departure delays due to bad weather).

- **Identifying customer waits** — Blueprints can also pinpoint stages in the process at which customers commonly have to wait (*Figure 8.5*), and where there are points of potentially excessive waits. These can then either be designed out of the process, or if that is not always possible, firms can implement strategies to make waits less unpleasant for customers (see the strategies discussed in Chapter 9 "Managing Demand and Capacity").

- **Service standards and targets** should be established for each activity to reflect customer expectations. They include specific times set for the completion of each task and the acceptable wait between each customer activity. Developing service blueprints gives marketing and operational personnel detailed process knowledge that can then be used to develop standards. The final service blueprint should contain key service standards for each front-stage activity, including the estimated time for the completion of a task and maximum customer wait times in between tasks. Standards should then be used to set targets for service delivery teams to ensure that service processes perform well against customer expectations.

Figure 8.5 Long waiting lines indicate operational problems that need to be addressed

Blueprinting the Restaurant Experience: A Three-Act Performance

To illustrate how the blueprinting of a high-contact, people-processing service can be done, we examine the dinner experience for two at Chez Jean, an upscale restaurant that enhances its core food service with a variety of other supplementary services (*Figure 8.6*). A rule of thumb in full-service restaurants is that the cost of purchasing the food ingredients represents about 20–30% of the price of the meal. The balance can be seen as the fees that customers are willing to pay for a great dining experience that includes "renting" tables and chairs in a pleasant setting, the food preparation services of expert chefs and their kitchen equipment, and serving staff to wait on them in the dining room.

Most service processes can be divided into three main steps:

1. **Pre-process stage** where the preliminaries occur, such as making a reservation, parking the car, getting seated and being presented with the menu.

2. **In-process stage** where the main purpose of the service encounter is accomplished, such as enjoying the food and drinks in a restaurant.

3. **Post-process stage** where the activities necessary for the closing of the encounter happens, such as getting the check and paying for dinner.

It is important to differentiate these stages as customers tend to have different objectives and sensitivities in these stages. For example, research in the context of restaurants found that people are more upset about a delay during the pre-process or post-process stages than the in-process stage[3]. Also, the pre- and post-process stages typically are not the core of the service and customers want efficiency and convenience in those stages (e.g., a convenient way to get a reservation, and getting the check and payment done quickly when one wants to leave the restaurant), whereas the in-process stage has to deliver the core benefits of the service.

In *Figure 8.6*, we use a more theatrical terminology of these three acts to represent the three stages to connect to the theatre analogy perspective discussed in Chapter 2, and to emphasize the drama and experience dimension of this service process.

The key components of the blueprint in *Figure 8.6*, reading from top to bottom, are:

1. Definition of standards for each front-stage activity (only a few examples are actually stated in the figure).

2. Principal customer actions (illustrated by pictures).

3. Physical and other evidence for front-stage activities (stated for all steps).

4. Line of interaction.

5. Front-stage actions by customer-contact personnel.

6. Line of visibility.

7. Back-stage actions by customer-contact personnel.

8. Support processes involving other service personnel.

9. Support processes involving information technology.

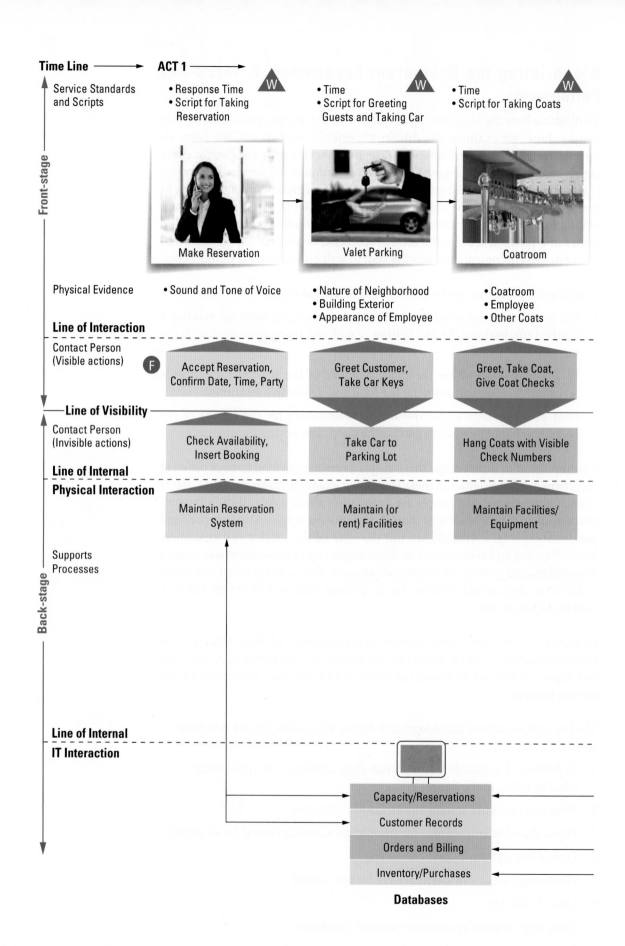

Figure 8.6 Blueprinting a full-service restaurant experience

- Time
- Order Accuracy
- Script for Serving Drinks

- Punctuality vs. Reservation
- Script for Seating

ACT II ⟶

- Time
- Script for Greeting Guests, Taking Order

- Time
- Script for Wine Service

Cocktails → **Seating** → **Order Food and Wine** → **Wine Service**

- Cocktail Lounge Decor
- Furnishings
- Table Setting
- Staff, Other Customers

- Dining Room Decor
- Appearance/Demeanor of Staff
- Table Setting
- Other Guests

- Wine Quality

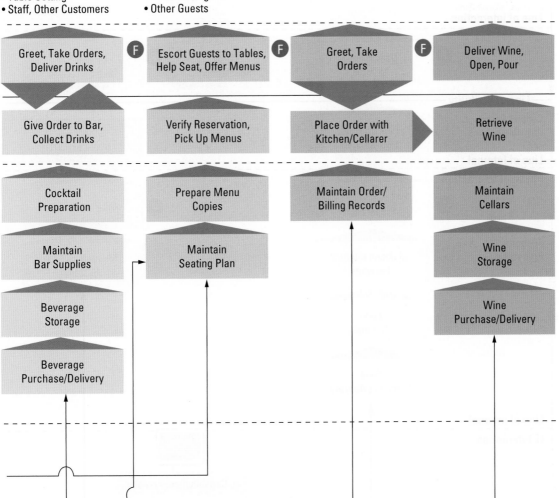

Greet, Take Orders, Deliver Drinks **F**

Escort Guests to Tables, Help Seat, Offer Menus **F**

Greet, Take Orders **F**

Deliver Wine, Open, Pour

Give Order to Bar, Collect Drinks

Verify Reservation, Pick Up Menus

Place Order with Kitchen/Cellarer

Retrieve Wine

Cocktail Preparation

Prepare Menu Copies

Maintain Order/ Billing Records

Maintain Cellars

Maintain Bar Supplies

Maintain Seating Plan

Wine Storage

Beverage Storage

Wine Purchase/Delivery

Beverage Purchase/Delivery

KEY

F Points Fail

W Risk of Excessive Wait (Standard times should specify limits.)

Managing the Customer Interface **299**

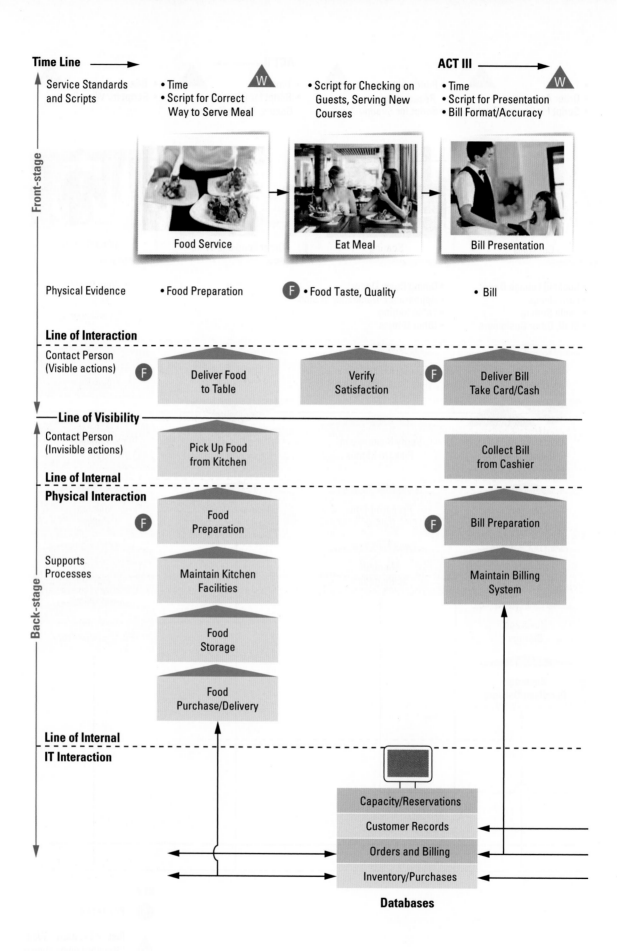

Figure 8.6 (Continued)

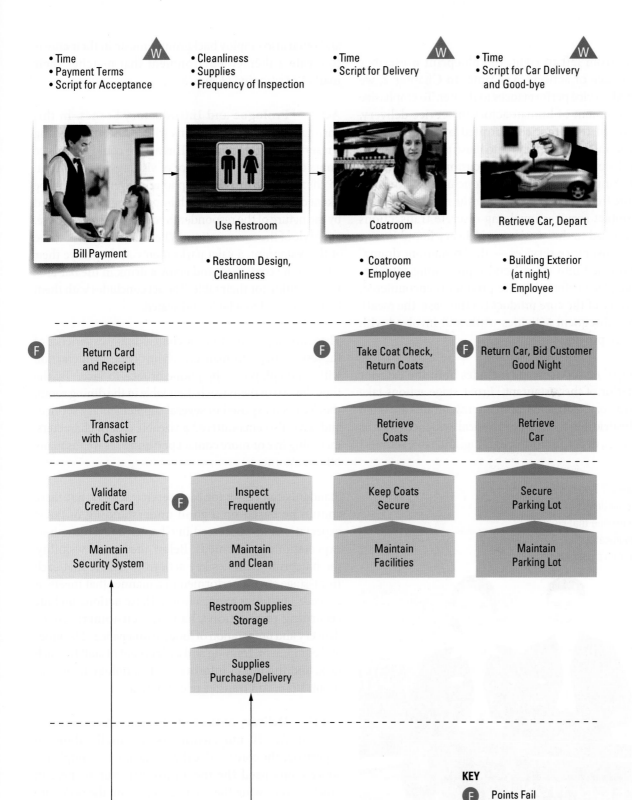

- Time
- Payment Terms
- Script for Acceptance

W

- Cleanliness
- Supplies
- Frequency of Inspection

- Time
- Script for Delivery

W

- Time
- Script for Car Delivery and Good-bye

W

Bill Payment

Use Restroom

Coatroom

Retrieve Car, Depart

- Restroom Design, Cleanliness

- Coatroom
- Employee

- Building Exterior (at night)
- Employee

F **Return Card and Receipt**

F **Take Coat Check, Return Coats**

F **Return Car, Bid Customer Good Night**

Transact with Cashier

Retrieve Coats

Retrieve Car

Validate Credit Card

F **Inspect Frequently**

Keep Coats Secure

Secure Parking Lot

Maintain Security System

Maintain and Clean

Maintain Facilities

Maintain Parking Lot

Restroom Supplies Storage

Supplies Purchase/Delivery

KEY

F Points Fail

W Risk of Excessive Wait (Standard times should specify limits.)

Reading from left to right, the blueprint prescribes the sequence of actions over time. In Chapter 2, we compared service performances to theater. To emphasize the involvement of human actors in service delivery, we followed the practices adopted by some service organizations by using pictures to illustrate each of the 14 principal steps involving our two customers, beginning with making a reservation and concluding with their departure from the restaurant after the meal. Like many high-contact services involving discrete transactions — as opposed to the continuous delivery found in, say, utility or insurance services — the "restaurant drama" can be divided into three "acts", representing activities that take place before the core product is encountered, the delivery of the core product (in this case, the meal), and the subsequent activities while still involved with the service provider.

The "stage" or servicescape includes both the exterior and interior of the restaurant. Front-stage actions take place in a very visual environment; restaurants are often quite theatrical in their use of physical evidence (such as furnishings, décor, uniforms, lighting, and table settings)

Figure 8.7 Two hosts welcome diners in a servicescape that clearly communicates the restaurant's positioning

and often also employ background music in their efforts to create a themed environment that matches their market positioning (*Figure 8.7*).

Act I — Prologue and Introductory Scenes. In this particular drama, Act I begins with a customer making a reservation by telephone. This action could take place hours or even days in advance of visiting the restaurant. In theatrical terms, the telephone conversation can be likened to a radio drama, with impressions being created by the nature of the respondent's voice, speed of response, and style of the conversation. When our customers arrive at the restaurant, a valet parks their car, they leave their coats in the coatroom, and enjoy a drink in the bar area while waiting for their table. The act concludes with them being escorted to a table and seated.

These five steps constitute the couple's initial experience of the restaurant performance, each involving an interaction with an employee — by phone or face-to-face. By the time the two of them reach their table in the dining room, they've been exposed to several supplementary services and have also encountered a sizeable cast of characters, including five or more contact personnel, as well as many other customers.

Standards can be set for each service activity, but these should be based on a good understanding of guest expectations (as discussed in Chapter 2 regarding how expectations are formed). Below the line of visibility, the blueprint identifies key actions to ensure that each front-stage step is performed in a manner that meets or exceeds customer expectations. These actions include recording reservations, handling customers' coats, delivery and preparation of food, maintenance of facilities and equipment, training and assignment of staff for each task, and the use of information technology to access, input, store, and transfer relevant data.

Act II — Delivery of the Core Product. As the curtain rises on Act II, our customers are finally about to experience the core service they came for. For simplicity, we've condensed the meal into just four scenes. In practice, reviewing the menu and placing the order are two separate activities; meantime, meal service proceeds on a course-by-course basis. If you were actually running a restaurant yourself, you'd need to go into greater detail to identify each of the many steps involved in what is often a tightly scripted drama. Assuming all goes well, the two guests will have an excellent meal, well served in a pleasant atmosphere, and perhaps a fine wine to enhance it. But if the restaurant fails to satisfy their expectations (and those of its many other guests) during Act II, it is going to be in serious trouble. There are numerous potential fail points. Is the menu information accurate? Is everything listed on the menu actually available this evening? Will explanations and advice be given in a friendly and non-condescending manner for guests who have questions about specific menu items or are unsure about which wine to order?

After our customers decide on their meals, they place their orders with the server, who must then pass on the details to personnel in the kitchen, bar, and billing desk. Mistakes in transmitting information are a frequent cause of quality failures in many organizations. Bad handwriting, unclear verbal requests, or a wrong entry into a handheld wireless ordering device can lead to incorrect preparation or delivery of the wrong items altogether.

Figure 8.8 The billing process should be quick and painless to ensure customer convenience

In the subsequent scenes of Act II, our customers may evaluate not only the quality of food and drink — the most important dimension of all — but also how promptly it is served (not too quickly, for guests do not want to feel rushed!) and the style of service. Even if the server can perform the job correctly, the experience of the customer can still be spoiled if the server is disinterested, unfriendly, or has an overly casual behavior.

Act III — The Drama Concludes. The meal may be over, but much is still taking place both front-stage and back-stage as the drama moves to its close. The core service has now been delivered, and we'll assume that our customers are happily digesting. Act III should be short. The action in each of the remaining scenes should move smoothly, quickly, and pleasantly, with no shocking surprises at the end. Most customers' expectations would probably include the following:

- An accurate, intelligible bill is presented promptly as soon as the customer requests it (*Figure 8.8*).

- Payment is handled politely and expeditiously (with all major credit cards accepted).

- The guests are thanked for their patronage and invited to come again.

- Customers visiting the restrooms find them clean and properly supplied.

- The right coats are promptly retrieved from the coatroom.

- The customer's car is brought to the door without much of a wait, in the same condition as when it was left. The attendant thanks them again and bids them a good evening.

Identifying Fail Points

Running a restaurant is a complex business and much can go wrong. A good blueprint should draw attention to the points in service delivery where things are particularly at risk of going wrong. From a customer's perspective, the most serious fail points, marked in our blueprint by *an F in a circle*, are those that will result in the failure to access or enjoy the core product. They involve items such as the reservation ("Could the customer get through by phone?", "Was a table available at the desired time and date?," or "Was the reservation recorded accurately?") and seating ("Was a table available when promised?").

Since service delivery takes place over time, there is also the possibility of delays between specific actions that require the customers to wait. Common locations for such waits are identified on the blueprint by *a W within a triangle*. Excessive waits will annoy customers. In practice, every step in the process — both front-stage and back-stage — has some potential for failures and delays. In fact, failures often lead directly to delays (e.g., orders that were never passed on) or time spent correcting mistakes.

David Maister coined the acronym OTSU ("opportunity to screw up") to stress the importance of thinking through all the things that might go wrong in the delivery of a particular service[4]. It's only by identifying all the possible OTSUs associated with a particular process that service managers can put together a delivery system that is designed to avoid such problems.

Fail-Proofing to Design Fail Points Out of Service Processes

⟳ LO 4

Understand how to use fail-proofing to design fail points out of service processes.

Once fail points have been identified, careful analysis of the reasons for failure in service processes is necessary. This analysis often reveals opportunities for fail-proofing certain activities in order to reduce or even eliminate the risk of errors[5].

One of the most useful Total Quality Management (TQM) methods in manufacturing is the application of *poka-yokes* or fail-safe methods to prevent errors in the manufacturing processes. The term poka-yoke is derived from the Japanese words *poka* (inadvertent errors) and *yokeru* (to prevent). Richard Chase and Douglas Steward introduced this concept to fail-safe service processes[6]. Server poka-yokes ensure that service employees do things correctly, as asked, in the right order and at the right speed. Examples include surgeons whose surgical instrument trays have individual indentations for each instrument. For a given operation, all of the instruments are nested in the tray so it is clear if the surgeon has not removed all instruments from the patient before closing the incision (*Figure 8.9*).

Some service firms use poka-yokes to design frequently occurring service failures out of the service processes, and to ensure that certain steps or standards in the customer–staff interaction are followed. A bank ensures eye contact by requiring tellers to record the customer's eye color on a checklist at the start of a transaction. Some firms place mirrors at the exits of staff areas and frontline staff can then automatically check their appearance before greeting a customer. At one restaurant, servers place round coasters in front of those diners who have ordered a decaffeinated coffee and square coasters in front of the others, and Starbucks barristers are trained to repeat their customers' orders to ensure that the correct coffee is served.

Designing poka-yokes is part art and part science as most of the procedures seem trivial, but this is actually a key advantage of this method. A three-step approach for effectively using poka-yokes includes systematically collecting data on problem occurrence, analyzing the root causes, and establishing preventive solutions. We describe this process in the context of preventing failures caused by customers in *Service Insights 8.3* later in this chapter.

Setting Service Standards and Targets

⟲ LO 5

Know how to set service standards and performance targets for customer service processes.

The service blueprint, combined with discussions with customers and frontline employees, helps firms to see which service and process attributes are important to customers at each touchpoint. Through both formal research and on-the-job experience, service managers can learn the nature of customer expectations at each step in the process. As outlined in Chapter 2, customers' expectations range across a spectrum — referred to as the zone of tolerance — from desired service (an ideal) to a threshold level of merely adequate service.

Those aspects of the service process that require the attention of management (i.e., attributes that are most important to customers and most difficult to manage) should be the basis for setting standards. Here, service providers should design standards for each step sufficiently high to satisfy and even delight customers; if that's not possible, then they will need to modify customer expectations. These standards might include time parameters, the script for a technically correct performance, and prescriptions for appropriate style and demeanor. Our restaurant blueprint shows key standards for each touch point. As the axiom goes, "What is not measured is not managed", standards must be expressed in ways that permit objective measurement. Process performance needs to be monitored against standards, and compliance targets need to be determined. Importantly, even soft and intangible (but important) service attributes need to be made measurable. This is often achieved through using service process indicators that try to capture the essence of, or at least approximate, these important attributes.

For example, in a retail banking context, the attribute "responsiveness" can be operationalized as "processing time to approve a loan application". Service standards are then ideally based on customer expectations and policy decisions which, in turn, are based on how these expectations can be met cost effectively. In cases where standards do not meet customer needs, expectations need to be managed (e.g., when dealing with exceptional cases, expected application approval times can be communicated by service employees verbally).

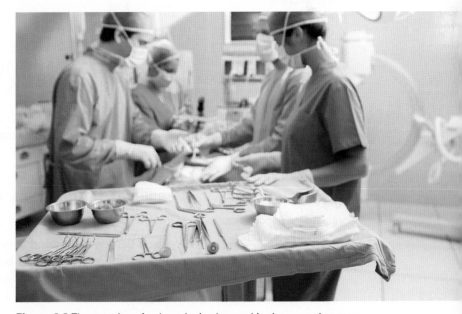

Figure 8.9 The practice of poka-yoke is observed in the operating room

Finally, performance targets define specific process and/or team performance targets (e.g., 80% of all applications within 24 hours) for which team leaders will be held accountable for. *Figure 8.10* shows the relationship between indicators, standards, and targets.

The distinction between standards and performance targets is important. As they are subsequently used for evaluating staff, branch and/or team performance, it makes the setting of standards and targets highly sensitive and political. By separating standards and targets, the firm can be "hard" about reflecting customer expectations in the performance standards, but "realistic" about what the teams actually can deliver.

In practice, management can stand firm on setting the right standards (i.e., according to customer needs and expectations), and go easy on negotiating performance targets that reflect operational reality (i.e., it may not be possible to consistently achieve the standards). This separation of standards and targets can be important for three reasons. First, the correct (i.e., customer-driven) standards get communicated to and internalized by the organization. Second, when implemented well, process owners and department or branch managers will, over time, raise their performance levels through continuous and incremental improvements to bring them more in line with customer expectations. Third, it facilitates buy-in and support for the (tough) service standards as it also provides latitude to management and staff[7].

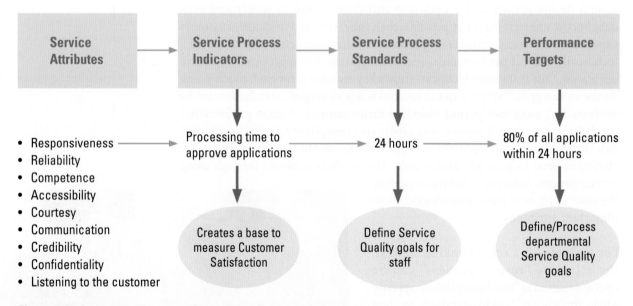

Figure 8.10 Setting standards and targets for customer service processes

⊃ **LO 6**

Appreciate the importance of consumer perceptions and emotions in service process design.

Consumer Perceptions and Emotions in Service Process Design

As Jason Barger, author and consultant, said: "People will forget what you said, people will forget what you do, but people will never forget how you made them feel". Therefore, service processes also need to be designed[8] with emotional intelligence.

Sriram Dasu and Richard Chase highlighted key principles about sequencing service encounters based on their in-depth research in designing emotionally smart processes[9]:

1. **Start strong.** Ideally, service firms should try to provide consistently high performance at each step. In reality, however, many service performances are inconsistent. Nevertheless, it is always important to start and finish strong. The opening scenes of a service drama are particularly important because customers' first impressions can affect their evaluations of quality during the later stages of the service delivery. Perceptions of their service experiences tend to be cumulative. If a few things go badly at the outset, customers may simply walk out. Even if they stay, they may now be looking for other things that aren't quite right. On the other hand, if the first few steps go well, their zone of tolerance may increase so they are more willing to overlook minor mistakes later on in the service performance.

2. **Build an improving trend.** People in general like things to keep moving in a positive direction. Thus, a service encounter that is perceived to start at an adequate level and then builds up in quality is generally rated better than one that starts well but declines at the end[10].

3. **Create a peak.** If you want to improve the perception of your service, you are better off making one step sensational and the other steps merely adequate. Customers tend to remember the peak! For example, the Sea World in Orlando could spend more money on various attractions, but the thing that counts — the signature Shamu the Whale show — must be done to perfection.

4. **Get bad experiences over with early.** Unpleasant news (e.g., about delays), discomfort (e.g., as part of medical treatments), unpleasant tasks (e.g., completing registration forms), and unavoidable long waits should be early in the experience, not at the end. This way, customers avoid the dread of pain or aggravation, and these negative aspects of the experience are less likely to dominate the memory of the entire service encounter.

5. **Segment pleasure, combine pain.** Since an event is perceived as longer when it is segmented or broken up into separate steps, service processes should extend the feeling of pleasurable experiences by dividing them and combining unpleasant experiences into a single event as far as possible.

6. **Finish strong.** Performance standards should not be allowed to fall off toward the end of service delivery. Rather, the finish should be strong — think of rock concerts which always conclude with big hits, comedians who save their best jokes for the end, and fireworks close with an amazing array of colors lighting the sky and a deafening finale. Ending on a high note is an important aspect of every service encounter, even if it is just a cheerful and affirmative: "Have a nice day!"

7. **Emotionprints.** In order to manage the customer experience well and implement the principles for sequencing service processes, firms can also map the expected associated emotions at each stage of the service processes. Flowcharts that describe how customers feel are called emotionprints. For example, it can be anticipated that expectant mothers will feel happy and excited when they first see the ultrasound photo of their baby (*Figure 8.11*). On the other hand, they may also be anxious during a test for abnormalities in a fetus. Hence, hospitals can anticipate common customer emotions at each step in a process and train their staff to react accordingly. An attitude of celebration would include cheering and applauding. On the other hand, faced with an emotionally negative situation in the service process, staff could show compassion, listen attentively and speak softly[11].

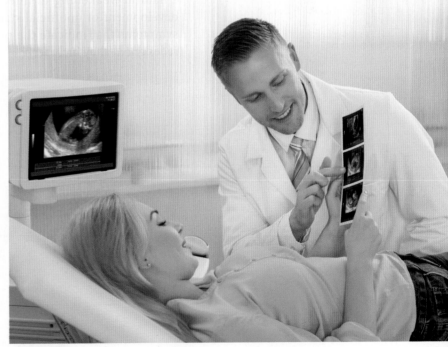

Figure 8.11 A doctor rejoices together with an expectant mother

Finally, our restaurant example was deliberately chosen to illustrate a familiar high-contact, people-processing service. However, many possession-processing services (such as repair or maintenance) and information-processing services (such as insurance or accounting) involve far less contact with customers, because much of the action takes place back-stage. In these situations, a failure committed front-stage is likely to be viewed even more seriously by customers as it represents a higher proportion of the customer's service encounters with a company. Furthermore, the firm has fewer subsequent opportunities to create a favorable impression.

⊃ **LO 7**
Explain the necessity for service process redesign.

SERVICE PROCESS REDESIGN

Service processes become outdated over time as changes in technology, customer needs, added service features, new service offerings, and even changes in legislation make existing processes inefficient or irrelevant. Mitchell T. Rabkin MD, former president of Boston's Beth Israel Hospital (now Beth Israel-Deaconess Medical Center, a teaching hospital of Harvard Medical School), characterized the problem as "institutional rust" and declared: "Institutions are like steel beams — they tend to rust. What was once smooth, shiny and nice tends to become rusty[12]". He suggested two main reasons for this deterioration of processes. The first involves changes in the external environment that make existing practices obsolete, and thus, require the redesign of underlying processes — or even the creation of brand-new processes — in order for the organization to remain relevant and responsive. In healthcare, such changes may reflect new forms of competition, legislation, technology, health insurance policies, and evolving customer needs (*Figure 8.12*).

The second reason for institutional rusting occurs internally. Often, it reflects a natural weakening of internal processes, creeping bureaucracy, or the development of unofficial standards (*Service Insights 8.1*). There are many symptoms that indicate the processes are not working well and need to be redesigned. They include:

Figure 8.12 Healthcare can be redesigned to better meet customers' needs

SERVICE INSIGHTS 8.1
Rooting Out Unofficial Standards in a Hospital

One of the distinctive characteristics of Mitchell T. Rabkin's 30-year tenure as president of Boston's Beth Israel Hospital[13] was his policy of routinely visiting all areas of the hospital. He usually did so unannounced and in a low-key fashion. No one working at the hospital was surprised to see Dr. Rabkin drop by at almost any time of the day or night. His natural curiosity gave him unparalleled insights into how effectively service procedures were working and the subtle ways in which things could go wrong. As the following story reveals, he discovered that there is often a natural deterioration of messages over time.

One day, I was in the EU (emergency unit), chatting with a house officer (physician) who was treating a patient with asthma. He was giving her medication through an intravenous drip. I looked at the formula for the medication and asked him, "Why are you using this particular cocktail?" "Oh," he replied, "that's hospital policy." Since I was certain that there was no such policy, I decided to investigate.

What had happened went something like this. A few months earlier, Resident (physician) A says to Intern B, who is observing her treat a patient: "This is what I use for asthma." On the next month's rotation, Intern B says to new Resident C: "This is what Dr. A uses

for asthma." The following month, Resident C says to Intern D, "This is what we use for asthma." And finally, within another month, Intern D is telling Resident E, "It's hospital policy to use this medication."

As a result of conversations like these, well-intentioned but unofficial standards keep cropping up. It's a particular problem in a place like this, which isn't burdened by an inhuman policy manual where you must look up the policy for everything you do. We prefer to rely on people's intelligence and judgment and limit written policies to overall, more general issues. One always has to be aware of the growth of institutional rust and to be clear about what is being done and why it is being done.

- A lot of information exchange is needed with the customer and between different service units as the data available is not useful.

- A high ratio of checking or control activities to value-adding activities.

- Increased processing of exceptions.

- Growing number of customer complaints about inconvenient and unnecessary procedures.

Service Process Redesign Should Improve Both Quality and Productivity

Managers in charge of service process redesign projects should look for opportunities to achieve a quantum leap in both productivity and service quality at the same time[14]. *Service Insights 8.2* shows how Singapore's National Library Board did just that.

⮞ LO 8
Understand how service process redesign can help improve both service quality and productivity.

In this digital age, libraries have suffered from reduced usage. The National Library Board of Singapore (NLB) has had to work hard to change people's views of the library being a place with rows of shelves full of old books and unfriendly staff. NLB transformed its library services[15] through the clever use of the latest technologies to expand its services, go virtual, encourage the use of its libraries, and promote lifelong learning for its members, all while dramatically increasing productivity. At the core of that transformation was the radical redesign of its service.

One of the many examples of how NLB used advanced technology to redesign processes is its electronic library management system (ELiMS) which is based on radio frequency identification (RFID). In fact, NLB was the first public library in the world to prototype RFID, an electronic system for automatically identifying items. It uses RFID tags, or transponders contained in smart labels consisting of a silicon chip and coiled antenna. They receive and respond to radio frequency queries from an RFID transceiver, which enables remote automatic storage, retrieval, and sharing of information. Unlike barcodes which need to be manually scanned, RFID simply broadcasts its presence and automatically sends data about the item to electronic readers. This technology is already in use in mass transit cashless ticketing systems, ski resort lift passes, and security badges for controlled access to buildings.

NLB installed RFID tags in over 10 million of its books, making it one of the largest users of RFID tags in the world. After redesigning the processes with RFID, customers don't have to spend time waiting anymore; they can check out the book themselves using the self-service kiosks, and books can be returned simply at any book drop at any library in its system. From the outside, the book drop looks like an ATM, but with a large hole covered by a flap. A user simply places the book in the box below the flap, the book is scanned using RFID, and a message on the screen instantly confirms that the book has been recorded as "returned" in the user's account.

NLB recently introduced self-service reservation lockers at one of its library branches that allow its users to self-collect their loaned items booked online. The system will trigger an email or text message notification to the user that the books have been deposited into the locker. After the user has collected the item, the reservation locker will communicate to the back-end system to register the loan.

To further enhance convenience and productivity, NLB has been moving toward completely side-stepping the handling of physical books — library members can now download some 800,000 e-books and 600 e-magazines for free from its website. Another recent innovation was a dispensing machine for some of its most popular books.

And what are the results of NLB's rigorous redesigning of service processes? Highly satisfied users, a world-class library highly-regarded by librarians from around the world, and it is featured in case studies at top business schools such as Harvard Business School and INSEAD.

Examining service blueprints is an important step in identifying such opportunities and then redesigning the ways in which tasks are performed. Redesign efforts typically focus on achieving the following four key objectives, and ideally, redesign efforts should achieve all four simultaneously:

1. Reduced number of service failures.

2. Reduced cycle time from customer initiation of a service process to its completion.

3. Enhanced productivity.

4. Increased customer satisfaction.

Service process redesign often involves reconstruction, rearrangement, and substitution of service processes. These efforts typically include[16]:

- **Examining the service blueprint with key stakeholders.** By closely examining blueprints of existing services, managers can identify problems in a service process and discover ways to improve it. Each of the stakeholders in a process (i.e., customers, frontline employees, support staff, and IT teams) should be invited to review the blueprint with the purpose of brainstorming for ideas on how to improve the process. This involves identification of missing or unnecessary steps and changes in sequence. Stakeholders also highlight ways in which developments in information technology, equipment, and new methods offer advantages.

For example, Avis does research each year on what factors car renters care about the most. The company breaks down the car rental process into more than 100 incremental steps, including making reservations, finding the pickup counter, getting to the car, driving it, returning it, paying the bill, and so forth. Because Avis knows customers' key concerns, it claims it can quickly identify ways to improve their satisfaction while also driving the firm's productivity. What travelers most desire is to get their rental car quickly and drive away, so the firm has designed its processes to achieve that goal. "We're constantly making little enhancements around the edges," says Scott Deaver, the company's then-Executive Vice President for Marketing. Obviously, Avis is living up to its tagline, "We Try Harder", which the company has employed for some 40 years. "It's not a slogan," says Deaver, "it's in the DNA of the place."

- **Eliminating non-value adding steps.** Often, activities at the front-end and backend processes of services can be streamlined with the goal of focusing on the benefit-producing part of the service encounter. The outcomes of such process redesigns typically include increased productivity and customer satisfaction at the same time.

For example, a customer wanting to rent a car is not interested in filling out forms, processing payment, or waiting for the returned car to be checked. Service redesign tries to eliminate such steps that customers view as non-value adding. Now, some car rental companies allow customers to rent a car online and pick it up from a designated car park, where a large electronic board lists the name of the customer, the car, and the parking lot numbers. The key is in the car, and the only interaction with a car rental employee is at the exit when driving the car out of the car park where the customer's driving license is checked and the contract is signed (including the customer confirming the condition of the car). When returning the car, it is simply parked at an allocated area at the rental company's car park, the key is dropped into a safe deposit box, the final bill is deducted from a predetermined customer credit card and emailed to the billing address, and the customer does not have to come into contact with service personnel.

- **Addressing bottlenecks in the process.** Bottlenecks and resulting customer waits are a feature of many service processes.[17] It is the step in the service process with the lowest throughput rate that determines the effective capacity of the entire process. For an efficient process, ideally all the steps should have the same capacity so that none of the stations form a bottleneck or is idle. The objective is to design a balanced process in which the processing times of all the steps are approximately the same, and consumers "flow" smoothly through the process without having to wait at any one step.

Determining the processing time and capacity for each step in the blueprint allows one to see the actual capacity available in each step. One way to identify bottlenecks is to simply observe where customers have to wait. Once bottlenecks are identified, management can address them by devoting more and better resources, and/or redesigning the process and its tasks to increase capacity (see also Chapter 9 "Balancing Demand and Capacity" for other ways to manage service capacity).

- **Shifting to self-service.** Significant productivity and sometimes even service quality gains can be achieved by increasing self-service (*Figure 8.13*). For example, decades ago, FedEx already aimed and succeeded in shifting more and more of its transactions from its call centers to its website, thus reducing the number of employees in its call centers by tens of thousands of people[18]. Businesses are also taking advantage of smartphones and tablets to shift to self-service. One example is Fish & Co., an innovative seafood restaurant chain in Southeast Asia and the Middle East which replaced its menu with an iPad so that customers can perform self-service ordering. An app shows all the delicious food available with lots of drilldown information if desired, and allows diners to send their orders directly to the kitchen. At the backend, the app links to the restaurant's point-of-sale system to complete the order. Customers can have fun by connecting to social media websites like Facebook and sharing their meal orders and comments with their friends. The app also has features that up-sell menu items and combine dishes with recommended side orders[19].

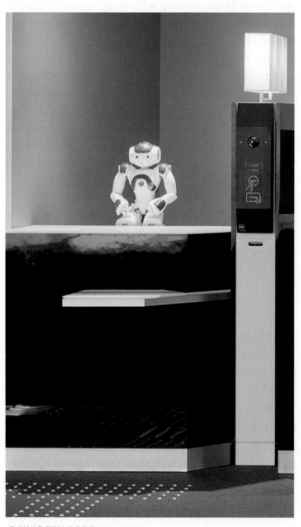

Although not self-service in the traditional sense, robots will increasingly be deployed to serve customers, and customers need to feel comfortable interacting with robots in very much the same way they learned to interact with ATMs and websites. For example, the Bank of Tokyo Mitsubishi UFJ in Tokyo will use robots to greet their customers, answer basic questions, and guide them to the correct service counter. Nao, a 58-centimeter-tall robot model, can analyze customers' facial expressions and behaviors, and answer the most basic questions related to customer-service. Bank spokesman Kazunobu Takahara said: "We can ramp up communication with our customers by adding a tool like this." The robot costs around $8,000, a fraction of the costs of having frontline employees performing these tasks, and it can speak up to 19 languages in preparation for the Tokyo 2020 Olympics[20]!

Figure 8.13 Here is a look at Nao, the 58-centimeter-tall humanoid robot that can analyze customers' facial expressions and behaviors, and answer the most basic questions related to customer-service

CUSTOMER PARTICIPATION IN SERVICE PROCESSES

LO 9
Understand the levels of customer participation in service processes.

Service process redesign for productivity and efficiency often calls for customers to become more involved in the delivery of the service. Blueprinting helps to specify the role of customers and to identify the extent of contact between them and service providers.

Levels of Customer Participation

Customer participation refers to the actions and resources supplied by customers during service production, including mental, physical, and even emotional inputs[21]. Some degree of customer participation in service delivery is unavoidable in many services that involve real-time contact between customers and providers. However, the extent of such participation varies widely and can be divided into three broad levels[22].

Figure 8.14 Possession-processing services have little customer involvement

Low Participation Level. With a low participation level, employees and systems do all the work. Service products tend to be standardized. In situations where customers come to the service factory, all that is needed is the customers' physical presence. Examples include visiting a movie theater or taking a bus. In possession-processing services, such as routine cleaning or maintenance, customers can remain entirely uninvolved with the process apart from providing access to service providers and making payment (*Figure 8.14*).

Moderate Participation Level. With a moderate participation level, customers' inputs are required to assist the firm in creating and delivering the service, and in providing a degree of customization. These inputs may include the provision of information, personal effort, or even physical possessions. When getting their hair washed and cut, customers must let the stylist know what they want and cooperate during the different steps in the process. If a client wants an accountant to prepare a tax return, she must first pull together information and physical documentation that the accountant can use to prepare the return correctly and then be prepared to respond to any questions that the latter may have.

Figure 8.15 Yoga classes are services that require high participation from the customer

High Participation Level. With a high participation level, customers work actively with the provider to co-produce the service. Service cannot be created without the customer's active participation (*Figure 8.15*). In fact, if customers fail to assume this role effectively and don't perform certain mandatory tasks, they will jeopardize the quality of the service outcome. Marriage counseling and educational services fall into this category. In health-related services, especially those related to the improvement of the patient's physical condition, such as rehabilitation or weight loss, customers work under professional supervision. Here, the patient has to play an active part to help, perhaps by closely following a dietary and exercise plan provided by the doctor. Successful delivery of many B2B services require customers and providers to work together closely as members of a team, such as in management consulting and supply chain management services.

Customers as Service Co-Creators

⊃ LO 10

Be familiar with the concept of service customers as "co-creators" and the implications of this perspective.

Customers are involved in service processes and can be thought of as service co-creators. Value is created when the customer and service providers interact during production, consumption and delivery of the service. This means that customers are actively participating in the process, and that their performance affects the quality and productivity of output. Therefore, service firms need to look at how customers themselves can contribute effectively to value creation, and firms need to educate and train customers so that they have the skills and motivation needed to perform their tasks well[23].

Reducing Service Failures Caused by Customers

In addition to educating customers, poka-yokes can be used to develop systems that make customers perform their roles effectively in service processes. Stephen Tax, Mark Colgate, and David Bowen found that customers cause about one-third of all service problems[24]. Therefore, firms should focus on preventing customer failures as is described in *Service Insights 8.3*.

SERVICE INSIGHTS 8.3

A Three-Step Approach to Preventing Customer Failures

Fail-safe methods (or poka-yokes) need to be designed not only for employees but also for customers, especially when customers participate actively in the creation and delivery processes. Customer poka-yokes focus on preparing the customer for the encounter (including getting them to bring the right materials for the transaction and to arrive on time, if applicable), understanding and anticipating their role in the service transaction, and selecting the correct service or transaction.

A good way is to use the following three-step approach to prevent customer-generated failures:

1. Systematically collect information on the most common failure points.

2. Identify their root causes. It is important to note that an employee's explanation may not be the true cause. Instead, the cause must be investigated from the customer's point of view. Human causes of customer failure include lack of needed skills, failure to understand their role, and insufficient preparation. Some processes are complex and unclear. Other causes may include weaknesses in the design of the servicescape or self-service technology (e.g., "unfriendly" user machines and websites).

3. Create strategies to prevent the failures that have been identified. The five strategies listed below may need to be combined for maximum effectiveness.

   (a) Redesign the customer involvement in the process (e.g., redesign customers' role as well as processes). For example, aircraft lavatory doors must be locked in order for the lights to be switched on. ATMs use beepers so that customers do not forget to retrieve their cards at the end of their transaction. In future, customer identification with cards and PINs at ATMs are likely to be replaced by biometric identification

   (e.g., retina reading combined with voice recognition) and thereby designing lost card or forgotten PIN problems out of the process and increasing customer convenience.

   (b) Use technology. For example, some hospitals use automated systems that send short text messages or emails to patients to confirm and remind them of their appointments, and inform them on how to reschedule an appointment if required.

   (c) Manage customer behavior. For example, one may print dress code requests on invitations, send reminders of dental appointments, or print user guidelines on customer cards (e.g., "Please have your account and pin number ready before calling our service representatives").

   (d) Encourage "customer citizenship" (e.g., customers help one another to prevent failure, like in weight-loss programs).

   (e) Improve the servicescape. For example, many firms forget that customers need user-friendly directional signs to help them find their way around, failing which, they might become frustrated.

Helping customers to avoid failure can become a source of competitive advantage, especially when companies increasingly use self-service technologies (SST).

Source

Stephen S. Tax, Mark Colgate, and David E. Bowen (2006), "How to Prevent Customers from Failing," *MIT Sloan Management Review,* Vol. 47, Spring, pp. 30–38.

SELF-SERVICE TECHNOLOGIES

The ultimate form of involvement in service production is for customers to undertake a specific activity on their own, using facilities or systems provided by the service supplier. In effect, the customer's time and effort replaces that of a service employee. In the case of Internet- and app-based services, customers even provide their own terminals.

Consumers are faced with an array of self-service technologies (SSTs) that allow them to produce a service without direct service employee involvement[25]. SSTs include automated banking terminals, self-service scanning at supermarket checkouts, self-service gasoline pumps, and automated telephone systems such as phone banking, automated hotel checkout, self-service train ticketing machines (*Figure 8.16*), and numerous Internet- and app-based services.

Information-based services lend themselves particularly well to the use of SSTs and include not only supplementary services such as getting information, placing orders and reservations, and making payments, but also the delivery of core products in fields such as banking, research, entertainment, and self-paced education. Even consultation and sales processes, traditionally carried out face-to-face, have been transformed into self-service processes with the use of electronic recommendation agents (*Service Insights 8.4*)[26].

Many companies have developed strategies designed to encourage customers to serve themselves through the Internet and apps. They hope to divert customers from using more expensive alternatives such as face-to-face contact with employees, use of intermediaries such as brokers and travel agents, or voice-to-voice telephony. Using service blueprints (*Figure 8.17*) helps to visualize and design self-service processes.

Increasingly, customers also help each other in peer-to-peer problem solving, facilitated by online brand communities and firm-hosted platforms. Research has shown that encouraging customers to help themselves by posting their questions, and to help others by responding to peer questions reduces the resources a firm has to expand on traditional customer support services. Promoting peer-to-peer customer interactions is a strategic lever to increase the efficiency and effectiveness of a firm's support service[27].

Nevertheless, not all customers take advantage of SSTs. Matthew Meuter and his colleagues observe: "For many firms, often the challenge is not managing the technology but rather getting consumers to try the technology[28]."

Figure 8.16 Tourists appreciate easy-to-understand instructions when traveling abroad and making payment for train tickets

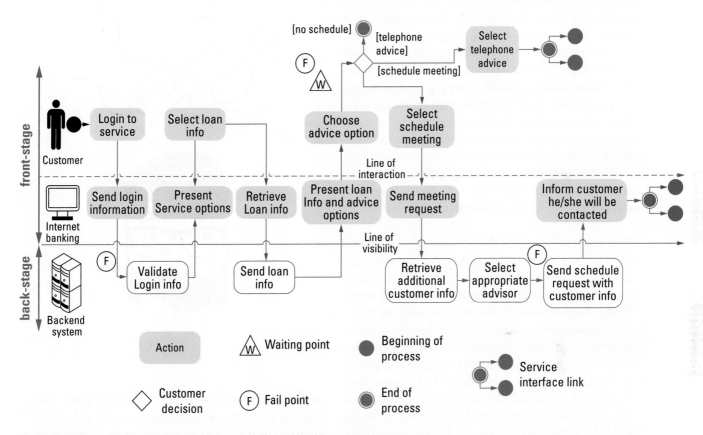

Figure 8.17 Blueprint for a self-service Internet-delivered banking process

Source

Lia Patrício, Raymond P. Fisk, João Falcão e Cunha, and Larry Constantine (2011), "Multilevel Service Design: From Customer Value Constellation to Service Experience Blueprinting," *Journal of Service Research*, Vol. 14, No. 2, pp. 180–200; Reprinted by Permission of SAGE Publications, Inc.

SERVICE INSIGHTS 8.4

Making Electronic Recommendation Agents More Effective

Consumers often face a bewildering array of choices when purchasing goods and services from online vendors. One way in which these "e-tailers" try to assist consumers is to offer electronic recommendation agents as part of their service. Recommendation agents are low-cost "virtual salespeople" designed to help customers make their selections from among large numbers of competing offerings. These recommendation agents generate rank-ordered lists according to predicted consumer preferences. However, research by Lerzan Aksoy shows that many existing recommendation agents rank options in different ways than customers do. For example, they weigh product attributes differently from customers, and they use alternative decision strategies that do not match the simple rules of thumb used by customers.

The research simulated the selection of a cell phone from among 32 alternatives, described on a website as each having differing features relating to price, weight, talk time, and standby time. The study results demonstrated that it helps consumers to use a recommendation agent that thinks like them, either in terms of attribute weights or decision strategies. When the ways in which agents work are completely dissimilar, consumers may actually be worse off than if they had simply used a randomly ordered list of options. Even though the subjects in this research tended to listen to the agent's recommendations, those who felt it had a dissimilar decision strategy and dissimilar attribute weights from their own, were less likely to come back to the website, recommend it to friends, or believe that the site had met their expectations well.

In conclusion, to make recommendation agents add value to the customer and enhance sales and repeat business, firms need to closely understand their customers' decision-making strategies, attributes, and attribute weightings (refer to Chapter 2 on multi-attribute models in consumer decision making, and Chapter 3 on determinant attributes).

Source

Lerzan Aksoy, Paul N. Bloom, Nicholas H. Lurie, and Bruce Cooil (2006), "Should Recommendation Agents Think Like People?" *Journal of Service Research*, Vol. 8, May, pp. 297–315.

Customer Benefits and Adoption of Self-Service Technology

Given the significant investment in time and money required for firms to design, implement, and manage SSTs, it's critical for service marketers to understand how consumers decide between using an SST option and relying on a human provider. Multiple attitudes drive customer intentions to use a specific SST, including overall attitudes toward related service technologies, attitudes toward the specific service firm and its employees, and importantly, the overall perceived benefits, convenience, costs, and ease of use customers see in using an SST[29]. That is, firms need to recognize that SSTs present both advantages and disadvantages for their customers. Key advantages of using SSTs include[30]:

- Greater convenience, including time savings, faster service, flexibility of timing (e.g., through 24/7 availability), and flexibility of location (e.g., many ATMs). Customers love SSTs when they bail them out of difficult situations, often because SST machines are conveniently located and accessible 24/7. As *Figure 8.18* shows, a website is as close as the nearest computer or smartphone, making this option much more accessible than the company's physical sites. If you need cash urgently, wouldn't you be glad that you can obtain cash at one of the many ATMs in town rather than having to hunt for a bank branch?

- Greater control over service delivery, more information, and higher perceived level of customization.

- Lower prices and fees.

Success at the customer interface requires an understanding of what target customers want from an interaction. Sometimes a well-designed SST can deliver better service than a human being. Said one customer about the experience of purchasing convenience store items from a new model of automated vending machine, "A guy in the store can make a mistake or give you a hard time, but not the machine. I definitely prefer the machine[31]." Many SSTs enable users to get detailed information and complete transactions faster than they could through face-to-face or telephone contact. Experienced travelers rely on SSTs to save time and effort at airports, rental car facilities, and hotels. A Wall Street Journal article summarized the trend — "Have a Pleasant Trip: Eliminate Human Contact[32]." In short, many customers like SSTs when they work well and especially when customers have to use them frequently.

Customers may derive fun, enjoyment, and even spontaneous delight from SST usage. For example, children take a lot of delight in doing self-scanning at supermarket checkouts or making orders on tablets in restaurants as they find this activity enjoyable.

However, there are always some consumers who feel uncomfortable with SSTs, feel anxious and stressed, or may view service encounters as social experiences and prefer to deal with people. Even after an initial trial, not all customers will continue using an SST. It is important that the first trial is satisfying, and customers feel confident that they can use the SST effectively in the future. If this is not the case, customers are likely to go back to using traditional, frontline employee-provided services. Some retail banks, for example, use "greeters" in their branches to assist customers in migrating to in-branch SSTs. This not only helps customers to overcome technology anxiety and ensures a successful first trial, but also builds confidence in their ability to use the SST again[33].

In sum, customers love SSTs when they are easy to use, perform better and are cheaper than the alternative of being served by a service employee. However, not all customers are comfortable with using SSTs.

Figure 8.18 A man pays for a transaction with his mobile phone at an Internet kiosk. This makes visiting companies online more convenient than going to the actual site

Customer Disadvantages and Barriers of Adoption of Self-Service Technology

Customers hate SSTs when they fail. Users get angry when they find that self-service machines are out of service, their PIN numbers are rejected, websites are down, or tracking numbers do not work. Even when SSTs do work, customers get frustrated by poorly designed technologies that make service processes difficult to understand and use. A common complaint is the difficulty in navigating one's way around a website or completing online registrations and forms that keep rejecting their entries.

Users also get frustrated when they themselves mess up, due to errors such as forgetting their passwords, failing to provide information as requested, or simply hitting the wrong button (*Figure 8.19*). Self-service logically implies that customers can cause their own dissatisfaction. However, even when it is the customers' own fault, they may still blame the service provider for not providing a simpler and more user-friendly system and then, on the next occasion, revert to the traditional human-based system[34].

A key problem with SSTs is that so few of them include effective service recovery systems. In too many instances, when the process fails, there is no simple way to solve the problem on the spot. Typically, customers are forced to telephone, email or make a personal visit to the service company to solve the problem, which may be exactly what they were trying to avoid in the first place!

In sum, the challenge for the service firm is to design SSTs to be as "idiot-proof" as possible, mitigate common customer errors, use customer poka-yokes, and even design service recovery processes for customers so that they can help themselves should things go wrong[35].

Figure 8.19 Customers feel frustrated when they get stuck in poorly designed online self-service processes

Assessing and Improving SSTs

Mary Jo Bitner suggests that managers should put their firms' SSTs to the test by asking the following basic questions[36]:

- **Does the SST work reliably?** Firms must make sure that SSTs work as promised and the design is user-friendly. Southwest Airlines' online ticketing system has set a high standard for simplicity and reliability. It boasts the highest percentage of online ticket sales of any airline — a clear evidence of customer acceptance!

- **Is the SST better than the interpersonal alternative?** If it doesn't save time or provide ease of access, cost savings, or some other benefit, then customers will continue to use the familiar interpersonal choice. Amazon.com's success reflects its efforts to create a highly personalized yet efficient alternative to visiting a retail store[37], which has become the most preferred way of browsing and buying books today. The fast growth of e-books will only accelerate this trend.

- **If the SST fails, are systems in place to recover the service?** It's critical for firms to provide systems, structures, and recovery technologies that will enable prompt service recovery when things go wrong (*Figure 8.20*). Most banks display a phone number at their ATMs, giving customers direct access to a 24-hour customer service center where they can talk to a "real person" if they have questions or run into difficulties. Supermarkets that have installed self-service checkout lanes usually assign one employee to monitor the lanes; this practice combines security with customer assistance. In telephone-based service systems, well-designed voicemail menus include an option for customers to reach a customer service representative.

Figure 8.20 As a fail-safe measure, departmental stores normally have employees on standby near self-checkout lanes to assist if there are problems

Designing a website to be easy to use and virtually failure-proof is no easy task and can be very expensive, but it is through such investments that companies can encourage self-service and create loyal users. *Service Insights 8.5* describes the emphasis on user-friendliness of CarePages.

Managing Customers' Reluctance to Change

Increasing the customers' participation level in a service process, or shifting the process entirely to self-service using SSTs, requires the firm to change customer behavior. This is often a difficult task as customers resent being forced to use SST[38]. *Service Insights 8.6* identifies ways of addressing customer resistance to change, particularly when the innovation is a radical one.

LO 12
Know how to manage customers' reluctance to change their behaviors in service processes, including the adoption of SSTs.

SERVICE INSIGHTS 8.5
CarePages Creates an Exceptional User Experience

When his sister's five-day old baby, Matthew, underwent surgery at the University of Michigan Medical Center in early 1998 to correct a life-threatening heart defect, Mark Day was more than a thousand miles away at Stanford, studying for a PhD in engineering. Feeling isolated, knowing nothing about the heart, and wanting to do something useful, Mark turned to medical information on the Internet, which was just beginning to hit its stride. Within a few weeks, he had created a simple website that family and friends could access. He edited the information he had gathered and uploaded

Copyright © 2016, CarePages, Inc.

it to the site, together with bulletins on Matthew's condition and how he was responding to treatment. "It was a very simple site," Mark declared later. "If I had paid somebody else to do it for me, it probably wouldn't have cost more than a few hundred dollars." To minimize the need for emailing, Mark added a bulletin board so that people could send messages to his sister Sharon and her husband, Eric.

To everyone's surprise, the site proved exceptionally popular. News spread by word-of-mouth and the site recorded hundreds of daily visitors, with more than 200 different people leaving messages for the family.

Two years and three operations later, Matthew was a happy healthy toddler. His parents, Eric and Sharon Langshur decided to create a company, TLContact. com, to commercialize Mark's concept as a service for patients and their families. They invited Mark to join the company as chief technology officer.

Recognizing that TLC's patient sites, known as CarePages, would be accessed by a wide array of individuals, many of whom would be under stress, Mark and his team placed a premium on ease of use. He commented: "It's very difficult to create a piece of software that's really user friendly. It takes an incredible amount of skill, effort, and time to develop something that's usable, functional, and scalable — meaning that it can be expanded and built upon without failing." The total cost of creating the initial functioning website was close to half a million dollars. By 2015, CarePages is an online community with over a million unique visitors a month, coming together to share the challenges, hopes and triumphs of anyone facing a life-changing health event. CarePages.com offered a variety of resources and support tools for living a more compassionate life. Private-labeled CarePages websites were also offered by over 625 US and Canadian healthcare facilities. CarePages had a simple, singular mission — to ensure that no one faces a health challenge alone. Have a look at www. carepages.com on CarePage's services.

Source

Christopher Lovelock, "CarePages.com (A)" 2007; www.carepages.com, accessed May 4, 2015; www.carepages.com, accessed September 15, 2015.

SERVICE INSIGHTS 8.6
Managing Customers' Reluctance to Change

Customer resistance to changes in familiar processes and long-established behavior patterns can thwart attempts to improve productivity and even quality. The following six steps can help smooth the path of change.

1. **Develop customer trust.** It's more difficult to introduce productivity-related changes when people are distrustful of the initiator, as they often are in the case of large, seemingly impersonal institutions. Customers' willingness to accept change may be closely related to the degree of goodwill they bear toward the firm.

2. **Understand customers' habits and expectations.** People often get into a routine of using a particular service, with certain steps being taken in a specific sequence. In effect, they have their own individual service script or flowchart in mind. Innovations that disrupt deeply rooted routines are more likely to face resistance. Aligning new processes more closely with customers' habits and expectations enhances the chances of success.

3. **Pre-test new procedures and equipment.** To determine probable customer response to new procedures and equipment, marketing researchers can employ concept and laboratory testing and/or field testing. If service personnel are going to be replaced by automatic equipment, it's essential to create designs that customers of almost all types and backgrounds will find easy to use. Even the phrasing of instructions needs careful thought. Unclear or complex instructions may discourage customers with poor reading skills.

4. **Publicize the benefits.** Introduction of self-service equipment or procedures requires consumers to perform part of the task themselves. Although this additional "work" may be associated with such benefits as extended service hours, time savings, and (in some instances) monetary savings, these benefits are not necessarily obvious — they have to be promoted. Customers have to be informed about the innovation, their interest aroused, and specific benefits to customers clarified of using a new delivery system.

5. **Teach customers to use innovations and promote trial.** Assigning service personnel to demonstrate new equipment and answer questions — providing reassurance as well as educational assistance — is a key element in gaining acceptance of new procedures and technology. The costs of such demonstration programs can be spread across multiple outlets by moving staff members from one site to another if the innovation is rolled out sequentially across the various locations. For Web-based innovations, firms can consider to provide access to email, chat, or even telephone-based assistance. Promotional incentives such as price discounts, loyalty points, or lucky draws may also help to stimulate trial. Once customers have tried a self-service option (particularly an electronically-based one) and find that it works well, they will be more likely to use it regularly in the future.

6. **Monitor performance and continue to seek improvements.** Introducing quality and productivity improvements is an ongoing process, especially for SSTs. It is important to monitor utilization, frequency of transaction failures (and their fail points), and customer complaints over time. Service managers have to work hard to continuously improve SSTs and keep up the momentum so that SSTs can achieve their full potential and not left to become white elephants.

Once the nature of the changes has been decided, marketing communications can help prepare customers for the change, explaining the rationale, the benefits, and what customers will need to do differently in the future.

CONCLUSION

In this chapter, we emphasized the importance of designing and managing service processes which are central in creating the service product and significantly shaping the customer experience. We covered in detail blueprinting as a powerful tool to understand, document, analyze, and improve service processes. Blueprinting helps to identify and reduce service fail points and provides important insights for service process redesign.

An important part of process design is to define the roles customers should play in the production of services. Their level of desired participation needs to be determined, and customers need to be motivated and taught to play their part in the service delivery to ensure customer satisfaction and firm productivity. The increasing importance of SSTs and strategies to increase their adoption were also discussed.

CHAPTER SUMMARY

LO1 From the customer's perspective, services are experiences. From the organization's perspective, services are the processes that are designed and managed to create the desired experience for customers. Processes are the underlying architecture of services.

LO2 Flowcharting is a technique for displaying the nature and sequence of the different steps in delivering a service to the customer. It is a simple way to visualize the total customer service experience. Blueprinting is a more complex form of flowcharting, specifying in detail how service processes are constructed, including what is visible to the customer and all that goes on in the back-office. Blueprints facilitate the detailed design and redesign of customer service processes.

LO3 A blueprint typically has the following design elements:

- The **front-stage activities** that map the overall customer experience, the desired inputs and outputs, and the sequence in which the delivery of that output should take place.
- The **physical evidence** the customer can see and use to assess service quality.
- The **line of visibility** clearly separates what customers experience and can see front-stage, and the back-stage processes customers can't see.
- The **back-stage activities** that must be performed to support a particular front-stage step.
- The **support processes and supplies** where support processes are typically provided by the information system, and supplies are needed for both front- and back-stage steps.
- **Fail points** are where there is a risk of things going wrong and affecting service quality. Fail points should be designed out of a process (e.g., via the use of poka-yokes), and firms should have backup plans for failures that are not preventable.
- Common **customer waits** in the process and points of potential excessive waits. These should then either be designed out of the process, or if that is not possible, firms can implement strategies to make waits less unpleasant.
- **Service standards and targets** should be established for each activity, reflecting customer expectations. This includes specific times to be set for the completion of each task and the acceptable wait between each customer activity.

LO4 A good blueprint identifies fail points where things can go wrong. Fail-safe methods, also called poka-yokes, can then be designed to prevent and/or recover such failures for both employees and customers. A three-step approach can be used to develop poka-yokes:
1. Collect information on the most common fail points.
2. Identify the root causes of those failures.
3. Create strategies to prevent the failures that have been identified.

LO5 Service blueprints help to set service standards that should be high enough to satisfy customers. As standards need to be measurable, important but subjective or intangible service attributes need to be operationalized. This can often be achieved through service process indicators that capture the essence or at least approximate these attributes. Once standards are decided, performance targets can be set.

LO6 Service processes need to be designed with emotional intelligence. Key principles about sequencing service include:

- Start strong. The opening scenes of a service drama are particularly important, because customers' first impressions can affect their evaluations of quality during later stages of service delivery.
- Build an improving trend. All things being equal, it is better to start a little lower and build a little higher than to start a little higher and fall off a little at the end.
- Create a peak. Customers tend to remember the peak!
- Get bad experiences over with earlier on so that negative aspects of the experience are less likely to dominate the memory of the entire service encounter.
- Segment pleasure but combine pain. Service processes should extend the feeling of pleasurable experiences by dividing them up throughout the experience, and combining unpleasant experiences into a single event.
- Finish strong. Ending on a high note is an important aspect of every service encounter, even if it is just a cheerful and affirmative "Have a nice day".

A tool that helps to manage customer emotions is emotionprints, which documents likely customer emotions at each stage of the service process. The objective is to manage the customer experience well.

LO7 Changes in technology, customer needs, and service offerings require customer service processes to be redesigned periodically. Symptoms indicating that a process is not working well include:
- A lot of information exchange is required; the data available is not useful.
- A high ratio of checking or control activities to value-adding activities.
- Increased processing of exceptions.
- Growing numbers of customer complaints about inconvenient and unnecessary procedures.

LO8 Service process redesign efforts aim to:
1. Reduce number of service failures.
2. Reduce cycle time.
3. Improve productivity.
4. Increase customer satisfaction.

Service process redesign includes reconstruction, rearrangement, or substitution of service processes. These efforts typically include:
- Examining the service blueprint with key stakeholders — customers, frontline employees, support staff and IT teams are invited to review the blueprint and to brainstorm for ideas on how to improve the process.
- Elimination of non-value adding steps.
- Reducing bottlenecks and balancing process capacity.
- Shifting to self-service.

LO9 Understand the levels of customer participation in service processes, which can range from low, to moderate and high.

LO10 Customers are often involved in service processes as co-producers and can therefore be thought of as "service co-creators". Their performance affects the quality and productivity of output. Therefore, service firms need to educate and train customers so that they have the skills and motivation needed to perform their tasks well.

LO11 The ultimate form of customer involvement is self-service. Most people welcome SSTs that offer more convenience (i.e., time savings, faster service, 24/7 availability, and more locations), cost savings, and better control, information, and customization. However, poorly designed technology and inadequate education in how to use SSTs can cause customers to reject SSTs.

Three basic questions can be used to assess the potential for success of an SST and to improve it:
- Does the SST work reliably?
- Is the SST better for customers compared to other service delivery alternatives?
- If the SST fails, are there systems in place to recover the service?

LO12 Increasing the customers' participation level in a service process or shifting the process entirely to self-service requires the firm to change customer behavior. There are six steps to guide this process and reduce customer reluctance to change:
- Develop customer trust.
- Understand customers' habits and expectations.
- Pretest new procedures and equipment.
- Publicize the benefits of changes.
- Teach customers to use innovations and promote trial.
- Monitor performance and continue to seek improvements.

Review Questions

1. How does blueprinting help us to better understand the service process from the perspective of the key actors (i.e., customers and the employees from different service departments and functional areas) in a serviced process?

2. What are the typical design elements of a service blueprint?

3. How can fail-safe methods be used to reduce service failures?

4. Why is it important to develop service standards and targets?

5. How can consumer perceptions and emotions be considered in the design of service processes?

6. Why is it necessary to periodically redesign service processes, and what are the typical symptoms of a service process that is not working well?

7. What are the four key objectives of service process redesign?

8. What efforts are typically involved in service process redesign?

9. Why does the customer's role as a cocreator need to be designed into service processes?

10. Explain what factors make customers like and dislike self-service technologies (SSTs).

11. How can you test whether an SST has the potential to be successful, and what can a firm do to increase its chances of customer adoption?

Application Exercises

1. Review the blueprint of the restaurant visit in *Figure 8.6*. Identify several possible "OTSUs" ("opportunity to screw up") for each step in the front-stage process. Consider possible causes underlying each potential failure and suggest ways to eliminate or minimize these problems.

2. Prepare a blueprint for a service you are familiar with. On completion, consider (a) the tangible cues or indicators of quality from the customers perspective, considering the line of visibility; (b) whether all steps in the process are necessary; (c) the extent to which standardization is possible and advisable throughout the process; (d) the location of potential fail points and how they could be designed out of the process and what service recovery procedures could be introduced; and (e) the potential measures of process performance.

3. Think about what happens in a doctor's office when a patient comes for a physical examination. How much participation is needed from the patient in order for the process to work smoothly? If a patient refuses to cooperate, how can that affect the process? What can the doctor do in advance to ensure the patient cooperates in the delivery of the process?

4. Review the tools and templates Coleman Associates used to redesign healthcare clinics at www. patientvisitredesign.com. How do these tools and templates map against the key learnings from this chapter. What additional insights can you gain for service process redesign in general?

5. Observe supermarket shoppers who use self-service checkout lanes, and compare them to those who use the services of a checker. What differences do you observe? How many of those conducting self-service scanning appear to run into difficulties, and how do they resolve their problems?

6. Identify three situations in which you use self-service delivery. For each situation, what is your motivation for using self-service delivery, rather than having service personnel do it for you?

7. What actions could a bank take to encourage more customers to bank by the Internet, through apps and the ATMs rather than visiting a branch?

8. Identify one website that is exceptionally user-friendly and another that is not. What are the factors that make for a satisfying user experience in the first instance, and a frustrating one in the second? Specify recommendations for improvements in the second website.

Endnotes

1   To analyze, improve and design end-to-end customer journey using bottom-up (data driven) and top down judgment driven approaches, see: Alex Rawson, Ewan Duncan, and Conor Jones (2013), "The Truth About Customer Experience: Touchpoints Matter, But It's the Full Journey that Really Counts," *Harvard Business Review*, Vol. 91, No. 9, pp. 90–98.

2   G. Lynn Shostack (1984), "Designing Services That Deliver," *Harvard Business Review*, January–February, pp. 133–39; Jane Kingman-Brundage (1989), "The ABCs of Service System Blueprinting," in M.J. Bitner and L. A. Crosby (eds.), *Designing a Winning Service Strategy.* Chicago: American Marketing Association; Lia Patrício, Raymond P. Fisk, and João Falcão Cunha (2008), "Designing Multi-Interface Service Experiences: The Service Experience Blueprint," *Journal of Service Research*, Vol. 10, No. 4, pp. 318–334.

   For an excellent approach to designing and mapping complex service systems, see: Lia Patrício, Raymond P. Fisk, João Falcão e Cunha, and Larry Constantine (2011), "Multilevel Service Design: From Customer Value Constellation to Service Experience Blueprinting," *Journal of Service Research*, Vol. 14, No. 2, pp. 180–200.

   An additional tool that helps to visualize service operations, processes and interactions involving networks of entities is the Process-Chain-Network (PCN) analysis, see: Scott E. Sampson (2012), "Visualizing Service Operations", *Journal of Service Research*, Vol. 15, No. 2, pp. 182–198.

3   Laurette Dubé-Rioux, Bernd H. Schmitt, and France Leclerc (1991), "Consumers' Affective Responses to Delays at Different Phases of a Service Delivery," *Journal of Applied Social Psychology*, Vol. 21, No. 10, pp. 810–820.

4   David Maister, now President of Maister Associates, coined the term OTSU ("opportunity to screw up") while teaching at Harvard Business School.

5   For descriptions of how poka-yokes can be used to improve business operations, see: Sameer Kumar, Brett Hudson and Josie Lowry (2010), "Consumer Purchase Process Improvements in E-tailing Operations," *International Journal of Productivity and Performance Management*, Vol. 59, No. 4, pp. 388–403; Sameer Kumar, Angelena Phillips and Julia Rupp (2009), "Using Six Sigma DMAIC to Design a High-quality Summer Lodge Operation," *Journal of Retail & Leisure Property*, Vol. 8, No. 3, pp. 173–191.

6   This section is based in part on Richard B. Chase and Douglas M. Stewart (1994), "Make Your Service Fail-Safe," *Sloan Management Review*, Vol. 35, Spring, pp. 35–44.

7   This section was adapted from Jochen Wirtz and Monica Tomlin (2000), "Institutionalizing Customer-driven Learning through Fully Integrated Customer Feedback Systems," *Managing Service Quality*, Vol. 10, No. 4, pp. 205–215.

8   Parts of this section were based on: Sriram Dasu and Richard B. Chase (2013), *The Customer Service Solution: Managing Emotions, Trust, and Control to Win Your Customer's Business.* New York: McGraw Hill. This book provides an excellent overview of designing service processes with emotional intelligence.

9   Adapted from: Sriram Dasu and Richard B. Chase (2013), *The Customer Service Solution: Managing Emotions, Trust, and Control to Win Your Customer's Business.* New York: McGraw Hill, pp. 134–135.

   We added the item "start strong" based on the following research: Eric J. Arnould and Linda L. Price (1993), "River Magic: Extraordinary Experience and the Extended Service Encounter," *Journal of Consumer Research*, Vol. 20, June, pp. 24–25; Richard B. Chase and Sriram Dasu (2014), "Experience Psychology – A Proposed New Subfield of Service Management," *Journal of Service Management*, Vol. 25, No. 5, pp. 574–577.

10 David E. Hansen and Peter J. Danaher (1999), "Inconsistent Performance during the Service Encounter: What's a Good Start Worth?" *Journal of Service Research*, Vol. 1, February, pp. 227–235; Richard B. Chase and Sriram Dasu (2001), "Want to Perfect Your Company's Service? Use Behavioral Science." *Harvard Business Review*, Vol. 79, June, pp. 79–84.

   A recent study also showed that a service failure at the end of an extended service encounter has a stronger impact on overall satisfaction than a failure earlier in the process; see: Ina Garnefeld and Lena Steinhoff (2013), "Primary versus Recency Effects in Extended Service Encounters," *Journal of Service Management*, Vol. 24, No. 1, pp. 64–81.

11 Sriram Dasu and Richard B. Chase (2010), "Designing the Soft Side of Customer Service," *MIT Sloan Management Review*, Vol. 52, No. 1, pp. 33–39.

12 Mitchell T. Rabkin, MD, cited in Christopher H. Lovelock (1994), *Product Plus.* New York: McGraw-Hill, pp. 354–355.

13 Christopher Lovelock (1994), *Product Plus*. New York: McGraw-Hill, p. 355.

14 See, for example, Michael Hammer and James Champy, *Reengineering the Corporation: A Manifesto for Business Revolution*. Rev. ed., New York: Harper Business.

For a nice documentation of a service process redesign cum introducing cross-functional teams, see: Agneta Larsson, Mats Johansson, Fredrik Bååthe, and Sanna Neselius (2012), "Reducing Throughput Time in a Service Organization by Introducing Cross-Functional Teams," *Production Planning & Control*, Vol. 23, No. 7, pp. 571–580.

15 Kah Hin Chai, Jochen Wirtz, and Robert Johnston (2009), "Using Technology to Revolutionize the Library Experience of Singaporean Readers," in Christopher Lovelock, Jochen Wirtz, and Patricia Chew, eds. *Essentials of Services Marketing*. Singapore: Prentice Hall, pp. 534–536; http://www.nlb.gov.sg, accessed May 4, 2015; Email interview with Lee Kee Siang, Chief Information Officer, NLB, conducted on June 5, 2015.

16 This section is partially based on Leonard L. Berry and Sandra K. Lampo (2000), "Teaching an Old Service New Tricks – The Promise of Service Redesign," *Journal of Service Research,* Vol. 2, No. 3, pp. 265–275. Berry and Lampo identified the five service redesign concepts: self-service, direct service, preservice, bundled service, and physical service. We expanded some of these concepts in this section to embrace more of the productivity enhancing aspects of process redesign.

17 Parts of this section were adapted from: Robert Johnston, Graham Clark, and Michael Shulver (2012), *Service Operations Management: Improving Service Delivery*. 4th ed., Essex, United Kingdom: Pearson Education.

18 Leonard L. Berry and Sandra K. Lampo (2000), "Teaching an Old Service New Tricks – The Promise of Service Redesign," *Journal of Service Research*, Vol. 2, No. 3, February, pp. 265–275.

19 Victoria Ho (2011), "Businesses Swallow the Tablet and Smile," *The Business Times*, March 14.

20 Atsuko Fukase (2015), "Robots to Greet Customers at Japanese Bank", *The Wall Street Journal*, January 13. http://blogs.wsj.com/japanrealtime/2015/01/13/robots-to-greet-customers-at-japanese-bank, accessed May 3.

21 Amy Risch Rodie and Susan Schultz Klein (2000), "Customer Participation in Services Production and Delivery," in T. A. Schwartz and D. Iacobucci, eds. *Handbook of Service Marketing and Management*. Thousand Oaks, CA: Sage Publications, pp. 111–125.

22 Mary Jo Bitner, William T. Faranda, Amy R. Hubbert, and Valarie A. Zeithaml (1997), "Customer Contributions and Roles in Service Delivery," *International Journal of Service Industry Management*, Vol. 8, No. 3, pp. 193–205.

23 There is a large body of literature dealing with customer co-creation of value. Key articles include: Atefeh Yazdanparast, Ila Manuj and Stephen M. Swartz (2010), "Co-creating Logistics Value: A Service-Dominant Logic Perspective," *The International Journal of Logistics Management*, Vol. 21, No. 3, pp. 375–403; Evert Gummesson, Robert F. Lusch and Stephen L. Vargo (2010), "Transitioning from Service Management to Service-Dominant Logic," *International Journal of Quality and Service Sciences*, Vol. 2, No. 1, pp. 8–22; Kristina Heinonen, Tore Strandvik and Karl-Jacob Mickelsson (2010), "A Customer-Dominant Logic of Service," *Journal of Service Management*, Vol. 21, No. 4, pp. 531–548; Robert F. Lusch, Stephen L. Vargo and Matthew O'Brien (2007), "Competing Through Service: Insights from Service Dominant Logic," *Journal of Retailing*, Vol. 83, No. 1, pp. 5–18; Stephen L. Vargo and Robert F. Lusch (2008), "Service-Dominant Logic: Continuing the Evolution," *Journal of the Academy of Marketing Science*, Vol. 36, No. 1, pp. 1–10. Loic Ple and Ruben Chumpitaz Caceres (2010), "Not Always Co-Creation: Introducing Interactional Co-Destruction of Value in Service-Dominant Logic" *Journal of Services Marketing*, Vol. 24, No. 6, pp. 430–437.

Additional important research on customer participation in service processes is published in: Kimmy Wa Chan, Chi Kin (Bennett) Yim, and Simon S.K. Lam (2010), "Is Customer Participation in Value Creation a Double-Edged Sword? Evidence from Professional Financial Services Across Cultures," *Journal of Marketing*, Vol. 74, No. 3, pp. 48–64; Andrew S. Gallan, Cheryl Burke Jarvis, Stephen W. Brown, and Mary Jo Bitner (2013), "Customer Positivity and Participation in Services: An Empirical Test in a Health Care Context," *Journal of the Academy of Marketing Science*, Vol. 41, No. 3, pp. 338–356; Thomas Eichentopf, Michael Kleinaltenkamp, and Janine van Stiphout (2011), "Modelling Customer Process Activities in Interactive Value Creation," *Journal of Service Management*, Vol. 22, No. 5, pp. 650–663; Beibei Dong, K. Sivakumar, Kenneth R. Evans, and Shaoming Zou (2015), "Effect of Customer Participation on Service Outcomes: The Moderating Role of Participation Readiness," *Journal of Service Research*, Vol. 18, No. 2, pp. 160–176.

24 Stephen S. Tax, Mark Colgate, and David E. Bowen (2006), "How to Prevent Customers from Failing," *MIT Sloan Management Review*, Vol. 47, Spring, pp. 30–38.

25 Matthew L. Meuter, Amy L. Ostrom, Robert I. Roundtree, and Mary Jo Bitner (2000), "Self-Service Technologies: Understanding Customer Satisfaction with Technology-Based Service Encounters," *Journal of Marketing*, Vol. 64, July, pp. 50–64.

26 Gerard Haübl and Kyle B. Murray (2003), "Preference Construction and Persistence in Digital Marketplaces: The Role of Electronic Recommendation Agents," *Journal of Consumer Psychology*, Vol.13, No. 1, pp. 75–91; Lerzan Aksoy, Paul N. Bloom, Nicholas H. Lurie, and Bruce Cooil (2006), "Should Recommendation Agents Think Like People?" *Journal of Service Research*, Vol. 8, May, pp. 297–315.

27 Sterling A. Bone, Paul W. Fombelle, Kristal R. Ray, and Katherine N. Lemon (2015), "How Customer Participation in B2B Peer-to-Peer Problem-Solving Communities Influences the Need for Traditional Customer Service," *Journal of Service Research*, Vol. 18, No. 1, pp. 23–38.

28 Matthew L. Meuter, Mary Jo Bitner, Amy L. Ostrom, and Stephen W. Brown (2005), "Choosing Among Alternative Service Delivery Modes: An Investigation of Customer Trial of Self-Service Technologies," *Journal of Marketing*, Vol. 69, April, pp. 61–83.

29 A large number of studies examined the attitudes and perceptions that drive the adoption of SSTs. Important studies include: James M. Curran (2003), Matthew L. Meuter, and Carol G. Surprenant, "Intentions to Use Self-Service Technologies: A Confluence of Multiple Attitudes," *Journal of Service Research*, Vol. 5, February, pp. 209–224; Joel E. Collier and Daniel L. Sherrell (2010), "Examining the Influence of Control and Convenience in a Self-Service Setting," *Journal of the Academy of Marketing Science*, Vol. 38, No. 4, pp. 490–509; Jeffrey S. Smith, Mark R. Gleim, Stacey G. Robinson, William J. Kettinger, and Sung-Hee 'Sunny' Park (2014), "Using an Old Dog for New Tricks: A Regulatory Focus Perspective on Consumer Acceptance of RFID Applications," *Journal of Service Research*, Vol. 17, No. 1, pp. 85–101; Katja Gelbrich and Britta Sattler (2014), "Anxiety, Crowding, and Time Pressure in Public Self-Service Technology Acceptance", *Journal of Service Marketing*, Vol. 28, No. 1, pp. 82–94; Toni Hilton, Tim Hughes, Ed Little and Ebi Marandi (2013), "Adopting Self-Service Technology to Do More with Less," *Journal of Service Marketing*, Vol. 27, No. 1, pp. 3–12; Joel E. Collier and Sheryl E. Kimes, "Only if it is Convenient: Understanding How Convenience Influences Self-Service Technology Evaluation," *Journal of Service Research*, Vol. 16, No. 1, pp. 39–51.

30 Pratibha A. Dabholkar (1996), "Consumer Evaluations of New Technology-Based Self-Service Options: An Investigation of Alternative Models of Service Quality," *International Journal of Research in Marketing*, Vol.13, pp. 29–51; David G. Mick and Susan Fournier (1998), "Paradoxes of Technology: Consumer Cognizance, Emotions, and Coping Strategies," *Journal of Consumer Research*, Vol. 25, September, pp. 123–43; Mary Jo Bitner, Stephen W. Brown, and Matthew L. Meuter (2000), "Technology Infusion in Service Encounters," *Journal of the Academy of Marketing Science*, Vol. 28, No. 1, pp. 138-149; Dabholkar *et al.*, 2003, op. cit. Maria Åkesson, Bo Edvardsson, and Bård Tronvoll (2014), "Customer Experience from a Self-Service System Perspective," *Journal of Service Management*, Vol. 25, No. 5, pp. 677–698; Meuter et al,. 2000; Mary Jo Bitner (2001), "Self-Service Technologies: What Do Customers Expect?" *Marketing Management*, Spring, pp. 10–11.

31 Jeffrey F. Rayport and Bernard J. Jaworski (2004), "Best Face Forward," *Harvard Business Review*, Vol. 82, December.

32 Kortney Stringer (2002), "Have a Pleasant Trip: Eliminate All Human Contact," *Wall Street Journal*, October 31.

33 Cheng Wang, Jennifer Harris, and Paul Patterson (2013), "The Roles of Habit, Self-Efficacy, and Satisfaction in Driving Continued Use of Self-Service Technologies: A Longitudinal Study," *Journal of Service Research*, Vol. 16, No. 3, pp. 400–414.

If an SST is perceived as delivering service quality, it has a positive impact on the intention to return to a retail store; see Hyun-Joo Lee, Ann E. Fairhurst and Min-Young Lee (2009), "The Importance of Self-Service Kiosks in Developing Consumers' Retail Patronage Intentions," *Managing Service Quality*, Vol. 19, No. 6, pp. 687–701.

34 Neeli Bendapudi and Robert P. Leone (2003), "Psychological Implications of Customer Participation in Co-Production," *Journal of Marketing*, Vol. 67, January, pp. 14–28.

35 Zhen Zhu, Cheryl Nakata, K. Sivakumar, and Dhruv Grewal (2013), "Fix It or Leave It? Customer Recovery from Self-Service Technology Failures," *Journal of Retailing*, Vol. 89, No. 1, pp. 15–29.

36 Bitner, 2001, op. cit.

37 Brad Stone (2013), *The Everything Store: Jeff Bezos and the Age of Amazon*. Little, Brown and Company.

38 Machiel J. Reinders, Pratibha A. Dabholkar, and Ruud T. Frambach (2008), "Consequences of Forcing Consumers to Use Technology-Based Self-Service," *Journal of Service Research*, Vol. 11, No. 2, pp. 107–123.

CHAPTER 09 Balancing Demand and Capacity

Balancing the supply and demand sides of a service industry is not easy, and whether a manager does it well or not makes all the difference.

W. Earl Sasser
Professor at Harvard Business School

They also serve who only stand and wait.

John Milton
English poet, 1608–1674

LEARNING OBJECTIVES (LOs)

By the end of this chapter, the reader should be able to:

⮕ **LO 1** Know the different demand–supply situations that fixed capacity firms may face.

⮕ **LO 2** Describe the building blocks of dealing with the problem of fluctuating demand.

⮕ **LO 3** Understand what is meant by **productive capacity** in a service context.

⮕ **LO 4** Be familiar with the basic ways to **manage capacity**.

⮕ **LO 5** Recognize that demand patterns vary by segment, so that segment-specific variations in demand can be predicted.

⮕ **LO 6** Be familiar with the five basic ways to **manage demand**.

⮕ **LO 7** Understand how to use the marketing mix elements of price, product, place, and promotion to smooth out fluctuations in demand.

⮕ **LO 8** Know how to use waiting lines and queuing systems to inventory demand.

⮕ **LO 9** Understand how customers perceive waits and how to make waiting less burdensome for them.

⮕ **LO 10** Know how to use reservations systems to inventory demand.

⮕ **LO 11** Be familiar with strategic approaches to utilize residual surplus capacity even after all other options of matching demand and capacity have been exhausted.

OPENING VIGNETTE

Summer on the Ski Slopes

It used to be that ski resorts shut down once the snow melted and no skiing could be done. The chairlifts stopped operating, the restaurants closed, and the lodges were locked and shuttered until the next winter. However, some ski operators realized over time that a mountain offers summer pleasures too, so they kept lodging and restaurants open for hikers and picnickers. Some even built alpine slides — curving tracks in which wheeled toboggans could run from the top of the mountain to the base — thus creating demand for tickets on the ski lifts.

The arrival of the mountain biking craze created opportunities for equipment rentals as well as chairlift rides. Killington Resort in Vermont has long encouraged summer visitors to ride to the summit, see the view, and eat at the mountaintop restaurant. Now, it also enjoys business in renting out mountain bikes and related equipment such as helmets. Next to the base lodge, where racks of skis are available for rental in winter, the summer visitor can now choose from rows of mountain bikes. Usually, bikers use the specially equipped chairlifts to carry their bikes up to the top of the mountain, and then ride them down the marked trails. Once in a while, a biker will reverse the process and choose to ride up the mountain. Avid hikers do the same; they climb to the top through the trails, get some refreshments from the restaurant, and then take the chairlift back down to the base.

Most large ski resorts look for a variety of additional ways to attract guests to their hotels and rental homes during the summer. Mont Tremblant in Québec, for instance, is located next to a beautiful lake. In addition to swimming and other water sports, the resort offers visitors activities such as a championship golf course, tennis, rollerblading, and specially designed activities for children. Hikers and mountain bikers ride the lifts up the mountain. This is a wonderful example of how service development and marketing generated demand for an otherwise idle service capacity!

FLUCTUATIONS IN DEMAND THREATEN PROFITABILITY

Many services with limited capacity face wide swings in demand. In the opening vignette, this wide swing of demand is caused by the change in seasons. This is a problem because service capacity usually cannot be kept aside for sale at a later date. The effective use of expensive productive capacity is one of the secrets of success in such businesses. The goal should be to utilize staff, labor, equipment, and facilities as **productively** as possible. By working with managers in operations and human resources, service marketers may be able to develop strategies to bring demand and capacity into balance, in ways that create benefits for customers as well as to improve profitability for the business.

LO 1

Know the different demand-supply situations that fixed capacity firms may face.

From Excess Demand to Excess Capacity

For fixed capacity firms, the problem is a familiar one. "It's either feast or famine for us!" sighs the manager. "In peak periods, we're disappointing prospective customers by turning them away. And in low periods when our facilities are idle, our employees are standing around looking bored, and we're losing money." In other words, demand and supply are not in balance.

At any given moment, a fixed-capacity service may face one of the four following conditions (*Figure 9.1*):

- **Excess demand** — The level of demand exceeds maximum available capacity, resulting in some customers being denied service and business is lost.
- **Demand exceeds optimum capacity** — No one is turned away, but conditions are crowded and customers are likely to perceive a deterioration in service quality and may feel dissatisfied.
- **Demand and supply are well balanced** at the level of optimum capacity — Staff and facilities are busy without being overworked, and customers receive good service without delays.
- **Excess capacity** — Demand is below optimum capacity and productive resources are underutilized, resulting in low productivity. Low usage also poses a risk that customers may find the experience disappointing or have doubts about the viability of the service.

Sometimes optimum and maximum capacities are one and the same. At a live theater performance or sports event, a full house looks grand and is exciting for the performers or the players and the audience. It creates a more satisfying experience for all. With most other services however, you probably feel that you get better service if the facility is not operating at full capacity. The quality of restaurant service for instance, often deteriorates when every table is occupied, because the staff is rushed and there is a greater likelihood of errors or delays. If you are traveling alone in an aircraft with high-density seating, you tend to feel more comfortable if the seat next to you is empty. When repair and maintenance shops are fully scheduled, delays may result if there is no slack in the system to allow for unexpected problems in completing particular jobs.

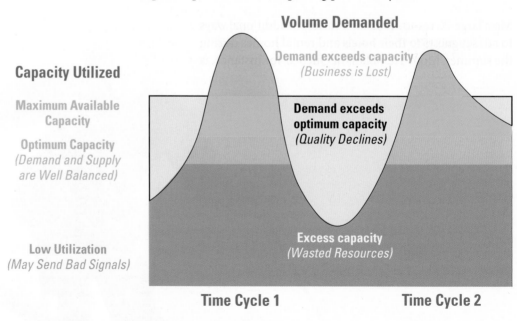

Figure 9.1 Implications of variations in demand relative to capacity

Building Blocks of Managing Capacity and Demand

There are two basic approaches to the problem of fluctuating demand. One is to adjust the level of capacity to meet variations in demand. This approach requires an understanding of what constitutes productive capacity and how it may be increased or decreased on an incremental basis. The second approach is to manage the level of demand. This requires a good understanding of demand patterns and drivers on a segment-by-segment basis, so that firms can use marketing strategies to smooth out variations in demand. Most service firms use a mix of both approaches[1].

Figure 9.2 shows the four building blocks that provide an integrative approach to balancing capacity and demand. The remainder of this chapter is organized along these four building blocks.

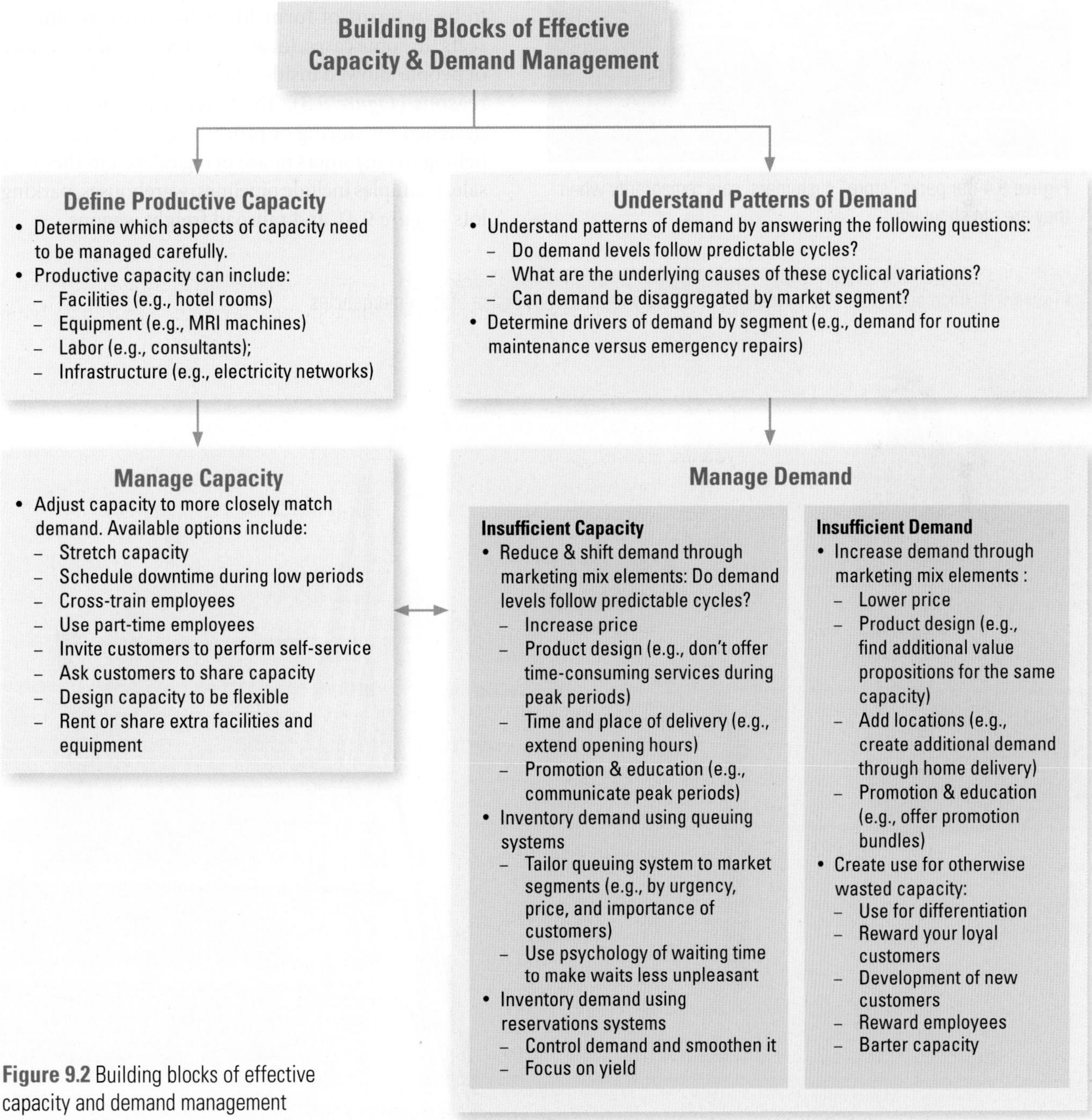

⊃ **LO 2**
Describe the building blocks of dealing with the problem of fluctuating demand.

PART 3

Building Blocks of Effective Capacity & Demand Management

Define Productive Capacity
- Determine which aspects of capacity need to be managed carefully.
- Productive capacity can include:
  - Facilities (e.g., hotel rooms)
  - Equipment (e.g., MRI machines)
  - Labor (e.g., consultants);
  - Infrastructure (e.g., electricity networks)

Understand Patterns of Demand
- Understand patterns of demand by answering the following questions:
  - Do demand levels follow predictable cycles?
  - What are the underlying causes of these cyclical variations?
  - Can demand be disaggregated by market segment?
- Determine drivers of demand by segment (e.g., demand for routine maintenance versus emergency repairs)

Manage Capacity
- Adjust capacity to more closely match demand. Available options include:
  - Stretch capacity
  - Schedule downtime during low periods
  - Cross-train employees
  - Use part-time employees
  - Invite customers to perform self-service
  - Ask customers to share capacity
  - Design capacity to be flexible
  - Rent or share extra facilities and equipment

Manage Demand

Insufficient Capacity
- Reduce & shift demand through marketing mix elements: Do demand levels follow predictable cycles?
  - Increase price
  - Product design (e.g., don't offer time-consuming services during peak periods)
  - Time and place of delivery (e.g., extend opening hours)
  - Promotion & education (e.g., communicate peak periods)
- Inventory demand using queuing systems
  - Tailor queuing system to market segments (e.g., by urgency, price, and importance of customers)
  - Use psychology of waiting time to make waits less unpleasant
- Inventory demand using reservations systems
  - Control demand and smoothen it
  - Focus on yield

Insufficient Demand
- Increase demand through marketing mix elements :
  - Lower price
  - Product design (e.g., find additional value propositions for the same capacity)
  - Add locations (e.g., create additional demand through home delivery)
  - Promotion & education (e.g., offer promotion bundles)
- Create use for otherwise wasted capacity:
  - Use for differentiation
  - Reward your loyal customers
  - Development of new customers
  - Reward employees
  - Barter capacity

Figure 9.2 Building blocks of effective capacity and demand management

DEFINING PRODUCTIVE SERVICE CAPACITY

When we refer to managing capacity, we implicitly mean productive capacity. This term refers to the resources or assets that a firm can use to create goods and services that are typically key cost components and therefore need to be managed carefully. In a service context, productive capacity can take several forms, including facilities, equipment, labor, and infrastructure.

Figure 9.4 Car parks "store" customers' cars temporarily when they are out shopping

1. **Facilities** that are critical to capacity management can relate to those that are designed to "hold" customers and those that hold goods. The former is used for people-processing services or mental stimulus processing services. Examples include medical clinics, hotels, passenger aircrafts, and college classrooms. The primary capacity constraint is likely to be in terms of furnishings like beds, rooms, or seats. In some cases, local laws may limit the number of people allowed inside a facility for health or safety reasons (*Figure 9.3*). The latter relates to facilities designed for storing or processing goods that either belong to customers or are being offered to them for sale. Examples include pipelines, warehouses, parking lots (*Figure 9.4*), and railroad freight wagons.

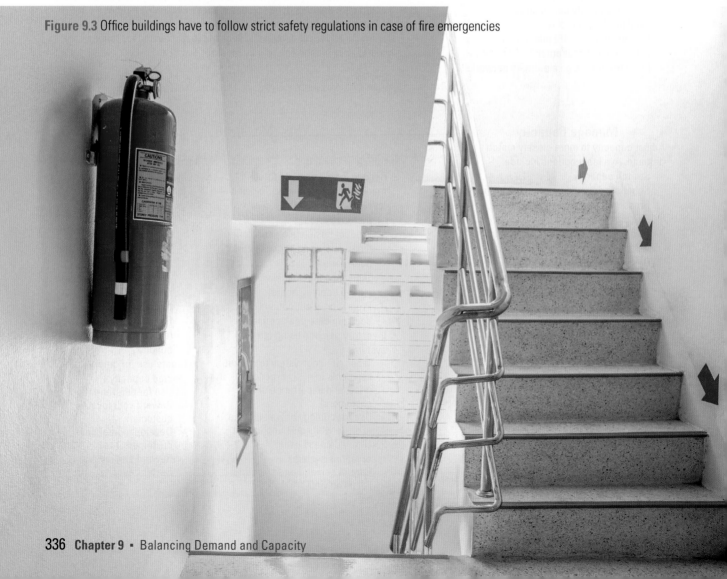

Figure 9.3 Office buildings have to follow strict safety regulations in case of fire emergencies

2. **Equipment** used to process people, possessions, or information may encompass a large range of items and can be very situation-specific — diagnostic equipment (*Figure 9.5*), airport security detectors, toll gates, bank ATMs, and "seats" in a call center are among the many items whose absence in sufficient numbers for a given level of demand can bring service to a crawl, or even a complete stop.

3. **Labor** is a key element of productive capacity in all high-contact services and many low-contact ones (*Figure 9.6*). If staffing levels are not sufficient, customers might be kept waiting or service will become rushed. Professional services are especially dependent on highly skilled staff to create high value-added, information-based output. Abraham Lincoln captured it well when he remarked that "A lawyer's time and expertise are his stocks in trade."

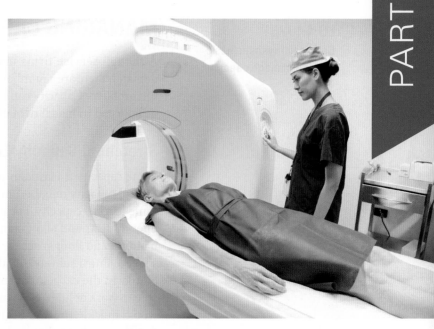

Figure 9.5 Productive capacity is expressed in terms of available hours for MRI scanning equipment

Infrastructure capacity can also be critical. Many organizations are dependent on access to sufficient capacity in the public or private infrastructure to be able to deliver quality service to their own customers. Capacity problems of this nature may include congested airways that lead to air traffic restrictions on flights, traffic jams on major highways, and power failures (or "brown outs" caused by reduced voltage).

Financial success in capacity-constrained businesses is, in large measure, a function of the management's ability to use productive capacity — labor, equipment, facilities, and infrastructure — as efficiently and as profitably as possible. In practice, however, it is difficult to achieve this ideal all the time. Not only do demand levels vary, often randomly, but the time and effort required to process each person or thing may vary widely at any point in the process. In general, processing times for people are more varied than for objects or things, reflecting the varying levels of preparedness ("I've lost my credit card"), argumentative versus cooperative personalities ("If you won't give me a table with a view, I'll have to ask for your supervisor"), and so forth. Furthermore, service tasks are not necessarily homogeneous. In both professional services and repair jobs, diagnosis and treatment times vary according to the nature of the customers' problems.

Figure 9.6 Restaurants need to ensure sufficient manpower to meet customer demands

MANAGING CAPACITY

Although service firms may encounter capacity limitations due to varying demand, there are a number of ways in which capacity can be adjusted to reduce the problem. Capacity can be stretched or shrunk, and the overall capacity can be adjusted to match demand.

Stretching Capacity Levels

Some capacity is elastic in its ability to absorb extra demand. Here, the actual level of capacity remains unchanged, and more people are being served with the same level of capacity. For example, the normal capacity for a subway car may offer 40 seats and allow standing room for another 60 passengers with enough handrail and floor space for all. At rush hour, however, up to 200 people could squeeze into a subway car, although under sardine-like conditions (*Figure 9.7*). Similarly, the capacity of service personnel can be stretched and staff may be able to work at high levels of efficiency for short periods of time. However, staff would quickly tire and begin to provide poor service if they had to work that fast for a prolonged period of time.

Another way to stretch capacity is to utilize the facilities for longer periods. For example, some banks extend their opening hours during weekdays and even open on weekends. Universities may offer evening classes, and weekend and summer programs.

Lastly, the average amount of time customers (or their possessions) spend in process may be reduced. Sometimes, this is achieved by minimizing slack time. For example, a restaurant can buzz tables, seat arriving diners and present menus fast, and the bill can be presented promptly to a group of diners relaxing at the table after a meal[2]. In other instances, it may be achieved by cutting back the level of service — say, offering a simpler menu at busy times of the day.

Figure 9.7 Rush hour crowd stretches the capacity of train services

Adjusting Capacity to Match Demand

Unlike stretching capacity, adjusting capacity involves tailoring the overall level of capacity to match variations in demand — a strategy also known as **chasing demand**. There are several actions that managers can take to adjust capacity as needed[3]. These actions are from the easiest to implement, to the more difficult:

1. **Schedule downtime during periods of low demand.** To make sure that 100% of capacity is available during peak periods, maintenance, repair, and renovations should be conducted when demand is expected to be low. Employees should also take their holidays during such periods.

2. **Cross-train employees.** Even when the service delivery system appears to be operating at full capacity, some physical elements — and their attendant employees — may be under-utilized. If employees can be cross-trained to perform a variety of tasks, they can be shifted to bottleneck points whenever needed, thereby increasing total capacity. In supermarkets, for instance, the manager may call on stockers to operate cash registers when lines become too long. Likewise, during slow periods, the cashiers may be asked to help stock shelves (*Figure 9.8*).

3. **Use part-time employees.** Many organizations hire extra workers during their busiest periods. Examples include postal workers and retail store associates during the Christmas season, extra staff for tax preparation service firms at the end of the financial year, and additional hotel employees during holiday periods and for major conventions.

4. **Invite customers to perform self-service.** If the number of employees is limited, capacity can be increased by involving customers in the co-production of certain tasks. One way to do this is by adding self-service technologies such as electronic kiosks at the airport for airline ticketing and check-in, or automated check-out stations at supermarkets.

Figure 9.8 Supermarket employees are cross-trained as cashiers and stockers

5. **Ask customers to share.** Capacity can be stretched by asking customers to share a unit of capacity normally meant for one individual. For instance, at busy airports and train stations, where the supply of taxis is sometimes insufficient to meet demand, travelers going in the same direction may be given the option of sharing a ride at a reduced rate.

6. **Create flexible capacity.** Sometimes, the problem is not the overall capacity but in the mix available to serve the needs of different market segments. One solution lies in designing physical facilities to be flexible[4]. For example, the tables in a restaurant can be all two-seaters. When necessary, two tables can be combined to seat four, or three tables combined to seat six. An airline may have too few seats in the economy class even though there are empty seats in the business class cabin on any given flight. Facing tough competition from Airbus, Boeing received what it described in jest as "outrageous demands" from potential customers when it was designing its 777 airliner. The airlines wanted an aircraft where galleys as well as the lavatories with their plumbing could be relocated almost anywhere in the cabin within a matter of hours.

Boeing gulped at the demands but managed to come up with solutions. Airlines can now rearrange the passenger cabin of the "Triple Seven" within hours and reconfigure it with varying number of seats allocated to the different classes.

7. **Rent or share extra facilities and equipment.** To reduce spending on fixed assets, a service business may be able to rent extra space or machines during peak times. Two firms with complementary demand patterns may enter into formal sharing agreements. For example, some universities rent out student accommodation to visitors during the peak holiday season when their own students have their summer break and the first-year students have not moved into the campus yet.

LO 5

Recognize that demand patterns vary by segment, so that segment-specific variations in demand can be predicted.

UNDERSTAND PATTERNS OF DEMAND

Now let's look at the other side of the equation. In order to effectively manage demand for a particular service, managers need to understand that demand often differs by market segment.

Random fluctuations are usually caused by factors beyond management's control. However, analysis will sometimes reveal that a predictable demand cycle for one segment is concealed within a broader, seemingly random pattern. This fact illustrates the importance of breaking down demand on a segment-by-segment basis. For instance, a repair and maintenance shop that services industrial electrical equipment may already know that a certain proportion of its work consists of regularly scheduled contracts to perform preventive maintenance (*Figure 9.9*). The balance may come from "walk-ins" and emergency repairs. Although it might seem hard to predict or control the timing and volume of

Figure 9.9 Scheduled maintenance checks at a power plant

such work, further analysis might show that walk-in business is more prevalent on some days of the week than others, and that emergency repairs are frequently requested, following damage sustained during thunderstorms, which tend to be seasonal in nature and can often be forecast a day or two in advance. Understanding demand patterns allows the firm to schedule less preventive maintenance work on the days with high anticipated demand of typically more profitable emergency repairs.

To understand the patterns of demand by segment, research should begin by getting some answers to a series of important questions about the patterns of demand and their underlying causes (*Table 9.1*).

Table 9.1 Questions About Demand Patterns and Their Underlying Causes

1. **Do demand levels follow a predictable cycle?**
   If so, is the duration of the *demand cycle*:
   - One *day* (varies by hour)
   - One *week* (varies by day)
   - One *month* (varies by day or by week)
   - One *year* (varies by month or by season or reflects annual public holidays)
   - Another period

2. **What are the underlying causes of these cyclical variations?**
   - Employment schedules
   - Billing and tax payment/refund cycles
   - Wage and salary payment dates
   - School hours and vacation
   - Seasonal changes in climate
   - Occurrence of public or religious holidays
   - Natural cycles, such as coastal tides

3. **Do demand levels seem to change randomly?**
   If so, could the underlying causes be:
   - Day-to-day changes in the weather
   - Health events whose occurrence cannot be pinpointed exactly
   - Accidents, fires, and certain criminal activities
   - Natural disasters (e.g., earthquakes, storms, mudslides, and volcanic eruptions)

4. **Can demand for a particular service over time be disaggregated by market segment to reflect such components as follows?**
   - Use patterns by a particular type of customer or for a particular purpose
   - Variations in the net profitability of each completed transaction

Most cycles influencing demand for a particular service vary in length from one day to 12 months. In many instances, multiple cycles operate simultaneously. For example, demand levels for public transport may vary according to the time of the day (highest during commute hours), day of week (less traveling to work on the weekends but more leisure travel), and season of year (more traveling by tourists in the summer, as seen in *Figure 9.10*). The demand for service during the peak period on a Monday in summer is likely to be very different from the demand during the peak period on a Saturday in winter, reflecting day-of-week and seasonal variations jointly.

No strategy for smoothing demand is likely to succeed unless it is based on an understanding of why customers from a specific market segment choose to use the service when they do. For example, it's difficult for hotels to convince business travelers to remain on Saturday nights since few executives do business over the weekend. Instead, hotel managers may do better to promote weekend use of their facilities for conferences or leisure travel. Attempts to get commuters to shift their travel to off-peak periods will probably fail, since such travel is determined by people's employment hours. Instead, efforts should be directed at employers to persuade them to adopt flexi-time or staggered working hours.

Figure 9.10 In summer, many tourists flock to Cologne, Germany to take in its rich heritage

Keeping good records of each transaction helps enormously when it comes to analyzing demand patterns based on past experiences. Best practice queuing systems supported by sophisticated software can automatically track customer consumption patterns by the type of customer, service requested, and date and time of day. Where relevant, it is also useful to record weather conditions and other special factors such as a strike, an accident, a big convention in town, a price change, or the launch of a competing service that might have influenced demand.

MANAGING DEMAND

 LO 6
Be familiar with the five basic ways to **manage demand**.

Once we have understood the demand patterns of the different market segments, we can proceed to manage demand. There are five basic approaches:

- Take no action and leave demand to find its own levels.
- Reduce demand during peak periods.
- Increase demand during low periods.
- Inventory demand using a queuing system.
- Inventory demand using a reservations system.

The first approach, **take no action**, has the virtue of simplicity but little else. Eventually customers learn from experience or word-of-mouth when they can expect to stand in line to use a service and when it will be available without delay. The trouble is that they may also learn to find out about a competitor who is more responsive, and low off-peak utilization cannot be improved unless action is taken. The other four proactive approaches are, therefore, far superior and profitable strategies.

Table 9.2 links these five approaches to the two problematic situations of excess demand and excess capacity. Many service businesses face both situations at different points in the cycle of demand and should consider use of the interventionist strategies described. Next in this section, we will discuss how marketing mix elements can help to shape demand levels, as well as how to inventory demand first through waiting lines and queuing systems, and second through reservation systems.

Table 9.2 Alternate Demand Management Strategies for Different Capacity Situations

	Capacity Situation	
Approaches in Managing Demand	**Insufficient Capacity (Excess Demand)**	**Insufficient Demand (Excess Capacity)**
Take no action	• Results in unorganized queuing (may irritate customers and discourage future use)	• Capacity is wasted (customers may have a disappointing experience for services such as theater)
Manage demand through marketing mix elements	Reduce demand in peak periods: • Higher prices will increase profits. • Change product elements (e.g., don't offer time-consuming services during peak times). • Modify time and place of delivery (e.g., extend opening hours). • Communication can encourage use in other time slots, (Can this effort be focused on less profitable and less desirable segments?). • Note that demand from highly profitable segments should still be stimulated, and priority to capacity should be given to those segments. Demand reduction and shifting should primarily be focused on lower yield segments	Increase demand in low periods: • Lower prices selectively (try to avoid cannibalizing existing business; ensure that all relevant costs are covered). • Change product elements (find alternative value propositions for service during low seasons). • Use communications and variation in products and distribution (but recognize extra costs, if any, and make sure that appropriate trade-offs are made between profitability and use levels).
Inventory demand using a queuing system	• Match appropriate queue configuration to service process. • Consider priority system for most desirable segments and make other customer shift to off-peak period. • Consider separate queues based on urgency, duration and premium pricing of service. • Shorten customer's perceptions of waiting time and make their waits more comfortable.	• Not applicable, but the queuing system can still collect data on number and type of transactions and customers served. The same applied to reservations systems below.
Inventory demand using a reservations system	• Focus on yield and reserve capacity for less price sensitive customers. • Consider a priority system for important segments. • Make other customers shift to off-peak periods.	• Clarify that capacity is available and let customers make reservations at their preferred time slots.

Marketing Mix Elements Can Be Used to Shape Demand Patterns

LO 7
Understand how to use the marketing mix elements of price, product, place, and promotion to smooth out fluctuations in demand.

Several marketing mix variables can be used to stimulate demand during periods of excess capacity, and decrease or shift around demand during periods of insufficient capacity. Price is often the first variable to be proposed for bringing demand and supply into balance. However, changes in product, distribution strategy, and communication efforts can also be used to reshape demand patterns. Although each element is discussed separately, effective demand management efforts often require changes in several elements concurrently.

Use Price and Non-monetary Costs to Manage Demand. One of the most direct ways to balance supply and demand is through the use of pricing. The lure of lower prices may encourage at least some people to change the timing of their behavior, whether for shopping, travel, or sending in equipment for repair. Non-monetary costs may have a similar effect too. For instance, customers who dislike spending time waiting in crowded and unpleasant conditions will try to come during less busy periods.

For the monetary price of a service to be effective as a demand management tool, managers must have some sense of the shape and slope of a product's demand curve. They must understand how the quantity of the service demanded responds to the increases or decreases in the price per unit at a particular point in time. It's important to determine whether the demand curve for a specific service varies sharply from one time period to another. For instance, will the same person be willing to pay more for a weekend stay in a hotel on Cape Cod in summer than in winter when the weather can be freezing cold? The answer is probably yes. If so, very different pricing schemes may be needed to fill capacity in each time period.

Complicating matters further, there are typically separate demand curves for different segments within each time period (e.g., business travelers are usually less price sensitive than tourists, as discussed in Chapter 6 on service pricing).

One of the most difficult tasks facing service marketers is to determine the nature of all these different demand curves. Historical data (often from revenue management systems), research, trial and error, and analysis of parallel situations in other locations or in comparable services, are all ways of understanding the situation. Many service businesses explicitly recognize the existence of different demand curves by designing distinct products with physical and non-physical design elements (or rate fences) for their key segments, each priced at levels appropriate to the demand curve of a particular segment. In essence, each segment receives a variation of the basic product, with value being added to the core service through supplementary services to appeal to higher paying segments. For instance, in computer and printing service firms, product enhancement takes the form of faster turnaround time and more specialized services. In each case, the objective is to maximize the revenues received from each segment.

However, when capacity is limited, the goal in a profit-seeking business should be to ensure that as much capacity as possible is utilized by the most profitable segments available at any given time. For instance, airlines hold a certain number of seats for business passengers paying full fare, and place restrictive conditions on excursion fares for tourists (using non-physical rate fences such as requiring advance purchase and a Saturday night stay) in order to prevent business travelers from taking advantage of cheap fares designed to attract tourists who can help fill the aircraft. Pricing strategies of this nature are known as revenue management and are discussed in Chapter 6.

Change Product Elements. Sometimes, pricing alone will be ineffective in managing demand. The opening vignette is a good case in point — in the absence of skiing opportunities, no skiers would buy lift tickets on a midsummer's day at any price. It is the same for a variety of other seasonal businesses. Thus, educational institutions offer weekend and summer programs for adults and senior citizens, small pleasure boats offer cruises in the summer and a dockside venue for private functions in winter months. These firms recognize that no amount of price discounting is likely to develop business when it is out of season, and that a new service product targeted at different segments is instead needed to encourage demand.

There can even be variations in the product offering during the course of a 24-hour period. Some restaurants provide a good example of this, marking the passage of the hours with the changing of menus and levels of service, variations in lighting and decor, opening and closing of the bar, and the presence or absence of entertainment. The goal is to appeal to different needs within the same group of customers, to reach out to different customer segments, or to do both, according to the time of day. Product elements can also be changed to increase capacity during peak periods — for example, the lunch menu is designed to contain only dishes that can be prepared quickly during the busy lunch period.

Modify Place and Time of Delivery. Rather than seeking to modify the demand for a service that continues to be offered at the same time in the same place, firms can also respond to market needs by modifying the time and place of delivery. The following basic options are available:

- **Vary the times when the service is available.** This strategy reflects changing customer preference by day of week, by season, and so forth. Theaters and cinema complexes often offer matinees on weekends when people have more leisure time throughout the day. During the summer, cafes and restaurants may stay open later as people are generally inclined to enjoy the longer balmier evenings outdoors. Shops may extend their opening hours in the weeks leading up to Christmas or during school holidays.

- **Offer the service to customers at a new location.** One approach is to operate mobile units that take the service to customers, rather than requiring them to visit fixed-site service locations. Mobile car wash services, in-office tailoring services, home-delivered meals and catering services, and vans equipped with primary care medical facilities are examples of this. A cleaning and repair firm that wishes to generate business during low demand periods might offer free pickup and delivery of movable items that need servicing.

Promotion and Education. Even if other variables of the marketing mix remain unchanged, communication efforts alone may be able to help facilitate smooth demand. Signage, advertising, publicity, and sales messages can be used to educate customers about peak periods and encourage them to make use of the service at off-peak times when there will be fewer delays[5]. Examples include the US Postal Service requests to "Mail Early for Christmas", public transport messages urging non-commuters — such as shoppers or tourists — to avoid the cramped conditions of commuting hours during peak periods, and communications from sales representatives for industrial maintenance firms advising customers of periods when preventive maintenance work can be done quickly. In addition, management can ask service personnel (or intermediaries such as travel agents) to encourage customers with flexible schedules to consider off-peak travel periods.

Changes in pricing, product characteristics, and distribution must be communicated clearly. If a firm wants to obtain a particular response to the variations in the marketing mix elements, it must fully inform customers about their options. As discussed in Chapter 7, short-term promotions that combine both pricing and communication elements as well as other incentives may provide customers with attractive incentives to shift the timing of service usage.

Not all demand is desirable. In fact, some requests for service are inappropriate and make it difficult for the organization to respond to the legitimate needs of its target customers. For example, many calls to emergency numbers such as 911 are not cases that the fire department, the police, or ambulance services should be dispatched to. Such calls make it difficult for the organization to respond to the actual emergency cases. *Service Insights 9.1* shows how a marketing campaign was used to reduce undesirable demand and free up capacity. Discouraging undesirable demand through marketing campaigns or screening procedures will not eliminate random fluctuations in the remaining demand. However, it may help to keep peak demand levels within the service capacity of the organization.

SERVICE INSIGHTS 9.1
Discouraging Demand for Non-emergency Calls

Have you ever wondered what it's like to be a dispatcher for an emergency telephone service such as 911? People differ widely in what they consider to be an emergency.

Imagine yourself in the huge communications room at Police Headquarters in New York. A gray-haired sergeant is talking patiently by phone to a woman who has dialed 911 because her cat has run up a tree and she's afraid it will get stuck there. "Ma'am, have you ever seen a cat skeleton in a tree?" the sergeant asks her. "All those cats get down somehow, don't they?" After the woman has hung up, the sergeant turns to a visitor and shrugs. "These kinds of calls keep pouring in," he says. "What can you do?"

The trouble is, when people call the emergency number with complaints about noisy parties next door, pleas to rescue cats, or requests to turn off leaking fire hydrants, they may be slowing the response times to cases that actually involve fires, heart attacks, or violent crimes.

At one point, the situation in New York City became so bad that officials were forced to develop a marketing campaign to discourage the public from making inappropriate requests for emergency assistance through the 911 number. What seemed like an emergency to the caller — a beloved cat stuck up a tree, a noisy party preventing a tired person from getting much needed sleep — was not a life (or property) threatening situation that the city's emergency services were poised to resolve. A communications campaign

using a variety of media, was developed to urge the public not to call 911 unless they were reporting a dangerous emergency. For help in resolving other matters, they were asked to call their local police station or other city agencies. The ad shown below appeared on New York buses and subways.

LO 8

Know how to use waiting lines and queuing systems to inventory demand.

INVENTORY DEMAND THROUGH WAITING LINES AND QUEUING SYSTEMS

As seen in the previous section, there are a variety of tactics for balancing demand and supply. But what's a manager to do when the possibilities for shaping demand and adjusting capacity have been exhausted, and yet supply and demand are still out of balance? Not taking any action and leaving customers to sort things out on their own is no recipe for customer satisfaction. Rather than allowing matters to degenerate, customer-oriented firms must try to develop strategies to ensure order, predictability, and fairness. Therefore, for services which regularly face demand that exceeds capacity, managers often need to take steps to inventory demand.

Demand can be inventoried in two ways: (1) by asking customers to wait in line, usually on a first-come, first-served basis, or by offering customers more advanced queuing systems (e.g., systems that take into account urgency, price, or importance of the customer), and (2) by offering customers the opportunity of reserving or booking service capacity in advance. We will discuss the wait line and queuing systems in this section, and reservation systems in the next.

Waiting Is a Universal Phenomenon

Waiting is something that occurs everywhere. Waiting lines — known to operations researchers (and the British) as "queues" — occur whenever the number of arrivals at a facility exceeds the capacity of the system to process them. In a very real sense, queues are basically a symptom of unresolved capacity management problems. Analysis and modeling of queues is a well-established branch of operations management. Queuing theory has been traced back to 1917, when a Danish telephone engineer was charged with determining how large the switching unit in a telephone system had to be to keep the number of busy signals within reason[6].

Nobody likes to wait, or to be kept waiting (*Figure 9.11*). It's boring, time-wasting, and sometimes physically uncomfortable, especially if there is nowhere to sit or if you are outdoors. Almost every organization faces the problem of waiting lines somewhere in its operation. People are kept waiting on the phone, listening to recorded messages like "Your call is important to us", they line up with their supermarket carts to check out their grocery purchases, and they wait for their bills after a restaurant meal. They sit in their cars waiting to enter drive-in car washes and to pay at toll booths. Some physical queues are geographically dispersed. Travelers wait at many different locations for the taxis they have ordered by phone to arrive and pick them up.

A survey in the US revealed that the waiting lines most dreaded by Americans are those in doctors' offices (cited by 27%) and in government departments that issue motor vehicle registrations and drivers' licenses (26%), followed by grocery stores (18%) and airports (14%)[7]. Situations that make it even worse at retail check-outs include slow or inefficient cashiers, a shopper who changes her mind about an item that has already been rung up, or one who leaves the line to run back for an item. It doesn't take long before people start to lose their cool — One-third of Americans say they get frustrated after waiting in line for 10 minutes or less, although women report more patience than men and are more likely to chat with others to pass the time while waiting.

Physical and inanimate objects wait for processing too. Customers' emails sit in customer service staff's inboxes, appliances wait to be repaired, and checks wait to be cleared at a bank. In each instance, a customer may be waiting for the outcome of that work — an answer to an email, an appliance that is working again, and a check credited to a customer's balance.

Managing Waiting Lines

The problem of reducing customer waiting time often requires a multi-pronged approach, as seen by the approach taken by Disney, described in *Service Insights 9.2*. Increasing capacity by simply adding more space or staff is not always the best solution in situations where customer satisfaction must be balanced against cost considerations. Like Disney, managers should consider a variety of ways, including:

1. Rethinking the design of the queuing system (i.e., queue configuration and virtual waits).

2. Tailoring the queuing system to different market segments (e.g., by urgency, price, or importance of the customer).

3. Managing customers' behavior and their perceptions of the wait (i.e., use the psychology of waiting to make waits less unpleasant).

4. Installing a reservations system (e.g., use reservations, booking, or appointments to distribute demand).

5. Redesigning processes to shorten the time of each transaction (e.g., by installing self-service machines).

Points 1 to 4 are discussed in the next few sections of this chapter. Point 5 is discussed in Chapter 8 on customer service process redesign.

Disney Turns Queue Management Into a Science

Have you ever been in a queue at Disneyland? Very often, we may not realize how long we have been waiting as they are many sights to see while queuing. We may be watching a video, playing with interactive technology and touch screens stationed along the way, looking at other customers enjoying themselves, or reading the various posters on the wall, and enjoying comfort in the form of fans and shade that help us cool off. As our waits are occupied and comfortable, we may not realize that a long time has passed. Disney's theme park line management is an extension of their entertainment philosophy!

At Disney World's "Dumbo the Flying Elephant" ride, children and their parents can play in an interactive room resembling a circus tent. While playing, these children are also waiting for a buzzer to signal their turn to go onto the outdoor line for the ride. These children playing in the tent don't have the perception of waiting in line, but that is exactly what they are doing!

Disney has taken the management of waiting lines to another level. At Walt Disney World, there is a Disney Operational Command Center, where the technicians are monitoring the queues to make sure that they are not too long and people are moving along. To them, patience is not a virtue in the theme park business. Inside the Command Center, they have computer programs, video cameras, digital maps of the park, and other tools to help them spot where there might be queues that are too long. Once there is a wait problem, they will send a staff to fix the problem immediately. The problem may be dealt with in several ways. For example, they could send a Disney character to entertain the waiting customers. Alternatively, they could deploy more capacity. For example, if there is a long queue for the boat ride, then they will deploy more boats so that the queue moves faster. Disney World is divided into different lands. If there is less crowd in one land compared to another, they may re-route a mini-parade towards that area, so that the crowds will follow and the crowd distribution becomes more even. They have also added video games to waiting areas.

With the Command Center in place, they have managed to increase the average number of rides a visitor to Magic Kingdom normally takes, from nine rides to 10 rides. Disney will continue to experiment with different types of technology to help them manage customer waiting time. They are experimenting with smartphone technology and the Walt Disney World° app to see how it can be used to help manage waiting lines. Disney does all this in the hopes that customers will not be frustrated by the waits, and thus return more often.

Source

Brooks Barnes (2010), "Disney Tackles Major Theme Park Problem: Lines," *The New York Times*, December 27, http://www.nytimes.com/2010/12/28/business/media/28disney.html; Eamon McNiff, Sarah Lang, and Kimberly Launier (2014), "Disney Theme Parks Reimagining the Wait in Line," *ABC News*, April 23; https://itunes.apple.com/en/app/my-disney-experience-walt/id547436543?mt=8, all accessed April 6, 2015.

Different Queue Configurations

There are different types of queues, and the challenge for managers is to select the most appropriate type. *Figure 9.11* shows diagrams of several types you may have experienced yourself.

- In **single line sequential stages**, customers proceed through several serving operations, as in a cafeteria. Bottlenecks may occur at any stage where the process takes longer to execute than at previous stages. Many cafeterias have lines at the cash register because the cashier takes longer to calculate how much you owe and to return change, than the servers take to slap food on your plate.

- **Parallel lines to multiple servers** offer more than one serving station, allowing customers to select one of several lines in which to wait. Banks and ticket windows are common examples. Fast food restaurants usually have several serving lines in operation at busy times of day, with each offering the full menu. A parallel system can have either a single stage or multiple stages. The disadvantage of this design is that lines may not move at equal speed.

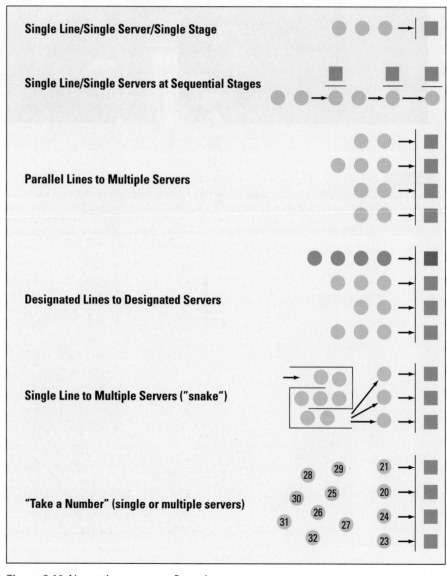

Figure 9.11 Alternative queue configurations

Figure 9.12 Post offices use the single line to multiple servers approach to control human traffic

How many times have you chosen what looked like the shortest line only to watch in frustration as the lines on either side of you moved at twice the speed of yours, because someone in your line has a complicated transaction?

- A **single line to multiple servers**, commonly known as a "snake." This type of waiting line solves the problem of the parallel lines to multiple servers moving at different speeds. This method is commonly used at post offices and airport check-ins (*Figure 9.12*).

- **Designated lines** involve assigning different lines to specific categories of customers. Examples include express lines for five items or less and regular lines at supermarket check-outs, and different check-in stations for first class, business class, and economy class airline passengers.

- **Taking a number** saves customers the need to stand in a queue. This procedure allows them to sit down and relax, or to guess how long the wait will be and do something else in the meantime — although at the risk of losing their place if earlier customers are served faster than expected. Users of this method include large travel agents, government offices, and outpatient clinics in hospitals.

- Restaurants often have **wait lists** where people put their names down and wait until their name is announced. There are four common ways of wait listing: (1) party size seating, where the number of people is matched to the size of the table; (2) VIP seating, which involves giving special rights to favored customers; (3) call-ahead seating, which allows people to phone before arriving on-site to hold a place on the wait list; and (4) large party reservations. If customers are familiar with wait listing techniques, they are likely to view them to be fair. If not, VIP seating is viewed as especially unfair by guests who don't enjoy the priority treatment[8].

Figure 9.13 Single queuing systems in cafes usually have more than one cash register stations

Queues can also be a combination of different approaches. For instance, a cafeteria with a single serving line might offer two cash register stations at the final stage (*Figure 9.13*). Similarly, patients at a small medical clinic might visit a single receptionist for registration, proceed sequentially through multiple channels for testing, diagnosis, and treatment, and conclude by returning to a single line for payment at the receptionist's desk.

Research suggests that selecting the most suitable type of queue is important to customer satisfaction. Anat Rafaeli and her colleagues found that the way queues in a waiting area are laid out can produce feelings of injustice and unfairness in customers. Customers who waited in parallel lines to multiple servers reported significantly higher agitation and dissatisfaction with the fairness of the service delivery process than customers who waited in a single line ("snake") to access multiple servers. This result was despite the fact that both groups of customers waited the same amount of time and were involved in completely fair service processes[9]. The issue of perceived fairness arises as waiting customers are often very conscious of their own progress towards getting served. Perhaps you've watched resentfully as other diners who arrived at a busy restaurant later than you were given priority and leapfrogged the line. It doesn't seem fair — especially when you are hungry!

Virtual Waits

One of the problems associated with waiting in line is the waste of time this involves for customers. The "virtual queue" strategy is a creative way of taking the physical waiting out of the wait altogether. Instead, customers register their place in line on a terminal, which estimates the time at which they will reach the front of the virtual line and should return to claim their place[10]. Sushi Tei, a restaurant chain, implemented a self-service touch screen terminal where guests can simply select the party size, which allows the restaurant to match table sizes, enter their cell phone number, and then go shopping (*Figure 9.14*). Diners will receive a text message confirming their booking, and the message contains a link where they can view in real time how many parties are still ahead of them in the queue. They will be called by an automated system five minutes before their table is available, and diners can confirm their booking (by pressing "1"), ask for an additional 15 minutes until they will reach back to the restaurant (by pressing "2"), or they can cancel their booking if they have made alternative plans (by pressing "3"). The restaurant has a long queue on weekend evenings, but this system helps them keep customers loyal and extends the time it operates at full capacity on busy days.

Service Insights 9.3 describes the virtual queuing systems used in two very different industries — a theme park and a call center.

Figure 9.14 An innovating queuing system allows customers to enter a virtual queue for a table

SERVICE INSIGHTS 9.3
Waiting in a Virtual Queue

Disney is well known for its efforts to give its theme park visitors information on how long they may have to wait to ride a particular attraction, and for entertaining guests while they are waiting in line. However, the company found that the long waits at its most popular attractions were still a major source of dissatisfaction and thus created an innovative solution.

The virtual-queue concept was first tested at Disney World. At the most popular attractions, guests were able to register their place in line with a computer and were then free to use the wait time visiting other places in the park. Surveys showed that guests who used the new system spent more money, saw more attractions, and had significantly higher satisfaction. After further refinement, the system, now named Fastpass, was introduced at the five most popular attractions at Disney World, and was subsequently extended to all Disney parks worldwide. It is now used by more than 50 million guests a year.

Fastpass is easy to use. When guests approach a Fastpass attraction, they are given two clear choices — obtain a Fastpass ticket there and return at a designated time, or wait in a standby line. Signs indicate how long the wait is in each instance. The wait time for each line tends to be self-regulating, because a large difference between the two will lead to increasing numbers of people choosing the shorter line. In practice, the virtual wait tends to be slightly longer than the physical one. To use the Fastpass option, guests insert their park admission ticket into a special turnstile and receive a Fastpass ticket stating a return time. Guests have some flexibility because the system allows them a 60-minute window beyond the printed return time.

Just like the Fastpass system, call centers also use virtual queues. There are different types of virtual queuing systems for call centers. The first-in, first-out queuing system is very common. When callers call in, they will hear a message that informs them of the estimated wait time for the call to be taken by an agent. The caller can (1) wait in the queue and get connected to an agent when his turn arrives or (2) choose to receive a call back. When the caller chooses the latter option, he has to enter his telephone number and tell his name. He then hangs up the phone and his virtual place in the queue is kept. When he is nearly at the head of the queue, the system calls the customer back and puts him at the head of the queue where an agent will attend to him next. In both situations, the customer is unlikely to complain. In the first situation, it is the customer's choice to wait in the queue, and he can still do something else as he already knows the estimated wait time. In the second situation, the person does not have to wait for very long on the phone after the call back, before reaching an agent. The call center also benefits as fewer frustrated customers will take up the valuable time of the agents by complaining about how long they had to wait. In addition, firms also reduce aborted or missed calls from customers.

Source

Duncan Dickson, Robert C. Ford, and Bruce Laval (2005), "Managing Real and Virtual Waits in Hospitality and Service Organizations," *Cornell Hotel and Restaurant Administration Quarterly*, Vol. 46, February, pp. 52–68; "Virtual Queue," Wikipedia, www.en.wikipeidao.org/wiki/virtual_queuing; A FASTPASS Guide for Disneyland and California Adventure, http://dlrprepschool.com/a-fastpass-guide-for-disneyland-and-california-adventure, accessed March 25, 2015.

The concept of virtual queues has many potential applications. Cruise ships, all-inclusive resorts, and restaurants can use this strategy if customers are willing to provide their cell phone numbers or remain within buzzing range of a firm-operated pager system.

Queuing Systems Can Be Tailored to Market Segments

Although the basic rule in most queuing systems is "first come, first served", not all queuing systems are organized in that way. Market segmentation is sometimes used to design queuing strategies that set different priorities for different types of customers. Allocation to separate queuing areas may be based on any of the following:

- **Urgency of the job.** At many hospital emergency units, a nurse is assigned to greet incoming patients, and decide which patients require priority medical treatment and which patients can be safely asked to register, sit down and wait for their turn.

- **Duration of service transaction.** Banks, supermarkets, and other retail services often have "express lanes" for shorter, less complicated tasks.

- **Payment of a premium price.** Airlines usually offer separate check-in lines for first-, business-, and economy-class passengers, with a higher ratio of personnel to passengers in the first- and business-class lines, resulting in reduced waits for those who paid more for their tickets. At some airports, premium passengers may also enjoy faster lanes for the security check.

- **Importance of the customer.** Members of frequent flyer clubs frequently get priority wait-listing. For example, the next available seat is given to a platinum card holder of the airline's loyalty program, and these members can also jump the queue with priority access to call centers, and even when travelling economy class, members of frequent flyer clubs can use the shorter business class check-in lines.

⊃ LO 9

Understand how customers perceive waits and how to make waiting less burdensome for them.

CUSTOMER PERCEPTIONS OF WAITING TIME

People don't like wasting their time on unproductive activities any more than they like wasting money. Customer dissatisfaction with delays in receiving service often can stimulate strong emotions, even anger[11]. In fact, it has been found that if customers are dissatisfied with the wait, they must be more satisfied with the service to have the same level of loyalty as customers who were satisfied with the wait[12].

The Psychology of Waiting Time

Research shows people often think they waited longer for a service than they actually did. For instance, studies of public transportation use have shown that travelers perceive the time spent waiting for a bus or train as passing 1.5 to 7 times more slowly than the time actually spent traveling in the vehicle[13].

Savvy service marketers recognize that customers experience waiting time in different ways, depending on the circumstances. Why are some willing to wait for 50% of their time at an amusement park, but complain when they have to wait for 20 minutes for a taxi? David Maister and other researchers have the following suggestions on how to use the psychology of waiting to make waits less stressful and unpleasant[14]:

- **Unoccupied time feels longer than occupied time.** The noted philosopher William James observed, "Boredom results from being attentive to the passage of time itself." When you are sitting around with nothing to do, time seems to crawl. The challenge for service organizations is to give customers something to do or to distract them while waiting. For example, BMW car owners can wait in comfort in BMW service centers where waiting areas are furnished with designer furniture, large-screen TVs, Wi-Fi, magazines, and freshly brewed cappuccinos. Many customers even bring their own entertainment in the form of a smart phone or tablet.

  Some restaurants manage the waiting problem by inviting dinner guests to have a drink in the bar until their table is ready (that approach makes money for the house as well as keeps the customer occupied). In similar fashion, guests waiting in line for a show at a casino may find themselves queuing in a corridor lined with slot-machines.

- **Solo waits feel longer than group waits.** It is nice to wait with people you know, and talking to them is one way of helping to pass the time while waiting. However, not everyone is comfortable talking to a stranger.

- **Physically uncomfortable waits feel longer than comfortable waits.** "My feet are killing me!" is one of the most often heard comments when people are forced to stand in line for a long time. Whether they are seated or standing, waiting seems more burdensome if the temperature is too hot or too cold, if it's drafty or windy, or if there's no protection from rain or snow.

- **Pre- and post-process waits feel longer than in-process waits.** Waiting to buy a ticket to enter a theme park is different from waiting to ride on a roller coaster once you're in the park.

- **Unfair waits are longer than equitable waits.** Perceptions about what is fair or unfair sometimes vary from one culture or country to another. In the US, Canada, or Britain, people may expect everybody to wait their turn in line and are likely to get irritated if they see others jumping ahead or being given priority for no apparent reason. When people perceive the wait as fair, it reduces the negative effect of waiting.

- **Unfamiliar waits seem longer than familiar ones.** Frequent users of a service know what to expect and are less likely to worry while waiting. New or occasional users, in contrast, are often nervous, wondering not only about the probable length of the wait but also about what happens next.

- **Uncertain waits are longer than known, finite waits.** Although any wait can be frustrating, we can tend to mentally prepare ourselves to a wait of a known length. It's the unknown that keeps us on edge. Imagine waiting for a delayed flight and not being told how long the delay will be. You don't know whether you have the time to get up and walk about in the terminal, whether to stay at the gate in case the flight is called any minute, and whether you will make your connecting flight on the other end.

- **Unexplained waits are longer than explained waits.** Have you ever been in a subway or an elevator that has stopped for no apparent reason, without any announcements telling you why? In addition to uncertainty about the length of the wait, there's added worry about what is going to happen. Has there been an accident on the line? Will you be stuck there for hours?

- **Anxiety makes waits seem longer.** Can you remember waiting for someone to show up at the arranged meeting time or rendezvous, and worrying about whether you had gotten the time or location correct? While waiting in unfamiliar locations, especially outdoors and at night, people often worry about their personal safety.

- **The more valuable or important the service, the longer people will wait.** People will queue up overnight under uncomfortable conditions to get good seats to a major concert or sports event expected to sell out fast.

INVENTORY DEMAND THROUGH RESERVATIONS SYSTEMS

As an alternative, or in addition, to waiting lines, reservations systems can be used to inventory demand. Ask someone what services come to mind when you talk about reservations and they will most likely cite airlines, hotels, restaurants, car rentals, and theaters. Use synonyms like "bookings" or "appointments" and they may add haircuts, visits to professionals such as doctors and consultants, vacation rentals, and service calls to fix anything from a broken refrigerator to a temperamental laptop. There are many benefits in having a reservations system:

- Customer dissatisfaction due to excessive waits can be avoided. One aim of reservations is to guarantee that service will be available when customers want it. Customers who hold reservations should be able to count on avoiding a queue, because they have been guaranteed service at a specific time.

- Reservations allow demand to be controlled and smoothed out in a more manageable way. A well-organized reservations system allows the organization to deflect demand for service from a first-choice time to earlier or later times, from one class of service to another ("upgrades" and "downgrades"), and even from first-choice locations to alternative ones, and thereby overall contributing to higher capacity utilization.

- Reservations systems enable the implementation of revenue management and serve to pre-sell a service to different customer segments (see Chapter 6 on revenue management). For example, requiring reservations for normal repair and maintenance allows management to make sure that some capacity will be kept free for handling emergency jobs. Since these are unpredictable, higher prices can be charged and these bring with them higher margins.

- Data from reservation systems also help organizations to prepare operational and financial projections for future periods. Systems vary from a simple appointments book using handwritten entries for a doctor's office to a central, computerized data bank for an airline's global operations.

The challenge in designing reservation systems is to make them fast and user-friendly for both staff and customers. Many firms now allow customers to make their own reservations on a self-service basis via their websites and smartphones. Whether they are talking to a reservations agent or making their own bookings, customers want quick answers about whether a service is available at a preferred time and at what price. They also appreciate it if the system can provide further information about the type of service they are reserving. For instance, can a hotel assign a specific room on request, or at least assign a room with a view of the lake rather than one with a view of the parking lot? Some businesses now even charge a fee for making a reservation (see *Service Insights 9.4*).

Of course, problems arise when customers fail to show up or when service firms overbook. Marketing strategies for dealing with these operational problems include requiring a deposit, canceling non-paid reservations after a certain time, and providing compensation to victims of overbooking were discussed in Chapter 6 on revenue management.

SERVICE INSIGHTS 9.4
Pay to Get That Hard-To-Get Table Reservation!

Today's Epicure is an exclusive online company that helps customers get table reservations at the most popular dining spots in New York, such as Carbone, Lafayette, or The NoMad, where only people who are "somebody" or have the right connections can secure a table. Even then, it can take several months of patient planning. The company is able to get a table on a specific day, and on short notice. Currently, the company focuses on areas where it is difficult to get reservations, namely New York City, Philadelphia, and the Hamptons. Individuals pay a membership fee of $1,000 to join and $125 per month for access to the service.

Pascal Riffaud, the entrepreneur behind this idea, was president of Personal Concierge International, a leading company providing exclusive concierge services in the US. During his work experience as president of Personal Concierge, Riffaud built a large network of contacts with exclusive restaurants, allowing him to obtain those hard-to-get reservations.

His clients were delighted with his service and kept flooding him with requests for reservations. However, similar to earlier start-ups, there have been protests from restaurant owners who felt these types of services were upsetting their reservation systems and also selling their tables for a price. Even though these services cancel unsold reservations, restaurant owners feel these could have been sold to other customers who really wanted a table. As more start-ups offer similar service (see www.Table8.com and www.resy.com in Los Angeles), restaurants may have to rethink the way they handle reservations!

Source

"Would You Pay $1,000 for a Dinner Reservation? Meet the Scalper Selling Table Spots at New York's Hottest Restaurants," by Daily Mail Reporter, www.dailymail.co.uk/femail/article-2384867/Meet-Pascal-Riffaud-Today-s-Epicures-scalper-selling-table-spots-New-Yorks-hottest-restaurants.html#ixzz3VOp1ZlDb, https://www.todaysepicure.com, http://resy.com, all accessed March 25, 2015.

Reservations Strategies Should Focus on Yield

Increasingly, service firms are looking at their "yield" —the average revenue received per unit of capacity. Yield analysis forces managers to recognize the opportunity cost of selling capacity for a given date to a customer from one market segment when another might subsequently yield a higher rate. Think about the following problems facing sales managers for different types of service organizations with capacity limitations:

- Should a hotel accept an advance booking from a tour group of 200 room nights at $140 each, when some of these same room nights might possibly be sold later at short notice to business travelers at the full posted rate of $300?

- Should a railroad with 30 empty freight cars accept an immediate request for a shipment worth $1,400 per car or hold the cars for a few more days in the hopes of getting a priority shipment that would be twice as valuable?

- Should a print shop process all jobs on a first-come, first-served basis, with a guaranteed delivery time for each job, or should it charge a premium rate for "rush" work, and tell customers with "standard" jobs to expect some variability in completion dates?

Decisions on such problems deserve to be handled with a little more sophistication than just resorting to "the bird in the hand is worth two in the bush" formula. Good information based on detailed record-keeping of past usage supported by current market intelligence is the key to allocating the inventory of capacity among different segments. The decision to accept or reject business should be based on realistic estimates of the probabilities of obtaining higher rated business and on the awareness of the need to maintain established (and desirable) customer relationships. We discussed the more sophisticated approach of revenue management systems for allocating capacity to different "rate buckets" and setting prices in Chapter 6 "Setting Prices and Implementing Revenue Management".

LO 11

Be familiar with strategic approaches to utilize residual surplus capacity even after all other options of matching demand and capacity have been exhausted.

CREATE ALTERNATIVE USE FOR OTHERWISE WASTED CAPACITY

Even after professional management of capacity and demand, most service firms will still experience periods of excess capacity. However, not all unsold productive capacity has to be wasted, as alternative "demand" can be created by innovative firms. Many firms take a strategic approach to the disposition of anticipated surplus capacity, allocating it in advance to build relationships with customers, suppliers, employees, and intermediaries[15]. Possible uses for otherwise wasted capacity include:

- **Use capacity for service differentiation.** When capacity utilization is low, service employees can go all the way to truly "wow" their customers. A firm that wants to build customer loyalty and market share should use a slack in operations to focus on outstanding customer service. This can include extra attention paid to the customer, allocation of preferred seating, and the likes.

- **Reward your best customers and build loyalty.** This can be done through special promotions as part of a loyalty program, while ensuring that existing revenues are not cannibalized.

- **Customer and channel development.** Provide free or heavily discounted trials for prospective customers and for intermediaries who sell to end customers.

- **Reward employees.** In certain industries such as restaurants, beach resorts, or cruise lines, capacity can be used to reward employees and their families to build loyalty. This can improve employee satisfaction and provide employees an understanding of the service as experienced from the customer's perspective and thereby raising performance.

- **Barter free capacity.** Service firms often can save costs and increase capacity utilization by bartering capacity with their own suppliers. Among the most widely bartered services are advertising space or airtime, airline seats, and hotel rooms.

CONCLUSION

Because many capacity-constrained service organizations have heavy fixed costs, even modest improvements in capacity utilization tend to have a significant effect on the bottom line. In this chapter, we have shown how managers can manage productive capacity and demand and improve customers' waiting and queuing experiences. Managing capacity and demand for a service at a particular place and time closely links back to what we learned in past chapters, including decisions on product elements and tiering of service seen in Chapter 4, place and time of service delivery seen in Chapter 5, revenue management as discussed in Chapter 6, promotion and education as discussed in Chapter 7, and designing and balancing the capacity of service processes as discussed in Chapter 8.

CHAPTER SUMMARY

LO1 At any one time, a firm with limited capacity can face different demand–supply situations:
- Excess demand.
- Demand that exceeds ideal capacity.
- Well-balanced demand and supply.
- Excess capacity.

When demand and supply are not in balance, firms will have idle capacity during low periods, but have to turn away customers during peak periods. This situation impedes the efficient use of productive assets and erodes profitability. Firms, therefore, need to try and balance demand and supply through adjusting capacity and/or demand.

LO2 The building blocks for effective capacity and demand management are:
- Define productive capacity.
- Use capacity management tools.
- Understand demand patterns and drivers by customer segment.
- Use demand management tools.

LO3 When we refer to managing capacity, we implicitly mean productive capacity. There are several different forms of productive capacity in services:
- Physical facilities for processing customers.
- Physical facilities for processing goods.
- Physical equipment for processing people, possessions, or information.
- Labor.
- Infrastructure.

LO4 **Capacity** can be managed in a number of ways, including **stretching capacity** and **adjusting capacity**.

Stretching capacity means that some capacity is elastic and more people can be served with the same capacity through crowding (e.g., in a subway car), extending operating hours, or speeding up customer processing times.

Adjusting capacity involves to more closely match demand by:
- Scheduling downtime during low periods.
- Cross-training employees.
- Using part-time employees.
- Inviting customers to perform self-service.
- Asking customers to share capacity.
- Designing capacity to be flexible.

- Renting or sharing extra facilities and equipment.

LO5 To manage **demand** effectively, firms need to understand demand patterns and drivers by market segment. Different segments often exhibit different demand patterns (e.g., routine maintenance versus emergency repairs). Once firms have an understanding of the demand patterns of their market segments, they can use marketing strategies to reshape those patterns.

LO6 Demand can be managed in the following five basic ways:
- Take no action, and leave demand to find its own levels.
- Reduce demand during peak periods.
- Increase demand during low periods.
- Inventory demand through waiting lines and queuing systems.
- Inventory demand through reservation systems.

LO7 The following marketing mix elements can be used to help smooth out fluctuations in demand:
- Use price and nonmonetary customer costs to manage demand.
- Change product elements to attract different segments at different times.
- Modify the place and time of delivery (e.g., through extended opening hours).
- Promotion and education (e.g., "mail early for Christmas").

LO8 **Waiting line** and **queuing systems** help firms inventory demand over short periods of time. There are different types of queues with their respective advantages and applications. Queuing systems include single line with sequential stages, parallel lines to multiple servers, single line to multiple servers, designated lines, taking a number, and wait list.

Not all queuing systems are organized on a "first come, first served" basis. Rather, good systems often segment waiting customers by:
- Urgency of the job (e.g., hospital emergency units).
- Duration of the service transaction (e.g., express lanes).
- Premium service based on a premium price (e.g., first-class check-in counters).

- Importance of the customer (e.g., frequent travelers get priority wait listing).

LO9 Customers don't like wasting their time waiting. Firms need to understand the **psychology of waiting** and take active steps to make waiting less frustrating. We discussed 10 possible steps, including:
- Keeping customers occupied or entertained while waiting.
- Informing customers how long the wait is likely to be.
- Providing them with an explanation of why they have to wait.
- Avoiding perceptions of unfair waits.

LO10 Effective **reservations systems** inventory demand over a longer period of time and offer several benefits. They:
- Help to reduce or even avoid customers waiting in queues and thereby avoid dissatisfaction due to excessive waits.
- Allow the firm to control demand and smooth it out.
- Enable the use of revenue management to focus on increasing yield by reserving scarce capacity for higher-paying segments, rather than selling off capacity on a "first come, first served" basis.

LO11 Even after professional management of capacity and demand, most service firms will still experience periods of excess capacity. Firms can take a strategic approach to the use of surplus capacity, including:
- Use capacity for service differentiation. When capacity utilization is low, service employees can go all the way to truly "wow" their customers.
- Reward your best customers and build loyalty (e.g., through special promotions as part of a loyalty program).
- Customer and channel development (e.g., provide free or heavily discounted trials).
- Reward employees (e.g., excess capacity in restaurants, beach resorts, or cruise lines can used to reward loyal employees and their families).
- Barter free capacity (e.g., service firms can consider bartering excess capacity for advertising space, airline seats, and hotel rooms).

Review Questions

1. What is the difference between ideal capacity and maximum capacity? Provide examples of a situation where (a) the two might be the same and (b) the two are different.

2. Describe the building blocks for managing capacity and demand.

3. What is meant by productive capacity in services?

4. Why is capacity management particularly important for service firms?

5. What actions can firms take to adjust capacity to be more closely matched to demand?

6. How can firms identify the factors that affect demand for their services?

7. What actions can firms take to adjust demand to match capacity more closely?

8. How can marketing mix elements be used to reshape demand patterns?

9. What do you see as the advantages and disadvantages of the different types of queues for an organization serving large numbers of customers? For which type of service might each of the queuing types be more suitable?

10. How can firms make waiting more pleasant for their customers?

11. What are the benefits of having an effective reservation system?

12. How can service firms use residual service capacity after all strategies of matching supply and demand have been exhausted?

Application Exercises

1. Explain how flexible capacity can be created in each of the following situations: (a) a local library, (b) an office-cleaning service, (c) a technical support helpdesk, (d) an Interflora franchise.

2. Identify some specific examples of firms in your community (or region) that significantly change their product and/or marketing mix in order to increase patronage during low demand periods.

3. Select a service organization of your choice, and identify its particular patterns of demand with reference to the checklist provided in *Table 9.1* and answer: (a) What is the nature of this service organization's approach to capacity and demand management? (b) What changes would you recommend in relation to its management of capacity and demand and why?

4. Review the 10 suggestions on the psychology of waiting. Which are the most relevant in (a) a supermarket; (b) a city bus stop on a rainy, dark evening; (c) a doctor's office; and (d) a ticket line for a football game expected to be a sell-out?

5. Give examples, based on your own experience, of a reservation system that worked really well and of one that worked really badly. Identify and examine the reasons for the success and failure of these two systems. What recommendations would you make to both firms to improve (or further improve, in the case of the good example) their reservation systems?

Endnotes

1. Kenneth J. Klassen and Thomas R. Rohleder (2001), "Combining Operations and Marketing to Manage Capacity and Demand in Services," *The Service Industries Journal*, Vol. 21, April, pp. 1–30.

2. Breffni M. Noone, Sheryl E. Kimes, Anna S. Mattila, and Jochen Wirtz (2007), "The Effect of Meal Pace on Customer Satisfaction," *Cornell Hospitality Quarterly*, Vol. 48, No. 3, pp. 231–245; Breffni M. Noone, Jochen Wirtz and Sheryl E. Kimes (2012), "The Effect of Perceived Control on Consumer Responses to Service Encounter Pace: A Revenue Management Perspective," *Cornell Hospitality Quarterly*, Vol. 53, No. 4, pp. 295–307.

3. Based on material in James A. Fitzsimmons and M. J. Fitzsimmons (2008), *Service Management: Operations, Strategy, and Information Technology.* 6th ed., New York: Irwin McGraw-Hill; W. Earl Sasser, Jr. (1976), "Match Supply and Demand in Service Industries," *Harvard Business Review*, Vol. 54, November–December, pp. 133–140.

4. See also the discussion on bottlenecks in service processes and how to balance the capacity in each of the steps in a customer service process (Chapter 8, "Designing Service Processes") to maximize overall process capacity.

5. Kenneth J. Klassen and Thomas R. Rohleder (2004), "Using Customer Motivations to Reduce Peak Demand: Does It Work?" *The Service Industries Journal*, Vol. 24, September, pp. 53–70.

6. http://en.wikipedia.org/wiki/Queueing_theory, accessed March 25, 2015.

7. The Case Bank's survey were reported in: "Contactless Payments in a 'blink,'" http://www.cr80news.com/news-item/contactless-payments-in-a-blink/, accessed on March 25, 2015.

8. Kelly A. McGuire and Sheryl E. Kimes (2006), "The Perceived Fairness of Waitlist-Management Techniques for Restaurants," *Cornell Hotel and Restaurant Administration Quarterly*, Vol. 47, May, pp. 121–134.

9. Anat Rafaeli, G. Barron, and K. Haber (2002), "The Effects of Queue Structure on Attitudes," *Journal of Service Research*, Vol. 5, November, pp. 125–139.

10. Duncan Dickson, Robert C. Ford, and Bruce Laval (2005), "Managing Real and Virtual Waits in Hospitality and Service Organizations," *Cornell Hotel and Restaurant Administration Quarterly*, Vol. 46, February, pp. 52–68.

11. Ana B. Casado Diaz and Francisco J. Más Ruiz (2002), "The Consumer's Reaction to Delays in Service," *International Journal of Service Industry Management*, Vol. 13, No. 2, pp. 118–140.

12. Frederic Bielen and Nathalie Demoulin (2007), "Waiting Time Influence on the Satisfaction-Loyalty Relationship in Services," *Managing Service Quality*, Vol. 17, No. 2, pp. 174–193.

13. Jay R. Chernow (1981), "Measuring the Values of Travel Time Savings," *Journal of Consumer Research,* Vol. 7, March, pp. 360–371. This entire issue of Journal of Consumer Research was devoted to the consumption of time.

14. This section is based on David H. Maister (1986), "The Psychology of Waiting Lines," in J. A. Czepiel, M. R. Solomon, and C. F. Surprenant, eds. *The Service Encounter.* Lexington, MA: Lexington Books/D.C. Heath, pp. 113–123; Peter Jones and Emma Peppiat (1996), "Managing Perceptions of Waiting Times in Service Queues," *International Journal of Service Industry Management*, Vol. 7, No. 5, pp. 47–61; Clay M. Voorhees, Julie Baker, Brian L. Bourdeau, E. Deanne Brocato, and J. Joseph Cronin, Jr. (2009), "Moderating the Relationships Among Perceived Waiting Time, Anger and Regret," *Journal of Service Research*, Vol. 12, No. 2, November, pp. 138–155; Kelly A. McGuire, Sheryl E. Kimes, Michael Lynn, Madeline E. Pullman and Russell C. Lloyd (2010), "A Framework for Evaluating the Customer Wait Experience," *Journal of Service Management*, Vol. 21, No. 3, pp. 269–290.

    See also the findings for wait situations in stressful service encounters such as dental appointments by Elizabeth Gelfand Miller, Barbara E. Kahn, and Mary Frances Luce (2008), "Consumer Wait Management Strategies for Negative Service Events: A Coping Approach," *Journal of Consumer Research*, Vol. 34, No. 5, pp. 635–648.

    For customer abandoning of waits for service: Narayan Janakiraman, Robert J. Meyer, and Stephen J. Hoch (2011), "The Psychology of Decisions to Abandon Waits for Service," *Journal of Marketing Research*, Vol. 48, December, pp. 970–984.

15. Irene C.L. Ng, Jochen Wirtz, and Khai Sheang Lee (1999), "The Strategic Role of Unused Service Capacity," *International Journal of Service Industry Management*, Vol. 10, No. 2, pp. 211–238.

CHAPTER
10

Crafting the Service Environment

Managers…need to develop a better understanding of the interface between the resources they manipulate in atmospherics and the experience they want to create for the customer.

Jean-Charles Chebat and Laurette Dubé
Professors of Marketing at HEC Montréal Business School and McGill University, Montréal, respectively

Restaurant design has become as compelling an element as menu, food and wine…in determining a restaurant's success.

Danny Meyer
New York City restaurateur and CEO of
Union Square Hospitality Group

LEARNING OBJECTIVES (LOs)

By the end of this chapter, the reader should be able to:

➲ **LO 1**　Recognize the four core purposes service environments fulfill.

➲ **LO 2**　Know the theoretical foundation from environmental psychology that helps us understand how customers and employees respond to service environments.

➲ **LO 3**　Be familiar with the integrative servicescape model.

➲ **LO 4**　Know the three main dimensions of the service environment.

➲ **LO 5**　Discuss the key ambient conditions and their effects on customers.

➲ **LO 6**　Determine the roles of spatial layout and functionality.

➲ **LO 7**　Understand the roles of signs, symbols, and artifacts.

➲ **LO 8**　Know how service employees and other customers are part of the servicescape.

➲ **LO 9**　Explain why designing an effective servicescape has to be done holistically and from the customer's perspective.

OPENING VIGNETTE
The Guggenheim Museum in Bilbao

When the Guggenheim Museum in Bilbao in northern Spain opened its doors to the public, there was praise for it from all over the world. Designed by the influential and famous Canadian-American architect Frank Gehry, it had a fascinating architecture hailed as "the greatest building of our time". It put Bilbao, a previously unheard of place, on the world map as a tourist destination. Once an industrial area with a shipyard, large warehouse districts, and a river filled with a century of waste from factories that lined its shores, the entire city was transformed with the museum being the first step of the city's redevelopment plan. Such a transformation is now even called the "Bilbao effect", and is being studied to understand how this kind of "wow" effect architecture can help transform a city.

The design features of the museum have a number of meanings and messages. It is shaped like a ship and blends in with the environment of the river. The museum is a mixture of regular forms built in stone, curved forms made of titanium, and huge glass walls that allow natural light to penetrate the museum and provide visitors inside the building with a view of the surrounding hills. Outside, the titanium panels have been arranged to look like fish scales, keeping in tune with the image of being by the Nervion River. A 43-foot-tall terrier topiary made of pots of fresh pansies and a large spider sculpture, called "Maman" by the 20th century leading sculptor Louise Bourgeois, greets visitors.

From the museum's huge, metal-domed atrium, patrons can visit 19 other galleries connected by curved walkways, glass lifts, and stairways. Even the design of the galleries hints at what visitors can expect inside. The rectangular-shaped galleries have limestone-covered walls. The rectangle is a more conventional shape, and these galleries hold the classic art collections. The irregularly shaped galleries hold collections of selected living artists. In addition, there are special galleries with no structural columns so that large artworks can be displayed. The structures of these galleries are also a work of art that comes from a specially designed and planned servicescape.

While not all servicescapes are great works of architecture, the Guggenheim Museum in Bilbao is. It is an attention-grabbing medium that shapes the expectations of its visitors. They can look forward to an awesome experience at the museum.

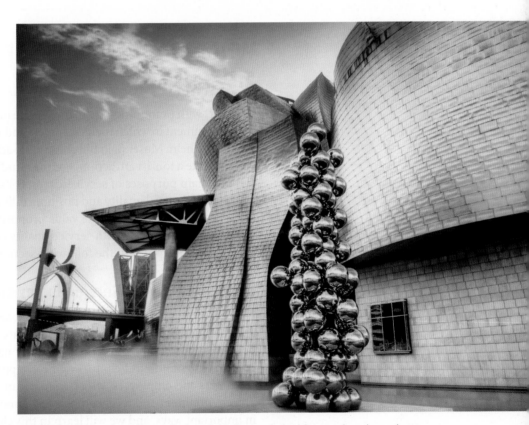

Figure 10.1 The extraordinary design of the Guggenheim Museum has drawn large amounts of praise and crowds.

SERVICE ENVIRONMENTS — AN IMPORTANT ELEMENT OF THE SERVICE MARKETING MIX

The physical service environment that customers experience plays a key role in shaping the service experience and enhancing (or undermining) customer satisfaction, especially in high-contact people-processing services[1]. Disney theme parks are often cited as vivid examples of service environments that make customers feel comfortable and highly satisfied and leave a long-lasting impression. In fact, organizations such as hospitals, hotels, restaurants, and offices of professional service firms have come to recognize that the service environment is an important element of their services marketing mix and overall value proposition.

Designing the service environment is an art that involves a lot of time and effort, and it can be expensive to implement. Service environments, also called servicescapes, relate to the style and appearance of the physical surroundings and other experiential elements encountered by customers at service delivery sites[2]. Once designed and built, service environments are not easy to change. *Figure 10.2* provides an overview of the key topics covered in this chapter. Note that we focus on the key dimensions of service environments in the servicescape model and not much on its others aspects.

⊃ LO 1
Recognize the four core purposes service environments fulfill.

WHAT IS THE PURPOSE OF SERVICE ENVIRONMENTS?

Let's start with examining why many service firms take so much trouble to shape the environment in which their customers and service personnel will interact. For the Guggenheim Museum in Bilbao, it was to address several of the city's problems and to create a tourist attraction. For the museum and many service firms, there are four main purposes of servicescapes: (1) shape customers' experiences and behaviors; (2) signal quality and position, differentiate and strengthen the brand; (3) be a core component of the value proposition; and (4) facilitate the service encounter and enhance both service quality and productivity. We discuss each of these four purposes in the following sections.

Shape Customers' Service Experiences and Behaviors

For organizations that deliver high-contact services, the design of the physical environment and the way in which tasks are performed by customer-contact personnel play a vital role in shaping the nature of customers' experiences. Physical surroundings help to "engineer" appropriate feelings and reactions in customers and employees, which in turn can help to build loyalty to the firm[3]. The environment and its accompanying atmosphere can affect buyer behavior in important ways, and we will learn in this chapter how the design elements of the service environment can make customers feel excited or relaxed, help them find their way in complex servicescapes such as hospitals or airports, and shape their quality perceptions and important outcomes such as buying behavior, satisfaction, and repeat purchase.

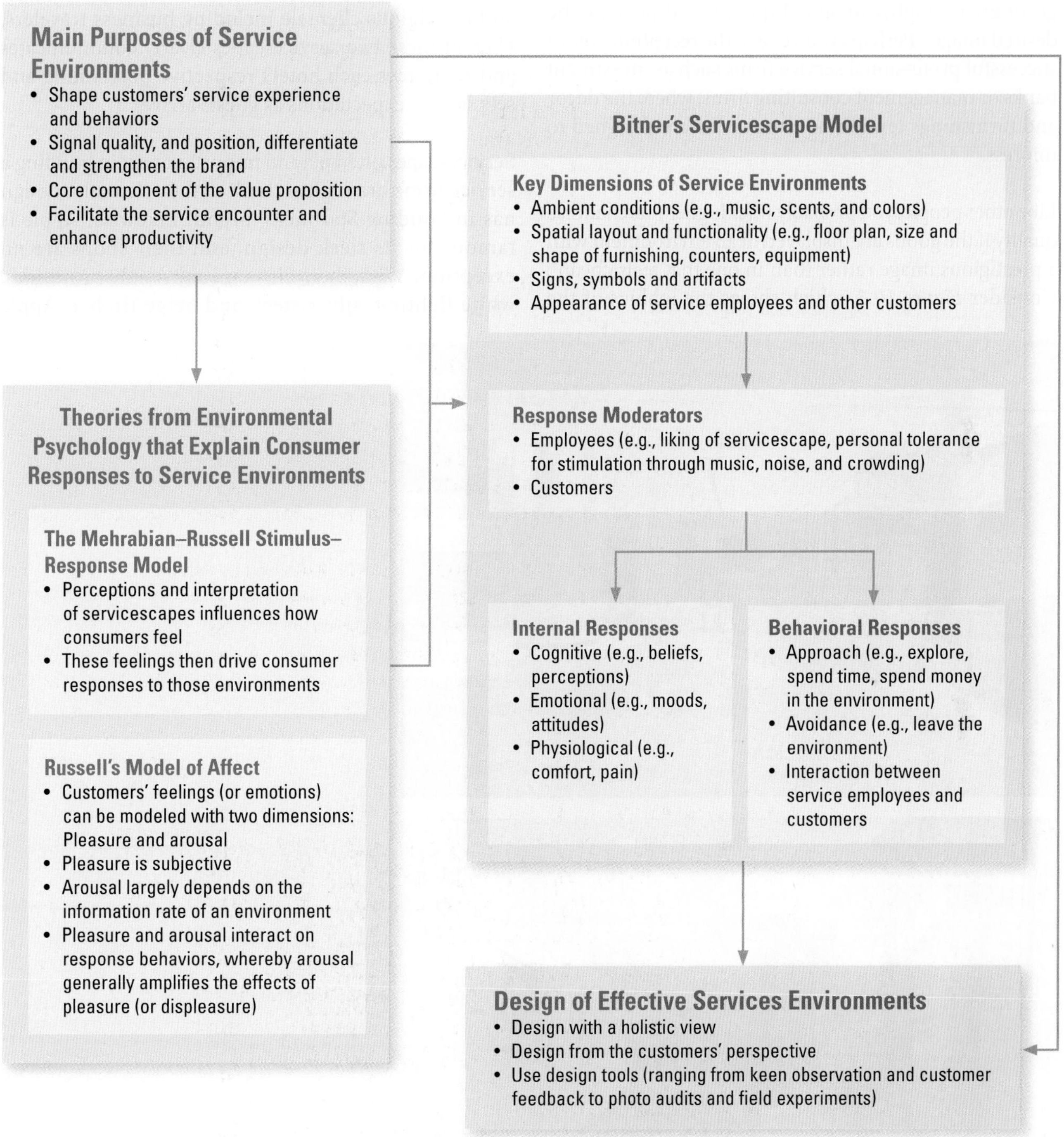

Main Purposes of Service Environments
- Shape customers' service experience and behaviors
- Signal quality, and position, differentiate and strengthen the brand
- Core component of the value proposition
- Facilitate the service encounter and enhance productivity

Theories from Environmental Psychology that Explain Consumer Responses to Service Environments

The Mehrabian–Russell Stimulus–Response Model
- Perceptions and interpretation of servicescapes influences how consumers feel
- These feelings then drive consumer responses to those environments

Russell's Model of Affect
- Customers' feelings (or emotions) can be modeled with two dimensions: Pleasure and arousal
- Pleasure is subjective
- Arousal largely depends on the information rate of an environment
- Pleasure and arousal interact on response behaviors, whereby arousal generally amplifies the effects of pleasure (or displeasure)

Bitner's Servicescape Model

Key Dimensions of Service Environments
- Ambient conditions (e.g., music, scents, and colors)
- Spatial layout and functionality (e.g., floor plan, size and shape of furnishing, counters, equipment)
- Signs, symbols and artifacts
- Appearance of service employees and other customers

Response Moderators
- Employees (e.g., liking of servicescape, personal tolerance for stimulation through music, noise, and crowding)
- Customers

Internal Responses
- Cognitive (e.g., beliefs, perceptions)
- Emotional (e.g., moods, attitudes)
- Physiological (e.g., comfort, pain)

Behavioral Responses
- Approach (e.g., explore, spend time, spend money in the environment)
- Avoidance (e.g., leave the environment)
- Interaction between service employees and customers

Design of Effective Services Environments
- Design with a holistic view
- Design from the customers' perspective
- Use design tools (ranging from keen observation and customer feedback to photo audits and field experiments)

Figure 10.2 Organizational framework

Signal Quality, and Position, Differentiate and Strengthen the Brand

Services are often intangible and customers cannot assess their quality well. So customers use the service environment as an important quality proxy, and firms go to great lengths to signal quality and portray the desired image[4]. Perhaps you've seen the reception area of successful professional service firms such as investment banks or management consulting firms, where the decor and furnishings tend to be elegant and are designed to impress.

Like other people, you probably infer higher merchandise quality if the goods are displayed in an environment with a prestigious image rather than in one that feels cheap[5]. Consider *Figure 10.3*, which shows the lobbies of the Generator Youth Hostel in London and The Fairmont Express in Victoria, British Columbia, Canada. These are two different types of hotels catering to two very different target segments. The Generator caters to younger guests who love fun and have low budgets, and the Fairmont Express caters to a more mature, affluent, and prestigious clientele including business travelers. Each of these two servicescapes clearly communicates and reinforces each hotel's respective positioning and sets service expectations as guests arrive.

Servicescapes often play an important part in building a service firm's brand. Just think of the role outlet design has in building Starbucks' brand! Likewise, Apple is famous for its sleek design, and their shops are no exception. With their airy and minimalist interiors, white lighting, silver steel, and beige timber, Apple

Figure 10.3 Compare the two hotel lobbies; different types of hotels have very different target segments

Stores create a bright, open and futuristic servicescape that provides a carefree and casual atmosphere. Apple's flagship stores feature dramatic locations such as inside the Louvre in Paris, or a 40-foot-high glass cylinder in Shanghai. Apple's retail operations are an important part of its business — it has 453 retail stores in 16 countries; of its 43,000 employees in the US, 30,000 work at Apple Stores, and its sales per square foot of $4,551 per annum in 2014 were the highest of any retailer in the US[6]! The Apple Stores' ability to deliver a consistent, differentiated and high-quality service experience reinforces Apple's brand image, and is consistent with the upmarket and high-quality positioning of its products.

Core Component of the Value Proposition

The servicescape can even be a core component of a firm's value proposition. Consider how effectively many amusement parks use the servicescape concept to engineer their visitors' service experiences as they come to these parks to enjoy the environment and the rides. The clean environment of Disneyland or the LEGOLAND® Windsor Resort (*Figure 10.4*), in addition to employees in colorful costumes all contribute to the sense of fun and excitement that visitors encounter upon arrival and throughout their visit.

Resort hotels illustrate how servicescapes can become a core part of the value proposition. Club Med's villages,

Figure 10.4 In LEGOLAND®, the servicescape is part of the value proposition

designed to create a totally carefree atmosphere, may have provided the original inspiration for "getaway" holiday environments. New destination resorts are not only far more luxurious than Club Med, but they also draw inspiration from theme parks to create fantasy environments both indoors and outdoors. Perhaps the most extreme examples can be found in Las Vegas. Facing competition from numerous casinos in other locations, Las Vegas has repositioned itself away from being a purely adult destination, to a somewhat more wholesome entertainment destination where families too can have fun. The gambling is still there, but many of the huge hotels recently built (or rebuilt) have been transformed by adding visually attractive features like erupting "volcanoes," (*Figure 10.5*) mock sea battles, and striking reproductions of Paris, the pyramids of Egypt, and Venice and its canals.

Figure 10.5 At the Mirage Hotel and Casino in Las Vegas, an erupting volcano is part of the servicescape

Facilitate the Service Encounter and Enhance Productivity

Service environments are often designed to facilitate the service encounter and to increase productivity. For example, childcare centers use toy outlines on walls and floors to show where toys should be placed after use. In fast-food restaurants and school cafeterias, strategically located tray-return stands and notices on walls remind customers to return their trays. As shown in Bangalore Express Restaurant (*Figure 10.6*), environments can be designed to optimize the use of expensive rental space. Finally, *Service Insights 10.1* shows how the design of hospitals helps patients recover and employees perform better.

Figure 10.6 Bangalore Express City, a restaurant in the city of London, is designed to optimize expensive rental space

SERVICE INSIGHTS 10.1
The Hospital Servicescape and Its Effects on Patients and Employees

Thankfully, most of us do not have to stay in hospitals[7]. If it should happen, we hope our stay will allow us to recover in a suitable environment. But what is considered suitable in a hospital?

Patients may contract infections while in hospital, feel stressed by the contact with many strangers, and yet become bored without much to do, dislike the food, or be unable to rest well. All these factors may delay a patient's recovery. Medical workers usually work under demanding conditions and may contract infectious diseases, be stressed by the emotional labor of dealing with difficult patients, or be at risk of injury when exposed to various types of medical equipment. Research has shown that greater care in designing the hospital servicescape reduces these risks and contributes to patients' well-being and recovery, as well as staff welfare and productivity. The recommendations include:

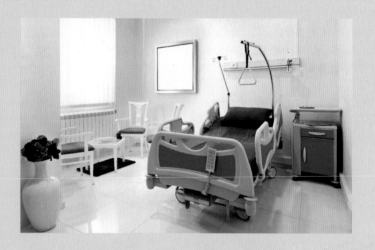

- **Provide single-bed rooms.** These can lower the number of infections caught in the hospital, improve rest and sleep quality by lessening disturbance caused by other patients sharing the room, increase patient privacy, facilitate social support by families, and even improve communication between staff and patients.

- **Reduce noise levels.** This leads to decreased stress levels for staff, and improved sleep for patients.

- **Provide distractions for patients,** including areas of greenery and nature for them to visit or see from their beds, personalized televisions with headphones to avoid disturbing others, the Internet access for tablets and smartphones, and perhaps a reading room with a library with newspapers, magazines, and books. These can all aid in patients' recovery.

- **Improve lighting,** especially access to natural light. A lighted environment increases cheerfulness in the building. Natural lighting can lead to a reduced length of stay for patients. Hospital staff can work better under proper lighting and make fewer errors.

- **Improve ventilation** and air filtration to reduce the transmission of airborne viruses and improve the overall air quality in the building.

- **Develop user-friendly "wayfinding" systems.** Hospitals are complex buildings, and it can be frustrating for many first-time and infrequent visitors when they cannot find their way, especially when rushing to see a loved one who has been hospitalized.

- **Design the layout** of patient care units and the location of nurse stations to reduce unnecessary walking within the building, and the fatigue and time wastage that can cause. This way, the quality of patient care can be improved. Well-designed layouts also enhance staff communication and activities.

A well-designed service environment makes customers feel good, boosts their satisfaction, and allows the firm to influence their behavior (e.g., adhering to the service script and prompting impulse purchases). As service quality is often difficult to assess, customers frequently use the service environment as an important quality signal; therefore, the service environment can play a major part in shaping customers' perception of a firm's image and positioning, and can even be a core part of the firm's value proposition. Finally, a well-designed service environment will enhance the productivity of the service operation.

THE THEORY BEHIND CONSUMER RESPONSES TO SERVICE ENVIRONMENTS

⊃ LO 2

Know the theoretical foundation from environmental psychology that helps us understand how customers and employees respond to service environments.

We now understand why service firms take so much effort to design the service environment. But why does the service environment have such important effects on people and their behaviors? The field of environmental psychology studies how people respond to particular environments, and we can apply its theories to better understand and manage how customers behave in different service settings.

Feelings are a Key Driver of Customer Responses to Service Environments

Two important models help us better understand consumer responses to service environments. The first, the Mehrabian–Russell Stimulus–Response Model holds that our feelings are central to how we respond to different elements in the environment. The second, Russell's Model of Affect, focuses on how we can better understand those feelings and their implications on response behaviors.

The Mehrabian–Russell Stimulus–Response Model. *Figure 10.7* displays a simple yet fundamental model of how people respond to environments. The model holds that the conscious and unconscious perception and interpretation of the environment influences how people feel in that setting[8]. People's feelings in turn drive their responses to that environment. Feelings are central to the model, which posits that feelings, rather than perceptions or thoughts, drive behavior. Similar environments can lead to very different feelings and subsequent responses.

Figure 10.7 Model of environmental responses

For example, we may dislike being in a crowded department store with lots of other customers, find ourselves unable to get what we want as quickly as we wish, and thus seek to avoid that environment. We don't simply avoid an environment because of the presence of many people around us; rather we are deterred by the unpleasant feeling of crowding, of people being in our way, of lacking perceived control, and of not being able to get what we want at our pace. However, if we were not in a rush and felt excited about being part of the crowd during seasonal festivities in the very same environment, then we might derive feelings of pleasure and excitement that would make us want to stay and enjoy the experience. In environmental psychology research, the typical outcome variable studied is the "'approach' or 'avoidance'" of an environment. In services marketing, we can add a long list of additional outcomes that a firm might want to manage, including how much time and money people spend, and how satisfied they are with the service experience after they have left the firm's premises.

Russell's Model of Affect. Given that affect or feelings are central to how people respond to an environment, we need to understand those feelings better. For this, Russell's Model of Affect (*Figure 10.8*) is widely used. It

suggests that emotional responses to environments can be described along the two main dimensions of pleasure and arousal[9]. Pleasure is a direct, subjective response to the environment, depending on how much an individual likes or dislikes the environment. Arousal refers to how stimulated the individual feels, ranging from deep sleep (lowest level of internal activity) to highest levels

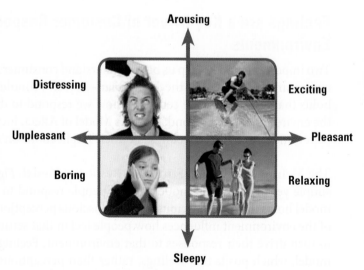

Figure 10.8 The Russell Model of Affect

of adrenaline in the bloodstream, for example, when bungee-jumping (highest level of internal activity). The arousal quality of an environment is much less subjective than its pleasure quality. Arousal quality depends largely on the information rate or load of an environment. For example, environments are stimulating (i.e., have a high information rate) when they are complex, include motion or change, and have novel and surprising elements. A relaxing environment with a low information rate has the opposite characteristics.

But how can feelings and emotions be explained by only two dimensions? Russell separates the cognitive, or thinking, part of emotions from these two underlying emotional dimensions. Thus, the emotion of anger about a service failure is modeled as high arousal and high displeasure. This locates it in the distressing region in our model, combined with a cognitive attribution process. When a customer attributes a service failure to the firm — that is, he thinks it is the firm's fault this happened, it was under their control, and they firm did not do much to prevent it from happening — then this powerful cognitive attribution process feeds directly into high arousal and displeasure. Similarly, most other emotions can be dissected into their cognitive and affective components.

The strength of Russell's model of affect is its simplicity as it allows a direct assessment of how customers feel while they are in the service environment. Therefore, firms can set targets for the affective states they want their customers to be in. For example, a roller coaster operator wants its customers to feel excited (which is a relatively high arousal environment combined with pleasure), a spa may want customers to feel relaxed a bank pleasant and so on. Later on in this chapter, we discuss how service environments can be designed to deliver the types of service experiences desired by customers.

Affective and Cognitive Processes. Affect can be caused by sensing, perceptions, and cognitive processes of any degree of complexity. However, the more complex a cognitive process becomes, the more powerful its potential impact on affect is. For example, a customer's disappointment with service level and food quality in a restaurant (a complex cognitive process, in which perceived quality is compared to previously held service expectations) cannot be compensated by a simple cognitive process such as the subconscious perception of pleasant background music. Yet this doesn't mean that simple cognitive processes, such as the subconscious perception of scents or music, are unimportant. In practice, the large majority of people's service encounters are routine, with little high-level cognitive processing. We tend to function on "autopilot" and follow our service scripts when doing routine transactions such as using a bus or subway, or entering a fast-food restaurant or a bank. Most of the time, it is the simple cognitive processes that determine how people feel in the service setting. Those include the conscious and even subconscious perceptions of space, colors, scents, and so on. However, should higher levels of cognitive processes be triggered — for instance, through something surprising in the service environment — then it's the interpretation of this surprise that determines people's feelings[10].

Behavioral Consequences of Affect. At the most basic level, pleasant environments result in "approach" behaviors and unpleasant ones result in "avoidance" behaviors. Arousal acts as an amplifier of the basic effect of pleasure on behavior. If the environment is pleasant, increasing arousal can generate excitement, leading to a stronger positive response. Conversely, if a service environment is inherently unpleasant, increasing arousal levels would move customers into the "distressed" region. For example, loud and fast-paced music would increase the stress levels of shoppers trying to make their way through crowded aisles on a pre-Christmas Friday evening. In such situations, retailers should try to lower the information load of the environment.

Finally, customers have strong affective expectations of some services. Think of experiences such as a romantic candlelight dinner in a restaurant, a relaxing spa visit, or an exciting time at the stadium. When customers have strong affective expectations, it is important that the environment be designed to match those expectations[11].

LO 3

Be familiar with the integrative servicescape model.

The Servicescape Model — An Integrative Framework

Building on the basic models in environmental psychology, Mary Jo Bitner developed a comprehensive model that she named the "servicescape"[12]. *Figure 10.9* shows the main dimensions identified in service environments: (1) ambient conditions, (2) space/functionality, and (3) signs, symbols and artifacts. As individuals tend to perceive these dimensions holistically, the key to effective design is how well each individual dimension fits together with everything else.

Bitner's model shows that there are customer, and employee-response moderators. This means that the same service environment can have different effects on different customers, depending on who they are and what they like — after all, beauty lies in the eyes of the beholder and is subjective. For example, rap music or an opera may be sheer pleasure to some customer segments, but torture to others.

An important contribution of Bitner's model is the inclusion of employee responses to the service environment. After all, employees spend much more time there than customers, and it's important that designers are aware of how a particular environment enhances (or at least, does not reduce) the productivity of the frontline personnel and the quality of service they deliver[13].

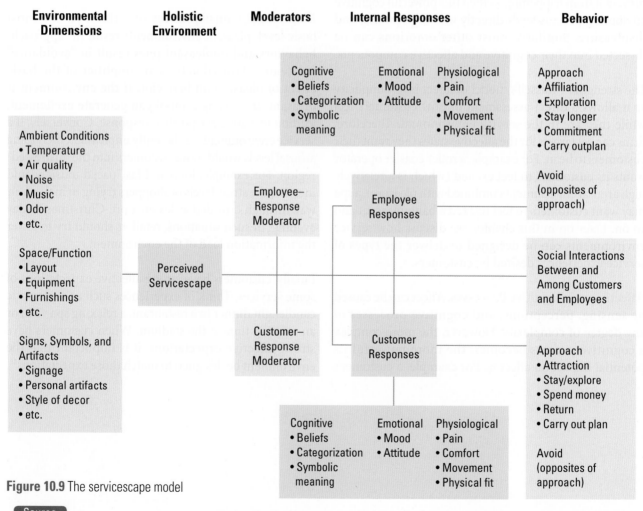

Figure 10.9 The servicescape model

Source

Reprinted with permission from *Journal of Marketing*, published by the American Marketing Association, Mary Jo Bitner, Servicescapes: The Impact of Physical Surroundings on Customers and Employees, 56 (April).

Internal customer and employee responses can be grouped into cognitive responses (e.g., quality perceptions and beliefs), emotional responses (e.g., feelings and moods), and physiological responses (e.g., pain and comfort). These internal responses lead to overt behavioral responses such as avoiding a crowded supermarket, or responding positively to a relaxing environment by staying longer and spending extra money on impulse purchases. It's important to understand that the behavioral responses of customers and employees must be shaped in ways that aid the production and purchase of high-quality services. Consider how the outcomes of service transactions may differ in situations where both customers and frontline staff feel stressed rather than relaxed and happy.

DIMENSIONS OF THE SERVICE ENVIRONMENT

⤵ **LO 4**
Know the three main dimensions of the service environment.

Service environments are complex and have many design elements. *Table 10.1* gives an overview of the design elements that might be encountered in a retail outlet. In this section, we focus on the main dimensions of the service environment in the servicescape model, which are the ambient conditions, space and functionality, signs, symbols, and artifacts[14].

Table 10.1 Design Elements of a Retail Store Environment

Dimensions	Design Elements	
Exterior facilities	• Architectural style • Size of building • Color of building • Exterior walls and exterior signs • Storefront • Marquee • Lawns and gardens	• Window displays • Entrances • Visibility • Uniqueness • Surrounding stores • Surrounding areas • Congestion • Parking and accessibility
General interior	• Flooring and carpeting • Color schemes • Lighting • Scents • Odors (e.g., tobacco smoke) • Sounds and music • Fixtures • Wall composition • Wall textures (paint, wallpaper) • Ceiling composition	• Temperature • Cleanliness • Width of aisles • Dressing facilities • Vertical transportation • Dead areas • Merchandise layout and displays • Price levels and displays • Cash register placement • Technology, modernization
Store layout	• Allocation of floor space for selling, merchandise, personnel, and customers • Placement of merchandise • Grouping of merchandise • Workstation placement • Placement of equipment • Placement of cash register	• Waiting areas • Traffic flow • Waiting queues • Furniture • Dead areas • Department locations • Arrangements within departments
Interior displays	• Point-of-purchase displays • Posters, signs, and cards • Pictures and artwork • Wall decorations • Theme setting • Ensemble	• Racks and cases • Product display • Price display • Cut cases and dump bins • Mobiles
Social dimensions	• Personnel characteristics • Employee uniforms • Crowding	• Customer characteristics • Privacy • Self-service

Source

Adapted from: Barry Berman and Joel R. Evans, *Retail Management — A Strategic Approach*, 8th edition, Upper Saddle River, NJL Prentice Hall, 2001, p. 604; L.W. Turley and Ronald E. Milliman (2000), "Atmospheric Effects on Shopping Behavior: A Review of the Experimental Literature," *Journal of Business Research*, Vol. 49, pp. 193–211.

LO 5

Discuss the key ambient conditions and their effects on customers.

The Effect of Ambient Conditions

Ambient conditions refer to characteristics of the environment that pertain to your five senses. Even when they're not noted consciously, they may still affect a person's emotional well-being, perceptions, even attitudes, and behaviors. They are composed of literally hundreds of design elements and details that must work together if they are to create the desired service environment[15]. The resulting atmosphere creates a mood that is perceived and interpreted by the customer. Ambient conditions are perceived both separately and holistically, and include music, sounds and noise, scents and smells, color schemes and lighting, and temperature and air movement. Clever design of these conditions can elicit desired behavioral responses among consumers. Consider the innovative thinking underlying the new trend to transform dental clinics into relaxing dental spas, as described in *Service Insights 10.2*.

Let's next discuss a number of important ambient dimensions, beginning with music.

Music can have powerful effects on perceptions and behaviors in service settings, even if played at barely audible volumes. The various structural characteristics of music such as tempo, volume, and harmony are perceived holistically, and their effect on internal and behavioral responses is moderated by respondent characteristics (e.g., younger people tend to like different music and therefore respond differently from older people to the same piece of music)[16]. Numerous research studies have found that fast-tempo and high volume music increases arousal levels, which can then lead to customers increasing the pace of various behaviors[17]. People tend to adjust their pace, either voluntarily or involuntarily, to match the tempo of music. This means that restaurants can speed up table turnover by increasing the tempo and volume of the music and serve more diners during the course of the busy lunch hour, or slow diners down with slow beat music and softer volume to keep evening diners longer in the restaurant and increase beverage revenues. A restaurant study conducted over eight weeks showed that the customers who dined in a slow-music environment spent longer in the restaurant than the individuals in a fast-music condition. As a result, beverage revenue increased substantially when slow-beat music was played[18].

Likewise, studies have shown that shoppers walked less rapidly and increased their level of impulse purchases when slow music was played. Playing familiar music in a store was shown to stimulate shoppers, thereby reduce their browsing time, whereas playing unfamiliar music induced shoppers to spend more time there[19]. In situations that require waiting for service, effective use of music may shorten the perceived waiting time and increase customer satisfaction. Relaxing music proved effective in lowering stress levels in a hospital's surgery waiting room. Pleasant music has even been shown to enhance customers' perceptions of service personnel[20].

SERVICE INSIGHTS 10.2
Cutting the Fear Factor at the Dentist

Dentistry is not a service that most people look forward to. Some patients simply find it uncomfortable, especially if they have to remain in a dental chair for a long period of time. Many are afraid of the pain associated with certain procedures, while others risk their health by not going to the dentist at all. Now, some practitioners are embracing "spa dentistry" where juice bars, neck rubs, foot massages, and even scented candles and the sound of wind chimes are used to pamper patients and distract them from necessarily invasive treatments inside their mouths.

"It's not about gimmicks," says Timothy Dotson, owner of the Perfect Teeth Dental Spa in Chicago, as a patient breathed strawberry-scented nitrous oxide. "It's treating people the way they want to be treated. It helps a lot of people overcome fear." His patients seem to agree. "Nobody likes coming to the dentist, but this makes it so much easier," remarked one woman as she waited for a crown while a heated massage pad was kneading her back.

Hot towels, massages, aromatherapy, coffee, fresh cranberry-orange bread, and white wine spritzers reflect dentists' efforts to meet changing consumer expectations, especially at a time when there is growing consumer demand for esthetic care to whiten and correct teeth, in a bid to achieve that perfect smile. The goal is to entice patients who might otherwise find visiting the dentist stressful. Many dentists who offer spa services do not charge extra, arguing that their cost is more than covered by repeat business and patient referrals.

In Houston, Max Greenfield has embellished his Image Max Dental Spa with fountains and modern art. Patients can change into a robe, sample eight different aromas of oxygen, and meditate in a relaxation room decorated like a Japanese garden. The actual dental area features lambskin leather chairs, hot aromatherapy towels, and a procedure known as "bubble gum jet massage" that uses air and water to clean teeth.

Although dental offices from Los Angeles to New York are adopting spa techniques, some question whether this touchy-feely approach is good dentistry or just a passing fad. "I just can't see mingling the two businesses together," remarked the dean of one university dental school.

Source

Adapted from "Dentists Offer New Services to Cut the Fear Factor," Chicago Tribune syndicated article, February 2003.

Providing the right mix of music to restaurants, retail stores, and even call centers has become an industry in its own right. Mood Media, the market leader in this space, provides music to over 300,000 commercial locations in the US. It tailors its playlists to outlets such as Christian bookstores, black barbershops, and bilingual malls where Anglo and Hispanic customers mingle, and uses "day parting" to target music to their clients' segments such as daytime mothers or after-school teens[21].

Would it surprise you to learn that music can also be used to deter the wrong type of customer? Many service environments, including subway systems, supermarkets, and other publicly accessible locations, attract individuals who are not bona fide customers. Some are jaycustomers (see Chapter 13) whose behavior causes problems for management and a firm's target customers alike. In the United Kingdom, an increasingly popular strategy for driving such individuals away is to play classical music (*Figure 10.10*), which is apparently unpleasant to vandals' and loiterers' ears. Co-op, a UK grocery chain, has been experimenting with playing music outside its outlets to stop teenagers from hanging around and intimidating customers. Its staff are equipped with a remote control and, as reported by Steve Broughton of Co-op, "can turn the music on if there's a situation developing and they need to disperse people[22]."

The London Underground (subway) system has probably made the most extensive use of classical music as a deterrent. Thirty stations pump out Mozart and Haydn to discourage loitering and vandalism. A London Underground spokesperson reports that the most effective deterrents are anything written by Mozart or those sung by Pavarotti. According to Adrian North, a psychologist researching the link between music and behavior at Leicester University, unfamiliarity is a key factor in driving people away. When the target individuals are unused to strings and woodwind, Mozart will do. However, for the more musically literate loiterer, an atonal barrage is likely to work better. For instance, North tormented Leicester's students in the union bar who tended to linger long beyond closing time with what he describes as "computer-game music". It cleared the place[23]!

Figure 10.10 Classical music can be used to deter vandals and loiterers

Scent is the next important ambient dimension. Ambient scent or smell pervading an environment may or may not be consciously perceived by customers and is not related to any particular product. The presence of scent can have a strong impact on mood, feelings, and evaluations, and even purchase intentions and in-store behaviors[24]. We experience the power of smell when we are hungry and get a whiff of freshly baked croissants long before we pass a local bakery. This smell makes us aware of our hunger and points us to the solution (i.e., walk into the bakery and get some food). Other examples include the smell of freshly baked cookies on Main Street in Disney's Magic Kingdom to relax customers and provide a feeling of warmth, or the smell of potpourri in Victoria's Secret stores creating the ambiance of a lingerie closet.

Figure 10.11 Aromatherapy can induce a state of relaxation and rejuvenation

Olfaction researcher Alan R. Hirsch, Managing Director of the Smell & Taste Treatment and Research Foundation based in Chicago, is convinced that at some point in the future we will understand scents so well that we will be able to use them to manage people's behaviors[25]. Service marketers are interested in how to make you hungry and thirsty in the restaurant, relax you in a dentist's waiting room, and energize you to work out harder in a gym. In aromatherapy, it is generally accepted that scents have special characteristics and can be used to solicit certain emotional, physiological, and behavioral responses (*Figure 10.11*). *Table 10.2* shows the generally assumed effects of specific scents on people. In service settings, research has shown that scents can have significant impact on customers' perceptions, attitudes, and behaviors. For example:

- Gamblers plunked 45% more quarters into slot machines when a Las Vegas casino was scented with a pleasant artificial smell. When the intensity of the scent was increased, spending jumped by 53%[26].

Table 10.2 Aromatherapy – The Effects of Selected Fragrances on People

Fragrance	Aroma Type	Aromatherapy Class	Traditional Use	Potential Psychological Effect on People
Eucalyptus	Camphoraceous	Toning, stimulating	Deodorant, antiseptic, soothing agent	Stimulating and energizing
Lavender	Herbaceous	Calming, balancing, soothing	Muscle relaxant, soothing agent, astringent	Relaxing and calming
Lemon	Citrus	Energizing, uplifting	Antiseptic, soothing agent	Soothing energy levels
Black pepper	Spicy	Balancing, soothing	Muscle relaxant, aphrodisiac	Balancing people's emotions

Source

http://www.aromatherapy.com/, accessed April 25, 2015; Dana Butcher (1998), "Aromatherapy—Its Past & Future." *Drug and Cosmetic Industry*, Vol. 16, No. 3, pp. 22–24; Shirley Price and Len Price, *Aromatherapy for Health Professionals*, 4th ed., Mattila, A. S., and Wirtz, J. (2001), Congruency of Scent and Music as a Driver of In-Store Evaluations and Behavior. *Journal of Retailing*, Vol. 77, pp. 273–289.

- People were more willing to buy Nike sneakers and pay more for them — an average of $10.33 more per pair — when they tried on the shoes in a floral-scented room. The same effect was found even when the scent was so faint that people could not detect it, that is, the scent was perceived unconsciously[27].

Service firms have recognized the power of scent and increasingly made it a part of their brand experience. For example, Westin Hotels uses a white tea fragrance throughout its lobbies, and Sheraton scents its lobbies with a combination of fig, clove, and jasmine. As a response to the trend of scenting servicescapes, professional service firms have entered the scent marketing space. For example, Ambius, a Rentokil Initial company, offers scent-related services such as "sensory branding", "ambient scenting", and "odor remediation" for retail, hospitality, healthcare, financial services, and other services. Firms can outsource their servicescape scenting to Ambius, which offers one-stop solutions ranging from consulting, designing exclusive signature scents for a service firm, to managing the ongoing scenting of all the outlets of a chain[28]. Clients of Mood Media, a leading provider of music, scents, and signage for commercial establishments, can choose their ideal ambient scent from a library of 1,500 scents[29]!

Although there is overwhelming evidence for the potentially powerful effects scent can have on customers' experiences and behaviors, it has to be implemented with caution. The ambient scent has to fit the service context and the target audience (very much as discussed for music). Furthermore, a recent study suggests that simple scents whereby the researchers used a simple orange scent in a retail environment can have an excellent impact on sales per customer, whereas more complex scents such as basil-orange with green tea used as a complex scent in this study, did not do better than unscented environments. In this study, both scents were perceived as equally pleasant, but the simple scent helped in consumer decision-making (consumers spent less time deciding which items to buy), whereas the complex scent did not (consumers spent as much time deciding as in the no scent condition). The researchers concluded that complex scents cannot be fluently processed by consumers and require too much cognitive effort, which subsequently has a negative effect on consumer decision-making and perceptions[30].

Finally, as we will discuss later in this chapter, servicescapes have to be seen holistically, which means no one of its dimensions can be optimized in isolation. This also applies to scent. For example, *Service Insights 10.3* shows that even the arousal dimensions of scent and music interact, they need to be considered in conjunction to elicit the desired customer responses.

While these findings are derived only from a few research projects, they suggest that managers need to carefully match their scents to their context, and probably should favor simpler rather than more complex scents. In any case, using field experiments, monitoring sales and shopper behaviors and perceptions would be an excellent way to optimize the ambient scent in any particular servicescape.

SERVICE INSIGHTS 10.3
Match and Mismatch of Scent and Music in the Servicescape

Whether a certain type of background enhances consumer responses depends on the ambient scent of the service environment. Using a field experiment, Anna Mattila and Jochen Wirtz manipulated two types of pleasant music and scent in a gift store, which differed in their arousing qualities. Consumer impulse purchasing and satisfaction were measured for the various music and scent conditions.

The experiment used two compact discs from the Tune Your Brain™ series by Elizabeth Miles, an ethnomusicologist. The low-arousal music was the *Relaxing Collection* featuring slow-tempo music, while the high-arousal music from the *Energizing Collection* featured fast-tempo music. Similarly, scent was manipulated to have high or low arousal quality. Lavender was used for the low-arousal scent because of its relaxing and calming properties. Grapefruit was used for the high-arousal scent because of its stimulating properties, which can refresh, revive, and improve mental clarity and alertness, and can even enhance physical strength and energy.

The results of this experiment show that when the arousal qualities of music and ambient scent were matched, consumers responded more favorably. The figures below show these effects clearly. For instance, scenting the store with a low-arousal scent (lavender) combined with slow-tempo music led to higher satisfaction and more impulse purchases as compared to using that scent with high-arousal music. Playing fast-tempo music had a more positive effect when the store was scented with grapefruit (high-arousal scent) as compared to lavender. This study showed that when environmental stimuli act together to provide a coherent atmosphere, consumers in that environment will respond more positively.

Note: Both charts are on a scale from 1 to 7, with 7 being the extreme positive response. The solid-line circles show the match conditions, where both music and scent are either stimulating or relaxing, and the intermitted-line circles show the mismatch conditions, in which one stimulus is relaxing and the other is stimulating (ie., relaxing music and stimulating scent, or stimulating music and relaxing scent).

Figure 10.12 the effect of scent and music on satisfaction

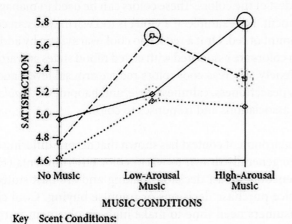

Figure 10.13 The effect of scent and music on impulse purchases

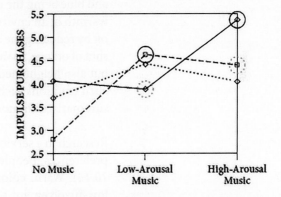

Note: Both charts are on a scale from 1 to 7, with 7 being the extreme positive response. The solid-line circles show the match conditions, where both music and scent are either stimulating or relaxing, and the intermitted-line circles show the mismatch conditions, in which one stimulus is relaxing and the other is stimulating (i.e., relaxing music and stimulating scent or stimulating music and relaxing scent).

Source

Adapted from Anna S. Mattila and Jochen Wirtz (20010, "Congruency of Scent and Music as a Driver of In-Store Evaluations and Behavior," *Journal of Retailing*, Vol. 77, pp. 273–289.

In addition to music and scent, researchers have found that **colors** have a strong impact on people's feelings[31]. Color is "stimulating, calming, expressive, disturbing, impressionable, cultural, exuberant, symbolic. It pervades every aspect of our lives, embellishes the ordinary, and gives beauty and drama to everyday objects[32]."

The de facto system used in psychological research is the Munsell System, which defines colors in the three dimensions of hue, value, and chroma[33]. **Hue** is the pigment of the color (i.e., the name of the color: red, orange, yellow, green, blue, or violet). **Value** is the degree of lightness or darkness of the color, relative to a scale that extends from pure black to pure white. **Chroma** refers to hue intensity, saturation, or brilliance; high chroma colors have a high intensity of pigmentation in them and are perceived as rich and vivid, whereas low chroma colors are perceived as dull.

Hues are classified into warm colors (red, orange and yellow hues) and cold colors (blue and green), with orange (a mix of red and yellow) being the warmest, and blue being the coldest of the colors. These colors can be used to manage the warmth of an environment. For example, if a violet is too warm, you can cool it off by reducing the amount of red. Or if a red is too cool, warm it up by adding a shot of orange[34]. Warm colors are associated with elated mood states and arousal, but also heightened anxiety, whereas cool colors reduce arousal levels and can elicit emotions such as peacefulness, calmness, love, and happiness[35]. *Table 10.3* summarizes common associations and responses to colors.

Research in a service environment context has shown that despite differing color preferences, people are generally drawn to warm color environments (*Figure 10.14*). Warm colors encourage fast decision-making and are best suited for low-involvement service purchase decisions or impulse buying. Cool colors are favored when consumers need time to make high-involvement purchase decisions[36].

Table 10.3 Common Associations and Human Responses to Colors

Color	Degree of Warmth	Nature Symbol	Common Association and Human Responses to Color
Red	Warm	Earth	High energy and passion; can excite and stimulate emotions, expressions, and warmth
Orange	Warmest	Sunset	Emotions, expressions, and warmth
Yellow	Warm	Sun	Optimism, clarity, intellect, and mood enchancing
Green	Cool	Growth, grass, and trees	Nurturing, healing, and unconditional love
Blue	Coolest	Sky and ocean	Relaxation, serenity, and loyalty
Indigo	Cool	Sunset	Meditation and spirituality
Violet	Cool	Violet flower	Spirituality, reduces stress, can create an inner feeling of calm

Source

Sara O. Marberry and Laurie Zagon, *The Power of Color—Creating Healthy Interior Spaces* (New York: John Wiley, 1995), 18; Sarah Lynch, *Bold Colors for Modern Rooms: Bright Ideas for People Who Love Color* (Gloucester, MA: Rockport Publishers, 2001), 24–29.

Figure 10.14 Bright and warm colors are usually used in environments with children to provide an attractive and cheery effect

An early example of using color schemes to enhance the service experience was the HealthPark Medical Center in Fort Meyers, Florida, which combined full-spectrum color in its lobby with unusual lighting to achieve a dreamlike setting. The lobby walls were washed with rainbow colors by using an arrangement of high-intensity blue, green, violet, red, orange, and yellow lamps. Craig Roeder, the lighting designer for the hospital, explained, "It's a hospital. People walk into it worried and sick. I tried to design an entrance space that provides them with light and energy — to 'beam them up' a little bit before they get to the patient rooms[37]."

A recent example of effective color and lighting are the new cabin designs in the Boeing 787 Dreamliner and Airbus A350 and models. In the past, cabin lights were either on or off, but with the new light-emitting diode (LED) technology a wide range of lighting palette is available. Designers start to experiment to illuminate the cabin in all kinds of hues, and ask questions such as: "Does a pinkish-purple glow soothe and calm passengers when boarding better than an amber warmth?" or "Can lighting be used to prevent jet lag as much as possible?" The Finnair A350 cabin has two dozen light settings aligned with the different stages of a long-haul flight such as featuring a 20-minute "sunset". It also aligns colors with the destination by featuring warmer, amber colors when flying into Asia, and cooler "Nordic blue" hues when arriving in Finland. Similarly, Virgin Atlantic has a few mainsettings on its 787 flights, including rose-champagne for boarding, purple-pink for drinks, amber for dinner, a silver glow for overnight sleep, and a waking color. According to Nik Lusardi, the design manager at Virgin Atlantic: "We've always wanted to create a different kind of atmosphere aboard our aircraft, and light plays exactly into our hands. ...You can get people energized or you can relax people very, very quickly[38]."

Figure 10.15 Uncomfortable chairs in a lecture theater make it harder for students to concentrate

Although we have an understanding of the general effects of colors, their use in any specific context needs to be approached with caution. For example, a transportation company in Israel decided to paint its buses green as part of an environmentalism public relations campaign. Reactions to this seemingly simple act from multiple groups of people were unexpectedly negative. Some customers found the green color as hampering service performance because the green buses blended in with the environment and were more difficult to see; some felt that the green was esthetically unappealing and inappropriate as it represented undesirable notions such as terrorism or opposing sports teams[39].

Spatial Layout and Functionality

⊃ LO 6
Determine the roles of spatial layout and functionality.

In addition to ambient conditions, spatial layout and functionality are other key dimensions of the service environment. As a service environment generally has to fulfill specific purposes and customer needs, spatial layout and functionality are particularly important.

Spatial layout refers to the floor plan, size and shape of furnishings, counters, and potential machinery and equipment, and the ways in which they are arranged. **Functionality** refers to the ability of those items to facilitate the performance of service transactions. Both dimensions affect the user-friendliness and the ability of the facility to service customers well. Tables that are too close in a café, counters in a bank that lack privacy, uncomfortable chairs in a lecture theatre (*Figure 10.15*), and lack of parking space can all leave negative impressions on customers, affect the service experience and buying behavior, and consequently, the business performance of the service facility.

Signs, Symbols, and Artifacts

Many things in the service environment act as explicit or implicit signals to communicate the firm's image, help customers find their way (e.g., to certain service counters, departments, or the exit), and to convey the service script (e.g., for a queuing system). In particular, first-time customers will automatically try to draw meaning from the environment to guide them through the service processes[40].

Examples of explicit signals include signs, which can be used (1) as labels (e.g., to indicate the name of the department or counter), (2) for giving directions (e.g., to certain service counters, entrance, exit, way to lifts and toilets), (3) for communicating the service script (e.g., take a queue number and wait for it to be called, or clear the tray after your meal), and (4) for reminders about behavioral rules (e.g., switch off or turn your mobile devices to silent mode during a performance, or smoking/non-smoking areas). Signs are often used to teach behavioral rules in service settings. Singapore, which strictly enforces rules in many service settings, especially in public buildings and on public transport, is sometimes ironically referred to as a "fine" city (*Figure 10.16*). Contrast these signs to the more creative and perhaps equally effective signs used by Singapore's Changi Airport at the entrance of its butterfly garden (*Figure 10.17*). Some signs are quite interesting and may be obvious, but other signs need the person to think a little before understanding the meaning.

Figure 10.16 Singapore is a "fine" city

Figure 10.17 Changi Airport uses a creative sign to manage visitor behavior in its butterfly garden

Table 10.4 provides an overview of the benefits well-designed signage can provide to customers and service organizations.

Table 10.4 Benefits Well-Designed Signage for Customers and Service Organizations

Potential Benefits of Well-developed Signage

For Customers

- Be informed, up-to-date, oriented, free to move about, guided along prepared paths, emotionally stimulated
- Creates familiarity with the servicescape
- Helps to participate with greater ease in the service process
- Increases confidence and reassurance while following signage; provides higher levels of perceived control during the service encounter
- Reduces tension, confusion, feeling lost, wrong turns and requests for information
- Reduces time to reach the desired goal as efficiently as possible

For the Service Organization

- Direct, inform and manage the flow and the behavior of customers
- Improve the quality of service provided and increase customer satisfaction
- Reduce information-giving by frontline employees
- Help frontline employees to work with fewer interruptions
- Attract and excite curiosity, help to strengthen the corporate image
- Differentiate the firm from the competition

Source

Adapted from: Angelo Bonfani (2013), "Towards an Approach to Signage Management Quality (SMQ)," *Journal of Services Marketing*, Vol. 27, No. 4, pp. 312–321.

The challenge for servicescape designers is to use signs, symbols, and artifacts to guide customers clearly through the process of service delivery, and to teach the service script in as intuitive a manner as possible. This task assumes particular importance in situations in which there is a high proportion of new or infrequent customers (e.g., airports and hospitals), and/or a high degree of self-service with no or only a few service employees available to guide customers through the process (e.g., a self-service bank branch).

Customers become disoriented when they cannot derive clear signals from a servicescape, leading to anxiety and uncertainty about how to proceed and how to obtain the desired service. Customers can easily feel lost in a confusing environment and experience anger and frustration as a result. Think about the last time you were in a hurry and tried to find your way through an unfamiliar hospital, shopping center, or a large government office where the signs and other directional cues were not intuitive to you. At many service facilities, customers' first point of contact is likely to be the car park. As emphasized in *Service Insights 10.4*, the principles of effective environment design apply even in such a very mundane environment.

SERVICE INSIGHTS 10.4
GUIDELINES FOR PARKING DESIGN

Car parks play an important role at many service facilities[41]. Effective use of signs, symbols, and artifacts in a parking lot or garage helps customers find their way, manages their behavior, and portrays a positive image for the sponsoring organization.

- **Friendly warnings** — all warning signs should communicate a customer benefit. For instance, "Fire lane — for everyone's safety we ask you not to park in the fire lane."

- **Safety lighting** — good lighting that penetrates all areas makes life easier for customers and enhances safety. Firms may want to draw attention to this feature with notices stating that "Parking lots have been specially lit for your safety."

- **Help customers remember where they left their vehicle** — forgetting where one left the family car in a large parking structure can be a nightmare. Many car parks have adopted color-coded floors to help customers remember which level they parked on. In addition, many car parks also mark sections with special symbols, such as different kinds of animals. This helps customers to not only remember the level, but also the section where the car is parked. Boston's Logan Airport goes two steps further. Each level has been assigned a theme associated with Massachusetts, such as Paul Revere's Ride, Cape Cod, or the Boston Marathon. An image is attached to each theme — a male figure on horseback, a lighthouse, or a female runner. While waiting for the elevator, travelers hear music that is tied to the theme for that level; in the case of the Boston Marathon floor, it's the theme song from *Chariots of Fire,* an Oscar-winning movie about an Olympic runner.

- **Maternity parking** — handicapped spaces are often required by law but require the display of special stickers on the vehicle. A few thoughtful organizations have special expectant mother parking spaces, painted with a blue/pink stork. This strategy demonstrates a sense of caring and understanding of customer needs.

- **Fresh paint** — curbs, cross walks, and lot lines should be repainted regularly before any cracking, peeling, or disrepair become evident. Pro-active and frequent repainting give positive cleanliness cues and projects a positive image.

LO 8

Know how service employees and other customers are part of the servicescape.

People Are Part of the Service Environment Too

The appearance and behavior of both service personnel and customers can strengthen or weaken the impression created by a service environment, and some academics argue that these social dimensions should be explicitly considered when assessing the quality of servicescapes[42]. Dennis Nickson and his colleagues use the term "aesthetic labor" to capture the importance of the physical image of service personnel who serve customers directly[43]. Employees at Disney theme parks are called cast members. Whether the staff are acting as Cinderella, one of the seven dwarfs, or as the park cleaner or the person managing Buzz Lightyear's Tomorrowland booth, these cast members must dress up and look the part. Once dressed up, they must "perform" for the guests.

Likewise, marketing communications may seek to attract customers who will not only appreciate the ambience created by the service provider but will actively enhance it by their own appearance and behavior. In hospitality and retail settings, newcomers often survey the array of existing customers before deciding whether to patronize the establishment. Consider *Figure 10.18*, which shows the interior of two restaurants. Imagine that you have just entered each of these two dining rooms. How does each restaurant position itself within the restaurant industry? What sort of dining experience can you expect? And what are the clues you use to make your judgments? In particular, what assumptions do you make from looking at the customers who are already seated in each restaurant?

Figure 10.18 Distinctive servicescapes – from table settings, furniture, and room design to other customers present in the servicescape – create different customer expectations of these two restaurants

PUTTING IT ALL TOGETHER

⊃ **LO 9**
Explain why designing an effective servicescape has to be done holistically and from the customer's perspective.

Although individuals often perceive particular aspects or individual design features of an environment, it is the total configuration of all those design features that determines consumer responses. That is, consumers perceive service environments holistically.

Design With a Holistic View

Whether a dark, glossy wooden floor is the perfect flooring depends on everything else in that service environment, including the type, color scheme and materials of the furniture, the lighting, the promotional materials, the overall brand perception, and positioning of the firm. Servicescapes have to be seen holistically, which means no dimension of the design can be optimized in isolation, because everything depends on everything else.

As the design of the environment needs to be planned as a whole, it is more like an art. Therefore, professional designers tend to focus on specific types of servicescapes. For example, a handful of famous interior designers do no other projects but create hotel lobbies around the world. Similarly, there are design experts who focus exclusively on restaurants, bars, clubs, cafes and bistros, or retail outlets, or healthcare facilities, and so forth[44].

Design From a Customer's Perspective

Many service environments are built with an emphasis on esthetic values, and designers sometimes forget the most important factor to consider when designing service environments — the customers who will be using them. Ron Kaufman, the founder of Up Your Service! College, experienced the following design flaws in two new high-profile service environments:

A new Sheraton Hotel just had opened in Jordan without clear signage that would guide guests from the ballrooms to the restrooms. The signs that did exist were etched in muted gold on dark marble pillars. More "obvious" signs were apparently inappropriate amidst such elegant décor. Very swish, very chic, but who were they designing it for?

At a new airport lounge in a major Asian city, a partition of colorful glass hung from the ceiling. My luggage lightly brushed against it as I walked inside. The entire partition shook and several panels came undone. A staff member hurried over and began carefully reassembling the panels. (Thank goodness nothing broke.) I apologized profusely. "Don't worry," she replied, "This happens all the time." An airport lounge is a heavy traffic area. People are always moving in and out. Kaufman keeps asking "What were the interior designers thinking? Who were they designing it for?

"I am regularly amazed," declared Kaufman, "by brand new facilities that are obviously 'user unfriendly'!" He draws the following key learning point: "It's easy to get caught up in designing new things that are 'cool', 'elegant' or 'hot'. But if you don't keep your customer in mind throughout, you could end up with an investment that's not[45]."

Along a similar vein, Alain d'Astous explored environmental aspects that irritate shoppers. His findings highlighted the following problems:

- **Ambient conditions** (ordered by level of irritation):
  - Store is not clean.
  - Too hot inside the store or the shopping center.
  - Music inside the store is too loud.
  - Bad smells in the store.

- **Environmental design variables:**
  - No mirror in the dressing room.
  - Unable to find what one needs.
  - Directions within the store are inadequate.
  - Arrangement of store items has been changed in a way that confuses customers.
  - Store is too small.
  - Losing one's way in a large shopping center[46] (*Figure 10.19*).

To design servicescapes from the customer's perspective, managers have to understand how their customers use it. An in-depth study in the context of a highly functional and utilitarian service, a public transport systems, showed that consumers use servicescapes in three main ways, namely[47]: (1) identifying the resources in the environment and trying to understand the objects and persons in the service environment as resources and how they can be used (e.g., searching for a bus stop, timetable, map, or bus; approaching staff or other customers); (2) sense-making, which is the process of giving meaning to and comprehending the resources previously identified (e.g., trying to understand maps and timetables); and (3) using the resources to attain their consumption goals (e.g., finding ones way in the subway system). The implications of these findings are clear: Servicescapes should be designed to support customers to attain their consumption goals by making the designs intuitive (i.e., easy to sense), meaningful (i.e., easy to understand), and easy to use[48].

Of course, for hedonic services, customers use the service environment for additional objectives; they want to experience what they came for when they entered the servicescape (e.g., have fun, relax, or socialize). In this context, contrast Kaufman's experiences and d'Astou's findings with the Disney example in *Service Insights 10.5*. What conclusions do you draw?

Figure 10.19 Badly designed shopping centers affect the shopping experience

SERVICE INSIGHTS 10.5
DESIGN OF DISNEY'S MAGIC KINGDOM

Walt Disney was one of the undisputed champions of designing service environments. His tradition of amazingly careful and detailed planning has become one of his company's hallmarks, and is visible everywhere in its theme parks. For example, Main Street is angled to make it seem longer upon entry into the Magic Kingdom than it actually is. With a myriad of facilities and attractions strategically located at each side of the street, this makes people look forward to the relatively long journey to the Castle. However, looking down the slope from the Castle back toward the entrance makes Main Street appear shorter than it really is, relieving exhaustion and rejuvenating guests. It encourages strolling, which minimizes the number of people who take the buses and so eliminates the threatening problem of traffic congestion.

Meandering sidewalks with multiple attractions keep guests feeling entertained by both the planned activities and also by watching other guests; trash bins are aplenty and always in sight to convey the message that littering is prohibited; and the repainting of facilities is a routine procedure that signals a high level of maintenance and cleanliness.

Disney's servicescape design and upkeep help to script customer experiences and create pleasure and satisfaction for guests, not only in its theme parks but also in its cruise ships and hotels.

Source

Lewis P. Carbone and Stephen H. Haeckel (1994), "Engineering Customer Experiences," *Marketing Management*, Vol. 3, No. 3, Winter, pp. 10–11; Kathy Merlock Jackson, *Walt Disney, A Bio-Bibliography* (Westport, CT: Greenwood Press, 1993), 36–39, Andrew Lainsbury, *Once Upon an American Dream: The Story of Euro Disneyland* (Lawrence KS, Kan: University Press of Kansas, 2000), 64–72. See also: Disney Institute, *Be Our Guest: Perfecting the Art of Customer Service* (New York: Disney Enterprises, 2011).

As a manager, how can you determine how customers use the servicescape, and which of its aspects irritate them and which do they like? Among the tools you can use are:

- **Keen observation** of customers' behavior and responses to the service environment by management, supervisors, branch managers, and frontline staff.

- **Feedback and ideas from frontline staff and customers** using a variety of research tools ranging from scanning social media, using suggestion boxes, focus groups, and surveys. The latter are often called environmental surveys if they focus on the design of the service environment.

- **Photo audit** is a method of asking customers (or mystery shoppers) to take photographs of their service experience. These photographs can later be used as a basis for further interviews of their experience, or included as part of a survey about the service experience[49].

- **Field experiments** which can be used to manipulate specific dimensions in an environment so that the effects can be observed. For instance, researchers can experiment with various types of music and scents, and then measure the time and money customers spend in the environment. Laboratory experiments using pictures or videos, or other ways to simulate real-world service environments (such as virtual tours via computers) can be effectively used to examine the impact of changes in design elements that cannot be easily manipulated in a field experiment. Examples include testing of different color schemes, spatial layouts, or styles of furnishing.

- **Blueprinting** or flowcharting (as described in Chapter 8) can be extended to include the physical evidence in the environment. Design elements and tangible cues can be documented as the customer moves through each step of the service delivery process. Photos can supplement the map to make it more vivid.

Table 10.5 A Visit to the Movies: The Service Environment as Perceived by the Customer

Steps in the Service Encounter	Design of the Service Environment	
	Exceeds Expectations	**Fails Expectations**
Locate a parking lot	Ample room in a bright place near the entrance, with a security officer protecting your valuables	Insufficient parking spaces, so patrons have to park in another lot
Queue up to obtain tickets	Strategic placement of mirrors, posters of upcoming movies, and entertainment news to ease perception of long wait, if any; movies and time slots easily seen; ticket availability clearly communicated	A long queue and having to wait for a long while; difficult to see quickly what movies are being shown at what time slots and whether tickets are still available
Check tickets to enter the theater	A very well-maintained lobby with clear directions to the theater and posters of the movie to enhance patrons' experience	A dirty lobby with rubbish strewn and unclear or misleading directions to the movie theater
Go to the restroom before the movie starts	Sparkling clean, spacious, brightly lit, dry floors, well-stocked, nice décor, clear mirrors wiped regularly	Dirty, with an unbearable odor; broken toilets; no hand towels, soap, or toilet paper; overcrowded; dusty and dirty mirrors
Enter the theater and locate your seat	Spotless theater; well designed with no bad seats; sufficient lighting to locate your seat; spacious, comfortable chairs, with drink and popcorn holders on each seat; and a suitable temperature	Rubbish on the floor, broken seats, sticky floor, gloomy and insufficient lighting, burned-out exit signs
Watch the movie	Excellent sound system and film quality, nice audience, an enjoyable and memorable entertainment experience overall	Substandard sound and movie equipment, uncooperative audience that talks and smokes because of lack of "No Smoking" and other signs; a disturbing and unenjoyable entertainment experience overall
Leave the theater and return to the car	Friendly service staff greet patrons as they leave; an easy exit through brightly lit and safe parking area, back to the car with the help of clear lot signs	A difficult trip, as patrons squeeze through a narrow exit, unable to find the car because of no or insufficient lighting

Source

Adapted from Albrecht, S. (1996). "See Things from the Customer's Point of View—How to Use the 'Cycles of Service' to Understand What the Customer Goes Through to Do Business with You." *World's Executive Digest*, December, pp. 53–58.

Table 10.5 shows an examination of a customer's visit to a movie theater, identifying how different environmental elements at each step exceeded or failed to meet expectations. The service process was broken up into steps, decisions, duties, and activities, all designed to take the customer through the entire service encounter. The more a service company can see, understand, and experience the same things as its customers, the better equipped it will be to realize errors in the design of its environment and to further improve what is already functioning well.

CONCLUSION

The service environment plays a major part in shaping customers' perception of a firm's image and positioning. As service quality is often difficult to assess, customers frequently use the service environment as an important quality signal. A well-designed service environment makes customers feel good and boosts their satisfaction and allows the firm to influence their behavior (e.g., adhering to the service script and impulse purchasing) while enhancing the productivity of the service operation.

CHAPTER SUMMARY

⊃ **LO1** Service environments fulfill four core purposes. Specifically, they:
- Shape customers' experiences and behaviors.
- Play an important role in determining customer perceptions of the firm, and its image and positioning. Customers often use the service environment as an important quality signal.
- Can be a core part of the value proposition (e.g., as for theme parks and resort hotels).
- Facilitate the service encounter and enhance productivity.

⊃ **LO2** Environmental psychology provides the theoretical underpinning for understanding the effects of service environments on customers and service employees. There are two key models:
- The Mehrabian–Russell Stimulus–Response model holds that environments influence peoples' affective state (or emotions and feelings), which in turn drives their behavior.
- Russell's Model of Affect holds that affect can be modeled with the two interacting dimensions of pleasure and arousal, which together determine whether people approach, spend time and money in an environment, or whether they avoid it.

⊃ **LO3** The servicescape model, which builds on the above theories, represents an integrative framework that explains how customers and service staff respond to key environmental dimensions.

⊃ **LO4** The servicescape model emphasizes three dimensions of the service environment:
- Ambient conditions (including music, scents, and colors).
- Spatial layout and functionality.
- Signs, symbols, and artifacts.

⊃ **LO5** Ambient conditions refer to those characteristics of the environment that pertain to our five senses. Even when not consciously perceived, they still can affect people's internal and behavioral responses. Important ambient dimensions include:
- Music — its tempo, volume, harmony, and familiarity shape behavior by affecting emotions and moods. People tend to adjust their pace to match the tempo of the music.
- Scent — ambient scent can stir powerful emotions and relax or stimulate customers.
- Color — colors can have strong effects on

people's feelings with warm (e.g., a mix of red and orange) and cold colors (e.g., blue) having different impacts. Warm colors are associated with elated mood states, while cold colors are linked to peacefulness and happiness.

⊃ **LO6** Effective spatial layout and functionality are important for efficiency of the service operation and enhancement of its user-friendliness.
- Spatial layout refers to the floor plan, size and shape of furnishing, counters, potential machinery and equipment, and the ways in which they are arranged.
- Functionality refers to the ability of those items to facilitate service operations.

⊃ **LO7** Signs, symbols, and artifacts help customers to draw meaning from the environment and guide them through the service process. They can be used to:
- Label facilities, counters, or departments.
- Show directions (e.g., to entrance, exit, elevator, toilet).
- Communicate the service script (e.g., take a number and watch it to be called).
- Reinforce behavioral rules (e.g., "please turn your cell phones to silent").

⊃ **LO8** The appearance and behavior of service employees and other customers in a servicescape can be part of the value proposition and can reinforce (or detract from) the positioning of the firm.

⊃ **LO9** Service environments are perceived holistically. Therefore, no individual aspect can be optimized without considering everything else, making designing service environments an art rather than a science.
- Because of this challenge, professional designers tend to specialize on specific types of environments, such as hotel lobbies, clubs, healthcare facilities, and so on.
- Beyond esthetic considerations, the best service environments should be designed with the customer's perspective in mind, guiding them smoothly through the service process.
- Tools that can be used to design and improve servicescapes include careful observation, feedback from employees and customers, photo audits, field experiments, and blueprinting.

Review Questions

1. What are the four main purposes service environments fulfill?

2. Describe how the Mehrabian–Russell Stimulus–Response Model and Russell's Model of Affect explain consumer responses to a service environment.

3. What is the relationship or link between Russell's Model of Affect and the servicescape model?

4. Why can it happen that different customers and service staff respond vastly different to the same service environment?

5. Explain the dimensions of ambient conditions and how each can influence customer responses to the service environment.

6. What are the roles of signs, symbols, and artifacts?

7. What are the implications of the fact that environments are perceived holistically?

8. What tools are available for aiding our understanding of customer responses, and for guiding the design and improvement of service environments?

Application Exercises

1. Identify firms from three different service industries where the service environment is a crucial part of the overall value proposition. Analyze and explain in detail the value that is being delivered by the service environment in each of the three industries.

2. Visit a service environment, and have a detailed look around. Experience the environment and try and feel how the various design elements shape what you feel and how you behave in that setting.

3. Select a bad and a good waiting experience and contrast the two situations with respect to the service environment and other people waiting.

4. Visit a self-service environment and analyze how the design dimensions guide you through the service process. What do you find most effective for you, and what seems least effective? How could that environment be improved to further ease the 'way-finding' for self-service customers?

5. Take a camera and conduct a photo audit of a specific servicescape. Photograph examples of excellent and very poor design features. Develop concrete suggestions how this environment could be improved.

Endnotes

1   See also Hooper and Coughlan (2013) who show that the quality of a service environment should be modeled as a separate construct which precedes overall service quality perceptions; Daire Hooper and Joseph Coughlan (2013), "The Servicescape as an Antecedent to Service Quality and Behavioral Intentions," *Journal of Services Marketing*, Vol. 27, No. 4, pp. 271–280.

2   The term *servicescape* was coined by Mary Jo Bitner (1992) in her paper "Servicescapes: The Impact of Physical Surroundings on Customers and Employees," *Journal of Marketing*, Vol. 56, pp. 57–71.

3   Madeleine E. Pullman and Michael A. Gross (2004), "Ability of Experience Design Elements to Elicit Emotions and Loyalty Behaviors," *Decision Sciences*, Vol. 35, No. 1, pp. 551–578.

    A recent study in a retail context has shown that retail shops which were remodeled experienced an increase in sales and continued to outperform shops there were not remodeled. Interestingly, customers acquired in the remodelled shops had spent more than customers acquired before the remodeling, and overall, had more positive attitudes towards the retailer. See: Tracy S. Dagger and Peter J. Danaher (2014), "Comparing the Effect of Store Remodeling on New and Existing Customers," *Journal of Marketing*, Vol. 78, No. 3, pp. 62–80.

4   Anja Reimer and Richard Kuehn (2005), "The Impact of Servicescape on Quality Perception," *European Journal of Marketing*, Vol. 39, No. 7/8, pp. 785–808.

5   Julie Baker, Dhruv Grewal, and A. Parasuraman (1994), "The Influence of Store Environment on Quality Inferences and Store Image," *Journal of the Academy of Marketing Science*, Vol. 22, No. 4, pp. 328–339.

6   Barbara Thau (2014), "Apple and the Other Most Successful Retailers by Sales per Square Foot," *Forbes*, May, http://www.forbes.com/sites/barbarathau/2014/05/20/apple-and-the-other-most-successful-retail-stores-by-sales-per-square-foot/, accessed April 25, 2015; Yukari Iwatani Kane and Ian Sherr, "Secrets from Apple's Genius Bar: Full Loyalty, No Negativity," *The Wall Street Journal*, June 12, 2011, http://www.wsj.com/articles/SB10001424052702304563104576364071955678908, accessed April 25, 2015; http://en.wikipedia.org/wiki/Apple_Store, accessed April 25, 2015.

7   Roger Ulrich, Craig Zimring, Xiaobo Quan, Anjali Joseph, and Ruchi Choudhary (2004). The Role of the Physical Environment in the Hospital of the 21st Century: A Once-in-a-Lifetime Opportunity. Report to the Center for Health Design for the Designing the 21st Century Hospital Project, funded by the Robert Wood Johnson Foundation. (September).

    For a review of the literature on hospital design effects on patients, see: Karin Dijkstra, Marcel Pieterse, and Ad Pruyn (2006), "Physical Environmental Stimuli That Turn Healthcare Facilities into Healing Environments Through Psychologically Mediated Effects: Systematic Review," *Journal of Advanced Nursing*, Vol. 56, No. 2, pp. 166–181. See also the painstaking effort the Mayo Clinic extends to lowering noise levels in their hospitals: Leonard L. Berry and Kent D. Seltman, *Management Lessons from Mayo Clinic: Inside One of the World's Most Admired Service Organization* (New York: McGraw Hill, 2008), 171–172. For a study on the effects of servicescape design in a hospital setting on service workers' job stress and job satisfaction, and subsequently, their commitment to the firm, see: Janet Turner Parish, Leonard L. Berry, and Shun Yin Lam (2008), "The Effect of the Servicescape on Service Workers," *Journal of Service Research*, Vol. 10, No. 3, pp. 220–238.

8   Robert J. Donovan and John R. Rossiter (1982), "Store Atmosphere: An Environmental Psychology Approach," *Journal of Retailing*, Vol. 58, No. 1, pp. 34–57.

9   James A. Russell (1980), "A Circumplex Model of Affect," *Journal of Personality and Social Psychology*, Vol. 39, No. 6, pp. 1161–1178.

10 Jochen Wirtz and John E.G. Bateson (1999), "Consumer Satisfaction with Services: Integrating the Environmental Perspective in Services Marketing into the Traditional Disconfirmation Paradigm," *Journal of Business Research*, Vol. 44, No. 1, pp. 55–66.

11 Jochen Wirtz, Anna S. Mattila, and Rachel L.P. Tan (2007), "The Moderating Role of Target-Arousal on the Impact of Affect on Satisfaction — An Examination in the Context of Service Experiences," *Journal of Retailing*, Vol. 76, No. 3, pp. 347–365; Jochen Wirtz, Anna S. Mattila, and Rachel L. P. Tan (2007), "The Role of Desired Arousal in Influencing Consumers' Satisfaction Evaluations and In-Store Behaviours," *International Journal of Service Industry Management*, Vol. 18, No. 2, pp. 6–24.

12 Mary Jo Bitner (1992), "Servicescapes: The Impact of Physical Surroundings on Customers and Employees," *Journal of Marketing*, Vol. 56, April, pp. 57–71.

13 When servicescapes are designed or redesigned, it is important to use cross-functional teams as there are

significant perception gaps between managers and frontline employees, and the latter's perspective is important for servicescapes to facilitate productive and effective service delivery; see: Herman Kok, Mark Moback and Onno Omta (2015), "Facility Design Consequences of Different Employees' Quality Perceptions," *The Service Industries Journal*, Vol. 35, No. 3, pp. 152–178.

14 For a comprehensive review of experimental studies on the atmospheric effects refer to: L.W. Turley and Ronald E. Milliman (2000), "Atmospheric Effects on Shopping Behavior: A Review of the Experimental Literature," *Journal of Business Research*, Vol. 49, pp. 193–211.

15 Patrick M. Dunne, Robert F. Lusch and David A. Griffith, *Retailing*, 8th ed. (Orlando, FL: Hartcourt, 2013).

16 Steve Oakes (2000), "The Influence of the Musicscape Within Service Environments," *Journal of Services Marketing*, Vol. 14, No. 7, pp. 539–556.

17 Morris B. Holbrook and Punam Anand (1990), "Effects of Tempo and Situational Arousal on the Listener's Perceptual and Affective Responses to Music," *Psychology of Music*, Vol. 18, pp. 150–162; and S.J. Rohner and R. Miller (1980), "Degrees of Familiar and Affective Music and Their Effects on State Anxiety," *Journal of Music Therapy*, Vol. 17, No. 1, pp. 2–15.

18 Laurette Dubé and Sylvie Morin (2001), "Background Music Pleasure and Store Evaluation Intensity Effects and Psychological Mechanisms," *Journal of Business Research*, Vol. 54, pp. 107–113

19 Clare Caldwell and Sally A. Hibbert (2002), "The Influence of Music Tempo and Musical Preference on Restaurant Patrons' Behavior," *Psychology and Marketing* 19, No. 11, pp. 895–917.

20 For a review of the effects of music on various aspects of consumer responses and evaluations see: Steve Oakes and Adrian C. North (2008), "Reviewing Congruity Effects in the Service Environment Musicscape," *International Journal of Service Industry Management*, Vol. 19, No. 1, pp. 63–82.

21 See www.moodmedia.com for in-store music solutions provided by Mood Media, and *The Economist*, "Christmas Music: Dreaming of a Hip-Hop Christmas," December 14, 2013, p. 36.

22 This section is based on: *The Economist*, "Classical Music and Social Control: Twilight of the Yobs," January 8th, 2005, p. 48.

23 *Ibid.*

24 Eric R. Spangenberg, Ayn E. Crowley, and Pamela W. Henderson (1996), "Improving the Store Environment: Do Olfactory Cues Affect Evaluations and Behaviors?" *Journal of Marketing*, Vol. 60, April, pp. 67–80; Paula Fitzerald Bone and Pam Scholder Ellen (1999), "Scents in the Marketplace: Explaining a Fraction of Olfaction," *Journal of Retailing*, Vol. 75, No. 2, pp. 243–262; Jeremy Caplan (2006), "Sense and Sensibility," *Time*, Vol. 168, No. 16, pp. 66–67.

25 Alan R. Hirsch (1997), "Dr. Hirsch's Guide to Scentsational Weight Loss," UK: Harper Collins, January, pp. 12–15. http://www.smellandtaste.org/, accessed April 25, 2015.

26 Alan R. Hirsch (1995), "Effects of Ambient Odors on Slot Machine Usage in a Las Vegas Casino," *Psychology and Marketing*, Vol. 12, No. 7, pp. 585–594.

27 Alan R. Hirsch and S.E. Gay (1991), "Effect on Ambient Olfactory Stimuli on the Evaluation of a Common Consumer Product," *Chemical Senses*, Vol. 16, p. 535.

28 See Ambius' website for details of its scent marketing, ambient scenting and sensory branding services at: http://www.ambius.com/ambius-catalogs/scent/index.html, accessed April 24, 2015.

29 *The Economist*, "Christmas Music: Dreaming of a Hip-Hop Christmas," December 14, 2013, p. 36.

30 Andreas Herrmann, Manja Zidansek, David E. Sprott, and Eric R. Spangenberg (2013), "The Power of Simplicity: Processing Fluency and the Effects of Olfactory Cues on Retail Sales," *Journal of Retailing*, Vol. 89, No. 1, pp. 30–43.

31 Ayn E. Crowley (1993), "The Two-Dimensional Impact of Color on Shopping," *Marketing Letters*, Vol. 4, No. 1, pp. 59-69; Gerald J. Gorn, Amitava Chattopadhyay, Jaideep Sengupta, and Shashank Tripathi (2004), "Waiting for the Web: How Screen Color Affects Time Perception," *Journal of Marketing Research*, Vol. XLI, May, pp. 215–225; Iris Vilnai-Yavetz and Anat Rafaeli (2006), "Aesthetics and Professionalism of Virtual Servicescapes," *Journal of Service Research*, Vol. 8, No. 3, pp. 245–259.

32 Linda Holtzschuhe, *Understanding Color — An Introduction for Designers*, 3rd ed. (New Jersey: John Wiley, 2006), p. 51.

33 Albert Henry Munsell, *A Munsell Color Product* (New York: Kollmorgen Corporation, 1996).

34 Linda Holtzschuhe, *Understanding Color — An Introduction for Designers,* 3rd ed. (New Jersey: John Wiley, 2006).

35 Heinrich Zollinger, *Color: A Multidisciplinary Approach.* (Zurich: Verlag Helvetica Chimica Acta (VHCA) Weinheim, Wiley-VCH, 1999), pp. 71–79.

36 Joseph A. Bellizzi, Ayn E. Crowley, and Ronald W. Hasty (1983), "The Effects of Color in Store Design," *Journal of Retailing,* Vol. 59, No. 1. pp. 21–45.

37 Sara O. Marberry and Laurie Zagon, *The Power of Color – Creating Healthy Interior Spaces* (New York: John Wiley & Sons, 1995), 38.

38 Justin Bachman (2015), "Airlines Add Mood Lighting to Chill Passengers Out: New Boeing and Airbus Models Offer Cabin Designers Splashy Ways to Engage Passengers with Light," Bloomberg Business, http://www.bloomberg.com/news/articles/2015-04-22/airlines-add-mood-lighting-to-chill-passengers-out, accessed April 24, 2015.

39 Anat Rafaeli and Iris Vilnai-Yavetz, "Discerning Organizational Boundaries Through Physical Artifacts," in N. Paulsen and T. Hernes, eds. *Managing Boundaries in Organizations*: Multiple Perspectives (UK: Basingstoke, Hampshire, Macmillan, 2003); Anat Rafaeli and Iris Vilnai-Yavetz (2004), "Emotion as a Connection of Physical Artifacts and Organizations," *Organization Science*, Vol. 15, No 6, pp. 671-686; and Anat Rafaeli and Iris Vilnai-Yavetz, "Managing Organizational Artifacts to Avoid Artifact Myopia," in A. Rafaeli and M. Pratt, eds., *Artifacts and Organization: Beyond Mere Symbolism* (Mahwah, NJ: Lawrence Erlbaum Associates Inc., 2005), 9–21.

40 For an excellent review of the quality of signage management, see: Angelo Bonfani (2013), "Towards an Approach to Signage Management Quality (SMQ)," *Journal of Services Marketing*, Vol. 27, No. 4, pp. 312–321.

41 Lewis P. Carbone and Stephen H. Haeckel (1994), "Engineering Customer Experiences," *Marketing Management,* Vol. 3, No. 3, Winter, pp. 9–18; Lewis P. Carbone, Stephen H. Haeckel and Leonard L. Berry (2003), "How to Lead the Customer Experience," *Marketing Management,* Vol. 12, No. 1, Jan/Feb, p. 18; Leonard L. Berry and Lewis P. Carbone (2007), "Build Loyalty Through Experience Management," *Quality Progress*, Vol. 40, No. 9, September, pp. 26–32.

42 Roscoe Hightower, Jr. and Mohammad Shariat (2009), "Servicescape's Hierarchical Factor Structure Model," *Global Review of Business and Economic Research*, Vol.

5, No. 2, pp. 375–398; Roscoe Hightower, Jr. (2010), "Commentary on Conceptualizing the Servicescape Construct in 'A Study of the Service Encounter in Eight Countries,'" *Marketing Management Journal*, Vol. 20, Spring, No. 1, pp. 75–86.

43 Dennis Nickson, Chris Warhurst, and Eli Dutton (2005), "The Importance of Attitude and Appearance in the Service Encounter in Retail and Hospitality," *Managing Service Quality,* Vol. 2, pp. 195–208.

44 Christine M. Piotrowski, *Designing Commercial Interiors* (New York: John Wiley & Sons, Inc., 2007); Martin M. Pegler, *Cafes & Bistros* (New York: Retail Reporting Corporation, 1998); Paco Asensio, *Bars & Restaurants.* (New York: HarperCollins International, 2002); Bethan Ryder, *Bar and Club Design* (London: Laurence King Publishing, 2002).

45 Ron Kaufman, "Service Power: Who Were They Designing it For?" *Newsletter*, May 2001, http://Ron Kaufman.com.

46 Alan d'Astous (2000), "Irritating Aspects of the Shopping Environment," *Journal of Business Research,* Vol. 49, pp. 149–156. See also: K. Douglas Hoffman, Scott W. Kelly, and Beth C. Chung (2003), "A CIT Investigation of Servicscape Failures and Associated Recovery Strategies," *Journal of Services Marketing,* Vol. 17, No. 4, pp. 322–40.

47 Jörg Pareigis, Per Echeverri, and Bo Edvardsson (2012), "Exploring Internal Mechanisms Forming Customer Servicescape Experiences," *Journal of Service Management*, Vol. 23, No. 5, pp. 677–695.

48 Interestingly, visual complexity in environments hinders shoppers' information processing, and thereby reduces their satisfaction. This finding is especially applicable in utilitarian service contexts, and also suggest that it is better for service organizations to reduce complexity in servicescape design and make it easy for customers to sense and process a servicescape. This finding is well-aligned with the study by Jörg Pareigis, Per Echeverri, and Bo Edvardsson (2012); see: Ulrich R. Orth, Frauke Heinrich, and Keven Malkewitz (2012), "Servicescape Interior Design and Consumer Personality Impressions," *Journal of Services Marketing*, Vol. 26, No. 3, pp. 194–203; Ulrich R. Orth and Jochen Wirtz (2014), "Consumer Processing of Interior Service Environments," *Journal of Service Research*, Vol. 17, No. 3, pp. 296–309.

49 Madeleine E. Pullman and Stephani K.A. Robson (2007), "Visual Methods: Using Photographs to Capture Customers' Experience with Design," *Cornell Hotel and Restaurant Administration Quarterly*, Vol. 48, No. 2, pp. 121–144.

CHAPTER 11 Managing People for Service Advantage

Quintessentially we are a people-based company. You couldn't find another consumer brand as dependent on human behavior.

Howard Schultz
CEO of Starbucks

The old adage "People are your most important asset" is wrong. The right people are your most important asset.

Jim Collins
Consultant, teacher, and author of
best-selling book "Good to Great"

Customer satisfaction results from the realization of high levels of value compared to competitors… Value is created by satisfied, committed, loyal, and productive employees.

**James I. Heskett, W. Earl Sasser, Jr.,
and Leonard L. Schlesinger**
Current and former professors at
Harvard Business School

LEARNING OBJECTIVES (LOs)

By the end of this chapter, the reader should be able to:

⊃ **LO 1** Explain why service employees are so important to the success of a firm.

⊃ **LO 2** Understand the factors that make the work of frontline staff so demanding and often difficult.

⊃ **LO 3** Describe the cycles of failure, mediocrity, and success in HR for service firms.

⊃ **LO 4** Understand the key elements of the Service Talent Cycle of successful HR management in service firms.

⊃ **LO 5** Know how to attract, select, and hire the right people for service jobs.

⊃ **LO 6** Explain the key areas in which service employees need training.

⊃ **LO 7** Understand the role of internal marketing and communications.

⊃ **LO 8** Understand why empowerment is so important in many frontline jobs.

⊃ **LO 9** Explain how to build high-performance service delivery teams.

⊃ **LO 10** Know how to integrate teams across departments and functional areas.

⊃ **LO 11** Know how to motivate and energize service employees so that they will deliver service excellence and productivity.

⊃ **LO 12** Understand what a service-oriented culture is.

⊃ **LO 13** Know the difference between service climate and culture, and describe the determinants of a climate for service.

⊃ **LO 14** Explain the qualities of effective leaders in service organizations.

⊃ **LO 15** Understand different leadership styles, the importance of role modeling and focusing the entire organization on the frontline.

Fortunately, his training had prepared him to deal with all types of customers.

OPENING VIGNETTE
Cora Griffith — The Outstanding Waitress[1]

Cora Griffith, a waitress for the Orchard Café at the Paper Valley Hotel in Appleton, Wisconsin, is superb in her role, appreciated by first-time customers, famous with her regular customers, and revered by her coworkers. Cora loves her work — and it shows. Comfortable in a role that she believes is the right one for her, Cora follows nine rules of success:

1. **Treat Customers Like Family.** First-time customers are not allowed to feel like strangers. Cheerful and proactive, Cora smiles, chats, and includes everyone at the table in the conversation. She is as respectful to children as she is to adults, and makes it a point to learn and use everyone's name. "I want people to feel like they're sitting down to dinner right at my house. I want them to feel they're welcome, that they can get comfortable, and that they can relax. I don't just serve people, I pamper them."

2. **Listen First.** Cora has developed her listening skills to the point that she rarely writes down customers' orders. She listens carefully and provides a customized service: "Are they in a hurry? Or do they have a special diet or like their selection cooked in a certain way?"

3. **Anticipate Customers' Wants.** She refills beverages and brings extra bread and butter in a timely manner. One regular customer, for example, who likes honey with her coffee, gets it without having to ask. "I don't want my customers to have to ask for anything, so I always try to anticipate what they might need."

4. **Simple Things Make the Difference.** She manages the details of her service, monitoring the cleanliness of the utensils and their correct placement. The fold for napkins must be just right. She inspects each plate in the kitchen before taking it to the table. She provides crayons for small children to draw pictures while waiting for the meal. "It's the little things that please the customer," she says.

5. **Work Smart.** Cora scans all her tables at once, looking for opportunities to combine tasks. "Never do just one thing at a time," she advises. "And never go from the kitchen to the dining room empty-handed. Take coffee or iced tea or water with you." When she refills one glass of water, she refills others. When clearing one plate, she clears others. "You have to be organized, and you have to keep in touch with the big picture."

6. **Keep Learning.** Cora makes it an ongoing effort to improve existing skills and learn new ones.

7. **Success Is Where You Find It.** Cora is content with her work. She finds satisfaction in pleasing her customers, and she enjoys helping other people enjoy. Her positive attitude is a positive force in the restaurant. She is hard to ignore. "If customers come to the restaurant in a bad mood, I'll try to cheer them up before they leave." Her definition of success: "To be happy in life."

8. **All for One, One for All.** Cora has been working with many of the same coworkers for more than eight years. The team supports one another on the crazy days when 300 conventioneers come to the restaurant for breakfast at the same time. Everyone pitches in and helps. The wait staff cover for one another, the managers bus the tables, and the chefs garnish the plates. "We are like a little family," Cora says. "We know each other very well and we help each other out. If we have a crazy day, I'll go in the kitchen towards the end of the shift and say, 'Man, I'm just proud of us. We really worked hard today.'"

9. **Take Pride in Your Work.** Cora believes in the importance of her work and in the need to do it well. "I don't think of myself as 'just a waitress'...I've chosen to be a waitress. I'm doing this to my full potential, and I give it my best. I tell anyone who's starting out: 'Take pride in what you do'. You're never just an 'anything', no matter what you do. You give it your all...and you do it with pride."

Cora Griffith is a success story. She is loyal to her employer and dedicated to her customers and coworkers. A perfectionist who seeks continuous improvement, Cora's enthusiasm for her work and unflagging spirit creates an energy that radiates through the restaurant. She is proud of being a waitress, proud of 'touching lives'. Says Cora: "I have always wanted to do my best. However, the owners really are the ones who taught me how important it is to take care of the customer and gave me the freedom to do it. The company always has listened to my concerns and followed up. Had I not worked for the Orchard Café, I would have been a good waitress, but I would not have been the same waitress."

⊃ **LO 1**

Explain why service
employees are so important
to the success of a firm.

SERVICE EMPLOYEES ARE EXTREMELY IMPORTANT

The quality of a service firm's staff — especially those working in customer-facing positions — plays a crucial role in determining market success and financial performance. Frontline employees are a key input for delivering service excellence and competitive advantage. The market and financial results of managing people effectively for service advantage can be phenomenal. That's why the *People* element of the **7 Ps** is so important.

Among the most demanding jobs in service businesses are the frontline jobs. Employees working in these customer-facing jobs span the boundary between inside and outside of the organization. They are expected to be fast and efficient in executing operational tasks, as well as to be courteous and helpful when dealing with customers.

Behind most of today's successful service organizations stands a firm commitment to effective management of human resources (HR), including recruitment, selection, training, motivation, and retention of employees. Organizations that display this commitment understand the economic payoff from investing in their people. These firms are also characterized by a distinctive culture of service leadership and role modeling by its top management. Good HR strategies allied with strong management leadership at all levels often lead to a sustainable competitive advantage. It is probably harder for competitors to duplicate high-performance human assets compared to any other corporate resource.

Highly capable and motivated people are at the center of service excellence and productivity. Cora Griffith in our opening vignette is a powerful demonstration of a frontline employee delivering service excellence and productivity, and at the same time having high job satisfaction. Many of the pointers in Cora Griffith's "nine rules of success" are the result of good HR strategies for service firms. After reading this chapter, you will know how to get HR right in service firms, and how to get satisfied, loyal, motivated, and productive service employees. The organizing framework for this chapter is provided in *Figure 11.1*.

Frontline Employees Are Important. They:

- Are a core part of the service product
- Are the service firm in the eyes of the customer
- Are a core part of the brand, deliver the brand promise
- Sell, cross-sell and up-sell
- Are a key driver of customer loyalty
- Determine productivity

HR in Service Firms Is Challenging

Frontline Work Is Difficult & Stressful
- Boundary spanning positions
- Link the inside of the organization to the outside world
- Have conflicting roles that cause role stress:
  - Organization/client conflict
  - Person/role conflict
  - Inter-client conflict
- Require emotional labor

Basic Models of HR in Service Firms
- Cycle of Failure
  - Low pay, low investment in people, high staff turnover
  - Result in customer dissatisfaction, defection, and low margins
- Cycle of Mediocrity
  - Large bureaucracies; offer job security but little scope in the job itself
  - No incentives to serve customers well
- Cycle of Success
  - Heavy investment in recruitment, development, and motivation of frontline employees
  - Employees are engaged and productive
  - Customers are satisfied and loyal, margins are improvedpleasure (or displeasure)

How to Get HR Right — The Service Talent Cycle

Hire the Right People
- Be the preferred employer and compete for talent market share
- Intensify the selection process to identify the right people for the organization and given job
  - Conduct multiple structured interviews
  - Use personality tests
  - Observe candidate behavior
  - Give applicants a realistic preview of the job

Enable the Frontline
Training & Development
- Conduct extensive training on:
  - Organizational culture, purpose, & strategy
  - Interpersonal and technical skills
  - Product/service knowledge
- Reinforce training to shape behaviors
- Use internal communications/marketing to shape the service culture and behaviors
- Professionalize the frontline

Empower the Frontline
- Provide discretion to find solutions to service problems and customization of service delivery
- Set appropriate levels of empowerment depending on the business model and customer needs
- Empowerment requires: (1) information about performance, (2) knowledge that enables contribution to performance, (3) power to make decisions, and (4) performance-based rewards.

Organize Frontline Employees into Effective Service Delivery Teams
- Use cross-functional teams that can service customers from end-to-end
- Structure teams for success (e.g., set goals, carefully select members with the right skills)
- Integrate teams across departments and functional area (e.g., cross-postings, and internal campaigns such as "walk a mile in my shoes" and "a day in the field")

Motivate the Frontline
- Energize and motivate employees with a full set of rewards
- Rewards should include pay, performance bonuses, satisfying job content, feedback and recognition, and goal accomplishment

Service Culture, Climate, & Leadership

Service Culture
- Shared perceptions of what is important in an organization
- Shared values and beliefs of why those things are important

Climate for Service
- Climate is culture translated into policies, practices, and procedures
- Shared perception of practices and behaviors that get rewarded

Leadership
- Qualities of effective leaders
- Leadership styles that focus on basics versus transformation
- Strong focus on frontline

Figure 11.1 Organizing framework — managing people for service advantage

Service Personnel as a Source of Customer Loyalty and Competitive Advantage

Almost everybody can recount a dreadful experience they had with a service business. If pressed, many of these same people can also recount a really good service experience. Service personnel usually feature prominently in such dramas. They either feature in roles as uncaring, incompetent, mean-spirited villains, or in roles as heroes who went out of their way to help customers by anticipating their needs and resolving problems in a helpful and empathetic manner. You probably have your own set of favorite stories, featuring both villains and heroes — and if you're like most people, you probably talk more about the former than the latter.

From a customer's perspective, the encounter with service staff is probably the most important aspect of a service. From the firm's perspective, the service levels and the way service is delivered by frontline personnel can be an important source of differentiation as well as competitive advantage. Among the reasons why service employees are so important to customers and the firm's competitive positioning are that the frontline:

- **Is a core part of the product.** Often, the service employees are the most visible element of the service. They deliver the service, and greatly affect service quality.

- **Is the service firm.** Frontline employees represent the service firm, and from a customer's perspective, they are the firm.

- **Is the brand.** Frontline employees and the service they provide are often a core part of the brand. It is the employees who determine whether the brand promise is delivered[2].

- **Affects sales.** Service personnel are often critically important for generating sales, cross-sales, and up-sales.

- **Is a key driver of customer loyalty.** Frontline employees play a key role in anticipating customers' needs, customizing the service delivery (*Figure 11.2*), and building personalized relationships with customers[3]. An effective performance of these activities should ultimately lead to increased customer loyalty.

- **Determines productivity.** Frontline employees have heavy influence on the productivity of frontline operations.

The story of Cora Griffith and many other success stories of how employees showing discretionary effort have reinforced the truism that highly motivated people are at the core of service excellence[4]. Increasingly, they are a key factor in creating and maintaining competitive positioning and advantage.

The intuitive importance of the effect of service employees on customer loyalty was integrated and formalized by James Heskett and his colleagues in their pioneering research on what they call the **Service–Profit Chain** (Chapter 1 illustrates the chain in more detail). It demonstrates the chain of relationships among (1) employee satisfaction, retention and productivity; (2) service value; (3) customer satisfaction and loyalty; and (4) revenue growth and profitability for the firm[5]. Unlike manufacturing, "shop-floor workers" in services (i.e., frontline staff) are in constant contact with customers, and there is solid evidence showing that employee satisfaction and customer satisfaction are highly correlated[6]. Therefore, this chapter focuses on how to have satisfied, loyal, and productive service employees who care.

Figure 11.2 Service personnel represent the firm and often build personal relationships with their customers

Figure 11.3 The pleasant personality of call center staff can result in a positive "moment of truth," where a firm's service quality will be viewed positively

The Frontline in Low-Contact Services

Much research in service management relates to high-contact services. However, many services are moving towards using low-contact delivery channels such as call centers, where contact is voice-to-voice rather than face-to-face. A growing number of self-service transactions no longer involve frontline staff. As a result, a large and increasing number of customer contact employees work by telephone or email, never meeting customers face-to-face. In the light of these trends, are frontline employees really all that important for such services?

Most people do not call the service hotline or visit the service center of their cell phone service operator or credit card companies more than once or twice a year. However, these occasional service encounters are absolutely critical — they are the "moments of truth" that drive a customer's perceptions of the service firm (*Figure 11.3*). Also, it is likely that these interactions are not about routine transactions, but about service problems and special requests. These very few instances of contact determine whether a customer thinks, "Your customer service is excellent! When I need help, I can call you, and this is one important reason why I bank with you!", or "Your service stinks. I don't like interacting with you, and I am going to switch away from your bank when I get the chance!"

Given that technology is relatively commoditized, the service delivered by the frontline, whether it is face-to-face, "ear to ear," or via email, Twitter or chat, is highly visible and important to customers and, therefore, a critical component of a service firm's marketing strategy.

LO 2

Understand the factors that make the work of frontline staff so demanding and often difficult.

FRONTLINE WORK IS DIFFICULT AND STRESSFUL

The Service–Profit Chain needs high-performing, satisfied employees to achieve service excellence and customer loyalty (see Chapter 1 for a detailed discussion). However, these customer-facing employees work in some of the most demanding jobs in service firms. Perhaps you have worked in one or more of such jobs, which are common in the healthcare, hospitality, retail, and travel industries. There is a story that became viral about a JetBlue flight attendant who abruptly quit his job after 28 years of service as a flight attendant. Apparently, he was fed up with a difficult passenger with a bag problem, who had sworn at him. He scolded the passenger publicly over the airplane intercom, announced that he had had enough, and opened the emergency slide to get off the plane[7]. This is an example of how stress can affect a person at work. Let's discuss the main reasons why these jobs are so demanding (and you can relate these to your own experience, while recognizing there may be differences between working part-time for short periods and working full-time as a career).

Service Jobs Are Boundary Spanning Positions

The organizational behavior literature refers to service employees as *boundary spanners*. They link the inside of an organization to the outside world, operating at the boundary of the company. Due to the position they occupy, boundary spanners often have conflicting roles. In particular, customer contact personnel must attend to both operational and marketing goals. This multiplicity of roles in service jobs often leads to role conflict and role stress, which we will discuss next[8].

Sources of Role Conflict

There are three main causes of role conflict and role stress in frontline positions: organization/client, person/role, and interclient conflicts.

Organization/Client Conflict. Customer contact personnel must attend to both operational and marketing goals. They are expected to delight customers, which takes time, and yet they have to be fast and efficient at operational tasks[9]. In addition, they are often expected to do selling, cross-selling, and up-selling. For instance, it is common to hear customer contact personnel suggest: "Now would be a good time to open a separate account to save for your children's education"; or "For only $35 more per night, you can upgrade to the executive floor."

Finally, customer contact personnel can even be responsible for enforcing rate integrity and pricing schedules that might be in direct conflict with customer satisfaction (e.g., "I am sorry, but we don't serve ice water in this restaurant, although we do have an excellent selection of still and carbonated mineral waters," or "I am sorry, but we cannot waive the fee for the bounced check for the third time this quarter.") This type of conflict is also called the two-bosses dilemma, where service employees have the unpleasant choice between enforcing the company's rules or satisfying customer demands. The problem is especially acute in organizations that are not customer-oriented.

Figure 11.4 Emotional labor and forced smiles can be difficult for service employees

Person/Role Conflict. Service staff may have conflicts between what their job requires and their own personalities, self-perception, and beliefs. For example, the job may require staff to smile and be friendly even to rude customers (see also the section on jaycustomers in Chapter 12). V. S. Mahesh and Anand Kasturi note from their consulting work with service organizations around the world that thousands of frontline staff, when asked, consistently tend to describe customers with a pronounced negative flavor — frequently using phrases such as "over-demanding," "unreasonable," "refuse to listen," "always want everything their way, immediately," and also "arrogant[10]."

Providing quality service requires an independent, warm, and friendly personality. These traits are more likely to be found in people with higher self-esteem. However, many frontline jobs are seen as low-level jobs that require little education, offer low pay, and very little career advancement. If an organization is not able to "professionalize" their frontline jobs and move away from this image, these jobs may be inconsistent with staff's self-perception and lead to person/role conflicts.

Interclient Conflict. Conflicts between customers are not uncommon (e.g., smoking in non-smoking sections, jumping queues, talking on a cell phone in a movie theater, or being excessively noisy in a restaurant), and it is usually the service staff that are summoned to call the offending customer to order. This is a stressful and unpleasant task, as it is difficult and often impossible to satisfy both sides.

In conclusion, frontline employees may perform triple roles, satisfying customers, delivering productivity, and generating sales. Although employees may experience conflict and stress, they are still expected to smile and be friendly towards the customer. We call this emotional labor, which in itself is an important cause of stress. Next, let's look at emotional labor in more detail.

Emotional Labor

The term *emotional labor* was first used by Arlie Hochschild in her book *The Managed Heart*[11]. Emotional labor arises when a discrepancy exists between how frontline staff feel inside and the emotions that management requires them to show in front of customers. Frontline staff are expected to have a cheerful disposition, be genial, compassionate, sincere or even self-effacing — emotions that can be conveyed through facial expressions, gestures, tone of voice, and choice of words. To make matters worse, it is the authentic display of positive emotions rather than surface acting (e.g., "faking" emotions) that affects customer satisfaction[12]. Although some service firms make an effort to recruit employees with such characteristics, there will inevitably be situations when employees do not feel such positive emotions, yet are required to suppress their true feelings in order to conform to customer expectations (*Figure 11.4*). As Pannikkos Constanti and Paul Gibbs point out, "the power axis for emotional labor tends to favor both the management and the customer, with the front line employee…being subordinate." thus creating a potentially exploitative situation[13].

Dilbert by Scott Adams. © Universal Uclick All Rights Reserved.

Figure 11.5 Dibert Encoutners Emotional Labor at the Bank

The stress of emotional labor is nicely illustrated in the following, probably apocryphal story: A flight attendant was approached by a passenger with "Let's have a smile." She replied with "Okay. I'll tell you what, first you smile and then I'll smile, okay?" He smiled. "Good," she said. "Now hold that for 15 hours," and walked away[14]. *Figure 11.5 captures emotional labor with humor.*

Firms need to be aware of ongoing emotional stress among their employees and make sure that their employees are trained to deal with emotional stress and cope with pressure from customers, as well as get support from their team leaders. If not, employees will use a variety of ways to resist the stress of emotional labor[15]. For example, because of Singapore Airlines' reputation for service excellence, its customers tend to have high expectations and can be very demanding. This puts considerable pressure on its frontline employees. The commercial training manager of Singapore Airlines (SIA) explained:

> *We have recently undertaken an external survey and it appears that more of the "demanding customers" choose to fly with SIA. So the staff are really under a lot of pressure. We have a motto: "If SIA can't do it for you, no other airline can." So we encourage staff to try to sort things out, and to do as much as they can for the customer. Although they are very proud, and indeed,*

> *protective of the company, we need to help them deal with the emotional turmoil of having to handle their customers well, and at the same time, feel they're not being taken advantage of. The challenge is to help our staff deal with difficult situations and take the brickbats[16].*

Service Sweatshops?

Rapid developments in information technology (IT) are permitting service businesses to make radical improvements in business processes and even completely reengineer their operations. These developments sometimes result in wrenching changes in the nature of work for existing employees. In some instances, deployment of new technology and methods can dramatically change the nature of the work environment (*Service Insights 11.1*). In other instances, face-to-face contact is replaced by use of the Internet or call center–provided services, and firms have redefined and relocated jobs, created new employee profiles for recruiting purposes, and sought to hire employees with a different set of qualifications.

As a result of the growing shift from high-contact to low-contact services, a large and increasing number of customer contact employees work by telephone or email, never meeting customers face-to-face. For example, a remarkable 3% of the total US workforce is now employed in call centers as customer service representatives (CSRs).

At best, when well-designed, such jobs can be rewarding, and often offer parents and students flexible working hours and part-time jobs (some 50% of call center workers are single mothers or students). In fact, it has been shown that part-time workers are more satisfied with their work as CSRs than full-time staff, and perform just as well[17]. At worst, these jobs place employees in an electronic equivalent of the old-fashioned sweatshop. Even in the best-managed call

Figure 11.6 Work in customer contact centers is intense! Yet, how customer service representatives perform often determines how a firm's service quality is perceived by customers.

centers (also often called "customer contact centers") the work is intense (see *Figure 11.6*), with CSRs expected to deal with up to two calls a minute (including trips to the toilet and breaks) and under a high level of monitoring. There is also significant stress from customers themselves, because many are irate at the time of contact.

Research on call centers found that intrinsically motivated agents suffered less customer stress[18]. As we will discuss in this chapter, some of the keys to success in this area involve screening applicants to make sure they already know how to present themselves well on the telephone and have the potential to learn additional skills, training them carefully, and giving them a well-designed working environment.

SERVICE INSIGHTS 11.1

Counting the Seconds — Performance Measurement of Frontline Employees

Retailers have come under tremendous pressure to cut costs, and labor is their biggest controllable expense. It is no wonder then that business is booming for the Operations Workforce Optimization (OWO) unit, which was recently acquired by Accenture, the global consulting firm. The consulting and software company adapted time-motion concepts developed for manufacturing operations to service businesses, where it breaks down tasks such as working a cash register in a supermarket into quantifiable units and develops standard times to complete each unit or task. The firm then implements software to help its clients to monitor employee performance.

A spokesperson of a large retailer explained that they "expect employees to be at 100% performance to the standards, but we do not begin any formal counseling process until the performance falls below 95%." If a staff falls below 95% of the baseline score too many times, he or she is likely to be bounced to a lower-paying job or be fired. Employee responses to this approach can be negative. Interviews with cashiers of that large retailer suggest that the system has spurred many to hurry up and experience increased stress levels. Hanning, 25 years old, took a cashier job in one of the chain's stores in Michigan for $7.15 per hour in July 2007. She said she was "written up" three or four times for scores below 95%, and was told that she had to move to another department at a lower pay if her performance did not improve. She recalled being told,

"Make sure you're just scanning, grabbing, bagging." She resigned after almost one year on the job.

The customers' experience can also be negatively affected. Gunter, 22 years old, says he recently told a longtime customer that he could not chat with her anymore as he was being timed. He said, "I was told to get people in and out." Other cashiers said that they avoided eye contact with shoppers and hurried along those customers who may take longer to unload carts or make payment. A customer reported, "Everybody is under stress. They are not as friendly. I know elderly people have a hard time making change because you lose your ability to feel. They're so rushed at checkout that they don't want to come here."

OWO recommends that retailers adjust time standards to account for customer service and other variables that can affect how long a particular task should take, but the interviews seem to suggest that quite a number of firms focus on productivity first. One clothing and footwear chain calculated that they could save $15,000 per annum for every second cut from the checkout process, and another installed fingerprint readers at the cash registers so that cashiers can sign in directly at their individual workplaces and not at a central time clock, which saves minutes of wasted time according to a former director of a major retailer. OWO says that its methods can cut labor costs by 5% to 15%.

Source

Vanessa O'Connell (2008), "Seconds Counts as Stores Trim Costs," *The Wall Street Journal*, November 17.

⊃ **LO 3**
Describe the cycles of
failure, mediocrity, and
success in HR for service
firms.

CYCLES OF FAILURE, MEDIOCRITY, AND SUCCESS

After having discussed the importance of frontline employees and how difficult their work is, let's look at the big picture of how poor, mediocre, and excellent firms set up their frontline employees for failure, mediocrity, or success. All too often, poor working environments translate into dreadful service, with employees treating customers the way their managers treat them. Businesses with high employee turnover are often stuck in what has been termed the **Cycle of Failure**. Others, which offer job security but little scope for personal initiative and are heavily rule- and procedure-based, may suffer from an equally undesirable **Cycle of Mediocrity**. However, if managed well, there is potential for a virtuous cycle in service employment, called the **Cycle of Success**[19].

The Cycle of Failure

In many service industries, the search for productivity is carried out with a vengeance and frequently leads to simplifying work routines and hiring workers as cheaply as possible to perform repetitive work tasks that require little or no training. Among consumer services, departmental stores, fast-food restaurants, and call center operations are often cited as examples in which this problem abounds (although there are notable exceptions). The cycle of failure captures the implications of such a strategy, with its two concentric but interactive cycles: one involving failures with employees; the second, with customers (*Figure 11.7*).

The employee **Cycle of Failure** begins with a narrow design of jobs to accommodate low skill levels, an emphasis on rules rather than service, and the use of technology to control quality. Low wages are paid, accompanied by little investment in employee selection and training. Consequences include bored employees who lack the ability to respond to customer problems, who become dissatisfied, and who develop a poor service attitude. The results for the firm are low service quality and high employee turnover. Because of weak profit margins, the cycle repeats itself with the hiring of more low-paid employees to work in this unrewarding atmosphere (*Figure 11.8*). Some service firms can reach such low levels of employee morale that frontline staff become hostile towards customers and may even engage in "service sabotage" as described in *Service Insights 11.2*.

Figure 11.8 Employees in the cycle of failure are bored and dissatisfied

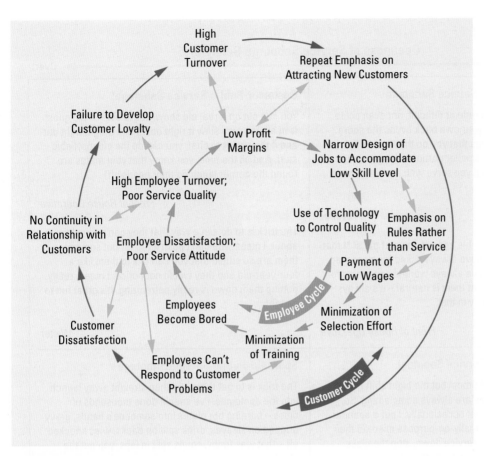

Figure 11.7 The Cycle of Failure

Source

© 1991 from MIT *Sloan Management Review*/Massachusetts Institute of Technology. All rights reserved. Distributed by Tribune Content Agency.

SERVICE INSIGHTS 11.2

Service Sabotage by the Frontline

The next time you are dissatisfied with the service provided by a service employee — in a restaurant, for example — it's worth pausing for a moment to think about the consequences of complaining about the service. You might just become the unknowing victim of a malicious case of service sabotage, such as having something unhygienic added to one's food.

There is a fairly high incidence of service sabotage by frontline employees. Lloyd Harris and Emmanuel Ogbonna found that 90% of their interviewees accepted that frontline behavior with malicious intent

to reduce or spoil the service — service sabotage — is an everyday occurrence in their organizations.

Harris and Ogbonna classify service sabotage along two dimensions: covert-overt and routinized-intermittent behaviors. Covert behaviors are concealed from customers, whereas overt actions are purposefully displayed often to coworkers and sometimes also to customers. Routinized behaviors are ingrained into the culture, whereas intermittent actions are sporadic, and less common. Some true examples of service sabotage classified along these two dimensions appear in *Figure 11.9*. Another study showed that if customers are abusive in any way, some employees will retaliate!

Openness of Service Sabotage Behaviors

Covert ◄───► Overt

"Normality" of Service Sabotage Behaviors — Routinized ▲ / Intermittent ▼

Customary-Private Service Sabotage

Many customers are rude or difficult, not even polite like you or I. Getting your own back evens the score. There are lots of things that you do that no one but you will ever know – smaller portions, doggy wine, a bad beer – all that and you serve with a smile! Sweet revenge!

Waiter

It's perfectly normal to file against some of the s**t that happens. Managers have always asked for more than fair and customers have always wanted something for nothing. Getting back at them is natural – it's always happened, nothing new in that.

Front of House Operative

Customer-Public Service Sabotage

You can put on a real old show. You know – if the guest is in a hurry, you slow it right down and drag it right out and if they want to chat, you can do the monosyllabic stuff. And all the time, you know that your mates are round the corner laughing their heads off!

Front of House Operative

The trick is to do it in a way that they can't complain about. I mean, you can't push it too far but some of them are so stupid that you can talk to them like a four-year-old and they would not notice. I mean, really putting them down is really patronizing. It's great fun to watch!

Waiter

Sporadic-Private Service Sabotage

I don't often work with them but the night shift here really gets to me. They are always complaining. So, to get back at them, just occasionally, I put a spanner in the works – accidentally-on-purpose misread their food orders, slow the service down, stop the glass washer so that they run out – nothing heavy.

Senior Chef

I don't know why I do it. Sometimes it's simply a bad day, a lousy week, I dunno – but kicking someone's bags down the back stairs is not that unusual – not every day – I guess a couple of times a month.

Front of House Supervisor

Sporadic-Public Service Sabotage

The trick is to get them and then straight away launch into the apologies. I've seen it done thousands of times – burning hot plates into someone's hands, gravy dripped on sleeves, drink spilt on backs, wigs knocked off – that was funny, soups split in laps, you get the idea!

Long Serving General Attendant

Listen, there's this rule that we are supposed to greet all customers and smile at them if they pass within 5 meters. Well, this ain't done 'cos we think it's silly but this guy we decided to do it to. It started off with the waiters – we'd all go up to him and grin at him and say "hello." But it spread. Before you know it, managers and all have cottoned on and this poor chap is being met and greeted every two steps! He doesn't know what the hell is going on! It was so funny – the guy spent the last three nights in his room – he didn't dare go in the restaurant

Housekeeping Supervisor

Figure 11.9 Examples of service sabotage

Source

Lloyd C. Harris and Emmanuel Ogbonna (2002), "Exploring Service Sabotage: The Antecedents, Types, and Consequences of Frontline, Deviant, Antiservice Behaviors," *Journal of Service Research*, Vol. 4, No. 3, pp. 163–183; Ramana Kumar Madupalli and Amit Poddar (2014), "Problematic Customers and Customer Service Employee Retaliation," *Journal of Service Marketing*, Vol. 28, No. 3, pp. 244–255.

The customer **Cycle of Failure** begins with heavy organizational emphasis on attracting new customers, who become dissatisfied with employee performance and the lack of continuity implicit in continually changing faces due to high staff turnover. Because these customers fail to become loyal to the supplier, they turn over as quickly as the staff, requiring an ongoing search for new customers to maintain sales volume. The departure of discontented customers is especially worrying in the light of what we know about the greater profitability of a loyal customer base (see Chapter 12 on customer loyalty).

Managers' excuses and justifications for perpetuating the cycle of failure tend to focus on employees:
- "You just can't get good people nowadays."
- "People today just don't want to work."
- "To get good people would cost too much and you can't pass on these cost increases to customers."
- "It's not worth training our frontline people when they leave you so quickly."
- "High turnover is simply an inevitable part of our business. You've got to learn to live with it.[20]"

Too many managers ignore the long-term financial effects of low-pay/high turnover human resource strategies. Part of the problem is the failure to measure all relevant costs. In particular, three key cost variables are often omitted: (1) the cost of constant recruiting, hiring, and training (which is as much a time cost for managers as it is a financial cost); (2) the lower productivity of inexperienced new workers; and (3) the costs of constantly attracting new customers (which requires extensive advertising and promotional discounts). Also frequently ignored are two revenue variables: (1) future revenue streams that might have continued for years, but are lost when unhappy customers take their business elsewhere; and (2) the potential income lost from prospective customers who are turned off by negative word of mouth. Finally, there are less easily quantifiable costs of disruptions to service while a job remains unfilled, and the loss of the departing employee's knowledge of the business (and potentially his/her customers as well).

The Cycle of Mediocrity

The **Cycle of Mediocrity** is another potentially vicious employment cycle (*Figure 11.10*). You are most likely to find it in large, bureaucratic organizations. These are often typified by state monopolies, industrial cartels, or regulated oligopolies in which there's little market pressure from more agile competitors to improve performance, and in which fear of entrenched unions may discourage management from adopting more innovative labor practices.

In such environments, service delivery standards tend to be prescribed by rigid rulebooks, oriented towards standardized service and operational efficiencies, and prevention of both employee fraud and favoritism toward specific customers. Job responsibilities tend to be narrowly and unimaginatively defined, tightly categorized by grade and scope of responsibilities, and further rigidified by union work rules. Salary increases and promotions are largely based on how long the person has been working in the organization. Successful performance in a job is often measured by the absence of mistakes, rather than by high productivity or outstanding customer service. Employee training focuses on learning the rules and the technical aspects of the job, not on improving human interactions with customers and coworkers. Since employees are given very little freedom to do

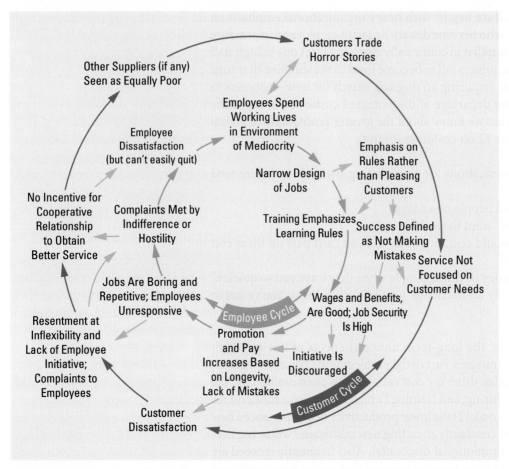

Figure 11.10 The Cycle of Mediocrity

Source

Christopher Lovelock, "Managing Services: The Human Factor" in W. J. Glynn and J. G. Barnes, eds., *Understanding Service Management* (Chichester, UK: John Wiley & Sons), 228.

their work in the way they think is necessary or suitable, jobs tend to be boring and repetitive. However, unlike the Cycle of Failure, most positions provide adequate pay and often good benefits, combined with high job security. Thus, employees are reluctant to leave. This lack of mobility is compounded by an absence of marketable skills that would be valued by organizations in other fields.

Customers find such organizations frustrating to deal with. Faced with bureaucratic hassles, lack of service flexibility, and unwillingness of employees to make an effort to serve them well, customers can become resentful. There is little incentive for customers to cooperate with the organization to achieve better service. When they complain to employees who are already unhappy, the poor service attitude becomes worse. Employees may

then protect themselves through mechanisms such as withdrawal into indifference, overtly playing by the book, or countering rudeness with rudeness.

It's not surprising that dissatisfied customers sometimes display hostility toward service employees who feel trapped in their jobs and who are powerless to improve the situation. However, customers often remain with the organization as there is nowhere else for them to go, either because the service provider holds a monopoly or because all other available players are perceived as equally bad or worse. The net result is a vicious cycle of mediocrity in which unhappy customers continually complain to sullen employees (and also to other customers) about poor service and bad attitudes, generating greater defensiveness and lack of caring on the part of the staff.

The Cycle of Success

Some firms reject the assumptions underlying the cycles of failure or mediocrity. Instead, they take a long-term view of financial performance, seeking to prosper by investing in their people in order to create a **Cycle of Success** (*Figure 11.11*).

As with failure or mediocrity, success applies to both employees and customers. Better pay and benefits attract good quality staff. Broadened job designs are accompanied by training and empowerment practices that allow frontline staff to control quality. With more focused recruitment, intensive training, and better wages, employees are likely to be happier in their work and provide higher-quality service. Lower turnover means that regular customers appreciate the continuity in service relationships and are more likely to remain loyal. With greater customer loyalty, profit margins tend to be higher, and the organization is free to focus its marketing efforts on reinforcing customer loyalty through customer retention strategies. These strategies are usually much more profitable than strategies for attracting new customers.

A powerful demonstration of a frontline employee working in the Cycle of Success is waitress Cora Griffith (featured in the Opening Vignette of this chapter). Even public service organizations in many countries are increasingly working toward creating their own cycles of success, and offer their users good quality service at a lower cost to the public[21].

When we look at the three cycles, it is of course ideal for firms to be operating under the conditions in the Cycle of Success. However, firms operating under the other two cycles can still survive if some element of their offering meets customer expectations. For example, in a restaurant context, customers may be dissatisfied with the service provided by the staff, but if they are willing to accept it because they like the restaurant's quality of food and location, then that element has met their expectations. Nevertheless, for long-run profitability and success, firms should ideally move toward the Cycle of Success.

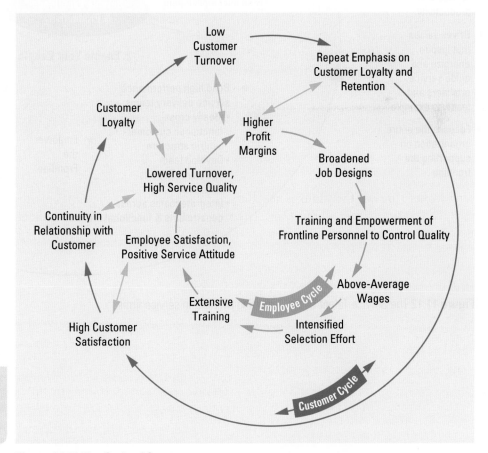

Figure 11.11 The Cycle of Success

LO 4

Describe the cycles of failure, mediocrity, and success in HR for service firms.

HUMAN RESOURCE MANAGEMENT — HOW TO GET IT RIGHT?

Any rational manager would like to operate in the Cycle of Success. In this section, we'll discuss HR strategies that can help service firms to move toward that goal. Specifically, we'll discuss how firms can hire, motivate, and retain engaged service employees who are willing and able to deliver service excellence, productivity, and sales. *Figure 11.12* shows the Service Talent Cycle which is our guiding framework for successful HR practices in service firms. We will discuss the recommended practices one by one in this section.

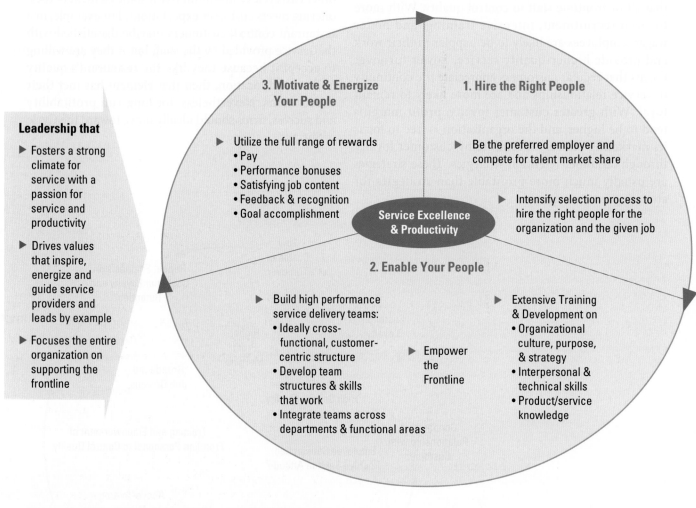

Leadership that

► Fosters a strong climate for service with a passion for service and productivity

► Drives values that inspire, energize and guide service providers and leads by example

► Focuses the entire organization on supporting the frontline

3. Motivate & Energize Your People

► Utilize the full range of rewards
• Pay
• Performance bonuses
• Satisfying job content
• Feedback & recognition
• Goal accomplishment

1. Hire the Right People

► Be the preferred employer and compete for talent market share

► Intensify selection process to hire the right people for the organization and the given job

Service Excellence & Productivity

2. Enable Your People

► Build high performance service delivery teams:
• Ideally cross-functional, customer-centric structure
• Develop team structures & skills that work
• Integrate teams across departments & functional areas

► Empower the Frontline

► Extensive Training & Development on
• Organizational culture, purpose, & strategy
• Interpersonal & technical skills
• Product/service knowledge

Figure 11.12 The Service Talent Cycle — getting HR right in service firms

Hire the Right People

⊃ **LO 5**
Know how to attract, select, and hire the right people for service jobs.

It is naïve to think that it's sufficient to satisfy employees. Employee satisfaction should be seen as necessary but not sufficient for having high-performing staff. For instance, a recent study showed that employee effort is a strong driver of customer satisfaction over and above employee satisfaction[22]. As Jim Collins said, "The old adage 'People are the most important asset' is wrong. The *right* people are your most important asset." We would like to add: "…and the wrong people are a liability that is often difficult to get rid of." Getting it right starts with hiring the right people. Hiring the right people includes competing for applications from the best employees in the labor market, then selecting from this pool the best candidates for the specific jobs to be filled.

Be the Preferred Employer. To be able to select and hire the best people, they first have to apply for a job with you and then accept your job offer in preference over others (the best people tend to be selected by several firms). Service firms have a brand in the labor market too, and potential candidates tend to seek companies that are good to work for and have an image that's congruent with their own values and beliefs[23]. Job seekers regularly approach current and former employees for information and can easily learn about salaries, benefits, working climate, and even interview questions[24]. A lot of internal company information can also be found online. For example, Glassdoor.com had over 500, 000 company and job reviews in 2014, providing potential employees good insights into what it would be like to work for a particular firm[25]. That means, a firm has to first compete for talent market share, or as global consulting firm McKinsey & Company calls it, "the war for talent[26]".

To effectively compete in the labor market means having an attractive value proposition for prospective employees. This typically includes a good image in the community as a place to work, being seen as delivering high-quality products and services, and being a good corporate citizen and engaging in relevant corporate social responsibility (CSR)[27], which together make employees feel proud to be part of the team. Furthermore, the compensation package cannot be below average — top people expect above average packages. In our experience, it takes a salary in the range of the 60th to 80th percentile of the market to attract top performers to top companies (*Figure 11.13*). However, a firm does not have to be a top paymaster, if other important aspects of the value proposition are attractive. In short, understand the needs of your target-employees and get your value proposition right. See *Service Insights 11.3* on how Google has managed to remain one of the best companies in the world to work for in the last few years. As Netflix describes the most basic element of its talent management philosophy: "The best thing you can do for employees — a perk better than football or free sushi — is hire only "A" players to work alongside them. Excellent colleagues trump everything else." That is, just having a reputation for having the best people working in the firm itself is itself a powerful value proposition to prospective candidates[28].

Figure 11.13 A firm does not need to pay top dollars to attract top performers

© Randy Glasbergen.
www.glasbergen.com

"I'm offering you a six-figure salary. Three figures on the 15th of the month and three figures on the 30th."

SERVICE INSIGHTS 11.3

Google, the Preferred Employer

Google was voted number 1 in *Fortune's* 100 Best Companies to work for in 2015 for the sixth year. The immediate question on people's minds will be: Why so? What makes it one of the best? What kind of culture does the company have? What kind of benefits do the employees enjoy? What are its employees like?

Employees of Google are called Googlers. They are widely perceived as fun-loving and interesting people. At the same time, when it comes to work, they are achievement-oriented and driven. Google has a culture of being innovative, unconventional, different, and fun, and in line with this, its employees are given the freedom to work independently. Google's experience thus far suggests that pampering employees actually results in increased productivity and profitability. Certainly, Googlers seem willing to work long hours for the company.

What kind of benefits do Googlers enjoy? The list is long, but top on the list is gourmet food for free, and this is just the appetizer! At the company's headquarters in Mountain View, California, the "campus" offers many free amenities, including Wi-Fi enabled shuttle buses, motorized scooters to get around, car washes, and oil changes. If Googlers are interested in buying hybrid cars, they get a $5,000 subsidy for that. Googlers have five free on-site doctors, unlimited sick days, free flu shots, a gym to work out at, and a pool to do laps in with lifeguards on duty. For more domestic activities, there are free on-site laundry services or one can drop off their laundry at the dry cleaners. There are also childcare services, and new parents (including dads, domestic partners, adoptive parents, and surrogate parents) can get fully paid baby bonding time for up to 12 weeks. For leisure and sports, one can play a game of pool, do some rock climbing on the wall, or play a game of volleyball at the beach volleyball pit. The list goes on. As a result, Googlers can spend long and productive hours at work. However, it must be noted that the benefits offered to employees working at other Google offices tend to be less significant.

Google has an engineering headquarters in Zurich, Switzerland. This building was partly designed by the engineers who work there. Life there is just as fun. There are meeting places that are designed to look like Swiss chalets and igloos. People can get from one floor to another using fireman poles, and there is a slide that allows them to reach the cafeteria very quickly. There are other areas like a games room, a library in the style of an English country house, and an aquarium where staff can lie in a bath of red foam and look at the fishes if they feel stressed out.

"The slide gets people to the cafeteria quickly."

Because the firm is seen as such a desirable place to work, it can be extremely selective in its recruiting, hiring only the best and the brightest. This may work particularly well for its engineers, who tend to get the most kudos. However, despite the company's stellar reputation as an employer, some observers question whether this very positive environment can be maintained as the company grows and its workforce matures.

Source

http://fortune.com/best-companies, accessed May 11, 2015; www.google.com.sg/about/careers/lifeatgoogle/benefits, accessed May 11, 2015; Jane Wakefield, "Google Your Way to a Wacky Office," *BBC News Website*, March 13 2008, http://news.bbc.co.uk/2/hi/7290322.stm, accessed May 11, 2015.

Select the Right People. There's no such thing as the perfect employee (*Figure 11.14*). Different positions are often best filled by people with different skill sets, styles, and personalities. Different brands have different personalities, and it is important that there is a good employee-brand fit so that it is natural for employees to deliver service that supports the firm's espoused image, and that their behavior is perceived as authentic by their customers[29]. The recruitment and selection processes should be explicitly designed to encourage a good employee-brand fit[30]. This includes the recruitment advertising to explicitly display key brand attributes and firm positioning, and to encourage potential candidates to reflect on their fit with the firm; to design selection methods to convey brand values to allow employees to make a self-assessment of their fit; and to ensure recruiters are proactively looking out for brand fit and potential misfit.

For example, The Walt Disney Company assesses prospective employees in terms of their potential brand fit ("Is magic, fun, and happiness your world?") and then for on-stage or backstage work. On-stage workers, known as cast members, are given to those people with the looks, personalities, and skills to match the job.

What makes outstanding service performers so special? Often it is the things that *cannot* be taught. It is the qualities that are intrinsic to the people, and qualities they would bring with them to any employer. As one study of high performers observed:

Figure 11.15 Social media screening has become an important part of selecting the right employees

© MARK ANDERSON, WWW.ANDERTOONS.COM

"According to your LinkedIn profile you're a focused, disciplined achiever. According to your Facebook photos you prefer Jack Daniels and are pretty comfortable with your body."

Figure 11.14 There's no such thing as a perfect employee

GLASBERGEN

"Allen is an incredible, wonderful, fun, generous, exciting, kind, loving, brilliant, very special human being. This personal reference from your dog is quite impressive."

Energy...cannot be taught, it has to be hired. The same is true for charm, for detail orientation, for work ethic, for neatness. Some of these things can be enhanced with on-the-job training... or incentives... But by and large, such qualities are instilled early on[31].

HR managers have also discovered that while good manners and the need to smile and make eye contact can be taught, warmth itself cannot be learnt. The only realistic solution is to ensure that the organization's recruitment criteria favors candidates with naturally warm personalities. Jim Collins emphasizes that "the right people are those who would exhibit the desired behaviors anyway, as a natural extension of their character and attitude, regardless of any control and incentive system[32]."

The logical conclusion is that service firms should devote great care to attracting and hiring the right candidates. Increasingly, the top companies are using employee analytics to improve their ability to attract and retain the best talent. Employee analytics are similar to customer analytics; for example, it is able to predict who would be a better performer. They can also use analytics to place the right employees in the right job[33]. Apart from the use of data analysis, let's next review some tools to help you identify the right candidates for a given firm and job, and perhaps even more importantly, reject candidates that are not a good fit.

Tools to Identify the Best Candidates

Excellent service firms use a number of approaches to identifying the candidates with the best fit in their applicant pool.[34] These approaches include interviewing applicants, observing behavior, conducting personality tests, and providing applicants with a realistic job preview.

Use Multiple, Structured Interviews. To improve hiring decisions, successful recruiters like to employ structured interviews built around job requirements, and to use more than one interviewer. People tend to be more careful in their judgments when they know that another individual is also judging the same applicant. Another advantage of using two or more interviewers is that it reduces the risk of "similar to me" bias — we all like people who are similar to ourselves (*Figure 11.16*).

Observe Candidate Behavior. The hiring decision should be based on the behavior that recruiters observe, not just the words they hear. As John Wooden said: "Show me what you can do, don't tell me what you can do. Too often, the big talkers are the little doers[35]." Behavior can be directly or indirectly observed by using behavioral simulations or assessment center tests that use standardized situations in which applicants can be observed to see whether they display the kind of behaviors the firms' clients would expect. In addition, past behavior is the best predictor of future behavior: Hire the person who has won service excellence awards, received many compliment letters, and has great references from past employers.

Conduct Personality Tests. Many managers hire employees based on personality. Personality tests help to identify traits related to a particular job. For example, willingness to treat customers and colleagues with courtesy, consideration, and tact; perceptiveness of customer needs; and ability to communicate accurately and pleasantly are traits that can be measured. It's better to hire upbeat and happy people, because customers report higher satisfaction when being served by more satisfied staff[36]. Research has also shown that certain traits such as being hardworking and the belief in one's capabilities to manage situations result in strong employee performance and service quality[37]. Hiring decisions based on such tests tend to be accurate, especially in identifying and rejecting unsuitable candidates.

Figure 11.16 Is the "similar to me" bias coming into play?

For example, the Ritz-Carlton Hotels Group uses personality profiles on all job applicants. Employees are selected for their natural predisposition for working in a service context. Inherent traits such as a ready smile, a willingness to help others, and an affinity for multi-tasking enables them to go beyond learned skills. An applicant to Ritz-Carlton shared her experience of going through the personality test for a job as a junior-level concierge at the Ritz-Carlton Millenia, Singapore. Her best advice: "Tell the truth. These are experts; they will know if you are lying," and then she added:

> On the big day, they asked if I liked helping people, if I was an organized person and if I liked to smile a lot. "Yes, yes and yes," I said. But I had to support it with real life examples. This, at times, felt rather intrusive. To answer the first question for instance, I had to say a bit about the person I had helped — why she needed help, for example. The test forced me to recall even insignificant things I had done, like learning how to say hello in different languages, which helped to get a fix on my character.[38]

Apart from intensive interview-based psychological tests, cost–effective Internet-based testing kits are available. Here, applicants enter their test responses to a web-based questionnaire, and the prospective employer receives the analysis, the suitability of the candidate, and a hiring recommendation. Developing and administering such tests has become a significant service industry in its own right. A leading global supplier of such assessment products, SHL Talent Measurement (a unit of CEB), serves over 20,000 organizations in 30 languages in over 110 countries. Have a look at its website to see the tests that are available.

Give Applicants a Realistic Preview of the Job. During the recruitment process, service companies should let candidates know the reality of the job, thereby giving them a chance to "try on the job"[39] and assess whether it's a good fit or not. At the same time, recruiters can observe how candidates respond to the job's realities. Some candidates may withdraw if they realize the job is not a good match for them. At the same time, the company can manage new employees' expectations of their job. Many service companies adopt this approach. For example, Au Bon Pain, a chain of French bakery cafes, lets applicants work for two paid days in one of its cafés prior to the final selection interview. Here, managers can observe candidates in action, and candidates can assess whether they like the job and the work environment[40]. In the ultimate recruitment and interview process, Donald Trump worked with the NBC network to produce the reality TV series, *The Apprentice*, where the winner received the chance to join the Trump organization and manage a project selected by Trump himself. See *Service Insights 11.4* on how Southwest Airlines uses a combination of interviews and other selection tools to identify the right candidates with the right attitude and a personality that fits the Southwest culture from its vast pool of applicants.

LO 6

Explain the key areas in which service employees need training.

Train Service Employees Actively

If a firm has good people, investments in training and development can yield outstanding results. Having a good career development program for employees helps them to feel they are valued and taken care of, and in turn, they will work to meet customers' needs, resulting in customer satisfaction, loyalty, and ultimately, profitability for the firm[41]. Service champions show a strong commitment to training in words, dollars, and action. Employees of Apple retail stores, for example, are given intensive training on how to interact with customers, phrase words in a positive rather than negative way, and what to say when customers are emotional. Employees are supposed to help customers solve problems rather than sell[42]. As Benjamin Schneider and David Bowen put it, "The combination of attracting a diverse and competent applicant pool, utilizing effective techniques for hiring the most appropriate people from that pool, and then training the heck out of them would be gangbusters in any market[43]."

Training Contents. There are many aspects in a firm that service employees need to be trained on. Service employees need to learn:

- **Organizational Culture, Purpose, and Strategy.** Start strong with new hires, and focus on getting emotional commitment to the firm's core strategy, and promote core values such as commitment to service excellence, responsiveness, team spirit, mutual respect, honesty and integrity. Use managers to teach, and focus on "what", "why", and "how", rather than the specifics of the job[44]. For example, new recruits at Disneyland attend the "Disney University Orientation". It starts with a detailed discussion of the company history and philosophy, the service standards expected of cast members, and a comprehensive tour of Disneyland's operations[45].

SERVICE INSIGHTS 11.4

Hiring at Southwest Airlines

Southwest hires people with the right attitude and with personality that matches its corporate personality. Humor is the key. Herb Kelleher, Southwest's legendary former CEO and now chairman said, "I want flying to be a helluva of fun!" "We look for attitudes; people with a sense of humor who don't take themselves too seriously. We'll train you on whatever it is you have to do, but the one thing Southwest cannot change in people is inherent attitudes." Southwest has one fundamental, consistent principle — hire people with the right spirit. Southwest looks for people with other-oriented, outgoing personalities, individuals who become part of an extended family of people who work hard and have fun at the same time.

Southwest's painstaking approach to interviewing continues to evolve in the light of experience. It is perhaps at its most innovative in the selection of flight attendants. A day-long visit to the company usually begins with applicants being gathered in a group. Recruiters watch how well they interact with each other (another chance for such observation will come at lunchtime).

Then comes a series of personal interviews. Each candidate has three one-on-one "behavioral-type" interviews during the course of the day. Based on input from supervisors and peers in a given job category, interviewers target eight to 10 dimensions for each position. For a flight attendant, these might include a willingness to take initiative, compassion, flexibility, sensitivity, sincerity, a customer service orientation, and a predisposition to be a team player. Even humor is "tested". Prospective employees are

Airport: Costa Rica - San Jose - Juan Santamaría Intl (SJO / MROC) © Carlos Rojas V

typically asked, "Tell me how you recently used your sense of humor in a work environment. Tell me how you have used humor to defuse a difficult situation."

Southwest describes the ideal interview as "a conversation", in which the goal is to make candidates comfortable. "The first interview of the day tends to be a bit stiff, the second is more comfortable, and by the third they tell us a whole lot more. It's really hard to fake it under those circumstances." The three interviewers don't discuss candidates during the day but compare notes afterwards, so that it reduces the risk of bias.

To help select people with the right attitude, Southwest invites supervisors and peers (with whom future candidates will be working) to participate in the in-depth interviewing and selection process. In this way, existing employees buy into the recruitment process and feel a sense of responsibility for mentoring new recruits and helping them to become successful in the job (rather than wondering, as an interviewer put it, "who hired this turkey?"). More unusually, it invites its own frequent flyers to participate in the initial interviews for flight attendants and to tell the candidates what they, the passengers, value.

The interviewing team asks a group of potential employees to prepare a five-minute presentation about themselves, and gives them plenty of time to prepare. As the presentations are delivered, the interviewers don't watch just the speakers. They watch the audience to see which applicants are using their time to work on their own presentations and which are enthusiastically cheering on and supporting their potential coworkers. Unselfish people who will support their teammates are the ones who catch Southwest's eyes, not the applicants who are tempted to polish their own presentations while others are speaking.

By hiring the right attitude, the company is able to foster the so-called Southwest spirit — an intangible quality in people that causes them to want to do whatever it takes and to want to go that extra mile whenever they need to. Southwest itself goes the extra mile for its employees and has never laid anyone off, even after it decided to close reservations centers in three cities in 2004 to cut costs. Management knows that the airline's culture is a key competitive advantage.

Source

Kevin and Jackie Freiberg, *Nuts! Southwest Airlines' Crazy Recipe for Business and Personal Success* (New York: Broadway Books, 1997), 64–69; Christopher Lovelock, *Product Plus* (New York: McGraw-Hill, 1994), 323–326; Barney Gimbel (2005), "Southwest's New Flight Plan," *Fortune,* May 16, pp. 93–98.

SERVICE INSIGHTS 11.5

Coaching in a Call Center

Coaching is a common method employed by services leaders to train and develop staff. Dial-A-Mattress' Jennifer Grassano was a bedding consultant (BC) for three days a week, and a coach to other BCs for one day a week. She focused on staff whose productivity and sales performance were slumping.

Her first step was to listen in on the BCs' telephone calls with customers. She would listen for about an hour and take detailed notes on each call. The BCs understood that their calls may be monitored, but they received no advance notice, as that would defeat the purpose.

Grassano conducted a coaching session with the staff member, in which strengths and areas for improvements were reviewed. She knew how difficult it is to maintain a high energy level and convey enthusiasm when handling some 60 calls per shift. She

liked to suggest new tactics and phrasings "to spark up their presentation". One BC was not responding effectively when customers asked why one mattress was more expensive than another. Here, she stressed the need to paint a picture in the customer's mind:

Customers are at our mercy when buying bedding. They don't know the difference between one coil system and another. It is just like buying a carburetor for my car. I don't even know what a carburetor looks like. We have to use very descriptive words to help bedding customers make the decision that is right for them. Tell the customer that the more costly mattress has richer, finer padding with a blend of silk and wool. Don't just say the mattress has more layers of padding.

About two months after the initial coaching session, Grassano conducted a follow-up monitoring session with that BC. She then compared the BC's performance before and after the coaching session to assess the effectiveness of the training.

Grassano's experience and productivity as a BC gave her credibility as a coach. "If I am not doing well as a BC, then who am I to be a coach? I have to lead by example. I would be much less effective if I was a full-time trainer." She clearly relishes the opportunity to share her knowledge and pass on her craft.

Source

Leonard L. Berry, *Discovering the Soul of Service — The Nine Drivers of Sustainable Business Success* (New York: The Free Press, 1999), 171–172. Dial-a-Mattress merged with two other companies and today is called: 1800Mattress.com; see http://en.wikipedia.org/wiki/1800Mattress.com, accessed May 11, 2015.

- **Interpersonal and Technical Skills.** Interpersonal skills tend to be generic across service jobs, and include visual communications skills such as making eye contact, attentive listening, understanding body language, and even facial expressions, and reading customers' needs. Technical skills include all the required knowledge related to processes (e.g., how to handle a merchandized return), machines (e.g., how to operate the terminal, or cash machine), and rules and regulations related to customer service processes. Creativity in designing solutions and solving problems is also required in non-routine encounters and service recovery. Both technical and interpersonal skills are *necessary* but neither is enough for optimal job performance on its own[46].

- **Product/Service Knowledge.** Knowledgeable staff are a key aspect of service quality. They must be able to explain product features effectively and also position the product correctly. For example, all the products are openly displayed for customers to try out at an Apple retail store. Staff members need to be able to answer questions about any of the product's features, usage, and any other aspects of service like maintenance, service bundles, and so on. See also *Service Insights 11.5* on how Jennifer Grassano coached individual staff members in a call center on how to paint pictures in the customer's mind.

Reinforce Training to Shape Behaviors. Of course, training has to result in observable changes in behavior. If staff do not apply what they have learnt, the investment is wasted. Learning is not only about becoming smarter, but about changing behaviors and improving decision-making. To achieve this, practice and reinforcement are needed. Supervisors play a crucial role by following up regularly on learning objectives, for instance, meeting with staff to reinforce key lessons from recent complaints and compliments (*Figure 11.17*).

Another example of constant reinforcement is Ritz-Carlton's approach. It translated the key product and service requirements of its customers into the Ritz-Carlton Gold Standards, which include a credo, motto, three steps of service, and 12 service values (see *Service Insights 11.6*) Ritz-Carlton's service values are split into different levels.

Service values 10, 11, and 12 represent functional values such as safety, security, and cleanliness. Ritz-Carlton refers to the next level of excellence as emotional engagement, which covers values 4 through to 9. They relate to learning and professional growth of its employees, teamwork, service, problem solving and service recovery, innovation, and continuous improvement. Besides the guests' functional needs and emotional engagement, the third level is "Ritz-Carlton Mystique," which relates to values 1, 2, and 3. This level aims to create unique, memorable, and personal guest experiences, which Ritz-Carlton believes can only occur when employees deliver on the guests' expressed and unexpressed wishes and needs, and when they strive to build lifetime relationships between Ritz-Carlton and its guests. The three levels are reflected in the Sixth Diamond in Ritz-Carton's gold standards as a new benchmark in the hospitality industry and the three levels for achieving both employee and customer engagement[47].

Tim Kirkpatrick, Director of Training and Development of Ritz-Carlton's Boston Common Hotel said, "The Gold Standards are part of our uniform, just like your name tag. But remember, it's just a laminated card until you put it into action[48]." To reinforce these standards, every morning briefing includes a discussion directly related to the standards. The aim of these discussions is to keep the Ritz-Carlton philosophy at the center of its employees' minds.

Figure 11.17 Morning briefings by a supervisor offer effective training opportunities.

SERVICE INSIGHTS 11.6
Ritz-Carlton's Gold Standards

Gold Standards

Our Gold Standards are the foundation of The Ritz-Carlton Hotel Company, LLC. They encompass the values and philosophy by which we operate and include:

The Credo

The Ritz-Carlton Hotel is a place where the genuine care and comfort of our guests are our highest mission. We pledge to provide the finest personal service and facilities for our guests who will always enjoy a warm, relaxed, yet refined ambience.

The Ritz-Carlton experience enlivens the senses, instills well-being, and fulfills even the unexpressed wishes and needs of our guests.

The Motto

At The Ritz-Carlton Hotel Company, LLC, "We are Ladies and Gentlemen serving Ladies and Gentlemen." This motto exemplifies the anticipatory service provided by all staff members.

Three Steps of Service

1. A warm and sincere greeting. Use the guest's name.
2. Anticipation and fulfillment of each guest's needs.
3. Fond farewell. Give a warm good-bye and use the guest's name.

Service Values: I Am Proud to Be Ritz-Carlton

1. I build strong relationships and create Ritz-Carlton guests for life.
2. I am always responsive to the expressed and unexpressed wishes and needs of our guests.
3. I am empowered to create unique, memorable, and personal experiences for our guests.
4. I understand my role in achieving the Key Success Factors, embracing Community Footprints, and creating The Ritz-Carlton Mystique.
5. I continuously seek opportunities to innovate and improve The Ritz-Carlton experience.
6. I own and immediately resolve guest problems.
7. I create a work environment of teamwork and lateral service so that the needs of our guests and each other are met.
8. I have the opportunity to continuously learn and grow.
9. I am involved in the planning of the work that affects me.
10. I am proud of my professional appearance, language, and behavior.
11. I protect the privacy and security of our guests, my fellow employees, and the company's confidential information, and assets.
12. I am responsible for uncompromising levels of cleanliness and creating a safe and accident-free environment.

The 6th Diamond

Mystique
Emotional Engagement
Functional

The Employee Promise

At The Ritz-Carlton, our Ladies and Gentlemen are the most important resource in our service commitment to our guests.

By applying the principles of trust, honesty, respect, integrity, and commitment, we nurture and maximize talent to the benefit of each individual and the company.

The Ritz-Carlton fosters a work environment where diversity is valued, quality of life is enhanced, individual aspirations are fulfilled, and The Ritz-Carlton Mystique is strengthened.

Source

http://www.ritzcarlton.com/en/about/gold-standards, accessed March 2, 2016.

Internal Communications to Shape the Service Culture and Behaviors

In addition to having a strong training platform, it takes a significant communications effort to shape the culture and get the message to the troops. Service leaders use multiple tools to build their service culture, ranging from internal marketing and training, to core principles, and company events and celebrations. Internal communications to employees (often also referred to as internal marketing) play a vital role in maintaining and nurturing a corporate culture founded on specific service values.

Well-planned internal marketing efforts are especially necessary in large service businesses that operate in widely dispersed sites, sometimes around the world. Even when employees work far from the head office, they still need to be kept informed of new policies, changes in service features, and new quality initiatives. Communications may also be needed to nurture team spirit and support common corporate goals across national frontiers. Consider the challenge of maintaining a unified sense of purpose at the overseas offices of companies such as Citibank, Air Canada, Marriott, or Starbucks, where people from different cultures who speak different languages must work together to create consistent levels of service.

Effective internal communications are an excellent complimentary tool to training that can help ensure efficient and satisfactory service delivery, achieve productive and harmonious working relationships, and build employee trust, respect, and loyalty. Commonly used media include internal newsletters and magazines, videos, Intranets, email, face-to-face briefings, and promotional campaigns using displays, prizes, and recognition programs.

LO 7
Understand the role of internal marketing and communications.

PART 3

Professionalizing the Frontline. Training and learning professionalizes the frontline, and move these individuals away from the common (self)-image of being in low-end jobs that have no significance. Well-trained employees feel and act like professionals. A waiter who knows about food, cooking, wines, dining etiquette, and how to effectively interact with customers (even complaining ones), feels professional, has a higher self-esteem, and is respected by his customers. Training and internal communications are therefore extremely effective in reducing person/role stress, and in enabling and energizing front line employees.

Empower the Frontline

⊃ **LO 8**

Understand why empowerment is so important in many frontline jobs.

After being the preferred employer, selecting the right candidates, and training them well, the next step is to empower the frontline[49] and encourage them to show proactive customer service performance that can go beyond the call of duty[50]. Virtually all breakthrough service firms have legendary stories of employees who recovered failed service transactions, or walked the extra mile to make a customer's day, or avoid some kind of disaster for that client (as an example, see *Service Insights 11.7* — Empowerment at Nordstrom). To allow this to happen, employees have to be empowered. Nordstrom trains and trusts its employees to do the right thing and empowers them to do so. Its employee handbook has only one rule: "Use good judgment in all situations."

Good judgment is important as it is a fine line between going the extra mile for a customer and service sweethearting, whereby employees unnecessarily and potentially, illicitly waive bills or give freebies to boost their unit's satisfaction rating or avoid confrontation with a customer who is in the wrong (see also Chapter 13 on jaycustomers)[51]. It is therefore important that employees are self-directed, especially in service firms because frontline staff frequently operate on their own, face-to-face with their customers, and it tends to be difficult for managers to closely monitor their behavior[52].

For many services, providing employees with greater discretion (and training in how to use their judgment) enables them to provide superior service on the spot, rather than taking time to get permission from supervisors. Empowerment looks to frontline staff to find solutions to service problems, and to make appropriate decisions about customizing service delivery. It is therefore not surprising that research has linked high empowerment to higher customer satisfaction[53].

When Are High Levels of Empowerment Appropriate?

Advocates claim that the empowerment approach is more likely to yield motivated employees and satisfied customers than the "production-line" alternative, in which management designs a relatively standardized system and expects workers to execute tasks within narrow guidelines. However, David Bowen and Edward Lawler suggest that different situations may require different solutions, declaring that "both the empowerment and production-line approaches have their advantages... and... each fits certain situations. The key is to choose the management approach that best meets the needs of both employees and customers." Not all employees are necessarily eager to be empowered, and many employees do not seek personal growth within their jobs, and would prefer to work to specific directions rather than to use their own initiative. Research has shown that a strategy of empowerment is most likely to be appropriate when most of the following factors are present within the organization and its environment:

SERVICE INSIGHTS 11.7
Empowerment at Nordstrom

Van Mensah, a men's clothes sales associate at Nordstrom, received a disturbing letter from one of his loyal customers. The gentleman had purchased some $2,000 worth of shirts and ties from Mensah, and mistakenly washed the shirts in hot water. They all shrank. He was writing to ask Mensah's professional advice on how he should deal with his predicament (the gentleman did not complain and readily conceded the mistake was his).

Mensah immediately called the customer and offered to replace those shirts with new ones at no charge. He asked the customer to mail the other shirts back to Nordstrom — at Nordstrom's expense. "I didn't have to ask for anyone's permission to do what I did for that customer," said Mensah. "Nordstrom would rather leave it up to me to decide what's best."

Middlemas, a Nordstrom's veteran said to employees, "You will never be criticized for doing too much for a customer, you will only be criticized for doing too little. If you're ever in doubt as to what to do in a situation, always make a decision that favors the customer before the company." Nordstrom's Employee Handbook confirms this. It reads:

Welcome to Nordstrom

We're glad to have you with our Company. Our number one goal is to provide outstanding customer service.

Set both your personal and professional goals high.

We have great confidence in your ability to achieve them.

Nordstrom Rules:

Rule#1: Use your good judgment in all situations. There will be no additional rules.

Please feel free to ask your department manager, store manager, or division general manager any question at any time.

Source

Robert Spector and Patrick D. McCarthy, *The Nordstrom Way to Customer Service Excellence: The Handbook for Becoming the "Nordstrom" of Your Industry,* 2nd ed. (New York: John Wiley & Sons, 2012).

- The firm offers personalized, customized service and is based on competitive differentiation.

- The firm has extended relationships with customers rather than short-term transactions.

- The organization uses technologies that are complex and non-routine in nature.

- Service failures often are non-routine and cannot be designed out of the system. Frontline employees have to respond quickly to recover the service.

- The business environment is unpredictable and surprises are to be expected.

- Existing managers are comfortable with letting employees decide independently for the benefit of both the organization and its customers.

- Employees have a strong need to grow and deepen their skills in the work environment, are interested in working with others, and have good interpersonal and group process skills[54].

Requirements for Empowering the Frontline. The production-line approach to managing people is based on the well-established **control** model of organization design and management. There are clearly defined roles, top–down control systems, hierarchical pyramid structures, and an assumption that the management knows best. Empowerment, by contrast, is based on the **involvement** (or **commitment**) model, which assumes that employees can make good decisions, and produce good ideas for operating the business, if they are properly socialized, trained, and informed. This model also assumes that employees can be internally motivated to perform effectively and that they are capable of self-control and self-direction.

Schneider and Bowen emphasize that "empowerment isn't just 'setting the frontline free' or 'throwing away the policy manuals'. It requires systematically redistributing four key ingredients throughout the organization, from the top downwards[55]." The four features are:

- **Information** about organizational, team, and individual performance (e.g., operating results and measures of competitive performance).

- **Knowledge** that enables employees to understand and contribute to organizational, team, and individual performance (e.g., problem-solving skills).

- **Power** to make decisions that influence work procedures and organizational direction (e.g., through quality circles and self-managing teams) at the higher level, and transaction-specific decisions (e.g., decisions regarding customization for a customer and service recovery) at the micro level.

- **Rewards** based on organizational, team, and individual performance, such as bonuses, profit sharing, and stock options.

In the control model, the four features are concentrated at the top of the organization, while in the involvement model, these features are pushed down through the organization. In restaurants, for example, management often schedules servers for shifts they would rather not take, and worse, the least-productive servers can be scheduled on the most profitable shifts. To solve both issues, the Boston-based restaurant chain Not Your Average Joe's pushed all four features of empowerment to the front line. The restaurant developed a performance rating system that tracks and communicates sales and customer satisfaction (measured by tips or directly) data for each server (giving them information and knowledge). Based on their ranking, employees can now self-select their preferred shifts and restaurant sections through a self-service online system (providing them with decision-making power and rewards). This system empowers and rewards high performers, fosters a culture of performance, saves each restaurant manager between three to five hours of scheduling work per week, and makes restaurants more profitable[56].

Levels of Employee Involvement. The empowerment and production-line approaches are at opposite ends of a spectrum that reflects increasing levels of employee involvement as additional information, knowledge, power, and rewards are pushed down to the front line. Management needs to determine the appropriate level of empowerment for its business model and customers' needs. Empowerment can take place at several levels:

- **Suggestion Involvement** empowers employees to make recommendations through formalized programs. McDonald's, often portrayed as an archetype of the production-line approach, listens closely to its frontline. Did you know that innovations ranging from Egg McMuffin, to methods of wrapping burgers without leaving a thumbprint on the bun, were invented by employees?

- **Job Involvement** represents a dramatic opening up of job content. Jobs are redesigned to allow employees to use a wider array of skills. In complex service organizations such as airlines and hospitals where individual employees cannot offer all facets of a service, job involvement is often accomplished through the use of teams. To cope with the added demands accompanying this form of empowerment, employees require training, and supervisors need to be reoriented from directing the group to facilitating its performance in supportive ways.

- **High Involvement** gives even the lowest-level employees a sense of involvement in the company's overall performance. Information is shared. Employees develop skills in teamwork, problem solving, and business operations, they participate in work-unit management decisions, and are a source of learning and innovation for the organization[57]. Frontline employees are involved in designing and implementing new services, and rewards are performance-based[58].

Southwest Airlines illustrates a high-involvement company, promoting common sense and flexibility. It trusts its employees and gives them the latitude, discretion, and authority they need to do their jobs. The airline has eliminated inflexible work rules and rigid job descriptions, so its people can assume ownership for getting the job done and enabling flights to leave on time, regardless of whose "official" responsibility it is. This gives employees the flexibility to help each other when needed. As a result, they adopt a "whatever it takes" mentality. Southwest mechanics and pilots feel free to help ramp agents load bags. When a flight is running late, it's not uncommon to see pilots helping passengers in wheelchairs to board the aircraft, assisting operations agents by taking boarding passes, or helping flight attendants clean the cabin between flights. All of these actions are their way of adapting to the situation and taking ownership for getting customers on board more quickly. In addition, Southwest employees apply common sense, not rules, when it's in the best interests of the customer.

Rod Jones, assistant chief pilot, recalls a captain who left the gate with a senior citizen who had boarded the wrong plane. The customer was confused and very upset. Southwest asks pilots not to go back to the gate with an incorrectly boarded customer. In this case, the captain was concerned about this individual's well-being. "So, he adapted to the situation." says Jones. "He came back to the gate, deplaned the customer, pushed back out, and gave us an irregularity report. Even though he broke the rules, he used his judgment and did what he thought was best. And we said, 'Attaboy!'[59]"

Build High-Performance Service-Delivery Teams

A team has been defined as "a small number of people with complementary skills who are committed to a common purpose, set of performance goals, and approach for which they hold themselves mutually accountable[60]." The nature of many services requires people to work in teams, often across functions, in order to offer seamless customer service.

Traditionally, many firms were organized by functional structures — for example, one department is in charge of consulting and selling (e.g., selling a subscription contract with a cell phone), another is in charge of customer service (e.g., activation of value-added services and change of subscription plans), and yet another is in charge of billing. This structure prevents internal service teams from viewing end customers as their own, and this structure can also mean poorer teamwork across functions, slower service, and more errors between functions. When customers have service problems, they easily fall between the cracks.

LO 9
Explain how to build high performance service delivery teams.

Figure 11.18 Lack of cooperation within a team will lead to problems in the company

"We're a Limited Partnership. We're limited by Allen's pessimism, Elizabeth's abrasive personality, and Dave's refusal to work weekends."

Empirical research has confirmed that frontline employees themselves regard the lack of interdepartmental support as an important factor in hindering them from satisfying their customers (*Figure 11.18*)[61]. Because of these problems, service organizations in many industries need to create cross-functional teams with the authority and responsibility to serve customers from the beginning of the service encounter to the end. Such teams are also called self-managed teams[62].

The Power of Teamwork in Services. Teams, training, and empowerment go hand-in-hand. Effective teams and their leaders facilitate communication among team members, sharing of knowledge, and alignment[63]. By operating like a small, independent unit, service teams take on more responsibility and require less supervision than the more traditional functionally organized customer service units. Furthermore, teams often set higher performance targets for themselves than supervisors would. Within a good team, the pressure to perform is high[64].

Some academics even feel that too much emphasis is placed on hiring "individual stars", and too little attention is paid to hiring staff with good team abilities and the motivation to work cooperatively. Stanford professors Charles O'Reilly and Jeffrey Pfeffer emphasize that how well people work in teams is often as important as how good people are, and that stars can be outperformed by others through superior teamwork[65].

At Customer Research Inc. (CRI), a progressive and successful marketing research firm, team members' feelings are illustrated in the following quotes:

- "I like being on the team. You feel like you belong. Everyone knows what's going on."
- "We take ownership. Everyone accepts responsibility and jumps in to help."
- "When a client needs something in an hour, we work together to solve the problem."
- "There are no slugs. Everyone pulls their weight[66]."

Team ability and motivation are crucial for the effective delivery of many types of services, especially those involving individuals who each play specialist roles. For example, healthcare services heavily depend on effective teamwork of many specialists (*Figure 11.19*).

Structure Service-Delivery Teams for Success. It's not easy to make teams function well. If people are not prepared for team work, and the team structure isn't set up right, a firm risks having initially enthusiastic team members who lack the competencies that teamwork requires. The skills needed include not only cooperation, listening to others, coaching and encouraging one another, but also an understanding of how to air their differences professionally, tell one another the hard truths, and ask the tough questions. All these require training[67]. Management also needs to set up a structure that will move the teams towards success, which includes the following[68]:

- Identify what the team will achieve. Goals need to be defined and shared with the team members.

- Select team members with care. All the skills needed to achieve the goal must be found within the team.

- Monitor the team and its team members, and provide feedback. This aligns individual and team goals with those of the organization.

- Keep team members informed of goal achievement, update them, and reward them for their efforts and performance.

- Coordinate and integrate with other teams, departments, and functions to achieve the overall company objectives (see the next section for details).

Integrate Teams Across Departments and Functional Areas

 LO 10
Know how to integrate teams across departments and functional areas.

Even if service delivery teams work well, we find many firms in which individuals and teams from different departments and functional areas have conflicts with each other. Marketers may see their role as one of continually adding value to the product offering, enhancing its appeal to customers, and stimulating sales. However, operations managers may see their job as cutting down on "extras" to reflect the reality of service constraints — such as staff and equipment — and the need to control cost. HR wants to control headcount and payroll, and IT is struggling with many changing demands as it often controls the information backbone of many services processes.

Part of the challenge of service management is to ensure that the different departments and functions cooperate with the other. The potential ways to reduce conflict and break down the barriers between departments include:

1. Transferring individuals internally to other departments and functional areas, allowing them to develop a more holistic perspective and being able to view issues from the different perspectives of the various departments.

2. Establishing cross-departmental and -functional project teams (e.g., for new service development or customer service process redesign).

3. Having cross-departmental/functional service delivery teams.

4. Appointing individuals whose job it is to integrate specific objectives, activities, and processes between departments. For example, Robert Kwortnik and Gary Thompson suggest forming a department in charge of "service experience management" that integrates marketing and operations[69].

5. Carrying out internal marketing and training, and integration programs (see the Southwest Airlines example).

6. Having top management's commitment to ensure that the overarching objectives of all departments are integrated.

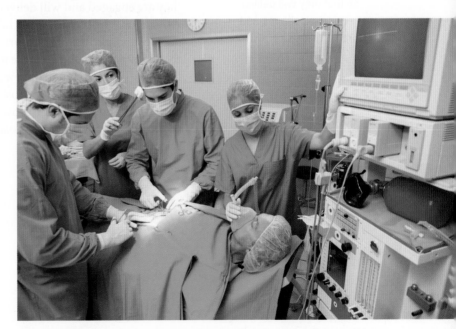

Figure 11.19 Surgical teams work under particularly demanding conditions

A great example of a firm with a strong culture and strong integration across functions is Southwest Airlines, which continuously uses new and creative ways to strengthen its culture. Southwest's Culture Committee members are zealots when it comes to the continuation of Southwest's family feel. The committee represents everyone from flight attendants and reservationists to top executives, as one participant observed: "The Culture Committee is not made up of Big Shots; it is a committee of Big Hearts." The Culture Committee members are not out to gain power. They use the power of the Southwest spirit to better connect people to the cultural foundations of the company. The committee works behind the scenes to foster Southwest's commitment to its core values. The following are examples of events held to reinforce Southwest's cultures.

- **Walk a Mile in My Shoes.** This program helped Southwest employees gain an appreciation for other people's jobs. Employees were asked to visit a different department on their day off and to spend a minimum of six hours on the "walk". These participants were rewarded not only with transferable roundtrip passes, but also with goodwill and increased morale.

- **A Day in the Field.** This activity is practiced throughout the company all year long. For example, Barri Tucker, then a senior communications representative in the executive office, once joined three flight attendants working a three-day trip. Tucker gained by experiencing the company from a new angle and by hearing directly from customers. She was able to see how important it is for corporate headquarters to support Southwest's frontline employees.

- **Helping Hands.** Southwest sent out volunteers from around the system to lighten the load of employees in the cities where Southwest was in direct competition with United's Shuttle. This not only built momentum and strengthened the troops for the battle with United, it also helped rekindle the fighting spirit of Southwest employees[70].

Motivate and Energize People

⟳ **LO 11**

Know how to motivate and energize service employees so that they will deliver service excellence and productivity.

Once a firm has hired the right people, trained them well, empowered them, and organized them into effective service delivery teams, how can it ensure that they are engaged and will deliver? Staff performance is a function of ability and motivation[71]. Effective hiring, training, empowerment, and teams give a firm able people; and performance appraisal and reward systems are key to motivating them. Service staff must get the message that providing quality service efficiently holds the key for them to be rewarded. Motivating and rewarding strong service performers are some of the most effective ways of retaining them (*Figure 11.20*). Staff quickly pick up that those who get promoted are the truly outstanding service providers, and that those who get fired are those who do not deliver at the customer level.

However, a major reason why service businesses fail is because they do not utilize the full range of available rewards effectively. Many firms think in terms of money as reward, but it does not pass the test of an effective motivator. Receiving a fair salary is a hygiene factor rather than a motivating factor. Paying more than what is seen as fair only has short-term motivating effects, and wears off quickly. On the other hand, bonuses that are contingent on performance have to be earned again and again, and therefore they tend to be more lasting in their effectiveness. Other, more lasting rewards are the job content itself, recognition and feedback, and goal accomplishment.

Job Content. People are motivated and satisfied simply by knowing they are doing a good job. They feel good about themselves, and like to reinforce that feeling. This is true especially if the job:

- Has a variety of different activities.
- Requires the completion of "whole" and identifiable pieces of work.
- Is seen as significant in the sense that it has an impact on the lives of others.
- Comes with autonomy and flexibility.
- Provides direct and clear feedback about how well employees did their work (e.g., grateful customers and sales performance).

Feedback and Recognition. Humans are social beings, and they derive a sense of identity and belonging to an organization from the recognition and feedback they receive from the people around them — their customers, colleagues, and superiors. If employees are recognized and thanked for service excellence beyond what happens during formal performance appraisal meetings, they will want to continue achieving it. If done well, the star employee of the month-type of awards recognize excellent performances and can be highly motivating.

Positive emotions are contagious. Employees are highly satisfied and motivated when they work in jobs where they can make a positive impact on others. Hence, putting employees in touch with end-users and letting them hear positive feedback from customers can be very motivating[72]. Positive effects were observed even if frontline employees just saw pictures of customers or read stories of the "wow" experiences customers had[73].

Figure 11.20 Rewarding employees according to their performances is essential to the success of a business

Goal Achievement. Goals focus people's energy. Achieving important goals is a reward in itself. Goals that are specific, difficult but attainable, and accepted by the staff are strong motivators (*Figure 11.21*). They result in higher performance as compared to no goals, or vague goals ("do your best"), or goals that are impossible to achieve[74]. In short, well-communicated and mutually accepted goals are effective motivators.

The following are important points to note for effective goal setting:

- When goals are seen as important, achieving the goals is a reward in itself.

- Goal accomplishment can be used as a basis for giving rewards, including bonuses, feedback, and recognition as part of formal performance appraisals. Feedback and recognition from peers can be given faster, more cheaply and effectively than pay, and have the additional benefit of gratifying an employee's self-esteem.

- Service employee goals that are specific and difficult must be set publicly to be accepted. Although goals must be specific, they can be something intangible like improved employee courtesy ratings.

- Progress reports about goal accomplishment (feedback), and goal accomplishment itself must be public events (recognition), if they are to gratify employees' esteem needs.

- It is mostly unnecessary to specify the means to achieve goals. Feedback on progress while pursuing the goal serves as a corrective function. As long as the goal is specific, difficult but achievable, and accepted, goal pursuit will result in goal accomplishment, even in the absence of other rewards.

Charles O'Reilly and Jeffrey Pfeffer conducted in-depth research on why some companies can succeed over long periods of time in highly competitive industries without having the usual sources of competitive advantage such as barriers of entry or proprietary technology. They concluded that these firms did not succeed by winning the war for talent (although these firms were hiring extremely carefully for fit), "but by fully using the talent and unlocking the motivation of the people" they already had in their organizations[75].

The Role of Labor Unions

Labor unions and service excellence do not seem to gel. The power of organized labor is widely cited as an excuse for not adopting new approaches in both service

Figure 11.21 When people are focused on goal achievement, it will motivate and energize them

and manufacturing businesses. "We'd never get it past the unions," managers say, wringing their hands and muttering darkly about restrictive work practices. Unions are often portrayed as villains in the press, especially when high-profile strikes inconvenience millions. Many managers seem to be rather antagonistic towards unions.

Contrary to the negative view presented above, many of the world's most successful service businesses are, in fact, highly unionized; Southwest Airlines is one example. The presence of unions in a service company is not an automatic barrier to high performance and innovation, unless there is a long history of mistrust, acrimonious relationships, and confrontation.

Jeffrey Pfeffer has observed wryly that "the subject of unions and collective bargaining is... one that causes otherwise sensible people to lose their objectivity[76]." He urges a pragmatic approach to this issue, emphasizing that "the effects of unions depend very much on what *management* does". The higher wages, lower turnover, clearly established grievance procedures, and improved working conditions often found in highly unionized organizations can yield positive benefits in a well-managed service organization. Furthermore, management consultation and negotiation with union representatives are essential if employees are to accept new ideas (conditions that are equally valid in non-unionized firms). The challenge is to jointly work with unions, to reduce conflict, and to create a climate for service[77].

SERVICE CULTURE, CLIMATE, AND LEADERSHIP

So far, we have discussed the nuts and bolts of HR in service firms. To close this chapter, we take a look at the leader's role in nurturing an effective service culture within the organization. Let's start with defining culture and climate for service.

Building a Service-Oriented Culture

 LO 12
Understand what a service-oriented culture is.

Service firms that strive to deliver service excellence need a strong service culture[78] that is continuously reinforced and developed by management to achieve alignment with the firm's strategy[79]. **Organizational culture** concerns the basic assumptions and values that guide organization action; it includes:

- Shared perceptions or themes regarding what is important in the organization.
- Shared values about what is right and wrong.
- Shared understanding about what works and what doesn't.
- Shared beliefs and assumptions about why these beliefs are important.
- Shared styles of working and relating to others.

Transforming an organization to develop and nurture a new culture along each of these five dimensions is no easy task for even the most gifted leader. It's doubly difficult when the organization is part of an industry that prides itself on deeply rooted traditions, with many different departments run by independent-minded professionals in different fields who are attuned to how they are perceived by fellow professionals in the same field at other institutions. This situation is often found in the nonprofit world, such as colleges and universities, major hospitals, and large museums.

Leonard Berry advocates a value-driven leadership that inspires and guides service providers[80]. Leadership should bring out the passion for serving. It should also tap the creativity of service providers, nourish their energy and commitment, and give them a fulfilled working life. An essential feature of a strong service culture is a strong belief in the importance of delivering superior customer value and service excellence. Some of the core values Berry found in excellent service firms included excellence, innovation, joy, teamwork, respect, integrity, and social profit (see *Service Insights 11.8* for an example of a value statement). These values are part of the firm's culture. Berry further boils down the definition of **service culture** to two points:

- Shared perceptions of **what** is important in an organization
- Shared values and beliefs of **why** those things are important.

It is the responsibility of the leaders to create a service culture with values that inspire, energize, and guide service providers.

As Zappos, the legendary US online retailer, had grown, its leaders felt it was important to explicitly define the core values that determined its service culture, brand, and business strategy. These are the ten core values that Zappos lives by:

1. Deliver WOW Through Service,
2. Embrace and Drive Change,
3. Create Fun and a Little Weirdness,
4. Be Adventurous, Creative, and Open-Minded,
5. Pursue Growth and Learning,
6. Build Open and Honest Relationships With Communication,
7. Build a Positive Team and Family Spirit,
8. Do More With Less,
9. Be Passionate and Determined,
10. Be Humble.

Tony Hsieh, CEO and founder of Zappos, describes in his book *Delivering Happiness: A Path to Profits, Passion and Purpose* in detail each of these 10 values and why they are important.

Source

http://www.zappos.com/d/about-zappos-culture, accessed May 12, 2015; Tony Hsieh, *Delivering Happiness: A Path to Profits, Passion and Purpose* (New York, NY: Business Plus, 2010).

LO 13

Know the difference between service climate and culture, and describe the determinants of a climate for service.

A Climate for Service

While culture is more overarching and values-focused, **organizational climate**[81] is the part of the organization's culture that can be felt and seen. Employees rely heavily on their perceptions of what is important by noting what the company and their leaders do, not so much what they say.

Employees gain their understanding of what is important through the daily experiences they have with the firm's human resource, operations, marketing and IT policies, practices, and procedures. It is culture translated into more concrete aspects that can be experienced by the employees, which then in turn drives employee behavior and customer outcomes[82]. In short, climate represents the shared perceptions of employees about the practices, procedures, and types of behaviors that get supported and rewarded in a particular setting.

As a climate must relate to something specific — for instance, to service, support, innovation, or safety — multiple climates often coexist within a single organization. Essential features of a climate for service include clear marketing goals and a strong drive and support to be the best in delivering superior customer value or service quality[83].

LO 14

Explain the qualities of effective leaders in service organizations.

Qualities of Effective Leaders in Service Organizations

Leaders are responsible for creating a culture and climate for service. Why are some leaders more effective than others in bringing about a desired change in culture and climate?

Many commentators have written on the topic of leadership. It has even been described as a service in its own right. The late Sam Walton, founder of the Wal-Mart retail chain, highlighted the role of managers as "servant leaders[84]". The following are some qualities that effective leaders in a service organization should have:

- Love for the business. Excitement about the business will encourage individuals to teach the business to others and to pass on to them the art and secrets of operating it.

- Many outstanding leaders are driven by a set of core values that are related to service excellence and performance they pass on in the organization[85]. Service quality is seen as a key foundation for success.

- Recognizing the key part played by employees in delivering service, service leaders need to believe in the people who work for them and pay special attention to communicating with employees.

- Effective leaders are able to ask great questions and get answers from the team, rather than just relying on themselves to dominate the decision-making process[86].

- Role model the behaviors they expect of their teams.

- Effective leaders have a talent for communicating with others in a way that is easy to understand. They know their audiences and are able to communicate even complicated ideas in simple terms accessible to all[87]. Effective communication is a key skill to inspire an organization to create success.

Rakesh Karma warns against excessive emphasis on charisma in selecting CEOs, arguing that it leads to unrealistic expectations[88]. He notes that unethical behavior may occur when charismatic but unprincipled leaders induce blind obedience in their followers, and cites the illegal activities stimulated by the leadership of Enron, which eventually led to the company's collapse. Of course, there is also the risk of prominent leaders becoming too externally focused at the risk of their internal effectiveness. A CEO who enjoys an enormous income (often through the exercise of huge stock options), maintains a princely lifestyle, and basks in widespread publicity may even turn off low-paid service workers at the bottom of the organization. Jim Collins concludes that a leader does not require a larger-than-life personality. Leaders who aspire to take a company to greatness, he says, need to have personal humility blended with intensive professional will, ferocious resolve, and a willingness to give credit to others while taking the blame to themselves[89].

Finally, in hierarchical organizations, it's often assumed that leadership at the top is sufficient. However, as Sandra Vandermerwe points out, forward-looking service businesses need to be more flexible. Today's greater emphasis on using teams within service businesses means that:

> [L]eaders are everywhere, disseminated throughout the teams. They are found especially in the customer facing and interfacing jobs in order that decision-making will lead to long-lasting relationships with customers... leaders are customer and project champions who energize the group by virtue of their enthusiasm, interest, and know-how[90].

Leadership Styles, Focus on the Basics, and Role Modeling

Service climate research has contrasted two leadership styles: Management of the "basics" as compared to transformational leadership that sets strategy and drives change[91]. Research has shown that the persistent management of the basics and endless details create a strong climate for service. Leaders who demonstrate a commitment to service quality, set high standards, recognize and remove obstacles, and ensure the availability of resources required to do it — create a strong climate for service. This basic leadership style seems mundane compared to transformational leadership, yet according to James Heskett and his colleagues, both are needed, a recognition of the "importance of the mundane" and providing a strong service vision that inspires and motivates the troops[92].

One of the traits of successful leaders is their ability to role model the behavior they expect of managers and other employees, and thereby focus the organization on the basics. Often, this requires the approach known as "management by walking around", popularized by Thomas Peters and Robert Waterman in their book *In Search of Excellence*[93]. When Herb Kelleher was CEO of Southwest Airlines, no one was surprised to see him turn up at a Southwest maintenance hanger at two in the morning or even to encounter him working an occasional stint as a flight attendant. Walking around involves regular visits, sometimes unannounced, to various areas of the company's operation. This approach provides insights into both back-stage and front-stage operations, the ability to observe and meet both employees and customers, and an opportunity to see how corporate strategy is implemented at the frontline.

LO 15

Understand different leadership styles, the importance of role modeling and focusing the entire organization on the frontline.

Periodically, this approach may lead to a recognition that changes in a firm's strategy are needed. Encountering the CEO on such a visit can also be motivating for service personnel. It also provides an opportunity for role modeling good service. *Service Insights 11.9* describes how the CEO of a major hospital learned the power of role modeling early in his tenure.

Empirical research in the hotel industry demonstrates why it is important for management to walk the talk. Judi McLean Park and Tony Simons conducted a study of 6,500 employees at 76 Holiday Inn hotels to determine whether workers perceived that their hotel managers showed behavioral integrity using measures such as "My manager delivers on promises", and "My manager practices what he preached". These statements were correlated with employee responses to questions such as "I am proud to tell others I am part of this hotel", and "My coworkers go out of the way to accommodate guests' special requests", and then to revenues and profitability.

The results were stunning. They showed that behavioral integrity of a hotel's manager was highly correlated to employees' trust, commitment, and willingness to go the extra mile. Furthermore, of all manager behaviors measured, it was the single most important factor driving profitability. In fact, a mere one-eight point increase in a hotel's overall behavioral integrity score on a five-point scale was associated with a 2.5% increase in revenue, and a $250,000 increase in profits per hotel per year[94].

SERVICE INSIGHTS 11.9
A Hospital President Learns the Power of Role Modeling

During his 30-year tenure as president of Boston's Beth Israel Hospital (now Beth Israel-Deaconess Medical Center), Mitchell T. Rabkin, MD, was known for regularly spending time making informal visits to all parts of the hospital. "You learn a lot from 'management by walking around'," he said. "And you're also seen. When I visit another hospital and am given a tour by its CEO, I watch how that CEO interacts with other people, and what the body language is in each instance. It's very revealing. Even more, it's very important for role modeling." To reinforce that point, Dr. Rabkin liked to tell the following story:

People learn to *do* as a result of the way they see you and others *behave*. An example from the Beth Israel that's now almost apocryphal — but *is* true — is the story of the bits of litter on the floor.

One of our trustees, the late Max Feldberg, head of the Zayre Corporation, asked me one time to take a walk around the hospital with him and inquired, "Why do you think there are so many pieces of paper scattered on the floor of this patient care unit?"

"Well, it's because people don't pick them up," I replied. He said, "Look, you're a scientist. We'll do an experiment. We'll walk down this floor and we'll pick up every other piece of paper. And then we'll go upstairs, there's another unit, same geography, statistically the same amount of paper, but we won't pick up anything."

So this 72-year-old man and I went picking up alternate bits of the litter on one floor and nothing on the other. When we came back 10 minutes later, virtually all the rest of the litter on the first floor had been removed and nothing, of course, had changed on the second.

And "Mr. Max" said to me, "You see, it's not because *people* don't pick them up, it's because *you* don't pick them up. If you're so fancy that you can't bend down and pick up a piece of paper, why should anybody else?"

Source
Christopher Lovelock, *Product Plus: How Product + Service = Competitive Advantage* (New York: McGraw-Hill, 1994).

Focusing the Entire Organization on the Frontline

A strong service culture is one where the entire organization focuses on the frontline, understanding that it is the lifeline of the business. The organization understands that today's, as well as tomorrow's, revenues are largely driven by what happens at the service encounter. In firms with a passion for service, top management show through their actions that what happens at the frontline is crucially important to them, by being informed and actively involved. They achieve this by regularly talking to and working with frontline staff and customers. Mark Frissora, CEO of car rental company Hertz, expressed this as follows:

> *I often hear people say, "As a CEO, you can't get too involved in the day-to-day operations of your business. That's micromanaging." My response is, "I have to get 'too involved' in the business because I'm setting the strategy. If I don't understand the business, then I'm a poor manager and I've failed as a leader." It's critical that leaders spend a lot of time where the work actually gets done.[95]*

Many actually spend significant amounts of time at the frontline serving customers. For example, Disney World's management spends weeks every year in frontline staff job such as sweeping the streets, selling ice-cream, or working as a ride attendant, in order to gain a better appreciation and understanding of what really happens on the ground[96]. Service leaders are not only interested in the big picture, but they focus on the details of the service, they see opportunities in nuances which competitors might consider trivial, and they believe the way the firm handles little things sets the tone for how it handles everything else.

Zappos focuses all new recruits on the frontline by ensuring that everyone who is hired in its headquarters goes through the same training their call center employees (called "Customer Loyalty Team") go through. Whether they hire an accountant, lawyer, or software developer, regardless of seniority, they go through exactly the same training program. It takes four weeks and covers the company history, the importance of customer service, the long-term vision of the company, and Zappos' philosophy about company culture. Following this training, all new hires work for two weeks in the call center taking customer calls. According to its CEO Tony Hsieh: "This goes back to our belief that customer service shouldn't just be a department, it should be the entire company[97]."

Figure 11.22 shows the inverted pyramid, which highlights the importance of the frontline. It shows that the role of top management and middle management is to support the frontline in their task of delivering service excellence to their customers.

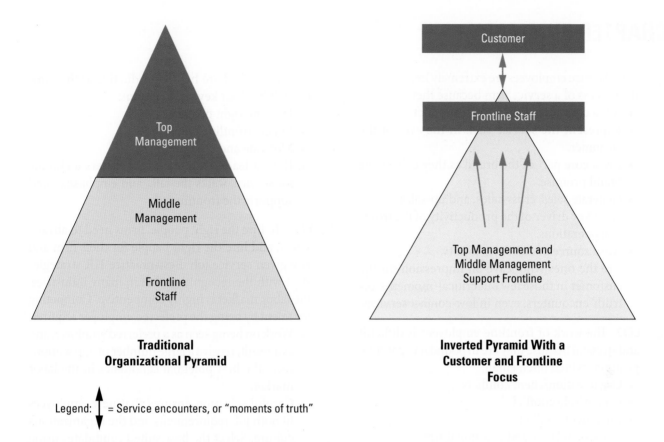

Legend: ↕ = Service encounters, or "moments of truth"

Figure 11.22 The inverted organizational pyramid

CONCLUSION

The quality of a service firm's people — especially those working in customer-facing positions — plays a crucial role in determining market success and financial performance. That's why the *People* element of the **7 Ps** is so important. Successful service organizations are committed to the effective management of human resources, and work closely with marketing and operations managers to balance what might otherwise prove to be conflicting goals. They recognize the value of investing in HR and understand the costs resulting from high levels of turnover. In the long run, offering better wages and benefits may be a more financially viable strategy than paying less to employees who have no loyalty and soon defect.

The market and financial results of managing people effectively for service advantage can be phenomenal. Good HR strategies allied with strong management leadership at all levels often lead to a sustainable competitive advantage. It is probably harder to duplicate high-performing human assets than any other corporate resource.

CHAPTER SUMMARY

LO1 Service employees are extremely important to the success of a service firm because they:
- Are a core part of the service product.
- Represent the service firm in the eyes of the customer.
- Are a core part of the brand as they deliver the brand promise.
- Generate sales, cross-sales, and up-sales.
- Are a key driver of the productivity of the frontline operations.
- Are a source of customer loyalty.
- Are the ones who leave an impression on the customer in those few but critical 'moments-of-truth' encounters, even in low-contact services.

LO2 The work of frontline employees is difficult and stressful because they are in boundary spanning positions which often entail:
- Organization/client conflicts
- Person/role conflict
- Interclient conflicts
- Emotional labor and emotional stress

LO3 We used three types of cycles involving frontline employees and customers to describe how firms can be set up for failure, mediocrity, and success:
- The **Cycle of Failure** involves a low pay and high employee turnover strategy, and as a consequence, results in high customer dissatisfaction and defections which depress profit margins.
- The **Cycle of Mediocrity** is typically found in large bureaucracies, offering job security but not much scope in the job itself. There is no incentive to serve customers well.
- Successful service firms operate in the **Cycle of Success**, where employees are satisfied with their jobs and are productive, and as a consequence, customers are satisfied and loyal. Higher profit margins allow investment in the recruitment, development and motivation of the right frontline employees.

LO4 The Service Talent Cycle is a guiding framework for successful HR strategies in service firms, helping them to move their firms into the Cycle of Success. Implementing the service talent cycle correctly will give firms highly motivated employees who are willing and able to deliver service excellence and go the extra mile for their customers, and are highly productive at the same time. It has four key prescriptions:
- Hire the right people.
- Enable frontline employees.
- Motivate and energize them.
- Have a leadership team that fosters a climate for service, walks the talk, and emphasizes and supports the frontline.

LO5 To hire the right people, firms need to attract, select, and hire the right people for their firm and any given service job. Best-practice HR strategies start with the recognition that in many industries, the labor market is highly competitive. Competing for talent by being the preferred employer requires:
- Work on being seen as a preferred employer, and as a result, receive a large number of applications from the best potential candidates in the labor market.
- Careful selection ensures that new employees fit both job requirements and the organization's culture. Select the best-suited candidates using screening methods such as multiple structured interviews, observation, personality tests, and providing realistic job previews.

To enable their frontline employees, firms need to:

LO6 Conduct painstakingly extensive training on (1) the organizational culture, purpose, and strategy; (2) interpersonal and technical skills; and (3) product/service knowledge.

LO7 Use internal communications (also referred to as "internal marketing") to reinforce the firm's service culture and get the message to everyone in the company. An effective mix of internal communications tools should be used (e.g., emailers, magazines, videos, briefings, and promotional campaigns using displays, prices, and recognition programs.

LO8 Empower the frontline so they can respond with flexibility to customer needs and non-routine encounters and service failures. Empowerment and training will give employees the authority, skills, and self-confidence to use their own initiative in delivering service excellence.
- Empowerment needs to be set at the appropriate level for the business model and customer needs. It ranges from the low level of empowerment

in the "production-line" approach for highly standardized services to a high level of decision authority for the frontline in more complex and customized services.

- Empowerment requires systematically distributing four key features: (1) information about organizational, team, and individual performance; (2) knowledge that enables employees to understand and contribute to performance; (3) power to make decisions; and (4) performance-based rewards.

LO9 Organize frontline employees into effective service delivery teams (often cross-functional) that can serve their customers from end-to-end.

LO10 Integrate service delivery teams across departments and functional areas. To be successful, the marketing, operations, human resource, and IT management functions need to be tightly integrated, and work closely together in well-coordinated ways. Integration means that the key deliverables and objectives of the various functions are not only compatible but also mutually reinforcing.

- Ways to improve integration include (1) internal transfers across functional areas, (2) cross-functional project teams, (3) cross-functional service delivery teams, (4) appointing individuals to integrate objective, activities and processes between departments, (5) training, internal marketing and campaigns (such as "walk a mile in my shoes" and "a day in the field"), and (6) management commitment that ensures that the overarching objectives of all functions are integrated.

LO11 Finally, energize and motivate employees with a full set of rewards, ranging from pay, performance bonuses, satisfying job content, feedback and recognition, to goal accomplishment.

LO12 A **service culture** describes the basic assumptions and values that guide organization action. It can be boiled down to two points:

- Shared perceptions of **what** is important in an organization, and
- Shares values and beliefs of **why** those things are important.

An essential feature of a service-oriented culture is a strong belief in the importance of delivering superior value and service excellence. It builds employee understanding and support for the organization's goals that lead to those outcomes.

Exemplary leaders understand the powerful, unifying effect of focusing on customers and creating a service culture with values that inspire, energize and guide service providers.

LO13 A **service climate** is the surface layer on top of the culture. Climate is culture translated into the more concrete aspects that can be experienced by employees and includes the policies, practices, and procedures of HR, operations, marketing, and IT. Climate also represents the shared perceptions of employees about the practices and behaviors that get rewarded in an organization.

LO14 Service leaders should have the following qualities:

- Love for the business.
- A set of core values that are related to service excellence and performance they pass on to the organization. Service quality is seen as a key foundation for success.
- A strong belief in the people who work for them, and recognition of the importance of the frontline.
- Ability to ask great questions and get answers from their teams.
- Role model the behaviors they expect of their teams.
- Effective communication skills that allow leaders to inspire the organization to create success.

LO15 A leadership style that focuses on the basics and details creates a strong climate for service typically involves leaders to demonstrate a commitment to quality, to set high standards, recognize and remove obstacles, and ensure the availability of resources required to do it. This leadership seems mundane compared to transformational leadership, which sets strategy and drives change, but both are needed for a strong climate for service.

A strong service culture focuses on the frontline. Leaders show by their actions that what happens at the frontline is crucially important to them. It is the role of top and middle management to support the frontline in delivering service excellence to their customers.

Review Questions

1. Why are service personnel so important for service firms?

2. There is a trend of service delivery moving from high-contact to low-contact. Are service employees still important in low-contact services? Explain.

3. What is emotional labor? Explain the ways in which it may cause stress for employees in specific jobs. Illustrate with suitable examples.

4. What are the key barriers for firms to break the Cycle of Failure and move into the Cycle of Success? How should an organization trapped in the Cycle of Mediocrity proceed?

5. List five ways in which investment in hiring and selection, training, and ongoing motivation of employees will have a positive impact on customer satisfaction for organizations like (a) a restaurant, (b) an airline, (c) a hospital, and (d) a consulting firm.

6. Describe the key components of the Service Talent Cycle.

7. What can a service firm do to become a preferred employer, and as a result, receive a large number of applications from the best potential candidates in the labor market?

8. How can a firm select the best-suited candidates from a large number of applicants?

9. What are the key types of training service firms should conduct?

10. Identify the factors needed to make service teams successful in (a) an airline, (b) a restaurant, and (c) a customer contact center. What are the factors that favor a strategy of employee empowerment?

11. How can frontline employees be effectively motivated to deliver service excellence?

12. How can a service firm build a strong service culture that emphasizes service excellence and productivity?

13. What is the relationship among organizational culture, climate for service and leadership?

14. Why is role modeling a desirable quality in service leaders?

Application Exercises

1. An airline runs a recruiting advertisement for cabin crew that shows a picture of a young boy sitting in an airline seat and clutching a teddy bear. The headline reads: "His mom told him not to talk to strangers. So what's he having for lunch?" Describe the types of personalities you think would be (a) attracted to apply for the job by that ad, and (b) discouraged from applying.

2. Consider the following jobs: emergency department nurse, bill collector, computer repair technician, supermarket cashier, dentist, kindergarten teacher, prosecuting attorney, waiter in a family restaurant, waiter in an expensive French restaurant, stockbroker, and undertaker. What type of emotions would you expect each of them to display to customers in the course of doing their job? What drives your expectations?

3. Use the Service Talent Cycle as a diagnostic tool on a successful and an unsuccessful service firm you are familiar with. What recommendations would you prescribe to each of these two firms?

4. Think of two organizations you are familiar with, one with a very good climate for service, and one with very poor service climate. Describe the factors that contributed to shaping those climates. What factors do you think contributed most and why?

5. Which issues do you see as most likely to create boundary spanning problems for employees in a customer contact center at a major Internet service provider? Select four issues and indicate how you would mediate between operations and marketing to create a satisfactory outcome for all three groups.

6. Identify the factors needed to make service teams successful in (a) an airline, (b) a restaurant, and (c) a customer contact center.

7. Profile an individual whose leadership skills have played a significant role in the success of a service organization, identifying personal characteristics that you consider important.

Endnotes

1   Adapted from Leonard L. Berry, *Discovering the Soul of Service — The Nine Drivers of Sustainable Business Success* (New York: Free Press, 1999), pp. 156–159.

2   Recent research focuses on how strategically aligning frontline employees and their behaviors with a firm's brand positioning strengthens brand equity, see: Nancy J. Sirianni, Mary Jo Bitner, Stephen W. Brown, and Naomi Mandel (2013), "Branded Service Encounters: Strategically Aligning Employee Behavior with the Brand Positioning," *Journal of Marketing*, Vol. 77, No. 6, pp. 108–123.

3   Liliana L. Bove, and Lester W. Johnson (2001), "Customer Relationships with Service Personnel: Do We Measure Closeness, Quality or Strength?" *Journal of Business Research*, Vol. 54, pp. 189–197; Magnus Söderlund and Sara Rosengren (2008), "Revisiting the Smiling Service Worker and Customer Satisfaction," *International Journal of Service Industry Management*, Vol. 19, No. 5, pp. 552–574; Anat Rafaeli, Lital Ziklik, and Lorna Doucet (2008), "The Impact of Call Center Employees' Customer Orientation Behaviors and Service Quality," *Journal of Service Research*, Vol. 10, No. 3, pp. 239–255.

4   The following study established the link between extra-role effort and customer satisfaction; for example, Carmen Barroso Castro, Enrique Martín Armario, and David Martín Ruiz (2004), "The Influence of Employee Organizational Citizenship Behavior on Customer Loyalty," *International Journal of Service Industry Management*, Vol.15, No. 1, pp. 27–53.
There is a large body of research that documented how and why employees have such a strong impact on customers' satisfaction and future behaviors. Recent studies include: Alicia A. Grandey, Lori S. Goldberg, and S. Douglas Pugh (2011), "Why and When do Stores With Satisfied Employees Have Satisfied Customers," *Journal of Service Research*, Vol. 14, No. 4, pp. 397–409; Heiner Evanschitzky, Christopher Groening, Vikas Mittal, and Maren Wunderlich (2011), "How Employer and Employee Satisfaction Affect Customer Satisfaction: An Application to Franchise Services," *Journal of Service Research*, Vol. 14, No. 2, pp. 136–148; Gabriel Gazzoli, Murat Hancer, and BeomCheol (Peter) Kim (2013), "Explaining Why Employee-Customer Orientation Influences Customers' Perceptions of the Service Encounter," *Journal of Service Management*, Vol. 24, No. 4, pp. 382–400; Cécile Delcourt, Dwayne D. Gremmler, Allard C.R. van Riel, and Marcel van Birgelen (2013), "Effects of Perceived Employee Emotional Competence on Customer Satisfaction and Loyalty: The Mediating

Role of Rapport," *Journal of Service Management*, Vol. 24, No. 1, pp. 5–24; Kumar Rakesh Ranjan, Praveen Sugathan, and Alexander Rossmann (2014), "A Narrative Review and Meta-Analysis of Service Interaction Quality: New Research Directions and Implications" *Journal of Services Marketing*, Vol. 29, No. 1, pp. 3–14.

5   James L. Heskett, Thomas O. Jones, Gary W. Loveman, W. Earl Sasser, Jr., and Leonard A. Schlesinger (1994), " Putting the Service Profit Chain to Work," *Harvard Business Review*, Vol. 72, March–April, pp. 164–174.

6   Benjamin Schneider and David E. Bowen (1993), "The Service Organization: Human Resources Management is Crucial," *Organizational Dynamics*, Vol. 21, No. 4, Spring, pp. 39–52.

7   http://www.fiveguysproductions.com/2010/08/just-little-excitement-on-my-flight.html, "Just a Little Excitement on my Flight Today," posted on August 9, 2010, accessed May 11, 2015.

8   David E. Bowen and Benjamin Schneider, "Boundary-Spanning Role Employees and the Service Encounter: Some Guidelines for Management and Research" in J. A. Czepiel, M. R. Solomon, and C. F. Surprenant, eds., *The Service Encounter* (Lexington, MA: Lexington Books, 1985), pp. 127–148.

For a recent study on the effects of stress on employee performance and how this effect can be mitigated, see: Kimmy Wa Chan and Echo Wen Wan (2012), "How Can Stressed Employees Deliver Better Customer Service: The Underlying Self-Regulation Depletion Mechanism," *Journal of Marketing*, Vol. 76, No. 1, pp. 119–137.

9   Conflicting goals (e.g., short average call duration and customer satisfaction) set by the organization are also a key cause of burnout, see: Michael Rod and Nicholas J. Ashill (2013), "The Impact of Call Centre Stressors on Inbound and Outbound Call-Center Agent Burnout," *Managing Service Quality*, Vol. 23, No. 3, pp. 245–264; Benjamin Piers William Ellway (2014), "Is The Quality-Quantity Trade-Off in Call Centres a False Dichotomy?," *Managing Service Quality*, Vol. 24, No. 3, pp. 230–251.

For a recent study on selling in a call center service context, see: Claudia Jasmand, Vera Blazevic, and Ko de Ruyter (2012), "Generating Sales While Providing Service: A Study of Customer Service Representatives' Ambidextrous Behavior," *Journal of Marketing*, Vol. 76, No. 1, pp. 20–37.

10 Vaikakalathur Shankar Mashesh and Anand Kasturi (2006), "Improving Call Centre Agent Performance: A UK-India Study Based on the Agents' Point of View," *International Journal of Service Industry Management,* Vol. 17, No. 2, pp. 136–157.

On potentially conflicting goals, see also: Detelina Marinova, Jun Ye and Jagdip Singh (2008), "Do Frontline Mechanisms Matter? Impact of Quality and Productivity Orientations on Unit Revenue, Efficiency, and Customer Satisfaction," *Journal of Marketing,* Vol. 72, No. 2, pp. 28–25.

11 Arlie R. Hochschild, *The Managed Heart: Commercialization of Human Feeling* (Berkeley: CA, University of California Press, 1983).

12 Won-Moo Hur, Tae-Won Moon, and Yeon Sung Jung (2015), "Customer Response to Employee Emotional Labor: The Structural Relationship Between Emotional Labor, Job Satisfaction, and Customer Satisfaction," *Journal of Services Marketing,* Vol. 29, No. 1, pp. 71–80.

13 Panikkos Constanti and Paul Gibbs (2005), "Emotional labor and Surplus Value: The Case of Holiday 'Reps'," *The Service Industries Journal,* Vol. 25, January, pp. 103–116.

14 Arlie Hochschild (1982), "Emotional Labor in the Friendly Skies," *Psychology Today,* June, pp. 13–15.

15 Michel Rod and Nicholas J. Ashill (2009), "Symptoms of Burnout and Service Recovery Performance," *Managing Service Quality,* Vol. 19, No. 1, pp. 60–84; Jody L. Crosno, Shannon B. Rinaldo, Hulda G. Black and Scott W. Kelley (2009), "Half Full or Half Empty: The Role of Optimism in Boundary-Spanning Positions," *Journal of Service Research,* Vol. 11, No. 3, pp. 295–309.

Recent research has linked emotional exhaustion to turnover intentions, see: Tobias Kraemer and Matthias H.J. Gouthier (2014), "How Organizational Pride and Emotional Exhaustion Explain Turnover Intentions in Call Centers," *Journal of Service Management,* Vol. 25, No. 1, pp. 125–148.

Note that there is emotional contagion for both positive and negative emotions from service employees to customers; therefore how frontline employees deal with stress is important for the customer experience. See: Jiangang Du, Xiucheng Fan, and Tianjun Feng (2011), "Multiple Emotional Contagions in Service Encounters," *Journal of the Academy of Marketing Science,* Vol. 39, No. 3, pp. 449–466.

Emotional support seems particularly important when employees have to deal with unreasonable and dysfunctional customers; see: Taeshik Gong, Youjae Yi, and Jin Nam Choi (2014), "Helping Employees Deal with Dysfunctional Customers: The Underlying Employee Perceived Justice Mechanism," *Journal of Service Research,* Vol. 17, No. 1, pp. 102–116.

For how frontline staff resist emotional labor, see: Jocelyn A. Hollander and Rachel L. Einwohner (2004), "Conceptualizing Resistance," *Sociological* Forum, Vol. 19, No. 4, pp. 533–554; Diane Seymour (2000), "Emotional Labour: A Comparison Between Fast Food and Traditional Service Work," *International Journal of Hospitality* Management, Vol. 19, No. 2, pp. 159–171; Peter John Sandiford and Diane Seymour (2011), "Reacting to the Demands of Service Work: Emotional Resistance in the Coach Inn Company," *The Service Industries Journal,* Vol. 31, No. 7–8, May, pp. 1195–1217.

16 Jochen Wirtz and Robert Johnston (2003), "Singapore Airlines: What It Takes to Sustain Service Excellence — A Senior Management Perspective," *Managing Service Quality,* Vol. 13, No.1, pp. 10–19; and Loizos Heracleous, Jochen Wirtz, and Nitin Pangarkar, *Flying High in a Competitive Industry: Secrets of the World's Leading Airline.* (Singapore: McGraw-Hill, 2009).

17 Dan Moshavi and James R. Terbord (2002), "The Job Satisfaction and Performance of Contingent and Regular Customer Service Representatives — A Human Capital Perspective," *International Journal of Service Industry Management,* Vol. 13, No. 4, pp. 333–347.

18 Vaikalathur Shankar Mahesh and Anand Kasturi (2006), "Improving Call Centre Agent Performance," *International Journal of Service Industry Management,* Vol. 17, No. 2, pp. 136–157.

19 The terms "Cycle of Failure" and "Cycle of Success" were coined by Leonard L. Schlesinger and James L. Heskett (1991), "Breaking the Cycle of Failure in Services," *Sloan Management Review,* Vol. 31, Spring, pp. 17–28. The term, "Cycle of Mediocrity" comes from Christopher H. Lovelock, "Managing Services: The Human Factor," in W.J. Glynn and J.G. Barnes, eds. *Understanding Services Management* (Chichester, UK: John Wiley & Sons, 1995), p. 228.

20 Leonard Schlesinger and James L. Heskett (1991), "Breaking the Cycle of Failure," *Sloan Management Review,* Vol. 31, Spring, pp. 17–28.

21 Reg Price and Roderick J. Brodie (2001), "Transforming a Public Service Organization from Inside out to Outside in," *Journal of Service Research,* Vol. 4, No. 1, pp. 50–59.

22 Mahn Hee Yoon (20010, "The Effect of Work Climate on Critical Employee and Customer Outcomes," *International Journal of Service Industry Management,* Vol. 12, No. 5, pp. 500–521

23 Tor W. Andreassen and Even J. Lanseng (2010), "Service Differentiation: A Self-Image Congruency Perspective on Brand Building in the Labor Market," *Journal of Service Management*, Vol. 21, No. 2, pp. 212–236.

24 Kathleen A. Keeling, Peter J. McGoldrick and Henna Sadhu (2013), "Staff Word-of-Mouth (SWOM) and Retail Employee Recruitment" *Journal of Retailing*, Vol. 89, No. 1, pp. 88–104.

25 www.glassdoor.com and http://en.wikipedia.org/wiki/Glassdoor, accessed on May 7, 2015.

26 Charles A. O'Reilly III and Jeffrey Pfeffer, *Hidden Value — How Great Companies Achieve Extraordinary Results with Ordinary People* (Boston, MA: Harvard Business School Press, 2000), 1.

27 Being seen as a good company and engaging in corporate social responsibility is increasingly seen as important in both labor and consumer markets. See also: Daniel Korschun, C.B. Bhattavharya, and Scott D. Swain (2014), "Corporate Social Responsibility, Customer Orientation, and the Job Performance of Frontline Employees," *Journal of Marketing*, Vol. 78, No. 3, pp. 20–37.

28 Patty McCord (2014), "How Netflix Reinvented HR," *Harvard Business Review*, Vol. 92, No. 1/2, pp. 70–76.

29 Nancy J. Sirianni, Mary Jo Bitner, Stephen W. Brown, and Naomi Mandel (2013), "Branded Service Encounters: Strategically Aligning Employee Behavior with the Brand Positioning," *Journal of Marketing*, Vol. 77, No. 6, pp. 108–123; Birgit Löndorf and Adamantios Diamantopoulos (2014), "Internal Branding: Social Identify and Social Exchange Perspectives on Turning Employees into Brand Champions," *Journal of Service Research*, Vol. 17, No. 3, pp. 310–325.

It also has shown that frontline employees have varying mental models of the meaning of customer service — ranging from satisfying the customers' needs efficiently, filling sales quota to forming a mutually beneficial relationship. The mental model of employees therefore should fit the firm's marketing strategy and positioning. See: Rita Di Mascio (2010), "The Service Models of Frontline Employees," *Journal of Marketing*, Vol. 74, No. 4, pp. 63–80.

30 Scott A. Hurrell and Dora Scholarios (2014), "'The People Make the Brand': Reducing Social Skills Gaps Through Person-Brand Fit and Human Resource Management Practices," *Journal of Service Research*, Vol. 17, No. 1, pp. 54–67. This study has also shown that a firm that recruits based on person-brand fit leads to their employees having better identification with the brand and smaller skills gaps.

31 Bill Fromm and Len Schlesinger, *The Real Heroes of Business* (New York: Currency Doubleday, 1994), 315–316.

32 Jim Collins (1999), "Turning Goals into Results: The Power of Catalytic Mechanisms," *Harvard Business Review*, Vol. 77, July–August, p. 77.

33 Thomas H. Davenport (2010), Jeanne Harris and Jeremy Shapiro, "Competing on Talent Analytics," *Harvard Business Review*, October, pp. 52–58.

34 This section was adapted from: Benjamin Schneider and David E. Bowen, *Winning the Service Game* (Boston, MA: Harvard Business School Press, 1995), 115–126.

35 John Wooden, *A Lifetime of Observations and Reflections On and Off the* Court (Chicago, IL: Lincolnwood, 1997), 66.

36 For a review of this literature see Benjamin Schneider (1991), "Service Quality and Profits: Can You Have Your Cake and Eat It, Too? *Human Resource Planning*, Vol. 14, No. 2, pp. 151–157.

37 There is a large literature on the effects of and how to select employees based on personality. Important and recent research includes: Tom J. Brown, John C. Mowen, D. Todd Donovan, and Jane W. Licata (2002), "The Customer Orientation of Service Workers: Personality Trait Effects on Self- and Supervisor Performance Ratings," *Journal of Marketing Research*, Vol. 39, No. 1, pp. 110–119; Salih Kusluvan, Zeynep Kusluvan, Ibrahim Ilhan, and Lutfi Buyruk (2010), "The Human Dimension: A Review of Human Resources Management Issues in the Tourism and Hospitality Industry," *Cornell Hospitality Quarterly*, Vol. 51, No. 2, May, pp. 171–214; Hui Liao and Aichia Chuang (2004), "A Multilevel Investigation of Factors Influencing Employee Service Performance and Customer Outcomes," *Academy of Management Journal*, Vol. 47, No. 1, pp. 41–58; Androniki Papadopoulou-Bayliss, Elizabeth M. Ineson, and Derek Wilkie (2001), "Control and Role Conflict in Food Service Providers," *International Journal of Hospitality Management*, Vol. 20, No. 2, pp. 187–199; Michael J. Tews, Kathryn Stafford, and J. Bruce Tracey (2011), "What Matters Most? The Perceived Importance of Ability and Personality for Hiring Decisions," Cornell Hospitality Quarterly, Vol. 52, No. 2, pp. 94–101; John E.G. Bateson, Jochen Wirtz, Eugene F. Burke and Carly J. Vaughan (2014), "Sifting to Efficiently Select the Right Service Employees," *Organizational Dynamics*, Vol. 43, pp. 312–320.

38 Serene Goh, "All the Right Staff," and Arlina Arshad, "Putting Your Personality to the Test," *The Straits Times*, Singapore, September 5, 2001, p. H1.

39   This section was adapted from Leonard L. Berry, *On Great Service — A Framework for Action* (New York: The Free Press, 1995), pp. 181–182.

40   Leonard Schlesinger and James L. Heskett (1991), "Breaking the Cycle of Failure," *Sloan Management Review*, Vol. 32, No. 3, Spring, pp. 17–28.

41   Donald W. Jackson Jr. and Nancy J. Sirianni (2009), "Building the Bottom Line by Developing the Frontline: Career Development for Service Employees," *Business Horizons*, Vol. 52, pp. 279–287; Timothy R. Hinkin and J. Bruce Tracey (2010), "What Makes It So Great? An Analysis of Human Resources Practices among Fortune's Best Companies to Work For," *Cornell Hospitality Quarterly*, Vol. 51, No. 2, May, pp. 158–170; Rick Garlick (2010), "Do Happy Employees Really Mean Happy Customers? Or Is There More to the Equation? *Cornell Hospitality Quarterly*, Vol. 51, No. 3, August, pp. 304–307.

42   Yukari Iwatani Kane and Ian Sherr, "Secrets From Apple's Genius Bar: Full Loyalty, No Negativity," *The Wall Street Journal*, June 15, 2011, http://www.wsj.com/articles/SB10001424052702304563104576364071955678908, accessed May 11, 2015.

43   Benjamin Schneider and David E. Bowen, *Winning the Service Game* (Boston, MA: Harvard Business School Press, 1995), 131.

44   Leonard L. Berry, *Discovering the Soul of Service — The Nine Drivers of Sustainable Business Success* (New York: The Free Press, 1999), 161; Pep Simo, Mihaela Enache, Jose M. Sallan, and Vicenc Fernandez (2014), "Relations Between Organizational Commitment and Focal and Discretionary Behaviors," *The Service Industries Journal*, Vol. 34, No. 5, pp. 422–438.

45   Disney Institute, *Be Our Guest: Perfecting the Art of Customer Service* (New York: Disney Enterprises, 2011), updated edition.

46   David A. Tansik, "Managing Human Resource Issues for High Contact Service Personnel," in *Service Management Effectiveness*, eds. D.E. Bowen, R. B. Chase, T.G. Cummings, and Associates (San Francisco: Jossey-Bass, 1990), pp. 152–176; Kelly M. Wilder, Joel E. Collier, and Donald C. Barnes (2014), "Tailoring to Customers' Needs: Understanding How to Promote an Adaptive Service Experience With Frontline Employees," *Journal of Service Research*, Vol. 17, No. 4, pp. 446–459.

Recent research has even focused on how obese frontline employees can counter a negative stereotype (e.g., perceived lack of energy) with lower customer evaluations of frontline transactions. The research found that outwards expression of joviality (e.g., displaying an attitude of being "jolly" and "fun") can attenuate negative effects of obesity. Likewise, sending strong signals of quality of the encounter (e.g., paying extra attention to facility cleanliness, merchandise neatness, and displaying employee accomplishments) reduced the negative effects of obesity on customer perceptions. Training can help employees to to use these tactics. See: Kelly O. Cowart and Michael K. Brady (2014), "Pleasantly Plum: Offsetting Negative Obesity Stereotypes for Frontline Employees," *Journal of Service Research*, Vol. 90, No. 3, pp. 365-378.

47   Joseph A. Mitchelli, *The New Gold Standard: 5 Leadership Principles for Creating a Legendary Customer Experience Courtesy of The Ritz-Carlton Hotel Company* (New York: McGraw Hill, 2008), 61–66 and 191–197.

48   Paul Hemp (2002), "My Week as a Room-Service Waiter at the Ritz," *Harvard Business Review*, Vol. 80, June, pp. 8–11.

49   Parts of this section are based on David E. Bowen, and Edward E. Lawler, III (1992), "The Empowerment of Service Workers: What, Why, How and When," *Sloan Management Review*, Vol. 33, Spring, pp. 32–39.

50   For important recent research on discretionary employee behavior in the frontline see: Steffen Raub and Hui Liao (2012), "Doing the Right Thing Without Being Told: Joint Effects of Initiative Climate and General Self-Efficacy on Employee Proactive Customer Service Performance," *Journal of Applied Psychology*, Vol. 97, No. 3, pp. 651–667; Jeroen Schepers, Tomas Falk, Ko de Ruyter, Ad de Jong, and Maik Hammerschmidt (2012), "Principles and Principals: Do Customer Stewardship and Agency Control Compete or Complement When Shaping Frontline Employee Behavior?" *Journal of Marketing*, Vol. 76, No. 6, pp. 1–20.

51   Michael K. Brady, Clay M. Voorhees, and Michael J. Brusco (2012), "Service Sweethearting: Its Antecedents and Customer Consequences," *Journal of Marketing*, Vol. 76, No. 2, pp. 81–98.

52   Dana Yagil (2002), "The Relationship of Customer Satisfaction and Service Workers' Perceived Control — Examination of Three Models," *International Journal of Service Industry Management*, Vol. 13, No. 4, pp. 382–398.

53   Graham L. Bradley and Beverley A. Sparks (2000), "Customer Reactions to Staff Empowerment: Mediators and Moderators," *Journal of Applied Social Psychology*, Vol. 33, Spring, pp. 32–39.

54   David E. Bowen, and Edward E. Lawler, III (1992), "The Empowerment of Service Workers: What, Why, How and When," *Sloan Management Review*, Vol. 33, Spring, pp. 32–39.

55   Benjamin Schneider and David E. Bowen, *Winning the Service Game* (Boston, MA: Harvard Business School Press, 1995), p. 250.

56   The system is described in: Serguei Netessine and Valery Yakubovich (2012), "The Darwinian Workplace," *Harvard Business Review*, Vol. 90, May, pp. 25–28. Karan Girotra and Serguei Netessine (2014), "Four Paths to Business Model Innovation: The Secret to Success Lies in Who Makes the Decisions When and Why," *Harvard Business Review*, Vol. 92. No. 7/8, pp. 96–103.

57   Jun Ye, Detelina Marionova, and Jagdip Singh (2012), "Bottom-Up Learning in Marketing Frontlines: Conceptualization, Processes, and Consequences," *Journal of the Academy of Marketing Science*, Vol. 40, No. 6, pp. 821–844.

58   Susan Cadwallader, Cheryl Burke Jarvis, Mary Jo Bitner, and Amy L. Ostrom (2010), "Frontline Employee Motivation to Participate in Service Innovation Implementation," *Journal of the Academy of Marketing Science*, Vol. 38, No. 2, pp. 219–239.

59   This paragraph is based on Kevin Freiberg and Jackie Freiberg, *Nuts! Southwest Airlines' Crazy Recipe for Business and Personal Success* (New York: Broadway Books, 1997), pp. 87–88.

60   Jon R. Katzenbach and Douglas K. Smith (1993), "The Discipline of Teams," *Harvard Business Review*, Vol. 71, March–April, p. 112.

61   Andrew Sergeant and Stephen Frenkel (2000), "When Do Customer Contact Employees Satisfy Customers?" *Journal of Service Research, Vol. 3*, No. 1, August, pp. 18–34.

62   Ad de Jong, Ko de Ruyter, and Jos Lemmink (2004), "Antecedents and Consequences of the Service Climate in Boundary-Spanning Self-Managing Service Teams," *Journal of Marketing*, Vol. 68, April, pp. 18–35.

63   For the effects and drivers of alignment between leaders and their service delivery teams see: Alexander Benlian (2014), "Are We Aligned…Enough? The Effects of Perceptual Congruence Between Service Teams and Their Leaders on Team Performance," *Journal of Service Research*, Vol. 17, No. 2, pp. 212–228.

64   Leonard L. Berry, *On Great Service — A Framework for Action*, p. 131.

65   Charles A. O'Reilly III and Jeffrey Pfeffer, *Hidden Value — How Great Companies Achieve Extraordinary Results with Ordinary People,* (Boston, MA: Harvard Business School Press, 2000), p. 9.

66   Leonard L. Berry, *Discovering the Soul of Service — The Nine Drivers of Sustainable Business Success*, p. 189.

67   Schneider and Bowen, *Winning the Service Game*, 141; Leonard L. Berry, *On Great Service — A Framework for Action*, p. 225.

68   Mike Osheroff (2007), "Teamwork in the Global Economy," *Strategic Finance*, Vol. 88, No.8, February, pp. 25, 61.

69   Robert J. Kwortnik Jr. and Gary M. Thompson (2009), "Unifying Service Marketing and Operations With Service Experience Management," *Journal of Service Research*, Vol. 11, No. 4, pp. 389–406.

70   Adapted from Kevin and Jackie Freiberg, *Nuts! Southwest Airlines' Crazy Recipe for Business and Personal Success* (New York: Broadway Books, 1997), pp. 165–168.

71   This section is based on Schneider and Bowen, *Winning the Service Game*, pp. 145–173.

72   Linda Nasr, Jamie Burton, Thorsten Gruber, and Jan Kitshoff (2014), "Exploring the Impact of Customer Feedback on the Well-Being of Service Entities: a TSR Perspective," *Journal of Service Management*, Vol. 25, No. 4, pp. 531–555; Regina-Viola Frey, Tomás Bayón, and Dirk Totzek (2013), "How Customer Satisfaction Affects Employee Satisfaction and Retention in a Professional Service Context," *Journal of Service Research*, Vol. 16, No. 4, pp. 503–517.

73   Adam M. Grant (2011), "How Customers Can Rally Your Troops," *Harvard Business Review*, June, pp. 96–103.

74   A good summary of goal setting and motivation at work can be found in Edwin A. Locke and Gary Latham, *A Theory of Goal Setting and Task Performance,* (Englewood Cliffs, NJ: Prentice Hall, 1990).

75   Charles A. O'Reilly III and Jeffrey Pfeffer, *Hidden Value — How Great Companies Achieve Extraordinary Results with Ordinary People,* (Boston, MA: Harvard Business School Press, 2000), p. 232.

76 Jeffrey Pfeffer, *Competitive Advantage Through People,* (Boston, MA: Harvard Business School Press, 1994), pp. 160–163.

77 Jody Hoffer Gittell, Andrew von Nordenflycht, and Thomas A. Kochan (2004), "Mutual Gains for Zero Sum? Labor Relations and Firm Performance in the Airline Industry," *Industrial and Labor Relations Review,* Vol. 57, No. 2, pp. 163–180.

78 This section is based, in part, on Benjamin Schneider and David E. Bowen, *Winning the Service Game.* Boston: Harvard Business School Press, 1995; David E. Bowen and Benjamin Schneider (2014), "A Service Climate Synthesis and Future Research Agenda," *Journal of Service Research,* Vol. 17, No. 1, pp. 5–22.

79 The authors of the following paper emphasize the role of alignment between tradition, culture and strategy that together form the basis for the firms HR practices: Benjamin Schneider, Seth C Hayes, Beng-Chong Lim, Jana L. Raver, Ellen G. Godfrey, Mina Huang, Lisa H. Nishii, and Jonathan C. Ziegert (2003), "The Human Side of Strategy: Employee Experiences of a Strategic Alignment in a Service Organization," *Organizational Dynamics,* Vol. 32, No. 2, pp. 122–141.

A study exploring the fit of company culture with the national context the firm operates in found that a good fit improves firm performance. For example, cultural values of stability, people orientation, and detail orientation and outcomes are significantly more important to Japanese retailers compared to their US counterparts. The study showed that a firm operating in countries with different cultural values show lower performance. See: Cynthia Webster and Allyn White (2010), "Exploring the National and Organizational Culture Mix in Service Firms," *Journal of the Academy of Marketing Science,* Vol. 38, No. 6, pp. 691–703.

80 Leonard L. Berry, *On Great Service — A Framework for Action* (New York: The Free Press, 1995), pp. 236-237; Leonard L. Berry and Kent D. Seltman, *Management Lessons from Mayo Clinic: Inside One of the World's Most Admired Service Organization* (McGraw Hill, 2008).

The following study emphasized the importance of the perceived ethical climate in driving service commitment of service employees: Charles H. Schwepker Jr. and Michael D. Hartline (2005), "Managing the Ethical Climate of Customer-Contact Service Employees," *Journal of Service Research,* Vol. 7, No. 4, pp. 377–397.

81 For an excellent review of the extant service climate literature and related constructs, see: David E. Bowen and Benjamin Schneider (2014), "A Service Climate Synthesis and Future Research Agenda", *Journal of Service Research,* Vol. 17, No. 1, pp. 5–22.

For a meta-analysis review that integrates service climate into the service profit chain with customer outcomes (satisfaction and loyalty) and the financial performance of the firm (sales and profit growth), see: Ying Hong, Hui Liao, Jia Hu, and Kaifeng Jiang (2013), "Missing link in the service profit chain: A meta-analytic review of the antecedents, consequences, and moderators of service climate," *Journal of Applied Psychology,* Vol. 98, No. 2, pp. 237-267.

82 For example, two recent studies linked service climate to service innovation and to customer loyalty, respectively. See: Ping-Jen Kao, Peiyu Pai, Tingling Lin, and Jun-Yu Zhong (2015), "How Transformational Leadership Fuels Employee' Service Innovation Behavior,",= The Service Industries Journal, Vol. 35, No. 7–8, pp. 448–466; Mei-Ling Wang (2015), "Linking Service Climate to Customer Loyalty," *The Service Industries Journal,* Vol. 35, No. 7–8, pp. 403–414.

83 Hans Kasper (2002), "Culture and Leadership in Market-oriented Service Organisations," *European Journal of Marketing,* Vol. 36, No. 9/10, pp. 1047–1057; Ronald A. Clark, Michael D. Hartline, and Keith C. Jones (2009), "The Effects of Leadership Style on Hotel Employees' Commitment to Service Quality," *Cornell Hospitality Quarterly,* Vol. 50, No. 2, pp. 209–231.

84 James L. Heskett, W. Earl Sasser, Jr., and Leonard A. Schlesinger, *The Service Profit Chain* (New York: Free Press, 1997), p. 236.

85 Leonard L. Berry, *Discovering the Soul of Service* (New York,: The Free Press, 1999), 44, 47. See also D. Micheal Abrashoff (2001), "Retention Through Redemption," *Harvard Business Review,* February, pp. 136–141, which provides a fascinating example on successful leadership in the US Navy.

86 Hamm, J. (2006). The five messages leaders must manage. *Harvard Business Review,* Vol. 84, May, pp. 115–123.

87 Blagg, D. and Young, S. (2001). What makes a leader? *Harvard Business School Bulletin,* February, pp. 31–36.

88 Rakesh Karma (2002), "The Curse of the Superstar CEO," *Harvard Business Review,* Vol. 80, September, pp. 60–66.

89 Jim Collins (2001), "Level 5 Leadership: The Triumph of Humility and Fierce Resolve," *Harvard Business Review,* Vol. 79, January, pp. 66–76.

90 Sandra Vandermerwe, *From Tin Soldiers to Russian Dolls.* Reprint edition (Oxford, UK: Butterworth-Heinemann, 1993), p. 129.

91 This section was adapted from: David E. Bowen and Benjamin Schneider (2014), "A Service Climate Synthesis and Future Research Agenda," *Journal of Service Research*, Vol. 17, No. 1, pp. 5–22. This article provides a detailed review of the research that underlies this section.

92 James L. Heskett, Thomas O. Jones, Gary W. Loveman, W. Earl Sasser, Jr., and Leonard A. Schlesinger (1994), "Putting the Service Profit Chain to Work," *Harvard Business Review,* Vol. 72, March–April, p. 164.

93 Thomas J. Peters and Robert H. Waterman, *In Search of Excellence* (New York: Harper & Row, 1982), p. 122.

94 Tony Simons (2002), "The High Cost of Lost Trust," *Harvard Business Review*, Vol. 80, September, pp. 2–3.

95 Rik Kirkland (2013), "Leading in the 21st Century: An Interview with Hertz CEO Mark Frissora," *McKinsey Quarterly*, November.

96 Catherine DeVrye, *Good Service Is Good Business*, (Upper Saddle River, NJ: Prentice Hall, 2000), p. 11.

97 Tony Hsieh, *Delivering Happiness: A Path to Profits, Passion and Purpose* (New York: Business Plus, 2010), p. 153.

PART 4

The Services Marketing Framework

Part I

Understanding Service Products, Consumers, and Markets

1. Creating Value in the Service Economy
2. Understanding Service Consumers
3. Positioning Services in Competitive Markets

Part II

Applying the 4 Ps of Marketing to Services

4. Developing Service Products and Brands
5. Distributing Services Through Physical and Electronic Channels
6. Service Pricing and Revenue Management
7. Service Marketing Communications

Part III

Managing the Customer Interface

8. Designing Service Processes
9. Balancing Demand and Capacity
10. Crafting the Service Environment
11. Managing People for Service Advantage

Part IV

Developing Customer Relationships

12. Managing Relationships and Building Loyalty
13. Complaint Handling and Service Recovery

Part V

Striving for Service Excellence

14. Improving Service Quality and Productivity
15. Building a World-Class Service Organization

Figure IV Organizing framework for services marketing

DEVELOPING CUSTOMER RELATIONSHIPS

Part IV focuses on developing customer relationships through building loyalty, effective complaint handling and service recovery for long-term profitability. It consists of the following two chapters:

CHAPTER 12

Managing Relationships and Building Loyalty

Chapter 12 focuses on achieving profitability through creating relationships with customers from the right segments, and then finding ways to build and reinforce their loyalty using the Wheel of Loyalty as an organizing framework. This chapter closes with a discussion of customer relationship management (CRM) systems.

CHAPTER 13

Complaint Handling and Service Recovery

Chapter 13 examines how effective complaint handling and professional service recovery can be implemented. It starts with a review of consumer complaining behavior and the principles of effective service recovery. Service guarantees are discussed as a powerful way of institutionalizing effective service recovery and as an effective marketing tool that signals high-quality service. The chapter also discusses how to deal with jaycustomers who take advantage of service recovery policies and abuse the service in other ways.

CHAPTER 12 Managing Relationships and Building Loyalty

The first step in managing a loyalty-based business system is finding and acquiring the right customers.

Frederick F. Reichheld,
Author, strategist, and fellow of Bain & Company

Strategy first, then CRM.

Steven S. Ramsey,
Former senior partner with Accenture,
current executive vice president with IRi

LEARNING OBJECTIVES (LOs)

By the end of this chapter, the reader should be able to:

◗ **LO 1** Recognize the important role customer loyalty plays in driving a service firm's profitability.

◗ **LO 2** Calculate the lifetime value (LTV) of a loyal customer.

◗ **LO 3** Understand why customers are loyal to a particular service firm.

◗ **LO 4** Know the core strategies of the Wheel of Loyalty that explain how to develop a loyal customer base.

◗ **LO 5** Appreciate why it is so important for service firms to target the "right" customers.

◗ **LO 6** Use service tiering to manage the customer base and build loyalty.

◗ **LO 7** Understand the relationship between customer satisfaction and loyalty.

◗ **LO 8** Know how to deepen the relationship through cross-selling and bundling.

◗ **LO 9** Understand the role of financial and non-financial loyalty rewards in enhancing customer loyalty.

◗ **LO 10** Appreciate the power of social, customization, and structural bonds in enhancing loyalty.

◗ **LO 11** Understand what factors cause customers to switch to a competitor, and how to reduce such switching.

◗ **LO 12** Know why loyalty programs and customer relationship management (CRM) systems are important enablers of delivering loyalty strategies.

◗ **LO 13** Understand the part played by CRM systems in delivering customized services and building loyalty.

OPENING VIGNETTE
Caesars Entertainment's Customer Relationship Management

Caesars Entertainment (formerly Harrah's Entertainment) is the world's largest gaming company with its number of key brands, including Caesars, Harrah's, Horseshoe, and the London Clubs family of casinos.[1] It is a leader in the use of highly sophisticated loyalty programs. Harrah's was first to launch a tiered customer loyalty program in the gaming industry, which covers all Caesars Entertainment's brands today. It has four tiers in its loyalty program — Gold, Platinum, Diamond, and Seven Stars (which is by invitation only). The program is integrated across nearly all its properties and services. Customers identify themselves (and earn points) at every touchpoint throughout the company, ranging from its gaming tables, restaurants, hotels, to gift shops and shows. The points collected can be used to obtain cash, merchandise, lodging, show tickets, vacations, and events.

What is special about Caesars Entertainment is not its loyalty program, but what it does with the information gathered about its customers when they use their cards to earn points. At the backend, the firm has linked all its databases from casino management, hotel reservations, and events to allow it to have a holistic view of each of its customers. It now has detailed data on over tens of millions of customers, and knows each customer's preferences and behaviors. These range from how much they spend on each type of game and their likes in food and drinks, to entertainment and lodging preferences. All tthis information about the customer is captured in real time.

Caesars Entertainment uses this data to drive its marketing and on-site customer service. For example, if a Diamond card holder on slot machine 278 signals for service, a Caesars associate is able to ask, "The usual, Mr. Jones?" and then track the time it takes for a server to fill the guest's request. In another example, when a customer wins a jackpot, Caesars can tailor a customer-specific reward to celebrate that win. Caesars also knows when a customer is approaching his maximum gaming limit on a particular evening and when the customer is likely to stop playing. Just before the limit is reached, Caesars can offer him a heavily discounted ticket in real time via text message for a show with available seats. This keeps the customer on the premises (and spending), and makes him feel valued as he gets a very special deal just when he wanted to stop playing. At the same time, it uses otherwise wasted capacity in its shows and restaurants.

Likewise, when a customer makes a call to its call center, the staff have detailed real-time information about a customer's preferences and spending habits, and can then tailor promotions that cross-sell or up-sell its services. Caesars does not do blanket promotions that target all its customers at the same time, which is, according to Caesars' Chairman, President, and CEO Gary Loveman, "a margin eroding nightmare". Rather, it uses highly targeted promotions that create the right incentives for each of its different customers. It also uses control groups to measure the success of a promotion in dollars and cents, and to further fine-tune its campaigns.

With its data-driven customer relationship management (CRM), Caesars is able to transform customer interactions into personal and differentiated ones. This enabled Harrah's, the first brand in the group to launch the Total Rewards Program, to increase the share-of-wallet of its Total Rewards card holders to an impressive 50%, up from 34% before its CRM program was implemented.

THE SEARCH FOR CUSTOMER LOYALTY

Targeting, acquiring, and retaining the "right" customers is at the core of many successful service firms. In Chapter 3, we discussed segmentation and positioning. In this chapter, we emphasize the importance of focusing on desirable, loyal customers within the chosen segments, and then taking the pains to build and maintain their loyalty through well-conceived relationship marketing strategies. The objective is to build relationships and to develop loyal customers who will contribute to a growing volume of business with the firm in future. *Figure 12.1* provides the organizing framework for this chapter.

Loyalty is an old-fashioned word that has traditionally been used to describe fidelity and enthusiastic devotion to a country, a cause, or an individual. Loyalty in a business context describes a customer's willingness to continue patronizing a firm over the long run, preferably on an exclusive basis, and recommending the firm's products to friends and associates. Customer loyalty extends beyond purchasing behavior, and includes preference, liking, and future intentions.

"Defector" was a nasty word during wartime. It describes disloyal people who sell out, betray their own side, and go over to the enemy. Even when they defected toward "our" side, rather than away from it, they are still suspect. In a marketing context, the term *defection* is used to describe customers who drop off a company's radar screen and transfer their purchases to another supplier. Not only does a rising defection rate indicate that something is wrong with quality (or that competitors offer better value), it may also be signaling a fall in profits. Big customers don't necessarily disappear overnight; they often may signal their mounting dissatisfaction by steadily reducing their purchases and shifting part of their business elsewhere.

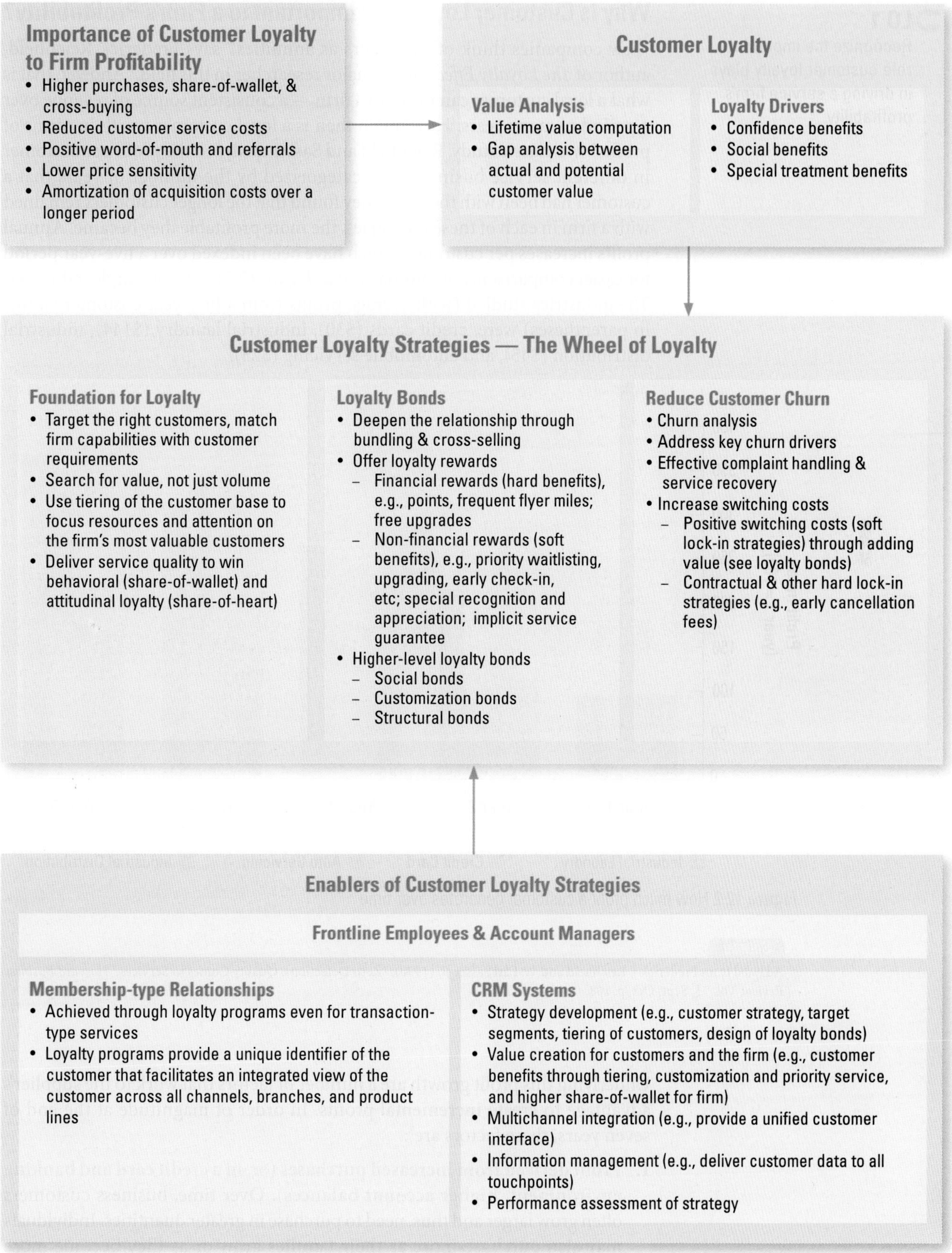

Importance of Customer Loyalty to Firm Profitability
- Higher purchases, share-of-wallet, & cross-buying
- Reduced customer service costs
- Positive word-of-mouth and referrals
- Lower price sensitivity
- Amortization of acquisition costs over a longer period

Customer Loyalty

Value Analysis
- Lifetime value computation
- Gap analysis between actual and potential customer value

Loyalty Drivers
- Confidence benefits
- Social benefits
- Special treatment benefits

Customer Loyalty Strategies — The Wheel of Loyalty

Foundation for Loyalty
- Target the right customers, match firm capabilities with customer requirements
- Search for value, not just volume
- Use tiering of the customer base to focus resources and attention on the firm's most valuable customers
- Deliver service quality to win behavioral (share-of-wallet) and attitudinal loyalty (share-of-heart)

Loyalty Bonds
- Deepen the relationship through bundling & cross-selling
- Offer loyalty rewards
  - Financial rewards (hard benefits), e.g., points, frequent flyer miles; free upgrades
  - Non-financial rewards (soft benefits), e.g., priority waitlisting, upgrading, early check-in, etc; special recognition and appreciation; implicit service guarantee
- Higher-level loyalty bonds
  - Social bonds
  - Customization bonds
  - Structural bonds

Reduce Customer Churn
- Churn analysis
- Address key churn drivers
- Effective complaint handling & service recovery
- Increase switching costs
  - Positive switching costs (soft lock-in strategies) through adding value (see loyalty bonds)
  - Contractual & other hard lock-in strategies (e.g., early cancellation fees)

Enablers of Customer Loyalty Strategies

Frontline Employees & Account Managers

Membership-type Relationships
- Achieved through loyalty programs even for transaction-type services
- Loyalty programs provide a unique identifier of the customer that facilitates an integrated view of the customer across all channels, branches, and product lines

CRM Systems
- Strategy development (e.g., customer strategy, target segments, tiering of customers, design of loyalty bonds)
- Value creation for customers and the firm (e.g., customer benefits through tiering, customization and priority service, and higher share-of-wallet for firm)
- Multichannel integration (e.g., provide a unified customer interface)
- Information management (e.g., deliver customer data to all touchpoints)
- Performance assessment of strategy

Figure 12.1 Organizing framework for managing relationships and building loyalty

⊃ **LO 1**

Recognize the important role customer loyalty plays in driving a service firm's profitability.

Why Is Customer Loyalty So Important to a Firm's Profitability?

"Few companies think of customers as annuities," says Frederick Reichheld, author of *The Loyalty Effect*, and a major researcher in this field.[2] And yet, that is what a loyal customer can mean to a firm — a consistent source of revenue over a period of many years. How much then is a loyal customer worth in terms of profits? In a classic study, Reichheld and Sasser analyzed the profit per customer in different service businesses, as categorized by the number of years that a customer had been with the firm. They found that the longer customers remained with a firm in each of these industries, the more profitable they became. Annual profits increases per customer, which have been indexed over a five-year period for easier comparison, are summarized in *Figure 12.2* for a few sample industries. The industries studied (with average profits from a first-year customer shown in parentheses) were: credit cards ($30), industrial laundry ($144), industrial distribution ($45), and automobile servicing ($25).

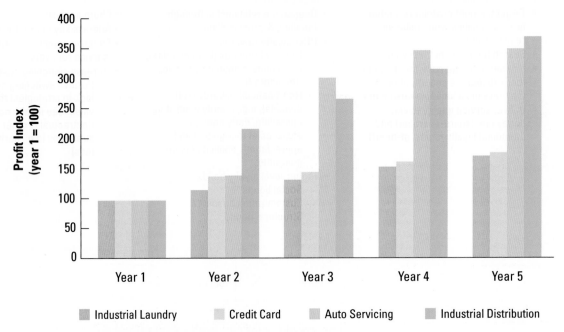

Figure 12.2 How much profit a customer generates over time

`Source`

Adapted from Frederick J. Reichheld and W. Earl Sasser Jr. (1990), "Zero Defections: Quality Comes to Services," *Harvard Business Review*, Vol. 73, Sept–Oct, p. 108.

Underlying this profit growth are a number of factors that work to the supplier's advantage to create incremental profits. In order of magnitude at the end of seven years, these factors are[3]:

1. **Profit derived from increased purchases (or, in a credit card and banking environment, higher account balances).** Over time, business customers often grow larger and thus, need to purchase in greater quantities. Individuals may also purchase more as their families grow or as they become more affluent. Both types of customers may be willing to consolidate their purchases with a single supplier who provides high-quality service, resulting in what we call a high share-of-wallet.

2. **Profit from reduced customer service costs.** As customers become more experienced, they make fewer demands on the supplier (for instance, they have less need for information and assistance, and make use of self-service options more). They may also make fewer mistakes when involved in operational processes, thus contributing to greater productivity.

3. **Profit from referrals to other customers.** Positive word-of-mouth recommendations are like free sales and advertising, saving the firm from having to invest as much money in these areas.

4. **Profit from lower price sensitivity that allow a price premium.** New customers often benefit from introductory promotional discounts, whereas long-term customers are more likely to pay regular prices, and when they are highly satisfied they tend to be less price sensitive.[4] Moreover, customers who trust a supplier may be more willing to pay higher prices at peak periods or for express work.

5. **Acquisition costs can be amortized over a longer period.** The upfront costs of attracting new buyers can be amortized over many years. These customer acquisition costs can be substantial and can include sales commissions, advertising and promotions costs, administrative costs of setting up an account, and sending out welcome packages and sign-up gifts.

Figure 12.3 shows the relative contribution of each of these different factors over a year period, based on an analysis of 19 different product categories (both goods and services). Reichheld argues that the economic benefits of customer loyalty noted above often explain why one firm is more profitable than a competitor. As a response, Reichheld and Sasser popularized the term **zero defections**, which they describe as keeping every customer the company can serve profitably.[5]

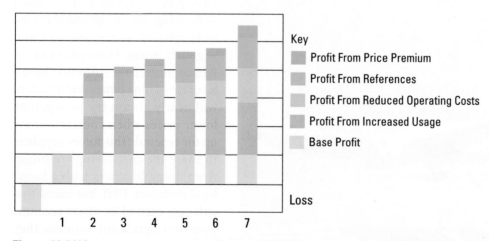

Figure 12.3 Why customers are more profitable over time

Source

Adapted from Frederick J. Reichheld and W. Earl Sasser Jr. (1990), "Zero Defections: Quality Comes to Services," *Harvard Business Review*, Vol. 73, September–October, p. 108.

Assessing the Value of a Loyal Customer

One of the challenges you are likely to face in your work is to determine the costs and revenues associated with serving customers to different market segments at different points in their customer lifecycles, and to predict future profitability. For insights on how to calculate customer value, see "Worksheet for Calculating Customer Lifetime Value".[6]

Recent studies have also shown that the profit impact of a customer may vary dramatically depending on the stage of the service product lifecycle. For instance, referrals by satisfied customers and negative word-of-mouth from "defected" customers have a much greater effect on profit in the early stages of the service product's lifecycle — when the name of the game is acquisition of new customers — than in later stages, where the focus is more on generating cash flow from the existing customer base.[7]

Finally, it's a mistake to assume that loyal customers are always more profitable than those who make one-time transactions.[8] On the cost side, not all types of services incur heavy promotional expenditures to attract a new customer. Sometimes, it is more important to invest in a good retail location that will attract walk-in traffic. Unlike banks, insurance companies, and other "membership" organizations that incur costs for review of applications and account setup, many service firms face no such costs when a new customer first seeks to make a purchase.

On the revenue side, loyal customers may not spend more than one-time buyers, and in some instances, they may even expect price discounts. Finally, profits do not necessarily increase with time for all types of customers.[9] In most mass market business-to-customer (B2C) services — such as banking, mobile phone services, or hospitality — customers cannot negotiate prices. However, in many B2B contexts, large customers have a lot of bargaining power and therefore will nearly always try to negotiate lower prices when contracts come up for renewal. This forces suppliers to share the cost savings resulting from doing business with a large, loyal customer. DHL has found that although each of its major accounts generates significant business, they yield below average margins. In contrast, DHL's smaller, less powerful accounts provide significantly higher profitability (*Figure 12.4*).[10]

Figure 12.4 DHL prices differently for different market segments

Worksheet for Calculating Customer Lifetime Value

Calculating customer value is an inexact science that is subject to a variety of assumptions. You may want to try varying these assumptions to see how it affects the final figures. Generally speaking, revenues per customer are easier to track on an individualized basis than are the associated costs of serving a customer, unless (1) no individual records are kept and/or (2) the accounts served are very large and all account-related costs are individually documented and assigned.

Acquisition Revenues Less Costs

If individual account records are kept, the initial application fee paid and initial purchase (if relevant) should be found in these records. Costs, by contrast, may have to be based on average data. For instance, the marketing cost of acquiring a new client can be calculated by dividing the total marketing costs (advertising, promotions, selling, etc.) devoted toward acquiring new customers by the total number of new customers acquired during the same period. If each acquisition takes place over an extended period of time, you may want to build in a lagged effect between when marketing expenditures are incurred and when new customers come on board. The cost of credit checks—where relevant—must be divided by the number of new customers, not the total number of applicants, because some applicants will probably fail this hurdle. Account set-up costs will also be an average figure in most organizations.

Annual Revenues and Costs

If annual sales, account fees, and service fees are documented on an individual-account basis, account revenue streams (except referrals) can be easily identified. The first priority is to segment your customer base by the length of its relationship with your firm. Depending on the sophistication and precision of your firm's records, annual costs in each category may be directly assigned to an individual account holder or averaged for all account holders in that age category.

Value of Referrals

Computing the value of referrals requires a variety of assumptions. To get started, you may need to conduct surveys to determine (1) what percentage of new customers claim that they were influenced by a recommendation from another customer and (2) what other marketing activities also drew the firm to that individual's attention. From these two items, estimates can be made of what percentage of the credit for all new customers should be assigned to referrals.

Net Present Value

Calculating net present value (NPV) from a future profit stream will require choice of an appropriate annual discount figure. (This could reflect estimates of future inflation rates.) It also requires assessment of how long the average relationship lasts. The NPV of a customer, then, is the sum of the anticipated annual profit on each customer for the projected relationship lifetime, suitably discounted each year into the future.

Acquisition		Year 1	Year 2	Year 3	Year n
Initial Revenue	*Annual Revenues*				
Application fee[a]	Annual account fee[a]				
Initial purchase[a]	Sales				
	Service fees[a]				
	Value of referrals[b]				
Total Revenues					
Initial Costs	*Annual Costs*				
Marketing	Account management				
Credit check[a]	Cost of sales				
Account setup[a]	Write-offs (e.g., bad debts)				
Less total costs					
Net Profit (Loss)					

[a] If applicable.
[b] Anticipated profits from each new customer referred (could be limited to the first year or expressed as the net present value of the estimated future stream of profits through year *n*); this value could be negative if an unhappy customer starts to spread negative word-of-mouth that causes existing customers to defect.

The Gap Between Actual and Potential Customer Value

For profit-seeking firms, the potential profitability of a customer should be a key driver in marketing strategy. As Alan Grant and Leonard Schlesinger said, "Achieving the full profit potential of each customer relationship should be the fundamental goal of every business... Even using conservative estimates, the gap between most companies' current and full potential performance is enormous."[11] They suggest an analysis of the following gaps between the actual and potential value of customers:

- What is the current purchasing behavior of customers in each target segment? What would be the impact on sales and profits if they exhibited the ideal behavior profile of (1) buying all services offered by the firm, (2) using these to the exclusion of any purchases from competitors, and (3) paying full price?

- On average, how long do customers remain with the firm? What impact would it have if they remained customers for life?

As we showed earlier, the profitability of a customer often increases over time. Management's task is to design and implement marketing programs that increase loyalty — including share-of-wallet, up-selling, and cross-selling — and identify the reasons why customers defect and then take corrective action. The active management of the customer base and customer loyalty is also referred to as **customer asset management**.[12]

⊃ **LO 3**

Understand why customers are loyal to a particular service firm.

Why Are Customers Loyal?

After understanding how important loyal customers can be for the bottom line of a service firm, let's explore what it is that makes a customer loyal. Customers are not automatically loyal to any one firm. Rather, we need to give our customers a reason to consolidate their buying with us and then stay with us. We need to create value for them to become and remain loyal.

Relationships can create value for individual consumers through factors such as inspiring greater confidence, offering social benefits, and providing special treatment (*Service Insights 12.1*). We will next discuss how we can systematically think about creating value propositions for our customers to become loyal using the Wheel of Loyalty.

SERVICE INSIGHTS 12.1
How Customers See Relational Benefits in Service Industries

What benefits do customers see themselves receiving from an extended relationship with a service firm? Researchers seeking answers to this question conducted two studies. The first consisted of in-depth interviews with 21 respondents from a broad cross-section of backgrounds. Respondents were asked to identify service providers that they used on a regular basis, and then were invited to identify and discuss any benefits they received as a result of being a regular customer. Among the comments were:

- "I like him [hair stylist]… He's really funny and always has lots of good jokes. He's kind of like a friend now."

- "I know what I'm getting — I know that if I go to a restaurant that I regularly go to, rather than taking a chance on all of the new restaurants, the food will be good."

- "I often get price breaks. The little bakery that I go to in the morning, every once in a while, they'll give me a free muffin and say, 'You're a good customer, it's on us today.'"

- "You can get better service than drop-in customers… We continue to go to the same automobile repair shop because we have gotten to know the owner on a kind of personal basis, and he…can always work us in."

- "Once people feel comfortable, they don't want to switch to another dentist. They don't want to train or break a new dentist in."

After evaluating and grouping the comments, the researchers designed a second study in which they collected 299 survey questionnaires. The respondents were told to select a specific service provider with whom they had a strong, established relationship. Then they were asked to assess the extent to which they received each of the 21 benefits (derived from an analysis of the first study) as a result of their relationship with the specific provider they had identified. Finally, they were asked to assess the importance of these benefits for them. A factor analysis of the results showed that most of the benefits that customers derived from relationships could be grouped into three categories. The first and most important group involved what the researchers labeled confidence benefits, followed by social benefits, and lastly, special treatment.

- **Confidence benefits** included feelings by customers that in an established relationship, there was less risk of something going wrong, greater confidence in correct performance, and the ability to trust the provider. Customers experienced lowered anxiety when purchasing because they knew what to expect, and they typically received the firm's highest level of service.

- **Social benefits** embraced mutual recognition between customers and employees, being known by name, having a friendship with the service provider, and enjoyment of certain social aspects of the relationship.

- **Special treatment benefits** included better prices, discounts on special deals that were unavailable to most customers, extra services, higher priority when there was a wait, and faster service than most customers.

Source

Kevin P. Gwinner, Dwayne D. Gremler, and Mary Jo Bitner (1998), "Relational Benefits in Services Industries: The Customer's Perspective," *Journal of the Academy of Marketing Science,* Vol. 26, No. 2, pp. 101–114.

⊃ LO 4

Know the core strategies of the Wheel of Loyalty that explain how to develop a loyal customer base.

THE WHEEL OF LOYALTY

Building customer loyalty is difficult. Just try and think of all the service firms you are loyal to. Most people cannot think of more than perhaps a handful of firms they truly like (i.e., give a high share-of-heart) and to whom they are committed to going back (i.e., give a high share-of-wallet). This shows that although firms put enormous amounts of money and effort into loyalty initiatives, they often are not successful in building true customer loyalty. We use the Wheel of Loyalty shown in *Figure 12.5* as an organizing framework to discuss how to build customer loyalty as discussed in the following sections.

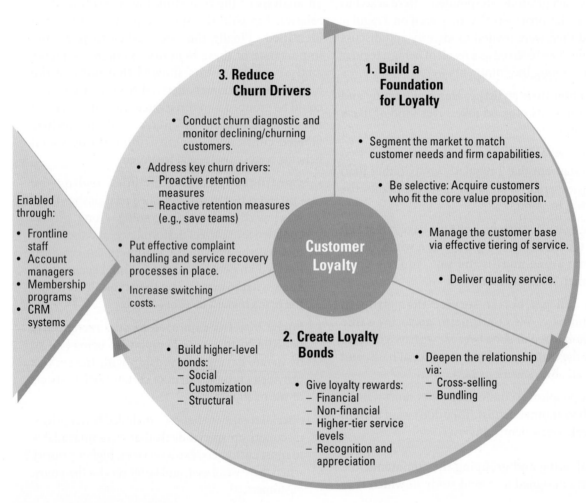

Figure 12.5 The Wheel of Loyalty

BUILDING A FOUNDATION FOR LOYALTY

Many elements are involved in creating long-term customer relationships and loyalty. In Chapter 3, we discussed segmentation and positioning. In this section, we emphasize the importance of focusing on serving several desirable customer segments, and then taking the pains to build and maintain their loyalty through carefully thought-out relationship marketing strategies.

Target the Right Customers

Loyalty management starts with segmenting the market to match customer needs and firm capabilities. "Who should we be serving?" is a question that every service business needs to raise periodically. Not all customers offer a good fit with the organization's capabilities, delivery technologies, and strategic direction. Companies need to be selective about the segments they target if they want to build successful customer relationships. Managers must think carefully about how customer needs relate to operational elements such as speed and quality, and the physical features and appearance of service facilities. They also need to consider how well their service personnel can meet the expectations of specific types of customers, in terms of both personal style and technical competence.[13]

Leaders are picky about acquiring only the right customers, which are those for whom their firms have been designed to deliver truly special value. Acquiring the right customers often brings long-term revenues and continued growth from referrals. It can also enhance employees' satisfaction, whose daily jobs are improved when they can deal with appreciative customers. Attracting the wrong customers typically results in costly churn, a diminished company reputation, and disillusioned employees.

The result of carefully targeting customers by matching the company capabilities and strengths with customer needs should be a superior service offering in the eyes of those customers who value what the firm has to offer. As Frederick Reichheld said, "The result should be a win–win situation, where profits are earned through the success and satisfaction of customers, and not at their expense."[14] Building customer loyalty starts with identifying and targeting the right customers.

⊃ LO 5
Appreciate why it is so important for service firms to target the "right" customers.

Search for Value, Not Just Volume

Too many service firms continue to focus on the **number** of customers they serve without giving sufficient attention to the **value** of each customer.[15] For example, Starwood Hotels & Resorts found that their top 2% of guests generated a whopping 30% of its profits![16] Generally speaking, heavy users who buy more frequently and in larger volumes are more profitable than occasional users. Roger Hallowell makes this point nicely in a banking context:

> *A bank's population of customers undoubtedly contains individuals who either cannot be satisfied, given the service levels and pricing the bank is capable of offering, or will never be profitable, given their banking activity (their use of resources relative to the revenue they supply). Any bank would be wise to target and serve only those customers whose needs it can meet better than its competitors in a profitable manner. These are the customers who are most likely to remain with that bank for long periods, who will purchase multiple products and services, who will recommend that bank to their friends and relations, and who may be the source of superior returns to the bank's shareholders.*[17]

Ironically, it is often the firms that are highly focused and selective in their customer acquisition — rather than those that focus on unbridled acquisition — that are growing fast over long periods. *Service Insights 12.2* shows how the Vanguard Group, a leader in the mutual funds industry, designed its products and pricing to attract and retain the right customers for its business model.

Also, relationship customers are by definition not buying commodity services. Service customers who buy strictly based on lowest price (a minority in most markets) are not good target customers for relationship marketing in the first place. They are deal-prone, continuously seeking the lowest price on offer, and switch brands easily.

SERVICE INSIGHTS 12.2

Vanguard Discourages the Acquisition of "Wrong" Customers

© The Vanguard Group, Inc., used with permission.

The Vanguard Group is a growth leader in the mutual fund industry that built its $3 trillion in managed assets by 2015 by painstakingly targeting the right customers for its business model.[18] Its share of new sales, which was around 25%, reflected its share of assets or market share. However, it had a far lower share of redemptions (customer defections in the fund context), which gave it a market share of net cash flows of 55% (new sales minus redemptions), and this made it the fastest growing mutual fund in its industry.

How did Vanguard achieve such low redemption rates? The secret was in its careful acquisition, and its product and pricing strategies, which encouraged the acquisition of the "right" customers.

John Bogle, Vanguard's founder, believed in the superiority of index funds and that their lower management fees would lead to higher returns over the long run. He offered Vanguard's clients unparalleled low management fees through a policy of not trading (its index funds hold the market they are designed to track), not having a sales force, and only spending a fraction of what its competitors did on advertising. Another important part of keeping its costs low was its aim to discourage the acquisition of customers who were not long-term index holders.

Bogle attributes the high customer loyalty Vanguard has achieved to a great deal of focus on customer redemptions. "I watched them like a hawk," he explained, and he analyzed them more carefully than new sales to ensure that Vanguard's customer acquisition strategy was on course. Low redemption rates meant that the firm was attracting the right kind of loyal, long-term investors. The inherent stability of its loyal customer base has been key to Vanguard's cost advantage. Bogle's pickiness became legendary. He scrutinized individual redemptions with a fine-tooth comb to see who let the wrong kind of customers on board. When an institutional investor redeemed $25 million from an index fund bought only nine months earlier, he regarded the acquisition of this customer as a failure of the system. He explained, "We don't want short-term investors. They muck up the game at the expense of the long-term investor." At the end of his chairman's letter to the Vanguard Index Trust, Bogle repeated, "We urge them [short-term investors] to look elsewhere for their investment opportunities."

This care and attention to acquiring the right customers is famous. For example, Vanguard once turned away an institutional investor who wanted to invest $40 million because the firm suspected that the customer would churn the investment within the next few weeks, creating extra costs for existing customers. The potential customer complained to Vanguard's CEO, who in turn not only supported the decision, but also used it as an opportunity to reinforce to his teams why they needed to be selective about the customers they accept.

Furthermore, Vanguard introduced a number of changes to industry practices that discouraged active traders from buying its funds. For example, Vanguard did not allow telephone transfers for index funds, redemption fees were added to some funds, and the standard practice of subsidizing new accounts at the expense of existing customers was rejected because the practice was considered as disloyal to its core investor base. These product and pricing policies in effect turned away heavy traders, but made the fund extremely attractive for long-term investors.

Finally, Vanguard's pricing was set up to reward loyal customers. For many of its funds, investors pay a one-time fee upfront, which goes into the funds themselves (and not to Vanguard) to make up to all current investors for the administrative costs of selling new units. In essence, this fee subsidizes long-term investors, and penalizes short-term investors. Another novel pricing approach was the creation of its Admiral shares for loyal investors, which carried a lower expense fee than ordinary shares (0.15% instead of 0.18% per year).

Source

Adapted from Frederick F. Reichheld, *Loyalty Rules! How Today's Leaders Build Lasting Relationships* (Boston: MA, Harvard Business School Press, 2001), 24–29, 84–87, 144–145; www.vanguard.com, accessed March 12, 2012.

Different segments offer different value for a service firm. Like investments, some types of customers may be more profitable than others in the short term, but others may have greater potential for long-term growth. Similarly, the spending patterns of some customers may be stable over time, while others may be more cyclical, for example, spending heavily in boom times but cutting back sharply in recessions. A wise marketer seeks a mix of segments in order to reduce the risks associated with volatility in demand.[19]

In many cases, David Maister emphasizes, marketing is about getting *better* business, not just *more* business.[20] For instance, the caliber of a professional firm is measured by the type of clients it serves and the nature of the tasks on which it works. Volume alone is no measure of excellence, sustainability, or profitability. In professional services such as consulting firms or legal partnerships, the mix of business attracted may play an important role in both defining the firm and providing a suitable mix of assignments for staff members at different levels in the organization.

Finally, managers shouldn't assume that the "right customers" are always big spenders. Depending on the service business model, the right customers may come from a large group of people that no other supplier is doing a good job of serving. Many firms have built successful strategies on serving customer segments that had been neglected by established players, which didn't see them as being "valuable" enough. Examples include Enterprise Rent-A-Car, which targets customers who need a temporary replacement car. It avoided the more traditional segment of business travelers targeted by its principal competitors. Similarly, Charles Schwab focused on retail stock buyers, and Paychex provides small businesses with payroll and human resource services.[21]

⊃ **LO 6**
Use service tiering to manage the customer base and build loyalty.

Manage the Customer Base Through Effective Tiering of Service

Marketers should adopt a strategic approach to retaining, upgrading, and even ending relationships with customers. Customer retention involves developing long-term, cost-effective links with customers for the mutual benefit of both parties, but these efforts need not necessarily target all the customers of a firm with the same level of intensity. Research has confirmed that customer profitability and return on sales can be increased by focusing a firm's resources on top-tier customers.[22] Furthermore, different customer tiers often have quite different service expectations and needs. According to Valarie Zeithaml, Roland Rust, and Katharine Lemon, it's critical for service firms to understand the needs of customers within different profitability tiers and adjust their service levels accordingly.[23]

Just as service product categories can be tiered to reflect the level of value included (e.g., first, business, and economy class in air travel; see Chapter 4, p. 142), so can groups of customers. In the latter instance, service tiers can be developed around the levels of profit contribution of different groups of customers and their needs (including sensitivities to variables such as price, comfort, and speed), and identifiable personal profiles such as demographics. Zeithaml, Rust, and Lemon illustrate this principle through a four-level pyramid (*Figure 12.6*).

- **Platinum.** These customers form a very small percentage of a firm's customer base, but are heavy users and tend to contribute a large share of the profits. This segment is usually less price sensitive, but expects higher service levels in return, and it is likely to be willing to invest in and try new services.

- **Gold.** The gold tier includes a larger percentage of customers than the platinum, but individual customers contribute less profit than platinum customers. They tend to be slightly more price sensitive and less committed to the firm.

- **Iron.** These customers provide the bulk of the customer base. Their numbers give the firm economies of scale. Hence, they are important so that a firm can build and maintain a certain capacity level and infrastructure, which is often needed for serving gold and platinum customers well. However, iron customers on their own may only be marginally profitable. Their level of business is not enough to justify special treatment.

- **Lead.** Customers in this tier tend to generate low revenues for a firm, but often still require the same level of service as iron customers, which turns them into a loss-making segment from a firm's perspective.

The precise characteristics of customer tiers vary, of course, from one type of business to another, and even from one firm to another. *Service Insights 12.3* provides an illustration from the marketing research industry.

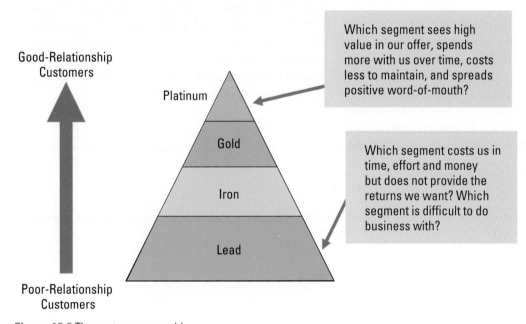

Figure 12.6 The customer pyramid

Source

Adapted from Valerie A. Zeithaml, Roland T. Rust, and Katherine N. Lemon (2001), "The Customer Pyramid: Creating and Serving Profitable Customers," *California Management Review*, Vol. 43, No. 4, Summer, Figure 1, pp. 118–142.

SERVICE INSIGHTS 12.3

Tiering the Customers of a Market Research Agency

Tiering its clients helped a leading US market research agency understand its customers better. The agency defined **platinum clients** as large accounts that were not only willing to plan a certain amount of research work during the year, but were also able to commit to the timing, scope, and nature of their projects, which made capacity management and project planning much easier for the research firm. The acquisition costs for projects sold to these clients were only 2%–5% of project values (as compared to as much as 25% for clients who required extensive proposal work and project-by-project bidding). Platinum accounts were also more willing to try new services, and buy a wider range of services from their preferred provider. These customers were generally very satisfied with the research agency's work and were willing to act as references for potential new clients.

Gold accounts had a similar profile to platinum clients, except that they were more price sensitive, and were more inclined to spread their budgets across several firms. Although these accounts had been clients for many years, they were not willing to commit their research work for a year in advance even though the research firm would have been able to offer them better quality and priority in capacity allocation.

Iron accounts spent moderate amounts on research, and commissioned work on a project basis. Selling costs were high, as these firms tended to send out requests-for-proposals (RFPs) to a number of firms for all their projects. They sought the lowest price, and often did not allow for sufficient time for the research firm to perform a good quality job.

Lead accounts sought only isolated, low-cost projects that tended be "quick and dirty" in nature, with little opportunity for the research firm to add value or to apply its skill sets appropriately. Sales costs were high as the client typically invited several firms to quote. Furthermore, as these firms were inexperienced in conducting research and in working with research agencies, selling a project often took several meetings and required multiple revisions to the proposal. Lead accounts also tended to be high maintenance because they did not understand research work well; they often changed project parameters, scope, and deliverables midstream and then expected the research agency to absorb the cost of any rework, thus further reducing the profitability of the engagement.

Source

Adapted Valarie A Zeithaml, Roland T Rust, and Katharine N Lemon (2001), "The Customer Pyramid: Creating and serving profitable customers," *California Management Review; Berkeley*, Vol. 43, No. 4, Summer, pp. 127–128.

Customer tiers are typically based on profitability and their service needs. Rather than providing the same level of service to all customers, each segment receives a service level that is customized based on its requirements and value to the firm. For example, the platinum tier is provided some exclusive benefits that are not available to other segments. The benefit features for platinum and gold customers should be designed to encourage them to remain loyal because these customers are the very ones competitors would like to steal most.

Marketing efforts can be used to encourage an increased volume of purchases, upgrading the type of service used, or cross-selling additional services to any of the four tiers. However, these efforts have different thrusts for the different tiers, as their needs, usage behaviors, and spending patterns are usually very different. Among the segments for which the firm already has a high share-of-wallet, the focus should be on nurturing, defending, and retaining these customers, possibly by use of loyalty programs.[24]

In contrast, among lead tier customers at the bottom of the pyramid, the options are to either to move them to the iron segment (e.g., through increasing sales, increasing prices, and/or cutting servicing costs) or to end the relationship with them. Migration can be achieved through a combination of strategies, including up-selling, cross-selling, and setting base fees and price increases. For example, imposing a minimum fee that is waived when a certain level of revenue is generated may encourage customers who use several suppliers to consolidate their buying with a single firm instead. Another way to move customers from the lead tier to the iron tier is to encourage them to use low-cost service delivery channels. For instance, lead tier customers may be charged a fee for face-to-face interactions but the fee is waived when such customers use electronic channels. In the cellular telephone industry, for example, low-use mobile users can be encouraged to use prepaid packages that do not require the firm to send out bills and collect payment, which also eliminates the risk of bad debts on such accounts.

Divesting or terminating customers comes as a logical consequence of the realization that not all existing customer relationships are worth keeping.[25] Some relationships may no longer be profitable for the firm because they cost more to maintain than the contributions they generate. Some customers no longer fit the firm's strategy, either because that strategy has changed or because the customers' behavior and needs have changed.

Figure 12.7 Many banks are increasingly pushing their customers toward online transactions

Occasionally customers are "fired" outright (although the concern for due process is still important). Capital One 360 is the fast-food model of consumer banking — it is about as no-frills as it gets. It only has a handful of basic products, and it lures low-maintenance customers with no minimum balance nor fees and slightly higher interest rates for its savings accounts and lower interests on its home loans. To offset that generosity, its business model pushes its customers toward online transactions (*Figure 12.7*), and the bank routinely fires customers who don't fit its business model. When a customer calls too often (the average customer phone call costs the bank $5.25 to handle), or wants too many exceptions to the rule, the bank's sales associates will say, "Look, this doesn't fit you. You need to go back to your community bank and get the kind of contact you're comfortable with." As a result, its cost per account are much lower than industry average.[26]

Other examples where customers get fired include students who are caught cheating in examinations, or country club members who consistently abuse the facilities or other people. In some instances, termination may be less confrontational. Banks wishing to divest themselves of certain types of accounts that no longer fit their corporate priorities have been known to sell them to other banks (one example is credit card holders who receive a letter in the mail telling them that their account has been transferred to another card issuer).

Just as investors need to dispose of poor investments and banks may have to write off bad loans, each service firm needs to examine its customer portfolio regularly and consider ending unsuccessful relationships. Of course, legal and ethical considerations will determine how to take such actions. For example, a bank may introduce a minimum monthly fee for accounts with a low balance (e.g., below $1,000), but for social responsibility considerations, waive this fee for customers on social security.

Customer Satisfaction and Service Quality Are Prerequisites for Loyalty

⊃ **LO 7**
Use service tiering to manage the customer base and build loyalty.

The foundation for building true loyalty lies in customer satisfaction. Highly satisfied or even delighted customers are more likely to consolidate their buying with one supplier, spread positive word-of-mouth, and become loyal apostles of a firm.[27] In contrast, dissatisfaction drives customers away and is a key factor in switching behavior.

The satisfaction–loyalty relationship can be divided into three main zones: defection, indifference, and affection (*Figure 12.8*). The **zone of defection** occurs at low satisfaction levels. Customers will switch if switching costs are high or there are no viable or convenient alternatives. Extremely dissatisfied customers can turn into "terrorists" providing an abundance of negative word-of-mouth for the service provider.[28] The **zone of indifference** is found at moderate satisfaction levels. Here, customers are willing to switch if they find a better alternative. Finally, the **zone of affection** is located at very high satisfaction levels, where customers have such high attitudinal loyalty that they do not look for alternative service providers. Customers who praise the firm in public and refer others to the firm are described as "apostles".

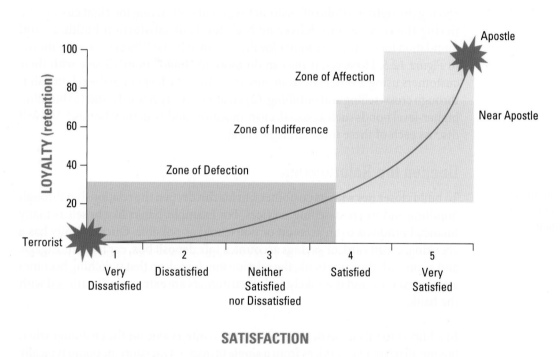

Figure 12.8 The customer satisfaction–loyalty relationship

Source

Adapted from Thomas O. Jones and W. Earl Sasser, Jr. (1995), "Why Satisfied Customers Defect," *Harvard Business Review*, November–December, p. 91.

True loyalty is often defined as combining both behavioral and attitudinal loyalty, also referred to as **share-of-wallet** and **share-of-heart**. Behavioral loyalty includes behaviors such as buying again, a high share-of-wallet, providing positive word-of-mouth, and attitudinal loyalty refers to a true liking and emotional attachment of the firm, service, and brand.

It is important to note though that satisfaction can be seen as a necessary but not sufficient driver of true customer loyalty. Satisfaction alone does not explain a large amount of variance in loyalty behaviors, and has to be seen in combination with other factors such as switching costs and customer knowledge (e.g., knowledgeable customers feel more confident in switching and have lower risk perceptions),[29] how the firm compares to competitors (e.g., if a firm is seen as offering the best value proposition compared to that of the next best alternative provider,[30] switching makes little sense and customers keep buying), and the loyalty bonds as discussed in the next section.

STRATEGIES FOR DEVELOPING LOYALTY BONDS WITH CUSTOMERS

Having the right portfolio of customer segments, attracting the right customers, tiering the service, and delivering high levels of satisfaction builds a solid foundation for creating customer loyalty as shown in the Wheel of Loyalty shown in *Figure 12.5*. However, firms can do more to "bond" more closely with their customers using a variety of strategies, including (1) deepening the relationship through cross-selling and bundling, (2) creating loyalty rewards, and (3) building higher-level bonds such as social, customization, and structural bonds.[31] We will discuss each of these three strategies next.

Deepen the Relationship

⟲ **LO 8**
Know how to deepen the relationship through cross-selling and bundling.

To build closer ties with its customers, firms can deepen the relationship through bundling and/or cross-selling services. For example, banks like to sell as many financial products to an account or household as possible. Once a family has a checking, credit card, or savings account, a safe deposit box, car loan, mortgage, and so on with the same bank, the relationship is so deep that switching becomes a major exercise and is unlikely, unless customers are extremely dissatisfied with the bank.

In addition to raising switching costs, there is often value for the customer when buying all particular services from a single provider. One-stop shopping typically is more convenient than buying individual services from different providers. When having many services with the same firm, the customer may achieve a higher service tier and receive better services, and sometimes service bundles do come with price discounts.

Encourage Loyalty Through Financial and Nonfinancial Rewards

⊃ **LO 9**
Understand the role of financial and nonfinancial loyalty rewards in enhancing customer loyalty.

Few customers buy only from only one supplier. This is especially true in situations where service delivery involves separate transactions (such as a car rental) instead of being continuous in nature (as with insurance coverage). In many instances, consumers are loyal to several brands (sometimes described as "polygamous loyalty") but avoid others. In such instances, the marketing goal is to strengthen the customer's preference for one brand over others and to gain a greater share of the customer's spending in that service category. Once acquired, it tends to be the reward-based bonds (often offered through a loyalty program) that entice customers to spend more money and increase a firm's share-of-wallet.[32] Incentives that offer rewards based on the frequency of purchase, value of purchase, or a combination of both, represent a basic level of customer bonding. These rewards can be **financial** and **non-financial** in nature.

Financial Rewards. Financial rewards are customer incentives that have a financial value (also called "hard benefits"). These include discounts on purchases, loyalty program rewards such as frequent flier miles (*Figure 12.9*), and the cash-back programs provided by some credit card issuers.

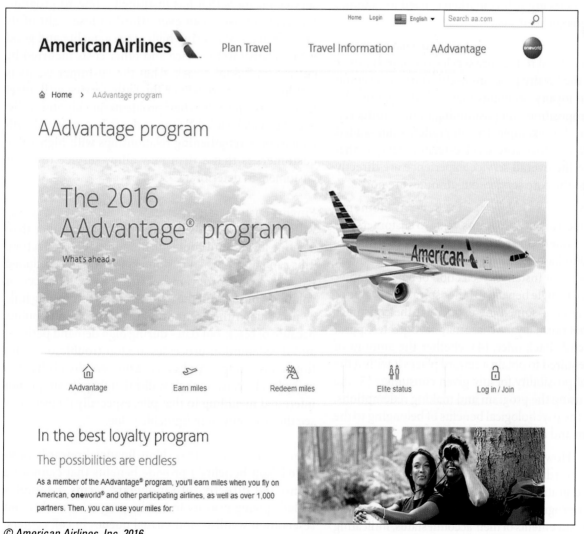

© American Airlines, Inc. 2016

Figure 12.9 American Airlines uses its AAdvantage program to promote customer loyalty

Besides airlines and hotels, an increasing number of service firms ranging from retailers (such as department stores, supermarkets[33], book shops, and gas stations), telecommunications providers, café chains, to courier services and cinema chains have launched similar reward programs in response to the increasing competitiveness of their markets. Although some provide their own rewards — such as free merchandise, vehicle upgrades, or free hotel rooms at vacation resorts — many firms denominate their awards in miles that can be credited to a selected frequent flyer program. In fact, air miles have become a form of promotional currency in the service sector.[34]

Research in the credit card industry suggests that financial rewards–based loyalty programs strengthen the customers' perception of the value proposition, and lead to increased revenues due to higher usage levels and fewer defections.[35] To assess the potential of a loyalty program to alter normal patterns of behavior, Grahame Dowling and Mark Uncles argue that marketers need to examine three psychological effects:[36]

- **Brand loyalty versus deal loyalty.** To what extent are customers loyal to the core service (or brand) rather than to the loyalty program itself? Marketers should focus on loyalty programs that directly support the value proposition and positioning of the product in question. For example, free upgrades, value-added services, or other core service-related benefits that enhance the overall service experience are directly linked to the core service, but air miles are not.

- **How buyers value rewards.** Several elements determine a loyalty program's value to customers: (1) the cash value of the redemption rewards (if customers had to purchase them); (2) the range of choice among rewards — for instance, a selection of benefits rather than just a single benefit; (3) the aspirational value of the rewards — something exotic that the consumer would not normally purchase may have greater appeal than a cash-back offer; (4) whether the amount of usage required to obtain a reward places it within the realm of possibility for any given consumer; (5) the ease of using the program and making redemptions; and (6) the psychological benefits of belonging to the program and accumulating points.

- **Timing.** How soon can benefits from participating in the rewards program be obtained by customers? Deferred gratification tends to weaken the appeal of a loyalty program. One solution is to send customers periodic statements of their account status, indicating progress toward reaching a particular milestone and promoting the rewards that might be forthcoming when that point is reached.

Interestingly, if a firm has loyalty program partners, (e.g., an airline may partner credit card companies, hotels, car rental firms, where loyalty program points can also be earned with these companies), satisfaction with the core service can have a positive impact on buying from program partners. In the same way, satisfaction with the service of program partners can have a positive impact on the buying of the core service.[37] It is therefore important for firms to be selective in choosing loyalty program partners.

Of course, even well-designed reward programs by themselves are not enough to keep a firm's most desirable customers. If you are dissatisfied with the quality of service, or believe that you can get better value from another provider, you may quickly become disloyal. No service business that has instituted a reward program for frequent users can ever afford to lose sight of its broader goals of offering high service quality and good value relative to the price and other costs incurred by customers.[38] Sometimes, what the customer wants is just for the firm to deliver the basic service well, meet their needs, and solve their problems quickly and easily, and they will be loyal.[39] One of the risks associated with a focus on strengthening relationships with high-value customers is that a firm may allow service to other customers to deteriorate.

Finally, customers can even get frustrated especially with financial rewards–based programs, so rather than creating loyalty and goodwill, they breed dissatisfaction! This can happen when customers feel they are excluded from a reward program because of low balances or volume of business, if the rewards are seen as having little or no value, if they cannot redeem their loyalty points because of black-out dates during high demand periods, and if redemption processes are too troublesome and time-consuming.[40] And some customers already have so many loyalty cards in their wallet that they are simply not interested in adding to that pile, especially if customers see them as only of marginable value.

Non-financial Rewards. Non-financial rewards (also called "soft benefits") provide benefits that cannot be translated directly into monetary terms. Examples include giving priority to loyalty program members on reservation waitlists and virtual queues in call centers.

Some airlines provide benefits such as higher baggage allowances, priority upgrading, access to airport lounges, and the like, to its frequent flyers even when they are only flying in economy class.

Important intangible rewards include special recognition and appreciation. Customers tend to value the extra attention given to their needs and appreciate the efforts to meet their occasional special requests. High-tier loyalty program members also tend to enjoy an implicit service guarantee. That is, when things go wrong, frontline employees will pay extra attention to their most valuable customers and see that the service is recovered to their satisfaction.

Many loyalty programs also provide important status benefits to customers in the top-tiers who feel part of an elite group (e.g., the Seven Stars card holders with Caesars in our opening vignette) and enjoy their special treatment.[41] Tiered loyalty programs in particular can provide powerful incentives and motivation for customers to achieve the next higher level of membership, which often leads to a higher share-of-wallet for the preferred provider.

Non-financial rewards, especially if linked to higher-tier service levels, are typically more powerful than financial ones as the former can create tremendous value for customers. Unlike financial rewards, non-financial rewards directly relate to the firm's core service and improve the customers' experience and value perception. In the hotel context for example, redeeming loyalty points for free gifts does nothing to enhance the guest experience. However, getting priority for reservations, early check-in, late check-out, upgrades, and receiving special attention and appreciation will make your stay more pleasant, leave you with the fuzzy warm feeling that this firm appreciates your business, and makes you want to come back.[42]

Service Insights 12.4 describes how British Airways has designed its Executive Club, effectively combining financial and non-financial loyalty rewards.

Small businesses often don't run formal loyalty programs but can still employ effective bonds. For example, they can use informal loyalty rewards that may take the form of periodically giving regular customers a small treat as a way of thanking them, reserving their favorite table in a restaurant context, paying them special attention, and the like.

Unlike some frequent flyer programs, in which customer usage is measured simply in miles, Executive Club members of British Airways (BA) receive both **air miles** toward redemption of air travel rewards and **points** toward silver or gold tier status for travel on BA. With the creation of the OneWorld alliance with American Airlines, Qantas, Cathay Pacific, and other airlines, Executive Club members have been able to earn miles (and sometimes points) by flying these partner airlines, too.

As shown in *Table 12.1*, silver and gold cardholders are entitled to special benefits such as priority reservations and a superior level of on-the-ground service. For instance, even if a gold cardholder is only traveling in economy class, he or she will be entitled to first-class standards of treatment at check-in, in the airport lounges and boarding. Miles will not expire as long as the frequent flyer account has at least one transaction in every 36 months (after which they expire), but tier status is valid for only 12 months beyond the membership year in which it was earned. This means that the right to special privileges must be re-earned each year. The objective of awarding tier status is to encourage passengers who have a choice of airlines to concentrate their travel on BA, rather than to join several frequent flyer programs and collect mileage awards from all of them. Few passengers travel with such frequency that they will be able to obtain the benefits of gold tier status (or its equivalent) on more than one airline.

Points given also vary according to the class of service. Longer trips earn more points than shorter ones. However, tickets at deeply discounted prices may earn fewer miles and no points at all. To reward purchase of higher-priced tickets, passengers earn points at up to 2.5 times the economy rate if they travel in club (business class), and up to triple the rate in first class.

Although the airline makes no promises about complimentary upgrades, Executive Club members of BA are more likely to receive such invitations than other passengers. Tier status is an important consideration when employees decide who to upgrade on an overbooked flight. Unlike many airlines, BA tends to limit upgrades to situations in which a lower class of cabin is overbooked. They do not want frequent travelers to believe that they can plan on buying a less expensive ticket and then automatically receive an upgrade.

BA has even created a Household Account that allows for up to six family members who live at the same address to pool their miles and allow them to make full use of the collective balance.

Table 12.1 Selected Benefits Offered by British Airways to Its Most Valued Passengers

Benefit	Bronze-Tier Members	Gold-Tier Members
Reservations		Dedicated gold phone line
Reservation assurance		If flight is full, a guaranteed seat in economy when booking full fare ticket at least 24 hours in advance and checking in at least one hour in advance
Priority waitlist and standby	Higher priority	Highest priority
Check-in desk	According to class of travel	First (regardless of travel class)
Lounge access	According to class of travel	First class departure lounge for passenger and one guest, regardless of travel class; use of arrival lounges; lounge access anytime, allowing use of lounges even when not flying BA intercontinental flights
Special services assistance		Dedicated direct line to customer support staff; problem solving beyond that accorded to other BA travelers
Bonus air miles	+25%	+100%
Upgrade for two		Free upgrade to next cabin for member and companion after earning 2,500 tier points in one year; another upgrade for two after 3,500 points in same year.
Partner cards		Upon reaching 5,000 points, the member will receive two Executive Club Silver cards and one Gold Partner so that the benefits can be shared with loved ones.
Special privilege		Concorde Room access at Heathrow Terminal 5 and New York JFK Terminal 7 after earning 5,000 points
Life time membership		Upon earning 35,000 points, Gold membership status will be awarded for life.

Source

British Airways Executive Club benefits, https://www.britishairways.com/en-gb/executive-club/tiers-and-benefits/compare-the-tiers, accessed July 1, 2015.

LO 10

Appreciate the power of social, customization, and structural bonds in enhancing loyalty.

Build Higher-Level Bonds

One objective of loyalty rewards is to motivate customers to combine their purchases with one provider or at least make it the preferred provider. However, reward-based loyalty programs are quite easy for other suppliers to copy, and they rarely provide a sustained competitive advantage. In contrast, higher-level bonds tend to offer a more sustained competitive advantage. We next discuss the three main types of higher-level bonds (1) social, (2) customization, and (3) structural bonds.

Social Bonds. Have you ever noticed how your favorite hairdresser addresses you by name when you go for a haircut, or how she asks why she hasn't seen you for a long time and hopes everything went well when you were away on a long business trip? Social bonds and related personalization of service are usually based on personal relationships between providers and customers. Social bonds are more difficult to build than financial bonds and may take longer to achieve, but they are also harder for other suppliers to replicate for that same customer. A firm that has created social bonds with its customers has a better chance of retaining them for the long term because of the trust the customers place in the staff. [43] When social bonds include shared relationships (*Figure 12.10*) or experiences between customers, such as in country clubs or educational settings, they can be a major loyalty driver for the organization. [44]

Figure 12.10 A knowledgeable and charismatic lecturer helps build social bonds with students

Figure 12.11 Starbucks' employees are encouraged to learn their customers' preferences

Customization Bonds. These bonds are built when the service provider succeeds in providing customized service to its loyal customers. For example, Starbucks' employees are encouraged to learn their regular customers' preferences and customize their service accordingly (*Figure 12.11*). Many large hotel chains capture the preferences of their customers through their loyalty program databases. Firms offering customized service are likely to have more loyalty customers, so that, when customers arrive at their hotel for example, they find their individual needs have already been anticipated, from the preferred room type (e.g., smoking vs. non-smoking) and bed type (e.g., twins or king size), to the kind of pillow they like and the newspaper they want to read in the morning. Among many other benefits, Fairmont Hotels & Resorts' loyalty program provides its members with jogging shoes and apparel of the right size, and yoga mats and stretch bands waiting in the guests' rooms at their arrival.[45] When a customer becomes used to this special service level, he or she may find it difficult to adjust to another service provider who is not able to customize the service (or at least immediately, as it takes time for the new provider to learn about someone's needs and preferences).[46]

Structural Bonds. Structural bonds are frequently seen in B2B settings. They are created by getting customers to align their way of doing things with the supplier's own processes, thus linking the customer to the firm. This situation makes it more difficult for competitors to draw them away. Examples include joint investments in projects and sharing of information, processes and equipment.

Structural bonds can be created in a B2C environment, too. For instance, some car rental companies offer travelers the opportunity to create a customized account on the firm's website and mobile app, where they can retrieve details of past trips, including pick-up and return locations, the types of cars, insurance coverage, billing address, credit card details, and so forth. This simplifies the task of making new bookings. Once customers have integrated their way of doing things with the firm's processes, structural bonds are created, linking the customer to the firm and make it more difficult for competition to draw them away.

Have you noticed that while all these bonds tie a customer closer to the firm, they also deliver the confidence, social, and special treatment benefits that customers desire? (Refer to *Service Insights 12.1*)? In general, bonds will not work well in the long term unless they generate value for the customer!

LO 11
Understand what factors cause customers to switch to a competitor and how to reduce such switching.

STRATEGIES FOR REDUCING CUSTOMER DEFECTIONS

So far, we have discussed drivers of loyalty and how to tie customers more closely to the firm. A complementary approach is to understand the drivers of customer defections, also called customer churn, and work on eliminating or at least reducing those drivers.

Analyze Customer Defections and Monitor Declining Accounts

A first step is to understand the reasons for customer switching. Susan Keveaney conducted a large-scale study across a range of services and found several key reasons why customers switch to another provider (*Figure 12.12*).[47] These were:
- Core service failures (44% of respondents).
- Dissatisfactory service encounters (34%).
- High, deceptive, or unfair pricing (30%).
- Inconvenience in terms of time, location, or delays (21%).
- Poor response to service failure (17%).

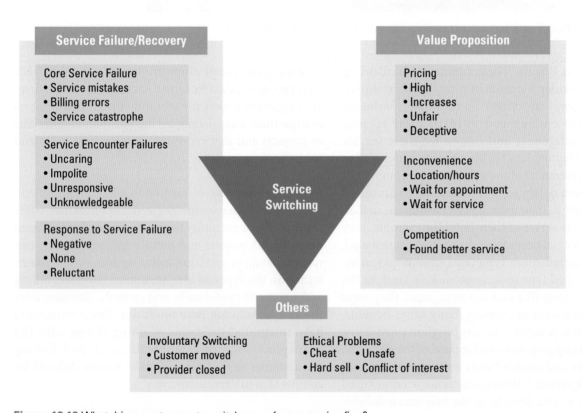

Figure 12.12 What drives customers to switch away from a service firm?

Source

Adapted from Susan M. Keaveney (1995), "Customer Switching Behavior in Service Industries: An Exploratory Study," *Journal of Marketing*, Vol. 59, April, pp. 71–82.

Many respondents decided to switch after a series of related incidents, such as a service failure followed by an unsatisfactory service recovery. Other important factors that drive switching include overall dissatisfaction with the current service provider and the perception that it has an inferior performance on important attributes compared to the best alternative provider.[48]

Progressive service firms regularly conduct what is called **churn diagnostics** to gain a better understanding of why customers defect. This includes the analysis of data from churned and declining customers, exit interviews (call center staff often have a short set of questions they ask when a customer cancels an account), and in-depth interviews of former customers by a third-party research agency, which typically yield a more detailed understanding of churn drivers.[49]

Some firms even try to predict churn of individual accounts. For example, cell phone service providers use **churn alert systems**, which monitor the activity in individual customer accounts with the objective of predicting impending customer switching. Important accounts at risk are flagged and efforts are made to keep the customer, such as sending a voucher and/or having a customer service representative call the customer to check on the health of the customer relationship and initiate corrective action if needed.

Address Key Churn Drivers

Keaveney's findings underscore the importance of addressing some general churn drivers by delivering quality service (see Chapter 14), minimizing inconvenience and other non-monetary costs, and having fair and transparent pricing (Chapter 6). In addition to these generic drivers, there are often industry-specific churn drivers as well. For example, handset replacement is a common reason for cellular phone service subscribers to discontinue an existing relationship, as new subscription plans usually come with heavily subsidized brand-new handsets. To prevent handset-related churn, many providers now offer proactive handset replacement programs, where their current subscribers are offered to buy heavily discounted handsets at regular intervals. Some providers even provide handsets for free to high-value customers or against the redemption of loyalty points.

In addition to such proactive retention measures, many firms also use reactive measures. These include specially trained call center staff called **save teams**, who deal with customers who intend to cancel their accounts. The main job of save team employees is to listen to customer needs and issues, and try to address them with the key focus of retaining the customer. However, you need to be careful on how to reward save teams — see *Service Insights 12.5*.

Implement Effective Complaint Handling and Service Recovery Procedures

Effective complaint handling and excellent service recovery are crucial for keeping unhappy customers from switching providers. Well-managed firms make it easy for customers to voice their problems and respond with suitable service recovery strategies. In that way, customers will remain satisfied, and this will reduce the intention to switch.[50] We will discuss in depth on how to do that effectively in Chapter 13.

SERVICE INSIGHTS 12.5
Churn Management Gone Wrong

America Online (AOL) found itself on the wrong end of churn management when about 300 of its subscribers filed complaints with the New York state attorney general's office, saying that AOL had ignored their demands to cancel the service and stop billing them. After an investigation by the State of New York, AOL eventually agreed to pay $1.25 million in penalties and costs, and to change some of its customer service practices to settle the case.

What went wrong? AOL had been rewarding its call center employees for "saving" customers who called in to cancel their service. Employees could earn high bonuses if they were able to persuade half or more of

such customers to stay with the firm. As claimed by the attorney general's office, this may have led AOL's employees to make it difficult to cancel service. As a response, AOL agreed in a settlement to have service cancellations requests recorded and verified by a third-party monitor, and to provide up to months' worth of refunds to all New York subscribers who claim that their cancellations had been ignored (AOL did not admit to any wrongdoing in that settlement). The New York's Attorney General at the time said, "This agreement helps to ensure that AOL will strive to keep its customers through quality service, not stealth retention programs."

Source

The Associated Press, "AOL to Pay $1,25M to Settle Spitzer Probe," *USA Today,* August 25, 2005, p. 5B.

Increase Switching Costs

Another way to reduce churn is to increase switching costs.[51] Many services have natural switching barriers. For example, it is a lot of work for customers to change their primary banking account, especially when many direct debits, credits, and other related banking services are tied to that account, plus many customers are reluctant to learn about the products and processes of a new provider.[52] Firms can increase these switching costs further by focusing on providing added value to customers through increased convenience, customization, priority (collectively called "positive switching costs" or "soft lock-in strategies") to tie a customer closer to the firm and make switching more costly. Such strategies have been shown to be more effective in generating both attitudinal and behavioral loyalty than the "hard lock-in strategies" discussed next.[53]

Hard lock-in strategies refer to switching costs that are created by having contractual penalties for switching, such as the transfer fees payable to some brokerage firms for moving shares and bonds to another financial institution. Cellular phone service providers often impose contractual penalties if a contract is cancelled during a lock-in period. However, firms need to be careful so that they are not seen as holding their customers hostage. A firm with high switching barriers and poor service quality is likely to generate negative attitudes and bad word-of-mouth. At some point, the last straw is reached and a customer will have had enough and continue to switch service providers even with significant switching costs, or at the first opportune moment, for example, when a contract expires.[54]

ENABLERS OF CUSTOMER LOYALTY STRATEGIES

⊃ **LO 12**
Know why loyalty programs and CRM systems are important enablers of delivering loyalty strategies.

As you can see, most strategies discussed in the Wheel of Loyalty require an in-depth understanding of its customers to actively improve their loyalty. Enablers of customer loyalty strategies provide this understanding and include the creation of "membership-type" of relationships such as through loyalty programs and CRM systems, account managers, and frontline employees. Before discussing these enablers, let's focus on the fundamental difference between strategies intended to produce a single transaction (i.e., transaction marketing) and those designed to create extended relationships with customers (relationship marketing).

Customer Loyalty in a Transactional Marketing Context

A **transaction** is an event during which an exchange of value takes place between two parties. One transaction or even a series of transactions don't necessarily constitute a relationship, which requires mutual recognition and knowledge between the parties. When each transaction between a customer and a supplier is essentially discrete and anonymous, with no long-term record kept of a customer's purchasing history, and little or no mutual recognition between the customer and employees, then no meaningful marketing relationship can be said to exist. This is true for many services, ranging from passenger transport to food service, or visits to a movie theater, in which each purchase and use is a separate event.

Customer loyalty strategies in a transactional marketing context have to focus mostly on the foundation strategies of the Wheel of Loyalty, such as segmenting the market and matching customer needs with firm capabilities, and delivering high service quality. However, most other strategies require a good understanding of a firm's customer behavior. For example, unless a firm knows the consumption behavior of individual customers, it cannot apply tiering of service, loyalty rewards, customization, personalization, churn management, and the like. For all those strategies, a firm has to have individual customer data, which is the case in relationship marketing.

Relationship Marketing

The term **relationship marketing** has been widely used to describe the type of marketing activity designed to create extended relationships with customers. Ideally, both the firm and the customer have an interest in a deeper engagement and higher value-added exchange. A firm may have transactions with some customers who have neither the desire nor the need to make future purchases, while working hard to move others up the loyalty ladder.[55] Evert Gummesson identified no fewer than 30 types of relationships. He advocates **total relationship marketing**, describing it as:

> ...marketing based on relationships, networks, and interaction, recognizing that marketing is embedded in the total management of the networks of the selling organization, the market, and society. It is directed to long-term, win-win relationships with individual customers, and value is jointly created between the parties involved.[56]

Relationship marketing requires a membership-type relationship. The next section shows that some service industries naturally have a membership-type relationship, whereas others have to work hard to create them.

Creating "Membership-Type" Relationships as Enablers for Loyalty Strategies

The nature of the current relationship with customers can be analyzed by asking first — does the supplier enter into a formal "membership" relationship with customers, as with telephone subscriptions, banking, and the family doctor? Or is there no defined relationship? Second, is the service delivered on a continuous basis, as in insurance, broadcasting, and police protection? Or is each transaction recorded and charged separately? *Table 12.2* shows the matrix resulting from this categorization, with examples in each category. A **membership relationship** is a formalized relationship between the firm and an identifiable customer, which often provides special benefits to both parties.

Discrete transactions in which each use involves a payment to the service supplier by an essentially "anonymous" consumer, are typical of services such as transport, restaurants, cinemas, and shoe repairs. The problem for marketers of such services is that they tend to be less informed about who their customers are and what use each customer makes of the service, than their counterparts in membership-type organizations. Managers in businesses that sell discrete transactions have to work a little harder to establish relationships.

In small businesses such as hair salons, frequent customers are (or should be) welcomed as "regulars" whose needs and preferences are remembered. Keeping formal records of customers' needs, preferences, and purchasing behavior is useful even for small firms, because it helps employees to avoid asking the same questions on each service occasion, allowing them to personalize the service given to each customer, and also enables the firm to anticipate future needs. In addition, selling the service in bulk (for instance, a theater series subscription or a commuter ticket on public transport) can also transform discrete transactions into membership relationships, but don't necessarily allow for more customer insight and deployment of more sophisticated loyalty strategies.

In large companies with substantial customer bases, transactions can still be transformed into relationships by offering extra benefits to customers who choose to register with the firm (loyalty programs for hotels, airlines, and car rental firms, and mobile apps for café

Table 12.2 Relationships with Customers

| Nature of Service Delivery | Type of Relationship Between the Service Organization and Its Customers | |
	Membership Relationship	No Formal Relationship
Continuous delivery of service	• Insurance • Cable TV subscription • College enrollment • Banking	• Radio station • Police protection • Lighthouse • Public highway
Discrete transactions	• Long-distance calls from subscriber phone • Theater series subscription • Travel on commuter ticket • Repair under warranty • Health treatment for HMO member	• Mail service • Toll highway • Movie theater • Public transportation • Restaurant

chains fall into this category). Having a loyalty program in place enables a firm to know who its current customers are, to capture their service transactions and preferences. This is valuable information for service delivery, allowing customization and personalization, and for segmentation and tiering of service purposes. For transaction-type businesses, loyalty reward programs, in combination with CRM systems, become a necessary enabler for implementing the strategies discussed in the Wheel of Loyalty.

Novices often equate loyalty points with loyalty programs. However, the most valuable aspect of loyalty programs for both the customer and the firm are often all the other benefits a firm's loyalty strategy brings with it. As discussed in the context of the Wheel of Loyalty, it is often the benefits of the loyalty program that enhance the core service (from priority to customization) and have the highest value. You may ask, why then don't firms do away with the points and focus on these other benefits? The answer has to do with consumer psychology — we all need a little incentive to sign up, install an app, provide information, and carry a loyalty card. For a firm to gain a system-wide view across outlets (and often, across countries), channels, and services, the only unique identifier that is reliable is typically a loyalty card (or membership card number) or a mobile app connected to a cell phone number. All other unique identifiers such as name, passport numbers, and address have been shown to be problematic, as names and addresses can be misspelled and passport numbers change. Therefore, it is often good to view the points (or air miles) of a loyalty program as a little incentive for customers to sign up and identify themselves at reservations, check-ins, and purchases, through their loyalty program membership number, card, or mobile app. The real customer (and firm) benefits are then delivered through the other bonds as described in the Wheel of Loyalty.

Of course, the loyalty program and loyalty strategies have to be delivered, and that typically happens through CRM systems that capture, analyze and deliver the relevant information to frontline employees and account managers (in B2B contexts, or top-tier consumer segments). Frontline employees were discussed in Chapter 11, and the role of CRM systems in delivering loyalty strategies are discussed next.

CRM: CUSTOMER RELATIONSHIP MANAGEMENT

Service marketers have understood for some time the power of CRM, and certain industries have applied it for decades. Examples include the corner grocery store, the neighborhood car repair shop, and providers of banking services to high net-worth clients. However, mention CRM and immediately, costly and complex information technology (IT) systems and infrastructure come to mind. But CRM actually signifies the whole process by which relations with the customers are built and maintained.[57] It should be seen as an enabler of the successful implementation of the Wheel of Loyalty. Let's first look at CRM systems before we move to a more strategic perspective.

> **LO 13**
> Understand the part played by customer relationship management (CRM) systems in delivering customized services and building loyalty.

Common Objectives of CRM Systems

Many firms have large numbers of customers (sometimes millions), many different touchpoints (for instance, tellers, call-center staff, self-service machines, apps, and websites), and at multiple geographic locations. At a single large facility, it's unlikely that a customer will be served by the same frontline staff on two consecutive visits. In such situations, managers historically lacked the tools to practice relationship marketing. Today, CRM systems allow customer information to be captured and delivered to the various touchpoints. From a customer perspective, well-implemented CRM systems can offer a unified customer interface that delivers customization and personalization. This means that at each transaction, the relevant account details, knowledge of customer preferences and past transactions, or history of a service problem are at the fingertips of the person serving the customer. This can result in a vast service improvement and increased customer value.

From a company's perspective, CRM systems allow the company to better understand, segment, and tier its customer base, better target promotions and cross-selling, and even implement churn alert systems that signal if a customer is in danger of defecting.[58] *Service Insights 12.6* highlights some common CRM applications.

SERVICE INSIGHTS 12.6
Common CRM Applications

- **Data collection.** The system captures customer data such as contact details, demographics, purchasing history, service preferences, and the like.

- **Data analysis.** The data captured is analyzed and grouped by the system according to the criteria set by the firm. This is used to tier the customer base and tailor service delivery accordingly.

- **Sales force automation.** Sales leads, cross-sell and up-sell opportunities can be effectively identified and processed, and the entire sales cycle from lead generation to the closing of sales and provision of after-sales services can be tracked and facilitated through the CRM system.

- **Marketing automation.** Mining of customer data allows the firm to target its market. A good CRM system enables the firm to achieve one-to-one marketing and cost savings, often in the context of loyalty and retention programs. This results in increasing the return on investment (ROI) on its marketing expenditure. CRM systems also allow firms to assess the effectiveness of marketing campaigns through the analysis of responses.

- **Call center automation.** Call center staff have customer information at their fingertips and can improve their service levels to all customers. Caller ID and account numbers also allow call centers to identify the customer tier the caller belongs to, and to tailor the service accordingly. For example, platinum callers get priority in waiting loops.

What Does a Comprehensive CRM Strategy Include?

Rather than viewing CRM as a technology, we subscribe to a more strategic view of CRM that focuses on the profitable development and management of customer relationships.[59] *Figure 12.13* provides an integrated framework of five key processes involved in a CRM strategy.

1. **Strategy development** involves the assessment of business strategy, including articulation of the company's vision, industry trends, and competition. The business strategy is typically the responsibility of top management. For CRM to have a positive impact on a firm's performance, the firm's strategy is key.[60] Therefore, business strategy should guide the development of customer strategy, including the choice of target segments, customer base tiering, the design of loyalty bonds, and churn management as discussed in the Wheel of Loyalty.

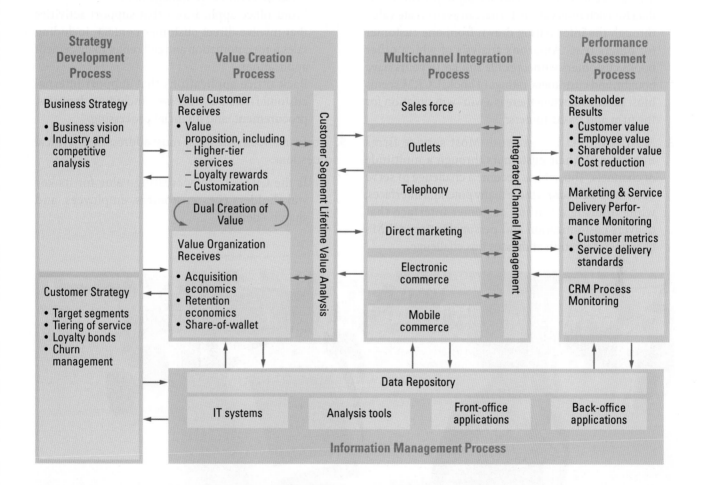

Figure 12.13 An integrated framework for CRM strategy

Source

Adapted from Adrian Payne and Pennie Frow (2005), "A Strategic Framework for Customer Relationship Management," *Journal of Marketing*, Vol. 69, October, pp. 167–176.

2. **Value creation** translates business and customer strategies into specific value propositions for customers and the firm. The value created for customers includes all the benefits that are delivered through priority tiered services, loyalty rewards, customization, and personalization. The value created for the firm includes reduced customer acquisition and retention costs, increased share-of-wallet, and reduced customer serving costs. Customers need to participate in CRM (e.g., through volunteering their personal information) for them to benefit from the firm's CRM strategy. For instance, only if your driver's license, billing address, credit card details, and car and insurance preferences are stored in a car rental's CRM system, then you benefit from the increased convenience of not having to provide those data for each reservation. Firms can even create value through the information drawn from one customer for others (e.g., Amazon's analysis of which other books customers with a profile similar to yours have bought, and customers' ratings of books). CRM seems most successful when there is a win–win situation for the firm and its customers.[61]

3. **Multi-channel integration.** Most service firms interact with their customers through a multitude of channels. Thus, it has become a challenge to serve customers well across these many potential interfaces, while offering a unified customer interface that delivers customization and personalization. CRM's channel integration addresses this challenge.

4. **Information management.** Service delivery across many channels depends on the firm's ability to collect customer information from all channels, integrate it with other relevant information, and make the relevant information available to the frontline (or to the customer in a self-service context) at the various touchpoints (*Figure 12.14*). The information management process includes:
   - The data repository that contains all the customer data.
   - IT systems including IT hardware and software.
   - Analytical tools such as data mining packages.
   - Specific application packages such as campaign management analysis, credit assessment, customer profiling, churn alert systems, and even customer fraud detection and management.
   - Front-office applications that support activities that involve direct customer contact, including sales force automation and call center management applications.
   - Back-office applications that support internal customer-related processes, including, logistics, procurement, and financial processing.

5. **Performance assessment** must address three critical questions:
   - Is the CRM strategy creating value for its key stakeholders (i.e., customers, employees, and shareholders)?

Figure 12.14 Airport self check-in kiosks represent another service touchpoint that needs to be integrated into an airline's CRM system

– Are the marketing objectives (ranging from customer acquisition, share-of-wallet, retention to customer satisfaction) and service delivery performance objectives (e.g., call center service standards such as call waiting time, abortion, and first-time resolution rates) being achieved?

– Is the CRM process itself performing up to expectations? Are the relevant strategies being set, is customer and firm value being created, is the information management process working effectively, and is integration across customer service channels being achieved effectively? The performance assessment process should drive the continuous improvement of the CRM strategy itself.

Common Failures in CRM Implementation

Unfortunately, the majority of CRM implementations have failed in the past.[62] According to the Gartner Group, the CRM implementation failure rate is 55%, and Accenture claims it to be as high as 60%. A key reason for this high failure rate is that firms often equate installing CRM systems with having a customer relationship strategy. They forget that the system is just a tool to enhance the firm's customer servicing capabilities, and is not the strategy in itself.

Furthermore, CRM cuts across many departments and functions (e.g., from customer contact centers and online services, to branch operations, employee training, and IT departments), programs (ranging from sales and loyalty programs to launching of new services, and cross-selling initiatives), and processes (e.g., from credit line authorization to complaint handling and service recovery). The wide-ranging scope of CRM implementation, and the unfortunate reality that it is often the weakest link that determines the success of an implementation, shows the challenge of getting it right. Common reasons for CRM failures include:

- **Viewing CRM as a technology initiative.** It's easy to let the focus shift toward technology and its features, whereby the IT department takes the lead in devising the CRM strategy rather than top management or marketing. This often results in a lack of strategic direction, understanding of customers and markets during implementation.

- **Lack of customer focus.** Many firms implement CRM without the ultimate goal of enhancing the service value and enabling consistent service delivery for valued customers across all customer service processes and delivery channels.

- **Insufficient appreciation of customer LTV.** The marketing of many firms is not sufficiently structured around the vastly different profitability of different customers. Furthermore, servicing costs for different customer segments are often not well-captured (e.g., by using activity-based costing as discussed in Chapter 6).

- **Inadequate support from top management.** Without ownership and active involvement from top management, the CRM strategic intent will not survive the implementation intact.

- **Failing to re-engineer business processes.** It is nearly impossible to implement CRM successfully without redesigning customer service and back-office processes. Many implementations fail because CRM is fitted into existing processes, rather than redesigning the processes to fit a customer-centric CRM implementation. Redesigning also requires change management and employee involvement and support, which are often lacking.

- **Underestimating the challenges in data integration.** Firms frequently fail to integrate customer data that are usually scattered all over the organization. A key to unlocking the full potential of CRM is to make customer knowledge available in real time to all employees who need it.

Finally, firms can put their CRM strategies at substantial risk if customers believe that CRM is used in a way that is harmful to them.[63] Examples include feeling that they are not being treated fairly (for example, not being offered attractive promotions that are offered to new accounts but not to existing customers), and potential privacy concerns. Being aware of and actively avoiding these pitfalls is a first step toward a successful CRM implementation.

How to Get CRM Implementation Right

Despite the many horror stories of millions of dollars sunk into unsuccessful CRM projects, more firms are getting it right. "No longer a black hole, CRM is becoming a basic building block of corporate success," argue Darrell Rigby and Dianne Ledingham.[64] Seasoned McKinsey consultants believe that even CRM systems that have been implemented but have not yet shown results can still be turned around. They recommend taking a step back and focusing on how to build customer loyalty, rather than focusing on the technology itself.[65] Rather than using CRM to transform entire businesses through the wholesale implementation of the CRM model shown in *Figure 12.13*, service firms should focus on clearly defined problems within their customer relationship cycle. These narrow CRM strategies often reveal additional opportunities for further improvements which, when taken together, can evolve into broad CRM implementation extending across the entire company.[66] Likewise, Rigby, Reichheld, and Schefter recommend focusing on the customer strategy and not the technology, posing the question:

> *If your best customers knew that you planned to invest $130 million to increase their loyalty…, how would they tell you to spend it? Would they want you to create a loyalty card or would they ask you to open more cash registers and keep enough milk in stock? The answer depends on the kind of company you are and the kinds of relationships you and your customers want to have with one another.[67]*

Among the key issues managers should debate when defining their customer relationship strategy for a potential CRM system implementation are:

1. How should our value proposition change to increase customer loyalty?

2. How much customization or one-to-one marketing and service delivery is appropriate and profitable?

3. What is the incremental profit potential of increasing the share-of-wallet with our current customers? How much does this vary by customer tier and/or segment?

Figure 12.15 CRM can help companies create two-way channels with customers

4. How much time and resources can we allocate to CRM right now?
5. If we believe in CRM, why haven't we taken more steps in that direction in the past? What can we do today to develop customer relationships without spending a lot on technology?[68]

Answering these questions may lead to the conclusion that a CRM system may currently not be the best investment or the highest priority, or that a scaled-down version may suffice to deliver the intended customer strategy. In any case, we emphasize that the system is merely a tool to drive the strategy, and thus must be tailored to deliver that strategy (*Figure 12.15*).

CONCLUSION

Many elements are involved in gaining market share, increasing share-of-wallet, and cross-selling other products and services to existing customers, and creating long-term loyalty. We used the Wheel of Loyalty as an organizing framework, which starts with a solid foundation that includes targeting the right portfolio of customer segments, attracting the right customers, tiering the service, and delivering high levels of satisfaction. Second, to truly build loyalty, a firm needs to develop close bonds with its customers that ideally deepen the relationship through cross-selling and bundling, and add value to the customer through loyalty rewards and higher-level bonds including social, customization and structural bonds. Finally, a firm needs to identify and reduce the factors that result in "churn" — the loss of existing customers and the need to replace them with new ones.

Marketers need to pay special attention to those customers who offer the firm the greatest value, as they purchase its products with the greatest frequency and spend the most on premium services. CRM is a key enabler for the strategies discussed in the Wheel of Loyalty and is often integrated with loyalty programs. Loyalty programs help to create membership-type relationships with customers even in transaction-type businesses, which, together with effective CRM systems, enable marketers to track the behavior of high-value customers in terms of where and when they use the service, what service classes or types of products they buy, and how much they spend. With the relevant knowledge delivered at key service touchpoints, frontline employees, account managers and systems (e.g., ATMs, websites, and mobile apps) can deliver the high value-add benefits inherent in many of the loyalty bonds as discussed in this chapter. From a customer perspective, CRM can result in vast service improvements and increased customer value such as through customization and increased convenience.

CHAPTER SUMMARY

⮑ **LO1** Customer loyalty is an important driver of a service firm's profitability. The profits derived from loyal customers come from (1) increased purchases, (2) reduced operation costs, (3) referral of new customers, and (4) price premiums. Also, customer acquisition costs can be amortized over a longer period of time.

⮑ **LO2** To understand the profit impact of the customers, firms need to learn how to calculate the LTV of their customers. LTV calculations need to include (1) acquisition costs, (2) revenue streams, (3) account-specific servicing costs, (4) expected number of years the customer will stay with the firm, and (5) discount rate for future cash flows. Also note that it is not true that loyal customers are always more profitable as they may expect price discounts and higher service levels, both of which can reduce customer profitability.

⮑ **LO3** Customers are only loyal if there is a benefit for them to be so. Common benefits customers see in being loyal include:
- **Confidence benefits** such as feeling there is less risk of something going wrong and the ability to trust the provider.
- **Social benefits** such as being known by name, friendship with the service provider, and enjoyment of certain social aspects of the relationship.
- **Special treatment benefits** such as better prices, extra services, and higher priority.

⮑ **LO4** It is not easy to build customer loyalty. The **Wheel of Loyalty** offers a systematic framework that guides firms on how to do so. The framework has three components that follow a sequence.
- First, firms need to build a **foundation for loyalty** without which loyalty cannot be achieved. The foundation delivers confidence benefits to its loyal customers.
- Once the foundation is laid, firms can then create **loyalty bonds** to strengthen the relationship. Loyalty benefits deliver social and special treatment benefits.
- Finally, besides focusing on loyalty, firms have to work on reducing **customer churn**.

To build the foundation for loyalty, firms need to:

⮑ **LO5** Segment the market and **target the "right" customers**. Firms need to choose their target segments carefully and match them to what the firm can do best. Firms need to focus on customer value and fit, instead of just going for customer volume.

⮑ **LO6** Manage the customer base through **service tiering**, which divides the customer base into different value tiers (e.g., platinum, gold, iron, and lead). It helps to tailor strategies to the different service tiers. The higher tiers offer higher values for the firm, but also expect higher service levels. For the lower tiers, the focus should be on increasing profitability through building volume, increasing prices, cutting servicing costs, and as a last resort, even ending unprofitable relationships.

⮑ **LO7** Understand that the foundation for loyalty lies in **customer satisfaction**. The satisfaction loyalty relationship can be divided into three main zones: defection, indifference, and affection. Only highly satisfied or delighted customers who are in the zone of affection will be truly loyal. True loyalty covers both behavioral loyalty (share-of-wallet and referral behavior) and attitudinal loyalty (share-of-heart).

Loyalty bonds are used to build relationships with customers. There are three different types of customer bonds:

⮑ **LO8** Deepening the relationship bonds can be achieved through cross-selling and bundling that **deepen the relationships** and make switching more difficult, and often increase convenience through one-stop shopping.

⮑ **LO9** Loyalty reward-based programs aim at building share-of-wallet through **financial rewards** (e.g., loyalty points) and **non-financial rewards** (e.g., higher-tier service levels, priority service, recognition, and appreciation).

⮑ **LO10** Higher-level bonds include **social**, **customization**, and **structural bonds**. These bonds tend to be more difficult than reward-based bonds to be copied by competitors.

LO11 The final step in the Wheel of Loyalty is to understand what causes customers to leave, and then systematically reduce these **churn drivers**.

- Common causes for customers to switch include core service failures and dissatisfaction, perceptions that pricing is deceptive and unfair, inconvenience, poor response to service failures, and the overall perception that the provider has an inferior performance on key attributes compared to the best alternative provider.
- To prevent customers from switching, firms should analyze and address key reasons why their customers leave them, have good complaint handling and service recovery processes in place, and increase "positive" customer switching costs.

LO12 Most strategies discussed in the Wheel of Loyalty require an in-depth understanding of customers to actively improve loyalty. For example, unless a firm knows the consumption behavior of individual customers, it cannot apply tiering of service, customization, personalization, and churn management. Here, the "membership-type" relationships needed can be created even for transaction-type services through loyalty programs and CRM systems.

LO13 Finally, **CRM systems** should be seen as enabling the successful implementation of the Wheel of Loyalty. CRM systems are particularly useful when firms have to serve large numbers of customers across many service delivery channels. An effective CRM strategy includes five key processes:

- **Strategy development** such as the choice of target segments, tiering of service, and design of loyalty rewards.
- **Value creation** such as delivering benefits to customers through tiered services and loyalty programs (e.g., priority wait listing and upgrades).
- **Multi-channel integration** to provide a unified customer interface across many different service delivery channels (e.g., from the website to the branch office).
- **Information management**, which includes the data repository, analytical tools (e.g., campaign management analysis and churn alert systems), and front- and back-office applications.
- **Performance assessment**, which has to address these three questions:
  (1) Is the CRM creating value for customers and the firm?
  (2) Are its marketing objectives being achieved?
  (3) Is the CRM system itself performing according to expectations?
- Performance assessment should lead to continuous improvement of the CRM strategy and system.

Review Questions

1. Why is customer loyalty an important driver of profitability for service firms?

2. Why is targeting the "right customers" so important for successful customer relationship management?

3. How can you estimate a customer's LTV?

4. How do the various strategies described in the Wheel of Loyalty relate to one another?

5. How can a firm build a foundation for loyalty?

6. What is tiering of services? Explain why it is used and what are its implications for firms and their customers.

7. Identify some key measures that can be used to create customer bonds and encourage long-term relationships with customers.

8. Why are benefits related to the core service (e.g., customization, transaction convenience, and service priority) generally more effective in building loyalty than rewards that are unrelated to the core service (e.g., air miles)?

9. What is the role of churn management in an effective loyalty strategy, and what tools can be used to understand and reduce customer churn?

10. Why are loyalty programs often important of a customer loyalty strategy?

11. What is the role of CRM in delivering a customer relationship strategy?

Application Exercises

1. Identify three service businesses that you buy from on a regular basis. For each business, complete the following sentence: "I am loyal to this business because..."

2. What conclusions do you draw about (a) yourself as a consumer, and (b) the performance of each of the businesses in Exercise 1? Assess whether any of these businesses managed to develop a sustainable competitive advantage through the way it won your loyalty.

3. Identify two service businesses that you used several times but have now stopped to buy from (or plan to stop patronizing soon). Complete the sentence: "I stopped using (or will soon stop using) this organization as a customer because..."

4. What conclusions do you draw about yourself and the firms in Exercise 3? How could each of these firms avoid your defection? What could each of these firms do to avoid defections of customers with a profile similar to yours in the future?

5. Evaluate the strengths and weaknesses of two loyalty programs, each one from a different service industry. Assess how each program could be improved further.

6. Design a questionnaire and conduct a survey asking about two loyalty programs. The first is about a membership/loyalty programs your classmates or their families like best and keep them loyal to that firm. The second should be about a loyalty program that is not well perceived, and does not seem to add value to the customer. Use open-ended questions such as "What motivated you to sign up in the first place?", "Why are you using this program?", "Has participating in the program changed your purchasing/usage behavior in any way?", "Has it made you less likely to use competing suppliers?", "What do you think of the rewards available?", "Did membership in the program lead to any immediate benefits in the use of the service?", "What are the three things you like best about this loyalty program?", "What did you like least?", and "What are some suggested improvements?" Analyze what features make loyalty/membership programs successful, and what features do not achieve the desired results. Use the Wheel of Loyalty framework to guide your analysis and presentation.

7. Approach service employees in two or three firms with implemented CRM systems. Ask the employees about their experience interfacing with these systems, and whether or not the CRM systems (a) help them understand their customers better, and (b) lead to improved service experiences for their customers. Ask them about potential concerns and improvement suggestions they may have about their organizations' CRM systems.

Endnotes

1 James L. Heskett, W. Earl Sasser, and Joe Wheeler, *The Ownership Quotient* (Boston, MA: Harvard Business Press, 2008), pp. 9–13; www.totalrewards.com, accessed June 30, 2015.

Note that Caesars placed Caesars Entertainment Operating Co. into a prepackaged bankruptcy in January 2015, which was largely caused by high level of debt that was held by the company because of its privatization and follow-on acquisitions. Have a look how the court ruling penned out for Caesars.

2 Frederick F. Reichheld and Thomas Teal, *The Loyalty Effect* (Boston: Harvard Business School Press, 1996).

3 The first four factors were proposed by Frederick F. Reichheld and W. Earl Sasser, Jr. (1990), "Zero Defections: Quality Comes to Services," *Harvard Business Review*, Vol. 68, No. 5, October, pp. 105–111. The fifth factor was added by the authors of this book.

4 Christian Homburg, Nicole Koschate, and Wayne D. Hoyer (2006), "Do Satisfied Customers Really Pay More? A Study of the Relationship Between Customer Satisfaction and Willingness to Pay," *Journal of Marketing*, Vol. 69, April, pp. 84–96.

5 Frederick F. Reichheld and W. Earl Sasser, Jr. (1990), "Zero Defections: Quality Comes to Services," *Harvard Business Review*, Vol. 68, No. 5, October, pp. 105–111.

6 For a discussion on how to evaluate the customer base of a firm, see: Sunil Gupta, Donald R. Lehmann, and Jennifer Ames Stuart (2004), "Valuing Customers," *Journal of Marketing Research*, Vol. 41, No.1, pp. 7–18. An excellent overview of the metric of CLV and related concepts such as RFM (i.e., recency, frequency, and monetary spent), PCV (i.e., past customer value, also called customer profitability analysis [CPA]), and share-of-wallet is provided in: V. Kumar (2007), "Customer Lifetime Value — The Path to Profitability," *Foundations and Trends in Marketing*, Vol. 2, No. 1, pp. 1–96.

A review of when to use and how to measure CLV (a prospective perspective on customer LTV which attempts to predict future customer behaviors and discounts derived future cash flows) and CPA, which deploys a retrospective profitability analysis that measures the costs and revenues per customer in the past, is provided in: Morten Holm, V. Kumar, and Carsten Rohde (2012), "Measuring Customer Profitability in Complex Environments: An Interdisciplinary Contingency Framework," *Journal of the Academy of Marketing Science*, Vol. 30, No. 3, pp. 387–401.

7 John E. Hogan, Katherine N. Lemon, and Barak Libai, "What is the True Cost of a Lost Customer?" *Journal of Services Research*, Vol. 5, No. 3, pp. 196–208.

8 Grahame R. Dowling and Mark Uncles (1997), "Do Customer Loyalty Programs Really Work?," *Sloan Management Review*, Summer, pp. 71–81; Werner Reinartz and V. Kumar (2002), "The Mismanagement of Customer Loyalty," *Harvard Business Review*, Vol. 80, July, pp. 86–94.

9 Werner J. Reinartz and V. Kumar (2000), "On the Profitability of Long-Life Customers in a Non-contractual Setting: An Empirical Investigation and Implications for Marketing," *Journal of Marketing*, Vol. 64, October, pp. 17–35.

10 Jochen Wirtz, Indranil Sen, and Sanjay Singh, "Customer Asset Management at DHL in Asia," in J. Wirtz and C. Lovelock, eds. *Services Marketing in Asia — A Case Book* (Singapore: Prentice Hall, 2005), pp. 379–396.

11 Alan W. H. Grant and Leonard H. Schlesinger (1995), "Realize Your Customer's Full Profit Potential," *Harvard Business Review*, Vol. 73, September–October, pp. 59–75. See also Nicolas Glady and Christophe Croux (2009), "Predicting Customer Wallet Without Survey Data," *Journal of Service Research*, Vol. 11, No. 3, pp. 219–231.

12 Ruth Bolton, Katherine N. Lemon, and Peter C. Verhoef (2004), "The Theoretical Underpinnings of Customer Asset Management: A Framework and Propositions for Future Research," *Journal of the Academy of Marketing Science*, Vol. 32, No. 3, pp. 271–292.

13 It has even been suggested to let "chronically dissatisfied customer go to allow frontline staff focus on satisfying the 'right' customers," see: Ka-shing Woo and Henry K.Y. Fock (2004), "Retaining and Divesting Customers: An Exploratory Study of Right Customers, "At-Risk" Right Customers, and Wrong Customers," *Journal of Services Marketing*, Vol. 18, No. 3, pp. 187–197.

14 Frederick F. Reichheld, *Loyalty Rules — How Today's Leaders Build Lasting Relationships* (Boston: MA, Harvard Business School Press, 2001), 45.

15 Yuping Liu (2007), "The Long-Term Impact of Loyalty Programs on Consumer Purchase Behavior and Loyalty," *Journal of Marketing*, Vol. 71, No. 4, October, pp. 19–35.

16 Mark R. Vondrasek (2015), "Redefining Service Innovation at Starwood," *McKinsey Quarterly*, February.

17 Roger Hallowell (1996), "The Relationships of Customer Satisfaction, Customer Loyalty, and Profitability: An Empirical Study," *International Journal of Service Industry Management,* Vol. 7, No. 4, pp. 27–42.

18 This feature was adapted from Frederick F. Reichheld, Loyalty Rules! *How Today's Leaders Build Lasting Relationships* (Boston, MA: Harvard Business School Press, 2001), 24–29, 84–87, 144–145; John C. Bogle, *Don't Count On it! Reflections on Investment Illusions, Capitalism, 'Mutual' Funds, Indexing, Entrepreneurship, Idealism, and Heroes* (NJ: John Wiley & Sons, 2011); https://en.wikipedia.org/wiki/The_Vanguard_Group, accessed June 20, 2015.

19 Ravi Dhar and Rashi Glazer (2003), "Hedging Customers," *Harvard Business Review*, Vol. 81, May, pp. 86–92.

20 David H. Maister, *True Professionalism* (New York: The Free Press, 1997). (See especially Chapter 20).

21 David Rosenblum, Doug Tomlinson and Larry Scott (2003), "Bottom-Feeding for Blockbuster Business," *Harvard Business Review,* March, pp. 52–59.

22 Christian Homburg, Mathias Droll, and Dirk Totzek (2008), "Customer Prioritization: Does it Pay Off, and How Should It Be Implemented?" *Journal of Marketing,* Vol. 72. No. 5, pp. 110–130.

23 Valarie A. Zeithaml, Roland T. Rust, and Katharine N. Lemon (2001), "The Customer Pyramid: Creating and Serving Profitable Customers," *California Management Review,* Vol. 43, No. 4, Summer, pp. 118–142

24 Werner J. Reinartz and V. Kumar (2003), "The Impact of Customer Relationship Characteristics on Profitable Lifetime Duration," *Journal of Marketing,* Vol. 67, No. 1, pp. 77–99.

25 Vikras Mittal, Matthew Sarkees, and Feisal Murshed (2008), "The Right Way to Manage Unprofitable Customers," *Harvard Business Review,* April, pp. 95–102.

26 Elizabeth Esfahani, "How to Get Tough with Bad Customers," *ING Direct*, October 2004, and https://home.ingdirect.com/index.html, accessed August 5, 2011.

Capital One Financial Corporation purchased ING Direct in 2012 and rebranded it as Capital One 360 in 2013. The positioning of the firm remained unchanged and is focused on saving customers time and money by offering simple products at low costs; see https://home.capitalone360.com, accessed June 30, 2015.

27 Not only is there a positive relationship between satisfaction and share-of-wallet, but the greatest positive impact is seen at the upper extreme levels of satisfaction. For details, refer to: Timothy L. Keiningham, Tiffany Perkins-Munn, and Heather Evans (2003), "The Impact of Customer Satisfaction on Share-of-wallet in a Business-to-Business Environment," *Journal of Service Research,* Vol. 6, No. 1, pp. 37–50; See also: Neil A. Morgan, and Lopo Leotte Rego (2006), "The Value of Different Customer Satisfaction and Loyalty Metrics in Predicting Business Performance," *Marketing Science*, Vol. 25, No. 5, September– October, pp. 426–439; Beth Davis-Sramek, Cornelia Droge, John T. Mentzer, and Matthew B. Myers (2009), "Creating Commitment and Loyalty Behavior Among Retailers" What Are the Roles of Service Quality and Satisfaction?" *Journal of the Academy of Marketing Science*, Vol. 37, No. 4, pp. 440–454.; Ina Garnefeld, Sabrina Helm, and Andreas Eggert (2011), "Walk Your Talk: An Experimental Investigation of the Relationship Between Word of Mouth and Communicators' Loyalty," *Journal of Service Research*, Vol. 14, No. 1, pp. 93–107.

28 Florian v. Wangenheim (2005), "Postswitching Negative Word of Mouth," *Journal of Service Research,* Vol. 8, No. 1, pp. 67–78.

29 For a review of the satisfaction–loyalty link, see: V. Kumar, Ilaria Dalla Pozza, and Jaishankar Ganesh (2013), "Revisiting the Satisfaction-Loyalty Relationship: Empirical Generalizations and Directions for Further Research," *Journal of Retailing*, Vol. 89, No. 3, pp. 246–262.

For a review of the quantiative impact of customer satisfaction on various loyalty behaviors, see: Mittal, Vikas, and Carly Frennea (2010), "Customer Satisfaction: A Strategic Review and Guidelines for Managers," *MSI Fast Forward Series*, Marketing Science Institute, Cambridge, MA.

30 Absolute satisfaction scores are less important in determining loyalty behaviors compared to being seen as the best or preferred provider, see: Timothy L. Keiningham, Lerzan Aksoy, Alexander Buoye, and Bruce Cooil (2011), "Customer Loyalty Isn't Enough. Grow Your Share-of-wallet," *Harvard Business Review*, Vol. 89, No. 10, pp. 29–31; Timothy L. Keiningham, Lerzan Aksoy, Luke Williams, and Alexander Buoye, *The Wallet Allocation Rule: Winning the Battle for Share* (Hoboken, NJ: Wiley, 2015).

31 Leonard L. Berry and A. Parasuraman, "Three Levels of Relationship Marketing," in *Marketing Services —*

Competing through Quality (New York: The Free Press, 1991), pp. 136–142; and Valarie A. Zeithaml, Mary Jo Bitner, and Dwayne D. Gremler, *Services Marketing*, 6th ed., (New York: McGraw-Hill, 2012), Chapter 7.

32 Heiner Evanschitzky, B. Ramaseshan, David M. Woisetschlager, Verena Richelsen, Markus Blut, and Christof Backhaus (2012), "Consequences of Customer Loyalty to the Loyalty Program and to the Company," *Journal of the Academy of Marketing Science*, Vol. 40, No. 5, pp. 625–638; Michael Lewis (2004), "The Influence of Loyalty Programs and Short-Term Promotions on Customer Retention," *Journal of Marketing Research*, Vol. 41, August, pp. 281–292; Jochen Wirtz, Anna S. Mattila, and May Oo Lwin (2007), "How Effective Are Loyalty Reward Programs in Driving Share-of-wallet?" *Journal of Service Research*, Vol. 9, No. 4, pp. 327–334.

For an excellent review of the academic literature and effectiveness of loyalty programs, see: Tammo H. A. Bijmolt, Matilda Dorotic, and Peter C. Verhoef (2010), "Loyalty Programs: Generalizations on Their Adoption, Effectiveness and Design," *Foundations and Trends in Marketing*, Vol. 5, No. 5, pp. 197–258.

33 Richard Ho, Leo Huang, Stanley Huang, Tina Lee, Alexander Rosten, and Christopher S. Tang (2009), "An Approach to Develop Effective Customer Loyalty Programs: The VIP Program at T&T Supermarkets Inc," *Managing Service Quality*, Vol. 19, No. 6, pp. 702–720.

34 Katherine N. Lemon and Florian v. Wangenheim (2009), "The Reinforcing Effects of Loyalty Program Partnerships and Core Service Usage," *Journal of Service Research*, Vol. 11, No. 4, pp. 357–370; Frederick DeKay, Rex S. Toh, and Peter Raven (2009), "Loyalty Programs: Airlines Outdo Hotels," *Cornell Hospitality Quarterly*, Vol. 50, No. 3, pp. 371–382.

35 Ruth N. Bolton, P.K. Kannan, and Matthew D. Bramlett, "Implications of Loyalty Program Membership and Service Experience for Customer Retention and Value," *Journal of the Academy of Marketing Science*, Vol. 28, No. 1, pp. 95–108; Michael Lewis (2004), "The Influence of Loyalty Programs and Short-Term Promotions on Customer Retention," *Journal of Marketing Research*, Vol. 41, No. 3, pp. 281–292.

36 Dowling and Uncles (1997), "Do Customer Loyalty Programs Really Work?," *Sloan Management Review*, Vol. 38, No. 4, pp. 71–82.

37 Katherine N. Lemon and Florian v. Wangenheim (2009), "The Reinforcing Effects of Loyalty Program Partnerships and Core Service Usage," *Journal of Service Research*, Vol. 11, No. 4, pp. 357–370.

38 See for example: Iselin Skogland and Judy Siguaw (2004), "Are Your Satisfied Customers Loyal?," *Cornell Hotel and Restaurant Administration Quarterly*, Vol. 45, No. 3, pp. 221–234.

39 Matthew Dixon, Karen Freeman, and Nicholas Toman (2010), "Stop Trying to Delight Your Customers," *Harvard Business Review*, July–August, pp 116–122.

40 Bernd Stauss, Maxie Schmidt, and Adreas Schoeler (2005), "Customer Frustration in Loyalty Programs," *International Journal of Service Industry Management*, Vol. 16, No. 3, pp. 229–252.

41 On the perception of design of loyalty tiers, see: Xavier Drèze and Joseph C. Nunes (2009), "Feeling Superior: The Impact of Loyalty Program Structure on Consumers' Perceptions of Status," *Journal of Consumer Research*, Vol. 35, No. 6, pp. 890–905.

42 Concrete benefits related to the core service (e.g., priority early check-in and priority waitlisting) are more effective in driving customer gratitude and sales growth than status elevation without concrete benefits (i.e., the status is mostly symbolic). The latter can have a negative effect on profitability as they are more likely to increase customer entitlement perceptions, which in turn result in higher service costs; see: Hauke A. Wetzel, Maik Hammerschmidt, and Alex R. Zablah (2014), "Gratitude Versus Entitlement: A Dual Process Model of the Profitability Implications of Customer Prioritization," *Journal of Marketing*, Vol. 78, No. 2, pp. 1–19.

Furthermore, preferences for soft and hard benefits differ between customer segments, see: Praveen K. Kopalle, Yacheng Sun, Scott A. Neslin, Baohong Sun, and Vanitha Swaminathan (2012), "The Joint Sales Impact of Frequency Reward and Customer Tier Components of Loyalty Programs," *Marketing Science*, Vol. 31, No. 2, pp. 216–235. This study also found that customers experience "points pressure," which induces them to increase their spending with the firm as customers get closer to a reward or a higher service tier level. Finally, it found that both the loyalty points and service tiering have synergy and generate incremental sales.

43 Paolo Guenzi, Michael D. Johnson, and Sandro Castaldo, "A Comprehensive Model of Customer Trust in Two Retail Store," *Journal of Service Management*, Vol. 20, No. 3, pp. 290–316; Dwayne Ball, Pedro S. Coelho, and Manuel J. Vilares (2006), "Service Personalization and Loyalty," *Journal of Services Marketing*, Vol. 20, No. 6, pp. 391–403; Alessandro Arbore, Paolo Guenzi, and Andrea Ordanini (2009), "Loyalty Building, Relational Trade-offs and Key Service Employees: The Case of Radio DJs," *Journal of Service Management*, Vol. 20, No. 3, pp. 317–341.

44 Mark S. Rosenbaum, Amy L. Ostrom, and Ronald Kuntze (2005), "Loyalty Programs and a Sense of Community," *Journal of Services Marketing*, Vol. 19, No. 4, pp. 222–233; Isabelle Szmigin, Louise Canning, and Alexander E. Reppel (2005), "Online Community: Enhancing the Relationship Marketing Concept Through Customer Bonding," *International Journal of Service Industry Management*, Vol. 16, No. 5, pp. 480–496; Inger Roos, Anders Gustafsson, and Bo Edvardsson (2005), "The Role of Customer Clubs in Recent Telecom Relationships," *International Journal of Service Industry Management*, Vol. 16, No. 5, pp. 436–454; Dennis Pitta, Frank Franzak, Danielle Fowler, "A Strategic Approach to Building Online Customer Loyalty: Integrating Customer Profitability Tiers," *Journal of Consumer Marketing*, Vol. 23, No. 7, pp. 421–429; Nelson Oly Ndubisi (2007), "Relationship Marketing and Customer Loyalty," *Marketing Intelligence & Planning*, Vol. 25, No. 1, pp. 98–106.

45 https://www.fairmont.com/fpc/benefits, accessed July 20, 2015.

46 Rick Ferguson and Kelly Hlavinka (2006), "The Long Tail of Loyalty: How Personalized Dialogue and Customized Rewards Will Change Marketing Forever," *Journal of Consumer Marketing*, Vol. 23, No. 6, pp. 357–361.

47 Susan M. Keaveney (1995), "Customer Switching Behavior in Service Industries: An Exploratory Study," *Journal of Marketing*, Vol. 59, April, pp. 71–82.

48 Jochen Wirtz, Ping Xiao, Jeongwen Chiang, and Naresh Malhotra (2014), "Contrasting Switching Intent and Switching Behavior in Contractual Service Settings," *Journal of Retailing*, Vol. 90, No. 4, pp. 463–480.

49 For a more detailed discussion of situation-specific switching behavior, refer to: Inger Roos, Bo Edvardsson, and Anders Gustafsson (2004), "Customer Switching Patterns in Competitive and Noncompetitive Service Industries," *Journal of Service Research*, Vol. 6, No. 3, pp. 256–271.

50 Gianfranco Walsh, Keith Dinnie, and Klaus-Peter Wiedmann (2006), "How Do Corporate Reputation and Customer Satisfaction Impact Customer Defection? A Study of Private Energy Customers in Germany," *Journal of Services Marketing*, Vol. 20, No. 6, pp. 412–420.

51 Jonathan Lee, Janghyuk Lee, and Lawrence Feick (2001), "The Impact of Switching Costs on the Consumer Satisfaction-Loyalty Link: Mobile Phone Service in France," *Journal of Services Marketing*, Vol. 15, No. 1, pp. 35–48; Shun Yin Lam, Venkatesh Shankar, M. Krishna Erramilli, and Bvsan Murthy (2004), "Customer Value, Satisfaction, Loyalty, and Switching Costs: An Illustration from a Business-to-Business Service Context," *Journal of the Academy of Marketing Science*, Vol. 32, No. 3, pp. 293–311; Michael A. Jones, Kristy E. Reynolds, David L. Mothersbaugh, and Sharon Beatty (2007), "The Positive and Negative Effects of Switching Costs on Relational Outcomes," *Journal of Service Research*, Vol. 9, No. 4, pp. 335–355.

For an excellent review and meta-analysis of customer perception of switching costs, see: Doreén Pick and Martin Eisend (2014), "Buyers' Perceived Switching Costs and Switching: A Meta-Analytic Assessment of Their Antecedents," *Journal of the Academy of Marketing Science*, Vol. 42, No. 2, pp. 186–204.

52 Simon J. Bell, Seigyoung Auh, and Karen Smalley (2005), "Customer Relationship Dynamics: Service Quality and Customer Loyalty in the Context of Varying Levels of Customer Expertise and Switching Costs," *Journal of the Academy of Marketing Science*, Vol. 33, No. 2, pp. 169–183; Markus Blut, Sharon E. Beatty, Heiner Evanschitzky, and Christian Brock (2014), "The Impact of Service Characteristics on the Switching Cost-Customer Loyalty Link," *Journal of Retailing*, Vol. 90, No. 2, pp. 275–290.

53 Arvind Malhotra and Claudia Kubowicz Malhotra (2013), "Exploring Mobile Switching Behavior of US Mobile Service Customers," *Journal of Services Marketing*, Vol. 27, No. 1, pp. 13–24; Liane Nagengast, Heiner Evanschitzky, Markus Blut, and Thomas Rudolph (2014), "New Insights in the Moderating Effect of Switching Costs on the Satisfaction-Repurchase Behavior Link," *Journal of Retailing*, Vol. 90, No. 3, pp. 408–427.

54 Lesley White and Venkat Yanamandram (2004), "Why Customers Stay: Reasons and Consequences of Inertia in Financial Services," *International Journal of Service Industry Management*, Vol. 14, No. 3, pp. 183–194.

55 Johnson and Selnes proposed a typology of exchange relationships that included "strangers," "acquaintances," "friends," and "partners" and derived implications for customer portfolio management. For details, see: Michael D. Johnson and Fred Selnes (2002), "Customer Portfolio Management: Towards a Dynamic Theory of Exchange Relationships," *Journal of Marketing*, Vol. 68, No. 2, pp. 1–17.

56 Evert Gummesson, *Total Relationship Marketing* (Oxford: Butterworth-Heinemann, 1999), p. 24.

57 For an overview on CRM, see: V. Kumar and Werner J. Reinartz, *Customer Relationship Management: A Database Approach*. Hoboken (NJ: John Wiley & Sons, 2006); B. Ramaseshan, David Bejou, Subhash C. Jain, Charlotte Mason, and Joseph Pancras (2006), "Issues and Perspective in Global Customer Relationship Management," *Journal of Service Research*, Vol. 9, No. 2, pp. 195–207; V. Kumar, Sarang Sunder, and B. Ramaseshan (2011), "Analyzing the Diffusion of Global Customer Relationship Management: A Cross-Regional Modeling Framework," *Journal of International Marketing*, Vol. 19, No. 1, pp. 23–39.

58 Kevin N. Quiring and Nancy K. Mullen, "More Than Data Warehousing: An Integrated View of the Customer," in John G. Freeland, ed. *The Ultimate CRM Handbook — Strategies & Concepts for Building Enduring Customer Loyalty & Profitability* (New York: McGraw-Hill, 2002), pp. 102–108.

59 This section is adapted from: Adrian Payne and Pennie Frow (2005), "A Strategic Framework for Customer Relationship Management," *Journal of Marketing*, Vol. 69, October, pp. 167–176.

60 Martin Reimann, Oliver Schilke, and Jacquelyn S. Thomas (2010), "Customer Relationship Management and Firm Performance: The Mediating Role of Business Strategy," *Journal of the Academy of Marketing Science*, Vol. 38, No. 3, pp. 326–346. The authors found that the effect of CRM is fully mediated by the two basic strategic postures of firms: differentiation versus cost leadership. Furthermore, their study found that the effects of CRM on differentiation are stronger in highly commoditized industries compared to highly differentiated industries.

61 William Boulding, Richard Staelin, Michael Ehret, and Wesley J. Johnston (2005), "A Customer Relationship Management Roadmap: What Is Known, Potential Pitfalls, and Where to Go," *Journal of Marketing*, Vol. 69, No. 4, pp. 155–166.

62 This section is based on: Sudhir H. Kale (2004), "CRM Failure and the Seven Deadly Sins," *Marketing Management*, September/October, pp. 42–46.

63 See note 61.

64 Darrell K. Rigby, and Dianne Ledingham (2004), "CRM Done Right," *Harvard Business Review*, November, pp. 118–129.

65 Manuel Ebner, Arthur Hu, Daniel Levitt, and Jim McCrory, "How to Rescue CRM?" *The McKinsey Quarterly* 4 (Technology, 2002).

66 Darrell K. Rigby and Dianne Ledingham (2004), "CRM Done Right," *Harvard Business Review*, November, pp. 118–129.

67 Darrell K. Rigby, Frederick F. Reichheld, and Phil Schefter (2002), "Avoid the Four Perils of CRM," *Harvard Business Review*, February, p. 108.

68 Darrell K. Rigby, Frederick F. Reichheld, and Phil Schefter (2002), "Avoid the Four Perils of CRM," *Harvard Business Review*, February, p. 108.

Interestingly, research has shown that firms that implement CRM mostly because of competitive pressure reap less benefits from their CRM systems than firms that use CRM to proactively pursue their own strategic objectives, see: Bas Hillebrand, Jurriaan J. Nijholt, and Edwin J. Nijssen (2011), "Exploring CRM Effectiveness: An Institutional Theory Perspective," *Journal of the Academy of Marketing Science*, Vol. 39, No. 4, pp. 592–608.

Complaint Handling and Service Recovery

A complaint is a gift.

Claus Møller,
management consultant and author

Customers don't expect you to be perfect. They do expect you to fix things when they go wrong.

Donald Porter,
V.P. British Airways

To err is human; to recover, divine.

Christopher Hart, **James Heskett**, and **Earl Sasser**,
current and former professors at
Harvard Business School
(paraphrasing 18th-century poet Alexander Pope)

LEARNING OBJECTIVES (LOs)

By the end of this chapter, the reader should be able to:

⊃ **LO 1** Recognize the actions that customers may take in response to service failures.

⊃ **LO 2** Understand why customers complain.

⊃ **LO 3** Know what customers expect from the firm when they complain.

⊃ **LO 4** Understand how customers respond to effective service recovery.

⊃ **LO 5** Explain the service recovery paradox.

⊃ **LO 6** Know the principles of effective service recovery systems.

⊃ **LO 7** Be familiar with the guidelines for frontline employees on how to handle complaining customers and recover from a service failure.

⊃ **LO 8** Recognize the power of service guarantees.

⊃ **LO 9** Understand how to design effective service guarantees.

⊃ **LO 10** Know when firms should not offer service guarantees.

⊃ **LO 11** Be familiar with the seven groups of jaycustomers and understand how to manage them effectively.

OPENING VIGNETTE

Too Little, Too Late — JetBlue's Service Recovery

It was a terrible ice storm in the East Coast of the United States.[1] Hundreds of passengers were trapped for 11 hours inside JetBlue planes at the John F. Kennedy International Airport in New York. These passengers were furious. No one in JetBlue did anything to get the passengers off the planes. On top of that, JetBlue canceled more than 1,000 flights over six days, leaving even more passengers stranded. This incident canceled out much that JetBlue had done right to become one of the strongest customer service brands in the US. JetBlue was going to be ranked number four by *Business Week* in a list of top 25 customer service leaders. However, due to this incident, it was pulled from the rankings. What happened?

There was no service recovery plan. No one — not the pilot, flight attendants, nor station manager — had the authority to get the passengers off the plane. JetBlue's offer of refunds and travel vouchers did not seem to reduce the anger of the passengers, who had been stranded for so long. David Neeleman, JetBlue's CEO at the time, sent a personal email to all customers in the company's database to explain what caused the problem, apologized profusely,

and detailed its service recovery efforts. He even appeared on late-night television to apologize, and he admitted that the airline should have had better contingency planning. However, the airline still had a long way to go to repair the damage done to its reputation.

Slowly, the airline rebuilt its reputation, starting with its new Customer Bill of Rights. The bill required the airline to provide vouchers or refunds in certain situations when flights were delayed. Neeleman also changed JetBlue's information systems to keep track of the locations of its crew, and trained its staff at the headquarters to help out at the airport when needed. All these activities were aimed at climbing its way back up to the heights it fell from (*Figure 13.1*). By 2014, JetBlue Airways was back on the list of J. D. Power Customer Service Champions for many consecutive years. (J. D. Power and Associates conducts customer satisfaction research based on survey responses from millions of customers worldwide.) This shows that JetBlue's customers had finally forgiven the company for its service failure, and now support its efforts to deliver continued service excellence.

Figure 13.1 JetBlue's took active measures to win their customers back and are now on the list of J. D. Power Customer Service Champions for many years

CUSTOMER COMPLAINING BEHAVIOR

The first law of service quality and productivity might be: Do it right the first time. However, we can't ignore the fact that failures continue to occur, sometimes for reasons outside of the organization's control such as the ice storm that caused the JetBlue incident in our opening vignette.[2] Many "moments of truth" in service encounters are vulnerable to breakdowns. Distinctive service characteristics such as real-time performance, customer involvement, and people as part of the product can greatly increase the chance of service failures occurring. How well a firm handles complaints and resolves problems frequently determines whether it builds customer loyalty or it should just watch its customers take their business elsewhere. An overview of this chapter is provided in *Figure 13.2*.

Customer Response Options to Service Failure

LO 1

Recognize the actions that customers may take in response to service failures.

Chances are, you're not always satisfied with some of the services you receive. How do you respond to your dissatisfaction with these services? Do you complain informally to an employee, ask to speak to the manager, or file a formal complaint? Or perhaps you just mutter darkly to yourself, grumble to your friends and family, and choose an alternative supplier the next time you need a similar type of service?

If you are among those who do not complain to the firm about poor service, you are not alone. Research around the globe has shown that most people will choose not to complain, especially if they think it will do no good. *Figure 13.3* depicts the courses of action a customer may take in response to a service failure. This model suggests at least three major courses of action:

1. Take some form of public action (including complaining to the firm or to a third party, such as a customer advocacy group, a consumer affairs or regulatory agency, or even take the matter to the civil or criminal courts).
2. Take some form of private action (including abandoning the supplier).
3. Take no action (*Figure 13.4*).

It's important to remember that a customer can take any one or a combination of actions. Managers need to be aware that the impact of a defection can go far beyond the loss of that customer's future revenue stream. Angry customers often tell other people about their problems[3], and the Internet allows for unhappy customers to reach thousands of people by posting complaints on bulletin boards, blogs and even setting up their own websites to talk about their bad experiences with specific organizations.

Figure 13.4 Some customers may just be frustrated but do not take any action to complain, as seen here in an interaction with an online service

CAN'T YOU DO ANYTHING RIGHT?

GLASBERGEN

© Randy Glasbergen.   www.glasbergen.com

Understanding Customer Complaining Behavior

LO 2

Understand why customers complain.

To be able to effectively deal with dissatisfied and complaining customers, managers need to understand the key aspects of complaining behavior, starting with the questions posed below.

Customer Responses to Service Failure

- Take public action (complain to the firm, to a third party, take legal action)
- Take private action (switch provider, spread negative word-of-mouth)
- Take no action

Customer Expectations Once a Complaint Is Made

Customers expect fair treatment along three dimensions:
- Procedural justice: Customers expect a convenient, responsive, and flexible service recovery process
- Interactional justice: The recovery effort must be seen as genuine, honest, and polite
- Outcome justice: The restitution has to reflect the customer loss and inconveniences suffered

Customer Responses to an Effective Service Recovery

- Avoids switching, restores confidence in the firm
- The Service Recovery Paradox: An excellent recovery can even result in higher satisfaction and loyalty than if a service was delivered as promised

Customer Complaining

Why do customers complain?
- Obtain restitution or compensation
- Vent anger
- Help to improve the service
- For altruistic reasons

What proportion of unhappy customers complains?
- 5%–10% complain

Why don't unhappy customers complain?
- It takes time and effort
- The payoff is uncertain
- Complaining can be unpleasant

Who is most likely to complain?
- Higher socioeconomic class customers
- Customers with more product knowledge

Where do customers complain?
- Vast majority of complaints are made at the point of service provision (face-to-face or over the phone)
- Only a small proportion of complaints is sent via email, social media, websites, or letters

Principles of Effective Service Recovery Systems

- Make it easy for customers to provide feedback and reduce customer complaint barriers
- Enable effective service recovery: Make it (1) proactive, (2) planned, (3) trained, and (4) empowered
- Establish appropriate compensation levels: Set based on the (1) positioning of the firm, (2) severity of the service failure, and the (3) importance of the customer. Target for "well-dosed generosity"

Dealing with Complaining Customers:
- Act fast
- Acknowledge customer's feelings
- Don't argue
- Show understanding
- Clarify the facts
- Give customer the benefit of the doubt
- Propose steps to solve the problem
- Keep the customer informed
- Consider compensation
- Persevere to regain customer goodwill
- Improve the service system

Service Guarantees

- Institutionalize professional complaint handling & service recovery
- Drive improvement of processes
- Design: (1) unconditional, (2) easy to understand, (3) meaningful, (4) easy to invoke, (5) easy to collect on, & (6) credible
- Unsuitable for firms with (1) a reputation for excellence, (2) poor quality service, and (3) uncontrollable quality due to external factors (e.g., weather)

Jaycustomers

There are 7 types of jaycustomers:
- The Cheat
- The Thief
- The Rule Breaker
- The Belligerent
- The Family Feuders
- The Vandal
- The Deadbeat

- Jaycustomers cause problems for firms and can spoil the service experience of other customers.
- Firms need to keep track and manage their behavior, incl., as a last resort, blacklisting them from using the firm's facilities.

Figure 13.2 Organizing framework for managing complaints and service recovery

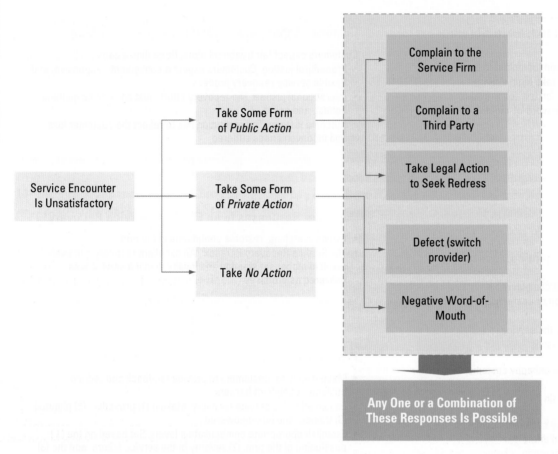

Figure 13.3 Customer response categories to service failures

Why Do Customers Complain? In general, studies of consumer complaining behavior have identified four main purposes for complaining:

1. **Obtain restitution or compensation.** Consumers often complain to recover some economic loss by seeking a refund, compensation, and/or have the service performed again[4].

2. **Vent their anger.** Some customers complain to rebuild self-esteem and/or to release their anger and frustration. When service processes are bureaucratic and unreasonable, or when employees are rude, deliberately intimidating or apparently uncaring, the customers' self-esteem, self-worth, or sense of fairness can be negatively affected. They may become angry and emotional.

3. **Help to improve the service.** When customers are highly involved with a service (e.g., at a college, an alumni association, or their main banking connection), they give feedback to try and contribute towards service improvements.

4. **For altruistic reasons.** Finally, some customers are motivated by altruistic reasons. They want to spare other customers from experiencing the same shortcomings, and they may feel bad if they fail to draw attention to a problem that will raise difficulties for others if it remains uncorrected.

What Proportion of Unhappy Customers Complain? Research shows that on average, only 5–10% of customers who have been unhappy with a service actually complain[5]. Sometimes the percentage is far lower. A review of the records of a public bus company showed that formal complaints occurred at the rate of about three complaints for every million passenger trips. Assuming two trips a day, a person would need 1,370 years (roughly 27 lifetimes) to make a million trips. In other words, the rate of complaints was incredibly low, especially since public bus companies are rarely known for service excellence. Although only a minority of dissatisfied customers complain, there's evidence that consumers across the world are becoming better informed, more self-confident, and more assertive about seeking satisfactory outcomes for their complaints.

Why Don't Unhappy Customers Complain? A number of studies have identified a number of reasons why customers don't complain. Customers may not want to take the time to write a letter, send an email, fill in a form, or make a phone call, particularly if they don't see the service as being important enough to be worth the effort. Many customers see the payoff as uncertain and believe that no one would be concerned about their problem or would be willing to deal with it, and that complaining is simply not worth their while. In some situations, people simply don't know where to go or what to do. Also, many people feel that complaining is unpleasant and may be afraid of confrontation, especially if the complaint involves someone whom the customer knows and may have to deal with again (*Figure 13.5*)[6].

Finally, complaining behavior can be influenced by role perceptions and social norms. Customers are less likely to voice complaints in service situations in which they perceive they have "low power" (the ability to influence or control the transaction)[7]. This is particularly true when the problem involves professional service providers such as doctors, lawyers, or architects. Social norms tend to discourage customer criticism of such individuals.

Who Is Most Likely to Complain? Research findings consistently show that people in higher socioeconomic levels are more likely to complain than those in the lower levels. They are better educated, have higher income, and are more socially involved, and this gives them the confidence, knowledge, and motivation to speak up when they encounter problems[8]. Furthermore, those who complain also tend to be more knowledgeable about the product in question.

Where Do Customers Complain? Studies show that the majority of complaints are made at the place where the service was received. One of the authors of this book completed a consulting project developing and implementing a customer feedback system. He found that an amazing 99% of customer feedback was given face-to-face or over the phone to customer service representatives. Less than 1% of all complaints were submitted via firms' websites, social media pages, email, letters, or feedback cards. A survey of airline passengers found that only 3% of respondents who were unhappy with their meal actually complained about it, and they all complained to the flight attendant. None complained to the company's headquarters or to a consumer affairs office[9]. Also, customers tend to use interactive channels such as face-to-face, or the telephone when they want a problem to be fixed, but use noninteractive channels to complain (e.g., email or websites) when they mainly want to vent their anger and frustration[10].

In practice, even when customers do complain, managers often don't hear about the complaints made to frontline employees. Without a formal customer feedback system, only a tiny proportion of the complaints may reach corporate headquarters[11]. If unhappy customers have already used other channels of complaint but their problem is not solved, then they are more likely to turn to online public complaining. This is due to "double deviation." The service performance already caused dissatisfaction in the first instance, and the resolution of the problem also failed.[12]

Figure 13.5 Customers often view complaining as difficult and unpleasant

What Do Customers Expect Once They Have Made a Complaint?

Whenever a service failure occurs, people expect to be treated fairly. However, research has shown that many customers feel that they have not been treated fairly nor received adequate compensation. When this happens, their reactions tend to be immediate, emotional, and enduring. In contrast, outcomes that are perceived as fair have a positive impact on customer satisfaction[13].

Stephen Tax and Stephen Brown found that as much as 85% of the variation in the satisfaction with a service recovery was determined by three dimensions of fairness (*Figure 13.6*)[14]:

- **Procedural justice** refers to the policies and rules that any customer has to go through to seek fairness. Customers expect the firm to take responsibility, which is the key to the start of a fair procedure, followed by a convenient and responsive recovery process. That includes flexibility of the system and consideration of customer inputs into the recovery process.

- **Interactional justice** involves the employees of the firm who provide the service recovery and their behavior toward the customer. It is important to give an explanation for the failure and to make an effort to resolve the problem. The recovery effort must also be seen as genuine, honest, and polite.

- **Outcome justice** concerns the restitution or compensation that a customer receives as a result of the losses and inconveniences caused by the service failure. This includes compensation for not only the failure, but also for the time, effort, and energy spent during the process of service recovery.

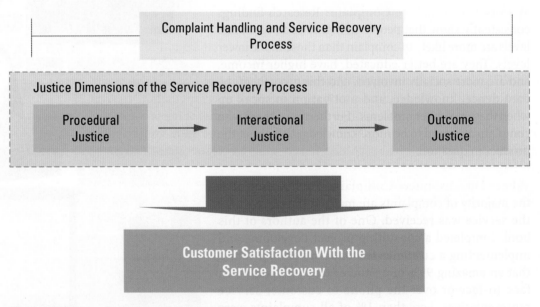

Figure 13.6 Three dimensions of perceived fairness in service recovery processes

Source

Adapted from Stephen S. Tax and Stephen W. Brown (1998), "Recovering and Learning from Service Failure," *Sloan Management Review*, Vol. 49, No. 1, Fall, pp. 75–88.

CUSTOMER RESPONSES TO EFFECTIVE SERVICE RECOVERY

➲ **LO 4**
Understand how customers respond to effective service recovery.

"Thank Heavens for Complainers" was the provocative title of an article about customer complaining behavior, which also featured a successful manager exclaiming, "Thank goodness I've got a dissatisfied customer on the phone! The ones I worry about are the ones I never hear from.[15]" Customers who do complain give a firm the chance to correct its problems (including some the firm may not even know of), restore relationships with the complainer, and improve future satisfaction for all.

Service recovery is a term for the systematic efforts by a firm to correct a problem following a service failure and to retain a customer's goodwill. Service recovery efforts play an important role in achieving (or restoring) customer satisfaction and loyalty[16]. In every organization, things that occur may have a negative impact on relationships with customers. The true test of a firm's commitment to customer satisfaction and service quality isn't in the advertising promises, but in the way it responds when things go wrong for the customer. Although complaints tend to have a negative effect on service personnel's commitment to customer service, employees with a positive attitude toward service and their own jobs are more likely to explore additional ways in which they can help customers, and view complaints as a potential source of improvement and to explore additional ways in which they can help customers[17].

Effective service recovery requires thoughtful procedures for resolving problems and handling disgruntled customers. It is critical for firms to have effective recovery strategies, as even a single service problem under the following conditions can destroy a customer's confidence in a firm:
- The failure is totally outrageous (e.g., blatant dishonesty on the part of the supplier).
- The problem fits a pattern of failure rather than being an isolated incident.
- The recovery efforts are weak, serving to compound the original problem rather than correct it[18].

The risk of defection is high, especially when there are a variety of competing alternatives available. One study of customer switching behavior in service industries found that close to 60% of all respondents who reported changing suppliers did so because of a service failure — 25% cited failures in the core service, 19% reported an unsatisfactory encounter with an employee, 10% reported an unsatisfactory response to a prior service failure, and 4% described unethical behavior on the part of the provider[19].

Impact of Effective Service Recovery on Customer Loyalty

When complaints are resolved satisfactorily, there is a much higher chance that the customers involved will remain loyal. In fact, research has shown that complainants who are satisfied with the service recovery experienced are 15 times more likely to recommend a company than dissatisfied complainants[20]. TARP research found that intentions to repurchase for different types of products ranged between 9–37% when customers were dissatisfied but did not complain. For a major complaint, the retention rate increased from 9% when dissatisfied customers did not complain, to 19% if the customer complained and the company offered a sympathetic ear but was unable to resolve the complaint to the satisfaction of the customer. If the complaint could be resolved to the satisfaction of the customer, the retention rate jumped to 54%. The highest retention rate of 82% was achieved when problems were fixed quickly — typically on the spot[21]!

We can conclude that complaint handling should be seen as a profit center, not a cost center. When a dissatisfied customer defects, the firm loses more than just the value of the next transaction. It may also lose a long-term stream of profits from that customer and from anyone else who is deterred from patronizing that firm as a result of negative comments from an unhappy friend. However, many organizations have yet to buy into the concept that it pays to invest in service recovery designed to protect those long-term profits[22].

The Service Recovery Paradox

LO 5

Explain the service recovery paradox.

The **service recovery paradox** describes the phenomenon where customers who experience an excellent service recovery after a failure feel even more satisfied than customers who had no problem in the first place[23]. For example, a passenger may arrive at the check-in counter and find there are no seats for him due to overbooking, even though he has a confirmed seat. To recover the service, the passenger is upgraded to a business class seat, at no additional cost. The customer ends up being more satisfied than before the problem had occurred.

The service recovery paradox may lead to the thinking that it may be good for customers to experience service failure so they can be delighted as a result of an excellent service recovery. However, this approach would be too expensive for the firm. It is also important to note that the service recovery paradox does not always apply. In fact, research has shown that the service recovery paradox is far from universal[24]. For example, a study of repeated service failures in a retail banking context showed that the service recovery paradox held for the first service failure that was recovered to customers' full satisfaction[25]. However, if a second service failure occurred, the paradox disappeared. It seems that customers may forgive a firm once, but become disillusioned if failures recur. The study also showed that customers' expectations were raised after they experienced a very good recovery; thus, excellent recovery becomes the standard they expect for dealing with future failures.

Whether a customer comes out delighted from a service recovery may also depend on the severity and "recoverability" of the failure — no one can replace spoiled wedding photos, a ruined holiday, or eliminate the consequences of a debilitating injury caused by service equipment. In such situations, it's hard to imagine anyone being truly delighted even when the most professional service recovery is conducted. Compare these examples with a lost hotel reservation for which the recovery is an upgrade to a better room — or even a suite. When poor service is recovered by delivery of a superior product, you're usually delighted and probably hope for another lost reservation in the future.

In conclusion, the best strategy is to do it right the first time. As Michael Hargrove puts it, "Service recovery is turning a service failure into an opportunity you wish you never had[26]." Unfortunately, empirical evidence shows that some 40–60% of customers reported dissatisfaction with the service recovery processes they experienced[27].

512 **Chapter 13** · Complaint Handling and Service Recovery

PRINCIPLES OF EFFECTIVE SERVICE RECOVERY SYSTEMS

LO 6
Know the principles of effective service recovery systems.

Recognizing that current customers are a valuable asset base, managers need to develop effective procedures for service recovery following unsatisfactory experiences. Unfortunately, many service recoveries fail and some of the common causes for failure are shown in *Service Insights 13.1*. Next, we discuss three guiding principles for how to get it right: (1) make it easy for customers to give feedback, (2) enable effective service recovery, and (3) establish appropriate compensation levels. A fourth principle, learning from customer feedback and driving service improvements, will be discussed in Chapter 14 in the context of customer feedback systems. The components of an effective service recovery system are shown in *Figure 13.7*[28].

SERVICE INSIGHTS 13.1
Common Service Recovery Mistakes

Here are some typical service recovery mistakes made by many organizations:

- **Managers disregard evidence that shows that service recovery provides a significant financial return.** In recent years, many organizations have focused on cost cutting, paying only lip service to retain their most profitable customers. On top of that, they have also lost sight of the need to respect all their customers.

- **Companies do not invest enough in actions that would prevent service issues.** Ideally, service planners address potential problems before they become customer problems. Although preventive measures don't eliminate the need for good service recovery systems, they greatly reduce the burden on frontline staff and the service recovery system in its entirety.

- **Customer service employees fail to display good attitudes.** The three most important things in service recovery are attitude, attitude, and attitude. No matter how well-designed and well-planned the service recovery system is, it won't work well without the friendly and proverbial smile-in-the-voice attitude from frontline staff.

- **Organizations fail to make it easy for customers to complain or give feedback.** Although some improvement can be seen, such as hotels and restaurants offering comment cards and links on their websites and apps, little is done to communicate their simplicity and value to customers. Research shows that a large proportion of customers are unaware of the existence of a proper feedback system that could help them get their problems solved.

Developing Customer Relationships **513**

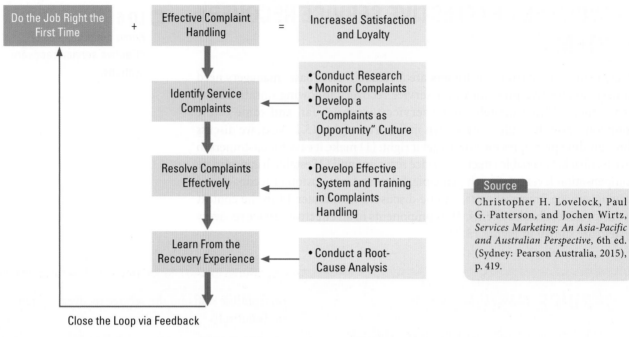

Figure 13.7 Components of an effective service recovery system

Source

Christopher H. Lovelock, Paul G. Patterson, and Jochen Wirtz, *Services Marketing: An Asia-Pacific and Australian Perspective*, 6th ed. (Sydney: Pearson Australia, 2015), p. 419.

Make It Easy for Customers to Give Feedback

How can managers overcome unhappy customers' reluctance to complain about service failures? The best way is to directly address the reasons for their reluctance. *Table 13.1* gives an overview of potential measures that can be taken to overcome those reasons we identified earlier. Many companies have improved their complaint-collection procedures by adding special toll-free phone lines (see *Figure 13.8* for a tongue-in-cheek example of what not to do), links on their websites and social media pages, and clearly displayed customer comment cards in their branches. In their customer communications, some companies feature service improvements that were the direct result of customer feedback under the motto "You told us, and we responded."

Table 13.1 Strategies to Reduce Customer Complaint Barriers

Complaint Barriers for Dissatisfied Customers	Strategies to Reduce These Barriers
Inconvenience • Difficult to find the right complaint procedure • Effort, for example, writing and mailing a letter	Make feedback easy and convenient: • Put customer service hotline numbers, email the website and/or postal addresses on all customer communications materials (letters, bills, brochures, website, phone book, yellow pages listings, etc.)
Doubtful payoff • Uncertain whether any or what action will be taken by the firm to address the issue the customer is unhappy with	Reassure customers that their feedback will be taken seriously and will pay off: • Have service recovery procedures in place and communicate this to customers, for example, in customer newsletter and website • Feature service improvements that resulted from customer feedback
Unpleasantness • Fear of being treated rudely • Fear of being hassled • Feeling embarrassed	Make providing feedback a positive experience: • Thank customers for their feedback (can be done publicly and in general by addressing the entire customer base) • Train service employees not to hassle and to make customers feel comfortable • Allow for anonymous feedback

Enable Effective Service Recovery

Recovering from service failures takes more than just pious expressions of determination to resolve any problems that may occur. It requires commitment, planning, and clear guidelines. Specifically, effective service recovery should be: (1) proactive, (2) planned, (3) trained, and (4) empowered.

Service Recovery Should Be Proactive. Service recovery is ideally initiated on the spot, preferably before customers have a chance to complain (see *Service Insights 13.1*). Service personnel should be sensitive to signs of dissatisfaction, and ask whether customers might be experiencing a problem. For example, the waiter may ask a guest who has only eaten half of his dinner: "Is everything all right, sir?" The guest may say, "Yes, thank you, I am not very hungry," or "The steak is well done but I had asked for medium-rare." The second response then gives the waiter a chance to recover the service, rather than have an unhappy diner leave the restaurant and potentially not return.

Recovery Procedures Need to Be Planned. Contingency plans have to be developed for service failures, especially for those that occur regularly and cannot be designed out of the system[29]. For example, revenue management practices in the travel and hospitality industries often result in overbooking, and travelers are denied boarding or hotel guests are "walked" even though they had confirmed seats or reservations. To simplify the task of frontline staff, firms should identify the most common service problems such as overbooking, and then develop solution sets for employees to follow. In contact centers, the customer service representatives have prepared scripts to guide them in a service recovery situation.

Recovery Skills Must be Taught. As a customer, you may quickly feel insecure at the point of service failure because things are not turning out as you had expected. So you look to an employee for assistance. However, are they willing and able to help you? Effective training builds confidence and competence among frontline staff[30], enabling them to turn distress into delight. With effective training of how to handle recovery solution sets for routine service failures (e.g., as in our hotel example in *Service Insights 13.2*) and for non-routine service failures, frontline staff can turn distress into delight with confidence and skill.

Recovery Requires Empowered Employees. Service recovery efforts should be flexible and employees should be empowered to use their judgment and communication skills to develop solutions that will satisfy complaining customers[31]. This is especially true for out-of-the-ordinary failures for which a firm may not have developed and trained solution sets. Employees need to be able to make decisions and spend money in order to resolve service problems promptly and recover customer goodwill. At the Ritz-Carlton and Sheraton hotels, employees are given the freedom to be proactive, rather than reactive. They take ownership of the situation and help resolve customers' problems to the best of their ability. In this day and age where online public complaining is gaining popularity, employees may even be empowered to respond online, for example, to complaints in the form of tweets, by tweeting back with a solution to resolve the problem. [32]

Figure 13.8 How not to treat unhappy customers

"Ok, how about this motto: 'If you are unhappy for any reason, we will feel really bad'."

SERVICE INSIGHTS 13.2

Effective Service Recovery in Action

The lobby is deserted. It's not hard to overhear the conversation between the front desk receptionist at the Marriott Long Wharf Hotel in Boston and the late-arriving guest.

"Yes, Dr. Jones, we've been expecting you. I know you are scheduled to be here for three nights. I'm sorry to tell you, sir, but we are booked solid tonight. A large number of guests we assumed were checking out did not. Where is your meeting tomorrow, sir?"

The doctor told the receptionist where it was.

"That's near the Omni Parker House! That's not very far from here. Let me call them and get you a room for the evening. I'll be right back."

A few minutes later the receptionist returned with the good news.

"They're holding a room for you at the Omni Parker House, sir. And, of course, we'll pick up the tab. I'll forward any phone calls that come here for you. Here's a letter that will explain the situation and expedite your check-in, along with my business card so you can call me directly here at the front desk if you have any problems."

The doctor's mood was moving from exasperation towards calm. But the receptionist was not finished with the encounter. He reached into the cash drawer. "Here is a $50 bill. That should more than cover your cab fare from here to the Parker House and back again in the morning. We don't have a problem tomorrow night, just tonight. And here's a coupon that will get you complimentary continental breakfast on our concierge level on the fifth floor tomorrow morning… and again, I am so sorry this happened."

As the doctor walks away, the hotel's night manager turns to the receptionist, "Give him about 15 minutes and then call to make sure everything went okay."

A week later when it was still a peak period for hotels in that city, the same guest who had overheard the exchange is in a taxi, *en route* to the same hotel. Along the way, he tells about the great service recovery episode he had witnessed the week before. The two travelers arrive at the hotel and make their way to the front desk, ready to check in.

They are greeted with unexpected news: "I am so sorry gentlemen. I know you were scheduled here for two nights. But we are booked solid tonight. Where is your meeting scheduled tomorrow?"

The would-be guests exchange a rueful glance as they give the receptionist their future plans. "That's near the Méridien. Let me call over there and see if I can get you a room. It won't but take a minute." As the receptionist walks away, the tale teller says, "I'll bet he comes back with a letter and a business card."

Sure enough, the receptionist returns to deliver the solution; it's not a robotic script but all the elements from the previous week's show are on display. What the tale teller thought was pure initiative from front desk receptionist the previous week, he now realizes was a planned, seemingly spontaneous yet predetermined response to a specific category of service problem.

Source

Adapted from: Ron Zemke and Chip R. Bell, *Knock Your Socks Off Service Recovery* (New York: AMACOM, 2000), 59–60.

How Generous Should Compensation Be?

Clearly, vastly different costs are associated with possible recovery strategies. How much compensation should a firm offer when there has been a service failure? Or would an apology be sufficient instead? The following rules of thumb can help managers to answer these questions:

- **What is the positioning of your firm?** If a firm is known for service excellence and charges a premium price for quality, then customers will expect service failures to be rare, so the firm should make a demonstrable effort to recover the few failures that do occur and be prepared to offer something of significant value. However, in a mass market business, customers are likely to accept an apology and rework of the service.

- **How severe was the service failure?** The general guideline is "let the punishment fit the crime". Customers expect little for minor inconveniences (in this case, often a sincere apology will do), but a much more significant compensation if there was major damage in terms of time, effort, annoyance, or anxiety was created by the failure[33].

- **Who is the affected customer?** Long-term customers and those who spend heavily at a service provider expect more, and it is worth making an effort to save their business. One-time customers tend to be less demanding, and have less economic importance to the firm. Hence, compensation can be less, but should still be fair. There is always the possibility that a first-time user will become a repeat customer if he or she is treated well.

The overall rule of thumb for compensation at service failures should be "well-dosed generosity." Being perceived as stingy adds insult to injury, and the firm will probably be better off apologizing than offering a minimal compensation. Overly generous compensation is not only expensive, customers may even interpret such a response negatively by raising questions in their minds about the soundness of the business and leading them to become suspicious about the underlying motives. Customers may worry about the implications for the employee as well as for the business. Also, overgenerosity does not seem to result in higher repeat purchase rates than simply offering a fair compensation[34]. There is also a risk that a reputation for overgenerosity may encourage dishonest customers to actively "seek" service failures[35]. In fact, what customers really want is often just a satisfactory solution to their service problem rather than bells and whistles[36]!

Dealing With Complaining Customers

Both managers and frontline employees must be prepared to deal with distressed customers, including jaycustomers who can become confrontational and behave in unacceptable ways towards service personnel who often aren't at fault in any way.

Good interactive skills combined with training and on-the-spot thinking are critical for frontline employees to deal with such situations. *Service Insights 13.3* provides specific guidelines for effective problem resolution, designed to help calm upset customers and to deliver a resolution that they will see as fair and satisfying[37].

 LO 7
Be familiar with the guidelines for frontline employees on how to handle complaining customers and recover from a service failure.

SERVICE INSIGHTS 13.3

Guidelines for the Frontline: How to Handle Complaining Customers and Recover From a Service Failure

1. **Act fast.** If the complaint is made during service delivery, then time is of the essence to achieve a full recovery. When complaints are made after the fact, many companies have established policies of responding within 24 hours, or sooner. Even when full resolution is likely to take longer, fast acknowledgment remains very important.

2. **Acknowledge the customer's feelings.** Do this either tacitly or explicitly (for example, "I can understand why you're upset"). This action helps to build rapport, the first step in rebuilding a bruised relationship.

3. **Don't argue with customers.** The goal should be to gather facts to reach a mutually acceptable solution, not to win a debate or prove that the customer is wrong. Arguing gets in the way of listening and seldom diffuses anger.

4. **Show that you understand the problem from each customer's point of view.** Seeing situations through the customers' eyes is the only way to understand what they think has gone wrong and why they're upset. Service personnel should avoid jumping to conclusions with their own interpretations.

5. **Clarify the facts and sort out the cause.** A failure may result from inefficiency of service, misunderstanding by customers, or the misbehavior of a third party. If you've done something wrong, apologize immediately in order to win the understanding and trust of the customer. The more the customer can forgive you, the less he or she will expect to be compensated. Don't be defensive; reacting defensively may suggest that the organization has something to hide or is reluctant to fully look into the situation.

6. **Give customers the benefit of the doubt.** Not all customers are truthful and not all complaints are genuine. However, customers should be treated as though they have a valid complaint until clear evidence proves that it is not true. If a lot of money is at stake (as in insurance claims or potential lawsuits), careful investigation needs to be carried out. If the amount involved is small, it may not be worth haggling over a refund or other compensation. However, it's still a good idea to check the records to see if there is a past history of dubious complaints by the same customer.

7. **Propose the steps needed to solve the problem.** When instant solutions aren't immediately available, tell customers how the firm intends to take action to deal with the problem. This also sets expectations about the time involved, so firms should be careful not to overpromise!

8. **Keep customers informed of progress.** Nobody likes being left in the dark. Uncertainty causes people to be anxious and stressed. People tend to be more accepting if they know what's going on and receive periodic progress reports. Therefore, people should be kept informed about what is going on regularly.

9. **Consider compensation.** When customers do not receive the service outcomes they believe they have paid for or have suffered serious inconvenience and/or loss of time and money because the service failed, either a monetary payment or some other compensation in kind (e.g., an upgrade on a flight or a free dessert in a restaurant) is appropriate. This type of recovery strategy may also reduce the risk of legal action by an angry customer. Service guarantees often lay out in advance what such compensation will be, and the firm should ensure that all guarantees are met.

10. **Persevere to regain customer goodwill.** When customers have been disappointed, one of the hardest things to do is to restore their confidence and keep the relationship going. Perseverance may be required to defuse customers' anger and to convince them that actions are being taken to avoid a recurrence of the problem. Truly exceptional recovery efforts can be extremely effective in building loyalty and referrals.

11. **Self-check the service delivery system and improve it.** After the customer has left, you should check to see whether the service failure was caused by accidental mistakes or system defects. Take advantage of every complaint to perfect the whole service system. Even if the complaint is found to be a result of a misunderstanding by customer, this implies that some part of your communication system is ineffective.

SERVICE GUARANTEES

One way for particularly customer-focused firms to institutionalize professional complaint handling and effective service recovery is through offering service guarantees. In fact, a growing number of companies offer customers a service guarantee, promising that if service delivery fails to meet predefined standards, the customer will be entitled one or more forms of compensation, such as an easy-to-claim replacement, refund, or credit. A well-designed service guarantee not only facilitates effective service recovery, but also institutionalizes learning from service failures and subsequent system improvements[38].

The Power of Service Guarantees

LO 8
Recognize the power of service guarantees.

Service guarantees are powerful tools for both promoting and achieving service quality for the following reasons[39]:

1. They force firms to focus on what their customers want and expect in each element of the service.

2. They set clear standards, telling customers and employees alike what the company stands for. Payouts to compensate customers for poor service cause managers to take guarantees seriously as they highlight the financial costs of quality failures.

3. They require the development of systems for generating meaningful customer feedback and acting on it.

4. They force service organizations to understand why they fail and encourage them to identify and overcome potential fail points.

5. They build "marketing muscle" by reducing the risk of the purchase decision and building long-term loyalty.

Figure 13.9 Hampton Inn includes its "100% satisfaction guaranteed" in its advertising

From the customer's perspective, the primary function of service guarantees is to lower the perceived risks associated with purchase[40]. The presence of a guarantee may also make it easier for customers to complain and more likely that they will do so, because they will anticipate that frontline employees will be prepared to resolve the problem and provide appropriate compensation. Sara Björlin Lidén and Per Skålén found that even when dissatisfied customers were unaware that a service guarantee existed before making their complaint, they were positively impressed to learn that the company has a preplanned procedure for handling failures and to find that their complaints were taken seriously.[41]

The benefits of service guarantees can be seen clearly in the case of Hampton Inn's "100% Hampton Guarantee" ("If you're not 100% satisfied, you don't pay"; see *Figure 13.9*). As a business-building program, Hampton's strategy of offering to refund the cost of the room to a guest who expresses dissatisfaction has attracted new customers and also served as a powerful retention device. People choose to stay at a Hampton Inn because they are confident they will be satisfied. At least as important,

the guarantee has become a vital tool to help managers identify new opportunities for quality improvement.

In discussing the impact on staff and managers, the vice president–marketing of Hampton Inn stated, "Designing the guarantee made us understand what made guests satisfied, rather than what *we thought* made them satisfied." It became imperative that everyone from reservationists and frontline employees, to general managers and personnel at corporate headquarters, listen carefully to guests, anticipate their needs to the greatest extent possible, and remedy problems quickly so that guests were satisfied with the solution. Viewing a hotel's function in this customer-centric way had a profound impact on the way the firm conducted business.

The guarantee "turned up the pressure in the hose," as one manager put it, showing where "leaks" existed, and providing the financial incentive to plug them. As a result, the "100% Hampton Guarantee" has had an important impact on product consistency and service delivery across the Hampton Inn chain, and it showed a dramatically positive effect on its financial performance.[42]

How to Design Service Guarantees

Some guarantees are simple and unconditional. Others appear to have been written by lawyers and contain many restrictions. Compare the examples in *Service Insights 13.4* and ask yourself which guarantees instill trust and confidence and would make you like to do business with that firm.

All three service guarantees — from L. L. Bean, MFA Group, and BBBK — are powerful, unconditional, and instill trust. The other guarantee is weakened by the many conditions attached to it. Hart argues that service guarantees should be designed to meet the following criteria[43]:

1. **Unconditional** — Whatever is promised in the guarantee must be totally unconditional and there should not be any element of surprise for the customer.

2. **Easy to understand and communicate** — The customer is clearly aware of the benefits that can be gained from the guarantee.

3. **Meaningful to the customer** in that the guarantee is on something important to the customer and the compensation should be more than adequate to cover the service failure[44].

4. **Easy to invoke** — It should be easy for the customer to invoke the guarantee.

5. **Easy to collect on** — If a service failure occurs, the customer should be able to easily collect on the guarantee without any problems.

6. **Credible** — The guarantee should be believable (*Figure 13.10*).

Is Full Satisfaction the Best You Can Guarantee?

Full satisfaction guarantees have generally been considered the best possible design. However, it has been suggested that the ambiguity associated with such guarantees can lead to the discounting of their perceived value. For example, customers may raise questions such as "What does full satisfaction mean?" or "Can I invoke a guarantee when I am dissatisfied, although the fault does not lie with the service firm?"[45] Attribute-specific guarantees (e.g., guaranteed delivery within 24 hours) are highly specific and therefore don't suffer from ambiguity, although their coverage is not comprehensive and limits their appeal. A hybrid version of the full satisfaction and attribute-specific guarantee, referred to as the "combined guarantee," addresses this issue. It combines the wide scope of a full satisfaction guarantee with the low uncertainty of attribute-specific performance standards. The combined guarantee has been shown to be superior to the pure full satisfaction or attribute-specific guarantee designs.[46] Specific performance standards are guaranteed (e.g., on-time delivery), but should the consumer be dissatisfied with any other element of the service, the full-satisfaction coverage of the combined guarantee applies. *Table 13.2* shows examples of the various types of guarantees.

LO 9
Understand how to design effective service guarantees.

Figure 13.10 To leave a clear stamp of service quality on customers, the guarantee must be unconditional, meaningful, credible, easily understood, invoked, and collectable

SERVICE INSIGHTS 13.4
Examples of Service Guarantees

United States Postal Service Express Mail Guarantee

Service Guarantee: Express Mail international mailings are not covered by this service agreement. Military shipments delayed due to customs inspections are also excluded. If the shipment is mailed at a designated USPS Express Mail facility on or before the specified deposit time for overnight delivery to the addressee, delivery to the addressee or agent will be attempted before the applicable guaranteed time. Signature of the addressee's agent, or delivery employee is required upon delivery. If a delivery attempt is not made by the guaranteed time and the mailer files a claim for a refund, the USPS will refund the postage unless the delay was caused by: proper retention for law enforcement purposes; strike or work stoppage; late deposit of shipment; forwarding, return, incorrect address, or incorrect ZIP code; delay or cancellation of flights; governmental action beyond the control of the Postal Service or air carriers; war, insurrection or civil disturbance; breakdowns of a substantial portion of the USPS transportation network resulting from events or factors outside the control of the Postal Service or Acts of God.

L. L. Bean's Guarantee

100% Guaranteed. Our products are guaranteed to give 100% satisfaction in every way. Return anything purchased from us at any time if it proves otherwise. We do not want you to have anything from L. L. Bean that is not completely satisfactory.

Our guarantee is based on something as simple as a handshake — the deal that you'll be satisfied with a purchase, and if you are not, we'll make it right. We guarantee that we'll hold up our end of the bargain. It's just how we do business. If your purchase isn't completely satisfactory, we're happy to accept your exchange or return at any time.

MFA Group Inc. (a Professional Recruitment Agency)

We "put our money where our mouth is," in two ways:

1. **Money back:** We offer an unconditional money back guarantee — if at any point during the search process you are unhappy with progress, simply address the fact with us and if you are still not 100% satisfied after that discussion, we will cheerfully and unconditionally, refund every cent you have paid as a retainer. No quibble, no hassle, guaranteed period.

2. **Twelve-month candidate guarantee:** All candidates placed by us are guaranteed for a full 12 months. If, during this period they leave your firm, for any reason whatsoever, we will conduct an additional search, completely free of charge, until a suitable replacement has been found.

The Bugs Burger Bug Killer Guarantee (a Pest Control Company)

- You don't owe us a penny until all the pests on your premises have been eradicated.
- If you're ever dissatisfied with the BBBK's service you will receive a refund for as much as 12 months of service — plus fees for another exterminator of your choice for the next year.
- If a guest spots a pest on your premises, the exterminator will pay for the guest's meal or room, send a letter of apology, and pay for a future meal or stay.
- If your premises are closed down because of the presence of roaches or rodents, BBBK will pay any fines, as well as all lost profit, plus $5000.

Source

Printed on back of Express Mail receipt, January 2006. (Note that USPS has dramatically improved its guarantee since.)

Printed in all L. L. Bean catalogs and on the company's website, http://global.llbean.com/guarantee.html, accessed August 26, 2015.

MGA Group's website, http://www.mfagroup.com/recruiting.htm, accessed June 1, 2009.

Reproduced in Christopher W. Hart (1990), "The Power of Unconditional Service Guarantees," *Harvard Business Review,* July–August.

Table 13.2 Types of Service Guarantees

Term	Guarantee Scope	Example
Single attribute-specific guarantee	One key attribute of the service is covered by the guarantee.	"Any of three specified popular pizzas is guaranteed to be served within 10 minutes of ordering on working days between 12 a.m. and 2 p.m. If the pizza is late, the customer's next order is free."
Multiattribute-specific guarantee	A few important attributes of the service are covered by the guarantee.	Minneapolis Marriott's guarantee: "Our quality commitment to you is to provide: • a friendly, efficient check-in; • a clean, comfortable room, where everything works; • a friendly efficient check-out. If we, in your opinion, do not deliver on this commitment, we will give you $20 in cash. No questions asked. It is your interpretation."
Full-satisfaction guarantee	All aspects of the service are covered by the guarantee. There are no exceptions.	Lands' End's guarantee: "If you are not completely satisfied with any item you buy from us, at any time during your use of it, return it and we will refund your full purchase price. We mean every word of it. Whatever. Whenever. Always. But to make sure this is perfectly clear, we've decided to simplify it further. GUARANTEED. Period."
Combined guarantee	All aspects of the service are covered by the full-satisfaction promise of the guarantee. Explicit minimum performance standards on important attributes are included in the guarantee to reduce uncertainty	Datapro Information Services guarantees "to deliver the report on time, to high quality standards, and to the contents outlined in this proposal. Should we fail to deliver according to this guarantee, or should you be dissatisfied with any aspect of our work, you can deduct any amount from the final payment which is deemed as fair."

Source

Wirtz, J. and Kum, D (2002). "Designing Service Guarantees — Is Full Satisfaction the Best You Can Guarantee?" *Journal of Services Marketing*, Vol. 15, No. 14, pp. 282–299.

LO 10
Know when firms should not
offer service guarantees.

Is It Always Beneficial to Introduce a Service Guarantee?

Managers should think carefully about their firm's strengths and weaknesses when deciding whether or not to introduce a service guarantee. There are a number of situations in which a guarantee may not be appropriate[47]:

- Companies that already have a strong reputation for service excellence may not need a guarantee. In fact, it can be incongruent with their image to offer one as it might confuse the market[48]. Rather, best practice service firms will be expected to do what's right without offering a service guarantee.

- In contrast, a firm whose service is currently poor must first work to improve its quality to a level above what is guaranteed. Otherwise, too many customers will invoke the guarantee with serious cost implications.

- Service firms whose quality is truly uncontrollable due to external forces would be foolish to consider a guarantee. For example, when Amtrak realized that it was paying out substantial refunds because it lacked sufficient control over its railroad infrastructure, it was forced to drop a service guarantee that included the reimbursement of fares in the event of unpunctual train service.

- In a market where consumers see little financial, personal, or physiological risk associated with purchasing and using a service, a guarantee adds little value but still costs money to design, implement, and manage.

In markets where there is little perceived difference in service quality among competing firms, the first firm to institute a guarantee may also be able to obtain a first-mover advantage and create value differentiation for its services. If more than one competitor already have guarantees in place, offering one may become a qualifier for the industry, and the only real way to make an impact is to launch a highly distinctive guarantee beyond what is already offered by competitors[49].

DISCOURAGING ABUSE AND OPPORTUNISTIC CUSTOMER BEHAVIOR

Throughout this chapter, we advocate that firms should welcome complaints and invocations of service guarantees and even encourage them. While we discussed the importance of professional complaint handling and service recovery, we have to acknowledge that not all complaints are honest. When firms have generous service recovery policies or offer guarantees, there is always the fear that some customers may take advantage of them. Also, not all complaining customers are right or reasonable in their behavior, and some may actually be the cause of complaints by other customers[50]. We refer to such people as **jaycustomers**.

Visitors to North America from other English-speaking countries are often puzzled by the term "jaywalker," a distinctively American word used to describe people who cross streets at unauthorized places or in a dangerous manner. The prefix "jay" comes from a 19th Century slang for a stupid person. We define a jaycustomer as someone who acts in a thoughtless or abusive way, causing problems for the firm, its employees, and other customers.

Customers who act in uncooperative or abusive ways are a problem for any organization. However, they have even more potential for mischief in service businesses, particularly those in which many other customers are present in the same service environment. As you know from personal experience, other people's behavior can affect your enjoyment of a service. If you like classical music and attend symphony concerts, you expect audience members to keep quiet during the performance, and to not spoil the experience for others by talking, coughing loudly or failing to turn off their cell phones. In contrast, a silent audience would be deadly during a rock concert or team sports event, where active audience participation adds to the excitement. However, there's a fine line between spectator enthusiasm and abusive behavior by supporters of rival sports teams. Firms that fail to deal effectively with customer misbehaviors risk damaging their relationships with all the other customers they'd like to keep.

However, opinions on this topic seem to polarize around two opposing views. One is denial: "the customer is king and can do no wrong." The other view sees the marketplace of customers as positively overpopulated with nasty people who cannot be trusted to behave in ways that self-respecting service providers should expect and require. The first viewpoint has received wide publicity in gung-ho management books and in motivational presentations to captive groups of employees. The second view often appears to be dominant among cynical managers and frontline employees who have been burned at some point by customer misbehaviors. As with many opposing viewpoints, there are important grains of truth in both perspectives. What is clear, however, is that no self-respecting firm wants an ongoing relationship with an abusive customer.

Every service has its share of jaycustomers. Jaycustomers are undesirable. At best, a firm should avoid attracting them in the first place, and at worst, a firm needs to control or prevent their abusive behavior. Let's first describe the main types of jaycustomers before discussing how to deal with them.

Seven Types of Jaycustomers

Defining a problem is the first step in resolving it, so let's start by considering the different types of jaycustomers.[51] We've identified seven broad categories and given them generic names, but many customer contact personnel have come up with their own special terms.

The Cheat. There are many ways in which customers can cheat service firms. Cheating ranges from writing complaint letters with the sole purpose of exploiting service recovery policies and cheating on service guarantees, to inflating or faking insurance claims and "wardrobing" (e.g., using an evening dress or tuxedo for an evening and then returning it back to the retailer)[52]. Fake returns have become more common and socially accepted, especially so with online retailers. One company reported that 1% of its customers who bought five or more items sent back 90% or more of their purchases[53]! The following quotes describe the thinking of these customers nicely in other contexts:

LO 11
Be familiar with the seven groups of jaycustomers and understand how to manage them effectively.

On checking in to a hotel I noticed that they had a "100% satisfaction or your money back" guarantee, I just couldn't resist the opportunity to take advantage of it, so on checking out I told the receptionist that I wanted a refund as the sound of the traffic kept me awake all night. They gave me a refund, no questions asked. These companies can be so stupid they need to be more alert. [54]

I've complained that service was too slow, too quick, too hot, too cold, too bright, too dark, too friendly, too impersonal, too public, too private... it doesn't matter really, as long as you enclose a receipt with your letter, you just get back a standard letter and gift coupon[55].

Firms cannot easily check whether a customer is faking dissatisfaction or truly is unhappy. At the end of this section, we will discuss how to deal with this type of consumer fraud.

The Thief. The thief jaycustomer has no intention of paying and sets out to steal goods and services (or to pay less than full price by switching price tickets, or contesting bills on baseless grounds). Shoplifting is a major problem in retail stores. What retailers euphemistically call "shrinkage" is estimated to cost them huge sums of money in annual revenues. Many services lend themselves to clever schemes for avoiding payment. For those with technical skills, it's sometimes possible to bypass electricity meters, access telephone lines free of charge, or bypass normal cable TV feeds. Riding free on public transportation, sneaking into movie theaters, or not paying for restaurant meals are also popular, not forgetting the use of fraudulent forms of payment such as using stolen credit cards or checks drawn on accounts without any funds. Finding out how people steal a service is the first step in preventing theft or catching thieves and, where appropriate, prosecuting them. However, managers should try not to alienate honest customers by degrading their service experiences. Provision must also be made for honest but absent-minded customers who forget to pay.

The Rulebreaker. Just as highways need safety regulations (including "Don't Jaywalk"), many service businesses need to establish rules of behavior for customers to guide them safely through the various steps of the service process. Some of these rules are imposed by government agencies for health and safety reasons. The sign found in many restaurants that states "No shirt, no shoes, no service" demonstrates a health-related regulation. Air travel provides one of the best examples of rules designed to ensure safety — there are few other environments outside prison where healthy, mentally competent, adult customers are quite so constrained (albeit for good reason).

In addition to enforcing government regulations, suppliers often impose their own rules to facilitate smooth operations, avoid unreasonable demands on employees, prevent misuse of products and facilities, protect themselves legally, and discourage individual customers from misbehaving. For instance, ski resorts are strict on careless skiers who pose risks to both themselves and others. Collisions can cause serious injury and even death. As such, ski patrol members must be safety-oriented and sometimes take on a policing role. Just as dangerous drivers can lose their licenses, dangerous skiers can lose their lift tickets (*Figure 13.11*). For example, at Vail and Beaver Creek in Colorado, ski patrollers once revoked nearly 400 lift tickets in just a single weekend. At Winter Park near

Denver, skiers who lose their passes for dangerous behavior may have to attend a 45-minute safety class before they can get their passes back. Ski patrollers at Vermont's Okemo Mountain may issue warnings to reckless skiers by attaching a bright orange sticker to their lift tickets. If pulled over again for inappropriate behavior, such skiers may be escorted off the mountain and banned for a day or more. "We're not trying to be Gestapos on the slopes," says the resort's marketing director, "just trying to educate people."

How should a firm deal with rulebreakers? Much depends on which rules have been broken. In the case of legally enforceable ones — theft, bad debts, or trying to take guns on an aircraft — the courses of action need to be laid down explicitly to protect employees and to punish or discourage wrongdoing by customers.

Company rules are a little more ambiguous. Are they really necessary in the first place? If not, the firm should get rid of them. Do they deal with health and safety? If so, educating customers about the rules should reduce the need for taking corrective action. The same is true for rules designed to protect the comfort and enjoyment of all customers. There are also unwritten social norms such as "thou shalt not cut in line," although this is a much stronger cultural expectation in the United States or Canada than in many countries, as any visitor to Paris or Hong Kong Disneyland can attest! Other customers can often be relied upon to help service personnel enforce rules that affect everybody else; they may even take the initiative in doing so.

There are risks attached to making lots of rules. The firm may become too inflexible and make it appear bureaucratic and overbearing. Instead of being customer-oriented, employees become like police officers, making sure that customers follow all the rules. However, the fewer the rules, the clearer the important ones can be.

Figure 13.11 Dangerous skiers are rule breakers who pose a danger to others and need to be policed

Figure 13.12 Confrontations between customers and service employees can easily escalate

The Belligerent. You've probably seen him (or her) in a store, at the airport, in a hotel or restaurant — red in the face and shouting angrily, or perhaps icily calm and mouthing insults, threats, and obscenities. Things don't always work as they should: machines break down, service is clumsy, customers are ignored, a flight is delayed, an order is delivered incorrectly, staff are unhelpful, or a promise is broken. Perhaps the customer in question is expressing resentment at being told to abide by the rules. Service personnel are often abused, even when they are not to blame. If an employee lacks the power to resolve the problem, the belligerent may become angrier still, even to the point of physical attack. Unfortunately, when angry customers rant at service personnel, the latter sometimes respond in kind, thus escalating the confrontation and reducing the likelihood of resolution (*Figure 13.12*).

Drunkenness and drug abuse add extra layers of complication. Organizations that care about their employees go to great efforts to develop skills in dealing with these difficult situations. Training exercises that involve role-playing help employees develop the self-confidence and assertiveness needed to deal with upset, belligerent customers (sometimes referred to as "irates"). Employees also need to learn how to defuse anger, calm anxiety, and comfort distress (particularly when there is good reason for the customer to be upset with the organization's performance).

"We seem to live in an age of rage," declared Stephen Grove, Raymond Fisk, and Joby John, noting a general decline in civility[56]. They suggest that rage behaviors are learned via socialization as appropriate responses to certain situations. Anger and dissatisfaction are qualitatively different emotions. Whereas dissatisfied customers had a feeling of unfulfillment or "missing out" and wanted to find out who or what was responsible for the event, angry customers were thinking how unfair the situation was, sought to get back at the organization, and wanted to hurt someone[57]. The problem of "Air Rage" has attracted particular attention in recent years due to the risks it poses to innocent people (*Service Insights 13.5*)[58].

What should an employee do when an aggressive customer brushes off attempts to defuse the situation? In a public environment, one priority should be to move the person away from other customers. Sometimes supervisors may have to settle disagreements between customers and staff members; at other times, they need to support the employee's actions. If a customer has physically attacked an employee, then it may be necessary to summon security officers or the police. Some firms try to conceal such events, fearing bad publicity. Others however, feel obliged to make a public stand on behalf of their employees, like the Body Shop manager who ordered an ill-tempered customer out of the store, telling her: "I won't stand for your rudeness to my staff."

Telephone rudeness poses a different challenge. Service personnel have been known to hang up on angry customers, but that action doesn't resolve the problem. For instance, bank customers tend to get upset upon learning that checks have been returned because the account is overdrawn (which means they've broken the rules), or that a request for a loan has been denied. One approach for handling customers who continue to shout at a telephone-based employee is for the latter to say firmly: "This conversation isn't getting us anywhere. Why don't I call you back in a few minutes when you've had time to digest the information?" In many cases, taking a break to think (and cool down) is exactly what's needed.

SERVICE INSIGHTS 13.5
Air Rage: Unruly Passengers Pose a Continuing Problem

Joining the term "road rage" — coined in 1988 to describe angry, aggressive drivers who threaten other road users — is "air rage," describing the behavior of violent, unruly passengers who endanger flight attendants, pilots, and other passengers. Incidents of air rage are perpetrated by only a tiny fraction of all airline passengers — reportedly about 5,000 times a year — but each incident in the air may affect the comfort and safety of hundreds of other people.

Although terrorism is an ongoing concern, out-of-control passengers pose a serious threat to safety too. On a flight from Orlando, Florida to London, a drunken passenger smashed a video screen and began ramming a window, telling fellow passengers they were about to "get sucked out and die." The crew strapped him down and the aircraft made an unscheduled landing in Bangor, Maine, where US marshals arrested him. Another unscheduled stop in Bangor involved a drug smuggler flying from Jamaica to the Netherlands. When a balloon filled with cocaine ruptured in his stomach, he went berserk, pounding a bathroom door to pieces and grabbing a female passenger by the throat.

On a flight from London to Spain, a passenger who was already drunk at the time of boarding became angry when a flight attendant told him not to smoke in the lavatory and then refused to serve him another drink. Later, he smashed her over the head with a duty-free vodka bottle before being restrained by other passengers (she required 18 stitches to close the wound). Other dangerous incidents have included throwing hot coffee at flight attendants, head-butting a copilot, trying to break into the cockpit, throwing a flight attendant across three rows of seats, and attempting to open an emergency door in flight.

On a US domestic flight with a tragic outcome, a violent passenger was restrained and ultimately suffocated by other passengers after he kicked through the cockpit door of an airliner 20 minutes before it was scheduled to land in Salt Lake City.

A growing number of carriers are taking air rage perpetrators to court. Northwest Airlines permanently blacklisted three violent travelers from flying on its aircraft. British Airways gives out "warning cards" to any passenger getting dangerously out of control. Celebrities are not immune to air rage. Rock star Courtney Love blamed her "potty mouth" after being arrested on arrival in London for disruptive behavior on board a flight from Los Angeles. Some airlines carry physical restraints to subdue out-of-control passengers until they can be handed over to airport authorities.

In April 2000, the US Congress increased the civil penalty for air rage from $1,100 to $25,000 in an attempt to discourage passengers from misbehaving. Criminal penalties — a $10,000 fine and up to 20 years in jail — can also be imposed for the most serious incidents. Some airlines have been reluctant to publicize this information for fear of appearing confrontational or intimidating. However, the visible implementation of anti-terrorist security precautions have made it more acceptable to tighten enforcement of procedures designed to control and punish air rage.

What causes air rage? Psychological feelings of a loss of control, or problems with authority figures may be causal factors for angry behavior in many service settings. Researchers suggest that air travel, in particular, has become increasingly stressful as a result of crowding and longer flights; the airlines themselves may have contributed to the problem by squeezing rows of seats more tightly together and failing to explain delays. Findings suggest that risk factors for air travel stress include anxiety and an anger-prone personality; they also show that traveling on unfamiliar routes is more stressful than traveling on a familiar one. Another factor may be restrictions on smoking. However, alcohol abuse underlies a majority of incidents!

Airlines are training their employees to handle violent individuals and to spot problem passengers before they start causing serious problems. Some carriers offer travelers specific suggestions on how to relax during long flights. Some airlines have also considered offering nicotine patches to passengers who are desperate for a smoke but are not allowed to light up. Increased security in the air may be curtailing rage behavior on board flights, but concern continues to grow about passenger rage on the ground. An Australian survey of airport employees found that 96% of airport staff had experienced air rage at work: 31% of agents experienced some form of air rage daily, and 15% of agents reported that they had been physically touched or assaulted by a passenger.

Source

Based on information from multiple sources, including: Daniel Eisenberg, "Acting Up in the Air," *Time*, December 21, 1998; "Air Rage Capital: Bangor Becomes Nation's Flight Problem Drop Point," *The Baltimore Sun*, syndicated article, September, 1999; Melanie Trottman and Chip Cummins, "Passenger's Death Prompts Calls for Improved 'Air Rage' Procedures," *The Wall Street Journal*, September 26, 2000; Blair J. Berkley and Mohammad Ala (2001), "Identifying and Controlling Threatening Airline Passengers, *Cornell Hotel and Restaurant Administration Quarterly*, Vol. 42, August–September, pp. 6–24; www.airsafe.com/issues/rage.htm, accessed August 26, 2015.

The Family Feuders. People who get into arguments with members of their own family — or worse, with other customers — make up a subcategory of belligerents we call "family feuders". Employee intervention may calm the situation or actually make it worse. Some situations require detailed analysis and a carefully thought-out response. Others, such as customers starting a food fight in an upscale restaurant, require an almost immediate response. Service managers in these situations need to be prepared to think on their feet and act fast.

The Vandal. Soft drinks are poured into bank cash machines; graffiti are scrawled on both interior and exterior surfaces; burn holes from cigarettes scar carpets, tablecloths, and bedcovers; bus seats are slashed and hotel furniture broken; customers' cars are vandalized; glass is smashed and fabrics are torn — the list is endless. Customers don't cause all of the damage, of course. Bored or drunk young people are the source of much exterior vandalism. Disgruntled employees have been known to commit sabotage. Much of the problem does originate with paying customers who choose to misbehave. Alcohol and drugs are sometimes the cause, at other times psychological problems may contribute, and carelessness can play a role. There are also occasions when unhappy customers, feeling mistreated by the service firm, try to take revenge in some way.

The best cure for vandalism is prevention. Improved security discourages some vandals (*Figure 13.13*). Good lighting helps, as well as open design of public areas. Companies can choose vandal-resistant surfaces and protective coverings for equipment, and rugged furnishings. Educating customers to use equipment properly (rather than fighting with it) and providing warnings about fragile objects can reduce the likelihood of abuse or careless handling. Finally, there are economic sanctions: security deposits or signed agreements in which customers agree to pay for any damage that they cause.

Figure 13.13 Installing surveillance cameras in public car parks can discourage vandalism

What should managers do if prevention fails and damage is done? If the perpetrator is caught, they should first clarify whether there are any extenuating circumstances (because accidents do happen). Sanctions for deliberate damage can range from a warning to prosecution. As far as the physical damage itself is concerned, it's best to fix it fast (within any constraints imposed by legal or insurance considerations). The general manager of a bus company had the right idea when he said: "If one of our buses is vandalized, whether it's a broken window, a slashed seat, or graffiti on the ceiling, we take it out of service immediately so nobody sees it. Otherwise you just give the same idea to five other characters who were too dumb to think of it in the first place!"

The Deadbeat. Leaving aside those individuals who never intended to pay in the first place (our term for them is "the thief"), there are many reasons why customers fail to pay for services they have received. They are the ones who delay payment. Once again, preventive action is better than a cure. A growing number of firms insist on pre-payment. Any form of ticket sale is a good example of this. Direct marketing organizations ask for your credit card number as they take your order, as do most hotels when you make a reservation. The next best thing is to present the customer with a bill immediately on completion of service. If the bill is to be sent by mail, the firm should send it fast, while the service is still fresh in the customer's mind.

Not every apparent delinquent is a hopeless deadbeat. Perhaps there's a good reason for the delay and acceptable payment arrangements can be worked out. A key question is whether such a personalized approach can be cost justified, relative to the results obtained by purchasing the services of a collection agency. There may be other considerations too. If the client's problems are only temporary, what is the long-term value of maintaining the relationship? Will it create positive goodwill and word-of-mouth to help the customer work things out? These decisions are judgment calls, but if creating and maintaining long-term relationships is the firm's ultimate goal, they are worth exploring.

Consequences of Dysfunctional Customer Behavior

Dysfunctional customer behavior has consequences for frontline staff, other customers, and the organization itself[59]. Employees who are abused may not only find their mood or temper negatively affected in the short run, but may eventually suffer long-term psychological damage. Their own behavior too, may take on negative dimensions, such as taking revenge on abusive customers. Staff morale can be hurt, with implications for both productivity and quality[60].

The consequences for customers can take both positive and negative forms. Other customers may rally to the support of an employee whom they perceive as having been abused; however, bad behavior can also be contagious, leading a bad situation to escalate as others join in. More broadly, being exposed to negative incidents can spoil the consumption experience for many customers. Companies suffer financially when demotivated employees no longer work as efficiently and effectively as before, or when employees are forced to take medical leave. There may also be direct financial losses from restoring stolen or damaged property, legal costs, and paying fraudulent claims.

As suggested in the earlier discussion of air rage, the nature of jaycustomer behavior is likely to be shaped by the characteristics of the service industry in which it occurs. *Service Insights 13.6* reports on a study of jaycustomers in the hospitality industry.

Dealing With Customer Fraud

Dishonest customers can take advantage of generous service recovery strategies, service guarantees, or simply a strong customer orientation in a number of ways. For example, they may steal from the firm, refuse to pay for the service, fake dissatisfaction, purposefully cause service failures to occur, or overstate losses at the time of genuine service failures. What steps can a firm take to protect itself against opportunistic customer behaviors?

Treating customers with suspicion is likely to alienate them, especially in situations of service failure. The president of TARP notes:

> *Our research has found that premeditated rip-offs represent 1–2% of the customer base in most organizations. However, most organizations defend themselves against unscrupulous customers by... treating the 98% of honest customers like crooks to catch the 2% who are crooks*[61].

Using this knowledge, the working assumptions should be, "If in doubt, believe the customer." However, as *Service Insights 13.7* shows, it's crucial to keep track of customers who repeatedly "experience service failures" and ask for compensation or invoke the firm's service guarantee. For example, one Asian airline found that the same customer lost his suitcase on three consecutive flights. The chances of this truly happening are probably lower than winning in the national lottery, so frontline staff were made aware of this individual. The next time he checked in his suitcase, the check-in staff followed the video image of the suitcase almost from check-in to pickup at the baggage claim carrousel at the traveler's destination. It turned out that a companion collected the suitcase and took it away while the traveler again made his way to the lost baggage counter to report his missing suitcase. This time, the police were waiting for him and his friend.

In another example, Continental Airlines consolidated some 45 separate customer databases into a single data warehouse to improve service and to also detect customer fraud. The airline found one customer who received 20 bereavement fares in 12 months off the same dead grandfather!

SERVICE INSIGHTS 13.6

Categorizing Jaycustomers in Hotels, Restaurants, and Bars

To learn more about dysfunctional customer behavior in the hospitality industry, Lloyd Harris and Kate Reynolds developed a research project to identify and categorize different types of misconduct. Open-ended interviews, typically lasting one hour (but sometimes longer) were conducted with 31 managers, 46 frontline employees, and 29 customers. These interviews took place in 19 hotels (all of which had restaurants and bars), 13 restaurants, and 16 bars. A purposive sampling plan was employed, with the goal of selecting informants with extensive participation in and insights of service encounters. All informants had encountered — or had perpetrated — what could be considered as jaycustomer behavior and were invited to give details of specific incidents. In total, the 106 respondents generated 417 critical incidents.

Based on analysis of these incidents, Harris and Reynolds codified eight types of behavior:

1. **Compensation letter writers** who deliberately and fraudulently wrote to centralized customer service departments with largely unjustified complaints in anticipation of receiving a check or gift voucher.

2. **Undesirable customers** whose behavior fell into three subgroups: (1) irritating behavior by "jaykids" and "jayfamilies;" (2) criminal behavior, typically involving drug sales or prostitution; and (3) homeless individuals who used an organization's facilities and stole other customers' refreshments.

3. **Property abusers** who vandalized facilities and stole items — often to keep as souvenirs.

4. **(Off-duty) service workers** who know how to work the system to their own advantage as customers and deliberately disrupt service encounters, either for financial gain or simply to cause problems for frontline staff.

5. **Vindictive customers** who are violent towards people or property, possibly because of some perceived injustice.

6. **Oral abusers** include professional complainers seeking compensation, and "ego hunters" who take pleasure in offending frontline staff and other customers.

7. **Physical abusers** who physically harm frontline staff.

8. **Sexual predators** — often acting in groups — engage in sexual harassment of frontline personnel either verbally or behaviorally.

Some of these behaviors, such as letter writing and property abuse, are covert in nature (i.e., not evident to others at the time they are committed). Certain underlying causes assert themselves across multiple categories; they include desire for personal gain, drunkenness, personal psychological problems, and negative group dynamics.

Table 13.3 shows the percentage of employees and customers reporting incidents within each category. Rather remarkably, with the exception of the "undesirable customers" category, the incidents in the customer column are all self-reports of the respondents' own misbehavior.

The verbatim reports of jaycustomer behavior recorded in this study make for somber, even scary reading. In particular, they demonstrate especially the challenges posed to management and staff by manipulative customers seeking personal financial gain, and by the abusive behavior of individuals, sometimes acting in groups and fueled by alcohol, who appear unconstrained by traditional societal norms.

Table 13.3 Percentage of Respondents Reporting Incidents by Category

Category	Employees (%)	Customers (%)
Compensation letter writers	30	20
Undesirable customers	39	47
Property abusers	51	20
[Off-duty] service workers	11	11
Vindictive customers	30	22
Oral abusers	92	70
Physical abusers	49	20
Sexual predators	38	0

Source

Lloyd C. Harris and Kate L. Reynolds (2004), "Jaycustomer Behavior: An Exploration of Types and Motives in the Hospitality Industry," *Journal of Services Marketing*, Vol. 18, No. 5, pp. 339–357.

To be able to effectively detect consumer fraud, maintaining a central database of all compensation payments, service recoveries, returned goods, and any other benefits given to customers based on special circumstances are needed (i.e., such transactions cannot be retained only at the local or branch level, but must be captured in a centralized system), and it is important to merge customer data across departments and channels for detecting unusual transactions and the systems that allow them[62].

Research has shown that customers who think they were treated unfairly in any way (refer to our earlier discussion regarding distributive, procedural, and interactive fairness) are much more likely to take advantage of a firm's service recovery effort. In addition, consumers tend to take advantage of large firms more often than small ones — customers think that large firms can easily afford the recovery costs. Also, one-time customers are much more likely to cheat than loyal customers, and customers who do not have a personal relationship with service employees are more likely to take advantage of service recovery policies.

Service guarantees are often used as payouts in service recovery, and it has been shown that the amount of a guarantee payout (e.g., whether it is a 10% or 100% money-back guarantee) had no effect on consumer cheating. It seems that customers who cheat for a 100 percent refund also cheat for 10%, and that customer who does not cheat for 10% also won't do so for 100%. However, repeat purchase intention significantly reduced cheating intent. A further finding was that customers were also reluctant to cheat if the service quality provided was truly high compared to when it was just satisfactory[63].

These findings suggest a number of important managerial implications:

1. Firms should ensure that their service recovery procedures are fair.

2. Large firms should recognize that consumers are more likely to cheat on them and have robust fraud detection systems in place.

3. Firms can implement and thus reap the bigger marketing benefits of 100% money-back guarantees without worrying that the large payouts would increase cheating by much.

4. Guarantees can be offered to regular customers or as part of a membership program, because repeat customers are unlikely to cheat on service guarantees.

5. Truly excellent services firms have less to worry about cheating than the average service provider.

SERVICE INSIGHTS 13.7
Tracking Down Guests Who Cheat

As part of its guarantee tracking system, Hampton Inn has developed ways to identify guests who appeared to be cheating — using aliases or various dissatisfaction problems to invoke the guarantee repeatedly in order to get the cost of their room refunded. Guests showing high invocation trends receive personalized attention and follow-up from the company's Guest Assistance Team. Wherever possible, senior managers telephone these guests to ask about their recent stays. The conversation might go as follows: "Hello, Mr. Jones. I'm the director of guest assistance at Hampton Inn, and I see that you've had some difficulty with the last four properties you've visited. Since we take our guarantee very seriously, I thought I'd give you a call and find out what the problems were."

The typical response is dead silence! Sometimes the silence is followed by questions of how headquarters could possibly know about their problems. These calls have their humorous moments as well. One individual, who had invoked the guarantee 17 times in what appeared to be a trip that took him across the US and back was asked, "Where do you like to stay when you travel?" "Hampton Inn," came the enthusiastic response. "But," said the executive making the call, "our records show that the last 17 times you have stayed at a Hampton Inn, you have invoked the 100% Satisfaction Guarantee." "That's why I like them!" proclaimed the guest (who turned out to be a long-distance truckdriver on a per diem for his accommodation expenses).

Source
Christopher W. Hart and Elizabeth Long, *Extraordinary Guarantees* (New York: AMACOM, 1997).

CONCLUSION

Encouraging customer feedback provides an important means of increasing customer satisfaction and retention. It is an opportunity to get into the hearts and minds of the customer. In all but the worst instances, complaining customers are indicating that they want to continue their relationship with the firm, but also that all is not well and they expect the company to make things right. Here, service firms need to develop effective strategies to recover from service failures so that they can maintain customer goodwill. That is vital for the long-term success of the company.

Having professional and generous service recovery systems does not mean "the customer is always right" and that the firm is open to customer abuse. Rather, it is important for the benefit of all (i.e., other customers, service employees and the service firm) to effectively deal with jaycustomers.

CHAPTER SUMMARY

○ **LO1** When customers are dissatisfied, they have several alternatives. They can take some form of:
- Public action (e.g., complain to the firm, a third party, or even take legal action).
- Private action (e.g., switch to another provider and/or spread negative word-of-mouth).
- Take no action.

○ **LO2** To effectively recover from a service failure, firms need to understand customer complaining behavior and motivations and also what customers expect in response.
- Customers typically complain for any combination of the following four reasons; they want: (1) restitution or compensation, (2) vent their anger, (3) help to improve the service, and (4) spare other customers from experiencing the same problems (i.e., they complain for altruistic reasons).
- In practice, most dissatisfied customers do not complain as they may not know where to complain, and find it takes too much effort and is unpleasant, and perceive the payoffs of their effort as uncertain.
- The people who are most likely to complain tend to be better educated, have higher income, are more socially involved, and have more product knowledge.
- Customers are most likely to complain at the point of service provision (face-to-face and over the phone). Only a small proportion of complaints is made via other channels such as email, social media, websites, or letters.

○ **LO3** Once customers make a complaint, they expect firms to deal with them in a fair manner along three dimensions of fairness:
- Procedural fairness — customers expect the firm to have a convenient, responsive, and flexible service recovery process.
- Interactional justice — customers expect an honest explanation, a genuine effort to solve the problem, and polite treatment.
- Outcome justice — customers expect a compensation that reflects the loss and inconvenience suffered as a result of the service failure.

○ **LO4** Effective service recovery can avoid customer switching and restore confidence in the firm in many cases. When customers complain, they give the firm a chance to correct problems, restore the relationship with the complainer, and improve future satisfaction. Service recovery is therefore an important opportunity to retain a valued customer.

○ **LO5** The **service recovery paradox** describes the phenomenon where customers who experience an excellent service recovery after a failure feel even more satisfied than customers who had no problem in the first place. However, it is important to note that this paradox does not always apply. It is still best to get it right the first time rather than providing expensive service recovery.

○ **LO6** Effective service recovery systems should:
- Make it easy for customers to give feedback (e.g., provide hotline numbers, email addresses, and social media channels on all communications materials) and encourage them to provide feedback.
- Enable effective service recovery by making it (1) proactive, (2) pre-planned, (3) trained, and (4) empowered.
- Establish appropriate compensation levels. Compensation should be higher if (1) a firm is known for service excellence, (2) the service failure is serious, and (3) the customer is important to the firm.

○ **LO7** The guidelines for frontline employees to effectively handle customer complaints and service recovery include: (1) act fast; (2) acknowledge the customer's feelings; (3) don't argue with the customer; (4) show that you understand the problem from the customer's point of view; (5) clarify the truth and sort out the cause; (6) give customers the benefit of doubt; (7) propose the steps needed to solve the problem; (8) keep customers informed of progress; (9) consider compensation; (10) persevere to regain customer goodwill; and (11) check the service delivery system and improve it.

○ **LO8** Service guarantees are a powerful way to institutionalize professional complaint handling and service recovery. Service guarantees set clear standards for the firm, and they also reduce customers' risk perceptions and can build long-term loyalty.

⊃ **LO9** Service guarantees should be designed to be: (1) unconditional, (2) easy to understand and communicate, (3) meaningful to the customer, (4) easy to invoke, (5) easy to collect on, and (6) credible.

⊃ **LO10** Not all firms stand to gain from service guarantees. Specifically, firms should be careful offering service guarantees when: (1) they already have a reputation for service excellence; (2) service quality is too low and has to be improved first; (3) aspects of service quality are uncontrollable because of external factors (e.g., the weather); and (4) customers perceive low risk when buying the service.

⊃ **LO11** Not all customers are honest, polite and reasonable. Some may want to take advantage of service recovery situations, and others may inconvenience and stress frontline employees and other customers alike. Such customers are called jaycustomers.
- There are seven groups of jaycustomers: (1) the Cheat, (2) the Thief, (3) the Rule Breaker, (4) the Belligerent, (5) the Family Feuders, (6) the Vandal, and (7) the Deadbeat.
- Different types of jaycustomers cause different problems for firms and may spoil the service experience of other customers. Hence, firms need to manage their behavior, even if that means keeping track of how often a customer invokes a service guarantee, or as a last resort, blacklisting them from using the firm's facilities.

Review Questions

1. How do customers typically respond to service failures?

2. Why don't more unhappy customers complain? What do customers expect the firm to do once they have filed a complaint?

3. Why would a firm prefer its unhappy customers to come forward and complain?

4. What is the service recovery paradox? Under what conditions is this paradox most likely to hold? Why is it best to deliver the service as planned, even if the paradox does hold in a specific context?

5. How can a firm make it easy for dissatisfied customers to complain?

6. Why should a service recovery strategy be proactive, planned, trained, and empowered?

7. How generous should compensations related to service recovery be?

8. How should service guarantees be designed? What are the benefits of service guarantees over and above a good complaint handling and service recovery system?

9. Under what conditions is it not suitable to introduce a service guarantee?

10. What are the different types of jaycustomers and how can a service firm deal with such customers?

Application Exercises

1. Think about the last time you experienced a less-than-satisfactory service experience. Did you complain? Why? If you did not complain, explain why not.

2. When was the last time you were truly satisfied with an organization's response to your complaint. Describe in detail what happened and what made you satisfied.

3. What would be an appropriate service recovery policy for a wrongly bounced check for (a) your local savings bank, (b) a major national bank, (c) a private bank for high net-worth individuals? Please explain your rationale, and also compute the economic costs of the alternative service recovery policies.

4. Design an effective service guarantee for a service with high perceived risk. Explain (a) why and how your guarantee would reduce perceived risk of potential customers, and (b) why current customers would appreciate being offered this guarantee although they are already a customer of that firm and therefore are likely to perceive lower levels of risk.

5. How generous should compensation be? Review the following incident and comment. Then evaluate the available options, comment on each, select the one you recommend, and defend your decision.

"The shrimp cocktail was half frozen. The waitress apologized and didn't charge me for any of my dinner," was the response of a very satisfied customer about the service recovery he received. Consider the following range of service recovery policies a restaurant chain could set and try to establish the costs for each policy:
Option 1: Smile and apologize, defrost the prawn cocktail, return it, smile and apologize again.
Option 2: Smile and apologize, replace the prawn cocktail with a new one, and smile and apologize again.
Option 3: Smile, apologize, replace the prawn cocktail, and offer a free coffee or dessert
Option 4: Smile, apologize, replace the prawn cocktail, and waive the bill of $80 for the entire meal.
Option 5: Smile, apologize, replace the prawn cocktail, waive the bill for the entire dinner, and offer a free bottle of champagne.
Option 6: Smile, apologize, replace the prawn cocktail, waive the bill for the entire dinner, offer a free bottle of champagne, and give a voucher valid for another dinner, to be redeemed within three months.

6. Identify the possible behavior of jaycustomers for a service of your choice. How can the service process be designed to minimize or control the behavior of jaycustomers?

Endnotes

1 "An Extraordinary Stumble at JetBlue," *Business Week*, March 5, 2007, http://www.bloomberg.com/bw/stories/2007-03-04/an-extraordinary-stumble-at-jetblue, accessed August 22, 2015.

2 Even failures by other customers also have an impact on how a firm's customers feel about the firm, see: Wen-Hsien Huang (2010), "Other-Customer Failure: Effects of Perceived Employee Effort and Compensation on Complainer and Non-Complainer Service Evaluations," *Journal of Service Management*, Vol. 21, No. 2, pp. 191–211.

3 Roger Bougie, Rik Pieters, and Marcel Zeelenberg (2003), "Angry Customers Don't Come Back, They Get Back: The Experience and Behavioral Implications of Anger and Dissatisfaction in Service," *Journal of the Academy of Marketing Science*, Vol. 31, No. 4, pp. 377–393; Florian v. Wangenheim (2005), "Postswitching Negative Word of Mouth," *Journal of Service Research*, Vol. 8, No. 1, pp. 67–78.

4 For research on cognitive and affective drivers of complaining behavior, see: Jean-Charles Chebat, Moshe Davidow, and Isabelle Codjovi (2005), "Silent Voices: Why Some Dissatisfied Consumers Fail to Complain," *Journal of Service Research*, Vol. 7, No. 4, pp. 328–342.

5 Stephen S. Tax and Stephen W. Brown (1998), "Recovering and Learning from Service Failure," *Sloan Management Review,* Vol. 49, No. 1, Fall, pp. 75–88.

6 A large body of literature has examined consumer complaining behavior. Important studies include: Jean-Charles Chebat, Moshe Davidow and Isabelle Codjovi (2005), "Silent Voices: Why Some Dissatisfied Consumers Fail to Complain," *Journal of Service Research*, Vol. 7, No. 4, pp. 328–342; Nancy Stephens and Kevin P. Gwinner (1998), "Why Don't Some People Complain? A Cognitive-Emotive Process Model of Consumer Complaining Behavior," *Journal of the Academy of Marketing Science*, Vol. 26, No. 3, pp. 172–189; Kelli Bodey and Debra Grace (2006), "Segmenting Service "Complainers" and "Non-Complainers" on the Basis of Consumer Characters," *Journal of Services Marketing*, Vol. 20, No. 3, pp. 178–187.

7 Cathy Goodwin and B.J. Verhage (1990), "Role Perceptions of Services: A Cross-Cultural Comparison with Behavioral Implications," *Journal of Economic Psychology,* Vol. 10, pp. 543–558.

8 Nancy Stephens, "Complaining," in Teresa A. Swartz and Dawn Iacobucci, eds. *Handbook of Services Marketing and Management* (Thousand Oaks, CA: Sage Publications, 2000), p. 291; Alex M. Susskind (2015), "Communication Richness: Why some Guest Complaints Go Right to the Top — and Others Don't," *Cornell Hospitality Quarterly*, Vol. 56, No. 3, pp. 320–331.

9 John Goodman (1999), "Basic Facts on Customer Complaint Behavior and the Impact of Service on the Bottom Line," *Competitive Advantage*, Vol. 8, June, No.1, pp. 1–5.

10 Anna Mattila and Jochen Wirtz (2004), "Consumer Complaining to Firms: The Determinants of Channel Choice," *Journal of Services Marketing,* Vol. 18, No. 2, pp. 147–155; Kaisa Snellman and Tiina Vihtkari (2003), "Customer Complaining Behavior in Technology-based Service Encounters," *International Journal of Service Industry Management,* Vol. 14, No. 2, pp. 217–231; Terri Shapiro and Jennifer Nieman-Gonder (2006), "Effect of Communication Mode in Justice-Based Service Recovery," *Managing Service Quality*, Vol. 16, No. 2, pp. 124–144.

11 Technical Assistance Research Programs Institute (TARP), *Consumer Complaint Handling in America; An Update Study, Part II* (Washington DC: TARP and US Office of Consumer Affairs, 1986).

12 Thomas M. Tripp and Yany Gregoire (2011), "When Unhappy Customers Strike Back on the Internet," *MIT Sloan Management Review*, Vol. 52, No. 3, Spring, pp. 37–44; Sven Tuzovic (2010), "Frequent (Flier) Frustration and the Dark Side of Word-of-Web: Exploring Online Dysfunctional Behavior in Online Feedback Forums," *Journal of Services Marketing*, Vol. 24, No. 6, pp. 446–457.

13 Kathleen Seiders and Leonard L. Berry (1990), "Service Fairness: What It Is and Why It Matters," *Academy of Management Executive,* Vol. 12, No. 2, pp. 8–20. For review on complaint handling and customer satisfaction, see: Katja Gelbrich and Holger Roschk (2011), "A Meta-Analysis of Organisational Complaint Handling and Customer Responses," *Journal of Service Research*, Vol. 14, No. 1, pp. 24–43.

See also Klaus Schoefer and Adamantios Diamantopoulos (2008), "The Role of Emotions in Transaction Perceptions of (In)Justice into Postcomplaint Behavioral Responses," *Journal of Service Research,* Vol. 11, No. 1, pp. 91–103; Yany Grégoire and Robert J. Fisher (2008), "Customer Betrayal and Retaliation: When Your Best Customers Become Your Worst Enemies," *Journal of the Academy of Marketing*

Science, Vol. 36, No. 2, pp. 247–261; Zheng Fang, Xueming Luo, and Minghua Jiang (2012), "Quantifying the Dynamic Effects of Service Recovery on Customer Satisfaction: Evidence from Chinese Mobile Phone Markets," *Journal of Service Research*, Vol. 16, No. 3, pp. 341–355; Ana Belén del Río-Lanza, Rodolfo Vázquez-Casielles, and Ana María Díaz-Martín (2009), "Satisfaction with Service Recovery: Perceived Justice and Emotional Responses", *Journal of Business Research*, Vol. 62, No. 8, pp. 775–781.

14 Stephen S. Tax and Stephen W. Brown (1998), "Recovering and Learning from Service Failure," *Sloan Management Review*, Vol. 49, No. 1, Fall, pp. 75–88;

See also Tor Wallin Andreassen (2000), "Antecedents of Service Recovery," *European Journal of Marketing*, Vol. 34, No. 1 and 2, pp. 156–175; Ko de Ruyter and Martin Wetzel (2002), "Customer Equity Considerations in Service Recovery," *International Journal of Service Industry Management*, Vol. 13, No. 1, pp. 91–108; Janet R. McColl-Kennedy and Beverley A. Sparks (2003), "Application of Fairness Theory to Service Failures and Service Recovery," *Journal of Service Research*, Vol. 5, No. 3, pp. 251–266; Jochen Wirtz and Anna Mattila (2004), "Consumer Responses to Compensation, Speed of Recovery and Apology After a Service Failure," *International Journal of Service Industry Management*, Vol. 15, No. 2, pp. 150–166.

For a meta-analysis of the effects of fairness on consumer responses, see: Chiara Orsingher, Sara Valentini, and Matteo de Angelis (2010), "A Meta-Analysis of Satisfaction with Complaint Handling in Services," *Journal of the Academy of Marketing Science*, Vol. 38, No. 2, pp. 169–186.

15 Oren Harari (1997), "Thank Heavens for Complainers," *Management Review*, Vol. 86, No. 3, March, pp. 25–29.

16 Tom DeWitt, Doan T. Nguyen, and Roger Marshall (2008), "Exploring Customer Loyalty Following Service Recovery," *Journal of Service Research*, Vol. 10, No. 3, pp. 269–281.

17 Simon J. Bell and James A. Luddington (2006), "Coping with Customer Complaints," *Journal of Service Research*, Vol. 8, No. 3, February, pp. 221–233.

18 Leonard L. Berry, *On Great Service: A Framework for Action* (New York: The Free Press, 1995), p. 94. For a meta-analysis on the customer attribution process and how to effectively manage customer attributions of service failures, see: Yves Van Vaerenbergh, Chiara Orsingher, Iris Vermeir, and Bart Larivière (2014), "A Meta-Analysis of Relationships Linking Service Failure Attributions to Customer Outcomes," *Journal of Service Research*, Vol. 17, No. 4, pp. 381–398.

19 Susan M. Keaveney (1995), "Customer Switching Behavior in Service Industries: An Exploratory Study," *Journal of Marketing*, Vol. 59, April, pp. 71–82.

20 Customer Care Measurement & Consulting (CCMC), *2007 National Customer Rage Study* (Customer Care Alliance, 2007).

21 Technical Assistance Research Programs Institute (TARP), *Consumer Complaint Handling in America; An Update Study, Part II* (Washington DC: TARP and US Office of Consumer Affairs, 1986). Since this study, CCMC and W. P. Carey School of Business, Arizona State University (ASU) have conducted six follow-on studies, known as the "Customer Rage Studies," to explore important, emerging trends in the customer experience related to complaining behavior and service recovery. For highlights of the latest study, "The 2013 Customer Rage Study," see: http://www.customercaremc.com/wp/wp-content/uploads/2014/01/KeyFindingsFrom2013NationalCustomerRageSurvey.pdf.

Not addressing a service failure or dissatisfaction with a service recovery effort has been shown to result in various negative customer responses, including revenge, rage, and opportunistic behaviors, see: Yany Grègoire, Daniel Laufer and Thomas M. Tripp (2010), "A Comprehensive Model of Customer Direct and Indirect Revenge: Understanding the Effects of Perceived Greed and Customer Power," *Journal of the Academy of Marketing Science*, Vol. 38, No. 6, pp. 738–758.

22 For a discussion on how to quantify complaint management profitability, see: Bernd Stauss and Andreas Schoeler (2004), "Complaint Management Profitability: What do Complaint Managers Know?" *Managing Service Quality*, Vol. 14, No.2/3, pp. 147–156.

For a comprehensive treatment of all aspects of effective complaint management, see: Bernd Stauss and Wolfgang Seidel, *Complaint Management: The Heart of CRM* (Mason, OH: Thomson, 2004); and Janelle Barlow and Claus Møller, *A Complaint Is a Gift*. 2nd ed. (San Francisco, CA: Berrett-Koehler Publishers, 2008).

23 Celso Augusto de Matos, Jorge Luiz Henrique, and Carlos Alberto Vargas Rossi (2007), "Service Recovery Paradox: A Meta-Analysis," *Journal of Service Research*, Vol. 10, No. 1, pp. 60–77; Randi Priluck and Vishal Lala (2009), "The Impact of the Recovery Paradox on Retailer-Customer Relationships," *Managing Service Quality*, Vol. 19, No. 1, pp. 42–59.

24 Stefan Michel and Matthew L. Meuter (2008), "The Service Recovery Paradox: True but Overrated?" *International Journal of Service Industry Management*, Vol. 19, No. 4, pp. 441–457.

Other studies also confirmed that the service recovery paradox does not hold universally; Tor Wallin Andreassen (2001), "From Disgust to Delight: Do Customers Hold a Grudge?" *Journal of Service Research,* Vol. 4, No. 1, pp. 39–49; Michael A. McCollough, Leonard L. Berry, and Manjit S. Yadav (2000), "An Empirical Investigation of Customer Satisfaction after Service Failure and Recovery," *Journal of Service Research,* Vol. 3, No. 2, pp. 121–137; James G. Maxhamm III (2001), "Service Recovery's Influence on Consumer Satisfaction, Positive Word-of-Mouth, and Purchase Intentions," *Journal of Business Research,* Vol. 54, No. 1, pp. 11–24; Chihyung Ok, Ki-Joon Back, and Carol W. Shankin (2007), "Mixed Findings on the Service Recovery Paradox," *The Service Industries Journal,* Vol. 27, No. 5, pp. 671–686.

25   James G. Maxham III and Richard G. Netemeyer (2002), "A Longitudinal Study of Complaining Customers' Evaluations of Multiple Service Failures and Recovery Efforts," *Journal of Marketing,* Vol. 66, No. 4, pp. 57–72.

26   Michael Hargrove, cited in Ron Kaufman, Up Your Service! (Singapore: Ron Kaufman Plc. Ltd., 2005), p. 225.

27   Steven S. Tax and Steven W. Brown (1998), "Recovering and Learning from Service Failure," *Sloan Management Review,* Vol. 40, No. 1, pp. 75–88; Stephen S. Tax, Stephen W. Brown, and Murali Chandrashekaran (1998), "Customer Evaluation of Service Complaint Experiences: Implications for Relationship Marketing," *Journal of Marketing,* Vol. 62, No. 2, Spring, pp. 60–76.

     For a study in the online environment, see: Betsy B. Holloway and Sharon E. Beatty (2003), "Service Failure in Online Retailing: A Recovery Opportunity," *Journal of Service Research,* Vol. 6, No. 1, pp. 92–105.

28   For a discussion on how to quantify complaint management profitability, see: Bernd Stauss and Andreas Schoeler (2004), "Complaint Management Profitability: What Do Complaint Managers Know?" *Managing Service Quality,* Vol. 14, No.2/3, pp. 147–156.

     For a comprehensive treatment of all aspects of effective complaint management, see: Bernd Stauss and Wolfgang Seidel, *Complaint Management: The Heart of CRM* (Mason, OH: Thomson, 2004); and Janelle Barlow and Claus Möller, *A Complaint Is a Gift,* 2nd ed. (San Francisco, CA: Berrett-Koehler Publishers, 2008).

29   Christian Homburg and Andreas Fürst (2005), "How Organizational Complaint Handling Drives Customer Loyalty: An Analysis of the Mechanistic and the Organic Approach," *Journal of Marketing,* Vol. 69, July, pp. 95–114.

30   Ron Zemke and Chip R. Bell, *Knock Your Socks Off Service Recovery* (New York: AMACOM, 2000), p. 60.

31   Barbara R. Lewis, "Customer Care in Services," in W.J. Glynn and J.G. Barnes, eds. *Understanding Services Management* (UK: Chichester, Wiley 1995), pp. 57–89. Prior rapport between employees and customers has also been shown to improve service recovery satisfaction, see: Tom DeWitt and Michael K. Brady (2003), "Rethinking Service Recovery Strategies: The Effect of Rapport on Customer Responses to Service Failure," *Journal of Service Research,* Vol. 6, No. 2, pp. 193–207.

32   Josh Bernoff and Ted Schadler (2010), "Empowered," *Harvard Business Review,* Vol. 88, July–August, No. 7/8, pp. 95–101.

33   The incremental impact of increasing compensation depends on whether customer accept the value proposition of the service delivered (i.e., the service provided value-in-use to the customer). If not, high levels of compensation are required to achieve post-complaint satisfaction; see: Katja Gelbrich, Jana Gäthke and Yany Grégoire (2015), "How Much Compensation Should a Firm Offer for a Flawed Service? An Examination of the Nonlinear Effects of Compensation on Satisfaction," *Journal of Service Research,* Vol. 18, No. 1, pp. 107–123.

34   Rhonda Mack, Rene Mueller, John Crotts, and Amanda Broderick (2000), "Perceptions, Corrections and Defections: Implications for Service Recovery in the Restaurant Industry," *Managing Service Quality,* Vol. 10, No. 6, pp. 339–46.

35   Jochen Wirtz and Janet R. McColl-Kennedy (2010), "Opportunistic Customer Claiming During Service Recovery," *Journal of the Academy of Marketing Science,* Vol. 38, No. 5, pp. 654–675.

36   Matthew Dixon, Karen Freeman, and Nicholas Toman (2010), "Stop Trying to Delight Your Customers: To Really Win Their Loyalty, Forget the Bells and Whistles and Just Solve Their Problems", *Harvard Business Review,* Vol. 88, No. 7/8, pp. 116–122.

37   A comprehensive assessment tool of service recovery performance comprises of the following nine dimensions: (1) Apology, (2) Compensation, (3) Explanation, (4) Follow-up, (5) Facilitation, (6) Speed of Response, (7) Courtesy, (8) Effort, and (9) Problem-solving. The tool is called the CURE scale (CUstomer REcovery scale), which organizations can use to identify the impact of these service recovery actions on customer responses; see: Rania Mostafa, Cristiana

R. Lages, and Maria Sääksjärvi (2014), "The CURE Scale: A Multidimensional Measure of Service Recovery Strategy," *Journal of Services Marketing*, Vol. 28, No. 4, pp. 300–310.

38 For an excellent review of extant academic literature on service guarantees see: Jens Hogreve and Dwayne D. Gremler (2009), "Twenty Years of Service Guarantee Research," *Journal of Service Research*, Vol. 11, No. 4, pp. 322–343.

39 Christopher W. L Hart (1988), "The Power of Unconditional Service Guarantees," *Harvard Business Review*, Vol. 66, July–August, No. 4, pp. 54–62.

40 L.A. Tucci and J. Talaga (1997), "Service Guarantees and Consumers' Evaluation of Services," *Journal of Services Marketing*, Vol. 11, No. 1, pp. 10–18; Amy Ostrom and Dawn Iacobucci (1998), "The Effect of Guarantees on Consumers' Evaluation of Services," *Journal of Services Marketing*, Vol. 12, No. 5, pp. 362–78.

41 Sara Björlin Lidén and Per Skålén (2003), "The Effect of Service Guarantees on Service Recovery," *International Journal of Service Industry Management*, Vol. 14, No. 1, pp. 36–58.

42 Christopher W. Hart and Elizabeth Long, *Extraordinary Guarantees* (New York: AMACOM, 1997).

43 Christopher W. Hart, "The Power of Unconditional Service Guarantees."

44 For a scientific discussion on the optimal guarantee payout amount, see: Tim Baker and David A. Collier (2005), "The Economic Payout Model for Service Guarantees," *Decision Sciences*, Vol. 36, No. 2, pp. 197–220.

45 McDougall, Gordon H., Terence Levesque, and Peter VanderPlaat (1998), "Designing the Service Guarantee: Unconditional or Specific?" *Journal of Services Marketing*, Vol. 12, No. 4, pp. 278–293; Jochen Wirtz (1998), "Development of a Service Guarantee Model," *Asia Pacific Journal of Management*, Vol. 15, No. 1, pp. 51–75.

46 Jochen Wirtz and Doreen Kum (2001), "Designing Service Guarantees — Is Full Satisfaction the Best You can Guarantee?" *Journal of Services Marketing*, Vol. 15, No. 4, pp. 282–299

47 Amy L. Ostrom and Christopher Hart, "Service Guarantee: Research and Practice," in T. Schwartz and D. Iacobucci, ed., *Handbook of Services Marketing and Management* (Thousand Oaks, CA: Sage Publications, 2000), pp. 299–316.

48 Jochen Wirtz, Doreen Kum, and Khai Sheang Lee (2000), "Should a Firm with a Reputation for Outstanding Service Quality Offer a Service Guarantee?" *Journal of Services Marketing*, Vol. 14, No. 6, pp. 502–512.

For the impact of implicit service guarantees on business performance, see: Hyunju Shin and Alexander E. Ellinger (2013), "The Effect of Implicit Service Guarantees on Business Performance," *Journal of Services Marketing*, Vol. 27, No. 6, pp. 431–442.

49 For a decision support model and deciding whether to have a service guarantee, and if yes, on how to design and implement it, see: Louis Fabien (2005), "Design and Implementation of a Service Guarantee," *Journal of Services Marketing*, Vol. 19, No. 1, pp. 33–38.

50 A large body of literature has examined the behavior of jaycustomers. Important studies include: Ray Fisk, Stephen Grove, Lloyd C. Harris, Kate L. Daunt, Dominique Keeffe, Rebekah Russell-Bennett, and Jochen Wirtz (2010), "Customers Behaving Badly: A State of the Art Review, Research Agenda and Implications for Practitioners," *Journal of Services Marketing*, Vol. 24, No. 6, pp. 417–429; Lloyd C. Harris and Kate L. Reynolds (2004), "Jaycustomer Behavior: An Exploration of Types and Motives in the Hospitality Industry," *Journal of Services Marketing*, Vol. 18, No. 5, pp. 339–357; Kate L. Reynolds and Lloyd C. Harris (2009), "Dysfunctional Customer Behavior Severity: An Empirical Examination," *Journal of Retailing*, Vol. 85, No. 3, pp. 321–335; Kate L. Daunt and Harris C. Lloyd (2011), "Customers Acting Badly: Evidence from the Hospitality Industry," *Journal of Business Research*, Vol. 64, No. 10, pp. 1034–1042.

51 This section is adapted and updated from Christopher Lovelock, *Product Plus* (New York: McGraw-Hill, 1994), Chapter 15. For an additional discussion of jaycustomers, see: Leonard L. Berry and Kathleen Seiders (2008), "Serving Unfair Customers," *Business Horizons*, Vol. 51, No. 1, pp. 29–37.

52 There is a large body of literature on opportunistic customer behavior. Important studies include: Harris, Lloyd C., and Kate L. Reynolds (2003), "The Consequences of Dysfunctional Customer Behavior," *Journal of Service Research*, Vol. 6, No. 2, pp. 144–161; Jochen Wirtz and Janet R. McColl-Kennedy (2010), "Opportunistic Customer Claiming During Service Recovery," *Journal of the Academy of Marketing Science*, Vol. 38, No. 5, pp. 654–675; Chu Wujin, Eitan Gerstner, and James D. Hess (1998), "Managing Dissatisfaction: How to Decrease Customer Opportunism by Partial Refunds," *Journal of Service Research*, Vol. 1, No. 2, pp. 140–155.

Important research exploring opportunism in the B2B context includes: Steven H. Seggie, David A. Griffith, and Sandy D. Jap (2013), "Passive and Active Opportunism in Interorganizational Exchange," *Journal of Marketing*, Vol. 77, No. 6, pp. 73–90; Qiong Wang, Julie Juan Li, William T. Ross Jr., and Christopher W. Craighead (2013), "The Interplay of Drivers and Deterrents of Opportunism in Buyer-Supplier Relationships," *Journal of the Academy of Marketing Science*, Vol. 41, No. 1, pp. 111–131; Lloyd C. Harris (2008), "Fraudulent Return Proclivity: An Empirical Analysis," *Journal of Retailing*, Vol. 84, No. 4, pp. 461–476. Some customers are out to take full advantage of return policies.

53 The Economist (2013), "Online Retailing, Return to Santa: E-commerce Firms have a Hard Core of Costly, Impossible-to-please Customers," December 21, p. 103.

54 Kate L. Reynolds and Lloyd C. Harris (2005), "When Service Failure Is Not Service Failure: An Exploration of the Forms and Motives of 'Illegitimate' Customer Complaining," *Journal of Services Marketing*, Vol. 19, No. 5, p. 326.

55 Harris, Lloyd C. and Kate L. Reynolds (2004), "Jaycustomer Behavior: An Exploration of Types and Motives in the Hospitality Industry," *Journal of Services Marketing*, Vol. 18, No. 5, p. 339.

56 Stephen J. Grove, Raymond P. Fisk, and Joby John (2004), "Surviving in the Age of Rage," *Marketing Management*, Vol. 13, March/April, pp. 41–46.

57 Roger Bougie, Rik Pieters, and Marcel Zeelenberg (2003), Angry Customers Don't Come Back, They Get Back: The Experience and Behavioral Implications of Anger and Dissatisfaction in Services," *Journal of the Academy of Marketing Science*, Vol. 31, No. 4, pp. 377–393.

Further important studies on customer rage include: Jiraporn Surachartkumtonkun, Paul G. Patternson, and Janet R. McColl-Kennedy (2013), "Customer Rage Back-Story: Linking Needs-Based Cognitive Appraisal to Service Failure Type," *Journal of Retailing*, Vol. 89, No. 1, pp. 72–87; Thomas M. Tripp and Yany Grégoire (2011), "When Unhappy Customers Strike Back on the Internet," *Sloan Management Review*, Vol. 52, No. 3, pp. 1–10; Stephen J. Grove, Gregory M. Pickett, Scott A. Jones, and Michael J. Dorsch (2012), "Spectator Rage as the Dark Side of Engaging Sport Fans: Implications for Service Marketers," *Journal of Service Research*, Vol. 15, No. 1, pp. 3–20.

58 Blair J. Berkley and Mohammad Ala (2001), "Identifying and Controlling Threatening Airline Passengers, *Cornell Hotel and Restaurant Administration Quarterly*, Vol. 42, August–September, pp. 6–24.

59 Lloyd C. Harris and Kate L. Reynolds (2003), "The Consequences of Dysfunctional Customer Behavior," *Journal of Service Research*, Vol. 6, November, pp. 144–161; Lloyd C. Harris, and Kate L. Reynolds (2004), "Jaycustomer Behavior: An Exploration of Types and Motives in the Hospitality Industry," *Journal of Services Marketing*, Vol. 18, No. 5, pp. 339–357.

60 Recent research has explored how firms can help their frontline employees to deal with the job stress related to illegitimate and unreasonable dysfunctional customer behavior: Taeshik Gong, Youjae Yi, and Jin Nam Choi (2014), "Helping Employees Deal with Dysfunctional Customers: Employee Perceived Justice Mechanism," *Journal of Service Research*, Vol. 17, No. 1, pp. 102–116.

61 John Goodman (1990), quoted in "Improving Service Doesn't Always Require Big Investment," *The Service Edge*, July–August, p. 3.

62 Jill Griffin, "What Your Worst Customers Teach You About Loyalty," January 24, 2006, http://www.marketingprofs.com/6/griffin5.asp, accessed August 22, 2015.

63 Jochen Wirtz and Doreen Kum (2004), "Consumer Cheating on Service Guarantees," *Journal of the Academy of Marketing Science,* Vol. 32, No. 2, pp. 159–175; Jochen Wirtz and Janet R. McColl-Kennedy (2010), "Opportunistic Customer Claiming During Service Recovery," *Journal of the Academy of Marketing Science*, Vol. 38, No. 5, pp. 654–675; Heejung Ro and June Wong (2012), "Customer Opportunistic Complaints Management: A Critical Incident Approach," *International Journal of Hospitality Management*, Vol. 31, No. 2, pp. 419–427.

For additional research on how to manage opportunistic customers and jaycustomers, see: Lloyd C. Harris and Kate Daunt (2013), "Managing Customer Misbehavior: Challenges and Strategies," *Journal of Services Marketing*, Vol. 27, No. 4, pp. 281–293.

PART 5

The Services Marketing Framework

Part I

Understanding Service Products, Consumers, and Markets

1. Creating Value in the Service Economy
2. Understanding Service Consumers
3. Positioning Services in Competitive Markets

Part II

Applying the 4 Ps of Marketing to Services

4. Developing Service Products and Brands
5. Distributing Services Through Physical and Electronic Channels
6. Service Pricing and Revenue Management
7. Service Marketing Communications

Part III

Managing the Customer Interface

8. Designing Service Processes
9. Balancing Demand and Capacity
10. Crafting the Service Environment
11. Managing People for Service Advantage

Part IV

Developing Customer Relationships

12. Managing Relationships and Building Loyalty
13. Complaint Handling and Service Recovery

Part V

Striving for Service Excellence

14. Improving Service Quality and Productivity
15. Building a World-Class Service Organization

Figure V Organizing framework for services marketing

STRIVING FOR SERVICE EXCELLENCE

Part V focuses on service quality and productivity, and how firms can achieve service leadership. It consists of the following two chapters:

CHAPTER 14

Improving Service Quality and Productivity

Both productivity and quality are necessary and related to financial success in services. Chapter 14 discusses how to diagnose quality shortfalls using the gaps model, and reviewing strategies to close quality gaps. Customer feedback systems are introduced as an effective tool for systematically listening to and learning from customers. Productivity is concerned with bringing down costs, and key approaches for increasing productivity are discussed.

CHAPTER 15

Building a World-Class Service Organization

Chapter 15 covers the characteristics of world-class service organizations and introduces four levels of service performance — service loser, nonentity, professional, and service leader. An audit tool that helps to assess the performance level of an organization is provided. We discuss how to move a service organization to achieve higher levels of performance. The chapter closes with a discussion on the impact of customer satisfaction on financial performance and shareholder value.

Improving Service Quality and Productivity

Not everything that counts can be counted, and not everything that can be counted, counts.

Albert Einstein,
Theoretical physicist and Nobel Prize winner

Improve quality and you automatically improve productivity. You capture the market with lower price and better quality. You stay in business and you provide jobs. It's so simple.

W. Edwards Deming,
Engineer, statistician, professor, and management consultant, and father of the Total Quality Management movement

Our mission remains inviolable: Offer the customer the best service we can provide; cut our costs to the bones; and generate a surplus to continue the unending process of renewal.

Joseph Pillay,
Former Chairman,
Singapore Airlines

LEARNING OBJECTIVES (LOs)

By the end of this chapter, the reader should be able to:

⊃ **LO 1** Explain the relationships between service quality, productivity, and profitability.

⊃ **LO 2** Be familiar with the different perspectives of service quality.

⊃ **LO 3** Demonstrate how to use the Gaps Model for diagnosing and addressing service quality problems.

⊃ **LO 4** Differentiate between hard and soft measures of service quality.

⊃ **LO 5** Explain the common objectives of effective customer feedback systems.

⊃ **LO 6** Describe key customer feedback collection tools.

⊃ **LO 7** Be familiar with hard measures of service quality and control charts.

⊃ **LO 8** Select suitable tools to analyze service problems.

⊃ **LO 9** Understand return on quality and determine the optimal level of reliability.

⊃ **LO 10** Define and measure service productivity.

⊃ **LO 11** Understand the difference between productivity, efficiency, and effectiveness.

⊃ **LO 12** Recommend the key methods to improve service productivity.

⊃ **LO 13** Know how productivity improvements impact quality and value.

⊃ **LO 14** Understand how to integrate all the tools to improve the quality and productivity of customer service processes.

⊃ **LO 15** Explain how TQM, ISO 9000, Six Sigma, and the Malcolm-Baldrige and EFQM approaches relate to managing and improving service quality and productivity.

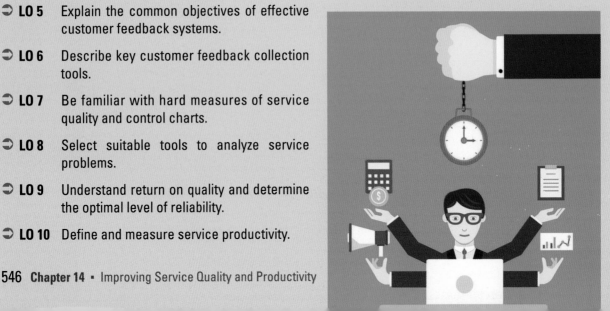

OPENING VIGNETTE

Improving Service Quality in a Ferry Company

Sealink British Ferries, whose routes linked Britain to Ireland and several European countries, was a poor service quality provider.[1] Its top–down, military-style structure focused on the operational aspects of ship movements, but not on the quality of customers' experiences. Sealink was then acquired by the Swedish company Stena Line, one of the world's largest car-ferry operators today. Compared to Sealink, Stena had a whole department devoted to improving its service quality.

Before the takeover, Sealink did not focus on punctual or reliable operations, and ferries were often late. Customer complaints were ignored, and there was little pressure from customer service managers to improve the situation. After the takeover, things started to change. The ferry operator solved the problem of late departures and arrivals by concentrating on individual problem areas. On one route, for instance, the port manager involved all operational staff and gave each person responsibility over a particular aspect of the improvement process, thus creating employee "ownership." They kept detailed records of each sailing, together with the reasons for late departures. They also kept track of their competitors' performance. In this way, staff members in the different job positions had close links with one another. Customer service staff also learnt from experience. Within two years, the Stena ferries on this route were operating at close to 100% punctuality.

On-board service was another area singled out for improvement. Historically, customer service managers did what was convenient for staff rather than customers, including scheduling staff meal breaks at times when customer demand for service was greatest. As one observer noted, "customers were ignored during the first and last half hour on board, when facilities were closed… customers were left to find their own way around [the ship]… Staff only responded to customers when [they] initiated a direct request and made some effort to attract their attention."

Personnel from each on-board functional area had to choose a particular area for service quality and productivity improvements, and worked in small groups to achieve this. Initially, some teams were more successful than others, resulting in inconsistent levels of service from one ship to another. Subsequently, managers shared ideas and experiences, learning from each other's' successes and failures, and made further changes on their individual ships. Key changes during the first two years contributed to eventual success in achieving consistent service levels on all sailings and ferries. Together, the employees have come up with almost 1,500 improvement ideas since 2006.

By 2015, Stena Line has become one of the world's largest ferry operators with 35 ships sailing on 22 routes, carrying over seven million passengers and 1.5 million vehicles each year. A leader in all its markets, Stena places emphasis on constant service and product improvement. Says the company's website:

> Customers must have the best possible experience when they choose Stena Line for travel, holidays, relaxation or freight transport. The focus is firmly on constantly improving the service by, among other things, developing new and innovative products and services that create value for customers.

INTEGRATING SERVICE QUALITY AND PRODUCTIVITY STRATEGIES

The Stena Line success story in the opening vignette is an excellent example that shows how improving service quality and productivity can turn a failing business around. We will learn in this chapter that quality and productivity are twin paths in creating value for both customers and organizations. An overview of this chapter is provided in *Figure 14.1*.

Let's next delve deeper and examine the relationships between service quality, productivity, and profitability.

Service Quality, Productivity, and Profitability[2]

The individual relationships between service productivity, customer satisfaction (i.e., excellence) and profitability, are shown in *Figure 14.2*. When examining the individual links, one can see that, everything being equal, higher customer satisfaction should improve the bottom line through higher repeat purchases, share-of-wallet, and referrals. Likewise, everything being equal, higher productivity should lead to higher profitability as costs are reduced.

The relationship between productivity and customer satisfaction is more complex. There is the general notion of a service productivity–customer satisfaction tradeoff. However, although the relationships between productivity, service quality, and profitability can conflict, there are examples where productivity gains and customer satisfaction are aligned. For example, if a service firm redesigns customer service processes to be leaner, faster, and more convenient by eliminating non-value-adding work steps, then both productivity and customer satisfaction should improve, and both should have a direct and indirect positive effect on profitability. An example would be serve-it-yourself yogurt stores, which substitute relatively inexpensive and easy-to-use self-serve machines for multiple human contact people. In this case, there is a positive impact on profitability through increased productivity and increased customer satisfaction, resulting in higher customer loyalty.

In contrast, if productivity improvements result in changes in the service experience that customers do not like, customer satisfaction will drop. For example, getting service employees to work faster may make customers feel rushed and unwanted. Likewise, replacing a human agent in a customer contact center with an interactive voice response system to reduce headcount, doubling class sizes to increase the productivity of university professors, and reducing the frequency of trains to increase load factors can all have negative implications for the customer experience. In these cases, there is a tradeoff to be expected, whereby in the short term, productivity enhancements have an immediate and direct positive effect on profitability. However, these productivity enhancements lead to lower customer satisfaction which, over the medium to long term, are likely to lead to lower customer loyalty and referrals. This means that these productivity improvements have a positive direct effect on profitability, but also a negative indirect effect (via customer satisfaction).

Integrating Service Quality & Productivity
- Quality and productivity are twin paths to creating value for customers and firms
- Service quality and productivity improvements can reinforce, be independent or even counter each others' impact on profitability

What Is Service Quality?
- Customer defined
- Consistently meeting or exceeding customer expectations

The Gaps Model
The Gaps Model helps to identify the causes of quality problems at the macro level through a gap analysis:
- Gap 1: The Knowledge Gap
- Gap 2: The Policy Gap
- Gap 3: The Delivery Gap
- Gap 4: The Communications Gap
- Gap 5: The Perceptions Gap
- Gap 6: The Service Quality Gap

Each of the gaps has distinct causes. Prescriptions are provided on how to address the causes of each gap.

Measuring Service Quality

Customer Feedback
- Referred to as "soft measures"

Objectives:
- Assess and benchmark performance
- Improve performance by cementing strengths and improving weaknesses
- Create a customer-oriented service culture and a culture for change

Use a mix of tools to obtain reliable, and actionable feedback, such as:
- Surveys, feedback cards, & online/mobile messages, complaints & compliments
- Mystery shopping
- Focus groups and service reviews
- Online reviews and discussions

Operational Measures
- Process & outcome measures
- Referred to as "hard measures"
- Relate to process activities and outcomes that can be counted, timed or measured (e.g., system uptime, on-time departure, service response time, and failure rates)

Analysis, Reporting, & Dissemination of Customer Feedback & Operational Measures
- Daily morning briefings to the frontline
- Monthly service performance updates to process owners & service teams
- Quarterly service performance reviews to middle management & process owners
- Annual service performance reports to top management & entire firm

Analyzing Service Quality Problems
Analytical tools:
- Fishbone diagram to conduct root cause analysis
- Pareto charts to identify key fail points & root causes
- Blueprinting

Return on quality:
- Assess costs and benefits of quality initiatives
- Importance-performance matrix
- Optimal level of reliability depends on cost of service recovery

Systematic Approaches to Improving Service Quality & Productivity

Nine-step approach to service process improvement:
- Determine priority processes for improvement
- Set targets for (a) customer satisfaction, (b) defects, (c) cycle-time, and (d) productivity improvements
- Identify key elements of quality
- Assess process performance
- Identify quality gaps
- Identify root causes of gaps
- Improve process performance
- Control and fine-tune
- Start again, the journey is the destination...

Widely-used organization-wide systematic approaches:
- Total quality management (TQM)
- ISO 9000 Certification
- Six Sigma (i.e., DMAIC)
- Malcolm-Baldrige and EFQM Approaches

Measuring & Improving Service Productivity

Defining and measuring productivity:
- Productivity: output/input
- Efficiency: compared to a standard (i.e., "do things right")
- Effectiveness: compared to a goal (i.e., "do the right things")
- All three have to be balanced

Productivity improvement strategies:
- Generic productivity strategies (i.e., "doing the same things better, faster, cheaper")
- Customer-driven approaches (e.g., shifting time of demand, using lower cost service delivery channels, and self-service)
- Outsourcing to third parties
- Monitor potential customer implications of productivity enhancement

Figure 14.1 Improving service quality and productivity

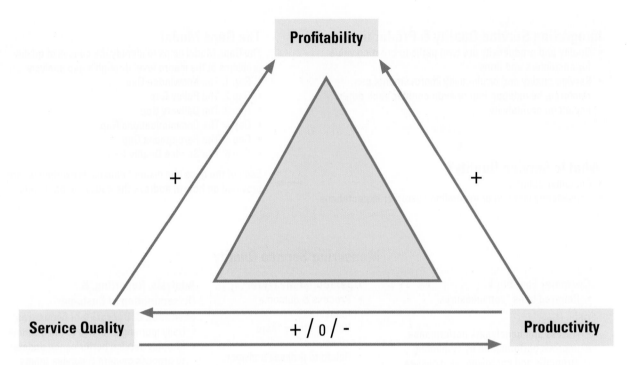

Figure 14.2 The service quality–productivity–profit triangle

Likewise, marketing strategies designed to improve customer satisfaction can prove costly and disruptive if the implications for operations and human resources have not been carefully thought through. For example, replacing an interactive voice response system with human agents in a customer contact center and increasing head count, reducing class sizes to improve the learning experience of students, and increasing the frequency of trains to increase passenger convenience) will have medium to long-term positive direct effects on profitability via customer loyalty. However, these changes will also have an immediate negative indirect effect on profitability via reduced productivity. The net result on profitability in both cases depends on the relative impact of the direct and indirect effects.

Finally, some quality improvements may not have any implications on productivity (e.g., improving a process in the front office that does not change the cost of providing it) and vice versa (e.g., improving efficiency of back office operations that do not have implications for customer touch points). In these cases, there is only a single positive effect of productivity improvements on profitability, or of customer satisfaction improvements on profitability.

One can see that the relationship between productivity and customer satisfaction can be positive, neutral, or negative. In broad terms, quality focuses on the benefits created for the customer's side of the equation, and productivity addresses the financial costs incurred by the firm, and if not properly integrated, these two foci can be in conflict. The bottom line is that service quality and productivity improvement strategies must be considered jointly, not in isolation. Let's next examine how to improve service quality before we turn to productivity.

WHAT IS SERVICE QUALITY?

⊃ **LO 2**
Be familiar with the different perspectives of service quality.

What do we mean when we speak of service quality? **Quality** can mean different things to people according to the context[3]. Common perspectives on quality include the manufacturing-based approach. It is primarily concerned with engineering and manufacturing practices and typically means delivery against measurable standards within certain tolerance levels (e.g., tolerance levels for weld seams in car manufacturing). In services, we would say that quality is operations-driven. It focuses on the conformance to internally developed specifications, and they tend to be tightly aligned with productivity and cost-containment goals.

Service researchers argue that the nature of services requires a distinctive approach in defining and measuring service quality. The intangible, multifaceted nature of many services makes it harder to evaluate the quality of a service compared to a good (*Figure 14.3*). As customers are often involved in service production, a distinction needs to be drawn between the **process** of service delivery (what Christian Grönroos calls functional quality) and the actual **output** (or outcome) of the service (what he calls technical quality)[4]. Grönroos and others also suggest that the perceived quality of a service is the result of an evaluation process in which customers compare their perceptions of service delivery and its outcome to what they expect. Therefore, we define service quality from the user's perspective as a high standard of performance that consistently meets or exceeds customer expectations (see Chapter 2 for a detailed discussion of the customer perspective of service quality).

Figure 14.3 Service quality can be difficult to manage for the fussy diner.

IDENTIFYING AND CORRECTING SERVICE QUALITY PROBLEMS

After understanding what service quality is, let's explore a model that allows us to identify and correct service quality problems at the overall firm level.

The Gaps Model in Service Design and Delivery

⊃ **LO 3**

Demonstrate how to use the Gaps Model for diagnosing and addressing service quality problems.

Valarie Zeithaml, A. Parasuraman, and Leonard Berry identified four potential gaps within the service organization that may lead to the fifth and most serious final gap — the difference between what customers expected and what they perceived was delivered[5]. *Figure 14.4* extends and refines their framework to identify a total of six types of gaps that can occur at different points during the design and delivery of a service performance.

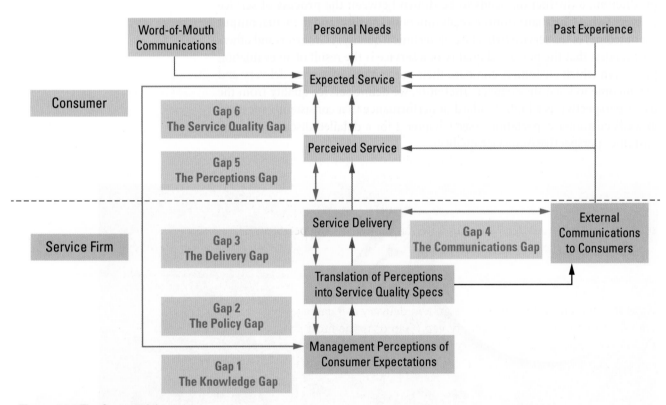

Figure 14.4 The Gaps model

Source

Adapted from the original five-gaps model developed by Parasuraman, A., Zeithaml, V. A., & Berry, L. L. "A conceptual model of service quality and its implications for future research". *Journal of Marketing* 49, Fall 1985 41–50; Zeithaml, V. A., Bitner, M. J., & Gremler, D. *Services Marketing: Integrating Customer Focus Across the Firm* (p. 46.). NY: McGraw Hill/Irwin, 2006. A further gap (Gap 5) was added by Christoper Lovelock (1994), *Product Plus* (p. 112). NY: McGraw Hill.

Let's explore the six gaps in more detail:

- Gap 1: The **knowledge gap** is the difference between what senior management believes customers expect and what customers actually need and expect.

- Gap 2: The **policy gap** is the difference between management's understanding of customers' expectations and the service standards they set for service delivery. We call it the policy gap because the management has made a policy decision not to deliver what they think customers expect. Reasons for setting standards below customer expectations are typically cost and feasibility considerations.

- Gap 3: The **delivery gap** is the difference between specified service standards and the service delivery teams' actual performance on these standards.

- Gap 4: The **communications gap** is the difference between what the company communicates, and what the customer understands and subsequently experiences. This gap is caused by two sub gaps[6]. First, the *internal* communications gap is the difference between what the company's advertising and sales personnel think are the product's features, performance, and service quality level, and what the company is actually able to deliver. Second, the *external* communications gap (also referred to as the overpromise gap) can be caused by advertising and sales personnel being assessed by the sales they generate. This can lead them to overpromise in order to generate sales.

- Gap 5: The **perceptions gap** is the difference between what is actually delivered and what customers feel they have received because they are unable to accurately judge service quality accurately.

- Gap 6: The **service quality gap** is the difference between what customers expect to receive and their perception of the service that is actually delivered.

In this model, Gaps 1, 5, and 6 represent external gaps between the customer and the organization. Gaps 2, 3, and 4 are internal gaps occurring between various functions and departments within the organization.

Key Ways to Close the Gaps in Service Quality

Gaps at any point in the service design and delivery can damage relationships with customers. The service quality gap (Gap 6) is the most critical. Hence, the ultimate goal in improving service quality is to close or narrow this gap as much as possible. To achieve this, service organizations usually need to first work on closing the other five gaps depicted in *Figure 14.4*. Improving service quality requires identifying the specific causes of each gap and then developing strategies to close them.

The strength of the gaps model is that it offers generic insights and solutions that can be applied across industries. We summarize a series of generic prescriptions for closing the six quality gaps in *Table 14.1*. These prescriptions are a good starting point to think about how to close specific gaps in an organization, and later in this chapter, we will discuss the nuts and bolts on how to do this at the micro, or process level.

Table 14.1 Suggestions for Closing Service Quality Gaps

Gap 1: The Knowledge Gap

Suggestion: Educate Management About What Customers Expect

- Implement an effective customer feedback system that includes satisfaction research, complaint and compliment content analysis, customer panels, and online monitoring.
- Sharpen market research procedures including questionnaire and interview design, sampling, and field implementation, and periodically repeat research studies.
- Increase interactions between customers and senior management (e.g., programs such as "a day in the field" and senior management taking calls in customer contact centers).
- Improve upward communications, and facilitate and encourage communication between frontline employees and management.

Gap 2: The Policy Gap

Suggestion: Establish the Right Service Products, Processes and Standards That Are Based on Customer Needs and Expectations

- Get the products and customer service processes right:
  - Use a rigorous, systematic, and customer-centric process for designing and redesigning service products and customer service processes.
  - Standardize repetitive work tasks to ensure consistency and reliability by substituting hard technology for human contact and improving work methods (soft technology).
- Set, communicate, and reinforce measurable customer-oriented service standards for all work units:
  - Establish a set of clear service quality goals for each step in the service delivery that are challenging, realistic, and explicitly designed to meet customer expectations.
  - Ensure that employees understand and accept these goals, standards, and priorities.
- Develop tiered service products that meet customer expectations:
  - Consider premium, standard, and economy-level products to allow customers to self-segment according to their needs, or
  - Offer customers different levels of service at different prices.

Gap 3: The Delivery Gap

Suggestion: Ensure That Performance Meets Standards

- Ensure that customer service teams are motivated and are able to meet service standards:
  - Improve recruitment with a focus on employee-job fit; select employees for the abilities and skills needed to perform their job well.
  - Train employees on the technical and soft skills needed to perform their assigned tasks effectively, including interpersonal skills, especially for dealing with customers under stressful conditions.
  - Clarify employee roles and ensure that employees understand how their jobs contribute to customer satisfaction; teach them about customer expectations, perceptions, and problems.
  - Build cross-functional service teams that can offer customer-centric service delivery and problem resolution, including effective service recovery.
  - Empower managers and employees in the field by pushing decision-making power down the organization.
  - Measure performance, provide regular feedback, and reward customer service team performance as well as individual employees and managers for attaining quality goals.
- Install the right technology, equipment, support processes, and capacity:
  - Select the most appropriate technologies and equipment for enhanced performance.
  - Ensure that employees working on internal support jobs provide good service to their own internal customer, the frontline personnel.
  - Balance demand against productive capacity.
- Manage customers for service quality:
  - Educate customers to perform their roles and responsibilities in a service delivery effectively.
- Effectively align intermediaries and third parties involved in service delivery:
  - Align objectives, performance, costs and rewards with intermediaries (e.g., as in outsourced service delivery in customer contact centers or airline check in counters).
  - Monitor and incentivize service quality.

Gap 4: The Communications Gap

Suggestion: Close the Internal and External Communications Gaps by Ensuring That Communication Promises Are Realistic and Correctly Understood by Customers

- Ensure that communications content sets realistic customer expectations, and educate managers responsible for sales and marketing communications about operational capabilities:
  - Seek inputs from frontline employees and operations personnel when new communications programs are developed.
  - Let service providers preview advertisements and other communications before customers are exposed to them.
  - Get sales staff to involve operations staff in face-to-face meetings with customers.
  - Develop internal educational and motivational campaigns to strengthen understanding and integration among the marketing, operations, and human resource functions, and to standardize service delivery across different locations.
- Align incentives for sales teams with those of service delivery teams. This will avoid the problem where the sale teams focus exclusively on generating sales (e.g., through overpromising) and neglect customer satisfaction (e.g., through disappointed expectations).
- Be specific with promises and manage customers' understanding of communication content:
  - Pre-test all advertising, brochures, telephone scripts, and website content to see if target audience interprets them as the firm intends (if not, revise and retest). Make sure the advertising content reflects service characteristics most important to customers. Let them know what is and is not possible, and why.
  - Identify and explain, in real time, the reasons for shortcomings in service performance, highlighting those that cannot be controlled by the firm.
  - Document beforehand what tasks and performance guarantees are included in an agreement or contract.

Gap 5: The Perception Gap

Suggestion: Tangibilize and Communicate the Service Quality Delivered

- Make service quality tangible and communicate the service quality delivered:
  - Develop service environments and physical evidence cues that are consistent with the level of service provided.
  - For complex and credence services, keep customers informed during service delivery on what is being done, and give debriefings after the delivery so customers can appreciate the quality of service received.
  - After completion of the work, explain what work was performed in relation to a specific billing statement.
  - Provide physical evidence (e.g., for repairs, show customers the damaged components that were removed).

Gap 6: The Service Gap

Suggestion: Close Gaps 1 to 5 to Consistently Meet Customer Expectations

- Gap 6 is the accumulated outcome of all the preceding gaps. It will be closed when Gaps 1 to 5 have been addressed.

Source

Adapted and extended from Valarie A. Zeithaml, A. Parasuraman, and Leonard L. Berry, *Delivering Service Quality: Balancing Customer Perceptions and Expectations* (New York: The Free Press, 1990), Chapters 4–7; and Valarie A. Zeithaml, Mary Jo Bitner, and Dwayne D. Gremler, *Services Marketing: Integrating Customer Focus Across the Firm.* 5th ed. (New York: McGraw-Hill, 2013), Chapter 2. The remaining prescriptions were developed by the authors.

MEASURING SERVICE QUALITY

We now understand the gaps model and the generic prescriptions on how to close the six quality gaps. Let us next discuss how to use measurement to guide our service quality improvement efforts. It is commonly said that "what is not measured is not managed." Without measurement, managers cannot be sure whether service quality gaps exist, let alone what types of gaps, where they exist, and what potential corrective actions should be taken. And, of course, measurement determines whether goals for improvement are met after changes have been implemented.

⊃ **LO 4**

Differentiate between hard and soft measures of service quality.

Soft and Hard Service Quality Measures

Customer-defined standards and measures of service quality can be grouped into two broad categories: "soft" and "hard". Soft standards and their measures are those that cannot be easily observed and are typically gathered by talking to customers. Soft standards provide direction, guidance, and feedback to employees on how to achieve customer satisfaction, and they can be quantified by measuring customer perceptions and beliefs[7]. SERVQUAL (as seen in Chapter 2) is an example of a sophisticated soft measurement system, and we will discuss a variety of other customer feedback tools later in this chapter.

Hard standards and measures, in contrast, are typically process activities and outcomes that can be counted, timed, or measured. Such measures may include how many orders were filled correctly, the time required to complete a specific task, how many minutes customers had to wait in line at a particular stage in the service delivery, how many trains arrived late, how many bags were lost, the temperature of a particular food item, how many telephone calls were dropped while customers were on hold, or how many patients made a complete recovery following a specific type of surgery. Standards are often set with reference to the percentage of occasions on which a particular measure is achieved. The challenge for service marketers is to ensure that operational measures of service quality reflect customer needs and wants.

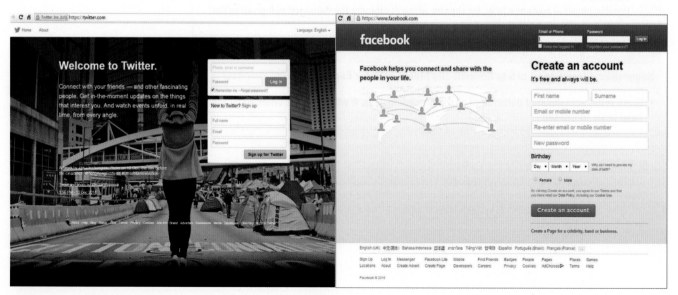

Figure 14.5 Social media such as Facebook and Twitter have been deployed by organizations to gather valuable feedback from customers

Organizations that are known for service excellence make use of both soft and hard measures (*Figure 14.6*). These organizations are good at listening to both their customers and their customer-contact employees. The larger the organization, the more important it is to create formalized feedback systems using a variety of professionally designed and implemented customer feedback and research procedures. We will next give you an overview of soft measures in the section on customer feedback, followed by a section on hard measures.

LEARNING FROM CUSTOMER FEEDBACK

How can companies measure their performance against soft standards of service quality? According to Leonard Berry and A. Parasuraman:

> [C]ompanies need to establish ongoing listening systems using multiple methods among different customer groups. A single service quality study is a snapshot taken at a point in time and from a particular angle. Deeper insight and more informed decision-making come from a continuing series of snapshots taken from various angles and through different lenses, which form the essence of systematic listening[9].

In this section, we discuss how customer feedback[8] can be systematically collected, analyzed, and disseminated to relevant departments via an institutionalized customer feedback system to achieve customer-driven learning and service improvements.[10]

Key Objectives of Effective Customer Feedback Systems

"It is not the strongest species that survive, nor the most intelligent, but the ones most responsive to change," wrote Charles Darwin. Similarly, many strategists have concluded that in increasingly competitive markets, the best competitive advantage for a firm is to learn and change faster than its competition[11]. This notion is echoed by Jack Welch, former CEO of General Electric, who said when he outlined his strategy for the 21st century, "We have only two sources of competitive advantage: First, the ability to learn more about our customers faster than the competition, and second, the ability to turn that learning into action faster than the competition".

Customer feedback is a key input for becoming and remaining a customer-driven learning organization, and effective customer feedback systems facilitate fast learning. Their objectives typically fall into the following three main categories:

1. **Assessment and Benchmarking of Service Quality and Performance.** The objective is to answer the question "How satisfied are our customers?" This objective includes learning about how well a firm performed in comparison to its main competitor(s), in comparison to the previous year (or quarter, or month), whether investments in certain service aspects have paid off in terms of customer satisfaction, and where the firm wants to be the following year. Often, a key objective of comparison against other units (branches, teams, service products, competitors) is to motivate managers and service staff to improve performance, especially when the results are linked to compensation.

    Benchmarking does not only have to be with companies from the same industry. For example, Southwest Airlines benchmarked Formula One pit-stops for speedy turnaround of aircraft; Pizza Hut benchmarked FedEx for on-time package delivery; and Ikea examined the military for excellence in coordination and logistics management.

LO 5
Explain the common objectives of effective customer feedback systems.

2. **Customer-Driven Learning and Improvements.** Here, the objective is to answer the questions, "What makes our customers happy or unhappy?" and "What are our strengths we want to cement, and what are our weaknesses we need to improve on?" For this, more specific or detailed information on processes and products is required to guide a firm's service improvement efforts and to pinpoint which areas have possible high returns for quality investment.

3. **Creating a Customer-Oriented Service Culture.** This objective is concerned with bringing the "voice of the customer" into the organization, focusing the organization on customer needs and customer satisfaction, and rallying the entire organization towards a service quality culture. It also includes fostering a culture of continuous improvement and change.

Of the three objectives just discussed, firms seem to do well on the first point, but often miss great opportunities in the other two. Neil Morgan, Eugene Anderson, and Vikas Mittal concluded in their research on customer satisfaction information usage (CSIU) the following:

> *Many of the firms in our sample do not appear to gain significant customer-focused learning benefits from their CS [customer satisfaction] systems, because they are designed to act primarily as a control mechanism [i.e., for assessment and benchmarking]. ...[Firms] may be well served to re-evaluate how they deploy their existing CSIU resources. The majority of CSIU resources...are consumed in CS data collection. This often leads to too few resources being allocated to the analysis, dissemination, and utilization of this information to fully realize the potential payback from the investment in data collection[12].*

Use a Mix of Customer Feedback Collection Tools

LO 6

Describe key customer feedback collection tools.

Renee Fleming, soprano and America's beautiful voice, once said: "We singers are unfortunately not able to hear ourselves sing. You sound entirely different to yourself. We need the ears of others — from outside." Likewise, firms need to listen to the voice of the customer. *Table 14.2* gives an overview of typically used feedback tools and their ability to meet various requirements. Recognizing that different tools have different strengths and weaknesses, service marketers should select a mix of customer feedback collection tools that jointly deliver the needed information. As Leonard Berry and A. Parasuraman observed, "Combining approaches enables a firm to tap the strengths of each and compensate for weaknesses.[13]"

Figure 14.6 Qualitative and quantitative feedback collection tools complement each other.

Total Market, Annual, and Transactional Surveys. **Total market surveys** and **annual surveys** typically measure satisfaction with all major customer service processes and products[14]. The level of measurement is usually high, with the objective of obtaining a global index or indicator of overall service satisfaction for the entire firm. This could be based on indexed (e.g., using various attribute ratings) and/or weighted data (e.g., weighted by core segments and/or products).

Overall indices such as these tell us how satisfied customers are, but not why they are happy or unhappy.

There are limits to the number of questions that can be asked about each individual process or product. For example, a typical retail bank may have 30–50 key customer service processes (e.g., from car loan applications and cash deposits at the teller to online banking). Because of the sheer number of processes, many surveys have room for only one or two questions per process (e.g., how satisfied are you with our ATM services?) and cannot address issues in greater detail.

In contrast, transactional surveys, also called intercept surveys, are typically conducted after customers have

Table 14.2 Strengths and Weaknesses of Key Customer Feedback Collection Tools

Collection Tools	Level of Measurement			Actionable	Representative, reliable	Potential for Service Recovery	First-hand Learning	Cost-Effectivness
	Firm	Process	Transaction Specific					
Total market survey (including competitors)	●	○	○	○	●	○	○	○
Annual survey on overall satisfaction	●	◐	○	○	●	○	○	○
Transactional survey	●	●	◐	◐	●	○	○	○
Service feedback cards and messages	◐	●	●	◐	◐	●	◐	●
Mystery shopping	○	◐	●	●	○	○	◐	○
Unsolicited feedback (e.g., Complaints)	○	◐	●	●	○	●	◐	●
Focus group discussions	○	◐	●	●	○	◐	●	◐
Service reviews	○	◐	●	●	○	●	●	◐
Online reviews and discussions (e.g., Reviews and social media postings)	○	◐	●	●	○	●	●	●
Legend:	● Meets requirements fully; ◐ moderately; ○ hardly at all							

Source

Adapted from Jochen Wirtz and Monica Tomlin (2000), "Institutionalizing Customer-driven Learning through Fully Integrated Customer Feedback Systems," *Managing Service Quality*, Vol. 10, No. 4, p. 210.

completed a specific transaction (*Figure 14.7*). At this point, if time permits, they may be queried about the process in some depth. In the case of the bank, all key attributes and aspects of ATM services could be included in the survey, including some open-ended questions, such as "liked best," "liked least," and "suggested improvements." Such feedback is more actionable, can tell the firm why customers are happy or unhappy with the service, and usually yields specific insights on how customer satisfaction can be improved.

Many market research agencies offer cost-effective email, SMS, electronic terminals, and app-based transactional survey tools. For example, hotel guests receive an automated email or message with a link to an online survey after checking out. Monthly online reports are then automatically generated for the hotel group at the overall level, for each of the individual hotels in a chain, and even for individual units within each hotel (e.g., front desk, rooms, room service, restaurants, spa, and gym). Such solutions are fully automated and can therefore be provided at a low cost of as little as US$100 per hotel per month in a large chain.

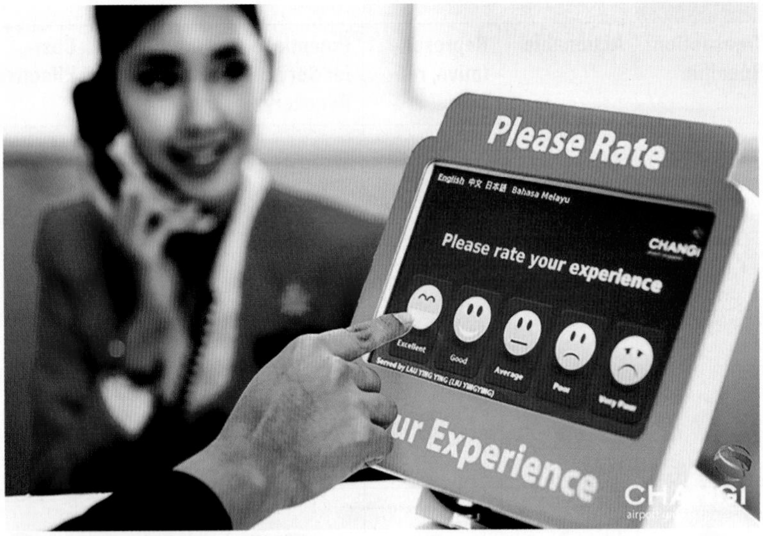

Similarly, point-of-transaction surveys on touchscreen terminals allow the measurement of customer satisfaction on key attributes immediately after a transaction has taken place (*Figure 14.8*). Again, the collection, analysis and reporting are fully automated and cost-effective, and the analysis can even be broken down to the individual service employee as they sign out of their service terminals.

All three survey types are representative and reliable when designed properly. Representativeness and reliability are required for:

Photo Credit: Changi Airport Group

Figure 14.7 Transactional surveys are typically conducted following service delivery

1. Accurate assessments of where the company, a process, branch, team, or individual stands relative to quality goals. It is important to have a representative and reliable sample, to ensure that observed changes in quality scores are not the result of sample biases and/or random errors.

2. Evaluations of individual service employees, service delivery teams, branches, and/or processes, especially when incentive schemes are linked to such measures. The methodology has to be water-tight if staff are to trust and buy into the results, especially when surveys deliver bad news.

The potential for service recovery is important and should, if possible, be designed into feedback collection tools. However, many surveys promise anonymity, making it impossible to identify and respond to dissatisfied respondents. In personal encounters or telephone surveys, interviewers can be instructed to ask customers whether they would like the firm to get back to them on dissatisfying issues.

Figure 14.8 Point-of-transaction terminals have become common in airports, hotels and government offices around the world.

and in-depth insights for coaching, training, and performance evaluation.

As the number of mystery calls or visits is typically small, no individual survey is reliable or representative. However, if a particular staff member performs well (or poorly) month after month, managers can infer with reasonable confidence that this person's performance is good (or poor).

Unsolicited Customer Feedback. Customer complaints, compliments, and suggestions can be transformed into a stream of information that can be used to help monitor quality, and highlight improvements needed to the service design and delivery. Complaints and compliments are rich sources of detailed feedback on what makes customers unhappy and what delights them.

Like feedback cards, unsolicited feedback is not a reliable measure of overall customer satisfaction, but it is a good source of ideas for improvement. If the objective of collecting feedback is mainly to get ideas on what to

Service Feedback Cards, Online and Mobile Messages. These powerful and inexpensive tools involve providing customers the opportunity to use feedback cards, online forms, e-mail, text messaging or apps[15] to provide feedback, typically to a central customer feedback unit (*Figure 14.9*). For example, a feedback card can be attached to each housing loan approval letter or to each hospital invoice. These cards are a good indicator of process quality and yield specific feedback on what works well and what doesn't. However, customers who are delighted or very dissatisfied are likely to be overrepresented among the respondents, which affects the reliability and representativeness of this tool.

Mystery Shopping. Service businesses often use "mystery shoppers" to determine whether frontline staff display desired behaviors (*Service Insights 14.1*). Banks, retailers, car rental firms, and hotels are among the industries actively using mystery shoppers. For example, the central reservation offices of a global hotel chain may appoint a research agency to conduct a large-scale monthly mystery caller survey to assess the skills of individual associates in relation to the phone sales process. Actions such as the correct positioning of the various products, up-selling and cross-selling, and closing the deal are measured. The survey also examines the quality of the phone conversation on criteria such as "a warm and friendly greeting" and "establishing rapport with the caller." Mystery shopping provides highly actionable

Figure 14.9 The widespread use of SMS text messaging allows for convenient mobile feedback

Mystery shopping is a good method for checking whether frontline employees display the desired and trained behaviors and follow the specified service procedures, but don't use customer surveys for this. Ron Kaufman, founder of Up Your Service! College, describes a service experience:

"We had a wonderful ride in the hotel car from the airport. The driver was so friendly. He gave us a cold towel and a cool drink. He offered a choice of music, talked about the weather, and made sure we were comfortable with the air conditioning. His smile and good feelings washed over us, and I liked it!"

"At the hotel, I signed the guest registration and gave my credit card. Then the counter staff asked me to complete another form." It read:

Kaufman continued: "As I read the form, all the good feelings fell away. The driver's enthusiasm suddenly seemed a charade. His concern for our well-being became just a checklist of actions to follow. His good mood was merely an act to meet the standard, not a connection with his guests. I felt like the hotel's quality control inspector, and I did not like it. If the hotel wants my opinion, make me an advisor, not an inspector. Ask me: What did you enjoy most about your ride from the airport? (I had told them about their wonderful driver). What else could we do to make your ride even more enjoyable? (I'd have recommended offering the use of a cell phone)."

LIMOUSINE SURVEY

To consistently ensure the proper application of our quality standards, we value your feedback on our limousine service:

1. Were you greeted by our airport representative?	YES/NO
2. Were you offered a cold towel?	YES/NO
3. Were you offered cold water?	YES/NO
4. Was a selection of music available?	YES/NO
5. Did the driver ask you about the air conditioning?	YES/NO
6. Was the driver driving at a safe speed?	YES/NO

Room Number: _____

Limo Number: _____ Date: _____

improve (rather than for benchmarking and/or assessing staff), reliability and representativeness are not needed, and more qualitative tools such as complaints/compliments or focus groups generally suffice.

Detailed customer complaint and compliment letters, recorded telephone conversations, and direct feedback from employees can also serve as an excellent tool for communicating internally what customers want, and allowing employees and managers at all levels to "listen" to customers first hand. Such learning is much more powerful for shaping the thinking and customer orientation of service staff than using "clinical" statistics and reports. For example, Singapore Airlines prints excerpts from complaint and compliment letters in its monthly employee magazine. Southwest Airlines shows video footage of customers providing feedback to service staff in their training sessions. Seeing actual customers giving comments about their service (positive and negative) leaves a much deeper and lasting impression on staff than any statistical analysis, and encourages them to further improve.

For complaints, suggestions, and inquiries to be useful as research input, they have to be funneled into a central collection point, logged, categorized, and analyzed[16]. That requires a system for capturing customer feedback where it is made, and then reporting it to a central unit. Some firms use a simple Intranet site to record all feedback received by any staff member. Coordinating such activities is not a simple matter, due to the many entry points, including the firm's own frontline employees who may be in contact with customers face-to-face, by telephone, or via mail or email, intermediary organizations acting on behalf of the original supplier, and managers who normally work backstage, but who are contacted by a customer seeking higher authority,

Figure 14.10 Service reviews being conducted with an important B2B customer

Focus Group Discussions and Service Reviews. Both tools give specific insights on potential service improvements and ideas. Typically, focus groups are organized by key customer segments or user groups to drill down on the needs of these users. Service reviews are in-depth, one-on-one interviews that are usually conducted once a year with a firm's most valuable customers (*Figure 14.10*). Typically, a senior executive of the firm visits the customer and discusses issues such as how well the firm performed the previous year and what should be maintained or changed. The senior executive then goes back to the organization and discusses the feedback with his or her account managers, and then both write a letter back to the client detailing how the firm will respond to that customer's service needs and how the account will be managed the following year. Apart from providing an excellent learning opportunity (especially when the reviews across all customers are compiled and analyzed), service reviews focus on the retention of the most valuable customers and get high marks for service recovery potential.

Online Reviews and Discussions. User-generated content and data can increasingly provide rich insights into quality perceptions of a firm and its competitors, and how these comparisons vary over time at an increasingly granular attribute and temporal level[17]. Sentiment analysis of postings and automated text processing often allows real-time insights into changes in consumer perceptions[18]. As one study showed, monitoring online sentiments has been shown to be a leading indicator of offline brand tracking surveys and even stock market prices[19]. Online monitoring tools combined with big data analytics allow real time sensing of information, location-based and user-generated content will be analyzed increasingly using techniques such as text mining, image processing and classification, social geotagging, human annotations, and geo-mapping[20].

However, such analyses should be seen as augmenting more traditional tools such as surveys and focus groups. Consider the following example. A high-quality, high-priced grab-and-go-food business showed high growth (i.e., their customers must have loved what they offer), but online reviews were critical (e.g., "If you have money to spare, you could do worse", and "The prices are seriously whacked"), and its rating on an important review website was only three out of five stars.

One of the co-owners then attended a meeting with the elite reviewers of this site and, to his surprise, found these reviewers looked nothing like their customers, who tended to be professionals in their 30s and older. These reviewers were mostly in their 20s, had ample spare time to write free reviews, and seemed much less affluent than the firm's customers. The co-owner learned from his conversations with these reviewers that they were highly price sensitive and were not willing to pay premium prices for premium food, which were factors that undoubtedly colored their reviews. In fact, they liked the food, but they downgraded the business as they felt the price was too high. The management of this firm responded to these findings with increasing investment in traditional focus groups to ensure that they respond to the needs of their core market[21]. Not relying too much on online user-generated content seems especially important if a firm's core target segments are expected to differ from the people who post their comments online.

Analysis, Reporting, and Dissemination of Customer Feedback

Choosing the relevant feedback tools and collecting customer feedback is meaningless if the company is unable to disseminate the information to the relevant parties to take action. Hence, to drive continuous improvement and learning, a reporting system needs to deliver feedback and its analysis to frontline staff, process owners, branch or department managers, and top management. *Figure 14.11* provides an overview of which information should go to different key stakeholders in the organization. It also illustrates nicely how the different tools complement each other: the top-level tools provide the benchmarking over time and against competition, and the lower-level tool allows us to identify what ratings go up or down, and generate insights and ideas on how the service can be improved.

The feedback loop to the frontline should be immediate for complaints and compliments, as is practiced in a number of service businesses where complaints, compliments and suggestions are discussed with staff during a daily morning brief. In addition, we recommend three types of service performance reports to provide the necessary information for service management and team learning:

1. A monthly **Service Performance Update** provides process owners with timely feedback on customer comments and operational process performance. Here, the verbatim feedback should be passed on to the process managers who can in turn discuss them with their service delivery teams.

2. A quarterly **Service Performance Review** provides process owners and branch or department managers with trends in process performance and service quality.

3. An annual **Service Performance Report** gives top management a representative assessment of the status and long-term trends relating to customer satisfaction with the firm's services.

These reports should be short and reader-friendly, focus on key indicators and provide an easily understood commentary for the people in charge to act on. In addition to customer feedback, these reports should also contain key operational measures as discussed in the next section.

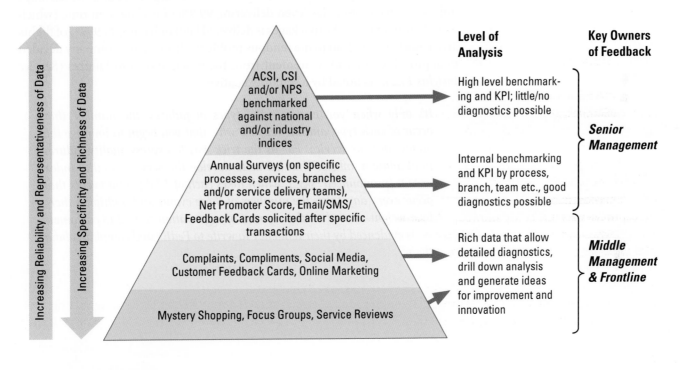

Figure 14.11 Mapping reporting of tools to levels of management

LO 7
Be familiar with hard
measures of service quality
and control charts.

HARD MEASURES OF SERVICE QUALITY

Having learnt about the various tools for collecting soft service quality measures, let's explore hard measures in detail. Hard measures typically refer to operational processes or outcomes and include data such as uptime, service response times and failure rates. In a complex service operation, multiple measures of service quality will be recorded at many different points. In low-contact services where customers are not deeply involved in the service delivery process, many operational measures apply to backstage activities that have only a second-order effect on customers.

FedEx was one of the first service companies to understand the need for a firm-wide index of service quality that embraced all the key activities that affect customers. By publishing a single, composite index on a frequent basis, senior managers hoped that all FedEx employees would work toward improving quality. The firm recognized the danger of using percentages as targets, because they might lead to complacency. In an organization as large as FedEx, which ships millions of packages a day, even delivering 99.9% of packages on time (which would mean one in 1,000 packages is delivered late) or having 99.999% of flights arrive safely would lead to horrendous problems. Instead, the company decided to approach quality measurement from the baseline of zero failures (*Service Insights 14.2*). As noted by a senior executive:

> *It's only when you examine the types of failures, the number that occur of each type, and the reasons why, that you begin to improve the quality of your service. For us the trick was to express quality failures in absolute numbers. That led us to develop the Service Quality Index or SQI [pronounced "sky"], which takes each of 12 different events that occur every day, takes the numbers of those events and multiplies them by a weight...based on the amount of aggravation caused to customers — as evidenced by their tendency to write to FedEx and complain about them[22].*

SERVICE INSIGHTS 14.2

FedEx's Approach to Listening to the Voice of the Customer

"We believe that service quality must be mathematically measured," declared Frederick W. Smith, Chairman, President, and CEO of FedEx Corporation. The company has a commitment to clear quality goals, and continuously measures its progress against those goals. This practice forms the foundation for its approach to quality.

FedEx initially set two ambitious quality goals: 100% customer satisfaction for every interaction and transaction, and 100% service performance on every package handled. Customer satisfaction was measured by the percentage of on-time deliveries, which referred to the number of packages delivered on time as a percentage of total package volume. However, as things turned out, the percentage of on-time delivery was an internal standard that was not synonymous with customer satisfaction.

As FedEx had systematically cataloged customer complaints, it was able to develop what CEO Smith calls the "Hierarchy of Horrors", which referred to the eight most common complaints by customers: (1) wrong day delivery, (2) right day, late delivery, (3) pick-up not made (4) lost package, (5) customer misinformed, (6) billing and paperwork mistakes, (7) employee performance failures, and (8) damaged packages. In other words, the design of this "hard" index reflected the findings of extensive "soft" customer research. The "Hierarchy of Horrors" was the foundation on which FedEx build its customer feedback system.

FedEx refined the list of "horrors" and developed its SQI, a 12-item measure of satisfaction and service quality from the customers' viewpoint. The raw numbers of each event are multiplied by a weight that highlights the seriousness of that event for customers (*Table 14.3*). The result is a point score for each item. The points are then added up to generate that day's index. Like a golf score, the lower the index, the better the performance. However, unlike golf, the SQI involves substantial numbers — typically six figures — reflecting the huge numbers of packages shipped

Table 14.3 Composition of FedEx's Service Quality Index (SQI)

Failure Type	Weighting Factor x No. of Incidents = Daily Points
Late delivery—right day	1
Late delivery—wrong day	5
Tracing requests unanswered	1
Complaints reopened	5
Missing proofs of delivery	1
Invoice adjustments	1
Missed pickups	10
Lost packages	10
Damaged packages	10
Aircraft delays (minutes)	5
Overgoods (packages missing labels)	5
Abandoned calls	1
Total failure points (SQI)	225

daily. The total SQI and all its 12 items are tracked daily, so that a continuous index can be computed.

An annual goal is set for the average daily SQI, based on reducing the occurrence of failures over the previous year's total. To ensure a continuing focus on each separate component of the SQI, FedEx established 12 Quality Action Teams, one for each component. The teams were charged with understanding and correcting the root causes underlying the observed problems.

In addition to the SQI, which has been modified over time to reflect changes in procedures, services, and customer priorities, FedEx uses a variety of other ways to capture feedback.

Customer Satisfaction Survey. This telephone survey is conducted on a quarterly basis with several thousand randomly selected customers, stratified by its key segments. The results are relayed to senior management on a quarterly basis.

Targeted Customer Satisfaction Survey. This survey covers specific customer service processes and is conducted on a semiannual basis with clients who have experienced one of the specific FedEx processes within the last three months.

FedEx Center Comment Cards. Comment cards are collected from each FedEx storefront business center.

The results are tabulated twice a year and relayed to managers in charge of the centers.

Online Customer Feedback Surveys. FedEx has commissioned regular studies to get feedback for its online services, such as package tracking, as well as ad hoc studies on new products.

The information from these various customer feedback measures has helped FedEx to maintain a leadership role in its industry and played an important role in enabling it to receive the prestigious Malcolm Baldrige National Quality Award.

Source

"Blueprints for Service Quality: The Federal Express Approach," *AMA Management Briefing* (New York: American Management Association, 1991), 51–64; Linda Rosencrance (2000), "BetaSphere Delivers FedEx Some Customer Feedback," *Computerworld*, Vol. 14, No. 14, p. 36; Madan Birla, *Fedex Delivers: How the World's Leading Shipping Company Keeps Innovating and Outperforming the Competition* (John Wiley, 2005), 91–92; Madan Birla, *FedEx Delivers: How the World's Leading Shipping Company Keeps Innovating and Outperforming the Competition* (Wiley, 2013), ISBN-13: 978-0471715795.

How can we show performance on hard measures? For this, **control charts** are a simple method of displaying performance over time against specific quality standards. The charts can be used to monitor and communicate individual variables or an overall index. Since they are visual, trends are easily identified. *Figure 14.12* shows an airline's performance on the important hard standard of on-time departures. The trends displayed suggest that this issue needs to be addressed by management, as its performance is erratic and not satisfactory. Of course, control charts are only as good as the data on which they are based.

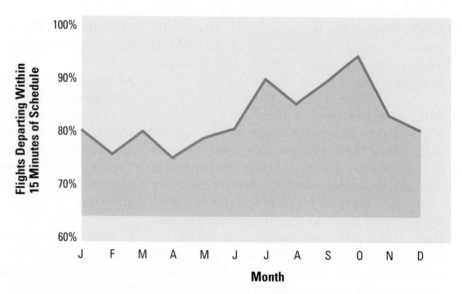

Figure 14.12 Control chart for departure delays showing percentage of flights departing within 15 minutes of schedule

TOOLS TO ANALYZE AND ADDRESS SERVICE QUALITY PROBLEMS

⊃ **LO 8**
Select suitable tools to analyze service problems.

After having assessed service quality using soft and hard measures, how can we now drill deeper to identify common causes of quality shortfalls and take corrective actions? When a problem is caused by controllable, internal forces, there's no excuse for allowing it to recur. After all, maintaining customers' goodwill after a service failure depends on keeping promises made to the effect of "we're taking steps to ensure that it doesn't happen again!" With prevention as a goal, let's look briefly at some tools for determining the root causes of specific service quality problems.

Root Cause Analysis: The Fishbone Diagram

The cause-and-effect analysis uses a technique first developed by Japanese quality expert, Kaoru Ishikawa. Groups of managers and staff brainstorm all the possible reasons that might cause a specific problem. The reasons are then grouped into one of five groupings — Equipment, Manpower (or People), Material, Procedures, and Other — on a cause-and-effect chart, popularly known as a fishbone diagram due to its shape. This technique has been used initially in manufacturing but is now widely used for services.

To apply this tool better to service organizations, we show an extended framework that has eight instead of five groupings[23]. "People" has been further broken down into "Front-Stage Personnel" and "Backstage Personnel". This highlights the fact that front-stage service problems are often experienced directly by customers, whereas backstage failures tend to show up more obliquely through a ripple effect.

In addition, "Information" has been separated from "Procedures", recognizing the fact that many service problems result from information failures. For example, these failures are often because front-stage personnel do not readily have the required information or do not tell customers what to do and when to do it.

"Customers" were added as a further source of root causes. In manufacturing, customers do not really affect the day-to-day operations. However, in a high-contact service, they are involved in front-stage operations. If they don't play their own role correctly, they may reduce service productivity and cause quality problems for themselves and other customers. For instance, an aircraft can be delayed if a passenger tries to board at the last minute with an oversized suitcase, which then has to be loaded into the cargo hold. An example of the extended fishbone is shown in *Figure 14.13*, displaying 27 possible reasons for late departures of passenger aircraft[24].

Once all the main potential causes for flight delays have been identified, it is necessary to assess how much impact each cause has on actual delays. This can be established using frequency counts in combination with Pareto analysis, which is discussed next.

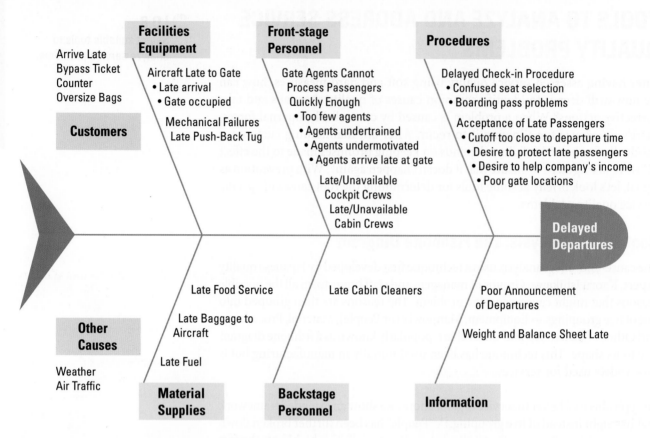

Figure 14.13 Cause-and-effect chart for flight departure delays

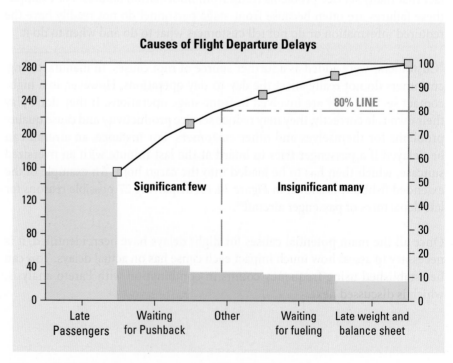

Figure 14.14 Pareto analysis of causes of flight departure delays

Pareto Analysis

Pareto Analysis (so named after the Italian economist who first developed it) identifies the main causes of observed outcomes. It separates the important from the trivial and helps a service firm to focus its improvement efforts on the most important problem areas. This type of analysis underlies the so-called 80/20 rule, because it often reveals that around 80% of the value of one variable (in this instance, the number of service failures) is caused by only 20% of the causal variables (i.e., the number of possible causes as identified by the fishbone diagram). By combining the fishbone diagram and Pareto analysis, we can identify the main causes of service failure.

In the airline example, findings showed that 88% of the company's late departing flights from the airports it served were caused by only four (15%) of all the possible factors (*Figure 14.14*). In fact, more than half of the delays were caused by a single factor: acceptance of late passengers (i.e., situations when the staff held a flight for one more passenger who was checking in after the official cutoff time).

On such occasions, the airline made a friend of the passenger who was late — possibly encouraging a repeat of this undesirable behavior on future occasions — but risked alienating all the other passengers who were already onboard, waiting for the aircraft to depart. Other major delays included waiting for pushback (a vehicle must arrive to pull the aircraft away from the gate), waiting for fueling, and delays in signing the weight and balance sheet (a safety requirement relating to the distribution of the aircraft's load that the captain must follow on each flight).

However, further analysis showed significant variations in the reasons from one airport to another (*Figure 14.15*). This finding suggests that the individual airport teams should set slightly different priorities for improvements.

Blueprinting — A Powerful Tool for Identifying Fail Points

Fishbone diagrams and Pareto analyses tell us the causes and importance of quality problems. Blueprints allow us to drill down further to identify where exactly in a service process the problem was caused. As described in Chapter 8, a well-constructed blueprint enables us to visualize the process of service delivery by showing the sequence of front-stage interactions that customers experience as they encounter service providers, facilities, and equipment, together with supporting backstage activities, which are hidden from the customers and are not part of their service experience.

Blueprints can be used to identify the potential fail points where failures are most likely to occur, and they help us to understand how failures at one point (such as the incorrect entry of an appointment date) may have

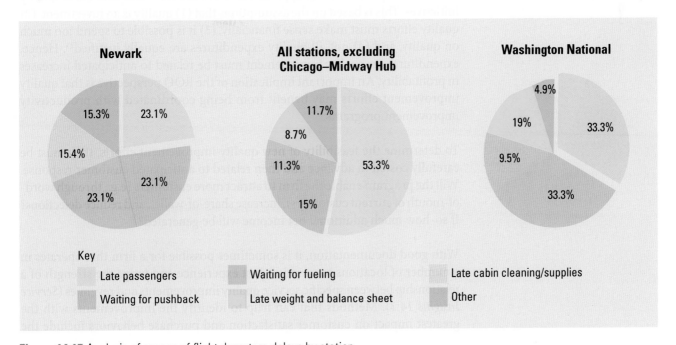

Figure 14.15 Analysis of causes of flight departure delays by station

a ripple effect on the later stages of the process (i.e., the customer arrives at the doctor's office and is told the doctor is unavailable). By adding frequency counts to the fail points in a blueprint, managers can identify the specific types of failures that occur most frequently and thus need urgent attention. Knowing what and where things can go wrong is an important first step in preventing service quality problems.

One desirable solution is to design fail points out of the system (see Chapter 8 for a discussion of the poka-yokes technique). In the case of failures that cannot easily be designed out of a process or are not easily prevented (such as problems related to weather or the public infrastructure), solutions may revolve around development of contingency plans and service recovery guidelines (see Chapter 13 on how to design service recovery policies and procedures).

LO 9

Understand return on quality and determine the optimal level of reliability.

RETURN ON QUALITY

We now understand how to drill down to specific quality problems, and we can use what we learnt from Chapter 8 on how to design and redesign improved service processes. However, the picture is incomplete without understanding the financial implications related to quality improvements. Many firms pay a lot of attention on improving service quality; however, quite a few of them have been disappointed by the results. Even firms recognized for service quality efforts have sometimes run into financial difficulties. This is partly because they spent too lavishly on quality improvements that customers do not value or even recognize. In other instances, such results show poor or incomplete execution of the quality program itself.

Assess Costs and Benefits of Quality Initiatives

A return on quality (ROQ) approach assesses the costs and benefits of quality initiatives. This is based on the assumptions that (1) quality is an investment, (2) quality efforts must make sense financially, (3) it is possible to spend too much on quality, and (4) not all quality expenditures are equally justified[25]. Hence, expenditures on quality improvement must be related to anticipated increases in profitability. An important implication of the ROQ perspective is that quality improvement efforts may benefit from being coordinated with productivity improvement programs.

To determine the feasibility of new quality improvement efforts, they must be carefully costed in advance and then related to anticipated customer response. Will the program enable the firm to attract more customers (e.g., through word-of-mouth of current customers), increase share-of-wallet, and reduce defections? If so, how much additional net income will be generated?

With good documentation, it is sometimes possible for a firm that operates in a number of locations to examine past experience and judge the strength of a relationship between specific service quality improvements and revenues (*Service Insights 14.3*). Methods that can help to identify the improvements with the greatest impact on customer satisfaction and purchase behaviors include the

SERVICE INSIGHTS 14.3

Quality of Facilities and Room Revenues at Holiday Inn

To find out the relationship between product quality and financial performance in a hotel context, Sheryl Kimes analyzed three years of quality and operational performance data from 1,135 franchised Holiday Inn hotels in the United States and Canada.

Indicators of product quality came from the franchisor's quality assurance reports. These reports were based on unannounced, semi-annual inspections by trained quality auditors who were rotated among different regions, and inspected and rated different quality dimensions of each hotel. Sheryl Kimes used 12 of these quality dimensions in her study: two relating to the guest rooms (bedroom and bathroom) and 10 relating to commercial areas (e.g., exterior, lobby, public restrooms, dining facilities, lounge facilities, corridors, meeting area, recreation area, kitchen, back of house). Each quality dimension usually included 10–12 individual items that could be passed or failed. The inspector noted the number of defects for each dimension and the total number for the entire hotel.

Holiday Inn Worldwide also provided data on the revenue per available room (RevPAR) at each hotel. To adjust for differences in local conditions, Kimes analyzed sales and revenue statistics obtained from thousands of US and Canadian hotels, and reported in the monthly Smith Travel Accommodation Reports (a widely used service in the travel industry). This data enabled Kimes to calculate the RevPAR for the immediate midscale competitors of each Holiday Inn hotel. The results were then used to make the RevPARs comparable across all Holiday Inns in the sample.

For the purposes of the research, if a hotel had failed at least one item in an area, it was considered "defective" in that area. The findings showed that as the number of defects in a hotel increased, the RevPAR decreased. Quality dimensions that showed quite a strong impact on RevPAR were the exterior, the guest room, and the guest bathroom. Even a single defect resulted in a statistically significant reduction in RevPAR. However, the combination of defects in all three areas showed an even larger effect on RevPAR over time. Kimes calculated that the average annual revenue impact on a defective hotel was a revenue loss of $204,400 compared to a non-defective hotel.

Using a Return on Quality perspective, the results showed that the main focus of increased expenditures on housekeeping and preventive maintenance should be the hotel exterior, the guest rooms, and bathrooms.

Source

Sheryl E. Kimes (1999), "The Relationship between Product Quality and Revenue per Available Room at Holiday Inn," *Journal of Service Research*, Vol. 2, November, pp. 138–144.

importance-performance matrix (see *Figure 14.16* for an example), multiple regression analyses that establish the attributes with the highest impact on overall satisfaction, and a new method called marginal utility analysis (MUA) which uses direct questioning of customers on their improvement priorities (e.g., "if you could make an improvement…which four would be your top priorities")[26].

Determine the Optimal Level of Reliability

How far should we go in improving service reliability? A company with poor service quality can often achieve big jumps in reliability with relatively modest investments in improvements. As illustrated in *Figure 14.17*, initial investments in reducing service failure often bring dramatic results. At some point, however, diminishing returns set in as further improvements require increasing the initial levels of investment, and can even become prohibitively expensive. What level of reliability should we then target?

Typically, the cost of service recovery is lower than the cost of an unhappy customer. This suggests that service firms should increase reliability up to the point that the incremental improvement equals the cost of service recovery (which is the actual cost of failure). Although this strategy results in a service that is less than 100% failure-free, the firm can still aim to satisfy 100% of its target customers by ensuring that either they receive the service as planned or, if a failure occurs, they obtain a satisfying service recovery.

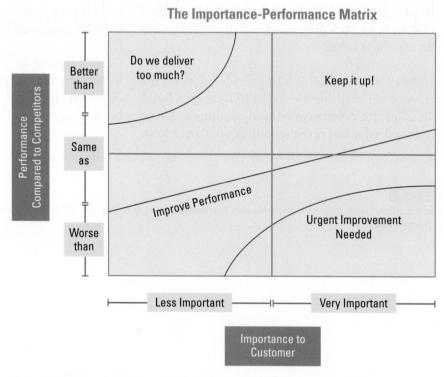

Figure 14.16 The importance-performance matrix compares a firm's service performance against competition and customer needs.

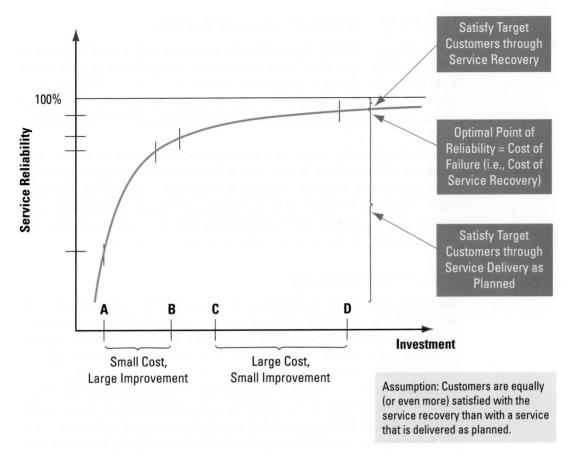

Figure 14.17 When does improving service reliability become uneconomical?

DEFINING AND MEASURING PRODUCTIVITY

⊃ LO 10
Define and measure service productivity.

Historically, services have lagged behind manufacturing in productivity growth, but research by the McKinsey Global Institute shows that five of the seven largest contributors to labor productivity growth in the United States since 2000 have been service industries, including retail and wholesale trade, finance and insurance, administrative support, and scientific and technical services[27]. Clearly, advances in technology enable dramatic improvements in productivity! We highlighted in the introduction of this chapter that we need to look at quality and productivity improvement strategies together rather than in isolation. A firm needs to ensure that it can deliver quality experiences more efficiently to improve its long-term profitability. Let's first discuss what productivity is and how it can be measured.

Defining Productivity in a Service Context

Simply defined, productivity measures the amount of output produced relative to the amount of input used. Hence, improvements in productivity are reflected by an increase in the ratio of outputs to inputs. An improvement in this ratio might be achieved by cutting the resources required to create a given volume of output, and/or by increasing the output obtained from a given level of inputs.

What do we mean by "input" in a service context? Input varies according to the nature of the business. It may include labor, materials, energy, and capital (consisting of land, buildings, equipment, information systems, and financial assets). The intangible nature of service performances makes it more difficult to measure the productivity of service industries than that of manufacturing. The problem is especially acute for information-based services.

Measuring Productivity

Measuring productivity is difficult in services when the output is frequently difficult to define. In a people-processing service such as a hospital, we can look at the number of patients treated in the course of a year and the hospital's "census" or average bed occupancy. However, how do we take into account the different types of medical activities performed, such as the removal of cancerous tumors, treatment of diabetes, or setting of broken bones? What about the differences between patients? How do we judge the inevitable difference in outcomes? Some patients get better, some develop complications, and sadly, some even die. Relatively few standardized medical procedures offer highly predictable outcomes.

The measurement task is perhaps simpler in possession-processing services, since many quasi-manufacturing are performing routine tasks with easily measurable inputs and outputs. Examples include garages that change a car's oil and rotate its tires, or fast-food restaurants that offer limited and simple menus. However, the task gets more complicated when the garage mechanic has to find and repair a water leak, or when we are dealing with a French restaurant known for its varied and exceptional cuisine. What about information-based services? How should we define the output of an investment bank or a consulting firm?

Independent of these more detailed considerations, labor productivity (e.g., revenue per employee, value-added per employee, and number of customers served per employee) and asset productivity (e.g., return on assets) are frequently used measures to capture productivity at a high level.

Service Productivity, Efficiency, and Effectiveness

LO 11
Understand the difference between productivity, efficiency, and effectiveness.

When we look at the issue of productivity, we need to distinguish among productivity, efficiency, and effectiveness[28]. **Productivity** refers to the output one can get from a certain amount of inputs (e.g., labor and asset productivity). **Efficiency** involves comparison to a standard which is usually time-based. It is a measure of how well you do things. For example, how long does it take for an employee to perform a particular task compared to industry average or some other standard? The faster the task can be completed, the higher the efficiency. **Effectiveness** can be defined as the degree to which an organization meets its goals and desired outcomes, which would typically include customer satisfaction (*Figure 14.18*). Peter Drucker expressed it succinctly: "Efficiency is doing the thing right. Effectiveness is doing the right thing."

Figure 14.18 A counselor needs to take his time in a session so that patients can gain greater benefit from their group therapy

Classical techniques of productivity and efficiency measurement focus on outputs and benchmarking, rather than outcomes. This means that productivity and efficiency are stressed, but effectiveness is neglected. In freight transport for instance, a ton-mile of output for freight that is delivered late is treated the same for productivity purposes as a similar shipment delivered on time. Similarly, suppose a hairdresser usually serves three customers per hour. However, she can increase her output to one every 15 minutes by reducing conversation with the customer and by rushing them. Even if the haircut itself is just as good, the delivery process may be perceived as functionally inferior, leading customers to rate the overall service experience less positively (*Figure 14.19*). In this example, productivity and efficiency have been achieved, but not effectiveness.

In the long run, organizations that are more effective in consistently delivering outcomes desired by customers should be able to command higher prices for their output, and build a loyal and profitable customer base. Therefore, there is a need to place emphasis on effectiveness and outcomes (including quality and value generated for customers) in addition to productivity and efficiency[29].

Figure 14.19 Productivity for the firm may result in customer frustration when they cannot easily talk to service personnel

Copyright 2003 by Randy Glasbergen.
www.glasbergen.com

"If you're losing patience with our endless automated system and need to run outside and scream, press 44. If you're feeling better now and wish to continue, press 45..."

IMPROVING SERVICE PRODUCTIVITY

Intense competition in many service sectors pushes firms to continually seek ways to improve their productivity.[30] This section discusses various sources of and possible approaches to productivity gains.

Generic Productivity Improvement Strategies

 LO 12
Recommend the key methods to improve service productivity.

Traditionally, operations managers have been in charge of improving service productivity and their focus can be summed up as achieving the same output "better, faster and cheaper". This approach typically centers on actions such as:

- Careful cost control at every step in the process. Many senior managers subscribe to the saying, "Costs are like fingernails: You have to cut them constantly."

- Reduce the waste of materials and labor.

- Train and motivate employees to do things faster, better, and more efficiently. As a result, employees should work more productively (note that faster is not necessarily better if it leads to mistakes or unsatisfactory work that has to be redone).

- Broaden the variety of tasks that a service worker can perform (which may require revised labor agreements) so as to eliminate bottlenecks and wasteful downtime, by allowing managers to deploy workers wherever they are needed most.

- Improve capacity utilization through better matching of supply and demand, and/or match productive capacity to average levels of demand rather than at peak levels, so that workers and equipment are not underemployed for extended periods.

- Use machines, equipment, technology, and data that enable employees to work faster and/or to a higher level of quality.

- Install expert systems that allow paraprofessionals to take on work previously performed by more experienced individuals earning higher salaries.

- Redesign customer service processes to be more productive and effective (e.g., through lean six sigma)

- Replace service employees with automated machines and customer-operated self-service technologies (SSTs).

- Tier service levels to allocate resources better to more important customers.

- Outsource non-core activities that can be provided more cost-effectively by third parties.

Although improving productivity can be approached incrementally, major gains often require redesigning customer service processes. For example, it's time for service process redesign when customers face unbearably long waits, as often experienced in healthcare (*Figure 14.20*). We discussed service process redesign in depth in Chapter 8.

Figure 14.20 Long waiting times often indicate a need for service process redesign

Customer-Driven Approaches to Improve Productivity

In situations where customers are deeply involved in the service production process, operations managers should also examine how customer inputs can be made more productive. Marketing managers should be thinking about what marketing strategies should be used to influence customers to behave in more productive ways. Some of these strategies include:

- **Change the Timing of Customer Demand.** By encouraging customers to use a service outside of peak periods and offering them incentives to do so, managers can make better use of their productive assets and provide better service. The issues that relate to managing demand in capacity-constrained service businesses are discussed in detail in Chapter 9; revenue management strategies are explored in Chapter 6.

- **Encourage Use of Lower Cost Service Delivery Channels and Self-Service.** Shifting transactions to more cost-effective service delivery channels such as the Internet, through apps or self-service machines, improves productivity. It also helps in demand management by reducing the pressure on employees and certain types of physical facilities at peak hours. Many technological innovations are designed to get customers to perform tasks previously undertaken by service employees (*Figure 14.21*). The issues related to customers playing a more active role as co-producers of the service are discussed in detail in the context of service process design in Chapter 8.

- **Ask Customers to Use Third Parties.** In some instances, managers may be able to improve service productivity by delegating one or more service support functions to third parties. Specialist intermediaries may enjoy economies of scale, allowing them to perform the task more cheaply than the core service provider. This allows the service provider to focus on quality and productivity in its own area of expertise. An example of an intermediary is a travel agency. We discussed the use of intermediaries in detail in Chapter 5 in the context of distribution.

Figure 14.21 Self-service pumps with credit card readers have increased gas station productivity

How Productivity Improvements Impact Quality and Value

⟳ **LO 13**
Know how productivity improvements impact quality and value.

Managers would do well to examine productivity enhancements from the broader perspective of the business processes used to transform resource inputs into the outcomes desired by customers — especially for processes that not only cross departmental and sometimes geographic boundaries, but also link the backstage and front-stage areas of the service operation. Hence, as firms make productivity improvements, they need to examine the impact on the customer experience. See also our discussion on the service quality–productivity–profitability triangle at the beginning of this chapter.

Front-Stage Efforts to Improve Productivity. In high-contact services, many productivity improvements are quite visible. Some changes simply require acceptance by customers, while others require customers to adopt new patterns of behavior in their dealings with the organization. If substantial changes are proposed, then it makes sense to conduct market research first to determine how customers may respond. Failure to consider the effects on customers may result in a loss of business and cancel out anticipated productivity gains. Refer to Chapter 8 on how to manage and overcome customers' reluctance to change in service processes.

How Backstage Changes May Impact Customers. The marketing implications of backstage changes depend on whether they affect or are noticed by customers. If airline mechanics develop a procedure for servicing jet engines more quickly without incurring increased wage rates or material costs, the airline has obtained a productivity improvement that has no impact on the customer's service experience.

Other backstage changes, however, may have ripple effects that extend to the front-stage and affect customers. Marketers should be aware of proposed backstage changes, not only to identify such ripples but also to pre-empt customers. At a bank for instance, the decision to install new computers and printer peripherals may be due to plans to improve internal quality controls and reduce the cost of preparing monthly statements. However, this new equipment may change the appearance of bank statements and the time of the month when they are posted. If customers are likely to notice such changes, an explanation may be warranted. If the new statements are easier to read and understand, the change may be worth promoting as a service improvement.

A Caution on Cost Reduction Strategies. In the absence of new technology, most attempts to improve service productivity tend to center on efforts to eliminate waste and reduce labor costs. Cutbacks in front-stage staffing can mean that the remaining employees have to work harder and faster, or that there are insufficient personnel to serve customers promptly at busy times. Although employees may be able to work faster for a brief period of time, few can maintain a rapid pace for extended periods. They become exhausted, make mistakes, and treat customers in a cursory manner. Workers who are trying to do two or three things at once — for example, serving a customer face-to-face while simultaneously answering the telephone and sorting papers — may do a poor job of each task. Excessive pressure breeds discontent and frustration, especially among customer contact personnel who are caught in between trying to meet customer needs and attempting to achieve management's productivity goals.

A better way is to search for service process redesign opportunities that lead to drastic improvements in productivity and at the same time increase service quality. Biometrics is set to become a new technology that may allow for both (*Service Insights 14.4*).

SERVICE INSIGHTS 14.4

Biometrics — The Next Frontier in Driving Productivity and Service Quality?

Intense competitive pressures and razor-thin margins in many service industries do not allow firms the luxury of increasing costs to improve quality. Rather, the trick is to constantly seek ways to simultaneously achieve great improvements in service quality and efficiency at the same time. In the past, Internet and service apps have allowed many firms to do just that, and redefined industries including financial services, music distribution, and travel agencies. Biometrics may be the next major technology driving further service and productivity improvements in the service sector.

Biometrics is the authentication or identification of individuals based on a physical characteristic or trait. Physical characteristics include fingerprints, facial recognition, hand geometry and the structure of the iris, and traits include signature formation, keystroke patterns, and voice recognition. Biometrics, as something you are, is more convenient and more secure than something you know (passwords or pieces of personal information) or something you have (card keys, smart cards, or tokens). There is no risk of forgetting, losing, copying, loaning, or getting your biometrics stolen (*Figure 14.22*).

Applications of biometrics range from controlling access to service facilities (used by Disney World to provide access to season pass holders), voice recognition at call centers (used by the Home Shopping Network and Charles Schwab to enable fast and hassle-free client authentication), self-service access to safe deposit vaults at banks (used by the Bank of Hawaii and First Tennessee Bank), cashing in checks at supermarkets (used by Kroger, Food 4 Less, and BI-LO), and even in schools (for library

book issue and for debiting of catering accounts based on the child's finger-scan). The use of biometrics will become more prevalent.

Biometrics clearly have exciting applications. They are generally more secure, but if handled wrongly, the potential damage could also be far more serious. Even biometrics can be cloned. For example, fingerprints can be replicated (or "spoofed") from something a person has touched. Resetting a compromised password is merely a hassle, but what will happen if someone stole the digital version of your fingerprint or your retina? Perhaps, biometrics will be supplemented by additional safety features for the highest risk applications. Future service innovation will show where biometrics can add the highest value to service organizations and their customers.

Figure 14.22 Customers cannot forget or lose their biometrics!

Source

Jochen Wirtz and Loizos Heracleous (2005), "Biometrics Meets Services," *Harvard Business Review*, February, pp. 48–49; Loizos Heracleous and Jochen Wirtz (2006), "Biometrics — The Next Frontier in Service Excellence, Productivity and Security in the Service Sector," *Managing Service Quality*, Vol. 16, No. 1; *The Economist*, "Internet Security: Kill or Cure," September 7, 2013, p. 52.

INTEGRATION AND SYSTEMATIC APPROACHES TO IMPROVING SERVICE QUALITY AND PRODUCTIVITY

⮞ **LO 14**
Understand how to integrate all the tools to improve the quality and productivity of customer service processes.

We discussed a number of tools and concepts on how to improve service quality and productivity. *Table 14.4* integrated the key tools discussed into a generic nine-step framework you can use to structure your approach to improve the quality and productivity of a single customer service process. Such projects are typically conducted by experienced in-house teams or external consultants. However, the continual improvement of a process (as described in step 9) should typically be the responsibility of the process owner.

There are also systematic approaches that help service firms to achieve an organization-wide culture of becoming customer, service quality and productivity focused. In fact, much of the thinking, tools and concepts introduced in this chapter originate from these approaches, which include the Total Quality Management (TQM), ISO 9000, Six Sigma, and the Malcolm-Baldrige and European Foundation for Quality Management (EFQM) approaches. We briefly discuss each of these approaches and relate them to the service quality and productivity context in the following sections.

Total Quality Management

⮞ **LO 15**
Explain how TQM, ISO 9000, Six Sigma, and the Malcolm-Baldrige and EFQM approaches relate to managing and improving service quality and productivity.

Total Quality Management (TQM) was originally developed in Japan. It is probably the most widely-known approach to continuous improvement in manufacturing, and more recently, in service firms. TQM can help organizations to attain service excellence, increase productivity, and be a continued source of value creation through innovative process improvements[31].

Some concepts and tools of TQM can be applied directly to services. As discussed in this chapter, TQM tools such as control charts, Pareto analysis, blue prints, and fishbone diagrams are used by service firms with great results for monitoring service quality and determining the root causes of specific problems.

Twelve critical dimensions for successful implementation of TQM in a service context have been identified: (1) top management commitment and visionary leadership; (2) human resource management; (3) technical system, including service process design and process management; (4) information and analysis system; (5) benchmarking; (6) continuous improvement; (7) customer focus; (8) employee satisfaction; (9) union intervention and employee relations; (10) social responsibility; (11) servicescapes; and (12) service culture[32].

Table14.4 An Integrated Nine-Step Approach to Customer Service Process Improvement

Step	Objectives	Potential Tools to Apply
1	Determine priority processes for improvement and redesign	• Frequency count of process occurrence and number of complaints per process to identify priority processes • Use prioritization matrix (ease of implementation vs. potential business impact) to identify "low hanging fruits" with which to start a service improvement initiative
2	For the shortlisted processes, set targets for (1) customer satisfaction, (2) defects, (3) cycle-time, and (4) productivity improvements	• Benchmarking internally, against competition, best in class and world-class to determine targets for all four priorities • Decide the target level of performance (e.g., do you aim to be the best in your industry, or just catch up with industry average on those four priorities?) • Use a project charter to formalize the objectives of this customer service process redesign project
3	Identify key elements of quality in priority service processes and determine customer needs and expectations	• Use blueprinting to identify all touchpoints of a customer journey and the line of visibility to understand the customer view of a process • For each touch point, determine what quality means in the customer's eyes (e.g., use the five dimensions of service quality (see Chapter 2) to cover all important dimensions, review customer feedback, content analysis of compliments and complaints to understand drivers of customer delight and disgust, conduct focus groups)
4	Assess process performance	• Review hard, operational process measures (e.g., cycle times, customer waiting times, one-time resolution, etc.) • Measure customer perceptions of process performance (e.g., process-specific customer satisfaction surveys) • Interview frontline employees to obtain their view of what works and what doesn't, and what needs urgent improvement
5	Identify performance shortfalls and quality gaps	• Map customer needs and wants of the process against process performance measures to determine important performance and quality gaps. • Identify the main performance gaps, e.g., map frequency counts of service failures (and/or complaints) on service blueprints to understand where exactly service processes fail
6	Identify root causes of quality gaps	• Use the Gaps Model to capture all possible sources of gaps in customer's service quality perceptions • Use TQM tools to drill down on specific gaps, e.g., use Pareto charts to understand which fail points to focus on, use Fishbone diagrams to identify the exact causes of key fail points, and again use Pareto charts to identify the main root causes to be designed out of the processes
7	Improve process performance	• Use prescriptions from the Gaps Model to close each of the six gaps (see Table 14.1) • Use customer service design and redesign tools (see Chapter 8, including design fail points of the system through use of poka-yokes • Plan service recovery for fail points that cannot be designed out of the system (i.e., make it proactive, preplanned, trained and empowered, see Chapter 13)
8	Control and continuously fine-tune and further improve the process	• After redesign, monitor the performance of the redesigned process using operational measures and customer feedback • Make it a routine process at the new, high level of performance • Ask the process owner to fine-tune the process through incremental improvements (e.g., use Kaizen or other tools to get the process team to monitor and continually improve the process it is responsible for)
9	Start over, the journey is the destination…	• Create a culture of customer centricity, process improvement, and change by continuously working and redesigning customer service processes; become a customer-driven learning organization

ISO 9000 Certification

There are 162 countries that are members of ISO (the International Organization for Standardization based in Geneva, Switzerland), which promotes standardization and quality to facilitate international trade. ISO 9000[33] is all about quality management and it comprises requirements, definitions, guidelines, and related standards to provide an independent assessment and certification of a firm's quality management system. The official ISO 9000 definition of quality is: "The totality of features and characteristics of a product or service that bear on its ability to satisfy a stated or implied need. Simply stated, quality is about meeting or exceeding your customer's needs and requirements."

The ISO 9000 is comprised of a family of sub-standards family addressing various aspects of quality management. These standards provide guidance and tools for organizations who want to ensure their products and services consistently meet customers' requirements, and that quality is consistently improved.

To ensure quality, ISO 9000 uses many TQM tools and internalizes their use in participating firms and makes use of W. Edwards Deming's PDCA Cycle (i.e., Plan-Do-Act-Check Cycle).

Service firms generally adopted ISO 9000 standards later than manufacturing firms. Major service sectors that have adopted ISO 9000 certification include wholesale and retail firms, IT service providers, healthcare providers, consultancy firms, and educational institutions. By adopting the ISO 9000 standards, service firms can ensure that their services conform to customer expectations and achieve improvements in productivity.

Six Sigma

The Six Sigma approach was originally developed by Motorola to improve product quality and reduce warranty claims, and was soon adopted by other manufacturing firms to reduce defects in a variety of areas.

Subsequently, service firms embraced various Six Sigma strategies to reduce defects, reduce cycle times, and improve productivity[34]. As early as 1990, GE Capital applied Six Sigma methodology to reduce the backroom costs of selling consumer loans, credit card insurance, and payment protection. Its former president and COO Denis Nayden said:

> *Although Six Sigma was originally designed for manufacturing, it can be applied to transactional services. One obvious example is in making sure the millions of credit card and other bills GE sends to customers are correct, which drives down our costs of making adjustments. One of our biggest costs in the financial business is winning new customers. If we treat them well, they will stay with us, reducing our customer-origination costs.[35]*

Statistically, Six Sigma means achieving a quality level of only 3.4 defects per million opportunities (DPMO). To understand how stringent this target is, consider mail deliveries. If a mail service delivers with 99% accuracy, it misses 3,000 items out of 300,000 deliveries. But if it achieves a Six Sigma performance level, only one item out of this total will go astray.

Over time, Six Sigma has evolved from a defect reduction approach to an overall business improvement approach. As defined by Pande, Neuman, and Cavanagh:

> *Six Sigma is a comprehensive and flexible system for achieving, sustaining and maximizing business success. Six Sigma is uniquely driven by close understanding of customer needs, disciplined use of facts, data and statistical analysis, and diligent attention to managing, improving, and reinventing business processes[36].*

Process improvement and process design/redesign are two strategies that form the cornerstone of the Six Sigma approach. Process improvement strategies aim to identify and eliminate the root causes of service delivery problems, thereby improving service quality. Process design/redesign strategies act as a supplementary strategy to improvement strategy. If a root cause can't be identified or effectively eliminated within the existing processes, either new processes are **designed** or existing process are **redesigned** to fully or partially address the problem.

The most popular Six Sigma improvement tool for analyzing and improving business processes is the DMAIC model, shown in *Table 14.5*. DMAIC stands for:

- **D**efine the opportunities (including the problem, scope, and goals).
- **M**easure the current performance along key steps/inputs.
- **A**nalyze to identify root causes.
- **I**mprove the process and its performance.
- **C**ontrol the process to sustain the higher level of performance.

Table 14.5 Applying the DMAIC Model to Process Improvement and Redesign

	Process Improvement	Process Design/Redesign
Define	• Identify the problem • Define requirements • Set goals	• Identify specific or broad problems • Define goal/change vision • Clarify scope and customer requirements
Measure	• Validate problem/process • Refine problem/goal • Measure key steps/inputs	• Measure performance to requirements • Gather process efficiency data
Analyze	• Develop causal hypothesis • Identify root causes • Validate hypothesis	• Identify best practices • Assess process design • Refine requirements
Improve	• Develop ideas to measure root causes • Test solutions • Measure results	• Design new process • Implements new process, structures, and systems
Control	• Establish measures to maintain performance • Correct problems as needed	• Establish measures and reviews to maintain performance • Correct problems as needed

Source

Republished with permission of McGraw-Hill Companies from *The Six SIGMA Way: How GE, Motorola, and Other Top Companies Are Honing Their Performance* by Peter S. Pande, Roland R. Cavanagh, Robert P. Neuman, Copyright 2000; permission conveyed through Copyright Clearance Center, Inc.

Malcolm-Baldrige and EFQM Approaches

The Malcolm Baldrige National Quality Award (MBNQA) was developed by the National Institute of Standards and Technology (NIST) with the goal of promoting best practices in quality management, and recognizing and publicizing quality achievements among US firms. Countries other than the US have similar quality awards, of which the most widely used is probably the European Foundation for Quality Management (EFQM) approach[37].

While the framework is generic and does not distinguish between manufacturing and service organizations, the award has a specific service category, and the model can be used to create a culture of ongoing service improvements. Major services firms that have won the award include PricewaterhouseCoopers, Ritz-Carlton, FedEx, University of Wisconsin, Xerox Business Services, Boeing Aerospace Support, Caterpillar Financial Services Corp, and AT&T. Research has confirmed that employing this framework can improve organizational performance[38].

The Malcolm-Baldrige Model assesses firms on seven areas:

1. Leadership commitment to a service quality culture.

2. Planning priorities for improvements, including service standards, performance targets, and measurement of customer satisfaction, defects, cycle-time, and productivity.

3. Information and analysis that will aid the organization to collect, measure, analyze, and report strategic and operational indicators.

4. Human resources management that enables the firm to deliver service excellence, ranging from hiring the right people to development, involvement, empowerment, and motivation.

5. Process management, including monitoring, continuous improvement, and process redesign.

6. Customer and market focus that allows the firm to determine customer requirements and expectations.

7. Business results[39].

Which Approach Should a Firm Adopt?

As there are various approaches to systematically improving a service firm's service quality and productivity, the question of which approach should be adopted arises — TQM, ISO 9000, the Malcolm-Baldrige model, or Six Sigma? It is best to see these approaches as complementary and building on another, and not as mutually exclusive. TQM can be applied at differing levels of complexity, and basic tools such as flowcharting, frequency charts, and fishbone diagrams probably should be adopted by any type of service firm. Six Sigma and ISO 9000 seem to suit the next level of commitment and complexity, and focus on process improvements and compliance to performance standards, followed by the Malcolm-Baldrige Model or the EFQM approaches that offer comprehensive frameworks for organizational excellence. The complementarity of approaches can be seen in a study on educational institutions in *Service Insights 14.5*.

Any one of the approaches can be a useful framework for understanding customer needs, analyzing processes, and improving service quality and productivity. Firms can choose a particular program, depending on their own needs and desired level of sophistication. Each program has its own strengths, and firms can use more than one program to add on to the other. For example, the ISO 9000 program can be used for standardizing the procedures and process documentation, and the Six Sigma and Malcolm-Baldrige programs can then be used to improve processes and focus on performance improvement across the organization.

A key success factor of any of these programs depends on how well the particular quality improvement program is part of the overall business strategy. Service champions make best practices in service quality management a core part of their organizational culture[40]. The NIST, which organizes the Malcolm-Baldrige Award program, has an index called the "Baldrige Index" of Malcolm-Baldrige Award winners. It was observed that winners always outperformed the S&P 500 index[41]!

SERVICE INSIGHTS 14.5

TQM and ISO Certification in Educational Institutions

Higher educational institutions are increasingly competing for talented students and have started to accept that they have to be more customer-centric in their approach to increase student satisfaction. What is the meaning of service quality in a higher educational institution? A TQM model has been proposed with the following five variables that measure different dimensions of service quality in an institution of higher learning, and they suggest that these variables will increase student satisfaction:

- **Commitment of Top Management.** Top management has to "walk the talk" and make sure that what is preached in terms of educational excellence and service quality is really being practiced.

- **Course Delivery.** While institutions of higher learning hire people with expert knowledge, there is a need for such expert knowledge to be transmitted expertly, with passion.

- **Campus Facilities.** Attention needs to be focused on having excellent infrastructure and facilities for student learning as well as for their extracurricular activities. These facilities also have to be properly maintained.

- **Courtesy.** This is a positive attitude toward students that will create a friendly learning environment.

- **Customer Feedback and Improvement.** Continuous feedback from students can lead to improvements.

The researchers studied TQM in a mix of ISO-certified and non-ISO certified institutions, and found that ISO 9001:2000 certified institutions were adopting TQM faster and offered a better quality education than non-ISO certified institutions.

Their findings showed that while all five variables together did predict student satisfaction, two variables in particular were more important in affecting student satisfaction. The variables were top management commitment and campus facilities. Top management needs to be committed to quality assurance in making sure the other variables are in place to improve the student experience.

Figure 14.23 Higher learning increasingly focus on service quality

Source

P. B. Sakthivel, G. Rajendran, and R. Raju (2005), "TQM Implementation and Students' Satisfaction of Academic Performance," *The TQM Magazine*, Vol. 17, No. 6, pp. 573–589.

Ironically however, the two-time winner of the award and Six Sigma pioneer, Motorola, had suffered financially and lost market share, partly due to the firm's failure to keep up with new technology. Also, firms which implement one of these programs due to peer pressure or just as a marketing tool are less likely to succeed than firms which view these programs as important development tools[42]. Clearly, success cannot be taken for granted. Commitment, implementation and constant improvement that follow changing markets, technologies, and environments are keys for sustained success (*Figure 14.24*).

CONCLUSION

Enhancing service quality and improving service productivity are often two sides of the same coin, offering powerful potential to improve value for both customers and the firm. It is a key challenge for any service business to deliver service quality and satisfaction to its customers in ways that are cost-effective for the firm. Strategies to improve service quality and productivity should reinforce rather than counteract each other. In a world of continuous innovation and competitive markets, only few businesses can afford to spend more money (i.e., allow lower productivity) for better quality. Therefore, the name of the game is to seek improvements that offer a quantum leap in service quality and productivity at the same time.

Figure 14.24 When commitment and constant improvement meet head-on the challenge of changing markets, technology and environments, success is more likely.

CHAPTER SUMMARY

LO1 Quality and productivity are twin paths for creating value for customers and the firm. However, the relationship between productivity and customer satisfaction (and the net effects on profitability) can be positive, neutral, or negative, and therefore needs to be managed carefully.

LO2 There are different definitions of service quality. In this book, we adopt the customer-focused definition of service quality as consistently meeting or exceeding customer expectations.

LO3 The GAPS Model is an important tool to diagnose and address service quality problems at a macro level. We identified six gaps that can be the cause of quality shortfalls:
- Gap 1 — the knowledge gap.
- Gap 2 — the policy gap.
- Gap 3 — the delivery gap.
- Gap 4 — the communications gap.
- Gap 5 — the perceptions gap.
- Gap 6 — the service quality gap. It is the most important gap. In order to close Gap 6, the other five gaps have to be closed first.

We summarized a series of potential causes for each of the gaps and provided generic prescriptions for addressing the causes and thereby closing the gaps. These prescriptions take a holistic organization perspective.

LO4 There are both soft and hard measures of service quality. **Soft measures** are usually based on perceptions of and feedback from customers and employees. **Hard measures** relate to processes and their outcomes.

LO5 Feedback from customers (i.e., mostly soft measures) should be systematically collected via a **customer feedback system** (CFS). The key objectives of a CFS include:
- Assessment and benchmarking of service quality and performance.
- Customer-driven learning and improvement.
- Creating a customer-oriented service culture, and a culture for change.

LO6 Firms can use a variety of tools to collect customer feedback, including: (1) total market surveys, (2) annual surveys on overall satisfaction, (3) transactional surveys, (4) service feedback cards, and other transaction-specific feedback tools such as text-messaging, emails, and social media, (5) mystery shopping, (6) unsolicited customer feedback (e.g., compliments and complaints), (7) focus group discussions, (8) service reviews, and (9) online and social media monitoring.

A reporting system is needed to channel feedback and its analysis to the relevant parties to take action.

LO7 **Hard measures** relate to operational processes and outcomes, and can be counted, timed, or observed. **Control charts** are a simple method of displaying performance on hard measures over time against specific quality standards.

LO8 Key tools to analyze and address important service quality problems are:
- **Fishbone diagrams**, to identify the causes of quality problems.
- **Pareto analysis**, to assess the frequency of quality problems and identify the most common causes.
- **Blueprinting**, to exactly determine the location of fail points in a customer service process and then help to redesign the process.

LO9 There are financial implications of service quality improvements. A **return on quality** (ROQ) approach assesses the costs and benefits of specific quality initiatives. Firms should increase service reliability up to the point that the incremental improvement equals the cost of service recovery (which is the actual cost of failure). When a service failure occurs, customers receive a satisfying service recovery.

LO10 Productivity measures the amount of output produced relative to the amount of inputs used. An improvement in this ratio can be achieved by cutting the resources required to create a given volume of output, and/or by increasing the output obtained from a given level of inputs. Key inputs vary according to the industry and can include labor, materials, energy, and assets.

LO11 It is important to differentiate these three concepts:
- **Productivity** involves the amount of outputs based on a given level of inputs (e.g., input/output ratio).

- **Efficiency** is usually time-based and compared to a standard such as industry average (e.g., speed of delivery).
- **Effectiveness** refers to the degree a goal, such as customer satisfaction, is met.

Productivity and efficiency cannot be separated from effectiveness. Firms that strive to be more productive, efficient, and effective in consistently delivering customer satisfaction will be more successful.

LO12 Generic methods to improve productivity include:
- Cost control.
- Reduce waste of materials and labor.
- Train employees to work more productively.
- Broaden the job scope of employees to reduce bottlenecks and downtime.
- Improve capacity utilization.
- Provide employees with equipment and information that enables them to work faster and better.
- Install expert systems so that paraprofessionals can do the work previously done by higher-paid experts.
- Replace service employees by automated machines and customer-operated SSTs.
- Tier service levels to allocate resources better to more important customers.
- Outsource non-core activities that can be provided more cost-effectively by third parties

Customer-driven methods to improve productivity include:
- Change the timing of customer demand to better match capacity to demand.
- Encourage the use of lower-cost service delivery channels and replacing labor with machines and SSTs.
- Get customers to use more cost-effective third parties for parts of the service delivery.

LO13 When improvements are made to productivity, firms need to bear in mind that both front-stage and backstage improvements can have an impact on service quality and the customer experience.

LO14 A nine-step approach can be used to improve customer service processes. It includes:
- Determine priority processes for improvement (e.g., through a frequency count of process occurrence and number of complaints; use prioritization matrix).
- Set targets for customer satisfaction, defects, cycle-time and productivity improvements (e.g., through benchmarking and a project charter).
- Identify key elements of quality (e.g., through blue printing to identify touch points, and then use the five dimensions of quality together with customer and employee feedback to understand what quality means in the eyes of the customer).
- Assess process performance (e.g., through hard operational measures and soft customer feedback measures).
- Identify performance shortfalls and quality gaps (e.g., map customer needs and wants against process performance; map frequency count of service failures on service blueprints to understand where exactly service processes fail).
- Identify root causes of gaps (e.g., use the Gaps Model to capture all possible sources of gaps, and use TQM tools such as the Fishbone diagram, Pareto charts and service blueprints to drill down on specific gaps).
- Improve process performance (e.g., use the prescriptions of the Gaps Model for closing the quality shortfalls; use customer service process redesign tools as discussed in Chapter 8, and plan for service recovery as covered in Chapter 13).
- Control and fine-tune (i.e., monitor the performance of the redesigned process and fine-tune it further).
- Start over, the journey is the destination…

LO15 TQM, ISO 9000, Six Sigma, and Malcolm-Baldrige and European Foundation for Quality Management (EFQM) approaches are systematic and complementary approaches to managing and improving service quality and productivity. They integrate many of the tools discussed in this chapter.

Review Questions

1. Explain the relationships between service quality, productivity, and profitability.

2. Identify the gaps that can occur in service quality, and the steps that service marketers can take to prevent them.

3. Why are both soft and hard measures of service quality needed?

4. What are the main objectives of an effective customer feedback system?

5. What are the key customer feedback collection tools? What are the strengths and weaknesses of each of these tools?

6. What are the main tools service firms can use to analyze and address service quality problems?

7. Why is productivity more difficult to measure in service than in manufacturing firms?

8. How can you integrate all the tools in a nine-step approach to improve the quality and productivity of customer service processes?

9. How do concepts such as TQM, ISO 9000, and Six Sigma, Malcolm-Baldrige and EFQM approaches relate to managing and improving service quality and productivity?

Application Exercises

1. Consider your own recent experiences as a service consumer. On which dimensions of service quality have you most often experienced a large gap between your expectations and your perceptions of the service performance? What do you think the underlying causes might be? What steps should management take to improve quality?

2. Collect a few customer feedback forms and tools (customer feedback cards, questionnaires, online forms, and apps), and explain how the information gathered with those tools can be used to achieve the main objectives of effective customer feedback systems.

3. What key measures could be used for monitoring service quality, productivity, and profitability for a large pizza restaurant chain? Specifically, what measures would you recommend to such a firm to use, taking administration costs into consideration? Who should receive what type of feedback on the results and why? On which measures would you base a part of the salary scheme of branch level staff and why?

4. In what ways can you, as a consumer, help to improve productivity for at least three service organizations that you patronize? What distinctive characteristics of each service make some of these actions possible?

5. Do a literature search, and identify the critical factors for a successful implementation of ISO 9000 or (Lean) Six Sigma in service firms.

Endnotes

1   Adapted from Audrey Gilmore (1998), "Service Marketing Management Competencies: A Ferry Company Example," *International Journal of Service Industry Management*, Vol. 9, No. 1, pp. 74–92, www.stenaline.com, accessed September 1, 2015.

2   This section was adapted from Jochen Wirtz and Valarie Zeithaml, "Cost-Effective Service Excellence: Developing a Conceptual Framework," in Bartsch, Silke and Blümelhuber, Christian eds. *Always Ahead in Marketing: Offensiv, Digital, Strategisch* (Wiesbaden: Gabler Verlag, Germany, 2015), pp. 547–557.

3   For an integrative framework of quality that captures how firms and customers produce quality, see: Peter N. Golder, Debanjan Mitra, and Christine Moorman (2012), "What Is Quality? An Integrative Framework of Processes and States," *Journal of Marketing*, Vol. 76, No. 4, pp. 1–12.

4   Christian Grönroos, *Service Management and Marketing*. 3rd ed. (Chichester, NY: Wiley, 2007).

5   A. Parasuraman, Valarie A. Zeithaml, and Leonard L. Berry (1985), "A Conceptual Model of Service Quality and Its Implications for Future Research," *Journal of Marketing*, Vol. 49, Fall, pp. 41–50; Valarie A. Zeithaml, Leonard L. Berry, and A. Parasuraman (1988), "Communication and Control Processes in the Delivery of Services," *Journal of Marketing*, Vol. 52, April, pp. 36–58.

6   The sub-gaps in this model are based on the 7-gaps model by Christopher Lovelock, *Product Plus: How Product + Service = Competitive Advantage* (New York: McGraw-Hill, 1994), p. 112.

7   Valarie A. Zeithaml, Mary Jo Bitner, and Dwayne D. Gremler, *Services Marketing: Integrating Customer Focus Across the Firm*. 5th ed. (New York: McGraw-Hill, 2013), p. 261.

8   This section is based partially on Jochen Wirtz and Monica Tomlin (2000), "Institutionalizing Customer-driven Learning Through Fully Integrated Customer Feedback Systems," *Managing Service Quality,* Vol. 10, No. 4, pp. 205–215.

Additional reading on service quality measurement can be found in Ching-Chow Yang (2003), "Establishment and Applications of the Integrated Model of Service Quality Measurement," *Managing Service Quality*, Vol. 13, No. 4, pp. 310–324.

9   Leonard L. Berry and A. Parasuraman (1997), "Listening to the Customer — The Concept of a Service Quality Information System," *Sloan Management Review,* Vol. 38, Spring, pp. 65–76.

10   Customer listening practices have been shown to affect service performance, growth and profitability, see: William J. Glynn, Sean de Búrca, Teresa Brannick, Brian Fynes, and Sean Ennis (2003), "Listening Practices and Performance in Service Organizations," *International Journal of Service Industry Management,* Vol. 14, No. 3, pp. 310–330.

11   W. E. Baker, and J. M. Sinkula (1999), "The Synergistic Effect of Market Orientation and Learning Orientation on Organizational Performance," *Journal of the Academy of Marketing Science*, Vol. 27, No. 4, pp. 411–427.

12   Neil A. Morgan, Eugene W. Anderson, and Vikas Mittal (2005), "Understanding Firms' Customer Satisfaction information Usage," *Journal of Marketing*, Vol. 69, July, pp. 131–151.

13   Leonard L. Berry and A. Parasuraman (1997) provide an excellent overview of all key research approaches discussed in this section, plus a number of other tools in their paper, "Listening to the Customer — The Concept of a Service Quality Information System," *Sloan Management Review,* Vol. 38, Spring, pp. 65–76.

14   For a discussion on suitable satisfaction measures, see: Jochen Wirtz and Lee Meng Chung (2003), "An Examination of the Quality and Context-Specific Applicability of Commonly Used Customer Satisfaction Measures," *Journal of Service Research*, Vol. 5, May, pp. 345–355.

15   There have been mobile apps developed that can track customers' experiences in real time, supply instant information and are highly cost-effective, see: Emma K. Macdonald, Hugh N. Wilson, and Umut Konuş (2012), "Better Customer Insight — in Real Time," *Harvard Business Review*, Vol. 90, No. 9, pp. 90, pp. 102–108.

16   Robert Johnston and Sandy Mehra (2002), "Best-Practice Complaint Management," *Academy of Management Executive*, Vol. 16, No. 4, pp. 145–154.

17   Seshadri Tirunillai and Gerard J. Tellis (2014), "Mining Marketing Meaning from Online Chatter: Strategic Brand Analysis of Big Data Using Latent Dirichlet Allocation," *Journal of Marketing Science*, Vol. 51, No. 4, pp. 463–479.

18 Advanced analytical tools allow analysis and visualization of online posted reviews; see: Thomas Y. Lee and Eric T. Bradlow (2011), "Automated Marketing Research Using Online Customer Reviews," *Journal of Marketing Research*, Vol. 48, No. 5, pp. 881–894.

The technology for analyzing unstructured textual data (provided to the firm as customer feedback, or if posted online) is advancing rapidly. For a recent study exploring the use for customer feedback mapping on service blue prints, see: Francisco Villarroel Ordenes, Babis Theodoulidis, Jamie Burton, Thorsten Gruber, and Mohamed Zaki (2014), "Analyzing Customer Experience Feedback Using Text Mining: A Linguistics-Based Approach," *Journal of Service Research*, Vol. 17, No. 3, pp. 278–295.

19 Note, however, that there are differences across online media. For example, sentiments expressed in blogs tend to be more positive than those posted in other media such as forums; see: David A. Schweidel and Wendy W. Moe (2014), "Listening In on Social Media: A Joint Model of Sentiment and Venue Format Choice," *Journal of Marketing Research*, Vol. 51, No. 4, pp. 387–402.

20 Roland T. Rust and Ming-Hui Huang (2014), "The Service Revolution and the Transformation of Marketing Science," *Marking Science*, Vol. 33, No. 2, pp. 206-221; Anindya Ghose, Panagiotis G. Ipeirotis P.G., and Beibei Li (2012), "Designing Marketing Ranking Systems for Hotels on Travel Search Engines by Mining User-Generated and Crowdsourced Content," *Marketing Science*, Vol. 31, No. 3, pp. 493–520.

21 Duncan Simester (2011), "When You Shouldn't Listen to Your Critics," *Harvard Business Review*, Vol. 89, No. 6, p. 42.

22 Comments by Thomas R. Oliver (1990), then senior vice president, sales and customer service, Federal Express; reported in Christopher H. Lovelock, *Federal Express: Quality Improvement Program, Lausanne: International Institute for Management Development*.

23 Christopher Lovelock, *Product Plus: How Product + Service = Competitive Advantage* (New York: McGraw-Hill, 1994), p. 218.

24 These categories and the research data that follow have been adapted from information in D. Daryl Wyckoff (2001), "New Tools for Achieving Service Quality," *Cornell Hotel and Restaurant Administration Quarterly*, August–September, pp. 25–38.

25 Roland T. Rust, Anthony J. Zahonik, and Timothy L. Keiningham (1995), "Return on Quality (ROQ): Making Service Quality Financially Accountable," *Journal of Marketing*, Vol. 59, April, pp. 58-70; and

Roland T. Rust, Christine Moorman, and Peter R. Dickson (2002), "Getting Return on Quality: Revenue Expansion, Cost Reduction, or Both?" *Journal of Marketing*, Vol. 66, October, pp. 7–24.

26 Marginal utility analysis was found to outperform analyses based on importance-performance and regression analyses; see: Donald R. Bacon (2012), "Understanding Priorities for Service Attribute Improvement," *Journal of Service Research*, Vol. 15, No. 2, pp. 199–214.

27 Martin Neil Baily, Diana Farrell, and Jaana Remes (2006), "Where US Productivity is Growing." *The McKinsey Quarterly*, No. 2, pp. 10–12.

For EU data, see: Kristian Uppenberg and Hubert Strauss (2010), *Innovation and Productivity Growth in the EU Services Sector*. European Investment Bank, the publication is available at: http://www.eib.org/attachments/efs/efs_innovation_and_productivity_en.pdf

28 Kenneth J. Klassen, Randolph M. Russell, and James J. Chrisman (1998), "Efficiency and Productivity Measures for High Contact Services," *The Service Industries Journal*, Vol. 18, October, pp. 1–18; James L. Heskett, *Managing in the Service Economy* (New York: The Free Press, 1986).

For a review and discussion on service productivity, see: Christian Grönroos and Katri Ojasalo (2004), "Service Productivity: Towards a Conceptualization of the Transformation of Inputs into Economic Results in Services," *Journal of Business Research*, Vol. 57, No. 4, pp. 414–423.

29 Rust and Huang examined the tradeoff between using labor to provide service (which generally increases service quality and effectiveness) and using automation and technology (which increases productivity). Depending on the competitive positioning of a firm, different levels of optimal productivity emerge, see: Roland T. Rust and Ming-Hui Huang (2012), "Optimizing Service Productivity," *Journal of Marketing*, Vol. 76, No. 2, pp. 47–66.

30 For a more in-depth discussion on service productivity, refer to Cynthia Karen Swank (2003), "The Lean Service Machine," *Harvard Business Review*, Vol. 81, No. 10, pp. 123–129.

31 C. Mele and M. Colurcio (2006), "The Evolving Path of TQM: Towards Business Excellence and Stakeholder Value," *International Journal of Quality and Reliability Management*, Vol. 23, No. 5, pp. 464–489; C. Mele (2007), "The Synergic Relationship Between TQM and Marketing in Creating Customer Value," *Managing Service Quality*, Vol. 17, No. 3, pp. 240–258.

32 G. S. Sureshchandar, Chandrasekharan Rajendran, and R. N. Anantharaman (2001), "A Holistic Model for Total Service Quality," *International Journal of Service Industry Management,* Vol. 12, No. 4, pp. 378–412.

33 See the official website of (International Organization for Standardization (ISO) for detailed information on ISO: http://www.iso.org.

The ISO 9000 family of standards is described at: http://www.iso.org/iso/home/standards/management-standards/iso_9000.htm and an introduction is provided in the publication: ISO Central Secretariat (2009), *Selection and Use of the ISO 9000 Family of Standards.*" ISO, ISBN: 978-92-67-10494-2 (this book can be downloaded for free from the ISO 9000 website).

34 Jim Biolos (2002), "Six Sigma Meets the Service Economy," *Harvard Business Review,* Vol. 80, November, pp. 3–5.

35 Mikel Harry and Richard Schroeder, *Six Sigma — The Breakthrough Management Strategy Revolutionizing the World's Top Corporations.* (New York: Currency, 2000), p. 232.

36 Peter S. Pande, Robert P. Neuman, and Ronald R. Cavanagh, *The Six Sigma Way: How GE, Motorola, and Other Top Companies Are Honing Their Performance* (New York: McGraw-Hill, 2000).

37 The official website for the Malcolm Baldrige Award is http://www.nist.gov/baldrige.

The official website for the European Foundation for Quality Management (EFQM) it is http://www.efqm.org, and an overview of the EFQM model is provided at http://www.efqm.org/sites/default/files/overview_efqm_2013_v1.1.pdf.

38 Susan Meyer Goldstein and Sharon B. Schweikhart (2002), "Empirical Support for the Baldrige Award Framework in U.S. Hospitals," *Health Care Management Review,* Vol. 27, No. 1, pp. 62–75.

39 Allan Shirks, William B. Weeks, and Annie Stein (2002), "Baldrige-Based Quality Awards: Veterans Health Administration's 3-Year Experience," *Quality Management in Health Care,* Vol. 10, No. 3, pp. 47–54; National Institute of Standards and Technology, "Baldrige FAQs," http://www.nist.gov/baldrige/about/baldrige_faqs.cfm, accessed September 1, 2015.

40 Cathy A. Enz and Judy A. Siguaw (2000), "Best Practices in Service Quality," *Cornell Hotel and Restaurant Administration Quarterly,* October, pp. 20–29.

41 *Eight NIST Stock Investment Study* (Gaithersburg, MD: National Institute of Standards and Technology, March 2002).

42 Gavin Dick, Kevin Gallimore, and Jane C. Brown (2011), "ISO 9000 and Quality Emphasis: An Empirical study of Front-Room and Back Room Dominated Service Industries," *International Journal of Service Industry Management,* Vol. 12, No. 2, pp. 114–136; and Adrian Hughes and David N. Halsall (2002), "Comparison of the 14 Deadly Diseases and the Business Excellence Model," *Total Quality Management,* Vol. 13, No. 2, pp. 255–263.

CHAPTER 15 Building a World-Class Service Organization

Marketing is so basic that it cannot be considered a separate function... It is the whole business seen from the point of view of its final result, that is, from the customer's point of view. Concern and responsibility for marketing must, therefore, permeate all areas of the enterprise.

Peter Drucker[1],
Management consultant, educator, and author
Described as a founder of modern management

[T]he more short-term a company's focus becomes, the more likely the firm will be to engage in behavior that actually destroys value.

Don Peppers and **Martha Rogers**,
Founding partners of Peppers & Rogers Group
A customer-centric management consulting firm

Why is it so hard for so many to realize that winners are usually the ones who work harder, work longer, and as a result, perform better?" and "Big things are accomplished only through the perfection of minor details.

John Wooden,
Legendary former UCLA Basketball Team Coach
Harvard Business School
(paraphrasing 18th century poet Alexander Pope)

LEARNING OBJECTIVES (LOs)

By the end of this chapter, the reader should be able to:

➲ **LO 1** Know the characteristics of world-class service organizations and be familiar with the four levels of service performance.

➲ **LO 2** Understand what is required for moving a service firm from service loser to service leader.

➲ **LO 3** Know the long-term impact of customer centricity on profitability and shareholder value.

INTRODUCTION

You are almost at the end of this book and presumably also at the tail-end of your services marketing course. We hope the module exceeded your expectations, gave you new insights into the marketing (and management) of services, provided you with the tools and skills you need to succeed in our service economy of the future, as well as motivate and excite you to become a service champion yourself.

In this final chapter, we provide you with a summary of what a world-class service organization looks like. You can also use this summary as an assessment tool. This is followed by a discussion of the financial impact of being a service leader, and the chapter closes with a call to action on your part!

CREATING A WORLD-CLASS SERVICE ORGANIZATION

 LO 1

Know the characteristics of world-class service organizations and be familiar with the four levels of service performance.

How would one describe a breakthrough service organization? Having worked in the field of services marketing for decades, we observed that a number of characteristics are necessary (but may not be sufficient) for becoming and remaining a breakthrough service organization. Let's next analyze more comprehensively how firms can be categorized into four performance levels, and how they can then move up the performance ladder.

From Losers to Leaders: Four Levels of Service Performance

Service leadership is not based on outstanding performance within a single dimension. Rather, it reflects excellence across multiple dimensions. In an effort to capture this performance spectrum, we need to evaluate the organization within each of the three functional areas described earlier — marketing, operations, and human resources. *Table 15.1* categorizes service performers into four levels: loser, nonentity, professional, and leader[2]. At each level, there is a brief description of a typical organization across 12 dimensions.

Under the marketing function, we look at the role of marketing, competitive appeal, customer profile, and service quality. Under the operations function, we consider the role of operations, service delivery (front-stage), backstage processes, productivity, and introduction of new technologies. Finally, under the human resources function, we examine the role of HRM, workforce, and frontline management. Obviously, there are overlaps between these dimensions and across functions. There may also be differences in the relative importance of some dimensions in different industries and across different delivery systems. For instance, human resource management tends to play a more prominent strategic role in high-contact services. The goal of this overall service performance framework is to generate insights into how service leaders perform so well and what needs to be changed in organizations that are not performing as well as they might.

If you want to do an in-depth appraisal of a company in a specific industry, you may find it useful to view *Table 15.1* as a point of departure, modifying some of the elements to create a customized assessment tool.

Table 15.1 Four levels of service performance assessment tool

Level	1. Loser	2. Nonentity
Marketing Function		
Role of Marketing	Tactical role only; advertising and promotions lack focus; no involvement in product or pricing decision	Uses mix of selling and mass communication, using simple segmentation strategy; makes selective use of price discounts and promotions; conducts and tabulates basic satisfaction surveys
Competitive Appeal	Customers patronize a firm for reasons other than performance	Customers neither seek nor avoid the firm
Customer profile	Unspecified; a mass market to be served at a minimum cost	One or more segments whose basic needs are understood
Service Quality	Highly variable, usually unsatisfactory. Subservient to operations priorities	Meets some customer expectations; consistent on one or two key dimensions, but not all
Operations Function		
Role of Operations	Reactive; cost oriented	The principal line management function creates and delivers product, focuses on standardization as key to productivity, and defines quality from internal perspective
Service Delivery (front-stage)	A necessary evil. Locations and schedules are unrelated to preferences of customers, who are routinely ignored	Sticklers for tradition; "If it ain't broke, don't fix it"; tight rules for customers; each step in delivery runs independently
Back-stage Operations	Divorced from front-stage operations; cogs in a machine	Contributes to individual frontstage delivery steps but organized separately; unfamiliar with customers
Productivity	Undefined; managers are punished for failing to stick within budget	Based on standardization; rewarded for keeping costs below budget
Introduction of New Technology	Late adopter, under duress, when necessary for survival	Follows the crowd when justified by cost savings
Human Resources Function		
Role of Human Resources	Supplies low-cost employees who meet minimum skill requirements for the job	Recruits and trains employees who can perform competently
Workforce	Negative constraints: poor performers, do not care, disloyal	Adequate resources, follows procedures but uninspired; turnover often high
Frontline Management	Controls workers	Controls the process

3. Professional	4. Leader	Assessment Score
Marketing Function		
Has clear positioning strategy against competition; uses focused communications with distinctive appeals to clarify promises and educate customers; pricing is based on value; monitors customer usage and operates loyalty programs; uses a variety of research techniques to measure customer satisfaction and obtain ideas for service enhancements; works with operations to introduce new delivery systems	Innovative leader in chosen segments, known for marketing skills; brands at product/process level; conducts sophisticated analysis of relational databases as inputs to one-to-one marketing and proactive account management; uses state-of-the-art research techniques; uses concept testing, observation, and lead customers as inputs to new-product development; close to operations/HR	
Customers seek out the firm based on its sustained reputation for meeting customer expectations	Company's name is synonymous with service excellence; its ability to delight customers raises expectations to levels that competitors can't meet	
Groups of individuals whose variation in needs and value to the firm are clearly understood	Individuals are selected and retained based on their future value to the firm, including their potential for new service opportunities and their ability to stimulate innovation.	
Consistently meets or exceeds customer expectations across multiple dimensions	Raises customer expectations to new levels; improves continuously	
	Subtotal	
Operations Function		
Plays a strategic role in competitive strategy; recognizes a trade-off between productivity and customer-defined quality; willing to outsource; monitors competing operations for ideas, threats	Recognized for innovation, focus, and excellence; an equal partner with marketing and HR management; has in-house research capability and academic contacts; continually experimenting	
Driven by customer satisfaction, not tradition; willing to customize, embrace new approaches; emphasis on speed, convenience, and comfort	Delivery is a seamless process organized around the customer; employees know whom they are serving; focuses on continuous improvement	
Process is explicitly linked to front-stage activities; sees role as serving "internal customers," who, in turn, serve external customers	Closely integrated with front-stage delivery, even when geographically far apart; understands how own role relates to the overall process of serving external customers; continuing dialog	
Focuses on reengineering backstage processes; avoids productivity improvements that will degrade customers' service experience; continually refining processes for efficiency	Understands the concept of return on quality; actively seeks customer involvement in productivity improvement; ongoing testing of new processes and technologies	
An early adopter when IT promises to enhance service for customers and provide a competitive edge	Works with technology leaders to develop new applications that create first-mover advantage; seeks to perform at levels competitors cannot match	
	Subtotal	
Human Resources Function		
Invests in selective recruiting, ongoing training; keeps close to employees, promotes upward mobility; strives to enhance the quality of working life	Sees the quality of employees as a strategic advantage; the firm is recognized as outstanding place to work; HR helps top management to nurture culture	
Motivated, hard-working, allowed some discretion in choice of procedures, offers suggestions	Innovative and empowered; very loyal, committed to the firm's values and goals; creates procedures	
Listens to customers; coaches and facilitates workers	Source of new ideas for top management; mentors, workers to enhance career growth, value to firm	
	Subtotal	
	Total Score	

Legend: Score each area from '1' to '4' depending on the performance level of the organization that is being assessed. Average the scores for each function, and then average the functions to obtain the total assessment score.

A score of "3.5 and above" indicates excellent performance; a score from "2.5 to 3.4" indicates good performance, a score from "1.5 to 2.4" indicates average to poor performance, and a score of "1.4 and lower" indicates very poor performance.

Note: This framework was inspired by, and expands upon, work in service operations management by Richard Chase and Robert Hayes.

Service Losers. These firms are at the bottom of the barrel from customer, employee and managerial perspectives, and get failing grades in marketing, operations, and HRM. Customers patronize them for reasons other than performance, typically because there is no viable alternative, which is one reason why service losers continue to survive. Managers of such organizations may even see service delivery as a necessary evil. New technology is introduced only under duress, and the uncaring workforce is a negative constraint on performance.

Service Nonentities. Although their performance still leaves much to be desired, service nonentities have eliminated the worst features of losers. Nonentities are dominated by a traditional operations mindset, typically based on achieving cost savings through standardization. Their marketing strategies are unsophisticated, and the roles of human resources and operations might be summed up, respectively, by the philosophies "adequate is good enough" and "if it ain't broke, don't fix it". Managers may talk about improving quality and other goals, but are unable to set clear priorities to have a clear direction, nor gain the respect and commitment of their employees (*Figure 15.1*). Several such firms are often found competing in a lackluster fashion within a given marketplace, and you might have difficulty distinguishing one from the others. Periodic price discounts tend to be the primary means of trying to attract new customers.

Service Professionals. Service professionals are in a different league from nonentities and have a clear market positioning strategy. Customers within the target segments seek out these firms based on their sustained reputation for consistently meeting expectations. Marketing is sophisticated, using targeted communications and pricing based on value to the customer. Research is used to measure customer satisfaction and obtain ideas for service enhancement. Operations and marketing work together to introduce new delivery systems, and recognize the trade-off between productivity and customer-defined quality. There are explicit links between backstage and front-stage activities, and the firm has a much more proactive, investment-oriented approach to HRM than is found among nonentities.

Service Leaders. These organizations are breakthrough service organizations, world-class service leaders, and are the *crème de la crème* of their respective industries. Where service professionals are good, service leaders are outstanding. When we think of service leaders, we think of Amazon, McKinsey, Ritz Carlton, Southwest Airlines, Starbucks, and Zappos. Their company names are synonymous with service excellence and the ability

Figure 15.1 Dilbert's boss loses focus — and his audience

to delight customers. Service leaders are recognized for their innovation in each functional area of management as well as for their superior internal communications and coordination among these three functions — often the result of a relatively flat organizational structure and the extensive use of teams. As a result, service delivery is a seamless process organized around the customer.

Marketing efforts by service leaders make extensive use of customer relationship management (CRM) systems that offer strategic insights about customers, who are often addressed on a one-to-one basis. Concept testing, observation, and contacts with lead customers are employed in the development of new, breakthrough services that respond to previously unrecognized needs. Operations specialists work with technology leaders around the world to develop new applications that will create a first mover advantage, and enable the firm to perform at levels that competitors cannot hope to reach for a long time to come. Senior executives see quality of employees as a strategic advantage. HRM works on building and maintaining a service-oriented culture and creating an outstanding working environment that simplifies the task of attracting and retaining the best people (*Figure 15.2*)[3]. The employees themselves are committed to the firm's values and goals. Because they are engaged, empowered, and quick to embrace change, they are an ongoing source of new ideas and they continuously drive improvement.

Moving to a Higher Level of Performance

Almost all companies want to be service leaders. We want to win our customers' loyalty and we want our customers to say good things about us. If we can achieve these objectives, we will increase our market share, our shareholder value, and our share of community goodwill. These are powerful reasons for moving to a higher performance level[4]. This view is becoming widely accepted, and in most markets we can find companies moving up the performance ladder through conscious efforts to improve and coordinate their marketing, operations, and HRM functions, in a bid to establish more favorable competitive positions and better satisfy their customers.

It requires human leaders at all levels of an organization to take a service firm in the right direction, set the right strategic priorities, and ensure the relevant strategies are implemented throughout the organization. And the various chapters throughout this book discuss exactly how you can do that. You now have the tools, concepts, and theories to help you become a change agent in your organization.

LO 2
Understand what is required for moving a service firm from service loser to service leader.

Figure 15.2 Creating an outstanding work environment attracts and retains the best people

LO 3

Know the long-term impact of customer centricity on profitability and shareholder value.

CUSTOMER SATISFACTION AND CORPORATE PERFORMANCE

The philosophy of this book has been all about customer centricity and creating value for customers as a long-term core strategy. This perspective permeates many of the key concepts and models you have learned in this book, including the Service-Profit Chain, the Cycle of Success, the Service Talent Cycle, the Wheel of Loyalty, and the Gaps Model. We therefore feel it is fitting to end this book with a final piece of evidence that long-term perspective and customer centricity will pay off financially.

There's convincing evidence of strategic links between the level of customer satisfaction with a firm's service offerings and overall firm performance. Researchers from the University of Michigan found that on average, every 1% increase in customer satisfaction is associated with a 2.4% increase in a firm's return on investment (ROI)[5]. Analysis of companies' scores on the American Customer Service Index (ACSI) shows that, on average, among publicly traded firms, a 5% change in the ACSI score is associated with a 19% change in the market value of common equity[6]. In other words, by creating more value for the customer, as measured by increased satisfaction, the firm creates more value for its owners (see *Service Insights 15.1*).

SERVICE INSIGHTS 15.1

Customer Satisfaction and Wall Street — High Returns and Low Risk!

Does a firm's customer satisfaction levels have anything to do with its stock price? This was the research question Claes Fornell and his colleagues wanted to answer. More specifically, they examined whether investments in customer satisfaction led to excess stock returns (see *Figure 15.3*), and if so, whether these returns were associated with higher risks as would be predicted by finance theory.

The researchers built two stock portfolios, one hypothetical back-dated portfolio and a real-world portfolio that tracked stock market performance in real time over several years. Both portfolios consisted of only firms that did well in terms of their customer satisfaction ratings, as measured by the American Customer Satisfaction Index (ACSI).

The ACSI-based portfolios were rebalanced once a year on the day when the annual ACSI results were announced. Only firms in the top 20% in terms of customer satisfaction ratings were included (firms were either retained if they already were in the top

20% last year, or firms that improved their satisfaction ranking into the top 20% were added to the portfolio). Firms that fell below the 20% cut-off were sold. The return and risk of both portfolios were measured and their risk-adjusted returns were then compared to broad market indices such as the S&P 500 and NASDAQ.

Their findings are striking for managers and investors alike! Fornell and his colleagues discovered that the ACSI-based portfolios generated significantly higher risk-adjusted returns than their market benchmark indices and outperformed the market. Changes in the ACSI ratings of individual firms were significantly related to their future stock price movement, and as another study showed, even CEO compensation[7].

However, simply publishing the latest data on the ACSI index did not immediately move share prices as efficient market theory would have predicted. Instead, share prices seemed to adjust slowly over time as firms published other results (perhaps earnings data or other "hard" facts which may lag behind changes in customer satisfaction). A recent study in a retail context confirmed this time lag, whereby increases in customer satisfaction were shown to lag operational improvements, and profits lagged increases in customer satisfaction. Therefore, becoming a service champion requires a longer term perspective[8].

The conclusion is that acting faster than the market to changes in the ACSI index generated excess stock returns. This finding represents a stock market imperfection, but it is consistent with research in marketing, which holds that satisfied customers improve the level and the stability of cash flow.

In a later study, Lerzan Aksoy and her colleagues built on these findings and also confirmed that a portfolio based on ACSI data outperformed the S&P 500 index over a 10-year period and delivered risk-adjusted abnormal returns.

For marketing managers, the findings of both studies confirm that investments (or "expenses" — if you talk to accountants) into managing customer relationships and the cash flows they produce are fundamental to the firm's, and therefore shareholders' value creation.

Figure 15.3 Can customer satisfaction data help to outperform the market?

Although the results are convincing, be careful should you want to exploit this apparent market inefficiency and invest in firms that show high increases in customer satisfaction in future ACSI releases — your finance friends will tell you that efficient markets learn fast! You will know this has happened when you see stock prices move as a response of future ACSI releases. You can learn more about the ACSI at www.theacsi.org.

Source

Claes Fornell, Sunil Mithas, Forrest V. Morgeson III, and M.S. Krishnan (2006), "Customer Satisfaction and Stock Prices: High Returns, Low Risk," *Journal of Marketing*, Vol. 70, January, pp. 3–14. Lerzan Aksoy, Bruce Cooil, Christopher Groening, Timothy L. Keiningham, and Atakan Yalçin (2008), "The Long-Term Stock Market Valuation of Customer Satisfaction," *Journal of Marketing*, Vol. 72, No. 4, pp. 105–122.

CONCLUSION

You are at the end of this book. We hope it exceeded your expectations, gave you new insights into the marketing (and management) of services, provided you with the tools and skills you need to succeed. Transforming an organization and maintaining service leadership is no easy task for even the most gifted leader. We hope that having worked through this book will help you to become a more effective marketer and leader in any service organization. We also hope we not only managed to equip you with the necessary knowledge, understanding, and insights, but also with the beliefs and attitudes about what propels a firm to service leadership. If this book motivated and excited you to become a service champion yourself, we as authors have achieved our objectives.

If you are interested in reading more, have a look at the Appendix where we provide some of our favorite books and resources on services marketing and management. If you have feedback and suggestions on how to further improve this book, do contact us via www.JochenWirtz. com or sg.linkedin.com/in/jochenwirtz. We'd love to hear from you!

We started each chapter with inspirational quotes, and we like to end the book with a final quote by Tony Robins: "*It's not knowing what to do, it's doing what you know.*" On this note, we wish you enjoyment, fulfillment, and success in applying what you've learned.

CHAPTER SUMMARY

LO1 There are four levels of service performance, and only the last two follow the key learnings from this book:

- **Service losers.** They are poor performers in marketing, operations, and HRM. Service losers survive because monopoly situations give customers little choice but to buy from them.
- **Service nonentities.** Their performance leaves much to be desired, but they have eliminated the worst features of losers.
- **Service professionals.** They have a clear market position, and customers in target segments seek them out based on their sustained reputation for meeting expectations. They are solid performers in marketing, operations, and HR, and the functions are tightly integrated.
- **Service leaders.** They are the breakthrough service champions, the *crème de la crème* of their respective industries. Their company names are synonymous with service excellence and an ability to delight customers.

- We contrasted the description and actions of a service leader against professionals, nonentities, and losers along the three functional areas in *Table 15.1*. Service leadership requires high performance across a number of dimensions, including their sophistication of marketing, managing, and motivating employees, and continuously improving service quality and productivity.

LO2 It requires human leaders at all levels of an organization to take a service firm in the right direction, and ensure that the relevant strategies are implemented throughout the organization. And the various chapters throughout this book discuss exactly how you can do that. You now have the tools, concepts, and theories to help you become a change agent in your organization.

LO3 A service leader's adoption of a long-term perspective and customer centricity pays off financially. There is solid empirical evidence that high customer satisfaction (compared to an organization's peer group) leads to superior financial returns.

Review Questions

1. How are the four levels of service performance defined? Based on your own service experiences, provide an example of a company for each category.

2. Is there evidence that improving customer satisfaction leads to improved financial returns for shareholders?

Application Exercises

1. Select a company you know well, and obtain additional information from a literature review, website, company publication, blog, and so on. Evaluate the company on as many dimensions of service performance as you can, identifying where you believe it fits on the service performance spectrum shown in *Table 15.1*.

2. Based on all you've learned from this book, what do you believe are the key drivers of success for service organizations? Try and develop an integrative causal model that explains the important drivers of success for a service organization.

APPENDIX: Further Resources on Services Marketing and Management

Below is a list of books, websites and resources we find useful. This list is not exhaustive, but we hope it provides a starting point for anyone who is interested in delving deeper into this exciting topic. We also list some earlier books as they are classics and are still highly relevant. We apologize should we have missed important sources and, if so, let us know and we will update the list in the next edition.

Books (in alphabetical order by surname of the first author):

- Janelle Barlow and Claus Moller (2008), *A Complaint is a Gift*. 2nd ed., Berrett-Koehler Publishers.
- Jonah Berger (2013), *Contagious: Why Things Catch On*. Simon & Schuster.
- Leonard L. Berry and Kent D. Seltman (2008), *Management Lessons from Mayo Clinic: Inside One of the Most Admired Service Organizations*, McGraw-Hill.
- Sriram Dasu and Richard B. Chase (2013), *The Customer Service Solution: Managing Emotions, Trust, and Control to Win Your Customer's Business*, McGraw-Hill.
- Thomas J. DeLong, John J. Gabarro, and Robert J. Lees (2007), *When Professionals Have to Lead: A New Model for High Performance*. Harvard Business School Press.
- James A. Fitzsimmons and Mona J. Fitzsimmons (2013), *Service Management: Operations, Strategy, Information Technology*. 8th ed., McGraw-Hill.
- Frances Frei and Anne Morriss (2012), *Uncommon Service: How to Win by Putting Customers at the Core of Your Business*. Harvard Business Review Press.
- James L. Heskett, W. Earl Sasser, Jr., and Joe Wheeler (2008), *The Ownership Quotient*, Harvard Business School Press.
- James L. Heskett, W. Earl Sasser, Jr., and Leonard A. Schlesinger (2015), *What Great Service Leaders Know and Do: Creating Breakthroughs in Service Firms*. Berrett-Koehler Publishers.
- Tony Hsieh (2013), *Delivering Happiness: A Path to Profits, Passion, and Purpose*. Grand Central Publishing

- Robert Johnston, Graham Clark, and Michael Shulver (2012), *Service Operations Management: Improving Service Delivery*. 4th ed., Prentice Hall.
- Ron Kaufman (2012), *Uplifting Service: The Proven Path to Delighting Your Customers, Colleagues, and Everyone Else You Meet*. Evolve Publishing.
- Robert F. Lusch and Stephen L. Vargo (2014), *Service-Dominant Logic: Premises, Perspectives, Possibilities*. Cambridge University Press.
- Richard L. Oliver (2010), *Satisfaction: A Behavioral Perspective on the Consumer*. 2nd ed., M.E. Sharpe.
- Roland T. Rust, Katherine N. Lemon and Das Narayandas (2005), *Customer Equity Management*. Pearson Prentice Hall.
- Laurie Young (2005), *Marketing the Professional Service Firm*. John Wiley & Sons.
- Valarie A. Zeithaml, Mary Jo Bitner, and Dwayne D. Gremler (2012), *Services Marketing: Integrating Customer Focus Across the Firm*. 6th ed., McGraw-Hill.
- Valarie A. Zeithaml, Stephen W. Brown, Mary Jo Bitner, and Jim Sala (2014), *Profiting from Services and Solutions: What Product-Centric Firms Need to Know*. Business Expert Press.

Leading service research centers and their websites (in alphabetical order):

- The Cambridge Service Alliance at the University of Cambridge in England (http://cambridgeservicealliance.eng.cam.ac.uk)
- The Center for Excellence in Service of Robert H. Smith School of Business at University of Maryland (www.rhsmith.umd.edu/ces)
- The Center for Services Leadership at the W. P. Carey School of Business at Arizona State University (http://wpcarey.asu.edu/csl)
- The Institute of Service Excellence at the Singapore Management University (http://ises.smu.edu.sg)
- The Service Research Center at Karlstad University in Sweden (www.ctf.kau.se)

Listing of other resources:

There are a number of websites and blogs of firms with in-depth service expertise and leading service providers, but blogs and their contents and focus change fast. We therefore list a few companies you can follow on LinkedIn or search for their websites and blogs;

- Firms: Accenture, Disney Institute, Forrester, McKinsey & Company, Salesforce.com, UP! Your Service College.[9]

- For a listing of leading service-related blogs see: *50 Customer Experience Blogs You Should Be Reading*, available at http://www.ngdata.com/50-customer-experience-blogs-you-should-be-reading.

- Service design and innovation uses many different tools and methods originating from various disciplines. Several websites provide further resources, for example, ServiceDesignTools.org and ServiceDesignThinking.com.

Endnotes

1. Peter Drucker did not regard himself as a marketer, yet his writing has had profound impact on the marketing field and discipline. The opening quote is discussed further in: Frederick E. Webster Jr. (2009), "Marketing IS management: The wisdom of Peter Drucker," *Journal of the Academy of Marketing Science,* Vol. 37, No. 1, pp. 20–27.

2. The operations perspective was originally developed by: Richard B. Chase and Robert H. Hayes (1991), "Beefing Up Operations in Service Firms," *Sloan Management Review,* Fall, pp. 15–26. The framework shows in this chapter has been significantly extended to incorporate the marketing and HR functions, and has been updated.

3. Claudia H. Deutsch, "Management: Companies Scramble to Fill Shoes at the Top," *nytimes.com,* November 1, 2000.

4. This book provides you with the tools and knowledge to develop a winning services marketing strategy and with key tools to shape HR, operations, and IT towards service excellence. In addition, there are a number of audit tools and checklists you can consult to assess a service organization. They include:

   James L. Heskett, W. Earl Sasser, and Leonard A. Schlesinger, *The Value Profit Chain: Treat Employees Like Customers and Customers Like Employees.* (New York: Free Press, 2003), Appendix B: The Value Profit Chain Audit, pp. 318–337.

   James L. Heskett, W. Earl Sasser, and Joe Wheeler, *The Ownership Quotient: Putting the Service Profit Chain to Work for Unbeatable Competitive Advantage.* (Boston, MA: Harvard Business Press, 2008), Appendix B: Audition Ownership, pp. 193–203.

   The European Foundation for Quality Management (EFQM) has detailed assessment sheets for all dimensions of the EFQM Model. They can be downloaded free-of-charge from http://www.efqm.org/efqm-model/efqm-model-in-action-0.

5. Eugene W. Anderson and Vikas Mittal (2000), "Strengthening the Satisfaction-Profit Chain," *Journal of Service Research,* Vol. 3, November, pp. 107–120.

6. Claes Fornell, Sunil Mithas, Forrest V. Morgeson III, and M.S. Krishnan (2006), "Customer Satisfaction and Stock Prices: High Returns, Low Risk," *Journal of Marketing,* Vol. 70, January, pp. 3–14.

7. A large-scale empirical study based on the ACSI showed that CEOs benefit if their firms outperform their peer group in terms of customer satisfaction in form of higher annual bonuses over and above what was explained by typical financial performance metrics and key control variables; see: Vincent O'Connel and Don O'Sullivan (2011), "The Impact of Customer Satisfaction on CEO Bonuses", *Journal of the Academy of Marketing Science,* Vol. 39, No. 6, pp. 828–845.

8. The authors estimated that a 20% increase in operational investments to improve service resulted in an immediate drop in operating profits, which only in the next year resulted in an increase in profit of twice the drop experienced in the year of investment; see: Heiner Evanschitzky, Florian v. Wangenheim, and Nancy V. Wünderlich (2012), "Perils of Managing the Service Profit Chain: The Role of Time Lags and Feedback Loops", *Journal of Retailing,* Vol. 88, No. 3, pp. 356–366.

9. Disclosure: One of the authors (Jochen Wirtz) has a small equity stake in UP! Your Service College and was involved in the early development and positioning of the college.

PART 6

Case Studies

Sullivan Ford Auto World

Christopher H. Lovelock

A young healthcare manager unexpectedly finds herself running a family-owned car dealership in financial trouble. She is very concerned about the poor performance of the service department and wonders whether a turnaround is possible.

Viewed from Wilson Avenue, the Sullivan Ford Auto World dealership presented a festive sight. Flags waved, and strings of triangular pennants in red, white, and blue fluttered gaily in the late afternoon breeze. Rows of new model cars and trucks gleamed and winked in the sunlight. Geraniums graced the flowerbeds outside the showroom entrance. A huge rotating sign at the corner of Wilson Avenue and Route 78 sported the Ford logo and identified the business as Sullivan Ford Auto World. Banners below urged "Let's Make a Deal!"

Inside the handsome, high-ceilinged showroom, four of the new model Fords were on display — a dark-green Explorer SUV, a red Mustang convertible, a white Focus sedan, and a red Ranger pickup truck. Each vehicle was polished to a high sheen. Two groups of customers were chatting with salespeople, and a middle-aged man sat in the driver's seat of the Mustang, studying the controls.

Upstairs in the comfortably furnished general manager's office, Carol Sullivan-Diaz finished running another spreadsheet analysis on her laptop. She felt tired and depressed. Her father, Walter Sullivan, had died of a sudden heart attack four weeks earlier at the age of 56. As executor of his estate, the bank had asked her to temporarily assume the position of general manager of the dealership. The only visible change that she had made to her father's office was installing an all-in-one laser printer, scanner, copier, and fax, but she had been very busy analyzing the current position of the business.

Sullivan-Diaz did not like the look of the numbers on the printout. Auto World's financial situation had been deteriorating for 18 months, and had been running in the red for the first half of the current year. New car sales had declined, dampened in part by the poor macro-economic environment. Margins had been squeezed by promotions and other efforts to move new cars off the lot. Reflecting rising fuel prices, industry forecasts of future sales were discouraging, and so were her own financial projections for Auto World's sales department. Service revenues, which were below average for a dealership of this size, had also declined, although the service department still made a small surplus.

Had she had made a mistake last week, Carol wondered, in turning down Bill Froelich's offer to buy the business? Admittedly, the amount was substantially below the offer from Froelich that her father had rejected two years earlier, but the business had been more profitable then.

THE SULLIVAN FAMILY

Walter Sullivan purchased a small Ford dealership in 1993, renaming it Sullivan's Auto World, and had built it up to become one of the best known in the metropolitan area. In 2009, he borrowed heavily to purchase the current site at a major suburban highway intersection, in an area of the city with many new housing developments.

There had been a dealership on the site, but the buildings were 30 years old. Sullivan had retained the service and repair bays but torn down the showroom in front of them and replaced it with an attractive modern facility. On moving to the new location, which was substantially larger than the old one, he renamed his business Sullivan Ford Auto World.

Everybody seemed to know Walter Sullivan. He was a consummate showman and entrepreneur, appearing in his own radio and television commercials, and was active in community affairs. His approach to car sales emphasized promotions, discounts, and deals in order to maintain volume. He was never happier than when making a sale.

Carol Sullivan-Diaz, 28, was the eldest of Walter and Carmen Sullivan's three daughters. After obtaining a bachelor's degree in economics, she went on to take an MBA degree and then embarked on a career in healthcare management. She was married to Dr. Roberto Diaz, a surgeon at St. Luke's Hospital. Her 20-year-old twin sisters, Gail and Joanne, who were students at the state university, lived with their mother.

In her own student days, Sullivan-Diaz had worked part time in her father's business on secretarial and book-keeping tasks, and as a service writer in the service department, so she was quite familiar with the operations of the dealership. While at business school, she decided on a career in healthcare management. After graduation, she worked as an executive assistant to the president of St. Luke's, a large teaching hospital. Two years later, she joined Heritage Hospitals, a large multi-hospital facility that also provided long-term care, as the assistant director of marketing, a position she had held for almost three years. Her responsibilities included designing new services, complaint handling, market research, and introducing an innovative day-care program for hospital employees and neighborhood residents.

Carol's employer had given her a six-week leave of absence to put her father's affairs in order. She doubted that she could extend that leave much beyond the two weeks still remaining. Neither she nor other family members were interested in making a career of running the dealership. However, she was prepared to take time out from her healthcare career to work on a turnaround if that seemed a viable proposition. She had been successful in her present job and believed it would not be difficult to find another health management position in the future.

THE DEALERSHIP

Like other car dealerships, Sullivan Ford Auto World operated both sales and service departments, often referred to in the trade as "front end" and "back end" respectively. Both new and used vehicles were sold, since a high proportion of new car and van purchases involved trading in the purchaser's existing vehicle. Auto World would also buy well-maintained used cars at auctions for resale. Purchasers who decided that they could not afford a new car would often buy a "preowned" vehicle instead, while shoppers who came in looking for used cars could sometimes be persuaded to buy new ones. Before being put on sale, used vehicles were carefully

serviced, with parts being replaced as needed. They were then thoroughly cleaned by a detailer whose services were hired as required. Dents and other blemishes were removed at a nearby body shop, and occasionally, the vehicle's paintwork was resprayed too.

The front end of the dealership employed a sales manager, seven salespeople, an office manager, and a secretary. One of the salespeople had given notice and would be leaving at the end of the following week. The service department, when fully staffed, consisted of a service manager, a parts supervisor, nine mechanics, and two service writers. The Sullivan twins often worked part-time as service writers, filling in at busy periods, when one of the other writers was sick or on vacation, or when — as currently — there was an unfilled vacancy. The job entailed scheduling appointments for repairs and maintenance, writing up each work order, calling customers with repair estimates, and assisting customers when they returned to pick up their cars and pay for the work that had been done.

Sullivan-Diaz knew from her own experience as a service writer that it could be a stressful job. Few people liked to be without their car, even for a day. When a car broke down or was having problems, the owner was often nervous about how long it would take to get it fixed and, if the warranty had expired, how much the labor and parts would cost. Customers were quite unforgiving when a problem was not fixed completely on the first attempt and they had to return their vehicle for further work.

Major mechanical failures were not usually difficult to repair, although parts replacement costs might be expensive. It was often the "little" things, like water leaks and wiring problems, that were the hardest to diagnose and correct, and it might be necessary for the customer to return two or three times before such a problem was resolved. In these situations, parts and material costs were relatively low, but labor costs mounted up quickly, being charged at $75 an hour. Customers could sometimes be quite abusive, yelling at service writers over the phone or arguing with service writers, mechanics, and the service manager in person.

Turnover in the service writer job was high, which was one reason why Carol — and more recently her sisters — had often been pressed into service by their father to "hold the fort", as he described it. More than once, she had seen an exasperated service writer respond sharply to a complaining customer or hang up on one who was abusive over the telephone. Gail and Joanne were currently taking turns to cover the vacant position, but there were times when both of them had classes and the dealership had only one service writer on duty.

By national standards, Sullivan Ford Auto World stood towards the lower end of medium-sized dealerships, selling around 1,100 cars a year, equally divided between new and used vehicles. In the most recent year, its revenues totaled $26.6 million from new and used car sales and $2.9 million from service and parts — down from $30.5 million and $3.6 million respectively, in the previous year. Although the unit value of car sales was high, the margins were quite low, with margins for new cars being substantially lower than those for used ones. Industry guidelines suggested that the contribution margin (known as the departmental selling gross) from car sales should be about 5.5% of sales revenues, and from service, around 25% of revenues. In a typical dealership, 60% of the selling gross would traditionally come from sales and 40% from service, but the balance was shifting from sales to service. The selling gross was then applied to fixed expenses, such as administrative salaries, rent or mortgage payments, and utilities.

For the most recent 12 months at Auto World, Sullivan-Diaz had determined that the selling gross figures were 4.6% and 24%, respectively, both of them lower than those in the previous year and were insufficient to cover the dealership's fixed expenses. Her father had made no mention of financial difficulties, and she had been shocked to learn from the bank after his death that Auto World had been two months behind in mortgage payments on the property. Further analysis also showed that accounts payable had also risen sharply in the previous six months. Fortunately, the dealership held a large insurance policy on Sullivan's life, and the proceeds from this was more than sufficient to bring mortgage payments up to date, pay down all overdue accounts, and leave some funds for future contingencies.

OUTLOOK

The opportunities for expanding new car sales did not appear promising, given declining consumer confidence and recent layoffs at several local plants, which were expected to hurt the local economy. However, promotional incentives had reduced the inventory to manageable levels. From discussions with Larry Winters, Auto World's sales manager, Sullivan-Diaz had concluded that costs could be cut by not replacing the departing sales representative, maintaining inventory at its current

reduced level, and trying to make more efficient use of advertising and promotion. Although Winters did not have Walter's exuberant personality, he had been Auto World's leading sales representative before being promoted, and had shown strong managerial capabilities in his current position.

As she reviewed the figures for the service department, Sullivan-Diaz wondered what potential might exist for improving its sales volume and selling gross. Her father had never been very interested in the parts and service business, seeing it simply as a necessary adjunct of the dealership. "Customers always seem to be miserable back there," he had once remarked to her. "But here in the front end, everybody's happy when someone buys a new car." The service facility was not easily visible from the main highway, being hidden behind the showroom. Although the building looked old and greasy, the equipment itself was modern and well-maintained. There was sufficient capacity to handle more repair work, but a higher volume would require hiring one or more new mechanics.

Customers were required to bring cars in for servicing before 8.30 a.m. After parking their cars, customers entered the service building by a side door and waited for their turn to see the service writers, who occupied a cramped room with peeling paint and an interior window overlooking the service bays. Customers stood while work orders for their cars were prepared. Ringing telephones frequently interrupted the process. Filing cabinets containing customer records and other documents lined the far wall of the room.

If the work were of a routine nature, such as an oil change or tune-up, the customer was given an estimate immediately. For more complex jobs, they would be called with an estimate later in the morning once the car had been examined. Customers were required to pick up their cars by 6.00 p.m. on the day the work was completed. On several occasions, Carol had urged her father to computerize the service work order process, but he had never acted on her suggestions, so all orders continued to be handwritten on large yellow sheets, with carbon copies.

The service manager, Rick Obert, who was in his late forties, had held the position since Auto World opened at its current location. The Sullivan family considered him to be technically skilled, and he managed the mechanics effectively. However, his manner with customers could be gruff and argumentative.

CUSTOMER SURVEY RESULTS

Another set of data that Sullivan-Diaz had studied carefully was the results of the customer satisfaction surveys that were mailed to the dealership monthly by a research firm retained by Ford USA.

Purchasers of all new Ford cars were sent a questionnaire by email within 30 days of making the purchase and asked to use a five-point scale to rate their satisfaction with the dealership sales department, vehicle preparation, and the characteristics of the vehicle itself.

The questionnaire asked how likely the purchaser would recommend the dealership, the salesperson, and the manufacturer to someone else. Other questions asked if the customers had been introduced to the dealer's service department and been given explanations on what to do if their cars needed service. Finally, there were some classification questions relating to customer demographics.

A second survey was sent to new car purchasers nine months after they bought their cars. This questionnaire began by asking about satisfaction with the vehicle and then asked customers if they had taken their vehicles to the selling dealer for service of any kind. If so, respondents were then asked to rate the service department on 14 different attributes — ranging from the attitudes of service personnel to the quality of the work performed — and then to rate their overall satisfaction with service from the dealer.

Customers were also asked about where they would go in the future for maintenance service, minor mechanical and electrical repairs, major repairs in those same categories, and bodywork. The options listed for service were the selling dealer, another Ford dealer, "some other place", or "do it yourself". Finally, there were questions about overall satisfaction with the dealer sales department and the dealership in general, as well as the likelihood of their purchasing another Ford product and buying it from the same dealership.

Dealers received monthly reports summarizing customer ratings of their dealership for the most recent month and for several previous months. To provide a comparison of how other Ford dealerships performed, the reports also included regional and national rating averages. After analysis, completed questionnaires were returned to the dealership. Since these included each customer's name, a dealer could see which customers were satisfied and which were not.

In the 30-day survey of new purchasers, Auto World achieved better than average ratings on most dimensions. One finding that puzzled Carol was that almost 90% of respondents answered "yes" when asked if someone from Auto World had explained what to do if they needed service, but less than a third said they had been introduced to someone in the service department. She resolved to ask Larry Winters about this discrepancy. The nine-month survey findings disturbed her. Although vehicle ratings were in line with national averages, the overall level of satisfaction with service at Auto World was consistently low, placing it in the bottom 25% of all Ford dealerships. The worst ratings for service concerned promptness of writing up orders, convenience of scheduling the work, convenience of service hours, and appearance of the service department. On length of time to complete the work, availability of needed parts, and quality of work done ("Was it fixed right?"), Auto World's rating was close to the average. For interpersonal variables such as attitude of service department personnel, politeness, understanding of customer problems, and explanation of work performed, its ratings were relatively poor.

When Sullivan-Diaz reviewed the individual questionnaires, she found that there was a wide degree of variation between customers' responses on these interpersonal variables, ranging all the way across a five-point scale from "completely satisfied" to "very dissatisfied." Curious, she went to the service files and examined the records for several dozen customers who had recently completed the nine-month surveys. At least part of the ratings could be explained by which service writers the customer had dealt with. Those who had been served two or more times by her sisters for instance, gave much better ratings than those who had dealt primarily with Jim Fiskell, the service writer who had recently quit.

Perhaps the most worrying responses were those relating to customers' likely use of Auto World's service department in the future. More than half indicated that they would use another Ford dealer or "some other place" for maintenance service (such as oil change, lubrication, or tune-up) or for minor mechanical and electrical repairs. About 30% would use another source for major repairs. The rating for overall satisfaction with the selling dealer after nine months was below average and the customer's likelihood of purchasing from the same dealership again was a full point below that of buying another Ford product.

OPTIONS

Sullivan-Diaz pushed aside the spreadsheets she had printed out and shut down her laptop. It was time to go home for dinner. She saw the options for the dealership as basically twofold: either prepare the business for an early sale at what would amount to a distress price, or take a year or two to try to turn it around financially. In the latter instance, if the turnaround succeeded, the business could subsequently be sold at a higher price than it presently commanded, or the family could install a general manager to run the dealership for them.

Bill Froelich, owner of another nearby dealership and three more in nearby cities, had offered to buy Auto World for a price that represented a fair valuation of the net assets, according to Auto World's accountants, plus $500,000 in goodwill. However, the rule of thumb when the auto industry was enjoying good times was that goodwill should be valued at $1,200 per vehicle sold each year. Carol knew that Froelich was eager to develop a network of dealerships in order to achieve economies of scale. His prices on new cars were very competitive and his nearest dealership clustered several franchises — Ford, Lincoln, Volvo, and Jaguar — on a single large property.

AN UNWELCOME DISTURBANCE

As Carol left her office, she spotted the sales manager coming up the stairs leading from the showroom floor. "Larry," she said, "I've got a question for you."

"Fire away!" replied the sales manager.

"I've been looking at the customer satisfaction surveys. Why aren't our sales reps introducing new customers to the folks in the Service Department? It's supposedly part of our sales protocol, but it only seems to be happening about one-third of the time!"

Larry Winters shuffled his feet. "Well, Carol, basically I leave it to their discretion. We tell them about service, of course, but some of the guys on the floor feel a bit uncomfortable taking folks over to the service bays after they've been in here. It's quite a contrast, if you know what I mean."

Suddenly, the sound of shouting arose from the floor below.

A man of about 40, wearing a windbreaker and jeans, was standing in the doorway yelling at one of the salespeople.

The two managers could catch snatches of what he was saying, in between various obscenities:

> *…Three visits… still not fixed right… service stinks… who's in charge here?"* Everybody else *in the showroom stopped what they were doing and turned to look at the newcomer.*

Winters looked at his young employer and rolled his eyes. "If there was something your dad couldn't stand, it was guys like that, yelling and screaming in the showroom and asking for the boss. Walt would go hide out in his office! Don't worry, Tom'll take care of that fellow and get him out of here. What a jerk!"

"No," said Sullivan-Diaz, "I'll deal with him! One thing I learned when I worked at St. Luke's was that you don't let people yell about their problems in front of everybody else. You take them off somewhere, calm them down, and find out what's bugging them."

She stepped quickly down the stairs, wondering to herself, "What else have I learned in healthcare that I can apply to this business?"

Exhibit 1 Marketing cars is a different proposition to marketing services for the same vehicles.

Study Questions

1. How does marketing cars differ from marketing service for those same vehicles?

2. Compare the sales and service departments at Auto World.

3. From a consumer's perspective, what useful parallels do you see between operating a car sales and service dealership, and operating health services?

4. What advice would you give to Carol Sullivan-Diaz?

Dr. Beckett's Dental Office

Lauren K. Wright

A dentist seeks to differentiate her practice on the basis of quality. She constructs a new office and redesigns the practice to deliver high-quality service to her patients and to improve productivity through increased efficiency. However, it's not always easy to convince patients that her superior service justifies higher fees that are not always covered by insurance.

MANAGEMENT COMES TO DENTISTRY

"I just hope the quality differences are visible to our patients," mused Dr. Barbro Beckett as she surveyed the new office that housed her well-established dental practice. She had recently moved to her current location from an office she felt was too cramped to allow her staff to work efficiently — a factor that was becoming increasingly important as the costs of providing dental care continued to rise. While Dr. Beckett realized that productivity gains were necessary, she did not want to compromise the quality of service her patients received.

The classes Dr. Beckett took in dental school taught her a lot about the technical side of dentistry but nothing about the business side. She received no formal training in the mechanics of running a business or understanding customer needs. In fact, professional guidelines discouraged marketing or advertising of any kind. That had not been a major problem 22 years earlier, when Dr. Beckett started her practice, since profit margins had been good then. But the dental care industry had changed dramatically. Costs rose as a result of labor laws, malpractice insurance, and the constant need to invest in updating equipment and staff training as new technologies were introduced. Dr. Beckett's overhead was now between 70 and 80% of revenues before accounting for her wages or office rental costs.

At the same time, there was also a movement in the US to reduce healthcare costs to insurance companies, employers, and patients, by offering "managed health care" through large health maintenance organizations (HMOs). The HMOs set the prices for various services by putting an upper limit on the amount their doctors and dentists could charge for various procedures. The advantage to patients was that their health insurance covered virtually all costs. But the price limitations meant that HMO doctors and dentists would not be able to offer certain services that might provide better quality care but were more expensive. Dr. Beckett had decided not to become an HMO provider as the reimbursement rates were only 80–85% of what she normally charged for treatments. At these rates, she felt that she could not provide high-quality care to patients.

These changes presented some significant challenges to Dr. Beckett, who wanted to offer the highest level of dental care rather than being a low-cost provider. With the help of a consultant, she decided her top priority was differentiating her practice on the basis of quality. She and her staff developed an internal mission statement that reflected this goal. The mission statement (prominently displayed in the back office) read, in part: *It is our goal to provide superior dentistry in an efficient, profitable manner within the confines of a caring, quality environment.*

Since higher quality care was more costly, Dr. Beckett's patients often had to pay fees for costs not covered by their insurance policies. Therefore, if the quality differences were not substantial, they might decide to switch to an HMO dentist or another lower-cost provider.

REDESIGNING THE SERVICE DELIVERY SYSTEM

The move to a new office gave Dr. Beckett a unique opportunity to rethink almost every aspect of her service. She wanted the work environment to reflect her own personality and values as well as providing a pleasant place for her staff to work.

Facilities and Equipment

Dr. Beckett first looked into office spaces available in the Northern California town where she practiced. She didn't find anything she liked, so she hired an architect from San Francisco to design a contemporary office building with lots of light and space. This increased the building costs by $100,000 but Dr. Beckett felt it would be a critical factor in differentiating her service.

Dr. Beckett's new office was Scandinavian in design, reflecting her Swedish heritage and attention to detail. The waiting room and reception area were filled with modern furniture in muted shades of brown, grey, green, and purple. Live plants and flowers were abundant, and the walls were covered with art. Classical music played softly in the background. Patients could enjoy a cup of coffee or tea, and browse through the large selection of current magazines and newspapers while waiting for their appointments.

The treatment areas were both functional and appealing. There was a small, soundproof conference room at the front of the office where children could watch movies or play with toys while their parents were being treated. Educational videos and pamphlets were available here to demonstrate different dental procedures and explain what patients needed to do to maximize their treatment outcomes.

The chairs in the examining rooms were covered in leather and were very comfortable. Each room had a large window that allowed patients to watch birds eating at the feeders that were filled each day. There were also attractive mobiles hanging from the ceiling to distract patients from the unfamiliar sounds and sensations they might experience. Headphones were available with a wide selection of music.

The entire back-office staff (including Dr. Beckett) wore uniforms in cheerful shades of pink, purple, and blue that matched the office décor. Dr. Beckett's dental degrees were prominently displayed, along with certificates from various programs that she and her staff had attended to update their technical skills. All the equipment in the treatment rooms was modern and spotlessly clean. Each room had a chair-side computer monitor where both patients and staff could view digital x-rays and photos while discussing treatment options. The digital x-rays provided many benefits, including reduced radiation emissions (80% less than traditional x-rays), high-quality images that could be viewed immediately, and digital storage and transmission capabilities. The hygienists used a tool called a DIAGNOdent during teeth cleaning procedures. The DIAGNOdent is a non-invasive laser that scanned teeth for decay and detected cavities that were just starting to develop so that they could be treated at a very early stage (*Exhibit 1*).

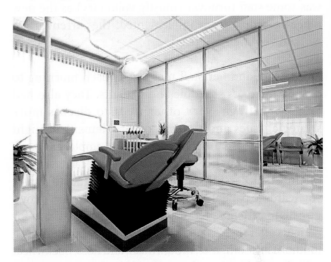

Exhibit 1 A modern, state-of-the-art treatment room projects a professional image to visiting patients.

Service Personnel

There were eight employees in the dental practice, including Dr. Beckett (who was the only dentist.) The seven staff members were separated by job functions into "front-office" and "back-office" workers. Front-office duties (covered by two employees) included receptionist and secretarial tasks, and financial/budgeting work. The back office was divided into hygienists and chairside assistants.

The three chairside assistants helped the hygienists and Dr. Beckett with treatment procedures. They had specialized training for their jobs but did not need a college degree. The two hygienists handled routine exams and teeth cleaning, as well as some treatment procedures. In many dental offices, hygienists tend to act like *prima donnas* because of their education (a bachelor's degree in addition to specialized training) and experience. According to Dr. Beckett, such an attitude could destroy any possibility of teamwork among the office staff. She felt very fortunate that her hygienists viewed themselves as part of a larger team that worked together to provide quality care to patients.

Dr. Beckett valued her friendships with staff members and also understood that they were a vital part of the service delivery. "90% of patients' perceptions of quality come from their interactions with the front desk and the other employees — not from the staff's technical skills," she stated. When Dr. Beckett began to redesign her practice, she discussed her goals with the staff and involved them in the decision-making process. The changes meant new expectations and routines for most employees, and some were not willing to adapt. There was some staff turnover (mostly voluntary) as the new office procedures were implemented. The current group worked very well as a team.

Dr. Beckett and her staff met briefly each morning to discuss the day's schedule and patients. They also had longer meetings every other week to discuss more strategic issues and resolve any problems that might have developed. During these meetings, employees made suggestions about how to improve patient care. Some of the most successful staff suggestions included "thank you" cards to patients who referred other patients; follow-up calls to patients after major procedures; a "gift" bag for patients after they'd had their teeth cleaned containing a toothbrush, toothpaste, mouthwash, and floss; buckwheat pillows and blankets for patient comfort during long procedures; coffee and tea in the waiting area; and a photo album in the waiting area with pictures of staff and their families (*Exhibit 2*).

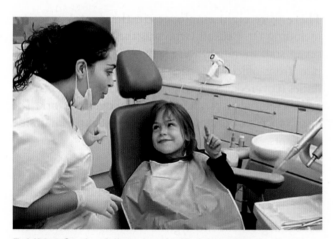

Exhibit 2 Service delivery is enhanced through customized interaction with patients both young and old.

The expectations for staff performance (in terms of both technical competence and patient interactions) were very high. However, Dr. Beckett provided her employees with many opportunities to update their skills by attending classes and workshops. She also rewarded their hard work by giving monthly bonuses if business had been good. Since she shared the financial data with her staff, they could see the difference in revenues if the schedule was slow or patients were dissatisfied. This provided an extra incentive to improve service delivery. The entire office also went on trips together once a year (paid for by Dr. Beckett); spouses were welcome to participate but had to cover their own trip expenses. Past destinations for these excursions had included Hawaii and Washington, D.C.

Procedures and Patients

With the help of a consultant, all the office systems (including billing, ordering, lab work, and patient treatment) were redesigned. One of the main goals was to standardize some of the routine procedures so that error was reduced and all patients would receive the same level of care. Specific times were allotted for each procedure and the staff worked very hard to see that these targets were met. Office policy specified that patients should be kept waiting no longer than 20 minutes without being given the option to reschedule, and employees often called patients in advance if they knew there would be a delay. They also attempted to fill in cancellations to make sure office capacity was maximized. Staff members substituted for each other when necessary or helped with tasks that were not specifically in their job descriptions in order to make things run more smoothly.

Dr. Beckett's practice included about 2,000 "active" patients (and many more who came infrequently). They were mostly white collar workers with professional jobs (university employees, healthcare workers, and managers/owners of local establishments.) She did no advertising; all of her new business came from positive word of mouth by current patients. Dr. Beckett's practice was so busy that patients often had to wait three to four months for a routine cleaning and exam (if they didn't already have their appointments automatically scheduled every six months), but they didn't seem to mind the delay.

The dentist believed that referrals were a real advantage as new patients didn't come in "cold". She did not have to sell herself because they had already been told about her service by friends or family. All new patients were required to have an initial exam so that Dr. Beckett could do a needs assessment and educate them about her service. She believed this was the first indication to patients that her practice was different from others they had experienced.

THE BIGGEST CHALLENGE

"Redesigning the business was the easy part," Dr. Beckett sighed. "Demonstrating the high level of quality to patients is the hard job." She said it was especially difficult since most people disliked going to the dentist, or felt that it was an inconvenience and came in with a negative attitude. Dr. Beckett tried to reinforce the idea that quality dental care depended on a positive long-term relationship between patients and the dental team. The website for the practice (*http://www.mychicodentist.com*) was designed to emphasize this concept. This philosophy was also reflected in a section of the patient mission statement hanging in the waiting area:

> *We are a caring, professional dental team serving motivated, quality-oriented patients interested in keeping healthy smiles for a lifetime. Our goal is to offer a progressive and educational environment. Your concerns are our focus.*

Although Dr. Beckett enjoyed her work, she admitted it could be difficult to maintain a positive attitude. The job required precision and attention to detail, and the procedures were often painful for patients. She often felt as though she were "walking on eggshells" because she knew patients were anxious and uncomfortable, which made them more critical of her service delivery. It was not uncommon for patients to say negative things to Dr. Beckett even before treatment began (such as "I really hate going to the dentist — it's not you, but I just don't want to be here!"). When this happened, she reminded herself that she was providing quality service whether patients

appreciated it or not. "The person will usually have to have the dental work done anyway," she remarked, "So I just do the best job I can and make them as comfortable as possible." Even though patients seldom expressed appreciation for her services, she hoped that she made a positive difference in their health or appearance that would benefit them in the long run.

Exhibit 3 A team of closely-knit professionals working under the guidance of a clear, common mission statement can help overcome the most negative pre-conceived notions about visiting the dentist.

Study Questions

1. Which of the seven elements of the services marketing mix are addressed in this case? Give examples of each "P" you identify.

2. Why do people dislike going to the dentist? Do you feel Dr. Beckett has addressed this problem effectively?

3. How do Dr. Beckett and her staff educate patients about the service they are receiving? What else could they do?

4. What supplementary services are offered? How do they enhance service delivery?

5. Contrast your own dental care experiences with those offered by Dr. Beckett's practice. What differences do you see? Based on your review of this case, what advice would you give to (a) your current or former dentist, and (b) Dr. Beckett?

6. Evaluate Dr. Beckett's website (*http://www.mychicodentist.com*). What strengths do you think the website has? What improvements would you suggest?

Bouleau & Huntley: Cross-selling Professional Services

Jochen Wirtz and Suzanne Lowe

A professional firm specializing in pension fund audits seeks to extend the firm's relationships with existing clients in the Philippines by offering consulting services. But the first attempt at cross-selling is a flop. What has gone wrong and why?

Juan Miguel Duavit, a new partner and co-director in the Manila office of Bouleau & Huntley, pondered over what had gone wrong earlier in the day at his meeting with National Metals Corporation, a Philippines-based major metals manufacturer, where his carefully prepared consulting presentation had been greeted with a bewildered silence.

THE FIRM

Duavit, 42, had joined Bouleau & Huntley three months earlier, in January 2015. Bouleau & Huntley was a multi-national corporation with headquarters in New York that specialized in pension funds auditing and human resources management. Its Manila office had been serving clients in the Philippines for the past 17 years.

The firm was founded in 1923 by Robert Bouleau, a New York actuary, and William Huntley, an insurance executive, who had noted that American corporations were rapidly creating new pension funds for their executives. The two men recognized this trend would create vast new opportunities for a professional firm that could advise firms properly and audit their plans every year, as required by US laws at the time.

Within 10 years, Bouleau & Huntley had become the leader of a new profession, with a well-established presence in the US. Subsequently, it began opening offices overseas. By 2015, Bouleau & Huntley was a worldwide firm with 45 offices, 335 partners, and revenues in excess of $1.6 billion. The firm continued to flourish with its combination of high-quality professionalism and aggressive marketing. New divisions had been launched in four areas closely related to pension funds: executive compensation, personnel management, insurance consulting, and re-insurance consulting.

Expansion into the Philippines

The Philippines had a Retirement Act, the Republic Act No. 7641, which required that an employee facing compulsory retirement at age 65 must receive from his employer a retirement benefit based on his final monthly salary and the number of years worked with the firm. Most companies turned to the private insurance industry for pension schemes.

Having repeatedly been sought out by various prestigious clients in the Philippines, Bouleau & Huntley opened its Manila office in 1998. By 2015, the office had 13 partners and 130 employees in the Philippines, operating from its headquarters in Metro Manila, with small satellite offices in Cebu and Luzon. The firm's total revenues in the Philippines were 552 million peso (approximately $12.2 million)[1].

© 2016 by Jochen Wirtz and Suzanne Lowe; Jochen Wirtz is Professor of Marketing, National University of Singapore. Suzanne Lowe is President, Expertise Marketing LLC.

The authors gratefully acknowledge the Professor Christopher Lovelock for his contribution to earlier versions of this case. Furthermore, the authors thank Professor Leonardo R. Perez Jr., Chairman, Marketing Management Department, College of Business & Economics, De La Salle University; Tom Sablak, FSA, MAAA, EA, FCA, Principal at Buck Consultants LLC; Debbie Smith, Partner, National Professional Standards; Anna Dourdourekas, National Partner in Charge, Ethical Standards, Grant Thornton LLP; and to Pressy Santos-Rowe (a former fellow student at the London Business School of the first author) for their feedback and assistance with the writing of this case.

1 The peso is the Philippine currency. The exchange rate in July 2015 was 100 peso = US $2.21

The firm's mission for its Philippines office, as stated by its geographic director, Jose Arellano, was "to serve large international companies active in the Philippines and to develop a national clientele among leading Filipino companies". In keeping with Bouleau & Huntley's firm-wide growth goals for selected lines of business in its total portfolio of services, the Manila office had been assigned the task of experimenting with expansion into other types of professional activities that could be adopted worldwide throughout Bouleau & Huntley.

Duavit Changes Jobs

Duavit had graduated from the prestigious University of Philippines (UP). After a two-year stint with Oracle Corporation as a brand manager, he spent two years in the US, obtaining an MBA from the Wharton School. Upon returning to the Philippines, he joined the glass division of Glasscore, holding several jobs in marketing and strategic planning over a four-year period. Through a UP classmate, he was recruited by the Manila office of Ascent Strategic Consultants (ASC), where he enjoyed a very successful career for 12 years, spending the last seven as a partner in ASC. However, over time, he began to feel restless. His personal interest in the "soft" side of consulting problems, dealing with people rather than profits and efficiency alone, was not shared by the leadership in ASC.

It was through Jose Arellano, one of his neighbors in the plush Sangun district, that Duavit first became familiar with Bouleau & Huntley. Both men served on the board of the private school attended by their children and had come to know each other socially. Over dinner one evening, Arellano suggested that his friend think seriously about joining Bouleau & Huntley. "I've been working with our strategy committee in New York to develop new lines of professional activity," he told Duavit. "We believe strategy consulting is a natural added service line that our current clients would find valuable. What you have done with ASC is of real interest to us, and I am sure you would enjoy working with our personnel management and compensation partners." Warming to his theme, Arellano continued:

> We've been hugely successful in our major activity of pension fund auditing. Worldwide, we have 350 Fortune 500 companies as our steady clients. Historically, it's been a very profitable business, enjoying steady growth as the pension funds themselves grow in size. However, this has attracted new competition and the business

> is becoming more price-sensitive than in the past. In addition, it is heavily influenced either positively or negatively by regulatory and national political decisions totally beyond our control.

> In the Philippines, we have decided to explore entering new professional areas, such as the strategy and general management consulting that you know so well. We think the synergies of cross-selling your strategy consulting services with our main line of pension fund auditing services are obvious. There are two international trends that have informed our thinking about this idea.

> One is that large strategy consulting firms like the Boston Consulting Group and McKinsey & Company are beginning to sell strategy work in what they call emerging markets like the Philippines. Also, as I'm sure you are aware, the Big Four accounting firms are forbidden from selling strategy work to their audit clients in the US. But they recognize that in Europe and many Asian countries, the rules are looser, and they are working hard to offer "one-stop-shopping" to their clients.

> It won't surprise you that we are keen to capture our share of the strategy consulting market, and to consolidate our hold on our pension audit clients, before the strategy consultancies or Big Four accounting firms can take away our market share. With someone like you on board, and with the team we will help you build, it should be possible to bring new value to our pension fund audit clients, generate additional cash flow from them, gain new clients for the firm, and protect our competitive advantage.

Duavit and Arellano discussed these opportunities further in conversations during the subsequent months, and confirmed their mutual interest. Both men agreed that a vast potential existed in the Philippines among leading Filipino companies, as well as with the Asian affiliates of multi-national groups headquartered in Manila. Arellano made several calls and exchanged confidential emails with the managing director and several senior partners of the firm about hiring Duavit on a quasi-equal basis to himself, in recognition of his extensive experience and in anticipation of expected cross-selling results.

Finally, over lunch at the Manila Hotel one day, Arellano answered Duavit's discerning questions about the cross-selling environment at Bouleau & Huntley. Arellano provided Duavit with several examples that the firm, although new at cross-selling in the Philippines, had successfully supported cross-selling in other countries and regions. Arellano offered Duavit an immediate directorship, a new departure for Bouleau & Huntley, as well as a compensation package so generous it was "impossible to refuse". Not only would Duavit receive a fixed compensation equal to his current total remuneration, but there was a provision for a large bonus (up to 30% of his salary) on incremental business from existing clients, and up to 50% for the successful acquisition of new clients.

Working at Bouleau & Huntley

Duavit joined the Manila office of Bouleau & Huntley in January 2015. His new colleagues welcomed him warmly, but he was surprised to find them somewhat reticent about discussing their own clients. Duavit ascribed this to professional respect for confidentiality. He set to work, following up several leads of his own. By March 2015, he brought in two new consulting clients. He was also involved in arranging for Bouleau & Huntley to audit a supplementary pension fund that one of his former employers was creating for its senior executives. He had started building a team of four younger consultants, including one bright young man who, after spending two years in Bouleau & Huntley's compensation practice, had decided to move on to strategic work.

Duavit was already looking forward to the day when he could propose that this enthusiastic consultant should become the first junior partner of the new Manila practice. Despite these early successes, he remained concerned by the reserved attitude among his colleagues. One day when he was having lunch with three of them, he answered their questions about his work at ASC. Describing a project he had directed the previous year to reorganize a major oil company, he encountered a mixture of disbelief and incomprehension.

"Do you mean that you and your colleagues actually restructured this enormous company last year?" one of them asked.

"Yes," Duavit replied, "We helped them simplify their structure, reduce the number of levels from 11 to 6, and even helped them relocate 482 people, saving about 644 million peso (US$14.2 million) in overhead costs. Then,

we streamlined their management information and planning system. Total fees amounted to 81 million peso (US$1.8 million) for 15 months of continued work by a team that ranged in size from four to seven consultants."

"Hey, what happened to their pension funds?" interjected another of his colleagues.

"Nothing, I believe," responded Duavit, slightly surprised. "Do you want an introduction to their CEO to sell him a pension fund audit?"

"No, we were just curious about the name of the guy who set up their last pension fund," another replied.

Despite his successful selling and high-quality client work in his first three months at the firm, Duavit was surprised to see that his kind of work did not interest them at all. He made a mental note to work harder to understand better the obscure workings of his actuarial colleagues' assignments. He also marveled at the enormous fees the firm charged for what seemed to him was tedious, arcane, and repetitive work. He was also deeply impressed by two things: their extensive use of standardized software systems that seemed to be doing all the work, and the ease with which they obtained repeat business year after year without any need for the costly and time-consuming "developmental" work required in his own type of consulting. All his pension auditing colleagues did was send a letter of renewal at the end of each year, with a prepared space for the company to sign. It seemed so easy! One Friday afternoon, just before 5.00 p.m., Duavit was beginning to check a 50-page report due at the client's the following Monday and he still had to write a proposal before going home for the weekend. Two of his partner colleagues poked their heads in at his open doorway. They were carrying their briefcases and were evidently leaving for home. Quickly sizing up the situation, one of them, Victor Vasquez, remarked cheerily, "My dear *pare* [the Filipino equivalent of 'pal' or 'chap'], you're obviously in the wrong business! You should have gotten an actuarial degree like us, instead of wasting your time at Wharton! See you on Monday! Cheers!"

Duavit immediately sent Arellano an email outlining his concerns that his new colleagues didn't seem very enthusiastic to help him build the firm's Philippines strategy-consulting revenues. Isn't cross-selling a strategic mandate, he asked Arellano? Arellano replied promptly, and promised to encourage Vasquez (and other Bouleau & Huntley actuaries) to introduce Duavit to their pension fund audit clients.

A PRESENTATION AT NATIONAL METALS CORPORATION

Two weeks later, Duavit felt Arellano's support was finally coming to fruition. Vasquez had agreed to introduce him to his largest client, National Metals Corporation, a company involved in refining and marketing copper, chromium, and nickel. Since Duavit had led an ASC consulting team for Amix, a large mill for primary and semi-finished iron and steel in Indonesia several years earlier, he knew the metals business and was certain that he could do something beneficial for Vasquez's client.

Vasquez and Duavit briefly communicated about an upcoming meeting that Vasquez had arranged. Duavit generally described his plan to present a brief overview of his work to the client. Although he didn't say so directly, he felt certain Vasquez understood his real goals, which were to impress Vasquez's client, and seek an introduction to one of his colleagues.

At National Metals Corporation's main administrative offices in Makati City, Vasquez led Duavit along a series of tortuous corridors to the office of Carlos Aseniero. Duavit was a bit surprised to find that his colleague's principal contact was a harassed-looking little man in a cluttered office. Aseniero greeted them politely and cleared several files off the chairs so the two visitors could sit down.

After the introductions were made and Vasquez had confirmed that the audit report would be ready on the promised date, Duavit launched into his presentation. He delivered a thorough but succinct analysis of five years of published figures, complete with diagrams he had prepared that very morning. He compared overall profitability, days of inventory, and asset rotation for National Metals Corporation against three of its main Asian competitors. Duavit concluded what he considered to be a stimulating 15-minute presentation by inviting Aseniero to introduce him to the appropriate National Metals colleague who could make use of Bouleau & Huntley's strategic consulting services to help the company increase market share and improve profitability.

Expecting an interested response, Duavit was amazed to be greeted by complete silence in the room. Not only Aseniero, but also Vasquez appeared somewhat bewildered by what they had just heard.

Seeking to regain the initiative, Duavit asked Aseniero, "Do you think that your boss would be interested in pursuing these issues further?"

Looking slightly ill at ease, Aseniero replied, "You have to understand that my office reports to the assistant finance director, reflecting the immense amounts of money the company is investing in this pension fund. The fund is also used as collateral for some of the company's borrowings. I don't believe that my boss, Mr. Perez, participates in strategy discussions with our board. Of course, I could ask him to arrange an appointment with our director general [CEO], but I'm told he's a very busy man."

"Thank you, Mr. Aseniero," Vasquez said, rising to his feet and holding out his hand. "My colleague and I really appreciate your willingness to take time out of your busy schedule."

Duavit also shook hands with Aseniero and thanked him, but found it difficult to hide his disappointment. The two partners left the office and retraced their way back to the reception area.

"What happened?" Duavit asked as the two of them climbed back into Vasquez's new top-of-the range Audi. "I thought that I gave him a very convincing line. Wasn't he interested? Or did he simply not understand?"

Vasquez eased the Audi out of the parking lot and frowned. "Duavit, I owe you an apology. I didn't really understand what you wanted to present to Aseniero, nor did I have a good grasp of your expertise. I didn't support you very well in that meeting. I think your presentation overwhelmed him rather than impressed him. And it made us look like we hadn't done our homework about what our client needs. I'll never be that unprepared again!"

Duavit remained silent for a time. It was becoming clear to him that, despite Arellano's individual encouragement to Vasquez, the actuarial partners in general appeared to be more interested in using him and his work to bring in new clients for their own practice, rather than the other way around. Duavit also realized that he and Vasquez didn't really understand each other's perspectives at all. Yet, he liked what Jose Arellano had told him about Bouleau & Huntley's combination of professionalism and aggressive marketing. Obviously, a lot still needed to be done before the synergies he and Arellano had dreamed about could be achieved.

"Well, let's use this situation to help us improve," Duavit said eventually, as Vasquez accelerated onto Ayala Avenue. "Victor, let's think this experience through and decide, together with our other partners, what we should do differently to implement our firm's cross-selling strategies. I know we want to succeed as a team. Our clients depend on us to bring them value, and today we acted pretty tactically. What do you think?"

"I agree, Juan," Vasquez answered. "In fact, Jose has given me the task of setting up the agenda for our yearly Manila Partners meeting in Makati City next month. I still have nothing finalized for the morning of the third day. Let's work together to present our ideas on cross-selling key strategies and propose cross-selling processes that could be used by all the partners to improve their results. How much time do you think we'll need?"

APPENDIX: THE AUDITING AND CONSULTING WORLD IN 2015

Until the 1970s, auditing firms focused mostly on auditing activities. However, with the rise of information technology (IT), many firms including the Big Six (now Big Four) accounting firms branched into IT and management consulting. Soon, revenues from consulting activities far exceeded their auditing revenues.

Things came to a head after the collapse and bankruptcy of the energy giant, Enron, in December 2001 and the document-destruction scandal and subsequent indictment of its auditor Arthur Andersen, by the US Justice Department. Arthur Andersen's dual role of auditor and consultant for Enron put it in the spotlight, raising concern about the issue of conflict of interest from serving corporate managers and auditing (i.e., protecting public interest).

Critics argued that the provision of non-audit services by audit firms could interfere with the independence of auditors and compromise the quality of their audits. In fact, a few academic studies found that there was more "creative accounting" among companies

that also engaged their auditors in large consulting projects than in firms that made little use of their auditors for non-auditing related services. As a result, Ernst & Young's decision to sell off its consulting arm two years before the Enron collapse to Gemini Consulting was hailed as a stroke of genius. After the Enron incident, PricewaterhouseCoopers (rebranded firm-wide in 2010 as PwC) sold its PwC Consulting unit to IBM Corporation, while Andersen Worldwide sold its IT consulting practices on a piecemeal basis.

Inevitably, over the next decade, the world's economies shifted, making more 'mundane' work like operations management and auditing attractive again for big accounting and management consultancies. Also by mid-2015, cross-selling of pension fund auditing and consultancy services appeared to present much less of a conflict (independence or other). Pension funds were generally managed separately from the other financial aspects of a business. Thus, unlike auditing of accounts, pension fund auditing was not concerned with the operations of a firm. Hence, it would be easier for pension fund auditors to maintain independence after appropriate vetting by their firms, even if their firm provided consultancy services to their audit clients. Nevertheless, Bouleau & Huntley would have to be sensitive to potential independence, or conflict of interest issues and how its activities were perceived in the market.

Study Questions

1. What do you see as the key differences between pension fund auditing and management consulting? How good is the fit between the two?

2. Evaluate the visit to National Metals Corporation. What happened?

3. What are the lessons of this experience?

4. What actions should Bouleau & Huntley take now?

Uber: Competing as Market Leader in the US versus Being a Distant Second in China

Jochen Wirtz and Christopher Tang

ABSTRACT

Uber allowed people to book and share rides in private cars via their smartphones. With its headquarters in the US, it operates in 60 countries and has a strong presence in the Asia–Pacific region. This case study explores Uber's development and growth, first in the US, then its global expansion and subsequent foray into China. Despite enjoying international success with deep penetration in major cities, Uber flopped in the Chinese market. What were the reasons for its failure in China, given its spectacular performance in many other countries?

INTRODUCTION

Uber was founded in 2009 by Travis Kalanick (current Chief Executive Officer) and Garrett Camp (Co-Founder) in San Francisco. Its business model rested on the use of an app to call for a driver at any time and location (*Exhibit 1*). Uber managed to build a spectacular network of drivers and passengers in just three years, thriving in what some people term as an "instant-gratification economy", powered by the smartphone as the remote control for life. "If we can get you a car in five minutes, we can get you anything in five minutes," Kalanick said[1].

© 2016 by Jochen Wirtz and Christopher Tang. Jochen Wirtz is Professor of Marketing at the National University of Singapore, and Christopher Tang is a UCLA Distinguished Professor and the holder of the Edward W. Carter Chain in Business Administration.

The authors thank Chia En Celeste for her excellent assistance with the data collection, analysis, and writing of this case study.

1 Vanity Fair covered an interview with Travis Kalanick in December 2014; this article's insights can be found throughout the Uber case study: http://www.vanityfair.com/news/2014/12/uber-travis-kalanick-controversy

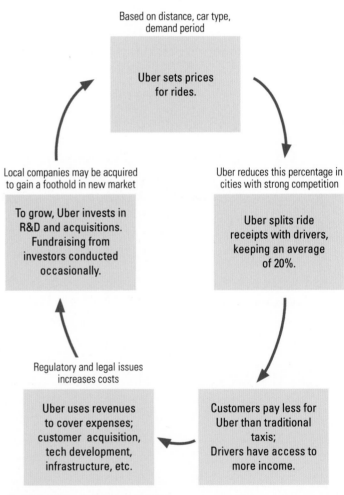

Based on distance, car type, demand period

Uber sets prices for rides.

Uber reduces this percentage in cities with strong competition

Uber splits ride receipts with drivers, keeping an average of 20%.

Customers pay less for Uber than traditional taxis; Drivers have access to more income.

Regulatory and legal issues increases costs

Uber uses revenues to cover expenses; customer acquisition, tech development, infrastructure, etc.

Local companies may be acquired to gain a foothold in new market

To grow, Uber invests in R&D and acquisitions. Fundraising from investors conducted occasionally.

Exhibit 1 Uber's Business Model

Source

Forbes: http://www.forbes.com/sites/aswathdamodaran/2014/06/10/a-disruptive-cab-ride-to-riches-the-uber-payoff; accessed October 27, 2015.

Expanding outside of the US, Uber was a threat to taxi services in Europe and Asia, triggering protests in France, Germany, and India. Despite resulting government scrutiny, tighter regulations and disputes with local taxi companies, Uber's disruptive business model successfully posed an effective challenge to taxi monopolies in the countries it operated in. As of August 2015, Uber clinched the title of the most valuable startup in the world, valued at $51 billion.

Enjoying first mover advantage in app-enabled transportation services and ridesharing, Uber was far more successful in its number of users and drivers than its main American competitor, Lyft. Lyft positioned itself as a more informal, community-centered way to travel, with the expectation that drivers and shotgun-riding passengers would strike up a conversation during the ride. By being a late entrant to the market entering three years after Uber, Lyft managed to operate in only 65 American cities by the end of 2015. In contrast, Uber had been operating in a total of 300 large cities in 60 countries. Both companies offered a myriad of services at different price points (*Exhibit 2*).

China, with a projection of 221 cities containing a population of one million or more, was a highly attractive market for any internationally-minded taxi company. Uber pioneered its taxi service in Shanghai in 2013. Entering difficult markets was not new to Uber, which had previously successfully navigated diverse markets in the UK, India, and South Africa. Nevertheless, Uber encountered unique roadblocks in China — strong competitors, existing low-cost taxi services, and a lack of know-how to navigate around local regulations and even corrupt officials. Uber also faced tough competition from a much larger local player, Didi-Kuaidi (known locally as 滴滴打车). Didi boasted more than one million drivers in 360 cities in China, whereas Uber only had about 100,000 drivers in 20 cities.

Exhibit 2 A Comparison of Uber and Lyft's Services in the US

Uber	Lyft
UberX The least expensive Uber service. Seats four riders. Drivers use everyday cars that are 2,000 or newer	**Lyft** The lowest cost service. A request for a Lyft will send to you a four-seater car
UberXL Seats at least six passengers. An UberXL car will be an SUV or a Minivan. Higher fare price than UberX	**Lyft Plus** A car that seats six or more passengers. Slightly more expensive than Lyft
UberPOOL Share your ride with another person and split the cost	**Lyft Line** A ridesharing service that pairs you with other passengers who are traveling along the same route. Similar to a carpool
UberPlus/UberSelect A luxury sedan that seats up to four riders. Expect a BMW, Mercedes, Audi, etc., with a leather interior	
UberBLACK Uber's executive luxury service. Commercially registered and insured livery vehicles, typically a black SUV or luxury sedan	

Services are sorted according to fares in ascending order. Information adapted from http://www.ridesharingdriver.com

UBER'S GROWTH

The first conceptualization of Uber's business model started in Paris in 2008, when founders Kalanick and Camp could not get a cab after returning from a conference. The two discussed solving the problem with a mobile app — push a button and get a car.

In 2009, UberCab was born. After downloading its app, registering and entering credit-card information, customers could summon a car with the press of a button. G.P.S. took care of the location, and the cost was automatically charged to the customer's credit card, with tips included. It did not take long for the company to run into regulatory issues when the San Francisco Municipal Transportation Agency objected to the use of "cab" in UberCab's name a few months after its launch, given its operation without a taxi license.

After changing its name to Uber, things went on an upward trajectory. Valued at $60 million after only six months of operation, Uber received support not just from angel investors and venture capitalists, but also from prominent celebrities like Ashton Kutcher (founder of A-Grade Investments), Jay Z (co-founder of Roc-A-Fella Records), and Jeff Bezos (founder of Amazon).

Uber faced many obstacles and criticism in its early years. One criticism was directed at the "surge pricing" model, which referred to the practice of charging customers higher prices at peak hours. It garnered a lot of attention during a snowstorm in New York in December 2013, when rates increased up to eight times its standard rates, attracting a flood of negative publicity. Kalanick defended this practice with economics — it reflected demand and supply at any given point in time, and effectively allocated capacity to customers who were willing to pay even during super-peak periods. To ameliorate public outrage, Uber eventually tweaked its pricing model and limited fare hikes to a maximum of 2.8 times the normal fares in the face of snowstorms in New York[2]. Uber proudly announced in January 2015 that it had more than 160,000 active drivers in the US who provided more than a million rides a day.

Uber's operations covered 75% of the US population, and even as it sets its sights on international markets, it remained focused on growth at home. Its efforts were mainly channeled towards building a strong network of drivers and improving service for consumers. These efforts paid off — 40,000 US drivers joined Uber in December 2014 alone; service efficiency saw improvements with 91% of UberX rides arriving in less than 10 minutes in Philadelphia; and the demand for Uber peaked when people celebrate and consume alcohol, testifying to Uber's position as a "better late-night option". Uber also started to pay more attention to corporate social responsibility. For example, its program UberMILITARY led to the hiring of 10,000 veterans — ex-military personnel — as drivers, while the use of UberPOOL was calculated to save more than 13,000 gallons of fuel each month in San Francisco alone[3]. By stretching its network of drivers to different demographic segments in society, offering alternative ridesharing options and reducing waiting time, Uber was able to build on network effects for drivers and loyalty among consumers, making it difficult for competitors to enter and grow in its markets.

LYFT'S RISE AND RIVALRY

Lyft was founded in 2012 by John Zimmer and Logan Green, launched primarily as a low-cost competitor to Uber. Its focus was on short, urban rides. Lyft logged an impressive 2.2 million rides in December 2014, with revenues for that year estimated at $130 million. In May 2015, Lyft was valued at $2.5 billion[4], its promising growth bolstered by estimates of 2015 revenues to be $796 million, an impressive 512% jump from 2014.

While Uber touted its iconic black cars to differentiate its luxury services for professionals (*Exhibit 2*), Lyft adorned its cars with a pink moustache (*Exhibit 3*), which had become an identifying factor for the company when driving down the streets of San Francisco[5]. This was accompanied by the greeting of all Lyft passengers with a fist bump. While these tongue-in-cheek communications

2 The Guardian covered the revision in surge pricing by Uber in http://www.theguardian.com/technology/2015/jan/26/uber-surge-pricing-new-york-snowstorm

3 Uber Expansion, not officially affiliated with Uber, provides a range of statistics pertaining to Uber's expansion in this page: http://uberexpansion.com/2015-uber-data-stats

4 Business Insider website reported on the $2.5 billion valuation on 15 May 2015; the whole article can be found here: http://www.businessinsider.sg/carl-icahn-invests-150-million-in-lyft-2015-5/#.VicRavkrLIV

5 Wired Magazine reports on the changing of Lyft's most prominent quirks in January 2015, with reasons: http://www.wired.com/2015/01/lyft-finally-ditching-furry-pink-mustache

The original version of the carstache. Retrieved from http://cdn. arstechnica.net/wp-content/uploads/2012/07/Pinkout81-640x426.jpg

Lyft's new moustache, termed a "glowstache". Retrieved from http:// www.autorentalnews.com/fc_images/news/l-lyft-moustache.jpg

Exhibit 3 Lyft's Pink Carstaches

were successful in positioning Lyft differently, Lyft's top management announced plans to tone down the *carstache* and scrap the fist bump practice in January 2015. This decision was made with the realization that what worked in the West Coast would not work in Lyft's plans to expand to other cities in the US, or even internationally.

Regardless of Lyft toning down its practices, it still prided itself on its friendliness and laidback driving experience when compared to Uber. An internal presentation from March 2015 that was leaked to Bloomberg revealed its criticisms of Uber for its "top-down model", "exclusive mentality", and "anti-social culture"[6]. On the other hand, Lyft claimed its growth to be bottom-up and led by drivers through positive word-of-mouth marketing, 32% of whom were female. All in all, Lyft believed itself to be a "trusted brand" delivering a "social experience" with memorable quirks — the *carstache* being one of them.

Apart from its more relaxed brand image, Lyft mainly positioned itself as a lower-cost alternative to Uber. Since 2014, the company announced big price cuts — they first cut prices by 20% in early 2014 and then reduced them again by 10% in May[7]. Lyft also used a surge-pricing

model; to ward off potential criticism, it provided discounts of 10–15% during off-peak hours. While both companies engaged in aggressive price cutting strategies whenever they operated in the same city, Lyft drivers typically charged — and earned — less than Uber drivers (*Exhibit 4*), which was consistent with Lyft's positioning of being a lower cost alternative.

While Lyft enjoyed strong branding and was expected to spend a generous 60.5% of its revenue on marketing in December 2015, its operations were not as entrenched as Uber's. One example can be seen in its attempts to break into New York's tight network of taxis in July 2014, where Uber had already operated for three years. A public exposé occurred, in which the company was issued a cease-and-desist letter by the New York State Department of Financial Services just days before it planned to open operations[8], for non-compliance with safety requirements and licensing criteria. Uber also aggressively cut the price of its UberX service by 20% that week, to price itself significantly lower than regular taxis just before Lyft entered the market. The bottom line of Lyft and Uber's rivalry was that the latter enjoyed a first-mover advantage and, having established a presence in major cities beforehand, benefited from network effects and sufficient margins which allowed it to cut prices when needed, to erect barriers to entry and slow down the growth of competitors. Uber's significantly higher market valuation also helped to raise more capital each funding

---

6 Eric Newcomer and Leslie Picker (2015), "Leaked Lyft Document Reveals a Costly Battle With Uber", Bloomberg Businessweek. Retrieved from http://www.bloomberg.com/news/articles/ 2015-04-30/leaked-lyft-document-reveals-a-costly-battle-with-uber

7 Vator talks about Lyft's model with respect to prices and Uber's response in 2 articles written in 2014: http://vator.tv/news/2014-04-24-lyft-takes-off-hits-24-new-cities-in-one-day and http://vator.tv/news/2014-03-18-lyft-counters-surge-pricing-by-reducing-off-peak-fares

8 To follow Lyft's saga in New York City in July 2014, the time period it decided to offer its services to Hong Kong, read Bloomberg Businessweek's exposé on the issue: http://www.bloomberg.com/news/articles/2014-07-10/lyft-not-authorized-for-new-york-days-before-start-due

Seattle
UberX: $13.17
Lyft: $11.21

San Francisco
UberX: $14.65
Lyft: $13.42

Dallas
UberX: $11.45
Lyft: $11.19

New York City
UberX: $29.34
Lyft: $28.62

Miami
UberX: $14.38
Lyft: $12.30

Source
Adapted from http://time.com/money/3959091/uber-lyft-price-per-trip; accessed October 27, 2015.

Exhibit 4 Average Income of Uber and Lyft Drivers per Trip in Selected Cities.

round — it raised $1 billion in July 2015 while Lyft raised only half the amount in the same year. This helped sustain any losses in operations in an era of price cuts.

Finally, Lyft tried to expand fast — it raised $250 million in 2014 and another $530 million in March 2015, with the main goal of expanding internationally and entering less competitive markets without already entrenched competitors.

DIDI

In China, Uber found itself in the position of the much smaller late entrant. Here, Didi was the clear leader. Didi-Kuaidi, referred to as Didi by the public, was the product of a merger between Didi Dache and Kuaidi Dache, two of China's leading taxi-hailing apps. In February 2015, the merged entity was valued at $6 billion, and doubled to $12 billion by September in the same year[9]. Didi's services covered 80% of China's huge market of 800 million city dwellers (*Exhibit 5*), being a deep-pocketed dominant player reaping the network-leveraging dividends of having drivers and customers hooked on to its product early.

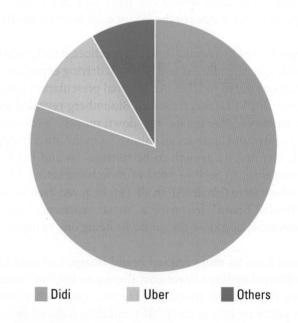

■ Didi   ■ Uber   ■ Others

Exhibit 5 Market Share of App-Based Car-Hire Services in China

Source
Adapted from http://fortune.com/2015/09/30/will-china-be-ubers-waterloo, accessed October 10, 2015.

9 Gerry Shih (2015), "China taxi apps Didi Dache and Kuaidi Dache announce $6 billion tie-up", Reuters. Retrieved from http://www.reuters.com/article/2015/02/14/us-china-taxi-merger-idUSKBN0LI04420150214

Didi was also far more successful than Uber in the aspect of legal legitimacy, acquired from its local connections[10]. Didi enjoyed backing from powerful Chinese government investors, the most notable one being the China Investment Corporation, China's sovereign fund in charge of managing foreign exchange reserves. These well-connected investors opened up opportunities for Didi at the expense of its competitors, which included working with regulators. A success was commemorated in October 2015, when Didi became the first car-hailing app to be awarded an official license in Shanghai. This authorization was hailed as a landmark decision, allowing Didi to operate its ride-hailing business in the city without any fear of legal infringements[11]. It assuaged concerns among taxi drivers, as one revealed in September 2015, "I worry all the time about being caught and fined by the government. My biggest concern is policy uncertainties." With this formal recognition, more drivers were certain to sign on with Didi *vis-à-vis* its competitors, which could not provide the same level of regulatory security.

From the beginning, Didi pursued an aggressive strategy to lure as many drivers to its app as possible. Didi spent $700 million on rewards to taxi drivers between 2013 and 2014, attracting both new drivers and switching drivers from existing taxi companies with monetary incentives. So important were taxi companies as a source of growth that the sales team in Didi even went to the streets to promote their app to cabbies. By allowing its mobile apps to be used by taxi drivers as an additional channel to attract more passengers, Didi sought to convert these drivers to work for them exclusively during peak hours by offering more attractive rates and bonuses. This method of attracting and converting drivers with the use of incentives allowed Didi to swiftly convert a large number of taxi drivers, quickly scaling their operations in other cities. It also highlights the main difference between Didi and Uber's business model — Didi started out with taxi drivers adopting its app, before adding non-traditional transport services to its portfolio while Uber started out with the intention of disrupting the taxi industry itself by replacing its services.

Part of Didi's fast growth was also due to tweaking and expanding its business model to meet unique local demands. For example, urban dwellers frequently looked for a compromise between overcrowded public transportation and the high cost of driving to work themselves, which led Didi to introduce Hitch as a service offering in its app, which was a group ride-sharing service along preset routes. Hitch was for casual drivers who wanted to recoup some gas money and toll fees on their daily commute — by inputting their start and end points into the app, Hitch connected them with nearby passengers heading in the same direction, allowing them to share the ride. This was different from the more traditional taxi-type service as drivers had control over where the ride ended, and they did not make a profit off the service — passengers only paid for the cost of gas and tolls. This allowed for fares that were 30–40% lower than those of regular taxis. For Didi, Hitch encouraged consumers to try Didi's services at a low cost, therefore, opening a pathway for them to convert to the more expensive for-profit taxi service eventually.

Clearly, Didi understood the local market's needs well enough to carry out effective customer segmentation to target the differentiated needs in its product development. This allowed for the building of customer loyalty to the main corporate brand, and the greater willingness to try *and* switch between Didi's various services, depending on the occasion of travel.

UBER'S RESPONSE TO DIDI'S MULTIPLE SERVICE OFFERINGS

Uber had prioritized China as a key market for expansion, and it was befuddling to the company to be in a distantly second position. Uber to Didi in China was like Lyft to Uber in the US. In a cruel twist of fate, Didi recently invested $100 million in Lyft in September 2015, forming an international ride-sharing partnership.

Uber managed to capture only 11.5% of the Chinese market, but experts did not find it surprising given China's unique institutional structures. Greg Tarr, partner at CrossPacific Capital, commented, "When you have great technology and a great business model but don't understand some of those local business premises... West Coast aggressiveness will only get you so far. China is such a different animal in terms of dealing with the local culture, the protectionism and the fact that you don't have local investors." This demonstrated the need for

---

10 Deborah Findling (2015), "What stands between Uber and success in China?", CNBC. Retrieved from http://www.cnbc.com/2015/09/15/what-stands-between-uber-and-success-in-china.htm

11 "In the race for legal legitimacy," (2015) *Wall Street Journal.* Retrieved from http://www.wsj.com/articles/chinas-didi-kuaidi-gets-license-to-ride-in-shanghai-1444288510?alg=y

Uber to better understand the Chinese market, rather than merely transplanting its San Francisco model of attracting American drivers and dealing with local regulations. Uber thus attempted to work closely with China's Ministry of Transport by setting up servers in China, in an effort to obtain an internet service company license by sharing data with local transport authorities.

Reformation in Uber's marketing strategy in China was a priority, and steps were taken to set up local teams to localize logistics, including language and support services. At consumers' requests, Uber strategically partnered with Chinese search giant Baidu, ditching Google Maps for Baidu maps into its app. Baidu also prominently advertised Uber on its main page with a prominent "Get a Car" button, linking it to Uber's app. Partnerships with Alibaba also allowed Uber to use the simpler and non-credit card-based payment mechanism of Alipay[12]. This was important as many Chinese residents did not own credit cards.

Uber competed vigorously with Didi on many other fronts to attract drivers to sign on with their companies. Both offered bonuses for drivers who hit ride targets, in a bid to extend geographical coverage and reduce wait times. This was based on an industry-wide understanding that spending cash to build an operational base as quickly as possible leveraging on economies of scale was the only way to win in China. As Didi's President, Jean Liu, revealed, "By using subsidies to get more cars on the road… waiting times were shortened, fares became cheaper, more users were drawn on to the platform and drivers on the platform. We have already created such a virtuous circle of increased orders, customer retention."[13]

To try and respond more effectively to Didi's diversification of services, Uber looked beyond its typical car-ordering model that worked so well in other international markets. In August 2014, Uber announced the implementation of People's Uber, where drivers offered "non-profit" rides to carpooling passengers who only paid for the cost of gas and maintenance. This was Uber's version of Didi's Hitch, competing directly to attract people who wanted low cost rides.

Uber seemed to be playing catch-up rather than setting trends in the China market. The race to grab market share was critical because it was understood that whoever got ahead first would remain the dominant player for a long time. Uber had to decide how to effectively compete with a much larger competitor, where to side-step competition and innovate new services, and where and how to go head-on with Didi.

---

12 The Market Mogul covers Didi's triumph over Uber in the Chinese market in a short read: http://themarketmogul.com/didi-kuaidi-crushes-uber-in-the-chinese-market

13 Financial Times reports on the intensive cash burning on subsidies in the China market by Didi and Uber in http://www.ft.com/intl/cms/s/0/e85cc5fa-5473-11e5-8642-453585f2cfcd.html#axzz3oPUktNrd

Study Questions

1. How could Uber retain its dominant position in the US market? Are there services and/or geographic niche markets where Uber should accommodate Lyft?

2. How could Uber effectively compete with Didi? Should it compete head-on in China, or should it side-step competition by focusing on niche markets through service innovation, and geographic expansion within China?

CASE 05

Banyan Tree: Designing and Delivering a Branded Service Experience

Jochen Wirtz

Banyan Tree Hotels & Resorts had become a leading player in the luxury resort and spa market in Asia. As part of its growth strategy, Banyan Tree had launched new brands and brand extensions that included resorts, spas, residences, destination club memberships, and retail outlets. Now, the company was preparing to aggressively grow its global footprint in the Americas, Caribbean, Europe, and the Middle East while preserving its distinctive Asian identity and strong brand image of Banyan Tree.

A brand synonymous with private villas, tropical garden spas, and retail galleries promoting traditional craft, Banyan Tree Hotels & Resorts received its first guest in 1994 in Phuket, Thailand. Since then, it had grown into a leading manager and developer of niche and premium resorts, hotels, and spas in Asia–Pacific.

Despite having minimal advertising, Banyan Tree achieved global exposure and a high level of brand awareness through the company's public relations and global marketing programs. Much interest was also generated by the company's socially responsible business values and practices caring for the social and natural environments. To gain a wider customer base, the company introduced Angsana in 2000, a contemporary brand at a slightly lower price point that also appeals to families.

As the resorts market became increasingly crowded with similar competitive offerings, lured by the success of Banyan Tree, the company had to contemplate expanding its business and preserving its distinct identity. Banyan Tree and Angsana resorts were expanding geographically outside of Asia and also into the urban hotel market in major cities throughout the world[1]. With around 30 hotels and resorts scheduled to open over the next five years, Banyan Tree faced the challenge of translating and maintaining the success of a niche Asian hospitality brand into various market segments on a global scale.

COMPANY BACKGROUND

By October 2015, Banyan Tree Holdings Ltd (BTHR) managed and/or had ownership interests in 38 resorts and hotels, 67 spas, 79 retail galleries, and three golf courses in 28 countries. Since its establishment in 1994, the company's flagship brand, Banyan Tree, had won a mindboggling 1,200 international tourism, hospitality, design, and marketing awards, some of which included "2014 Forbes Travel Guide Award", "Top 10 Hotels In Mexico" in 2014 by the US News for Banyan Tree Mayakoba, "Best Spa Resort in China" in 2014 for Banyan Tree Lijiang from the 7th Annual TTG China Travel Award, "National Geographic Traveler" award for Banyan Tree Yangshuo in 2014, and "Best Spa Operator" at the 25th Annual TTG Travel Awards 2014 (for the 10th consecutive year), for Banyan Tree Spa[2].

The support and feedback of the management of Banyan Tree Hotels & Resorts in the writing of this case is gratefully acknowledged.

1 Note that Banyan Tree has a significant property units that are typically in close proximity of its resorts. As part of its property development it launched a new brand, Casia, which targets the Asian middle class. This case study focuses on the Banyan Tree brand.

2 The complete list of awards won by Banyan Tree can be found on the company's Web site at *www.banyantree.com*.

BTHR was founded by Ho Kwon Ping, a travel enthusiast and former journalist, and his wife Claire Chiang, a strong advocate of corporate social responsibility. Prior to entering the hotels and resorts business, Ho spent some 15 years managing the family business, which was into everything imaginable, such as commodities, food products, consumer electronics, and property development. It competed mainly on cost, and was not dominant in any particular country or industry. Meanwhile, Chiang was deeply involved in sociology and social issues.

The closing of a factory in Thailand one year after its opening — because it lost out to other low-cost producers in Indonesia — was the last straw for Ho, who then realized that a low-cost strategy was not only difficult to follow but would also lead them nowhere. Determined to craft out something proprietary that would allow the company to become a price maker rather than a price taker, Ho decided that building a strong brand was the only way for him to maintain a sustainable competitive advantage.

The idea of entering the luxury resorts market was inspired by the gap in the hotel industry that giant chains such as the Hilton and Shangri-La could not fill. There was a market segment that wanted private and intimate accommodation, but without the expectation of glitzy chain hotels. This was fueled by the sharp price gap between the luxurious Aman Resorts and other resorts in the luxury resorts market. For example, in 2004, the Amanpuri in Thailand, one of Aman's resorts, charged a rack rate for its villas ranging from US$650 to more than US$7,000 a night, whereas the prices of other luxury resorts, such as the Shangri-La Hotel and Phuket Arcadia Beach Resort by Hilton in Thailand were priced below US$350.

Noticing the big difference in prices between Aman Resorts and the other resorts in the luxury resorts market, Ho saw potential for offering an innovative niche product that could also bridge the price gap in this market. Ho and Chiang had backpacked throughout the world in their youth, and were seasoned travelers themselves.

Hotel Business – Outlook

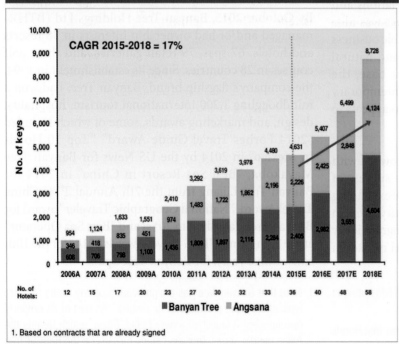

Highlights

→ CAGR of 17% based on contracts completion dates.

→ Room keys to grow almost 2 folds to over 8,700.

→ More than 90% of additional keys is managed only with no equity.

Source

Banyan Tree Holdings Limited. 2Q15 & 1H15 Results Briefing, www.SGX.com, http://infopub.sgx.com/FileOpen/Results_Briefing-2Q15.ashx?App=Announcement&FileID=364840, accessed October 1, 2015.

Their extensive travel experience is evident in their non-conforming beliefs that resorts should provide more than just accommodation. Ho and Chiang hit upon the idea of building a resort comprising individual villas, with locally-inspired architectural design, positioned as a romantic and intimate escapade for guests. Banyan Tree moved its positioning into the higher end of the luxury market, and by 2015, its rack rates for its basic category were typically between US$600 and US$1,200 for the resort in Phuket, and between €900 and €3,500 for the resort in the Seychelles.

Operations at Banyan Tree began with only one resort in Phuket, situated on a former mining site once deemed too severely ravaged to sustain any form of development by a United Nations Development Program planning unit and the Tourism Authority of Thailand. It was a bold decision, but the company, together with Ho, Chiang, and Ho's brother Ho Kwon Cjan, restored it after extensive rehabilitation works costing a total of US$250 million. The Banyan Tree Phuket was so successful when it was finally launched that the company worked quickly to build two other resorts, one on Bintan Island in Indonesia, and the other at Vabbinfaru Island in the Maldives. The company has never looked back since. Even though Asia's travel industry experienced periodic meltdowns such as during the Asian economic crisis in 1997/8, the September 11 attacks on the World Trade Center in 2001, the dot.com crisis in 2001/2, severe acute respiratory syndrome (SARS) in 2003, the Indian Ocean tsunami on December 26, 2004, the World Economic Crisis in 2008/9, and the Euro Crisis from 2011 through to 2015, no employee was retrenched; instead, Banyan Tree grew its number of resorts and rooms aggressively, and its room rates rose steadily.

BRAND ORIGINS

Known as *Yung Shue Wan* in the local dialect, Banyan Tree Bay was a fishing village on Lamma Island in Hong Kong, where Ho and Chiang lived for three idyllic years before Ho joined the family business. Despite the village's modest and rustic setting, they remembered it to be a sanctuary of romance and intimacy. The large canopies of the Banyan Tree also showed semblance of the shelter afforded by Asia's tropical rainforests. Ho and Chiang thus decided to name their resort Banyan Tree, and position it as a "Sanctuary for the Senses".

THE SERVICE OFFERING

Unlike most other resorts then, Banyan Tree resorts comprised individual villas that came with a private pool, Jacuzzi, or spa treatment room, each designed to offer guests exclusivity and utmost privacy. For example, a guest could skinny-dip in the private pool within his villa without being seen by other guests, putting him in a world of his own (*Exhibit 1*).

Exhibit 1 A world of privacy in a double pool villa at Banyan Tree Phuket

All Banyan Tree hotels and resorts were designed around the concept of providing "a sense of place" to reflect and enhance the culture and heritage of the destination. This is reflected in the architecture, furnishings, landscape, vegetation, and the service they offer. To create a sense of exotic sensuality and ensure the privacy of its guests, the resorts are designed to blend into the natural landscape of the surrounding environment, and use the natural foliage and boulders as its privacy screen (see *Exhibit 2* showing Banyan Tree Seychelles). The furnishings of Banyan Tree villas were deliberately native to convey the exoticism of the destination with its rich local flavor and luxurious feel. The spa pavilions in Seychelles were constructed around the large granite boulders and lush foliage to offer an outdoor spa experience in complete privacy. The resorts' local flavor was also reflected in the services offered, some of which were unique to certain resorts. Employees were allowed to vary the service delivery process according to local culture and practices, as long as these were consistent with the brand promise of romance and intimacy. Thus, in Phuket for instance, a couple could enjoy dinner on a traditional Thai long

Exhibit 2 Banyan Tree Seychelles blends well into its natural environment

Exhibit 3 The Banyan Tree Spa Pavilion with a view

tail boat accompanied by private Thai musicians while cruising, instead of dining in a restaurant. Banyan Tree Phuket also offers wedding packages in which couples were blessed by Buddhist monks. In the Maldives, wedding ceremonies could be conducted underwater among the corals. Guests could also choose to dine in a castaway sandbank with only their private chefs and the stars for company, and watch the sunset toasting champagne on a Turkish gulet upon returning from a trip watching a school of spinner dolphins.

Products and services were conceived with the desired customer experience in mind. Banyan Tree launched themed packages across their hotels, such as "Sense of Rejuvenation" with a focus on wellness, spa, and detox, and "Sense of Romance" for couples. These themed packages varied from resort to resort, to incorporate the unique experiences each location had to offer, but they would have some common features, such as a couple spa treatment, couple dining concepts, and the special decoration of the couples' villas with lit candles, incense oil burners, flower petals spread throughout the room, and a chilled bottle of champagne or wine. The couple would be presented with a variety of aromatic massage oils and bath salts to further inspire intimate moments.

Another draw of the resorts was the Banyan Tree Spa, found at every Banyan Tree property. The pioneer of the tropical garden spas concept, Banyan Tree Spas offered a variety of aromatic oil massages, and face and body beauty treatments using traditional Asian therapies, with a choice of indoors or outdoors treatment. The spa products used were natural, indigenous products made from local herbs and spices. Non-clinical in concept, Banyan Tree Spas relied mainly on the "human touch" instead of energy-consuming high-tech equipment. The

spa experience was promoted as a sensorial, intimate experience that would rejuvenate the "body, mind, and soul," and was mainly targeted at couples who would enjoy their treatments together.

In line with Banyan Tree's ethos of conserving local culture and heritage, and promoting cottage crafts, Chiang founded the Banyan Tree Gallery, a retail outlet showcasing indigenous crafts. Banyan Tree Gallery outlets were set up in each resort. Items sold were made by local artisans, and included traditionally woven handmade fabrics, garments, jewelry, handicrafts, tribal art, and spa accessories, such as incense candles and massage oils, which guests could use at home to recreate the Banyan Tree experience.

Banyan Tree Gallery embarked on projects to support the various communities in the locations Banyan Tree resorts are situated, and worked closely with village cooperatives and not-for-profit craft marketing agents to provide gainful employment to artisans. While acting as a marketing channel for Asian crafts like basket weaving, hill tribe cross-stitching and lacquer ware, Banyan Tree Gallery also educated its customers about the crafts with an accompanying write-up. In the course of Banyan Tree Gallery's operations, the community outreach extended from across Thailand to Laos, Cambodia, India, Nepal, Sri Lanka, Indonesia, Malaysia, and Singapore.

The result of Banyan Tree's efforts was "a very exclusive, private holiday feeling", as described by one guest. Another guest commented, "It's a treat for all the special occasions like honeymoons and wedding anniversaries. It's the architecture, the sense of place and the promise of romance."

Exhibit 4 A contemporary Asian shopping experience with a strong sense of corporate responsibility at Banyan Tree Gallery

MARKETING BANYAN TREE

In the first two years Banyan Tree was launched, the company's marketing communications was managed by an international advertising agency. The agency also designed the Banyan Tree logo shown in *Exhibit 5* and, together with the management, came up with the marketing tagline "Sanctuary for the Senses".

Though furnished luxuriously, Banyan Tree resorts were promoted as providing romantic and intimate "smallish" hotel experiences, rather than luxurious accommodation as touted by most competitors then. "Banyan Tree Experiences" was marketed as intimate private moments. The resorts saw themselves as setting the stage for guests to create those unforgettable memories.

BANYAN TREE

Exhibit 5 The Banyan Tree logo

When Banyan Tree was first launched, extensive advertising was carried out for a short period of time to gain recognition in the industry. Subsequently, the company scaled down on advertising and kept it minimal, mainly in high-end travel magazines in key markets. The advertisements were visual in nature, with succinct copy showcasing the awards and accolades won. *Exhibit 6* shows a Banyan Tree advertisement highlighting the award-winning Banyan Tree Spa.

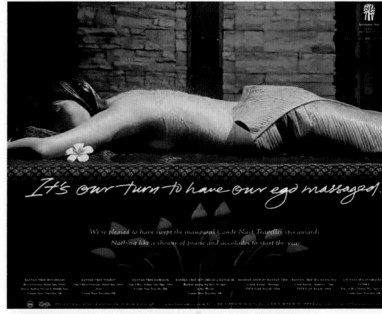

It's our turn to have our ego massaged.

Exhibit 6 An advertisement showcasing "Spa of the Year" award from Conde Nast Traveller

Brand awareness for Banyan Tree was generated largely through public relations and global marketing programs. For example, relationships with travel editors and writers were cultivated to encourage visits to the resorts. This helped to increase editorial coverage on Banyan Tree, which management felt was more effective in conveying the "Banyan Tree Experience" from an impartial third-party perspective. Its website www.banyantree.com increasingly drove online bookings, and provided vivid information on the latest offerings of Banyan Tree's fast-growing portfolio.

The management of marketing activities was centralized at its headquarters in Singapore in order to maintain consistency in brand building. BTHR appointed a few key wholesalers in each targeted market, and worked closely with them to promote sales. Rather than selling through wholesale and retail agents that catered to the general market, BTHR chose to work only with agents specializing in exclusive luxury holidays targeted at wealthy customers. Global exposure was also achieved through Banyan Tree's membership in the Small Luxury Hotels (LX) and Leading Hotels of the World (LW). Targeting high-end consumers, they represent various independent exclusive hotels, and have sales offices in major cities around the world.

The end of 2007 marked a new stage of Banyan Tree's global expansion, with the launch of its own GDS code "BY". GDS is a Global Distribution System that is used by travel providers to process airline, hotel, car rental reservations across 640,000 terminals of travel agents, and other distribution partners around the world. Prior to BY, Banyan Tree was represented by its marketing partners, Leading Hotels of the World (LW) and Small Luxury Hotels (LX). Thereafter, Banyan Tree had its unique identity on the GDS code, further strengthening its brand presence and customer ownership. Banyan Tree then had enough critical mass to ensure the economic feasibility of a GDS private label. The acquisition of its own GDS code meant that Banyan Tree was transitioning from a relatively small regional player to a global brand in the eyes of the travel industry.

BRAND VALUES

Banyan Tree embraced certain values, such as actively caring for the natural and human environment, revitalizing local communities, which in turn created pride and respect among staff. The company hoped to build the brand on values that employees and customers could identify with and support as part of their own life values. A dedicated corporate social responsibility committee, headed by Chiang and featuring general managers and valued associates from each resort, was formed to focus on these issues with both a regional overview and simultaneously local perspectives. Thus, the company worked actively to preserve, protect, and promote the natural and human environments in which the Banyan Tree resorts were located. In 2009, Banyan Tree Global Foundation was launched as a separate entity to enhance governance and institutional safeguards for funding of sustainability projects.

PRESERVING THE ENVIRONMENT

Resorts were built using local materials as far as possible, and at the same time minimizing the impact on the environment. At Banyan Tree Bintan, for example, the 70 villas located in a rainforest were constructed around existing trees, cutting down as few trees as possible, to minimize the impact the resort had on the natural environment. The villas were built on stilts and platforms to avoid cutting trees, and possible soil erosion. At Banyan Tree Maldives Vabbinfaru and Banyan Tree Seychelles, fresh water supply was obtained by the more expensive method of desalination, instead of extracting water from the underground water-table, which risked long-term disruption of the ecological system. Toiletries such as shampoo, hair conditioner, bath foam, and body lotion, provided in the resorts were non-toxic and biodegradable, and filled in reusable containers made from celadon or ceramic. Refuse was recycled where possible or otherwise treated through an in-house incinerator system. Waste water was also treated and recycled in the irrigation of resort landscapes.

Through the retail arm Banyan Tree Gallery, the human environment efforts were evident in the active sourcing of traditional crafts from indigenous tribes to provide gainful employment. These employment opportunities provided a source of income for the tribes, and at the same time, preserve their unique heritage.

In line with the Banyan Tree Group's Green Imperative initiative, Banyan Tree Gallery constantly used eco-friendly and recycled materials in the development of its merchandise. Examples included photo frames made using discarded telephone directories, elephant dung paper stationary, and lead-free celadon and ceramic spa amenities. Unique collections like the black resin turtles stationery range and leaf-inspired merchandise were created to promote environmental awareness and were accompanied by a write-up to educate the consumer on the targeted conservation campaign. In support of animal rights, the galleries did not carry products made from shell or ivory.

Besides trying to conduct business in an environmentally responsible manner, BTHR actively pursued a number of key initiatives, including its Greening Communities program. Greening Communities was launched in 2007 as a challenge for properties to raise awareness for climate change by planting 2,000 trees per year. It planted 28,321 trees in the first two years of the program. For example, Banyan Tree Lijiang planted some 20,000 fruit trees to create additional income for families of the supporting community. While trees will absorb carbon dioxide and improve the quality of the environment, the main goal of this program was to engage local communities, associates, and guests to share the cause of climate change, and actions that can reduce our collective carbon footprint. The program had planted 358,885 trees by end-2014, far exceeding its target of 286,272.

CREATING BRAND OWNERSHIP AMONG EMPLOYEES

All Banyan Tree employees were trained to the basic standards of five-star service establishments, which included greeting guests, remembering their first names, and anticipating their needs. In addition, some employees got a taste of the "Banyan Tree Experience" as part of their training. The management believed that the stay would help employees understand better what guests will experience, and, in return, enhance their delivery of special experiences for the guests.

Although management imposed strict rules in the administration of the resorts, employees were empowered to exercise creativity and sensitivity. For example, the housekeeping teams were not restricted by a standard bed decoration. Rather, they were given room for creativity although they had general guidelines for turning the bed to keep in line with the standards of a premium resort. Banyan Tree invested liberally in staff welfare — employees were taken to and from work in air-conditioned buses, and had access to various amenities including good-quality canteens, medical services, and childcare facilities. Staff dormitories had televisions, telephones, refrigerators, and attached bathrooms.

The company's generous staff welfare policies apparently paid off. Ho said, "The most gratifying response is the sense of ownership that our staff began to have. It's not a sense of financial ownership, but they actually care about the property. In our business, service and service standards do not always mean the same thing as in a developed country, where standards are measured by efficiency and productivity, by people who are already quite well-versed in a service culture. We operate in places that, sometimes, have not seen hotels. People come from villages. What we need — more than exact standards — is for them to have a sense of hospitality, a sense that the guest is an honored person who, by virtue of being there, is able to give a decent livelihood to the people who work. This creates a culture in which everybody is friendly and helpful."

INVOLVING GUESTS IN ENVIRONMENTAL CONSERVATION

Part of the company's corporate social responsibility initiatives were designed to encourage environmental conservation and help ecological restoration. To create greater environmental awareness, Banyan Tree organized activities that involved interested guests in their research and environmental preservation work. In the Maldives, for instance, guests were invited to take part in the coral transplantation program (see *Exhibit 7* for a picture of guest involvement in the long-running coral planting program). Guests who participated in the program were then encouraged to return several years later to see the progress of their efforts. Guests were also offered free marine biology sessions, allowing them to learn more about the fascinating marine life and its conservation. Guests also had an opportunity to take part in the Green Sea Turtle Headstarting Projects. The response from guests was tremendously positive.

Banyan Tree established The Green Imperative Fund (GIF) to further support community-based and environmental initiatives in the regions where it has a presence. Guests were billed US$2 per room night at Banyan Tree properties and US$1 at Angsana properties (of which they could opt out if they wished) for this fund and the company matched it dollar for dollar. Details of the program were communicated to guests through various methods, including sand-filled turtles and in-villa turndown gifts.

Exhibit 7 A guest participates in planting corals at the Banyan Tree Maldives and Angsana Ihuru Maldives

Guests were generally happy to know that their patronage contributed to meaningful causes, like the construction of new schools for the local community, the restoration of coral reefs, and also helped ensure the longevity of local village crafts.

INVOLVING THE LOCAL COMMUNITY

In addition to engaging local craftsmen to produce indigenous art and handicrafts for sale at its galleries, Banyan Tree also involved the local community in all aspects of its business, even as the resorts were being built. Villas were constructed with as much indigenous material as possible, most of which was supplied by local traders. Traditional arts and handicrafts that complemented the villas' aesthetics were also purchased from local artisans.

The company believed in building profitable resorts that would benefit the surrounding environment and contribute to local economies through the creation of employment and community development projects. As such, besides providing employment for the local community, the company also brought business to the local farmers and traders by making it a point to purchase fresh produce from them. Whenever possible, the company supported other regional tourism ventures that would benefit the wider local community and enhance the visitor's experience. The Banyan Tree Maldives Marine Laboratory is a prime example, being the first fully equipped private research facility to be fully funded and operated by a resort. The Lab seeks to lead conservation efforts in the Maldives to protect and regenerate coral and marine life for the future of the tourism industry as well as to promote awareness and education of this field to the local community.

Recognizing that the disparity in lifestyles and living standards between guests and the local community might create a sense of alienation within the local community, a Community Relations Department was set up to develop and manage community outreach programs. After consultations with community stakeholders, a number of funding scholarships for needy children were given, a school and childcare center were built, lunches and parties for the elderly were hosted, and local cultural and religious activities were supported.

One of BTHR's formalized programs was Seedlings, which aimed to help young adults from local communities, and motivate them and provide the means for completing their education to successfully enter the labor force as adults. This program benefitted the community at large as it provided the next generation with educational opportunities to break the poverty cycle[3].

GROWING BANYAN TREE

In 2002, BTHR took over the management of a city hotel in the heart of Bangkok from Westin Hotel Company. The hotel was rebranded as Banyan Tree Bangkok, after extensive renovation works were completed to upgrade the hotel's facilities, build new additional spa amenities and a Banyan Tree Gallery. This was the first Banyan Tree hotel to be located in the city area, unlike the other beachfront Banyan Tree properties. Banyan Tree planned to open city hotels in Seoul, Shanghai, and Hangzhou, and Angsana also expanded into Morocco and Laos.

As the Banyan Tree brand became established, the company began expanding its network of spas and retail outlets. Standalone Banyan Tree Spas and Banyan Tree Galleries were set up as separate ventures, independent of Banyan Tree hotels and resorts, in various cities such as Singapore, Shanghai, Sydney, India, and Dubai, operating either in other hotels, cruise ships, or as standalone outlets.

In addition to the Spa Academy in Phuket which opened in 2001, and to support its fast-growing spa business, Banyan Tree opened two new spa academies in Lijiang, China and Bangkok, Thailand in 2007.

After establishing a foothold in the luxury resorts market, BTHR introduced the Angsana brand in response to the demand from hotel operators in Asia that were keen to introduce spa services in their hotels. As the positioning of these hotels did not fit that of Banyan Tree, the company decided to launch a new brand, Angsana, a more contemporary and affordable brand than Banyan Tree, to run as standalone spa businesses in other hotels.

---

3 Detailed information on BTHR's CSR activities can be found at http://www.banyantree.com/csr.

The first Angsana Spa was opened in 1999 at Dusit Laguna, one of several hotels at Laguna Phuket, an integrated resort development with shared facilities located at Bang Tao Bay in Thailand. The Angsana Spa was so well received that the company quickly set up five other such spas in various hotels in Thailand. In 2000, BTHR opened its first Angsana Resort & Spa complete with an Angsana Gallery, located less than one kilometer away from Banyan Tree Bintan in Indonesia.

In 2003, Banyan Tree launched The Museum Shop by Banyan Tree — a joint partnership with Singapore's National Heritage Board to showcase Asia's rich and diverse cultural heritage through unique museum-inspired merchandise. Designed to inspire and educate shoppers, The Museum Shop by Banyan Tree made history more accessible and approachable to the layperson. Although it eventually disposed of all museum shops, Banyan Tree had 79 retail outlets, ranging from Banyan Tree Galleries, Heritage Collection by Banyan Tree, Elements by Banyan Tree, and Angsana Galleries by 2015.

Banyan Tree Galleries are the retail outlets supporting the hotels, while Banyan Tree Spa Galleries support the spa outlets, selling more spa-focused merchandise such as signature aromatherapy amenities, essential oils, candles, and body care products.

Exhibit 9 Angsana Ihuru Maldives

THE ROAD AHEAD

To diversify its geographic spread, Ho had started to venture into locations in South America (the first resort in Mexico opened in 2009), southern Europe, and the Middle East, where he hoped to replicate Banyan Tree's rapid success. However, given the higher costs of doing business in the Americas and Europe, would the same strategy that had brought fame and success to Banyan Tree in Asia be workable in the rest of the world? Ho's ultimate vision was "to string a necklace of Banyan Tree Resorts around the world; not quantity, but a number of jewels that form a chain around the world". By the second half of 2015, Banyan Tree had signed management contracts that would increase the total numbers to 66 hotels and resorts, 117 spas, and 115 galleries across 33 countries by 2019. Of the properties under development, the majority were resorts and/or integrated resorts.

While expanding the company's network of hotels and resorts, spas, and retail outlets, Ho had to be mindful of the brands' focus and be careful not to dilute the brands. He also had to consider the strategic fit of the company's portfolio of brands, which comprised Banyan Tree and Angsana (*Exhibit 9*), and more recently, a significant property arm that develops and sells villas and serviced apartment units that are typically in close proximity of its resorts. As part of this property development, it launched a new brand, Cassia, an exciting and bold new proposition in the serviced apartment sector which targets the Asian middle class.

Banyan Tree certainly stood out among its competitors in the resorts industry when it was first launched. Since then, its success had attracted various competitors who offer similar products and services. Thus, it was imperative that Banyan Tree retained its competitive advantage to prevent losing its distinctive position in the market, bringing Banyan Tree to the Americas, Europe, and the Middle East. How could Banyan Tree address those issues?

1. What are the main factors that contributed to Banyan Tree's success?

2. Evaluate Banyan Tree's brand positioning and communications strategies. Can Banyan Tree maintain its unique positioning in an increasingly overcrowded resorts market?

3. Discuss whether the brand portfolio of Banyan Tree, Angsana, and Cassia, as well as the product portfolio of beach resorts, services residences, city hotels, spas, galleries, and museum shops fit as a family. What are your recommendations to Banyan Tree for managing these brands and products in future?

4. What effect does the practice of corporate social responsibility have on brand equity?

5. What potential problems do you foresee bringing Banyan Tree to the Americas, Europe, and the Middle East? How could Banyan Tree address those issues?

Kiwi Experience

Mark Colgate

How do you manage a business where customers are unlikely to buy again? Answer: the Kiwi Experience Way! This case explores how to truly get inside the heads of your target market, how to build a culture of service excellence, and how other customers can add as much to the experience as the employees — but only if you encourage them to do so.

"Are you ready for a most excellent adventure?" shouted Rob, the driver of the Kiwi Experience bus, as it climbed to the top of an extinct volcano on a beautiful sunny morning in Auckland. It was the start of another trip around New Zealand, for the driver and the bus, as well as the 40 like-minded travelers, who were unprepared for the burst of enthusiasm as the panoramic view unveiled itself.

Virtually all of the travelers were unaware and unsure of what to expect from this trip. They had never traveled on Kiwi Experience before, although all had heard of the company through various mediums before they bought their tickets. This knowledge had somewhat reduced their uncertainty.

One of the passengers, Rory Gillies, a 23-year-old Scotsman, had heard much about Kiwi Experience while traveling around Australia. He was curious to find out what made this bus service so successful and so different to others offered in New Zealand. As they boarded the bus after taking in the sights of Auckland, Rory approached Rob the driver.

"Have you been busy this summer?" Rory asked. "I haven't stopped" replied Rob, "and what's more, I can only remember once or twice when my bus has not been full!" "So what does Kiwi Experience do that makes it so successful then?" continued Rory. "If I told you, it would ruin the trip for you," Rob suggested, "but jump on and maybe I'll give you a few ideas along the way".

© 2016 by Mark Colgate

Mark Colgate is Professor of Service Excellence at the Gustavson School of Business, University of Victoria. The support and feedback of the management of Kiwi Experience in the writing of this case is gratefully acknowledged. All statistics on Zealand's tourism industry were taken from http://www.stats.govt.nz/tourism.

COMPANY BACKGROUND

Kiwi Experience (KE) is an adventure transport network formed in December 1988 by three partners. The first bus left in late 1989. They recently celebrated their 25th birthday, and more than 400,000 passengers have now had a Kiwi Experience.

The concept behind the venture was to create a coach transport network that was neither an express point-to-point service nor an inflexible coach tour. Instead, they set out to create a transport tour experience which had the advantages of both. This meant that KE was going to offer the flexibility of the traditional express service, in that customers could get on or off the bus where they wanted, in addition to the guidance, information, and access to excitement-orientated places that a good adventure tour would offer, without the inherent drawbacks of either service.

This was an innovation in the marketplace and the first of its kind in the world. In fact, the concept was so original that in the beginning, staff at KE had to spend much of their time explaining the concept to potential customers. Clarifying to clients that KE passengers can get on and off the coach wherever they like (on a pass that lasts for six months), yet they are still part of an adventure trip that takes them to places off the beaten track. Since their inception, more than 90% of customers break their journey at some point, which proves this concept has been popular with travelers. Today, many copies of the KE concept can be seen all over the world.

Neil Geddes, one of the founders of the company, outlines the KE concept:

> I have always thought that a coach was a great way to get around, as meeting people is one of the fun things about traveling. But I could

never understand the fact that everyone is stuck on one coach, and you all had to do the same things. I don't believe you can create the ideal holiday for more than just the one person — this is why KE was invented.

The company's service offering is specifically designed for backpackers, adventurers, and other like-minded travelers. This means that KE is developed around the high-volume, low-margin business where minimizing cost is key.

Although KE has no specific target market in terms of age (they believe a backpacker tends to be defined in terms of lifestyle rather than age), it is the 18 to 30 age group which travels on KE the most, with 18 to 22 being the most common age range. Similarly, many nationalities travel on KE with backpackers from the UK, Germany, the US, Canada, Denmark, Switzerland, and Nordic countries making up the bulk of customers. Less than 1% of customers actually come from New Zealand itself.

NEW ZEALAND AS A TOURIST DESTINATION

In 2015, New Zealand hosted a total of three million international visitors aged 15 years and above (compared to 1.6 million in 1999, and 2.5 million in 2014). This number is up dramatically from 2014, and as New Zealand Tourism has worked hard to recover from the 2007 financial crisis that hit it hard. Total international visitor expenditure in 2014 reached NZ$10.3 billion; this was up from $9.6 billion in 2013. New Zealand's current share of international tourism is small at only 1–2% but given the size of the country, they do incredibly well.

New Zealand is marketed abroad as a "clean, green" adventure playground, with beautifully natural destinations such as Milford Sound, Abel Tasman National Park, or the Tongariro Alpine Crossing. Activities such as bungee jumping or whale watching exemplify typical tourist attractions, marketed primarily to individuals and small-group travelers. Of course, the Lord of the Rings and The Hobbit movies have also added international attraction to New Zealand as a destination.

As a growing labor-intensive industry, tourism generates an increasingly wide range of jobs for New Zealanders. The number of equivalent full-time jobs supported directly by tourism in New Zealand was approximately 168,000 in 2014, about 7.8% of the workforce.

GROWTH OF KIWI EXPERIENCE

KE has grown rapidly since its creation. Although some of the increase in passengers is undoubtedly due to the growth in visitors to New Zealand, the percentage increase of passengers traveling on KE is well above the percentage increase in overseas visitors. In fact, the number of KE passengers has increased faster than the growth of international visitors. KE is clearly taking the larger slice of a growing market.

In fact, KE has grown to a size the original owners never thought possible; they now have 30 buses and more than 40 drivers. They thought they had reached market saturation a few years ago; however, the idea of a backpacking holiday and the types of people undertaking backpacking holidays has grown immensely over the last few years. The Kiwi Experience directors' limited definition of backpacking has had to be broadened to encompass the demographic who now travel on KE. For instance, professionals who only have three weeks' holiday are now opting for a backpacker-style holiday around New Zealand.

Exhibit 1 Iconic Kiwi Experience Bus

THE "EXPERIENCE"

"How did you enjoy Waitomo Caves?" Rob asked Rory at a stop *en route* to Rotorua. "Amazing," he replied. "I saw the caves while blackwater rafting, and I really enjoyed the candlelight walk you took us all on through the Ruakuri Scenic Reserve to see the glow worms. It didn't stop there though; later on, a group of us from the coach went down to the Waitomo Tavern for a few drinks — I feel a bit rough today!" Rob laughed. Rory, he thought, was slowly coming to grips with what the KE was all about.

The Kiwi Experience concept is based on being the best in the market for people who want to see the real New Zealand. Backpacking is all about traveling, meeting other people, getting value for money, and getting involved in the local environment and culture. The service KE offers allows them to do just that; it allows backpackers to choose where and on what they want to spend their money on, at a price they can afford.

When Neil Geddes was asked what makes the KE so good, he had a simple reply.

> We ensure we give the customer what they want better than anyone else. Our service is not designed around what is good for the drivers; it is designed around what is good for the customer. We are close to our market, we are proud to be close to our market. When we [the directors of KE] travel, we stay in backpackers hostels, so as to learn and understand what the market wants. That is how we ensure that we always offer the best possible service for our clients. That is our core strength.

KE tries to get all people working within the business interacting with customers. For example, there was a BBQ at a backpacker's hostel in Auckland recently at which KE had their accountants and other staff meet the guests. In general, this group of staff does not usually come in direct contact with customers, but this event gave them a better understanding of who KE's customers are, and where they come from.

Being first in the marketplace has also helped, as it has meant that KE has gained a lead in understanding what their target market wants and how to service these needs effectively. This understanding has led KE staff to comprehend that it is both the driver of the coach and the interaction between backpackers, which help create the "KE Experience".

The Drivers

"The drivers are the single most important people in our company, we know that," states Neil Geddes. Their market research has shown the driver makes or breaks a KE trip. This is why KE undertakes a very comprehensive and strict selection process for its drivers, along with a very thorough training program.

The first thing the directors look for when selecting drivers is a certain type of person — they must be fun, young, and adventurous. They must have an outgoing personality and be proud to show off New Zealand. While this means that most drivers are from New Zealand, it is not necessarily always the case. Secondly, they must have extensive driving experience as it is critical they are a safe driver.

KE receives hundreds of applications for their driver jobs; one of the reasons is the pay. The drivers are rewarded nicely for doing their job well, particularly through bonuses and commission they may receive at the end of each trip. However, only very few drivers fit the strict selection criteria that KE have. The drivers must undergo a series of driving tests and interviews before they are selected. Even then, they may not necessarily get the job.

All prospective drivers are then taken on a 'dummy' trip around New Zealand. The drivers are asked to take notes of the various activities that are on offer and record any other information that may assist them in doing their job effectively. After this initial training, drivers are taken on a proper KE trip, where they observe how an experienced driver operates. The prospective driver could be asked to take over the driving or the commentary at any moment in time. Only when the drivers perform satisfactorily in these two tests will they then be taken on as a KE staff member.

Driving a KE bus is a highly rewarding job, but a stressful one too. There are many responsibilities placed on a driver apart from having to safely drive 40 people around the whole of New Zealand. These include:

- Providing informative and knowledgeable commentary.
- Booking all accommodation every night.
- Ensuring people on the bus interact as much as possible.
- Socializing as much as possible among the passengers.
- Organizing group meals and other group activities (*Exhibit 2*).
- Organizing paid excursions.
- Undertaking regular checks and maintenance (e.g., cleaning) of the bus.
- Listening to and responding to customer complaints.

Exhibit 2 A Kiwi Experience costume party organized by one of its drivers

Because of the above factors, drivers of KE buses rarely last three years within the company. Not all leave because of the intensive nature of the job; many leave because they obtain other jobs elsewhere.

Each driver is debriefed by an operations manager after each trip. This enables the operations manager to understand how tired the driver is, and whether he or she should be taken off the duty roster for a couple of weeks. An exhausted driver cannot provide the best service for the customers on the bus, and this will only harm the reputation of both the driver and KE in the long run. An experienced operations manager can easily spot when a certain driver needs a rest. The drivers are also required to fill out a survey at the end of each trip that asks them how the trip went and the problems they encountered. The survey also includes a section which enables the driver to make recommendations to improve the overall quality of the KE.

It is clear, therefore, that the drivers are the single most important asset that KE possesses. Their enthusiasm, knowledge, and personality will have a huge impact on customers' perception of the overall quality of the trip, and of KE as a whole.

Customer Interaction

Market research has shown the interaction between the customers on the bus is the second most important part of a KE trip. Backpackers generally enjoy meeting other like-minded people, which is the nature of their trip. In fact, many backpackers travel for the specific purpose of meeting new friends and acquaintances. Therefore, it is important that KE manages this interaction well to ensure this occurs.

KE does several things to ensure they achieve the correct customer mix on the buses, and that customers interact well together (beyond the normal interaction which would occur). Firstly, KE ensures, as best they can, that they and their booking agents do not book people who would not be suited to this kind of experience on the bus. For example, the older travelers may not be interested in some of things the KE does. This strategy is important as it prevents potential customers from having a negative experience on the trip. These customers' negative experience could also influence the experience the other customers on the bus are having. Ultimately, it may well lead to negative word-of-mouth for KE.

One way the company ensures this occurs is by sending representatives from their booking agents on tour to help them understand the types of people who would enjoy traveling with KE. Secondly, the drivers are trained to notice any passengers on the bus who are affecting the quality of the service other passengers are receiving. The driver will then take appropriate action. For example, in extreme cases, the driver may ask certain passengers to leave the bus, with a full refund being offered to encourage them to do so. In this case, KE has realized that it is important to remove people from the bus who may be influencing the enjoyment of a significant proportion of other customers.

Finally, the driver encourages social interaction between the customers on the bus. This enables different customers to meet each other and form bonds and friendships at an early stage within the trip. This may increase the positive experiences customers have on their bus, which should positively impact on the impression customers have on the overall trip. The drivers usually encourage interaction through group meals and social activities in the evening, for example, fancy dress competitions (pictured above).

ADVERTISING AND WORD-OF-MOUTH

"Why did you choose Kiwi Experience anyway?" Rob asked Rory, as the inter-Islander ferry pulled away from the Wellington Harbour on its three-and-a-half hour trip to Picton in the South Island. "I never really planned to; before I left Scotland, I'd always planned to hire a Campervan," replied Rory.

"So what made you change your mind then?" quizzed Rob. "I kept hearing of KE when I was traveling around Australia," said Rory. "Every time I stopped at a backpackers, I'd meet at least one person who would have a Kiwi Experience story to tell. Then when I came to New Zealand, KE did a slide show in the Backpackers I was staying at, and that really swung it for me!"

Many service organizations can rely on repeat purchases to maintain and enhance their profitability. For example, airlines often have passengers who have flown with them many times before. For KE, however, this is not the case. It is very unusual for passengers to travel with KE for a second time. KE relies heavily on new and referral customers for virtually all of their sales. Promoting and stimulating word-of-mouth is vitally important.

KE has realized this and promotes heavily in its target market and, wherever possible, attempts to stimulate word-of-mouth. One thing KE has realized is that it is important to advertise overseas. Backpackers often start searching for information well before they have left their own country to come to New Zealand, a fact that Neil Geddes acknowledges:

> A significant amount of our customers look for travel options well before they come near New Zealand. Most people mistakenly believe that backpackers turn up and make up their mind when they get in New Zealand. In fact, around 25% of customers buy their KE ticket overseas. For us, therefore, it is important to advertise overseas.

Other research KE has undertaken shows that 75% of customers have heard of KE before they enter New Zealand. This assists in sales since customers are familiar with the service before they purchase it. Word-of-mouth accounts for some of the people who have heard of KE before they enter the country, but a large percentage of customers hear of KE through other advertising. For example, KE places leaflets in backpackers' and youth hostels along commonly visited destinations that backpackers visit before they come to New Zealand, such as Hawaii, Sydney, Bangkok, and Fiji.

Once the backpackers are in New Zealand, then the advertising really starts. KE uses people called 'street fighters' — backpackers who hand out brochures at railway terminals and bus stations throughout the gateway cities of Auckland and Christchurch. They also spread the word through backpacker hostels. KE prefers recruiting backpackers who have had the "Experience" as they are informed, motivated, and credible communicators who can sell the KE service better than anyone else. KE, it seems, really does fight for every customer they get.

The distinctive branding that KE uses on their leaflets and brochures certainly helps get their advertisements noticed. *Exhibits 3* and *4* show their new brand logo and ad execution launched a few years ago. Their brand research revealed a profile of their target market which helped to shape their new brand:

> 18 to 35-year-old men and women. They have a sense of anticipation; they crave the unknown and are seeking total adventure. The thought of meeting new people is an essential criteria in their choice of holiday... They spend time wondering what the dynamic of the group might

Exhibit 3 Kiwi Experience logo

Exhibit 4 An advertisement from Kiwi Experience

be, and the 'unknown' is a thrill for them. They are free of the day-to-day rat race and they yearn to be their hedonistic selves. Each day is a new feeling, a new experience... There is little time for thinking on this holiday, only time for doing! These men and women love a laugh — they love the sensation of not taking anything too seriously (there will be other times in their life when they will have to be grown-up)... Right now life is about living — to the max.

KE also holds slide shows in backpackers' hostels in Auckland and Christchurch to persuade consumers who are still unsure about which mode of transport to use around New Zealand. These slide shows are an attempt to make the service which KE offers more tangible, and to reduce the perceived risk customers may have about taking the trip.

KE also creates their own propaganda letters, called "Bullsheets", which they send to their major booking agents in New Zealand. This enables agents to be better informed about the service KE offers. Finally, KE tries to ensure their service is mentioned in popular travel guides such as *Lonely Planet*, which is widely read by backpackers (although the most recent write-up of Kiwi Experience was less than complimentary).

KE ensures that word-of-mouth will be positive by monitoring the performance of their service at all times. KE does this by surveying customers on every single bus. One of the directors and the operations manager will read these surveys so as to monitor what is happening. They then use these surveys to improve their service to the marketplace. Although their core experience has basically remained the same, they continually try and add value to their service.

This strategy has worked, says Neil Geddes:

We have always had a strong and loyal customer following that is proud to have traveled with us, and proud to tell other people about KE. That is the one good thing about the backpacker market, they enjoying giving good information to other travelers. We rely on a huge rate of first time users and we achieve that by having good word-of-mouth.

In essence, KE attempts to create positive word-of-mouth by always ensuring they offer a consistently high quality of service.

COMPETITION

"There goes our rivals," screamed Rob, as another bus whisked past the KE bus as they approached Franz Joseph Glacier. A huge "Boooo" was released from the passengers and various faces were pulled as the competition disappeared in the distance. "They weren't hanging about," stated Rory. "They have got to get back in Auckland as soon as possible, no time to look at the scenery!" replied Rob. "Yeah right, it is not as if it's important or anything," laughed Rory.

The competition KE faces comes from many places. Direct competition comes from another national backpacker coach services, several 'regional' backpacker buses, and other tour buses and coach services that travel around New Zealand. In the past, KE's single biggest competition was the alternative national backpacking bus, Magic Bus. This bus service was created by the national coach company whose market had been diminished by the introduction of KE in 2013. However, KE purchased Magic Bus and now, KE dominates the market even more.

However, a new national competitor has emerged, Stray Bus. This new competition emerged in the absence of Magic Bus. Their target market is slightly older with the trips slightly longer than KE's, and is less of a party bus although overall, their trips are very similar. *Exhibit 5* shows a comparison of some of the similar trips and prices the two companies offer. The debate about which bus company to take, even how to travel around New Zealand, is a heated one amongs travelers. See http://backpackercompare.com/nz-backpacker-bus/ for updated discussion on Stray Bus versus KE!

Exhibit 5 Kiwi Experience and Stray Bus: Comparison of trips and prices for 2015

Company	Pass	Length of Trip	Price in $NZ
Kiwi Experience	All of New Zealand	25	1,895
Stray Bus	All of New Zealand	30	1,995
Kiwi Experience	Auckland to Christchurch	22	1,696
Stray Bus	Auckland to Christchurch	21	1,455

The other backpacking bus services that exist operate in other very specific regions of New Zealand; there are currently three of these in operation. Most of these bus services were in existence before KE was created. Since the introduction of KE, and the competition that followed, these buses have been hit badly as passengers have favored a national bus pass over a regional one.

The third type of competition comes from other national bus companies that either offer express services to different points in New Zealand, or specific tours around New Zealand that do not allow the passenger to get on and off the bus wherever they desire. These buses pose a threat to KE, but a smaller one compared to the backpacking buses as they tend to attract different market segments.

The fourth type of competition comes from other modes of transport that can be taken around New Zealand. The main sources of this type of competition are rental campervans and cars, especially in the winter when a large number of unused cars and campervans are 'dumped' into the market. However, customers with different psychographic, behavioral, and demographic (particularly in terms of income) variables are likely to use rental cars or campervans compared to those types of people who would use backpacker buses.

The domestic airlines in New Zealand are not a large threat to KE as it is a relatively small country; they really only pose a threat over longer distances. In fact, KE has attempted to overcome any possible threat from the airlines by creating strategic alliances with them. For example, one of the national passes KE offers includes an Air New Zealand flight from Christchurch to Auckland. KE also offers other similar passes. The railway network in New Zealand offers little competition as it is limited in its coverage.

The final form of competition to Kiwi Experience is from other countries. Most travelers have a limited time to spend on holiday and must therefore make decisions about where to spend their time. In this case, New Zealand competes with countries like Australia, the US, Fiji, Thailand, and most recently South Africa, which has become a larger threat. Staff at KE are aware they must promote New Zealand as well as KE itself.

One of KE's major appeals is the enormous amount of paid excursions and activities that are on offer. From swimming with dolphins to aerobatic flights, the list is endless. By purchasing a KE bus ticket, a passenger is also entitled to discounts on many activities throughout New Zealand.

The activities offered on the KE are important to the organization for a variety of reasons. First, it helps KE differentiate itself from other competitors, since some activities and discounts are exclusive to KE. This is one way that KE attempts to exceed the expectations customers may have, even before the start of the trip. Secondly, backpackers are usually adventurers who are looking for excitement and activities that will challenge them. By offering these activities, KE is fulfilling these customer needs. Finally, these activities also provide an additional source of revenue, since KE is paid a commission for bringing passengers to these activities by the service operator. This enables KE to earn incremental income from their passengers.

One risk for KE is that these activities do not always match or offer the same quality of service that KE offers. If an activity that is offered turns out to be of low quality, it will reflect poorly on KE since they recommended it. Therefore, it is important that KE ensures that a constant (excellent) standard of quality is maintained so as to protect their brand image. Neil Geddes states how KE attempts to achieve this:

> We assess every single activity that we offer, and we monitor their performance continuously. We ask questions on a customer questionnaire regarding the paid excursions they undertook. We also ensure every activity is up to adequate safety standards, beyond those of legal requirements, and we get feedback from our drivers on the quality of these activities.

ADVENTURE ACTIVITIES

Rory's face was white as he approached the bus. "Are you ready to go?" asked Rob. "Just about, the skydiving was incredible, but I feel a bit dizzy," replied Rory. "Wait until you do the bungee in Queenstown, then you'll know what dizzy means," Rob stated. "No thanks," said Rory, "I think I've had enough excitement to last me a lifetime."

MEMORABILIA

"Okay, everyone, squeeze in together!" shouted the photographer along the Queenstown waterfront. All the passengers on the KE bus shuffled together to ensure they all appeared in the photo. "Rob, jump in at the front!" shouted Rory, "We can't have a group photograph without you!" Rob was reluctantly pushed into the photograph, and the picture was taken. Queues quickly formed to order a copy of the photo (*Exhibit 6*).

Exhibit 6 A recent Kiwi Experience group photo from Queenstown

Souvenirs and memories of the KE trip are a small but important part of KE. Not only do they provide additional revenue for the organization, they are also positive reminders of the KE trip, which hopefully will generate loyalty and positive word-of-mouth for a long time. Memorabilia can take the form of T-shirts, sweatshirts, baseball caps, and group photographs.

FLEXIBILITY AND VALUE FOR MONEY

"I'm going to leave the bus here in Queenstown," stated Rory to Rob. "A group of us are going to hang around here for a few weeks, and take in the amazing scenery." "Great idea," said Rob. "Make sure you book yourself on the bus; one comes through here every day in the summer." "Thanks for a great time," added Rory, "Maybe you'll be driving the next bus we catch!"

If there is one thing that the management of KE constantly strives for, it is greater frequency of its bus services. This is because they have realized that the more often the buses operate, the more flexible their service becomes. This increases its attractiveness to potential customers. KE offers daily departures for about four months of the year (from January to April) and four to five times a week throughout the rest of the year (although some of the more off-beat routes run less frequently). However, KE has learned to stay flexible and change their departure dates quickly. As they are in a high-volume, low-margin business, they must always be fluid in the way they operate. This has sometimes led to customers being stuck in various places for longer times than they had planned.

One way this flexibility is created is through the reservation system, which can tell KE where their customers are, where they got off the bus, and for how long. This enables customer flows to be managed effectively and ensures that the buses are as full as possible. This is important to KE as it only makes any significant amount of profit on the last 15% of their business. This is due to the fact that they work on very fine breakevens, which are significantly higher than traditional package tours. The reservation system is not faultless though, and every now and then, overbooking and underbooking occur (where they tell a backpacker the bus is full when in fact, it is not).

Market research has shown that value for money is the third most important aspect of the KE trip. The price of the tickets, along with the activities offered, and the flexibility and the quality of the service means that many backpackers often feel they are obtaining value from KE. To date, KE has managed to maintain this perception, and it is the one of the fundamental reasons for KE's success.

However, KE does not intend to stand still. Neil Geddes knows that in order to stay ahead of the competition, they must always improve their service offering:

> We are our own biggest threat, being seen as mainstream, or not leading edge, or by becoming a service that is perceived as not being for independent travelers. We must continually move with the market to ensure we offer the best possible experience for our customers.

The challenges for KE are clear and present. They need to be seen as leading edge but not mainstream. They also need to ensure they avoid being labeled a "booze bus", which its competitor Contiki suffers from. Finding high-quality bus drivers is always a constant source of worry, as is the reservation system.

"Hey, Rory!" shouted Rob, as Rory walked toward his backpackers. "Did you ever work out the answer to your question?" Rory turned around and looked puzzled. "What question?" he said. "Oh, you mean the one about why Kiwi Experience is so successful?"

"That's it! Did you ever work it out?" asked Rob. "Yeah I think I did... no, I know I did," Rory said forcefully. "It's just difficult to express it all, maybe one day I'll put it down on paper," he stated.

"Well, don't forget to mention me if you ever do," laughed Rob.

Study Questions

1. How does Kiwi Experience maintain a continual customer focus?

2. What role does culture and leadership play in the success of Kiwi Experience?

3. Brainstorm as to how other service companies might get customers to pay a more active role (rather than passive) in the service experience.

The Accra Beach Hotel: Block Booking of Capacity during a Peak Period

Sheryl E. Kimes and Jochen Wirtz

Cherita Howard, sales manager for the Accra Beach Hotel, a 175-room hotel on the Caribbean island of Barbados, was debating what to do about a request from the West Indies Cricket Board. The Board wanted to book a large block of rooms more than six months ahead during several of the hotel's busiest times, and was asking for a discount. In return, it promised to promote the Accra Beach in all its advertising materials and television broadcasts as the host hotel for the upcoming West Indies Cricket Series, an important international sporting event.

THE HOTEL

The Accra Beach Hotel and Resort had a prime beachfront location on the south coast of Barbados, just a short distance from the airport and the capital city of Bridgetown. Located on 3½ acres of tropical landscape and fronting one of the best beaches on Barbados, the hotel featured rooms offering panoramic views of the ocean, pool, or island.

The centerpiece of its lush gardens was the large swimming pool, which had a shallow bank for lounging as well as a swim-up bar. In addition, there was a squash court and a fully equipped gym. Golf was also available only 15 minutes away at the Barbados Golf Club, with which the hotel was affiliated.

The Accra Beach had two restaurants and two bars, as well as extensive banquet and conference facilities. It offered state-of-the-art conference facilities to local, regional, and international corporate clientele, and had hosted a number of large summits in recent years. Three conference rooms, which could be configured in a number of ways, served as the setting for large corporate meetings, training seminars, product displays, dinners, and wedding receptions. A business center provided guests with Internet access, faxing capabilities, and photocopying services.

Exhibit 1 Beach view of the Accra Beach Hotel

Note: Certain data have been disguised. Unless otherwise indicated, all currencies are in US dollars.

Exhibit 2 Pool view of The Accra Beach Hotel

The hotel's 141 standard rooms were categorized into three groups — Island View, Pool View, and Ocean View — and there were also 24 Ocean View Junior Suites, four two-bedroom and six Penthouse Suites, each decorated in tropical pastel prints and handcrafted furniture. All rooms were equipped with cable/satellite TV, air-conditioning, ceiling fans, hairdryer, coffee percolator, direct-dial telephone, bathtub/shower and a balcony.

Standard rooms were configured with either a king-size bed or two twin beds in the Island and Ocean View categories, while the Pool Views had two double beds. The eight Penthouse Suites and four two-bedroom Suites, which all offered ocean views, contained all the features listed for the standard rooms as well as added comforts. They were built on two levels, featuring a living room with a bar area on the third floor of the hotel and a bedroom accessed by an internal stairway on the fourth floor. These suites also had a bathroom containing a Jacuzzi, shower stall, double vanity basin, and a skylight.

The 24 Junior Suites were fitted with a double bed or two twin beds, as well as a living room area with a sofa that converted to another bed.

HOTEL PERFORMANCE

The Accra Beach enjoyed a relatively high occupancy rate, with the highest occupancy rates achieved from January through March and the lowest generally during the summer (*Exhibit 3*). Their average rate followed a

Exhibit 3 Accra Beach Hotel Monthly Occupancy Rate

Year	Month	Occupancy
2 Years Ago	January	87.7%
2 Years Ago	February	94.1%
2 Years Ago	March	91.9%
2 Years Ago	April	78.7%
2 Years Ago	May	76.7%
2 Years Ago	June	70.7%
2 Years Ago	July	82.0%
2 Years Ago	August	84.9%
2 Years Ago	September	64.7%
2 Years Ago	October	82.0%
2 Years Ago	November	83.8%
2 Years Ago	December	66.1%
Last Year	January	87.6%
Last Year	February	88.8%
Last Year	March	90.3%
Last Year	April	82.0%
Last Year	May	74.7%
Last Year	June	69.1%
Last Year	July	76.7%
Last Year	August	70.5%
Last Year	September	64.7%
Last Year	October	71.3%
Last Year	November	81.7%
Last Year	December	72.1%

similar pattern, with the highest room rates ($150 to $170) being achieved from December through March but relatively low rates ($120) during the summer months (*Exhibit 4*). The hotel's RevPAR (revenue per available room — a product of the occupancy rate times the average room rate) showed even more variation, with RevPARs exceeding $140 from January through March, but falling to less than $100 from June through October (*Exhibit 5*). The rates on the Penthouse suites ranged from $310 to $395, while those on the junior suites ranged from $195 to $235.

Exhibit 4 Accra Beach Hotel Average Daily Room Rate

Year	Month	Average Room Rate (in US$)
2 Years Ago	January	$159.05
2 Years Ago	February	$153.73
2 Years Ago	March	$157.00
2 Years Ago	April	$153.70
2 Years Ago	May	$144.00
2 Years Ago	June	$136.69
2 Years Ago	July	$122.13
2 Years Ago	August	$121.03
2 Years Ago	September	$123.45
2 Years Ago	October	$129.03
2 Years Ago	November	$141.03
2 Years Ago	December	$152.87
Last Year	January	$162.04
Last Year	February	$167.50
Last Year	March	$158.44
Last Year	April	$150.15
Last Year	May	$141.79
Last Year	June	$136.46
Last Year	July	$128.49
Last Year	August	$128.49
Last Year	September	$127.11
Last Year	October	$132.76
Last Year	November	$141.86
Last Year	December	$151.59

Note: Includes standard rooms and suites.

Exhibit 5 Accra Beach Hotel Revenue per Available Room (RevPAR)

Year	Month	Revenue per Available Room (in US$)
2 Years Ago	January	$139.49
2 Years Ago	February	$144.66
2 Years Ago	March	$144.28
2 Years Ago	April	$120.96
2 Years Ago	May	$110.45
2 Years Ago	June	$96.64
2 Years Ago	July	$100.15
2 Years Ago	August	$102.75
2 Years Ago	September	$79.87
2 Years Ago	October	$105.80
2 Years Ago	November	$118.18
2 Years Ago	December	$101.05
Last Year	January	$141.90
Last Year	February	$148.67
Last Year	March	$143.02
Last Year	April	$123.12
Last Year	May	$105.87
Last Year	June	$94.23
Last Year	July	$98.55
Last Year	August	$90.59
Last Year	September	$82.24
Last Year	October	$94.62
Last Year	November	$115.89
Last Year	December	$109.24

Note: RevPAR refers to revenue per available room and is computed by multiplying the room occupancy rate (Exhibit 1) with the average room rate (Exhibit 2).

The hotel has traditionally promoted itself as a resort destination, but in the last few years, it has been promoting its convenient location and has therefore attracted many business customers. Cherita works extensively with tour operators and corporate travel managers. The majority of hotel guests were corporate clients from companies such as Barbados Cable & Wireless, and the Caribbean International Banking Corporation (*Exhibit 6*). The composition of hotel guests had changed drastically over the past few years. Traditionally, the hotel's clientele had been dominated by tourists from the UK and Canada, but in the past few years, the percentage of corporate customers had increased dramatically. The majority of corporate customers come for business meetings with local companies. The Accra Beach Hotel has twice been named "Hotel of the Year" by the Barbados Hotel Association.

Sometimes, guests who were on vacation (particularly during the winter months) felt uncomfortable finding themselves surrounded by business people. As one vacationer puts it, "There's just something weird about being on vacation and going to the beach and then seeing suit-clad business people chatting on their cell phones." However, the hotel achieved a higher average room rate from business guests than vacationers, and had found the volume of corporate business to be much more stable than that from tour operators and individual guests.

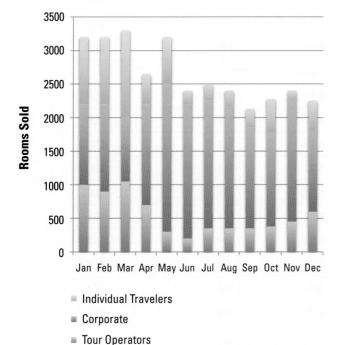

Exhibit 6 Accra Beach Hotel – Market Segments

THE WEST INDIES CRICKET BOARD

Cherita Howard, the hotel's sales manager, had been approached by the West Indies Cricket Board (WICB) about the possibility of the Accra Beach Hotel serving as the host hotel for next spring's West Indies Cricket Home Series, an important international sporting event among cricket-loving nations. The location of this event rotated among several different Caribbean nations, and Barbados would be hosting the next one, which would feature visiting teams from India and New Zealand.

Cherita and Jon Martineau, general managers of the hotel, both thought the marketing exposure associated with hosting the teams would be very beneficial for the hotel, but were concerned about accepting the business as they knew from past experience that many of the desired dates were usually very busy days for the hotel. They were sure the rate that the WICB was willing to pay would be lower than the average rate of $140–$150 they normally achieved during these times. In contrast to regular guests, who could usually be counted upon to have a number of meals at the hotel, team members and officials would probably be less likely to dine at the hotel as they would be on a per diem budget. Also, they worried about how the hotel's other guests might react to the presence of the cricket teams. Still, the marketing potential for the hotel was substantial. The WICB had promised to list the Accra Beach as the host hotel in all promotional materials and during its televised matches.

The West Indies Home Series was divided into three parts, and each would require bookings at the Accra Beach Hotel. The first part pitted the West Indies team against the Indian team and would run from April 24 to May 7. The second part featured the same two teams and would run from May 27 to May 30. The final part showcased the West Indies team against the New Zealand team and would run from June 17 to June 26.

The WICB wanted 50 standard rooms for the duration of each part and was willing to pay $110 per night per room. They also specified that each team had to be housed on a single floor of the hotel. In addition, the WICB insisted that laundry service for team uniforms (cricket teams typically wear all-white clothing) and practice gear be provided at no additional charge for all team members. Cherita estimated that it will cost the hotel about $20 per day if they can do the laundry in-house, but about $200 per day if they have to send it to an outside source.

Cherita called Ferne Armstrong, the reservations manager of the hotel, and asked her what she thought. Like Cherita, Ferne was concerned about the possible displacement of higher-paying customers, but offered to do further investigation into the expected room sales and associated room rates for the desired dates. Since the dates were over six months in the future, Ferne had not yet developed forecasts. However, she was able to provide data on room sales and average room rates from the same days of the previous year (*Exhibit 7*).

Soon after Cherita returned to her office to analyze the data, she was interrupted by a phone call from the head of the WICB wanting to know the status of his request. She promised to have an answer for him before the end of the day. As soon as she hung up, Jon Martineau called and chatted about the huge marketing potential of being the host hotel.

Cherita shook her head and wondered, "What should I do?"

Exhibit 7 Standard Room Sales and Average Daily Room Rates for Same Periods in Previous Year

Date of WICB Home Series	Standard Rooms Sold in Last Year During the Same Period	Average Daily Room Rate (ADR) in US$
Part 1		
4/24	141	$129
4/25	138	$120
4/26	135	$128
4/27	134	$135
4/28	123	$133
4/29	128	$124
4/30	141	$119
5/1	141	$124
5/2	141	$121
5/3	139	$122
5/4	112	$118
5/5	78	$126
5/6	95	$130
5/7	113	$138
Part II		
5/27	99	$131
5/28	114	$132
5/29	114	$136
5/30	125	$136
Part III		
6/17	124	$125
6/18	119	$122
6/19	112	$126
6/20	119	$111
6/21	125	$110
6/22	116	$105
6/23	130	$106
6/24	141	$101
6/25	141	$110
6/26	125	$115

Note: ADR excludes VAT.

Study Questions

1. What factors lead to variations in demand for rooms at a hotel such as the Accra Beach?

2. Identify the various market segments currently served by the hotel. What are the pros and cons of seeking to serve customers from several segments?

3. What are the key considerations facing the hotel as it reviews the booking requests from the West Indies Cricket Board[1]?

4. What action should Cherita Howard take and why?

---

1 For simplification of calculations, assume that each room will hold only one occupant. i.e., 50 rooms equate to 50 cricket players.

Aussie Pooch Mobile

Lorelle Frazer

After creating a mobile service that washes dogs outside their owners' homes, a young entrepreneur has successfully franchised the concept. Her firm now has almost 200 franchises in many parts of Australia, as well as up to 30 in other countries. She and her management team are debating how best to plan future expansion.

Elaine and Paul Beale drew up in their four-wheel drive outside 22 Ferndale Avenue, towing a bright blue trailer with red and white lettering. As Aussie Pooch Mobile franchisees whose territory covered four suburbs of Brisbane, Australia, they were having a busy day. It was only 1.00 p.m., and they had already washed and groomed 16 dogs at 12 different houses. Now they were at their last appointment — a 'pooch party' of 10 dogs at Number 22, where five other residents of the street had arranged to have their dogs washed on a biweekly basis.

Prior to their arrival outside the house, there had been ferocious growling and snarling from a fierce-looking Rottweiler. But when the animal caught sight of the brightly colored trailer, he and two other dogs in the yard bounded forward eagerly to the chain link fence, in a flurry of barking and wagging tails.

Throughout the residential areas of Brisbane and in a number of other Australian cities, dogs of all shapes and sizes were being washed and groomed by Aussie Pooch Mobile franchisees. By mid-2015, the company had grown to more than 165 franchisees, and claimed to be "Australia's premier mobile dog wash and care company". A key issue facing its managing director, Christine Taylor, and members of the management team was how to plan and shape future expansion (*Exhibit 1*).

FOUNDING AND EXPANSION

Located in Burpengary, Queensland, just north of Brisbane, Aussie Pooch Mobile Pty Ltd. (APM) was

Exhibit 1 Chris Taylor with dogs

founded in 1991 by Christine Taylor, then aged 22. Taylor had learned customer service early, working in her parents' bait and tackle shop from the age of eight. Growing up in an environment with dogs and horses as pets, she knew she wanted to work with animals, and learned dog grooming skills from working in a local salon. At 16, Taylor left school and began her own grooming business on a part-time basis, using a bathtub in the family garage. Since she was still too young to drive, her parents would take her to pick up the dogs from their owners. She washed and groomed animals at home and then returned them.

Once Taylor had learned to drive and bought her own car, she decided to take her service to the customers. So she went mobile, creating a trailer in which the dogs could be washed outside their owners' homes, and naming the fledgling venture "The Aussie Pooch Mobile". Soon, it became a full-time job. Eventually, she found she had more business than she could handle alone, so she hired assistants. The next step was to add a second trailer. Newly married, she and her husband David McNamara ploughed their profits into the purchase of additional trailers and gradually expanded until they had six mobile units.

The idea of franchising came to Taylor when she found herself physically constrained by a difficult pregnancy:

> *David would go bike riding or head to the coast and have fun with the jet ski and I was stuck at home and felt like I was going nuts, because I'm a really active person. I was hungry for information on how to expand the business, so I started researching other companies and reading heaps of books and came up with franchising as the best way to go, since it would provide capital and also allow a dedicated group of small business people to help expand the business further.*

As existing units were converted from employees to franchisee operations, Taylor noticed they quickly became about 20% more profitable. Initially, APM focused on Brisbane and the surrounding region of southeast Queensland. Subsequently, it expanded into New South Wales and South Australia in 1995; Canberra, Australian Capital Territory (ACT) in 1999, and Victoria in 2000 (*Exhibit 2*). Expansion into Western Australia came in mid-2004.

In 1996, a New Zealand division of the firm was launched in Tauranga, a small city 200 kilometers southeast of Auckland, under the name Kiwi Pooch Mobile. In 2000, Taylor expanded operations into New Caledonia through a master franchise agreement, launching "La Pooch Mobile". In 2001, Aussie Pooch Mobile was launched in the UK, beginning with a town in northern England. Soon, there were four operators under a master franchisee. The following year saw the official launch of The Pooch Mobile Malaysia, also under a master franchisee. When setting up the company's presence in

the US in 2006, Taylor offered the master franchise to a top performing Australian master franchisee to provide them with further opportunities to grow.

By mid-2015, the company had 167 mobile units in Australia, with 60 located in Queensland, 52 in New South Wales, 19 in Victoria, 14 in South Australia, 14 in Western Australia, and eight in the Australian Capital Territory. The Aussie Pooch Mobile group bathed more than 20,000 dogs each month, and had an annual turnover of approximately $7.5 million.

APM was a member of the Franchise Council of Australia and complied with the Franchising Code of Conduct. The management team consisted of Christine Taylor as managing director and David McNamara as director responsible for overseeing trailer design and systems support. Each state had its own manager and training team. The central support office also housed staff who provided further assistance to managers and franchisees.

APM's expansion benefitted from the leverage provided by several master franchisees, who had obtained the rights to work a large territory and sell franchises within it. Said Taylor:

> *I look at the business as if it's my first child. I see it now starting to come of age where it wants to go alone, but still needs me to hold its hand a little bit, whereas initially it needed me there the whole time. With the support staff we have in place, the business is now gaining the support structure it needs to work without me. This is what I am aiming towards. I appreciate that a team of people can achieve much more than one person alone.*

THE SERVICE CONCEPT

Aussie Pooch Mobile specialized in bringing its dog washing services to customers' homes. Dogs were washed in a hydrobath installed in a specially designed trailer, which was parked in the street. The trailer had partially open sides and a roof to provide protection from sun and rain (*Exhibit 3*). Apart from flea control products and a few grooming aids, APM did not attempt to sell dog food and other pet supplies initially. The company had resisted the temptation to diversify into other fields to focus on their niche in the dog bathing industry. "We did not want to be a jack of all trades because you'll never be good at anything," declared Taylor. "We now have an exclusive

Exhibit 2 APM expanded into the different states in Australia

Exhibit 3 Dog trailer image

range of products that customer demand has driven us to providing, but we still work closely with vets and pet shops, and are by no means a pet shop on wheels. We are more like a specialist dog care service that provides needed items with professional advice."

In contrast to retail pet service stores, where customers brought their animals to the store or kennel, APM brought the service to customers' homes, with the trailer parked outside on the street. The use of hydrobath equipment, in which warm, pressurized water was pumped through a shower head, enabled operators to clean dogs more thoroughly than would be possible with a garden hose. The bath was designed to rid the dog of fleas and ticks, improve its skin condition as well as clean its coat and eliminate smells. Customers supplied water and electrical power.

The fees paid by customers varied from $22 to $70 per dog, depending on breed and size, condition of coat and skin, behavior, and geographic location, with discounts for multiple animals at the same address. At 'pooch parties', a concept developed at APM, the homeowner acting as host typically received a discount on their dog wash at the discretion of the operator. Additional services, for which an extra fee was charged, included aromatherapy baths, doggy facials, and doggy massages. These services ranged from $4 to $10. Additional dog grooming and clipping was available for $10 to $50 per dog depending on the breed and condition of the animal.

Operators also offered free advice to customers about their dogs' diet and health care, including issues such as ticks and skin problems. They encouraged customers to have their dogs bathed on a regular basis. Most customers made appointments once every two or four weeks.

Exhibit 3

Services offered in 1990	Services offered in 2015
Hydrobath	Hydrobath
Brush	Brush
Nail cut	Nail cut
Ear Clean	Ear Clean
Eye clean	Eye clean
Chamois dry	Chamois dry
Deodorise	Deodorise
Own brand solutions	Own brand solutions — expanded
	Blow Dry
	Retail own brand products
	Retail products
	Medicated washes
	Worming
	Massage for dogs
	Aromatherapy for dogs
	Doggy Facials
	Clipping (hair cutting)

A SATISFIED CUSTOMER

The process of bathing a dog involved a sequence of carefully coordinated actions, as exemplified by Elaine Beal's treatment of Zak the Rottweiler. "Hello my darling, who's a good boy?" crooned Elaine as she patted the enthusiastic dog, placed him on a leash, and led him out through the gate to the footpath on that warm, sunny day. Paul busied himself connecting hoses and electrical cords to the house, while Elaine began back-combing Zak's coat in order to set it up for the water to get underneath. She then led the now placid dog to the hydrobath inside the trailer, where he sat patiently while she removed his leash and clipped him to a special collar in the bath for security. Meanwhile, the water had been heating to the desired temperature.

Over the next few minutes, Elaine bathed the dog, applied a medicated herbal shampoo to his coat, and rinsed him thoroughly with the pressure-driven hose. After releasing

Zak from the special collar and reattaching his leash, she led him out of the hydrobath and onto the footpath, where she wrapped him in a chamois cloth and dried him. Next, she cleaned the dog's ears and eyes with disposable baby wipes, all the time continuing to talk soothingly to him. She checked his coat and skin to ensure there were no ticks or skin problems, gave his nails a quick clip, and sprayed a herbal conditioner and deodorizer onto Zak's now gleaming coat and brushed it in. Returning Zak to the yard and removing the leash, Elaine patted him and gave him a large biscuit, specially formulated to protect the animal's teeth.

THE AUSTRALIAN MARKET

Australia's population of 23.7 million in 2015 was small in relation to the country's vast land area of 7.7 million km². A federal nation, Australia was divided into six states — New South Wales (NSW), Victoria, Queensland, South Australia, Western Australia, and the island of Tasmania — as well as two territories: the large but thinly populated Northern Territory, and the small Australian Capital Territory (ACT), which contained the federal capital, Canberra, and its suburbs. The average annual earning for employed persons was $77,000.

With much of the interior of the continent uninhabitable and many other areas inhospitable to permanent settlement, most of the Australian population was concentrated in a narrow coastal band running clockwise from Brisbane on the southeast coast through Sydney and Melbourne, to Adelaide, the capital of South Australia. Some 2,700 kilometers (1,600 miles) to the west lay Perth, known as the most isolated city in the world. A breakdown of the population by state and territory is shown in *Exhibit 4*. The northern half of the country was in the tropics, Brisbane and Perth enjoyed a sub-tropical climate, and the remaining major cities had a temperate climate. Melbourne was known for its sharp fluctuations in temperature.

There were about 3.4 million domestic dogs in the country in 2009, and approximately 36% of the nation's eight million households owned at least one. Western Australia had the lowest proportion of dogs per population, while Tasmania had the highest. In 2011, it was estimated that Australians spent an estimated $3.6 billion on dog-related goods and services, of which 30% went to dog food, 37% to veterinary services, 15% to dog products and equipment, and 17% to other services, including washing and grooming (*Exhibit 5*).

Exhibit 4 Population of Australia by State and Territory, March 2011

State/Territory	Population (000)
New South Wales	7,618.2
Victoria	5,938.1
Queensland	4,779.4
South Australia	1,698.6
Western Australia	2,591.6
Tasmania	516.6
Australian Capital Territory	390.8
Northern Territory	244.6
Australia Total	**23,781.2**

Source

Australian Bureau of Statistics 2015.

Exhibit 5 Distribution of Consumer Expenditures on Dog-related Goods and Services 2010

Product/Service	Allocation
Dog Food	31%
Vet Charges	44%
Dog Services	21%
Pet Purchases	4%
Total dog-related expenditure	**$3.6 billion**

Source

Australian Companion Animal Council, '*The Pet Care Industry to the Australian Economy: 7th Edition 2010*' Report.

FRANCHISING IN AUSTRALIA

Australia was home to a number of internationally known franchise operators, including Hertz Rent-a-Car, Avis, McDonald's, KFC, Pizza Hut, Subway, Kwik Kopy, and Snap-on Tools. In contrast, most Burger King outlets operated under the name Hungry Jack's, an acquired Australian chain with significant brand equity.

By the beginning of the 21st century, the Australian franchising sector had reached a stage of early maturity. McDonald's, KFC, and Pizza Hut opened their first outlets in Australia in the 1970s. These imported systems were followed by many home-grown business format franchises such as Just Cuts (hairdressing), Snap Printing, Eagle Boys Pizza, and VIP Home Services, all of which grew into large domestic systems and then expanded internationally, principally to New Zealand and Southeast Asia.

In 2014, Australia boasted more than 1,100 business-format franchise systems holding an estimated 79,000 outlets. Although the US had many more systems and outlets, Australia had more franchisors per capita, reflecting the relative ease of entry into franchising in this country.

Most of the growth in franchising occurred in business format franchising as opposed to product franchising. Business-format franchises provided franchisees with a full business system and the rights to operate under the franchisor's brand name, whereas product franchises merely allowed independent operators to supply a manufacturer's product, such as car dealerships or soft-drink bottlers.

Typically, franchisees were required to pay an upfront franchise fee (averaging $30,000 in service industries and $40,000 in retailing) for the right to operate under the franchise system within a defined geographic area. This initial fee was included in the total start-up cost of the business (ranging from around $89,000 in the service sector to more than $275,000 in the retail industry). In addition, franchisees paid a royalty on all sales, and an ongoing contribution toward advertising and promotional activities designed to build brand awareness and preference. Would-be franchisees who lacked sufficient capital might be able to obtain bank financing against personal assets such as property or an acceptable guarantor.

FRANCHISING TRENDS

The rapid growth of franchising globally had been stimulated in part by demographic trends, including the increase in dual-income families, which had led to greater demand for outsourcing of household services such as lawn mowing, house cleaning, and pet grooming. Some franchise systems offered multiple concepts under a single corporate brand name. For instance, VIP Home Services had separate franchises available in lawn mowing, cleaning, car washing, and rubbish removal. Additional growth came from conversion of existing individual businesses to a franchise format. For instance, Eagle Boys Pizza had often approached local pizza operators and offered them the opportunity to join this franchise. Almost half the franchise systems in Australia were in retail trade (27% non-food and 18% food). Other large and growing industries were administration and support services (15%) and other services (11%), as shown in *Exhibit 6*. Most franchisees were former white-

Exhibit 6 Distribution of Franchise Systems in Australia by Industry

Industry	Percentage
Retail trade	27.1
Accommodation and food services (includes food retail, fast food, coffee shops, etc.)	18.1
Administration and support services (includes travel agencies, office services, domestic and industrial cleaning, gardening services, lawn mowing, etc.)	14.7
Other services (includes personal services, pet services, auto repairs and servicing, IT services, etc.)	10.5
Education and training	6.9
Rental, hire, and real estate services	6.4
Arts and recreation services	3.4
Financial and insurance services	3.3
Professional, scientific and technical	2.9
Construction	2.1
Transport, postal, and warehousing	1.2
Information media and telecommunications	1.0
Healthcare and social assistance	1.0
Wholesale trade	0.6
Manufacturing	0.4
Electricity, gas, water, and waste services	0.4
Total	**100.0**

Source

Franchising Australia 2014, Asia-Pacific Centre for Franchising Excellence, Griffith University.

collar workers or blue-collar supervisors who craved independence and a lifestyle change.

Over the years, Australia's franchising sector had experienced a myriad of regulatory regimes. Finally in 1998, in response to perceived problems in many franchising systems, the federal government introduced a mandatory Franchising Code of Conduct, administered under what is now the *Competition and Consumer Act 2011* (formerly the *Trade Practice Act*). Among other things, the Code required that potential franchisees be given full disclosure about the franchisor's background and operations prior to signing a franchise agreement. In contrast, the franchising sector in the US faced an inconsistent set of regulations that varied from one state to another. In the UK, there were no specific franchising regulations beyond those applying to all corporations operating in designated industries.

Master franchising arrangements had become common in Australian franchise systems. Under master franchising, a local entrepreneur was awarded the rights to subfranchise the system within a specific geographic area, such as an entire state. Because of Australia's vast geographic size, it was difficult for a franchisor to monitor franchisees who were located far from the head office. The solution was to delegate many of the tasks normally handled by the franchisor itself, to master franchisees instead. This made them responsible for recruiting, selecting, training, and monitoring franchisees in their territories as well as overseeing marketing and operations.

Not all franchisees proved successful, and individual outlets periodically failed. The main reasons for failure appeared to be poor choice of location or territory, and a franchisee's own shortcomings. In addition to the technical skills required in a given field, success often hinged on of the franchisees' sales and communication abilities. Disputes in franchising were not uncommon, but could usually be resolved internally without recourse to legal action. The causes of conflict most frequently cited by franchisees related to franchise fees and alleged misrepresentations made by the franchisor. In contract, franchisors cited conflicts based on lack of compliance with the system by franchisees.

FRANCHISING STRATEGY AT AUSSIE POOCH MOBILE

New APM franchisees were recruited through newspaper advertisements and 'advertorials' as well as by word-of-mouth. The concept appealed to individuals who sought to become self-employed on their own. Interested individuals were invited to meet with a representative of the company to learn more. If they wished to proceed further, they had to complete an application form and submit a refundable deposit of $250 to hold a particular area for a maximum of four weeks, during which the applicant could further investigate the characteristics and prospects of the designated territory. This fee was credited to the purchase cost of the franchise if the applicant decided to proceed, or returned if the applicant withdrew the application. A new franchise in 2015 cost $35,820, excluding the federal goods and services tax (GST), (up from $34,700 in 2010, $24,000 in 2002, and $19,500 in 1999). *Exhibit 7* identifies how APM costed out the different elements.

Exhibit 7 Aussie Pooch Mobile: Breakdown of Franchise Purchase Cost

Item		Cost (2015)
Initial training		$2,500.00
Initial franchise fee and documents		803.88
Guaranteed income		4,800.00
Exclusive territory plus trailer registration		10,900.00
Fixtures, fittings, stock, insurance, etc.:		
Aussie Pooch Mobile trailer and hydrobath	$12,064.30	
Consumables (shampoo, conditioner, etc.)	2,000.00	
Retail products	350.00	
Insurance	300.00	14,714.30
Initial advertising		2,000.00
Communications levy		100.00
Total franchise cost (excluding GST)		**$35,818.18**

SELECTION REQUIREMENTS FOR PROSPECTIVE FRANCHISEES

APM had set a minimum educational requirement of passing Year 10 of high school (or equivalent) for prospective franchisees. Taylor noted that successful applicants tended to be outdoors people who shared four characteristics:

> *They are motivated and outgoing. They love dogs, and they want to work for themselves. Obviously, being great with dogs is one part of the business — our franchisees understand that the dog's even an extended member of the customer's family — but it's really important that they can handle the bookwork side of the business as well, because that's basically where your bread and butter is made.*

Other desirable characteristics included people skills and patience, as well as good telephone etiquette. Would-be franchisees also required a valid driver's license, access to a vehicle that was capable of towing a trailer, and the ability to do this type of driving in an urban setting. Originally, Taylor had expected that most franchisees would be relatively young, with parents willing to buy their children a franchise and set them up with a job, but in fact, only about half of all franchisees were aged 21–30; 40% were aged 31–40 and 10% were in their forties or fifties. About 60% were female.

Potential franchisees were offered a trial work period with an operator to see if they liked the job and were suited to the business, including possessing skills with animals and people as well as sufficient physical fitness.

HOW THE FRANCHISE WORKED

In return for the franchise fee, successful applicants received the rights to a geographically defined franchise, typically comprising about 12,000 homes. Franchisees also obtained an APM trailer with all necessary products and solutions to service the first 100 dogs, as well as red uniform shirts and cap, advertising material, and stationery. The trailer was built to industrial grade standards. Its design included many refinements developed by APM in consultation with franchisees to simplify the process of dog washing and enhance the experience for the animals. Operators were required to travel with a mobile phone, which they had to pay for themselves.

In addition to franchised territories, APM had approximately 30 company-owned outlets. These were operated by representatives who leased the territory and equipment and in return, paid APM 25% of the gross weekly revenues (including GST). The reps generally were individuals who either could not currently afford the start-up cost or were evaluated by the company for their suitability as franchisees. Typically, reps either became franchisees within 12 months or have left the company.

ASSISTING FRANCHISEES, OLD AND NEW

The franchisor provided two weeks' pre-opening training for all new franchisees, and representatives also spent time with each one to help them open their new territories. Training topics included operational and business procedures, effective use of the telephone, hydrobathing techniques, dog grooming techniques, and information on dog health and behavior. Franchisees were given a detailed operations manual containing instructions on running the business in accordance with company standards.

To help new franchisees get started, APM placed advertisements in local newspapers for a period of 10 weeks. It also prepared human interest stories for distribution to these newspapers. Facebook and Google AdWords, along with other website advertising, was carried out. Other promotional activities at the time of launch included distributing pamphlets in the territory, and writing to local vets and pet shops to inform them of the business. APM guaranteed new franchisees a weekly income of $600 for the first eight weeks, and paid for a package of insurance policies for six months, after which the franchisee became responsible for the coverage.

Ongoing support by the franchisor included marketing efforts, Facebook networking within their area, monthly newsletters, a telephone hotline service for advice, an insurance package, regular (but brief) field visits, and additional training. If a franchisee fell sick or wished to take a vacation, APM would offer advice on how to best deal with this situation, wherever possible, providing a trained person to help out. It also organized periodic meetings for franchisees in the major metropolitan areas, at which guest presenters spoke on topics relating to franchise operations. Previous guest speakers included veterinarians, natural therapists, pharmacists, and accountants. Once a year, a conference was organized, and they had trade stalls and guest speakers from within the group as well as external speakers. At this conference, any new products, systems, and services were introduced.

To further support individual franchisees, APM formed a Facebook forum, allowing operators to share ideas among themselves, with a team leader keeping an eye on things to ensure this forum remained positive. Each franchisee was assigned to a franchise area development manager (FADM). The FADM facilitated communications between franchisees and the support office. Regular interaction was achieved through face-to-face contact, group meetings, and via phone and email to discuss different issues within the company. The FADM's undertook training twice yearly to help improve systems and communications within the franchise. They were provided with strategies and training to help support their groups to ensure all their KPI's were met.

FEES

In return for these services and support from the franchisors, franchisees paid a royalty fee of 10% of their gross weekly income, in addition to a $34 (including GST) flat fee per week. Prior to 2014, franchisees had paid an advertising levy of 2.5% instead of the flat fee component. Income was reported on a weekly basis and fees had to be paid weekly. In addition to these fees, operating costs for a franchisee included car-related expenses, purchase of consumable products such as shampoo, insurance, telephone, and stationery. *Exhibit 8* shows the average weekly costs that a typical franchisee might expect to incur.

Franchisees included several couples, like the Beales, but Taylor believed that having two operators work together was not really efficient, although it could be companionable. Paul Beal, a retired advertising executive, had other interests and did not always accompany Elaine. Some couples split the work, with one operating three days a week, and the other worked three or even four days. All franchisees were required to be substantially involved in the hands-on running of the business; some had more than one territory and employed additional operators to help them.

Exhibit 8 Average Annual Operating Expenses for an Aussie Pooch Mobile Franchisee based on $55,000 turnover

Expense Categories	Cost
Consumable products	$2,880
Car registration	430
Car insurance	500
Fuel	3,360
Insurances	1,151
Repairs and maintenance	1,104
Phones, stationery, etc.	1,920
Communications levy	624
Franchise royalties	5,500
Flat fee	1,607
Total	$19,076

ADVERTISING AND MARKETING

Aussie Pooch Mobile had a national website and Facebook page, and paid for Google AdWords to promote its national website. It promoted a single telephone number nationwide in Australia, staffed by an answering service 24 hours a day, seven days a week. Customers paid only a local call charge of 25 cents to access this number. They could leave their name and telephone number, which would then be electronically sorted and forwarded via alphanumeric pagers to the appropriate franchisee, who would then return the call to arrange a convenient appointment time. Customers were also able to send a message direct to an operator from the website.

APM offered its franchisees expert advice on local advertising and promotions, and also made promotional products and advertising templates available to franchisees who were also encouraged to setup their own Facebook pages. Other corporate communications activities included maintaining the website, www.aussiepm.com.au; distributing public relations releases to the media; and controlling all aspects of corporate identity such as trailer design, business cards, and uniforms.

"I try to hold the reins pretty tightly on advertising matters," said Taylor. APM's franchise agreement required individual franchisees to submit their plans for promotional activity for corporate approval. She shook her head as she remembered an early disaster, involving an unauthorized campaign by a franchisee who had placed an offer of a free dog wash in a widely distributed coupon book. Unfortunately, this promotion had set no expiration date or geographic restriction, with the result that customers were still presenting the coupon more than a year later, across several different franchise territories.

With APM's approval, some franchisees had developed additional promotional ideas. For example, Elaine and Paul Beal wrote informative articles and human interest stories about dogs for their local newspaper. When a client's dog died, Elaine sent a sympathy card and presented the owner with a small tree to plant in memory of the pet. Franchisees also provided a Pet Report Card to their clients accompanied by a retail promotional flyer.

DEVELOPING A TERRITORY

Obtaining new customers and retaining existing ones was an important aspect of each franchisee's work. The brightly colored trailer often attracted questions from passers-by and presented a useful opportunity to promote the service. Operators could ask satisfied customers to recommend the service to their friends and neighbors. Encouraging owners to increase the frequency of washing their dogs was another way to build business. Knowing that a dog might become lonely when its owner was absent and was liable to develop behavioral problems, Elaine Beal sometimes recommended the acquisition of a 'companion pet'. As Paul remarked, "Having two dogs is not twice the trouble, it halves the problem!"

However, to maximize profitability, franchisees also had to operate as efficiently as possible, minimizing time spent in non-revenue producing activities such as travel, setup, and socializing. As business grew, some franchisees employed additional operators to handle the excess workload, so that the trailer might be in service for extended hours, seven days a week. Eventually, a busy territory might be split, with a portion sold off to a new franchisee.

APM encouraged this practice. The company had found that franchisees reached a comfort zone of about 50 to 80 dogs a week, and then their business stopped growing because they could not physically wash any more dogs. Franchisees could set their own price when selling all or part of a territory, and APM helped them to coordinate the sale. When a territory was split, a franchisee usually was motivated to rebuild the remaining half to its maximum potential.

COMPETITION

Although many dog owners had traditionally washed their animals themselves (or had not even bothered), there was a growing trend towards paying a third party to handle this task. Dog washing services fell into two broad groups. One consisted of fixed-site operations to which dog owners brought their animals for bathing. The locations for these businesses included retail sites in suburban shopping areas, kennels, and service providers' own homes or garages. The second type of competition, which had grown in popularity in recent years, consisted of mobile operations that traveled to customers' homes.

With few barriers to entry, there were numerous dog washing services in most major metropolitan areas. The majority of dog washing services in Australia were believed to be standalone operations, but there were other franchisors in addition to Aussie Pooch Mobile. Of these, the most significant appeared to be Jim's Dogwash and HydroDog.

JIM'S DOGWASH

One of Australia's best-known locally developed franchisors was Melbourne-based Jim's Group, which described itself as providing quality mobile grooming and care for dogs throughout Australia and New Zealand. The company had originated with a mowing service started by Jim Penman in Melbourne in 1982, when he abandoned ideas of an academic career after his PhD thesis was rejected. In 1989, Penman began franchising the service, known as Jim's Mowing, as a way to facilitate expansion. The business grew rapidly, using master franchisees in different regions to recruit and manage individual franchisees. Over the years, an array of other home-related services were launched under the Jim's brand, including Jim's Fencing, Jim's Pool Care, Jim's Cleaning, Jim's Bookkeeping, and Jim's Car Detailing.

Jim's Dogwash made its debut in 1996, employing a bright red, fully enclosed trailer emblazoned with a logo that showed Jim with a dog. It had 57 franchises in Australia, and two franchisees in New Zealand. Jim's expansion strategy had been achieved in part by creating smaller territories than APM, and pricing them relatively inexpensively, in order to stimulate recruitment of new franchisees.

A territory, typically encompassing about 6,000 residences, sold from $13,000 up to $19,000 which included GST. A trailer could be purchased for $18,500 or rented at $400 per month (both including GST). Ongoing franchise fees included a flat monthly royalty (rather than royalties being calculated on a percentage of sales) of $438 including GST; an advertising levy, also set as a flat monthly fee of $165 including GST; and a $7 per lead fee including GST. Jim's fee for washing a dog including blow drying averaged $65 per dog. In recent years, Jim's Dogwash started offering aromatherapy, and also sold pet food and accessories.

BLUE WHEELERS

Another franchised dog washing operation was Blue Wheelers (formerly Hydrodog), based in the Gold Coast, Queensland. Hydrodog commenced operations in 1994 and sold its first franchise in 1996. In 2012, the franchise renamed itself Blue Wheelers and diversified its brand by introducing a new franchise called Dash Dog Wash, which provided a purely dog wash service only. Blue Wheelers continued to offer the full range of dog washing and grooming services. By 2015, Blue Wheelers had 178 franchise units across Australia with one master franchisee operating in Western Australia. Dash Dog Wash was still in the 'puppy' stage of development with only three units operating. The distribution of franchise units across both franchises was broken down as follows: A new Hydrodog franchise unit cost $24,950 (including

State/Territory	Blue Wheelers	Dash Dog Wash
ACT	4	0
New South Wales	51	1
Northern Territory	4	1
Queensland	40	0
South Australia	18	0
Tasmania	3	0
Victoria	36	1
Western Australia	22	0
Total	178	**3**

GST) in 2002, of which $10,800 was accounted for by the initial franchise fee for a 10,000-home territory. By 2011, the franchise fee had increased to $41,950 plus GST; this included the trailer, equipment, launch promotions, and everything a franchisee needed to start their business. The territory size had also changed, with a minimum of 5,000 homes, although most territories included more than that number, and were based on a designated suburb. By 2015, the Blue Wheelers franchise fee was $46,990 based on a minimum of 5,000 homes, and the Dash Dog Wash franchise fee was $29,990 based on 10,000 homes. On average, the company washed about 45,000 dogs per month with average earnings per franchisee between $1,100 and $2,500 per week.

Blue Wheeler's dog grooming services, which included blow drying, ranged in price from $35 to $90. In addition to their dog grooming services, franchisees sold dog food products, including dry biscuits and processed meats (pork, chicken, beef, or kangaroo), as well as dog toys and other accessories. They did not offer aromatherapy, facials, or massages. Both franchises charged franchisees a flat management fee instead of a royalty: $140 (plus GST) per week for Dash Dog Wash and $175 (plus GST) per week for Blue Wheelers.

DEVELOPING A STRATEGY OF GROWTH FOR THE FUTURE

For the directors of Aussie Pooch Mobile, managing continued expansion presented an ongoing challenge. However, as Chris Taylor pointed out, "You can be the largest but you may not be the best. Our focus is on doing a great job and making our franchisees successful."

To facilitate expansion outside its original base of southeast Queensland, APM appointed a franchise sales manager in Sydney for the New South Wales market, and another in Melbourne for both Victoria and South Australia. One question was whether to adopt a formal strategy of appointing master franchisees. Currently, there were master franchises in Queensland (Gold Coast), New South Wales (Wollongong and Campbelltown), and Western Australia.

Also, Taylor had long been attracted to the idea of expanding internationally. In 1996, the company had licensed a franchisee in New Zealand to operate a subsidiary named Kiwi Pooch Mobile. However, there was only one unit operating by early 2002, and she wondered how best to increase this number. Another subsidiary had been established as a master franchise in the French province of New Caledonia, a large island northeast of Australia. Launched in late 2000 under the name of La Pooch Mobile, it had one unit. Another master franchise territory had been established in Malaysia in late 2001, and there were two units operating by 2002.

In 2001, APM had granted exclusive rights for operation in the UK to a British entrepreneur who operated under the name The Pooch Mobile. Thus far, 12 units were operating in the English county of Lincolnshire, 200km (125 miles) north of London. This individual noted that English people traditionally washed their dogs very infrequently, often as little as once every two to three years, but once they had tried The Pooch Mobile, they quickly converted to becoming monthly clients, primarily for the hygiene benefits.

In 2004, the regional master franchisee from the Gold Coast in Queensland moved to Denver, Colorado, to open The Pooch Mobile in the US. The Pooch Mobile has since expanded to Las Vegas and Hawaii. The US market is strong, and dog owners have readily embraced the dog washing concept.

As the company grew, the directors knew it was likely to face increased competition from other providers of dog washing services. But as one successful franchisee remarked: "Competition keeps us on our toes. It's hard being in the lead and maintaining the lead if you haven't got anybody on your tail."

1. How did Christine Taylor succeed in evolving the local dog washing service she developed as a teenager into an international franchise business?

2. Compare and contrast the tasks involved in recruiting new customers and recruiting new franchisees.

3. From a franchisee's perspective, what is the advantage offered by belonging to the APM franchise rather than going it alone?

4. In planning for future expansion, how should Christine Taylor evaluate the market potential of Australia versus that of overseas? What strategies do you recommend and why?

CASE 09 Shouldice Hospital Limited (Abridged)

James Heskett and Roger Hallowell

Two shadowy figures, enrobed and in slippers, walked slowly down the semi-darkened hall of the Shouldice Hospital. They did not notice Alan O'Dell, the hospital's managing director, and his guest. Once they were out of earshot, O'Dell remarked good-naturedly, "By the way they act, you'd think our patients own this place. And while they're here, in a way they do." Following a visit to the five operating rooms, O'Dell and his visitor once again encountered the same pair of patients still engrossed in discussing their hernia operations, which had been performed the previous morning.

HISTORY

An attractive brochure that was recently printed, although neither dated nor distributed to prospective patients, described Dr. Earle Shouldice, the founder of the hospital:

> *Dr. Shouldice's interest in early ambulation stemmed, in part, from an operation he performed in 1932 to remove the appendix from a seven-year-old girl and the girl's subsequent refusal to stay quietly in bed. In spite of her activity, no harm was done, and the experience recalled to the doctor the postoperative actions of animals upon which he had performed surgery. They had all moved about freely with no ill effects.*

By 1940, Shouldice had given extensive thought to several factors that contributed to early ambulation following surgery. Among them were the use of a local anesthetic, the nature of the surgical procedure itself, the design of a facility to encourage movement without unnecessarily causing discomfort, and the post-operative regimen. With these things in mind, he began to develop a surgical technique for repairing hernias[1] that was superior to others; word of his early success generated demand.

Professor James Heskett prepared the original version of this case, "Shouldice Hospital Limited," HBS No. 683-068. This version was prepared jointly by Professor James Heskett and Roger Hallowell (MBA 1989, DBA 1997). HBS cases are developed solely as the basis for class discussion. Cases are not intended to serve as endorsements, sources of primary data, or illustrations of effective or ineffective management.

Dr. Shouldice's medical license permitted him to operate anywhere, even on a kitchen table. However, as more and more patients requested operations, Dr. Shouldice created new facilities by buying a rambling 130-acre estate with a 17,000-square-foot main house in the Toronto suburb of Thornhill. After some years of planning, a large wing was added to provide a total capacity of 89 beds.

Dr. Shouldice died in 1965. At that time, Shouldice Hospital Limited was formed to operate both the hospital and clinical facilities under the surgical direction of Dr. Nicholas Obney. In 1999, Dr. Casim Degani, an internationally recognized authority, became surgeon-in-chief. By 2004, 7,600 operations were performed per year.

THE SHOULDICE METHOD

Only external (vs. internal) abdominal hernias were repaired at Shouldice Hospital. Thus most first-time repairs, "primaries" were straightforward operations requiring about 45 minutes. The remaining procedures involved patients suffering recurrences of hernias

---

1 Most hernias, known as external abdominal hernias, are protrusions of some part of the abdominal contents through a hole or slit in the muscular layers of the abdominal wall, which is supposed to contain them. Well over 90% of these hernias occur in the groin area. Of these, by far the most common are inguinal hernias, many of which are caused by a slight weakness in the muscle layers brought about by the passage of the testicles in male babies through the groin area shortly before birth. Aging also contributes to the development of inguinal hernias. Because of the cause of the affliction, 85% of all hernias occur in males.

previously repaired elsewhere[2]. Many of the recurrences and very difficult hernia repairs required 90 minutes or more.

In the Shouldice method, the muscles of the abdominal wall were arranged in three distinct layers, and the opening was repaired, each layer in turn, by overlapping its margins as the edges of a coat might be overlapped when buttoned. The end result reinforced the muscular wall of the abdomen with six rows of sutures (stitches) under the skin cover, which was then closed with clamps that were later removed. (Other methods might not separate muscle layers, often involved fewer rows of sutures, and sometimes involved the insertion of screens or meshes under the skin.)

A typical first-time repair could be completed with the use of pre-operative sedation (sleeping pill) and analgesic (pain killer) plus a local anesthetic, an injection of Novocain in the region of the incision. This allowed immediate post-operative patient ambulation and facilitated rapid recovery.

The Patients' Experience

Most potential Shouldice patients learned about the hospital from previous Shouldice patients. Although thousands of doctors had referred patients, doctors were less likely to recommend Shouldice because of the generally regarded simplicity of the surgery, often considered a "bread and butter" operation. Typically, many patients had their problem diagnosed by a personal physician, and then contacted Shouldice directly. Many more made this diagnosis themselves.

The process experienced by Shouldice patients depended on whether or not they lived close enough to the hospital to visit the facility to obtain a diagnosis. Approximately 10% of Shouldice patients came from outside the province of Ontario, most of them from the US. Another 60% of patients lived beyond the Toronto area. These out-of-town patients often were diagnosed by mail using the Medical Information Questionnaire shown in *Exhibit 1*. Based on information in the questionnaire, a Shouldice surgeon would determine the type of hernia the respondent had and whether there were signs that some risk might be associated with surgery (for example, an overweight or heart condition, or a patient who had suffered a heart attack or a stroke in the past six months to a year, or whether a general or local anesthetic was required). At this point, a patient was given an operating date and sent a brochure describing the hospital and the Shouldice method. If necessary, a sheet outlining a weight-loss program prior to surgery was also sent. A small proportion was refused treatment, either because they were overweight, represented an undue medical risk, or because it was determined that they did not have a hernia.

Arriving at the clinic between 1.00 p.m. and 3.00 p.m. the day before the operation, a patient joined other patients in the waiting room. He or she was soon examined in one of the six examination rooms staffed by surgeons who had completed their operating schedules for the day. This examination required no more than 20 minutes, unless the patient needed reassurance. (Patients typically exhibited a moderate level of anxiety until their operation was completed.) At this point, it occasionally was discovered that a patient had not corrected his or her weight problem; others might be found not to have a hernia at all. In either case, the patient was sent home.

After checking administrative details, about an hour after arriving at the hospital, the patient was directed to the room number shown on his or her wrist band. Throughout the process, patients were asked to keep their luggage (usually light) with them.

All patient rooms at the hospital were semiprivate, containing two beds. Patients with similar jobs, backgrounds, or interests were assigned to the same room to the extent possible. Upon reaching their rooms, patients busied themselves unpacking, getting acquainted with roommates, shaving themselves in the area of the operation, and changing into pajamas.

At 4.30 p.m., a nurse's orientation provided the group of incoming patients with information about what to expect, including the need for exercise after the operation and the daily routine. According to Alan O'Dell, "Half are so nervous they don't remember much." Dinner was then served, followed by further recreation, and tea and cookies at 9.00 p.m. Nurses emphasized the importance of attendance at that time because it provided an opportunity for pre-operative patients to talk with those whose operations had been completed earlier that same day.

---

2 Based on tracking of patients over more than 30 years, the gross recurrence rate for all operations performed at Shouldice was 0.8%. Recurrence rates reported in the literature for these types of hernia varied greatly. However, one text stated, "In the United States, the gross rate of recurrence for groin hernias approaches 10%."

Patients to be operated on early were awakened at 5.30 a.m. to be given pre-op sedation. An attempt was made to schedule operations for roommates at approximately the same time. Patients were taken to the pre-operation room where the circulating nurse administered Demerol, an analgesic, 45 minutes before surgery. A few minutes prior to the first operation at 7.30 a.m., the surgeon assigned to each patient administered Novocain, a local anesthetic, in the operating room. This was in contrast to the typical hospital procedure in which patients were sedated in their rooms prior to being taken to the operating rooms.

Upon completion of their operation, during which a few patients were "chatty" and fully aware of what was going on, patients were invited to get off the operating table and walk to the post-operation room with the help of their surgeons. According to the Director of Nursing:

> Ninety-nine percent accept the surgeon's invitation. While we use wheelchairs to return them to their rooms, the walk from the operating table is for psychological as well as physiological [blood pressure, respiratory] reasons. Patients prove to themselves that they can do it, and they start their all-important exercise immediately.

Throughout the day after their operation, patients were encouraged by nurses and housekeepers alike to exercise. By 9.00 p.m. on the day of their operations, all patients were ready and able to walk down to the dining room for tea and cookies, even if it meant climbing stairs, to help indoctrinate the new "class" admitted that day. On the fourth morning, patients were ready for discharge.

During their stay, patients were encouraged to take advantage of the opportunity to explore the premises and make new friends. Some members of the staff felt that the patients and their attitudes were the most important element of the Shouldice program. According to Dr. Byrnes Shouldice, son of the founder, a surgeon on the staff, and a 50% owner of the hospital:

> Patients sometimes ask to stay an extra day. Why? Well, think about it. They are basically well to begin with. But they arrive with a problem and a certain amount of nervousness, tension, and anxiety about their surgery. Their first morning here, they're operated on and experience a sense of relief from something that's been bothering them for a long time. They are immediately able to get around, and they've got a three-day holiday ahead of them with a *perfectly good reason to be away from work with no sense of guilt. They share experiences with other patients, make friends easily, and have the run of the hospital. In summer, the most common after-effect of the surgery is sunburn.*

The Nurses' Experience

Thirty-four full-time-equivalent nurses staffed Shouldice each 24-hour period. However, during non-operating hours, only six full-time-equivalent nurses were on the premises at any given time. While the Canadian acute-care hospital average ratio of nurses to patients was 1:4, at Shouldice, the ratio was 1:15. Shouldice nurses spent an unusually large proportion of their time in counseling activities. As one supervisor commented, "We don't use bedpans." According to a manager, "Shouldice has a waiting list of nurses wanting to be hired, while other hospitals in Toronto are short-staffed and perpetually recruiting."

The Doctors' Experience

The hospital employed 10 full-time surgeons and eight part-time assistant surgeons. Two anesthetists were also on site. The anesthetists floated among cases except when general anesthesia was in use. Each operating team required a surgeon, an assistant surgeon, a scrub nurse, and a circulating nurse. The operating load varied from 30 to 36 operations per day. As a result, each surgeon typically performed three or four operations each day.

A typical surgeon's day started with a scrubbing shortly before the first scheduled operation at 7.30 a.m. If the first operation was routine, it usually was completed by 8.15 a.m. At its conclusion, the surgical team helped the patient walk from the room and summoned the next patient. After scrubbing, the surgeon could be ready to operate again at 8.30 a.m. Surgeons were advised to take a coffee break after their second or third operation. Even so, a surgeon could complete three routine operations and a fourth involving a recurrence and still be finished in time for a 12.30 p.m. lunch in the staff dining room.

Upon finishing lunch, surgeons not scheduled to operate in the afternoon examined incoming patients. A surgeon's day ended by 4.00 p.m. In addition, a surgeon could expect to be on call one weekday night in 10 and one weekend in 10. Alan O'Dell commented that the position appealed to doctors who "want to watch their children grow up. A doctor on call is rarely called to the hospital and has regular hours." According to Dr. Obney:

SHOULDICE HOSPITAL

7750 Bayview Avenue
Box 379, Thornhill, Ontario L3T 4A3 Canada
Phone (418) 889-1125

(Thornhill - One Mile North Metro Toronto)

MEDICAL INFORMATION

Patients who live at a distance often prefer their examination, admission and operation to be arranged all on a single visit — to save making two lengthy journeys. The whole purpose of this questionnaire is to make such arrangements possible, although, of course, it cannot replace the examination in any way. Its completion and return will not put you under any obligation.

Please be sure to fill in both sides.

(continued on next page)

This information will be treated as confidential.

FAMILY NAME (Last Name) | FIRST NAME | MIDDLE NAME

STREET & NUMBER (or Rural Route or P.O. Box) | Town/City | Province/State

County | Township | Zip or Postal Code | Birthdate: Month | Day | Year

Telephone Home _____ Work _____ | If none, give neighbour's number _____ | Married or Single | Religion

NEXT OF KIN: Name | Address | Telephone #

INSURANCE INFORMATION: Please give name of Insurance Company and Numbers. | Date form completed

HOSPITAL INSURANCE: (Please bring hospital certificates) | OTHER HOSPITAL INSURANCE

O.H.I.P. Number | BLUE CROSS Number | Company Name / Policy Number

SURGICAL INSURANCE: (Please bring insurance certificates) | OTHER SURGICAL INSURANCE

O.H.I.P. Number | BLUE SHIELD Number | Company Name / Policy Number

WORKMEN'S COMPENSATION BOARD | Approved Yes / No | Social Insurance (Security) Number

Claim No. | Name of Business | Are you the owner? Yes / No If Retired – Former Occupation

Occupation

How did you hear about Shouldice Hospital? (If referred by a doctor, give name & address)

Are you a former patient of Shouldice Hospital? | Yes | No | Do you smoke? | Yes | No

Have you ever written to Shouldice Hospital in the past? | Yes | No

What is your preferred admission date? (Please give as much advance notice as possible)

No admissions Friday, Saturday or Sunday.

FOR OFFICE USE ONLY

Date Received | Type of Hernia | Weight Loss _____ lbs.

Consent to Operate ☐ | Special Instructions | Approved
Heart Report ☐

Referring Doctor Notified | | Operation Date

Exhibit 1 Medical information questionnaire.

PLEASE BE ACCURATE: Misleading figures, when checked on a admission day, could mean postponement of your operation till your weight is suitable.

HEIGHT............ft..........ins.   WEIGHT.............lbs.Nude   Recent gain?.........lbs.
                                      or just pyjamas   Recent loss?.........lbs.

Waist (muscles relaxed)...............ins.   Chest (not expanded).................ins.

GENERAL HEALTH

Age..........years   is your health now GOOD ☐ ,   FAIR ☐ ,   or POOR ☐

Please mention briefly any severe past illness – such as a "heart attack" or a "stroke", for example, from which you have now recovered (and its approximate date)...............

We need to know about other present conditions, even though your admission is NOT likely to be refused because of them.

Please tick ☑ any condition for which you are having regular treatment:

Blood Pressure ☐
Excess body fluids ☐
Chest pain ("angina") ☐
Irregular Heartbeat ☐
Diabetes ☐
Asthma & Bronchitis ☐
Ulcers ☐
Anticoagulants ☐
(to delay blood-clotting or to "thin the blood")
Other. .... ☐

Name of any prescribed pills, tablets or capsules you take regularly -

Did you remember to MARK AN "X" on your body chart to show us where each of your hernias is located?

THIS CHART IS FOR EXPLANATION ONLY

Ordinary hernias are mostly either at the navel ("belly-button") - or just above it

or down in the groin area on either side

An "incisional hernia" is one that bulges through the scar of any other surgical operation that has failed to hold - wherever it may be.

THIS IS YOUR CHART – PLEASE MARK IT!

(MARK THE POSITION OF EACH HERNIA YOU WANT REPAIRED WITH AN "X")

APPROXIMATE SIZE...
Walnut (or less)
Hen's Egg or Lemon
Grapefruit (or more)

ESSENTIAL EXTRA INFORMATION
Use only the sections that apply to your hernias and put a ✓ in each box that seems appropriate.

NAVEL AREA (AND JUST ABOVE NAVEL) ONLY
Is this navel (bellybutton) hernia your FIRST one?   Yes ☐   No ☐

If it's NOT your first, how many repair attempts so far? ☐

GROIN HERNIAS ONLY

	RIGHT GROIN		LEFT GROIN	
	Yes	No	Yes	No
Is this your FIRST GROIN HERNIA ON THIS SIDE?	☐	☐	☐	☐

How many hernia operations in this groin already?   Right ☐   Left ☐   ☐

DATE OF LAST OPERATION

INCISIONAL HERNIAS ONLY (the ones bulging through previous operation scars)
Was the original operation for your Appendix? ☐ , or Gallbladder? ☐
or Stomach? ☐ , or Prostate? ☐ , or Hysterectomy? ☐ , or Other?............... ☐

How many attempts to repair the hernias have been made so far? ☐

Exhibit 1 (Continued)

When I interview prospective surgeons, I look for experience and a good education. I try to gain some insight into their domestic situation and personal interests and habits. I also try to find out why a surgeon wants to switch positions. And I try to determine if he's willing to perform the repair exactly as he's told. This is no place for prima donnas.

Dr. Shouldice added:

Traditionally, a hernia is often the first operation that a junior resident in surgery performs. Hernia repair is regarded as a relatively simple operation compared to other major operations. This is quite wrong, as is borne out by the resulting high recurrence rate. It is a tricky anatomical area and occasionally very complicated, especially to the novice or those doing very few hernia repairs each year. But, at Shouldice Hospital, a surgeon learns the Shouldice technique over a period of several months. He learns when he can go fast and when he must slow down. He develops a pace and a touch. If he encounters something unusual, he is encouraged to consult immediately with other surgeons. We teach each other and try to encourage a group effort. And he learns not to take risks to achieve absolute perfection. Excellence is the enemy of good.

Chief Surgeon Degani assigned surgeons to an operating room on a daily basis by noon of the preceding day. This allowed surgeons to examine the specific patients whom they were to operate on. Surgeons and assistants were rotated every few days. Cases were assigned to give doctors a non-routine operation (often involving a recurrence) several times a week. More complex procedures were assigned to more senior and experienced members of the staff. Dr. Obney commented:

If something goes wrong, we want to make sure that we have an experienced surgeon in charge. Experience is most important. The typical general surgeon may perform 25 to 50 hernia operations per year. Ours perform 750 or more.

The 10 full-time surgeons were paid a straight salary, typically $144,000[3]. In addition, bonuses to doctors were distributed monthly. These depended on profit,

individual productivity, and performance. The total bonus pool paid to the surgeons in a recent year was approximately $400,000. Total surgeon compensation (including benefits) was approximately 15% more than the average income for a surgeon in Ontario.

Training in the Shouldice technique was important because the procedure could not be varied. It was accomplished through direct supervision by one or more of the senior surgeons. The rotation of teams and frequent consultations allowed for an ongoing opportunity to appraise performance and take corrective action. Wherever possible, former Shouldice patients suffering recurrences were assigned to the doctor who performed the first operation "to allow the doctor to learn from his mistake." Dr. Obney commented on being a Shouldice surgeon:

A doctor must decide after several years whether he wants to do this for the rest of his life because, just as in other specialties — for example, radiology — he loses touch with other medical disciplines. If he stays for five years, he doesn't leave. Even among younger doctors, few elect to leave.

THE FACILITY

The Shouldice Hospital contained two facilities in one building — the hospital and the clinic. On its first level, the hospital contained the kitchen and dining rooms. The second level contained a large, open lounge area, the admission offices, patient rooms, and a spacious glass-covered Florida room. The third level had additional patient rooms and recreational areas. Patients could be seen visiting each other's rooms, walking up and down hallways, lounging in the sunroom, and making use of light recreational facilities ranging from a pool table to an exercycle. Alan O'Dell pointed out some of the features of the hospital:

The rooms contain no telephone or television sets. If a patient needs to make a call or wants to watch television, he or she has to take a walk. The steps are designed specially with a small rise to allow patients recently operated on to negotiate the stairs without undue discomfort. Every square foot of the hospital is carpeted to reduce the hospital feeling and the possibility of a fall. Carpeting also gives the place a smell other than that of disinfectant.

---

3 All monetary references in the case are to Canadian dollar. US$1 equaled C$1.33 on February 23, 2004.

This facility was designed by an architect with input from Dr Byrnes Shouldice and Mrs W. H. Urquhart (the daughter of the founder). The facility was discussed for years, and many changes in the plans were made before the first concrete was poured. A number of unique policies were also instituted. For example, parents accompanying children here for an operation stay free. You may wonder why we can do it, but we learned that we save more in nursing costs than we spend for the parent's room and board.

Patients and staff were served food prepared in the same kitchen, and staff members picked up food from a cafeteria line placed in the very center of the kitchen. This provided an opportunity for everyone to chat with the kitchen staff several times a day, and the hospital staff to eat together. According to O'Dell, "We use all fresh ingredients and prepare the food from scratch in the kitchen."

The Director of Housekeeping pointed out:

I have only three on my housekeeping staff for the entire facility. One of the reasons for so few housekeepers is that we don't need to change linens during a patient's four-day stay. Also, the medical staff doesn't want the patients in bed all day. They want the nurses to encourage the patients to be up socializing, comparing notes [for confidence], encouraging each other, and walking around, getting exercise. Of course, we're in the rooms straightening up throughout the day. This gives the housekeepers a chance to josh with the patients and to encourage them to exercise.

The clinic housed five operating rooms, a laboratory, and the patient recovery room. In total, the estimated cost to furnish an operating room was $30,000. This was considerably less than for other hospitals, which require a bank of equipment with which to administer anesthetics for each room. At Shouldice, two mobile units were used by the anesthetists when needed. In addition, the complex had one "crash cart" per floor for use if a patient should suffer a heart attack or stroke.

ADMINISTRATION

Alan O'Dell described his job:

We try to meet people's needs and make this as good a place to work as possible. There is a strong concern for employees here. Nobody is fired. [This was later reinforced by Dr. Shouldice, who described a situation involving two employees who confessed to theft in the hospital. They agreed to seek psychiatric help and were allowed to remain on the job.] As a result, turnover is low.

Our administrative and support staff are non-union, but we try to maintain a pay scale higher than the union scale for comparable jobs in the area. We have a profit-sharing plan that is separate from the doctors'. Last year, the administrative and support staff divided up $60,000.

If work needs to be done, people pitch in to help each other. A unique aspect of our administration is that I insist that each secretary is trained to do another's work and in an emergency is able to switch to another function immediately. We don't have an organization chart. A chart tends to make people think they're boxed in jobs[4], I try to stay one night a week, having dinner and listening to the patients, to find out how things are really going around here.

Operating Costs

The 2004 budgets for the hospital and clinic were close to $8.5 million[5] and $3.5 million, respectively[6].

THE MARKET

Hernia operations were among the most commonly performed operations on males. In 2000, an estimated 1,000,000 such operations were performed in the US alone. According to Dr. Shouldice:

---

4 The chart in Exhibit 2 was prepared by the case writer, based on conversations with hospital personnel.

5 This figure included a provincially mandated return on investment.

6 The latter figure included the bonus pool for doctors.

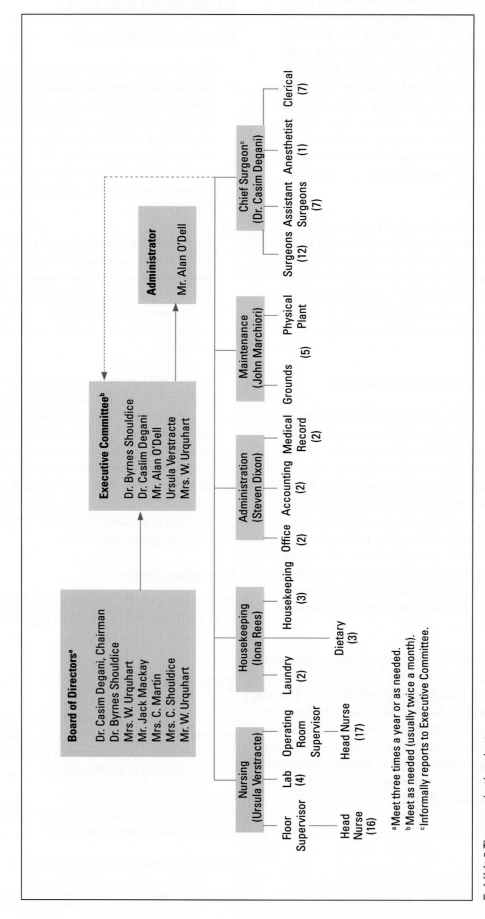

Board of Directors[a]

Dr. Casim Degani, Chairman
Dr. Byrnes Shouldice
Mrs. W. Urquhart
Mr. Jack Mackay
Mrs. C. Martin
Mrs. C. Shouldice
Mr. W. Urquhart

Executive Committee[b]

Dr. Byrnes Shouldice
Dr. Caslim Degani
Mr. Alan O'Dell
Ursula Verstracte
Mrs. W. Urquhart

Administrator

Mr. Alan O'Dell

Nursing
(Ursula Verstracte)

Lab (4)

Operating Room Supervisor

Head Nurse (17)

Floor Supervisor

Head Nurse (16)

Housekeeping
(Iona Rees)

Laundry (2)

Dietary (3)

Housekeeping (3)

Administration
(Steven Dixon)

Office (2)

Accounting (2)

Medical Record (2)

Maintenance
(John Marchiori)

Grounds

Physical Plant (5)

Chief Surgeon[c]
(Dr. Casim Degani)

Surgeons (12)

Assistant Surgeons (7)

Anesthetist (1)

Clerical (7)

[a]Meet three times a year or as needed.
[b]Meet as needed (usually twice a month).
[c]Informally reports to Executive Committee.

Exhibit 2 The organization chart.

When our backlog of scheduled operations gets too large, we wonder how many people decide instead to have their local doctor perform the operation. Every time we've expanded our capacity, the backlog has declined briefly, only to climb once again. Right now, at 2,400, it is larger than it has ever been and is growing by 100 every six months.

The hospital relied entirely on word-of-mouth advertising, the importance of which was suggested by the results of a poll carried out by students of DePaul University as part of a project (*Exhibit 3* shows a portion of these results). Although little systematic data about patients had been collected, Alan O'Dell remarked that "if we had to rely on wealthy patients only, our practice would be much smaller."

Patients were attracted to the hospital, in part, by its reasonable rates. Charges for a typical operation were four days of hospital stay at $320 per day, and a $650 surgical fee for a primary inguinal (the most common hernia). An additional fee of $300 was assessed if general anesthesia was required (in about 20% of cases). These charges compared to an average charge of $5,240 for operations performed elsewhere.

Round-trip fares for travel to Toronto from various major cities on the North American continent ranged from roughly $200 to $600.

The hospital also provided annual checkups to alumni, free of charge. Many occurred at the time of the patient reunion. The most recent reunion, featuring dinner and a floor show, was held at a first-class hotel in downtown Toronto and was attended by 1,000 former patients, many from outside Canada.

Direction: For each question, please place a check mark as it applies to you.

1. Sex — Male 41 (95.34%); Female 2 (4.65%)

2. Age — 20 or less ___; 21–40: 4 (9.30%); 41–60: 17 (39.54%); 61 or more: 22 (51.16%)

3. Nationality

Directions: Please place a check mark in nation you represent and please write in your province, state or country where it applies.

Canada 38 — Province 88.37%
America 5 — State 11.63%
Europe ___ — Country ___
Other ___

4. Education level — Elementary 5 (11.63%); High School 18 (41.86%); College 1980 (30.23%); Graduate work 7 (16.28%)

5. Occupation ___

6. Have you been overnight in a hospital other than Shouldice before your operation? Yes 31; No 12

7. What brought Shouldice Hospital to your attention?

Friend 23 (53.49%) Doctor 9 (20.93%) Relative 7 (16.28%) Article ___ Other 4 (Please explain) 9.30%

8. Did you have a single 25 (58.14%) or double 18 (41.86%) hernia operation?

9. Is this your first Annual Reunion? Yes 20 (46.51%) No 23 (53.49%)
If no, how many reunions have you attended? ___
2-5 reunions – 11 47.63%
6-10 reunions – 5 21.73%
11-20 reunions – 4 12.39%
21-36 reunions – 3 13.05%

10. Do you feel that Shouldice Hospital cared for you as a person?
Most definitely 37 (86.05%) Definitely 6 (13.95%) Very little ___ Not at all ___

11. What impressed you the most about your stay at Shouldice? Please check one answer for each of the following.

	Very Important	Important	Somewhat Important	Not Important
A. Fees charged for operation and hospital stay	10	3	6	24
B. Operation Procedure	33 (76.74%)	9 (20.93%)	1 (2.33%)	
C. Physician's Care	31 (72.10%)	12 (27.90%)	-	-
D. Nursing Care	28 (65.12%)	14 (32.56%)	1 (2.32%)	
E. Food Service	23 (53.48%)	11 (25.59%)	7 (16.28%)	2 (4.65%)
F. Shortness of Hospital Stay	17 (39.53%)	15 (34.88%)	8 (18.60%)	3 (6.98%)
G. Exercise; Recreational Activities	17 (39.53%)	14 (32.56%)	12 (27.91%)	-
H. Friendships with Patients	25 (58.15%)	10 (23.25%)	5 (11.63%)	3 (6.98%)
I. "Shouldice Hospital hardly seemed like a hospital at all."	25 (58.14%)	13 (30.23%)	5 (11.63%)	

12. In a few words, give the MAIN REASON why you returned for this annual reunion.

Exhibit 3 Shouldice Hospital annual patient reunion data

PROBLEMS AND PLANS

When asked about major questions confronting the management of the hospital, Dr. Shouldice cited a desire to seek ways of increasing the hospital's capacity while, at the same time, maintaining control over the quality of service delivered, the future role of government in the operation of the hospital, and the use of the Shouldice name by potential competitors. As Dr. Shouldice put it:

I'm a doctor first and an entrepreneur second. For example, we could refuse permission to other doctors who want to visit the hospital. They may copy our technique and misapply it or misinform their patients about the use of it. This results in failure, and we are concerned that the technique will be blamed. But we're doctors, and it is our obligation to help other surgeons learn. On the other hand, it's quite clear that others are trying to emulate us. Look at this ad (Exhibit 4).

This makes me believe that we should add to our capacity, either here or elsewhere. Here, we could go to Saturday operations and increase

our capacity by 20%. Throughout the year, no operations are scheduled for Saturdays or Sundays, although patients whose operations are scheduled late in the week remain in the hospital over the weekend. Or, with an investment of perhaps $4 million in new space, we could expand our number of beds by 50% and schedule the operating rooms more heavily.

Exhibit 4 Advertisement by a Shouldice competitor.

However, given government regulations, do we want to invest more in Toronto? Or should we establish another hospital with similar design, perhaps in the US? There is also the possibility that we could diversify into other specialties offering similar opportunities such as eye surgery, varicose veins, or diagnostic services (e.g., colonoscopies).

For now, we're also beginning the process of grooming someone to succeed Dr. Degani when he retires. He's in his early 60s, but, at some point, we'll have to address this issue. And for good reason, he's resisted changing certain successful procedures that I think we could improve on. We had quite a time changing the schedule for the administration of Demerol to patients to increase their comfort level during the operation. Dr. Degani has opposed a Saturday operating program on the premise that he won't be here and won't be able to maintain proper control.

Exhibit 5 The Shouldice Hospital grounds a haven for rest and recuperation.

Alan O'Dell added his own concerns:

How should we be marketing our services? Right now, we don't advertise directly to patients. We're even afraid to send out this new brochure we've put together, unless a potential patient specifically requests it, for fear it will generate too much demand. Our records show that just under 1% of our patients are medical doctors, a significantly high percentage. How should we capitalize on that? I'm also concerned about this talk of Saturday operations. We are already getting good utilization of this facility. And if we expand further, it will be very difficult to maintain the same kind of working relationships and attitudes. Already there are rumors floating around among the staff about it. And the staff is not pleased.

The matter of Saturday operations had been a topic of conversation among the doctors as well. Four of the older doctors were opposed to it. While most of the younger doctors were indifferent or supportive, at least two who had been at the hospital for some time were particularly concerned about the possibility that the issue would drive a wedge between the two groups. As one put it, "I'd hate to see the practice split over the issue."

Delwarca Software Remote Support Unit

Roy D. Shapiro and Paul E. Morrison

Jack McKinnon stood up from his desk to stretch for a moment and take a break from writing his analysis and proposal to his boss. In front of him and to his left and right, he could easily see the workstations and employees of Delwarca Software's Remote Support Unit, separated from each other by low partitions and configured like his in the open office layout of Delwarca's corporate headquarters in Waltham, Massachusetts. It was a comfortable, busy, and orderly scene with a murmur of voices and frequent ringing phones. However, McKinnon was deeply concerned that customer service performance in his unit was getting worse, not better.

In May 2012, McKinnon had been the manager of Delwarca's Remote Support unit for nearly a year, responsible for day-to-day operations, training, and supervision. McKinnon reported to the head of Software Support, who reported in turn directly to the president. In November 2011, McKinnon had responded to a customer service problem that seemed to be slowly eroding Delwarca's customer base. He changed the way incoming calls were handled in an effort to reduce customer waiting time on the telephones, and improve their perception of customer service, while at the same time trying to reduce Delwarca's costs. Now it was the time to analyze the results of the new procedure, called "Rapid ID", and make recommendations.

DELWARCA SOFTWARE

Delwarca provided supply chain management software globally to large, sophisticated corporate clients that had chosen to assemble their systems from various "best-of-breed" software programs. These independently operating systems usually supplemented and were integrated using software written and supported in-house by the corporation's own IT departments. This choice contrasted sharply with the popular corporate strategy of sourcing large and complicated Enterprise Resource Planning (ERP) systems from giant ERP firms such as SAP and Oracle.

The decision to integrate independent, disparate programs created some of the typical customer problems that triggered the need for support services from Delwarca. These problems included unexpected interaction effects with non-Delwarca software (including software sourced from other vendors as well as software written by the customer's IT staff); software–hardware interaction problems or performance concerns; the usual crashing or freezing of software; processing failures; attacks by malware; and installing and testing upgrades and patches.

Delwarca delivered its customer support through four separate units: (1) Software Development, which wrote new code or modified existing code; (2) Field Support, whose employees went on-site as needed for installation, training, upgrades, and trouble-shooting; (3) Critical Support, whose employees responded very rapidly using Delwarca's highest level of employee expertise to help customers with disasters such as unscheduled downtime, urgent malware and criminal issues, or time-critical processing malfunctions; and (4) Remote Support, which provided less time-critical support. Examples of less time-critical issues could be unexpectedly slow transaction processing times, intermittent failures to supply accurate reports, difficulties in writing custom reports, advice about "work-arounds" when integrating independent programs, interpreting Delwarca manuals, preparing for taking systems offline, or tracking down the origin of intermittent error messages.

THE REMOTE SUPPORT UNIT

Historically, nearly all of Delwarca's customers had been US-based corporations with IT offices in the US. With increasing globalization among its customers, Delwarca provided more support outside US business hours each year and was considering setting up separate European and East Asian offices, but had not done so yet for the relatively non-urgent work done by Remote Support. Up to this date, outside the US, Delwarca had provided non-urgent support using local Field and Critical Support units, but Delwarca was considering changing Remote Support staffing to provide 24-hour coverage.

As a result, in October 2011, Remote Support was fully staffed from 8.00 a.m. to 8.00 p.m. EST Monday to Friday. Apart from McKinnon and a supervisor, Remote Support employees were divided into two different levels of expertise: 12 Associates, who ranged from the newly hired to about four years of experience, and seven Senior Associates, who were the most skilled. Associates were paid from $40,000 to $66,000 per year plus benefits and overhead which averaged 26%, and Senior Associates were paid $70,000 to $90,000 per year plus benefits and overhead which averaged 23%. Remote Support employees had two 15-minute breaks and one half-hour lunch period per day, and were scheduled to be in the office eight hours per day. Breaks and lunch were scheduled to be sure that there were no periods when, as a result of multiple individual decisions about when to go on lunch or break, telephone coverage would be unexpectedly low. Unlike many call centers, Remote Support employees had no other tasks than resolving called-in problems, so between calls they had little to do. (See *Exhibit 1* for their schedule and the average incoming call volume by hour tracked during three months — August to October 2011). Calls during this period averaged 174.1 per day. The Remote Support unit did not experience significant call volume seasonality; there were some minor variations from day to day from Monday to Friday, but not enough to change the unit's staffing schedule.

Exhibit 1 Staff Schedule and Call Arrival Rate by Hour (August–October 2011)

Hour starting	Associates	Sr. Associate	Calls
8:00 AM	3	2	6.2
9:00 AM	7	4	14.8
10:00 AM	8	5	17.0
11:00 AM	8	5	16.8
12:00 PM	6	4	13.2
1:00 PM	6	4	14.4
2:00 PM	9	5	18.5
3:00 PM	8	5	18.1
4:00 PM	8	4	16.0
5:00 PM	7	4	14.2
6:00 PM	7	4	14.1
7:00 PM	7	3	10.8
			174.1

PRE-RAPID ID PROCEDURES

Prior to the new "Rapid ID" process McKinnon started in November 2011, a customer call was first taken by an operator who verified the corporate customer account, the identity, and the contact information of the caller. (In a tiny percentage of the cases, the operators decided that the customer actually needed to reach Delwarca's Critical Support unit and forwarded the call there.) The caller was then placed on hold waiting to be answered by the next available Associate, receiving an automated update while on hold every 90 seconds estimating how much time remained until someone picked up the call. The customer stayed on hold for the next available Associate even if a Senior Associate became available. The Associate answering the call verified that Remote Support was the appropriate Delwarca unit, and attempted to resolve the problem. If the Associate was able to resolve the call, the caller left the system. After the call, the Associate recorded notes on the call in the customer's Customer Relationship Management (CRM) database, and was then available to take another call.

If either the Associate or the customer believed that the Associate had not been able to resolve the problem, the customer was given the option of being put on hold again for the next available Senior Associate, or being called back when a Senior Associate was available. Virtually all of these customers chose to be put on hold rather than wait to be called back. After the call, Senior Associates also recorded notes in the customer's records. Unlike the more junior Associates, Senior Associates were always able to resolve the customer calls.

Customers did have the option of requesting a specific Senior Associate by name when their call was first picked up by the Operator, and 22% of all incoming calls made this request. (See *Exhibit 2* for average on-hold, talking, and note-taking time — in call centers usually called the Average Handling Time (AHT) — before Rapid ID and under Rapid ID, and *Exhibit 3* for the percentage of calls received and resolved by Associates and Senior Associates before and after the new Rapid ID procedure.) No matter which path customers took through the system, their priority in all queues was set by the time of "arrival" initially to the operator, when the call was "time-stamped" by the telecom system and was served thereafter by first-come first-served line discipline.

Exhibit 2 On-Hold and Talk Time, pre-Rapid ID and Rapid ID*

	Pre-Rapid ID	Rapid ID
Operator	1	1
Hold for Director	N/A	4
Talk to Director	N/A	2
Calls to Associate		
On hold to Associate	35.6	7.1
Talk to Associate	30.2	27.4
Forwarded to Sr. Associate		
On hold to Sr. Associate	23.7	38.5
Talk to Sr. after Associate	19.1	17.2
Directed to Sr. Associate		
On hold to Sr. Associate	N/A	49.8
Talk to Sr. Associate	N/A	23.6
Calls requesting specific Sr.		
On hold to Sr. Associate	24.9	57.8
Talk to Sr. Associate	21.6	24.4

* *"Take time" does not include entering notes.*

Exhibit 3 Percentage Calls Resolved by Associates and Sr. Associates

	Pre-Rapid ID	Rapid ID
Calls sent to Associates	78	54
Calls "directed" to Sr. Assoc.	N/A	18
Calls resolved by Assoc.	40	35
Calls forwarded to Sr. Associate	38	19
Calls requesting specific Sr. Assoc.	22	28

In general, surveys and conversations with customers showed that customers believed Delwarca's support was technically competent, but they were very dissatisfied with the long wait times. One irate caller who insisted on speaking to McKinnon told him, "Trust me, if I had a choice, I'd call anyone else on earth! We call you guys 'Deadwacko' — calling Remote is like being trapped in a zombie movie where they're all lurching away from you while you're trying to catch just one of them!" Customers acknowledged that with their phones on mobile headset they accomplished other work while waiting for service, but they still felt that waiting time, and total time in the system, was far too long.

THE RAPID ID PROCEDURE

Jack McKinnon joined Delwarca in 2005 as a programmer, had moved to Critical Support in 2008, was promoted to Supervisor there, and then became a Supervisor in Remote Support in July 2010 with the expectation of taking over from the Manager there. McKinnon had been promoted to Manager in Remote Support in June 2011 with the directive to reduce customer dissatisfaction within tight budgetary constraints. His boss told him, "Anyone can improve customer service by spending more money — it takes brains to do it spending less."

Under the Rapid ID procedure introduced in November 2011, an operator took the incoming call as before. The call was placed on hold and then taken by one of two highly experienced Associates (nicknamed "The Sorting Hats" by the staff) who made a quick initial assessment of the customer's requirements, and sent the call to either an Associate or a Senior Associate as appropriate. (This reduced Associate headcount available for regular calls by 1 FTE.) This "Director Associate" did not try to resolve the customer call. If an Associate could not resolve the call, the customer could still be forwarded to a Senior Associate. Customers requesting a specific Senior Associate made this request to the operator, and these were routed directly to that Senior Associate without speaking to a Director Associate.

McKinnon had hoped that the new, streamlined system would reduce waiting time and total customer time in the system by sending more calls directly to the Remote Support employee who could resolve them in a single call. The ultimate goal of the change was to improve perceived customer service. He also hoped to resolve more calls using the less expensive Associates. In October 2011 while preparing for the change, he told his Associates staff, "If you get the call, it should be one you can handle. Be confident, and work it through with the customer. If you need to take a little more time when you're working with them, that's OK — stretching a little is one way to learn."

BUMPS ON THE HIGHWAY

McKinnon was quite dissatisfied with the results of Rapid ID's first six months (*Exhibit 2* reports pre-Rapid ID data from May to October 2011, and Rapid ID data from November 2011 to May 2012; see *Exhibit 4* for the revised schedule for Associates and Senior Associates as of May 2012). During Rapid ID's first three months, McKinnon had hoped that performance problems would be temporary, but the second quarter under Rapid ID had not improved. Feedback directly from customers and from Delwarca employees in contact with customers told him that customers were more upset than ever with their time in the system. He did not consider himself an overly sensitive person, but his stomach clenched with tension every time he recalled a short, angry comment from one of his highest-performing Senior Associates: "We're the best people here and we're being run to death. By the time the customers get off hold and get to talk to us, they first want to rip some skin off our backs because they're just so angry. I've never had abuse like this, and frankly I don't think it's my fault. I don't know how much more we're going to want to take."

Exhibit 4 Staff Schedule and Call Arrival Rate by Hour (March–May 2012)

Hour starting	Associates*	Sr. Associate	Calls
8:00 AM	3	2	6.7
9:00 AM	6	5	16.0
10:00 AM	7	5	18.4
11:00 AM	7	5	18.1
12:00 PM	6	4	14.3
1:00 PM	6	5	15.6
2:00 PM	7	6	20.0
3:00 PM	7	6	19.5
4:00 PM	6	5	17.3
5:00 PM	6	5	15.3
6:00 PM	5	4	15.2
7:00 PM	4	4	11.7
			188.0

* Two experienced Associates covered the 10-hour day working part-time as "Directors," reducing Associate capacity by 1 FTE.

In total headcount, not much had changed. McKinnon had been able to reduce Associates by one while creating two part-time Director roles, but had felt compelled to hire an additional Senior Associate to cope with the workload. McKinnon was aware of several aspects of the work processes in Remote Support that might help him explain the results. Some of these he had known from his work before he became Manager, and others he had learned about as Rapid ID was carried out.

First, the Directors sometimes classified incoming calls as Associate/Senior Associate, meaning that they expected that the best resolution would occur when the customer had worked on the problem with an Associate who could solve or answer part of it, and then handed the case over to a Senior Associate for final resolution. The Directors reasoned that if at least part of the work could be completed on a relatively difficult case, Delwarca would benefit in two ways: first, the Associate would learn more from a challenging case, which would be developmental. The Associate might even be able to resolve the call, though the Directors did not expect this. In addition, if part of the problem could be handled in this way, less Senior Associate time overall might be needed to reach final resolution.

As shown in *Exhibit 3*, the Directors were sending 54% of all incoming calls to the Associates, but only 35% of all incoming calls were resolved by them; 18% of all calls were directed straight to the Senior Associates, but an additional 19% of all calls proceeded from Associates on to Senior Associates; 28% of total calls requested a specific Senior Associate.

This highlighted a second, unwelcome finding: more customers than ever were asking to go directly to a named Senior Associate. McKinnon had hoped that this percentage would decline as more customers experienced final resolution working only with an Associate, partly because he wanted Associates, not Senior Associates, used whenever possible, and partly because these requests for specific Senior Associates played havoc with his capacity planning. He knew that a variety of reasons could trigger these direct requests. First, while a call ended when the issue was "resolved", it was common on complicated issues for the customer to need or want follow-on conversations at a later date, or for the Senior Associate to want the customer to call back with a status report.

Third, it had been the case for years that Delwarca employees in both Field Support and Critical Support sometimes suggested to their customers that the customer call a specific individual in Remote Support for some aspect of assistance with a Field or Critical situation, or again for non-urgent but useful follow-up work or status checks. They suggested Senior Associates, whom they were more likely to know since Senior Associates had usually been with Delwarca longer, and because Senior Associates were much more likely to be able to resolve "their" customers' problems quickly, and so were less likely to embarrass the "referring" Delwarca employee. To some extent then, McKinnon's Senior Associates were informally teaming with Field and Critical Support employees.

Fourth, McKinnon was aware that some staff believed that establishing working relationships with customers extending across numerous issues and calls were helpful to the customer (since the Remote Support person got to know the customer employee and their problems better) and also to the Delwarca employee, who became somewhat less easily replaced within Delwarca, or who might be more likely to be offered an attractive job within a customer organization.

McKinnon had also collected information on call productivity among his staff (*Exhibit 5*). He had been aware that different employees in both groups often completed calls in very different amounts of time. He wondered how he could take advantage of this, or if instead, it was a problem for him. If it was a problem, he realized there were various approaches he could take to a solution. He did know that Associates took about the same amount of time on calls whether they were able to resolve them or not; when he asked several of them about this pattern, they told him that sometimes they could resolve calls very quickly, and sometimes it took quite an effort but they were able to work out a solution; and that when they could not resolve the calls, they could

sometimes realize that quite soon, and sometimes only after chewing on a problem for a long time before giving up. This pattern of call times averaging out regardless of outcome seemed to be true whether the Associate tended to below-average or above-average amounts of time on the call.

McKinnon knew that his boss wanted a detailed set of recommendations to address the problem of customer dissatisfaction in Remote Support. He knew that the stakes were high. He had been brought into Remote Support and promoted to Manager in order to improve operations and customer perceptions. His reorganization had improved some aspects of service, but mostly was not a success. Now a year later, he'd better get this one right, for Delwarca and for his own prospects at the company.

Exhibit 5 Minutes per call for Associates and Senior Associates*

Associate	Min/Call	Sr Associate	Min/call
Aronson	50.0	Dubois	13.6
Chedekel	24.3	Fluker	18.8
Filali	22.6	Kalinowsky	33.1
Herren	28.2	Mian	18.5
Kroshian	18.5	Puri	24.1
McNamara	25.3	Rice	15.8
Pierce	37.8	Sacks	44.6
Shah	40.8		
Wagoner	18.0		
Zuller	28.5		
Average:	29.4		24.1

* Includes time taking notes

Study Questions

1. Draw the process flow diagrams for the unit before Rapid ID and after. What changed?

2. What is the capacity utilization of the Remote Support Unit, and how is this affecting waiting times?

3. What would be the effect on capacity utilization of improving the productivity of the latest productive two Associate and two Senior Associates to the current Rapid ID average?

4. What is the labor cost per call taken by Associates and by Senior Associates? What is the cost per resolved call by Associates and by Senior Associates?

5. Why do you think system performance in terms of waiting time changed as it did? Why did customer behavior changed as it did?

6. If you were Jack McKinnon, what would you continue to do, and what should you stop doing?

CASE 11 Red Lobster

Christopher H. Lovelock

A peer review panel of managers and service workers from a restaurant chain must decide whether or not a waitress has been unfairly fired from her job.

"It felt like a knife going through me!" declared Mary Campbell, 53, after she was fired from her waitressing job at a restaurant in the Red Lobster chain. Instead of suing for what she considered unfair dismissal after 19 years of service, Campbell called for a peer review, seeking to recover her job and three weeks of lost wages.

Three weeks after the firing, a panel of employees from different Red Lobster restaurants was reviewing the evidence and tried to determine whether the server had, in fact, been unjustly fired for allegedly stealing a guest comment card completed by a couple of customers whom she had served.

PEER REVIEW AT DARDEN INDUSTRIES

Red Lobster was owned by Darden Industries, which also owned other restaurant chains like Olive Garden, Longhorn Steakhouse, The Capital Grill, Bahama Breeze, and Seasons 52. The company has about 1,900 restaurants serving 400 million meals a year. Red Lobster, which has more than 180,000 employees, had adopted a policy of encouraging peer review of disputed employee firings and disciplinary actions several years earlier. The company's key objectives were to limit worker lawsuits and ease workplace tensions.

Advocates of the peer review approach, which had been adopted at several other companies, believed it was a very effective way of constructively channeling the pain and anger employees felt after being fired or disciplined by

© 2009 by Christopher H. Lovelock, updated 2016 by Jochen Wirtz.

This case is based on information in a story by Margaret A. Jacobs in the Wall Street Journal. Real names have been changed.

their managers. By reducing the incidence of lawsuits, a company could also save on legal expenses.

A Darden spokesperson stated that the peer review program had been "tremendously successful" in keeping valuable employees from unfair dismissal. Each year, about 100 disputes ended up in peer review, with only 10 subsequently resulting in lawsuits. Red Lobster managers and many employees also credited peer review with reducing racial tensions. Ms. Campbell, who said she had received dozens of calls of support, chose peer review over a lawsuit not only because it was much cheaper, but "I also liked the idea of being judged by people who know how things work in a little restaurant".

THE EVIDENCE

The review panel included a general manager, an assistant manager, a server, a hostess, and a bartender, who had all volunteered to review the circumstances of Mary Campbell's firing. Each panelist had received peer review training and was receiving regular wages plus travel expenses. The instructions to the panelists were simply to do what they felt was fair.

Campbell had been fired by Jean Larimer, the general manager of the Red Lobster in Marston, where Campbell worked as a restaurant server. The reason given for the firing was that Campbell had asked the restaurant's hostess, Eve Taunton, for the key to the guest comment box and stole a card from it. The card had been completed by a couple of guests whom Campbell had served and seemed dissatisfied with their experience at the restaurant. Subsequently, the guests learned that their comment card, which complained that their prime rib of beef was too rare and their waitress was "uncooperative", had been removed from the box.

Jean Larimer's Testimony

Larimer, who supervised 100 full- and part-time employees, testified that she had dismissed Campbell after one of the two customers complained angrily to her and her supervisor. "She [the guest] felt violated," declared the manager, "because her card was taken from the box and her complaint about the food was ignored." Larimer drew the panel's attention to the company rule book, pointing out that Campbell had violated the policy that forbade removal of company property.

Mary Campbell's Testimony.

Campbell testified that the female customer had requested that her prime rib be cooked "well done" and then subsequently complained that it was fatty and undercooked. The waitress told the panel that she had politely suggested that "prime rib always has fat on it", but arranged to have the meat cooked some more. However, the woman still seemed unhappy. She poured some steak sauce over the meat, but then pushed away her plate without eating all the food. When the customer remained displeased, Campbell offered her a free dessert. But the guests decided to leave, paid the bill, filled out the guest comment card, and dropped it in the guest comment box.

Admitting she was consumed by curiosity, Campbell asked Eve Taunton, the restaurant's hostess, for the key to the box. After removing and reading the card, she pocketed it. Her intent, she declared, was to show the card to Ms. Larimer, who had earlier been concerned that the prime rib served at the restaurant was overcooked, not undercooked. However, she forgot about the card and later, accidentally threw it out.

Eve Taunton's Testimony

At the time of the firing, Taunton, a 17-year-old student, was working at Red Lobster for the summer. "I didn't think it was a big deal to give her [Campbell] the key," she said. "A lot of people would come up to me to get it."

THE PANEL DELIBERATES

Having heard the testimony, the members of the review panel had to decide whether Ms. Larimer had been justified in firing Ms. Campbell. The panelists' initial reactions to the situation were split by rank, with the hourly workers supporting Campbell and the managers supporting Larimer. But then the debate began in earnest in an effort to reach consensus.

Exhibit 1 The restaurant scene becomes the testing ground for the validity of peer review

Study Questions

1. What are the marketing implications of this situation?

2. Evaluate the concept of peer review. What are its strengths and weaknesses? What type of environment is required to make it work well?

3. Review the evidence. Do you believe the testimony presented?

4. What decision would you make and why?

CASE 12

Raleigh & Rosse: Measures to Motivate Exceptional Service

Robert Simons and Michael Mahoney

Grasping the iconic "golden horseshoe" door handle, CEO Linda Watkins strode into Raleigh & Rosse's Palm Springs, California store and surveyed the sales floor. Ambient lighting was subdued while hidden halogen ceiling lamps artfully spotlighted merchandise and signage. Display cases made from polished exotic woods projected visual warmth and sophistication. A harpist played Mozart crisply in the background. It was just over a week into January 2010, and the store, swept clean of holiday decorations, had bright spring colors on display. Watkins noticed many sales associates engaged with customers, but foot traffic was below expectations for a Saturday afternoon. Her cellphone rang.

"Linda, I got your voicemail. Raleigh & Rosse is being sued by its sales associates in a class action lawsuit?" asked Brian Rosse. He could barely contain his anger. Watkins moved to a quiet corner of the sales floor.

"Sorry, Brian. R&R was served notice late Friday," she said. "Looks like it's a rehash of the 'working off the clock' charges that we dealt with last year. Logan [R&R's general counsel] isn't too worried about the merits."

"But think about the negative publicity, the damage to our brand and image!"

"We've already engaged our PR agency to work on communications strategy. This is not great news, Brian, but I'm determined to find a way to manage it. Why don't we discuss the details and the legal strategy with Logan on Monday?" Watkins said.

Rosse calmed down a bit. He asked about last week's sales numbers.

"Overall, still weak. Miami and Chicago looked good, but most stores are struggling," explained Watkins. "Less than 60% of our associates met sales-per-hour targets this week."

"As if 2009 wasn't bad enough," he groaned. Watkins had to agree.

INDUSTRY BACKGROUND

The luxury goods industry is rooted in Europe, where craftsmen organized in small workshops created unique pieces for royal patrons. Most workshops were family owned, with skills and traditions passed down through generations. Historically, luxury goods distribution in the US was limited; if a wealthy customer wanted to buy a Dior gown, she would be invited to Paris to attend the semi-annual showing of the collection, where she would choose her designs and then be custom fitted for her one-of-a-kind purchase.

Luxury goods distribution in the US began to change after World War II. Couture houses licensed designs to high-end department stores, which opened up a new middle market for luxury apparel. The luxury goods market experienced a dramatic shift in the 1980s when luggage producer Louis Vuitton listed on the New York and Paris Stock Exchanges, acquired champagne producer Veuve Clicquot and the legendary fashion firm House of Givenchy, and merged with vintner/distiller Moet-Hennessy, creating a global luxury powerhouse. Louis Vuitton also disrupted traditional luxury distribution channels by creating its own retail outlets and buying out its distributors in the US. Many other European fashion groups followed suit in establishing their own US retail networks.

From 1995 to 2007, worldwide luxury goods industry revenue more than doubled. The global recession of

2008–2009 slammed the industry; Bain & Company estimated global industry revenues in 2009 at $214 billion, down 8% from the prior year, and down 10% from the industry revenue peak in 2007. Europe and the Americas represented 68% of revenues in 2009. The US was the largest single luxury goods market at $57 billion, with New York City alone generating revenues of $12.5 billion. In 2009, the luxury goods market was roughly split into four equal categories: apparel (27% of revenues), accessories such as handbags, leather goods, silk scarves (24%), perfume, and cosmetics (24%), and "hard luxury goods" such as jewelry and watches (19%). Nearly two-thirds of industry revenues were controlled by 35 brands, including Giorgio Armani, Chanel, Gucci, Hermes, Prada, Rolex, and Louis Vuitton Moet Hennessy.

COMPANY BACKGROUND

Raleigh and Rosse (R&R) was a privately held specialty retailer of luxury goods, including clothing, handbags, accessories, footwear, jewelry, fragrances, and watches for both men and women. The firm was founded by Michael Raleigh and Conor Rosse, two stable boys from Skibbereen, Ireland. As youngsters, they immigrated to the US in 1891, landing in New York City. Twelve years later, they opened a saddlery and equestrian shop. The store established a reputation for customer service among its well-heeled clientele. In the 1920s, R&R began importing a broader selection of leather goods such as footwear, luggage, and handbags from England, France, and Italy. In the 1950s and 1960s, the company broadened its merchandise mix to include high-end watches and designer clothing. Michael Raleigh's son Kevin succeeded the founders and led the firm's gradual expansion throughout the Northeast and Midwest, creating a national network of 17 US retail locations by the 1970s. R&R's main competitors at this time were high-end department stores such as Nordstrom, Saks Fifth Avenue, and Neiman Marcus.

While traditional department store retailers struggled to maintain market share in the luxury goods category in the 1990s as European luxury houses opened their own retail outlets in the US, R&R grew rapidly under the leadership of Brian Rosse, grandson of cofounder Conor Rosse. By 2007, R&R owned 38 retail locations with average revenue per square foot of $1,200 — significantly higher than the industry average of $675. But growth in luxury goods retailing outside the US, particularly in Asia, was exploding, and R&R was missing out. In 2007, R&R recruited Linda Watkins to succeed

Exhibit 1 Key points in R&R History

1903	First store opens in New York, selling saddlery and other equestrian goods
1920s	Other leather goods added, including luggage, handbags, and footware
1946	Kevin Raleigh becomes CEO
1952	Chicago store opening
1950s-1970s	• Merchandise mix expands to apparel, accessories, jewelry, watches, perfumes. • National expansion brings store total to 17 by 1975. • Revenues exceed $100 million
1987	Brian Rosse becomes CEO
1989-2007	• Aggressive US expansion program brings store total to 38. Revenues reach $524.2 million in 2007. • Launch of "Ownership Culture" programs in 1992-94 • Named "Top 100 Employer" by *Fortune* Magazine in 2002 • Former sales associate successfully sues R&R for wrongful termination, 2004 • *Fortune* publishes article criticizing R&R practices which leads to New York State Department of Labor investigation and settlement, 2005 • Brian Rosse hires Linda Watkins to replace him as CEO and becomes chairman, 2007
2008-January 2010	• Global economic downturn hits luxury retailers hard and R&R harder than competitors • Class action suit filed against R&R over SPH issues

Brian Rosse as the CEO, the first non-family member to lead R&R. A 25-year luxury retailing executive, she spearheaded Louis Vuitton's successful entry into Japan in the 1990s, and was most recently EVP of its Asia–Pacific region. Watkins expected to take R&R public to fuel its international expansion ambitions, but the global financial crisis of 2008 had derailed those plans. *Exhibit 1* presents a timeline of key points in company history; *Exhibit 2* provides R&R's core financial and other data for five years ending in 2009.

The Raleigh & Rosse Approach to Customer Service

Extraordinary customer service engendering deep customer loyalty was always a core value at R&R. In company literature, Kevin Raleigh described customer service as "a calling, a vocation to serve our clients at the highest level of devotion." Each R&R store was overseen by a store manager, and producing positive customer service evaluations was as important to that manager's

Exhibit 2 R&R Five-Year Statistical Summary ($000, except Stores & Facilities figures)

	2005	2006	2007	2008	2009
Operations					
Net Sales	$374,550	$437,784	$524,400	$482,448	$ 400,432
Total Costs & Expenses	$329,604	$380,872	$456,228	$453,501	$390,421
Earnings Before Income Taxes	$44,946	$56,912	$68,172	$28,947	$10,011
Net Earnings	$14,982	$17,074	$20,976	$4,824	$2,803
Stores & Facilities					
Company-Owned Stores	30	34	38	38	38
Total Square Footage (in sq ft)	330,000	377,400	437,000	437,000	437,000

performance evaluations as revenue and income generation. A core function of store managers was to hire, train, and continually motivate the sales associates — staff who worked the sales floor — who reported to them. It was at the sales associate level that most of the customer service was actually carried out.

Among R&R sales associates, it was common practice to drive to another store location to retrieve an out-of-stock item or drive to a customer's home to deliver an item. Stories of customer-service heroics permeated the R&R culture. Kathi Erdmann, a senior sales associate at R&R's flagship store in Manhattan, described some of her service requests:

> My clients are busy. I often run errands for them — once it was all the way to Boca Raton. I've packed a client's suitcases for a two-month safari. I spent part of my vacation in London hunting down a pair of Manolo Blahnik shoes for a client. One client called from work to ask me to pick something out of her closet and bring it to her office for an event that evening — she gave me the security access code to her apartment.

For R&R sales associates, client gratitude and loyalty meant greater earning potential. In 2007, the average R&R sales associate earned $63,000 in salary and commission (compared to an industry average of $50,000). Top performing associates could earn double that amount.

The exceptional service effort paid off for R&R by attracting a loyal base of ultra-wealthy clients. In 2005, the wealthiest 5% of Americans accounted for 53% of R&R revenues. Since luxury retailers rarely discounted prices and most luxury retailers could access the same luxury goods brands, the customer's experience was a primary competitive differentiator for R&R.

R&R recognized that extraordinary customer service might not always be defined the same way in each market. When Kevin Raleigh opened his boutique in Chicago in 1952 — the first store outside of the Northeast — the store struggled until he understood how these clients' expectations were different: "Chicago was an eye-opening experience for us. We thought we understood what great customer service meant, but Chicago's culture and client expectations were different from what we were accustomed to. We learned the valuable lesson that customer service must be fine-tuned in each store and, ultimately, tailored to each individual client." Beverly Hills store manager Callie Saloman described how her staff kept in touch with clients: "Our modus operandi is personalized service. We write thank-you letters when customers shop at our store. We have detailed files on all our customers, and if they haven't bought anything in a while, we'll send a handwritten note that subtly references the customer's tastes and preferences based on buying history."

Before the rapid expansion of its retail locations beginning in 1989, R&R relied on members of the Raleigh and Rosse families to manage its stores and ensure that the staff met customer service expectations. But in the early 1990s, CEO Brian Rosse recognized the need for a more scalable and formulaic set of HR policies and practices. Working with HR Director Gavin Rosse (his cousin) and a trusted subset of store managers, he developed and introduced the "R&R Ownership Culture."

The R&R Ownership Culture

When he ascended to the CEO's chair in 1987, Brian Rosse was concerned about maintaining R&R's distinctive reputation as he launched new strategic initiatives designed to significantly grow the firm's US retail locations.

Luxury retailing was booming. As we opened new stores, clients who had heard or read about us flocked to experience R&R for themselves. But I worried that our associates would become complacent and fail to honor our commitment to serve our clients. And we had to make sure that new members of our team shared our values.

Beginning in 1992, Rosse introduced the firm's "Ownership Culture" program — a set of initiatives and policies to create a more entrepreneurial and accountable environment. Among other things, R&R:

- Changed the hiring profile for its sales associates, shifting away from experienced sales professionals to recruiting ambitious recent college graduates with a strong work ethic seeking a career in retailing. The company invested heavily in "R&R University" to train sales associates in best practices and immerse them in the pro-customer culture.

- Maintained its policy of promoting from within, which increased the overall experience level of its middle management team while motivating its associates by exposing them to opportunities for advancement.

- Revamped its sales associates' commission system, which enabled unprecedented earnings potential of $100,000 or more for its top sales associates — revolutionary among specialty retailers.

- Invested in IT systems that provided store managers with extensive analysis of their store's operations, and increased the managers' authority to use these systems to optimize merchandise mix for their stores.

- Granted store managers significant autonomy on staffing, scheduling, and other aspects of sales associate performance. The firm's investment in customer relationship management and sales force automation systems aimed at the goal of enabling store managers to optimize their stores' staffing levels and to increase sales associates' productivity.

Rosse expected his store managers to "own their business", and store managers expected R&R sales associates to "own their relationships".

SPH: The Sales-Per-Hour Program

The heart of the Ownership Culture was the Sales-Per-Hour (SPH) measurement system. Prior to the introduction of SPH, sales associates were measured on their weekly sales, and store managers were measured using a dashboard of 11 metrics, including weekly store revenues and gross margin per square foot, specific revenue targets for various product categories, and a customer satisfaction metric based on written customer complaints and compliments.

Rosse recognized that historically all store managers had been family members (and owners). But expansion meant that non-family members would soon become store managers. He needed to instill and reinforce an entrepreneurial spirit in store managers that would permeate the store. And he wanted a simple, common metric that would more closely align associates and store managers. Thus, SPH was born.

Each store manager and associate was given a target SPH — sales minus merchandise returned by clients, divided by hours worked — based on his or her hourly wage ($14 to $18 per hour) and department. In 2009, a typical R&R sales associate had a $412 target SPH —meaning that he or she needed to generate at least $16,400 in sales revenue during an average 40-hour week. The actual SPH for the past two weeks appeared on each associate's paycheck. As one former associate put it, "I was reminded every two weeks what really counted at R&R. You saw your SPH and you knew what kind of week you'd be in for next week. I generally knew my numbers, but some weeks I dreaded opening my paycheck. Sounds crazy, doesn't it?"

If the actual SPH was higher than the target SPH, then the associate would be paid a 7.35% commission on net sales in lieu of an hourly wage. (*Exhibit 3* provides examples of the impact of SPH and reported hours on sales associates' performance measurement and compensation.) If the SPH was below the target, the employee would be paid his or her hourly wage. Failure to meet the target SPH resulted in decreased hours and, eventually, termination. Meeting or exceeding the target SPH meant more or better hours (when client traffic was heavier), and a better chance for promotion. At monthly store meetings, store managers would publicly review SPH performance versus target for all associates, and reward top performers with prizes and other incentives.

To generate an impressive SPH, associates had to be on the sales floor selling. But to provide the exemplary customer service expected from an R&R associate, they had to be available to serve clients off the floor. However, if these "non-selling" hours were formally recorded, SPH would decrease.

R&R recognized that associates spent time performing "non-selling" activities, such as restocking, merchandising (arranging & displaying merchandise), and attending internal meetings. Associates were compensated at their hourly wage rate for "non-selling" time, and the hours were excluded from the SPH calculation. But distinctions between "selling time" and "non-selling time" were vague and sometimes confusing (as described in an internal memo in *Exhibit 4*). "Doing whatever it takes" to satisfy a client meant associates might perform a wide range of activities which would be challenging to categorize in advance. Store managers' SPH included the total of all "selling" and "non-selling" hours.

Consequences of the SPH Program: 2004–2007

Soon after Brian Rosse introduced the "Ownership Culture", R&R was celebrated as a retail industry leader. R&R's superlative reputation for customer service combined with its generous commission plan attracted

bright, ambitious associates that fueled the company's expansion. In 2002, the company was named one of the "Top 100 Employers to Work For" by Fortune magazine. When it opened its highly anticipated Las Vegas store in 2003, over 1,000 people applied for 25 positions. Between 1995 and 2007, when luxury goods industry revenues doubled, R&R grew by more than 225%.

But life on the R&R sales floor wasn't always easy. R&R store managers cultivated an intense work environment. There were frequent sales contests, such as a "dinner for two" prize to the associate who sold the most multiple-item purchases in a given day. These contests helped to keep associates motivated on a daily basis. At monthly store meetings, store managers read aloud customer testimonial letters and rewarded associates on the spot with merchandise prizes. Repeated honorees were recognized as "Client All Stars"; they received their

Exhibit 3 Examples of Sales Associate Compensation Calculations

The following illustrates R&R sales associates' compensation model.

Assumptions:

Guaranteed base salary	$14.42 / hour
Sales Per Hour (SPH) target	$412
Sales per week target	$412 x 40 hrs = $16,484
Commission rate	7.35%, paid if SPH > $412

Example 1:

A sales associate works 50 hours and generates weekly sales of $17,000. The table below shows how compensation would vary if she reported working 40 rather than 50 hours.

Sales	$17,000	$17,000
Hours Reported	40	50
Sales Per Hour	$425	$340
Weekly Earnings	$1,250	$721
	($17,000 x 7.35%)	(50 hrs x $14.42)

A sales associate earns substantially more if she underreports her hours, thereby improving her SPH and qualifying for commission pay.

Example 2:

A sales associate works 50 hours and generates weekly sales of $15,000

Sales	$15,000	$15,000
Hours Reported	40	50
Sales Per Hour	$375	$300
Weekly Earnings	$576	$721
	(40 hrs x $14.42)	(50 hrs x $14.42)

In this case, if the sales associate reports all of her hours, she will earn more. But her SPH drops further below target. A substandard SPH can result in fewer scheduled hours, inferior shifts, substantial peer pressure, and possible termination.

```
TO:          ALL R&R STORE MANAGERS
FROM:        R&R CORPORATE OFFICE
SUBJECT:     CLARIFICATION OF COMPENSATORY WORK ACTIVITIES
DATE:        JULY 1, 2004
```

It has been long established business practice at R&R to pay all employees for time worked. Because superlative customer service demands that our employees respond to a wide variety of customer requests, it is not possible to describe all examples of work activities. This memo will review some common R&R practices that warrant employee compensation.

"Hand deliveries" – merchandise that is picked up by an associate at one store and delivered to another store. If the associate performs this task during regular work hours, then the associate remains on time clock. If the associate makes the delivery enroute to or from work, the associate may be entitled to be paid for time in excess of their normal commute. "Hand deliveries" that facilitate a personal sale are considered part of the selling process and regular "selling-time" would be paid. If an employee has been requested to pick up and deliver merchandise for a customer that is not a personal customer, their time would be compensated at "non-selling" time.

"Home deliveries" – merchandise that is delivered to a customer's home, office, hotel, airport, etc. The same criteria as "hand deliveries" applies.

There are many activities that are part of the selling and customer service process. There efforts are to be performed at the workplace. Also, when work is performed outside of the workplace (i.e. at home), then, depending on the circumstances, an associate may be entitled to be paid on the clock.

- Time spent finding merchandise from other stores via the telephone
- Stock assignments, floor moves and "picking up dead wood"
- Promotional activities and customer correspondence (i.e. Thank You notes, addressing sale notices)
- Workplace committees, including Store Spirit committee, Service Excellence Committee and Employee Recognition committee tasks and activities
- R&R University seminars and training
- Mandatory Store Meetings.

This partial list is not a comprehensive list of all possible job related activities. The intent is to clarify and illustrate compensatory work activities at R&R.

framed photo hung above the customer service desk and additional discounts on clothing. The pressure to become an All Star could sometimes result in undesirable behavior, such as "sharking", a term used to describe associates who stole credit for sales made by others.

One dispute landed in court. In 2004, a jury awarded $350,000 to a former R&R associate who claimed that she was wrongfully terminated because other associates posted anonymous comments claiming that she stole from them by falsely crediting herself with their commissions. An R&R store manager testified, "Our associates are intensely focused on serving our clients. It can be a very demanding and stressful job. If we fail to meet a client's expectations, R&R will lose that relationship. So we expect our associates to do whatever it takes. And sometimes that means that our associates aren't as respectful to each other as I would like them to be. But ultimately, it's our clients who are the final arbiters. And we measure client satisfaction by SPH."

Efforts to improve SPH led some managers and associates to manipulate the system. As an R&R associate described it:

> Brian Rosse says 'Own your business, own your customer relationships.' Everyone tells you that calling past customers for new business is important, handwritten thank-you cards are important, home delivery is important, taking a client's alterations to an outside tailor when the R&R tailor is backed up is important. No one says you have to do all of these extra things for clients on your own time. Each associate needs to figure it out for him- or herself. If you figure it correctly, you'll see that the system is working for you.

A newly hired associate in Washington, DC had a hard time adjusting to some of the R&R practices. "The first time I came to one of the many mandatory Saturday morning store meetings and I saw the sign 'Do not sign in', I assumed that [my managers] were telling the truth when they said that the system was down. But the system always seemed to be down on Saturday mornings. When I tried to log in anyway, my manager stopped me and accused me of not being 'a team player.'" Commenting on the variety of tasks she was expected to perform "off hours", she stated: "You couldn't complain, because then your manager would schedule you for bad hours, your SPH would fall, and then you'd be out the door."

Veteran associate Annie Simonds from Philadelphia explained it this way: "Initially you think, 'I've got to log in for every minute I'm here.' Then you find that you're at the bottom of the SPH ranking. Someone whispers in your ear, 'You know, you're only hurting yourself.' It's understood. There's pressure on store managers to give people with the best SPH the best hours, the best shifts. No one ever tells you 'If you log all of your hours, you'll get screwed,' but people here are smart. The people who don't get it, they leave. It's a Darwinian culture here."

Store managers sporadically forwarded to senior management concerns that associates had raised about "working off the clock". On several occasions, associates expressed their dissatisfaction by completing an "Ask Brian" comment form that allowed them to confidentially raise issues with senior executives. Each time, the corporate HR staff investigated the complaint, and the store manager in question responded that there must have been a misunderstanding.

During and after the 2004 wrongful termination lawsuit, the media took greater interest in R&R's sales floor culture. In an ironic twist, Fortune magazine published an unflattering story about R&R, spotlighting some of its store practices, just three years after it named R&R one of its "Best Employers". In the article, Brian Rosse responded to the criticism: "Our primary focus is always our client, and our employees love to serve them. R&R is a special place. A lot of our associates say 'I want to work here every day.' Sometimes associates complain that they can't get enough hours. Listen, during the busy times we all have to work hard. Frankly, I think that sometimes we don't work hard enough. That might sound harsh, but it's true. We're not slave drivers, we're not that kind of company. We have the lowest employee turnover in our industry. Our people are proud to be R&R associates and to serve our clients. They are well-compensated for their exemplary customer service."

The Fortune article triggered a three-month investigation by the New York State Department of Labor. The department found that R&R had violated state wage and hour laws in its failure to record all time worked, and to pay associates for performing certain activities. The agency ordered R&R to improve timekeeping systems and audit compliance, to pay back wages to affected employees, and to pay associates in the future for time spent on tasks such as attending internal meetings, home deliveries, and writing thank-you notes. Although the agency did not specify the number of affected employees or the amount of back wages owed, the New York Times reported that R&R could be liable for as much as $50 million.

2008–2009: Recession, then a Lawsuit

In the economic downturn of 2008 and 2009, worldwide luxury goods industry revenues dropped by 10%, and US luxury goods industry revenues fell by more than 14%. The slowdown had a particularly heavy impact on R&R, which, unlike most of its competitors, operated exclusively in the US.

CEO Linda Watkins indicated that, while some competing retailers were downsizing workforces, R&R needed to hold in place as much resources as possible. In a March 2008 internal newsletter, she wrote: "Our client relationships are our long-term assets. We have to maintain them, even during these difficult times. Although we have suspended new-store openings and implemented a hiring freeze, we have not laid off staff and do not plan to do so." At the same time, pressure on associates and store managers intensified to meet and exceed SPH targets; poor performance resulted in dismissal for associates and store managers alike. R&R senior management believed that the strength of its customer relationships and the value of its customer service would be severely tested, but ultimately would lead the company back to growth.

In 2009, the luxury goods industry showed signs of recovery, but R&R revenues continued to decline. On January 4, 2010, R&R sales associates filed a class action lawsuit under the Federal Fair Labor Standards Act (FLSA) alleging that R&R repeatedly and continuously violated state and federal wage and hour laws by coercing employees to work "off the clock". The plaintiffs sought damages equal to twice the amount of unpaid wages, plus additional punitive damages. In addition to the financial consequences, the lawsuit threatened to damage R&R's reputation irretrievably.

Linda Watkins considered her options. Of course, R&R would vigorously defend itself against the lawsuit. The firm's General Counsel assured her that following the 2007 New York State investigation, R&R had taken the corrective actions as mandated in the consent decree.

The risk of a potential $200 million judgment against R&R, combined with the reputational risk from a prolonged, high-profile lawsuit, forced Watkins to consider a potential settlement. She expected that the plaintiffs would demand substantial changes to elements of the "Ownership Culture" and SPH as part of any settlement. R&R's "Ownership Culture" and SPH had served the company well during its period of rapid growth, and Brian Rosse fervently believed that it was the essential driver of its success. In early 2008, Watkins recruited Bill Schwartz (a former colleague from Louis Vuitton) as her Senior Vice President for Human Resources to support international expansion efforts. Watkins had to admit that Schwartz had been skeptical from the start about several aspects of the Ownership Culture, especially SPH. He had questioned whether R&R's prior success had obscured critical flaws of its performance management system; perhaps other factors had been overlooked or underestimated. He had privately suggested to Watkins that she consider a "balanced scorecard" approach to performance management, but recognized the political risks in challenging one of R&R's "sacred cows". But 2008 — and then 2009 — had been taken up with more pressing financial concerns.

Watkins suspected that R&R's revenues for the first quarter of 2010 would continue their downward trajectory, while industry analysts predicted US same-store revenue growth for publicly traded competitors Tiffany & Co., Coach, and Gucci Group.

Watkins needed to make some decisions quickly and wondered how she should respond.

Study Questions

1. What is the cause of the problems described in this case? How serious are these problems? How would you quantify the potential financial risk to R&R?

2. Are R&R employees pressured inappropriately by the sales-per-hour system or by management?

3. How effective is the memo in Exhibit 4 in clarifying the distinction between "sell" and "non-sell" time?

4. How would you redesign compensation and performance appraisal systems at R&R? Is the sales-per-hour system an effective measure of customer satisfaction? Are R&R's HR policies and practices fully aligned with its business strategy?

CASE
13 Singapore Airlines: Managing Human Resources for Cost-effective Service Excellence

Jochen Wirtz and Loizos Heracleous

Singapore Airlines (SIA) has managed and organized its human resources (HR) to achieve sustainable competitive advantage and outperform other airlines in its peer group for decades. The case describes the role of HR in SIA's pursuit of the apparent conflicting objectives of service excellence and cost-effectiveness at the same time through its approach to recruitment, selection, training, motivation, and retention of its employees.

"At the end of the day, it's the software, people like us, who make the real difference."

Patrick Seow, Senior Rank Trainer,
Singapore Airlines Training School,
and Inflight Supervisor

"In Singapore, we always want to be the best in a lot of things. SIA is no different. …a lot of things that we have been taught from young, from our Asian heritage…filial piety, the care and concern, hospitality, and of course, the most important part is trying, if we can, to do whatever we can to please the customer. And how do we do it? Sometimes, people just wonder "How do you guys manage to do it with limited time and resources on a flight", yet we manage to do it somehow. Call us magicians."

Lim Suet Kwee, Assistant Manager of
Cabin Crew Performance Management,
and Former Senior Flight Stewardess

This case is based on the following earlier publications: Loizos Heracleous and Jochen Wirtz (2010), "Singapore Airlines' Balancing Act – Asia's Premier Carrier Successfully Executes a Dual Strategy: It Offers World-Class Service and is a Cost Leader", *Harvard Business Review*, Vol. 88, No. 7/8, July-August, 145–149. Loizos Heracleous, Jochen Wirtz, and Nitin Pangarkar (2009), *Flying High in a Competitive Industry: Cost-Effective Service Excellence at Singapore Airlines.* McGraw-Hill Education (Asia). Jochen Wirtz, Loizos Heracleous and Nitin Pangarkar (2008), "Managing Human Resources for Service Excellence and Cost Effectiveness at Singapore Airlines", *Managing Service Quality*, Vol. 18, No. 1, 4–19; and on interviews conducted with Singapore Airlines by Jochen Wirtz in 2015.

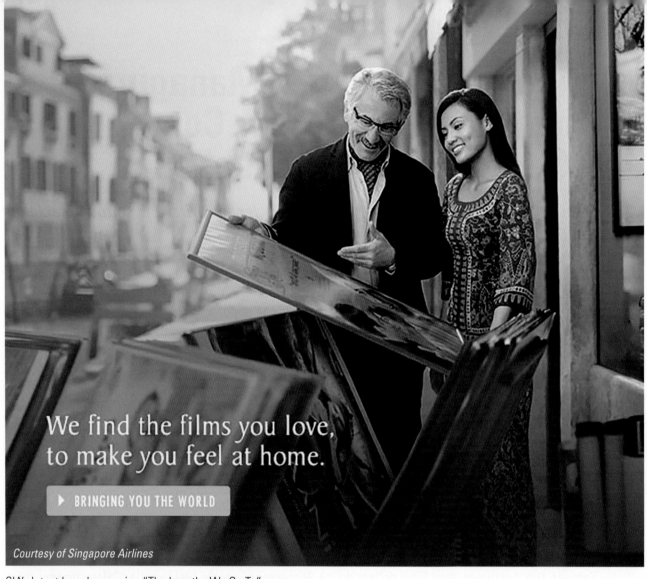

SIA's latest brand campaign "The Lengths We Go To"

SIA's International Culinary Panel (ICP) Cookbook

SIA's Business Class Seat on the A330 aircraft

HR AND COST-EFFECTIVE SERVICE EXCELLENCE AT SINGAPORE AIRLINES

Over the past four decades, SIA has earned a stellar reputation in the fiercely competitive commercial aviation business by providing customers with high-quality service and dominating the business travel segments. SIA has been the most awarded airline in the world for many years. For example, it won the World's Best Airline Award 23 out of the 24 times it has been nominated, from the prestigious UK travel magazine *Condé Nast Traveler*, and it won Skytrax's Airline of the Year award three times over the past decade. These awards are a reflection of SIA's customer focus — according to Mr. Tan Pee Teck, senior vice president (Product and Services), "It's not just consistency that we need to maintain, but also an overall elevation in the average standard of service to a higher threshold, because the expectations of frequent flyers especially will rise in tandem."

One key element of SIA's competitive success is that it manages to navigate skillfully between poles that most companies think of as distinct: delivering service excellence in a cost-effective way. SIA's costs are below all other full-service airlines, and in fact, its cost levels are so low, they are comparable to those of budget airlines. From 2001 to 2009, SIA costs per available seat kilometer were just 4.6 cents. According to a 2007 International Air Transport Association study, the costs for full-service European airlines were 8 to 16 cents, for US airlines 7 to 8 cents, and for Asian airlines 5 to 7 cents per available seat kilometer. SIA had even lower costs than most low-cost carriers in Europe and the US, which ranged from 4 to 8 cents and 5 to 6 cents respectively.

A key challenge of implementing business-level strategies, such as effective differentiation at SIA (through service excellence and innovation) combined with superior levels of operational efficiency, is the effective alignment of functional strategies such as human resources (HR), marketing, or operations with the business-level strategy. The focus of this case is on how HR practices, a crucial aspect of most service businesses, contribute to SIA's success through creating capabilities that support the company's strategy.

Five interrelated and mutually supportive elements inherent in SIA's HR strategy (*Figure 1*), along with leadership and role modeling by top management, play a key role in SIA's ability to deliver its business strategy

of service excellence in a cost-effective way. Let us next take a closer look at how the five elements work and complement each other.

Figure 1 The Five Core Elements of SIA's HR Strategy

Source

This model was derived from the authors' interviews with SIA's senior management and service personnel.

STRINGENT SELECTION AND RECRUITMENT PROCESS

HR strategy begins with recruitment, where SIA adopts a highly rigorous and strict selection process. Senior managers emphasize that SIA looks for cabin crew who can empathize with passengers and are cheerful, friendly, and humble. Cabin crew applicants are required to meet a multitude of criteria starting with an initial screening looking at age ranges, academic qualifications, and physical attributes.

The subsequent recruitment interviews comprise of four rounds. In round 1 (10 applicants at a time), applicants are asked to introduce themselves and answer a question posed by the interviewers. They are assessed on their command of English, confidence, and grooming. In round 2 (six applicants at a time), the candidates are divided into two groups and given a topic to debate. Applicants are assessed on their ability to work as a team and whether they are able to present their arguments in a logical and convincing manner. For the second half of the interview, applicants are given passages to read to test their enunciation. In round 3, one-on-one interviews with management are carried out to assess the candidate's aptitude and suitability for the position. In the final round, also called the grooming round, a uniform test allows the interviewers to assess the look of the applicant in SIA's *sarong kebaya*. This evaluation includes the posture, gait, and general appearance of the applicant in the uniform.

From the 18,000 applications received annually, only some 600 to 900 new cabin crew are hired to cover turnover rates of 10%, including both voluntary and directed attrition, and company growth. After the initial training, new crew are carefully monitored for the first six months of flying through monthly reports from the inflight supervisors during this probationary period. Usually, around 75% of them are confirmed for an initial five-year contract, some 20% have their probation extended, and the rest leave the company.

This meticulous selection process ensures with reasonable certainty that SIA hires applicants with the desired attributes, with a selection rate of 3–4% of its applicant pool. Despite the stringent procedures and strict rules about appearance and behavior, many educated young people around the region apply to join SIA due to the perceived social status and glamour associated with SIA's cabin crew. SIA's reputation as a service leader in the airline industry and an extensive and holistic developer of talent enables it to have its pick of applicants. Many school leavers and graduates view SIA as a desirable company to work for, and as an opportunity to move to more lucrative jobs in other companies after having worked with SIA typically for two five-year contracts or more.

EXTENSIVE INVESTMENT IN TRAINING AND RETRAINING

SIA places considerable emphasis on training, which is one of its focal points in its human resource strategy. According to a senior manager for human resource development, "SIA invests huge amounts of money in infrastructure and technology, but ultimately, you need people to drive it. At SIA, we believe that people actually do make a difference, so the company has in place a very comprehensive and holistic approach to developing our human resources. Essentially, we do two types of training, namely functional training and general management-type training." Almost half of SIA spending is on functional training and retraining.

Even though training is often emphasized as a key element of success in service industries, SIA remains the airline with the highest emphasis on this aspect. Newly recruited cabin crew are required to undertake intensive 15-week training courses — the longest and most comprehensive in the industry. SIA's training aims to enable cabin crew to provide gracious service reflecting warmth and friendliness, while maintaining an image of authority and confidence in the passengers' minds. SIA's holistic training includes not only safety and functional issues but also beauty care, gourmet food, wine appreciation, as well as the art of conversation. Even during economic downturns and crises, SIA keeps up its heavy emphasis on training. Mr. Goh Choon Phong, CEO of SIA said: "We will continue to invest heavily in the training and development of our people to bring out the best in them, even in the most difficult of times."

As SIA's reputation for service excellence grows stronger, its customers tend to have even higher expectations, which increases the pressure on its frontline staff. According to a commercial training manager, the motto of SIA is: "If SIA can't do it for you, no other airline can. The challenge is to help the staff deal with difficult situations and take the brickbats. The company helps its staff deal with the emotional turmoil of having to satisfy and even please very demanding customers, without feeling that they are being taken advantage of." Former CEO Dr. Cheong Choong Kong also commented: "To the company, training is forever and no one is too young to be trained, nor too old."

Continuous training and retraining have been vital to SIA in sustaining service excellence by equipping staff with an open mindset, to accept change and development, and to deliver the new services that SIA introduces regularly. SIA group has four training schools — corporate learning and three core functional areas of cabin crew, flight operations, and engineering. SIA Corporate Learning Centre (CLC) offers general management training under the purview of its HR division. CLC provides executive and leadership programs for all staff with the objective of generating effective managers and visionary leaders. In addition, CLC also drives customer service training and functional training for commercial areas.

SIA's training programs (about 70% of which are in-house) develop 12,000 people a year. Often, training is aimed to support internal initiatives such as the Transforming Customer Service (TCS) program involving staff in five key operational areas: cabin crew, engineering, ground services, flight operations, and sales support. According to a senior manager for HR development, "To ensure that the TCS culture is promoted company-wide, it is also embedded into all management training. The program aims at building team spirit among our staff in key operational areas so that together, we will make the whole journey as pleasant and seamless as possible for our passengers. One has to realize that it is not just the ticketing or reservations people and the cabin crew who come into contact with our passengers. The pilots, station managers, and station engineers have a role in customer service as well, because from time to time, they do come into contact with passengers." She also added, "But TCS is not just about people. In TCS, there is the 40–30–30 rule, which is a holistic approach to people, processes (or procedures) and products. SIA focuses 40% of the resources on training and invigorating our people, 30% on reviewing processes and procedures, and 30% on creating new product and service ideas."

SIA's leadership and relationship management with staff play a key role in the success of its training initiatives. As a project manager in SIA's new service development puts it, "I see myself first as a coach and second as a team player." SIA managers often assume the role of mentors and coaches to guide new employees, rather than just being managers and superiors.

SIA also adopts a job rotation approach to allow management to obtain a more holistic picture of the organization. Rotating to other departments every two to three years enables managers to develop a deeper understanding of operations at other areas of the organization. This practice promotes a corporate outlook, reduces the likelihood of inter-department conflicts, and facilitates change and innovation, as people bring fresh perspectives and approaches to their new roles. Constant job rotation is a core part of employee learning and development.

BUILDING HIGH-PERFORMANCE SERVICE DELIVERY TEAMS

The nature of the working environment on board requires people to work effectively as a team to deliver service excellence. In fact, effective teams are often a pre-requisite to service excellence. In view of this, SIA aims to create *esprit de corps* among its cabin crew. The 7,700 crew members are formed into 'wards'. Each ward consists of about 180 crew, led by a 'ward-leader' who acts as a counsellor to guide and develop the crew members.

Ward leaders issue newsletters for their teams, and organize face-to-face sessions and activities with their ward members. These activities include inter-ward games, overseas bonding sessions, and full-day engagement sessions on the ground.

The ward leaders learn about their ward members' individual strengths and weaknesses, and acts as counsellors to whom they can turn to for help or advice. There are also 'check trainers' who often fly with the teams to inspect performance and generate feedback that aids the team's development. According to an assistant manager of training, "Team leaders are able to monitor and point out what can be improved in the crew, team leaders are the ones to evaluate the crew, monitor staff development, staff performance, and supervise them. They see the feedback and monitor back the performance."

According to Mr. Sim Kay Wee, former senior vice president (cabin crew), "The interaction within each of the teams is very strong. As a result, when team leaders do staff appraisal, they really know the staff. You would be amazed how meticulous and detailed each staff record is, even though there are 7,700 of them. We can pinpoint any staff's strengths and weaknesses easily. So, in this way, we have good control; and through this, we can ensure that the crew delivers the promise. If there are problems, we will know about them and we can send them for retraining. Those who are good will be selected for promotion."

In addition, SIA organizes activities that reach out to the wider crew population. The management staff have frequent interactions with crew members at the Control Centre (where crew report for work) over food and drinks. The senior crew members are invited for full-day engagement sessions with the management.

SIA's cabin crew engages even in some seemingly unrelated activities; for example, the performing arts circle for talented employees where, during the biennial cabin crew gala dinner, they raised over half a million dollars for charity. Currently, there are 30 diverse groups whose activities cover arts, sports, music, dance, and community service. These interest groups provide an avenue for crew members to come together to pursue their passions outside of work. This helps crew members to further develop team spirit. The company believes that such activities encourage empathy for others, an appreciation of the finer things in life, camaraderie and teamwork, and therefore, supports cabin crew members who set up interest groups.

EMPOWERMENT OF FRONTLINE TO DELIVER SERVICE QUALITY

Over time, the soft skills of flight crew and other service personnel get honed, leading to service excellence that is difficult to replicate, not only in terms of how the service is delivered, but also in terms of the mindset that supports this delivery. Virtually all outstanding service firms have legendary stories of employees who recovered failed service transactions, walked the extra mile to make a customer's day, or averted some kind of disaster for a customer. A senior manager (crew performance) shared such a story:

> This particular passenger was a wheelchair-bound lady in her eighties, was very ill, suffering from arthritis. She was traveling from Singapore to Brisbane. What happened was that a stewardess found her gasping for air owing to crippling pain. The stewardess used her personal hot-water bottle as a warm compress to relieve the passenger's pain and knelt to massage the lady's legs and feet for 45 minutes. By that time, the lady's feet were actually swollen. The stewardess offered her a new pair of flight support stockings without asking her to pay for them. She basically took care of the old lady throughout the trip, seven to eight hours. When the old lady got back to Brisbane, her son called the hotel in which the crew were staying to try and trace this stewardess to thank her personally. He then followed up with a letter to us. I don't know if training contributes to it, or if it is personal. I mean, you don't find people who'd do this purely as a result of training, I think. We find the right people, give them the right support, give them the right training, and with the right support, people will do this kind of thing." Such thoughtful actions are part of the culture at SIA. According to a senior manager crew performance, the crew members "are very proud to be part of the SIA team, very proud of the tradition and very proud that SIA is held up as a company that gives excellent care to customers. So they want to live up to that.

Employees need to feel empowered in order to expend discretionary effort. It is pertinent that employees are able to make decisions independently, as frontline staff frequently have to handle customers on their own, since it is not feasible or even desirable for managers to constantly monitor employees' actions. At SIA, senior management emphasize that staff must have a clear concept of the boundaries of their authority and that it is the responsibility of management to communicate and explain the empowerment limits. Empowerment of the front line is especially important during service recovery processes and in situations where customers have special needs.

MOTIVATING STAFF THROUGH REWARDS AND RECOGNITION

Rewards and recognition is one of the key levers that any organization can use to encourage appropriate behavior, emphasize both positive as well as undesirable practices, and recognize excellence. SIA employs various forms of rewards and recognition including interesting and varied job content, symbolic actions, performance-based share options, and a significant percentage of variable pay components linked to individual staff contributions and company's financial performance. SIA keeps base salaries low by offering employees bonuses of up to 50% of their annual base salary, a formula that is hardwired and depends on SIA's profitability. The numerous international accolades received by the airline over the years, including "Best airline," "Best cabin crew service," and "Asia's most admired company", serve as further sources of motivation.

The company also holds company-wide meetings to keep staff updated about latest developments, and circulates newsletters. As an assistant manager cabin crew performance noted, "It's about communication. For example, if we add a new service at check-in, we will talk to the people involved before, during, and after implementation. We will discuss the importance and the value of it, and make sure everyone is aware of what we are doing and why. It helps to give staff pride in what they do."

Communication also aids in recognizing service excellence. Staff going the extra mile receive recognition through honors such as the annual CEO Transforming Customer Service (TCS) Awards. A former senior vice president cabin crew stressed the importance of recognition: "We know that a pat on the back, a good ceremony, photographs and write-ups in the newsletters can be more motivating than mere financial rewards; hence, we put in a lot of effort to ensure that heroes and heroines are recognized for their commitment and dedication."

Finding the right people and creating a service-oriented culture are key. A senior manager crew performance said, "Here, there are some intangibles. I think what makes it special is a combination of many things. First, you've got to ensure that you find the right people for the job, and after that, training matters a great deal: the way you nurture them, the way you monitor them and the way you reward them. The recognition you give need not necessarily be money. I think another very important ingredient is the overall culture of cabin crew, the fact that you have people who really are very proud of the tradition. And I think a lot of our senior people — and it rubs off on the junior crew — take pride in the fact that they helped build up the airline; they are very proud of it and they want to ensure that it remains that way." A senior manager (crew performance) added, "Among other contributing factors is a deeply ingrained service culture not just among the cabin crew but also in the whole company. I think it goes back to the early 1970s when the airline was set up. A very, very strong service culture throughout the whole organization, very strong commitment from top management. We take every complaint seriously. We respond to every compliment and complaint. We try to learn from the feedback; it's a never-ending process."

SIA's reward and evaluation system is highly aligned with the desired behaviors. The key element is "on board assessment", which encompasses image (grooming and uniform turnout), service orientation (crew's interaction and passenger handling capabilities), product knowledge and job skills, safety and security knowledge and adherence to procedures, work relationship (spirit of team work), and for the crew member in charge, additional factors of people management skills and pre-flight briefing sessions. The Appendix provides information on how cabin crew are evaluated.

SIA offers about average pay by Singaporean standards, which is low by global standards. Occasionally, there have been disputes between SIA group management and the labor unions. In 2007, the airline was in the spotlight again when the Air Line Pilots' Association Singapore (ALPA-S) disagreed with the management's proposed salary rate for pilots flying the Airbus A380, and the case had to be settled by the Industrial Arbitration Court.

BEYOND HUMAN RESOURCES

For four decades, SIA has managed to achieve what many others in the aviation industry can only dream of — cost-effective service excellence and sustained superior performance. Understanding the underpinnings of SIA's competitive success has important implications for organizations more broadly. One of the key implications concerns strategic alignment, in particular, aligning human resource practices to a company's competitive strategy.

At SIA, the human resource management practices outlined above enable the development of service excellence, customer orientation, adaptability and cost consciousness capabilities, which in turn support its dual strategy of differentiation through service excellence and low cost.

The SIA experience highlights how training and development should be employed in order to achieve a holistically developed workforce that can effectively support the company's strategy. Key questions for leaders therefore are: What sort of behaviors and attitudes do our reward and evaluation systems encourage? Are these aligned with what is needed to support our strategy? Do we train and develop our people in a way that develops the right capabilities to support our strategy? Do we go beyond technical training to address attitudes and ways of thinking?

No organization can stand still. The recent socio-economic crises at the macro-level, and the fast growth of high-quality full-service airlines in the Middle East (e.g., Emirates, Etihad, and Qatar Airways) and Asian budget carriers (e.g., AirAsia) at the industry level, mean that SIA not only needs to sustain its focus on achieving cost-effective service excellence, but also re-examine and re-invent some ingredients of its recipe for success.

1. Describe what is so special about SIA's five elements of its successful HR practices?

2. Evaluate the effectiveness of each element's contribution towards SIA's leadership in service excellence and cost-effectiveness.

3. Despite evidence that such practices help service firms achieve higher company performance, many organizations have not managed to execute them as effectively. Why do you think that is the case?

4. Why do you think are US full-service airlines largely undifferentiated low-quality providers? What are the reasons that none of the full-service airlines positioned itself and delivers as a high service quality provider?

5. Some of SIA's HR practices would be frowned upon in the US and Europe (e.g., having cabin crew on time-based contracts that are renewable every five years). Is this fair competition (i.e., desired competition between regulatory frameworks, as was favored by Margaret Thatcher, former prime minister of the UK), or is it arbitration of regulatory environments that encourage a "race to the bottom" in terms of employee rights?

6. How do people feel if they are working in a culture that focuses so intensely on customers, but cuts costs to the bone internally?

7. View https://www.youtube.com/watch?v=mIkNzhM2b70 (Across the World with the Singapore Girl) and http://youtu.be/P5sGKR6NJBw (Singapore Airlines SQ Girl), and discuss how these videos might be perceived by SIA cabin crew.

Courtesy of Singapore Airlines

Singapore Girls participating in the Heritage Parade during Singapore's National Day Parade 2015

APPENDIX: CABIN CREW PERFORMANCE MANAGEMENT (PM) QUESTIONS

1. **How is the cabin crew area structured and how does this influence the PM system?**

   Cabin crew are formed into 45 groups known as Wards, each headed by a Ward Leader (WL). Each Ward consists of approximately 180 crew, comprising of crew of all ranks. The WL is primarily responsible for monitoring the performance, coaching & developing, establishing rapport & communication and the welfare of crew of CS rank and below. WLs report to a Ward Management Leader (WML), who typically has five WLs under his/her supervision. Inflight Supervisors (IFS) come under the management of WMLs.

2. **Describe the performance management tool/ process that you use to monitor your cabin crew.**

   The performance of a crew member is measured through 'on-board assessments' (OBA) carried out by a more senior crew member on the same flight. Elements assessed in OBA are:

   a) Image — on grooming and uniform turnout

   b) Service Orientation — crew's interaction and passenger handling capabilities

   c) Product Knowledge and Job Skills — crew's performance with the various bar and meal services and crew's familiarity with procedures/ job and product knowledge

   d) Safety and Security — knowledge and adherence to safety and security procedures

   e) Work Relationship — to assess crew's general attitude and teamwork/team-spirit

   f) People Management Skills — supervisory and man-management skills, development of junior crew; ability to plan and co-ordinate the various services

   **Section f is applicable only to the crew-in-charge*

3. **How frequently do the assessments occur?**

   It varies from rank and is tracked over a Financial Year (FY).
   a) Inflight supervisor — two OBAs per FY
   b) All other cabin crew — six OBAs per FY

4. **What degree of alignment is there between the company values and the areas assessed?**

   The company's core values are embedded in the elements assessed in the OBAs, such as service orientation and product knowledge (pursuit of excellence), safety and security (safety), and work relationship and people management (teamwork).

5. **How do you train assessors and what level of on-going training occurs to ensure rater consistency?**

   All crew promoted to supervisory rank have to attend a one-day appraisal workshop where they are taught the basics of assessment, and are coached on the use of the OBA form. There's also an ongoing process to review all OBAs that have been improperly done and pick out appraisers who habitually give extreme ratings for follow-up by the ward leaders.

Dr. Mahalee Goes to London: Global Client Management

Christopher H. Lovelock

A senior account officer at an international bank is about to meet a wealthy Asian businessman who seeks funding for a buyout of his company. The prospective client has already visited a competing bank.

It was a Friday in mid-February and Dr. Kadir Mahalee, a wealthy businessman from the Southeast Asian nation of Tailesia, was visiting London on a trip that combined business and pleasure. Dr. Mahalee held a doctorate from the London School of Economics and had earlier been a professor of international trade and government trade negotiator. He was the founder of Eximsa, a major export company in Tailesia. Business brought him to London every two to three months. These trips provided him with the opportunity to visit his daughter, Leona, the eldest of his four children, who lived in London. Several of his 10 grandchildren were attending college in Britain. He was especially proud of his grandson, Anson, who was a student at the Royal Academy of Music. In fact, he had scheduled this trip to coincide with a violin recital by Anson at 2.00 p.m. on this particular Friday.

The primary purpose of Dr. Mahalee's visit was to resolve a delicate matter regarding his company. He had decided to retire and wished to make arrangements for the company's future. His son Victor was involved in the business and ran Eximsa's trading office in Europe. However, Victor was in poor health and was unable to take over the firm. Dr. Mahalee believed that a group of loyal employees would be interested in buying his company, if the necessary credit could be arranged.

Before leaving Tailesia, Dr. Mahalee discussed the possibility of a buyout with his trusted financial adviser, Pascal Huet, who recommended he talk to several banks in London due to the potential complexity of the business deal:

The London banks are experienced in buyouts. Also, you need a bank that can handle the credit for the interested buyers in New York and London, as well as Asia. Once the buyout takes place, you'll have significant cash to invest. This would be a good time to review your estate plans as well.

Referring Dr. Mahalee to two competing firms, The Trust Company and Global Private Bank, Lee added:

I've met an account officer from Global who called on me several times. Here's his business card; his name is Michael Johnston. I've never done any business with him, but he did seem quite competent. Unfortunately, I don't know anyone at the Trust Company, but here's their address in London.

After checking into the Savoy Hotel in London the following Wednesday, Dr. Mahalee called up Johnston's office. Since Johnston was out, Dr. Mahalee spoke to the account officer's secretary, introduced himself briefly, and arranged to stop by Global's Lombard Street office around mid-morning on Friday.

On Thursday, Dr. Mahalee visited The Trust Company. The two people he met were extremely pleasant and had spent some time in Tailesia. They seemed very knowledgeable about managing estates, and gave him some good recommendations about handling his complex family affairs. However, they were clearly less experienced in handling business credit, his most urgent need.

The next morning, Dr. Mahalee had breakfast with Leona. As they parted, she said, "I'll meet you at 1.30 p.m. in the lobby of the Savoy, and we'll go to the recital together. We mustn't be late if we want to get front-row seats."

On his way to Global Private Bank, Dr. Mahalee stopped at Mappin & Webb's jewelry store to buy his wife a present for their anniversary. His shopping was pleasant and

© 2012 Christopher H. Lovelock; updated 2016 by Jochen Wirtz.

leisurely. He purchased a beautiful emerald necklace that he knew his wife would like. When he emerged from the jewelry store, he was caught in an unexpected snow flurry. He had difficulty finding a taxi and his arthritis started acting up, which meant that walking to the nearest Tube station was out of the question. At last, he caught a taxi and arrived at the Lombard Street location of Global Bancorp around noon. After going into the street-level branch of Global Retail Bank, he was redirected by a security guard to the Private Bank offices on the second floor.

He arrived at the Private Bank's nicely appointed reception area at 12.15 p.m. The receptionist greeted him and contacted Johnston's secretary, who came out promptly to see Dr. Mahalee, and declared:

> *Mr. Johnston was disappointed that he couldn't be here to welcome you, Dr. Mahalee, as he had a lunch appointment with one of his clients that was scheduled over a month ago. He expects to return at about 1.30 p.m. In the meantime, he has asked another senior account officer, Sophia Costa, to assist you.*

Sophia Costa, 41, was a vice president of the bank and had worked for Global Bancorp for 14 years (two years longer than Michael Johnston). She had visited Tailesia once, but had not met Dr. Mahalee's financial adviser nor any member of the Dr. Mahalee family. An experienced relationship manager, Costa was knowledgeable about offshore investment management and fiduciary services. Michael Johnston had looked into her office at 11.45 a.m. and asked her if she would cover for him in case a prospective client, a Dr. Mahalee, whom he had expected to see earlier, should happen to arrive. He told Costa that Dr. Mahalee was a successful Tailesian businessman planning for his retirement, but that he had never met the prospect personally, and then rushed off to lunch.

The phone rang in Costa's office, and she reached across the desk to pick it up. It was Johnston's secretary. "Dr. Mahalee is in reception, Ms. Costa."

Exhibit 1 Receiving a client on short notice would require a bank's vice president to rely on all her expertise and experience to clinch the deal.

Study Questions

1. Prepare a flowchart of Dr. Mahalee's service encounters.

2. Putting yourself in Dr. Mahalee's shoes, how do you feel (both physically and mentally) after speaking with the receptionist at Global? What are your priorities right now?

3. As Sophia Costa, what action would you take in your first five minutes with Dr. Mahalee?

4. What would be a good outcome of the meeting for both the client and the bank? How should Costa try to bring about such an outcome?

The Royal Dining Membership Program Dilemma

Sheryl E. Kimes, Rohit Verma, Christopher W. Hart, and Jochen Wirtz

The Royal Dining membership program is highly popular with diners and generates significant revenues. However, it might be displacing regular, full-price paying customers and could have a negative effect on the painstakingly built and maintained high-end luxury image of the Hong Kong Grand Hotel. In addition, quite a few managers and servers expressed unhappiness with the program, the conflicts it creates with diners and the type of customers it attracts.

Erica Liu, Program Manager for the Royal Dining (RD) Membership Program at the Hong Kong Grand Hotel, hung up the phone after a call from a disgruntled customer. Just then, Jerome Tan, Vice President of Hotel Operations, walked into her office. "I tell you, Jerome," sighed Erica, "I've been getting calls from customers complaining about all the rules we have for the RD program. It's driving me nuts." "Tell me about it," Jerome replied. "These RD members really annoy our staff. All they're looking for is free stuff. I heard the ultimate one yesterday. Some guy walked into the Cantonese Café with 10 little kids and wanted them all to eat for free! Yes, we have a rule that kids under five can eat for free, but not the whole city! It turned out it was his son's birthday party. Can you believe that?" Erica sighed again. "I guess that means we're going to have to create another rule for members to complain about. I mean, I think it's a great program and all, and it definitely brings in a lot of business, but how are we going to deal with all these problems?"

THE HONG KONG GRAND LAUNCHES A DINING MEMBERSHIP PROGRAM

The Hong Kong Grand, a 140-room landmark hotel on Hong Kong Island, opened in the late 1800s and was considered a national monument. It was one of the world's well-known grand hotels and had received numerous awards, including Best Luxury Hotel and Best Hotel in Asia. Its guest list has included luminaries such as Queen Elizabeth II, Bill Gates, and James Michener, and it was one of the most photographed sites in Hong Kong. The hotel had four restaurants, ranging from the 56-seat Hollywood Road Deli to the fine-dining 112-seat Kabuki. All the restaurants took reservations and were open for lunch and dinner. The adjoining convention center, the second largest meeting space in Hong Kong, provided an ideal setting for upscale conferences, and the adjoining

Exhibit 1 The Hong Kong Grand's Restaurants

Restaurant Name	Cuisine	Restaurant Type	Average Check (HK$)	Number of Seats	à la Carte or Buffet	Average Lunch Duration (hours)	Average Dinner Duration (hours)	Hours of Operation for each Meal
Cantonese Café	Local/Buffet	Local/Buffet	$76	106	Both	1.0	1.0	5
Kabuki	Japanese	Fine Dining	$250	112	à la Carte	1.0	1.5	5
Hollywood Road Deli	American Style	Casual	$104	56	à la Carte	0.5	0.5	5
Dragon Boat	International	Smart casual	$109	72	Both	1.0	1.0	5

Sheryl E. Kimes, Rohit Verma and Christopher Hart are with the Cornell University School of Hotel Management, and Jochen Wirtz is with the National University of Singapore.

The names of the hotel, restaurants and membership program have been disguised.

shopping mall offered a multitude of shopping and dining options. For more information on the Hong Kong Grand restaurants (*Exhibit 1*).

The ownership of the Hong Kong Grand had changed recently. Previously, the company that owned the shopping center also owned the hotel, and had restricted the number of restaurants that operated in the mall. Once they sold the hotel, that restriction was lifted and the hotel restaurants had to contend with much more vigorous competition and as a result, its restaurants were often empty. As a response, the Hong Kong Grand launched the Royal Dining (RD) membership program.

The RD program was designed to encourage Hong Kong residents to dine in the restaurants at a discounted rate. With a food cost as a percentage of sales that averaged 32% of gross revenue, even a 50% discount yielded a reasonable gross margin. In addition, the RD program required the purchase of annual memberships, which provided a substantial revenue stream with practically no variable cost.

THE ROYAL DINING MEMBERSHIP PROGRAM

The RD membership program offered members the opportunity to receive discounted meals and rooms at the restaurants and bars located in The Hong Kong Grand. The program was an immediate hit. Within the first year, more than 1,000 memberships were sold. Local residents welcomed the opportunity to dine at the four hotel restaurants at major discounts. The hotel's restaurant revenue increased sharply from the added sales. By 2015, the program had a total of 4,200 members.

The RD membership card gave customers a 50% discount when two adults dined at one table and ordered at least one dish per person (starter, main course, or set menu). Typically, members dined for free; their dining companions paid for the meal. If members dined alone, they received only a 10% discount. The discount was calculated on the total food bill and did not include beverages, taxes, or service charges. It also was not available for takeaway orders or private dining events. Children dining with members also received the discount. Children under five ate for free in the buffet restaurant. In addition, special children's menus were available in the à la carte restaurants (see *Exhibit 2* for the complete program rules).

Exhibit 2 Royal Dining Membership Rules

Royal Dining annual membership fee: HKS$1,588 (ca. US$205)	
PRICE REDUCTION SCHEDULE:	
Member plus 1 guest (2 adults)	50%*
Member plus 2 guests (3 adults)	33%
Member plus 3 guests (4 adults)	25%
Member plus 4 guests or more (up to a total of 10 adults)	20%
Member dining alone	10%

* 50% discount is applicable only when there are two adult dining parties at a table and when a minimum of two food items are ordered (e.g., one set menu and one starter, or one main course and one starter). Two dining parties may not necessarily order a main course but at least two starter orders are required. In the event that only one food item is ordered for sharing and there are two parties dining, a 10% discount is applicable instead of the 50% discount. Members and their guests have to order a dish per person in order to enjoy the varying discounts. Side dishes are excluded from this discount benefit.

Conditions:

- The price-reduction structure is calculated on the total food bill only, excluding beverages, government taxes and service charge. Reduction does not apply to private dining and take-away.
- One card per table, per party, per occasion. Not valid with any other discounts or promotions.
- A 10% reduction will also be applied to bar snacks, where applicable.

OTHER BENEFITS

- A flat 20% discount will be given to members during Chinese New Year black-out dates when dining with a minimum of five or more people at one table at all restaurants except Kabuki.
- One Special Occasion voucher for 50% discount on total food bill in any one of the hotel's restaurants, when dining in a party of six to 12 people. Not available during Chinese New Year period, from the eve to the 15th day of Chinese New Year.
- Discounted room rates at the Hong Kong Grand (subject to availability)
- Birthday and wedding vouchers, and discounts at several stores in the hotel.

The card came with other benefits, including discounted room rates at the Hong Kong Grand (subject to availability), birthday and wedding vouchers, and discounts at several stores. Members could not use the card on Valentine's Day, Mother's Day, Christmas Eve, Christmas Day, and the first few days of the Chinese New Year. Although RD program rules stated that restaurants could restrict seating availability during busy periods, this was rarely done.

Exhibit 3 Royal Dining Membership

Membership Type	Number of Members	% Active Cards	Average Visits p.a.	Average Party Size	Average % Discount
RD–Traditional	78	71%	6.7	2.4	35%
RD–Epicure	641	76%	6.5	2.7	38%
Credit Card–Traditional	3,214	28%	3.5	2.5	35%
Credit Card–Epicure	310	20%	2.5	2.6	32%
Totals	4,243	49%	4.8	2.5	35%

Types of Memberships

Two types of memberships were available: Royal Dining Traditional (HK$1,588 per year) and Royal Dining Epicure (HK$2,588 per year). The majority of members opted for the Epicure membership as it included a free night at the hotel.

In addition, RD cards were given for free to all premium members of a well-known credit card company. The credit card company paid the Hong Kong Grand a discounted rate (HK$275 per year) for each member in the Traditional program and HK$400 per year for Epicure memberships, which were given only to their most valued customers. Both The Hong Kong Grand and the credit card company saw a mutually beneficial partnership evolving from the alliance of the two highly regarded brands. About 85% of all members were premium customers of the credit card company and thus, did not pay for their RD cards. Of the credit card members, 3,214 were Traditional members and 310 were Epicure members (*Exhibit 3*).

Not surprisingly, the purchased RD cards had a higher likelihood of being used — about 75% — and were used more frequently — about once every month-and-a-half — than those given to credit card holders. The 25% of credit card members who used their memberships used it at an average of once every four months. The average party size was comparable (about 2.5 customers); as was the average net revenue — HK$225 — except for the credit card Epicure members, whose average revenue was HK$325. The average discount for all RD transactions was 35% (*Exhibit 3*)[1].

The percentage of restaurant revenue derived from the RD program ranged from under 3% at the Hollywood Road Deli to over 60% at Kabuki (*Exhibit 4*).

Competing Programs

Food and dining out were important parts of Hong Kong's national identity. Along with shopping, eating out was often seen as a national pastime. Indeed, Hong Kong has frequently been referred to as a "gourmet paradise" and "the World's Fair of food"[2]. In response to RD, several other hotels had developed dining programs in an attempt to emulate The Hong Kong Grand and tie into the local passion for eating out.

Exhibit 4 Royal Dining Program Share of Restaurant Revenue

Restaurant	Last Financial Year Revenue (Millions of HK$)	% of Revenue from:	
		RD Members	Credit Card Members
Hollywood Road Deli	$23.3	3.4%	2.4%
Dragon Boat	$20.1	4.0%	5.9%
Kabuki	$53.5	42.8%	19.6%
Cantonese Café	$15.4	1.3%	1.4%

---

1 For a list of commonly used restaurant terminology, see Appendix A.

2 https://en.wikipedia.org/wiki/Hong_Kong_cuisine

THE PROGRAM DILEMMA

After finishing a meeting, Susan Li, Vice President of Finance, decided to stop by Erica Liu's office to say hello. Jerome Tan was there and the two were in a heated conversation that abruptly stopped when she knocked. "Let me guess. The two of you are arguing about the RD program again!" Their looks confirmed her suspicion. "I don't see why you have so many problems with it. It's produced a lot of incremental revenue that has boosted our bottom line." (See *Exhibits 5 to 7*.)

"But Susan," Jerome exclaimed, "the RD members are displacing lots of our regular customers, especially during busy periods, and we're practically giving away free meals. I feel that we should develop other programs to fill the restaurants and increase revenue — without all these cheapskates." Erica jumped in. "Jerome, I keep telling you this, but you're forgetting about all the money these people spend to become members. That is pure profit — hardly any cost involved. And the members deserve to get value for their money — or they won't renew their annual memberships. What do we give them, though? More rules that make them feel like anything *but* members. I'm telling you, I can understand why they complain."

"Erica, you just don't know what it's like to be working in the restaurants," Jerome replied. "These RD members are so pushy and always ask for more, more, more — and they try to game the system. For example, remember that rule about how only one discount card per table can be presented, even if there are two parties and each of them is a member? Well, since we have so many members, it's pretty common for several people at the table to have membership cards. And then, they all want to use their cards so they can save more money. When we tell them that it's against the rules, they say it's unfair because it penalizes people for dining together, that if they had come as couples and sat at separate tables, each table would have received a 50% discount. To get around the rule, guess what they're doing?" Pausing for effect, he said, "I'll tell you what they do. They show up separately and then ask to be seated at adjacent tables. Once seated, they push the tables together and try to get double the discount! How do you handle that situation if you're the server? Doesn't exactly fit with the ambience we're trying so hard to create, does it? And it does a number on the servers' attitudes." (See *Exhibit 8* for sample comments.)

Exhibit 5 Table Configuration of Hong Kong Grand Restaurants

Table Size	Cantonese Café	Kabuki	Hollywood Road Deli	Dragon Boat
			Tables	
2	5	2	16	8
4	20	15	3	12
5	0	0	0	0
6	0	0	2	0
8	2	2	0	1
10	0	0	0	0
Bar		10		
Tempura		Table for 10		
Teppanyaki		Table for 12		

Exhibit 6 Number of Customers for Each Restaurant by Meal Period and Day of Week

	Cantonese Café	Kabuki	Hollywood Road Deli	Dragon Boat
Average Number of Lunch Customers				
Monday	195	298	250	203
Tuesday	190	336	291	228
Wednesday	228	327	333	254
Thursday	228	344	333	269
Friday	244	370	375	277
Saturday	325	242	375	306
Sunday	244	225	354	337
Average Number of Dinner Customers				
Monday	325	190	260	170
Tuesday	358	249	286	198
Wednesday	293	257	286	161
Thursday	341	272	286	246
Friday	317	372	312	359
Saturday	317	327	312	320
Sunday	325	301	234	218

Exhibit 7 Average Revenue for Each Restaurant by Meal Period and Day of Week

	Cantonese Café	Kabuki	Hollywood Road Deli	Dragon Boat
Average Lunch Revenue				
Monday	$17,937	$39,107	$26,692	$25,563
Tuesday	$17,199	$42,576	$27,485	$30,170
Wednesday	$16,166	$38,231	$30,791	$29,003
Thursday	$16,751	$44,450	$32,208	$27,484
Friday	$18,052	$46,411	$35,783	$30,596
Saturday	$15,404	$40,234	$38,381	$28,890
Sunday	$19,227	$39,324	$41,110	$27,629
Average Dinner Revenue				
Monday	$20,754	$100,088	$21,437	$21,581
Tuesday	$25,671	$81,638	$25,738	$22,238
Wednesday	$24,438	$96,045	$20,451	$29,778
Thursday	$25,664	$109,375	$32,395	$28,136
Friday	$31,273	$113,909	$47,283	$31,160
Saturday	$28,678	$126,059	$40,559	$29,790
Sunday	$18,986	$112,027	$28,715	$24,368

Exhibit 8 Sample Server Comments about the Royal Dining Program

- "My RD customers love the program. For many of them, this is the only reason they come out to The Dragon Boat."
— *Dragon Boat*

- "I am sick of this program! I hate having to explain the rules to people trying to use multiple cards per table."
— *Cantonese Café*

- "While it's sometimes tough to have to explain rules to customers, I have to admit that the program benefits the restaurant and helps make my job more secure and earn more service fees and tips." — *Kabuki*

- "I think it's embarrassing! I'm working at the Hong Kong Grand and I have to deal with tacky discounts?!" — *Kabuki*

- "I'm sure it makes sense to management but dealing with customers who don't understand how the program works is the worst. The rules should be more clear to the customers."
— *Hollywood Road Deli*

- "The RD discount ruins the tip. I work for half as much!"
— *Dragon Boat*

Jerome was getting visibly upset. The more upset he got, the more flustered Erica became. Her program was adversely affecting people whose attitudes and behavior were vital to creating the dining experience. As Susan tried to calm him down, Carmen Teo, Vice President of Marketing walked in. "I heard you from my office around the corner! I thought I'd better come down before someone had to call security!" she said with a laugh. Erica quickly said, "What do you think of the RD program, Carmen?" Carmen thought for a long moment and then said, "I certainly can see the point of the program, but I just don't know. We spend so much money trying to build and maintain our luxury image — and then we offer a discount program that is very much at odds with it. I know it generates profits that we otherwise would never see, but what are the costs? Our guests pay a lot to be here and expect a wonderful experience. I don't know if we can provide this experience when we have coupon-wavers in there with them."

Jerome chimed in. "Especially when our customers have become so much more creative in getting around the rules." Erica agreed, saying, "Yes, and that's why we have so many rules now — and that's why I get so many calls complaining about them! Again, these people are spending a lot of money for their memberships and we're making it very difficult for them! I can see why they're annoyed."

Carmen said, "The question we need to think about is how to provide good value to our RD members that keeps the revenue flowing, while protecting the hotel from possible abuses of the program and negative impact on the guest experience. The answers are anything but obvious."

Susan jumped in, "Let me give you an alternative view. We have owners who are very much focused on the bottom line. Imagine their reaction if we suddenly dumped the program. I'm thinking that maybe we should extend the discount to beverages since our cost of sales is so much lower. Right now, our food cost percentage is 32%, but the beverage cost percentage is only 24%. I think it would be a strong contributor to financial performance." Jerome groaned. "But Susan, one of the only things that I can possibly see as a good thing for this program is that while we're basically giving the food away, we at least get a decent profit from the beverages. That would cost us more money!"

Erica checked her watch and noticed that she and Jerome were due at another meeting. "Well, it's nice that we're all in agreement. Anyone want to take over my job?"

Erica shook her head as she walked out the door and thought about the meeting she would have with the hotel executive committee in two days. Jerome, Carmen and Susan all were members, and high on the meeting's agenda was the future of the RD program. She thought to herself, "I need to present a comprehensive analysis of the program's costs and benefits and recommendations about where to go from here. How will I resolve all the differing views?"

"Better get to work," Erica thought, as she reached for a bottle of aspirin.

Study Questions

1. In Erica Liu's shoes, what would you present to the executive committee?

2. As Erica Liu, what analyses would you run to assess the financial performance of the RD membership program?

3. What effect does the RD membership program have on the brand and value perception of its local customers in Hong Kong and its full-paying hotel guests and diners? How could the hotel address these issues?

4. Review the rules set for the RD program. How would you go about setting rules for the program that protected the hotel against abuse, but does not make RD members feel that the program is unnecessarily restrictive and difficult to use?

5. How could negative server attitudes towards RD customers be handled?

APPENDIX A
RESTAURANT TERMINOLOGY

- Cover: A customer

- Average check: The average amount paid per customer

- Party: The number of customers at a particular table

- Total check: The total check amount from a party

- Server: A waiter or waitress

- Seat occupancy: The percentage of seats occupied during a given period.

- Table occupancy: The percentage of tables occupied during a given period.

- Revenue per available seat hour (RevPASH): Total revenue divided by the number of seat-hours available.

- Meal duration: The length of a meal. Varies based on the type of restaurant and the meal period (e.g., lunch, dinner). Dinners average 150% the time spent at lunch.

- Meal period: The length of time that the restaurant is open for a given meal. Depending upon the part of the world, most restaurants offer lunch from 11.00 a.m. to 2.30 p.m. or 3.00 p.m., while dinner is typically offered from 5.30 p.m. or 6.00 p.m. until 10.00 p.m.

- Restaurant types (in the context of The Hong Kong Grand):

  - Fine dining: Full service, sit-down restaurant with a comprehensive menu and served in a fairly luxurious setting. High average check per person. The type of restaurant that most people visit a few times per year.

  - Upscale casual: Full service, sit-down restaurant with a comprehensive menu and served in a casual setting. High average check per person. The type of restaurant that people might visit once a month.

  - Casual: Full service, sit-down restaurant with a somewhat limited menu and served in a casual setting. Moderate average check per person. The sort of restaurants that people might visit once a month.

  - Fast casual: Limited service restaurant with a fairly limited menu. Customers can either take their food with them or eat it in the restaurant. These restaurants are fairly casual with a low to moderate average check. The type of restaurant that most people might visit a few times per month.

  - Quick service (Fast-food): Limited service restaurant with a limited menu. Customers can either take their food with them or eat it in the restaurant. These restaurants are very casual with a low average check. The type of restaurant that most people might visit on a weekly basis.

CASE 16
Starbucks: Delivering Customer Service

Youngme Moon and John Quelch

Starbucks, the dominant specialty-coffee brand in North America, must respond to recent market research indicating that the company is not meeting customer expectations in terms of service. To increase customer satisfaction, the company is debating a plan that would increase the amount of labor in its stores and theoretically increase speed of service. However, the impact of the plan (which would cost $40 million annually) on the company's bottom line is unclear.

In mid-2002, Christine Day, Starbucks' senior vice president of administration in North America, sat in the seventh-floor conference room of Starbucks' Seattle headquarters and reached for her second cup of toffee nut latte. The handcrafted beverage — a buttery, toffee-nut-flavored espresso concoction topped with whipped cream and toffee sprinkles — had become a regular afternoon indulgence for Day ever since its introduction earlier that year.

As she waited for her colleagues to join her, Day reflected on the company's recent performance. While other retailers were still reeling from the post-9/11 recession, Starbucks was enjoying its 11th consecutive year of 5%, or higher, comparable store sales growth, prompting its founder and chairman, Howard Schultz, to declare: "I think we've demonstrated that we are close to a recession-proof product[1]."

Day, however, was not feeling nearly as sanguine, in part because Starbucks' most recent market research had revealed some unexpected findings. "We've always taken

great pride in our retail service," said Day, "but according to the data, we're not always meeting our customers' expectations in the area of customer satisfaction."

As a result of these concerns, Day and her associates had come up with a plan to invest an additional $40 million annually in the company's 4,500 stores, which would allow each store to add the equivalent of 20 hours of labor a week. "The idea is to improve speed of service and thereby increase customer satisfaction," said Day.

In two days, Day was due to make a final recommendation to both Schultz and Orin Smith, Starbucks' CEO, about whether the company should move forward with the plan. "The investment is the EPS (earnings per share) equivalent of almost seven cents a share," said Day. In preparation for her meeting with Schultz and Smith, Day had asked one of her associates to help her think through the implications of the plan. Day noted, "The real question is, do we believe what our customers are telling us about what constitutes 'excellent' customer service? And if we deliver it, what will the impact be on our sales and profitability?"

1 Jake Batsell, "A Grande Decade for Starbucks," The Seattle Times, June 26, 2002.

COMPANY BACKGROUND

The story of how Howard Schultz managed to transform a commodity into an upscale cultural phenomenon had become the stuff of legends. In 1971, three coffee fanatics — Gerald Baldwin, Gordon Bowker, and Ziev Siegl — opened a small coffee shop in Seattle's Pike Place Market. The shop specialized in selling whole arabica beans to a niche market of coffee purists.

In 1982, Schultz joined the Starbucks marketing team. Shortly thereafter, he traveled to Italy, where he became fascinated with Milan's coffee culture, in particular, the role the neighborhood espresso bars played in Italians' everyday social lives. Upon his return, the inspired Schultz convinced the company to set up an espresso bar in the corner of its only downtown Seattle shop. As Schultz explained, the bar became the prototype for his long-term vision:

> The idea was to create a chain of coffeehouses that would become America's "third place." At the time, most Americans had two places in their lives — home and work. But I believed that people needed another place, a place where they could go to relax and enjoy others, or just be by themselves. I envisioned a place that would be separate from home or work, a place that would mean different things to different people.

A few years later, Schultz got his chance when Starbucks' founders agreed to sell him the company. As soon as Schultz took over, he immediately began opening new stores. The stores sold whole beans and premium-priced coffee beverages by the cup and catered primarily to affluent, well-educated, white-collar patrons (skewed female) between the ages of 25 and 44. By 1992, the company had 140 such stores in the Northwest and Chicago and was successfully competing against other small-scale coffee chains such as Gloria Jean's Coffee Bean and Barnie's Coffee & Tea.

That same year, Schultz decided to take the company public. As he recalled, many Wall Street types were dubious about the idea: "They'd say, 'You mean, you're going to sell coffee for a dollar in a paper cup, with Italian names that no one in America can say? At a time in America when no one's drinking coffee? And I can get coffee at the local coffee shop or doughnut shop for 50 cents? Are you kidding me?'"

Ignoring the skeptics, Schultz forged ahead with the public offering, raising $25 million in the process. The proceeds allowed Starbucks to open more stores across the nation. By mid-2002, Schultz had unequivocally established Starbucks as the dominant specialty-coffee brand in North America. Sales had climbed at a compound annual growth rate (CAGR) of 40% since the company had gone public, and net earnings had risen at a CAGR of 50%. The company was now serving 20 million unique customers in well over 5,000 stores around the globe and was opening on average three new stores a day. (See *Exhibits 1* to *3* for company financials and store growth over time.)

What made Starbucks' success even more impressive was that the company had spent almost nothing on advertising to achieve it. North American marketing primarily consisted of point-of-sale materials and local-store marketing and was far less than the industry average. (Most fast-food chains had marketing budgets in the 3% to 6% range.)

For his part, Schultz remained as Chairman and Chief Global Strategist in control of the company, handing over day-to-day operations in 2002 to CEO Orin Smith, a Harvard MBA (1967) who joined the company in 1990.

THE STARBUCKS VALUE PROPOSITION

Starbucks' brand strategy was best captured by its "live coffee" mantra, a phrase that reflected the importance the company attached to keeping the national coffee culture alive. From a retail perspective, this meant creating an "experience" around the consumption of coffee, an experience that people could weave into the fabric of their everyday lives.

There were three components to this experiential branding strategy. The first component was the coffee itself. Starbucks prided itself on offering what it believed to be the highest quality coffee in the world, sourced from the Africa, Central and South America, and Asia–Pacific regions. To enforce its exacting coffee standards, Starbucks controlled as much of the supply chain as possible: It worked directly with growers in various countries of origin to purchase green coffee beans. It oversaw the custom-roasting process for the company's various blends and single-origin coffees. It controlled distribution to retail stores around the world.

The second brand component was service, or what the company sometimes referred to as "customer intimacy." "Our goal is to create an uplifting experience every time you walk through our door," explained Jim Alling, Starbucks' Senior Vice President of North American

---

2 Batsell.

Exhibit 1 Starbucks' financials, FY 1998 to FY 2002 (in million $).

	FY 1998	FY 1999	FY 2000	FY 2001	FY 2002
Revenue					
Co-owned North American	1,076.8	1,375.0	1,734.9	2,086.4	2,583.8
Co-owned International (UK, Thailand, Australia)	25.8	48.4	88.7	143.2	209.1
Total company-operated retail	1,102.6	1,423.4	1,823.6	2,229.6	2,792.9
Specialty operations	206.1	263.4	354.0	419.4	496.0
Net revenues	1,308.7	1,686.8	2,177.6	2,649.0	3,288.9
Cost of goods sold	578.5	747.6	961.9	1,112.8	1,350.0
Gross profit	730.2	939.2	1,215.7	1,536.2	1,938.9
Joint-venture income[a]	1.0	3.2	20.3	28.6	35.8
Expenses:					
Store operating expense	418.5	543.6	704.9	875.5	1,121.1
Other operating expense	44.5	54.6	78.4	93.3	127.2
Depreciation & amortization expense	72.5	97.8	130.2	163.5	205.6
General & administrative expense	77.6	89.7	110.2	151.4	202.1
Operating expenses	613.1	785.7	1,023.8	1,283.7	1,656.0
Operating profit	109.2	156.7	212.3	281.1	310.0
Net income	68.4	101.7	94.5	181.2	215.1
% Change in monthly comparable store sales[b]					
North America	5%	6%	9%	5%	7%
Consolidated	5%	6%	9%	5%	6%

Source

Adapted from company reports and Lehman Brothers, November 5, 2002.

[a] Includes income from various joint ventures, including Starbucks' partnership with the Pepsi-Cola Company to develop and distribute Frappuccino and with Dreyer's Grand Ice Cream to develop and distribute premium ice creams.

[b] Includes only company-operated stores open 13 months or longer.

Exhibit 2 Starbucks' store growth.

	FY 1998	FY 1999	FY 2000	FY 2001	FY 2002
Total North America	1,755	2,217	2,976	3,780	4,574
Company-operated	1,622	2,038	2,446	2,971	3,496
Licensed stores[a]	133	179	530	809	1,078
Total international	131	281	525	929	1,312
Company-operated	66	97	173	295	384
Licensed stores	65	184	352	634	928
Total stores	1,886	2,498	3,501	4,709	5,886

Source
Company reports.

[a] *Includes kiosks located in grocery stores, bookstores, hotels, airports, and so on.*

Exhibit 3 Additional data, North American company-operated stores (FY2002).

	Average
Average hourly rate with shift supervisors and hourly partners	$9.00
Total labor hours per week, average store	360
Average weekly store volume	$15,400.00
Average ticket	$3.85
Average daily customer count, per store	570

Source
Company reports.

retail. "Our most loyal customers visit us as often as 18 times a month, so it could be something as simple as recognizing you and knowing your drink or customizing your drink just the way you like it."

The third brand component was atmosphere. "People come for the coffee," explained Day, "but the ambience is what makes them want to stay." For that reason, most Starbucks had seating areas to encourage lounging, and layouts that were designed to provide an upscale yet inviting environment for those who wanted to linger. "What we have built has [a] universal appeal," remarked Schultz. "It's based on the human spirit, it's based on a sense of community, the need for people to come together[3]."

Channels of Distribution

Almost all of Starbucks' locations in North America were company-operated stores located in high traffic, high visibility settings, such as retail centers, office buildings, and university campuses[4]. In addition to selling whole-bean coffees, these stores sold rich-brewed coffees, Italian-style espresso drinks, cold-blended beverages, and premium teas. Product mixes tended to vary depending on a store's size and location, but most stores offered a variety of pastries, sodas, and juices, along with coffee-related accessories and equipment, music CDs, games, and seasonal novelty items. (About 500 stores even carried a selection of sandwiches and salads.)

Beverages accounted for the largest percentage of sales in these stores (77%); this represented a change from 10 years earlier, when about half of store revenues had come from sales of whole-bean coffees. (See *Exhibit 4* for retail sales mix by product type; see *Exhibit 5* for a typical menu board and price list.)

Starbucks also sold coffee products through noncompany-operated retail channels; these so-called "specialty operations" accounted for 15% of net revenues. About 27% of these revenues came from North American food-service accounts, that is, sales of whole bean and ground coffees to hotels, airlines, restaurants, and the like. Another 18% came from domestic retail store licenses that, in North America, were only granted when there was no other way to achieve access to desirable retail space (e.g., in airports).

---

3 Batsell.

---

4 Starbucks had recently begun experimenting with drive-throughs. Less than 10% of its stores had drive-throughs, but in these stores, the drive-throughs accounted for 50% of all business.

Exhibit 4 Product mix, North American company-operated stores (FY2002).

Retail Product Mix	Percent of Sales
Coffee beverages	77%
Food items	13%
Whole-bean coffees	6%
Equipment & accessories	4%

Source
Company reports.

The remaining 55% of specialty revenues came from a variety of sources, including international licensed stores, grocery stores and warehouse clubs (Kraft Foods handled marketing and distribution for Starbucks in this channel), and online and mail-order sales. Starbucks also had a joint venture with Pepsi-Cola to distribute bottled Frappuccino beverages in North America, as well as a partnership with Dreyer's Grand Ice Cream to develop and distribute a line of premium ice creams.

Day explained the company's broad distribution strategy:

Our philosophy is pretty straightforward — we want to reach customers where they work, travel, shop, and dine. In order to do this, we sometimes have to establish relationships with third parties that share our values and commitment to quality. This is a particularly effective way to reach newcomers with our brand. It's a lot less intimidating to buy Starbucks at a grocery store than it is to walk into one of our coffeehouses for the first time. In fact, about 40% of our new coffeehouse customers have already tried the Starbucks brand before they walk through our doors. Even something like ice cream has become an important trial vehicle for us.

Starbucks Partners

All Starbucks employees were called "partners." The company employed 60,000 partners worldwide, about 50,000 in North America. Most were hourly wage employees (called baristas), who worked in Starbucks retail stores. Alling remarked, "From day one, Howard has made clear his belief that partner satisfaction leads to customer satisfaction. This belief is part of Howard's DNA, and because it's been pounded into each and every one of us, it's become part of our DNA, too."

The company had a generous policy of giving health insurance and stock options to even the most entry-level partners, most of whom were between the ages of 17 and 23. Partly as a result of this, Starbucks' partner satisfaction rate consistently hovered in the 80% to 90% range, well above the industry norm,[5] and the company had recently been ranked 47th in the Fortune magazine list of best places to work, quite an accomplishment for a company with so many hourly wage workers.

In addition, Starbucks had one of the lowest employee turnover rates in the industry — just 70%, compared with fast-food industry averages as high as 300%. The rate was even lower for managers, and as Alling noted, the company was always looking for ways to bring turnover down further: "Whenever we have a problem store, we almost always find either an inexperienced store manager or inexperienced baristas. Manager stability is key. It not only decreases partner turnover but also enables the store to do a much better job of recognizing regular customers and providing personalized service. So our goal is to make the position a lifetime job."

To this end, the company encouraged promotion from within its own ranks. About 70% of the company's store managers were ex-baristas, and about 60% of its district managers were ex-store managers. In fact, upon being hired, all senior executives had to train and succeed as baristas before being allowed to assume their positions in corporate headquarters.

DELIVERING ON SERVICE

When a partner was hired to work in one of Starbucks' North American retail stores, he or she had to undergo two types of training. The first type focused on "hard skills," such as learning how to use the cash register and learning how to mix drinks. Most Starbucks beverages were handcrafted, and to ensure product quality, there was a pre-specified process associated with each drink. Making an espresso beverage, for example, required seven specific steps.

The other type of training focused on "soft skills." Alling explained:

In our training manual, we explicitly teach partners to connect with customers — to

5 Industrywide, employee satisfaction rates tended to be in the 50–60% range. Source: Starbucks, 2000.

Exhibit 5 Typical menu board and price list for a North American company-owned store.

Espresso Traditions Classic Favorites	Tall	Grande	Venti
Toffee Nut Latte	2.95	3.50	3.80
Vanilla Latte	2.85	3.40	3.70
Caffe Latte	2.55	3.10	3.40
Cappuccino	2.55	3.10	3.40
Caramel Macchiato	2.80	3.40	3.65
White Chocolate Mocha	3.20	3.75	4.00
Caffe Mocha	2.75	3.30	3.55
Caffe Americano	1.75	2.05	2.40

Espresso	Solo	Doppio	
Espresso	1.45	1.75	
Extras			
Additional Espresso Shot	.55		
Add flavored syrup	.30		
Organic milk & soy available upon request			

Frappuccino Ice Blended Beverages	Tall	Grande	Venti
Coffee	2.65	3.15	3.65
Mocha	2.90	3.40	3.90
Caramel Frappuccino	3.15	3.65	4.15
Mocha Coconut (limited offering)	3.15	3.65	4.15

Crème Frappuccino Ice Blended Crème	Tall	Grande	Venti
Toffee Nut Crème	3.15	3.65	4.15
Vanilla Crème	2.65	3.15	3.65
Coconut Crème	3.15	3.65	4.15

Tazo Tea Frappuccino Ice Blended Teas	Tall	Grande	Venti
Tazo Citrus	2.90	3.40	3.90
Tazoberry	2.90	3.40	3.90
Tazo Chai Crème	3.15	3.65	4.15

Brewed Coffee	Tall	Grande	Venti
Coffee of the Day	1.40	1.60	1.70
Decaf of the Day	1.40	1.60	1.70

Cold Beverages	Tall	Grande	Venti
Iced Caffe Latte	2.55	3.10	3.50
Iced Caramel Macchiato	2.80	3.40	3.80
Iced Caffe Americano	1.75	2.05	3.40

Cold Alternatives	Tall	Grande	Venti
Toffee Nut Crème	2.45	2.70	2.95
Vanilla Crème	2.20	2.45	2.70
Caramel Apple Cider	2.45	2.70	2.95
Hot Chocolate	2.20	2.45	2.70
Tazo Hot Tea	1.15	1.65	1.65
Tazo Chai	2.70	3.10	3.35

Whole Beans: Bold Our most intriguing and exotic coffees	1/2 lb	1 lb
Gold Coast Blend	5.70	10.95
French Roast	5.20	9.95
Sumatra	5.30	10.15
Decaf Sumatra	5.60	10.65
Ethiopia Sidame	5.20	9.95
Arabian Mocha Sanani	8.30	15.95
Kenya	5.30	10.15
Italian Roast	5.20	9.95
Sulawesi	6.10	11.65

Whole Beans: Smooth richer, more flavorful coffees	1/2 lb	1 lb
Espresso Roast	5.20	9.95
Decaf Espresso Roast	5.60	10.65
Yukon Blend	5.20	9.95
Café Verona	5.20	9.95
Guatemala Antigua	5.30	10.15
Arabian Mocha Java	6.30	11.95
Decaf Mocha Java/SWP	6.50	12.45

Whole Beans: Mild The perfect introduction to Starbucks coffees	1/2 lb	1 lb
Breakfast Blend	5.20	9.95
Lightnote Blend	5.20	9.95
Decaf Lightnote Blend	5.60	10.65
Colombia Narino	5.50	10.45
House Blend	5.20	9.95
Decaf House Blend	5.60	10.65
Fair Trade Coffee	5.95	11.45

Source

Starbucks location: Harvard Square, Cambridge, Massachusetts, February 2003.

enthusiastically welcome them to the store, to establish eye contact, to smile, and to try to remember their names and orders if they're regulars. We also encourage partners to create conversations with customers using questions that require more than a yes or no answer. So for example, "I noticed you were looking at the menu board — what types of beverages do you typically enjoy?" is a good question for a partner to ask.

Starbucks' "Just Say Yes" policy empowered partners to provide the best service possible, even if it required going beyond company rules. "This means that if a customer spills a drink and asks for a refill, we'll give it to him," said Day. "Or if a customer doesn't have cash and wants to pay with a check (which we aren't supposed to accept), then we'll give her a sample drink for free. The last thing we want to do is win the argument and lose the customer."

Most barista turnover occurred within the first 90 days of employment; if a barista lasted beyond that, there was a high probability that he or she would stay for three years or more. "Our training ends up being a self-selection process," Alling said. Indeed, the ability to balance hard and soft skills required a particular type of person, and Alling believed the challenges had only grown over time:

> Back in the days when we sold mostly beans, every customer who walked in the door was a coffee connoisseur, and it was easy for baristas to engage in chitchat while ringing up a bag. Those days are long gone. Today, almost every customer orders a handcrafted beverage. If the line is stretching out the door and everyone's clamoring for their coffee fix, it's not that easy to strike up a conversation with a customer.

The complexity of the barista's job had also increased over time; making a venti tazoberry and crème, for instance, required 10 different steps. "It used to be that a barista could make every variation of drink we offered in half a day," Day observed. "Nowadays, given our product proliferation, it would take 16 days of eight-hour shifts. There are literally hundreds of combinations of drinks in our portfolio."

This job complexity was compounded by the fact that almost half of Starbucks' customers customized their drinks. According to Day, this created a tension between product quality and customer focus for Starbucks:

> On the one hand, we train baristas to make beverages to our pre-established quality standards — this means enforcing a consistent process that baristas can master. On the other hand, if a customer comes in and wants it their way — extra vanilla, for instance — what should we do? Our heaviest users are always the most demanding. Of course, every time we customize, we slow down the service for everyone else. We also put a lot of strain on our baristas, who are already dealing with an extraordinary number of sophisticated drinks.

One obvious solution to the problem was to hire more baristas to share the workload. However, the company had been extremely reluctant to do this in recent years, particularly given the economic downturn. Labor was already the company's largest expense item in North America (*Exhibit 3*), and Starbucks stores tended to be located in urban areas with high wage rates. Instead, the company had focused on increasing barista efficiency by removing all non-value-added tasks, simplifying the beverage production process, and tinkering with the facility design to eliminate bottlenecks.

In addition, the company had recently begun installing automated espresso machines in its North American cafés. The verismo machines, which decreased the number of steps required to make an espresso beverage, reduced waste, improved consistency, and generated an overwhelmingly positive customer and barista response.

Measuring Service Performance

Starbucks tracked service performance using a variety of metrics, including monthly status reports and self-reported checklists. The company's most prominent measurement tool was a mystery shopper program called the "Customer Snapshot." Under this program, every store was visited by an anonymous mystery shopper three times a quarter. Upon completing the visit, the shopper would rate the store on four "Basic Service" criteria:

Service	Did the register partner verbally greet the customer?
	Did the barista and register partner make eye contact with the customer? Say "thank you"?
Cleanliness	Was the store clean? The counters? The tables? The restrooms?

Product quality Was the order filled accurately? Was the temperature of the drink within range? Was the beverage properly presented?

Speed of service How long did the customer have to wait?

The company's goal was to serve a customer within three minutes, from back-of-the-line to drink-in hand. This benchmark was based on market research which indicated that the three-minute standard was a key component in how current Starbucks customers defined "excellent service."

In addition to Basic Service, stores were also rated on "Legendary Service," which was defined as "behavior that created a memorable experience for a customer that inspired a customer to return often and tell a friend." Legendary Service scores were based on secret shopper observations of service attributes such as partners initiating conversations with customers, partners recognizing customers by name or drink order, and partners being responsive to service problems.

During 2002, the company's Customer Snapshot scores had increased across all stores (*Exhibit 6*), leading Day to comment, "The Snapshot is not a perfect measurement tool, but we believe it does a good job of measuring trends

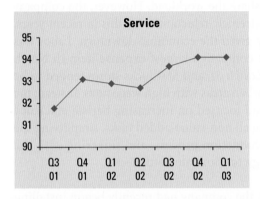

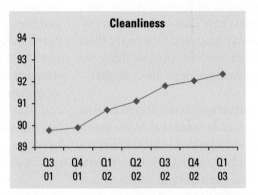

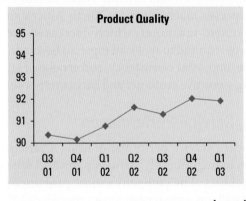

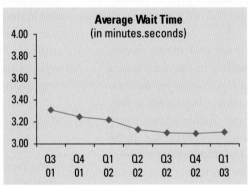

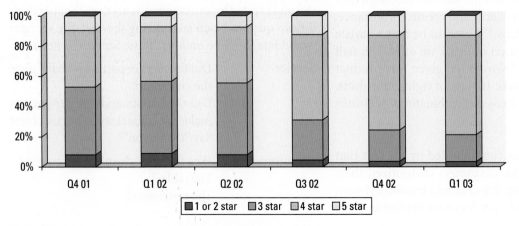

Exhibit 6 Customer Snapshot scores (North American stores)

over the course of a quarter. In order for a store to do well on the Snapshot, it needs to have sustainable processes in place that create a well-established pattern of doing things right so that it gets 'caught' doing things right."

COMPETITION

In the US, Starbucks competed against a variety of small-scale specialty-coffee chains, most of which were regionally concentrated. Each tried to differentiate itself from Starbucks in a different way. For example, Minneapolis-based Caribou Coffee, which operated more than 200 stores in nine states, differentiated itself on store environment. Rather than offer an upscale, pseudo-European atmosphere, its strategy was to simulate the look and feel of an Alaskan lodge, with knotty-pine cabinetry, fireplaces, and soft seating. Another example was California-based Peet's Coffee & Tea, which operated about 70 stores in five states. More than 60% of Peet's revenues came from the sale of whole beans. Peet's strategy was to build a super premium brand by offering the freshest coffee on the market. One of the ways it delivered on this promise was by "roasting to order," that is, by hand-roasting small batches of coffee at its California plant and making sure that all of its coffee shipped within 24 hours of roasting.

Starbucks also competed against thousands of independent specialty-coffee shops. Some of these independent coffee shops offered a wide range of food and beverages, including beer, wine, and liquor; others offered satellite televisions or Internet-connected computers. Still others differentiated themselves by delivering highly personalized service to an eclectic clientele.

Finally, Starbucks competed against donut and bagel chains such as Dunkin Donuts, which operated over 3,700 stores in 38 states. Dunkin Donuts attributed half of its sales to coffee and, in recent years, had begun offering flavored coffee and non-coffee alternatives, such as Dunkaccino (a coffee and chocolate combination available with various toppings) and Vanilla Chai (a combination of tea, vanilla, honey, and spices).

CAFFEINATING THE WORLD

The company's overall objective was to establish Starbucks as the "most recognized and respected brand in the world[6]." This ambitious goal required an aggressive growth strategy, and, in 2002, the two biggest drivers of company growth were retail expansion and product innovation.

Retail Expansion

Starbucks already owned close to one-third of America's coffee bars, more than its next five biggest competitors combined. (By comparison, the US's second-largest player, Diedrich Coffee, operated fewer than 400 stores.) However, the company had plans to open 525 company-operated and 225 licensed North American stores in 2003, and Schultz believed that there was no reason North America could not eventually expand to at least 10,000 stores. As he put it, "These are still the early days of the company's growth[6]."

The company's optimistic growth plans were based on a number of considerations:

- First, coffee consumption was on the rise in the US, following years of decline. More than 109 million people (about half of the US population) now drank coffee every day, and an additional 52 million drank it on occasion. The market's biggest growth appeared to be among drinkers of specialty coffee[8], and it was estimated that about one-third of all US coffee consumption took place outside of the home, in places such as offices, restaurants, and coffee shops (*Exhibit 7*).

- Second, there were still eight states in the US without a single company-operated Starbucks. In fact, the company was only in 150 of the roughly 300 metropolitan statistical areas in the nation.

- Third, the company believed it was far from reaching saturation levels in many existing markets. In the Southeast, for example, there was only one store for every 110,000 people (compared with one store for every 20,000 people in the Pacific Northwest). More generally, only seven states had more than 100 Starbucks locations.

6 Starbucks 2002 Annual Report.

7 Dina ElBoghdady, "Pouring It On: The Starbucks Strategy? Locations, Locations, Locations," The Washington Post, August 25, 2002.

8 National Coffee Association.

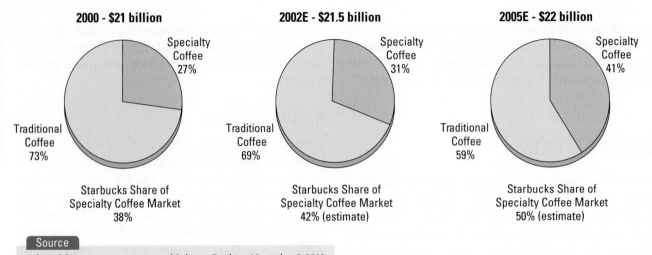

2000 - $21 billion	2002E - $21.5 billion	2005E - $22 billion
Specialty Coffee 27%	Specialty Coffee 31%	Specialty Coffee 41%
Traditional Coffee 73%	Traditional Coffee 69%	Traditional Coffee 59%
Starbucks Share of Specialty Coffee Market 38%	Starbucks Share of Specialty Coffee Market 42% (estimate)	Starbucks Share of Specialty Coffee Market 50% (estimate)

Source

Adapted from company reports and Lehman Brothers, November 5, 2002.

Other estimates[a] for the US retail coffee market in 2002:
- In the home, specialty coffee[b] was estimated to be a $3.2-billion business, of which Starbucks was estimated to have a 4% share.
- In the food-service channel, specialty coffee was estimated to be a $5-billion business, of which Starbucks was estimated to have a 5% share.
- In grocery stores, Starbucks was estimated to have a 7.3% share in the ground-coffee category and a 21.7% share in the whole-beans category.
- It was estimated that, over the next several years, the overall retail market would grow less than 1% per annum, but growth in the specialty-coffee category would be strong, with compound annual growth rate (CAGR) of 9–10%.
- Starbucks' US business was projected to grow at a CAGR of approximately 20% top-line revenue growth.

a The value of the retail coffee market was difficult to estimate, given the highly fragmented and loosely monitored nature of the market (i.e., specialty coffeehouses, restaurants, delis, kiosks, street carts, grocery and convenience stores, and vending machines).

b Specialty coffee includes espresso, cappuccino, latte, café mocha, iced/ice-blended coffee, gourmet coffee (premium whole bean or ground), and blended coffee.

Exhibit 7 Total US Retail coffee market (includes both in-home and out-of-home consumption)

Starbucks' strategy for expanding its retail business was to open stores in new markets while geographically clustering stores in existing markets. Although the latter often resulted in significant cannibalization, the company believed that this was more than offset by the total incremental sales associated with the increased store concentration. As Schultz readily conceded, "We self-cannibalize at least a third of our stores every day[9]."

When it came to selecting new retail sites, the company considered a number of criteria, including the extent to which the demographics of the area matched the profile of the typical Starbucks drinker, the level of coffee consumption in the area, the nature and intensity of competition in the local market, and the availability of attractive real estate. Once a decision was made to move forward with a site, the company was capable of designing, permitting, constructing, and opening a new store within 16 weeks. A new store typically averaged about $610,000 in sales during its first year; same-store sales (comps) were strongest in the first three years and then continued to comp positively, consistent with the company average.

Starbucks' international expansion plans were equally ambitious. Starbucks already operated over 300 company-owned stores in the UK, Australia, and Thailand, in addition to about 900 licensed stores in various countries in Asia, Europe, the Middle East, Africa, and Latin America. (Its largest international market was Japan, with close to 400 stores.) The company's goal was to ultimately have 15,000 international stores.

Product Innovation

The second big driver of company growth was product innovation. Internally, this was considered one of the most significant factors in comparable store sales growth, particularly since Starbucks' prices had remained relatively stable in recent years. New products were launched on a regular basis; for example, Starbucks introduced at least one new hot beverage every holiday season.

The new-product development process generally operated on a 12- to 18-month cycle, during which the internal research and development (R&D) team tinkered with product formulations, ran focus groups, and

9 ElBoghdady.

conducted in-store experiments and market tests. Aside from consumer acceptance, whether a product made it to market depended on a number of factors, including the extent to which the drink fit into the "ergonomic flow" of operations and the speed with which the beverage could be hand-crafted. Most importantly, the success of a new beverage depended on partner acceptance. "We've learned that no matter how great a drink it is, if our partners aren't excited about it, it won't sell," said Alling.

In recent years, the company's most successful innovation had been the 1995 introduction of a coffee and noncoffee-based line of Frappuccino beverages, which had driven same-store sales primarily by boosting traffic during non-peak hours. The bottled version of the beverage (distributed by PepsiCo) had become a $400-million[10] franchise; it had managed to capture 90% of the ready-to-drink coffee category due in large part to its appeal to non-coffee-drinking 20-somethings.

SERVICE INNOVATION

In terms of nonproduct innovation, Starbucks' stored-value card (SVC) had been launched in November 2001. This prepaid, swipeable smart card — which Schultz referred to as "the most significant product introduction since Frappuccino"[11] — could be used to pay for transactions in any company-operated store in North America. Early indications of the SVC's appeal were very positive: After less than one year on the market, about six million cards had been issued, and initial activations and reloads had already reached $160 million in sales. In surveys, the company had learned that cardholders tended to visit Starbucks twice as often as cash customers did and tended to experience reduced transaction times.

Day remarked, "We've found that a lot of the cards are being given away as gifts, and many of those gift recipients are being introduced to our brand for the first time. Not to mention the fact that the cards allow us to collect all kinds of customer-transaction data, data that we haven't even begun to do anything with yet."

---

10   Refers to sales at retail. Actual revenue contribution was much lower due to the joint-venture structure.

11   Stanley Holmes, "Starbucks' Card Smarts," BusinessWeek, March 18, 2002.

The company's latest service innovation was its T-Mobile HotSpot wireless Internet service, which it planned to introduce in August 2002. The service would offer high-speed access to the Internet in 2,000 Starbucks stores in the US and Europe, starting at $49.99 a month.

STARBUCKS' MARKET RESEARCH: TROUBLE BREWING?

Interestingly, although Starbucks was considered one of the world's most effective marketing organizations, it lacked a strategic marketing group. In fact, the company had no chief marketing officer, and its marketing department functioned as three separate groups — a market research group that gathered and analyzed market data requested by the various business units, a category group that developed new products and managed the menu and margins, and a marketing group that developed the quarterly promotional plans.

This organizational structure forced all of Starbucks' senior executives to assume marketing-related responsibilities. As Day pointed out, "Marketing is everywhere at Starbucks — it just doesn't necessarily show up in a line item called 'marketing.' Everyone has to get involved in a collaborative marketing effort." However, the organizational structure also meant that market- and customer-related trends could sometimes be overlooked. "We tend to be great at measuring things, at collecting market data," Day noted, "but we are not very disciplined when it comes to using this data to drive decision making." She continued:

> This is exactly what started to happen a few years ago. We had evidence coming in from market research that contradicted some of the fundamental assumptions we had about our brand and our customers. The problem was that this evidence was all over the place — no one was really looking at the "big picture." As a result, it took a while before we started to take notice.

Starbucks' Brand Meaning

Once the team did take notice, it discovered several things. First, despite Starbucks' overwhelming presence and convenience, there was very little image or product differentiation between Starbucks and the smaller coffee chains (other than Starbucks' ubiquity) in the minds of specialty coffeehouse customers. There was significant differentiation, however, between Starbucks and the independent specialty coffeehouses (Table A).

Table A Qualitative brand meaning: Independents vs. Starbucks.

Independents:
- Social and inclusive
- Diverse and intellectual
- Artsy and funky
- Liberal and free-spirited
- Lingering encouraged
- Particularly appealing to younger coffeehouse customers
- Somewhat intimidating to older, more mainstream coffeehouse customers

Starbucks:
- Everywhere—the trend
- Good coffee on the run
- Place to meet and move on
- Convenience oriented; on the way to work
- Accessible and consistent

Source

Starbucks, based on qualitative interviews with specialty coffeehouse customers.

More generally, the market research team discovered that Starbucks' brand image had some rough edges. The number of respondents who strongly agreed with the statement "Starbucks cares primarily about making money" was up from 53% in 2000 to 61% in 2001, while the number of respondents who strongly agreed with the statement "Starbucks cares primarily about building more stores" was up from 48% to 55%. Day noted, "It's become apparent that we need to ask ourselves, 'Are we focusing on the right things? Are we clearly communicating our value and values to our customers, instead of just our growth plans?'" (Table B).

Table B The top five attributes consumers associate with the Starbucks brand.

- Known for specialty/gourmet coffee (54% strongly agree)
- Widely available (43% strongly agree)
- Corporate (42% strongly agree)
- Trendy (41% strongly agree)
- Always feel welcome at Starbucks (39% strongly agree)

Source

Starbucks, based on 2002 survey.

The Changing Customer

The market research team also discovered that Starbucks' customer base was evolving. Starbucks' newer customers tended to be younger, less well educated, and in a lower income bracket than Starbucks' more established customers. In addition, they visited the stores less frequently and had very different perceptions of the Starbucks brand compared to more established customers (*Exhibit 8*).

Furthermore, the team learned that Starbucks' historical customer profile — the affluent, well-educated, white-collar female between the ages of 24 and 44 — had expanded. For example, about half of the stores in southern California had large numbers of Hispanic customers. In Florida, the company had stores that catered primarily to Cuban-Americans.

Customer Behavior

With respect to customer behavior, the market research team discovered that, regardless of the market — urban versus rural, new versus established — customers tended to use the stores the same way. The team also learned that, although the company's most frequent customers averaged 18 visits a month, the typical customer visited just five times a month (*Figure A*).

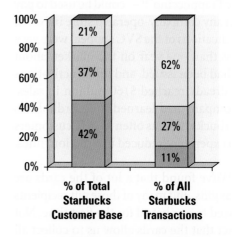

Figure A Customer visit

Exhibit 8 Starbucks' customer retention information.

% OF STARBUCKS' CUSTOMERS WHO FIRST STARTED VISITING STARBUCKS ...	
In the past year	27
1–2 years ago	20
2–5 years ago	30
5 or more years ago	23

Source

Starbucks, 2002. Based on a sample of Starbucks' 2002 customer base.

	New Customers (First Visited in the Past Year)	Established Customers (First Visited 5+ Years Ago)
Percent female	45	49%
Average age	36	40
Percent with college degree +	37	63
Average income	$65,000	$81,000
Average # cups of coffee/week (includes at home and away from home)	15	19
Attitudes toward Starbucks:		
High-quality brand	34%	51%
Brand I trust	30%	50%
For someone like me	15%	40%
Worth paying more for	8%	32%
Known for specialty coffee	44%	60%
Known as the coffee expert	31%	45%
Best-tasting coffee	20%	31%
Highest-quality coffee	26%	41%
Overall opinion of Starbucks	25%	44%

Source

Starbucks, 2002. "Attitudes toward Starbucks" measured according to the percent of customers who agreed with the above statements.

Measuring and Driving Customer Satisfaction

Finally, the team discovered that, despite its high Customer Snapshot scores, Starbucks was not meeting expectations in terms of customer satisfaction. The satisfaction scores were considered critical because the team also had evidence of a direct link between satisfaction level and customer loyalty (see *Exhibit 9* for customer satisfaction data).

Exhibit 9 Starbucks' customer behavior, by satisfaction level.

	Unsatisfied Customer	Satisfied Customer	Highly Satisfied Customer
Number of Starbucks Visits/Month	3.9	4.3	7.2
Average Ticket Size/ Visit	$3.88	$4.06	$4.42
Average Ticket Size/ Visit	1.1	4.4	8.3

Source

Self-reported customer activity from Starbucks survey, 2002.

While customer satisfaction was driven by a number of different factors (*Exhibit 10*), Day believed that the customer satisfaction gap could primarily be attributed to a service gap between Starbucks scores on key attributes and customer expectations. When Starbucks had polled its customers to determine what it could do to make them feel more like valued customers, "improvements to service" — in particular, speed-of-service — had been mentioned most frequently (*Exhibit 11*).

REDISCOVERING THE STARBUCKS CUSTOMER

Responding to the market research findings posed a difficult management challenge. The most controversial proposal was the one on the table before Day — it involved relaxing the labor-hour controls in the stores to add additional 20 hours of labor per week per store, at a cost of an extra $40 million per year. Not surprisingly, the plan was being met with significant internal resistance. "Our CFO is understandably concerned about the potential impact on our bottom line," said Day. "Each $6 million in profit contribution translates into a penny

To be read: 83% of Starbucks' customers rate a clean store as being highly important (90+ on a 100-point scale) in creating customer satisfaction.

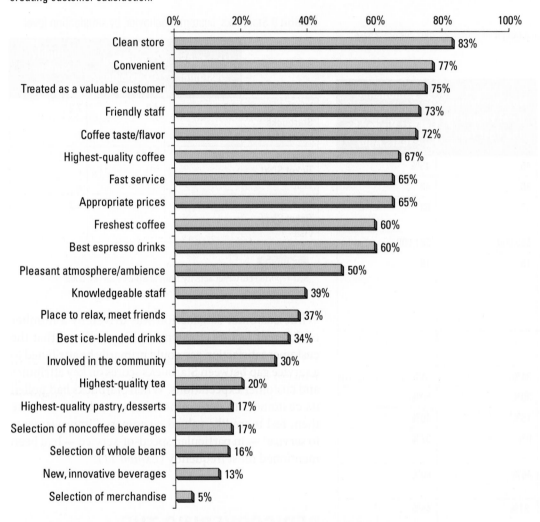

Exhibit 10 Importance Rankings of Key Attributes in Creating Customer Satisfaction

Exhibit 11 Factors driving "valued customer" perceptions

How could Starbucks make you feel more like a valued customer?	% Responses
Improvements to Service (total)	**34%**
Friendlier, more attentive staff	19%
Faster, more efficient service	10%
Personal treatment (remember my name, remember my order)	4%
More knowledgeable staff	4%
Better service	2%
Offer Better Prices/Incentive Programs (total)	**31%**
Free cup after X number of visits	19%
Reduce prices	11%
Offer promotions, specials	3%
Other (total)	21%
Better quality/variety of products	9%
Improve atmosphere	8%
Community outreach/charity	2%
More stores/more convenient locations	2%
Don't Know/Already Satisfied	**28%**

Source

Starbucks, 2002. Based on a survey of Starbucks' 2002 customer base, including highly satisfied, satisfied, and unsatisfied customers.

a share. But my argument is that if we move away from seeing labor as an expense to seeing it as a customer-oriented investment, we'll see a positive return." She continued:

We need to bring service time down to the three-minute level in all of our stores, regardless of the time of day. If we do this, we'll not only increase customer satisfaction and build stronger long-term relationships with our customers, we'll also improve our customer throughput. The goal is to move each store closer to the $20,000 level in terms of weekly sales, and I think that this plan will help us get there.

In two days, Day was scheduled to make a final recommendation to Howard Schultz and Orin Smith about whether the company should roll out the $40 million plan in October 2002. In preparation for this meeting, Day had asked Alling to help her think through the implications of the plan one final time. She mused:

We've been operating with the assumption that we do customer service well. But the reality is, we've started to lose sight of the consumer. It's amazing that this could happen to a company like us — after all, we've become one of the most prominent consumer brands in the world. For all of our focus on building the brand and introducing new products, we've simply stopped talking about the customer. We've lost the connection between satisfying our customers and growing the business.

Alling's response was simple: "We know that both Howard and Orin are totally committed to satisfying our retail customers. Our challenge is to tie customer satisfaction to the bottom line. What evidence do we have?"

Study Questions

1. What factors accounted for Starbucks' success in the early 1990s and what was so compelling about its value proposition? What brand image did Starbucks develop during this period?

2. Why have Starbucks' customer satisfaction scores declined? Has the company's service declined or is it simply measuring satisfaction the wrong way?

3. How has Starbucks changed since its early days?

4. Describe the ideal Starbucks customer from a profitability standpoint. What would it take to ensure that this customer is highly satisfied? How valuable to Starbucks is a highly satisfied customer?

5. Should Starbucks make the $40 million investment in labor in the stores? What's the goal of this investment? Is it possible for a mega-brand to deliver customer intimacy?

LUX*: Staging a Service Revolution in a Resort Chain

Jochen Wirtz and Ron Kaufman

ABSTRACT

LUX* was a successful hospitality group operating in the Indian Ocean as well as other locations. In its previous incarnation, the company suffered from poor financial performance, poor service quality and a weak brand. A change in the leadership of the company led the group through a transformation, which showed positive results within 12 months. This case study describes a service revolution that lead to rapid improvements in service culture and guest experience, which in turn lead to sustained financial improvements on a quarter-on-quarter basis.

INTRODUCTION

With its headquarters in Mauritius, the LUX* hospitality group operated a portfolio of eight resorts and a private island in the Indian Ocean (*Exhibit 1*). The brand

© 2016 by Jochen Wirtz and Ron Kaufman.

Jochen Wirtz is Professor of Marketing at the National University of Singapore. Ron Kaufman is founder and chairman of UP! Your Service Pte. Ltd.

The support and feedback of the management of LUX* is gratefully acknowledged, including Paul Jones, CEO; Julian Hagger, Chief Sales & Marketing Officer & Executive Director; Marie-Laure-Ah-You, Chief Strategy Officer; Nicolas Autrey, Chief Human Resources Officer; Nitesh Pandey, General Manager and Group Chief Innovation Officer; and Smita Modak, Group Training Manager; and Piers Schmidt, Founder of Luxury Branding. The authors also thank Arthur Lee who provided excellent assistance with the data collection, analysis and the writing of this case study.

All dollar amounts referred to in the text are in US Dollars unless otherwise indicated. The exchange rate used for all currency conversions is MUR100 to USD2.845.

promised guests a celebration of life through its new value proposition — luxury resort hospitality that is Lighter.Brighter.

What is the Lighter.Brighter hospitality? Established luxury hotels have come to be associated with stiff upper-lipped service and stuffy opulence. Lighter hospitality meant breaking away from these to offer a more effervescent experience without compromising on its upscale sensibilities. At the same time, LUX* wanted to brighten up guest experiences. For example, instead of having high prices for items from the mini-bar, LUX* wanted to encourage guests to enjoy themselves and just take from it what they fancy. To encourage this, LUX* lowered the prices of items in the mini-bar significantly. By being smarter in the way LUX* operated, both guests and business benefited.

Although LUX* was launched only four years ago, the group's resorts had been doing exceptionally well. Within a short span of time, LUX* successfully transformed its service culture. The group had seen 16 consecutive quarter-on-quarter improvements in its financial performance. The group's resorts also enjoyed a higher occupancy rate than the industry average in the destinations they operated in (measured quarterly by the Market Penetration Index, which compares the hotel's occupancy against its competitive set). The group's financial performance was mirrored by winning multiple accolades for service excellence, including "Indian Ocean Leading Hotel" for LUX* Maldives from World Travel Awards, "Best Resort Hotel Mauritius" for LUX* Belle Mare from International Hospitality Awards, and "Reunion Island's Leading Hotel" for LUX* Ile de la Réunion from World Travel Awards.

LUX* Belle Mare's Pool

LUX* Belle Mare's Beach

LUX* Belle Mare's Villa

LUX* Le Morne

LUX* Le Morne's Beach

Note: LUX* owns eight seaside resorts by the Indian Ocean. Each of them are fitted with an expansive infinity pool, stylish bars and ocean themed furnishings.

Exhibit 1 Some of the LUX* resorts in the Indian Ocean

THE DARK AGES

However, things were not always this rosy. Before LUX* was launched in 2011, the group was known as Naiade Resorts and the company suffered from poor financial health. None of its hotels were on the list of top 10 hotels on TripAdvisor in their geographic competitive sets. To top it off, the Naiade brand lacked clarity. Its brand name was used for nine different properties, ranging from three to five stars, creating an unclear positioning in the minds of consumers. Problems in its positioning became apparent when the global financial crisis struck in 2008–2009. This led to a large drop in occupancy and room rates (*Exhibit 2*). The group's troubles culminated in 2011 with a criminal case involving the high-profile murder of an Irish hotel guest.

Having witnessed prolonged economic turmoil and a criminal case, the motivation and morale of hotel employees were unprecedentedly low. Financially, the impact of these troubles cumulated in a downward trajectory in the company's performance from 2008 to 2010 (*Exhibit 3*). The company reported a loss in 2010.

After hitting rock bottom, management had to move fast, and Naiade Resorts achieved a turnaround within a very short span of time. By mid-2011, Naiade Resorts saw an improvement in its service and this quickly translated into improved financial performance. Since then, the company had witnessed substantive and consistent service culture improvement and financial performance growth. How did the group manage this turnaround so quickly?

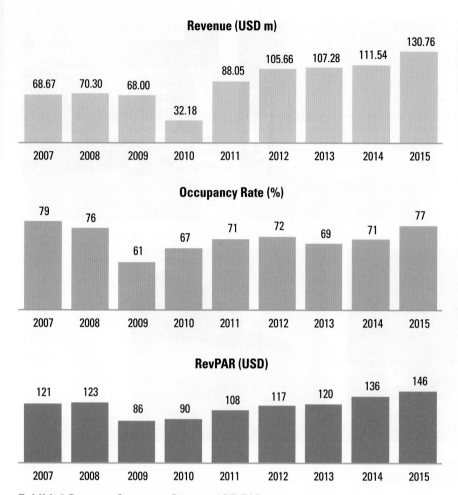

Revenue (USD m)

2007	2008	2009	2010	2011	2012	2013	2014	2015
68.67	70.30	68.00	32.18	88.05	105.66	107.28	111.54	130.76

Occupancy Rate (%)

2007	2008	2009	2010	2011	2012	2013	2014	2015
79	76	61	67	71	72	69	71	77

RevPAR (USD)

2007	2008	2009	2010	2011	2012	2013	2014	2015
121	123	86	90	108	117	120	136	146

Exhibit 2 Revenue, Occupancy Rates and REVPAR

EBITDA (USD m)

2007	2008	2009	2010	2011	2012	2013	2014	2015
21.26	14.20	10.55	2.73	18.92	18.98	22.02	25.10	29.56

Annual Profit (USD m)

2007	2008	2009	2010	2011	2012	2013	2014	2015
17.28	9.30	3.78	(0.68)	12.26	10.84	13.80	16.43	19.09

Note: Up till 2009, the financial year ended on 31 December. For 2010, all financial figures reported are for six months ending on 30 June 2010. From 2011 onwards, the financial year ended on 30 June.

Exhibit 3 Financial Performance of LUX*

LUX* TRANSFORMATION

The very first step in Naiade's transformation can be traced back to the second half of 2010. In dire straits then, the board of directors of Naiade Resorts made changes to the company's leadership, and appointed Paul Jones as CEO in October 2010.

Under Jones's leadership, many changes were introduced to the organization within the first 12 months of his appointment. They were aimed at rapidly improving the profitability of the business and creating a world-class brand so that it could expand internationally. However, this marked a difficult transitional period for Naiade Resorts, which was in financial doldrums. Every month, Naiade Resorts struggled to pay salaries. Some employees even wondered if the changes would sink the company further.

Observing how dire the situation was, Jones commented, "The numbers pre-2010 were alarming and the company was sinking fast and would have been bankrupt had it not been for the capital injection from shareholders. In addition, the properties were in poor shape and staff morale was exceedingly low".

Together with his team, Jones focused transformation efforts on four main areas through an integrated and congruent strategy (*Exhibit 4*). First, he looked into the company's core strategy as well as company values. Naiade Resorts' business model was shifted from one of owning hotels to managing them, following an asset-light strategy. Amongst others, the new model would reduce the company's cash outlay, as owning hotels can be highly capital extensive. For example, buying a modest-sized resort in Mauritius is estimated to cost upwards of 15 million. The new business model would reduce the company's risk exposure and allow it to expand at a faster rate. This shift provided a critical impetus for the company to concentrate on improving its service delivery.

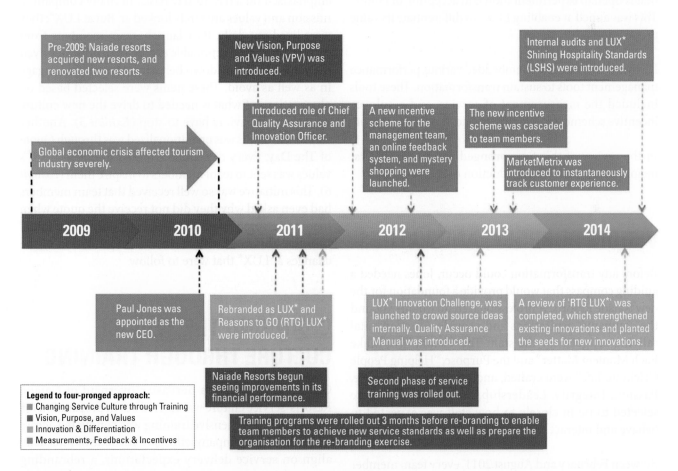

Note: *LUX*'s service revolution can be encapsulated by a four-pronged approach. After a change of leadership, Jones and his team swiftly introduced important changes in multiple areas that proved to be critical in turning the company around. The company has since continued to build on this momentum to continually improve.*

Exhibit 4 LUX*'s Four-Pronged Approach

To decide how to go forward, Paul Jones flew in the general managers from its resorts and the group's senior management from all over the world. The managers and executives from various levels made important decisions on the company. These include the company's new Vision, Purpose, and Values (VPV), a new name for the business, and redefining service standards. Many of these changes were implemented almost immediately after being agreed upon. This allowed for a progressive rollout of the company's new strategy.

Second, to engage and reinvigorate its staff in the transformation, the top management decided it had to build the company's service culture from scratch. This included extensive training across all levels of the organization, an alignment of expectations of service standards, and a psychological and tangible breakaway from the old Naiade Resorts.

Third, Jones leveraged a fledgling spirit of innovation to build an organization that is bold and open to ideas; one that is open to experimentation and accepting of failure. This was aimed at enabling LUX* to differentiate its value proposition.

Lastly, as CEO, Jones also embedded various performance management tools to sustain transformation. These tools included the measurement of service, and employee incentive schemes to realign a transformed organization.

In the review of this four-pronged approach, the first major change was the introduction of the new VPV.

VISION, PURPOSE, AND VALUES

Before any transformation could occur, Jones needed a guiding compass that would provide a foundation for the new Naiade Resorts. A professional credo would expound the company's aspirations and provide a fundamental rallying zeitgeist for the staff. The Vision, "We Make Each Moment Matter" and the Purpose, "Helping People Celebrate Life" were crafted, and the Values of "People, Passion, Integrity, Leadership, and Creativity" were selected to tie in closely to how staff was expected to behave and interact with guests.

Between February and August 2011, every team member of Naiade was called upon to participate in the VPV foundation course. The course was rolled out over three phases. In the first phase, the CEO personally visited each hotel to share with team members about the new VPV. Hand in hand with the CEO's visits, the general managers of the resorts rolled out engagement workshops to all team members, ensuring that everyone understood the VPV as the foundation of the group's operations. Finally, in the third phase, all staff members were asked to pledge to abide by the ideology.

To support this rollout process, Naiade Resorts developed communication collaterals to support what the staff had heard from its leaders. For example, a visual mnemonic representing the new values in the form of an open hand, was created. Also, the ideology of the group was translated into French, Creole, and Mandarin, the mother tongues of the majority of the employees. Beyond these initiatives, team members were encouraged to incorporate VPV into their lives outside of their work, such as making each moment matter for the staff's family and loved ones.

Even after its initial launch, VPV continued to be emphasized on a day-to-day basis. In many companies, mission and values are rarely looked at. But at LUX*, they were lived out daily. Post-launch, team members from each resort shared actionable examples of how they lived the values, by listing down behaviors they should engage in as well as avoid. These items were selected based on observations of what is needed to drive the new culture and which behaviors have to stop (Exhibit 5). Another way in which this was operationalized was through Quote of The Day. Every day, a quote linked to one of LUX*'s values was sent to team members to inspire them (Exhibit 6). This initiative was so well received that team members had even asked why they did not receive the quote when there were some operational hiccups during the initial roll-out. This new VPV formed the foundation of the changes at LUX* that were to follow.

CHANGING THE SERVICE CULTURE THROUGH TRAINING

Guided by the VPV, a pervasive overhaul of Naiade Resorts' service culture was carried out in preparation for its rebranding. Extensive training was conducted across all levels of the company, efforts were made to internally align on service delivery expectations, a rebranding exercise also provided a much needed psychological and tangible fresh start for the employees, and initiatives were introduced to sustain the transformation.

Exhibit 5 Actionable examples from employees on how they live by LUX*'s Values

People		Passion		Integrity		Leadership		Creativity	
Should Do	Should Not Do	Should Do	Should Not Do	Should Do	Should Not Do	Should Do	Should Not Do	Should Do	Should Not Do
Always thank guests when they are leaving	Argue/bad attitude/ rude	Go beyond expectations	Allow laziness to take over	Report any wrongdoing	Participate in any wrongdoings, no matter how insignificant they are	Always taking action	Act irresponsibly	Apply your own final touch	Dismiss colleagues' ideas disrespectfully
Be available to replace sick co-worker	Challenge the guest	Try to meet every guest request	Act in a frustrated or angry manner	Always say the truth regardless of circumstances	Not taking responsibility for a mistake	Attentive and prompt to act	Blame others when things go wrong	Surprise guests	Enter into a routine
Always be polite, caring and attentive	Ignore colleagues because you are busy	Care for the guest	See problems instead of opportunities in situations	Reporting every item found	Be involved in dishonest acts	Lead by example, be a role model & coach the employees, colleagues, team members	Behave in an autocratic manner	Go the extra mile by thinking out of the box & try to be innovative	Merely copy and replicate others' ideas

Note: After the introduction of the new VPV, employees from each resort listed behaviors that they considered to epitomize LUX's values. A sampling of the examples provided is shown above, in no particular order of importance.*

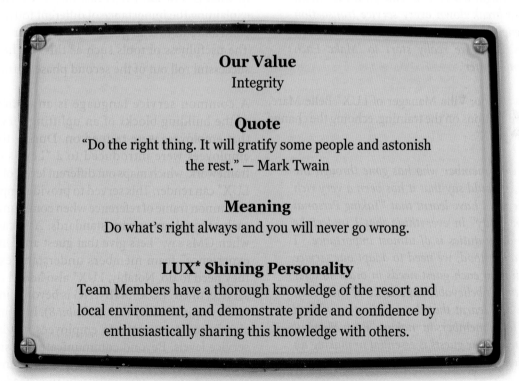

Our Value
Integrity

Quote
"Do the right thing. It will gratify some people and astonish the rest." — Mark Twain

Meaning
Do what's right always and you will never go wrong.

LUX* Shining Personality
Team Members have a thorough knowledge of the resort and local environment, and demonstrate pride and confidence by enthusiastically sharing this knowledge with others.

Note: A 'Quote of the Day' is sent to employees every day to remind them of LUX's values as well as to motivate and inspire them.*

Exhibit 6 An Example of a Quote of the Day

Comprehensive training permeated throughout the company. Apart from the senior managers who met to deliberate on the desired service standards — benchmarking against different industries — LUX* partnered with an external service provider to design and deliver training on fundamental service principles. The first course delivered an actionable service education that enabled team members to deliver service valued by guests. As part of the course, employees were introduced to the building blocks of an uplifting service culture. By breaking down an abstract concept like culture into smaller and more tangible parts, it was easier for the organization to achieve its desired culture. Such a training helped LUX* look beyond standard procedures to interact with guests to find out what they truly value. In doing so, LUX* was eventually able to deliver a unique experience to its guests.

Adarsh Grewal, HR and Training Manager at LUX* Le Morne, was one of the many employees who benefitted from the training. Adarsh commented on the training:

> When you break down everything you do daily and look at it from the eyes of your customer — internal or external; you begin to realize the value of every little step and the loopholes their absence might leave. Soon enough it becomes a habit to break down every service transaction and when it starts happening subconsciously, that is when we really start to 'Make Each Moment Matter'.

Nagassen Valadoo, Villa Manager of LUX* Belle Mare, shared his reflections on the training, echoing the change in culture at LUX*:

> As a team member who has gone through the course, I would say that it has been a very rich experience. I have learnt that "Taking Personal Responsibility" in everything that I undertake in my daily duties is of utmost importance. I have understood, we need to adapt our service according to each guest needs in order to offer them an Unbelievable experience of their stay. I have also learnt that the contribution of each of the team members in making "Each Moment Matter" for our guests is essential in making an experience memorable for them.

The training kicked off with an initiation workshop held for all 2,800 employees across the group. To roll out the training, more than 30 team members underwent a workshop to become certified course leaders. Hailing from diverse backgrounds, the trainers developed entirely in-house a customized version of the generic course materials from an external provider. This created the perception of the training as an internal LUX* product, improving receptivity from team members.

To make the materials more relatable for team members, the examples used were from best practice organizations in the hospitality industry. For instance, case studies of companies such as Disney, The Ritz-Carlton, and Singapore Airlines were used to illustrate service excellence.

The way the training was structured also contributed to the success of re-building the company's service culture. The course was rolled out in two phases with a gap of four months between the end of the first phase and the start of the second (*Exhibit 7*). Structuring the course in such a manner facilitated buy-in from staff as they were able to try out what they learnt in the first phase and then tried it out in their day-to-day work to see the value of the training. An example of this is the Perceptions Points analysis, which taught employees to focus on delivering service by first understanding guests' point of views and what they value rather than be bound by internal procedures. This analytical tool was applied to what is now known as Reasons to Go (RTG) LUX*, explaining the importance of different touch points that contribute to overall guest experience for each reason. The usefulness of tools such as this set the stage for a successful roll out of the second phase of training.

A common service language is an example of one of the building blocks of an uplifting service culture that employees were trained on. During the training, employees were introduced to a "Levels of Service" framework, which maps out different levels of service that LUX* can render. This served to provide employees with a common frame of reference when communicating with each other about service standards. As a case in point, when GMs say, "Let's give that guest an "Unbelievable" experience", team members understand exactly what they need to do. Notably, LUX* also added a 7th level of service, titled "LUX* SHINING is beyond unbelievable" to the original framework (*Exhibit 8*). In doing so, LUX* clearly communicated to employees its vision for its service levels. Beyond communicating desired service standards, LUX* helped employees to connect VPV to service standards, explaining why they needed to deliver on certain service standards based on their company beliefs. This took the form of a pledge that elegantly weaved VPV with service standards (*Exhibit 9*).

PHASE 1

- Introduction to six different levels of service
- Understand why service must continually improve
- Identify actions to improve service

- Learn to enhance service delivery by prioritizing customers' point of view and what they value.
- Analyze and improve service transactions in terms of critical touch points.

- Pledge to 'Take Personal Responsibility' to set the stage for team members to fully contribute to re-branding efforts.

PHASE 2

- Introduction to LUX* Shining Level of Service

- Understand how guests derive value in four different areas: primary product, delivery system, service mindset, and on-going relationships.
- Understand that the overall service experience is not just delivering service to guests when they are on the resort, but also when they interact prior and after their stay.

- Appreciate the use of appropriate communication styles in different contexts.

Note: To prepare the company for its new direction, employees underwent training in two different phases to learn more about building an uplifting service culture.

Exhibit 7 Training on Service Culture

OUR COMMON SERVICE LANGUAGE
The 7 Levels of Service at LUX*

LUX* SHINING is beyond Unbelievable

Unbelievable is **WOW**

Surprising is something special

Desired is what guests prefer

Expected is just average

Basic is the bare minimum

Criminal is below the bare minimum

Note: LUX* adapted the Levels of Service framework from its training partner, UP! Your Service College, and added a 7th Level of Service.

Exhibit 8 The 7 Levels of Service

As I believe in *'Consideration for People;'* I will always avoid **CRIMINAL** levels of service to my Guests and Colleagues.

As I believe in *'Serving with Passion;'* I cannot be satisfied with just giving **BASIC** level of service.

As I have pledged to *'Make Each Moment Matter'* for my Guests and Colleagues towards achieving our purpose of **'Helping People Celebrate Life;'** I must go beyond delivering only the **EXPECTED** level of service.

I expect myself and my colleagues always to be *Honest, Fair, Sincere and Authentic.* Together we will always *'Insist on Integrity.'*

Our belief *'Responsibility of Leadership;'* will Inspire me to **Lead by Example** in always delivering **DESIRED** level of service to my guests and colleagues.

My Curiosity and Imagination will drive my *'Creativity'* to deliver; when the opportunity arises; **SURPRISING** and **UNBELIEVABLE** levels of service to my guests and colleagues.

To uphold our promise and become a winning brand; I aim to deliver **LUX* SHINING** level of service to all our guests. I want to convince them that they have made a perfect choice for their vacation.

Exhibit 9 Weaving VPV Into Levels of Service

Three months after the launch of the course, Naiade Resorts was re-branded as LUX* Resorts and Hotels. On the December 3 2011, LUX* opened its doors to journalists and invited the finest magazines from around the world to stay in its resorts. A whole week of events was organized in Mauritius to celebrate the occasion. The launch of LUX* generated a very positive response from its key partners and the media, which helped to generate word-of-mouth.

Over time, the training became more comprehensive and covered five core areas (*Exhibit 10*). Service training continued to be delivered to both new team members as well as veterans. New hires were introduced to the content of the course as part of LUX*'s orientation program.

Almost 60–65% of the orientation's content was dedicated to service delivery, and preparing new team members to blend in seamlessly with experienced staff. For veterans, continual training on service culture helped to reinforce the learning. In follow-up sessions, participants shared how they had put the core learning to practice. Together, these revamped and intensified training and coaching programs helped to develop a strong learning culture and better-trained team members who contributed significantly to LUX*'s success.

Exhibit 10 LUX*'s Areas of Focus for Training

Area of Focus	Description
General Training	Ensured that team members were equipped to deal with operations and guest issues.
Service Culture	A large part of LUX*'s training efforts focused on building an uplifting service culture to deliver service that is truly world class.
Technical	Focused on training needed for staff to perform their jobs efficiently in different departments. A large part of the technical training was done in-house.
Leadership	Specific leadership development programs were targeted at different leadership levels in the company. Training was customized and delivered in partnership with training providers that had a strong focus in leadership.
Language	Language training was important to ensure that LUX* was able to customize their service experience to changing market mix — especially since the Chinese and Russian markets had seen fast growth in recent years.

INNOVATION AND DIFFERENTIATION

In order to deliver a truly Lighter.Brighter luxury resort experience, LUX* had to cultivate a service DNA that embraced the invariable experimentation failures along the way, and promote a culture that continually innovated and differentiated itself from the competition (see *Exhibit 11* on how employees embraced creativity).

During the development of LUX*, the management was bold and open to ideas. Paul Jones sought to instill in the LUX* DNA a spirit that is open to experimentation, continually innovating and accepting of failure. This

Exhibit 11 Employees exercise their own creativity in making guests feel special

meant that there were many ideas put to the test when the company re-branded, and even after the launch of LUX*. The company saw continual improvement of its service and performance as an imperative.

At the inception of LUX*, one idea that was experimented with is the use of theatre as an analogy to think about the hotel. Team members of the hotel were thought of as actors who performed while the general managers were producers who directed the show. LUX* intended to use this analogy to motivate staff to give more of themselves to guests. However, they soon realized that it was difficult to bring this idea to fruition. The analogy was confusing to guests, as well as team members.

On this matter, Sydney Pierre, Head of Worldwide Sales, shared:

> *The theatre analogy was a great concept and a game changer in terms of innovative operational approaches; however, the practicality of implementation was low and did not really make any difference to our tour operators.*

Echoing Sydney's thoughts was Caroline Gaud, Marketing Communication Manager, who said:

> *It was confusing for our partners and our guests; some of them expected to see a "show" playing at the resorts and were disappointed. The analogy was misunderstood and created too much confusion, therefore, we decided to get rid of it. Simplifying the brand concept was critical at this stage to raise awareness and attract guests.*

The team coined the term RTG LUX*, which stands for "reasons to go to LUX* and refers to the unique selling points of LUX* resorts. It bore testament to LUX*'s willingness to try and its innovative spirit. When creating LUX*, the leadership team had initially set a bold target of creating 50 RTG. This ambitious goal was met with difficulty, as there were many other initiatives that were concurrently being rolled out.

One RTG LUX* that was dropped was the Secret Bar, a pop-up bar. The bar was found in different parts of the resort at different times of the day and worked on an honor system – guests poured their own drinks and recorded what they consumed. Conceptually, the idea was brilliant but it was beset by operational challenges. One such challenge is that while serving themselves, spillage sometimes occurred, impacting the experience of subsequent guests. Although some properties were able to control the quality of the guest experience, it was difficult to achieve this across all properties. As a result, it had to be retired as a RTG LUX*. Nonetheless, it continues to be offered as a service in some properties that had managed to make it work.

Apart from quality, some RTG LUX* were withdrawn for reasons such as budget and logistics. Eventually, the list of RTG LUX* was organically narrowed down to 20. Some of these reasons became iconic and resonated very well with guests. One of the most documented RTG on social media and TripAdvisor was "Message In A Bottle".

XLuo, a TripAdvisor user, described his experience with Message In A Bottle as follows:

> *We found a total of four secret bottles around the island that include free bottle of wine, free*

pizza for in-villa dining, and free cocktails. We woke up every day around 6.00 a.m. to jog around the island and spend time to find these bottles hidden all around the island, and it was really a fun way to start every day on the island.

Epitomizing its emphasis on innovation was the decision to introduce the role of a Chief Quality Assurance and Innovation Officer. To stimulate innovation, the incumbent introduced the LUX* Innovation Challenge. Each year, a theme that revolves around business needs such as increasing the loyalty of guests and team members, and improving revenue is set. Teams in each resort as well as the head office then propose ideas, which are rolled-out upon approval. Towards the end of the year, the teams reconvene to present the results of their ideas to a jury. Subsequently, the winning idea is rolled-out across all the resorts, along with other promising ideas that had come out of this challenge.

A particularly impactful idea was FIESTA, which came in first place in the 2014 challenge on innovating to increase the loyalty of team members. FIESTA is a wide-ranging high engagement program that allows employees to benefit from activities in the following areas: *F*itness, *I*nnovation, *E*tiquette and *M*orale Week, *S*pa, *T*hank you, and *A*ward.

For example, Etiquette and Morale Week, the main highlight of the program and also the world's first, brings together young children of team members for three days for a series of activities. Examples of these activities are tennis classes, mocktail classes, recycling of plastic products, and dedicating poem writings to their parents to express gratitude. All in all, the event created a sense of pride and respect amongst the children for the work their parents do. This ground-up initiative had a significant impact on team member satisfaction (*Exhibits 12a* and *12b*) and also went on to win the Best Initiative in Human Resources at the 15th Edition of the Worldwide Hospitality Awards.

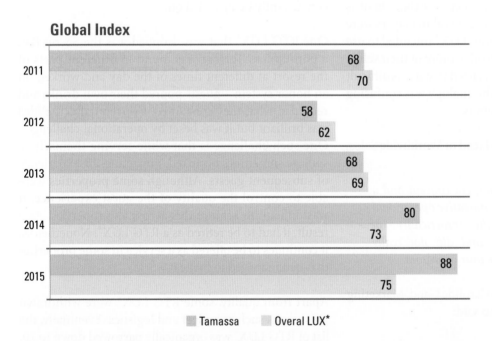

Global Index

	Tamassa	Overal LUX*
2011	68	70
2012	58	62
2013	68	69
2014	80	73
2015	88	75

Note: FIESTA was introduced in Tamassa and its impact on the loyalty of team members is reflected in the trend in its Global Index in comparison to other LUX resorts.*

The Global Index is a weighted index of 5 Dimensions of well-being at the workplace that are measured by LUX through its Team Member Satisfaction Survey. The higher the score of the index, the better the performance on these dimensions.*

Exhibit 12a The Impact of FIESTA

Exhibit 12b The Global Index — 5 Dimensions of well-being at the workplace

Dimension	Description
Vital Dimension	Team Member Morale. (State of mind: tense, depressed, happy, etc.)
Existential Dimension	Personal and Professional Accomplishment. (Training, Workload, and Resources)
Social Dimension	Interrelationships, Sense of Belonging, and Recognition.
Material Dimension	Physical Comfort at Work, Ergonomics, Salary, Benefits, Fun and Excitement.
Organizational Dimension	Internal Organization Perception and Degree of Engagement with LUX* Resorts' Vision, Purpose and Values.

LUX* was cognizant of the need to stay different and keep ahead of its competition. This spirit of constant innovation is also exemplified by the decision to review its RTG LUX* three years after its launch. The review served to formally define what a RTG LUX* is and critically evaluate the RTG — by identifying what was done well, what was not so successful and how to improve further. The value of each RTG was assessed using a 5D system (*Exhibit 13*) developed by LUX*.

Exhibit 13 The 5D System: Reasons to Go LUX*

Evaluation Filter	Guiding Questions
1. Does it **DELIVER** the brand experientially on property?	• Vision — Does it make a moment that matters? • Purpose — Does it help people to celebrate life? • Does it substantiate the promise of hospitality that is 'Lighter.Brighter'?
2. Does it **DEMONSTRATE** our creative principles?	• Does it banish thoughtless patterns? • Is it simple, fresh and sensory?
3. Does it **DRAMATISE** the brand concept?	• Does it celebrate 'Locale Life', our nature and culture? • Is it Light Luxury: lightweight and light-hearted?
4. Does it **DIFFERENTIATE** us from our competitors?	• Is it quirky, charming, or cool? • Is it generous, thoughtful, or surprising?
5. How well does it **DISSEMINATE** the word?	• Is it PR-able? • Is it sellable? • Is it shareable?

Note: The 5D system was developed by LUX* to evaluate current and future Reasons to go LUX*.

After the review, the management decided to focus on 11 RTG LUX* (*Exhibit 14*). They each appealed to different types of guests — families, couples, the young and young at heart, as well as niche audiences. These RTG made guests feel different and special. While one single reason may not have triggered guests to choose LUX*, the various reasons worked together to deliver an attractive proposition.

Exhibit 14 Eleven Reasons to go LUX*

Reasons to go LUX*	Description
Ici Exhibit 14a	A holiday without ice cream isn't a holiday at all so we created our own brand called 'ici'. An array of exotic, island flavors are served from retro-styled parlors and mobile carts while a fresh waffle cone is baked right in front of your eyes. Crunch. Munch. Perfect after lunch. (*Exhibit 14a*)
Café LUX*	We believe that great coffee is a must and not a luxury so at the heart of each resort, you'll find a Café LUX*. Enjoy our organic Island Blend, freshly roasted on-site, in a truly different café setting. Flat White or FrappeLux — they're perfect for a seaside sip and surf.
Phone Home	We believe that holidays should be stress and hassle-free, which is why if you explore our resorts you'll find a telephone box and inside a vintage VOIP phone. Here you can make local and international calls free of charge. We just ask one thing: Please do not call the office!
LUX* Me	LUX* Me is an integrated philosophy of well-being, offering a step by step path to an altogether healthier way of life. Naturally, in addition to al fresco classes, our personal trainers specialize in pilates, yoga and meditation classes as well as tailoring programs to you and your requirements. Now stretch!

Reasons to go LUX*	Description	Reasons to go LUX*	Description
Scrucap	We love a good Burgundy or vintage Bordeaux but the Indian Ocean's a long way from the vineyards of France so we've tapped South Africa for its most exciting contemporary wines. Cape blends survive the short journey in mint condition. Introducing 'Scrucap' and 'Popcap'. Not a corked wine in sight.	Message In A Bottle	You spot a lonely bottle hidden in a bush beside a sandy path. Inside this mysterious vessel, you find a scroll of paper, which reveals a special treat waiting for one lucky guest. Stay alert because it's only if you find the bottle that this daily surprise can be yours.
Cinema Paradiso	A large screen, fastened between two palms, flickers into life and you're transported to another world — of blockbusters, family classics and world cinema. It wouldn't be the movies without the nibbles, so there's fresh popcorn on the house, 'ici' ice cream and drinks served right to your beanbag. Curtain Up! (*Exhibits 14b and 14c*)	Thread Lightly	We can't always promise clear skies but, with your help, we can guarantee a clear conscience. LUX* cares about the destinations that are home to its properties. After all, memorable holidays shouldn't cost the earth and that's why we are doing our best to 'Thread Lightly' by offsetting 100% of the carbon emitted during your stay. It's one of a number of measures we're putting in place to help us leave a lighter footprint.
		Mamma Aroma	For as long as any of us can remember, amenities have been a staple in every hotel and resort bathroom around the world.
			Imagine hair lovingly nourished by deep conditioners; lazy baths scented with tropical oils; bodies gently burnished with a patina of sea salt scrub and sun-kissed skin glowing with the natural moisturizing properties of the island's products.
			LUX* Resorts & Hotels offers you, for your bath experience, something different: an element of surprise, a gasp of pleasure, and a nod to simplicity are behind our selection. And being considerate to the environment, our products and their packaging are as light on the planet as they are on the body.

Exhibit 14b

Exhibit 14c

Reasons to go LUX*	Description
Mamma Aroma	We have also worked with renowned aromatherapist Shirley Page to create an exclusive range of essential oils, using island ingredients- essences, flowers and spices that combine to create a magical world of fragrance. Used in our LUX* Me spa, the oils are also present in interior and linen scents.
Tree of Wishes **Exhibit 14d**	At every LUX* Resort & Hotel, you'll find a specially commissioned Tree of Wishes sculpture made by local artisans. Upon check-in, you'll be handed a unique ribbon featuring your initials and the date of your visit. Although not compulsory, you are invited to make a donation which will be made annually to a local children's charity. Tie the ribbon around one of the branches whilst making a wish. Whilst we can't guarantee your wish will come true, we can promise that once a year one lucky ribbon will be selected and the lucky person who placed it there will win a free holiday to LUX*. (*Exhibit 14d*)

Note: LUX staff places coupons for complimentary spa treatments, pedicure facial or massages in bottles around the beach. Some messages are written clues directing guests towards the Secret Bar, or offer an opportunity to enjoy a special dining experience for two on the beach. Guests who serendipitously stumble upon these bottles on the beach are in for a treat.*

Exhibit 15 Message In A Bottle

MEASUREMENT, FEEDBACK, AND INCENTIVES

In the transformation journey, measurement of service performance became a priority. Prior to Jones' tenure at LUX*, Naiade Resorts collected guest feedback using written forms and a quality assurance coordinator was appointed in each resort. This system placed certain limitations on what the company could do with feedback. These include delays in terms of consolidating feedback, a lack of central coordination of quality assurance, and hence, low visibility among top management, as well as difficulty in measuring service performance within and between the different properties of the group.

While a basic customer feedback system was in place, service measurement and feedback had become much more sophisticated under Jones' leadership. Within a month of recruiting the Chief Quality Assurance and Innovation Officer, LUX* went online with its feedback form. Although LUX* could not afford to invest heavily in an online feedback system at that point in time, it saw a basic online platform as a step in the right direction.

Another outcome of the review was an augmentation of the successful RTG. With Message In A Bottle (*Exhibit 15*), numerous improvements were made in various areas. Execution-wise, bottles were placed at different times to cater to guests with different sleep cycles.

To capture, develop and disseminate new ideas, LUX* created the LUX* Ideas Bank, a depository where ideas could be placed, shared, discussed, measured, and tested. Ideas were contributed by team members and scored. Promising ideas were developed into prototypes and evaluated again. Those ideas that passed the rigorous testing process were finally screened by a senior operator task force that selected them for implementation. This process created an innovation pipeline, allowing the company to launch three new RTG LUX* every quarter and thereby drove continual innovation.

With an online platform, LUX* had visibility on how each resort was performing in terms of service quality, and it also motivated employees to provide better service.

Soon after, LUX* launched a quality assurance manual based on standards of global best practices in hotel and hospitality management. It spelt out clear service targets in all areas of operations, right down to micro-moments such as the amount of time that the restaurant should take to hand guests the restaurant menu. This was accompanied by a mystery-shopping audit to check that standards were met.

In terms of external measurements, the company paid close attention to customer feedback and ratings on TripAdvisor (*Exhibit 16*). For instance, qualitative feedback on TripAdvisor was monitored and responded to by the management personally. The feedback was also discussed with department heads within LUX* when it concerned their line of work. The ratings were even monitored and tracked as part of selected employees' key performance indicators (KPI).

Throughout the transformation, the impact of the changes introduced was seen in the improvements in their financial performance such as the growth in their publicly reported quarterly revenue. This provided satisfaction for staff in the form of indirect feedback for what they had accomplished. In 2012, however, LUX*'s management also realized that there were only a few incentive schemes in place. Sometimes, the incentives did not serve the purpose of getting team members to focus on where they should. This prompted the management to review incentive plans to align the company in achieving its targets.

The new incentive schemes focused on three important things — Guest Experience, Team Member Engagement, and Earnings Before Interest, Taxes, Depreciation, and Amortization (EBITDA). This was rolled out first to the general managers of each resort in 2012. Subsequently, various schemes were developed for different groups of employees. A sample of the KPIs include targeted EBIDTA, targeted Trip Advisor scores, guest satisfaction related metrics, and a team member satisfaction index.

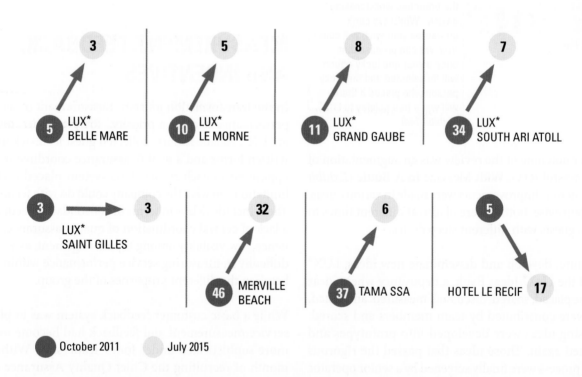

Note: This chart illustrates the change in ranking of LUX*'s resorts, from 2011 to 2015. The resorts are segmented by country, with the relevant LUX* resort ranked against other resorts listed on TripAdvisor. Note that TripAdvisor's ranking methodology changed in 2015 for LUX* Saint Gilles and Hotel Le Recif, using a much wider geographic region for the ranking. This lead to many more resorts being included in the ranking and it explains the drop for Hotel Le Recif.

Exhibit 16 LUX*'s Trip Advisor Rankings Within Each Country (2011 vs. 2015)

In Mauritius, an incentive scheme was extended to all Team Members. Under this scheme, the performance of individual hotels was linked to rewards for 2,000 frontline employees in Mauritius. By 2015, team members were given targets for EBITDA, TripAdvisor ratings, as well as MarketMetrix score (a measure of guest satisfaction). A bonus of 8% of the team member's basic monthly salary was paid when the KPIs were met. Paid out on a monthly basis, the bonus served as a tangible incentive to further motivate frontline staff to meet the company's goals.

While these tools served LUX* well, the group's ambitions have in a short few years evolved from turning around the company to becoming a leading international player. This also meant that some of its management tools had to evolve.

One tool that evolved was how LUX* measured customer satisfaction. In 2013, the LUX*'s online system evolved from a fairly basic system to one that is much more sophisticated. By partnering with MarketMetrix, LUX* was able to track customer experience almost instantaneously on a daily basis. Aspects of customer experience that were tracked included Check In and Check Out, Room, Food and Beverage, as well as Facilities and Amenities. Customer feedback was also taken so seriously that the CEO received metrics on customer satisfaction on his smart phone on a daily basis. LUX*'s partnership with MarketMetrix allowed it to not just benchmark itself across its resorts but also with its key competitors. This strong focus on customer satisfaction helped the company to better monitor and track its performance on a resort by resort basis, and within resorts, on a department by department level.

More recently, LUX* fine-tuned its internal quality standards and developed LUX* Shining Hospitality Standards (LSHS), which served as LUX*'s brand operational standards. In comparison to the LUX* Quality assurance manual, LSHS represented a shift from benchmarking against competitors to delivering service that was distinctively LUX*. For example, LSHS provided guidance to employees in terms of grooming and how they should interact with guests. A company-wide standard, LSHS was adapted to each resort in the form of standard operating procedures. Along with these changes in standards, LUX* also changed the way they tracked these standards such as using internal audits in place of mystery shopping.

FUTURE PLANS

Having successfully revolutionized its service through a four-pronged approach, LUX* was in 2015 in a much better position to implement its asset-light strategy. It already had signed a number of long-term management agreement for upcoming hotels in the Maldives and China.

By the end of 2016, LUX* expected to have close to a-third of its portfolio being owned by third-parties but managed by LUX*. Finally, LUX* entered into a franchise agreement to open Café LUX*, a RTG LUX* concept, outside the hotel. With its strong service culture, LUX* aimed to become more of a global company with a bigger footprint.

Study Questions

1. What were the main factors that contributed to LUX* Resort's successful service revolution?

2. What key challenges do you see in what LUX* did in carrying out its transformation? How were they addressed and what else could have been done?

3. What next steps do you think LUX* should take to cement its strong service culture, continue service innovation, and maintain its high profitability?

KidZania: Shaping a Strategic Service Vision for the Future

James L Heskett, Javier Renoso, and Karla Cabrera

Late in 2013, KidZania's management team under the leadership of Xavier Lopez Ancona held its latest meeting at the company's Mexico City headquarters to discuss the possible roll-out to other locations of new experiential learning concepts tested at its Cuicuilco kids' edutainment park.

The team had prepared itself over several months for what had become a complex discussion — based on 15 years of success developing and operating "parks" where children could role-play adult activities — about the direction the company should take. Having recently adopted experiential learning as its core strategy, the leadership team was challenged to understand what that meant in terms of priorities and tangible projects of the kind being brought to the company by potential partners as well as those tested at Cuicuilco. With initial operating results from Cuicuilco in hand, Lopez' team had evidence on which to base decisions about whether,

where, and how experiential learning initiatives should be introduced elsewhere in the KidZania global network. One important decision concerned the format for the first KidZania location in the US. In addition, franchising opportunities continued to arise. The two latest proposals were from Doha and London.

HISTORY OF KIDZANIA

While working in the toy industry in 1996, Luis Javier Laresgoiti visited a small childcare center, located in Raleigh, North Carolina, that incorporated themed role-playing activities. The children pretended they were visiting real-life destinations, and used fake money and groceries as part of their play. Upon returning to his home in Mexico, he formed a team with three of his friends to create a "city" for children that revolved around role-playing. Laresgoiti believed this concept would provide the perfect type of activity for the children of Mexico City who lacked an educational, fun, value-oriented and social entertainment center. The team formed a company and made plans to meet with developers and explore design options with architects.

After working together for a year, Laresgoiti introduced the group to Xavier Lopez Ancona, a friend from school who had attended business school at Northwestern University and was an executive at that time for GE Capital. Lopez's experience working with major corporations provided him with an extensive perspective for running a company. To make the envisioned city a reality from both a structural and financial standpoint, the group agreed that the concept had to be changed from a day care center to an entertainment and educational center. It would have to be large (4,000

Emeritus Professor James L. Heskett; Professor Javier Reynoso (Chair, Service Management Research & Education Group, EGADE Business School, Tecnologico de Monterrey, Mexico); and Senior Researcher Karla Cabrera (Service Management Research & Education Group, EGADE Business School, Tecnologico de Monterrey, Mexico) prepared this case with the assistance of Cammie Dunaway (KidZania Global CMO and US Pres ident). It was reviewed and approved before publication by a company designate. Funding for the development of this case was provided by Harvard Business School and not by the company. HBS cases are developed solely as the basis for class discussion. Cases are not intended to serve as endorsements, sources of primary data, or illustrations of effective or ineffective management.

All dollar amounts referred to in the text are in US Dollars unless otherwise indicated.

square meters or approximately 40,000 square feet), be able to accommodate 3,500 to 4,000 people per day over one or two shifts of eight hours each, be equally entertaining and educational, be built within a shopping mall (an existing, successful destination), and be created through a partnership with several established and highly recognizable companies functioning as sponsors. The sponsorship angle was particularly unique because it provided the group not only with the financial support it would need but also assistance in the design of activities, architecture, and interiors.

With significant investments from Lopez and a friend of his, the group began to implement its plan in February 1997. Soon after, they found an ideal site for the project in a major shopping center in the Santa Fe area of Mexico City. They hired an experienced design team to kickstart the planning and development process while they presented the idea to potential sponsors using sketches, renderings, 3D models, and a dynamic graphic identity package for what was then known as "La Ciudad de los Niños" ("The City of Children"). By the end of 1997, Lopez had tested the idea with 16 potential sponsors, all of which were major companies and whose brands aligned well with the concept of the project. Half of the companies expressed immediate interest and willingness to participate in the project.

In 1998, the team worked to acquire sponsors, complete the project's design, and obtain all the necessary permits. All of the final touches came together in 1999 and on September 1, "La Ciudad de los Niños" opened to the public. The park attracted 792,000 visitors during the first year (significantly more than the 400,000 that had been forecast), won industry accolades, and attracted investors, which in turn encouraged company growth. In part encouraged by the success of the concept, Larasgoiti sold his share in the venture and moved to Florida, where he opened a similar facility called Wannado. Ironically, it closed in 2011.

Based on ideas developed over more than five years in Mexico City, in February 2005, the team began working on a new city plan in Monterrey, Mexico's second-largest city, that enhanced the concept's environment, atmosphere, and activities. Many sponsors from Mexico City were eager to participate in the expanding company, and as plans for an updated location in Monterrey progressed, potential partners began contacting management with proposals for international opportunities. As a result, a franchise concept was developed, described in detail below. Under this program, the first franchise was granted to investors in Tokyo. Its facility became the first to open under the name of KidZania outside Mexico in October 2006.

As the company began to grow as an international entity, management, with the help of external consultants, arrived at the idea that each "city" (facility) could be part of a network comprising the "nation" of KidZania. This provided a framework for an expanded conceptual story of a nation founded by kids who saw how their parents had made many mistakes governing the real world; wrote a Declaration of Independence outlining six "rightz" to "be, know, create, share, care, and play"; composed both a national motto ("Get ready for a better world.") and a national anthem; and created a language. It also fueled the notion of franchise growth and an expansion of related project ideas. (See *Exhibit 1* for a list of KidZania locations).

In 2012, the company introduced a new outdoor automotive-based concept, with a stronger emphasis on driver education and citizenship, in Cuicuilco, a suburb of Mexico City. A concept that began with a passion to create a place for Mexican children to play among themselves while making a difference in their lives had now become a business concept that could inspire, educate, entertain, and empower children around the world.

A NATION IS BORN: THE KIDZANIA SERVICE CONCEPT

KidZania was conceived as an edutainment concept that invited children to role-play adult activities in realistically themed environments, programmed to mimic real-life. Built to a size scaled for kids (two-thirds of normal size), these environments were designed to imitate the inner workings of a typical city through the integration of recognizable destinations, real world products, and a functioning economy.

A Visitor's Experience

Under the KidZania service concept, every visitor to KidZania had the choice to participate in role-play activities, eat, and shop. Participation in the activities was varied in type and number depending on whether the visitor was a kid or an adult.

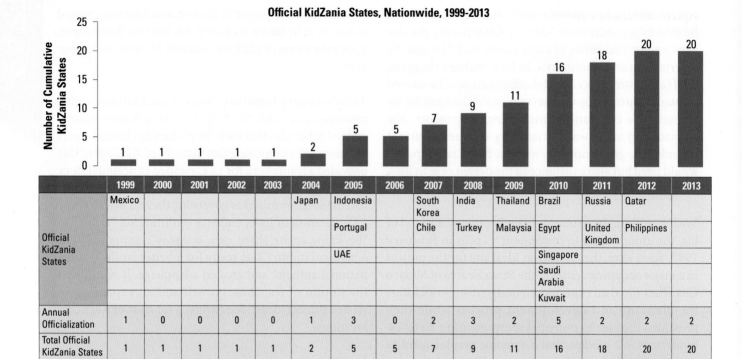

Official KidZania States, Nationwide, 1999-2013

Number of Cumulative KidZania States — bar chart values: 1 (1999), 1 (2000), 1 (2001), 1 (2002), 1 (2003), 2 (2004), 5 (2005), 5 (2006), 7 (2007), 9 (2008), 11 (2009), 16 (2010), 18 (2011), 20 (2012), 20 (2013)

	1999	2000	2001	2002	2003	2004	2005	2006	2007	2008	2009	2010	2011	2012	2013
Official KidZania States	Mexico					Japan	Indonesia		South Korea	India	Thailand	Brazil	Russia	Qatar	
							Portugal		Chile	Turkey	Malaysia	Egypt	United Kingdom	Philippines	
							UAE					Singapore			
												Saudi Arabia			
												Kuwait			
Annual Officialization	1	0	0	0	0	1	3	0	2	3	2	5	2	2	2
Total Official KidZania States	1	1	1	1	1	2	5	5	7	9	11	16	18	20	20

a *Year indicates when the license has been signed.*

Source
Company documents.

Exhibit 1 Official KidZania States and International Locations, 1999-2013a

To enter KidZania, visitors purchased a ticket (prices varied from $14 in Mexico City to $50 in Tokyo) at a branded airport ticket counter representing the entrance to each facility. Here, children and parents or guardians received RFID-enabled ID bracelets. These bracelets allowed adults to monitor the location of their children within KidZania at booths that were set up both inside and outside the actual facility. Each kid received 50 "kidZos" (Kidzania currency).

Upon entering, kids began learning a new language: "kai" (for hi), two fingers of the right hand arrayed over the heart for a greeting, "zanks" (thanks), and "Z-U", among others. Each KidZania facility was modeled to resemble a fully functional and realistic city. Children were guided through each activity under the supervision of a KidZania employee or "Zupervisor". Each activity had a runtime of approximately 25 minutes, and was carefully scripted for both Zupervisors and role-playing kids.

Those arriving at the park were classified into two categories: tourists and CitiZens. Tourists included children who were visiting KidZania for the first time as well as any adult. CitiZen, a status for which children had to apply after their first visit, was a special designation solely for repeat visitors to KidZania. These children were also referred to as "KidZanians", and were issued a "pazzport" as part of B•KidZanian, the Company's loyalty program. KidZanians had their passports stamped each time they visited a facility and at each establishment. As KidZanians received more stamps, they earned benefits such as expedited entry, increased salaries when performing a job at KidZania, discounted products, and invitations to special events. The loyalty program provided the means to drive traffic, repeat visits, and increased revenue by engaging parents with targeted offers and personalized recognition of the achievements of their CitiZens. It also enabled management to track preferences for various activities by age group. To date, about 400,000 PaZZports had been issued.

Children from four to 14 participated as workers, customers, spectators, or explorers. Those younger than four, and those above 14 and up to 16 years old did not participate in this manner. Instead, they participated in activities specially designed with their age group in mind. Adults with children over eight had the option of dropping their children off at KidZania, but adults with children younger than that had to join them inside the facility. Adults who wished to share in their kid's experience could become involved with activities as participants or spectators. They could also choose to spend time independently of their kids at spaces specially designed just for them, like the parent's lounge.

Activities offered to visitors represented common businesses, services, and industries that contributed to a conventional city's economy. Most of the activities in KidZania were designed as completely hands-on to provide the most contextual and engaging learning experiences. From police officer to dentist to restauranteur, each KidZania offered nearly 100 role-playing activities with a range of difficulty to meet the abilities and interests of every child. Kids worked to earn kidZos, KidZania's own currency, so they could pay for goods and services in KidZania city. Pilots navigated airplanes, television anchors read the news, police officers performed detective work, and chefs cooked up food. Getting started was simple: kids picked an occupation, learned about their job, donned a uniform, and started earning and spending kidZos, and, it was hoped, having fun.

When children and adults were ready to leave KidZania, they had to do so through the airport exit. This exit was a highly secure area in which the parent and child were cross-checked against the entry records before leaving.

The KidZania experience was reflected in 14 "brand qualities" subscribed to by its management: kid-centered, role-play based, reality-based, interactive, fun, thrilling, educational, skill developer, value promoter, safe, detail oriented, keep current, accessible to all, and sustainable. These brand qualities not only defined the organization's mission and offerings, but also served as a set of values by which the organization was to be managed. *Exhibit 2* contains several photos illustrating the KidZania service experience.

Withdrawing kidZos from ATM — KidZania Santa Fe, Mexico City

Airport ticket counters, KidZania Lisbon

Building in flames — KidZania Seoul

Main plaza — Kids running, KidZania Tokyo

Flight Simulator, KidZania Istanbul

Exhibit 2 Photos of KidZania Facilities in Different Countries

THE TARGET MARKET

KidZania's target visitor fell into one of four types of customer groups: young families with children three to 14 visiting mainly on weekends, holidays, and vacations; school groups attracted by the highly educational nature of the concept on weekdays; party groups attracted by special programming and food; and event groups that utilized KidZania after hours for gatherings, product launches, or for special programs such as summer camp.

KidZania catered to children ages three through 14 with most of its programming. It focused on kids from five to 11. Some of its programming was designed to be suitable for kids ages 11 to 14. Activities attractive to this older age group were generally more social in nature (e.g., Disco) or physically challenging (e.g., Climbing Building). KidZania also featured separate areas for toddlers, who were not yet ready for role-play, and adult visitors (parents, seniors, and teachers) who could spend their time in activities ranging from viewing children in the theatre productions to enjoying coffee and Internet access in the special parents' lounge.

KidZania's primary audience was families of middle to high socioeconomic levels. Kids from low-income families were also able to take advantage of price discounts that were offered as part of KidZania's corporate social responsibility program. All of KidZania's facilities and activities were designed to be accessible to visitors with mobility, viewing, hearing, or cognitive disabilities.

In addition, KidZania offered an alternative for educators to help children to use the expertise, skills, and values they acquired at school and practice them in a safe but realistic setting while sharing and cooperating with peers. Similarly, children who had experienced KidZania learning could practice this learning in their everyday lives.

The company was careful to direct all of its marketing activity to parents, not to kids. This helped dampen potential criticism of KidZania's role in introducing children to commercial activities.

Industry Partners

In addition to providing a valuable experience for children, the KidZania service concept also provided (and depended significantly upon) sponsorship opportunities for companies and institutions. Industry partners included corporations, non-governmental organizations (NGOs), and government institutions. Each contributed the economic resources for the design, build out, fit out, supplies, and know-how of each of the KidZania experiences. Partners brought the experience to life through the use of real products, services, processes, and technologies. KidZania's industry partners included many of the world's largest companies who additionally provided most of the supplies necessary for each activity, marketed and advertised the business and their association with it, and funded refurbishment. Industry partners ranged from major multinational brands like Coca Cola, Walmart, Toyota, DHL, and Sony to local companies like Telcel in Mexico (a major Telco), Yakult in Japan (yogurt company), and Qatar Airlines in Kuwait. KidZania had relationships with over 800 brands around the world. In-kind contributions and fees from partners represented about 30% of the revenue of a typical KidZania facility and about 40%–50% of the capital investment required. Capital investment ranged from $15 million (Monterrey and Jakarta, Indonesia) to $30 million (Dubai and Tokyo).

Each KidZania began with research about what children would like to see in the city. Some activities like firefighting were consistent across all facilities while some reflected local interests. Once a list of desirable activities was developed, the KidZania experience team created an outline of the content. The search then began for industry partners who could be a good fit with that content and could provide the knowledge to make it even more authentic. For example, in the first KidZania, the team knew they wanted an airplane activity. When they began meeting with American Airlines, the AA team decided it was necessary to provide a real airplane interior in which kids could work. Each partnership became a knowledge sharing activity between what KidZania's team knew about kids and what the partner knew about the best ways to bring its business to life. A list of some of KidZania's industry partners, and the activities they supported is shown in *Exhibit 3*.

THE SANTA FE OPERATION

The Santa Fe "Ciudad de los Niños" operated in roughly 40,000 square feet of space in the upscale Santa Fe shopping center in Mexico City.

The Offerings

The facility itself offered opportunities for role-playing of 80 different activities. Some of these required a minimum number of children to function properly. For example,

Exhibit 3 A Partial List of KidZania's Industry Partners in Santa Fe

Establishment	Activity	Industry Partner
Culinary School	Learn the basics of the Chef profession and learn and prepare a new recipe.	Herdez
Painting School	Learn an art discipline of choice, use authentic art supplies for painting a fresco on a wall or ceiling, paint on easels or color an illustration on paper.	Dixon Vinci
Secret Agent Training	Get training as an agent of the cities intelligence forces in a specially designed training facility and exercise the learned skills in a high rise building complex where a vertical descent down an elevator shaft is the final challenge.	Danone
University	Perform an enrollment process to get a student's ID and join a class of their choice in an undergraduate level. As students progress in their work experience, they can study a masters or a PhD degree, and receive higher salaries in kidZos as they finish higher degrees.	Anahuac University
City Bus Stop	At the bus stop, visitors board the city tour bus to know KidZania, its story, facts and its landmarks listening to a narration.	Cartoon Network
Bank	Cash kidZos checks provided at the airport's counters and perform bank transactions like opening an account, making a deposit or withdrawals and getting an account balance.	BBVA Bancomer
Hospital	Perform a liver transplant or a laparoscopy surgery in the operating rooms. Provide first aid services to an injured patient, taking her from the site of the accident to the emergency room in an ambulance. Bathe, change, dress, and feed newborn babies at the nursery room. Perform a general health check and sight test on patients to ensure their good health condition.	Hospital Angeles
Bottling Plant	Learn and execute the steps for producing a soft drink, from cleaning and filling the bottles with carbonated water and adding syrup, to placing a cap and labeling it.	Coca Cola
Chocolate Factory	Make a chocolate bar by mixing chocolate on a bowl, pouring it on a mold, cooling it down and packing it at the end of the process.	Nestle
Newspaper	Get an assignment to write for a section in a newspaper. Interview people as assigned and take pictures on the field to illustrate the story. Then, write the story at the news room integrating text and images, and print a copy of the newspaper for take away.	Reforma
TV Studio	Record a live TV program with audience on site, helping the cast to prepare for the program (wardrobe and makeup), performing in front of cameras setting up the scenery, operating cameras on the floor or audio, and video equipment in the control room.	Televisa
Beauty Salon	Provide customers with hairdressing, facials, makeup, and manicure services.	Jafra
Courier Service	Deliver and pick up parcels at different establishments around the city according to the assigned route. Kids also get the opportunity to send real letters to their friends or home.	DHL
Hotel	Welcome and check in hotel's guests at the front desk, set up a hotel room, making the bed and ensuring all amenities are in place, or set tables in a banquet hall.	Fiesta Americana
Vet Clinic	Learn concepts of animal health and perform a veterinarian task such as prescribing medicated pet food or performing a veterinary surgery.	Purina
Fire Station	Get training as fire fighter, then attend a fire alarm triggered at the Flamingo Hotel or a match factory, riding a fire truck along KidZania's streets to extinguish the fire with pressured-water hoses.	Seguros Bancomer
Burger Shop	Prepare a burger according to specified techniques for its ingredients and package.	McDonalds
Pizza Shop	Prepare an individual pizza, preparing the dough, pouring pizza sauce, and placing toppings according to specific instructions, then bake it, cut it and package it.	Domino's
Department Store	Customers have the opportunity to find products from different departments and buy them with the kidZos earned and saved.	Liverpool
Supermarket	Employees attend cash registries, serve in the different sections in the supermarket, like meat and poultry, fruits, vegetables, and pharmacy or restock shelves.	Walmart
Aviation Academy	Get aircraft pilot training in a state of the art flight simulator. Provide safety instructions to passengers in the cabin and provide them with the dining service.	American Airlines

Source
Company documents.

in the TV studio where kids aired a variety of programs including news reports, weather, and variety shows, kids were needed to operate the camera, work in the editing booth, and serve as reporters and news anchors. As a result, while an emphasis was placed on choice of activity by a child entering the facility, Zupervisors nevertheless were trained to suggest alternatives, depending on the need for role players in various activities and the desire to cut waiting times that reduced satisfaction.

Staffing

City staff were selected and encouraged to share eight qualities embedded in KidZania's core values: passion, creativity, quality, commitment, integrity, vision, motivation, and result orientation. These guiding principles shaped KidZania's corporate culture.

The success of KidZania relied on the staff's ability to make "the magic" happen: getting children involved in the realistic, thrilling and fun experiences of being an adult. The KidZania "experience" was centered on Zupervisors, typically 18 to 24-year-old undergraduate students or recent college graduates. More recently, they also included retired adults with a strong interest and experience in working with children, good energy, patience, and a service orientation, working on a part-time basis.

The KidZania experience relied on perfectly trained staff. As the organization grew and expanded internationally, KZ University was created to train local trainers with a focus on helping everyone understand the unique components of the KidZania brand experience as well as good customer service practices and operating procedures.

KidZania's turnover rate (83%) for frontline employees was lower than the average industry rate (120%). Efforts were ongoing to engage employees and encourage the sharing of best practice ideas. With that objective in mind, staff were rotated through various positions and had the opportunity to move between positions at an individual facility and headquarters, particularly in jobs that provided support to franchisees (described below).

Typically, a KidZania city required about 380 people to operate. About 130 of the employees were full-time. They included staff members who worked in point-of-sale positions selling food or merchandise. Approximately 40 people worked in general services including security, maintenance and IT. There were typically 15 to 20 people working in administrative functions like finance and procurement, and five in human resources. Each facility was led by a General Manager, called a Mayor, who was responsible for the overall facility P&L.

In addition, 250 part-time staff generally worked 4-hour shifts. They worked directly with the children to guide them through activities, communicate the key concepts, and help them to complete the job successfully. These "Zupervisors" also maintained their "establishment," doing light cleaning, restocking supplies, and setting up for each group. Staff members had to be selected and trained very carefully, with special attention to energy level and love for children. Training typically involved several days of classroom courses as well as three weeks of on-the-job training. The part-time staff received an hourly rate that ranged from the equivalent of $2 in Mexico to $10 in Japan. There were three levels each with different rates — a training level for three months followed by levels 1 and 2 Zupervisors. Labor costs were one of the most significant items on the unit level P&L, typically representing about 25%–30% of total revenue.

A chart showing the unit level organization for Santa Fe is presented in *Exhibit 4*. In its early years of operation, Santa Fe generated a great deal of publicity, and benefitted from a positive word-of-mouth that helped it maintain the traffic levels shown in *Exhibit 5*.

THE SERVICE CONCEPT EVOLVES: CUICUILCO

The development of the Cuicuilco facility represented a milestone in the evolution of KidZania. It was started in 2009 as a project requested by a local municipal government interested in promoting children's driver education. It opened in June 2012. It was based on the core KidZania service concept but offered new experiences to its visitors: driving and various aspects of citizenship. The facility, the largest opened to date, was outdoors and oriented around a system of roads, with most of the facility's grounds covered by tenting in case of inclement weather. The roads were navigated by scaled-down cars, and each child was assigned to different vehicles depending on age and experience. Each vehicle was designed with a low maximum speed and high safety standards in order to maintain an accident-free environment. After sufficient driving experience, children were able to upgrade from cars to trucks and buses.

ORGANIZATIONAL CHART
Kidzania KIDZANIA METROPOLITAN GOVERNMENT

SANTA FE

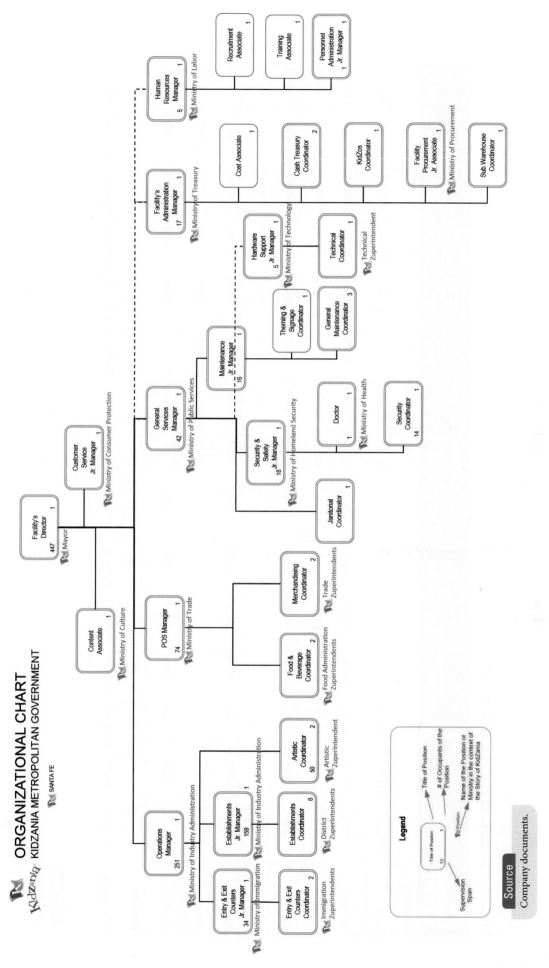

Legend

Title of Position → Title of Position

1 → # of Occupants of the Position

Position → Name of the Position or Ministry in the context of the Story of KidZania

12 → Supervision Span

Source
Company documents.

Exhibit 4 Organization Chart for Santa Fe

Exhibit 5 Historical Attendance Information for Santa Fe

Figures Expressed in MXP	1999	2000	2001	2002	2003	2004	2005	HISTORIC 2006	2007	2008	2009	2010	2011	2012	2013
SANTA FE															
Total Attendance	207,852	779,416	815,213	798,412	793,017	803,703	767,453	752,832	789,996	786,459	607,598	684,247	791,491	596,166	417,229
Families	156,215	493,529	462,723	433,367	452,091	460,411	430,669	421,364	426,173	417,510	319,650	341,677	365,940	306,636	246,771
Schools	28,430	211,458	289,839	289,136	263,395	271,801	277,236	286,900	287,668	281,248	217,166	240,567	296,491	218,077	112,013
Parties	9,877	26,084	18,511	16,287	16,388	18,620	17,419	17,720	18,717	19,706	20,534	25,171	25,445	22,613	17,716
Corporate	-	-	-	-	-	-	-	-	2,792	6,231	11,016	27,191	58,028	13,834	12,872
Events	13,330	33,010	12,315	27,014	28,297	26,330	19,654	26,848	31,252	38,465	11,346	21,869	16,483	6,887	1,500
Summer Camp	-	-	-	-	-	-	-	-	-	1,511	1,468	2,144	1,525	2,070	1,386
Pro Bono	-	15,335	31,825	32,608	32,846	26,541	22,475	-	23,394	21,788	26,418	25,628	27,579	26,049	24,971
Revenue															
Admissions	13,134,013	53,768,451	59,375,167	62,058,597	64,125,926	71,557,792	75,112,221	74,145,220	76,029,215	77,820,118	60,517,605	68,633,065	81,245,834	65,415,720	47,480,274

Source
Company documents.

In addition to driver education, Cuicuilco emphasized health, civics, community, and the environment. To transmit these topics, activities were redesigned and augmented. New ones were created. For example, the supermarket, a traditional KidZania establishment, was redesigned to include an activity in which children shopped for their groceries in a completely dark environment simulating the reality of a blind person. The facility also included a recyclables drop-off center, wind turbines, solar panels, and an electric power plant where children could learn about alternative energies and their impact on the environment. KidZania's focus on developing children's global citizenship, being empathetic and inclusive with those with different abilities, and awareness of issues like taking care of the environment was intended to enrich the KidZania service concept. However, it required not only much more space but also new kinds of partnerships.

Compared to the original Santa Fe concept, the 2012 facility at Cuicuilco (largely outdoors) required more employees, about 300 full-time and 500 part-time. It also required 23,435 square meters (or roughly 220,000 square feet) of indoor and outdoor space, higher equipment costs, and personnel costs that were 20%–25% of revenues. But it generated a higher operating profit. Because ticket prices had to be higher at Cuicuilco ($17) and there were more revenues from Industry partners, EBITDA margins were about 40%. Operating comparisons between Santa Fe and Cuicuilco are shown in *Exhibit 6*.

Challenges faced in the first few months of operation of Cuicuilco included managing a greater number of activities and staff. This contrasted to Santa Fe, where the biggest challenges in its first months of operation were learning the basics of operating an edutainment facility. In its first 12 months of operation, Cuicuilco attracted 729,000 people, substantially more than had been projected.

The Santa Fe facility required an investment of $8 million. It was financed with funds from industry partners (45%), equity (30%), and debt (25%). By comparison, Cuicuilco cost $38 million to build and equip. Its sources of financing were 30% from industry partners, 30% equity, and 40% debt.

FRANCHISING

The first KidZania franchised facility was opened in Tokyo in 2006. As franchised facilities began to develop along with those owned by KidZania, a detailed planning process, called "city planning", was refined. Excerpts from a document describing "city planning" are shown in *Exhibit 7*.

The original franchising agreement called for a payment by franchisees of $250,000 (later $650,000) in territory (countries or "nation states") fees, $250,000 (later $600,000) in facility fees and 5% of all ongoing revenue to KidZania. In return for the payments, KidZania agreed to provide intellectual property (name, logos, characters, story, music, and trademark registration); facility design (program development, master plan, design details, and theming); marketing materials; guidelines, manuals, and operating procedures; software; training; web design; and merchandise. Franchisees were required to secure the location, adapt the design locally, construct and fit out the facility, hire and train staff, market the concept and facility, secure industry partners, and operate the facility. There was significant supervision and oversight by KidZania both during development and ongoing operations. There was a system of regular audits and certifications that insured that the standards were consistently met. If there were significant breaches, the license could be revoked. This had not been necessary to date.

Interest among potential franchisees was strong. The first foreign entity to sign up was Japan, where KidZania was regarded as a good concept for Japanese families. Adjustments in the design of the park and the role-playing offerings to accommodate Japanese families included an even greater focus on educational content, including the addition of a University and a Kindergarten area for toddlers. These additions were a result of KidZania's ongoing research and commitment to continuous innovation. With each new facility, the company aimed to enhance the experience. After a successful opening in Tokyo, the KidZania brand became known in Asia. Others began approaching the company expressing a desire to franchise.

Even though the KidZania philosophy challenged adult customs, beliefs, and even laws in some countries, franchisees had found ways of adapting it to achieve acceptance among adults. Female kids, for example, were permitted to perform "jobs" in KidZania's Middle Eastern parks that their elders were prohibited from performing in the real world. KidZania's Middle Eastern facilities were among its most successful, something that management attributed to partnership with local franchisees.

Exhibit 6 Unit Financial Statements, Santa Fe and Cuicuilco, 2013

FIGURES IN MXN	Santa Fe TOTAL PY $	%	Cuicuilco TOTAL PY $	%
TOTAL ATTENDANCE	417,229	100.0 %	650,776	100.0 %
TOTAL PAYING ATTENDANCE	392,258	94.0 %	621,474	95.5 %
FAMILIES	246,771	59.1 %	342,242	52.6 %
SCHOOLS	112,013	26.8 %	185,245	28.5 %
PARTIES	17,716	4.2 %	28,717	4.4 %
CORPORATE EVENTS	14,372	3.4 %	64,673	9.9 %
CAMPS	1,386	0.3 %	597	0.1 %
PRO BONO	24,971	6.0 %	29,302	4.5 %
TOTAL PER CAPITA	175.17	100.0 %	228.31	100.0 %
ADMISSION	121.04	69.1 %	146.14	64.0 %
FOOD AND BEVERAGE	31.64	18.1 %	55.49	24.3 %
MERCHANDISING	12.94	7.4 %	17.60	7.7 %
PHOTO	5.55	3.2 %	4.89	2.1 %
LOYALTY	1.19	0.7 %	1.57	0.7 %
OTHERS	2.80	1.6 %	2.63	1.2 %
REVENUE	111,347,208	100.0 %	234,342,074	100.0 %
OPERATING REVENUE	68,710,417	61.7 %	141,891,567	60.5 %
INDUSTRY PARTNERS REVENUE	42,636,792	38.3 %	92,450,508	39.5 %
FRANCHISE REVENUE				
RETAIL REVENUE				
BUSINESS UNITS REVENUE				
COST OF GOODS SOLD	20,043,752	18.0 %	40,578,160	17.3 %
OPERATING COST OF GOODS SOLD	14,476,392	21.1 %	28,873,988	20.3 %
INDUSTRY PARTNERS COGS				
FRANCHISES COGS				
RETAIL COGS				
ROYALTY COGS	5,567,360	5.0 %	11,704,173	5.0 %
GROSS PROFIT	91,303,456	82.0 %	193,763,914	82.7 %
OPERATING EXPENSES	70,225,166	63.1 %	102,865,808	43.9 %
PAYROLL	44,478,913	39.9 %	68,780,304	29.4 %
RENT	8,779,845	7.9 %	9,168,413	3.9 %
UTILITIES	3,598,985	3.2 %	4,309,068	1.8 %
INSURANCE	358,104	0.3 %	577,152	0.2 %
SUPPLIES	2,816,602	2.5 %	2,208,247	0.9 %
MAINTENANCE	4,562,468	4.1 %	4,605,853	2.0 %
EXTERNAL OPERATING SERVICES	1,356,889	1.2 %	1,887,200	0.8 %
EXTERNAL PROFESSIONAL SERVICES	680,232	0.6 %	1,275,927	0.5 %
OPERATING TAXES	6,371	0.0 %	7,737	0.0 %
ALLOWANCE FOR DOUBTFUL ACCOUNTS				
NON DEDUCTIBLE	31,315	0.0 %	61,943	0.0 %
ADVERTISING	3,533,762	3.2 %	9,979,288	4.3 %
TRAVEL EXPENSES	21,679	0.0 %	4,677	0.0 %
OTHER EXPENSES				
EQUIPMENT LEASING				
EBITDA	21,078,290	18.9 %	90,898,106	38.8 %

Source
Company documents.

Exhibit 7 City Planning at KidZania

Selecting a Location

The market base for KidZania at city level requires a resident market size of three million people. The analysis of market size should consider the amount and type of competitors already operating in the city to reveal if the market's size can support additional development and explore pricing potential. It is also necessary to understand what the area's reputation is relative to tourism and what types of visitors are already frequenting businesses there. Also to be considered is if it the area is an appealing and considered an easy destination to get to.

KidZania facilities are best suited to a shopping mall that features an innovative tenant mix. Shopping malls are synergistic with the KidZania concept. They are strategically located and highly visible, offering good transport access, and large areas for parking. A situation indoors is preferable over outdoor entry venues because the position offers protection from inclement weather, is easier to maintain and easier to exert safety control. However, outdoors locations, as Cuicuilco, provide more realism and contribute to a more enjoyable experience.

The average size of a KidZania facility requires a footprint of 4,000 to 5,000 square meters and a total construction area of six to eight thousand square meters. The size reflects a mixture of visitor area, programming and back-office space and must include at least 50 to 60 establishments. Each KidZania facility must accommodate 1,800 to 2,000 visitors simultaneously, 3,500 to 4,000 visitors per day over one or two five-hour shifts of operation, and a yearly attendance of 400,000 to 800,000 visitors depending on the size of the facility.

Founding the City

After analyzing the market, an alliance is made with a local partner or a franchisee with global experience that provide the expertise to adapt the concept to local context. Every *Metropolis* (city) has a mixture of about 60 establishments, including mandatory (e.g., Airport, hospital, bank), optional (selected depending on the space available, e.g., go-karts), recommended (most popular) and switchable.

For each establishment there are a number of fun and educative activities designed for the kids. Local partners look for industry partners, consider the available space (e.g., driving experience or the stadium requires bigger spaces), cultural specificities (e.g., not including dogs in the UK facility) and, with the counseling of KidZania, make the final selection of establishments and activities.

All the activities are developed by KidZania to assure that the contents are attached to the experience learning guidelines and have a balance between learning and fun. Local partner input is crucial at this stage, and in some cases, its contributions led to the development of completely new experiences (e.g., Sleeping Institute in Korea).

The City Plan

The city's plan is one big environment made up of many small environments replicating a thematic mix of industry sectors. This is where the city comes to life. Establishments are the name for all the role-play locations independently if they take place at fabricated environments, in vehicular devices, or as part of independent activities within "common areas" of the city. The city plan is always arranged per four distinct city areas: city access, city center, suburbs, and industry clusters.

The role-play locations at KidZania are representative of the most common businesses, services, and industries that contribute to a conventional city's growing economy. These include: restaurants, retail, entertainment, media, public services, private services, transportation, and manufacturing.

The design of these scenarios physically replicates relevant areas or aspects of role-playing as dictated by the functional purpose of the environment or vehicle and follows a specially designed storyline supported by thematic components. These components collectively referred to as elements are occupationally related and include props, costumes, consumables, specialized equipment, and furnishings among others.

For each establishment KidZania provides detailed information to serve as a database and guide of the experience: activities, architecture design, theming, and fixed and variable elements. During the design of the city Experiential Learning fundamentals must be considered in order to provide the physical elements needed to create the experiences. For example, for the "University", a mandatory establishment in the city, KidZania specifies a foot print area between 50 and 60 square meters, provides a detailed description of all possible activities to be performed (e.g., "Bachelor degrees" in Health, "Administration" or "Engineering" or "postgraduate education"), the roles of Zupervisors, children, and adults (e.g., "professor", "student" and "observer", respectively), activity's duration (30 minutes), capacity (e.g., 12 children per hour), kidZo transactions (pay or purchase), giveaways (e.g., student card, career backpack), equipment (e.g. computers), uniforms for staff and children, theming props (e.g., human anatomy models), layout, accessibility components (e.g., wheel chair access for staff and visitors), etc. All these elements are aligned to offer children a fun experience while they learn about the role of a university in the society, strengthen values (e.g., honesty, preparing for an examination, and taking a test without cheating), and develop skills (e.g., children as students will require analytical thinking while solving doubts and answering exams).

City Staff

KidZania's corporate culture, completely service, and kid-oriented, makes the collaborators' selection and training crucial. As the CEO has mentioned: "If we are going to be an exceptional company is because of our people".

As a nation, KidZania faces the challenges of being multicultural and inclusive. Some of the best practices developed worldwide have been adapted to different cultural particularities. For example, in Jeddha, all Zupervisors must be women because men are not allowed to be physically in touch with children. In Cuicuilco, there are some blind Zupervisors performing specific activities associated with an effort to create a sightless experience for kids.

Safety and Security

KidZania takes great care to ensure the safety of its CitiZens, visitors and city workers going above and beyond standard safety and security practices. These practices include supervised access and exit monitored by a surveillance system and managed by security personnel; a well-trained security force to look out for the safety needs of the city and its people; an identification system of wireless radio frequency bracelets with a special identity chip that offers location tracking; the city's master plan provides for optimal precautionary considerations that include emergency exiting and signage, ambulance access, first aid location, and the position of each of its fire hydrants; in addition, all materials within the city are non-flammable or fire resistant and that nothing within reach features sharp textures, pointed corners, or expansive gaps that could cause injury. Areas frequented by KidZania's youngest visitors include the added consideration of non-toxicity in all materials specified.

Facility (Urban) Economics

Revenue. KidZania generates operating revenue through tickets (sold to families, schools, birthday parties, and corporations), food & beverage sales, photography, and merchandise. Admission prices vary based on relevant competitive and consumer factors, ranging from just over $15 in Monterrey to almost $60 per child in Japan. Prices also vary by age to provide discounts of ~35% to adults and toddlers who fall outside the target demographic. Children under the age of one enter free-of-charge and school groups receive a discount on the regular admission price. KidZania features a pay-one-price admission policy for entry that provides its visitors free access to all activities. Only food & beverage and merchandise locations require additional spending. Additional revenue comes from industry partners who pay an initial investment, an annual investment and remodeling fees when they wish to change or update their establishment design (see Capital Expenditures).

Expenses. General and administrative expenses consist of payroll costs composed of expenses from personnel working at the owned and operated facilities (see *Exhibits 6* and *8*) as well as employees at the corporate level; rent comprised of the rent paid for the owned and operated facilities located in the shopping malls as well as for the corporate offices in the US, Mexico, and Hong Kong; utilities and supplies including facility and office-related expenses such as telephones, the Internet, electricity, water, stationery, uniforms, etc.; marketing and PR expenses driven by marketing and PR initiatives at each facility and at the corporate level; travel primarily composed of the costs associated with the evaluation and development of both new owned and operated facilities as well as new licensed locations; external professional services primarily related to third party consulting and outsourced development services as well as architecture, tax, legal, auditing, and other outsourced services; and other expenses including maintenance costs, services, insurance expenses, leases, and other miscellaneous costs.

Capital Expenditures. Annual capital expenditures ("capex") can be broken down into two categories: maintenance and new facilities. Maintenance capital expenditures for the owned and operated facilities consist of remodeling expenses. The industry partner model enables KidZania to keep its maintenance capex relatively low. Industry partners not only typically pay for the upkeep of their establishments but also for any redesigns, leaving the company to only maintain the common grounds of each facility. New facility capex is made up of the costs to plan, design, and build out new owned and operated facilities.

> Source
> Compiled from company documents.

EXPERIENTIAL LEARNING

Competition that was increasing at a faster and faster pace globally (see below) combined with a more restrictive regulatory environment led KidZania's management to give increasing consideration to the expansion of the organization's mission and activities to include a greater emphasis on experiential learning. Experiential Learning involved education by direct experience or "doing" rather than rote or didactic learning. Research had shown that recall was higher after three weeks among people who had been told, shown, and experienced information as opposed to those who were only told or were told and shown. KidZania executives believed that its facilities' focus on role-play was particularly well aligned with the experiential learning approach to education. For example, rather than seeing a film on earning money and making decisions about spending, kids earned kidZos for the work they did, spent them on goods and services, and opened bank accounts where they could save kidZos and earn interest.

After the success of the educational and socially oriented ideas developed in Cuicuilco, KidZania's management adopted experiential learning as the core of the organization's service concept. As a result, experiential learning in KidZania was divided into two main blocks, general and specific learning. General learning fell into five main categories: How a City Works, Financial Literacy, The World of Work, Model CitiZenship, and Good Habits. Additionally, by participating in the activities and establishments, children were expected to develop expertise in understanding various industries and careers. It was hoped they would also develop necessary skills and good values. Specific learning areas were defined as: Expertise, Value Promotion, and Skills Development.

It was hoped that an increased emphasis on experiential learning at KidZania would strengthen the attractiveness of the service concept for a different mix of industry partners, providing them with a unique "experiential marketing" platform. For example, rather than a focus on just signage with logos, they could become a more integral part of the "story". This interactive and immersive environment would ensure that product interactions would be more meaningful and entertaining, while providing kids with ample opportunity to create a connection to the brand. If designed properly, these activities would reinforce KidZania's mission, and help to negate any criticism or misunderstanding about the commercialization of children.

For example, Walmart had been a partner for many years, sponsoring the grocery store in Santa Fe. This was a great way to teach children about the different sections of the supermarket as well as to practice adding up the cost of items as a customer or giving correct change as a clerk. Walmart wanted to go further, however, in helping kids understand the need to be empathetic to people with special needs. This was consistent with Walmart's own corporate goal to be a socially responsible company. As a result, at Cuicuilco KidZania created the Blind Awareness Center, where customers could shop or work in Walmart with special googles to stimulate the experience of being blind. To add to the children's experience, the Zupervisors

who worked in the establishment were themselves visually impaired. Similarly, JAFRA, a multinational beauty company that had long been a KidZania partner in the beauty salon activity, decided it wanted to teach kids the science in creating its products. So now kids could work as chemical engineers in its "cosmetics lab" at Cuicuilco, manufacturing customized cosmetic products, from development to packaging selection and decoration.

It was expected that experiential learning activities would require more detailed and complex design of activities. It would also require higher investments in media, complementary educational material (e.g., posters), and training. Designers faced the challenge of maintaining an optimal balance between learning and fun. Activities had to be adjusted to fit children's attention spans. While technology played a key role in the creation of children's experiences, one of the main objectives of experiential learning was promoting interaction among kids, avoiding the use of technology as a substitute for role-playing.

COMPETITION

While people inevitably compared KidZania with theme parks like Disney and Universal Studios, there were significant differences. For example, Disney was primarily a destination entertainment serving tourists who came from hundreds of miles away, and stayed three to five days. Most families visited Disney only one or two times in their lifetime, spending large sums of money. KidZania drew from a resident market, with families staying for five hours and coming multiple times during the year.

At Disney, the focus was on family fun with children interacting only with their families and primarily through rides and shows. At KidZania, children were largely free to pursue their own interests away from their parents. There was socialization and interaction with other children as they role-played together.

Disney focused on fantasy experiences and characters while KidZania focused on real life experiences. Because Disney was very capital intensive — with investment per facility of $1 to $2 billion — growth opportunities were limited to a handful of markets that could provide the necessary attendance. As a result, much of Disney's revenue growth came from licensing characters or other types of entertainment like movies and online games. By way of contrast, KidZania's facilities typically cost between $10 and $40 million, and could thrive in markets with as few as 700,000 children in a 90-minute radius.

That meant that growth could come from expanding to 90 to 100 cities that fit these criteria.

Both theme parks and KidZania did, however, compete with local establishments for visitors' time and money. Competing establishments included local operations such as zoos, movie theatres, concerts, sporting events, and museums. When potential customers decided where to spend time and money, they were influenced by such things as entertainment value, cost, time consumption, and proximity to home.

Perhaps KidZania's biggest source of competition was technology that fostered social networking among children. This could, however, present marketing opportunities. Cammie Dunaway, in charge of KidZania's global marketing, commented that "KidZania might be productively promoted to parents as a place for kids to get unplugged[1]." One Kidzanian remarked to a reporter in Kuwait that he would "much rather be at KidZania than in a virtual world…'What a boring thing, just touching a screen,' another added[2]."

KidZania's success to date and the fact that role-play could not be protected as intellectual property led other parties to attempt to replicate the business model, especially in Asia (where there were more than 50 copycats). But no one had had the success of KidZania in offering experiential learning. Competitors generally offered lower quality properties. Without adequate corporate sponsorship support, many of these struggled. They offered fewer, less frequently updated activities within their facilities. In addition, they often chose poor locations in small cities that could not support the traffic needed for the facilities to thrive. These more direct competitors were, however, getting savvier than in the past.

Other Challenges

In addition to increasing competition, KidZania faced a future characterized by changing market regulations, challenges in entering new markets, and the integration of new technologies. In particular, the digital revolution enveloping the world had significant implications for the organization and its service business concept. At the same time, the changing environment suggested the possibility of using new formats to introduce the public to KidZania. These shifting forces raised a number of questions in the minds of KidZania's leaders.

---

1 Rebeca Mead, "When I Grow Up," The New Yorker, January 19, 2015, p. 27.

2 Ibid., p. 28

- **Market regulations** — There was growing potential for greater parental resistance to overt marketing to children. The current regulatory environment associated with children's marketing could make it difficult to secure partnerships from "traditional" child-focused brands. This raised the question: How could KidZania adapt its business model, including industry partners, to face market regulations without losing profitability?

- **Entering into new markets** — What adjustments should KidZania make to enter into more sophisticated and crowded markets? In bigger markets, should KidZania open more than one facility? Why? Are smaller markets an expansion alternative for KidZania? What implications and risks must be considered?

- **Technology integration** — Greater sophistication of children and age compression could require adjustments to the core concept, integrating greater use and availability of technology into KidZania facilities, especially those aimed at children over the age of 10. How far should KidZania go in the integration of technology in its activities? How could KidZania best capitalize on the interactive essence of role-play based on technology?

- **Digital experiences** — Questions were raised by KidZania's leaders about the possibility of entering into services based on digital experiences. How could KidZania ensure that such digital experiences would maintain interactivity and experiential learning fundamentals? Without any prior expertise in digital experiences, what main aspects should KidZania consider before entering into a digital world?

- **New formats** — The company was also exploring new ways to extend the service experience outside the park through new formats and communication channels. This raised the questions: What new alternatives could be explored to extend the experiential learning experience? How could new formats and channels leverage KidZania's strategy of becoming the leader in experiential learning content?

RESULTS

KidZania's revenues and profits exhibited steady growth, as shown in the financial statements contained in *Exhibit 8* for the period 2010 through 2013. Both franchised and owned facilities continued to perform well, with franchising revenues comprising 25% of total revenues and a higher proportion of profits in 2013. This performance led to increasing expectations among the organization's major investors. It underlined the importance of initiatives to grow the KidZania Nation as well as those associated with experiential learning.

THE MANAGEMENT MEETING

Several items were on the agenda for the KidZania management meeting late in 2013. All were related to ways in which experiential learning could be expanded within KidZania's service concept and mission. First on the agenda was a consideration of the results of several tests of experiential learning activities at Cuicuilco. Management discussed the results of each to determine whether it should be rolled out to owned and franchised parks. It required an assessment of not only the financial potential of each but also the degree to which each activity enhanced experiential learning. The activities under consideration for inclusion in future KidZania "cities" were as follows:

1. The activities at Cuicuilco were divided into five theme areas: Driving Safety, Citizenship, Health and Wellness, Environmental Sensitivity, and Community. There was substantial support among members of the management group for including more government establishments as "partners". One benefit of this initiative would be improved relationships with government agencies that could exercise control over KidZania's offerings. Experience had shown that the selling cycle for such partnerships was longer and more onerous, and the contract period was shorter than KidZania's typical five-year contracts in other partnerships. A significant new initiative under consideration was the involvement of government agencies in creating activities centered around such entities as the tax office, customs, and the coin mint. Should it be added to offerings elsewhere?

2. The driving curriculum proved to be very popular at Cuicuilco. Should it be replicated elsewhere?

3. The Ecological House where children were to make environmentally friendly design decisions faced a lack of interest by industry partners at Cuicuilco. Did the idea warrant further exploration?

4. Should the blind Wal-Mart experience designed to sensitize children to a diverse range of personal differences be replicated elsewhere?

5. There was a proposal on the table to add a spa as part of the parents' lounge. Should it be explored further?

Supporting documentation for each of these initiatives is shown in *Exhibit 9*.

In addition, two new franchise proposals were before the group. They were for new facilities in Qatar and London. Information about each is contained in *Exhibit 10*. In addition to financial considerations, each would have to be assessed in terms of the degree to which they could carry out the demands created by the new emphasis on experiential learning and contribute further to the growth of the service concept.

Finally, further discussion was scheduled to determine which of the Santa Fe and Cuicuilco facility designs would be most suitable for KidZania's first facility in the US. It was anticipated that, unlike other non-Mexico parks, KidZania corporate would assume a significant share of the ownership of this facility.

Study Questions

1. Using service management best practices are criteria, which of the things KidZania is doing impressed you the most/the least, and why?

2. What are the risks in this business? How does KidZania's management ameliorate them?

3. What do you think are the main challenges and implications being faced regarding the changes in the service concept of KidZania, centered on experiential learning?

4. Considering the experience gained from all their current parks as well as the external forces including increasing competition, market regulations, diversity of potential new markets, and technology integration, what criteria should KidZania's management follow in selecting specific activities for its future "cities" to enhance experiential learning while remaining profitable?

Exhibit 8 Financial Statements for KidZania, 2010 through 2013 (in USD)

KZ CORPORATION FINANCIAL STATEMENTS	2010	2011	2012	2013
ATTENDANCE	**4,361,530**	**4,466,003**	**5,510,268**	**6,472,533**
TOTAL REVENUE	**27,368,627**	**25,993,847**	**51,871,401**	**47,906,339**
TOTAL OPERATION REVENUE	**10,171,733**	**11,575,021**	**15,765,830**	**20,315,180**
ADMISSION REVENUE	7,203,379	8,435,691	11,230,455	13,550,428
EVENTS REVENUE	172,550	-	-	-
FOOD & BEVERAGE REVENUE	1,650,586	1,933,567	3,332,718	4,347,321
MERCHANDISING REVENUE	886,465	1,042,471	975,853	1,444,445
PHOTOGRAPHY REVENUE	-	-	-	460,659
LOYALTY REVENUE	-	-	-	139,894
OTHER REVENUE	258,752	163,292	226,804	372,434
TOTAL INDUSTRY PARTNER	**7,168,339**	**5,948,797**	**19,319,321**	**13,592,690**
INDUSTRY PARTNER INITIAL INVESTMENT	1,705,735	853,984	11,617,763	1,765,309
INDUSTRY PARTNER OTHER	119,756	36,052	144,949	259,617
INDUSTRY PARTNER ANNUAL FEE	5,184,892	5,016,918	7,417,568	11,473,351
INDUSTRY PARTNER REMODELING REVENUE	157,956	41,843	139,040	94,413
FRANCHISE REVENUE	**10,028,555**	**8,148,006**	**13,238,324**	**11,673,977**
FEES	3,310,388	1,877,069	4,192,830	1,889,151
ROYALTIES	6,634,303	6,214,890	8,790,736	9,116,266
OTHER REVENUE	83,864	56,047	254,758	591,344
LOYALTY REVENUE	-	-	-	77,216
MERCHANDISING REVENUE	**-**	**322,024**	**3,547,926**	**2,324,492**
MERCHANDISING REVENUE	-	322,024	874,505	1,618,459
REDEMPTION REVENUE	-	-	230,401	282,847
KEY MATERIALS REVENUE	-	-	2,443,020	423,186
COST OF GOODS SOLD	**2,062,227**	**2,701,660**	**5,584,683**	**6,081,502**
ESTABLISHMENT CONSUMABLES	546,352	754,633	761,801	989,328
REDEMPTION	30,220	49,976	57,008	13,851
LOYALTY	-	-	210,932	110,645
FOOD & BEVERAGE	913,973	966,472	1,471,053	2,025,262
MERCHANDISING	436,927	685,623	3,018,024	2,507,370
PHOTOGRAPHY	-	-	-	309,008
EVENTS	97,538	-	-	-
FRANCHISES	37,217	244,956	65,866	126,037
ROYALTIES	-	-	-	-
GROSS PROFIT	**25,306,400**	**23,292,187**	**46,286,718**	**41,824,838**
% OF TOTAL REVENUE	92.5%	89.6%	89.2%	87.3%
OPERATION EXPENSES	**18,916,249**	**26,649,541**	**30,955,509**	**34,443,477**
PAYROLL	10,550,295	14,692,039	19,403,862	22,155,177
RENT	1,201,340	1,556,017	2,228,715	2,522,398
UTILITIES	711,779	858,946	1,058,839	1,193,109
SERVICES	463,176	507,357	683,300	684,013
MAINTENANCE	812,467	901,755	1,044,286	1,103,575
SUPPLIES	293,749	322,404	556,899	512,585
CORPORATE EXPENSES	3,094,223	4,291,190	2,677,478	3,575,182
MARKETING & PR EXPENSES	653,604	2,030,493	2,121,172	1,609,734
DOUBTFULL ACCOUNTS	-	-	-	-
TRAVEL EXPENSE	808,669	1,422,323	1,157,473	1,058,751
LEASES	326,854	67,018	23,487	28,951
EBITDA	**6,390,151**	**(3,357,354)**	**15,331,208**	**7,381,361**
% OF TOTAL REVENUE	23.3%	-12.9%	29.6%	15.4%

*2011 Negative EBITDA:
  First Year State USA Expenses
  Start operations of KSLP
  CUI Preop Expenses

Source
Company documents.

Exhibit 9 Information about initiatives to be Considered for Adoption at the December 2013 KidZania Management Meeting

| Establishment | | | | Activities Program | | | | | Industry Partner | | | |
Name	Ideal Footprint (sqm)	No. of Activities	Roles	Age Range	Duration (min)	Children per Hour	Adults per Hour	Staff Needed (regular season)	Industry Partner	Initial Fee (USD)	Annual Fee (USD)	2013 Attendance
Tax Office	20.00	2	• Tax contributor • Tax officer	7-16	10	48	0	1	SAT	100,400.00	57,900.00	28,768
Driving Street	190.00	1	• Driver	Children 4-9	10	72	0	2	AVIS	80,000.00	80,000.00	187,776
Natural Resources Research Lab	55.00	1	• Lab research assistant	Children 7-12	20	24	0	2	Seguros Bancomer	110,000.00	54,000.00	27,795
Supermarket	90.00	2	• Customer • Employee (cashier, aisles manager, shelf supply)	Children 4-12	20	15	0	2	Wal-Mart	95,000.00	95,000.00	26,783
Parents Spa	150.00	1	• Customer	Adults 16+	90	0	8	1	Fiesta Americana	176,000.00	99,000.00	3,351

Source
Company documents.

Exhibit 10 Information about KidZania's Two New Franchise Proposals

This exhibit shows information about two propositions to create a new franchise, the nature of the market, the proposed facility, a willingness to develop new experiential learning concepts, and estimates of potential traffic, revenue, and profit.

Proposal A

The first proposal was to establish KidZania in a major market in Europe. The franchisee would be a newly established affiliate of a limited corporation led by two entrepreneurs who had previously developed a wide range of property and leisure businesses across the market including a 24-hour restaurant; an iconic private members club for the media and entertainment business; a health & fitness club housing an organic supermarket and café and London's largest integrated medical center. The entrepreneurs were also involved in a number of charity projects ranging from education and wildlife conservation, to community sport and art.

The resident market size was over 20 million with a children's population between 0 and 14 of 3.6 million. Future population growth was expected to be moderate. There was also a sizable tourism market. Attendance forecasts for KidZania were around 700,000 annually. Because of the relative affluence of the market the expected children's ticket price would be approximately $41 in US currency.

The potential franchisees had identified a location in a well located and desirable mall that received over 47 million visitors a year.

The market was highly competitive with many entertainment and education offerings. Competition for school visits was extremely competitive with many reputable museums providing free attendance to school groups.

Development costs and rents in the market would be high. Labor costs were also a concern. As opposed to other KidZania locations which typically use a part time staff schedule of six hours per day, six days a week, this type of schedule would not work in this market due to difficulty of finding people willing to travel to work six days a week and the need to certify employees that work with children every year.

Proposal B

The second proposal came from a relatively small developing market in the Middle East. While the market would not normally fit with KidZania's requirements, the potential franchisee had close government relationships and made convincing arguments about the countries commitment to educational experiences.

The market size was 1.9 million with just over 290,000 children 0 and 14. The market, however, was growing rapidly and had one of the highest per capita average incomes in the world. Recently the government had created a specific plan to turn the country into a developed nation by 2030 with a focus on human, social, economic, and environmental development. There was a major desire and commitment to create new educational experiences for children as there were currently very few enrichment opportunities outside the classroom.

The potential franchisees had identified a location in a shopping center that was receiving 1.2 million visitors a year. They believed they could attract approximately 218,000 visitors a year to KidZania and charge admission fees equivalent to approximately $35 in US currency. They were very excited about the new educational content at Cuicuilco and felt they could receive significant government support both in sponsoring establishments and endorsing school field trips.

A comparison of the proposals is presented below:

	Proposal A	Proposal B
Market size	20,000,000	1,900,000
Children 0 and 14	3,600,000	290, 928
Assumed Penetration	3%	20%
Assumed Repeat		250%
Assumed Attendance	700,000	218,196
Location Footfall	47 Million	1.2 Million
Proposed Children's Ticket Price	$41	$35

Source
Company documents.

Additional Case Studies Available for Download

The following case studies are available for free download and class distribution on the Instructor's Resource Website for courses that adopt *Services Marketing: People, Technology, Strategy* (Eighth Edition).

Glossary

A

abstractness: refers to concepts such as financial security or investment-related matters, expert advice, or safe transportation that do not have one-to-one correspondence with physical objects.

activity-based costing (ABC): an approach to costing based on identifying the activities being performed and then determining the resources that each consumes.

adequate service: the minimum level of service that a customer will accept without being dissatisfied.

advertising: any paid form of non-personal communication by a marketer to inform, educate, or persuade members of target audiences.

arm's-length transactions: interactions between customers and service suppliers in which mail or telecommunications minimizes the need to meet face-to-face.

aromatherapy: is the practice of using the natural oils extracted from flowers, bark, stems, leaves, roots or other parts of a plant to enhance psychological and physical well-being.

attitude: a person's consistently favorable or unfavorable evaluations, feelings, and action tendencies toward an object or idea.

auction: a selling procedure managed by a specialist intermediary in which the price is set by allowing prospective purchasers to bid against each other for a product offered by a seller.

augmented product: core product (a good or a service) plus supplementary elements that add value for customers (*see also* **flower of service**).

B

backstage (or technical core): those aspects of service operations that are hidden from customers.

banner ads: small, rectangular boxes on websites that contain text and perhaps a picture to support a brand.

behavioral control: a customer can change the situation and ask for customization beyond what a firm typically offers.

behavioral segmentation: divides the market into groups based on their knowledge, attitudes, uses and responses to the product.

benchmarking: comparing an organization's products and processes to those of competitors or leading firms in the same or other industries to find ways to improve performance, quality, and cost-effectiveness.

benefit: an advantage or gain that customers obtain from the performance of a service or use of a physical good.

big data: is a term that describes the large volume of data — both structured and unstructured — that inundates a business on a day-to-day basis.

blog: a publicly accessible "web log" containing frequently updated pages in the form of journals, diaries, news listings, etc.; authors, known as bloggers, typically focus on specific topics.

blueprint: a visual map of the sequence of activities required for service delivery that specifies front-stage and backstage elements and the linkages between them.

boundary spanning: is a term to describe individuals within an innovation system who have, or adopt, the role of linking the organization's internal networks with external sources of information.

boundary-spanning positions: jobs that straddle the boundary between the external environment, where customers are encountered, and the internal operations of the organization.

brand: a name, phrase, design, symbol, or some combination of these elements that identifies a company's services and differentiates it from competitors.

branded house: refers to a company that uses a branding strategy in which the brand is equivalent to the company itself.

breakeven analysis: is an analysis to determine the point at which revenue received equals the costs associated with receiving the revenue.

business model: the means by which an organization generates income from sales and other sources through choice of pricing mechanisms and payers (e.g., user, advertiser or sponsor, other third parties), ideally sufficient to cover costs and create value for its owners. (Note: For nonprofits and public agencies, donations and designated tax revenues may be an integral part of the model.)

business-to-business (B2B) services: situation where one business makes a commercial transaction with another.

C

chain stores: two or more outlets under common ownership and control, and selling similar goods and services.

chasing demand: customers take advantage of price variation among channels and markets.

churn: loss of existing customer accounts and the need to replace them with new ones.

churn management: is the art of identifying the valuable customers, who are likely to churn from a company and executing proactive steps to retain them.

cognitive control: the customer understands why something happens and knows what will happen next (also known as predictive control).

communications gap: is the difference between what the company communicates, and what the customer understands and subsequently experiences.

company analysis: is a process carried out by investors to evaluate securities, collecting information related to the company's profile, products and services as well as profitability.

competition-based pricing: setting prices relative to those charged by competitors.

competitive advantage: a firm's ability to perform in ways that competitors cannot or will not match.

competitor analysis: is a critical part of your company marketing plan. With this evaluation, you can establish what makes your product or service unique — and therefore what attributes you play up in order to attract your target market.

complaint: a formal expression of dissatisfaction with any aspect of a service experience.

conjoint analysis: a research method for determining the utility values that consumers attach to varying levels of a product's attributes.

consumer surplus: is the difference between the total amount that consumers are willing and able to pay for a good or service.

consumption: purchase and use of a service or good.

control chart: a chart that graphs quantitative changes in service performance on a specific variable relative to a predefined standard.

control model of management: an approach based on clearly defined roles, top-down control systems, a hierarchical organizational structure, and the assumption that management knows best.

core competency: a capability that is a source of competitive advantage.

core products: company's products or services which are most directly related to their core competencies

corporate culture: shared beliefs, norms, experiences, and stories that characterize an organization.

corporate design: consistent application of distinctive colors, symbols, and lettering to give a firm an easily recognizable identity.

corporate social responsibility (CSR): is a form of corporate self-regulation integrated into a business model.

cost-based pricing: relating the price to be charged for a product to the costs associated with producing, delivering, and marketing it.

cost drivers: is the unit of an activity that causes the change in activity's cost. Cost driver is any factor which causes a change in the cost of an activity.

costs of service: cost of goods sold is the accumulated total of all costs used to create a product or service, which has been sold.

credence attributes: product characteristics that customers may not be able to evaluate even after purchase and consumption.

critical incident: a specific encounter between customer and service provider in which the outcome has proved especially satisfying or dissatisfying for one or both parties.

CRM system: information technology (IT) systems and infrastructure that support the implementation and delivery of a customer-relationship management strategy.

customer analysis: is a critical section of a company's business plan or marketing plan.

customer contact personnel: service employees who interact directly with individual customers, either in person or through mail and telecommunications.

customer defection: is the loss of clients or customers.

customer interface: all points at which customers interact with a service organization.

customer lifetime value (CLV): the net present value of the stream of future contributions or profits expected over each customer's purchases during his or her anticipated lifetime as a customer of a specific organization.

customer loyalty: is the key objective of customer relationship management and describes the loyalty which is established between a customer and companies, persons, products or brands.

customer needs analysis: is a means-end approach, meaning that product purchase decisions are the means to a value based goal or state.

customer participation: refers to the customer behaviors related to definition, production and delivery of a service, including mental, emotional, and physical behaviors.

customer relationship management (CRM): the overall process of building and maintaining profitable customer relationships by delivering superior customer value and satisfaction.

customer satisfaction: a short-term emotional reaction to a specific service performance.

customer service: is the provision of service to customers before, during and after a purchase.

customer service representatives (CSRs): interact with customers on behalf of an organization

customer training: training programs offered by service firms to teach customers about complex service products.

customization: tailoring service characteristics to meet each customer's specific needs and preferences.

cyberspace: a virtual reality without physical existence, in which electronic transactions or communications occur.

D

data analysis: is a process of inspecting, cleaning, transforming, and modeling data with the goal of discovering useful information, suggesting conclusions, and supporting decision-making.

data collection: is the process of gathering and measuring information on targeted variables in an established systematic fashion, which then enables one to answer relevant questions and evaluate outcomes.

data mining: extracting useful information about individuals, trends, and segments from often massive amounts of customer data.

data warehouse: a comprehensive database containing customer information and transaction data.

decisional control: the customer can choose between two or more standardized options without changing either option.

defection: a customer's decision to transfer brand loyalty from a current service provider to a competitor.

delivery channels: physical and electronic means by which a service firm (sometimes assisted by intermediaries) delivers one or more product elements to its customers.

delivery gap: is the difference between specified service standards and the service delivery teams' actual performance on these standards.

delivery processes: is a special process describing a complete and integrated approach for performing a specific project type.

demand curve: is a curve that shows the number of units the market will buy at different prices.

demand cycle: a period of time during which the level of demand for a sendee will increase and decrease in a somewhat predictable way before repeating itself.

demographic segmentation: dividing the market into groups based on demographic variables such as age, gender, family life cycle, family size, income, occupation, education, religion, or ethnic group.

dentistry: is a branch of medicine that is involved in the study, diagnosis, prevention, and treatment of diseases, disorders and conditions of the oral cavity, commonly in the dentition but also the oral mucosa, and of adjacent and related structures and tissues, particularly in the maxillofacial (jaw and facial) area.

desired service: the "wished for" level of service quality that a customer believes can and should be delivered.

direct marketing: is a form of advertising which allows businesses and nonprofit organizations to communicate directly to customers through a variety of media.

discounting: a strategy of reducing the price of an item below the normal level.

disintermediation: service firms that have achieved brand equity aim to migrate their customers and sales to lower cost channels to circumvent or remove intermediaries.

distributive justice: concerns the nature of a socially just allocation of goods in a society.

dynamic pricing: a technique, employed primarily by e-tailers to charge different customers different prices for the same products, based on information collected about their purchase history, preferences, and price sensitivity.

E

e-commerce: buying, selling, and other marketing processes supported by the Internet (*see also* **e-tailing**).

effectiveness: the degree to which an organization meets its goals and desired outcomes, which would typically include customer satisfaction.

efficiency: is the (often measurable) ability to avoid wasting materials, energy, efforts, money, and time in doing something or in producing a desired result.

emotional labor: expressing socially appropriate (but sometimes false) emotions toward customers during service transactions.

emotionprints: managing customer experience well and implement the principles for sequencing service processes.

employee involvement: the direct participation of staff to help an organization fulfill its mission and meet its objectives by applying their own ideas, expertise, and efforts towards solving problems and making decisions.

empowerment: authorizing employees to find solutions to service problems and make appropriate decisions about responding to customer concerns without having to obtain a supervisor's approval.

enhancing supplementary services: supplementary services that may add extra value for customers.

environmental psychology: is an interdisciplinary field focused on the interplay between individuals and their surroundings.

e-tailing: retailing through the Internet instead of through physical stores.

evidence management: is the administration and control of evidence related to an event so that it can be used to prove the circumstances of the event.

excess capacity: an organization's capacity to create service output that is not fully utilized.

excess demand: demand for a service at a given time that exceeds the organization's ability to meet customer needs.

expectations: internal standards that customers use to judge the quality of a service experience.

expert systems: interactive computer programs that mimic a human expert's reasoning to draw conclusions from data, solve problems, and give customized advice.

F

facilitating supplementary services: supplementary services that aid in the use of the core product or are required for service delivery.

fail point: a point in a process at which there is a significant risk of problems that can damage service quality (sometimes referred to humorously as an OTSU, short for "opportunity to screw up").

family feuders: people who get into arguments with members of their own family — or worse, with other customers — make up a subcategory of belligerents.

financial rewards: are customer incentives that have a financial value.

fishbone diagram: a chart-based technique that relates specific service problems to different categories of underlying causes (also known as a cause-and-effect chart).

fixed costs: costs that do not vary with production or sales revenue.

flat-rate pricing: quoting a fixed price for a service in advance of delivery.

flowchart: a visual representation of the steps involved in delivering service to customers (*see also* **blueprint**).

flower of service: a visual framework for understanding the supplementary service elements that surround and add value to the product core (*see also* **augmented product**).

focus group: a group, typically consisting of six to eight people and carefully preselected on certain characteristics (e.g., demographics, psychographics, or product ownership), who are convened by researchers for in-depth, moderator-led discussion of specific topics.

franchise: a contractual association between a franchiser (typically a manufacturer, wholesaler, or service organization) and independent businesspeople (franchisees) who buy the right to own and operate one or more units in the franchise system.

freemium: is a pricing strategy by which a product or service (typically a digital offering or application such as software, media, games or web services) is provided free of charge, but money (premium) is charged for proprietary features, functionality, or virtual goods.

frontline employees: people behind the counter, on the phone, in the cloud, and walking the floor — possess a large measure of control.

front-stage: those aspects of service operations and delivery that are visible or otherwise apparent to customers.

functionality: refers to the ability of those items to facilitate the performance of service transactions.

G

generality: items that comprise a class of objects, persons, or events — for instance, airline seats, flight attendants, and cabin service.

geographic segmentation: dividing a market into geographic units such as countries, regions, or cities.

global economy: economy of the world, considered as the international exchange of goods and services that is expressed in monetary units of account (money).

goal setting: is a major component of personal development and management literature.

goods: physical objects or devices that provide benefits for customers through ownership or use.

Gross Domestic Product (GDP): is the broadest quantitative measure of a nation's total economic activity.

H

halo effect: is a cognitive bias in which an observer's overall impression of a person, company, brand, or product influences the observer's feelings and thoughts about that entity's character or properties.

high-contact services: services that involve significant interaction among customers, service personnel, and equipment and facilities.

high-performance service-delivery teams: a small number of people with complementary skills who are committed to a common purpose, set of performance goals, and approach for which they hold themselves mutually accountable.

house of brands: refers to a branding strategy in which a parent company is home to multiple distinct brands.

human resource management (HRM): coordination of tasks related to job design, employee recruitment, selection, training, and motivation; also includes planning and administering other employee-related activities.

human resources (HR) departments: is a critical component of employee well-being in any business, no matter how small

I

image: a set of beliefs, ideas, and impressions held regarding an object.

impersonal communications: one-way communications directed at target audiences who are not in personal contact with the message source (including advertising, promotions, and public relations).

information-based services: all services in which the principal value comes from the transmission of data to customers; also includes mental stimulus processing and information processing (*see definitions*).

information management: infrastructure used to collect, manage, preserve, store and deliver information.

information processing: intangible actions directed at customers' assets.

information search: is a stage in the Consumer Decision Process during which a consumer searches for internal or external information.

in-process wait: a wait that occurs during service delivery.

inputs: all resources (labor, materials, energy, and capital) required to create service offerings.

intangibility: (*see* **mental intangibility** *and* **physical intangibility**).

intangible: something that is experienced and that cannot be touched or preserved.

integrated marketing communications (IMC): a concept under which an organization carefully integrates and coordinates its many communication channels to deliver a clear, consistent, and compelling message about the organization and its products.

interactional justice: is the degree to which the people affected by decision are treated by dignity and respect.

internal communications: all forms of communication from management to employees within an organization.

internal customers: employees who receive services from an internal supplier (another employee or department) as a necessary input to performing their own jobs.

internal marketing: marketing activities directed internally to employees to train and motivate them and instill a customer focus.

internal services: service elements within any type of business that facilitate creation of, or add value to, its final output.

Internet: a large public web of computer networks that connects users from around the world to each other and to a vast information repository.

interpersonal skills: the life skills we use every day to communicate and interact with other people, both individually and in groups.

inventory: for manufacturing, the physical output stockpiled after production for sale at a later date; for services, future output that has not yet been reserved in advance, such as the number of hotel rooms still available for sale on a given day.

involvement model of management: an approach based on the assumption that employees are capable of self-direction and, if properly trained, motivated, and informed, can make good decisions concerning service operations and delivery.

ISO 9000: is a quality management standard that presents guidelines intended to increase business efficiency and customer satisfaction.

J

jaycustomer: a customer who acts in a thoughtless or abusive way, causing problems for the firm, its employees, and other customers.

job involvement: the measure of the degree to which employee is involved in his job and takes part in decision-making.

K

knowledge gap: is the difference between what senior management believes customers expect and what customers actually need and expect.

L

labor union: is an organization intended to represent the collective interests of workers in negotiations with employers over wages, hours and working conditions.

levels of customer contact: the extent to which customers interact physically with the service organization.

life-time value (LTV): is a prediction of the net profit attributed to the entire future relationship with a customer.

loss leaders: is a pricing strategy where a product is sold at a price below its market cost to stimulate other sales of more profitable goods or services.

low-contact services: services that require minimal or no direct contact between customers and the service organization.

loyalty: a customer's commitment to continue patronizing a specific firm over an extended period of time.

M

market analysis: is a study of the dynamism of the market. It is the attractiveness of a special market in a specific industry.

market drivers: are the underlying forces that compel consumers to purchase products and pay for services.

market focus: the extent to which a firm serves few or many markets.

marketing automation: software platforms and technologies designed for marketing departments and organizations to more effectively market on multiple channels online and automate repetitive tasks.

marketing communications mix: a full set of communication tools (both paid and unpaid) available to marketers, including advertising, sales promotion, events, public relations and publicity, direct marketing, and personal selling.

marketing research: the systematic design, collection, analysis, and reporting of customer and competitor data and findings relevant to a specific marketing situation facing an organization.

marketplace: a location in physical space or cyberspace (*see definition*) where suppliers and customers meet to do business.

market segmentation: the process of dividing a market into distinct groups within each of which all customers share relevant characteristics that distinguish them from customers in other segments, and respond in similar ways; to a given set of marketing efforts.

market synergy: is when two marketing strategies are combined in an attempt to achieve a greater impact.

master franchising: delegating the responsibility for recruiting, training, and supporting franchisees within a given geographic area.

maximum capacity: the upper limit to a firm's ability to meet customer demand at a particular time.

medium-contact services: services that involve only a limited amount of contact between customers and elements of the service organization.

membership relationship: a formalized relationship between the firm and a specified customer that may offer special benefits to both parties.

mental impalpability: services that are sufficiently complex, multi-dimensional, or novel so much so that it is difficult for consumers.

mental intangibility: difficulty for customers in visualizing an experience in advance of purchase and understanding the process and even the nature of the outcome (*see also* **physical intangibility**).

mental-processing services: services to the customer's mind, such as news and entertainment.

mental stimulus processing: intangible actions directed at people's minds.

metaphors: is a figure of speech that identifies something as being the same as some unrelated thing for rhetorical effect, thus highlighting the similarities between the two.

mobile advertising: is the communication of products or services to mobile device and smartphone consumers.

mobile apps: is a software application developed specifically for use on small, wireless computing devices, such as smartphones and tablets, rather than desktop or laptop computers.

moment of truth: a point in service delivery at which customers interact with service employees or self-service equipment and the outcome may affect perceptions of service quality.

music: is an art form and cultural activity whose medium is sound and silence.

mystery shopping: a research technique that employs individuals posing as ordinary customers to obtain feedback on the service environment and customer–employee interactions.

N

needs-based segmentation: is a fascinating approach that helps get to the heart of what your customers want, and how to differentiate your offer to them.

needs: subconscious, deeply-felt desires that often concern long-term existence and identity issues.

negative disconfirmation: when product delivers less than expected.

negotiation flow: reaching an agreement on the service features and configuration, and the terms of the offer, so that a purchase contract can be closed. The objective is often to sell the right to use a service.

net present value (NPV): is the difference between the present value of cash inflows and the present value of cash outflows.

net value: the sum of all perceived benefits (gross value) minus the sum of all perceived outlays.

non-financial rewards: provide benefits that cannot be translated directly into monetary terms.

non-physical fences: differences in consumption, transaction, or buyer characteristics, but the service is basically the same.

non-searchability: fact that many of the service attributes cannot be searched or inspected before they are purchased.

North American Industry Classification System (NAICS): is used by business and government to classify business establishments according to type of economic activity in Canada, Mexico, and the United States of America.

North American Product Classification System (NAPCS): is a classification system used by Canada, Mexico, and the United States to classify products produced by industries in those countries.

O

offshoring: refers to services that are conducted in one country and consumed in another.

online advertising: also called online marketing or Internet advertising or web advertising, is a form of marketing and advertising which uses the Internet to deliver promotional marketing messages to consumers.

opportunity cost: the potential value of income or other benefits foregone as a result of choosing one course of action instead of other alternatives.

optimum capacity: a point beyond which a firm's efforts to serve additional customers will lead to a perceived decline in service quality.

organizational climate: employees' shared perceptions of the practices, procedures, and types of behaviors that are rewarded and supported in a particular setting.

organizational culture: shared values, beliefs, and work styles that are based on an understanding of what is important to the organization and why.

organization/client conflict: is a state of discord caused by the actual or perceived opposition of needs, values and interests between people working together.

original equipment manufacturers (OEMs): is misleading term used to describe a company that has a special relationship with computer and IT producers.

OTSU ("opportunity to screw up"): (*see* **fail point**).

outputs: the final outcome of the service delivery process as perceived and valued by customers.

outsourcing: is an arrangement in which one company provides services for another company that could also be or usually have been provided in-house.

P

Pareto analysis: an analytical procedure to identify what proportion of problem events is caused by each of several different factors.

people: customers and employees who are involved in service production.

people processing: services that involve tangible actions to people's bodies.

perception: a process by which individuals select, organize, and interpret information to form a meaningful picture of the world.

perceptions gap: is the difference between what is actually delivered and what customers feel they have received because they are unable to accurately judge service quality accurately.

perceptual control theory (PCT): is a model of behavior based on the principles of of negative feedback, but differing in important respects from engineering control theory.

perceptual map: a visual illustration of how customers perceive competing services.

performance assessment: is a form of testing that requires students to perform a task rather than select an answer from a ready-made list.

permission marketing: a marketing communications strategy that encourages customers to volunteer permission to a company to communicate with them through specified channels so they may learn more about its products and continue to receive useful information or something else of value to them.

personal communications: direct communications between marketers and individual customers that involve two-way dialog (including face-to-face conversations, phone calls, and email).

personal selling: two-way communications between service employees and customers designed to influence the purchase process directly.

person/role conflict: situation in which a person is expected to play two incompatible roles.

physical effort: undesired consequences to a customer's body resulting from involvement in the service delivery process.

physical environment: facilitates process delivery, and provides tangible evidence of a firm's image and service quality.

physical evidence: visual or other tangible clues that provide evidence of service quality.

physical fence: tangible product differences related to the different price.

physical intangibility: service elements that are not accessible to examination by any of the five senses; (more narrowly) elements that cannot be touched or preserved by customers.

placement-targeted ads: ads are not initiated by a search, but are simply displayed when a user browses a website.

platinum clients: accounts that were not only willing to plan a certain amount of research work during the year, but were also able to commit to the timing, scope and nature of their projects, which made capacity management and project planning much easier for the research firm.

podcasting: is a form of digital media that consists of an episodic series of audio, video, digital radio, PDF, or ePub files subscribed to and downloaded through web syndication or streamed online to a computer or mobile device.

poka-yokes: are fail-safe methods to prevent errors in service processes; server poka-yokes ensure service employees do things correctly in the right order and the right speed.

policy gap: is the difference between management's understanding of customers' expectations and the service standards they set for service delivery.

positioning: establishing a distinctive place in the minds of customers relative to the attributes possessed by or absent from competing products.

positive disconfirmation: when product delivers more than expected.

possession-processing services: services to the customer's physical possessions and includes repair and maintenance, freight transport, cleaning and warehousing.

possession-processing: tangible actions to goods and other physical possessions belonging to customers.

post-encounter stage: the final stage in the service purchase process, in which customers evaluate the service experienced, form their satisfaction/dissatisfaction judgment with the service outcome, and establish future intentions.

post-process wait: a wait that occurs after service delivery has been completed.

predicted service: the level of service quality a customer believes a firm will actually deliver.

pre-process wait: a wait before service delivery begins.

pre-purchase stage: the first stage in the service purchase process, in which customers identify alternatives, weigh benefits and risks, and make a purchase decision.

price bucket: an allocation of service capacity (e.g., seats) for sale at a particular price.

price bundling: is a strategy whereby a seller bundles together many different goods/items being sold and offers the entire bundle at a single price.

price customization: is the charging of different prices to end consumers based on a discriminatory variable.

price elasticity: the extent to which a change in price leads to a corresponding change in demand in the opposite direction. (Demand is described as price inelastic when changes in price have little or no effect on demand.)

price leader: a firm that takes the initiative on price changes in its market area and is copied by others.

price leadership: the setting of prices in a market by a dominant company, which is followed by others in the same market.

procedural justice: is the idea of fairness in the processes that resolve disputes and allocate resources.

process: a particular method of operations or series of actions, typically involving steps that need to occur in a defined sequence.

process quality: designed to support the entire product life cycle from inception, design and development.

product attributes: all features (both tangible and intangible) of a good or service that can be evaluated by customers.

product elements: all components of the service performance that create value for customers.

productive capacity: the amount of facilities, equipment, labor, infrastructure, and other assets available to a firm to create output for its customers.

productivity: how efficiently service inputs are transformed into outputs that add value for customers.

product: the core output (either a service or a manufactured good) produced by a firm.

promotion and education: all communication activities and incentives designed to build customer preference for a specific service or service provider.

psychographic segmentation: dividing a market into different groups based on personality characteristics, social class, or lifestyle.

psychological costs: is a pricing/marketing strategy based on the theory that certain prices have a psychological impact.

public relations: efforts to stimulate positive interest in a company and its products by sending out news releases, holding press conferences, staging special events, and sponsoring newsworthy activities put on by third parties.

Q

quality: the degree to which a service satisfies customers by consistently meeting their needs, wants, and expectations.

queue: a line of people, vehicles, other physical objects, or intangible items waiting their turn to be served or processed.

queue configuration: the way in which a waiting line is organized.

queuing theory: is the mathematical study of waiting lines, or queues.

R

rate fences: techniques for separating customers so that segments for whom the service offers high value are unable to take advantage of lower-priced offers.

reengineering: analysis and redesign of business processes to create dramatic performance improvements in such areas as cost, quality, speed, and customers' service experiences.

relationship marketing: activities aimed at developing long-term, cost-effective links between an organization and its customers for the mutual benefit of both parties.

reliability: ability to perform the promised service dependably and accurately.

rent: system of payment for the temporary use of something owned by someone else (hiring).

repositioning: changing the position a firm holds in a consumer's mind relative to competing services.

responsiveness: willingness to help customers and provide prompt service.

retail displays: presentations of merchandise, service experiences, and benefits in store windows and other locations.

retail gravity model: a mathematical approach to retail site selection that involves calculating the geographic center of gravity for the target population and then locating a facility to optimize customers' ease of access.

return on quality: financial return obtained from investing in service quality improvements.

revenue management: a pricing and product design strategy based on charging different prices to different segments at different times to maximize the revenue that can be derived from a firm's available capacity during a specific time frame (also known as yield management).

reverse auctions: is a type of auction in which the roles of buyer and seller are reversed.

risk perception: is the subjective judgement that people make about the characteristics and severity of a risk.

role: a combination of social cues that guides behavior in a specific setting or context.

role congruence: the extent to which both customers and employees act out their prescribed roles during a service encounter.

role theory: is a perspective in sociology and in social psychology that considers most of everyday activity to be the acting out of socially defined categories.

S

sales promotion: a short-term incentive offered to customers and intermediaries to stimulate faster or larger purchase.

satisfaction: a person's feelings of pleasure or disappointment resulting from a consumption experience when comparing a product's perceived performance or outcome in relation to his or her expectations.

script: a learned sequence of behaviors obtained through personal experience or communication with others.

script theory: is a psychological theory which posits that human behaviour largely falls into patterns.

search attributes: product characteristics that consumers can readily evaluate prior to purchase.

search engine advertising: is a form of Internet marketing that involves the promotion of websites by increasing their visibility in search engine results pages (SERPs) primarily through paid advertising.

segment: a group of current or prospective customers who share common characteristics, needs, purchasing behavior, or consumption patterns.

Self-Service Technology (SSTs): are technological interfaces allowing customers to produce services independent of involvement of direct service employee.

semi-variable costs: is a cost composed of a mixture of fixed and variable components. Costs are fixed for a set level of production or consumption, becoming variable after the level is exceeded.

service: an economic activity offered by one party to another, typically without transfer of ownership, creating value from rental of, or access to, goods, labor, professional skills, facilities, networks, or systems, singly or in combination.

service blueprint: (*see* **blueprint, flowchart**).

service concept: what the firm offers, to whom, and through what processes.

service delivery system: the part of the total service system during which final "assembly" of the elements takes place and the product is delivered to the customer; it includes the visible elements of the service operation.

service-dominant (S-D) logic: marketing inherited a model of exchange from economics, which had a dominant logic based on the exchange of "goods," which usually are manufactured output.

service economy: one or both of two recent economic developments.

service encounter: a period of time during which customers interact directly with a service.

service encounter stage: the second stage in the service purchase process in which the required service is delivered through interactions between customers and the service provider.

service factory: a physical site where service operations take place.

service failure: a perception by customers that one or more specific aspects of service delivery have not met their expectations.

service focus: extent to which a firm offers few or many services.

service guarantee: a promise that if service delivery fails to meet predefined standards, the customer is entitled to one or more forms of compensation.

service leadership: is both a leadership philosophy and set of leadership practices.

service model: an integrative statement that specifies the nature of the service concept (what the firm offers, to whom, and through what processes), the service blueprint (how the concept is delivered to target customers), and the accompanying business model (how revenues will be generated sufficient to cover costs and ensure financial viability).

service operations system: the part of the total service system in which inputs are processed and the elements of the service product are created.

service product: is a service that can be sold and that is performed within customer service.

service profit chain: a strategic framework that links employee satisfaction to performance on service attributes to customer satisfaction, then to customer retention, and finally to profits.

service quality: customers' long-term, cognitive evaluations of a firm's service delivery.

service quality gap: is the difference between what customers expect to receive and their perception of the service that is actually delivered.

service recovery paradox: is a situation in which a customer thinks more highly of a company after the company has corrected a problem with their service, compared to how he or she would regard the company if non-faulty service had been provided.

service recovery: systematic efforts by a firm after a service failure to correct a problem and retain a customer's goodwill.

servicescape: the design of any physical location where customers come to place orders and obtain service delivery.

service science: which integrates key disciplines required to design, improve, and scale service systems.

service sector: the portion of a nation's economy represented by services of all kinds, including those offered by public and nonprofit organizations.

services marketing mix: (*see* **seven (7) Ps**).

service tiering: branding which used to differentiates service levels.

SERVQUAL: a pair of standardized 22-item scales that measure customers' expectations and perceptions concerning five dimensions of service quality.

servuction: is a combination of the terms "service" and "production" — the servuction system refers to a part of the service organization's physical environment that is visible to and experienced by customers.

seven (7) Ps: seven strategic elements, each beginning with P, in the services marketing mix, representing the key ingredients required to create viable strategies for meeting customer needs profitably in a competitive marketplace.

sexual predators: is a person seen as obtaining or trying to obtain sexual contact with another person in a metaphorically "predatory" or abusive manner.

share of wallet: is a marketing term referring to the amount of the customer's total spending that a business captures in the products and services that it offers.

Six Sigma approach: is a disciplined, data-driven approach and methodology for eliminating defects (driving toward six standard deviations between the mean and the nearest specification limit) in any process — from manufacturing to transactional and from product to service.

social benefit: is the total benefit to society from producing or consuming a good/service.

social bonds: the personal relationships between service providers and customers that gives firms a better chance of retaining loyal customers.

social media: are computer-mediated tools that allow people or companies to create, share, or exchange information, career interests, ideas, and pictures/videos in virtual communities and networks.

social networking: is a social structure made up of a set of social actors (such as individuals or organizations), sets of dyadic ties, and other social interactions between actors.

spatial layout: refers to the floor plan, size and shape of furnishings, counters, and potential machinery and equipment, and the ways in which they are arranged.

standardization: reducing variation in service operations and delivery.

stickiness: a website's ability to encourage repeat visits and purchases by providing users with easy navigation, problem-free execution of tasks, and keeping its audience engaged with interactive communication presented in an appealing fashion.

sub-brands: a product or service whose character and brand values are distinct from, but related to, its parent brand.

supplementary services: support that is provided after the sale under warranty that supports the main offer.

sustainable competitive advantage: a position in the marketplace that cannot be taken away or minimized by competitors in the short run.

T

tangible: capable of being touched, held, or preserved in a physical form over time.

tangible cues: is a concrete symbol of the service offering. The facilities that customers visit or from which services are delivered, are a critical tangible part of the total service offering.

tangibilize: showing photographs and other graphics, videos, awards and recognitions, testimonials and other elements that make the organization's services more real or tangible.

target market: a part of the qualified available market with common needs or characteristics that a company decides to serve.

target segments: segments selected because their needs and other characteristics fit well with a specific firm's goals and capabilities.

teamwork: a dynamic process involving two or more healthcare professionals with complementary background and skills, sharing common health goals and exercising concerted physical and mental effort in assessing, planning, or evaluating patient care.

technical core: those aspects of service operations that are hidden from customers.

technical skills: the knowledge and abilities needed to accomplish mathematical, engineering, scientific or computer-related duties, as well as other specific tasks.

technology drivers: management philosophy that pushes for development of new goods or services based on a firm's technical abilities instead of proven demand.

telemarketing: the marketing of goods or services by means of telephone calls, typically unsolicited, to potential customers.

three-stage model of service consumption: a framework depicting how consumers move from a pre-purchase stage (in which they recognize their needs, search for and evaluate alternative solutions, and make a decision), to a service encounter search (in which they obtain service delivery), and then a post-encounter stage (in which they evaluate service performance against expectations).

time costs: an amount that has to be paid or given up in order to get something.

total costs: the sum of the fixed and variable costs for any given level of production.

Total Quality Management (TQM): is a comprehensive and structured approach to organizational management that seeks to improve the quality of products and services through ongoing refinements in response to continuous feedback.

traditional auctions: is a public sale, conducted by a professional auctioneer, at which (amongst other features) lots are normally sold to the highest bidder.

transactional marketing: is a business strategy that focuses on single, "point of sale" transactions.

transactional survey: a technique to measure customer satisfaction and perceptions of service quality while a specific service experience is still fresh in the customer's mind.

transaction: an event during which an exchange of value takes place between two parties.

U

undesirable demand: a request for service that conflicts with the organization's mission, priorities, or capabilities.

V

value-based pricing: the practice of setting prices based on what customers are willing to pay for the value they believe they will receive.

value creation: is the primary objective of any business entity.

value exchange: the transfer of benefits and solutions offered by a seller in return for financial and other value offered by a purchaser.

value-in-use: is the net present value (NPV) of a cash flow or other benefits that an asset generates for a specific owner under a specific use.

value proposition: a specified package of benefits and solutions that a company intends to offer and how it proposes to deliver them to customers, emphasizing key points of difference relative to competing alternatives.

vandalism: is an offense that occurs when a person destroys or defaces someone else's property without permission.

variability: a lack of consistency in inputs and outputs during the service production process.

variable costs: costs that depend directly on the volume of production or service transactions.

viral marketing: using the Internet to create word-of-mouth effects to support marketing efforts.

virtual queue: is a concept used in inbound call centers. Call centers use an Automatic Call Distributor (ACD) to distribute incoming calls to specific resources (agents) in the center.

W

wheel of loyalty: a systematic and integrated approach to targeting, acquiring, developing, and retaining a valuable customer base.

word-of-mouth: positive or negative comments about a service made by one individual (usually a current or former customer) to another.

Y

yield management: (*see* **revenue management**).

yield: the average revenue received per unit of capacity offered for sale.

Z

zone of affection: is located at very high satisfaction levels, where customers have such high attitudinal loyalty that they do not look for alternative service providers.

zone of defection: customers will switch unless switching costs are high or there are no viable or convenient alternatives.

zone of indifference: customers are willing to switch if they find a better alternative.

zone of tolerance: the range within which customers are willing to accept variations in service delivery.

Name Index

Subject Index

Services Marketing is available for various audiences:

Essentials of Services Marketing	Services Marketing: People, Technology, Strategy	Winning in Service Markets: Success Through People, Technology Strategy
Published by Pearson Education		

Suitable for:
- Polytechnic Students
- Undergraduate Students

Suitable for:
- Advanced Undergraduate Students
- Master's-Level/MBA Students

Suitable for:
- Executive Program/EMBA Participants
- Practitioners/Senior Management

Available in the following formats:
- Paperback
- E-book

Available in the following formats:
- Hardcover
- Paperback
- E-book
- Bundle of Paperback & E-book
- Rental 6 months

Available in the following formats:
- Hardcover
- Paperback
- E-book
- Bundle of Paperback & E-book

Services Marketing Series
- The content in terms of core theory, models and frameworks is largely the same across these publications. However, they are presented and designed to fit their particular target audiences.
- Services Marketing is available in some 26 languages and adaptations for key markets around the world.

Winning in Service Markets Series

Key chapters of Winning in Service Markets are available as stand-alone publications in e-book and paperback:
- Vol. 1: Understanding Service Consumers
- Vol. 2: Positioning Services in Competitive Markets
- Vol. 3: Developing Service Products & Brands
- Vol. 4: Pricing Services & Revenue Management
- Vol. 5: Service Marketing Communications
- Vol. 6: Designing Customer Service Processes
- Vol. 7: Balancing Demand & Capacity in Service Operations
- Vol. 8: Crafting the Service Environment
- Vol. 9: Managing People for Service Advantage
- Vol. 10: Managing Customer Relationships & Building Loyalty
- Vol. 11: Designing Complaint Handling & Service Recovery Strategies
- Vol. 12: Service Quality & Productivity Management
- Vol. 13: Building a World Class Service Organization (Assessment Tool)

Contact
- For orders of individual copies, course adoptions, bulk purchases: sales@wspc.com
- For orders for individual chapters, customized course packs: sales@wspc.com
- For adaptions or translation rights, permissions to reprint: rights@wspc.com
- For further information see: www.JochenWirtz.com
- For questions regarding contents: Jochen Wirtz, jochen@nus.edu.sg.